European
Accounting
Guide

MILLER

European
Accounting
Guide

Third Edition

Edited by
David Alexander and Simon Archer

HARCOURT BRACE PROFESSIONAL PUBLISHING

A Division of
Harcourt Brace & Company
SAN DIEGO   NEW YORK   CHICAGO   LONDON

ISBN: 0-15-606077-9

98 99 00 01 02 02 EBA 5 4 3 2 1

Preface

For many years, we have been involved with accounting in a specifically European context, as teachers, researchers, writers, or as practitioners. Twenty-five years ago, while one could write about "accounting in Europe," one could hardly have produced a book about "European accounting" as such, for national rules and practices were too diverse for such an expression to be easily understood. Today, although *European accounting* is certainly characterized by significant national diversities, the term has acquired a meaning. How has this come about? The answer lies in the development of the European Union and its impact not merely on its own member states but on Europe as a whole.

During the past two decades, the goal of creating a single European "economic space" has been progressively realized. This process did not end at midnight on December 31, 1992, both because the task of harmonization is incomplete and because new members will subsequently join the existing community. Nevertheless, the official commencement of the Single European Market on January 1, 1993 was a significant milestone in European history.

Accounting rules, practices, and concepts form an important part of the infrastructure of this single economic space. There are many reasons why it may be necessary or desirable to make comparisons of profitability, solvency, and other financial attributes of firms and sectors in different countries, including the functioning of capital markets and the capital allocation process, mergers and acquisitions, industrial relations, antitrust and competition surveillance, and taxation policy, just to name the most obvious. Therefore, the European Union (EU) has itself placed great emphasis on accounting harmonization, while recognizing that this is a slow process, since national idiosyncrasies in accounting are deeply rooted and intertwined with ideas and practices outside the confines of accounting itself. Thus, it is important to appreciate both the achievements in accounting harmonization and its present limitations.

To observers in countries outside Europe, the harmonization process may well appear lumbering and its results meager. For a number of European countries, however, both within and outside the EU, its implications have been dramatic. In addition to the major changes that occurred in, say, German financial reporting in the late 1980s, developments of similar magnitude have taken place in, for example, Italy and Spain in the early 1990s. Even greater changes are taking place in the former communist countries of Central and Eastern Europe. European countries outside the EU and hoping to join it or to enjoy a number of the benefits of membership are already aligning changes in their accounting rules with EU requirements.

When we started preparing the first edition of the Guide in 1990, it seemed to us that the production of a European accounting guide was a timely as well as fascinating project. The continuing developments just mentioned have made it imperative to produce successive editions, with chapters on countries not previously included, as well as many extensively revised chapters.

In previous editions, we have had some difficulty in deciding how to organize our coverage of Eastern Europe and which countries to include. Over time, these difficulties have increased rather than diminished. With the complete breakdown of centralist control (i.e., of the power of Moscow over the old USSR and beyond), the number of countries claiming nationhood and individuality has increased significantly, and within these countries the pace of accounting change and development has varied enormously.

Pressures of space and the degree of semi-repetition likely to arise force us to be selective in our country coverage. Our "sample" is wide-ranging and representative, but readers should not assume that any country is strictly typical of anything except itself. Differentiation is what nationhood and cultural heritage are all about.

We include chapters on the Czech Republic, Hungary, and Poland as countries closer to the European Union, both geographically and economically. The Baltic States distinguish themselves, and together justify the summary chapter provided here. Russia itself is too important to ignore, of course, and we also include a separate chapter on Belarus as an example—by no means extreme—of a country with an enormous road still to travel. For reasons of space, illustrative financial statements for the Baltic States, which are somewhat akin to EU formats, and for Belarus, which still follows the tradition shown for the Russian Federation formats, are excluded.

Two short overview comments by Derek Bailey are included in the appropriate places. We wish to place on record our great appreciation to Derek for his invaluable and enthusiastic assistance in the preparation of this section.

Throughout the book we have sought to provide the reader with not just an authoritative description of accounting rules and practices in each country but also an informed understanding of the processes affecting them.

We are grateful to our authors, whose expertise and effort have given the Guide its authoritative character, and to our publishers for their backing. We hope you will find the Guide both useful and interesting.

David Alexander
University of Hull

Simon Archer
University of Surrey

The editors wish to dedicate this volume to the memory of their dear friend and colleague Merete Christiansen, author of the chapters on Denmark in previous editions.

Contents

About the Editors

David Alexander teaches at the University of Hull, United Kingdom. He is the author or coauthor of major British and European textbooks on accounting.

Simon Archer, a former partner of Price Waterhouse, Paris, has had many years' experience working in Continental Europe. He is currently Professor at the University of Surrey, Guildford, United Kingdom.

European
Accounting
Guide

AN OVERVIEW OF
EUROPEAN ACCOUNTING

1. Introduction

1.1 Introductory Remarks

European Accounting Guide is a companion volume to the Miller *GAAP Guide* (guide to U.S. Generally Accepted Accounting Principles). It is, however, of necessity, a different kind of book. One reason for this is fairly obvious: not even the European Union of Fifteen, let alone the whole of Europe, constitutes a unified entity as far as accounting is concerned. The harmonization within the European Union of those institutional character- istics that directly affect financial accounting and reporting, namely, com- pany law and tax law, is far from complete. Thus, European accounting consists of nationally based sets of rules and practices, subject to a limited degree of harmonization in the case of European Union member states and most other countries, such as Norway, which by virtue of their member- ship in the European Economic Area have legal ties to the European Union that involve them in the same harmonization process.

There is, however, another reason for the differences between the two books, and this concerns the very concept of *generally accepted account- ing* principles (GAAP). GAAP is a concept that has its origins in a national system (that of the United States), in which neither the law nor govern- ment agencies seek to lay down detailed accounting rules. Instead, they lay down a few general principles and leave the promulgation of detailed rules or standards to the private sector, that is, to a body created by the account- ing profession and the business community. Because this body lacks legal authority, it must look elsewhere to find an authoritative basis for the standards that it sets.

It seeks this basis in the notion of general acceptance. Such a system for laying down national accounting rules owes much to the tradition of common law in the English-speaking countries. With one important ex- ception (the Netherlands), this rule-based system is not found in countries that do not share the common law. In these latter countries, detailed commercial codes provide the legal infrastructure of business activity, and accounting rules are part of that codified legal infrastructure. To apply the concept of "generally accepted accounting principles" to such accounting rules is potentially misleading. For what matters in these countries is not whether such rules are generally accepted, but whether they are the law; and these are different issues.

Nevertheless, the European Union Directives dealing with financial accounting and reporting may be considered not merely to constitute a minimalist core of accounting principles for the existing member states and their associates in the European Economic Area, but also to provide a focus for other European countries that wish to keep open the option to join the Union. There is no doubt that the principles adopted in the Directives are influential in such countries as Switzerland, the Czech Republic, Hungary, and Poland.

Another influence on European accounting is provided by the standards issued by the International Accounting Standards Committee (IASC). These standards have acquired a status as indicators of internationally acceptable practice that gives them an influence complementary to that of the EU Directives. In some countries, such as Italy, it is the practice to apply these International Accounting Standards (IAS) to issues not covered by a national standard. The possibility of conflict between IAS and the EU Directives has created a certain tension, which, together with the difficulties experienced in agreeing and implementing the Directives, has led to a view that the European Union should issue no more Accounting Directives but should support the international standard-setting efforts of the IASC. It seems that this latter view is prevailing. These matters, and the relevant institutions at both the European and international level, are discussed later in this chapter.

1.2 Accounting Harmonization and the Single European Market

As far as the members of the EU are concerned, accounting harmonization is an integral part of the development of the Union into a single "economic space." In this connection, a distinction needs to be made between two objectives of accounting harmonization. One is the establishment of a level playing field for enterprises competing within the single market, and the other is the promotion of an efficient, integrated capital market for the Union.

According to the principle of the level playing field, enterprises within the EU should be able to compete throughout the Union on equal terms as far as the legal and regulatory environment is concerned, being neither favored nor disfavored by particular requirements in individual member states. The application of this principle to financial reporting implies a need for the harmonization of financial reporting requirements—but not necessarily for the standard of financial reporting within the Union to be "leveled upward."

By contrast, the promotion of an efficient, integrated capital market has implications for the quality and quantity of financial disclosure provided by firms seeking capital in that market, so that arguably a need for "leveling upward" is implied. Much research has been carried out, both in order to measure the extent to which actors in capital markets derive information from published financial reports and to evaluate the effects of differences in accounting and reporting practices on this process. The evidence suggests that, while in many cases information contained in published financial reports may already be known to the market from other sources (such as analysts' reports), in some circumstances published financial reports do convey new information about capital market participants. The crucial role of financial reporting lies in the reduction of information asymmetries that may inhibit the entry of new participants into the market. The better the information provided in published financial reports, the more effective it can be in removing these information asymmetries and promoting market efficiency.

The integration of capital markets within the European Union implies that market participants situated in member state X do not find significant barriers to entry if they wish to seek capital from, or to provide capital to, market participants in member states Y or Z. One form of barrier to entry is the lack of consistency in financial reporting practice, especially if it is accompanied by substantial differences in the quantity and quality of information provided. Such differences represent one form of information asymmetry facing potential seekers of capital in other member states. Hence, in seeking to promote capital market integration, the harmonization program is concerned not just with the reduction of heterogeneity but with "leveling up."

The orientation of financial accounting and reporting toward meeting the information needs of participants in capital markets is associated with the requirement, stated in the Fourth Directive, that financial statements should give "a true and fair view of the company's assets, liabilities, financial position, and profit and loss." This requirement was written into the draft of the Directive only after the entry of the United Kingdom and the Republic of Ireland into the EU, and its inclusion has been a crucial and, in some respects, controversial factor in European accounting harmonization.

The harmonization process within the EU has also been affected by influences from outside the Union and particularly from the United States and other English-speaking countries whose attachment to "fair presentation" and "substance over form" has reinforced the position of the United Kingdom and Ireland. The major institutional influences on the development of European accounting are reviewed in the next section.

2. Institutional Influences on European Accounting

It is useful to consider institutional influences on European Accounting under three headings: national, European, and international institutions.

2.1 National Institutions

Relevant details about national law-making bodies, about national professional bodies of accountants and auditors, and about the creation of accounting regulations by such professional bodies will be found in the individual chapters on each country. The point to emphasize here is that the existence and importance of the national organizations cannot be ignored. Even within the EU, such national organizations have a responsibility to their members, close interrelationships with the local business (and political) communities, and often long and sometimes esoteric traditions. Indeed, in some countries, a number of national accounting bodies exist, each with its own particular constituency and ax to grind.

We must remember, therefore, as we look through our optimistic European spectacles, that the wishes, hopes, and fears of national and subnational accounting organizations must be taken into account.

2.2 European Institutions

The coordinating organization for the accountancy profession in Europe is the Fédération des Experts Comptables Européens, known as FEE. FEE formally began on January 1, 1987 and was formed by the merger of two earlier organizations, the Union Européenne des Experts Comptables, Economiques et Financiers (UEC), founded in 1951, and the Groupe d'Etudes des Experts Comptables de la CEE (Groupe d'Etudes), founded in 1961.

The main objectives of FEE have been stated as follows:

- To work generally toward the enhancement and harmonization of the practice of accountancy in the broadest sense.
- To promote cooperation among the professional accountancy bodies in Europe in relation to issues of common interest in both the public and private sectors.
- To represent the European accountancy profession at the international level.
- To be the sole consultative organization of the European accountancy profession in relation to the EC authorities.

The members of FEE are formally national professional bodies. Some thirty-four such bodies are members, representing more than twenty countries, including all EU member states. FEE is gradually increasing its role and influence as the "spokesperson" for European professional accounting bodies, and therefore for European accountants. Thus, it represents a regional grouping within the international Federation of Accountants (IFAC), a similarly constituted body with an international membership (see below). FEE does not intend to act as a standard-setting body but proposes to promote accounting harmonization in line with the policies of IFAC. The speed with which FEE emerges as a significant influence in its own right depends, of course, on the extent to which the member national accounting bodies are prepared to give up their own individual attempts at direct influence.

2.3 International Institutions

The International Federation of Accountants (IFAC) is the worldwide umbrella organization of accountancy bodies. It is independent of governmental or quasi-governmental control. Its stated purpose is "to develop and enhance a coordinated worldwide accountancy profession with harmonized standards." IFAC was created in 1973, and its constitution was formally approved in 1977. Perhaps the most important aspect of IFAC so far has been its relationship with the International Accounting Standards Committee (IASC). The IASC was also created in 1973, and all member bodies of IFAC are automatically members of IASC. IASC is independent and has total autonomy in the setting of international accounting standards. Its main objectives are:

- To formulate and publish in the public interest accounting standards to be observed in the presentation of financial statements and to promote their worldwide acceptance and observation.
- To work generally for the improvement and harmonization of regulations, accounting standards, and procedures relating to the presentation of financial statements.

3. Cultural Influences on European Accounting

When considering cultural influences, it is again useful to consider three categories—influences from within the existing EU members, influences from other European countries, and influences from the rest of the world. This division is merely one of convenience, however, and consistent with the structure of the Guide as a whole. Many attempts have been made in recent years to divide the world into accounting "zones." Such an analysis is in the end simplistic and approximate and not particularly helpful.

The Guide is divided into three major sections:

- The EU member states
- Other European Economic Area (EEA) countries and independents.
- The other countries formerly with centrally planned economies, which are in the process of adopting market economies and of developing accounting practices suited to such economies.

Four very general strands can be considered at this early stage, all of which influence (and explain) differences in specific practice and regulation.

3.1 The Relative Importance of Law

The question is the extent to which the "law of the land" determines the details of accounting and financial reporting. Tradition in the United Kingdom, for example, is that the law specifies general principles only, while in countries heavily influenced by the Roman Law tradition, the law tends to include more detail. Germany is often considered an example of the latter approach.

3.2 Prescriptiveness or Flexibility

If regulation is not specified in full detail in legislation, then two alternatives are still available. First, regulation might be created in detail by professional accounting bodies. Second, the broad regulation, whether created by legislation or by a professional accounting body, may be explicitly designed on the assumption that the *individual* expert, in each unique situation, can and should choose the appropriate course of action, within the broad parameters laid down. The principle of a "true and fair view" exemplifies this approach.

The distinction between prescriptiveness and flexibility is in practice relative rather than absolute. This is well illustrated by the nuances of distinction between "fair presentation" as applied in the United States and "a true and fair view" as applied in the United Kingdom. It might appear that these two terms refer to quite similar concepts. However, the full expression used in U.S auditors' reports is that the financial statements "present fairly . . . in accordance with generally accepted accounting principles" (GAAP), and especially with "promulgated GAAP" (i.e., the standards laid down by the Financial Accounting Standards Board and its predecessor bodies). Given the ever growing number of detailed and prescriptive Statements of Financial Accounting Standards, "fair presentation" in the United States can increasingly be considered as being a matter of formal compliance with a set of accounting rules. In other words, total compliance is arguably both a necessary and a sufficient condition for providing "fair presentation."

By contrast, "a true and fair view" in the United Kingdom has historically implied not just compliance with a set of accounting rules but also respect for an overriding principle or meta-rule that the financial statements, in the judgment of the preparer and the auditor, fairly reflect the economic substance of the situation reported upon, to which end a departure from one or more of the accounting rules may be called for. Total compliance with the rules has thus been considered as neither a sufficient nor even a necessary condition for providing a true and fair view. Legal opinions regarding the implications of the 1989 U.K. Companies Act, however, suggest that the significance of accounting standards in delineating a true and fair view is tending to increase, so that total compliance might now be considered a necessary (and even, perhaps, a sufficient) condition for providing a true and fair view. This remains to be tested in the courts. All the same, the degree of prescriptiveness, as measured by the volume of detailed, technical accounting standards, is still markedly less in the United Kingdom than in the United States.

3.3 The Providers of Finance

The roots of most of the accounting practices discussed in this Guide predate the arguments of recent years that accounting statements must satisfy the needs of a wide variety of users. Generally, the suppliers of finance to business were the only users seriously considered until late in this century (sometimes quite late). Different countries have different financial institutional structures and finance-raising traditions. It follows that accounting practice has adapted to suit the local dominant sources of finance. In some countries, tradition tends to focus on the shareholder, and therefore on profit and on the matching of expenses and revenues. Other countries have more active banking sectors and fewer shareholder investors. Accounting in those countries will tend to focus on creditors and, therefore, on the balance sheet and on the convention of prudence. Germany and Switzerland are often given as examples of this second approach.

A more obvious but less often quoted example of the influence of the provision of finance on financial reporting can be seen by considering the systems of Eastern Europe, as they emerge from a half-century during which all finance was provided by the state.

3.4 The Influence of Taxation

The scope and extent of the influence of taxation law on financial statements vary considerably. Perceptions of this are often simplistic and extremist. In reality, no country can justly claim that tax considerations do not influence published results, and no country can be accused of blindly taking tax-based results and publishing them just as they are. Within these nonexistent extremes, however, lies a quite real variety of tradition and practice. It is common in many countries, for instance, for some tax allowances to be claimable only if the identical figure from the tax computation is also used in the published financial statements.

3.5 Implications

The four strands of influence just described are, of course, to some extent interrelated. They are also—a crucial point too often forgotten—embedded in and emergent from the broad culture and "attitude to life" of each community to which they are applied. A number of important implications arise from this fact.

First, it helps us to understand the reasons why accounting philosophy and practice are what they are in each of the various states of Europe. Second, it carries an important message about the process of accounting harmonization or, more accurately, of movement toward harmonization within or beyond Europe. A true single European accounting way of thinking would imply a true single economic market and a common body of commercial law (which are both a long way away) embedded in a truly European culture. Third, we must remember that such interaction between accounting *per se* and its environment is a two-way process. Accounting needs to move as Europe moves. Accounting will be moved whether it likes it or not, as Europe moves.

At rock bottom, a fundamental question arises. We could conclude that the implication is that the ideal target of an accounting framework is theoretically attainable and that we must seek to move gradually and steadily toward it, though in full cognizance of the issues involved, which include the more general harmonization of company and commercial law with which accounting is intimately intertwined. Alternatively, we could conclude that such legal matters reflect different national histories with regard to business affairs and that a single European accounting framework would require a greater degree of homogeneity in approach than is likely in the near future or, arguably, even desirable. According to the latter way of thinking, harmonization would imply not ever-greater similarity but ever-greater recognition and mutual understanding across Europe of the different subcultures involved. This choice may appear semantic, but it is fundamental in its attitudinal and political implications.

4. The Non-European Influences

Before we explore the EU influences emerging, to use a convenient shorthand, "from Brussels," we should briefly consider the other international influences on financial reporting.

There is inevitably some direct influence from North America, as outlined above, if only because of its size and economic importance. More significant, however, is the existence and work of the International Accounting Standards Committee (IASC), already mentioned briefly. The IASC has issued an important series of standards (IASs). The IASC has operated throughout its existence in the knowledge that when the crunch came, it and its standards had no formal authority. It therefore has all along had to rely on persuasion and the quality of its analysis and argument. As a general comment, this can be seen to have had two major effects. First, the quality of logic and discussion in its publications has generally been high, and its conclusions—if sometimes debatable—have been feasible and clearly articulated. Second, however, the conclusions and recommendations of many of the published IAS documents often had to accommodate two or more alternative acceptable treatments, simply because both or all were already being practiced in countries that were members of IASC and were too significant to be ignored.

The disadvantages of this state of affairs are obvious and were well recognized by the IASC itself. Toward the end of the 1980s, the IASC decided it would attempt a more proactive approach, and early in 1989 it published an Exposure Draft (E32) on the comparability of financial statements. This proposed the elimination of certain treatments permitted by particular IASs and the expression of a clear preference for one particular treatment even where two alternatives were still to be regarded as acceptable.

Most of the proposed changes announced in E32 in 1989 have now been confirmed and incorporated in revised International Accounting Standards already published and operative for financial statements covering periods beginning on or after January 1, 1995. These changes, substantially in accordance with the E32 proposals, are summarized in Table 1.

Three issues proved rather more difficult. Table 2 sets out the proposals made by IASC on these issues in 1989. Table 3 gives the revised proposals made by IASC in 1991. Table 4 gives the actual requirements of the new International Accounting Standards operative from January 1, 1995.

Comparison of Tables 2, 3, and 4 will show that in two of the three cases, that is, assignment of costs to inventories and treatment of borrowing costs, the final proposals are the same as the original (1989) proposals, and in only one case, the treatment of development costs, does the revised

1991 (not the original) proposal persist. It appears that minds have changed several times.

It is important to put these apparently considerable changes and inconsistencies of attitude into context. First, as Table 1 shows, the majority of changes were agreed on and maintained. Second, these are complicated issues from a theoretical perspective, and genuine alternative arguments exist. Third, and perhaps most importantly, we must not forget that the Board, that is, the IASC, is not as such a decision-making mechanism. It is the *members* of IASC who collectively make the decisions, if necessary by voting, when consensus cannot be reached. The members are a small number of individuals, representing particular countries. Table 5 shows the Board members of IASC in 1998.

In 1995, the IASC entered into an agreement with the International Organization of Securities Commissions (IOSCO) to complete a "core set" of IASs by 1999 (since brought forward to 1998). With regard to the agreement, IOSCO's Technical Committee stated that completion of "comprehensive core standards acceptable to the Technical Committee" would allow it to "recommend endorsement" of those standards for "cross-border capital raising in all global markets." This position led to a conflict between IOSCO and IASC on the one hand and the U.S. SEC and FASB on the other.

The SEC's position is ostensibly one of qualified support for the IOSCO/IASC core standards project, but a close reading of its conditions for accepting IASs indicates that the Commission is in fact reserving its position. First, the core set must include enough standards to be considered a "comprehensive, generally accepted basis of accounting." Second, the standards must be of "high quality." This appears to mean that the standards must result in financial statements that are "comparable and transparent to users and provide for adequate disclosure." Finally, the standards must be "rigorously interpreted and applied." The SEC has expressed the intention that, once the core set of IASs has been completed, it will *consider* allowing the use of IASs in the financial statements of foreign companies registering with the SEC (in order to obtain a U.S. listing) without the current requirement of reconciling reported earnings and shareholders' equity to U.S. GAAP.

The uncertainty surrounding the likely outcome of the IASC's core standards project suggests that the position that there is no significant role

TABLE 1 *Some IASC Proposals in 1991*

Issues	Required or Benchmark Treatment	Allowed Alternative Treatment	Treatment Eliminated
Correction of fundamental errors and omissions, and adjustments resulting from accounting policy changes	• Adjust opening retained earnings (subject to certain exceptions) • Amend comparative information	• Include in income of the current period. • Present amended pro forma comparative information	
Recognition of revenue and net income on construction contracts	• Percentage of completion method • When the conditions for profit recognition are not met, recognize revenue to the extent of costs incurred that are recoverable		• Completed contract method
Measurement of property, plant, and equipment	• Measure at cost	• Measure at revalued amounts	
Measurement of property, plant, and equipment acquired in exchange for another asset	• Fair value for dissimilar assets acquired • Net carrying amount of asset given up for similar assets acquired		• Net carrying amount of asset given up for dissimilar assets acquired. • Fair value for similar assets acquired
Recognition of a revaluation increase relating to a revaluation decrease previously charged to income	• Recognize in income of the current period		• Recognize in shareholders' interests

Recognition of revenue on transactions involving the rendering of services	• Percentage of completion method • When the outcome of the contract cannot be reliably estimated, recognize revenue to the extent of costs incurred that are recoverable		• Completed contract method
Determining the cost of retirement benefits	• Accrued benefit valuation methods	• Projected benefit valuation methods	
Use of projected salaries in determining the cost of retirement benefits	• Incorporate an assumption about projected salaries		• Do not incorporate an assumption about projected salaries
Recognition of past service costs, experience adjustments and the effects of changes in actuarial assumption	• Recognize systematically over a period approximating the average of the expected remaining working lives of participating employees (subject to certain exceptions)		• Recognize in income of the current period as they arise
Recognition of foreign exchange gains and losses on long-term monetary items	• Recognize in income of the current period unless hedged		• Defer and recognize in income of current and future periods
Recognition of foreign exchange losses on the acquisition of an asset that result from a severe devaluation against which there is no practical means of hedging	• Recognize in income of the current period		• Recognize as part of the cost of the asset

(Table continues)

TABLE 1 *(Continued)*

Issues	Required or Benchmark Treatment	Allowed Alternative Treatment	Treatment Eliminated
Exchange rate for use in translating income statement items of foreign entities	• Exchange rates at the dates of the transactions (or average rate)		• Closing exchange rates
Treatment of differences on income statement items translated at other than the closing rate	• Recognize in shareholders' interests		• Recognize in income of the current period
Subsidiaries operating in hyperinflation economies	• Restate financial statements in accordance with IAS 29, "Financial Reporting in Hyperinflationary Economies," before translation		• Translate financial statements without prior restatement
Exchange differences on foreign operations integral to those of the parent	• Recognize in income of the period unless hedged	• Recognize as part of the cost of an asset when they result from a severe devaluation against which there is no practical means of hedging	• Defer and recognize in income of current and future periods
Accounting for business combinations	• Purchase method for acquisitions • Pooling of interests method for uniting of interests		• Pooling of interests meethod for acquisitons • Purchase method for uniting of interests

Positive goodwill	• Recognize as an asset and amortize to income on a systematic basis over its useful life. The amortization period should not exceed 5 years unless a longer period can be justified, which should not, in any case, exceed 20 years		• Adjust immediately to shareholders' interests
Negative goodwill	• Allocate over individual nonmonetary assets. After such an allocation, if negtive goodwill remains, treat as deferred income and recognize in income on a systematic basis as for positive goodwill	• Treat as deferred income and recognize in income on a systematic basis as for positive goodwill	• Adjust immediately to shareholders' interests
Measurement of minority interest arising on a business combination	• Measure at preacquisition carrying amounts	• Measure at postacquisition fair values	
Measurement of investment properties	• Measure at cost with depreciation	• Measure at revalued amounts	• Measure at cost without depreciation
Recognition of a realized gain previously recognized in revaluation surplus	• Transfer to retained earnings		• Recognize in income of the current period

From IASC Statement of Intent, 1991.

TABLE 2   *Some IASC Proposals in 1989 (extracted from E32)*

Issues	Required or Benchmark Treatment	Allowed Alternative Treatment	Treatment Eliminated
Assignment of cost to inventories	• FIFO and weighted average cost formulas	• LIFO formula	• Base stock formula
Development costs	• Recognize immediately as expenses	• Recognize as assets when they meet specified criteria	
Borrowing costs	• Recognize immediately as expenses	• Recognize as part of the cost of an asset if it takes a substantial period of time to get it ready for its intended use or sale	

for further standard setting at the European level (see Section 6 below) may be open to question.

5. The EU Directives

For many years the major method of engendering change across the EU has been by means of Directives. Once agreed (a process that can take more than 20 years), a Directive is a binding agreement by all the member states of the EU that they will introduce national legislation. It is important to clarify precisely what this means and what it does not mean. It does mean that all member states are required to implement the Directives. It does not mean that citizens or institutions within a member state are required to follow the Directive, unless and until the contents of the Directive are enacted by legislation within the state. Another important point is that each Directive exists not just in one language version but in each of the nine European Union languages. It is the language version applicable to a particular member state that is to be enacted into the law of that country. There may not be perfect semantic equivalence among differ-

TABLE 3 *Some Revised IASC Proposals, 1991 from IASC Statement of Intent 1991*

Issues	*Required or Benchmark Treatment*	*Allowed Alternative Treatment*	*LIFO and Base Stock Formulas*
Assignment of cost to inventories	• FIFO and weighted average cost formulas		• LIFO and base stock formulas
Development costs	• Recognize as assets when they meet specified criteria and as expenses when they do not meet criteria		• Recognize developments that meet the specified criteria as expenses
Borrowing costs	• Recognize as part of the cost of an asset if it takes a substantial period of time to get it ready for its intended use or sale; recognize as expense in other circumstances		• Recognize borrowing costs that meet criteria for capitalization as expenses

ent language versions of the Directives. Furthermore, when the contents of the national legislation following from a Directive differ from that Directive (either by restricting allowed options or by going against the terms of the Directive itself), it is the national legislation only that is legally binding within that state. If that national legislation fails to enact the Directive satisfactorily, the problem then potentially becomes an issue of European law.

5.1 The Accounting Directives

The fundamental EU Directive relating to financial reporting is the Fourth Company Law Directive of July 25, 1978. This relates to the accounts of limited companies. It was followed by the Seventh Company Law Direc-

TABLE 4 *IASC Changes to the Proposed Changes to the E32 Changes*

Issues	Required or Benchmark Treatment	Allowed Alternative Treatment	Treatment Eliminated
Assignment of cost to inventories	• FIFO and weighted average cost formulas	• LIFO formula	• Base stock formula
Development costs	• Recognize as assets when they meet specified criteria and as expenses when they do not meet criteria		• Recognize developments that do meet the specified criteria as expenses
Borrowing costs	• Recognize immediately as expenses	• Recognize as part of the cost of an asset if it takes a substantial period of time to get it ready for its intended use or sale	

Exracted from revised IASs issued 1993, operative from Jan. 1, 1995.

tive of June 13, 1983, which extends the principles of the Fourth Directive to the preparation of consolidated (group) accounts. The Fourth Directive seeks to provide a minimum of coordination of national provisions for the content and presentation of annual financial accounts and reports, of the valuation methods used within them, and of the rules for publication. It applies to "certain companies with limited liability"—broadly, all those above defined minimum size criteria—and aims to ensure that annual accounts disclose comparable and equivalent information.

The Fourth and Seventh Directives do not apply to the banking and insurance industries, but two industry-specific directives have been issued that are adaptations of the contents of the Fourth and Seventh directives to banking and insurance.

It is important to place the Fourth Directive into its historical context. It was drafted and debated over a period of some 10 years, beginning when the European Community had six members and ending when it had ten. The pre-Directive national characteristics of the accounting practices of

TABLE 5	*Board Members of IASC, 1997*
Australia	Japan
Canada	Malaysia
Federation of Swiss Industrial Holding Companies	Mexico
	Netherlands
France	Nordic Federation of
Germany	Public Accountants
India	South Africa
International Association of Financial Executives Institue	United Kingdom
	United States
International Coordinating Committee of Financial Analysts Associations	

the member states were significantly different, both in degree of sophistication and in direction. When appraising the success (or otherwise) of this Directive, we must measure its achievements against those at times startlingly diverse existing practices.

5.2 The True and Fair View

The key provision of the Fourth Directive is Article 2, reproduced in its entirety in Table 6. As some readers will recognize, the overriding requirement to show a true and fair view, over and above "the provisions of this Directive," is essentially taken from the philosophy and wording of the 1948 U.K. Companies Act. Also taken from the philosophy of the U.K. Companies Act is the fact that no attempt whatever is made to define "true and fair view." This article changed radically during the various drafts of the Directive. Its later interpretation, both in terms of the wording of resulting national legislation and, even more importantly, in terms of the philosophy of interpretation applied to it in practice in the various EU member states, has been highly varied. This, we suggest, is not surprising and reflects and illustrates the points made earlier about tradition and cultural influences being a vital consideration, both in understanding present practices and in predicting and influencing the future.

While the term *true and fair view* originated in U.K. company law, U.K. law does not spell out what the term means. The concept certainly does not

---
Table 6 *Article 2 of the Fourth Directive*
---

1. The annual accounts shall comprise the balance sheet, the profit and loss account and the notes on the accounts. These documents shall constitute a composite whole.

2. They shall be drawn up clearly and in accordance with the provisions of this Directive.

3. The annual accounts shall give a true and fair view of the company's assets, liabilities, financial position and profit or loss.

4. Where the application of the provisions of this Directive would not be sufficient to give a true and fair view within the meaning of paragraph 3, additional information must be given.

5. Where in exceptional cases the application of a provision of this Directive is incompatible with the obligation laid down in paragraph 3, that provision must be departed from in order to give a true and fair view within the meaning of paragraph 3. Any such departure must be disclosed in the notes on the accounts together with an explanation of the reasons for it and a statement of its effect on the assets, liabilities, financial position and profit or loss. The Member States may define the exceptional cases in question and lay down the relevant special rules.

6. The Member States may authorize or require the disclosure in the annual accounts of other information as well as that which must be disclosed in accordance with this Directive.

---

mean, for example, that assets must be stated at their current values, and it is generally applied within the context of the historical cost convention (as is its counterpart, *fair presentation*, in the United States). But it is clearly understood to exclude the use of hidden reserves and also to entail a distinction between write-downs of assets that are made for tax purposes and those that are made for financial reporting purposes. The latter need to have an economic rationale in terms of the loss or expiry of value. The existence of tax allowances in respect of a write-off is not, of itself, such a rationale, for one form of tax concession to businesses is to allow write-offs for tax purposes in excess of what is economically justified. In addition, providing a true and fair view is understood to imply that economic substance should prevail over legal form (as in the requirement to capitalize finance leases).

This orientation toward a true and fair view differs considerably from the tradition in most countries in mainland Europe, where the emphasis has been on a conservative statement of profits and net assets in order to prevent excessive dividend distributions, coupled with the use of tax rules for asset valuation and setting up reserves. These tax rules are normally conservative (i.e., they represent a form of concession with respect to calculating taxable profits), but some of them may have an opposite effect. For example, the former rule in Germany (now modified by the 1985 Accounting Directives Law) that the costs of funding employee pension liabilities were not tax deductible led to such liabilities being materially understated in published accounts. Whether their effects are conservative or otherwise, such practices are in any event clearly inconsistent with giving a true and fair view, and their use in preparing published financial statements seems baffling to persons educated to believe that such statements should provide a true and fair view. Conversely, people brought up to consider the use of financial statements in terms of constraints on dividends and of providing a basis for company taxation are equally baffled by the attachment of accountants from English-speaking countries to a concept of the true and fair view, which seems to elude satisfactory definition.

According to the thinking of the Germans, and to a certain extent of most other member states, the true and fair view is not an operational concept; accounting measurement rules are simply conventions that are agreed on by due democratic process, and if they allow hidden reserves, then such reserves are fair. From this standpoint, the idea that the results of such convention-laden calculations are "true" in the sense of being "representationally faithful" is bizarre. The conventions are considered to be part of a system of rules for governing the disposition of the wealth flows resulting from business activity and providing an equitable basis for dividends and taxation, while protecting creditors from overstatement of assets or overdistribution of dividends.

This is another example of the cultural divide mentioned at the start of this chapter, between the common law tradition and the tradition of codified law. In the former, definitions of such concepts are typically provided by courts in relation to specific situations, rather than by legislative texts intended to apply to many different situations. In the latter, the converse is true; the courts have a role of interpretation and clarification of legislative texts but not of providing situationally appropriate legal definitions. Thus, the tradition of economic liberalism of the English-speaking countries, the faith in markets and the suspicion of technocracy, go hand-in-hand with an essentially pragmatic common law tradition and a belief that the accounting profession can largely lay down its own rules in the form of "generally accepted accounting principles." By contrast, the coun-

---

TABLE 7   *Article 33(1) of the Fourth Directive*

---

1. The Member States may declare to the Commission that they reserve the power by way of derogation from Article 32 and pending subsequent coordination, to permit or require in respect of all companies or any classes of companies:

   (a) valuation by the replacement value method for tangible fixed assets with limited useful economic lives and for stocks;

   (b) valuation by methods other than that provided for in (a) which are designed to take account of inflation for the items shown in annual accounts, including capital and reserves;

   (c) revaluation of tangible fixed assets and financial fixed assets. Where national law provides for valuation methods as indicated in (a), (b) and (c), it must define their content and limits and the rules for their application. The application of any such method, the balance sheet and profit and loss account items concerned and the method by which the values shown are calculated shall be disclosed in the notes on the accounts.

---

tries of Continental Europe have less historical attachment to economic liberalism, more faith in technocracy, and a preference for explicit legal texts, which extends to the framing of accounting rules. Harmonization of accounting within the EU has involved bringing these two traditions into some degree of harmony, and it is in this respect that the inclusion of the true and fair requirement in the Fourth Directive was both crucial and controversial.

One school of thought about the true and fair view prevalent in some European countries argues that it represents the totality of all the detailed regulations. The opposite school of thought argues that the true and fair view represents precisely that extra element resulting from the integration of the various separate regulatory strands into a coherent whole. In other words, professional judgment about whether financial statements fairly represent that which they purport to represent can transcend particular regulatory requirements about the applications of accounting principles; thus, substance prevails over form. The U.K. tradition, embodied in the wording of the final version of the Fourth Directive, is firmly in the latter camp: correct following of every detailed regulation cannot, of itself, be relied on to give the adequate (true and fair) overall picture. Such a concept is alien to centuries of culture and tradition in some other areas of Europe. Individual national attitudes to this issue should emerge from the

---

TABLE 8   *Article 31 of the Fourth Directive*

---

1. The Member States shall ensure that the items shown in the annual accounts are valued in accordance with the following general principles:

    (a) the company must be presumed to be carrying on its business as a going concern;

    (b) the methods of valuation must be applied consistently from one financial year to another;

    (c) valuation must be made on a prudent basis, and in particular:

        (aa)   only profits made at the balance sheet date may be included,

        (bb)   account must be taken of all foreseeable liabilities and potential losses arising in the course of the financial year concerned or of a previous one, even if such liabilities or losses become apparent only between the date of the balance sheet and the date on which it is drawn up,

        (cc)   account must be taken of all depreciation, whether the result of the financial year is a loss or a profit;

    (d) account must be taken of income and charges relating to the financial year, irrespective of the date of receipt or payment of such income or charges;

    (e) the components of asset and liability items must be valued separately;

    (f) the opening balance sheet for each financial year must correspond to the closing balance sheet for the preceding financial year.

2. Departures from these general principles shall be permitted in exceptional cases. Any such departures must be disclosed in the notes on the accounts and the reasons for them given together with an assessment of their effect on the assets, liabilities, financial position and profit or loss.

---

relevant chapters. Some general implications for the future are discussed, or at least guessed at, later in this chapter.

5.3 Specific Provision of the Fourth Directive

The Fourth Directive defines and illustrates some detailed layouts and formats for published income statements and balance sheets. The content and sequence of presentation are precisely defined. Following from the diversity of the existing practice, however, two different formats for balance sheets and four for income statements are allowed. The Directive

---

TABLE 9 *Article 1 of the Seventh Directive*

---

1. A Member State shall require any undertaking governed by its national law to draw up consolidated accounts and a consolidated annual report if that undertaking (a parent undertaking):

   (a) has a majority of the shareholders' or members' voting rights in another undertaking (a subsidiary undertaking); or

   (b) has the right to appoint or remove a majority of the members of the administrative, management or supervisory body of another undertaking (a subsidiary undertaking) and is at the same time a shareholder in or member of that undertaking; or

   (c) has the right to exercise a dominant influence over an undertaking (a subsidiary undertaking) of which it is a shareholder or member, pursuant to a contract entered into with that undertaking or to a provision in its memorandum or articles of association, where the law governing that subsidiary undertaking permits its being subject to such contracts or provisions. A Member State need not prescribe that a parent undertaking must be a shareholder in or member of its subsidiary undertaking. Those Member States the laws of which do not provide for such contracts or clauses shall not be required to apply this provision; or

   (d) is a shareholder in or member of an undertaking, and:

   (aa) a majority of the members of the administrative, management or supervisory bodies of that undertaking (a subsidiary undertaking) who have held office during the financial year, during the preceding financial year and up to the time when the consolidated accounts are drawn up, have been appointed solely as a result of the exercise of its voting rights; or

   (bb) controls alone, pursuant to an agreement with other shareholders in or members of that undertaking (a subsidiary undertaking), a majority of shareholders' or members' voting rights in that undertaking. The Member States may introduce more detailed provisions concerning the form and contents of such agreements.

The Member States shall prescribe at least the arrangements referred to in (bb) above.

They may make the application of (aa) above dependent upon the holding's representing 20% or more of the shareholders' or members' voting rights.

However, (aa) above shall not apply where another undertaking has the rights referred to in subparagraphs (a), (b) or (c) above with regard to that subsidiary undertaking.

Table 10 *Candidates for Future Membership in the European Union as of 1998*

First Tranche	Second Tranche
Cyprus	Bulgaria
Czech Republic	Latvia
Estonia	Lithuania
Hungary	Romania
Poland	Slovakia
Slovenia	

Countries in the first tranche are expected to become members in the first few years of the 21st century. Those in the second tranche are perceived as requiring longer to meet the economic and institutional criteria for membership.

continues to prescribe requirements for particular items in the balance sheet and income statement. The other major consideration in this Directive concerns the rules of valuation. The major methodology is based firmly on the historic cost principle, that is, on "purchase price or production cost." However, the Directive also "allows national governments to allow" alternative valuation methods, as specified in Article 33(1) (see Table 7). Whichever valuation method is used, the general rules of Article 31 apply (see Table 8).

5.4 The Seventh Directive

The Seventh Directive applied and broadly extended the provisions of the Fourth Directive to the preparation and publication of consolidated accounts. Article 1(1) is reproduced in Table 9. The extent of the publication of consolidated accounts varied widely in the EU member states in pre-Seventh Directive days. This Directive required much development and change in some countries and very little in others.

6. Toward European Generally Accepted Accounting Principles?

We have pointed out that pre-EU accounting practices in the member states varied widely. The Fourth and Seventh Directives set out to harmonize these practices as far as possible, given the situation at the time. The extent to which practice had been harmonized by the late 1990s can be judged from the individual chapters later in this Guide. It has frequently been suggested that the Directives were always, and necessarily, seen very much as a first step. In retrospect, and given the divergences of practice and attitude discussed and illustrated throughout this volume, the point seems obvious, but the difficulties of going beyond this first step are also apparent.

Given that there is increasing recognition that the current EU accounting harmonization is obviously less than total in surface appearance, and where it does exist is often only skin deep, what is the way forward? This is a complicated issue, and the following brief sketch attempts to outline the major elements in general terms in a way that will not date too quickly.

It is generally recognized that formal Directives are not an effective way of moving forward. They are too cumbersome in approach and too time-consuming in development. As an alternative mechanism, a European Accounting Forum has been set up under the auspices of the EC Commission. This is intended as a gathering together of all major interested parties—the EC Commission, accounting standard-setting bodies, regulatory and government organizations, and business interest groups. The effectiveness of this forum seems to be highly uncertain, as perhaps was its original purpose.

One fundamental issue causing considerable uncertainty and aggravation concerns the relationship between *European* accounting and harmonization, and *international* accounting and harmonization. One school of thought would argue that to attempt further harmonization at the European level is merely to introduce an unnecessary and distracting middle layer into the wider movement toward greater international harmonization and comparability. The other school of thought, to which the European Commission once belonged, takes the view that Europe, consistent with its emergence as a single economic market, needs a single accounting and reporting framework within that market. The European Commission's current position is discussed below.

In April 1997, European Commissioner Mario Monti outlined what he termed "the Action Plan and Accounting Priorities" as follows. The Action Plan "covers all measures necessary to ensure that the full benefit of the Single Market is achieved before the introduction of the Single Currency in January 1999." Key problems to be addressed are "the incorrect or incomplete transposition of Community law into national law and the excessively complex nature of some national legislation," which are "two major factors in the Single Market's current inability to realise its full potential."

With regard to accounting, the Commissioner drew attention to a "new approach" adopted by the Commission in late 1995, with a view to "helping Europe's major companies gain access to capital on the world's markets." This new approach has as a principal objective keeping the Accounting Directives and IASs in line, so that companies operating at the global level can rely on one set of accounts throughout the world, an outcome that depends on the success of the IASC/IOSCO core standards project described in Section 4.

The approach will be pursued through closer cooperation and coordination, avoiding new European legislation as far as possible, but with a willingness to amend the Directives where necessary so that they are compatible with existing and new IASs. The Commission appears anxious to present the discrepancies between existing IASs and Accounting Directives as "very few and rather minor." However, while compliance with IASs may generally entail compliance with the Directives, the reverse is by no means necessarily the case because of the numerous options and derogation possibilities allowed by the latter. It is not clear, therefore, to what extent the process of cooperation and coordination will be a two-way one, with the IASC making efforts to accommodate a "European" perspective in framing IASs. In particular, the IASC's need to satisfy the criteria laid down by the SEC, as indicated in Section 4 above, would imply that the U.S. perspective will largely predominate over the European one in cases where the two differ.

If the core standards project fails to obtain SEC approval (and the SEC's reservations on this score imply that this is quite possible), then the willingness of the European Commission to align its accounting standard-setting activities with those of the IASC largely on the latter's terms will arguably have been ill-rewarded. Thus, one is left either doubting the wisdom of the European Commission's "new approach" to accounting or admitting that the inability of the European Union to attend effectively to accounting standard setting left it no viable alternative to accepting the uncertain hegemony of the IASC, and ultimately, perhaps, the hegemony of the SEC.

So where does this leave the prospects for European GAAP? We would summarize the position as follows:

- Practice among the EU members started from a diverse base.
- The achievements of the Fourth and Seventh Directives within the EU have been real but more successful at the presentation level than at the recognition, valuation, and philosophical levels. There is no European consensus on what a "true and fair view" means or implies.
- The organizational way forward—who or what will legislate or regulate: EU, Pan-European, or international dimension—is still unclear.
- The cultural dimension of accounting means that progress will of necessity be slow.
- The EU has recently acquired three new members (Austria, Finland, and Sweden). Additionally, a number of Baltic and Central and Eastern European countries have been accepted as candidates for membership (see Table 10). These countries will bring their own institutional and intellectual traditions into the Union and will influence, as well as be influenced by, European thinking on such matters as accounting.

The way forward, the crucial way and the only effective way, is through ever increasing mutual understanding of differences and of the reasons for them.

It is to this increase in mutual understanding that this Guide is dedicated.

Country Highlights
AUSTRIA

Common Legal Forms of Companies
- Aktiengesellschaft (AG)—Joint Stock corporation
- Gesellschaft mit beschränkter Haftung (GmbH)—Limited Liability Company
- Kommanditgesellschaft (KG)—Limited Partnership
- Offene Handelsgesellschaft (OHG) —General Partnership
- Einzelunternehmen—Sole Proprietorship

Sources of Financial Reporting Requirements
Austrian Commercial Code

Corporate Taxation
Corporate tax rate: 34 %

Auditing Requirements
All Aktiengesellschaften are subject to a statutory audit requirement. GmbHs are subject to a statutory audit requirement if two of the following three criteria are met in two consecutive years:

Total assets	> ATS 37 mio
Sales	> ATS 74 mio
Employees	> 50

Limited partnerships whose general partner is a limited liabiliy company are also subect to a statutory audit based on the above size criteria.

Organization of the Accounting and Auditing Professions
Certified Auditors (Beeidete Wirtschaftspruefer) and Tax Advisors (Steuerberater) are organized in the Austrian Chamber of Public Accountants (Kammer der Wirtschaftstreuhaender)—a self-regulating official organization.

Statutory audits may be performed only by certified auditors. Independence rules are defined in the Commercial Code and by professional regulations.

Constitution and Legal Systems
Austria is a Federal Republic within the European Union. The President of the Republic has a rather representative function and basically no governmental authority.

The constitution is based on a parliamentary democracy. The parliament—consisting of two houses: the National Council (Nationalrat) and the Federal Council (Bundesrat) is the legislative authority. The executive authority is exercised by the Federal Chancellor, who leads the Federal Government and the Ministers.

The legal system is based on Roman and German Law that dates from the late Middle Ages. Court decisions are to be based on existing law, the Courts have no right to establish or develop law. Court decisions do not set binding precedent. Unity of law is guaranteed, however, by the higher courts, which are expected to decide similar cases in a consistent manner.

Currency
Austrian Schilling (ATS); from 1999 onwards: euro

Official Languages
German

AUSTRIA

Helmut Maukner
Ernst & Young, Vienna

1. Background

1.1 Historical Development of Austrian Accounting Regulations

The history of Austrian Accounting Law dates back to 1863, when the General Commercial Code (*Allgemeines Handelsgesetzbuch, AHGB*) was introduced in the German Confederation, among which was the German speaking part of the Austrian Empire. Whereas the Commercial Code was developed further in Germany, where the German Commercial Code (*deutsches Handelsgesetzbuch, dHGB*) was enacted in 1900, the General Commercial Code remained in force in the first Austrian Republic after the collapse of the Austrian Empire. As a result of the *Anschluss* (annexation) of Austria to Germany in 1938, the German Law was set in force in Austria and by that the regulations ruling in Germany as of that date were set in force, including the German Commercial Code and the German Corporation Law (*deutsches Aktiengesetz, dAktG*). After the re-establishment of an independent Austria after World War II the German Commercial Code (then just called Commercial Code—*Handelsgesetzbuch, HGB*) and the German Corporation Law remained in force in Austria. The Corporation Law was slightly reformed and reissued in 1965 as Austrian Corporation Law (*oesterreichisches Aktiengesetz, oeAktG*).

Until 1990 the Commercial Code did not contain any specific rules regarding accounting principles, valuation, and the format of financial reporting. It referred only to general accounting principles, which, however, were nowhere codified. The advantage of this rudimentary codification was that there was room for an ongoing development of generally accepted accounting principles, and the legal regulations could remain unchanged for a long period of time. However, the Corporation Law contained more detailed regulations regarding valuation and the format of financial reporting, and these then were considered as interpretations of the more general regulations of the Commercial Code. By that, the accounting regulations contained in the Corporation Law were considered to be binding—at least to a certain extent—for all companies.

Compared with the development in other European countries, especially members of the European Union, the Austrian regulations were considered out of date in the 1980s. As a result of Austria's intention to join the European Union, the Commercial Code was revised in 1990 and a Third Book was introduced to the Commercial Code defining for the first time in more detail accounting regulations for all companies, regardless of their legal form. The new regulations were to a large extent in line with the Fourth and Seventh EC Directives. Among other completely new accounting concepts, the obligation for the preparation of group accounts was introduced and became effective for fiscal years beginning after December 31, 1993.

On January 1, 1994 the European Economic Area was set up and on January 1, 1995 Austria became a full member of the European Union. This required the full adaptation of the Fourth, Seventh, and Eighth EC Directives by the end of 1996. On May 23, 1996 the EU Adaptation Law (*EU-Gesellschaftsrechtsaenderungsgesetz, EU-GesRAeG*) was introduced. The new regulations became effective for fiscal years beginning after June 30, 1996.

1.2 The Influence of Tax Regulations on Commercial Accounting

Apart from the regulations included in the Commercial Code, specific regulations concerning bookkeeping and valuation are included in the tax law. However, one of the basic concepts of the Austrian tax law is the so-called "authoritative principle." According to this principle the commercial financial statements are the authoritative basis for tax accounts, which therefore do not form an independent set of accounts but are derived from the commercial accounts. Only where specific tax regulations require an accounting treatment different from the accounting regulations defined in the Commercial Code are differences between the commercial and the tax valuation accepted.

It is therefore a general practice to select tax optimal valuation principles for commercial accounting purposes, where options for different accounting treatments exist in the rulings of the Commercial Code. Moreover, some of the rulings of the Commercial Code specifically include an exception clause based on tax rulings (e.g. the reversal of write-offs (depreciation) is not obligatory if the written-down value is still accepted for tax purposes). Furthermore, tax regulations require the disclosure of tax-specific depreciations and reserves in the commercial accounts, which are then included as untaxed reserves in the commercial financial statements.

As a result of the influences of tax regulations on commercial accounts, there is a general tendency to reduce the value of assets to the minimum amount possible and to choose the highest value possible for liabilities, which leads to a predominance of the prudence principle compared with other accounting principles and thus a rather conservative valuation.

2. The Form and Content of Published Financial Statements

2.1 General

The form and content of financial statements as defined in the Austrian Commercial Code depends on the legal form and size of the reporting entity.

Sole proprietorships (*Einzelunternehmen*), general partnerships (*Offene Handelsgesellschaft, OHG*), and limited partnerships (*Kommanditgesellschaft, KG*), with at least one individual as a general partner have only minimal requirements for the form and content of financial statements. Regardless of their size they must prepare a balance sheet and a profit and loss statement only. There are basically no disclosure requirements for the income statement, the balance sheet must disclose separately fixed assets, current assets, prepaid expenses and deferred charges, equity, untaxed reserves, accruals, liabilities, and deferred income (§ 198 (1) HGB). A more detailed disclosure is required only in order to provide a true and fair view of the assets and liabilities and the earnings position of the company to the entrepreneur.

More detailed legal regulations exist for the form and content of financial statements of joint stock corporations (*Aktiengesellschaft, AG*) and limited liability companies (*Gesellschaft mit beschraenkter Haftung, GmbH*). These regulations also apply to general partnerships and limited partnerships with joint stock corporations and/or limited liability companies as the only general partner(s) (e.g. GmbH & Co KG, AG & Co). The financial statements comprise a balance sheet, a profit and loss statement, and notes to the financial statements. There are different levels of disclosure requirements, especially for disclosures in the notes, depending on the following size criteria, whereby any two of the three criteria must be met in two consecutive years; the categorization is then valid for the following fiscal year:

	Small	Medium-sized	Large
Total assets (ATS mio)	≤37	>37 and ≤150	>150
Sales (ATS mio)	≤74	>74 and ≤300	>300
Number of employees	≤50	>50 and ≤250	>250

Joint stock corporations, which are quoted on a stock exchange in the European Union or in the European Economic Area, are always deemed to be "large."

Medium-sized and large companies also must prepare a management report in addition to the financial statements.

Consolidated financial statements are to be prepared only if any two of the following three size criteria are met in two consecutive years; the categorization is then valid for the following fiscal year:

	If consolidated financial statements have not yet been prepared	If consolidated financial statements have already been prepared
	Added figures of all group companies	*Consolidated figures*
Total assets (ATS mio)	>450	>375
Sales (ATS mio)	>900	>750
Number of employees	>500	>500

The financial statements of all joint stock corporations and of medium-sized and large limited liability companies are subject to a statutory audit. In addition, an audit is required for the financial statements of those small limited liability companies that are legally obliged to have a supervisory board.

The form of financial statements once selected must be applied consistently, especially the classifications in the balance sheets and the income statements of succeeding years. Any changes in the form and disclosures are permitted only if the true and fair view is not deteriorated by such changes. The changes are to be explained in the notes to the financial statements.

A more detailed classification of assets, liabilities, income, and expenses than that defined by law is permitted. Even in this case the prescribed classification must be observed. Additional items may be added if their content is not covered by one of the items defined in the prescribed classification. Additional items are required if otherwise a true and fair view is not possible.

The prescribed classification may be condensed if the clarity of the presentation is thereby improved or individual items are considered to be immaterial. In any case, full details must then be disclosed in the notes to the financial statements. The main categories of assets and liabilities (indicated with letters and Roman numerals) and income and expenses (indicated with Arabic numbers) must in any case be disclosed in the balance sheet and the income statement, respectively.

2.2 Balance Sheet

The balance sheet is to be presented in the horizontal account format. Fixed assets, current assets, prepaid expenses, equity, untaxed reserves, accruals, liabilities, and deferred income are the main items of the balance sheet.

Fixed assets are defined as assets that are determined to be used permanently in the business. There are three main categories of fixed assets that must be disclosed separately:

I. Intangible Assets
II. Tangible Assets
III. Financial Assets

A fixed asset movement analysis is to be disclosed either in the balance sheet or in the notes. The movement analysis must provide information on the additions, disposals, and redisclosures, all at acquisition or production cost. Furthermore, the accumulated depreciation, the depreciation for the year, and the appreciation for the year are to be disclosed. Low value items that are written off immediately may be disclosed as disposal in the same year they are acquired.

According to § 224 (2) HGB, Intangible Assets are to be broken down further into:

1. Concessions, industrial property rights and similar rights, and advantages including licenses thereof derived
2. Goodwill
3. On-account payments for the acquisition of intangible assets

Tangible Assets are to be disclosed in further detail as follows:

1. Land, rights similar to land and buildings, including building on land owned by third parties
2. Technical equipment and machinery
3. Other equipment, furniture, and fixtures
4. On-account payments and assets under construction

The value of land is to be disclosed separately either in the balance sheet or in the notes.

Financial assets are to be broken down further into:

1. Investments in affiliated companies
2. Loans to affiliated companies
3. Investments in associated companies
4. Loans to associated companies
5. Marketable securities held as fixed assets
6. Other loans

Affiliated companies (*verbundene Unternehmen*) are all companies that are to be included in full in the consolidated financial statements of the ultimate parent company. This includes all companies in which the parent company possesses directly or indirectly more than 50% of the voting rights or is able to control the subsidiary by other methods (right to appoint or dismiss the majority of the members of the boards [this may be achieved either by specific clauses in the bylaws of the subsidiary or by contractual agreements with other shareholders], right to exercise a dominant influence based on a contractual agreement with the subsidiary) as well as all companies that are managed uniformly with the parent company and in which the parent company has—directly or indirectly—a participating interest that is assumed if the (direct or indirect) shareholding in the subsidiary is at least 20%.

Associated companies (*Unternehmen, mit denen ein Beteiligungsverhaeltnis besteht*) are companies in which a direct participation exists which is intended to serve own operating activities by means of a long-term association with these undertakings and which are not affiliated companies. An association is assumed when the shareholding is at least 20%.

Marketable securities are to be disclosed as fixed assets if it is intended to hold these securities in the long-term although not necessarily until maturity.

Receivables with a maturity of at least 5 years are to be disclosed as loans, whereby loans to affiliated companies and loans to associated companies are to be disclosed separately.

Current assets are defined as assets that are not determined to be used permanently in the business. There are four main categories of current assets that must be disclosed separately:

I. Inventories
II. Receivables and Other Assets
III. Marketable Securities and Investments
IV. Cash on Hand, Checks, Bank Deposits

Inventories are to be disclosed in further detail as follows:

1. Raw materials, supplies, and consumables
2. Partly finished products
3. Finished products and goods
4. Services not yet billable
5. Payments made on account

Receivables and Other Assets are to be further broken down by nature and by debtor as follows:

1. Trade accounts receivable
2. Receivables from affiliated companies
3. Receivables from associated companies
4. Other receivables and assets

Other Receivables and Assets are also included deferred charges.

Investments in affiliated companies disclosed under current assets are to be disclosed separately from other Marketable Securities and Investments.

No further breakdown is required for Cash on Hand, Checks, or Bank Deposits.

Expenditures made before the balance sheet date that are expenses of any following fiscal year are to be disclosed separately as Prepaid Expenses after Current Assets.

Equity is to be disclosed as the first item of the liability side of the balance sheet. It is to be broken down as follows:

I. Share capital
II. Capital reserves
III. Revenue reserves
IV. Retained earnings (thereof Profit brought forward/Losses brought forward)

The appropriated and the unappropriated part of Reserves is to be disclosed separately as a subheading of Capital Reserves. Revenue Reserves are to be split into the legal reserve, the statutory reserves, and other (free) reserves. Specific reserves according to tax regulations, which are to be presented separately in the financial statements, are disclosed as Untaxed Reserves. This includes the Valuation Reserve due to specific depreciation and other untaxed reserves.

Accruals are disclosed separately and split into the following categories, which also must be disclosed:

1. Accruals for Severance Payments
2. Accruals for Pensions
3. Tax Accruals
4. Other Accruals

The following categories of Liabilities must be disclosed:

1. Bonds
2. Liabilities to banks
3. On-account payments received for orders
4. Trade payables
5. Liabilities arising from the acceptance of bills of exchange and the issuance of promissory notes
6. Payables to affiliated companies

7. Payables to associated companies
8. Other liabilities

On-account payments received for orders may be offset with the respective inventory items to the extent the value of such inventory items exceeds the amount of the on-account payment received. The offset amount is to be disclosed separately.

Revenues received before the balance sheet date that represent income of any following period are to be disclosed separately as accrued income on the liability side of the balance sheet.

Commitments and Contingent Liabilities that are not included in accruals or liabilities are to be noted under the balance sheet.

2.3 Income Statement

There are two alternatives for the format of the income statement:

- The total cost format
- The cost of sales format

The difference between the two formats is only in the presentation of the operating income and expenses: the presentation format of the financial income and expenses, the extraordinary income and expenses, taxes on income, and the allocation to and release from reserves, respectively, is identical for both formats.

The total cost format presents a gross performance rather than only sales, and all operating expenses are disclosed by type. The individual lines to be disclosed under the total cost format for the operating activities of a company are as follows:

1. Sales
2. Changes in the stock of partly finished and finished goods as well as in services not yet billable
3. Other own work capitalized
4. Other operating income
5. Cost of material and other production related services received
6. Personnel expenses
7. Depreciation

8. Other operating expenses

9. Sub-total item 1 to 8

"Sales" include only revenue earned from normal business operations, that is, proce.eds from the sale of products, goods, or services that are typical for the business of the undertaking. Sales are shown net of any reductions such as discounts, bonuses, rebates, and net of any sales taxes.

Under "Changes in the stock of partly finished and finished goods as well as in services not yet billable," the difference to the prior year of the respective stock values as disclosed in the balance sheet is shown in the income statement. The item may thus be either positive or negative and comprises changes in quantities, cost, and allowances.

"Other own work capitalized" represents the cost for fixed assets manufactured by the company itself.

Sales, changes in the stock of partly finished and finished goods, as well as in services not yet billable and other own work capitalized represent the total operating performance of an undertaking.

"Other operating income" is to be split in the following subheadings:

(a) Income from the disposal of and the appreciation to fixed assets, with the exception of financial assets

(b) Income from the release of accruals

(c) Other

Cost of material and other production related services received include all expenses for raw material, supplies, and consumables, the total purchases of merchandise, as well as cost of purchased services that are directly related to production, such as services from subcontractors and also energy cost. The item must be broken down as follows:

(a) Cost of material

(b) Cost of services received

Personnel expenses include all expenses for personnel employed. Expenses for lease personnel are to be disclosed either as cost of services received or as other operating expenses. Personnel expenses are to be detailed as follows:

(a) Wages

(b) Salaries

(c) Expenses for severance payments

(d) Expenses for pension schemes

(e) Expenses for legally required social security contributions and remuneration related levies and compulsory contributions

(f) Expenses for other social benefits

Depreciation includes not only depreciation on fixed assets but also depreciation on current assets to the extent it exceeds the usual level of depreciation in the business. The item is therefore to be split as follows:

(a) Depreciation on intangible fixed assets, tangible assets, as well as amortization of the capitalized costs for the start-up and the expansion of the operation

(b) Depreciation on current assets, to the extent it exceeds the usual level of depreciation in the business

Any operating expenses not covered by one of the aforementioned income statement lines are to be disclosed as "Other operating expenses." This typically includes—among others—non-personnel-related marketing, selling and administration expenses, research and development expenses, rental expense, expenses for repair and maintenance, losses from the disposal of fixed assets, bad debt expense, and taxes other than taxes on income. The latter are to be disclosed under a separate subheading.

The cost of sales format of the income statement indicates only the actual sales performed, the expenses are disclosed in a cost center format. The individual lines to be disclosed under the cost of sales format for the operating activities of a company are as follows:

1. Sales
2. Cost of sales
3. Gross profit
4. Other operating income
5. Selling expenses
6. Administrative expenses
7. Other operating expenses
8. Subtotal item 1 to 7

Sales are defined in the same way as under the total cost format (compare above).

Cost of sales includes all cost necessary for the production of products, goods, or services sold, regardless of their type.

A subtotal is to be disclosed indicating the gross profit for the period under the cost of sales format.

Other operating income includes the same as in the total cost format. Also, the same subheadings are to be shown.

As a minimum requirement selling and administrative expenses are to be disclosed in the cost-of-sales format.

Any other operating expenses (e.g. research and development expenses, losses from the disposal of fixed assets) are disclosed as "other operating expenses." It is important to recognize that "other operating expenses" as defined under the cost of sales format differ significantly from "other operating expenses" under the total cost format.

Companies that apply the cost-of-sales format must disclose in the notes to the financial statements the cost of material and other production related services received and personnel expenses in the same way as required under the total cost format.

The cost-of-sales format is not much accepted in Austria. The reason for that is primarily the fact that the total cost format is more similar to the previous disclosure requirements as well as to the fact that Austrian companies try to reduce the published financial information to the minimal level necessary. The cost-of-sales format allows, however, much more insight into the earnings position of a company than the total cost method.

The financial income and expenses are to be disclosed at the minimum in the following detail (items numbered in accordance with the total cost format; the numbers are to be reduced by one for the cost-of-sales format):

10. Income from investments

11. Income from other marketable securities and loans

12. Other interest income and similar income

13. Income from the disposal of and the appreciation to financial assets and marketable securities disclosed as current assets

14. Expenses referring to financial assets and marketable securities disclosed as current assets

15. Interest expense and similar expenses

16. Subtotal items 10 to 15

Financial income and expenses from/to affiliated companies are to be disclosed separately. A separate disclosure is also required for the depreciation of financial assets and marketable securities disclosed as current assets. All this additional information can be given either directly in the income statement or in the notes.

The subtotals for operating income and expenses and for financial income and expenses add up to the result from ordinary business activities, which is to be disclosed as item no. 17.

The disclosure requirements for extraordinary items are as follows (the item numbers refer to the total cost format and are to be reduced by one for the cost-of-sales format):

18. Extraordinary income

19. Extraordinary expenses

20. Extraordinary result

Taxes on income are to be disclosed as item no. 21.

The result from ordinary business activities, the extraordinary result, and the taxes on income add up to the net income (loss) for the year (*Jahresueberschuss*) (*Jahresfehlbetrag*); item no. 22 in the total cost format).

The income statement is not finished with net income but also includes movements of the reserves, which are to be disclosed as follows (as above, items are numbered in accordance with the total cost format and are to be reduced by one for the cost-of-sales format):

23. Release of untaxed reserves

24. Release of capital reserves

25. Release of revenue reserves

26. Allocation to untaxed reserves

27. Allocation to revenue reserves

Further breakdowns are required in accordance with a more detailed disclosure of reserves in the balance sheet.

By considering the profit (losses) brought forward (item no. 28), the income statement concludes with Retained Earnings (item no.29).

2.4 Notes to the Financial Statements

The notes form an integral part of the financial statements and are to provide additional information for the interpretation of the balance sheet and the income statement in order to give a true and fair view of the reporting unit.

No format is described for the notes in the legal regulations. However, there is a general tendency to use the following structure for the notes:

- General information
- Accounting and valuation principles applied
- Explanatory notes to the balance sheet
- Explanatory notes to the income statement
- Other information

More and more it is becoming a general practice to cross-reference individual balance sheet and income statement items to the relating notes.

The basic information to be included in the notes for individual financial statements is defined in §§ 236–240 HGB; §§ 265 and 266 HGB define the basic content of the notes to group financial statements. There are, however, a number of additional regulations in the Commercial Code that also refer to disclosures to be given in the notes. Furthermore, certain disclosure requirements may be complied with either by additional remarks in the balance sheet or the income statement or by additional disclosures in the notes. The use of standard checklists is therefore highly recommended to ensure the completeness of the notes.

Key information to be included in the notes is as follows:

General information

- Legal framework of the financial statements
- Form and consistency of presentation and any changes compared with the previous year
- Any deviation from the true and fair view principle if it cannot be complied with according to conflicting compulsory legal requirements (the true and fair view principle is no overriding principle!)

Accounting and valuation principles applied

- Depreciation method and depreciation rates (or useful lives) applied for individual fixed asset categories
- Definition of production cost as applied for inventory valuation and/ or valuation of fixed assets
- Allowance policy
- Foreign currency translation method applied

Explanatory notes to the balance sheet

- Fixed asset movement analysis
- Amount due within 1 year included in loans
- Appreciations to financial assets not performed
- Accounts receivable due in more than 1 year (if not already disclosed directly in the balance sheet)
- Deferred income included in other accounts receivable
- Appreciations to marketable securities and investments included in current assets
- Details of share categories (for joint stock corporations only)
- Movement analysis of untaxed reserves
- Details of other accruals
- Liabilities due for payment after 1 year and after 5 years
- Liabilities secured by collaterals
- Deferred expenses included in other accounts payable
- Details of contingencies

Explanatory notes to the income statement

- Sales analysis by business segment and by geographic area
- Significant losses resulting from the disposal of fixed assets
- Income and expenses relating to prior periods, if significant
- Details of extraordinary income and expense
- Taxes on income relating to the result from ordinary business activities and to the extraordinary result, respectively
- Effect of the changes of untaxed reserves on the income tax expense
- Deferred tax assets capitalizable but not capitalized

Other information

- Details of affiliated companies
- Other financial commitments not disclosed in the balance sheet and not included in contingencies (e.g. lease and rental commitments)
- Average number of employees
- Members of the board
- Remuneration of the board members

The disclosure requirements in the notes are reduced for small companies.

2.5 Management Report

The management report represents a separate part of the annual reporting requirements and is not an integral part of the financial statements. Preparation of a management report is required only for large and medium-sized companies; small companies are exempted from the preparation of a management report (§ 243 (3) HGB).

Only limited regulations exist regarding the content of the management report. On an overall basis the report must provide a description of the development of the operational performance of the company in order to provide a true and fair view of the business operations (§ 241 (1) HGB).

Specific topics that must be dealt with in the management report are (§ 241 (2) HGB):

- Significant events subsequent to the balance sheet date
- Expected future development of the company/group
- Research and development activities
- Existing branches of the company

2.6 Consolidated Financial Statements

The form and content of consolidated financial statements are in general not different from the form and content of individual financial statements, with the following exceptions:

- Inventories are not to be broken down in further detail (see above) if this is not considered feasible under the circumstances (§ 251 (2) HGB).

- Untaxed reserves may be disclosed as revenue reserves, excluding the deferred taxes on such untaxed reserves that are to be included in the tax accruals (§ 253 (3) HGB).

- Minority interests are to be disclosed as a separate item within equity in the consolidated balance sheet and as a separate line after net income in the consolidated income statement (§ 259 HGB).

Furthermore, it is a common practice not to include the reserve movements in the consolidated income statement. Instead, an analysis of the shareholders' equity or of the revenue reserve will be included in the notes to the consolidated financial statements.

In accordance with § 251 (3) HGB and § 267 (3) HGB, the notes to the (single entity) financial statements and the notes to the consolidated financial statements as well as the management report to the (single entity) financial statements and the management report to the consolidated financial statements may be combined. This then requires that the (single entity) financial statements and the group financial statements always be presented together.

2.7 Audit Opinion and Audit Report

The wording of the (unqualified) Audit Opinion is defined by law as follows (§ 274 HGB):

"Based on my/our audit performed in accordance with professional duties, the accounting records and the financial statements/the consolidated financial statements comply with legal requirements. The financial statements/consolidated financial statements represent in compliance with generally accepted accounting principles, a true and fair view of the assets and liabilities, the financial position and the results of operations of the Company/the Group. The management report/group management report is in agreement with the financial statements/consolidated financial statements."

Explanatory comments or any conditional clauses are to be amended, if necessary. Should there be any objections, the Audit Opinion must be qualified or disclaimed.

Only the Audit Opinion is to be published with the Financial Statements. The Audit Report, which—in accordance with legal requirements and general practice—is a long form report including breakdowns and explanatory comments to the individual items of the financial statements, is directed only to the Supervisory Board and the Managing Board of the audited company.

Any facts that give reasonable doubt to the going concern of the company or that could have a significant negative impact on the company's development as well as any illegal acts are to be reported immediately. If none of these matters was noted in course of the audit, this is explicitly to be confirmed in the Audit Report.

The Audit Report must also include a section on adverse developments of the assets and liabilities, the financial position and the results of operations of the company, if any.

3. Accounting Principles and Practices

3.1 General Accounting Principles

Financial statements are to be prepared in accordance with GAAP. The key elements of Austrian GAAP as laid down in the Commercial Code are as follows:

General principles concerning the financial statements:

- Financial statements are to be prepared in a clear and easy-to-read format.
- Financial statements are to provide a true and fair view of the assets and liabilities, the financial position, and the earnings position of a company.
- Financial statements are to be complete, that is, they must include all assets, provisions and liabilities, expenses, and income, unless legal regulations require otherwise.
- Assets are not to be offset with provisions and liabilities, and income is not to be netted with expenses.

The general valuation principles are defined in the Commercial Code as follows:

- Consistency; that is, valuation principles are not to be changed from year to year.
- Going concern; that is, valuation is based on an assumed continuity of operations unless this is not supported by actual or legal circumstances.
- Valuation on an item-by-item basis; that is, assets and liabilities are to be valued on an individual basis rather than on a group basis and increases in value of one asset are not to be offset with decreases in value of another asset;
- Prudence, which is defined in more detail as follows:
  —Only profits already realized as of the balance sheet date are to be recognized (i.e. unrealized profits are not recognized).
  —All foreseeable risks and expected losses originating from the current fiscal year or preceding periods are to be recognized, even if such circumstances become known only after the balance sheet date but before the financial statements were completed.
  —Any devaluations are to be recognized, regardless whether there is a net profit or a net loss for the year.
- Accrual principle; that is, income and expenses are to be recognized regardless of when the relating cash flows occurred.
- Continuity; that is, the opening balance of a fiscal year must agree with the closing balance of the preceding year.

A deviation from these principles is allowed only when specific circumstances exist.

Valuation is based on the historical cost convention, with acquisition costs and production costs as the base values. Acquisition costs are defined as those expenses necessary to acquire an asset and to make it ready for operations, as far as such expenses are individually attributable to the asset. Acquisition costs also include incidentals and subsequent acquisition costs; purchase price reductions (such as rebates and cash discounts) are to be deducted. Production costs are defined as those expenses necessary to produce an asset, to extend it, or to significantly improve it beyond its original condition. A reasonable part of material overhead costs and production overhead costs may be included in production costs. For tax purposes, overhead costs are to be included. The calculation of overhead costs should be based on an average normal production capacity; excessive overhead costs due to idle capacity must not be included. Expenses for social services of the business and voluntary social expenses for pension plans and severance payments may also be included. General administration expenses and selling expenses must not be included in production costs. Interest capitalization is permitted only in connection with production costs to the extent the interest expenses refer to the financing of the production and only for the period of production.

Because of the authoritative principle, a widely applied approach is to use the minimum production cost as required for tax purposes and also for statutory accounting purposes. Accordingly, production costs generally consist of direct material and labor cost plus appropriate material and labor overhead costs. Other expense categories that may be included in production costs as used for valuation purposes including interest expenses are generally not capitalized, as the capitalization must also be performed for tax purposes if performed for statutory purposes.

3.2   Specific Valuation Principles

3.2.1   Expenses for the Foundation, Start-up, and Expansion of a Business

Expenses for the foundation of a business as well as expenses for raising equity must not be capitalized.

Expenses for the start-up and expansion of a business can be capitalized. If capitalized they are to be amortized with one-fifth of the total amount capitalized per annum at the minimum. When defining the amortization period, the prudence principle is to be observed.

3.2.2   Fixed Assets

As a general rule fixed assets are to be valued at acquisition costs or at production costs, reduced by accumulated depreciation. Intangible fixed assets (including goodwill) are to be capitalized only if acquired. Self-developed intangible fixed assets must not be capitalized.

Depreciation is to be calculated on the basis of a proper schedule. The Commercial Code does not define any depreciation method to be applied; however, for tax purposes, only the straight-line method of depreciation is accepted. As a result, depreciation is nearly exclusively calculated by using the straight-line method. In accordance with the respective tax regulations, it is general accounting practice not to calculate depreciation *pro rata temporis* but to charge a full annual depreciation for fixed asset additions in the first half of the year and half of the annual depreciation for additions in the second half of the year. Because of the authoritative principle (see Section 1.2, above), the estimated useful lives applied for defining depreciation rates are rather conservative.

Low value assets are fully written off in the year of acquisition and disclosed as addition and disposal in the movement schedule of fixed assets (see Section 2.2, above).

A permanent impairment of the value of a fixed asset requires a write-down to the fair value as of the balance sheet date, considering the usability of the asset in the company. For financial assets the write-down is also permitted if the impairment is not of a permanent nature.

The write-down must be reversed—considering the scheduled depreciation that would otherwise have been charged in the meantime—if the reason for the write-down no longer exists. The written-down value may, however, be retained if this is allowed under tax regulations, which is the case for all fixed assets, with the exception of investments. Consequently, it is a general practice not to reverse exceptional write-downs as a result of an impairment of value. The amount that would have to be reversed according to the general ruling is, however, to be disclosed in the notes.

Regarding government subsidies granted for the acquisition of fixed assets, no specific rulings are included in the Commercial Code. Also, accounting practice has not yet developed a generally accepted standard. Subsidies may either be directly deducted from acquisition cost, thus directly reducing the disclosed amount of fixed asset as well as the scheduled depreciation, or shown as a separate balance sheet item ("Subsidies") between untaxed reserves and accruals. This item is then amortized over the useful life of the asset; the amortization is normally included in other operating income. Both accounting methods result in the same income effect; the advantage of the second method (gross disclosure method) is the improved comparability and clarity. This is why the separate disclosure of subsidies is becoming the more accepted method.

3.2.3 Leases

There are no specific rulings in the Commercial Code concerning the treatment of leased assets. Because of the dominant influence of the tax regulations on statutory accounts, detailed tax regulations for the treatment of lease contracts are also applied for statutory accounting purposes.

Tax rulings differ between operating lease and finance lease. The lessor must include the leased asset in the balance sheet and depreciate it over its useful life in the case of an operating lease. A financial lease requires the capitalization and depreciation of the leased asset in the accounts of the lessee. Tax rulings assume—in general—a finance lease if the basic lease term is less than 40% or more than 90% of the useful life of the leased asset or if a bargain purchase option exists at the end of the lease term.

The inclusion of the leased asset in the accounts of the lessee is also required in the case that the lease asset is specifically designed for the use of the lessee.

Leasing contracts are in general set up in such a way as to meet the tax criteria for an operating lease. For operating lease contracts the lessee must disclose specific information in the notes: the minimum lease obligation due within one year and the minimum lease obligation payable within 5 years. The information is to be given in total for all commitments resulting from the use of tangible assets not disclosed in the balance sheet. Thus, this also includes payment obligations resulting from rental agreements.

3.2.4 Current Assets

General   The Commercial Code requires that current assets are valued at acquisition costs or production costs or at the lower market value.

A depreciation may also be performed if, in accordance with reasonable commercial considerations, it is necessary to avoid further depreciation in the near future. Such depreciation is to be disclosed separately in the income statement.

The depreciation must be reversed, if the market prices of current assets depreciated in the past increase again. The written-down value may, however, be retained if this is allowed under tax regulations, which is the case. Consequently it is a general practice to retain the lower value of depreciated current assets. The amount of depreciation that would have to be reversed according to the general ruling is, however, to be disclosed in the notes.

Inventories   The historical acquisition costs or production costs of inventories can either be calculated on the basis of actual costs per item on stock or by using weighted average prices. Any assumptions regarding the movements of inventory are allowed as long as they comply with generally accepted accounting principles. In practice only FIFO is applied, as LIFO and any other artificial methods are not accepted by the tax authorities.

Long-term production projects are also to be valued at production cost; however, general administrative expenses and selling expenses may be included in the capitalized production cost, provided a proper accounting system exists and no losses are expected for the completion of the contract. This accounting method can be considered an adapted completed-contract method. The percentage-of-completion method is not accepted under the rulings of the Austrian Commercial Code.

The market value of inventories is defined differently for individual inventory items: The historical costs of raw materials and supplies are to be compared with replacement costs; for semi-finished products, finished products, and work-in-progress the net realizable value less estimated costs to complete is defined as market. Merchandise is to be written down to the lowest of historical acquisition cost, replacement cost, or net realizable value. As a result of the prudence principle, a write-down to replacement costs is performed even if the net realizable value is above the historical cost.

Marketable Securities and Investments   Those marketable securities and investments that are disclosed as current assets are to be valued in accordance with the general valuation principles of current assets. Accordingly, they must be written down to the lower market value at the balance sheet date, regardless of whether the decline in value is of a permanent nature or not.

3.2.5 Accruals

The Commercial Code defines two types of accruals:

- Accruals for uncertain liabilities and for contingent losses resulting from pending contractual obligations
- Accruals for expenses, the character of which is exactly determinable and which relate to the reporting period or any preceding years (e.g. expenses for repair and maintenance necessary but not performed in the reporting period)

Whereas the first type of accruals is to be set up in any case, the second type of accruals is optional, except they are required by GAAP.

The Commercial Code furthermore lists some specific accruals that are to be set up in particular:

- Accrual for severance payments

- Accrual for pensions

- Accruals for fair dealing, unused holidays, jubilee payments, escheat obligations, and product liability risks

In general, accruals are to be set up with the amount necessary in accordance with reasonable commercial considerations. Specific reference is made to the prudence principle in connection with the valuation principles for accruals in the Commercial Code. As a result, accruals (except accruals for expenses) are already set up if the likelihood of an event is only possible.

Specific valuation rules exist for accruals for pension obligations, severance payments, and jubilee payments:

Accruals for pension obligations are to be based on an actuarial calculation. A detailed definition of the actuarial method to be applied is, however, not defined. As a result, there is significant room for judgment in the valuation of accruals for pensions. The most common method used is a present value calculation with a discount rate of 3.5–6%, based on current salary levels (i.e. future salary increases are not considered).

For income tax purposes a more restrictive calculation method is used that generally results in a lower accrual. This amount is then sometimes also used in the statutory accounts and the difference to the GAAP calculation is disclosed in the notes. This disclosure policy is considered acceptable if the difference is less than 25% of the pension accrual per GAAP calculation.

Furthermore, a transitional exception clause was introduced in 1992, when the new valuation principles had to be applied for the first time. The difference between the pension accrual at this time included in the books and the pension accrual according to the new valuation method can be amortized over a period of 20 years. The difference is either to be disclosed as a contingent liability under the balance sheet or to be included as a separate item in prepaid expenses (in this case the proper amount of the accrual for pensions is shown under accruals).

Accruals for severance payments (such payments are due when an employee retires or when an employee is dismissed) and similar obligations (e.g. jubilee payments, that is, payments due to employees after they have been with the firm for a defined period of time (e.g. 15, 20, 25, 30, 35 years) should preferably also be based on an actuarial computation. In practice a simplified calculation method is often used whereby the accrual for severance payments and the accrual for jubilee payments are based on a discounted value of expected future severance payments and jubilee payments using the current salary level (future salary increases are neglected).

Again, different rulings apply for income tax purposes: the accrual for severance payments is calculated as a fixed percentage of those severance payments that would be due if the employee would retire or would be dismissed as of the balance sheet date. The accrual for severance payments calculated in accordance with tax regulations is sometimes also used in the statutory accounts and the difference from the GAAP calculation is disclosed in the notes. This disclosure policy is considered acceptable if the difference is lower than 25% of the accrual for severance payments per GAAP calculation. An accrual for jubilee payments is currently not accepted for tax purposes.

3.2.6 Liabilities

Liabilities are to be valued at the amount to be repaid. Should it be agreed in advance that the amount repayable will be higher than the issuing amount, then the difference may be included as a separate item in prepaid expenses. The difference amount is then to be amortized in a systematic manner over the term of the liability.

3.2.7 Deferred Taxes

A deferred tax liability resulting from differences between the statutory result and the profit for tax purposes that will reverse in the future is to be recognized; a deferred tax asset may be recognized; if the asset is not recognized, the amount that could be capitalized is to be disclosed in the notes.

Differences that result from the movement in untaxed reserves are not considered for the deferred tax calculation. The effects of the movement of untaxed reserves on the taxes on income are, however, to be disclosed in the notes.

The tax rate to be used for the calculation of deferred taxes is the future tax rate that will be in effect when the temporary differences will reverse. Tax losses carried forward do not reveal a deferred tax asset.

3.2.8 Transactions in Foreign Currencies

Accounts receivable in foreign currencies are translated at the buying rate; accounts payable in foreign currencies are translated at the selling rate prevailing on the day they arise. A revaluation of such accounts receivable and accounts payable in foreign currencies at the balance sheet date takes place only if the translation at the exchange rate ruling at the balance sheet date results in a lower amount for accounts receivable or in a higher amount for accounts payable. In other words, only unrealized foreign exchange losses are realized, and unrealized foreign exchange gains are not realized.

Current bank accounts in foreign currencies are translated at the exchange rate ruling as of the balance sheet date.

3.3 Consolidation Principles

3.3.1 General

It was not until 1994 that the Commercial Code first required the preparation of consolidated financial statements. Although the importance of consolidated financial statements is generally recognized, they are still only informative financial statements from a legal point of view:

- Consolidated financial statements need to be approved neither by the supervisory board nor by the shareholders; they just have to take notice of them.
- Consolidated financial statements also do not form the basis for dividend payments, as the profit distribution is based on the individual financial statements of the parent company of a group.
- Consolidated financial statements are not the basis for the taxation of the group, as taxes on income are based on the individual financial statements.

Furthermore, a company is not obliged to prepare consolidated financial statements if it is a parent company of a sub-group, and consolidated financial statements that are in accordance with the Seventh EC Directive are prepared by its direct or indirect shareholding company.

The accounting and valuation principles applied in the consolidated financial statements must be followed by all companies included in the consolidation. The balance sheet date of the individual financial statements to be consolidated should be the same as the balance sheet date of the consolidated financial statements. Individual financial statements with a balance sheet date within a period of 3 months before the balance date of the consolidated financial statements are accepted, however, if significant events with an impact on the true and fair view of the consolidated financial statements are properly considered in the consolidated financial statements or at least reported in the notes to the financial statements.

3.3.2 Companies to Be Included in Consolidated Financial Statements

According to the relevant provisions of the Commercial Code (§ 244 HGB and § 247 HGB) the following companies must be included in the consolidated financial statements of a parent company:

- All companies that are managed under the direction of the parent company and in which the parent company holds a participating interest of at least 20%
- All companies in which the parent company and/or any of its subsidiary companies holds the majority of the voting rights
- All companies in which the parent company and/or any of its subsidiary companies has the right to appoint or dismiss the majority of the members of the boards
- All companies in which the parent company and/or any of its subsidiary companies has the right to exercise a dominant influence
- All companies in which the parent company and/or any of its subsidiary companies has the right—based on a contractual agreement with other shareholders of the respective company—to decide how the voting rights of shareholders, insofar as these voting rights are necessary to achieve a majority of votes together with the votes of the parent company and/or any of its subsidiary companies, shall be exercised for the appointment or dismissal of the majority of the members of the boards.

Companies whose operations differ significantly from the operations of the parent company (e.g. industrial company as a subsidiary of a bank) must not be included in the consolidated financial statements, if the inclusion would defeat the requirement to provide a true and fair view.

Companies may be excluded from the consolidated financial statements if:

- There exist considerable and persisting restrictions, which infringe on the parent companies' rights in respect of the net assets or the management of the respective company

- The information necessary for the preparation of the consolidated financial statements cannot be provided in due time or or can be provided only at unreasonable cost, considering the size of the respective company

- They are immaterial for the true and fair view of the group; the immateriality must be considered in respect not only on an individual basis but also in respect of all companies excluded from the consolidated financial statements.

3.3.3 Capital Consolidation

Full Consolidation   For all group companies that are under control of the parent company and/or any of its subsidiaries, a full consolidation is required; that is, assets and liabilities as well as income and expenses of the subsidiary are included in full in the consolidated financial statements.

There are two basic methods defined in the Commercial Code for the inclusion of the subsidiaries' assets and liabilities in the consolidated financial statements:

- Book value method

- Current value method

By applying the book value method the acquisition costs of the investment are set off against the (proportional) net equity of the subsidiary. The arising difference may be negative or positive.

A positive difference is primarily allocated to individual assets if the current value of such assets is greater than book value (the revaluation is done proportionally only, if the investment is less than 100%). A remaining positive difference is then disclosed as goodwill. If the remaining difference is considered to be marketable goodwill, the amortization period is defined with the useful life of the goodwill; otherwise the goodwill is to be amortized over a period of 5 years at the maximum. Alternatively, the goodwill can also be set off against reserves immediately, a method that is applied to a high extent by Austrian companies.

A negative difference is to be disclosed separately on the liability side of the balance sheet, unless either a negative trend of earnings as expected at the purchase date has realized or it is definite that the negative difference represents realized profits.

Under the current value method, assets and liabilities are revalued. The revaluation is, however, limited to the extent that (proportional) net assets equal the acquisition costs of the investment. A remaining positive difference between the acquisition costs of the investment and the revalued (proportionate) net assets of the subsidiary as well as a negative difference between the acquisition costs of the investment and the (proportionate) net assets is treated in the same way as under the book value method.

The current value method is rarely applied in Austria.

Capital consolidation is to be performed on either of the following dates:

- Date of acquisition of investment (whereby it is acceptable to use the beginning or the end of the fiscal year in which the acquisition took place instead of the exact acquisition date)

- Date of first inclusion in the consolidated financial statements (this may also be the date that the parent company has set up consolidated financial statements for the first time)

- Date when the requirements for consolidation were met (e.g. in the case of a consecutive purchase of shares)

Significant differences can occur as a result of different dates used.

Because of the late introduction of consolidated accounts in Austria, the capital consolidation for the majority of subsidiaries acquired before January 1, 1994 (i.e. the beginning of the fiscal year for which consolidated financial statements had to be prepared the first time) will have been performed as of this date, regardless of the actual acquisition date.

Proportional Consolidation   Under the concept of proportional consolidation, assets and liabilities as well as income and expenses are included in the consolidated financial statements only in proportion to the (direct and indirect) shareholding of the parent company.

Proportional consolidation may be applied for joint undertakings, where the parent company and/or a subsidiary and any third party shareholders manage the joint venture together and none of the shareholders has a dominant influence. The basic framework is the same as for full consolidation (see above).

At-Equity Consolidation   Companies that are not under the control of the parent company and/or any of the subsidiary companies but where the parent company and/or a subsidiary has a shareholding of at least 20% and exerts a significant influence on the business and financial policy are to be consolidated at equity.

The basic framework is the same as for full consolidation (see above), with the exception that at-equity consolidation means a one-line consolidation. A resulting goodwill may however be disclosed separately.

Deferred Taxes   Deferred taxes resulting from consolidation bookings, which will reverse in the future, are to be recognized regardless of whether it is a deferred tax asset or a deferred tax liability.

This is contrary to the rulings for deferred taxes in the individual financial statements (see Section 3.2.7). The deferred tax balance disclosed in the consolidated financial statements thus may be a mixture of different accounting principles applied for deferred taxes. Proper analyses should be given in the notes under these circumstances.

3.3.5 Translation of Financial Statements in Foreign Currency

There are no rulings in the Commercial Code for the translation of financial statements denominated in foreign currencies. A generally accepted accounting principle has also not yet developed. In practice, the closing rate method (all assets and liabilities as well as all income and expense items are translated at the exchange rate ruling at the balance sheet date) and the adapted closing rate method (all assets and liabilities are translated at the year-end rate, the income statement is translated at the average exchange rate of the fiscal year) are broadly used.

The treatment of translation differences shows a great variety of methods: Partly those differences are directly set off against reserves, others include the differences in the profit and loss account. A different treatment of the exchange differences with respect to their source can also be observed. Detailed explanations should therefore be included in the notes in order to allow a detailed understanding of the effects of the foreign exchange translation policy applied.

4. Expected Future Developments

The globalization of the economy has also an impact on the further development of accounting regulations. International investors request one international standard for the presentation of financial information regardless the nationality of the individual companies. The EC Directives failed to achieve such a unification within Europe, as there were too many options for alternative treatments within these Directives. More and more multinational companies therefore start to set up their accounts in accordance with either International Accounting Standards or U.S. GAAP, which are the regulations most accepted by the international investors. There is now an increasing demand that these international accounting concepts are accepted at least for group accounts also within the national accounting framework. It is expected that in Austria the application of International Accounting Standards and/or U.S. GAAP will be accepted as an alternative framework, at least for companies listed on the Stock Exchange. Where these standards comply with local regulations, a voluntary application can already be observed (e.g. the preparation of a cash-flow statement that is not yet compulsory under the existing accounting regulations).

Tax considerations will remain an important factor affecting the individual accounts, as it is not expected that the authoritative principle will be abandoned. It is therefore very likely that—contrary to the above outlined scenario for the regulations for group accounts of listed companies—accounting regulations for individual accounts will not undergo significant changes in the near future.

**Konzernabschluß und Jahresabschluß
der Austria Mikro Systeme International AG**
    Konzernbilanz
    Konzern-Gewinn- und Verlustrechnung
    Konzern-Geldflußrechnung
    Bilanz
    Gewinn- und Verlustrechnung
    Geldflußrechnung
    Zusammengefaßter Konzernanhang und Anhang

Austria Mikro Systeme International AG
Consolidated Financial Statements and
Individual Financial Statements
Consolidated Balance Sheet
Consolidated Income Statement
Consolidated Cash Flow Statement
Balance Sheet
Income Statement
Cash Flow Statement
Combined Notes to the Consolidated and Individual Financial Statements

Konzernbilanz
der Austria Mikro Systeme International AG
zum 31.12.1997 (in TATS)

		Anhang Nr.	31.12.1997	31.12.1996
Aktiva				
A.I.	Immaterielle Vermögensgegenstände	(1)	57.264	76.781
A.II.	Sachanlagen	(1), (3)	1.509.271	1.593.371
A.III.	Finanzanlagen	(1), (4)	39.408	40.884
A.	**Anlagevermögen**		**1.605.943**	**1.711.036**
B.I.	Vorräte	(5)	240.684	214.425
B.II.	Forderungen und sonstige Vermögensgegenstände	(6)	422.476	351.324
B.III.	Wertpapiere und Anteile	(7)	137.183	133.259
B.IV.	Kassenbestand, Guthaben bei Kreditinstituten	(8)	778.443	933.306
B.	**Umlaufvermögen**		**1.578.786**	**1.632.314**
C.	**Rechnungsabgrenzungsposten**		**7.718**	**8.280**
			3.192.447	**3.351.630**
Passiva				
A.I.	Grundkapital	(9)	300.000	300.000
A.II.	Kapitalrücklagen	(10)	740.799	740.799
A.III.	Gewinnrücklagen	(11)	436.659	432.236
A.IV.	Bilanzgewinn	(12)	30.756	30.669
A.V.	Ausgleichsposten für Anteile anderer Gesellschafter	(13)	358.191	425.285
A.	**Eigenkapital**		**1.866.405**	**1.928.989**
B.	**Zuschüsse**	**(15)**	**105.994**	**121.101**
C.1.	Rückstellungen für Abfertigungen	(16)	44.305	40.187
C.2.	Steuerrückstellungen	(17)	34.730	39.051
C.3.	Sonstige Rückstellungen	(18)	199.105	207.195
C.	**Rückstellungen**		**278.140**	**286.433**
D.	Verbindlichkeiten	(19)	933.700	1.005.721
E.	**Rechnungsabgrenzungsposten**		**8.208**	**9.386**
			3.192.447	**3.351.630**
Haftungsverhältnisse		(20)	124.244	100.731

Austria Mikro Systeme International AG
Consolidated Balance Sheet
as of 31.12.1997 (in TATS)

		Note No.	31.12.1997	31.12.1996
Assets				
A.I.	Intangible assets	(1)	57.264	76.781
A.II.	Tangible assets	(1), (3)	1.509.271	1.593.371
A.III.	Financial assets	(1), (4)	39.408	40.884
A.	**Fixed assets**		**1.605.943**	**1.711.036**
B.I.	Inventories	(5)	240.684	214.425
B.II.	Accounts receivable and other current assets	(6)	422.476	351.324
B.III.	Marketable securities and investments	(7)	137.183	133.259
B.IV.	Cash-on-hand, deposits at banks	(8)	778.443	933.306
B.	**Current assets**		**1.578.786**	**1.632.314**
C.	**Prepaid expenses**		**7.718**	**8.280**
			3.192.447	**3.351.630**
Liabilities and equity				
A.I.	Capital stock	(9)	300.000	300.000
A.II.	Capital reserves	(10)	740.799	740.799
A.III.	Revenue reserves	(11)	436.659	432.236
A.IV.	Retained earnings	(12)	30.756	30.669
A.V.	Adjustment for minority interests	(13)	358.191	425.285
A.	**Equity**		**1.866.405**	**1.928.989**
B.	**Subsidies**	**(15)**	**105.994**	**121.101**
C.1.	Provisions for severance payments	(16)	44.305	40.187
C.2.	Tax provisions	(17)	34.730	39.051
C.3.	Other provisions	(18)	199.105	207.195
C.	**Provisions**		**278.140**	**286.433**
D.	Liabilities	(19)	933.700	1.005.721
E.	**Deferred income**		**8.208**	**9.386**
			3.192.447	**3.351.630**
Contingent liabilities		(20)	124.244	100.731

Konzern-Gewinn- und Verlustrechnung der Austria Mikro Systeme International AG für das Geschäftsjahr 1997 (in TATS)

		Anhang Nr.	1997	1996
1.	Umsatzerlöse	(21)	1.656.920	1.793.915
2.	Veränderung des Bestands an fertigen und unfertigen Erzeugnissen sowie an noch nicht abrechenbaren Leistungen		38.009	-111.041
3.	Sonstige betriebliche Erträge	(22)	188.198	254.936
4.	Aufwendungen für Material und sonstige bezogene Herstellungsleistungen	(23)	-601.131	-574.379
5.	Personalaufwand	(24)	-643.985	-718.028
6.	Abschreibungen auf im materielle Vermögensgegenstände und Sachanlagen	(25)	-330.934	-355.991
7.	Sonstige betriebliche Aufwendungen	(26)	-308.096	-364.533
8.	Betriebsergebnis		-1.019	-75.121
9.	Erträge aus anderen Wertpapieren und Ausleihungen des Finanzanlagevermögens		1.766	1.941
10.	Sonstige Zinsen und ähnliche Erträge		40.745	41.532
11.	Erträge aus dem Abgang von Finanzanlagen und Wertpapieren des Umlaufvermögens		2.488	438
12.	Abschreibungen von Wertpapieren des Umlaufvermögens		-274	—
13.	Zinsen und ähnliche Aufwendungen		-41.730	-69.392
14.	Finanzergebnis	(27)	2.995	-25.481
15	**Ergebnis der gewöhnlichen Geschäftstätigkeit**		**1.976**	**-100.602**
16.	Außerordentliche Erträge	(28)	—	3.727
17.	Außerordentliche Aufwendungen	(28)	—	-15.268
18.	**Außerordentliches Ergebnis**		**0**	**-11.541**
19.	Steuern vom Einkommen und vom Ertrag	(30)	-34.560	6.579
20.	Jahresfehlbetrag		-32.584	-105.564
21.	Anteile anderer Gesellschafter am Jahresfehlbetrag		67.094	157.548
22.	Jahresüberschuß nach Anteilen anderer Gesellschafter (Anteil Austria Mikro Systeme International AG)		34.510	51.984

Austria Mikro Systeme International AG
Consolidated Income Statement for the fiscal year 1997
(in TATS)

		Note No.	*1997*	*1996*
1.	Sales	(21)	1.656.920	1.793.915
2.	Changes in the stock of partly finished and finished products and services not yet billable		38.009	-111.041
3.	Other operating income	(22)	188.198	254.936
4.	Cost of material and other production related services received -574.379	(23)	-601.131	
5.	Personnel expenses	(24)	-643.985	-718.028
6.	Depreciation on intangible and tangible fixed assets	(25)	-330.934	-355.991
7.	Other operating expenses	(26)	-308.096	-364.533
8.	Operating result		-1.019	-75.121
9.	Income from other securities and loans disclosed as financial assets		1.766	1.941
10.	Other interest and similar income		40.745	41.532
11.	Income from the disposal of financial assets and of marketable securities included in current assets		2.488	438
12.	Depreciation of marketable securities included in current assets		-274	—
13.	Interest and similar expenses		-41.730	-69.392
14.	Financial result	(27)	2.995	-25.481
15	**Result from ordinary business activities**		**1.976**	**-100.602**
16.	Extraordinary income	(28)	—	3.727
17.	Extraordinary expenses	(28)	—	-15.268
18.	**Extraordinary result**		**0**	**-11.541**
19.	Taxes on income	(30)	-34.560	6.579
20.	Net loss		-32.584	-105.564
21.	Net loss attributable to minority interests		67.094	157.548
22.	Net income excluding minority interests (attributable to Austria Mikro Systeme International AG)		34.510	51.984

Konzern-Geldflußrechnung der Austria Mikro Systeme International AG für das Geschäftsjahr 1997 (in TATS)

	1997	*1996*
Ergebnis der gewöhnlichen Geschäftstätigkeit	1.976	-100.602
Abschreibungen auf Vermögensgegenstände des Investitionsbereichs	331.208	355.991
Ergebnis aus dem Abgangvon Vermögensgegenständen des Investitionsbereichs	-462	-699
Auflösung von Zuschüssen	-36.047	-30.840
Veränderung der Vorräte, der Forderungen aus Lieferungen und Leistungen sowie anderer Aktiva	-66.062	158.192
Veränderung von Rückstellungen	-6.083	-67.819
Veränderung der Verbindlichkeiten (soweit nicht der Finanzierungstätigkeit zuzurechnen)	288	-81.929
Netto-Geldfluß aus der gewöhnlichen Geschäftstätigkeit	**224.818**	**232.294**
Zahlungen für Ertragsteuern	-67.557	-7.939
Netto-Geldfluß aus laufender Geschäftstätigkeit	**157.261**	**224.355**
Einzahlungen aus Anlagenabgang(ohne Finanzanlagen)	2.120	1.954
Einzahlungen aus Finanzanlagenabgang und sonstigen Finanzinvestitionen	2.394	2.803
Auszahlungen für Anlagenzugang(ohne Finanzanlagen)	-228.975	-320.800
Auszahlungen für Finanzanlagenzugang und sonstige Finanzinvestitionen	-918	-60.280
Netto-Geldfluß aus Investitionstätigkeit	**-225.379**	**-376.323**
außerordentliche Aufwendungen aus der Kapitalerhöhung	0	-519
Auszahlungen aus der Bedienung des Eigenkapitals	-30.000	-36.753
Erhaltene Zuschüsse	20.940	66.075
Einzahlungen aus der Aufnahme von Finanzkrediten	22.090	206.633
Auszahlungen für die Tilgung von Finanzkrediten	-95.577	-49.112
Netto-Geldfluß aus Finanzierungstätigkeit	**-82.547**	**186.324**
Zahlungswirksame Veränderung des Finanzmittel bestandes	**-150.665**	**34.356**
Finanzmittelbestand am Beginn der Periode	1.066.565	1.032.329
wechselkursbedingte Wertänderungendes Finanzmittelbestandes	-274	-120
Finanzmittelbestand am Ende der Periode	**915.626**	(778.443)
(davon Flüssige Mittel laut Bilanz)	(137.183)	**1.066.565**
(davon Wertpapiere des Umlaufvermögens)	(933.306)	(133.259)

Austria Mikro Systeme International AG Consolidated Cash Flow Statement for the fiscal year 1997 (in TATS)

	1997	1996
Result from ordinary business activities	1.976	-100.602
Depreciation on assets relating to investing activities	331.208	355.991
Result from the disposal of assets relating to investing activities	-462	-699
Release of subsidies	-36.047	-30.840
Change in inventories, trade debtors and other assets	-66.062	158.192
Change in provisions	-6.083	-67.819
Change in liabilities (excluding those relating to financing activities)	288	-81.929
Net cash flow from ordinary business activities	**224.818**	**232.294**
Payments for taxes on income	-67.557	-7.939
Net cash flow from current ordinary business activities	**157.261**	**224.355**
Payments received from the disposal of fixed assets (excluding financial assets)	2.120	1.954
Payments received from the disposal of financial assets and other financial investments	2.394	2.803
Payments made for the acquisition of fixed assets (excluding financial assets)	-228.975	-320.800
Payments made for the acquisition of financial assets and other financial investments	-918	-60.280
Net-Cash flow from investing activities	**-225.379**	**-376.323**
Extraordinary expenses for the capital increase	0	-519
Payments made for the servicing of equity	-30.000	-36.753
Subsidies received	20.940	66.075
Payments received resulting from borrowings	22.090	206.633
Payments made for the repayment of loans	-95.577	-49.112
Net-cash flow from financing activities	**-82.547**	**186.324**
Cash effective changes in liquid funds	**-150.665**	**34.356**
Liquid funds - at the beginning of the year	1.066.565	1.032.329
Effect of changes in exchange rates on liquid funds	-274	-120
Liquid funds—at the end of the year	**915.626**	(778.443)
(thereof cash-on-hand and deposits at banks)	(137.183)	**1.066.565**
(thereof marketable securities included in current assets)	(933.306)	(133.259)

Bilanz der Austria Mikro Systeme International AG zum 31.12.1997

		Anhang Nr.	31.12.1997 in ATS	31.12.1996 in TATS
Aktiva				
A.I.	Immaterielle Vermögensgegenstände	(2)	28.909.415,00	12.324
A.II.	Sachanlagen	(2), (3)	774.360.369,91	790.078
A.III.	Finanzanlagen	(2), (4)	569.746.421,60	571.222
A.	**Anlagevermögen**		**1.373.016.206,51**	**1.373.624**
B.I.	Vorräte	(5)	157.667.199,23	132.006
B.II.	Forderungen und sonstige Vermögensgegenstände	(6)	339.229.301,01	272.280
B.III.	Wertpapiere und Anteile	(7)	137.182.865,53	133.259
B.IV.	Kassenbestand, Guthaben bei Kreditinstituten	(8)	564.922.114,58	874.992
B.	**Umlaufvermögen**		**1.199.001.480,35**	**1.412.537**
C.	**Rechnungsabgrenzungsposten**		**3.784.740,00**	**3.693**
			2.575.802.426,86	**2.789.854**
Passiva				
A.I.	Grundkapital	(9)	300.000.000,00	300.000
A.II.	Kapitalrücklagen	(10)	740.799.390,01	740.799
A.III.	Gewinnrücklagen	(11)	459.031.000,00	402.031
A.IV.	Bilanzgewinn		30.755.574,76	30.669
A.	**Eigenkapital**		**1.530.585.964,77**	**1.473.499**
B.	**Unversteuerte Rücklagen**	**(14)**	**131.884.109,00**	**113.926**
C.	**Zuschüsse**	**(15)**	**9.136.010,00**	**10.207**
D.1.	Rückstellungen für Abfertigungen	(16)	44.304.576,00	40.187
D.2.	Steuerrückstellungen	(17)	34.730.000,00	36.940
D.3.	Sonstige Rückstellungen	(18)	164.468.348,08	173.612
D.	**Rückstellungen**		**243.502.924,08**	**250.739**
E.	**Verbindlichkeiten**	(19)	**652.660.801,10**	**932.097**
F.	**Rechnungsabgrenzungsposten**		**8.032.617,91**	**9.386**
			2.575.802.426,86	**2.789.854**
Haftungsverhältnisse		(20)	1.466.122,00	1.474

Austria Mikro Systeme International AG Balance Sheet as of 31.12.1997

		Note No.	31.12.1997 in ATS	31.12.1996 in TATS
Assets				
A.I.	Intangible assets	(2)	28.909.415,00	12.324
A.II.	Tangible assets	(2), (3)	774.360.369,91	790.078
A.III.	Financial assets	(2), (4)	569.746.421,60	571.222
A.	**Fixed assets**		**1.373.016.206,51**	**1.373.624**
B.I.	Inventories	(5)	157.667.199,23	132.006
B.II.	Accounts receivable and other assets	(6)	339.229.301,01	272.280
B.III.	Marketable securities and investments	(7)	137.182.865,53	133.259
B.IV.	Cash-on-hand, deposits at banks	(8)	564.922.114,58	874.992
B.	**Current assets**		**1.199.001.480,35**	**1.412.537**
C.	**Prepaid expenses**		**3.784.740,00**	**3.693**
			2.575.802.426,86	**2.789.854**
Liabilities				
A.I.	Capital stock	(9)	300.000.000,00	300.000
A.II.	Capital reserves	(10)	740.799.390,01	740.799
A.III.	Revenue reserves	(11)	459.031.000,00	402.031
A.IV.	Retained earnings		30.755.574,76	30.669
A.	**Equity**		**1.530.585.964,77**	**1.473.499**
B.	**Untaxed reserves**	**(14)**	**131.884.109,00**	**113.926**
C.	**Subsidies**	**(15)**	**9.136.010,00**	**10.207**
D.1.	Provisions for severance payments	(16)	44.304.576,00	40.187
D.2.	Tax provisions	(17)	34.730.000,00	36.940
D.3.	Other provisions	(18)	164.468.348,08	173.612
D.	**Provisions**		**243.502.924,08**	**250.739**
E.	Liabilities	(19)	652.660.801,10	932.097
F.	**Deferred income**		**8.032.617,91**	**9.386**
			2.575.802.426,86	**2.789.854**
Contingent liabilities		(20)	1.466.122,00	1.474

Gewinn- und Verlustrechnung der Austria Mikro Systeme International AG für das Geschäftsjahr 1997

		Anhang Nr.	*31.12.1997 in ATS*	*31.12.1996 in TATS*
1.	Umsatzerlöse	(21)	1.229.461.686,75	1.275.474
2.	Veränderung des Bestands an fertigen und unfertigen Erzeugnissen sowie an noch nicht abrechenbaren Leistungen		30.677.239,00	-91.360
3.	Sonstige betriebliche Erträge	(22)	71.127.068,70	76.156
4.	Aufwendungen für Material und sonstige bezogene Herstellungsleistungen	(23)	-426.887.558,67	-336.378
5.	Personalaufwand	(24)	-403.980.849,50	-395.645
6.	Abschreibungen auf immaterielle Vermögensgegenstände und Sachanlagen	(25)	-165.151.895,30	-161.277
7.	Sonstige betriebliche Aufwendungen	(26)	-206.300.233,24	-210.981
8.	Betriebsergebnis		128.945.457,74	155.989
9.	Erträge aus anderen Wertpapieren und Ausleihungen des Finanzanlagevermögens		1.765.960,00	1.941
10.	sonstige Zinsen und ähnliche Erträge		33.129.911,98	34.490
11.	Erträge aus dem Abgang von Finanzanlagen und Wertpapieren des Umlaufvermögens		2.488.375,00	438
12.	Abschreibungen von Wertpapieren des Umlaufvermögens		-274.324,00	—
13.	Zinsen und ähnliche Aufwendungen		-26.359.369,11	-20.669
14.	Finanzergebnis	(27)	10.750.553,87	16.200
15.	**Ergebnis der gewöhnlichen Geschäftstätigkeit**		**139.696.011,61**	**172.190**
16.	Außerordentliche Aufwendungen	(28)	—	-64.477
17.	**Außerordentliches Ergebnis**		**0,00**	**-64.477**
18.	Steuern vom Einkommen und vom Ertrag	(30)	-34.651.185,00	—
19.	**Jahresüberschuß**		**105.044.826,61**	**107.712**
20.	Auflösung unversteuerter Rücklagen	(14)	26.544,00	42.265
21.	Zuweisung zu unversteuerten Rücklagen	(14)	-17.984.527,00	-10.635
22.	Zuweisung zu Gewinnrücklagen		-57.000.000,00	-109.000
23.	**Jahresgewinn**		**30.086.843,61**	**30.342**
24.	Gewinnvortrag aus dem Vorjahr		668.731,15	327
25.	**Bilanzgewinn**		**30.755.574,76**	**30.669**

Austria Mikro Systeme International AG Income Statement for the fiscal year 1997

		Note No.	1997 in ATS	1996 in TATS
1.	Sales	(21)	1.229.461.686,75	1.275.474
2.	Changes in the stock of finished and partly finished products and services not yet billable		30.677.239,00	-91.360
3.	Other operating income	(22)	71.127.068,70	76.156
4.	Cost of material and other production related services received 336.378	(23)	-426.887.558,67	-
5.	Personnel expenses	(24)	-403.980.849,50	-395.645
6.	Depreciation on intangible and tangible fixed assets	(25)	-165.151.895,30	-161.277
7.	Other operating expenses	(26)	-206.300.233,24	-210.981
8.	Operating result		128.945.457,74	155.989
9.	Income from other securities and loans disclosed as financial assets		1.765.960,00	1.941
10.	Other interest and similar income		33.129.911,98	34.490
11.	Income from the disposal of financial assets andof marketable securities included in current assets		2.488.375,00	438
12.	Depreciation of marketable securities included in current assets		-274.324,00	—
13.	Interest and similar expenses		-26.359.369,11	-20.669
14.	Financial result	(27)	10.750.553,87	16.200
15.	**Result from ordinary business activities**		**139.696.011,61**	**172.190**
16.	Extraordinary expenses	(28)	—	-64.477
17.	**Extraordinary result**		**0,00**	**-64.477**
18.	Taxes on income	(30)	-34.651.185,00	—
19.	**Net income**		**105.044.826,61**	**107.712**
20.	Release of untaxed reserves	(14)	26.544,00	42.265
21.	Allocation to untaxed reserves	(14)	-17.984.527,00	-10.635
22.	Allocation to revenue reserves		-57.000.000,00	-109.000
23.	**Earnings of the year**		**30.086.843,61**	**30.342**
24.	Earnings brought forward from the previous year		668.731,15	327
25.	**Retained earnings**		**30.755.574,76**	**30.669**

Geldflußrechnung der Austria Mikro Systeme International AG für das Geschäftsjahr 1997 (in TATS)

	1997	*1996*
Ergebnis der gewöhnlichen Geschäftstätigkeit	139.696	172.189
Abschreibungen auf Vermögensgegenstände des Investitionsbereichs	165.426	161.277
Ergebnis aus dem Abgangvon Vermögensgegenständen des Investitionsbereichs	-462	—
Auflösung von Zuschüssen	-1.071	-1.071
Veränderung der Vorräte, der Forderungen aus Lieferungen und Leistungen sowie anderer Aktiva	-61.915	87.797
Veränderung von Rückstellungen	-5.026	-6.805
Veränderung der Verbindlichkeiten (soweit nicht der Finanzierungstätigkeit zuzuordnen)	37.454	-81.247
Netto-Geldfluß aus der gewöhnlichen Geschäftstätigkeit	**274.102**	**332.140**
Zahlungen für Ertragsteuern	-67.648	-7.939
Netto-Geldfluß aus laufender Geschäftstätigkeit	**206.454**	**324.201**
Einzahlungen aus Anlagenabgang(ohne Finanzanlagen)	1.606	—
Einzahlungen aus Finanzanlagenabgang und sonstigen Finanzinvestitionen	2.394	2.803
Auszahlungen für Anlagenzugang(ohne Finanzanlagen)	-167.164	-114.048
Auszahlungen für Finanzanlagenzugang und sonstige Finanzinvestitionen	-285.323	-28.253
Netto-Geldfluß aus Investitionstätigkeit	**-448.487**	**-139.498**
außerordentliche Aufwendungen aus der Kapitalerhöhung		-519
Auszahlungen aus der Bedienung des Eigenkapitals	-30.000	-36.000
Einzahlungen aus der Aufnahme von Finanzkrediten	22.090	188.338
Auszahlungen für die Tilgung von Finanzkrediten	-55.929	-49.112
Netto-Geldfluß aus Finanzierungstätigkeit	**-63.839**	**102.707**
Zahlungswirksame Veränderung des Finanzmittelbestandes	**-305.872**	**287.410**
Finanzmittelbestand am Beginn der Periode	1.008.251	720.841
wechselkursbedingte Wertänderungen des Finanzmittelbestandes	-274	—
Finanzmittelbestand am Ende der Periode	**702.105**	(564.922)
(davon Flüssige Mittel laut Bilanz)	(138.183)	**1.008.251**
(davon Wertpapiere des Umlaufvermögens)	(874.992)	(133.259)

Austria Mikro Systeme International AG Cash Flow Statement for the fiscal year 1997 (in TATS)

	1997	1996
Result from ordinary business activities	139.696	172.189
Depreciation on assets relating to investing activities	165.426	161.277
Result from the disposal of assets relating to investing activities	-462	—
Release of subsidies	-1.071	-1.071
Change in inventories, trade debtors and other assets	-61.915	87.797
Change in provisions	-5.026	-6.805
Change in liabilities (excluded those relating to financing activities)	37.454	-81.247
Net-cash flow from ordinary business activities	**274.102**	**332.140**
Payment for taxes on income	-67.648	-7.939
Net-cash flow from current business activities	**206.454**	**324.201**
Payments received from the disposal of fixed assets(excluding financial assets)	1.606	—
Payments received from the disposal of financial assets and other financial investments	2.394	2.803
Payments made for the acquisition of fixed assets(excluding financial assets)	-167.164	-114.048
Payments made for the acquisition of fixed assets and other financial investments	-285.323	-28.253
Net-cash flow from investing activities	**-448.487**	**-139.498**
Extraordinary expenses for the capital increase		-519
Payments made for the servicing of equity	-30.000	-36.000
Payments received resulting from borrowings	22.090	188.338
Payments made for the repayment of loans	-55.929	-49.112
Net-cash flow from financing activities	**-63.839**	**102.707**
Cash effective changes in liquid funds	**-305.872**	**287.410**
Liquid funds - at the beginning of the year	1.008.251	720.841
Effect of changes in exchange rates on liquid funds	-274	—
Liqudid funds - at the end of the year	**702.105**	(564.922)
(thereof cash-on-hand and deposits at banks)	(138.183)	**1.008.251**
(thereof marketable securities included in current assets)	(874.992)	(133.259)

Combined Notes to the Consolidated and Individual Financial Statements for the fiscal year 1997

General information

Basic Principles   The consolidated financial statements and the individual financial statements of Austria Mikro Systeme International AG as of 31.12.1997 are prepared according to the provisions of the Austrian Commercial Code (HGB). The new regulations introduced by the EU-Adaptation Law to the Commercial Code (EU-GesRÄG) were taken into account for the first time in 1997. The prior year figures were adjusted accordingly. In the following the notes to the financial statements are combined. In case an information refers to one of the two financial statements only, this is specifically indicated. In order to improve clarity, individual balance sheet and income statement items have been summarized. They are disclosed in detail in the notes. The income statements have been prepared in accordance with the „total cost" disclosure method. The cash flow statements have been established in accordance with the relevant expert opinion set up by the Austrian Chamber of Certified Public Accountants. In accordance with international practice the cash flows are classified therein into business-, investing- and financing activities. Liquid funds comprise cash-on-hand and deposits at banks as well as marketable securities included in current assets.

Consolidation

Consolidated companies   As in the prior year the consolidated financial statements comprise the parent company Austria Mikro Systeme International AG (herein referred to as "the Company") and the subsidiary company Thesys Gesellschaft für Mikroelektronik mbH, Erfurt, Germany (Thesys). 10 other subsidiaries were not included in the consolidated financial statements because they are in total not material in terms of providing a true and fair view of the assets and the liabilities, financial position and earnings situation of the Group. They render exclusively services to those group companies which are included in the consolidated financial statements and they do not effect external sales. The investments in these subsidiaries are accounted for at acquisition cost or at the lower book value and are disclosed as investments in affiliated companies. The investment held in South African Micro-Electronic Systems (Pty.) Ltd., Pretoria, South Africa (SAMES) was reduced from 51 % to 19 % in 1996. Therefore SAMES was no longer regarded a subsidiary and a deconsolidation was performed with effect of 30.9.1996. Hence, the prior year figures stated in the consolidated income statement also include those revenues and expenses of SAMES that incurred in the first nine months of the 1996 business year, so that the 1997 figures cannot be compared with those of the previous year.

Key figures of SAMES for the first 9 months of 1996
Sales   123.366
   (thereof external sales: MATS 116,1)
Operating result   -56.353
Result on ordinary activities   -77.637

Consolidation principles The financial statements of the companies included in the group financial statements were set up as at the balance sheet date of the consolidated financial statements and the same accounting and valuation policies were applied. Capital consolidation is carried out using the book value method. Thereby the acquisition costs for the investment in Thesys acquired on 18.10.1995 are set-off with the proportional capital of the subsidiary as of 31.10.1995. The negative difference resulting from this capital consolidation was disclosed in the balance sheet under other provisions in accordance with it s accounting implication. The respective provision was released in 1996, the revenue resulting thereof was allocated to other operating income. Inter-company accounts receivable and liabilities are eliminated in course of the consolidation. Sales and other operating income resulting from group-internal activities are offset against the corresponding expenses. Sales and services within the group are effected at market prices. Pursuant to their immaterial influence the elimination of profits resulting from inter-company transactions could be omitted. Tax deferrals were not necessary. The part of the equity and the net income of Thesys allotting to third parties are disclosed as separate items in the balance sheet and the income statement respectively.

Foreign currency translation

Accounts receivable and liabilities in foreign currencies Accounts receivable in foreign currencies are translated at the buying rate, liabilities are translated at the selling rate prevailing at the day they arise. If the translation at the exchange rate ruling at the balance sheet date results in a lower amount for accounts receivable, respectively a higher amount for liabilities, a provision is made for these unrealized losses.

Individual financial statements in foreign currencies All items of the financial statements of Thesys were - in consideration of the stable currency relation - translated at the average exchange rate prevailing in the respective year (1997: 100 DEM = 703.60 ATS; 1996: 100 DEM = 703.60 ATS).

Accounting and valuation principles

The accounting and valuation principles explained in the following have not been changed compared to the previous year. They apply - If not otherwise stated - both for the consolidated and the individual financial statements.

Intangible assets Acquired intangible assets are valued at acquisition cost and are depreciated on a straight-line basis over the respective asset life. The depreciable asset life is 4 to 10 years for the Company and 3 to 10 years for the Group. Self-developed intangible assets are not capitalised.

Tangible assets Tangible assets are valued at their acquisition costs. Tangible assets subject to wear an tear are depreciated on a straight-line basis in accordance with the assets´ normal economic life. For additions in the first half of the year a full annual depreciation is charged and for additions in the second half of the year half of the annual depreciation is charged. Low value assets are fully written off in the year of acquisition and disclosed as addition and disposal in the movement schedule of fixed assets.

Depreciable life of tangible fixed assets	
Buildings	30 years
Technical equipment and machinery	
—Plant facilities	10 years
—Other technical equipment and machinery	5 to 8 years
Other equipment, factory and office equipment	4 to 8 years

An impairment of the value of tangible assets, which exceeds the reduction in value considered by scheduled depreciation did not occur. Therefore an unscheduled deprecation was not performed.

Financial assets   Loans are valued at their nominal amounts, investments in affiliated companies and other financial assets are valued at their acquisition cost. Lower values at the balance sheet date are applied if the decline in value is predicted to be of a permanent nature. By making use of the respective option, potential appreciations were not performed.

Inventory   Raw materials and supplies as well as merchandise are valued at acquisition cost or at a lower market price. Unfinished and finished products as well as work in progress (unbilled services) are valued at production cost, which beside direct manufacturing cost and direct material cost also include proportional manufacturing and material overhead cost. Administration and selling cost as well as interest expenses are not capitalised. Production costs are calculated based on an average plant utilization, idle costs are eliminated. Sufficient allowances are made for inventory risks relating to slow-moving, obsolete or otherwise unsaleable items. In order to provide for contingent losses resulting from contractual obligations adequate write-offs are performed to the extent necessary.

Accounts receivable   Accounts receivable and other assets are valued at their nominal value. For identifiable specific risks write-offs are made. For the general bad debt risk is considered by a general bad debt allowance amounting to 1 % of all trade accounts receivable not provided for individually.

Marketable securities   Marketable securities included in current assets are valued at their acquisition cost or the lower stock exchange quotation By making use of the respective option, potential appreciations were not performed

Deferred taxes   Deferred tax assets referring to the individual financial statements of the companies included in the consolidation are not recognized.

Provisions   There were no commitments made for pension payments in the whole Group. Pension provisions are therefore not necessary. The provisions for severance payments are based on an actuarial computation, applying the mortality table by ETTL-PAGLER and using the following calculation parameter.

Calculation parameter for provisions for severance payments

Interest rate used	6%
Pension age	
—women	55 years
—men	60 years
Fluctuation factor	0,97

Liabilities the amount of which is uncertain, recognizable risks and contingent losses resulting from contractual obligations are considered by provisions to the amount necessary in accordance with reasonable commercial judgement.

Accounts payable   Accounts payable are stated at the value at which they are expected to be repaid.

Explanatory notes to the balance sheets

(1) Movements of fixed assets of the Group in 1997

in TATS	Gross acquisition and production costs				
	Balance 01.01.1997	*Additions*	*Reclassifi- cations*	*Disposals*	*Balance 31.12.1997*
Industrial property rights and similar rights and benefits as well as licences thereof	284.941	30.164	1.344	-3.012	313.437
Payments on account	141	3.061	345	—	3.547
Intangible assets	285.082	33.225	1.689	-3.012	316.984
Land and buildings	737.895	3.148	-7.460	-155	733.428
Technical equipment and machinery	2.138.507	154.802	36.725	-48.786	2.281.248
Other equipment, factory and office equipment	249.682	24.624	70	-8.555	265.821
Payments on account and construction in progress	43.443	13.176	-31.024	-190	25.405
Tangible assets	3.169.527	195.750	-1.689	-57.686	3.305.902
Investments in affiliated companies	2.254	1	—	—	2.255
Loans to affiliated companies	7.562	13.734	—	-2.394	18.902
Investments	2.958	0	—	—	2.958
Loans to associated companies	56.015	0	—	-13.734	42.281
Marketable securities	19.074	917	—	—	19.991
Financial assets	87.863	14.652	—	-16.128	86.387
Fixed assets	3.542.472	243.627	0	-76.826	3.709.273

in TATS	Depreciations				Net book value	
	Balance 01.01.1997	*Additions*	*Disposals*	*Balance 31.12.1997*	*Balance 31.12.1997*	*Balance 31.12.1996*
Industrial property rights and similar rights and benefits as well as licences thereof	208.301	54.431	-3.012	259.720	53.717	76.640
Payments on account	0	—	—	—	3.547	141

Intangible assets	208.301	54.431	-3.012	259.720	57.264	76.781
Land and buildings	169.300	23.290	—	192.590	540.838	568.595
Technical equipment and machinery	1.222.663	224.522	-47.668	1.399.517	881.731	915.844
Other equipment, factory and office equipment	184.193	28.691	-8.360	204.524	61.297	65.489
Payments on account and construction in progress	0	—	—	—	25.405	43.443
Tangible assets	1.576.156	276.503	-56.028	1.796.632	1.509.271	1.593.371
Investments in affiliated companies	0	—	—	0	2.255	2.254
Loans to affiliated companies	0	—	—	0	18.902	7.562
Investments	2.958	—	—	2.958	0	0
Loans to associated companies	42.281	—	—	42.281	0	13.734
Marketable securities	1.740	—	—	1.740	18.251	17.334
Financial assets	46.979	0	0	46.979	39.408	40.884
Fixed assets	1.831.436	330.934	-59.040	2.103.330	1.605.943	1.711.036

(2) Movements of fixed assets of the Company in 1997

in TATS	Gross acquisition and production costs				
	Balance 01.01.1997	*Additions*	*Reclassifi-cations*	*Disposals*	*Balance 31.12.1997*
Industrial property rights and similar rights and benefits as well as licences thereof	45.675	27.653	—	-3.012	70.316
Intangible assets	45.675	27.653	0	-3.012	70.316
Land and buildings	320.970	390	-8.635	—	312.725
Technical equipment and machinery	1.408.156	113.725	10.565	-42.842	1.489.604
Other equipment, factory and office					

equipment	189.440	17.329	—	-7.134	199.635
Payments on account and construction in progress	14.159	8.067	-1.930	—	20.296
Tangible assets	1.932.725	139.511	0	-49.976	2.022.260
Investments in affiliated companies	532.592	1	—	—	532.593
Loans to affiliated companies	7.562	13.734	—	-2.394	18.902
Investments	2.958	—	—	—	2.958
Loans to associated companies	56.015	0	—	-13.734	42.281
Marketable securities	19.074	917	—	—	19.991
Financial assets	618.201	14.652	0	-16.128	616.725
Fixed assets	2.596.601	181.816	0	-69.116	2.709.301

in TATS		*Depreciations*			*Net book value*	
	Balance 01.01.1997	Additions	Disposals	Balance 31.12.1997	Balance 31.12.1997	Balance 31.12.1996
Industrial property rights and similar rights and benefits as well as licences thereof	33.351	11.068	-3.012	41.407	28.909	12.324
Intangible assets	33.351	11.068	-3.012	41.407	28.909	12.324
Land and buildings	122.215	9.232	—	131.447	181.278	198.755
Technical equipment and machinery	867.767	127.700	-41.717	953.750	535.854	540.389
Other equipment, factory and office equipment	152.665	17.152	-7.115	162.702	36.933	36.775
Payments on account and construction in progress	0	—	—	0	20.296	14.159
Tangible assets	1.142.647	154.084	-48.832	1.247.899	774.361	790.078
Investments in affiliated companies	0	—	—	0	532.593	532.592
Loans to affiliated companies	0	—	—	0	18.902	7.562
Investments	2.958	—	—	2.958	0	0
Loans to associated						

companies	42.281	—	—	42.281	0	13.734
Marketable securities	1.740	—	—	1.740	18.251	17.334
Financial assets	46.979	0	0	46.979	569.746	571.222
Fixed assets	1.222.977	165.152	-51.844	1.336.285	1.373.016	1.373.624

(3) Tangible assets

in TATS	Group		Company	
	1997	*1996*	*1997*	*1996*
Real estate value of built-on land and vacant land	95.539	95.378	25.686	25.686

(4) Financial assets

The following Loan amounts are repayable in the respective following year:

in TATS	Group		Company	
	1997	*1996*	*1997*	*1996*
Loans to affiliated companies	2.577	2.394	2.577	2.394
Loans to associated companies	—	—	—	—
	2.577	2.394	2.577	2.394

Loans to affiliated companies comprise loans to subsidiaries not included in the consolidation.

Appreciations to marketable securities not performed amount in the Group and in the Company to TATS 578 (1996: TATS 781). No appreciations were possible for other items included in financial assets.

(5) Inventories in TATS

in TATS	Group		Company	
	1997	*1996*	*1997*	*1996*
Raw materials and supplies	59.882	68.025	24.505	27.730
Partly finished products	133.849	89.751	101.350	64.921
Finished products	22.106	25.606	9.596	13.040
Work in progress (unbilled services)	17.840	22.247	15.209	17.519
Payments on account	7.007	8.796	7.007	8.796
	240.684	214.425	157.667	132.006

Work in progress (unbilled services) refers to engineering projects for customers which have not been billed at the balance sheet date. The allowance for contingent losses directly set-off against the gross amount of work in progress amounts to TATS 30.134 (1996: TATS 33.160) for the Group and to TATS 28.681 (1996: TATS 33.160) for the Company.

(6) Accounts receivable

in TATS

	due within		*Total*	
	one year	*more than one year*	*1997*	*1996*
Accounts receivable trade	215.515		215.515	188.271
Accounts receivable to affiliated companies	42.361	(360)	(—)	42.361
(thereof accounts receivable trade)	(390)	37.342	(747)	
Other accounts receivable and other assets	164.600	—	164.600	125.711
	422.476	0	422.476	351.324

Group

in TATS

	due within		*Total*	
	one year	*more than one year*	*1997*	*1996*
Accounts receivable trade	159.944	—	159.944	143.867
Accounts receivable to affiliated companies	43.358	(1.387)	—	(—)
(thereoff from accounts receivable trade)	43.358	(1.387)	37.658	(1.063)
Other accounts receivable and other assets	135.927	—	135.927	90.755
	339.229	0	339.229	272.280

Company

The general bad debt provisions for receivables amount to TATS 1.798 (1996: TATS 1.734) for the Group and TATS 1.467 (1996: TATS 1.403) for the Company. They refer exclusively to accounts receivable trade. In the prior year all accounts receivable were due within one year.

The other accounts receivable and assets consist of the following:

in TATS	Group		Company	
	1997	*1996*	*1997*	*1996*
Loans	72.572	69.566	72.572	69.566
Accounts receivable from tax authorities	57.942	22.256	51.399	8.768
Grants receivable and investment allowances	18.173	11.253	7.105	1.965
other accounts receivable and assets	14.912	23.086	4.851	10.456
	164.600	125.711	135.927	90.755

They include assessed research support grants (TATS 18.173 in the Group resp. TATS 7.105 in the Company) as well as interest on securities (TATS 5.159 in the Group and TATS 5.159 in the Company), which do not become due for payment until after the balance sheet date.

(7) Marketable securities

The marketable securities mainly include fixed-interest bonds quoted at the stock exchange and investment fund certificates. Appreciations to marketable securities not performed amount to TATS 912 (1996: TATS 3.091) in the Group and in the Company.

(8) Liquid funds

Liquid funds consist of cash-on-hand and deposits at banks.

(9) Capital stock

The capital stock disclosed in both balance sheets equals to the share capital of Austria Mikro Systeme International AG and consists unchanged of 3.000.000 ordinary shares made out to the bearer each with a nominal value of ATS 100. A resolution of the founding shareholders passed on October 8, 1992 empowered the executive board of directors to raise the capital stock of the company by a nominal amount of ATS 125.000.000 by issuing new ordinary shares against cash payment or non-cash capital contribution, each with a nominal value of ATS 100 until June 30, 1997. Thus preference shares without voting rights could also be issued. The executive board of directors could establish the amount and conditions at which shares were issued in agreement with the supervisory board. This authorization was partly used in 1995 and a capital increase amounting to ATS 50.000 was concluded and executed. No further use was made of this authorizations.

(10) Capital reserves

in TATS	Group		Company	
	1997	*1996*	*1997*	*1996*
appropriated capital reserve	720.000	720.000	720.000	720.000
non-appropriated capital reserve	20.799	20.799	20.799	20.799
	740.799	740.799	740.799	740.799

(11) Revenue reserves

in TATS	Group		Company	
	1997	*1996*	*1997*	*1996*
Legal reserve	13.031	13.031	13.031	13.031
Other revenue reserves	423.628	419.205	446.000	389.000
	436.659	432.236	459.031	402.031

The untaxed reserves in the amount of TATS 131.884 (1996: TATS 113.926) and separately disclosed in the individual financial statements are disclosed under other revenue reserves in the Group's balance sheet according to § 253 (3) Austrian Commercial Code (HGB). Due to the nature of the parent company´s untaxed reserves and due to the tax situation of the subsidiary, a deduction of deferred taxes was not necessary.

The movement of the Group's revenue reserves was as follows:

in TATS	Group	
	1997	*1996*
Balance 1.1.	432.236	421.750
Earnings carried forward from the previous year	669	326
Net income excluding minority interests	34.510	51.984
Foreign currency translation differences	—	-10.466
Offsetting of goodwill	—	-689
	467.415	462.905
thereof disclosed under retained earnings	-30.756	-30.669
Balance 31.12.	436.659	432.236

The offsetting of goodwill in 1996 results from the acquisition of additional shares of Thesys Advanced Electronics GmbH, which occurred immediately before this company was merged with Thesys.

(12) Retained earnings

The retained earnings of the Group equal to the retained earnings of the Company.

(13) Adjustment for minority interests

The adjustment for minority interests corresponds to the part of the equity of Thesys not belonging to Austria Mikro Systeme International AG.

(14)   Untaxed reserves

The movement of untaxed reserves disclosed in the balance sheet of the Company was as follows:

in TATS		*Company*					
						1997	*1996*
		Investment allowance				*total*	*total*
	1994	*1995*	*1996*	*1997*			
Balance 1.1.	64.503	38.788	10.635	—		113.926	145.556
Additions	—	—	—	17.985		17.985	10.635
Release	27	—	—	—		27	42.265
Balance 31.12.	64.476	38.788	10.635	17.985		131.884	113.926

The effects of the movement of untaxed reserves with regard to taxes on income is explained in note (30).

(15) Subsidies

The subsidies result from a property development contribution as well as investment grants. They are released over the useful life of the respective assets. The resulting income is included in other operating income.

(16) Provisions for severance payments

in TATS	*Group*		*Company*	
	1997	*1996*	*1997*	*1996*
Balance 1.1.	40.187	34.655	40.187	34.655
Increase	5.048	5.532	5.048	5.532
Release	930	—	930	—
Balance 31.12.	44.305	40.187	44.305	40.187

The provision for severance payments for the Company calculated in accordance with the provisions of § 14 of the Austrian Income Tax Act (EStG) amount to TATS 41.471 (1996: TATS 37.448). These amounts are adequately funded by marketable securities. Total expenses for severance payments are explained in note (24).

(17) Provisions for taxes

The provisions for taxes represent taxes on income for 1997.

(18) Other provisions

in TATS	Group		Company	
	1997	**1996**	**1997**	**1996**
Risks	61.213	79.901	55.649	65.449
Contingent losses from contractual obligations	57.262	49.082	44.998	49.082
Outstanding charges	56.970	58.704	41.976	41.044
Personnel expenses	23.127	(4.875)	(18.252)	18.998
(thereof jubilee payments)	(4.239)	(14.759)	21.312	(4.256)
(thereof not consumed holidays)	(17.056)	17.527	(3.641)	(13.886)
Other provisions	533	510	533	510
	199.105	207.195	164.468	173.612

Provisions for risks include a possible claim of a guarantee given to a bank on behalf of SAMES. The provisions for contingent losses resulting from contractual obligations primarily relate to customer specific design services without proper financial refund. The provisions for outstanding charges for goods and services include outstanding suppliers' invoices and other expenditures not yet billed relating to the business year. Other provisions amounting to TATS 4.875 (1996: TATS 4.239) in the Group and TATS 4.256 (1996: TATS 3.641) in the Company are of a long-term nature.

(19) Liabilities:

in TATS	Group				
	due in			*total*	
	Less than one year	*more than one year and less than five years*	*more than five years*	*1997*	*1996*
Bank borrowings	223.813	(39.648)	377.303	(153.554)	85.252
(thereof secured by mortgages)	(31.134)	686.368	(224.336)	754.495	(263.984)
On-account payments received from customers	4.310	—	—	4.310	29.445

Accounts payable - trade	100.678	—	—	100.678	84.606
Accounts payable to affiliated companies	14.309	—	—	14.309	11.866
(thereof accounts payable trade)	(14.309)	(—)	(—)	(14.309)	(11.866)
Accounts payable to associated companies	5.952	—	—	5.952	—
(thereof accounts payable trade)	(5.952)	(—)	(—)	(5.952)	(—)
Other accounts payable	35.708	86.375		122.083	125.309
(thereof taxes)	(8.416)	(—)	(—)	(8.416)	(3.499)
(thereof social security contributions)	(13.799)	(—)	(—)	(13.799)	(12.729)
(thereof loans from the research development fund)	(2.060)	(86.375)	(—)	(88.435)	(93.795)
	384.770	**463.678**	**85.252**	**933.700**	**1.005.721**

Prior year maturities:

In the prior year bank borrowings due in less than one year amounted to TATS 258.164, due in 2-5 years to TATS 344.723 and due in more than 5 years to TATS 151.608.

The prior year amount of the research development fund loan included in other accounts payable (TATS 93.795) consists of a loan repayable in less than one year in the amount of TATS 27.450 and a loan due in 2-5 years in the amount of TATS 66.345.

The remaining liabilities in prior year were due in less than one year.

in TATS		Company			
		due in		*total*	
	Less than one year	*more than one year and less than five years*	*more than five years*	*1997*	*1996*
Bank borrowings	184.165	223.749	54.118	462.032	490.511
(thereof secured by mortgages)	(—)	(—)	(—)	(—)	(—)
On-account payments received from customers	4.310	—	—	4.310	3.039

Accounts payable - trade	55.226	—	—	55.226	31.590
Accounts payable to affiliated companies	21.329	—	—	21.329	297.617
(thereof accounts payable trade)	(21.329)	(—)	(—)	(21.329)	(13.212)
Accounts payable to associated companies	5.952	—	—	5.952	—
(thereof accounts payable trade)	(5.952)	(—)	(—)	(5.952)	(—)
Other accounts payable	17.437	86.375		!03.812	109.340
(thereof taxes)	(733)	(—)	(—)	(733)	(637)
(thereof social security contributions)	(8.037)	(—)	(—)	(8.037)	(7.199)
(thereof loans from the research development fund)	(2.060)	(86.375)	(—)	(88.435)	(93.795)
	288.419	310.124	54.118	652.661	932.097

Prior year maturities:

In the prior year bank borrowings due in less than one year amounted to TATS 183.476, due in 2-5 years TATS 211.166, and due in more than 5 years TATS 95.869.

The prior year amount of the research development fund loan included in other accounts payable due in less than one year amounts to TATS 27.450 and the amount due in 2-5 years was TATS 66.345.

The remaining liabilities in prior year were due in less than one year.

Bank borrowings include a revolving export financing loan (TATS 155.000), which due to its three-month notice period is disclosed under short-term accounts payable. The other accounts payable include social security contributions and other payroll related expenses (TATS 7.504 for the Group and TATS 4.584 for the Company) as well as net wages (TATS 5.437 for the Group and TATS 5.437 for AMS AG), as expenses which become due only after the balance sheet date.

(20) Contingent liabilities

in TATS	Group		Company	
	1997	*1996*	*1997*	*1996*
Guarantees	1.451	1.413	1.451	1.413
Bills of exchange	15	61	15	61

Investment supports and investment grants	122.778	99.257	—	—
	124.244	100.731	1.466	1.474

The guarantees (for the Group as well as the Company) represent a guarantee given on behalf of a German subsidiary to cover possible bank borrowings (TATS 706) and a compliance bond given on behalf of a customer (TATS 745). The contingent liabilities from investment supports and grants refer to supports and grants which were received in the years 1995 to 1997 and which have to be repaid if the retention period of three years is not met. This repayment risk is considered to be low.

Other financial commitments

Commitments resulting from the use of tangible assets not disclosed in the balance sheet

in TATS	Group		Company	
	1997	1996	1997	1996
Due in the following year	8.417	7.138	1.824	380
Due after one up to five years	3.219	26.663	1.750	—
Due within one to five years	11.636	33.801	3.574	380

The commitments result from leasing contracts.

Purchase order commitments

The purchase order commitments is of an usual extent.

Notes to the income statements

(21) Sales

Break-down according to product groups

in TATS	Group		Company	
	1997	*1996*	*1997*	*1996*
Production	1.373.780	1.513.629	1.069.145	1.122.617
Engineering	224.785	188.198	148.142	134.530
Other	61.951	95.192	14.387	21.226
Gross sales	1.660.516	1.797.019	1.231.674	1.278.373
Sales deductions	-3.596	-3.104	-2.212	-2.899
Net sales	1.656.920	1.793.915	1.229.462	1.275.474

Break-down according to market segments

in TATS	Group		Company	
	1997	*1996*	*1997*	*1996*
Communication	598.053	693.514	481.579	610.630
Industry	469.757	386.080	271.200	244.206
Automobile industry	268.254	230.781	238.575	205.825
Other	324.452	486.644	240.320	217.712
Gross sales	1.660.516	1.797.019	1.231.674	1.278.373
Sales deductions	-3.596	-3.104	-2.212	-2.899
Net sales	1.656.920	1.793.915	1.229.462	1.275.474

Break-down according to geographical areas

in TATS	Group		Company	
	1997	*1996*	*1997*	*1996*
Austria	87.433	68.368	81.607	65.097
Other EU-countries	964.038	961.111	713.250	755.065
Other European countries	167.266	163.003	161.105	150.054
Europe	1.218.737	1.192.482	955.962	970.216
Non-European countries	441.779	604.537	275.712	308.157
Gross sales	1.660.516	1.797.019	1.231.674	1.278.373

Sales deductions	-3.596	-3.104	-2.212	-2.899
Net sales	1.656.920	1.793.915	1.229.462	1.275.474

(22) Other operating income

in TATS	Group		Company	
	1997	1996	1997	1996
Income from the disposal of fixed assets excluding financial assets	462	699	462	(—)
Release of provisions	49.588	(51.428)	32.399	34.921
(thereof release of negative goodwill)		90.388	(—)	(—)
Supports and grants	63.385	67.283	22.091	25.370
Release of subsidies	36.047	30.840	1.071	1.071
Other operating income	38.716	65.726	15.104	14.794
	188.198	254.936	71.127	76.156

Other operating income mainly includes the release of allowances, gains from foreign exchange transactions and expenses recharged.

(23) Cost of material and other production related services received

in TATS	Group		Company	
	1997	1996	1997	1996
Cost of material	305.764	325.847	221.128	196.572
(thereof from affiliated companies)	(—)	(—)	(1.405)	(116)
Cost of services received	295.367	248.532	205.760	139.806
(thereof from affiliated companies)	(20.534)	(26.156)	(30.930)	(27.558)
	601.131	574.379	426.888	336.378

Cost of services received mainly include sub-contracting charges for the wafer-production and assembly as well as engineering services and energy consumed. Cost for engineering services are disclosed under this item for the first time. In previous years they were included under other operating expenses. Prior year figures were adjusted accordingly.

(24) Personnel expenses/employees

in TATS	Group		Company	
	1997	1996	1997	1996
Wages	120.864	132.062	89.147	90.283
Salaries	384.983	426.126	220.362	212.586
Expenses for severance payments	11.626	23.351	5.484	6.253

(thereof increase in provision for severance payments)	(4.117)	(5.532)	(4.117)	(5.532)
(thereof actual payments made)	(7.509)	(17.819)	(1.367)	(721)
Expenses for old age pension	—	2.644	—	—
Expenses for legally required social security contributions and salary related levies and compulsory contributions	124.501	124.316	87.168	84.677
Other social expenses	2.011	9.529	1.821	1.846
	330.934	718.028	403.981	395.645

The increase in the provision for severance payments refers with an amount of to TATS - 930 (1996: TATS 963) for the Group and the Company to the executive board of directors and other members of the company's management; no severance payments were made to the executive board of directors and other members of the company's management.

in TATS	Group		Company	
	1997	*1996*	*1997*	*1996*
Workers	399	451	275	289
(thereof working abroad)	(124)	(162)	(—)	(—)
Salaried	682	892	387	384
(thereof working abroad)	(300)	(513)	(5)	(5)
	1.081	1.343	662	673

(25) Depreciation

The depreciation expense for 1997 are analyzed in notes (1) and (2).

(26) Other operating expenses

in TATS	Group		Company	
	1997	*1996*	*1997*	*1996*
Taxes (excluding taxes on income)	6.295	6.004	5.662	3.328
Services provided by subsidiaries	47.248	45.456	51.954	45.456
Other operating costs	254.553	313.073	148.684	162.197
	308.096	364.533	206.300	210.981

The services provided by subsidiaries include other operating costs charged from those subsidiaries not included in the consolidation. In the previous years also cost for engineering services received was disclosed under this item. These are now included under "costs of services received"; the prior year figures were adjusted accordingly.

(27) Financial result

in TATS	Group		Company	
	1997	*1996*	*1997*	*1996*
Income from other securities and loans disclosed as financial assets	1.766	1.941	1.766	1.941
(thereof from affiliated companies)	(506)	(641)	(506)	(641)
Other interest income and similar income	40.745	41.532	33.130	34.490
(thereof from affiliated companies)	(—)	(—)	(—)	(—)
Income from the disposal of financial assets and of marketable securities included in current assets	2.488	438	2.488	438
(thereof from affiliated companies)	(—)	(—)	(—)	(—)
Depreciation of marketable securities included in current assets	274		274	(—)
(thereof from affiliated companies)	(—)	(—)	(—)	(—)
Interest and similar expenses	41.730	69.392	26.359	20.669
(thereof fromaffiliated companies)	(—)	(—)	(3.999)	(—)
	2.995	-25.481	10.751	16.200

(28) Extraordinary income

The extraordinary income in 1996 refers to income from the deconsolidation of SAMES.

(29) Extraordinary expenses

The extraordinary expenses in 1996 mainly incurred in connection with the restructuring of SAMES.

(30) Taxes on income

in TATS	Group		Company	
	1997	*1996*	*1997*	*1996*
Current taxes	34.560	-1.098	34.651	—
Deferred taxes	—	-5.481	—	—
	34.560	-6.579	34.651	—

In 1996 taxes in the amount of TATS 0 of the (negative) tax expense refer to the extraordinary result. The tax expense of the Company was reduced by TATS 6.106 on account of the changes in the untaxed reserves. Deferred tax assets which have however not been capitalised by making use of the respective option amount to TATS 11.717 (1996: TATS 11.147) in the Group and the Company.

Other matters

Companies, in which the Company has a share-holding interest of at least 20 %

Name and seat	Currency	Share-holding	Share-holders Equity	1997 Result
Austria Mikro SystemeInternational LTD (Camberley, United Kingdom)	GBP	100%	134.665	21.735
Austria Mikro Systeme International GmbH(Munich, Germany)	DM	100%	-342.615	-413.858
Austria Mikro SystemeInternational SARL(Vincennes, France)	FFR	100%	730.277	89.276
Austria Mikro Systeme International SRL (Milan, Italy)	LIT	100%	936.335.770	279.256.879
AMS Austria Mikro Systeme International INC.(Cupertino, USA)	USD	100%	88.139	4.129
Austria Mikro Systeme International Fejleszto Es Forgalmazo KFT. (Budapest, Hungary)	HUF	100%	15.462.201	344.425
Austria Mikro Systeme International LTD. (Hong Kong)	HKD	100%	169.903	78.987
Austria Mikro Systeme International S.L. (Barcelona, Spain)	ESP	100%	10.183.493	7.183.493
Integrated Circuit Design Centre (Proprietary) Ltd.Pretoria, South Africa)	ZAR	50%	1.000	-22
THESYS Gesellschaft für Mikroelektronik mbH(Erfurt, Germany)	DM	51,25%	93.115.828	-17.678.030

THESYS holds a 50% share in THESYS Intechna (Woronesh, Russia) and a 49% share in THESYS Mikropribor (Kiev, Ukraine). These joint ventures are only of minor importance for the net worth position and results of operations of the Group.

Relations to Affiliated companies

The 100 % subsidiaries of Austria Mikro Systeme International AG carry out market research as well as technical advisory work, they support the world-wide marketing and sale of products and represent an extension of the design capacity.

A commission agreement has been concluded between Austria Mikro Systeme International AG and Austria Mikro Systeme International SRL, Milan, as well as Austria Mikro

Systeme International S.L., Barcelona. In accordance with this agreement TATS 14.305 (1996: TATS 12.422) were expensed in 1997 by Austria Mikro Systeme International AG.

Service agreements based on the cost plus method have been concluded with all other subsidiaries. The charges resulting thereof amounted to TATS 32.943 (1996: TATS 33.034) and are disclosed under other operating costs.

In 1997 Austria Mikro Systeme International AG purchased engineering services from Austria Mikro Systeme International GmbH, Munich, amounting to TATS 15.850 (1996: TATS 19.384) and from Austria Mikro Systeme International Fejleszto Es Forgalmazo KFT., Budapest, amounting to TATS 4.684 (1996: TATS 6.472). These expenses are included in cost of services received.

Executive bodies of Austria Mikro Systeme International AG

Executive Board of Directors

Dipl.Ing. Horst Gebert (Chairman)

Mag. Johann Stritzelberger

Supervisory Board

Dipl.Ing. Guido Klestil (Chairman)

Prof. Dr. Hans Leopold (Deputy Chairman)

Mag. Hans Jörg Kaltenbrunner (Member of the executive committee)

Konstantin von Klitzing

Dr. Franz Kubik

Johann Eitner (Delegated by the employees´ council)

Ing. Peter Fink (Delegated by the employees´ council)

Dr. Günther Koppitsch (Delegated by the employees´ council)

Authorized Signatories

Dipl.Ing. Hartwin Breitenbach

Dr. Heimo Pirker

Dipl.Ing. Gerhard Richter

In a meeting held on February 23, 1998 the supervisory board of Austria Mikro Systeme International AG adopted the resolution to extend the executive board of directors by one person. Hans Jörg Kaltenbrunner takes over the function of the chairman of the executive board of directors from Horst Gebert, who resigns due to old age. The third member of the executive board has not yet been appointed.

Remuneration paid tothe members of the executive board and the supervisory board

The protection clause in accordance with § 241 of the Austrian Commercial Code (HGB) was applied regarding the disclosure of the remuneration paid to the members of the executive board. The remuneration for the supervisory board of Austria Mikro Systeme International AG amounted to TATS 325 (1996: TATS 325). No advances and loans were granted to members of the executive board or the supervisory board. No contingent liabilities were entered into in favor of this group of persons.

Proposal for profit distribution

The business year concludes with retained earnings of	ATS	30.755.574,76
The executive board of directors proposes to use the retained earnings as follows:		
Distribution of a dividend of ATS 10,- per share	ATS	30.000.000,00
Balance carried forward	ATS	755.574,76

Unterpremstätten, March 4, 1998

Executive Board of Directors

Dipl.Ing. Horst Gebert

Mag. Johann Stritzelberger

Auditor's Opinion

"Based on our audit performed in accordance with our professional duties, the accounting records, financial statements and group financial statements comply with legal requirements. The financial statements and the group financial statements represent in compliance with generally accepted accounting principles, a true and fair view of the assets and liabilities, the financial position and the results of operations of the Company and the Group. The management report combined with the management report of the Group is in agreement with the financial statements and the consolidated financial statements." Vienna, March 5, 1998

WIRTSCHAFTSPRÜFUNGS- UND STEUERBERATUNGSGMBH

Wolfgang Wildner

Helmut Maukner

(Austrian Certified Public Accountants)

Country Highlights
BELGIUM

Common Legal Forms of Companies

The following legal forms of business organization are defined in the Company Law:

- Public limited liability companies (*sociétés anonymes/naamloze vennootschap*)
- Private limited liability companies (*sociétés privées à responsabilité limitée/ besloten vennootschap met beperkte aansprakelijkheid*)
- Sole-proprietor limited liability companies (*société à responsabilité limitée/eenpersoons vennootschap met beperkte aansprakelijkheid*)
- Partnerships limited by shares (*sociétés en commandite par actions/commanditaire vennootschappen op aandelen*)
- Co-operatives (*sociétés coopératives/coöperatieve vennootschappen*). The Company Law allows two types of co-operative, namely co-operatives with limited liability and co-operatives with unlimited liability.
- Limited partnerships (*sociétés en commandite simple/gewone commanditaire vennootschappen*)
- General partnerships (*sociétés en nom collectif/vennootschappen onder firma*)

Sources of Financial Reporting

The Accounting Law on Bookkeeping and Financial Reporting for Industrial and Commercial Companies issued on July 17, 1975, together with the Royal Decrees that implement the Accounting Law are the sole source of binding regulation. The 1975 Act, together with the Royal Decrees, covers aspects of bookkeeping, the form and content of the annual accounts, valuation rules, disclosure requirements, and a basic standard chart of accounts. The Royal Decrees are also issued by Parliament, and they have the same status as a law.

A second source of accounting regulation, but not a binding one, in Belgium are the opinions issued by the Commission on Accounting Standards (*Commission des Normes Comptables*, CNC/*Commissie voor Boekhoudkundige Normen*, CBN).The opinions of the commission are authoritative pronouncements, but they do not have the force of the law.

Corporate Taxation

The starting point for calculation of the corporate income tax is the accounting profit. There is a strong link between accounting and taxation.

Auditing Requirements

An audit of the financial statements is required for all public limited liability companies, private limited liability companies, co-operatives, and partnerships limited by shares, which correspond to the criteria of large enterprises. A shareholder of a small or medium-sized company has the right to ask for an audit of the company. If a company has a workers' council, then an auditor must be appointed to report economic and financial information to the workers' council.

Organization of the Accounting and Auditing Profession

The profession is organized under the law of February 21, 1985. Two bodies are created by that law, namely the Institute of Auditors and the Institute of Accountants. The Higher Council of Accountancy has defined the functions of an auditor and an accountant and governs the relationship between the two Institutes. Only members of the Institute of Auditors may perform all functions with which public auditors are exclusively entrusted by law. The main task of members of the Institute of Accountants is to help small and medium-sized firms prepare their annual accounts and to give them legal and tax advice.

Constitution and Legal System

The legal system in Belgium is a codified law system. Laws are made by Parliament, and the government is responsible for their execution. As a result, Belgian accounting law is quite detailed and contains numerous requirements on bookkeeping, with valuation rules for specific items and prescribed formats, not only for the balance sheet and the profit and loss account, but also for the notes to the annual accounts.

Currency

- Belgian francs (BEF) until December 31, 1998
- Belgian francs and Euro from January 1, 1999 to July 1, 2002
- Euro from July 1, 2002

Official Languages

- Dutch
- French
- German

BELGIUM

Ann Jorissen
UFSIA, University of Antwerp, Belgium

1. A Brief History of Belgian Accounting Legislation

1.1 Introduction

By the mid-1970s, the existing Belgian legislation on companies' accounting and financial reporting was outdated and obsolete. In response to pressure from various users of accounting data (e.g. financial analysts, investors, employees) and to anticipated European legislation, on July 17, 1975 the Belgian legislature enacted the Law on Accounting and Companies' Annual Accounts. This basic law gave accounting a judicial status it had not had before, stating the fundamental principles by which annual accounts must abide, and also providing legal sanctions for the nonobservance of these principles.

The 1975 law, together with the Royal Decree of October 8, 1976 on companies' annual accounts and the Royal Decree of March 7, 1978 on a minimum standard chart of accounts, revolutionized accounting and financial reporting in Belgium. Since then, the 1975 law and these decrees have been amended several times.

Other laws and royal decrees have been passed in recent years. At the present stage in the development of accounting, financial reporting, audit requirements, and company law, it clearly can be asserted that the relevant European Directives have been completely implemented.

1.2 Early Belgian Accounting Legislation

The first legislation concerning accounting and financial reporting in Belgium can be traced back to the Napoleonic Code of Commerce of 1807. This code contained provisions regarding bookkeeping and served as the foundation for the elaboration of the basic Company Law of 1873, in which were regulated the issuance of stock, the statutes of the limited company, the disclosure of annual accounts, and the statute of the directors and commissioners. Since then, Belgian company law has been amended on several occasions, and this process led, eventually, to the so-called Coordinated Law of Companies of 1935, which remained in effect until it was superseded by the Royal Decree of October 8, 1976 on Companies' Annual Accounts. The more recent developments in company law will be examined later.

Section 9 of the coordinated Law of Companies of 1935 spelled out the various requirements with which companies had to comply regarding their bookkeeping and financial reporting. These requirements concerned only balance sheets and income statements and were minimal. The type of balance sheets companies had to prepare were often referred to as "pocket-sized" balance sheets, for, in order to meet the official requirements, companies had to publish only six items in their balance sheet: two on the asset side (fixed assets and accounts receivable) and four on the liability side (shareholders' equity, bond loans, secured debts, and unsecured debts). On the other hand, the only requirement regarding the income statement that the law imposed was that depreciation be "true and fair." Although a number of large companies went beyond those minimum legal requirements and disclosed additional information on a voluntary basis, this additional information often fell short of meeting users' needs and was not standardized.

These surprisingly limited disclosure requirements can be explained partly by historical and institutional factors. One of these is the existence in Belgium of a handful of quite powerful holding companies (such as the Société Générale established in 1822), which played a major role in financing the country's industrial sector. These holding companies were reluctant to disclose information to outsiders. In addition, only a small number of shares were in the hands of third parties, which explains why the general public showed little interest in those financial statements.

The remaining part of trade and industry in Belgium was and still is in the hands of small family-run companies. When those family-run companies needed extra financial sources to finance their growth or other investments, they always turned to banks and other financial institutions. There was no tradition for these companies to go public once they had reached a certain size. For that reason, stock exchanges in Belgium (Brussels, Antwerp, Liège, and Gent) were quite small and had only a few listed companies.

As a result, Belgian companies were and are to a large extent financed by banks and other creditors. Therefore, financial reporting in Belgium was viewed for a long time as providing information to creditors. Consequently, the emphasis was put on the balance sheet at the expense of the income statement in the belief that a positive net worth was the best protection a company could give its creditors. Indeed, disclosure requirements were imposed mainly on companies to protect creditors and insiders rather than to inform outside investors. In this context, the financial position of a company as shown on a conservative balance sheet took precedence over the detailed determination of its earnings.

This situation was reinforced by the fact that fiscal law dominated the financial reporting practices of Belgian firms up until 1975. In fact, Belgian firms published tax-biased accounts. The influence of taxation on financial reporting is further discussed in Section 3.2.

1.3 Toward a Comprehensive Accounting and Financial Reporting Legislation

1.3.1 Development up to 1975

From the late 1960s, financial analysts, accounting professionals, workers' councils, academics, and government agencies began to urge companies to disclose a broader range of information to the public. Among these pressure groups, workers' councils played a pivotal role in the process that led to the 1976 Royal Decree on accounting standards and financial reporting. The action of workers' councils can be traced back to the Economic and Social Conference of 1970, which called for a broadening of accounting disclosure requirements in Belgium and the provision of financial and economic information to workers' councils. The recommendations that emerged from that conference were embodied in the decree of November 27, 1973 (Royal Decree on Financial and Economic Information to Workers' Councils). The fundamental objective of this decree was to provide employees with a true and fair view of the economic and financial condition of their companies and to provide workers' councils with as much information as shareholders had.

After the Economic and Social Conference of 1970, several legislative committees were set up under the leadership of the Belgian government. These committees organized a series of hearings that allowed the accounting profession and different users of financial information (financial analysts, investors, academics) to present their views on the reform of the existing accounting legislation in Belgium. Various drafts of new accounting and financial reporting legislation were proposed by these committees.

Simultaneously, the European Commission was drafting its Fourth Directive, the purpose of which was to improve companies' accounting standards and to harmonize disclosure rules for annual accounts across member countries.

1.3.2   Crucial Legislation, 1975–1976

Drawing on the provisions of what later became the Fourth Directive, and on the various drafts proposed by the legislative committees set up in the early 1970s, the Belgian Parliament passed a law on July 17, 1975 calling for a major overhaul of accounting standards and financial reporting in Belgium. Detailed regulations concerning the reporting of corporate accounting data and the establishment of a minimum standard chart of accounts were later specified in the Royal Decrees of October 1976 and March 1978.

The Royal Decree of October 8, 1976 was a turning point in the history of accounting and financial reporting legislation in Belgium. As pointed out, the decree required corporations for the first time to divulge to the public a substantial amount of financial information: it defined the form and content of the annual accounts, the valuation rules, and the prescribed disclosure thereof. The disclosure of additional information in the income statement has had the greatest impact on accounting and reporting practice, because disclosure requirements before 1976 were quite limited in that respect.

Furthermore, it is interesting to note that the Belgian legislature attached great importance to the information to be disclosed in the notes to the balance sheet and the profit and loss account. The legislature even prescribed a format for these notes.

As Belgium has a tradition of a codified system of law, the accounting law of 1975 and the royal decrees have all the characteristics of this legal system. The accounting law and the accompanying royal decrees are quite detailed. They contain numerous requirements on bookkeeping, valuation rules, and the prescribed formats not only for the balance sheet and the profit and loss account but also for the notes. The Accounting Law and the Royal Decree of 1976 were later updated several times. An overview of these updates is included in Table 1.

TABLE 1 *Chronology of Accounting and*
Financial Reporting Legislation in Belgium

1807	Napoleonic Code of Commerce
May 18, 1873	Basic Company Law
July 22, 1913	Company Coordinated Law (Section 9, Article 75 spelled out the requirements with which companies had to comply regarding their bookkeeping and financial reporting)
July 9, 1935	Establishment of the Banking Commission: Royal Decree No. 18 on the legal status/control of banks and on the control of appeals to public saving (amended by the Laws of July 17, 1985 and of March 9, 1989)
November 30, 1935	Company Coordinated Law: new version (Section 9, article 77 spelled out the same requirements as those contained in Article 75 of the Law of July 22, 1913): this law has been amended several times
July 22, 1953	Establishment of the Public Auditors' Institute
November 27, 1973	Royal Decree on Financial and Economic Information to Workers' Councils (amended by the Royal Decrees of August 12, 1981 and of March 6, 1990)
July 17, 1975	Basic Law on Accounting and Companies' Annual Accounts (amended by the Laws of March 30, 1976 and March 24, 1978; the Royal Decree of December 15, 1978; the Law of July 1, 1983; the Royal Decree of January 16, 1986; the Law of July 12, 1989, and the Royal Decrees of December 30, 1991; August 6, 1993; August 4, 1996)
October 21, 1975	Establishment of the Accounting Standards Commission
October 8, 1976	Royal Decree on Companies' Annual Accounts (amended by the Royal Decrees of December 27, 1977; February 14 , 1979; September 12, 1983; March 5, 1985; November 6, 1987; March 6, 1990; December 30, 1991; December 3, 1993; August 4, 1996)
September 1, 1986	Royal Decrees on Annual Accounts and Consolidated Accounts of Holding Companies (amended by the Royal Decree of November 25,1991)
March 7, 1978	Royal Decree on a Minimum Standard Chart of Accounts (repealed by the Royal Decree of September 12, 1983)
November 12, 1979	Royal Decrees on Annual Accounts of Insur-

(Table continues)

(Table 1 continued)

October 19, 1981	ance companies (amended by the Royal Decree of November 17, 1997; August 4, 1996)
June 9, 1981	Royal Decree on a Minimum Standard Chart of Accounts for the oil industry
September 12, 1983	Royal Decree on a Minimum Standard Chart of Accounts (amended by the Royal Decree of November 6, 1987)
December 5, 1984	Law modifying the Company Coordinated Law of November 30, 1935 (last amendment)
February 21, 1985	Law on Public Auditing Function (revision of the Law of July 22, 1953); establishment of the Institute of Chartered Accountants
March 6, 1990	Royal Decree on Companies' Consolidated Accounts (amended by the Royal Decrees of December 30, 1991; December 3, 1993; April 27, 1995)
September 23, 1992	Royal Decree on Annual Accounts of Banks (amended by the Royal Decree of August 4, 1996)
August 4, 1996	Royal Decree on the Social Balance Sheet

1.3.3 Consolidated Accounts

As to the consolidated accounts, the law of July 17, 1975 stipulated that the government (formally, the King) could by royal decree oblige enterprises to establish and publish consolidated accounts. The first executive measure of this provision found its way into the Royal Decree of November 29, 1977. This decree imposes such requirements on holdings companies (*a*) which, on their own or through subsidiaries, have resorted to raising funds from the public; or (*b*) which have shareholdings worth either half their own equity or at least 500 million Belgian francs (BF).

This decree also deals with the nonconsolidated accounts of holding companies.

A second royal decree, that of September 1, 1986, related to the same companies. First, it adapted the decree of November 29, 1977 to recent changes in accounting legislation. Second, it incorporated into the first decree both the experience on consolidated accounts gained since 1977 and, to some extent, the European norm dealing with consolidation (the Seventh EC Directive of June 13, 1983). For holding companies, the Royal Decree of 1986 has been replaced by that of November 25, 1991.

Finally, the Royal Decree of March 6, 1990 sets up the rules that will regulate the drawing up of companies' consolidated accounts for industrial and commercial companies. Because the Belgian business community was not used to preparing consolidated accounts, the legislature chose to impose the obligation to prepare consolidated accounts up until 1999 on only very large groups. As a result, consolidated accounts are still of minor importance in Belgium. The individual accounts remain the most important source of financial company data.

1.3.4 Chronology of Accounting and Financial Reporting Legislation in Belgium

Table 1 summarizes the history of accounting and financial reporting legislation in Belgium, from the Napoleonic Code of commerce of 1807 until 1997.

1.3.5 The Commission for Accounting Standards

The Commission for Accounting Standards was created by the law of 1975 (*Commission des Normes Comptables/Commissie voor Boekhoudkundige Normen*). According to Article 14 of the law, the task of the commission is to give opinions to the government and Parliament as required, or on its own initiative, and to develop an accounting doctrine and to formulate the principles of proper accounting by way of opinion or recommendation. Since its establishment, the Commission on Accounting Standards has issued 37 bulletins. These bulletins contain opinions on the application of various articles of the Law of 1975 and the royal decrees. The opinions of the Commission are authoritative pronouncements but have no binding character.

1.4 Company Law

1.4.1 Origins

Belgian company law stems from a distant past. The Code of Commerce of 1807 took in most of the provisions already contained in the Order of Colbert of 1673. The Code of 1807 was revised by the Law of May 18, 1873, which remains the fundamental root of present company law. At the

(Table continues)

end of the past century, there was further modification by Royal Decree in 1935: some of the texts that still govern today date back to this period. Since 1949 there have been numerous reforms.

1.4.2   Company Form

In earlier days, many trade and industry activities were carried out by individuals or groups of individuals. During the past 10 years we have witnessed an evolution. Unlimited liability companies are little by little being abandoned. The limited liability companies are taking over in number. The most popular legal forms of business are the private limited liability company (±110,000 in 1996), the public limited liability company (±90,000 in 1996), and cooperative societies (±15,000 in 1996). Furthermore, there is a clear tendency for companies to create subsidiaries for various activities. This sometimes leads to the creation of holding companies.

The Belgian legislature has allowed the formation of "single person limited liability companies": this is an innovation introduced by the Law of July 14, 1985.

1.4.3   Reform of Company Law

A Reform Commission for company laws was set up in 1951 with a view to undertaking a reform of all outdated legislation. It was necessary to rethink old concepts. The same process was occurring in neighboring countries, which have all been proceeding, since the end of the Second World War, with a more or less complete overhaul of their legislation. The work of this commission continued up to 1968, although it was not until 10 years later that the government decided to deposit the project with the Chamber of Representatives (1979). As such, the project has had no follow-up on the parliamentary level.

It is important to note that the Belgian legislature is working on adapting the Company Law to European Directives as and when these become mandatory. But it is also taking initiatives that have been dictated by circumstances. Some texts stem from the works of the Reform Commission.

The Second EC Directive of December 13, 1976 provides for a harmonization of norms and procedures relative to the constitution, the minimum and the modifications of the capital of limited companies. One cannot say that Belgium was eager to assume its EC responsibilities regarding this matter. It took 8 years to adapt Belgian Company Law to the Second Directive (Law of December 5, 1984).

The 1984 law not only adapts Belgian Company Law to the Second Directive (see Section 3 for certain implications for the analyst), it also assures the transposition into Belgian law of the rules of the Fourth Directive that are directly linked with company law, especially

- The content and publication of the annual management report of directors accompanying the annual accounts
- The content and publication of the annual control report of statutory auditors (see below)
- The possibility of publishing abridged annual accounts
- The determination of distributable income (see Section 3)

1.5 Organization of the Auditing Profession

1.5.1 Introduction

In Belgium, the Institute of Auditors (*Institut des Réviseurs d'Entreprises* or *Institut van Bedeijfsrevisoren*) was created by the Law of July 22, 1953. The reform of the auditing profession was realized by the Law of February 21, 1985. This law appears to be a codification of procedures in force, containing the necessary specifications for rendering the former system in accordance with the Eighth EC Directive of April 10, 1984 (relative to the qualifications and work of auditors). This law also adapted the Belgian legislation to the Fourth Directive.

When the certification of annual accounts or other information is required by law, only recognized auditors are entitled to issue such certification.

In principle, all limited companies, private limited companies, cooperative companies, and limited partnerships with shares must appoint an auditor to control their annual accounts (including consolidated accounts). Small and medium-sized companies are exempt from this requirement. However, if a shareholder of a small or medium-sized company wants an audit of the company, the shareholder has the right to ask for it. Such audits of small and medium-sized companies might also be carried out by a member of the Institute of Accountants.

There are workers' councils in all Belgian companies and institutions that employ an average of more than one hundred workers annually. Economic and financial information must be provided to the workers' councils in accordance with the Royal Decree of November 27, 1973. A recognized auditor must be appointed to make a report to the workers' council, especially on the annual accounts and on the economic and financial information. This legal requirement represents a considerable extension of the social role of auditors: this is a peculiarity of the Belgian system.

The auditor has a control function. The auditor does not have the power to interfere with the management of the company. The Company Law provides that auditors be appointed from among the members of the Institute of Recognized Auditors. In order to be recognized as an auditor, the candidate must

- Be Belgian or resident in Belgium
- Be at least 25 years old and no older than 65
- Never have been deprived of civil and political rights
- Hold a university diploma of at least 4 years of study or be registered for 2 years on the roll of chartered accountants
- Have successfully passed an admission examination
- Have completed a 3-year training period with a professional auditor
- Have passed an aptitude exam at the end of the training period
- Have made an oath before the President of the Commerce Tribunal

1.5.2 *Attestation and Report of the Recognized Auditor (for the Annual General Meeting of Shareholders)*

The outcome of the auditor's work is an annual report, the content of which is specified by Article 65 of the Company Law of December 5, 1984 (this law anticipates the auditing reform). The auditor draws up for the general meeting of shareholders a detailed written report that specifically indicates:

- How they carried out their control and if they obtained from the administrators and managers of the company the explanations and information they requested

- Whether the accounting records are maintained and the annual accounts prepared in conformity with the legal and statutory requirements applicable in Belgium
- Whether in their opinion, the annual accounts give, taking into account the legal and statutory requirements that govern them, a true and fair view of the assets and liabilities, of the financial position and of the results of the company, and if the supplementary information given in the notes is adequate
- Whether the management report of the directors includes all information required by law and is in accordance with the annual accounts
- Whether the allocation of the profits proposed to the general meeting is in conformity with legal and statutory requirements
- Whether they have any knowledge at all of transactions or decisions made in violation of the statutes or of the Company Law

In their report, the auditors indicate and justify with precision any qualifications or objections that they consider necessary. Otherwise, they expressly mention that they have none at all to formulate. Obviously, Belgian law did not opt for a report in a brief and standardized form. The auditor's report must accompany any complete publication of the annual accounts.

The auditor's attestation must appear at the conclusion of the auditor's report; it concerns only the annual accounts. The law specifies that if the auditor has attested the annual accounts without formulating any qualifications, the text of the report can be replaced by the auditor's "attestation."

1.5.3 Types of Attestations (Audit Opinions)

The Company Law distinguishes three types of attestation:

- Attestation without qualification (if the annual accounts correspond to the legal and statutory requirements, if the rules of evaluation were applied in a consistent manner, and if all of the necessary information is given with clarity)
- Attestation with qualification (if the auditor cannot indicate agreement with the content or the form of one or several items of the annual accounts)

- The refusal to attest (when the auditor disapproves of the accounts because of disagreement with the managers on one or several essential points: no true and fair view)

2. The Form and Content of Published Financial Statements and Notes

2.1 Introduction

The regulated part of the annual report contains the financial statements of a company, which consist of a balance sheet, a profit and loss account, the notes to the accounts, and the "social" balance sheet. There is no requirement for other statements, such as sources and applications of funds or value added statements.

2.2 Disclosure

2.2.1   General Provisions

The annual accounts shall comprise the balance sheet, the income statement, and the notes to the accounts. These documents constitute a composite whole; they are stated in Belgian francs or, from 1999, Euros.

The annual accounts shall give a true and fair view of the enterprise's assets, liabilities, financial position, and result. They shall be prepared clearly and must set out systematically the nature and the amount of the enterprise's assets and rights, its debts and commitments, and its capital and reserves as of the balance sheet date, as well as the nature and the amount of its income and expense for the financial period then ended.

The opening balance sheet for each financial period shall correspond to the closing balance sheet for the preceding financial period. Any set-off between assets and liabilities, contingent assets and rights and contingent liabilities, or between income and expenses, shall not be permitted except as provided in the Accounting Decree (Royal Decree of October 1976, amended by Royal Decrees of September 1983 and November 1987).

2.2.2   Presentation of the Annual Accounts

The balance sheet and the income statement shall be drawn up in accordance with the layout provided in the Accounting Decree. The notes to the accounts shall contain the information and statements prescribed by the Accounting Decree.

Small and medium-sized enterprises (the accounting definition of these enterprises is given below) may, however, prepare their balance sheet and income statement in accordance with the abbreviated form provided for in the Accounting Decree, together with an abbreviated version of the notes.

Where assets or liabilities can be classified under more than one caption or subcaption of the balance sheet, and income or expenses under more than one caption or subcaption of the income statement, they shall be included under whichever item is most appropriate.

In order to provide more details, enterprises may further subdivide the prescribed captions and subcaptions in the notes. In order to comply with the true and fair view requirements, the nomenclature of captions preceded by a capital letter and subcaptions in the standard layout shall be adapted to the particular nature of the activity, the assets and liabilities, and the income and expenses of the enterprise.

2.2.3   Special Provisions Relating to the Annual Accounts

The balance sheet shall be prepared after appropriation, that is, after accounting for the results of appropriation, the result of the income statement, and the result brought forward. With respect to each caption and subcaption of the balance sheet and income statement, the amounts related to the corresponding item for the preceding financial period must be shown. Where the amounts of a financial period are not comparable with those of the preceding financial period, the figures of the preceding financial period may be adjusted in order to make them comparable: in that case the adjustments, where material, shall be disclosed and explained in the notes. Where the amounts of the preceding financial period are not adjusted, the notes must include the necessary details to allow comparison. Accumulated depreciation and amounts written off are deducted from the assets to which they relate.

The notes to the accounts shall state, by category, the contingent assets and liabilities not included in the balance sheet that may have a significant effect on the assets and liabilities or the financial position or result of the enterprise. Material contingent assets and liabilities that cannot be quantified shall be appropriately disclosed in the notes to the accounts.

2.2.4   The "Social" Balance Sheet

The Royal Decree of August 4, 1996 introduced the requirement to publish financial data concerning the workforce in the annual accounts. Whether or not this social balance sheet should be considered part of the notes to the balance sheet and profit and loss account or should be considered as a separate part of the annual accounts is still a matter of discussion.

This decree prescribed a standardized format. Companies that publish their annual accounts in abbreviated format may use the abbreviated format of the social balance sheet. Other companies must use the extended format of the social balance sheet.

The social balance sheet consists of four parts:

- Information on the number of people employed. A distinction is made among full-time employees, part-time employees, and temporary employees. For each category the number of hours worked is disclosed and also the total labor cost involved.
- A "labor movement" schedule. This part provides information on the number of new people hired and the number of people for whom labor contracts have been terminated and the reason for this termination.
- An overview of the use the company has made of government incentives and grants to create employment.
- Information on employee education programs. For each sex (male/female) an overview must be given of the number of hours of training and the costs involved.

2.3 Formats of Financial Statements

In the Appendix to this chapter, a real life example is given in the form of the financial statements of Petrofina, which include group accounts. The notes to the financial statements are also included.

The Fourth Directive allows member states to choose between a horizontal and a vertical balance sheet layout or to use both formats. Belgian legislation settles for the horizontal format. For the individual accounts, the law specifies a full format and an abridged version for the balance sheet. With regard to the profit and loss account, only the layouts in which the charges and the income are arranged by category are permitted for the individual accounts. Companies may choose between the horizontal and vertical form of presentation. For the profit and loss account of the consolidated accounts, layouts are allowed by category or by function. Each statement must include the comparative figures for the previous financial year.

Enterprises, irrespective of their legal form, that do not exceed more than one of the following criteria are allowed to present their annual accounts in abbreviated format:

- Personnel: 50
- Turnover: BF 200,000,000
- Balance sheet total: BF 100,000,000

If the number of employees exceeds 100, the enterprise must prepare its annual accounts using the full layout.

Individuals carrying on a commercial activity and general or limited partnerships with a turnover of less than BF 20 million may set up a simplified system of accounting, and they do not have to use the official formats, defined in the royal decrees, for the preparation of their annual accounts. (This turnover criterion is raised to BF 25 million for traders whose main activity is the retail sale of gaseous or liquid hydrocarbons for the propulsion of motor vehicles on public highways.)

With regard to the publication of the annual accounts, the following requirements exist:

1. Enterprises incorporated as companies or partnerships with varying degrees of limited liability (private limited liability companies, public limited liability companies, partnerships limited by shares, cooperative societies with limited liability) must publish their annual accounts by filing them with the National Bank of Belgium after approval by the general meeting (Article 80 of the Company Law)

2. For enterprises otherwise incorporated, one must make a distinction between those enterprises that are allowed to prepare their annual accounts using the abbreviated format and those enterprises that are obliged to use the full layout.

- The enterprises with an abbreviated format have no obligation to publish their annual accounts.

- The enterprises with a full layout must publish their annual accounts through filing with the National Bank of Belgium, except for individuals carrying on a commercial activity and general and limited partnerships of which all partners are individuals.

2.4 The Auditor's Report

The situation in Belgium with regard to auditing was described in Section 1.5. In the case of an unqualified audit report, only a short "attestation" need be published. Otherwise, the full text of the report should be published. An example of an unqualified attestation on the accounts of Petrofina is given in the Appendix.

3. Accounting Policies and Practices in Valuation and Income Measurement: Implications for the Analyst

3.1 Introduction

Since the enactment of the EC Fourth Directive into Belgian law, Belgian financial statements have been required to provide a "true and fair view." In Belgium's two main languages, French and Flemish, this phrase is translated as *une image fidele* and *een getrouw beeld*, respectively; that is to say, literally, "a faithful image" or "a true picture."

This concept was new to the Belgian world of preparers of financial statements and the profession. Until then, preparers, together with the profession, took a legal approach. If the annual accounts complied with the provisions of the law and the royal decrees and the prudence principle was respected, the annual accounts fulfilled all expectations. The notion of the predominance of the true and fair view over other dispositions of the Directive (Article 2, paragraph 5 of the Directive) is in Belgium, however, not interpreted to mean (as it is in the United Kingdom) that specific accounting rules should be overridden. Rather, the Belgian interpretation is similar to the French, namely that the notion of the true and fair view should be used to choose an accounting method when the specific rules leave a choice or are imprecise. This implies that when the balance sheet and the profit and loss account as such do not provide a true and fair view, it is sufficient to mention this in the notes in order to comply with the true and fair view. For this purpose, the notes to the accounts (*annexe*) must be considered an integral part of the financial statements. An example of this phenomenon can be found when, because of the influence of tax law, discussed below, the balance sheet and income statement by themselves may not give a true and fair view, and reference to the notes may be essential in order to be aware of the implications of this. In practice, preparers of financial information and the profession share the view that if they comply with those detailed legal rules, they prepare or certify financial statements that present a true and fair view.

3.2 The Influence of Tax Law on Published Accounts

Somewhat like France and Germany, but unlike the United Kingdom, the United States, and the Netherlands, Belgium has a tax regime under which the published annual accounts serve as the basis for corporate taxation.

Companies are obliged to provide the tax authorities with a balance sheet and a detailed income statement and are bound by their contents. At the same time, the tax authorities may discuss the contents of the financial statements and make adjustments to them to establish the tax basis. Companies naturally tend to draw up their accounts in a manner that will not lead to adjustments for tax purposes.

The first fiscal laws were issued in Belgium when it became independent in 1830. But only with the tax reform of 1913 was the concept of corporate income tax introduced. Because fiscal laws remained rather vague on the definition of taxable income, a rich body of tax regulations (issued by the tax authorities and the courts) was developed. For the first seventy years of the 20th century companies valued their assets, liabilities, costs, and revenues according to the fiscal rules in order to determine their taxable income. These fiscal rules became the *de facto* accounting rules, because company law did not mention any valuation rules. In this way a strong link was created between accounting and taxation, a link which still exists today.

Beginning in the mid-seventies a new situation emerged. Companies were faced with a complete new set of accounting rules with the introduction of the accounting law in 1975 and the existing set of fiscal rules, which companies had applied in the published annual accounts for years.

As companies were used to publishing only one set of annual accounts for public and fiscal purposes, they opposed the idea that they might have to prepare two sets of accounts. They considered this an administrative burden. As a solution to this conflict, the government chose to introduce the principle of fiscal neutrality.

The introduction of this principle was also a political choice because the government did not want the tax system and the computation of taxable income to be changed through the introduction of new accounting legislation. Fiscal neutrality is explained in the explanatory memorandum in the law of 1975 as follows: "The government does not want to change indirectly the impact of the current fiscal legislation through the introduction of this accounting legislation. The government will make sure that the fiscal neutrality is guaranteed and when necessary it shall take the necessary legal and administrative initiatives and measures." This principle is also discussed in the preamble to the Royal Decree of 1976 and in a fiscal administration circular dated March 31, 1978. Fiscal neutrality was to be achieved in the following way. The fiscal administration would accept for tax purposes all the rules of accounting law and the relevant royal decrees with regard to depreciation, write-offs, write-backs, provisions, and other valuation rules in order to determine the taxable amount unless expressly provided otherwise in the tax law.

In the preamble to the Royal Decree of October 18, 1976, Parliament expressed its will to permit fiscal rules to differ from accounting rules only in exceptional circumstances. So, according to Parliament, accounting law overrules fiscal law except concerning some special issues. In the beginning many distortions existed between fiscal law and accounting law. In order to eliminate these distortions, the government proceeded in several ways. First, it changed certain aspects of the fiscal law to bring it into line with accounting law. Second, items in accounting law were changed to harmonize with their fiscal treatment.

Almost 20 years after the introduction of the law on accounting and the principle of fiscal neutrality, one might say that fiscal neutrality has been achieved only in part. In many cases the fiscal law and fiscal administration accept the accounting rules. However, neutrality is constantly threatened by the fact that Parliament often uses fiscal law to stimulate economic activity. Moreover, such laws require registration in the books of the company as a precondition for obtaining the tax reliefs that provide such stimuli. Requirements of this sort result in tax-biased annual accounts.

With the implementation of the 7th Directive in Belgium, the concept of deferred taxes was introduced into Belgian accounting legislation. Article 40 of the Royal Decree of March 1991 states that "account shall be taken in the consolidated balance sheet and income statement of any difference arising on consolidation between the tax chargeable for the current financial period and for preceding financial periods and the amount of tax paid or payable in respect of those periods, provided it is probable that an actual charge to tax will arise within the foreseeable future for one of the consolidated enterprises. This future taxation must be recorded as a liability in the consolidated balance sheet." The legislature did not state explicitly which valuation methods for deferred taxes to use. Analyzing Article 40, however, one could say that the legislature is in favor of the liability approach and the partial method for recognizing timing differences.

3.3 Group Accounts

3.3.1 Introduction

As noted in Section 1, the requirement for holding companies to publish consolidated accounts was introduced in Belgium by the law of September 1, 1986. The Royal Decree of March 1990 introduced the obligation to prepare consolidated accounts for commercial and industrial enterprises.

Significant changes were made by the Royal Decree of March 8, 1990, and at the same time the required treatment in company accounts of financial fixed assets (participations in related companies, see Section 3.8.6) was harmonized with the rules for consolidated accounts. The Royal Decree of March 1990 was, above all, intended to clarify the definitions of relationships between business entities that are crucial in establishing the existence and membership of a group for the purpose of consolidation and equity accounting.

The requirement to consolidate applies to any company that meets the relevant criteria, irrespective of its legal form (public corporation, private limited liability company, limited partnership, etc.).

3.3.2 Scope of Consolidation

For the definition of the group concept, the Belgian legislature followed the criteria of the 7th Directive, which means that Belgium does not only have vertical groups but also consortia or horizontal groups. The determining factor for the existence of a group is the existence of a control relationship. In the decree on the individual accounts as well as in the decree on consolidated accounts, the group relations are defined on the basis of the concept of affiliated enterprises.

An enterprise's affiliated enterprises are defined as:

- An enterprise that it controls
- Enterprises that control it
- Enterprises with which it forms a consortium
- Other enterprises, which to the knowledge of management, are controlled by the enterprises referred to above (Royal Decree 1991, IV,A)

According to the legislation, control can be *de jure* or *de facto*. The wording of the Royal Decree of March 1990 is the following:

The control is *de jure* (consolidation decree, Article 2) and shall be presumed to be irrefutable in the following cases:

- where it results from the holding of the majority of the voting rights attached to all of the shares of the enterprise concerned.

- where a shareholder or member has the right to appoint or remove the majority of the board of directors or general management.

- where a shareholder or member has the power of control by virtue of the memorandum and articles of association of the enterprise concerned or agreements entered into with that enterprise.

- where pursuant to agreements entered into with other shareholders or members of the enterprise concerned, a shareholder or a member has the majority of the voting rights attached to all of the shares of that enterprise (these voting agreements are not constrained by form or content).

- in the event of joint control

Control is *de facto* where it derives from factors other than those referred to above. In the absence of evidence to the contrary, a shareholder or member of an enterprise is presumed to have *de facto* control over the enterprise if, at the two previous general meetings of the enterprise, the shareholder or member exercised voting rights representing the majority of the votes attached to the shares represented at those general meetings.

The consolidation decree defines the companies that should be included in the consolidated accounts (Royal Decree 1991, Article 5). The enterprises included in the consolidation are the consolidating enterprise and its affiliated enterprises or subsidiaries. The Royal Decree of 1991 also defines the concept of associated enterprises (this concept is not found in the royal decrees on individual accounts) as any enterprise other than an affiliated enterprise or joint subsidiary, in which an enterprise included in the consolidation holds a participating interest and exercises a significant influence on the orientation of management policy. According to the Royal Decree of 1991, significant influence shall be presumed (in the absence of evidence to the contrary), where the voting rights attached to the participating interest represent 20 percent or more of the voting rights of the shareholders or members of the enterprise.

3.3.3   Exemptions

With regard to the obligation of the parent company to prepare consolidated accounts, two exemptions are included in the consolidation decree, namely subconsolidation and small groups.

Subconsolidation   A company can be exempted from preparing consolidated accounts if that company is itself an affiliated enterprise of a parent company that prepares and publishes audited consolidated accounts and a consolidated annual report. The exemption is valid for two successive accounting years but can be renewed after two years. The exemption must be decided upon by the shareholders in their general meeting, respecting the conditions of Article 8 of the Royal Decree of 1991.

Small groups   A company is exempted from consolidation if it, and its subsidiaries, on a consolidated basis (after elimination of amounts payable and receivable and intragroup results), does not exceed more than one of the following limits:

Annual turnomver (VAT excluded) during the period	BEF 800 million
Balance sheet total	BEF 400 million
Average number of employees	250

For the financial periods beginning before January 1, 1999 these limits shall be increased to:

Annual turnover (VAT excluded) during the period	BEF 2000 million
Balance sheet total	BEF 1000 million
Average number of employees	500

Exceptions to the exemptions   The exemptions will not apply when all or part of the shares issued by one of the enterprises to be consolidated have been admitted to an official listing on a stock exchange in a European Union country. In spite of the presence of the exemption conditions, the consolidated accounts and directors' report must be prepared if those documents are required for the information of employees or their representatives (workers' councils) or by an administrative or judicial authority for its own purposes.

3.3.4   Exclusions from Consolidation

Further, the Belgian legislature introduced the following optional exclusions from the consolidation scope (nonmateriality, long-term control restriction, disproportionate expense or undue delay, intention of resale) and the following compulsory exclusions (divergent activities, the true and fair view principle, company in liquidation). In the case of an optional exclusion, the subsidiary will be reported on the consolidated balance sheet at cost or a revalued amount; in the case of a compulsory exclusion, the subsidiary will be included in the consolidated balance sheet according to the equity method. Although the legislature stated explicitly that these criteria for exclusion from the consolidation scope should be applied in a restrictive manner, practice shows that companies often make use of the true and fair view and the divergent activities clause to exclude subsidiaries from the consolidation scope.

3.3.5   The Equity Method (Equitization)

As well as being used for certain categories of subsidiary (see Section 3.3.4), equitization is required for associated companies. These are defined as companies in which an enterprise included in the consolidation holds a participation and over which it exercises a significant influence on the orientation of its management. This significant influence is presumed to exist (in the absence of proof to the contrary) if the voting rights attached to the participation represent 20% or more of the total voting rights of the investee company's shareholders.

3.3.6. Consolidation Methods

In order to prepare consolidated accounts, companies must use: full consolidation for subsidiaries, proportional consolidation for joint ventures, the equity method for associated companies, and the cost method for other companies, in which shares are held.

3.3.7 Valuation Rules for Consolidated Accounts

The valuation rules for consolidated accounts are identical to those of individual accounts. Differences are found with regard to consolidation differences, deferred taxation (see Section 3.2) and translation methods (see Section 3.4.2). Positive consolidation differences will be recorded under goodwill, and negative consolidation differences will be recorded under the equity of the group. Goodwill should be amortized over a period of five years; a negative consolidation difference will remain under equity.

3.4 Foreign Currency Translation

3.4.1 Introduction

The rules for foreign currency translation in the individual accounts of single entities are set out in an opinion (or Statement of Recommended Practice) issued by the Accounting Standards Commission in December 1987. As such, they are not legally binding, but departure from them would not normally be considered consistent with giving a true and fair view. For consolidated accounts, the relevant rules are set out in Part II, Section 3 of the Royal Decree of March 6, 1990, which is legally binding.

3.4.2 Foreign Currency Translation in Consolidated Accounts

With regard to the translation of annual accounts in foreign currencies, the consolidation decree allows two methods to be used, namely the monetary/nonmonetary method and the closing rate method. Translation differences in the case of the closing rate method are recorded only on the liability side of the balance sheet as part of the equity of the group. When the monetary/nonmonetary method is applied, translation differences are recorded in the profit and loss account as expenses or revenues. However, they can be treated as unrealized exchange differences.

3.4.3   *Foreign Currency Translation in Company Accounts*

The Commission for Accounting Standards has issued Bulletin No. 20 on the topic of foreign currency translation in company accounts. A brief summary is given here simply to indicate the general principles adopted.

All items that are expressed in a foreign currency should be translated into Belgian francs. A difference is made between monetary and nonmonetary items. Nonmonetary items should be translated into Belgian francs, when the transaction occurs, at the exchange rate of that date. The value of the nonmonetary items will not be influenced any more by changes in the exchange rate between the original currency and the Belgian franc.

Foreign currency monetary items are first recorded in the accounts at the relevant spot rate, unless they are specifically hedged, in which case the relevant forward rate should be used. In the case of an immediate and complete hedge, no exchange difference may arise.

At the balance sheet date, foreign currency monetary items must be valued at the spot rate of that moment. As a result, conversion differences will arise. Unrealized gains are not transferred to income (following the prudence principle) but are treated as a deferred income in the balance sheet. Following the same principle, unrealized losses are first offset against any balance of unrealized gains in the same currency, and any excess is transferred to income. Realized gains and losses from exchange differences are reported as such in the income statement.

In the same bulletin the Commission for Accounting Standards also issued advice with regard to the valuation of foreign currency forward contracts. For the valuation of those contracts a difference is made between forward contracts for hedging purposes and forward contracts for trading purposes.

3.5 Capital and Reserves

3.5.1   *Introduction*

Capital and reserves are divided into six main balance sheet headings:

- Capital
- Share premium
- Revaluation surpluses
- Reserves

- Profit and loss balance awaiting disposition
- Investment grants

Capital may be subdivided into capital subscribed and uncalled capital. The amounts of called-up capital still unpaid shall be accounted for as a receivable.

In addition to the share capital of corporations (shown at nominal value), the term covers the capital of noncorporations such as cooperatives and various forms of partnership.

Share premium or paid-in surplus is the difference between the issue price and the nominal or par value of shares. Share premium is not distributable.

Revaluation surplus arises on the revaluation of physical and financial fixed assets; the surpluses must be "certain but not realized." Such surpluses are not distributable but may effectively enter distributable reserves through being credited to income in line with depreciation charges in respect of the related assets. Alternatively, they may be capitalized if they are certain and durable, but account needs to be taken of the tax impact in case the related assets are realized.

3.5.2 Reserves

Reserves are divided into four categories:

- Legal reserves
- Unavailable (nondistributable) reserves
- Untaxed reserves
- Available (distributable) reserves

The legal reserve is a nondistributable reserve established by transferring at least 5% of annual net income until the reserve amounts to 10% of the share capital. Article 77 of the Company Law obliges companies to build up this legal reserve in the books of the company.

Unavailable reserves consist of two categories: an amount equal to the total of share capital repurchased and held as treasury stock and reserves that the shareholders' meeting cannot freely dispose of by normal majority. With regard to the first category, own shares may only be repurchased subject to the constitution of such a reserve of the appropriate amount (as in Germany). The effect of this is that the repurchase of the shares does not impair the total of the company's capital plus nondistributable reserves.

The untaxed reserves are equal to the realized gains and profits, after deduction of related deferred taxes, of which the tax exemption or tax deferral depends on their being retained within the enterprise. This is an example in which tax regulation dominates accounting regulation.

Available reserves are those over which the shareholders in general meeting have power of disposal. They are generally constituted by the disposition of the net income (profit and loss balance) for the year, after transfers to dividends payable and to other reserve categories as required by law or decided by the shareholders in general meeting.

The reserves are followed by the caption profit (losses) brought forward. This caption is used when the General Assembly approves that losses will be carried forward. In case of a profit this caption will be used when the definite appropriation (dividends or transfer to the reserves) is postponed to future financial periods.

3.5.3   Investment Grants

The Belgian government makes grants available to enterprises for various purposes, for example, when new employees are hired, interest subsidies, and grants for investing in new technology. All such grants except investment grants will be recorded as revenue in the year they relate to. Investment grants include grants from public authorities in respect of investment in fixed assets. After deduction of deferred taxes on such grants, the amount of the investment grant will be stated on the liability side of the balance sheet. These grants will be systematically released to the profit and loss account at the same rate as the depreciation of the related fixed assets, any remaining balance being released when the fixed assets are disposed of or taken out of service.

3.6 Liabilities and Provisions

Caption VII on the liability side of the balance sheet consists of provisions for risks and charges and deferred taxes.

3.6.1   Provisions for Risks and Charges

Four main categories of such provisions are recognized:

- Pensions and similar obligations
- Taxation
- Provisions for major repairs and maintenance
- Other provisions for risks and charges

3.6.2 Pension Obligations

Since January 1, 1986 pension promises made to the whole workforce or a part of it must be funded externally through a pension fund or by taking out an insurance contract. If the minimum funding requirements (stipulated in the Royal Decree of May 14 and 15, 1985) are met, then no pension provision will appear on the balance sheet of the employer. If there is a shortfall in the minimum funding level, a provision will appear on the balance sheet for that particular amount, unless the company is exempted from compliance with that minimum funding level, because the company complies with the transitional provisions foreseen in the Royal Decree of 1985. Provisions for pensions on the balance sheet will usually be used in case of pension commitments made to individuals and in the case of prepensions.

3.6.3 Provisions for Taxation

Provisions for taxes include provisions made to cover tax charges resulting from adjustments of taxable income or from changes in the method of computing taxes.

3.6.4 Major Repairs and Maintenance

The subcaption major repairs and maintenance is not foreseen in the layout of the Fourth Directive. When the future expense is certain but subject to estimation, it is acceptable to spread it over a number of years, corresponding to the periodicity of the repairs or maintenance in question. When the expenditure takes place, the balance of the provision is released to income, offsetting the charge.

It should be noted that in practice the amounts of the provisions are determined by the maximum allowed for tax purposes, rather than by what would be necessary to show a true and fair view.

3.6.5   Other Provisions for Risks and Charges

Other provisions for risks and charges include provisions for several types of situation, including the following:

- Risks under sales commitments
- Risks from futures markets in currencies or commodities
- Risks from orders placed or received for the supply of fixed assets
- Commitments relative to the acquisition or disposal of fixed assets
- Indemnities for redundancy to staff when closure of a company is certain but the amount of the indemnities is not yet established
- Warranties related to the supply of goods or services
- Items acquired in consideration for an annuity payment

The amounts of such provisions are likely to be tax-driven and may not necessarily represent what would be required to show a true and fair view.

3.6.6   Deferred Taxes

Only in the following circumstances will deferred taxes be presented on the balance sheet of the individual accounts:

1. Taxes deferred to later financial periods on investment grants obtained from public authorities for investment in fixed assets
2. Taxes deferred to later financial periods on gains on disposal of tangible and intangible fixed assets and of securities issued by Belgian public authorities, when the taxes on these gains are deferred
3. Foreign taxes of the same nature as the taxes referred to in items 1 and 2 deferred to later financial periods.

3.6.7 Financial Debts Due in More Than One Year

It should be noted that financial debts due in more than one year include the capitalized value of finance lease obligations (*contracts de location-financement* and similar), under which the lessee has an option to acquire the asset at the end of the contract. In this respect, the Belgian rules differ from those in France, where capitalization of finance leases is allowed in consolidated accounts only. See also Section 3.9.5.

For all debts due in more than one year, the current portion is classified as a current liability.

Article 27bis stipulates that all liabilities, except for leasing liabilities, should be valued at nominal value.

3.7 Assets: General Points on Principles of Valuation

These general points concern the definition of acquisition value or original (historical) cost and also revaluations.

Belgian accounting legislation provides that all assets are assessed at acquisition value, after deduction of depreciation and related reductions in value (excepting some particular cases discussed below).

Acquisition value refers to the purchase price, the production cost, or the assigned value that corresponds to the agreed value of contributions in kind.

1. The purchase price includes not only the purchase price, but also additional costs such as registration fee, transport costs, and installation costs.

2. The production cost includes not only the acquisition price, but also raw material, consumption supplies, and the costs of manufacturing directly chargeable to the product or range of products—just as the proportion of production costs (is) only indirectly chargeable to the same product or range of products, in that these costs can be ascribed to the usual period of manufacturing. It should be stressed that companies do not have to include all or part of the indirect costs of production in the cost price (in which case an explanation to that effect should be set out in the notes). Further, companies may include in the acquisition value of tangible and intangible fixed assets interest on capital borrowed to finance their acquisition or production, inasmuch as such interest relates to the period preceding the date on which such assets become ready for operation. Production cost of stocks and contracts in progress may include interest on capital borrowed to finance their production, inasmuch as such interest relates to stocks or contracts, the production or completion of which exceeds one year and relates to the normal production period for these stocks or the normal completion term for these contracts.

3. The share price corresponds to its agreed contractual/conventional value. This cannot exceed the market price of the assets at the moment of transfer of ownership.

3.7.1   Revaluation of Assets

A revaluation is permissible only for tangible fixed assets and financial assets. Enterprises may revalue these assets when it is considered that their value, as determined by reference to their usefulness to the enterprise, clearly and permanently exceeds their carrying value. Further, these assets may be revalued only to the extent that the surplus arising on revaluation can be justified by referrence to the profitability of the enterprise (Article 43, Royal Decree of 1976). Where revaluation relates to tangible fixed assets with a limited useful life, the surplus arising on revaluation should be depreciated in accordance with a predetermined plan in order to apportion the surplus over the estimated residual life of the assets in question.

The revaluation surplus is credited to the "Revaluation surpluses" heading in the capital and reserves section and held there as long as the assets to which they refer are not realized. These revaluation surpluses can nevertheless:

- Be taken to reserve to an amount not exceeding the depreciation on revaluation surplus
- Be incorporated into the capital
- Be withdrawn if they are discovered subsequently not to be funded, to an amount not exceeding the undepreciated figure

Intangible assets and stocks can no longer be subject to revaluation. "Revaluation surplus on intangible assets" accounts and "Revaluation surplus in stock" accounts are, however, retained in the accounting plan in order to register capital gains accruing from before the financial year that began on December 31, 1983.

3.8 Intangible Assets

3.8.1   Formation Expenses

The Belgian legislature created a separate caption for formation expenses. Falling under this heading are those expenses connected with formation, further development, or restructuring of a company, such as those incurred by setting up a company, an increase in capital, loan issue expenses, and restructuring expenses, if not charged against income in the period incurred.

Restructuring expenses may be recorded as assets when they are incurred insofar as they concern expenses (*a*) precisely defined, (*b*) relating to a substantial modification in the structure of the organization of the company, and (*c*) intended to have a favorable and long-lasting effect on the company's profitability. The fulfillment of these conditions must be set out in the notes.

Formation expenses are valued on a historical cost basis and are subject to amortization by annual installments of at least 20%, except for loan issue expenses, whose amortization can be spread out through the period of the loan.

3.8.2   Intangible Fixed Assets

Belgian accounting legislation distinguishes among the following intangibles:

1. Research and development costs: these are the costs of research, production, and development of prototypes, products, discoveries, and know-how relevant to the development of the company's future activities.

2. Franchises, patents, licenses, know-how, trademarks, and similar/simulated rights

3. Goodwill: Goodwill is defined as the excess of the acquisition cost of a company or a division/sphere of activities over and above the value of the assets and liabilities acquired—like the difference in a merger or takeover, for example, between the agreed share value and the net value of the assets and liabilities of the company being taken over

4. Installments paid on intangible assets.

Principles of Valuation   Intangible assets acquired by a third party or by the owners/second party are valued at their acquisition value. Those set up by the company itself are valued at their production cost. Intangible assets may not be subject to revaluation, dating from the financial year that started after December 31, 1983.

Interest expenses can be included under the acquisition value of intangible assets.

Tax-Permitted Methods of Amortization   For intangible assets with finite life, see the section on fixed assets. Amortization can be imposed on intangible assets with indefinite life. In this case, reductions in value must be imposed in order to take account of lasting depreciations/tax allowance.

Research and development costs and goodwill are generally amortized over a maximum of 5 years. If the period of amortization exceeds this term, it must be justified in the supplementary notes.

Complementary or special one-off amortization must be imposed when the accounting value exceeds the use value/recoverable amount as a result of changing economic or technological circumstances.

Declining Balance Depreciation   Since the 1989 tax reform, intangible assets may no longer be subject to declining balance depreciation, from the beginning of the 1991 tax year. The minimum period allowed for straight-line depreciation is fixed at 5 years; for research and development costs the minimum period is 3 years.

3.9 Tangible Fixed Assets

3.9.1   Introduction

Belgian accounting legislation distinguishes among the following categories of tangible fixed assets:

1.   Land and buildings
2.   Plant, machinery, and equipment
3.   Furniture and vehicles
4.   Leasing and other similar rights
5.   Other tangible assets
6.   Assets under construction and advance payments

For the subcaption "other tangible fixed assets," the legislature has presented the following definition:

(a)   Immovable property held in reserve for later use, dwellings, fixed assets which are idle or have been retired by the enterprise as well as any movable and immovable property, the use of which is granted to others by virtue of long term leases, building rights, rental or agricultural rental (except to the extent that the receivables arising from these contracts are to be included under caption V "Amounts receivable after one year" and caption VII "Amounts receivable within one year"). Immovable property acquired or constructed for resale is not included under this caption but recorded separately under stocks (caption VI);

(b) The expenses of improvements to immovable property rented by the enterprise, if they have not been charged to income in the period incurred.

3.9.2 Principles of Valuation

Fixed assets acquired or set up by the company itself are valued at their acquisition price. Valuation at replacement cost is no longer permitted. According to the Law of July 17, 1975, however, companies may apply the replacement price (by ministerial authorization). The revaluation of fixed assets is permitted.

3.9.3 Tax-Permitted Methods of Amortization

The depreciation plan must aim to spread the cost of fixed assets over their probable period of use and must be systematic. Accelerated depreciation can be applied in conformity with tax regulations.

Accounting legislation conforms with tax-permitted methods of amortization:

- Straight-line depreciation
- Declining balance depreciation
- Double straight-line depreciation (law of economic expansion)
- Accelerated depreciation on certain assets (e.g., energy-saving investments)

Additional or exceptional depreciation must be charged in respect of tangible fixed assets with a finite economic life if their net book value exceeds their value to the business, as a result of exceptional deterioration or changes in economic or technological conditions.

In accordance with the relevant tax regulations, accelerated depreciation may be used. Should this lead to a more rapid rate of depreciation than can be economically justified, however, the amount of the excess depreciation must be disclosed in the notes. (This disclosure requirement does not apply to assets acquired during financial years before December 31, 1983.)

3.9.4   Oil, Gas, and Other Mineral Resources

The accounting treatment of the acquisition and subsequent depreciation of a natural resource is set out in opinion No. 158/1 of the *Commission des Normes Comptables* (Accounting Standards Commission), published in December 1988. The acquisition of land that includes a natural resource is considered an acquisition of a tangible fixed asset. Its acquisition cost includes the costs of preparing it for effective exploitation.

A natural resource of unlimited life does not require any depreciation. In the case of limited life, depreciation is calculated on the basis of the units of production method. According to this method, the depreciation chargeable in respect of each unit produced is calculated by dividing the cost of acquisition by the estimated number of units likely to be produced in normal operating conditions. If the value to the business is lower than the net book value, an exceptional depreciation charge must be made.

Revaluation of natural resource assets is permitted.

3.9.5   Assets Held under Financial Lease Contracts

With regard to the definition of a financial lease contract, a distinction is drawn between immovable and movable property.

- With regard to immovable property, installments projected in the contract have to cover the capital invested by the lessor in the buildings, including interest and ancillary costs. Capital invested in the land by the lessor must not be covered through the installments of the contract. Such capital can be part of the price of the purchase option, which may be part of the contract. The price of the purchase option is never taken into account in determining whether or not a contract for immovable property is a financial lease contract.
- With regard to movable property, a contract qualifies as a financial lease contract when the installments envisaged, augmented by the price of the purchase option, cover the entire capital invested by the

lessor in the acquisition of property, including interest and ancillary costs. Where movable property is involved, the amount of the purchase option is taken into account in determining whether the total investment of the lessor is covered in the contract only when the price of the purchase option does not exceed an amount equal to 15% of the capital invested by the lessor.

Valuation Rules Financial lease contracts are valued as follows. The discounted value of installments envisaged in the contract should be reported on the asset side. This amount is called the capital value. The same amount is recorded on the liability side. The capital value is arrived at by using the interest rate stipulated in the leasing contract as the discount rate. The interest portion of the nominal value of the installments is reported as a financial cost in the year in which the installment is paid.

For the lessor, an amount corresponding to the lessee's lease liability (plus the present value of any amount receivable by the lessor at the end of the contract) is treated as a debtor, namely a trade-receivable due in more than one year (with the current portion being classified as a current trade receivable). The lessor's financial income from the lease transaction is equal to the rate of interest applied to the balance on capital outstanding. This balance receivable is calculated in a similar way to the lessee's balance payable, as described above.

Lease contracts that do not meet the criteria mentioned above are treated as operating leases and are not capitalized.

3.10 Financial Fixed Assets

3.10.1 Definitions

The caption "financial assets" includes participating interests and amounts receivable held in affiliated enterprises, enterprises linked by participating interests, and other enterprises.

For application of the Royal Decree of March 1990, the following are considered affiliated enterprises of an enterprise:

1. The enterprises that it controls
2. The enterprises that control it
3. The enterprises with which the enterprise forms a consortium
4. Other enterprises that, to the knowledge of management, are controlled by the enterprises referred to in 1, 2, and 3, above.

"Control over an enterprise" is defined in the Royal Decree of 1990 as the power *de jure* or *de facto* to exercise a decisive influence on the appointment of the majority of the board of directors or general management or on the orientation of the management policy.

According to the provisions of the Royal Decree, control *de jure* exists and shall be presumed to be irrefutable in the following situations:

1. When it results from the holding of the majority of the voting rights attached to all of the shares of the enterprise concerned

2. When a shareholder or member has the right to appoint or remove the majority of the board of directors or general management

3. When a shareholder or member has the power of control by virtue of the memorandum and articles of association of the enterprise concerned or agreements entered into with that enterprise

4. When, pursuant to agreements entered into with other shareholders or members of the enterprise concerned, a shareholder or member has the majority of the voting rights attached to all of the shares of that enterprise

5. In the event of joint control

The control is *de facto* where it results from other factors than those referred to above. In the absence of evidence to the contrary, a shareholder or member of an enterprise shall be presumed to have *de facto* control over the enterprise if, at the two previous general meetings of the enterprise, the shareholder or member has exercised voting rights representing the majority of the votes attached to the shares represented at those general meetings.

In the second category of the financial fixed assets the enterprises linked by participating interests are found. Enterprises linked by participating interests are those enterprises in which the holding of the rights is intended through establishing a lasting and specific relationship with these enterprises, to permit the enterprise to increase influence on the orientation of the management policy of these enterprises.

The following enterprises, if they are not affiliated enterprises, fall into the category "other enterprises linked by participating interest":

1. Those in which the enterprise or its subsidiaries have a participating interest

2. Those that, to the knowledge of management, have a direct participating interest in the enterprise or participating interest through subsidiaries

3. Those that, to the knowledge of management, are subsidiaries of enterprises mentioned under item 2.

In the absence of evidence to the contrary given in the notes to the accounts, the following are considered participating interests:

1. Possession of rights representing one-tenth of the capital or of a particular category of shares of an enterprise

2. Possession of rights representing a lower proportion than 10%

   a. when by addition of the rights held by the enterprise and its subsidiaries (...), this participating interest represents one-tenth of the capital or of a particular category of shares of the enterprise

   b. when the disposal of the shares or the exercise of the related rights are subject to agreements or unilateral commitments which the enterprise has entered into

Shares are reported under the subcaption "other financial assets" when the rights held in these enterprises are not considered participating interests but the holding is intended for a lasting relationship.

3.10.2   Valuation Rules for Financial Fixed Assets

Participations are valued at cost but may be revalued in appropriate cases. Write-downs must be made in cases on a durable impairment of value because of the situation, level on profitability, or future prospects of the company in which they are held. Such write-downs are reported as "exceptional items" in the income statement. Loans and advances are stated at nominal value.

Transaction costs incurred in acquiring financial fixed assets may be taken directly to the income statement.

3.10.3   Amounts Receivable in More than One Year

Amounts receivable must be valued at nominal value (Article 27bis). The current portion of such amounts receivable is reclassified as a current asset. In case of doubtful or incomplete collectability a write-down should be recorded.

3.11 Current Assets

3.11.1 Inventories

The sixth caption on the balance sheet includes stocks and contracts in progress. The following breakdown is presented on the balance sheet:

A. Stocks

1. Raw materials and consumables
2. Work in progress
3. Finished goods
4. Goods purchased for resale, which include goods purchased as such or after minor treatment
5. Immovable property acquired or constructed for resale
6. Advance payments

B. Contracts in progress

Contracts in progress include:

1. Work in progress, which is carried out for the account of third parties but has not yet been completed
2. Goods in progress, which are manufactured for the account of third parties and have not yet been delivered, except where these relate to standard production
3. Services that are performed for the account of third parties and have not yet been fulfilled, except where these relate to standard services

3.11.2 Valuation Rules

The general rule is that of the lower of cost and market value. If a write-down from cost to market value has been made and the market value subsequently increases, this increase must be reflected but not so that the value exceeds cost. Work in process is valued at production cost. These rules are also accepted for tax purposes.

Contracts-in-progress may be valued by using the percentage-of-completion method to recognize profit, when the profit may also be estimated with reasonable certainty. On the other hand, the completed contract method, under which no profit is recognized until completion, may be used. Different methods may be used for different contracts, provided this is done consistently for each contract and also providing the reasons are disclosed in the notes.

Cost may be determined by identifying individually the price of each item, or according to various cost-flow assumptions: weighted average, first-in-first-out (FIFO) or last-in-first-out (LIFO). If cost on a LIFO basis is substantially lower than market value, this fact should be mentioned in the notes. Standard cost is not accepted as such, and companies that use standard costs must adjust such costs so that they approximate one of the other types of cost just mentioned.

Cost is normally understood to include production overheads (full cost), but some or all of the indirect production overheads may be omitted, in which case this must be mentioned in the notes.

As well as write-downs of inventories from cost to market value if lower, as mentioned above, contracts-in-progress and work-in-process may have to be written down if the estimated total costs to complete exceed the net selling price.

The use of replacement cost for inventories was permitted under the Royal Decree of October 8, 1976 but later excluded by the Royal Decree of September 12, 1983.

Raw materials and consumables that are regularly replenished, whose quantity, value, and composition do not vary significantly from one period to another, and whose total amount is immaterial, may be recorded in the same way as small tools, described below.

3.11.3 Advances Received on Contracts-in-Progress

Advances received on contracts-in-progress are not deducted from the balance of the inventory accounts but are shown as current liabilities.

3.11.4 Small Tools

If small tools are regularly replenished, and their quantity, value, and composition do not vary significantly from one period to another, and their total amount is immaterial, they may be recorded at a fixed amount, with the cost of replenishment being recorded as an expense.

3.11.5   Short-Term Investments

Short-term investments are financial assets acquired for short-term trea-sury purposes and not as long-term investments. Deposits are stated at nominal value, while securities are stated following the rule of lower of cost or market value as described above for inventories.

Own shares acquired and held as treasury stock are classified under the caption "investments."

If an enterprise has bought bonds, they should be valued at acquisition price. The difference between the acquisition price and the redemption value shall be released to the income statement as a component of interest and added to or deducted from the acquisition cost of the securities on the basis of the actuarial yield.

3.12   Exceptional Items in the Income Statement

Exceptional items in the income statement include the following:

Exceptional income

- Write-backs of depreciation and of amounts written off against intan-gible and physical fixed assets
- Write-backs of amounts written off against financial fixed assets
- Write-backs of provisions for exceptional risks and charges
- Realized surpluses on disposal of fixed assets
- Other income

Exceptional charges

- Exceptional depreciation and write-offs against organization cost and intangible and tangible fixed assets
- Write-offs against financial fixed assets
- Provisions for exceptional risks and charges
- Losses on disposal of fixed assets
- Other charges
- Exceptional costs of restructuring, treated as deferred charges

The criterion for inclusion is that the item is such that it is not part of the normal activity of the business.

There is no distinction between "exceptional items" and "extraordinary items and prior year adjustments," and the items reported as "exceptional" in Belgium should not be equated with "extraordinary" items in the sense used in some other countries, although some of them may have this character.

4. Expected Future Developments

With the Royal Decree of March 1990 on Consolidated Accounts, a period of 15 years of development of financial accounting and reporting in Belgium reached its conclusion. During the 1970s and 1980s, it is probably fair to say that development of Belgian financial accounting lagged behind that of its neighbors in the Netherlands and in France. The decision taken in the mid-1970s to modernize Belgian accounting took time to come to fruition; similar decisions were taken in France in the late 1960s.

Consequently, the expected future developments in Belgian financial accounting and reporting are essentially consolidation of recent improvements. From the standpoint of the informational quality of Belgian financial statements, one major problem remains: the decision that accounting rules for financial reporting should follow tax accounting rules with resultant departures from a "true and fair view" being indicated in the notes. The experience of using published financial statements suggests that this is not a satisfactory solution. It is possible to find a way around this essentially legalistic problem by emancipating group accounts, as opposed to legal entity accounts, from the domination of tax accounting. However, it is not yet clear whether Belgian accounting will adopt this solution.

Useful Addresses

Institut des Experts Comptables
Rue Blanche 25
1050 Bruxelles
Belgium
Tel: +(2) 537.67.35
Fax: +(2) 537.53.63

FEE
Rue de la Loi 83
B-1040 Brussels
Belgium
Tel: +(2) 2310555
Fax: +(2) 231 1112

Institut des Réviseurs d'Entreprises
Avenue Marnix 22
1050 Bruxelles
Belgium
Tel: +(2) 512 5136
Fax: +(2) 512 7886

Financial Statements

GECONSOLIDEERDE BALANS

PER 31 DECEMBER 1995 EN 31 DECEMBER 1996

(in miljoenen BEF)

ACTIVA	1995		1996	
VASTE ACTIVA		205.761		221.714
II. IMMATERIELE VASTE ACTIVA *(pag. 73)*		2.809		3.232
III. CONSOLIDATIEVERSCHILLEN *(pag. 74)*		45		35
IV. MATERIELE VASTE ACTIVA *(pag. 74)*		196.009		211.594
A. Terreinen en gebouwen	25.134		28.548	
B. Installaties, machines, uitrusting, meubilair en rollend materieel	105.623		109.288	
C. Exploratie- en productie-installaties	53.623		53.802	
D. Leasing en soortgelijke rechten	1.350		1.169	
E. Overige materiële vaste activa	1.584		1.636	
F. Vaste activa in aanbouw en vooruitbetalingen	8.695		17.151	
V. FINANCIELE VASTE ACTIVA *(pag. 75)*		6.898		6.853
A. Ondernemingen waarop vermogensmutatie is toegepast				
1. Deelnemingen	4.338		4.107	
2. Vorderingen	251			
	4.589		4.107	
B. Andere ondernemingen				
1. Deelnemingen	1.662		2.189	
2. Vorderingen	647		557	
	2.309		2.746	
VLOTTENDE ACTIVA		132.017		149.932
VI. VORDERINGEN OP MEER DAN ÉÉN JAAR *(pag. 75)*		15.134		18.352
B. Overige vorderingen	15.134		18.352	
VII. VOORRADEN EN BESTELLINGEN IN UITVOERING *(pag. 76)*		45.033		48.176
VIII. VORDERINGEN OP TEN HOOGSTE ÉÉN JAAR *(pag. 76)*		65.575		77.203
A. Handelsvorderingen	58.688		69.140	
B. Overige vorderingen	6.887		8.063	
IX. GELDBELEGGINGEN		1.007		683
B. Overige beleggingen	1.007		683	
X. LIQUIDE MIDDELEN		1.969		2.599
XI. OVERLOPENDE REKENINGEN *(pag. 76)*		3.299		2.919
TOTAAL DER ACTIVA		**337.778**		**371.646**

(in miljoenen BEF)

PASSIVA	1995		1996	
EIGEN VERMOGEN *(pag. 77)*		122.207		133.069
I. KAPITAAL		43.293		43.293
A. Geplaatst kapitaal	43.293		43.293	
II. UITGIFTEPREMIES		24.310		24.314
IV. RESERVES		84.398		90.900
V. CONSOLIDATIEVERSCHILLEN		542		530
VI. OMREKENINGSVERSCHILLEN		- 30.853		- 26.462
VII. KAPITAALSUBSIDIES		517		494
BELANGEN VAN DERDEN *(pag. 78)*		4.890		5.658
VIII. BELANGEN VAN DERDEN	4.890		5.658	
VOORZIENINGEN EN UITGESTELDE BELASTINGEN *(pag. 78)*		42.259		46.949
IX. A. VOORZIENINGEN VOOR RISICO'S EN KOSTEN		28.111		29.415
1. Pensioenen en soortgelijke verplichtingen	11.340		11.984	
3. Grote herstellings- en onderhoudswerken	332		94	
4. Overige risico's en kosten	16.439		17.337	
B. UITGESTELDE BELASTINGEN		14.148		17.534
SCHULDEN		168.422		185.970
X. SCHULDEN OP MEER DAN ÉÉN JAAR *(pag. 80)*		43.948		48.855
A. Financiële schulden				
2. Niet-achtergestelde obligatieleningen	31.777		34.817	
3. Leasing en soortgelijke schulden	786		654	
4. Kredietinstellingen	10.698		12.567	
5. Overige leningen	687		817	
XI. SCHULDEN OP TEN HOOGSTE ÉÉN JAAR *(pag.81)*		118.510		130.633
A. Schulden op meer dan één jaar die binnen het boekjaar vervallen	5.825		1.200	
B. Financiële schulden				
1. Kredietinstellingen	19.473		27.439	
2. Overige leningen	8.552		6.405	
	28.025		33.844	
C. Handelsschulden				
1. Leveranciers	40.895		45.852	
2. Te betalen wissels	190		148	
	41.085		46.000	
E. Schulden met betrekking tot belastingen, bezoldigingen en sociale lasten				
1. Belastingen	23.459		28.296	
2. Bezoldigingen en sociale lasten	3.342		3.560	
	26.801		31.856	
F. Overige schulden	16.774		17.733	
XII. OVERLOPENDE REKENINGEN *(pag. 81)*		5.964		6.482
TOTAAL DER PASSIVA		337.778		371.646

BILANS CONSOLIDÉS

Aux 31 décembre 1995 et 31 décembre 1996

(En millions BEF)

ACTIF		1995		1996
Actifs immobilisés		205.761		221.714
II.　Immobilisations incorporelles *(page 73)*		2.809		3.232
III.　Écarts de consolidation *(page 74)*		45		35
IV.　Immobilisations corporelles *(page 74)*		196.009		211.594
A. Terrains et constructions	25.134		28.548	
B. Installations, machines, outillage,				
mobilier, matériel roulant	105.623		109.288	
C. Installations recherche-production	53.623		53.802	
D. Location-financement et droits similaires	1.350		1.169	
E. Autres immobilisations corporelles	1.584		1.636	
F. Immobilisations en cours	8.695		17.151	
V.　Immobilisations financières *(page 75)*		6.898		6.853
A. Entreprises mises en équivalence				
1. Participations	4.338		4.107	
2. Créances	251			
	4.589		4.107	
B. Autres entreprises				
1. Participations, actions et parts	1.662		2.189	
2. Créances	647		557	
	2.309		2.746	
Actifs circulants		132.017		149.932
VI.　Créances à plus d'un an *(page 75)*		15.134		18.352
B. Autres créances	15.134		18.352	
VII.　Stocks *(page 76)*		45.033		48.176
VIII.Créances à un an au plus *(page 76)*		65.575		77.203
A. Créances commerciales	58.688		69.140	
B. Autres créances	6.887		8.063	
IX.　Placements de trésorerie		1.007		683
B. Autres placements	1.007		683	
X.　Valeurs disponibles		1.969		2.599
XI.　Comptes de régularisation *(page 76)*		3.299		2.919
TOTAL DE L'ACTIF		337.778		371.646

(En millions BEF)

PASSIF		1995		1996
CAPITAUX PROPRES *(page 77)*		122.207		133.069
I. CAPITAL		43.293		43.293
A. Capital souscrit	43.293		43.293	
II. PRIMES D'ÉMISSION		24.310		24.314
IV. RÉSERVES		84.398		90.900
V. ÉCARTS DE CONSOLIDATION		542		530
VI. ÉCARTS DE CONVERSION		- 30.853		- 26.462
VII. SUBSIDES EN CAPITAL		517		494
INTÉRÊTS DE TIERS *(page 78)*		4.890		5.658
VIII. INTÉRÊTS DE TIERS	4.890		5.658	
PROVISIONS, IMPÔTS DIFFÉRÉS ET LATENCES FISCALES *(page 78)*		42.259		46.949
IX. A. PROVISIONS POUR RISQUES ET CHARGES		28.111		29.415
1. Pensions et obligations similaires	11.340		11.984	
3. Grosses réparations et entretiens	332		94	
4. Autres risques et charges	16.439		17.337	
B. IMPÔTS DIFFÉRÉS ET LATENCES FISCALES		14.148		17.534
DETTES		168.422		185.970
X. DETTES À PLUS D'UN AN *(page 80)*		43.948		48.855
A. Dettes financières				
2. Emprunts obligataires non subordonnés	31.777		34.817	
3. Dettes de location - financement				
et assimilées	786		654	
4. Etablissements de crédit	10.698		12.567	
5. Autres emprunts	687		817	
XI. DETTES À UN AN AU PLUS *(page 81)*		118.510		130.633
A. Dettes à plus d'un an échéant dans l'année	5.825		1.200	
B. Dettes financières				
1. Etablissements de crédit	19.473		27.439	
2. Autres emprunts	8.552		6.405	
	28.025		33.844	
C. Dettes commerciales				
1. Fournisseurs	40.895		45.852	
2. Effets à payer	190		148	
	41.085		46.000	
E. Dettes fiscales, salariales et sociales				
1. Impôts	23.459		28.296	
2. Rémunérations et charges sociales	3.342		3.560	
	26.801		31.856	
F. Autres dettes	16.774		17.733	
XII. COMPTES DE RÉGULARISATION *(page 81)*		5.964		6.482
TOTAL DU PASSIF		**337.778**		**371.646**

CONSOLIDATED BALANCE SHEET

AT DECEMBER 31, 1995 AND DECEMBER 31, 1996

(million BEF)

ASSETS	1995		1996	
FIXED ASSETS		205,761		221,714
II. INTANGIBLE FIXED ASSETS *(page 73)*		2,809		3,232
III. CONSOLIDATION ADJUSTMENTS *(page 74)*		45		35
IV. TANGIBLE ASSETS *(page 74)*		196,009		211,594
A. Land and buildings	25,134		28,548	
B. Plant, machinery, equipment,				
furniture and vehicles	105,623		109,288	
C. Exploration and Production assets	53,623		53,802	
D. Capital leases and similar				
commitments	1,350		1,169	
E. Other	1,584		1,636	
F. Assets under construction	8,695		17,151	
V. INVESTMENTS AND LOANS *(page 75)*		6,898		6,853
A. Companies accounted for under				
the equity method				
1. Investments	4,338		4,107	
2. Loans	251			
	4,589		4,107	
B. Other companies				
1. Investments	1,662		2,189	
2. Loans	647		557	
	2,309		2,746	
CURRENT ASSETS		132,017		149,932
VI. LONG TERM RECEIVABLE *(page 75)*		15,134		18,352
B. Other receivable	15,134		18,352	
VII. INVENTORIES *(page 76)*		45,033		48,176
VIII. ACCOUNTS RECEIVABLE *(page 76)*		65,575		77,203
A. Trade receivable	58,688		69,140	
B. Other	6,887		8,063	
IX. MARKETABLE SECURITIES		1,007		683
B. Other securities	1,007		683	
X: CASH		1,969		2,599
XI. DEFERRED CHARGES AND ACCRUED INCOME *(page 76)*		3,299		2,919
TOTAL ASSETS		337,778		371,646

(*million BEF*)

LIABILITIES AND STOCKHOLDER'S EQUITY		1995		1996
SHAREHOLDERS' EQUITY *(page 77)*			122,207	133,069
I. SHARE CAPITAL			43,293	43,293
A. ISSUED CAPITAL	43,293			43,293
II. SHARE PREMIUM			24,310	24,314
IV. RETAINED EARNINGS			84,398	90,900
V. CONSOLIDATION ADJUSTMENT			542	530
VI. CURRENCY TRANSLATION ADJUSTMENT			- 30,853	- 26,462
VII. INVESTMENT GRANTS			517	494
MINORITY INTERESTS *(page 78)*			4,890	5,658
VIII. MINORITY INTERESTS	4,890			5,658
PROVISIONS AND DEFERRED INCOME TAXES *(page 78)*			42,259	46,949
IX. A. PROVISIONS FOR LIABILITIES AND CHARGES			28,111	29,415
1. Pensions and similar commitments	11,340			11,984
3. Major repairs and maintenance	332			94
4. Other liabilities and charges	16,439			17,337
B. DEFERRED INCOME TAXES			14,148	17,534
LIABILITIES			168,422	185,970
X. LONG TERM LIABILITIES *(page 80)*			43,948	48,855
A. Financial				
2. Unsubordinated bonds and notes	31,777			34,817
3. Capital lease obligations	786			654
4. Banks and financial institutions	10,698			12,567
5. Others	687			817
XI. CURRENT LIABILITIES *(page 81)*			118,510	130,633
A. Long term debt - current portion	5,825			1,200
B. Financial debt				
1. Banks and financial institutions	19,473			27,439
2. Others	8,552			6,405
	28,025			33,844
C. Accounts payable				
1. Suppliers	40,895			45,852
2. Bills of exchange payable	190			148
	41,085			46,000
E. Taxes, salaries and social security contributions				
1. Taxes	23,459			28,296
2. Salaries and social security contributions	3,342			3,560
	26,801			31,856
F. Other	16,774			17,733
XII. ACCRUED CHARGES AND DEFERRED REVENUES *(page 81)*			5,964	6,482
TOTAL LIABILITIES AND SHAREHOLDERS' EQUITY			337,778	371,646

GECONSOLIDEERDE RESULTATENREKENING

PER 31 DECEMBER 1995 EN 31 DECEMBER 1996

(in miljoenen BEF)

		1995		1996
I.	BEDRIJFSOPBRENGSTEN *(pag.83)*		563.193	624.594
	A. Omzet	551.810		612.872
	C. Geproduceerde vaste activa	871		1.039
	D. Andere bedrijfsopbrengsten	10.512		10.683
II.	BEDRIJFSKOSTEN		- 531.613	- 587.012
	A. Handelsgoederen, grond- en hulpstoffen			
	1. Inkopen	- 234.813		- 271.623
	2. Wijziging in de voorraad	3.457		446
	3. Rechten en belastingen op producten	- 195.414		- 206.956
		- 426.770		- 478.133
	B. Diensten en diverse goederen	- 42.608		- 45.149
	C. Bezoldigingen, sociale lasten en pensioenen			
	(pag. 84)	- 27.119		- 27.462
	D. Afschrijvingen en waardeverminderingen op			
	immateriële en materiële vaste activa	- 26.059		- 26.489
	E. Waardeverminderingen op voorraden, bestel-			
	lingen in uitvoering en handelsvorderingen	- 232		- 361
	F. Voorzieningen voor risico's en kosten *(pag. 84)*	- 1.102		- 314
	G. Andere bedrijfskosten	- 7.723		- 9.104
III.	BEDRIJFSWINST		31.580	37.582
IV.	FINANCIELE OPBRENGSTEN *(pag. 85)*		3.282	2.549
	A. Opbrengsten uit financiële vaste activa	1.519		1.058
	B. Opbrengsten uit vlottende activa	956		1.026
	C. Andere financiële opbrengsten	807		465
V.	FINANCIELE KOSTEN *(pag. 85)*		- 7.800	- 6.453
	A. Kosten van schulden	- 6.062		- 5.576
	B. Waardeverminderingen op financiële activa	210		- 83
	C. Andere financiële kosten	- 1.948		- 794
VI.	WINST UIT DE GEWONE BEDRIJFSUITOEFENING			
	VOOR BELASTING		27.062	33.678

VII. UITZONDERLIJKE OPBRENGSTEN *(pag. 86)*			383	1.551
A. Terugneming van afschrijvingen en waardeverminderingen		230		
C. Terugneming van voorzieningen voor uitzonderlijke risico's en kosten		68		217
D. Meerwaarden bij de realisatie van vaste activa				
E. Andere uitzonderlijke opbrengsten		85		1.334
VIII. UITZONDERLIJKE KOSTEN *(pag. 86)*			- 2.210	- 1.893
A. Afschrijvingen en waardeverminderingen op immateriële en materiële vaste activa		- 274		- 154
C. Voorzieningen voor uitzonderlijke risico's en kosten		482		- 586
D. Minderwaarden bij de realisatie van vaste activa				
E. Andere uitzonderlijke kosten		- 2.418		- 1.153
IX. WINST VAN HET BOEKJAAR VOOR BELASTING			25.235	33.336
IXBIS. UITGESTELDE BELASTINGEN *(pag. 79)*			- 789	- 784
A. Overboeking naar de uitgestelde belastingen		- 789		- 784
B. Onttrekking aan de uitgestelde belastingen				
X. BELASTINGEN OP HET RESULTAAT *(pag. 81)*			- 12.180	- 16.791
A. Belastingen		- 12.180		- 16.791
XI. WINST VAN DE GECONSOLIDEERDE ONDERNEMINGEN			12.266	15.761
XII. AANDEEL IN HET RESULTAAT VAN DE ONDER- NEMINGEN WAAROP VERMOGENSMUTATIE IS TOEGEPAST			41	983
A. Resultaten winst		474		1.151
B. Resultaten verlies		- 433		- 168
XIII. GECONSOLIDEERDE WINST			12.307	16.744
XIV. AANDEEL VAN DERDEN IN HET RESULTAAT			699	696
XV. AANDEEL VAN DE GROEP IN HET RESULTAAT			11.608	16.048

RÉSULTATS CONSOLIDÉS

AUX 31 DÉCEMBRE 1995 ET 31 DÉCEMBRE 1996

(En millions BEF)

	1995		1996	
I. VENTES ET PRESTATIONS *(page 83)*		563.193		624.594
A. Chiffre d'affaires	551.810		612.872	
C. Production immobilisée	871		1.039	
D. Autres produits d'exploitation	10.512		10.683	
II. COÛTS DES VENTES ET PRESTATIONS		- 531.613		- 587.012
A. Approvisionnements et marchandises				
1. Achats	- 234.813		- 271.623	
2. Variations des stocks	3.457		446	
3. Droits et taxes sur produits	- 195.414		- 206.956	
	- 426.770		- 478.133	
B. Services et biens divers	- 42.608		- 45.149	
C. Rémunérations, charges sociales et pensions *(page 84)*	- 27.119		- 27.462	
D. Amortissements et réductions de valeur sur immobilisations incorporelles et corporelles	- 26.059		- 26.489	
E. Réductions de valeur sur stocks et créances commerciales	- 232		- 361	
F. Provisions pour risques et charges *(page 84)*	- 1.102		- 314	
G. Autres charges d'exploitation	- 7.723		- 9.104	
III. BÉNÉFICE D'EXPLOITATION		31.580		37.582
IV. PRODUITS FINANCIERS *(page 85)*		3.282		2.549
A. Produits des immobilisations financières	1.519		1.058	
B. Produits des actifs circulants	956		1.026	
C. Autres produits financiers	807		465	
V. CHARGES FINANCIÈRES *(page 85)*		- 7.800		- 6.453
A. Charges des dettes	- 6.062		- 5.576	
B. Réductions de valeur sur actifs financiers	210		- 83	
C. Autres charges financières	- 1.948		- 794	
VI. BÉNÉFICE COURANT AVANT IMPÔTS		27.062		33.678

VII.	PRODUITS EXCEPTIONNELS *(page 86)*		383	1.551
	A. Reprises d'amortissements et de réductions de valeur	230		
	C. Reprises de provisions pour risques et charges exceptionnels	68	217	
	D. Plus-values sur réalisation d'actifs immobilisés		1.334	
	E. Autres produits exceptionnels	85		
VIII.	CHARGES EXCEPTIONNELLES *(page 86)*		- 2.210	- 1.893
	A. Amortissements et réductions de valeur sur immobilisations incorporelles et corporelles	- 274	- 154	
	C. Provisions pour risques et charges exceptionnels	482	- 586	
	D. Moins-values sur réalisation d'actifs immobilisés			
	E. Autres charges exceptionnelles	- 2.418	- 1.153	
IX.	BÉNÉFICE DE L'EXERCICE AVANT IMPÔTS		25.235	33.336
IX.BIS	IMPÔTS DIFFÉRÉS *(page 79)*		- 789	- 784
	A. Transferts aux impôts différés	- 789	- 784	
	B. Prélèvements sur impôts différés			
X.	IMPÔTS SUR LE RÉSULTAT *(page 81)*		- 12.180	- 16.791
	A. Impôts courants	- 12.180	- 16.791	
XI.	BÉNÉFICE DES ENTREPRISES CONSOLIDÉES		12.266	15.761
XII.	QUOTE-PART DANS LE RÉSULTAT DES ENTREPRISES MISES EN ÉQUIVALENCE		41	983
	A. Résultats en bénéfice	474	1.151	
	B. Résultats en perte	- 433	- 168	
XIII.	BÉNÉFICE CONSOLIDÉ		12.307	16.744
XIV.	PART DES TIERS DANS LE RÉSULTAT		699	696
XV.	PART DU GROUPE DANS LE RÉSULTAT		11.608	16.048

CONSOLIDATED STATEMENT OF INCOME

AT DECEMBER 31, 1995 AND DECEMBER 31, 1996

(million BEF)

	1995		1996	
I. SALES AND OTHER OPERATING REVENUE *(page 83)*		563,193		624,594
A. Sales	551,810		612,872	
C. Internal capitalized expenses	871		1,039	
D. Other operating revenue	10,512		10,683	
II. COST AND EXPENSES		- 531,613		- 587,012
A. Supplies and goods				
1. Raw materials and products purchased	- 234,813		- 271,623	
2. Change in inventories	3,457		446	
3. Duties, taxes on products	- 195,414		- 206,956	
	- 426,770		- 478,133	
B. Services and other goods	- 42,608		- 45,149	
C. Personnel expenses *(page 84)*	- 27,119		- 27,462	
D. Depreciation, depletion and amortization	- 26,059		- 26,489	
E. Trade receivables and inventories				
(write-down) write-back	- 232		-361	
F. Provisions for liabilities and charges *(page 84)*	- 1,102		- 314	
G. Other operating expenses	- 7,723		- 9,104	
III. OPERATING PROFIT		31,580		37,582
IV. INVESTMENT INCOME *(page 85)*		3,282		2,549
A. Financial investments	1,519		1,058	
B. Current assets	956		1,026	
C. Other	807		465	
V. FINANCIAL EXPENSES *(page 85)*		- 7,800		- 6,453
A. Interest expense	- 6,062		- 5,576	
B. Current assets (write-down) write-back	210		- 83	
C. Other	- 1,948		- 794	
VI. CONSOLIDATED INCOME BEFORE EXCEPTIONAL ITEMS		27,062		33,678

VII. EXCEPTIONAL INCOME *(page 86)*		383		1,551
A. Depreciation and amortization reversals	230			
C. Provisions for liabilities and charges write-back	68		217	
D. Gain on disposal of fixed assets			1,334	
E. Other	85			
VIII. EXCEPTIONAL CHARGES *(page 86)*		- 2,210		- 1,893
A. Fixed assets depreciation and amortization	- 274		- 154	
C. Provisions for liabilities and charges	482		- 586	
D. Losses on disposal of fixed assets				
E. Other	- 2,418		- 1,153	
IX. CONSOLIDATED INCOME BEFORE TAXES		25,235		33,336
IXBIS. DEFERRED TAXES *(page 87)*		- 789		- 784
A. Deferred taxes	- 789		- 784	
X. TAXES ON INCOME *(page 91)*		- 12,180		- 16,791
A. Current taxes	- 12,180		- 16,791	
XI. NET INCOME OF CONSOLIDATED COMPANIES		12,266		15,761
XII. EQUITY IN NET INCOME OF AFFILIATED COMPANIES		41		983
A. Income	474		1,151	
B. Losses	- 433		- 168	
XIII. CONSOLIDATED NET INCOME		12,307		16,744
XIV. MINORITY INTERESTS		699		696
XV. GROUP NET INCOME		11,608		16,048

RESULTAATVERWERKING

(in miljoenen BEF)

RESULTAAT VAN HET BOEKJAAR	
a) Aandeel van de Groep	16.048
b) Aandeel van derden	696
Beschikbaar voor verdeling	16.744
Dividend van het boekjaar	9.301
Ter beschikking van de Raad van Bestuur, de Directie,	
het Kaderpersoneel en het Mecenaat	245
Reserves	6.502
Aandeel van derden	696
	16.744

CASH FLOW

De cash flow over het boekjaar bedraagt 45,1 miljard BEF tegenover 39,3 miljard BEF over het vorige.
Deze notie moet in de strikte betekenis geïnterpreteerd worden: ze is gedefinieerd als een resultaat vóór afschrijvingen en voorzieningen. Deze tabel toont de elementen, die na optelling bij het resultaat, de cash flow bepalen.

(in miljoenen BEF)

	1995	1996
Geconsolideerd resultaat	12.307	16.744
Afschrijvingen en waardeverminderingen op immateriële en		
materiële vaste activa (II.D.)	26.059	26.489
Waardeverminderingen op voorraden en handelsvorderingen (II.E.)	510	660
Terugnemingen van waardeverminderingen op voorraden (II.E.)	- 278	- 299
Terugnemingen van waardeverminderingen		
op handelsvorderingen (*pag. 86 E.*)	- 453	- 246
Voorzieningen voor risico's en kosten (II.F.)	1.102	314
Waardeverminderingen op financiële activa (V.B.)	-210	83
Uitgestelde belastingen (IXbis.)	789	784
Uitzonderlijke afschrijvingen en waardeverminderingen (VIII.A.)	274	154
Voorzieningen voor uitzonderlijke risico's en kosten (VIII.C.)	- 482	586
Terugnemingen van uitzonderlijke voorzieningen (VII.C.)	- 68	- 217
Terugnemingen van afschrijvingen en waardeverminderingen (VIII.A.)	- 230	—
GECONSOLIDEERDE CASH FLOW	39.320	45.052
Cash flow van de Groep	37.889	43.458

AFFECTATIONS DES RÉSULTATS

(En millions BEF)

RÉSULTATS DE L'EXERCICE	
a) Part du Groupe	16.048
b) Part des tiers	696
Disponible pour affectations	16.744
Dividende de l'exercice	9.301
Intéressement du Conseil, de la Direction, des Cadres et Mécénat	245
Réserves	6.502
Intérêts de tiers	696
	16.744

CASH-FLOW

Le cash-flow de l'exercice atteint 45,1 milliards BEF contre 39,3 milliards BEF pour l'exercice antérieur.

Cette notion doit être interprétée au sens strict: elle est définie comme le résultat avant amortissements et provisions. Le tableau suivant montre les éléments qui, ajoutés au résultat, permettent d'atteindre le cash-flow.

(En millions BEF)

	1995	1996
Résultats consolidés	12.307	16.744
Amortissements et réductions de valeur sur immobilisations incorporelles et corporelles (II.D.)	26.059	26.489
Réductions de valeur sur créances commerciales (II.E.)	510	660
Reprises de réductions de valeur sur stocks (II.E.)	- 278	- 299
Reprises de réductions de valeur sur créances commerciales *(page 88 E.)*	- 453	- 246
Provisions pour risques et charges (II.F.)	1.102	314
Réductions de valeur sur actifs financiers (V.B.)	- 210	83
Impôts différés (IXBIS.)	789	784
Amortissements et réductions de valeur exceptionnels (VIII.A.)	274	154
Provisions pour risques et charges exceptionnels (VIII.C.)	- 482	586
Reprises de provisions exceptionnelles (VII.C.)	- 68	- 217
Reprises d'amortissements et réductions de valeur (VII.A.)	- 230	-
CASH-FLOW CONSOLIDÉ	**39.320**	**45.052**
Cash-flow du Groupe	37.889	43.458

ALLOCATION OF NET INCOME

(million BEF)

NET INCOME FOR THE YEAR	
a) Group net income	16,048
b) Minority Interests	696
Available for allocation and distribution	16,744
Dividends	9,301
Bonuses to directors, senior management	
and donations to the Benevolent Fund	245
Allocation to retained earnings	6,502
Minority Interests	696
	16,744

CASH FLOW

The cash flow for the year was 45.1 billion BEF as opposed to 39.3 billion BEF in the previous year. This definition has to be strictly interpreted: the cash flow is defined as income before depreciation and provisions.
The following schedule reconciles the cash flow from net income.

(million BEF)

	1995	1996
Consolidated net income	12,307	16,744
Depreciation, depletion and amortization (II.D.)	26,059	26,489
Trade receivables write-down (II.E.)	510	660
Inventory write-backs (II.E.)	- 278	- 299
Trade receivables write-back (*page 84.E.*)	- 453	- 246
Provisions for liabilities and charges (II.F.)	1,102	314
Current assets (write-down) write-back (V.B.)	- 210	83
Deferred taxes (IXBIS.)	789	784
Exceptional depreciation and amortization (VIII.A.)	274	154
Provisions for exceptional liabilities and charges (VIII.C.)	- 482	586
Write-back of provisions for exceptional liabilities and charges (VII.C.)	- 68	- 217
Write-back of depreciation and of amounts written off (VII.A.)	- 230	—
CONSOLIDATED CASH FLOW	39,320	45,052
Group cash flow	37,889	43,458

VERMOGENSSTROMEN

(in miljoenen BEF)

	1995	1995
BEDRIJFSACTIVITEITEN		
Bedrijfswinst	31.580	37.582
Meerwaarden bij de realisatie van activa begrepen in de bedrijfswinst	- 186	0
Afschrijvingen en waardeverminderingen op immateriële en materiële vaste activa	26.059	26.489
Voorzieningen voor risico's en kosten	1.102	314
Waardeverminderingen op voorraden en klantenvorderingen	232	361
Bestedingen van waardeverminderingen op handelsvorderingen	- 453	- 246
Bruto zelffinancieringsmarge	58.334	64.500
Wijziging van het bedrijfskapitaal (1)	1.326	- 6.788
Netto vermogensstroom uit bedrijfsactiviteiten	**59.660**	**57.712**
INVESTERINGEN		
Investeringsuitgaven (2)	- 26.844	- 31.912
Opbrengsten uit de verkoop van materiële activa (3)	1.485	1.233
Kapitaalsubsidies	25	44
Netto vermogensstroom uit investeringen	**- 25.334**	**- 30.635**
FINANCIELE INVESTERINGEN		
Financiële investeringen	- 3.157	- 939
Opbrengsten uit de verkoop van financiële activa	490	1.555
Wijziging van de vorderingen op meer dan één jaar	- 2.369	- 2.266
Opbrengsten uit financiële vaste activa	1.519	1.058
Dividenden ontvangen van de ondernemingen waarop vermogensmutatie werd toegepast	331	656
Opbrengsten uit vlottende activa (4)	871	1.474
Netto vermogensstroom uit financiële investeringen	**- 2.315**	**1.538**
FINANCIERING		
Kapitaalverhogingen en uitgiftepremies	3	4
Kapitaalverhogingen en uitgiftepremies - derden	16	12
Wijziging van de financiële schulden op meer dan één jaar	- 4.296	1.965
Wijziging van de financiële schulden op ten hoogste één jaar	2.955	- 1.185
Resultaatverwerking boekjaar 1994 en 1995	- 7.663	- 8.415
Dividenden uitgekeerd aan derden	- 356	- 353
Kosten van de betaalde schulden (5)	- 6.603	- 6.874
Andere financiële kosten en opbrengsten (6)	- 1.206	- 142
Netto vermogensstroom uit financiering	**- 17.150**	**- 14.988**
BELASTINGEN		
Betaalde belastingen (toelichting XIII^TER.a.)	**- 12.046**	**- 13.563**
UITZONDERLIJKE ACTIVITEITEN		
Andere uitzonderlijke kosten	**- 2.333**	**181**
WIJZIGING VAN DE GELDBELEGGINGEN EN DE LIQUIDE MIDDELEN		
- Wijziging in de balans	- 345	306
- Monetaire wijzigingen en wijzigingen van de consolidatiekring	827	- 61
	482	**245**

De tabel van de vermogensstromen is uitgewerkt op basis van de effectieve stromen van het boekjaar. De wijzigingen in de consolidatiekring alsook de wijzigingen resulterend uit de monetaire schommelingen zijn in deze tabel niet vervat.

(1) Deze rubriek herneemt de voorraadwijzigingen, de handelsvorderingen en handelsschulden en de schulden met betrekking tot bezoldigingen en sociale lasten.
(2) Om tot de investeringsuitgaven te komen dienen van het bedrag van de investeringen van rubriek VII, 4de en de toelichting, nl. 33.714 miljoen BEF (30.441), te worden afgetrokken: de intercalaire interesten van 863 miljoen BEF (440), de financiële investeringen van 939 miljoen BEF (3.157).
(3) Dit bedrag vertegenwoordigt de som van de netto boekwaarden van de gerealiseerde immateriële en materiële vaste activa, nl. 1.233 miljoen BEF (1.299), van de meerwaarden vervat in het bedrijfsresultaat ten belope van 0 miljoen BEF (186).
(4) Onder deze rubriek is het bedrag begrepen van de opbrengsten uit vlottende activa van het boekjaar, nl. 1.026 miljoen BEF (956) en van de wijzigingen in de te ontvangen interesten van 448 miljoen BEF (-85).
(5) Dit bedrag vertegenwoordigt de som van de kosten van schulden van het boekjaar, nl. 5.576 miljoen BEF (6.062), van de intercalaire interesten voor 863 miljoen BEF (440) en van de wijzigingen in verschuldigde interesten van 435 miljoen BEF (101).
(6) Dit bedrag herneemt de andere financiële kosten van 794 miljoen BEF (1948) en de andere financiële opbrengsten van 465 miljoen BEF (807), onder aftrek van de omzettingsverschillen en de toegekende subsidies van het boekjaar.
N.B. De cijfers tussen haakjes hebben betrekking op het boekjaar 1995.

TABLEAU DES FLUX DE TRÉSORERIE

(En millions BEF)

	1995	1996
OPÉRATIONS D'EXPLOITATION		
Bénéfice d'exploitation	31.580	37.582
Plus-values sur ventes d'actifs comprises dans le bénéfice d'exploitation	- 186	0
Amortissements et réductions de valeur sur immobilisations incorporelles et corporelles	26.059	26.489
Provisions pour risques et charges	1.102	314
Reprises de réductions de valeur sur stocks et créances commerciales	232	361
Utilisations de réductions de valeur sur créances commerciales	- 453	- 246
Marge brute d'autofinancement	58.334	64.500
Variation du fonds de roulement d'exploitation[1]	1.326	- 6.788
Flux nets des opérations d'exploitation	**59.660**	**57.712**
OPÉRATIONS D'INVESTISSEMENT		
Dépenses d'investissement[2]	- 26.844	- 31.912
Produits des ventes d'actifs[3]	1.485	1.233
Subsides reçus en capital	25	44
Flux nets des opérations d'investissement	**- 25.334**	**- 30.635**
OPÉRATIONS D'INVESTISSEMENT FINANCIER		
Investissements financiers	- 3.157	- 939
Produits des cessions d'actifs financiers	490	1.555
Variation des créances à plus d'un an	- 2.369	- 2.266
Produits des immobilisations financières	1.519	1.058
Dividendes encaissés des entreprises mises en équivalence	331	656
Produits des actifs circulants[4]	871	1.474
Flux nets des opérations d'investissement financier	**- 2.315**	**1.538**
OPÉRATIONS DE FINANCEMENT		
Augmentations de capital et des primes d'émission	3	4
Augmentations de capital et des primes d'émission - tiers	16	12
Variations des dettes financières à plus d'un an	- 4.296	1.965
Variations des dettes financières à un an au plus	2.955	- 1.185
Distribution 1994, 1995	- 7.663	- 8.415
Dividendes distribués aux tiers	- 356	- 353
Charges des dettes payées[5]	- 6.603	- 6.874
Charges et produits financiers divers[6]	- 1.206	- 142
Flux nets des opérations de financement	**- 17.150**	**-14.988**
IMPÔTS		
Impôts payés (annexe XIII[TER]. a.)	**- 12.046**	**- 13.563**
OPÉRATIONS EXCEPTIONNELLES		
Autres charges et produits exceptionnels	**- 2.333**	**181**
VARIATIONS DE LA TRÉSORERIE ET DES VALEURS DISPONIBLES		
- Variation au bilan	- 345	306
- Variations monétaires et variations de périmètre	827	- 61
	482	**245**

Le tableau des flux de trésorerie est élaboré sur base des flux réels de l'exercice. Les modifications intervenues dans le périmètre de consolidation ainsi que les variations résultant des fluctuations monétaires en sont exclues.

(1) Cette rubrique reprend les variations de stocks, des créances et des dettes commerciales, et des dettes salariales et sociales.
(2) Pour obtenir les dépenses d'investissement, il convient de déduire du montant des investissements repris à la rubrique VII.4° de l'annexe, soit 33.714 millions BEF (30.441), les intérêts intercalaires de 863 millions BEF (440), et les investissements financiers de 939 millions BEF (3.157).
(3) Ce montant représente la somme de la valeur comptable nette des actifs corporels et incorporels cédés de 1.233 millions BEF (1.299), des plus-values comprises dans le résultat d'exploitation de 0 millions BEF (186).
(4) Est reprise sous cet intitulé la somme des produits des actifs circulants de l'exercice de 1.026 millions BEF (956) et de la variation des intérêts à recevoir de 448 millions BEF (- 85).
(5) Ce montant représente la somme des charges des dettes de l'exercice soit 5.576 millions BEF (6.062), des intérêts intercalaires s'élevant à 863 millions BEF (440) et de la variation des intérêts à payer de 435 millions BEF (101).
(6) Ce montant reprend les autres charges financières de 794 millions BEF (1.948) et les autres produits financiers de 465 millions BEF (807) desquels ont été déduits les résultats de change et les subsides reconnus dans l'année, et les provisions et réductions de valeur financières.
NB Les chiffres entre parenthèses concernent l'exercice 1995.

CONSOLIDATED STATEMENT OF CHANGES IN FINANCIAL POSITION

(million BEF)

	1995	1996
OPERATING ACTIVITIES		
Operating profit	31,580	37,582
Gain on disposal of fixed assets included in operating profit	- 186	0
Depreciation, depletion and amortization	26,059	26,489
Provisions for liabilities and charges	1,102	314
Inventory write-backs	232	361
Trade receivables write-backs	- 453	- 246
Self-financing gross margin	58,334	64,500
Net (increase) decrease in operating working capital[1]	1,326	- 6,788
Net cash provided by Operating activities	**59,660**	**57,712**
INVESTING ACTIVITIES		
Capital expenditures[2]	- 26,844	- 31,912
Proceeds from asset sales[3]	1,485	1,233
Investment grants received	25	44
Net cash used for investing activities	**- 25,334**	**- 30,635**
FINANCIAL INVESTING ACTIVITIES		
Financial capital expenditures paid	- 3,157	- 939
Proceeds from financial asset sales	490	1,555
Net change in long term receivables	- 2,369	- 2,266
Income from financial investments	1,519	1,058
Dividends received from companies accounted for under the equity method	331	656
Income from current assets received[4]	871	1,474
Net cash provided by financial investing activities	**- 2,315**	**1,538**
FINANCING ACTIVITIES		
Issuance of common stock	3	4
Issuance of common stock (Minority Interests)	16	12
Net change in long term debt	- 4,296	1,965
Net change in short term debt	2,955	- 1,185
Dividends paid	- 7,663	- 8,415
Dividends paid to Minority Interests	- 356	- 353
Interest on debt paid[5]	- 6,603	- 6,874
Other financial charges and income[6]	- 1,206	- 142
Net cash used for financial activities	**- 17,150**	**- 14,988**
TAXES		
Taxes paid (XIII^{TER}.a.)	- 12,046	- 13,563
EXTRAORDINARY CHARGES		
Other extraordinary charges	- 2,333	181
NET CHANGE IN CASH AND MARKETABLE SECURITIES		
- Balance sheet variation	- 345	306
- Effect of exchange rate changes and changes in the scope of consolidation	827	- 61
	482	245

This statement does not include the effect of changes in the consolidation scope and in exchange rates.
(1) This item includes the change in inventories, trade payables and receivables and social, salary, duty liabilities.
(2) Capital expenditures paid correspond to capital expenditures mentioned in note VII.4*, 33,714 million BEF (30,441) less the capitalized interest of 863 million BEF (440) , financial capital expenditures amounting to 939 million BEF (3,157).
(3) This amount represents the sum of the net book value of assets sold of 1,233 million BEF (1,299) , the gain on sales of assets which is included in the operating income of 0 million BEF (186).
(4) This includes the total amount of 1996 revenues derived from current assets of 1,026 million BEF (956) and the change in interests receivable of 448 million BEF (- 85).
(5) This amount includes interest payment on debts of 5,576 million BEF (6,062), capitalized interests of 863 million BEF (440) and the change in accrued interest expenses of 435 million BEF (101).
(6) This amount represents the sum of other financial charges of 794 million BEF (1,948), other financial income of 465 million BEF (807), less the exchange differences and the grants, which have been deducted.
NB Numbers enclosed in parentheses relate to 1995.

Notes to the Consolidated Financial Statements

These financial statements were developed using the guidelines of the Royal Decree of November 25, 1991, concerning the annual accounts of industrial holding companies. However, for accounting practices specific to the petroleum industry or those not yet implemented under Belgian accounting law, the Group has followed statement of "Financial Accounting Standards" (SFAS).

Accordingly, since 1991 PetroFina has applied SFAS 19 to account for its oil and gas exploration and production expenditures using the Successful Efforts method. Likewise, since 1992 the Group has applied SFAS 109 to value the provision for deferred taxes.

I. CRITERIA FOR CONSOLIDATION

Subsidiaries are defined as those companies over which the Group exercises significant economic or legal control. Minority shareholders' interests in the shareholders' funds of the consolidated companies are disclosed separately under the balance sheet heading "minority interests ".

Jointly controlled companies with a limited number of shareholders are proportionally consolidated.

Certain subsidiaries are excluded from the scope of the consolidation. This applies when a company's total capital employed, total assets and revenues amount to less than 1% of the total corresponding items in the consolidated balance sheet of the previous financial year, due to their immateriality to the Groups' financial position.

A subsidiary is not consolidated when effective control is significantly affected due to serious and long-term restrictions. Companies which are planned to be sold are treated likewise.

The equity method applies to companies in which the group holds between 20% to 50% of the capital and over which it exercises significant influence. The equity method, however, does not apply to companies in which the Group owns less than 100 million BEF of the shareholders' funds; their significance is deemed negligible.

When the investments are not covered by the above criteria they are shown in the consolidated financial statements at the book value of their parent company.

II. CONSOLIDATION SCOPE

A. On page 52 of this annual report the reader will find a list and summary of the main companies consolidated by the methods described above. A full list of consolidated companies and companies excluded from the scope of consolidation is available from the Public Relations and Communication Department of PetroFina s.a., rue de l'Industrie 52, B-1040 Brussels.

B. At December 31, 1996, those companies excluded from the consolidation scope because of restrictions affecting the exercise of control or due to their negligible significance represent less than 1% of all the consolidated companies' turnover, balance sheet totals and capital employed. Therefore there is no benefit in including these companies in the consolidation scope and in the valuation of the Group's assets, financial position or consolidated earnings.

C. Modifications to the scope of consolidation.

In March 1996, the Group sold to third parties its ownership interest (of 50%) in Finamont. This investment, being temporary in nature as of December 31, 1995, was excluded from the scope of consolidation and Finamont was accounted for under the equity method in 1995.

VI. VALUATION RULES

A. METHODS OF CONVERSION

Foreign currency transactions of consolidated companies are accounted for at the exchange rate prevailing on the date of transaction. Gains and losses resulting from the settlement of such transactions are recognized in the income statement. At December 31, foreign currency account balances are translated at yearend exchange rates unless hedged by forward foreign exchange contracts (in which case the forward exchange rate is used).

In the consolidation process, the balance sheets of foreign companies are converted into Belgian francs using the closing rate method. Under this method, all the assets and liabilities on the foreign companies' balance sheets are converted to Belgian francs at the year-end exchange rates, with the exception of shareholders' funds which are left at historical rates.

The income statement elements of foreign companies are converted at the average exchange rate of the year.

Differences arising from accounting as result of using exchange rates other than the closing rate (yearly average and historical rates) are recorded under the heading "Currency translation adjustment". The amount attributable to third parties is included under the heading "minority interests".

In 1995, the Group's valuation rules regarding exchange differences were modified. Exchange differences arising from the differences between the historical rates at which the foreign entities' retained earnings are translated and the rates at which the subsidiaries' income is distributed to the mother company are now directly recognized as income or expense in the income statement. Although the international accounting rules (IAS 21) and the American rules (SFAS 52) recommend recognizing the cumulative amounts of exchange differences in the income statement only at the time of disposal of the foreign entity or of reimbursement of the invested capital, the Board of Directors considers it prudent to recognize directly those exchange differences in the income statement due to the substantial amount of exchange adjustments in the Group's balance sheet.

This modification in the valuation rules produces an additional 851 million BEF of extraordinary expenses to the extent that it relates to elements that originate from previous accounting periods.

The results for 1996 were not affected by these new valuation rules.

B. DIFFERENCES ARISING FROM INITIAL CONSOLIDATION

Goodwill represents the excess of the cost of acquisition over the fair value of the Group's share in the net assets of the consolidated company existing at the date the company is consolidated for the first time. Goodwill is reported on the balance sheet and is amortized using the straight-line method over its useful economic life.

C. METHODS OF VALUATION AND RESTATEMENT

The consolidated balance sheet is based on the accounts as of December 31. The valuation rules used in the consolidated financial statements follow the valuation principles used by the parent company. The use of these standard accounting rules and valuation methods throughout all subsidiaries allows the consolidated accounts to be drawn up with no major restatement. Inter-company receivables and payables are eliminated, as well as capital gains made within the Group. Sales of raw materials and finished products between consolidated companies are stated at market prices.

1. Oil and gas exploration and production costs

The Group uses the Successful Efforts method whereby only those costs which have led to the discovery and development of economically recoverable reserves are capitalized.

Under this method:

- the costs of purchasing drilling rights or property rights are capitalized;

- the costs of exploration and geological, geophysical and seismic studies are expensed as incurred;

- dry hole costs are also expensed as incurred;

- the costs of drilling wells that are considered economically viable and the cost of developing them are capitalized and treated as assets.

2. Intangible assets and incorporation expenses

Incorporation expenses are charged to income in the year incurred. Intangible fixed assets with a limited life are amortized over their estimated useful economic life (between 5 and 10 years).

3. Tangible assets

Property, plant and equipment are valued at historical cost less accumulated depreciation. Depreciation is calculated on a straight-line basis over the useful economic life of the assets.

In certain circumstances, depreciation can be accelerated.

All fixed assets related to the production line of business are depreciated according to the unit of production method which is based on the proven and developed reserves.

Interest expenses incurred on debt used to finance property, plant and equipment under construction are capitalized.

Leases of property, plant and equipment which transfer all the risks and benefits of ownership in the leased assets to the consolidated subsidiary are classified as capital leases. Such leases are capitalised at the estimated present value of the underlying lease payments.

The corresponding rental obligations, net of financial charges, are reported either as long term or short term financial debt. Interest expense associated with these capital leases is charged to income over the contractual life of the lease.

Payments made under operating leases are charged in equal installments to income over the contractual period of the lease.

4. Investments

Investments reported on the balance sheet as "companies accounted for under the equity method" are valued on the basis of the Group's net interest in the equity of these companies.

Investments in "other companies" are shown at their acquisition cost. Reductions in value are recorded when the year-end review indicates that the decline in value is permanent in nature.

5. Inventories

Inventories are valued at the lower of cost or net realizable value. Crude, finished petroleum products and chemical products inventories are determined according to the LIFO method (last in/first out). All other inventories are valued at average cost.

The costs of finished products and products in progress includes raw material costs, direct costs and related production overhead costs but excludes any interest charges.

Net realizable value is defined as the estimated selling price (in the normal course of business) of an inventory item less the costs of completion and selling expenses.

6. Receivables and payables

Receivables and payables are accounted for at their nominal value, and valuation losses are recognized when the year-end valuation indicates that impairments are permanent in nature.

7. Marketable securities

Marketable securities are valued at the lower of cost or market.

8. Provisions

Provisions for liabilities and charges are established for clearly identifiable losses or expenses which are likely or certain by year-end but for which the actual amount can only be estimated.

a. The Group is subject to extensive legislation dealing with the environment and the restoration of industrial sites. Consequently, the Group has made a number of provisions based on the estimated future costs of cleaning up industrial sites. In making these provisions, the estimated future costs are not discounted to obtain a present value.

b. The majority of consolidated subsidiaries manage a number of pension plans, which cover most employee categories. The benefits provided by these pension plans are most often based on seniority and latest salary earned.

With the exception of Italy, Germany and Netherlands, the assets are managed by separate trustee administered Funds. In Belgium, pension obligations are managed by Fina Life, one of the consolidated companies. In each case, the Group takes into account the recommendations of independent experts regarding the actuarial value of the provisions.

c. In 1992, Fina, Inc. adopted SFAS 106 to make provisions for supplementary post-retirement health care benefits.

d. The provision for deferred taxes was established 0n the basis of rules defined under SFAS 109. According to SFAS 109, the company must value its provision for deferred taxes on the basis of all temporary differences between its taxable income and financial accounting income.

The provision for deferred taxes is reviewed each year to take account of the change in the tax base and any changes in the legislation. Deferred tax assets are reflected in the consolidated accounts only if they are reasonably likely to materialize in the foreseeable future.

9. Derivative financial instruments

The Group uses certain derivative financial instruments in managing risks inherent in the normal course of business. The Group uses swap agreements, forward foreign exchange rate contracts and options contracts to hedge its exposure to fluctuations in the prices of petroleum products and to help manage its interest rate and exchange rate exposures.

The Group does not use derivative financial instruments for trade or speculative purposes.

Both the market risk and credit risk which stem from the use of these derivative financial instruments can be considered negligible. The Group deals with internationally known companies, and consequently does not anticipate any failures which could impact its financial position or its net income.

Forward foreign exchange contracts are used to reduce the risk associated with transactions denominated in foreign currencies. Any gains or losses made on these contracts are offset by the corresponding gains or losses on the assets and liabilities being hedged.

The Group uses futures contracts and forward purchase commitments to reduce its exposure to fluctuations in the prices of crude oil, natural gas and petroleum products. Gains and losses related to these hedges are deferred and recognized in the income statement at the hedged transactions maturity. However, potential losses are directly recognized in the income statement.

The Group uses interest rate swap agreements to help to manage the balance between fixed rate and variable rate debt. The differentials between the amounts paid or received are spread over the life of the corresponding contracts and are considered as adjustments to interest expense.

10. Legal Proceedings

In the framework of its normal course of business, the Group is involved in various legal, fiscal and environmental proceedings. Given the advice of various legal experts, the Board of Directors determined that the outcome of these various legal proceedings will not have a significant impact on the Group's financial situation.

11. Research Costs

Research costs are charged to expense in the period incurred. Development costs of major projects are capitalized to the extent that the future revenues generated by these projects are sufficient to cover the costs of developing the projects. Capitalized development costs are amortized over a maximum period of 5 years.

12. During 1995, Fina Inc. adopted SFAS 121, "Accounting for the Impairment of Long-Lived Assets and for Long-Lived Assets to Be Disposed of".

Under SFAS 121, companies must evaluate their tangible assets by comparing future cash flows to book value. Impairment of the asset will be recognized when the book value exceeds the future cash flows. Fina Inc. incurred in 1995, before-tax, an additional 58.7 million USD (1.7 billion BEF) of depreciation, depletion and amortization primarily on its upstream assets.

This non-recurring expense had no impact on the 1995 consolidated financial statement. The Group had recognized this depreciation during previous years due to its valuation rules.

VII. FIXED ASSETS   *(million BEF)*

1° Fixed assets: geographical breakdown	1995	%	1996	%
Belgium	79,990	38.9	72,078	32.5
Other European countries	75,183	36.5	87,733	39.6
North America	48,057	23.4	58,847	26.5
Rest of the world	2,531	1.2	3,056	1.4
TOTAL	205,761	100.0	221,714	100.0
2° Fixed assets: segment breakdown	1995	%	1996	%
Exploration, Production	60,848	29.6	71,744	32.4
Refining, Marketing, Transportation	98,472	47.9	102,733	46.4
Chemicals	35,797	17.4	35,774	16.1
Paints	6,484	3.1	6,742	3.0
Other activities	4,160	2.0	4,721	2.1
TOTAL	205,761	100.0	221,714	100.0
3° Capital expenditures : geographical breakdown	1995	%	1996	%
Belgium	8,592	28.2	5,384	16.0
Other European countries	13,471	44.3	18,317	54.3
North America	7,335	24.1	9,465	28.1
Rest of the world	1,043	3.4	548	1,6
TOTAL	30,441	100.0	33,714	100.0

(million BEF)

4° Capital expenditures: segment breakdown	1995	%	1996	%	Budget 1997	%
Exploration, Production	12,288 (*)	40.4	17,964 (**)	53.3	17,354	46.6
Refining, Marketing, Transportation	8,098	26.6	9,164	27.1	10,046	27.0
Chemicals	8,093	26.6	3,799	11.3	7,983	21.4
Paints	807	2.6	1,235	3.7	1,161	3.1
Other activities	1,155	3.8	1,552	4.6	706	1.9
TOTAL	30,441	100.0	33,714	100.0	37,250	100.0

(*) includes depreciated exploration expenditures for 2,183 million BEF.   (**) includes depreciated exploration expenditures for 1,828 million BEF.

5° Capitalized interest on assets under construction included in capital expenditure	1995	1996
	440	863

VIII. INTANGIBLE ASSETS

(million BEF)

	Research and development expenses	Patents and licences	Customer goodwill	Other intangible assets	Total
A. GROSS AMOUNTS					
At December 31, 1995	1,022	2,279	2,310	3,520	9,131
Changes during the year:					
- Acquisitions	27	438	99	442	1,006
- Variations in scope					
- Disposals	- 124	- 25	- 310	- 133	- 592
- Transfers	40			-40	
- Exchange adjustments	1	67	61	43	172
At December 31, 1996	966	2,759	2,160	3,832	9,717
C. ACCUMULATED DEPRECIATION AND WRITE-DOWNS					
At December 31, 1995	- 713	- 1,595	- 1,854	- 2,160	- 6,322
Changes during the year:					
- Allocation for the year	- 146	- 92	- 199	- 154	- 591
- Variations in scope					
- Disposals	124	25	310	112	571
- Transfers	- 6			6	
- Exchange adjustments		- 66	- 40	- 37	- 143
At December 31, 1996	- 741	- 1,728	- 1,783	- 2,233	- 6,485
D. NET BOOK VALUE					
At December 31, 1996	225	1,031	377	1,599	3,232

VIIIBIS. Adjustments on Consolidation

(million BEF)

At December 31, 1995	45
Capital expenditures	2
Depreciation and amortization	- 13
Exchange adjustments	1
At December 31, 1996	35

IX. Tangible Assets

(million BEF)

	Land and buildings	Equipment Machinery, furniture, vehicles	Equipment Exploration, Production assets	Fixed assets held under leasing	Other tangible fixed assets	Assets under constru- tion	Total
A. Gross amounts							
At December 31, 1995	40,169	208,420	147,433	5,791	3,082	8,695	413,590
Changes during the year:							
- Acquisitions	3,886	12,572	6,960	2	195	8,153	31,768
- Variations in scope							
- Disposals	- 1,021	- 4,461	- 810	- 82	- 83		- 6,457
- Transfers	50	- 1		- 49			
- Exchange adjustments	2,120	8,208	14,240	874	186	303	25,931
At December 31, 1996	45,204	224,738	167,823	6,536	3,380	17,151	464,832
C. Accumulated depreciation and write-downs							
At December 31, 1995	- 15,035	- 102,797	- 93,810	- 4,441	- 1,498		- 217,581
Changes during the year:							
- Allocation for the year	- 1,688	- 12,521	- 11,299	- 261	- 271		- 26,040
- Variations in scope							
- Disposals	447	3,879	743	80	96		5,245
- Transfers	136	- 217		40	41		
- Exchange adjustments	- 516	- 3,794	- 9,655	- 785	- 112		- 14,862
At December 31, 1996	- 16,656	- 115,450	- 114,021	- 5,367	- 1,744		- 253,238
D. Net book value							
At December 31, 1996	28,548	109,288	53,802	1,169	1,636	17,151	211,594

X. INVESTMENTS AND LOANS

(million BEF)

	Purchase price	Write-downs	Loans	Accounted for on the equity method	Total
A. COMPANIES ACCOUNTED FOR UNDER THE EQUITY METHOD					
At December 31,1995	5,866	-23	251	-1,505	4,589
Changes during the year:					
- Acquisitions, capital increases	77				77
- Variations in scope					
- Sales	- 739		- 271	- 57	- 1,067
- Profits accounted for under the equity method				983	983
- Dividends received				-656	- 656
- Investment write-down		- 57			- 57
- Exchange adjustments	390	- 3	20	- 169	238
At December 31, 1996	5,594	-83	0	- 1,404	4,107
B. OTHER COMPANIES					
At December 31, 1995	4,357	- 2,695	647		2,309
Changes during the year:					
- Acquisitions, capital increases	841		21		862
- Variations in scope					
- Sales	- 346		- 142		- 488
- Investment write-down		- 15	- 11		- 26
- Exchange adjustments	47		42		89
At December 31, 1996	4,899	- 2,710	557		2,746

X^BIS. CURRENT ASSETS

A. LONG TERM RECEIVABLES

(million BEF)

	1995	1996
b) Investment of technical reserves relating to insurance operations	10,271	11,151
c) Other receivables	4,863	7,201
	15,134	18,352

B. **INVENTORIES** *(million BEF)*

	1995	1996
a) Petroleum products	24,121	27,581
b) Petrochemical products and paints	13,970	13,811
c) Other products and materials	6,942	6,784
	45,033	48,176

On December 31, 1993, PetroFina reduced the recorded cost of its crude oil and petroleum products inventory to their lower market values. In 1995 and 1996, the increase in market values of crude oil and petroleum products enabled PetroFina to partially recover the 1993 write-down, resulting in the recording of a BEF 300 million inventory revaluation for both years. The excess of replacement costs of crude oil and chemical products over LIFO costs at December 1996, was 6.2 billion BEF.

C. **ACCOUNTS RECEIVABLE** *(million BEF)*

1° *Trade receivables*	1995	1996
Trade receivables	61,188	71,957
Write-downs on trade receivables	-2,500	-2,817
	58,688	69,140

At December 31, 1995 and at December 31, 1996, accounts receivable factored with recourse, to various banks amounted to BEF 2.5 billion.

(million BEF)

2° *Other receivables*	1995	1996
Taxes and withholding taxes to be recovered	2,629	2,401
Receivables relating to exploration and production activities	478	587
Short-term financial loans	756	800
Other	3,024	4,275
	6,887	8,063

D. **DEFERRED CHARGES AND ACCRUED INCOME** *(million BEF)*

	1995	1996
- Proration of revenues accrued but not collected	1,091	686
- Charges relating to later years	2,180	2,205
- Valuation differences on guarantees and commitments	28	28
	3,299	2,919

XI.	LIABILITIES AND STOCKHOLDERS' EQUITY						

A.   EVOLUTION OF STOCKHOLDERS' EQUITY   *(million BEF)*

	Share capital	Share premium account	Retained earnings	Adjustments on consoli- dation	Currency translation adjustments	Capital grants	Total
At December 31, 1995	43,293	24,310	84,398	542	-30,853	517	122,207
Changes in the year:							
- Increases in the year		4			4.391	44	4.439
- Variations in scope				- 12			- 12
- Transfers to income						- 67	- 67
- Group net income			16,048				16,048
- Proposed distribution			- 9,546				- 9,546
At December 31, 1996	43,293	24,314	90,900	530	- 26,462	494	133,069

B.   SHARE CAPITAL

At December 31, 1996, the share capital of PetroFina S.A., totalled 43,293,266,488 BEF (represented by 23,252,863 shares), an increase of 767,144 BEF from December 31, 1995, as a result of the issuance of 412 shares. The conversion price per share has been allocated in respect of 1,862 BEF as share capital and the balance 8,392 BEF as share premium.

C.   SHARE PREMIUM ACCOUNT

This amounted to 24,313,802,250 BEF, an increase of 3,457,504 BEF from December 31, 1995, as a result of the exercice of 412 warrants attached to the 1991 bond issue reserved for personnel.

D.   RETAINED EARNINGS

The change in retained earnings is due to the movement in the allocations and deductions for the year, or a total of 16,048 million BEF and the transfer to the heading "other debt" (current liabilities) of the proposed allocation of dividends and directors' and staff bonuses (9,546 million BEF).

E.   ADJUSTMENTS ON CONSOLIDATION

This reflects adjustments on initial consolidation. The change for the year of 12 million BEF is a result of minor changes in the scope of the consolidation.

F.   CURRENCY TRANSLATION ADJUSTMENTS

Exchange adjustments arising in the valuation of subsidiaries' shareholders' funds when converted into Belgian francs at either historical or closing rates. The variation was substantially due to the decrease in the value of the dollar. The change in the year's results is mainly due to the appreciation of the US dollar, the Italian lira and the English pound.

In 1995, the Group's valuation rules regarding exchange differences were modified. Exchange differences arising from the difference between the historical rates at which the foreign entities' retained earnings are translated and the rates at which the subsidiaries' income is distributed to the mother company are now directly recognized as income or expense in the income statement.

In 1995, this modification in the valuation rules produced an additional 851 million BEF of extraordinary expenses.

In 1996, the change in valuation rules had no effect on the year's results.

Exchange Rates	1994	1995	1996
A. YEAR END RATE			
US Dollar	31.8375	29.4450	32.0050
Pound sterling	49.7550	45.6750	54.3925
Deutsch Mark	20.5535	20.5405	20.6020
French Franc	5.9555	6.0090	6.1150
Italian Lira	0.0196	0.0186	0.0210
B. AVERAGE RATE			
US Dollar	33.4312	29.5111	30.9551
Pound sterling	51.1491	46.5586	48.3487
Deutsch Mark	20.6060	20.5751	20.5798
French Franc	6.0249	5.9084	6.0521
Italian Lira	0.0207	0.0181	0.0201

G. INVESTMENT GRANTS

Investment grants from public authorities are depreciated at the same rate applied to the relevant investments. Grants received in 1996 amounted to 44 million BEF, 67 million BEF were transferred to "Other financial income".

H. MINORITY INTERESTS

This reflects minority interests in the fully consolidated subsidiaries, mainly the Minority Interests in Fina, Inc.

(million BEF)

	1995	1996
At beginning of year	4,848	4,890
Changes in the scope of consolidation	16	12
Minority interests' net income	699	696
Dividends paid to Minority Interests	-356	-353
Currency translation adjustments	-317	413
Year-end balance	4,890	5,658

The balance of currency translation adjustments represented - 530 million BEF at December 31, 1996 and -943 million BEF at December 31, 1995.

I. PROVISIONS AND DEFERRED INCOME TAXES

A. PROVISIONS FOR LIABILITIES AND CHARGES

(million BEF)

1. Pensions and similar commitments	1995	1996
Technical reserves from internal pension funds	9,563	9,964
Health care benefits (US companies)	1,777	2,020
	11,340	11,984

This represents provisions established by the Group to cover personnel benefits in the form of pensions and health care.

(million BEF)

3. Major repairs and maintenance	1995	1996
At beginning of year	240	332
Charge for the year	169	147
Utilization of previous provisions	- 62	- 421
Exchange adjustments	- 15	23
Other movements		13
Year-end balance	332	94

(million BEF)

4. Provisions for other liabilities and charges	1995	1996
a) Technical insurance provisions	4,564	4,033
b) Provisions for environmental costs and sites restoration	6,824	7,387
c) Other provisions for liabilities and charges	5,051	5,917
Year-end balance	16,439	17,337

B. DEFERRED TAXES

(million BEF)

4. Deferred income taxes	1995	1996
At beginning of year	14,191	14,148
Current allocation	880	1,453
Current utilization	- 91	- 669
Exceptional allocation	—	716
Transfer to tax assets	- 476	896
Exchange adjustments	- 324	1,034
Other movements	- 32	- 44
Year-end balance	14,148	17,534

XIII. Long term debt

(million BEF)

1° Analysis by category	1995		1996	
	Less than 5 years	More than 5 years	Less than 5 years	More than 5 years
- Bonds and notes	16,397	15,380	20,795	14,022
- Capital lease obligations	495	291	418	236
- Banks and financial institutions	7,246	3,452	1,979	10,588
- Other debt	7	680	19	798
TOTAL	24,145	19,803	23,211	25,644

2° Analysis by maturity	1995 *(million BEF)*	1996 *(million BEF)*
- 1997	1,136	—
- 1998	6,851	1,999
- 1999	3,234	2,235
- 2000	12,924	13,601
- 2001	2,449	5,376
- 2002	3,583	8,689
- 2003	6,069	7,349
- Later	7,702	9,606
	43,948	48,855

3° Analysis by currency	1995 *(%)*	1996 *(%)*
- Belgian francs	26	23
- US Dollars	67	75
- Pounds sterling	1	1
- French francs	1	1
- Other currencies	5	0
This analysis includes the effect of swap transactions	100	100

4° Analysis by nature	1995 *(million BEF)*		1996 *(million BEF)*	
a) Bonds and notes		31,777		34,817
b) Capital lease obligations		786		654
c) Banks and financial institutions		10,698		12,567
- fixed rates	5,668		2,945	
- variable rates	5,030		9,622	
d) Other loans		687		817
		43,948		48,855

5° Changes in the year	1995 *(million BEF)*	1996 *(million BEF)*
At beginning of year	50,384	43,948
New loans	2,424	13,877
Transfers to short term debt	- 5,825	- 1,200
Anticipated repayments	- 895	- 10,712
Exchange adjustments	- 2,004	2,942
Changes in the scope of consolidation	- 136	
At end of year	43,948	48,855

XIII [BIS]. **TOTAL FINANCIAL DEBT**

(million BEF)

	1995	1996
Debt of more than one year	43,948	48,855
Debt of more than one year maturing within the year	5,825	1,200
Financial debt of less than one year	28,025	33,844
	77,798	83,899
Cash and marketable securities	- 2,976	- 3,282
Net financial debt	74,822	80,617

XIII [TER]. **TAXES, SALARIES AND SOCIAL SECURITY CONTRIBUTIONS AND OTHER LIABILITIES**

A. **TAXES, SALARIES AND SOCIAL SECURITY CONTRIBUTIONS**

(million BEF)

	1995	1996
1° Taxes		
VAT payable	2,705	3,217
Income taxes payable (*)	6,346	10,135
Duties, taxes on petroleum products	13,124	13,503
Miscellaneous taxes	1,284	1,441
	23,459	28,296
2° Salaries and social security contributions	3,342	3,560
	26,801	31,856
(*) Income taxes payable		
- At beginning of year	6,324	6,346
- Charge included in the income statement	12,180	16,791
- Taxes paid during the year	- 12,046	- 13,563
- Variations in the scope of consolidation	- 1	-
- Exchange adjustments	- 111	561
Year-end balance	6,346	10,135

B. **OTHER LIABILITIES**

(million BEF)

	1995	1996
Proposed dividends and bonuses	8,415	9,546
Liabilities resulting from exploration and production operations	2,773	2,906
Other miscellaneous liabilities	5,586	5,281
	16,774	17,733

XIII [QUATER]. **ACCRUED CHARGES AND DEFERRED INCOME**

(million BEF)

	1995	1996
- Accrued charges		
• Interest payables	2,097	1,798
• Goods and services payables	2,143	2,445
- Deferred income	1,724	2,239
	5,964	6,482

XIV. STATEMENT OF INCOME

A. BREAKDOWN OF THE NON-RECURRENT ELEMENTS

The breakdown of the non-recurrent elements, by their different accounting headings, is as follows:

(million BEF)

	1995	1996
Non-recurrent capital gains on sales of assets (Other operating income)	186	—
Inventory write-backs (Trade receivables and inventories (write-down) write-back)	278	299
Taxes on non-recurrent elements (Taxes)	- 37	—
Total exceptional elements (Exceptional income and charges)	- 1,827	- 342
TOTAL	- 1,400	- 43
Minority Interests in the non-recurrent result	- 33	- 4
Group's share in the non-recurrent result	- 1,367	- 39
Group's share in the result	11,608	16,048
Group's share in the non-recurrent result	12,975	16,087

B. SALES AND OPERATING REVENUE BY SEGMENT

(million BEF)

1° SALES	Petroleum products		Chemicals		Paints		Other products		Total	
	1995	1996	1995	1996	1995	1996	1995	1996	1995	1996
Europe	357,067	400,163	46,314	42,160	24,841	25,411	6,097	6,426	434,319	474,160
North America	86,178	106,737	30,020	31,122			1,293	853	117,491	138,712
Africa and others										
TOTAL	443,245	506,900	76,334	73,282	24,841	25,411	7,390	7,279	551,810	612,872

2° FIXED ASSETS INTERNAL CAPITALIZED EXPENSES	Total	
	1995	1996
Europe	759	712
North America	112	327
TOTAL	871	1,039

3° OTHER OPERATING REVENUE	Total	
	1995	1996
Europe	9,197	9,752
North America	1,309	931
Rest of the world	6	—
TOTAL	10,512	10,683

(million BEF)

OTHER OPERATING REVENUE	1995	1996
Insurance premiums received from third parties	1,098	1,418
Transportation and pipeline revenues	1,478	1,428
Rental income	2,268	2,398
Gain or loss on sales of assets	186	—
Service fees, reinvoicing and processing fees	5,482	5,439
	10,512	10,683

(million BEF)

C. OPERATING EXPENSES	1995	1996
Services and other goods	42,608	45,149
Personnel expenses	27,119	27,462
Other operating expenses	7,723	9,104
TOTAL	77,450	81,715

D. PERSONNEL COSTS	Full consolidation		Proportional consolidation		Total	
	1995	1996	1995	1996	1995	1996
1. Personnel	*(number of employees)*					
Operational employees	3,948	3,923	512	438	4,460	4,361
Administrative employees	4,699	4,896	220	286	4,919	5,182
Management	3,992	3,807	282	238	4,274	4,045
TOTAL	12,639	12,626	1,014	962	13,653	13,588
2. Personnel costs	*(million BEF)*					
Salaries and direct social benefits	18,658	19,029	1,558	1,650	20,216	20,679
Employer's social security contributions	4,444	4,457	504	497	4,948	4,954
Employer's contribution to private insurance schemes	462	519	5	5	467	524
Other payroll costs	893	827	91	135	984	962
Pensions	386	246	118	97	504	343
TOTAL	24,843	25,078	2,276	2,384	27,119	27,462

(million BEF)

E. INVENTORIES AND TRADE RECEIVABLE (WRITE-DOWN) WRITE-BACK	1995	1996
Inventories (write-down), write-back	278	299
Trade receivable write-down	- 510	- 660
Trade receivable write-back	453	246
Losses on trade receivable written off during previous accounting periods	- 453	- 246
TOTAL	- 232	- 361

(million BEF)

F. PROVISIONS FOR LIABILITIES AND CHARGES	1995	1996
Provisions for major repairs and maintenance	- 108	274
Provisions for environmental costs and site restoration	- 302	- 495
Provisions for other liabilities and charges	69	- 8
Pension fund	- 852	- 1,013
Technical insurance provisions	91	928
TOTAL	- 1,102	- 314

(million BEF)

G. INVESTMENT INCOME	1995	1996
1. Financial investments Investment income includes dividends from investments which were neither consolidated nor accounted for under the equity method	1,519	1,058
2. Current assets Represents income relating to securities, cash and financial loans	956	1,026
3. Other Includes gains on disposal of current assets, capital and interest grants, exchange rate gains and other financial income	807	465

(million BEF)

H. FINANCIAL EXPENSES	1995	1996
1. Interest expenses Interest relating to short-term and long-term financial debt Capitalized interest relating to assets under construction	- 6,502 440	- 6,439 863
	- 6,062	- 5,576
2. Current assets (write-down) write-back Represents reductions in value of marketable securities and of non-commercial receivables	210	- 83
3. Other Includes reductions in value of sales of marketable securities and non-commercial receivables, commissions, financial costs, exchange rate losses, discount charges and other financial costs	- 1,948	- 794

In 1995, client discounts amounting to BEF 900 million were classified as other financial expenses. In 1996, they were reclassified as a reduction of sales as they were considered to be more akin to commercial rebates in nature.

I. EXCEPTIONAL ITEMS

(million BEF)

1. Exceptional charges	1995	1996
a) Fixed assets depreciation and amortization	- 274	- 154
c) Provisions for liabilities and charges		
- allocations	- 193	- 1,034
- uses	675	448
e) Other	- 2,418	- 1,153
TOTAL	- 2,210	- 1,893

In 1995, the exceptional depreciation charge of 0.3 billion BEF is broken down as follows: 0.1 billion BEF for the upstream sector and 0.2 billion BEF for the downstream sector.

Provisions for liabilities and charges include :

- Provisions for site restoration of 0.1 billion BEF in the upstream sector and provisions of 0.1 billion BEF for diverse legal proceedings in the paints line of business.
- In 1995, provisions for site restoration and provisions for restructuring costs that were recognized in previous accounting periods were utilized to the extent of 0.7 billion BEF. The related expenditures (of 0.7 billion BEF) were reported under the heading "other exceptional charges".

The other charges relate to :

- The recognition of 0.9 billion BEF of exchange losses resulting from the distribution of dividends following the modifications in valuation rules.
- The recognition of 0.9 billion BEF of restructuring costs and of early retirement benefits.
- Expenditures for site restoration and restructuring for which provisions were made in previous reporting periods (0.7 billion).

In 1996, fixed assets depreciation and amortization related to the European downstream sector.
Provisions for liabilities and charges include :

- Provisions for site restoration of 0.3 billion BEF and provisions for deferred taxes of 0.7 billion
- In 1996, provisions for site restoration and provisions for restructuring costs that were recognized in previous accounting periods were utilized to the extent of 0.4 billion. The related expenditures (of 0.4 billion) were reported under the heading «other charges»

The other charges concerned :

- Expenditures for site restoration and restructuring costs for which provisions have already been recorded in the previous year (0.4 billion).
- Expenditures for early retirement costs and restructuring costs.

(million BEF)

2. Exceptional income	1995	1996
a) Write-back of depreciation and amounts written off	230	
c) Write-back of provisions for extraordinary liabilities and charges	68	217
d) Gains on sales of assets		1,334
e) Other extraordinary income	85	
TOTAL	383	1,551

In 1995, exploration and production operations combined with refining and marketing operations accounted for BEF 300 million and BEF 100 million respectively of the reversal of amortization and provisions.

Gains on fixed asset disposals and reversals of provisions for liabilities and charges relate primarily to the European refining and marketing operations.

In 1996, the exceptional income mainly concerns the European downstream sector.

XV. OFF BALANCE SHEET GUARANTEES AND COMMITMENTS

(million BEF)

	1995	1996
1. CUSTOMS GUARANTEES GRANTED TO THIRD PARTIES	3,221	4,250
2. BANK GUARANTEES GRANTED TO NON-CONSOLIDATED COMPANIES	5,850	3,381
3. BANK GUARANTEES GRANTED TO THIRD PARTIES	870	6,273
4. PURCHASE COMMITMENTS FOR FIXED ASSETS	2,353	4,975
5. OPERATING LEASES		
Operating leases that deal with service station equipment or production facilities		
- 1996	2,624	
- 1997	2,373	2,626
- 1998	2,008	2,343
- 1999	1,535	2,102
- 2000	1,316	1,756
- 2001	959	1,430
- Later	4,183	5,690

XVI. FINANCIAL INSTRUMENTS

Amounts related to PetroFina's financial instruments were as follows :

(million BEF)

	December 31, 1995		December 31, 1996	
	Carrying amount	Fair value	Carrying amount	Fair value
BALANCE SHEET FINANCIAL INSTRUMENTS :				
Marketable securities	10,588	10,990	11,590	12,435
Debt	49,773	52,546	50,055	52,365
DERIVATIVE INSTRUMENTS :				
Interest rate swaps	350	- 993	99	- 510
Currency swaps	- 199	171	- 186	- 265
Forward foreign exchange contracts	- 108	- 108	- 175	- 175
Commodity contracts	2	2	208	208

All derivative financial instruments are off-balance sheet. However, the net receivable or payable positions related to such instruments are carried on the balance sheet.

PetroFina's notional amount of debt covered under interest rate swaps totaled approximately BEF 26.7 billion and BEF 22.3 billion, and under currency swaps totaled approximately BEF 7.1 billion and BEF 9.1 billion at December 31, 1996, and 1995, respectively. Amounts to be paid or received under these agreements are accrued on the balance sheet over the life of the swap agreements. The fair value of the swap agreements was not recognized in the consolidated financial statements since they are accounted for as hedges of the underlying debt instruments.

For the periods ended December 31, 1996 and 1995, PetroFina had forward foreign exchange buy contracts of BEF 34.3 billion and BEF 23.8 billion, respectively; and sell contracts of BEF 34.5 billion and BEF 23.9 billion, respectively. These contracts were principally in the U.S. dollar, German mark, French franc, Dutch gilder, and British pound. Gains and losses resulting from changes in the market value of these contracts are recognized in net income immediately. Because these contracts are of a short term nature (principally less than six months) their fair value and carrying value are approximately the same.

Also for the periods ended December 31, 1996 and 1995, the Company had crude oil and refined products futures and forward buy contracts of BEF 4.1 billion and BEF 1.4 billion, respectively; and sell contracts of BEF 1.6 billion and BEF 204 million, respectively. These contracts are recorded at fair value.

The Company also had futures contracts to sell natural gas as a hedge of equity production in the amount of BEF 620 million at December 31, 1996. Gains and losses on these contracts are deferred and included in the measurement of the related transaction, when the hedged transaction occurs. Derivative instruments related to natural gas activities were not significant at December 31, 1995.

The carrying value of cash and cash equivalents, accounts receivable, and accounts payable approximated their fair values due to the short term maturities of these instruments. The estimated fair values of other financial instruments, including debt and risk management instruments summarized above, have been determined using available market information and valuation methodologies, primarily discounted cash flow analysis.

XVII. A. FINANCIAL RELATIONS WITH DIRECTORS AND MANAGERS

Salaries attributed to staff in charge of daily management (three executive directors with permanent functions and nine General Managers) as well as the managers of the main subsidiaries amounted to 211,605,161 BEF.
In the 1996 profit allocation , the share of members of the Board of Directors and the nine General Managers was 104,600,000 BEF.

VERSLAG VAN HET COLLEGE VAN COMMISSARISSEN-REVISOREN

AAN DE GEWONE ALGEMENE VERGADERING VAN PETROFINA OVER DE GECONSOLIDEERDE JAARREKENING AFGESLOTEN PER 31 DECEMBER 1996

Mevrouwen, Mijne Heren,

In uitvoering van het mandaat dat u ons hebt toevertrouwd ingevolge de toepasselijke wettelijke bepalingen, hebben wij de eer u verslag uit te brengen over de geconsolideerde jaarrekening afgesloten per 31 december 1996.

De uitgevoerde controles zijn in overeenstemming met de algemene controlenormen van het Instituut der Bedrijfsrevisoren. De administratieve en boekhoudkundige organisatie en ook de procedures van interne controle werden voor de uitoefening van onze opdracht als voldoende beschouwd.

De aangestelden van de vennootschap hebben de gevraagde ophelderingen en inlichtingen verstrekt.

Bij onze controle van de rekeningen van de vennootschappen opgenomen in de consolidatie, hebben wij ons gesteund op documenten verschaft door de diensten van de diverse ondernemingen, gecontroleerd door bedrijfs-revisoren of gekwalificeerde buitenlandse confrators.

De geconsolideerde jaarrekening is opgesteld overeenkomstig de wettelijke en bestuursrechtelijke voorschriften die daarop van toepassing zijn. De waarderingsregels werden correct toegepast.

Het geconsolideerd jaarverslag bevat de door de wet vereiste inlichtingen en is in overeenstemming met de gecon-solideerde jaarrekening.

Tot besluit verklaren wij zonder voorbehoud, dat de geconsolideerde jaarrekening per 31 december 1996, waarvan het geconsolideerd balanstotaal 371.646 miljoen BEF en waarvan de resultatenrekening van het boekjaar afsluit met een geconsolideerde winst (aandeel van de Groep) van 16.048 miljoen BEF, een getrouw beeld geeft van het vermogen, de financiële toestand en de resultaten van de Groep, rekening houdend met de wettelijke en bestuurs-rechtelijke voorschriften en dat een passende verantwoording werd gegeven in de toelichting.

Brussel, 15 april 1997

Het College van Commissarissen-revisoren,

G. TIMMERMAN en K. VAN OOSTVELDT	M.C. VAES
Vennoten van KLYNVELD PEAT	Vennoten van DELOITTE & TOUCHE
MARWICK GOERDELER	Bedrijfsrevisoren B.C.V.
Bedrijfsrevisoren	

RAPPORT DU COLLEGE DES COMMISSAIRES-REVISEURS

À L'ASSEMBLÉE GÉNÉRALE ORDINAIRE DES ACTIONNAIRES DE PETROFINA SUR LES COMPTES ANNUELS CONSOLIDÉS ARRETÉS AU 31 DÉCEMBRE 1996.

Mesdames, Messieurs,

En exécution du mandat que vous nous avez confié conformément aux dispositions légales applicables en la matière, nous avons l'honneur de vous faire rapport sur les comptes consolidés arrêtés au 31 décembre 1996.

Nos contrôles ont été réalisés selon les normes générales de l'Institut des Reviseurs d'Entreprises. L'organisation administrative et comptable et les dispositifs de contrôle interne ont été jugés suffisants pour l'exercice de notre mission.

Nous avons obtenu des préposés de la société les explications et informations demandées.

Lors de notre révision des comptes des sociétés incluses dans la consolidation, nous nous sommes appuyés sur les documents fournis par les services des différentes sociétés, vérifiés par des reviseurs d'entreprises ou des confrères qualifiés à l'étranger.

Les comptes consolidés sont établis conformément aux dispositions légales et réglementaires qui les régissent. Les règles d'évaluation ont été appliquées d'une façon correcte.

Le rapport de gestion sur les comptes consolidés contient les informations requises par la loi et concorde avec les comptes annuels consolidés.

En conclusion, nous attestons sans réserve que les comptes annuels consolidés arrêtés au 31 décembre 1996, dont le total de bilan consolidé s'élève à 371.646 millions BEF et dont le compte de résultats se solde par un bénéfice consolidé de l'exercice (quote-part du Groupe) de 16.048 millions BEF, donnent une image fidèle du patrimoine, de la situation financière et des résultats du Groupe, compte tenu des dispositions légales et réglementaires qui les régissent et que les justifications données dans l'annexe sont adéquates.

Bruxelles, le 15 avril 1997

Le Collège des Commissaires-Reviseurs,

G. TIMMERMAN et K. VAN OOSTVELDT
Partners de KLYNVELD PEAT
MARWICK GOERDELER
Reviseurs d'Entreprises

M.C. VAES
Partner de DELOITTE & TOUCHE
Reviseurs d'Entreprises S.C.C.

REPORT OF THE JOINT STATUTORY AUDITORS

To THE ANNUAL GENERAL MEETING OF SHAREHOLDERS OF PETROFINA ON THE CONSOLIDATED ANNUAL ACCOUNTS FOR THE YEAR ENDED DECEMBER 31, 1996

Ladies and Gentlemen,

On completion of the audit assignment you entrusted to us in accordance with legal requirements we have the honour to report to you on the consolidated accounts as of December 31, 1996.

Our examination was made in accordance with the general auditing standards issued by the "Institut des Reviseurs d'Entreprises". The administrative and accounting organization and its system of internal controls have been considered adequate for the fulfilment of our mission.

The company's management supplied all explanations and information we requested.

Our examination of the financial statements of the companies included in the consolidation was based on documents supplied by the various companies and checked by company auditors or qualified auditors in the relevant country.

The consolidated accounts have been prepared in accordance with legal and statutoty requirements. Valuation rules have been applied correctly.

The Directors' report on the consolidated accounts contains the information required by law and is consistent with the consolidated annual accounts.

In conclusion, we certify without qualification, that the annual consolidated accounts as of December 31, 1996, with a balance sheet total of 371,646 million BEF and a statement of income showing consolidated net income for the year of 16,048 million BEF (Group's share), give a true and fair view of the assets and liabilities, the financial position and results of the Group, taking into account the applicable legal and statutory requirements, and that the supplementary information given in the notes is appropriate.

Brussels, April 15, 1997

The joint statutory auditors,

G. TIMMERMAN AND K. VAN OOSTVELDT	M.C. VAES
Partners of KLYNVELD PEAT	Partner DELOITTE TOUCHE
MARWICK GOERDELER	Corporate auditors
Corporate auditors	

Common Legal Forms of Companies

The two most common types of companies in Denmark are the public limited company (*Aktieselskab, or A/S*) and the private limited company (*Anpartsselskab, or ApS*), which are regulated by separate though very similar companies acts. A public limited company must have a share capital of at least DKK 500,000, while a private limited company must have a company capital of at least DKK 125,000.

Sources of Financial Reporting Requirements

Danish companies must file accounts in accordance with the Financial Statements Act (*Årsregnskabsloven*) and the Ministerial Order on Annual Accounts (*Årsregnskabsbekendtgørelsen*). All companies must publish their annual accounts by submitting them to the Danish Commerce and Companies Agency (*Erhvervs- og Selskabsstyrelsen*), an agency under the Ministry of Business and Industry. Companies listed on the stock exchange must furthermore comply with Danish accounting standards as published by the Institute of State-Authorized Public Accountants.

Corporate Taxation

The legislation on corporate taxation, which is completely independent of the legislation on financial statements, establishes rules concerning the calculation and payment of income tax by Danish companies. Corporate tax is 34% of taxable income.

Auditing Requirements

The financial statements of all public and private limited companies must be audited by at least one auditor who must be a state-authorized public accountant (*statsautoriseret revisor*) or a registered accountant (*registreret revisor*). Registered accountants are entitled to audit only the accounts of small and medium-sized companies or corporations. The financial statements of companies quoted on the stock exchange must always be audited by two auditors, of whom at least one must be a state-authorized public accountant.

Organization of the Accounting and Auditing Professions

There are two organisations of accountants in Denmark: the Institute of State-Authorized Public Accountants (*Foreningen af Statsautoriserede Revisorer,* or FSR) and the Institute of Registered Accountants (*Foreningen af Registrerede Revisorer,* or FRR), with around 2,000 and 4,000 practicing members, respectively. There is no legal requirement to the effect that accountants must be members of either institute to be entitled to carry out statutory auditing as required by legislation on financial statements and companies.

Constitution and Legal System

Denmark is a constitutional monarchy, with the powers of the monarch being purely formal in nature. The Danish Constitution divides power into legislative power, which lies with the monarch and the parliament, executive power, which lies with the government and the parliament, and judicial power, which lies with the courts of justice. The Danish parliament has 179 members elected in direct elections, which must be held at least every fourth year. All Danish citizens 18 years old and older have the right to vote. The prime minister and the government, who are formally appointed by the monarch, must not be opposed by a majority in parliament. Laws are enacted by parliament and enforced by the government. Ministers may, in pursuance of powers vested in them in legislation, issue orders such as the Ministerial Order on Annual Accounts.

Currency

Danish kroner (*danske kroner*), divisible into 100 øre (*øre*).

Official Language

The only official language in Denmark is Danish. Financial statements issued by Danish companies must be in Danish. Listed companies often publish their annual accounts in English as well.

DENMARK

Carsten K. Hansen
Copenhagen Business School

1. Background

1.1 History

The first known accounting regulation in Denmark was related to the kingdom and public administration in the sixteenth century, when the vassals and the nobility were obliged to render accounts concerning crown land. During the period of absolute monarchy and centralized administration, accounting requirements were extended. By 1840, all royal treasurers were required to keep books, and special royal cash controllers were appointed. Until the twentieth century, however, both the preparation and auditing of accounts were restricted to the state and municipal sectors.

The oldest limited companies in Denmark go back to the seventeenth century. The development of accounting at that time reflected the fact that Denmark relied mainly on agricultural production and fishing and that the capitalist society at that time lacked momentum. No accounting regulation existed, and when the first limited companies voluntarily published their annual accounts, considerable flexibility in the choice of accounting principles was observed. Gradually, the number of limited companies grew as a result of continuing industrialization. Around the beginning of the twentieth century there were about 1,000 limited companies, and by 1909 the number had increased to about 2,500. Financial scandals as well as the misuse of limited liability led to demands for the adoption of a limited companies act.

In 1908 one of the largest financial scandals in Denmark's financial history took place, involving Minister of Justice P. A. Alberti, who as chairman of a Danish savings bank gave himself up to the authorities, admitting to fraud and deception on an unprecedented scale. In 1909 a State-Authorized Public Accountants Act (*Lov om Statsautoriserede revisorer*) was passed as a consequence of the Alberti case. In this law the British/Dutch model based on an independent auditing profession was chosen over the German model based on a close relationship between the auditing profession and the banks, the so-called *Treuhandsgesellschaften*.

In Denmark, however, it was the state (Ministry of Trade and Shipping, later called the Ministry of Business and Industry) that was to authorize auditors rather than professional bodies, as in the United Kingdom.

In 1912 a Bookkeeping Act (*Bogføringsloven*) was adopted. Under its provisions all kinds of businesses were required to keep books relating to their financial affairs, the only important exceptions being farmers and craftsmen.

The growth of limited companies and problems relating to speculation and profiteering during the First World War increased the pressure for a limited companies act, and in 1917 Denmark introduced its first Limited Companies Act (*Aktieselskabsloven*). It was one of the last countries in Europe to do so. This law was influenced particularly by the German *Handelsgesetzbuch* of 1897, as well as by the newly adopted companies acts in Norway and Sweden. The accounting sections of the law, however, were framed in accordance with the English legal tradition by quoting a general clause as the only guideline for accounting practice. The law included only two sections regarding financial reporting and two sections regarding the audit. The law stated that limited companies must prepare a profit and loss account and a balance sheet showing the true position of the company in accordance with the best estimate of management. This formulation embodied the concept of "orderly and prudent business practice." The law applied to all limited companies, and it required the financial statements to be audited. All limited companies had to submit a copy of their financial statements to the public registry (*Aktieselskabsregisteret*, later called the Danish Commerce and Companies Agency, *Erhvervs- og Selskabsstyrelsen*). The only exception regarding publication was for family-owned companies, defined as companies that had ten or fewer shareholders and that were not open to inspection.

The Limited Companies Act of 1917 proved weak and ineffective, and during the 1920s attempts were made to introduce a new and stronger version. At that time, limited companies were primarily small and family-owned companies that were mainly debt financed; shareholders were relatively unimportant users of accounting information. The pressure for more accounting regulation, therefore, was rather weak, and a new Limited Companies Act was not adopted until 1930.

The Limited Companies Act of 1930 increased the amount of information that was to be presented in the financial statements. The requirements were embodied in a general clause, "orderly and prudent business practice," which became the leading principle of valuation. Prudence was emphasized to the extent that it allowed—perhaps even recommended—the creation of hidden reserves. The law also supported a prudent dividend policy in order to protect creditors by requiring that a legal reserve be set aside. Besides the general clause, the law included specific rules for revaluation, formation costs, and goodwill, but it went into no further detail about the items and formats of the accounts. The law was in force for more than 40 years, during which there were no major changes in accounting legislation.

Although the legal system of financial reporting remained unaltered from 1930 to 1973, accounting practice changed in several ways during these decades, with the accounting profession as one of the main driving forces.

One of the most significant changes began to make itself felt in the 1950s, when Danish companies moved from absorption costing to marginal costing. With marginal costing, inventory is valued at variable cost and the profit and loss account shows variable and fixed costs, the contribution margin being a subtotal if the vertical format is used. The driving force behind this development was the late Professor Palle Hansen (1911–1991), of the Copenhagen Business School, who was a strong advocate of the marginal costing principle for both management accounting and financial accounting purposes. During the 1960s marginal costing came to be used more and more and gradually established itself as a generally accepted accounting principle.

From 1917 to the Second World War, companies mainly used tax rules for the valuation of inventories, fixed assets, and so on, in the financial statements. In those days, tax law required only that the same inventory value be used in both statements, and the tax authorities would not accept higher depreciation charges (lower asset values) in the tax statement than in the financial statement. After the war a close relationship between tax rules and accounting rules continued, creating considerable confusion in Danish accounting practice. The problems increased when new tax rules were introduced during the 1950s and beyond, oriented toward fiscal objectives rather than income measurement. The auditing profession recommended that companies ignore tax rules in the financial statements but was divided about how to reflect this in the statements. Generally, the separation between the taxation and accounting concepts of profit was not completed until the implementation of the Fourth Directive in 1981.

After the Second World War, the German influence decreased and the accounting profession became more oriented toward the United Kingdom and the United States. During the 1960s the number of foreign groups establishing Danish subsidiaries, especially groups of U.S. origin, increased, and international audit firms like Arthur Andersen and Price Waterhouse set up affiliations in Denmark. U.S. and British accounting principles gradually penetrated Danish accounting practice (for example, the equity method and deferred taxation), and the international trends in financial accounting, especially the accounting developments taking place in the United Kingdom and the United States, became important driving forces for accounting changes.

In the late 1940s and afterwards, technological development initiated discussions related to the use of modern bookkeeping systems. The Bookkeeping Act and a relating order were revised in 1959, and in 1990, the Bookkeeping Order was revised once more to keep pace with developments in information technology.

During the 1960s demand grew for regulation of practicing unauthorized auditors, and in 1970 a second-tier group of auditors was created by the adoption of the Registered Public Accountants Act (*Lov om Registrerede Revisorer*). After the implementation of the Eighth Directive, registered public accountants were allowed to audit only small and medium-sized companies and groups.

As early as 1934 the Nordic countries decided to harmonize company law in Denmark, Finland, Norway, and Sweden, publishing a proposal in 1942. This proposal for a new companies act was never implemented, however, because of the Second World War. In 1957 the Danish parliament appointed a commission to draft a new limited companies act. The commission published a draft in 1964, which was never implemented because about that time the Nordic countries decided to continue their efforts to harmonize their company law. On the basis of these efforts and the expectation of future membership in the European Community (EC), a new proposal was put forward in 1969, and in 1973 the Limited Companies Act was replaced by two new acts relating to large and small limited companies, respectively: the Public Limited Companies Act and the Private Limited Companies Act. Its thirteen sections concerning financial reporting were primarily a codification of existing accounting practice and concentrated on broad-brush principles and requirements that did little to affect actual practice.

The most important changes were the following:

1. The directors' report became a mandatory part of financial reporting.
2. Specifications and notes regarding the accounts were introduced.
3. The notion of a group, which was for the first time defined in the legislation, was introduced. All Danish groups with a limited-liability parent company were now required to publish a consolidated balance sheet for the group as a whole or at least a so-called group statement, including information about intergroup outstandings and debt with the profit shown separately for the parent company and the subsidiaries. The auditor's report should cover both parent and group accounts.

The accounting regulation for public limited companies applied to private limited companies as well. The former privilege of nonpublication was withdrawn from family-owned companies, and all limited companies now had to prepare audited financial statements and to submit them to the Danish Commerce and Companies Agency, where they were open for inspection by anyone.

The former general clause "orderly and prudent business practice" was reformulated in modern terminology as "good accounting practice," the term used in all the Nordic Countries. "Prudence" was not mentioned in the general clause, but it remained an important concept.

In 1976 the auditing profession decided to join the International Accounting Standards Committee (IASC) and in subsequent years published the International Accounting Standards in Danish, with Danish comments, as a surrogate for national accounting standards. The International Accounting Standards are not legally enforceable and have not so far had the regulatory impact expected by the profession.

1.2 Recent History Leading to the Present Situation

Denmark became a member of the EC in 1973 and implemented the Fourth Directive in 1981,[1] being the first EC member state to do so. Accounting regulation was removed from the Limited Companies Acts, and a new Financial Statements Act, containing 68 sections, was promulgated.

Generally, the Financial Statements Act follows the Fourth Directive quite meticulously and takes advantage of the disclosure exemption rules in only a few cases. The directive is heavily represented, article by article. In cases in which it provides options (e.g., between the use of different valuation methods or formats), the Financial Statements Act generally includes the same options.

In 1990 the Seventh Directive was adopted in an amendment to the Financial Statements Act. At the same time the majority of disclosure rules and almost all the measurement rules relating to groups were removed from the act and incorporated in a special Financial Statements Order published by the Ministry of Industry (Commerce and Companies Agency).[2] A comparison between the accounting regulation of a single company (parent company) and that of groups exposes a shift of power involving the tactical level of accounting regulation. For single and parent companies, only rules regarding disclosure and sanctions are covered by the Financial Statements Order, whereas basic accounting principles and valuation principles are to be found in the Financial Statements Act. For groups, disclosure rules, basic accounting principles, and valuation principles are to be found in the Ministerial Order. Most regulation concerning groups is based on the Financial Statements Order. The separation between the act and the order was designed to avoid parliamentary involvement in highly technical matters concerning group accounting.

The most important innovations regarding group accounting were:

1. Small groups and subgroups do not need to prepare consolidated financial statements.
2. Under certain circumstances a subsidiary may be excluded from consolidation.
3. The consolidated financial statement must include notes.
4. The past equity method has become obligatory. The pooling of interests method is not acceptable.
5. The equity method must be used for associated undertakings in the consolidated financial statement and becomes an option in the financial statements of the parent company.
6. The treatment of the elimination difference (goodwill or negative goodwill) has changed (see Section 3.5).

The implementation of the Fourth and Seventh Directives brought significant changes in Danish accounting practice, for example, the number of notes, changes in formats, the introduction of true and fair view, but did not have as radical an effect as many had expected. Only a few major changes in valuation principles were required, and accounting practice continued to be relatively diverse. Danish accounting regulation remained fairly flexible.

The Financial Statements Act was revised in 1988, incorporating a transfer of the audit regulations from the Limited Companies Acts.

The Institute of State-Authorized Public Accountants (*Foreningen af Statsautoriserede Revisorer*, FSR) was forced to publish Danish Accounting Standards in 1988 and later. The approval or disapproval of Danish Accounting Standards was the responsibility of the FSR, although a hearing procedure took place before final adoption. After the financial collapse of Northern Feather (see details below), the government and parliament demanded a reorganization of the standard-setting process. The Accounting Panel was established under the leadership of the auditing profession but including representatives from producers and users. The FSR is still responsible for the issue of the standards, however, the Accounting Panel being an advisory body.

So far, the Copenhagen Stock Exchange has been reluctant to participate in the standard-setting process and to exercise any kind of control.

A number of revisions of the Financial Statements Act have been made in the 1990s, tightening disclosure requirements and introducing control as an obligation of the Danish Commerce and Companies Agency. The reason for these revisions was undoubtedly a series of major liquidations, first and foremost the winding up of Northern Feather in 1991. In the case of Northern Feather, accounting legislation in force was clearly violated, not least regarding the highly criticized handling of the breach of the consistency concept, the extent of which was scandalous.

Figure 1 shows the gradual development in accounting regulation, and Figure 2 presents an overview of existing accounting regulation. The scope of the Financial Statements Act has been widened and now includes partnerships and limited partnerships in which all partners and limited partners are public limited companies, limited partnership that have a public limited company as a general partner, and private limited companies or companies with a similar legal form or in which all partners and limited partners respectively are covered by the previous formulation.

In 1995 the Accounting Council, which is an advisory body under the Ministry of Business and Industry, carried out a number of studies to examine simplifying financial reporting for primarily small businesses.

FIGURE 1 *The Development of Danish Accounting Regulation*

1912	The first Bookkeeping Act
1917	The first Limited Companies Act
1930	The Limited Companies Act is revised.
1959	The Bookkeeping Act is revised.
	A Ministerial Order on the Accounting, Financial Statements and Preservation of Accounting Records of Commercial undertakings is issued.
1973	The Limited Companies Act is split into two acts: the Public Limited Companies Act and the Private Limited Companies Act.
1978	The Institute of State-Authorized Public Accountants publishes the International Accounting Standards in Danish.
1981	The sections dealing with annual accounts of limited companies are separated from the two limited companies acts, and the Financial Statements Act is adopted (implementation of the Fourth Directive).
1987	The Copenhagen Stock Exchange adopts the Information Obligations for Issuers of Listed Securities, in which it is stated that the financial statements of publicly listed companies must be in accordance with the highest level of accounting standard in the industry in which the company operates.
1988	The Financial Statements Act is revised: The chapter on auditing is transferred from the Limited Companies Acts to the Financial Statements Act.
1988	The first Danish Accounting Standard is published by the Institute of State-Authorized Public Accountants.
1989	The Information Obligations for Issuers of Listed Securities is revised
1990	The Ministerial Order on Accounting, Financial Statements and Preservation of Accounting Records of Commercial Undertakings is revised.
	A Ministerial Guideline Concerning Bookkeeping is issued.
1991	The Financial Statements Act is revised (the implementation of the Seventh Directive).
	A Ministerial Order relating to the Format of Annual Accounts and Group Accounts is adopted.
	A Ministerial Guideline concerning Group Accounts is issued.
1991	The Public Limited Companies Act is revised: The limit for information obligations concerning important shareholders is decreased from shareholders owning 10% of the share capital to shareholders owning 5% of the share capital.
1991	The Financial Statements Act is revised:
	— If a company changes its financial year, no financial period may exceed 12 months.
	— If a company changes its accounting policy, the accumulated change must be transferred directly to the equity and the comparative figures must be adjusted accordingly.
	— An outgoing auditor of a publicly listed company must immediately inform the Copenhagen Stock Exchange and must advise the newly elected auditor as to the reasons for leaving the auditorship of the company.
	— The auditor must attend the general meeting of publicly listed companies and answer questions relating to the annual accounts that are signed by him or her.

(Figure continues)

(Figure 1 continued)

— The auditor must verify that the board of directors follows the legislation laid down in the Limited Companies Acts and the Financial Statements Act.

— The financial report must be filed with the Danish Commerce and Companies Agency within 5 months after the end of the financial year.

1991   The Information Obligations for Issuers of Listed Securities is revised:

— A publicly listed company must follow the Danish Accounting Standards.

— Information must be given in the annual financial report if not all group companies are audited by at least one of the auditors of the parent company, their international affiliations, or a reputable international audit firm.

— The time limit for publishing the semiannual and annual reports is shortened.

1992   The Financial Statements Act is revised:

— Partnerships and limited partnerships must follow the act if all the partners or limited partners are companies covered by the law.

— The Danish Commerce and Companies Agency may request such information as is necessary in order to determine whether the act, provisions laid down pursuant to the act, and the company's articles of association have been complied with.

1992   The Public Limited Companies Act is revised:

— Information must be given at the annual general meeting and in the annual financial report concerning the position of the members of the board of directors in other public limited companies

1994   The Financial Statements Act is revised.

— The Danish Commerce and Companies Agency must carry out statistical tests to examine whether the companies follow the act and the provisions laid down pursuant to the act

— An Accounting Council is established as an advisory forum of the Ministry of Industry on accounting issues.

— Large companies must disclose auditing fees.

1996   An act on industrial and commercial businesses is adopted:

— Businesses with limited liability (cooperative societies) are covered by the provisions of the Financial Statements Act, though with a number of exemptions based on the special conditions applying to such undertakings.

1996   The Information Obligations for Issuers of Listed Securities are replaced by the rules governing issuers of securities listed by the Copenhagen Stock Exchange (*Regler for udstedere af børsnoterede værdipapirer på Københavns Fondsbørs A/S*)

1996   The Financial Statements Act and the Financial Statements Order are revised:

— Small companies need not prepare an annual report;

— Small companies need not incorporate the consequences of changed accounting practice into the opening balance of the year in which the change takes place. Instead they may include the sum relating to the change in their profit and loss account.

— Small companies need not explain expenses and income in their notes if they relate to a period before the balance sheet date (that is, the following year), provisions, expenses and income relating to previous years, and extraordinary expenses and income.

— The profit and loss account must no longer be submitted in the horizontal format, which was in fact also very rare in practice.

— It is specified that deferred tax must generally be set aside as provisions, though the sum of the deferred tax may still be indicated in a note.

— It is specified that provisions, write-downs, and reversals of provisions and write-downs must be included in the profit and loss account under the activities and functions to which they relate.

— It is specified that only income and expenses that do not relate to the ordinary operation of the company may be included under extraordinary items.

— The total financial impact of accounting estimates and changes of such estimates must be stated, and the estimate changes must be explained in the notes.

— The LIFO method for valuation of stocks must no longer be applied.

— It is specified that the net realisable value on the balance sheet date must be used in connection with write-down of current assets following the principle of lowest value.

— Tax on extraordinary result must be stated separately in the profit and loss account.

On the basis of these studies, the Financial Statements Act was amended once again in 1996, and a revised Ministerial Order on Annual Accounts was issued. The new order was an updated compilation of two previous orders. The Accounting Council considered the elimination or relaxation of a number of specific provisions relating to small businesses. However, it became evident that the EU directives do not permit such elimination or relaxation of quite a number of the provisions in question. Discussions in the Accounting Council gave the green light to initiating a thorough revision of the Financial Statements Act, primarily to establish whether the act is in keeping with the times or whether it needs revision. This work is still going on. The size criteria used for defining small and medium-sized enterprises that are neither government owned limited companies nor listed on the stock exchange were increased. Small businesses in particular but also medium-sized enterprises will benefit from a number of relaxations or exemptions (see Section 2.3). In certain circumstances, for example, small businesses may not need to prepare an annual report.

The amendments to the act also meant clarification of a number of provisions and limitation of a number of options, for example regarding research expenditure, deferred tax, provisions, write-down, extraordinary items, stocks, and work in progress. Finally, the Financial Statements Act now requires that government-owned companies abide by the rules and regulations on financial statements applying to listed companies.

FIGURE 2   *An Overview of Existing Accounting Regulation*

Laws and associated Ministerial Orders and Guidelines
- The Bookkeeping Act
- The Ministerial Order on Accounting, Financial Statements and Preservation of Accounting Records of Commercial Undertakings
- Ministerial Guideline Concerning Bookkeeping
- The Financial Statements Act
- The Ministerial Order relating to the Preparation, Filing, and Publication of Annual Accounts, etc. and Other Accounting Documents with the Danish Commerce and Companies Agency (Ministerial Order on Annual Accounts)
- Ministerial Guideline Concerning Group Accounts
- Special legislation exists concerning banks, insurance companies, mortgage credit institutions, and other credit institutions

Accounting Standards and Recommendations
- Danish Accounting Standards:
  - No. 1: Objective and Contents of the Annual Accounts
  - No. 2: Disclosure of Accounting Policies
  - No. 3: Changes in Accounting Policies and Accounting Estimates
  - No. 4: Contingent Liabilities and Events Occurring after the Balance Sheet Date
  - No. 5: Extraordinary Items
  - No. 6: Long-term Contracts
  - No. 7: Research and Development
  - No. 8: Inventories
  - No. 9: Foreign Currency Translation
  - No. 10: Tangible Fixed Assets
  - No. 11: Cash Flow Statements

  These standards are mandatory for publicly listed companies.
- Rules governing Issuers of Securities listed by the Copenhagen Stock Exchange. These obligations are mandatory for publicly listed companies.
- The International Accounting Standards
  Generally, these are recommended by the audit profession.
- Opinions issued by the Institute of State-Authorized Public Accountants (*Foreningen af Statsautoriserede Revisorer*, FSR)

Other Sources of Regulation
- *Revision & Regnskabsvæsen* (*Auditing & Accounting*, the professional journal of the FSR)
- *Revisorbladet* (*The Auditor's Journal*, the professional journal of the FRR (*Foreningen af Registrerede Revisorer*, FRR)
- Olaf Hasselager & Aksel Runge Johansen: *Årsregnskaber—Kommentarer til regnskabslovgivningen*. København: G.E.C. Gad 1992 (The standard commentary text concerning Danish accounting regulation)

In 1995 legislation concerning the Copenhagen Stock Exchange was amended, one result of which was the modernization of the structure of the stock exchange. In 1996 the rules applying to issuers of listed securities were modernized.

1.3 Driving Forces Behind the Development of Danish Accounting Regulation

Until the end of the 1950s Denmark was primarily an agricultural country; it is a relatively young industrial nation. Furthermore, most Danish companies are small, and most industries are light industry. Danish companies require only limited amounts of capital, and the main sources of capital are banks and similar financial institutions, although trade and other creditors also play an important role. Little state capital is invested in companies. About 250 Danish companies are listed on the Copenhagen Stock Exchange, which is the only stock exchange in Denmark. The Copenhagen Stock Exchange must be said to play a relatively minor role as a market for capital.

These are some of the factors that may help to explain why, until recently, accounting regulation has been liberal and featuring relatively limited though increasing professional self-regulation to support the loose legal regulation.

Developments during the past decade, however, seem to indicate that a change is taking place toward a growing and broader interest in accounting legislation and toward stricter accounting regulation, especially for publicly listed companies. The two main forces behind this change have been a number of completely unexpected liquidations of major companies in the late 1980s and early 1990s and, later on, growing internationalization. It appears that a fairly small but increasing number of listed companies base their accounting practices on International Accounting Standards.

2. The Form and Content of Published Financial Statements

2.1 Types of Financial Statement

In Denmark, both the parent company and the group as a whole must prepare and publish financial statements. Both sets of financial statements include a profit and loss account, balance sheet, and notes. The directors' report refers to the whole group, while the auditor's report covers both sets of financial statements.

The Financial Statements Act stresses that the directors' report should give a reliable statement concerning the development of the company, as well as supplementary information, should the financial statement be influenced by any exceptional circumstances or uncertainties. Six percent of publicly listed trade, service, and industrial groups discussed exceptional circumstances in their financial statements for 1996.

In addition, the directors' report must at a minimum include comments on:

1. Important events that have occurred subsequent to the end of the financial year

2. The company's expected future development

3. Research and development activities

4. The company's branches in foreign countries, if any

For listed companies, the directors' report must also state:

1. The result of the year compared with the expected result as publicized by the company in the course of the year, together with an explanation of any deviation in the result

2. The managerial positions occupied by members of the board of directors and the executive board in other companies, with the exception of fully owned subsidiaries

Normally, directors' reports of publicly listed companies go far beyond these minimum requirements. But the scope, the depth, and the precision vary considerably from company to company. A number of publicly listed trade, service, and industrial groups discuss topics related to environmental protection and standardization of quality. Twenty-five percent discussed state approval of their environmental policy and/or investments related to environmental protection, and thirty percent discussed ISO-Certification in their financial statements for 1996. As mentioned, small companies need notrepare and publish a directors' report.

According to the Financial Statements Act, no obligation exists to present any additional key figures or statements. The Copenhagen Stock

Exchange has published rules governing Issuers of Listed Securities listed by the Copenhagen Stock Exchange. The rules stress that the financial statement of a publicly listed company must include comparative key figures for the previous 4 years and a cash flow statement showing cash flow operations, investment activities, and financing transactions.

Furthermore, the Copenhagen Stock Exchange requires that the financial statements of publicly listed companies be in accordance with the highest level of accounting standards in the industry in which the company operates, and with generally accepted Danish accounting standards. At present the Danish Accounting Standards Nos. 1–11 are considered to be part of generally accepted Danish accounting practices. Foreign companies must meet these same obligations in relation to accounting standards in their home countries. The financial statement must also include an introductory description of the accounting policies used by the company, and the company must state whether the accounts are presented in compliance with generally accepted Danish accounting principles. Deviation from the above-mentioned obligations must be explained. An annual financial statement that is a summary of the financial report must be published when the board of directors has adopted the financial report. The Copenhagen Stock Exchange also requires that a semiannual financial statement be published.

2.3 Small and Medium-Sized Companies

As mentioned above, small companies in particular but also medium-sized companies or groups benefit from a number of relaxations and exemptions in accounting rules and regulations. The companies, which must not be listed by the stock exchange, must meet at least two of the following criteria:

	Small companies	*Medium-sized companies*
Balance sheet less than (DKK)	20 million	75 million
Net turnover less than (DKK)	40 million	150 million
Average number of employees during the financial year	50	250

2.4   Scope of Consolidation

A parent company must be a public or a private limited company or a partnership or a limited partnership, and a subsidiary may likewise have different legal forms, limited as well as unlimited.

Full consolidation takes place if one of the following criteria is met:

1. The company has the majority of the shareholders' voting rights in the other undertaking.

2. The company owns shares in another undertaking and:

    (a) has the right to appoint a majority of the management or supervisory board of the other undertaking; or

    (b) has the right to exercise a dominant influence over an undertaking pursuant to a contract or to a provision in its memorandum or articles of association; or

    (c) exercises dominant influence as a result of agreements with other investors; or

    (d) exercises *de facto* dominant influence.

As can be seen, "dominant influence" is the key criterion to determine whether there is a parent/subsidiary relationship. In accordance with the Seventh Directive, a subsidiary can be excluded from the consolidation under special circumstances. The subsidiary is then treated as "investment in a subsidiary" (a participating interest).

Before implementation of the Seventh Directive, all groups had to prepare and publish consolidated financial statements. Two general exceptions now exist:

1. Subgroups that are not publicly listed do not need to submit consolidated financial statements. A reference must be made in the financial statement of the parent company in which the subsidiary is consolidated.

2. Small groups in which none of the companies is publicly listed in an EU country do not need to submit consolidated financial statements, provided certain criteria are met.

2.5 Form of the Published Financial Statements

Denmark has adopted a liberal disclosure policy. Companies may choose freely between the two vertical formats of the profit and loss account provided by the Fourth Directive.

The mix of different formats makes it difficult for financial analysts to carry out cross-sectional analysis between companies. Comparability is obtainable only on an overall level.

Net turnover	XXXXX
Staff costs	XXXXX
Other costs except depreciation etc.	XXXXX
Depreciation and write-offs on tangible and intangible fixed assets	XXXXX

No Danish accounting standards deal with this problem of comparabilty. Some companies provide more detailed information than required, and there is sometimes a lack of consensus about where certain items should be included. For instance, provision for bad debts may be indicated as production cost, distribution cost, or as a general administrative charge. The seriousness of this problem is, as yet, unknown.

It is noteworthy too, that the EU formats of the profit and loss account do not correspond to Danish accounting traditions. Denmark had a long tradition of using the marginal costing principle for both management and financial accounting purposes. The use of marginal costing makes it possible to analyze the composition of variable and fixed costs. When the Fourth Directive was implemented, some people expected a shift toward absorption costing, but that took place only to a limited extent (see Table 1). The marginal costing era may have come to an end, however. The Danish Accounting Standard No. 8 on inventories recommends that, in addition to the direct production costs, the production cost should include overheads that have been incurred during the course of production and that are attributable to the goods in question. The Standard was adopted in 1993 after more than one year of discussion and is effective for financial statements covering financial years beginning on July 1, 1993 or later.

The formats make it difficult to show the distinction between variable and fixed costs. Here it should be remembered that most Danish companies are small or medium-sized, with relatively narrow bases of activity, which improves the usefulness of the contribution margin as a subtotal. In 1996, about 20% of publicly listed trade, service, and industrial companies disclosed a contribution margin. Most of the industrial companies did so by distinguishing between direct and indirect production costs. This can lead to errors if distribution costs include important groups of variable costs.

The marginal costing approach also explains another Danish phenomenon, namely a tradition of showing subtotals in the profit and loss account. Since EU harmonization, it has become far more difficult to present relevant subtotals, although Danish companies still try to do so, and a great variety of subtotals can be found. Therefore, financial analysts must reach their own conclusions concerning relevant subtotals.

A more detailed subdivision of the items in the financial statement is allowed, and new items may be added, provided that their contents are not included in any of the items prescribed by the formats. Items may be summarized if they are insignificant, or if a better overview is provided. This requires a note. In 1996 more than two-thirds of publicly listed companies included subdivisions, aggregations, or additions in their profit and loss accounts.

In Danish accounting practice a number of transactions come under the heading "extraordinary items," though the numerical proportion of such transactions is falling. Compared with the previous situation, there seems to be increasing consensus about the proper definition of extraordinary

TABLE 1 *Methods of Inventory Costing Used by Publicly Quoted Trade, Service, and Industrial Groups*

Finished goods	1992 No. (%)	1993 No. (%)	1994 No. (%)	1995 No. (%)	1996 No. (%)
Marginal costing	49 (44)	41 (38)	36 (32)	37 (32)	35 (29)
Absorption costing	21 (19)	29 (27)	38 (34)	44 (38)	50 (41)
Mixed principles	5 (5)	5 (5)	5 (4)	3 (3)	3 (2)
Other principles	7 (6)	6 (6)	6 (5)	6 (5)	6 (6)
No information/ not relevant	11 (10)	6 (6)	7 (6)	6 (5)	10 (8)
Not relevant, no finished goods	18 (16)	22 (20)	20 (18)	19 (17)	17 (14)
Total	111 (100)	109 (102)	112 (100)	115 (100)	121 (100)

Source: *ACCOUNT DATA - DK*, Copenhagen Business School.

items. In accordance with the Fourth Directive, the Financial Statements Act defines extraordinary items as items that are separate from ordinary activity. In accordance with IAS No. 8, Danish Accounting Standard No. 5 defines extraordinary items as gains and losses that derive from events or transactions that are distinct from the ordinary activities of the company and are therefore not expected to recur frequently or regularly. This Danish Accounting Standard has been mandatory for publicly listed companies for financial years beginning on July 1, 1990 or later. To an increasing extent, accounting practice pays attention to the time dimension in the definition of extraordinary items. One characteristic feature is that a decreasing number of Danish companies do not include gains and losses arising from the sale of tangible fixed assets as extraordinary items (Table 2). But the financial analyst should still be aware of the distinction between ordinary and extraordinary activities.

The format requirements concerning the balance sheet have not presented the same difficulties as the profit and loss account for accounting practice. Both the vertical and horizontal formats are allowed, though almost all companies use the horizontal format. It was new to Danish practice to disclose information concerning the age of debt. In practice, all companies divide debt into long-term debt and short-term debt. The short-term debt element of long-term debt, however, may be presented in at least two different ways: as an integral part of corresponding short-term debt items, or as a special item labeled "short-term part of long-term debt."

TABLE 2 *Treatment of Gains or Losses Arising from the Sale of Tangible Assets by Publicly Listed Trade, Service, and Industrial Groups*

	1992	*1993*	*1994*	*1995*	*1996*
	No. (%)	*No. (%)*	*No. (%)*	*No. (%)*	*No. (%)*
As ordinary item	41 (37)	43 (40)	45 (40)	44 (38)	57 (47)
As extraordinary item	9 (8)	7 (6)	6 (6)	7 (6)	3 (2)
As both ordinary and extraordinary item	9 (8)	14 (13)	16 (14)	21 (19)	11 (10)
No information/ not relevant	52 (47)	45 (41)	45 (40)	43 (37)	50 (41)
Total	111 (100)	109 (100)	112 (100)	115 (100)	121 (100)

Source: *ACCOUNT DATA - DK*, Copenhagen Business School.

Please note that Lundbeck A/S does not distinguish between short-term and long-term debt as being interest-bearing/non-interest-bearing.

The Financial Statements Order requires comparative figures for one year for the profit and loss account, the balance sheet, and some of the notes. The rules governing Issuers of Securities listed on the Copenhagen Stock Exchange require that the accounts must contain comparative figures for the previous year. In case of break of consistency, the comparative figures must be changed accordingly. Notes are compulsory for the financial statements of parent companies and for consolidated financial statement.

2.6   Statutory Audit and Audit Report

All public and private limited companies must be audited by at least one state-authorized public accountant or one registered public accountant. However, after the implementation of the Eighth Directive, registered public accountants are allowed to audit only small and medium-sized companies and groups. The audit report must confirm that the financial statement has been audited and state whether it is found to be in accordance with legal requirements and the articles of the company. An unqualified audit report signifies:

1. That the financial statement is correctly prepared in accordance with the books of the company and in accordance with existing values, rights and liabilities;

2. That the directors' report includes the information required by law and complies with any other requirements laid down in other provisions, including the requirement of detailed information about:

    — the financial development of the company;

    — extraordinary matters that have had major impact on the accounts; and

    — material uncertainty in connection with the preparation of the accounts;

3. That the profit and loss account, the balance sheet, and the notes meet the requirements concerning financial reporting laid down in legislation and other rules and regulations;

4. That the financial statement gives a true and fair view of the company's assets, liabilities, financial position, and profit or loss.

In recent years there has been much political debate concerning audit reports. A number of unexpected liquidations and crises in major Danish companies have undoubtedly contributed significantly to this debate. The concept of an expectation gap between the users of financial statements on one the hand and accountants on the other has often been mentioned, the result being that politicians wanted more nuanced audit reports than the typical "unqualified report" traditionally used. In addition, it seemed to be politically desirable to extend the number of cases in which auditors must make reservations in their reports. In light of this, the Danish Commerce and Companies Agency issued a new order on declarations by state-authorized and registered accountants, effective from May 1996. One result of this order is that, in line with international practice, Danish audit reports have become more extensive and that a number of basic matters have been specified. In connection with the order, the Commerce and Companies Agency has issued a number of guidelines concerning the order, titled "Guidelines on Audit Reports" (*Erklæringsvejledningen*). In addition, the Institute of State-Authorized Public Accountants (FSR) has revised Auditing Standard No. 7 concerning audit reports. FSR has issued 20 Danish Auditing Standards with auditing recommendations since 1978. Standard No. 7 of 1996, for instance, concerning the audit report, includes recommendations reflected in the audit report presented by Lundbeck A/S (see page 235).

An audit report *must* now comply with a specific format, and a number of *mandatory* headlines must be used in the report. The following elements must be included in a predetermined order:

1. Identification of the accounts audited;
2. Statement declaring that the accounts audited are in fact the accounts prepared by the executive board and the board of directors;
3. Statement concerning the audit made, including the organisation of the audit, etc;
4. Reservations, or a statement to the effect that the report contains no reservations;
5. Supplementary information;
6. Conclusion concerning the audit carried out.

Item 5 above, supplementary information, is new in Danish legislation, although supplementary information has often been included in audit reports in practice. The reason for introducing this new item in the audit report was to create a tool for use in situations in which more nuanced formulations are desirable and where an "unqualified opinion" would otherwise be given according to Danish practice. The auditor must, under a special heading in the report, draw the attention of the reader of the accounts to matters that are important in relation to the assessment of the result of the year, the financial position, or expectations concerning the future. An example of this would be cases in which there is uncertainty as to the continued operation of the company (going concern). In such a situation the auditor must give supplementary information even though the management may mention uncertainty as to the continued operation of the company in the annual report. The auditor may do so by mentioning the matter in the report, referring to the sections in the annual report or annual accounts where management mentions the uncertainty. It is, however, important to stress that supplementary information cannot replace a reservation.

If the auditor expresses a reservation in the audit report, the underlying matter must be stated and explained in a special section headed "Reservations." If no reservations are made, that is, the report is unqualified, the order goes a bit further than international practice in that it explicitly requires that the following appears clearly and in bold letters from the conclusion (for example in a separate line): "The audit has not given rise to any reservations" (see for example Lundbeck A/S page 235).

3. Accounting Policies and Practices in Valuation and Income Measurement: Implications for the Analyst

3.1 Fundamental Principles

In accordance with the Financial Statements Act, information must be given about valuation methods, methods of calculating depreciation, write-offs and revaluations, and the basis of foreign currency translation. Danish Accounting Standard No. 2 recommends that information be given about accounting practice in all areas that are important for a proper understanding of a financial statement. The information must be given in a separate section, before the profit and loss account, the balance sheet, and the notes.

Almost all publicly listed companies give some such information, but precise and exhaustive information is in rare cases still lacking. It is suggested that the financial analyst should read both this section and the notes carefully.

3.2 The True and Fair View

There is an overriding principle that the financial statement shall present a "true and fair view" of the assets and liabilities of the group and the company, its financial position, and of the profit and loss. Moreover, it legally obligatory to provide further information when the basic provisions of the law are not in themselves sufficient to present a true and fair view. Finally, it is obligatory to deviate from the law in cases in which the application of other provisions of the law do not meet the requirements of this generalclause. Such a deviation demands an explanation and information about its consequences for assets, liabilities, financial position, and profit. In practice, such deviations from statutory provisions, in order to give a true and fair view, seldom occur.

The true and fair view concept was somewhat different from the previous "good accounting practice," although both the Company Law Panel (*Det Selskabsretlige Panel*), which participated in the preparation for the Financial Statements Bill, and the auditing profession considered the two general clauses as practically identical. "Good accounting practice" was more an operational term than "a true and fair view." It was a process-oriented concept relating to the working methods normally used in the preparation of individual accounts. A true and fair view is a holistic concept relating to the desired attributes of the end-product as a whole, seen from the users' point of view.

3.3 The Prudence Principle

Generally, the prudence principle is deeply rooted in Danish accounting regulation and practice. In spite of its inherent conflict in relation to the true and fair view, and the general prohibition of the creation of hidden reserves, the prudence principle is heavily supported in law, which stresses "the lower of cost and market value" as a basic principle, based on the historical cost principle. Here the financial analyst should remember that both the typical financial structure of most Danish companies, which tends to stress the need for creditor protection, and the importance of the former

connection between accounting and taxation income have inevitably supported prudent accounting practice. At the same time, the financial analyst
should be aware that it is possible to revalue assets, as described in more
depth in subsequent sections.

The liberal accounting regulation therefore opens up a broad variety of
"true and fair views," from quite prudent ones to rather optimistic ones.
This sometimes makes time-series analysis and cross-sectional analysis
rather complicated to carry out.

3.4 The Principle of Consistency

According to the Financial Statements Act, consistency is one of the basic
accounting principles. In case of a breach of consistency, the annual
accounts for the year in which the change takes place must be prepared by
applying the new method. The total effect on the company's assets and
liabilities, its financial position, and profit or loss must be disclosed in the
notes. This also includes the effect on the tax on the profit or loss for the
year and deferred taxation. The opening balance sheet for the year in
which the change takes place must be adjusted accordingly.

Danish Accounting Standard No. 3 distinguishes between changes in
accounting method (break in consistency) and changes in accounting
estimates. According to the standard, a change in accounting method must
take place only:

1. If the change is a consequence of a law
2. If the change is a consequence of a Danish National Standard
3. If the change serves the general true and fair view clause in a better
   way than the old principle

Both concrete circumstances and international development may lead
to changes in accounting methods. In the event of changes of accounting
method, the following information must be given:

1. Confirmation that such a change has taken place
2. A description of the change
3. The reasoning behind the change
4. A description of the consequences of the change on assets, liabilities, financial position, and profit or loss

5. Confirmation that a corresponding change in the comparative figures of the last year or years has been made

The change must also be mentioned in the directors' report. Changes to accounting estimates normally affect the ordinary profit and loss figure. Significant changes must be described in the notes.

Many publicly listed companies (trade, service, and industrial) have adopted one or more changes in their accounting method in recent years, the main reason being the publication of new Danish accounting standards and growing internationalization. The vast majority of breaches of continuity are explained, and comprehensive descriptions are given of the impact on the result of the year, net capital and assets. Financial analysts must of course take such breaches of continuity into account.

3.5 Consolidated Financial Statements

In Denmark the most common method of business combination is for one company to become a subsidiary of another. In this situation the consolidation is based on the acquisition (purchase) method, and the subsidiary is consolidated at the time of acquisition (the past equity method). Before implementation of the Seventh Directive, most groups considered goodwill as merely a technical elimination difference between the cost of acquisition and the total capital employed in the subsidiary at the time of acquisition. Usually no revaluations of assets were considered, and the total difference was computed as goodwill. Implementation of the Seventh Directive requires revaluation of net assets at their fair value to the purchaser.

The elimination difference can be treated in different ways. It can be capitalized and depreciated as intangible assets, or eliminated directly against reserves. Even after the implementation of the Seventh Directive, only about 20% of the groups in question revalued net assets in 1996, the most commonly used method of elimination being elimination against reserves. Lundbeck A/S revalues its net assets.

Negative goodwill must appear separately as part of the total capital employed, offset against goodwill, or as a provision if it corresponds to a foreseeable loss or expense incurred in connection with the acquired subsidiary.

The pooling of interests method is not mentioned in the Financial Statements Act, but the Public Limited Companies Act presumes adoption of this method when a so-called legal merger takes place. A legal merger is a merger in which one of the companies continues the combined activities of all the merged undertakings by exchange of shares, and the other undertakings are legally dissolved.

One-line consolidation (the equity method, see Section 3.14 below) is used for nonconsolidated subsidiaries and associated undertakings. Joint ventures may be proportionally consolidated, but other methods may be used as well.

3.6 Foreign Currency Translation

The EU Directives do not deal with accounting problems related to foreign currency translation, and Denmark has no legal rules related to this.

Danish Accounting Standard No. 9 on foreign currency translation, which is by and large identical to IAS 21, is effective for annual accounts covering financial years beginning on July 1, 1995 or later, recommends that transactions in foreign currency be translated to Danish kroner by using the exchange rate at the date of the transaction and that the exchange rate at the end of the financial year is used for translation of transactions that are not yet completed. All translation differences must be disclosed in the profit and loss account.

Both realized and unrealized gains and losses are therefore reported in the profit and loss account. It should be noted, however, that a few listed companies do not disclose full information about their practice in this area, especially about where the differences are placed in the profit and loss account. The lack of such information makes it difficult for the financial analyst to evaluate the quality of earnings. In this area the financial analyst should carefully study the distinction between ordinary and extraordinary items, and movements on the equity account.

The standard also deals with hedged transactions including hedging of future transactions. Supplementary information about hedging or speculating policies and activities may be inadequate in some cases.

For subsidiaries that qualify as foreign entities, the net investment method is used. For subsidiaries that do not qualify as foreign entities the temporal method is used.

3.7 Capital and Reserves

The equity account consists of the following categories:

1. Subscribed capital: The nominal value of the share capital. The directors' report must include a list of all equity investors in possession of more than 5% of the share capital or of voting rights. The parent company and its subsidiaries may hold the parent company's own shares, up to a total maximum limit of 10% of the share capital or of voting rights.

2. Share premium account

3. Revaluation reserve

4. Reserves

    a. Net revaluation reserve arising through use of the equity method: Net revaluations concerning both unconsolidated subsidiaries and associated undertakings are placed here—their accumulated net results, eventual revaluations, exchange rate differences, etc.

    b. Reserve for own shares: Danish law allows own shares to be valued either at zero or at another unspecified value. Valuation at a value other than zero requires the creation of a parallel reserve of the same value. However, the most common practice is to value own shares at zero.

    c. Legal reserves: The Companies Law requires companies to keep sufficient reserves according to their financial position. The exact requirements are no longer prescribed.

    d. Reserves provided by the articles of association.

    e. Other reserve funds: Different types of reserve fund can be observed in practice, their titles dating mainly from the time before implementation of the Fourth Directive:

    —Disposition reserve fund

    —Common reserve fund

    —Exchange and security reserve fund

    —Extra reserve fund

    —Special reserve fund

    —Investment reserve fund

    f. Profit or loss brought forward

    g. Profit or loss for the financial year: Profit or loss for the financial year less dividend.

The financial analyst must carefully examine movements of the total capital employed. Items related to foreign currency translation can be shown either in the profit and loss account or directly as total capital employed. Revaluations or write-offs of revalued assets may be found as movements in the total capital employed, and goodwill may be offset directly against reserves. Since 1996 Danish law has required a note showing movements of the total capital employed concerning groups. This was in fact standard practice before the requirement was formalized.

Minority interests can be shown as part of the total capital employed, or as a separate item between the total capital employed and provisions for liabilities and charges. Most groups show minority interests as a separate item.

3.8 Provisions for Liabilities and Charges

Provisions for liabilities and charges are intended to cover losses, debts, or charges, the nature of which is clearly defined and which at the date of the end of the financial year are either likely to be incurred or are certain to be incurred but uncertain as to amount or date on which they will arise. Provisions for liabilities and charges must not be used to regulate the value of assets. Consequently, reserves for bad debts or write-offs on fixed assets do not qualify as provisions for liabilities and charges. Furthermore, provisions for liabilities and charges must not be used to create "hidden reserves." Important provisions for liabilities and charges must be explained in the notes. In recent years there has been much debate about provisions for restructuring and discontinued activities, since there is a certain confusion and lack of clarity regarding accounting practice in this respect. Many critics argue that the mention of provisions in annual accounts is not sufficiently precise, in that it is up to the user of the accounts to decide whether the figure concerned related to a provision, to a contingent liability, or perhaps to something else. It is also noteworthy that there is no specific Danish accounting standard concerning provisions in general, though there seems to be a need for such a standard. An exposure draft concerning income tax in annual accounts has been prepared but has not been adopted. The draft reflects to a great extent the content of IAS 12 (revised) and FAS 12.

In accounting practice, provision for deferred tax is the most common liability for provisions and charges. In the construction industry, guarantees, for example, are treated as provisions for liabilities and charges.

Negative goodwill, gains on sale and leaseback arrangements, and negative equity of subsidiaries may, in practice, also be treated as provisions for liabilities and charges. Sometimes the titles suggest a use in contravention of the legal requirements, and the financial analyst should carefully examine such provisions for liabilities and charges.

3.9 Property, Plant, and Equipment

By law, tangible fixed assets are valued at acquisition cost or production cost and amortized during their useful life. Production costs may include overheads and financial costs related to the production period, but few firms mention the inclusion of overheads and financial costs. Neither legislation nor the Danish Accounting Standard No. 10 does in fact regulate the choice of depreciation method or the useful life of different categories of assets. Accounting Standard No. 10 only establishes that the depreciation method must be such that it reflects the company's consumption of a tangible fixed asset as accurately as possible. Regarding estimation of useful life, considerable variation can be observed in practice.

Tangible assets may be revalued if the utility value of an asset has increased as a result of factors that do not seem to be temporary. Neither the Financial Statements Act nor Danish Accounting Standard No. 10 defines the concept of utility value. However, if revaluation is made, the accounting standard requires that both the evaluation and the revaluation are performed systematically on an asset-by-asset basis and for all assets that belong to the same category of fixed assets. If a depreciable asset is revalued, the depreciation must be based on the revaluation. Revaluations must not be shown in the profit and loss account before realization (sale). A special revaluation reserve exists as part of the equity account. If the value of a revalued asset drops, the revaluation reserve must be adjusted accordingly. When a revalued asset is sold, the revaluation reserve must be dissolved. According to Danish Accounting Standard No. 10, gains or losses arising from the disposal of a tangible fixed asset should generally be determined as the difference between the sales proceeds with the deduction of costs of dismantling, sale, and possible restoration and the book value at the time of disposal. This means that the revaluation (the part that has not been written off) is not shown as realized gain in the profit and loss account. In such a situation the company must transfer the revaluation directly from the revaluation reserve in the balance sheet to the so-called free reserves. As an exception to this, the gain or loss may be determined as the difference between the purchase price or production costs with the deduction of accumulated depreciation and the sales price. Danish Accounting Standard No. 10 specifies that gain or loss from the disposal of a tangible fixed asset must be included in the profit and loss account as part of the undertaking's ordinary operations unless the criteria for presentation as an extraordinary item are met (see Section 2.5).

In practice, revaluation is often seen in relation to land and buildings. Approximately 20% of Danish listed groups make such revaluations in any one year, and more than 40% had revaluation reserves in their balance sheets in 1996. Both the absolute and relateve numbers of groups with yearly revaluations seem to be almost constant. The reason for the revaluation of land and buildings probably lies in the existence of a public valuation system for tax purposes affecting land and buildings. Revaluations are carried out on all land and buildings each year for tax purposes on either a statistical basis or by official surveyors. The results of those revaluations are not automatically suitable for accounting purposes, but before implementation of the Fourth Directive, land and buildings were normally valued at those amounts, and they may also be used today as guidance in the valuation process.

Write-downs must be made if the useful value of an asset has declined as a result of factors that do not seem to be temporary. The company decides whether such write-downs shall be shown as part of "depreciation and write-offs" or as extraordinary charges. In Denmark no provision exists for uncertain declining values or for tax purposes.

Profit, assets, and equity all change when companies carry out revaluation. Most significant of these is the change in equity. The financial analyst must be aware of such revaluations, because they may distort both time-series analysis of the single group and cross-sectional analyses between different groups.

3.10 Financial Assets

In most respects the measurement rules relating to financial fixed assets other than investments in subsidiaries and associated undertakings follow the measurement rules for tangible fixed assets, but write-offs can be made even if a drop in value is only temporary.

Financial current assets are measured at the lower of cost or market value. Financial current assets that are publicly traded may be valued at their official price. The Financial Statements Act provides that unrealized gains must be placed in a revaluation reserve. In practice, however, a growing number of companies redefine the realization principle in accordance with IAS No. 25, and unrealized gains are shown in the profit and loss account. Hereby a symmetric treatment of gains and losses is established, in accordance with the matching principle and at the expense of the prudence principle.

In practice, some companies stick strictly to the historical cost principle, while others use the possibility of revaluation. The financial analyst should be aware of those differences.

3.11 Leasing

The only legal requirement concerning leasing is an obligation to show leasing liabilities in the notes. In practice, few groups show leasing assets and leasing liabilities in the balance sheet. It is impossible to know whether this indicates that the distinction between operational leases and financial leases in IAS No. 17 is not followed or that financial leasing is not very common. When IAS No. 17 was introduced in Denmark it was followed by some debate concerning the treatment of financial leasing. The FSR recommends both the legal requirements and the treatment according to IAS No. 17 and anticipates a gradual movement toward the approach of IAS No. 17.

3.12 Oil, Gas, and Other Mineral Resources

In Denmark no special accounting regulation exists in the area of oil, gas, and other mineral resources. DONG (Danish Oil and Natural Gas Company), one of the few Danish firms involved in oil and gas activities, uses the full cost principle.

3.13 Intangible Assets

As mentioned earlier, the prudence principle is an important one in both Danish accounting regulation and Danish accounting practice. The Danish Financial Statements Act and Danish Accounting Standard No. 7: Research and Development allow intangible assets bought from a third party to be capitalized. Development costs may also be capitalized. In practice, however, such a capitalization seldom occurs. Most companies expense intangible assets immediately. Capitalized intangible assets must be depreciated over a maximum of 5 years. A longer period of depreciation is permissible, but special arguments must be presented by the company. Intangible assets may not be revalued.

Write-downs must be made if the useful value of an asset has declined owing to factors that do not seem to be temporary. The company decides whether the write-offs shall be shown as part of "depreciation and write-offs" or as extraordinary charges. No provisions exist for uncertain declining values. Formation costs may not be capitalized. The financial analyst should be aware of companies changing policy from immediate expensing to capitalization and depreciation. In spite of relevant considerations related to the matching principle, it may be a sign of "creative accounting" aimed at restoration of equity.

The Danish Accounting Standard No. 7 concerning research and development is quite similar to IAS No. 9, but the Danish Standard does not recommend disclosure of total research and development costs.

3.14 Participating Interests

In the single company's financial statement, investments in subsidiaries and in associated undertakings may be treated in different ways, in accordance with the Financial Statements Act:

1. Historical cost
2. Intrinsic value in accordance with the general rules of valuation
3. The equity method

Before the implementation of the Seventh Directive, the equity method was allowed only for the treatment of investments in subsidiaries, and in practice both historical cost and intrinsic value were used also.

The equity method used in relation to associated undertakings is a new rule, resulting from the implementation of the Seventh Directive. Before harmonization, accounting practice was divided equally among three methods: historical cost, intrinsic value, and the equity method. At present the practice is changing dramatically toward the equity method, to avoid different treatment in the single company's financial statement and the consolidated financial statements.

Denmark permits combined taxation of the parent company and some or all of its wholly owned subsidiaries (joint taxation schemes). In the annual accounts the total tax amount may be divided among the different companies according to their pretax profit, or it may be charged to the parent company alone. When examining the financial statements of a parent company, the financial analyst should be aware of the treatment of profit from its subsidiaries.

Goodwill and negative goodwill are generally treated parallel to their treatment in the consolidated financial statements, so that profit or loss and the total capital employed will be similar in both the financial statements of the parent company and the consolidated financial statements.

No legal requirements are formulated in the case of a subsidiary that has negative equity. The negative equity may be offset against loans to the subsidiary. Eventually the negative equity is shown as a provision for liabilities and charges.

In the consolidated financial statements, investments in both unconsolidated subsidiaries and associated undertakings must be treated according to the equity method.

Before implementation of the Seventh Directive, no rules existed concerning joint ventures, and in accounting practice historical cost, one-line consolidation, and proportional consolidation could be observed. After EU harmonization, joint ventures may be proportionally consolidated, so companies may still choose freely among the different methods.

The financial analyst must be aware of the lack of regulation in this area and should also remember that Danish companies are often small companies with a relatively low capital strength in comparison with undertakings in other countries.

3.15 Inventories

As mentioned earlier, both marginal and absorption costing are allowed in Denmark according to the Financial Statements Act, and marginal costing is still the most widely used principle. Lundbeck A/S uses marginal costing (see page 225 under Stocks and Table 1). However, the Danish Accounting Standard No. 8 recommends absorption costing and that standard is effective for annual accounts covering financial years beginning on July 1, 1993 or later.

The financial analyst should be aware of the definition used. If turnover and production differ, the method used will influence profit, balance sheet, and total capital employed. Danish accounting regulations do not specify the criteria by which costs are judged to be variable or fixed. Neither do the regulations define the content of absorption cost. The Financial Statements Law allows weighted average, FIFO, and other similar methods to be used. No common practice in this area can be identified, because many companies omit detailed descriptions of the calculation principle. The Financial Statements Act requires the use of the lower of cost or market principle, where the net realizable value constitutes the upper limit. Inventories may be revalued to a limit of their replacement cost, but such a revaluation is seldom seen in practice. Nothing is said about interest during the production process. It is concluded that interest could be included in the valuation of inventory, though this is very rare in practice.

3.16 Profit on Construction Contracts

Income from sales of goods and services is realized when the goods or services are delivered and the risk is transferred to the customer. According to the Financial Statements Act, production bases can be used only through reference to the true and fair view. Danish Accounting Standard No. 6 concerning long-term contracts recommends that the percentage of completion method be used for long-term contracts. On account billings on the individual long-term contract should be deducted from the asset "Work in progress on behalf of third parties" if the on account billings relate to work already performed on the contract. On account billings exceeding work performed on the contract are recorded as advances from customers under current liabilities.

Today, most publicly listed firms that are involved in long-term contracts use the percentage of completion method, often with reference to the true and fair view.

3.17 Taxation

In Denmark the Fourth Directive established a separation between taxation and accounting, which was almost fully implemented by the end of 1985. Provision for deferred taxation is therefore necessary in Danish financial statements (Table 4). Accounting rules relating to taxation are summarized in Table 3.

Accounting practice is divided on the question whether deferred taxation due to timing differences should be shown fully or partly in the profit and loss account. The Financial Statements Act does not include rules on how to compute deferred taxation. The liability method is the method most commonly used.

TABLE 3 *Accounting Rules Relating to Taxation*

	Tax Payable	Deferred Taxation	Taxation Contingency[a]
Description	Tax to be paid	Owing to timing differences	Owing to possible realization at revalued book value
Information	In the accounts	In the accounts or in the notes	In the accounts or in the notes

[a] In a few areas Denmark taxes capital gains. If a taxable gain is made by selling an asset at its book value, a tax liability arises. A potential tax liability (a tax contingency) occurs when assets are revalued.

TABLE 4 *Treatment of Deferred Taxation by Publicly Listed Trade, Service, and Industrial Groups*

	1992 No. (%)	1993 No. (%)	1994 No. (%)	1995 No. (%)	1996 No. (%)
Tax payable	4 (4)	4 (4)	5 (4)	4 (3)	3 (3)
Tax payable and partial deferred taxation	35(31)	36 (33)	48 (43)	48 (42)	41 (34)
Tax payable and fully deferred taxation	62 (56)	59 (54)	47 (42)	52 (45)	64 (53)
Tax payable, fully deferred taxation, and contingent taxation	2 (1)	2 (1)	3 (2)	4 (3)	5 (4)
Taxation not specified	4 (4)	4 (4)	5 (5)	4 (4)	4 (3)
No information/ not relevant	4 (4)	4 (4)	4 (4)	3 (3)	4 (3)
Total	111 (100)	109 (100)	112 (100)	115 (100)	121 (100)

Source: *ACCOUNT DATA - DK*, Copenhagen Business School.

As mentioned earlier, taxation and accounting income differ considerably. Deferred taxation therefore often has a significant influence on the bottom line result in the profit and loss account, as well as on the division between equity and provisions. The financial analyst should pay attention to the principle used when time-series analysis and cross-sectional analysis are carried out.

Fully deferred taxation often includes the following timing differences between accounting and taxation:

1. Timing differences between accounting depreciation and tax-based depreciation. The tax rules are based on the declining balance sheet method.
2. Tax-based write-offs on inventories
3. Timing differences between accounting write-offs on bad debts and the tax-based write-offs.

Information concerning tax relating to extraordinary items is of special interest when the financial analyst is analyzing the sources of income. According to the Financial Statements Act, tax relating to extraordinary items must be indicated separately in the profit and loss account from 1996.

3.18 Pensions

Pension obligations are rarely seen in Danish Financial Statements. The Pension Act requires that pension obligations to be transferred to insurance companies, and most pension arrangements therefore are classified as "defined contribution" plans. Only directors may have pension agreements directly with their company. Pension obligations may exist owing to pension obligations in foreign subsidiaries. A few companies have set up pension funds. These pension obligations are either capitalized in the balance sheet or mentioned in the notes. The method of capitalization is seldom explained.

3.19 Government Grants

Government grants are an unregulated area. Neither the Financial Statements Act nor any Danish Accounting Standard deals with the treatment of government grants, and few companies disclose any information about the methods used.

4. Expected Future Developments

Even after the implementation of the Fourth and Seventh Directives, Danish accounting rules and regulations have remained fairly flexible. In light of this, it is not surprising that the auditing profession has been subject to criticism on some occasions. The criticism has focused mainly on self-regulation in the private sector in connection with the publication of accounting standards as a supplement to accounting legislation not being sufficiently effective and extensive.

However, it is beyond dispute that the publication of Danish accounting standards has increased the information value of the annual accounts published by companies listed on the Copenhagen Stock Exchange, not least in recent years. As mentioned above, the Stock Exchange demands that the standards be observed by listed companies. To this should be added the spin-off effect on nonlisted companies. It is difficult to assess the extent of this effect, which was foreseen in accounting circles. The number of Danish accounting standards is expected to increase in coming years. At present, four exposure drafts have been submitted for hearing: standards concerning directors' reports, investment properties, related party disclosures, and income taxes.

It is characteristic that almost all Danish standards are very close in content to comparable standards issued by IASC. Some analysts therefore think that a more radical approach should be adopted by toning down the importance of Danish accounting standards and attaching greater priority to the standards issued by IASC, which could perhaps even replace the Danish standards in the long term and become mandatory for listed companies. The Copenhagen Stock Exchange is not expected to show any interest in becoming involved in the formulation of Danish accounting standards in the future.

Though some uncertainty is sometimes seen regarding the future destiny and role of Danish accounting standards, it is a fact that the majority of annual accounts published by listed companies have become significantly more international in terms of both accounting principles and the extent of information published.

Within the next few years the Danish Financial Statements Act will be thoroughly revised and modernized. The act has been criticized for lacking overall objectives and definitions of basic concepts. Many accounting and auditing circles strongly advocate modernization of the Financial Statements Act to take place on the basis of a conceptual framework inspired by the conceptual framework applied by IASC and/or FASB. A new and more up-to-date act on financial statements is therefore anticipated, with broader social orientation than the present act, the cornerstones of which date back to 1981.

Notes

1. Companies must prepare financial statements in accordance with the law in respect of any financial year beginning on or after February 1, 1982.
2. Companies must prepare financial statements in accordance with the amended law and the order in respect of any financial year beginning on or after April 1, 1991.

Useful Addresses

Copenhagen Stock Exchange
Københavns Fondsbørs
Nikolaj Plads 6
DK-1007 Copenhagen K.
Denmark
Tel: +45 3393 3366
Fax: +45 3312 8613

The Danish Commerce and Companies Agency
Erhvervs- og Selskabsstyrelsen
Kampmannsgade 1
DK-1780 Copenhagen V.
Denmark
Tel: +45 3330 7700
Fax: +45 3330 7400

The Institute of Registered Public Accountants
Foreningen af Registrerede Revisorer (FRR)
Åmarksvej 1
DK-2650 Hvidovre
Denmark
Tel: +45 3634 4422
Fax: +45 3634 4444

The Institute of State-authorised Public Accountants
Foreningen af Statsautoriserede Revisorer (FSR)
Kronprinsessegade 8
DK-1306 Copenhagen K.
Denmark
Tel: +45 3393 9191
Fax: +45 3311 0913

Financial Statements

ACCOUNTING POLICIES

GENERAL

The annual accounts and the consolidated accounts have been prepared in accordance with the Danish Company Accounts Act and good accounting practice as well as generally accepted Danish accounting standards. The profit and loss account items for foreign subsidiaries are translated at the exchange rates ruling at the balance sheet date in accordance with the policy of previous years; translation at the exchange rates ruling at the transaction date appears from note 6.

The accounting policies for 1996 have been changed in the following areas:

- Securities are stated at the price ruling at the balance sheet date.
- Outstanding forward exchange contracts are stated at the price ruling at the balance sheet date.
- Mortgage debt and other interest-bearing debt are stated at the price ruling at the balance sheet date; thus capital losses arising from the raising of mortgage loans are no longer capitalised.

All value adjustments are, therefore, included in the profit and loss account under financial items.

The accumulated effect of the changes is taken to capital and reserves and the comparative figures have been restated in accordance with this new policy. The significance of the changes to the accounting figures is described in further detail in the comments on the accounts.

Otherwise, the accounting policies applied are consistent with those of the previous year.

CONSOLIDATION PRINCIPLES

The consolidated accounts comprise H. Lundbeck A/S (the parent company) and companies in which the parent company holds more than 50% of the voting rights or otherwise exercises a controlling influence. A Group overview is given in note 8.

Intercompany income and expenses, shareholdings, balances and dividends as well as unrealised intercompany profits on stocks are eliminated.

In the consolidated accounts, the book value of the parent company's shareholdings in the subsidiaries has been set off against the parent company's share of the subsidiaries' capital and reserves as calculated at the time when the Group relationship was established (past-equity method). In the consolidated accounts the difference arising from the set-off has been allocated to the assets and liabilities whose value, at the establishment of the Group relationship and in accordance with the Group's accounting policies, was higher or lower than the one at which they were recorded in the accounts of the subsidiaries. So far no other differences (goodwill) have been ascertained.

Newly acquired subsidiaries are included in the profit and loss account from the date of acquisition. Subsidiaries sold or wound up are included up to the time of sale or winding up.

TRANSLATION OF FOREIGN CURRENCIES

Receivables and debt denominated in foreign currencies are translated into Danish kroner at the rates of exchange ruling at the balance sheet date. Both realised and unrealised exchange adjustments are included in the profit and loss account.

Forward contracts outstanding at the balance sheet date are stated at the forward rate ruling at the balance sheet date, and exchange adjustments in relation to the contracted forward rates are included in the profit and loss account.

The profit and loss accounts and balance sheets of foreign subsidiaries are translated into Danish kroner at the rates of exchange ruling at the balance sheet date. A translation of the main items of the profit and loss account to the rates of the transaction date is given in note 6. The exchange-rate difference relating to the net assets of these subsidiaries at the beginning of the financial year is taken directly to capital and reserves.

STATEMENT OF SOURCES AND APPLICATION OF FUNDS

The statement of sources and application of funds is prepared according to the indirect method based on the profit for the year before tax. The statement of sources and application of funds shows the Group's cash flow with spe-

cial focus on the cash flow from operations and investments. Furthermore, the statement of sources and application of funds shows the year's change in interest-bearing net cash as well as the Group's liquidity position at year-end.

PROFIT AND LOSS ACCOUNT

NET TURNOVER

Net turnover comprises invoiced sales for the year less VAT, return goods and price reductions directly connected with sales.

Moreover, net turnover includes fees and licence income as well as non-refundable down payments received during the year. Large down payments received which represent an obligation to pay future costs are recorded on an accruals basis.

RESEARCH AND DEVELOPMENT COSTS

Research and development costs comprise costs attributable to the Group's research and development activities. As a principal rule, the Group charges research and development costs to the profit and loss account as they are incurred.

Research and development costs linked to product-related development loans are capitalised.

INCOME FROM SHAREHOLDINGS

The parent company's profit and loss account includes the parent company's proportional share of the subsidiaries' results after deduction of the year's change in unrealised intercompany profits. Shares of the net result recognised as income are transferred to the reserve for net revaluation according to the equity method to the extent that they exceed dividend received from the subsidiaries.

TAX

Tax on the profit or loss for the year comprises current tax, the year's adjustment of deferred tax and tax relating to income from shareholdings in subsidiaries.

The provision for deferred tax is the computed tax effect of the accumulated timing differences between amounts as stated in the accounts and as computed for taxation purposes.

THE BALANCE SHEET

INTANGIBLE FIXED ASSETS
Intangible fixed assets are stated at cost less accumulated amortisation and writedowns.

Capitalised research and development costs are written off on a straight-line basis in line with earnings over a period corresponding to the unexpired period of the lives of the relevant patents with a maximum of 20 years.

Leasehold improvements are written off over the term of the lease, with a maximum of 10 years.

TANGIBLE FIXED ASSETS
Tangible fixed assets are stated at cost plus any revaluations and less accumulated depreciation and writedowns.

Tangible fixed assets are depreciated on a straight-line basis over the expected lives of the assets as follows:

Buildings	30 years
Installations	10 years
Technical installations and machinery	3-10 years
Other fixtures and equipment	3-10 years

Improvements and acquisitions at a cost not exceeding DKK 50,000 are charged to the profit and loss account in the year of acquisition (DKK 30,000 in 1995).

FINANCIAL FIXED ASSETS
Shares in subsidiaries are stated in the parent company's accounts according to the equity method, ie at the equity value according to the accounts less unrealised intercompany profits.

Other capital holdings are valued at cost.

STOCKS
Raw materials, packaging and goods for resale are valued at the latest known cost at the balance sheet date, which corresponds essentially to cost computed according to the FIFO principle.

Work in progress and finished goods produced by the company are valued at cost, ie the cost of materials and direct production wages. Stocks do not include indirect production costs.

Writedown to net realisable value is made if it is lower than the acquisition or cost price, respectively.

SECURITIES
Securities are stated at the price ruling at the balance sheet date.

PROVISIONS
Provision for pension liabilities not covered by insurance is made as a liability under provisions. The statement of this liability is based on actuary calculations.

INTEREST-BEARING DEBT
Mortgage debt and other debt are listed at the price ruling at the balance sheet date. Other debt includes, among other things, loans from the Development Fund for the financing of research and development projects. For research projects in progress the loan will be written down if the company discontinues the development or fails to market the products concerned. Development loans relate to capitalised research and development costs.

RESULTATOPGØRELSE

	MODERSELSKAB				**KONCERNEN**	
1995 DKK mio.	1996 DKK mio.		Noter	1996 DKK mio.	1995 DKK mio.	
1.042,8	1.413,7	Nettoomsætning	1,6	2.326,4	1.852,6
469,1	534,2	Produktionsomkostninger	2	636,2	612,9
157,3	269,6	Distributionsomkostninger	2	608,7	426,5
160,8	202,5	Administrationsomkostninger	2,3	440,1	364,0
255,6	407,4	**Resultat før forskningsomkostninger**		641,4	449,2
221,2	331,0	Forskningsomkostninger	2	332,1	253,2
12,7	3,1	Andre driftsindtægter		6,7	16,6
5,9	2,1	Andre driftsudgifter		5,6	8,0
41,2	77,4	**RESULTAT AF PRIMÆR DRIFT**	6	310,4	204,6
		Indtægter af kapitalandele i			
155,3	234,8	dattervirksomheder før skat	5,8		
21,3	-2,6	Finansielle poster, netto	4	0,4	23,6
217,8	309,6	**RESULTAT FØR SKAT**		310,8	228,2
75,2	92,0	Skat af årets resultat	5	92,0	75,2
142,6	217,6	**ÅRETS RESULTAT**	6	218,8	153,0
		ÅRETS KONCERNRESULTAT FORDELES SÅLEDES:			
		Minoritetsinteressernes resultatandele		1,2	10,4
		H. Lundbeck A/S andel af årets koncernresultat		217,6	142,6
		ÅRETS KONCERNRESULTAT I ALT		218,8	153,0
		ÅRETS RESULTAT FOR H. LUNDBECK A/S **FORESLÅS FORDELT SÅLEDES:**			
22,0	0,0	Udlodning af udbytte			
9,6	5,7	Overskudsandel til medarbejdere for regnskabsåret			
		Overførsel til reserve for nettoopskrivning efter den			
11,4	30,4	indre værdis metode			
99,6	181,5	Overførsel til overført overskud			
142,6	217,6				

PROFIT AND LOSS ACCOUNT

PARENT COMPANY					GROUP	
1995 DKKm	1996 DKKm		Notes		1996 DKKm	1995 DKKm
1,042.8	1,413.7	Net turnover	1.6		2,326.4	1,852.6
469.1	534.2	Production costs	2		636.2	612.9
157.3	269.6	Distribution costs	2		608.7	426.5
160.8	202.5	Administration costs	2.3		440.1	364.0
255.6	407.4	**Profit before research and development costs**			641.4	449.2
221.2	331.0	Research and development costs	2		332.1	253.2
12.7	3.1	Other operating income			6.7	16.6
5.9	2.1	Other operating expenses			5.6	8.0
41.2	77.4	**OPERATING PROFIT**	6		310.4	204.6
155.3	234.8	Income from interests in subsidiaries, before tax	5.8			
21.3	-2.6	Financial items, net	4		0.4	23.6
217.8	309.6	**PROFIT BEFORE TAXES**			310.8	228.2
75.2	92.0	Tax on the profit for the year	5		92.0	75.2
142.6	217.6	**PROFIT FOR THE YEAR**	6		218.8	153.0
		THE GROUP PROFIT FOR THE YEAR IS DISTRIBUTED AS FOLLOWS:				
		Minority interests' share of the profit			1.2	10.4
		H. Lundbeck A/S' share of the Group profit for the year			217.6	142.6
		TOTAL GROUP PROFIT FOR THE YEAR			218.8	153.0
		THE PROFIT FOR THE YEAR OF H. LUNDBECK A/S IS PROPOSED TO BE DISTRIBUTED AS FOLLOWS:				
22.0	0.0	Distribution of dividend				
9.6	5.7	Employees' share of the profit for the financial year				
11.4	30.4	Transfer to reserve for net revaluation according to the equity method				
99.6	181.5	Transfer to profits carried forward				
142.6	217.6					

BALANCE PR. 31 DECEMBER

AKTIVER

MODERSELSKAB				KONCERNEN	
1995 DKK mio.	1996 DKK mio.		Noter	1996 DKK mio.	1995 DKK mio.
21,0	37,9	Forsknings- og udviklingsomkostninger		37,9	21,0
11,0	9,6	Indretning af lejede lokaler		15,2	15,8
32,0	47,5	IMMATERIELLE ANLÆGSAKTIVER	7	53,1	36,8
312,3	373,0	Grunde og bygninger		385,1	323,1
97,2	140,4	Tekniske anlæg og maskiner		186,3	137,0
112,2	101,5	Andre anlæg, driftsmateriel og inventar		139,8	153,5
114,0	146,6	Igangværende investeringer		148,3	115,5
635,7	761,5	MATERIELLE ANLÆGSAKTIVER	7	859,5	729,1
49,0	92,9	Kapitalandele i dattervirksomheder	8		
4,5	5,4	Andre kapitalandele	9	5,5	4,5
4,1	4,6	Andre tilgodehavender	9	7,7	6,8
31,6	14,6	Tilgodehavender hos dattervirksomheder	9		
89,2	117,5	FINANSIELLE ANLÆGSAKTIVER		13,2	11,3
756,9	926,5	ANLÆGSAKTIVER I ALT		925,8	777,2
54,2	73,1	Råvarer og hjælpematerialer		75,2	56,8
68,0	91,0	Varer under fremstilling		102,2	69,4
28,0	38,8	Fremstillede færdigvarer og handelsvarer		73,8	48,9
150,2	202,9	VAREBEHOLDNINGER		251,2	175,1
31,2	26,9	Tilgodehavender fra salg		426,8	346,8
235,6	336,6	Tilgodehavender hos dattervirksomheder			
104,4	118,6	Tilgodehavende udbytte			
2,3	4,4	Tilgodehavende selskabsskat		12,3	0,0
45,8	17,2	Andre tilgodehavender		43,4	70,9
3,5	2,2	Periodeafgrænsningsposter		12,9	11,7
422,8	505,9	TILGODEHAVENDER		495,4	429,4
431,9	417,6	VÆRDIPAPIRER		417,6	432,0
29,6	120,6	LIKVIDE BEHOLDNINGER		237,7	121,7
1.034,5	1.247,0	OMSÆTNINGSAKTIVER I ALT		1.401,9	1.158,2
1.791,4	2.173,5	AKTIVER I ALT		2.327,7	1.935,4

BALANCE SHEET AT 31 DECEMBER
ASSETS

PARENT COMPANY				GROUP	
1995 DKKm	1996 DKKm		Notes	1996 DKKm	1995 DKKm
21.0	37.9	Research and development costs		37.9	21.0
11.0	9.6	Leasehold improvements		15.2	15.8
32.0	47.5	**INTANGIBLE FIXED ASSETS**	7	53.1	36.8
312.3	373.0	Land and buildings		385.1	323.1
97.2	140.4	Technical installations and machinery		186.3	137.0
112.2	101.5	Other installations, operating equipment and fixtures		139.8	153.5
114.0	146.6	Assets in course of construction		148.3	115.5
635.7	761.5	**TANGIBLE FIXED ASSETS**	7	859.5	729.1
49.0	92.9	Shares in subsidiaries	8		
4.5	5.4	Other shareholdings	9	5.5	4.5
4.1	4.6	Other receivables	9	7.7	6.8
31.6	14.6	Accounts receivable from subsidiaries	9		
89.2	117.5	**FINANCIAL FIXED ASSETS**		13.2	11.3
756.9	926.5	**TOTAL FIXED ASSETS**		925.8	777.2
54.2	73.1	Raw materials and consumables		75.2	56.8
68.0	91.0	Work in progress		102.2	69.4
28.0	38.8	Finished goods and commercial goods		73.8	48.9
150.2	202.9	**STOCKS**		251.2	175.1
31.2	26.9	Trade debtors		426.8	346.8
235.6	336.6	Accounts receivable from subsidiaries			
104.4	118.6	Dividend receivable			
2.3	4.4	Corporation tax receivable		12.3	0.0
45.8	17.2	Other receivables		43.4	70.9
3.5	2.2	Prepayments and accrued expenses		12.9	11.7
422.8	505.9	**TOTAL RECEIVABLES**		495.4	429.4
431.9	417.6	**SECURITIES**		417.6	432.0
29.6	120.6	**CASH**		237.7	121.7
1,034.5	1,247.0	**TOTAL CURRENT ASSETS**		1,401.9	1,158.2
1,791.4	2,173.5	**TOTAL ASSETS**		2,327.7	1,935.4

BALANCE PR. 31 DECEMBER

PASSIVER

MODERSELSKAB				**KONCERNEN**	
1995 DKK mio.	1996 DKK mio.		Noter	1996 DKK mio.	1995 DKK mio.
110,0	110,0	Selskabskapital		110,0	110,0
14,7	14,7	Opskrivningshenlæggelser		14,7	14,7
		Reserve for nettoopskrivning efter			
25,5	56,2	den indre værdis metode			
785,1	966,5	Overført overskud		1.022,7	810,6
935,3	1.147,4	**H. LUNDBECK A/S ANDEL AF EGENKAPITALEN**	10	1.147,4	935,3
		Minoritetsinteressernes andel af egenkapitalen		5,2	4,0
		KONCERNENS SAMLEDE EGENKAPITAL	10	1.152,6	939,3
0,0	0,0	Hensættelse til pensioner		31,2	26,6
69,2	93,6	Hensættelse til eventualskat	11	107,5	75,7
69,2	93,6	**HENSÆTTELSER**		138,7	102,3
389,9	378,2	Prioritetsgæld		378,3	389,9
27,7	45,6	Anden gæld		53,2	40,9
10,3	94,4	Bankgæld		153,5	59,5
141,7	184,8	Gæld til dattervirksomheder			
569,6	703,0	**RENTEBÆRENDE GÆLD**	12	585,0	490,3
18,2	8,9	Gæld til dattervirksomheder			
84,5	94,6	Leverandørgæld		146,3	137,3
0,0	0,0	Selskabsskat		41,6	39,2
50,1	95,2	Merværdiafgift, skatter og feriepenge		136,6	92,7
31,6	25,1	Anden gæld		121,2	91,0
1,3	0,0	Periodeafgrænsningsposter		0,0	1,3
		Udbytte til minoritetsinteresser	10	0,0	10,4
31,6	5,7	Udbytte samt overskudsandel til medarbejdere	10	5,7	31,6
217,3	229,5	**IKKE-RENTEBÆRENDE GÆLD**		451,4	403,5
786,9	932,5	**GÆLD I ALT**	13	1.036,4	893,8
1.791,4	2.173,5	**PASSIVER I ALT**		2.327,7	1.935,4
		FORPLIGTELSER	16		

BALANCE SHEET AT 31 DECEMBER

LIABILITIES

1995 DKKm	1996 DKKm	PARENT COMPANY / GROUP	Notes	1996 DKKm	1995 DKKm
110.0	110.0	Share capital		110.0	110.0
14.7	14.7	Revaluation reserves		14.7	14.7
		Reserve for net revaluation according			
25.5	56.2	to the equity method			
785.1	966.5	Profit carried forward		1,022.7	810.6
935.3	1.147.4	**H. LUNDBECK A/S' SHARE OF**	10	1,147.4	935.3
		CAPITAL AND RESERVES			
		Minority interests' share of capital and reserves		5.2	4.0
		THE GROUP'S TOTAL CAPITAL AND RESERVES	10	1,152.6	939.3
0.0	0.0	Provisions for pensions		31.2	26.6
69.2	93.6	Provisions for deferred tax	11	107.5	75.7
69.2	93.6	**TOTAL PROVISIONS**		138.7	102.3
389.9	378.2	Mortgage debt		378.3	389.9
27.7	45.6	Other debt		53.2	40.9
10.3	94.4	Bank debt		153.5	59.5
141.7	184.8	Debt to subsidiaries			
569.6	703.0	**INTEREST-BEARING DEBT**	12	585.0	490.3
18.2	8.9	Debt to subsidiaries			
84.5	94.6	Trade creditors		146.3	137.3
0.0	0.0	Corporation tax		41.6	39.2
50.1	95.2	VAT, taxes and holiday pay commitments		136.6	92.7
31.6	25.1	Other debts		121.2	91.0
1.3	0.0	Accruals and deferred income		0.0	1.3
		Dividend to minority interests	10	0.0	10.4
31.6	5.7	Dividend and employees' share of the profit	10	5.7	31.6
217.3	229.5	**NON-INTEREST-BEARING DEBT**		451.4	403.5
786.9	932.5	**TOTAL DEBT**	13	1,036.4	893.8
1,791.4	2,173.5	**TOTAL LIABILITIES**		2,327.7	1,935.4
		CONTRACTUAL OBLIGATIONS	16		

PENGESTRØMSOPGØRELSE

	Noter	KONCERNEN 1996 DKK mio.	1995 DKK mio.
Årets resultat før skat		310,8	228,2
Hensættelser		5,0	1,2
Af- og nedskrivninger		84,3	77,7
CASH FLOW FRA DRIFT FØR ÆNDRING I DRIFTSKAPITAL		**400,1**	**307,1**
Tilgodehavender		-47,2	-143,0
Varebeholdninger		-78,4	-54,0
Ikke-rentebærende kortfristet gæld		78,0	27,0
ÆNDRING I DRIFTSKAPITAL		**-47,6**	**-170,0**
CASH FLOW FRA ORDINÆR DRIFT		**352,5**	**137,1**
Betalt selskabsskat		-71,2	-36,7
CASH FLOW FRA DRIFTSAKTIVITET		**281,3**	**100,4**
Anlægsinvesteringer		-231,4	-281,2
Salgssummer for solgte anlæg		9,6	9,3
Anden finansinvestering		-1,9	-2,2
CASH FLOW FRA INVESTERINGSAKTIVITET		**-223,7**	**-274,1**
CASH FLOW FRA DRIFTS- OG INVESTERINGSAKTIVITET		**57,6**	**-173,7**
Betalt udbytte til minoritetsinteresser		-10,3	-3,8
Betalt udbytte til aktionær		-22,0	0,0
Betalt overskudsandel til medarbejdere		-9,6	-7,4
CASH FLOW FRA FINANSIERINGSAKTIVITET FØR FORSKYDNINGER I RENTEBÆRENDE GÆLD*		**-41,9**	**-11,2**
ÆNDRING I RENTEBÆRENDE NETTOLIKVIDITET		**15,7**	**-184,9**
Ændring i rentebærende gæld*	14	86,3	268,7
NETTOÆNDRING I LIKVIDER		**102,0**	**83,8**
Likvider primo		553,7	471,2
Årets ændring		102,0	83,8
Valutakursomregning primo		-0,4	-1,3
LIKVIDER ULTIMO	15	**655,3**	**553,7**
Den rentebærende nettolikviditet ultimo kan opgøres således:			
Likvide beholdninger og værdipapirer		655,3	553,7
Rentebærende gæld		585,0	490,3
Valutakursomregning af rentebærende nettolikviditet		0,0	8,8
Rentebærende nettolikviditet ultimo		**70,3**	**54,6**
* Samlet cash flow fra finansieringsaktiviteter udgør		44,4	257,5

STATEMENT OF SOURCES AND APPLICATION OF FUNDS

GROUP

	Notes	1996 DKKm	1995 DKKm
Profit for the year		310.8	228.2
Provisions		5.0	1.2
Depreciation		84.3	77.7
CASH FLOW FROM OPERATIONS BEFORE CHANGE IN WORKING CAPITAL		400.1	307.1
Receivables		-47.2	-143.0
Stocks		-78.4	-54.0
Short-term non-interest-bearing debt		78.0	27.0
CHANGE IN WORKING CAPITAL		-47.6	-170.0
CASH FLOW FROM ORDINARY ACTIVITIES		352.5	137.1
Corporation tax paid		-71.2	-36.7
CASH FLOW FROM OPERATIONS		281.3	100.4
Capital expenditure		-231.4	-281.2
Proceeds from sales of assets		9.6	9.3
Other financial investments		-1.9	-2.2
CASH FLOW FROM INVESTMENTS		-223.7	-274.1
CASH FLOW FROM OPERATIONS AND INVESTMENTS		57.6	-173.7
Dividend paid to minority interests		-10.3	-3.8
Dividend paid for the year		-22.0	0.0
Employees' share of the profit paid		-9.6	-7.4
CASH FLOW FROM FINANCING BEFORE CHANGES IN INTEREST-BEARING DEBT*		-41.9	-11.2
CHANGE IN INTEREST-BEARING NET CASH		15.7	-184.9
Change in interest-bearing debt*	14	86.3	268.7
NET CHANGE IN CASH		102.0	83.8
Cash at 1 January		553.7	471.2
The year's changes		102.0	83.8
Currency translation at 1 January		-0.4	-1.3
CASH AT 31 DECEMBER	15	655.3	553.7
The interest-bearing net cash at 31 December is composed as follows:			
Cash and securities		655.3	553.7
Interest-bearing debt		585.0	490.3
Currency translation, interest-bearing net cash		0.0	8.8
Interest-bearing net cash at 31 December		70.3	54.6
*Total cash flow from financing amounts to		44.4	257.5

UNDERSKRIFTER

København, den 24. april 1997

D I R E K T I O N

Erik Sprunk-Jansen	Eva Steiness	Ib D. Christoffersen
Koncernchef,	Koncerndirektør	Fagdirektør, Økonomi
Adm. direktør		

B E S T Y R E L S E

Arne V. Jensen	Jørgen Fakstorp	Lars Bruhn
Formand	Næstformand	

Henrik Hertz	Bent Jakobsen	Sven Dyrløv Madsen

Jan Gottliebsen	Birgit Bundgaard Rosenmeier	Torben Skarsfeldt
Medarbejdervalgt	Medarbejdervalgt	Medarbejdervalgt

REVISIONSPÅTEGNING

Vi har revideret det af ledelsen aflagte koncernregnskab og årsregnskab for 1996 for H. Lundbeck A/S.

DEN UDFØRTE REVISION
Vi har i overensstemmelse med almindeligt anerkendte revisionsprincipper tilrettelagt og udført revisionen med henblik på at opnå en begrundet overbevisning om, at regnskaberne er uden væsentlige fejl og mangler. Under revisionen har vi ud fra en vurdering af væsentlighed og risiko efterprøvet grundlaget og dokumentationen for de i regnskaberne anførte beløb og øvrige oplysninger. Vi har herunder taget stilling til den af ledelsen valgte regnskabspraksis og de udøvede regnskabsmæssige skøn samt vurderet, om regnskabernes informationer som helhed er fyldestgørende.

Revisionen har ikke givet anledning til forbehold.

KONKLUSION
Det er vor opfattelse, at koncernregnskabet og årsregnskabet er aflagt i overensstemmelse med lovgivningens krav til regnskabsaflæggelsen, og at regnskaberne giver et retvisende billede af koncernens og moderselskabets aktiver og passiver, økonomiske stilling samt resultat.

København, den 24. april 1997

DELOITTE & TOUCHE
Statsautoriset Revisionsaktieselskab

Stig Enevoldsen	**Carsten Vaarby**
Statsautoriseret revisor	Statsautoriseret revisor

SIGNATURES

Copenhagen, 24 April 1997

THE BOARD OF MANAGEMENT

Erik Sprunk-Jansen	Eva Steiness	Ib D. Christoffersen
President	Executive Vice President	VP Finance

THE SUPERVISORY BOARD

Arne V. Jensen	Jørgen Fakstorp	Lars Bruhn
Chairman	Vice-Chairman	

Henrik Hertz	Bent Jakobsen	Sven Dyrløv Madsen

Jan Gottliebsen	Birgit Bundgaard Rosenmeier	Torben Skarsfeldt
Elected by employees	Elected by employees	Elected by employees

AUDITORS' REPORT

We have audited the accounts and the consolidated accounts of H. Lundbeck A/S for 1996 presented by the management.

BASIS OF OPINION

We have planned and conducted our audit in accordance with generally accepted audit standards to obtain reasonable assurance about whether the accounts are free of material mis-statement. Based on an evaluation of materiality and risk our audit has included an examination of evidence supporting the amounts and disclosures in the accounts. We have assessed the accounting policies applied and the estimates made by the management as well as evaluated the overall accounts presentation.

Our audit has not given rise to qualifications.

OPINION

In our opinion, the financial statements and the consolidated accounts have been presented in accordance with the accounting provisions of Danish legislation and give a true and fair view of the company's assets and liabilities, financial position and result.

Copenhagen, 24 April 1997

DELOITTE & TOUCHE
Statsautoriset Revisionsaktieselskab

Stig Enevoldsen	**Carsten Vaarby**
State-Authorised Public Accountant	State-Authorised Public Accountant
(Denmark)	(Denmark)

NOTES

1 NET TURNOVER

PARENT COMPANY

GROUP

1995 DKKm	1996 DKKm		1996 DKKm	1995 DKKm
282.2	263.0	Denmark	182.2	196.1
760.6	1,150.7	Exports	2,144.2	1,656.5
1,042.8	1,413.7	Total	2,326.4	1,852.6

2 PRODUCTION, DISTRIBUTION, ADMINISTRATION, RESEARCH AND DEVELOPMENT COSTS

Production, distribution, administration, and research and development costs include wages and salaries etc. as follows:

Employees:

PARENT COMPANY

GROUP

1995 DKKm	1996 DKKm		1996 DKKm	1995 DKKm
267.4	322.8	Wages and salaries	556.6	449.2
19.4	23.8	Contributions to pension schemes	37.6	29.1
2.6	4.7	Other social security costs	55.3	38.5
289.4	351.3	Total	649.5	516.8

Supervisory Board and Board of Management:

Total fees for the parent company's Supervisory Board for the financial year 1996 amount to DKK 1.3 million. Fees for the Supervisory Board for 1995 amounted to DKK 1.0 million.

Total salaries for the Group' Board of Management for the financial year 1996 amount to DKK 4.2 million. Salaries for the Group Board of Management for 1995 amounted to DKK 3.8 million.

Employees:

PARENT COMPANY

GROUP

1995 DKKm	1996 DKKm		1996 DKKm	1995 DKKm
892	1,007	Average number of persons employed in the financial year	1,829	1,545

Production, distribution, administration, and research and development costs include depreciation etc. and appear as follows:

PARENT COMPANY   **GROUP**

1995 DKKm	1996 DKKm		1996 DKKm	1995 DKKm
1.1	1.4	Intangible fixed assets	2.5	1.6
12.5	15.8	Land and buildings	16.3	12.6
13.7	14.0	Technical installations and machinery	19.7	16.9
33.4	29.9	Other installations, operating equipment and fixtures	47.1	47.5
60.7	61.1	Depreciation	85.6	78.6
0.4	0.0	Loss and gain on scrapping	-1.3	-0.9
61.1	61.1	Total	84.3	77.7

distributed as follows:

PARENT COMPANY   **GROUP**

1995 DKKm	1996 DKKm		1996 DKKm	1995 DKKm
35.4	36.0	Production	42.6	39.2
0.0	0.0	Distribution	4.0	2.7
14.5	13.8	Administration	25.7	23.9
11.2	11.3	Research and development	12.0	11.9
61.1	61.1	Total	84.3	77.7

3 AUDIT FEES

PARENT COMPANY   **GROUP**

1995 DKKm	1996 DKKm		1996 DKKm	1995 DKKm
0.7	0.7	Audit	2.6	2.1
0.4	0.6	Services other than audit	0.9	0.8
1.1	1.3	Total	3.5	2.9

NOTES

4 FINANCIAL ITEMS, NET

PARENT COMPANY   **GROUP**

1995 DKKm	1996 DKKm		1996 DKKm	1995 DKKm
44.4	33.7	Bank interest and securities, etc.	38.7	49.6
1.4	2.0	Interest income from subsidiaries		
30.4	16.1	Realised capital gains	16.1	30.4
2.8	5.5	Price adjustment, securities etc.	5.5	2.8
79.0	57.3	Total financial income	60.3	82.8
43.4	43.1	Bank interest and mortgage interest etc.	50.1	50.4
5.5	7.1	Interest expenses from subsidiaries		
8.8	9.7	Realised capital losses	9.8	8.8
57.7	59.9	Total financial expenses	59.9	59.2
21.3	-2.6	Financial items, net	0.4	23.6

5 TAX ON THE PROFIT FOR THE YEAR

PARENT COMPANY   **GROUP**

1995 DKKm	1996 DKKm		1996 DKKm	1995 DKKm
1.2	1.3	Tax due on the year's income	61.7	54.1
0.7	0.8	Adjustments relating to previous years	-0.3	0.7
		Corporation tax paid between jointly taxed		
-2.3	-2.7	subsidiaries and parent company		
59.5	68.2	Tax in subsidiaries		
16.1	24.4	Provision for deferred tax	30.6	20.4
75.2	92.0	Total	92.0	75.2

Taxes paid in the parent company for 1996 amount to DKK 3.7 million.

6 FOREIGN CURRENCY TRANSLATION OF SUBSIDIARIES' PROFIT AND LOSS ACCOUNTS AT THE EXCHANGE RATE RULING AT THE TRANSACTION DATE

Translation of subsidiaries' profit and loss accounts at the exchange rate ruling at the transaction date has the following effect on the key figures in the consolidated profit and loss account for 1996:

	Exchange rate ruling at the balance sheet date	Exchange rate ruling at the transaction date	Difference	Difference %
Turnover	2,326.4	2,315.4	-11.0	-0.5%
Operating profit	310.4	312.5	2.1	0.7%
Profit for the year	218.8	220.7	1.9	0.9%

NOTES

7 INTANGIBLE AND TANGIBLE FIXED ASSETS

GROUP:	Research and development costs	Leasehold improvements	INTANGIBLE FIXED ASSETS TOTAL	Land and buildings	Technical installations and machinery	Other installations, operating equipment and fixtures	Investments in progress	TANGIBLE FIXED ASSETS TOTAL	TOTAL
Purchase prices:									
Balance at 1.1.1996	21.0	20.6	41.6	415.3	224.7	301.7	115.5	1,057.2	1,098.8
Adjustment relating to changed accounting policies				-3.7		-4.0		-7.7	-7.7
Foreign currency translation	0.0	0.2	0.2	1.8	8.1	-0.2	0.3	10.0	10.2
Reclassification		1.7	1.7			-1.7		-1.7	0.0
Additions	16.9	0.6	17.5	75.5	62.1	43.8	134.2	315.6	333.1
Disposals	0.0	0.0	0.0	4.0	1.6	23.2	101.7	130.5	130.5
Purchase prices at 31.12.1996:	37.9	23.1	61.0	484.9	293.3	316.4	148.3	1,242.9	1,303.9
Revaluations	0.0	0.0	0.0	14.7	0.0	0.0	0.0	14.7	14.7
BALANCE AT 31.12.1996	37.9	23.1	61.0	499.6	293.3	316.4	148.3	1,257.6	1,318.6
Depreciation:									
Balance at 1.1.1996	0.0	4.7	4.7	99.2	87.7	148.2	0.0	335.1	339.8
Adjustment relating to changed accounting policies									
Foreign currency translation	0.0	0.0	0.0	0.1	1.1	-0.1	0.0	1.1	1.1
Reclassification		0.7	0.7			-0.7		-0.7	0.0
Additions	0.0	2.5	2.5	16.3	19.7	47.1	0.0	83.1	85.6
Disposals	0.0	0.0	0.0	1.1	1.5	17.9	0.0	20.5	20.5
Depreciation for the year	0.0	0.0	0.0	0.0	0.0	0.0	0.0	0.0	0.0
BALANCE AT 31.12.1996	0.0	7.9	7.9	114.5	107.0	176.6	0.0	398.1	406.0
BOOK VALUE AT 31.12.1996	37.9	15.2	53.1	385.1	186.3	139.8	148.3	859.5	912.6

7 INTANGIBLE AND TANGIBLE FIXED ASSETS - CONTINUED

PARENT COMPANY:	Research and development costs	Leasehold improvements	INTANGIBLE FIXED ASSETS TOTAL	Land and buildings	Technical installations and machinery	Other installations, operating equipment and fixtures	Investments in progress	TANGIBLE FIXED ASSETS TOTAL	TOTAL
Purchase prices:									
Balance at 1.1.1996	21.0	14.9	35.9	404.2	178.8	225.9	114.0	922.9	958.8
Adjustment relating to changed accounting policies				-3.7		-4.0		-7.7	-7.7
Additions	16.9	0.0	16.9	75.3	57.5	24.7	129.4	286.9	303.8
Disposals	0.0	0.0	0.0	4.0	1.7	6.3	96.8	108.8	108.8
Purchase prices at 31.12.1996:	37.9	14.9	52.8	471.8	234.6	240.3	146.6	1,093.3	1,146.1
Revaluations	0.0	0.0	0.0	14.7	0.0	0.0	0.0	14.7	14.7
BALANCE AT 31.12.1996	37.9	14.9	52.8	486.5	234.6	240.3	146.6	1,108.0	1,160.8
Depreciation:									
Balance at 1.1.1996	0.0	3.9	3.9	98.9	81.6	113.8	0.0	294.3	298.2
Adjustment relating to changed accounting policies									
Additions	0.0	1.4	1.4	15.8	14.0	29.9	0.0	59.7	61.1
Disposals	0.0	0.0	0.0	1.2	1.4	4.9	0.0	7.5	7.5
Depreciation for the year	0.0	0.0	0.0	0.0	0.0	0.0	0.0	0.0	0.0
BALANCE AT 31.12.1996	0.0	5.3	5.3	113.5	94.2	138.8	0.0	346.5	351.8
BOOK VALUE AT 31.12.1996	37.9	9.6	47.5	373.0	140.4	101.5	146.6	761.5	809.0

The official cash property value of the Danish recorded properties at 1 January 1996 or later is DKK 283.6 million.
The book value of mortgaged fixed assets in the parent company and the Group is DKK 305.5 million.

NOTES

8 SHARES IN SUBSIDIARIES

	Total	Purchase price	Acc. revaluations	Acc. writedowns
Book value at 1.1.1996	25.2	84.8	25.4	-85.0
Foreign currency translation at 1.1.1996	0.3		0.4	-0.1
Capital contribution	4.1	4.1		
Dividend paid by subsidiaries	-118.7		-115.5	-3.2
Profits in subsidiaries	185.3		145.8	39.5
Losses in subsidiaries	-18.7			-18.7
Total	77.5	88.9	56.1	-67.5
Of which is transferred for set-off against accounts receivable from subsidiaries	15.4			
Total	92.9			

8 SHARES IN SUBSIDIARIES - CONTINUED

Specified as follows:	Equity value at 31.12.1996 DKKm	Profit/loss for 1996 DKKm	Ownership	Equity value at 31.12.1995 DKKm	Profit/loss for 1995 DKKm
H. Lundbeck A/S, Norway	1.6	5.1	100%	-2.2	0.1
H. Lundbeck AB, Sweden	57.0	80.0	100%	33.7	68.1
OY H. Lundbeck AB, Finland	1.5	10.8	100%	1.5	10.2
Lundbeck EESTI AS, Estonia	0.5	0.5	100%	0.0	0.2
Lundbeck Pharma A/S, Denmark	0.7	3.6	100%	0.6	3.8
Lundbeck Medimerc A/S, Denmark			100%		-0.5
A/S Lundbeck Overseas, Denmark	10.8	2.2	100%	8.6	-0.3
Lundbeck Holding GmbH, Germany, including:	4.1	0.0	100%		
- Lundbeck Beteiligungs GmbH, Germany			100%		
- Promonta Lundbeck Arzneimittel Beteiligungs GmbH, Germany			50%		
- Promonta Lundbeck Arzneimittel GmbH & Co., Germany			50%		
LB Arzneimittel Produktrechte GmbH, Germany	0.1	0.0	51%	0.1	0.0
Lundbeck Group Limited, U.K., including:	1.1	-2.4	100%	3.0	-7.3
- Lundbeck Limited, U.K.			100%		
- Lundbeck Pharmaceuticals Limited, U.K.			100%		
Lundbeck Ireland Limited, Ireland	0.0	0.0	100%	0.0	0.0
Lundbeck B.V., the Netherlands	3.0	0.0	100%	3.1	3.0
Lundbeck N.V., Belgium	4.2	8.0	100%	2.9	8.5
Lundbeck S.A., France	2.3	6.6	100%	-4.3	-6.0
Lundbeck España S.A., Spain	3.5	3.9	100%	2.9	0.3
Lundbeck (Schweiz) AG, Switzerland	3.0	24.5	100%	3.3	21.4
Lundbeck Italia S.p.A., Italy	2.2	-0.6	100%	2.5	0.2
Lundbeck Arzneimittel Ges.m.b.H., Austria	2.4	11.0	100%	2.3	6.7
Lundbeck Hellas S.A., Greece	-13.9	-9.2	100%	-4.6	-5.5
Lundbeck South Africa (PTY) Limited, South Africa	0.4	0.0	100%	0.5	-0.2
Lundbeck Management (Canada) Inc., Canada, including:	2.3	4.3	100%	-1.9	-3.9
- Lundbeck Canada Inc., Canada			100%		
Lundbeck Australia (PTY) Limited, Australia	-5.3	-5.1	100%	-0.2	-0.8
Total	81.5	143.2		51.8	98.0
Total Group eliminations	-4.0	23.4		-26.5	-2.2
Book value year-end/Profit for the year	77.5	166.6		25.3	95.8

Group eliminations primarily constitute eliminations in respect of capitalised rights, unrealised intercompany profit on stocks and tax.

Furthermore, at year-end 1996, subsidiaries are being established in the following countries: Slovenia, Hungary, Poland, Russia, Latvia, New Zealand and Portugal.

NOTES

9 OTHER SHAREHOLDINGS AND OTHER RECEIVABLES

PARENT COMPANY				GROUP	
Other share-holdings	Receivables from subsidiaries	Other receivables		Share-holdings	Receivables
4.5	31.6	4.1	Accumulated historical cost at 1.1.1996	4.5	6.8
1.6	3.6	0.5	Additions during the year	1.7	1.0
-0.7	-20.6	0.0	Disposals during the year	-0.7	-0.1
5.4	14.6	4.6	Accumulated historical cost at 31.12.1996	5.5	7.7

10 CAPITAL AND RESERVES

	Share capital	Revaluation reserve	Reserves for net revaluation according to the equity method	Profits carried forward	PARENT COMPANY TOTAL	Minority interests' share	GROUP TOTAL	GROUP 1995
Capital and reserves 1.1.1996	110.0	14.7	25.5	789.9	940.1	4.0	944.1	835.6
Adjustment in connection with changed accounting policies				-4.8	-4.8		-4.8	-6.3
Adjusted capital and reserves 1.1.1996	110.0	14.7	25.5	785.1	935.3	4.0	939.3	829.3
Foreign currency translation			0.4	-0.2	0.2	-0.0	0.2	-1.0
Dividends from subsidiaries			-115.5	115.5	0.0		0.0	0.0
Profit for the year			145.8	71.8	217.6	1.2	218.8	153.0
Employees' share of the profit				-5.7	-5.7		-5.7	-9.6
Dividend for the financial year				0.0	0.0	0.0	0.0	-32.4
Capital and reserves 31.12.1996	110.0	14.7	56.2	966.5	1,147.4	5.2	1,152.6	939.3

The company capital of DKK 110.0 million is composed as follows:

A-shares, 187	100.0
B-shares, 1	10.0
	110.0

11 PROVISIONS FOR DEFERRED TAX

Timing differences between amounts as stated in the accounts and as computed for taxation purposes.

GROUP:	Balance at 1.1.1996	Adjustment in connection with changed accounting policies	Foreign currency translation	The year's movement	Balance at 31.12.1996
Intangible and tangible fixed assets	260.9	-7.7	3.6	13.5	270.3
Stocks	-19.6		-0.1	13.0	-6.7
Other untaxed reserves	-2.7	0.4		67.0	64.7
Total timing differences	238.6	-7.3	3.5	93.5	328.3
Provisions for deferred tax	78.2	-2.5	1.2	30.6	107.5

The year's movement includes provisions for deferred tax on the computed tax effect of differences between the year's computations for accounting purposes and for taxation purposes. Timing differences have been calculated as a net difference because deferred tax has been capitalised in respect of foreign subsidiaries.

PARENT COMPANY:	Balance at 1.1.1996	Adjustment in connection with changed accounting policies	The year's movement	Balance at 31.12.1996
Intangible and tangible fixed assets	216.5	-7.7	35.5	244.3
Stocks	-4.5		1.8	-2.7
Other untaxed reserves	-1.1	0.4	34.5	33.8
Total timing differences	210.9	-7.3	71.8	275.4
Provisions for deferred tax	71.7	-2.5	24.4	93.6

The year's movement includes provision for deferred tax on the computed tax effect of differences between the year's computations for accounting purposes.

12 LONG-TERM INTEREST-BEARING DEBT

Of the Group's total long-term interest-bearing debt of DKK 84.0 million, DKK 22.3 million falls due after 5 years.

NOTES

13 DEBT

PARENT COMPANY			GROUP	
1995 DKKm	1996 DKKm		1996 DKKm	1995 DKKm
378.2	30.8	Mortgage debt, long-term	30.8	378.2
27.7	45.6	Other debt	53.2	40.8
141.7	184.8	Debt to subsidiaries	0.0	0.0
547.6	261.2	Long-term interest-bearing debt	84.0	419.0
10.3	94.4	Bank debt	153.5	59.5
11.7	347.4	Mortgage debt, short-term	347.5	11.8
22.0	441.8	Short-term interest-bearing debt	501.0	71.3
569.6	703.0	Total interest-bearing debt	585.0	490.3
18.2	8.9	Debt to subsidiaries		
84.5	94.6	Trade creditors	146.3	137.3
0.0	0.0	Corporation tax	41.6	39.2
50.1	95.2	VAT, taxes and holiday pay	136.6	92.7
31.6	25.1	Other debt	121.2	91.0
1.3	0.0	Accruals and deferred income	0.0	1.3
		Dividend to minority interests	0.0	10.4
31.6	5.7	Dividend and employees' share of the profit	5.7	31.6
217.3	229.5	Short-term non-interest-bearing debt	451.4	403.5
786.9	932.5	Total debt	1,036.4	893.8
547.6	261.2	Long-term debt	84.0	419.0
239.3	671.3	Short-term debt	952.4	474.8
786.9	932.5	Total debt	1,036.4	893.8

14 CHANGE IN INTEREST-BEARING DEBT

GROUP

	1996 DKKm	1995 DKKm
Proceeds in connection with the raising of interest-bearing loans	346.1	563.3
Repayment of interest-bearing loans	-259.8	-294.6
Changes in interest-bearing debt, excl. exchange rate adjustments	86.3	268.7

15 CASH, YEAR-END

GROUP

	1996 DKKm	1995 DKKm
Securities, term to maturity less than 3 months	0.0	0.0
Securities, term to maturity more than 3 months	417.6	432.0
Securities entered as cash	417.6	432.0
Cash	237.7	121.7
Cash, year-end	655.3	553.7

16 CONTRACTUAL OBLIGATIONS

The parent company has assumed obligations amounting to DKK 142.5 million in the form of leases subject to special notice, commitments in connection with leasing of operating equipment, guarantee commitments and surety commitments and declarations of intent in relation to subsidiaries. Furthermore, the parent company is under an obligation to make capital contributions amounting to DKK 5.9 million, expected to be effected in 1997.

Subsidiaries have assumed liabilities totalling DKK 93.3 million in connection with leases and leasing of operating equipment. Furthermore, subsidiaries have assumed pension liabilities amounting to DKK 2.2 million. The Group has assumed no other obligations except such obligations to deliver as are usual in the industry and obligations ensuing from current joint research projects.

In 1994, H. Lundbeck A/S entered into a joint venture agreement with BYK Gulden Lomberg Chemische Fabrik GmbH about the foundation of the joint company Promonta Lundbeck Arzneimittel GmbH & Co. The agreement was made with a view to H. Lundbeck A/S taking over the partner's share when specified conditions have been fulfilled, however, not later than in the year 2009. At the same time and as part of the agreement, H. Lundbeck A/S has undertaken an obligation to purchase the share of the partner in the year 2009. A purchase price as at 31 December 1996 would be within the current financial scope of the Group. The purchase price is to be calculated on the basis of the agreement stipulating, among other things, that the purchase price will depend on the sales in Promonta-Lundbeck in the purchase year. Any excess price over the book values of assets and liabilities will be treated as goodwill.

FINLAND

Common Legal Forms of Companies

Sole trader (*Yksityisyrittäjä*). A person owns a business and is the only person responsible for it.

General partnership (*Avoin yhtiö*, AY). An association of two or more people who do business and bear the responsibility together.

Limited partnership (*Kommandiittiyhtiö*, KY). An association of one or more general partners and one or more limited (silent) partners. The general partner bears the responsibility for the debts of the firm. A limited partner is responsible for debts only up to the sum he or she has invested in the firm.

Limited company (*Yksityinen osakeyhtiö*, OY). A company of one or more shareholders who have limited responsibility. A private company whose shares are not for sale to the public.

Public limited company (*Julkinen osakeyhtiö*, OYJ). A company whose shares are quoted publicly on the Stock Exchange.

Co-operative society (*osuuskunta*). A co-operation owned by its members; equity is collected as membership fees.

Sources of Financial Reporting Requirements

- The Accounting Act (1336/1997) and the Accounting Decree (1337/1997), the Share Company Act (734/1978)
- Regulations and recommendations given by authorities such as the Accounting Board, Association of Authorized Public Accountants and Helsinki Stock Exchange.

Corporate Taxation

The Company Income Tax Act (*Elinkeinotuloverolaki*, EVL) regulates the company income taxation of all forms of companies. Taxation is tied to financial accounts. The same accounting and taxation rules are applied in profit calculation for all forms of companies. Calculation of income taxes differs in different forms of firms: in a sole trader, general partnership, and limited partnership, the owners of the business are pay taxes on company income as private individuals. The profit for the accounting period will be divided for tax purposes among the partners. Limited companies are treated as independent taxpayers. The rate of corporate income tax is now 28%.

Auditing Requirements

The Auditing Act (*Tilintarkastuslaki*, October 28, 1994/ 936) regulates the auditing obligatory in all companies except sole traders. In larger companies at least one or all auditors be certified as Authorized Public Accountant (KHT, *Keskuskauppakamarin hyväksymä tilintarkastaja*) or Approved Accountant (HTM, *hyväksytty tilimies*).

Organization of the Accounting and Auditing Profession

There are two kinds of authorized auditors and their organizations in Finland: Authorized Public Accountant (KHT, *Keskuskauppakamarin hyväksymä tilintarkastaja*) and Finnish Institute of Authorized Public Accountants (*KHT-yhdistys*); Approved Accountant (HTM, *hyväksytty tilimies*), and Association of Approved Accountants (*HTM-yhdistys*).

For financial accountants mainly working in firms of accountants there is an examination and a diploma given called Examination in Bookkeeping and Accounting (KLT, *Kirjanpidon ja laskentatoimen tutkinto*).

Constitution and Legal System

Finland represents a Roman Law country, where financial accounting and reporting are regulated by acts and decrees given by the Parliament, Ministries, and the President of Finland. Lower level regulations and recommendations are given by different authorities having an interest in accounting and reporting issues.

Currency

Finnish Mark. In recent legislation an expression of the "Finnish Currency" is used because of possible membership in EMU and the common European currency—the euro.

Official Languages

Finnish and Swedish. Annual reports are often published also in English. The official language of a Finnish company can be Finnish or Swedish, and often English is the official language for multinational companies.

FINLAND

Salme Näsi
Associate Professor of Accounting
University of Jyväskylä
Aila Virtanen
Senior Lecturer of Accounting
University of Jyväskylä, Finland

1. Background—A Brief History of Accounting in Finland from the Nineteenth Century to the Present Day

The roots of bookkeeping in Finland stretch back to the fourteenth and fifteenth centuries; even double-entry bookkeeping goes back as far as the seventeenth century. It was only in the second half of the nineteenth century, however, that bookkeeping was established by legislation in Finland.

Between 1809 and 1917 Finland was an autonomous Grand Duchy of the Tsarist Empire. In the first half of this period Finland was one of the most remote and impoverished countries in Europe. In the second half, the ideas of liberalism and entrepreneurial freedom started to spread throughout the country. Industrialization and urbanization began, and the country's economic life diversified and expanded. Storekeeping in the countryside became legal in 1859, and the number of merchants (storekeepers), both in urban communities and in the countryside, rose rapidly from 1860 until 1913.

Bookkeeping obligations at that time were based on the bankruptcy regulations prescribed in 1868. Bookkeeping mainly served the business proprietor in recording receivables, debts, and assets. It was not considered necessary to distinguish between the proprietor's private assets and those belonging to the business. Bookkeeping was designed to keep the business proprietor's property separate from that of other businesses and households.

The first share companies' act, which included some general bookkeeping and auditing requirements, was passed in 1895. The law precipitated the development of the accounting and auditing professions in Finland.

Several factors contributed to the development of financial accounting practice in the first two decades of the twentieth century: rapid growth in the number of corporations and co-operatives, inflation caused by World War I, and new legislation on company income taxation passed after Finland became independent in 1917. The profit and loss calculation (measurement of net income or net loss) became a central function of bookkeeping at that time.

Financial accounting in Finland is governed by specific accounting legislation. The first such law, *Laki kirjanpitovelvollisuudesta* (the Book-keeping Obligation Act), was passed in 1925. A few years later, in 1928, *Laki tilinpäätösten julkisuudesta* (the Publication of Financial Statements Act) was passed. The legislation did not define the form and content of financial statements but left this to the individual companies. The static balance equation theory (assets = liabilities + equity) formed the funda-mental basis of accounting at that time, contradicting the profit calculation function of bookkeeping. The balance sheet was the primary financial statement, and the annual income was measured as the change of equity during the accounting period.

Bookkeeping legislation was reformed in 1945. Wartime had increased state control over the economy, and one consequence of this was the need to have greater uniformity in company reporting practices. Companies now had to follow, in form and content, a model for financial statements set out in the new legislation. The 1945 legislation (*Kirjanpitolaki ja - asetus*; Bookkeeping Act and Decree) was still static by nature, being based on asset accounting, even though the main function of accounting was seen as the calculation of profit for the accounting period. Given this contradiction, a dynamic "expenditure–revenue theory of accounting" was outlined and propagated in Finland during the 1940s and 1950s by Profes-sor Martti Saario, the originator of the theory.

The expenditure–revenue theory is a dynamic accounting theory that places emphasis on annual profit calculation. The theory is coherently based on the realization principle for the recording of business transac-tions. There are three kinds of transactions: expenditures (associated with the acquisition of resources or factors of production), revenues (associated with the sale of goods and services), and monetary transactions (equity, loan, and other payments in the monetary process of the firm). The closing accounts are a matter of profit calculation, the core of which is divided into two parts:

1. The division of revenues into expenses and profit
2. The division of expenditures into expenses and assets (i.e., the division of expenditures between the profit and loss account and the balance sheet).

The second division is the most difficult and crucial task in annual profit calculation. Through the balance sheet, some expenditures are transferred to later years to be covered by later revenues. In the income statement, the aim is to match expenditures against corresponding revenues, that is, to follow the matching principle in annual profit measurement. In accordance with the conservatism concept, all expenditures that are no longer expected to generate revenues must be recorded in the profit and loss statement as expenses. The matching principle is theoretically clear, but in practice it is not so simple to apply. Depreciations of noncurrent assets were dependent on future revenue expectations.

It took almost 20 years before the expenditure–revenue theory and the new accounting thinking were officially sanctioned in legislation. The 1973 *Kirjanpitolaki ja -asetus* (Bookkeeping Act and Decree) conformed to the expenditure–revenue theory. Thanks to this dynamic accounting theory and legislation, income measurement was undoubtedly the main function of accounting, and the profit and loss statement was the primary financial statement for over twenty years in Finland. The profit and loss statement represented the company's result (profit or loss), and how it was composed. Expense items on the profit and loss statement followed a specific order of priority, based on Saario's cost priority theory proposed in 1949. The most prominent expense items deducted from sales revenues have been materials and supplies, external services, personnel expenses, and other variable costs and expenses. Listed under variable costs and expenses have been such fixed costs and expenses as personnel expenses, rents, and other fixed costs in the period. Operating revenues and expenses (and their surplus, operating profit or loss) were followed by depreciations, financial incomes and expenses, extraordinary incomes and expenses, and changes in provisions and other appreciations. After income tax subtraction, the residual "profit for the financial year" was available for distribution.

There was also a high degree of flexibility in annual income measurement. The most common permissible means of income smoothing were valuation adjustments (e.g., depreciations of noncurrent assets and valuation reserves of stock) and provisions. These means were used from the point of view of the company's income taxation and distribution of dividend to achieve the target annual result whenever there were enough revenues and expenditures to make such income smoothing possible.

Tax accounting rules have always had a considerable effect on financial accounting practices in Finland. This has been especially true since the 1968 *Elinkeinotuloverolaki* (EVL, the Company Income Tax Act). Company income tax legislation adopted expenditure–revenue theory concepts and tied taxation to accounting; that is, deductions and allowances were tax deductible, provided that corresponding entries were included in the profit calculation in the annual accounts. Accordingly, depreciations of fixed assets, for example, were usually made in accounting as maximum depreciations permitted by the Company Income Tax Act whenever the firm's result made this possible. Since the late 1980s, listed companies have presented depreciations of fixed assets systematically on the basis of a preset plan. Systematic depreciations represent the most common international practice and were therefore recommended in Finland by the Helsinki Stock Exchange and sanctioned by a single change made to accounting legislation in 1985.

The balance sheet has been of secondary importance in Finnish dynamic accounting thinking. It has been interpreted as a transfer account through which "capitalized" expenditures and other assets and liabilities are transferred to the following accounting period. The balance sheet does, however, show the financial position of the company at the moment when accounts are closed. Despite the secondary role of the balance sheet, financial statement analysis (including liquidity and solvency analysis based on the balance sheet information) has been a part of the Finnish accounting theory and practice.

By the time the bookkeeping legislation based on the theory described above was passed in 1973, there was an awareness that the internationalization of Finnish business life and the need for harmonization in accounting and reporting practices would soon lead to a new phase of accounting reform. In the 1980s most Finnish parent companies began to include a second set of financial statements prepared according to International Accounting Standards (IAS) in their annual reports. This "two sets of accounts system" was costly for companies, and it led to a lively debate about the need for international harmonization of Finnish financial accounting regulations. A government committee was appointed in 1989 to consider the reform of accounting legislation in order to establish international harmonization and the comparability of financial statements. New regulations, passed in December 1992, were to be followed in financial accounting and reporting practice from 1993 onward. This reform was a response to the needs of internationalized Finnish companies, but at the same time a means of preparing for Finland's probable membership in the European Union. New regulations were harmonized to a high degree with the EU's 4th and 7th Company Law Directives, even though the expenditure–revenue theory was retained as the theoretical basis for accounting.

Finland became a member of the EU in 1995. The 1992 accounting legislation reform was not complete enough to meet all the harmonization requirements for a member country, and therefore another committee was appointed in 1995 to determine how accounting legislation should be further revised. This committee gave its report in 1996, and the new accounting legislation, *Kirjanpitolaki* (the Accounting Act 1336/1997; hereafter abbreviated KPL 1997) and *Kirjanpitoasetus* (the Accounting Decree 1339/1997; hereafter abbreviated KPA 1997), was passed December 31, 1997 and took effect from the beginning of 1998. The structure of the new accounting legislation is displayed in Table 1.

The EU's Fourth and Seventh Company Law Directives have had a major impact on the Finnish accounting legislation reform work during the 1990s. Some rules not covered by the EU Directives, concerning for example financial leases and foreign currency exchange rates, are based on the IASC standards. Regulations on consolidated accounts were included in the share company legislation in 1983. Since the 1992 reform, regulations on group accounts have been included in their own chapter in accounting legislation.

The Accounting Act and Decree override all other relevant legislation and are applied in all forms of companies. Some additional, specific regulations are given in company legislation, for example in *Osakeyhtiölaki* (abbreviated OYL, Share Companies Act), passed in 1978, along with the latest reform passed in 1997. In addition to the legislature, other authorities issue regulations and recommendations on financial accounting and reporting in Finland. The most important authorities are *Kirjanpitolautakunta* (Financial Accounting Board), a legal institution affiliated with the Ministry of Trade and Industry; the organizations of the authorized public accountants, in particular *KHT-yhdistys* (the Association of Auditors Authorized by the Central Chamber of Commerce), the Finnish member of the IASC; and the Board of Directors of the Helsinki Stock Exchange, which gives disclosure recommendations especially for publicly owned companies.

TABLE 1   *Structure of the Finnish Accounting Legislation*

Accounting Act (*Kirjanpitolaiki* 1336/30.12.1997)

Chapter	*Heading*
1	General provisions
2	Recording of transactions and accounting bookkeeping documents
3	Closing annual accounts
4	Definitions of annual account items
5	Valuation and periodizing rules
6	Consolidated accounts
7	Accounting of person practising a profession
8	Miscellaneous provisions
9	Final provisions

Accounting Decree (*Kirjanpitoasetus* 1339/30.12.1997)

Chapter	
1	Layout of profit and loss accounts and the balance sheet
2	Operations report and notes
3	Consolidated profit and loss account and consolidated balance sheet
4	Notes on consolidated accounts
5	Specifications of the balance sheet and notes
6	Final provisions

---

2. Accounting Policies and Practices in Individual Companies' Accounts

2.1 Accounting Conventions and Contents of the Annual Accounts

The latest two reforms of accounting legislation in 1992 and 1997 have harmonized Finnish financial accounting regulations with the EU's Fourth and Seventh Company Law Directives. The expenditure–revenue theory has so far been retained as the fundamental basis for accounting norms and practices in Finland, even though transcribing international rules and principles may undermine or weaken the theoretical foundation of Finnish financial accounting.

The main principle revealed in the Finnish accounting legislation is "good accounting practice" (*hyvä kirjanpitotapa*). The Accounting Act of 1997 (KPL 1997, 1:3 §) states that "an accounting obligated company has to follow good accounting practice." The good accounting practice concept has no exact definition, but in Finland it is based on the following sources: (1) the expenditure–revenue theory, (2) accounting and other legislation, (3) rules and statements of the Financial Accounting Board, (4) statements and recommendations of auditors' and other accounting professionals' associations, and (5) general principles or conventions of accounting.

Since the 1992 reform Finnish accounting legislation also includes the "true and fair view" (*oikeat ja riittävät tiedot* or *oikea ja riittävä kuva*) concept, which emphasizes the informative nature of disclosure. Annual accounts should give a true and fair view concerning the result of operations and the economic position of the company. Inclusion of the true and fair view concept in the accounting rules represents a significant change in the spirit of Finnish financial accounting, based as it has been on the calculation of distributable profit. In practice, the true and fair view requirement has been interpreted in Finland to mean the disclosure of supplementary information in the notes if the true and fair view requirement is not otherwise fulfilled.

The following principles are copied from the EU's Fourth Council Directive (78/660/EEC Section 7, Valuation rules, Article 31), and explicitly stated in the Finnish Accounting legislation passed in 1997 as methods to be applied when closing and opening annual accounts: (1) presumption of going concern, (2) consistency in applying accounting principles and methods, (3) prudence regardless of the result of the financial year, (4) correspondence of the opening balance sheet to the closing balance sheet for the preceding financial year, (5) revenues and expenses relating to the financial year are included in accounts irrespective of the date of receipt or payment of revenue or expenditure, and (6) the components of asset and liability items must be valued separately (KPL 1997 3:3 §).

In Finland, the same accounting legislation is applied for all legal forms and sizes of company. Smaller private companies, however, have some lesser disclosure obligations than do large public companies. Annual accounts in Finland consist of (1) the profit and loss account, (2) the balance sheet, (3) notes, and (4) operations report. These elements of annual accounts must form a unified entirety (KPL 1997, 3:1 §). Following share company legislation, all public companies and larger private companies must prepare a cash flow statement that discloses the sources and uses of financial assets during the accounting period (OYL 1978, 9§).

2.2 Layout and Contents of the Profit and Loss Account

Five different layouts for the profit and loss account are specified in the Finnish accounting legislation (see Accounting Decree 1339/1997. KPA 1997, 1:1-5 §). Two alternative layouts (§1 and 2) are provided for business companies, and specific layouts for associations and foundations, for real estate companies and for persons practicing a profession. Companies must choose from two layouts: one that classifies expenses by nature and the other by function (see Appendix 1). These two layouts are uniform, with the two vertical profit and loss account models provided by the EU's Fourth Directive in Articles 23 and 25. Differences between the EU layouts and Finnish layouts are few and mostly of minor importance.

2.2.1 Classification and Content of Revenue and Expenses

The first item on the Finnish profit and loss statement is net turnover (*liikevaihto*), which comprises the amount derived from the sale of products and the provision of services falling within the company's ordinary activities. (KPL 1997, 4:1 §) The definition of net turnover is the same as in the EU's Article 28. In addition to realized sales revenues, it is also possible to recognize in annual accounts unrealized revenue (and corresponding costs) on the basis of the degree of completion of a product that needs a long production time (KPL 1997, 5:4 §). This method of recognizing revenue in annual accounts on the basis of completion can be applied, for example, to construction, shipbuilding, and machinery contracts that have a long completion time. This method is contrary to the realization principle and, depending on the interpretation, also to the EU's Fourth Directive (Article 31 (1) (c) (aa)), according to which valuation must be made on a prudent basis and only profits made at the balance sheet date may be included.

The Finnish Accounting Act (KPL 1997, 5:1 §) states that revenues in the accounting period are included on the profit and loss account, and expenditures that no longer produce corresponding revenue are subtracted as expenses from those revenues. Foreseeable expenditures and potential losses arising in the course of the financial year or of a previous year must also be taken into the profit and loss account.

The change (decrease or increase) in stocks of finished goods and work in progress and production costs of assets manufactured for a company's own use are either subtracted from or added to net sales. These items, too, are contrary to Finnish accounting theory, which emphasizes sale transactions as the source of sales revenue and the realization principle in recognizing revenues and costs.

The profit and loss account separates operating, financial, and extraordinary items following the model given in the EU's Fourth Directive. In the first alternative layout, operating expenses are classified by nature into raw materials and services, staff costs, depreciations and other value adjustments, and other operating charges. In the second layout, operating expenses are classified by function into purchase and manufacturing costs (cost of sales), distribution costs, administrative expenses, and other operating revenues and expenses.

Financial income and expenses are shown after the operating profit or loss. Financial income is reported with a separate indication of income derived from companies in the same group, from participating interests and from other noncurrent investments. Value adjustments of noncurrent and current financial investments are shown separately, and so are other interest and financial income and expenses under the heading of financial income and expenses

Extraordinary income and charges on the profit and loss account are generated by other transactions than ordinary operations. Extraordinary transactions are one-off by nature and significant by amount (KPL 1997, 4:2 §). The profit from the sale of a fixed asset, for example, should not be classified as an extraordinary item but should be included in net turnover.

2.2.2 Depreciations and Other Value Adjustments

The regulations concerning depreciations of tangible fixed assets (e.g., property, plant, and equipment) are brief in Finnish accounting legislation. The Accounting Act (KPL 1997, 5:5,1 §) states that the purchase price or production cost of tangible fixed and other long-term assets must be capitalized (recorded as an asset on the balance sheet) and deducted by depreciation expenses systematically over the periods in which the asset is in use. This regulation corresponds to Article 35 in the EU's Fourth Directive.

The Company Income Tax Law (EVL, passed in 1968) prescribes the maximum deductible rates of depreciation for different kinds of fixed assets and other long-term expenditures (EVL 30-45 §). Depreciations deductible in company income taxation may be higher than those calculated in annual accounts when systematic depreciation methods over the assets' useful economic lives are used. The difference between depreciations made systematically according to a preset plan and depreciations for taxation purposes is shown as an appropriation item ("a change in the difference of depreciations") on the profit and loss account just above the item for company income and other direct taxes. Depreciations made for taxation purposes must be recognized as expenses in accounting because deductions are tied in tax legislation to accounting (EVL 54,2 §). The cumulative difference between systematic and taxation depreciations is displayed in the liabilities on the balance sheet (See item B1, "Depreciation Difference" in Appendix 1).

The cost of a tangible asset with a useful economic life of three years or less (e.g. tools) is usually recorded as an expense for the acquisition year. This practice is based on rules in income tax legislation (EVL 33,1 §).

Finnish accounting legislation authorizes a prudent inclusion of formation expenses under "Assets" on the balance sheet. These expenses must be written off systematically within a maximum period of five years (KPL 1997, 5:7 §; compare the EU's Fourth Directive, Article 34 (1) (a)). The regulation limiting profit distribution when formation expenses have not been completely written off (compare 4th Directive 34 (1) (b)) is found in Finland in the Share Company Act (OYL 12:2,1a §).

Prudent capitalization of development expenditures and systematic write-offs within a maximum period of five years is possible according to the Finnish Accounting Act (KPL 1997, 5:8 §). A lengthening of the write-off period up to 20 years is possible, based on specific reasons and good accounting practice. The same rules for systematic write-offs and maximum periods of 5 years or duration of influence with a maximum of 20 years are to be applied also in acquisition cost of the goodwill of a company (see KPL 1997, 5:9 §). If other long-term expenditures (for example research expenditures) have been capitalized, they must be written off within a maximum of 5 years, with an opportunity again to extend the write-off period to the maximum of 20 years justified by good accounting practice (KPL 1997, 5:11 §).

Such long-term expenditures as patents, trademarks, operating licenses, and copyrights are usually allocated using the straight line method of depreciation, based on a maximum service or life span of ten years. This practice is based on tax regulations (EVL 37 §). The recommended life span for computer programs is 3–5 years.

Value adjustments to a fixed asset must be made if its future cumulative income is lower than its book value on the balance sheet. When this difference is permanent, it must be charged to the profit and loss account (KPL 1997, 5:13 §).

2.2.3 Appropriations

Appropriations consist of two items: "Change in the difference of depreciations" (see Section 2.2.2 above) and "Change in voluntary provisions." The latter is an appropriation item that affects the annual result (profit or loss) and is shown on the profit and loss account before company income taxes. Voluntary provisions are tax-related; an increase in provisions decreases the profit and taxes of the accounting period under consideration and vice versa. During the 1970s and 1980s Finnish legislation authorized several voluntary provisions that companies could make to achieve a desired profit level and to minimize company income taxes. The Accounting Act (KPL 1997, 5:15) still governs voluntary provisions, like investment, operations, and other provisions, but in taxation they were mostly abolished by the 1992 tax reform.

2.2.4 Company Income Taxes

The accrual-based total of company income and other direct taxes are subtracted from revenue to give the net profit, that is, the amount distributable to shareholders. The division of income taxes between profit on ordinary activities and extraordinary activities can be presented either on the profit and loss account or in the notes.

2.3 Layout and Contents of the Balance Sheet

Following the dynamic expenditure–revenue theory of accounting, the balance sheet is treated as a "transfer account" between two accounting periods and is of minor importance compared with the profit and loss account. Despite this theoretical minimization of the value of the balance sheet, it is used to display the financial position of the accounting entity at the moment of closing the annual accounts.

A common balance sheet layout for all types of firms and other accounting-obligated enterprises may be found in the accounting legislation (KPA

1997, 6 §). This layout is highly compatible with the EU's balance sheet layout given in the Fourth Directive, Section 3(9). It is the horizontal "gross" format, not the vertical "net current asset/liability" model shown in Section 3(10). Assets on the left-hand side of the balance sheet follow the liquidity order, the most liquid assets being at the end. Assets are categorized into fixed assets and current assets according to the use of each particular asset. Fixed assets are those that are meant to yield income over several accounting periods. Other assets are current. Fixed assets are grouped into intangible, tangible, and financial investments. Current assets are divided into stocks, receivables, financial securities, and money in cash and bank accounts. The right-hand side of the balance sheet lists financial sources used to fund the assets or to pay for the expenditures capitalized on the left-hand side. These sources are divided into four groups—equity, accumulated appropriations, obligatory provisions, and liabilities. They follow the order of pay-back of different types of capital, short-term debts with the shortest pay-back times being at the end.

2.3.1 Fixed Assets

The key concept for asset valuation in the Finnish legislation is "acquisition cost" (in Finnish *hankintameno*), which has been defined in the Accounting Act (KPL 1997, 4:5,1 §) as follows: "the acquisition cost includes the variable purchasing and manufacturing costs of an asset." This definition limits the acquisition cost to include only variable costs. It is the main rule even though the legislation authorizes the option of also including fixed purchasing and manufacturing costs in the acquisition cost if the share of fixed costs is significant compared to the variable purchase and manufacturing costs of the asset (KPL 1997, 4:5,2 §). The Finnish "acquisition cost" differs somewhat from the EU's "production cost." The definition of the latter is based on concepts of direct and indirect costs (Fourth Directive, Article 35. 3 (a) and (b)). In harmony with the Directives, the interest paid for a loan taken to finance the manufacturing of a fixed asset can be included in the acquisition cost of that particular asset (KPL 1997, 4:5,3 §).

Intangible assets include capitalized expenditures, such as formation, research, development, and goodwill expenditures. Depreciation regulations concerning these assets were considered in Section 2.2.2.

Tangible assets include land and water areas, buildings and structures, machinery and equipment, and other tangible assets. The book value of a tangible asset on the balance sheet reveals the difference between the acquisition cost (see the definition above) and accumulated depreciations made according to a preset plan. In individual company accounts no difference is made between financial and operating leases. Therefore, assets acquired by means of financial lease agreements are not presented as assets on the balance sheet. In consolidated accounts, however, financial lease agreement assets can be displayed on the consolidated balance sheet according to the 1997 Accounting Act (KPL 1997, 6:18 §).

Financial accounts deal with the acquisition cost of assets rather than their market values. Finnish accounting legislation permits an exception to this rule if the fair market value of a land or water area or security is permanently and significantly higher than its historical acquisition cost. Legislation then allows the accounting entity to adjust the value of that asset up to its estimated market value (KPL 1997, 5:17 §). The amount of revaluation must be added in the equity as a separate revaluation reserve. If the revaluation once made proves to be groundless, it must be cancelled. Revaluation principles, methods, and the assets revalued are shown in the notes to the financial statements (KPA 1997, 2:4,6 §).

Tangible assets that are constantly being replaced and the overall value of which is of secondary importance to the undertaking can be valued for a fixed quantity and fixed amount of money from one accounting period to another (KPL 1997, 5:5 §). The same rule concerns also valuation of inventory assets that have low purchare price and are constantly replaced (KPL 1997, 5:6 §).

2.3.2 Current Assets

Inventories should be subdivided into materials, work in progress, finished goods, and other inventories for sale. The main rule is that inventories are valued at variable purchasing and manufacturing costs. It is, however, possible to include fixed purchasing and manufacturing costs in inventory values, provided that their amount is relatively significant. This possibility is primarily intended for large companies that need to present their financial information in an internationally comparable way. FIFO and the lower of cost or market principle are generally followed in inventory valuation. The FIFO method is the only one approved in the Company Income Tax Act (EVL 14 §). In accounting it is possible to calculate the value of inventories by using the LIFO or weighted average cost instead of the FIFO method (KPL 1997, 5:6 §).

Receivables are shown on the balance sheet at their nominal value or at the lower probable value (KPL 1997. 5:2,1 §). Receivables must be subdivided into long-term and short-term receivables. The former fall due in more than one year and the latter in a year or sooner. Receivables consist of trade receivables, loan receivables, prepayments, and accrued income (KPL 1997, 4:7 §). Prepayments include expenditures incurred during this financial year but relating to subsequent financial years. Accrued income relates to this financial year but is due first during the next year.

According to Finnish accounting legislation, as well as IAS 21, foreign currency denominated receivables and liabilities and other obligations are converted into Finnish currency at the rate of exchange prevailing on the balance sheet date as quoted by the Bank of Finland. If the exchange rate for a foreign receivable, liability, or obligation is fixed based on an agreement or otherwise, this fixed rate can be used in conversion. If a receivable or liability, however, is long-term and matures in more than one year after the balance sheet date, the foreign currency exchange gain or loss can be taken into account in profit calculation first in the accounting period when the gain or loss is realized (KPL 1997, 5:3 §).

After short-term receivables on the balance sheet are financial investments, which include shares in affiliated undertakings, the company's own shares, and other financial investments. Financial investments must be valued at whichever is lower, the acquisition cost or the probable selling price to be attributed to them at the balance sheet date (KPL 1997,5:2,2 §).

2.3.3 Equity Capital

According to the Share Companies Act, the equity capital of corporations is to be divided into restricted equity, nonrestricted equity, and equity loan (OYL 1978, revised in 1997, 11:6). The distinction is made between restricted and nonrestricted equity capital to clearly define those funds distributable to shareholders. The same division should also be applied when preparing the consolidated balance sheet. Share capital, share premium, retained profits in reserve fund, and the revaluation reserve all belong to restricted equity, which cannot be paid out as dividends. Distributable equity, that is, unappropriated retained earnings and the net profit for the accounting period, form the maximum amount available to be paid as dividends. Changes in equity capital must be disclosed in the statements or in the notes. Subscribed, unpaid equity must be displayed as a separate item on the balance sheet (OYL 11:6).

2.3.4 Accumulated Appropriations

Accumulated appropriations after equity capital include two items: accelerated depreciations and voluntary provisions. According to the Accounting Act depreciations of fixed assets must be made systematically according to a preset plan (KPL 1997, 5:5 §). Companies are, however, permitted to make depreciations exceeding the planned depreciations, for specific reasons, like taxation (KPL 1997, 5:12 §). Accelerated depreciations present the accumulated difference between planned depreciations and depreciations in excess of plan.

According to the Accounting Act (KPL 1997, 5:15 §), voluntary provisions can be made for future investments, operations, or other purposes. The Company Income Tax Act reform of 1992 abolished almost all voluntary provisions. Currently voluntary provision for future operations is allowed to sole traders and on certain conditions for general and limited partnerships only, not for corporations. The accumulated depreciation difference in excess of plan and voluntary provisions are untaxed reserves. As a matter of fact they are partly liabilities (deferred income taxes) and partly shareholders' equity, depending on the current company income tax rate.

2.3.5 Provisions for Liabilities and Charges (Obligatory Provisions)

Finnish regulations concerning provisions for liabilities and charges (obligatory provisions) (KPL 1997, 5:14 §) correspond to the provisions of the EU's 4th Directive (Section 4, Article 20). The categorization of provisions on the balance sheet is also the same as in the EU's balance sheet layout. There are provisions for pensions, taxes, and other obligatory provisions (for example, warranty accruals and litigation settlements). In Finland, the total pension liability must be deducted from revenues and shown as an obligatory provision on the balance sheet by December 31, 2000. At present uncovered pension liabilities are often presented only in the notes.

2.3.6 Creditors

Debts are divided into long-term (noncurrent) and short-term (current), the latter falling due within one year from the date of the balance sheet. The short-term portion of long-term debt that is due within one year must also be disclosed as a current liability on the balance sheet. Foreign currency denominated liabilities are converted into Finnish currency using the same rules as in converting receivables (see Section 2.3.2 above).

Employee pensions are often organized through pension insurance companies or pension foundations. Pension loans in noncurrent liabilities mean that the company has borrowed back the money paid as pension insurance from insurance companies and foundations. It is recommended that pension liabilities be included on an accrual basis in the profit and loss statement and that uncovered pension liabilities be presented the same way as all other long-term debts on the balance sheet.

3. Accounting Policies and Practices for Consolidated Accounts

3.1 Regulations Concerning Group Accounts

Consolidated statements have been compulsory in Finland since the 1982 accounting period. Before the two latest accounting legislation reforms in 1992 and 1997, few regulations existed concerning consolidated accounts in Finland. There was something said about this subject in the Share Companies Act (OYL), but mostly regulations, recommendations, and guidelines were issued by various accounting authorities such as the Ministry of Trade and Industry (*Kauppa- ja teollisuusministeriö*), the Accounting Board (*Kirjanpitolautakunta*), the Association of Authorized Public Accountants (*KHT-yhdistys*), and the Board of Directors of the Helsinki Stock Exchange. Today the main regulations on consolidated accounts are in the Accounting Act (KPL 1997, Section 6) and Accounting Decree (KPA 1997, Section 3), but some additional regulations are still included in the Share Companies Act (OYL 1978).

3.2 The Scope and Purpose of Group Accounts

In accounting doctrine consolidated accounts serve three purposes. The first purpose is to present the net result and the financial position of the whole economic entity (the consolidated group). The second, and very important purpose, is to present the nonrestricted equity of the group, since it indicates the maximum amount available for cash dividends from the parent company. The third purpose, or the main principle to be followed in consolidation, is to give a true and fair view of the group with respect to its financial position and profitability. The main users of group accounting information are both existing and potential owners and creditors as well as other stakeholders.

In Finnish legislation the definition of a concern relationship is based on the group's power of control (*määräysvalta*). The obligation to draw up consolidated accounts is based on the power of control if an undertaking (a parent company) (1) has a majority of the shareholders' or members' voting rights in another undertaking (a subsidiary) and this majority of votes is based on ownership, membership, company articles, company agreement, or on other rules or an agreement comparable to them; or (2) has the right to appoint or remove a majority of the members of the administrative, management, or supervisory body of another undertaking (a subsidiary) and this right is based on the same factors as the majority of voting rights above (KPL 1997, 1:5 §).

Participating interest (*omistusyhteys*) means a right in the capital of another undertaking, which right creates a durable link between the undertakings and an intention to contribute to the companies' activities. Participating interest is normally constituted by 20 percent ownership of the share capital or equivalent (KPL 1997, 1:7 §). Participating interest companies do not belong to the concern group. An associated company (*osakkuusyritys*) is a participating interest company where an undertaking or a group has an ability to exercise significant influence (*huomattava vaikutusvalta*) based on the ownership of 20–50% of voting rights (KPL 1997, 1:8 §). Associated companies must be included in the consolidated accounts by using the equity method (KPL 1997, 6:13 §).

A parent company is obligated to prepare and include consolidated accounts in its annual accounts whether it is a public limited company, private limited company, general partnership or limited partnership, or other kind of undertaking (e.g. co-operative) carrying on industrial or commercial activities, excluding persons carrying on a trade. Small and medium-sized groups, measured by the sum of total net sales, the balance sheet total, or the total number of employees of the parent and subsidiaries, do not have to prepare consolidated accounts. The limits in Finnish legislation are the following: the balance sheet total 50 million FIM, turnover or equivalent 100 million FIM, and on average 250 employees (KPL 1997, 6:1,3 §). The size criteria correspond to the criteria in the EU's 4th Directive, Article 27 and Seventh Directive, Article 6(1). Finnish regulations concerning conditions for the preparation of consolidated accounts match the EU's consolidation provisions, bearing in mind that the Seventh Directive (Section 1) comprises several exemptions granted to member states.

Consolidated accounts shall comprise the consolidated balance sheet, the consolidated profit and loss account, and the notes to the accounts. In addition to these, the annual report of the parent company must include all important information on the development of the group's operations (KPL 1997, 6:2 §). Consolidated accounts shall be drawn up clearly, and the documents must constitute a composite whole.

3.3 Methods Applied in Producing Consolidated Financial Statements

Before the 1992 accounting legislation reform, Finnish multinational companies found it problematic to provide information for foreign shareholders and other stakeholders who were not familiar with Finnish accounting. In addition, there were problems in combining the financial accounts of foreign subsidiaries with the accounts of Finnish parent companies because of the accounting theory, legislation, and practice specific to Finland. Many of the largest Finnish multinational companies solved these problems by preparing their consolidated accounts according to the IAS 27 standards. The 1992 reform of the Finnish Accounting Act and Decree harmonized Finnish accounting legislation with international and, particularly, with European provisions to a very large extent. The 1997 accounting legislation reform then finally harmonized the rest of the prevailing differences with the European 4th and 7th Directives. The practical consequences will be seen later when the harmonized legislation is applied in accounting practice.

Consolidated accounts must show the profit or loss and financial position of the group of companies as if the undertakings included were a single accounting entity. The financial accounts of all undertakings should be converted before consolidation to apply the same accounting principles. The general rule is that subsidiaries should draw up their annual accounts at the same date as the annual accounts of the parent company. If a subsidiary's balance sheet date precedes the consolidated balance sheet date by more than three months, that subsidiary must draw up interim accounts for consolidation (KPL 1997, 6:5 §). This rule, like most of the Finnish legislation concerning consolidated accounts, corresponds to provisions in the Seventh Directive.

3.3.1   Elimination of Intercompany Transactions

Consolidated statements are prepared by combining the separate financial statements of the parent company and its subsidiaries and by eliminating the financial effects of all transactions between the members of the group. Intercompany revenues, expenses, internal profit distribution, and changes in internal contributions capitalized on the balance sheets of the undertakings included in the consolidation are to be eliminated from the consolidated profit and loss statement. Mutual receivables, debts, and capitalized internal contributions are to be eliminated from the consolidated balance sheet. Eliminations can be omitted in Finnish consolidated statements if they are not necessary for the true and fair view of the profit or loss and economic position of the concern (KPL 1997, 6:7 §).

"Accumulated appropriations" (accelerated depreciations and voluntary provisions) on the balance sheet and the "change of appropriations" on the profit and loss account are usually divided between equity and deferred income taxes on the consolidated balance sheet and between profit for the accounting period and change in deferred taxes on the consolidated profit and loss account.

3.3.2   Elimination of Internal Ownership of Shares: Consolidation Aktiva and Passiva

The parent company's ownership of a subsidiary's shares is an internal matter and must therefore be eliminated from the consolidated balance sheet. The purchase or acquisition method (*hankintamenomenetelmä*) is applied in the capital set-off (KPL 1997, 6:8 §). Under conditions stated in the accounting legislation (KPL 1997, 6:9 §), the pooling method (*yhdistelmämenetelmä*) can also be used in setting off the internal ownership of shares. The purchase method means that internal ownership is eliminated by setting off the purchase price of a subsidiary's shares in the books of the parent company against the parent company's share of shareholders' equity on the subsidiary's balance sheet at the date of acquisition.

If the parent company purchased the subsidiary's shares at price higher than the corresponding proportion of the shareholders' equity on the subsidiary's balance sheet at the time of acquisition, the difference is called *consolidation aktiva*. In consolidated statements this *aktiva* shall as far as possible be attributed to the subsidiary's assets and liabilities. Any residue from the consolidation *aktiva* that cannot be attributed to assets or liabilities, is shown as a separate item in intangible assets, "consolidation goodwill," on the consolidated balance sheet.

The consolidation goodwill has to be written off in consolidated accounts systematically over a maximum of five years. If the duration of influence of goodwill, however, is longer than five years, then the amortizing period can be lengthened up to 20 years. The depreciation of the consolidation goodwill is recorded on the profit and loss account under "Depreciations and Value Adjustments."

In contrast to consolidation *aktiva* a consolidation *passiva* may arise. This will be the case if the purchase price of the subsidiary's shares is lower than the parent company's share of the subsidiary's shareholders' equity at the date of acquisition. The consolidation *passiva* should be divided as far as possible between the balance sheet items that have generated the *passiva*. Any remaining amount of consolidated *passiva* is called the "consolidation reserve." The consolidation reserve will be recorded as a revenue on the consolidated profit and loss account in subsequent accounting periods against corresponding expenditures and losses in the subsidiaries' profit and loss account or against a realized revenue (KPL 1997, 6:9,5 §). The consolidation reserve is shown on the consolidated balance sheet as a separate item preceding creditors.

3.3.3 Separation of Minority Interests

According to the EU's Seventh Directive (Article 23) the amount of any profit or loss attributable to shares in subsidiary undertakings included in the consolidation held by persons other then the undertakings included in the consolidation shall be shown on the consolidated profit and loss account as a separate item with an appropriate heading. In the same way the amount attributable to shares in subsidiary undertakings held by persons other than the undertakings included in the consolidation shall be shown on the consolidated balance sheet as a separate item with an appropriate heading (Article 21). In Finland this heading is minority interest (*vähemmistöosuus*) both on the profit and loss account and on the balance sheet (KPL 1997, 6:7 §). On the profit and loss account the minority interest is displayed just above the bottom-line profit for the financial year. On the balance sheet the minority interest is shown separately after equity.

3.3.4   Consolidation of Associated Companies

An associated company relationship is based on the concepts of participating interest and significant influence. These concepts refer to an ownership of 20–50% of the equity voting rights and an ability to exercise a significant influence over the operating and financial policy of an undertaking not included in the consolidation. Regulations concerning the consolidation of associated companies correspond with the provision given in the Seventh Directive (Article 33).

Equity accounting or the one-line consolidation method is applied when including associated companies in the consolidated accounts. When an associated company is consolidated for the first time, the acquisition cost of its shares is recorded on the consolidated balance sheet. In the following years, investment in the associated company's shares is increased by the investor's share of undistributed profits (or losses) and subtracted by dividends and other profits achieved from the associated company calculated cumulatively since the first inclusion of that associated company. It is possible to leave an associated company out of consolidation if it does not affect the true and fair view of the results and financial position of the group. Information on why associated companies are not included and the effects of this decision on the financial result and equity of the group should be included in the notes (KPL 1997, 6:12 and 13 §).

3.3.5   Conversion of Foreign Subsidiary Statements

There are no rules in the Seventh Directive concerning the conversion of a foreign subsidiary's annual account items into Finnish marks for consolidated accounts. In Finnish legislation conversion norms are given. The use of the closing exchange rate quoted by the Bank of Finland is recommended for converting balance sheet items of foreign subsidiaries into Finnish currency. The profit and loss account should be converted by using the average rate of the accounting period (KPL 1997, 6:6 §). The same methods are to be used for conversion in the the the notes. Other methods based on good accounting practice and providing a true and fair view can also be used in conversion.

3.3.6   Financial Leasing Agreement

Financial leasing provisions in Finnish accounting legislation correspond with IAS 17 standards (accounting for leases). If the risks and benefits have to a significant extent passed to the leaseholder, the lessor can record the commodity as an asset sold in the accounts, and the leaseholder can record it as an acquisition. In cases of sale and lease back, the profit or loss from the sale is divided in the consolidated accounts over the duration of the leasing agreement.

3.3.7 Notes on Consolidated Accounts

Three long paragraphs in the Accounting Decree (KPA 1997, 4:1-4 §) deal with notes in consolidated accounts; all three list the matters that must be shown in the notes. The consolidated accounts should, where applicable, include information corresponding to the information in the notes of an individual company, information concerning the principles by which the accounts have been prepared, information about subsidiaries and associated companies, together with other additional information. The Share Company Act also contains some requirements for the notes in consolidated accounts.

3.3.8 Cash Flow Statement

The consolidated accounts must include the group's cash flow statement if the parent company is a public share company or a private one that according to the Accounting Act is obligated to draw up consolidated accounts. In 1983 the Accounting Board issued general instructions on how to prepare this statement, either on a "cash flow" or "net working capital flow" basis. In each case the sources and uses of funds must be disclosed. Sources are income, loans, and equity financing, and uses are investments, repayment of capital, and distribution of profit. No standard form is required for presenting the consolidated statement of changes in financial position, but the Association of Authorized Public Accountants has given recommendations as to how it should be prepared.

3.4 The Auditor's Report

Auditors' reports as published in Finnish annual reports are formal and often uninformative from a user's point of view. Regulations on auditing and auditors were earlier included in other legislation (for example in the Share Company Act), but a specific Auditing Act (Tilintarkastuslaki) was passed and came into force in the beginning of 1995. There are regulations concerning the authorization and registration of auditors, the obligations for auditing, the contents of auditing, qualifications, development and control of auditors and so on.

Financial Statements

The layouts of the Profit and Loss Account (KPA 1:1 §, KPA 1:2 §) and the Balance Sheet (KPA 1:6 §) in Finland (in Finnish and in English)

Profit and Loss Account (KPA 1:1)

1. LIIKEVAIHTO
2. Valmiiden ja keskeneräisten tuotteiden varastojen muutos
3. Valmistus omaan käyttöön
4. Liiketoiminnan muut tuotot
5. Materiaalit ja palvelut
   (a) Aineet, tarvikkeet ja tavarat:
      (aa) Ostot tilikauden aikana

      (ab) Varastojen muutos
   (b) Ulkopuoliset palvelut
6. Henkilöstökulut
   a) Palkat ja palkkiot
   b) Henkilösivukulut
      ba) Eläkekulut
      bb) Muut henkilösivukulut
7. Poistot ja arvonalentumiset
   a) Suunnitelman mukaiset poistot
   b) Arvonalentumiset pysyvien vastaavien hyödykkeistä
   c) Vaihtuvien vastaavien poikkeukselliset arvonalenemiset
8. Liiketoiminnan muut kulut
9. LIIKEVOITTO (-TAPPIO)
10. Rahoitustuotot ja -kulut
   a) Tuotot osuuksista saman konsernin yrityksissä
   b) Tuotot osuuksista omistusyhteysyrityksissä
   c) Tuotot muista pysyvien vastaavien sijoituksista
   d) Muut korko- ja rahoitustuotot
   e) Arvonalentumiset pysyvien vastaavien rahoitusarvopapereista
   f) Arvonalentumiset vaihtuvien vastaavien rahoitusarvopapereista
   g) Korkokulut ja muut rahoituskulut
11. VOITTO (TAPPIO) ENNEN SATUNNAISERIÄ

1. NET TURNOVER
2. Changes in stocks of finished goods and in work in progress
3. Production for own use
4. Other operating income
5. Raw materials and consumables:
   (a) Raw materials, supplies and goods
      (aa) Purchases during the financial period

      (ab) Changes in inventories
   (b) External charges
6. Staff costs
   a) Wages and salaries
   b) Social security costs
      ba) Pension costs
      bb) Other social security costs
7. Debreciations and value adjustments
   a) Debreciations according to plan
   b) Value adjustments in respect of fixed assets
   c) Value adjustments in respect of current assets
8. Other operating charges
9. OPERATING PROFIT (LOSS)
10. Financial income and expenses
   a) Income from affiliated undertakings
   b) Income from participating interests
   c) Income from other investments forming part of the fixed assets
   d) Other interest and financial income
   e) Value adjustments in respect of financial assets held as fixed assets
   f) Value adjustmenst in respect of financial assets held as current assets
   g) Interest and other financial expenses
11. PROFIT (LOSS) BEFORE EXTRAORDINARY ITEMS

12. Satunnaiset erät
    a) Satunnaiset tuotot
    b) Satunnaiset kulut
13. VOITTO (TAPPIO) ENNEN TILIN-
    PÄÄTÖSSIIRTOJA JA VEROJA
14. Tilinpäätössiirrot
    a) Poistoeron muutos
    b) Vapaaehtoisten varausten muutos
15. Tuloverot
16. Muut välittömät verot
17. TILIKAUDEN VOITTO (TAPPIO)

12. Extraordinary items
    a) Extraordinary income
    b) Extraordinary charges
13. PROFIT (LOSS) BEFORE
    APPROPRIATIONS AND TAXES
14. Appropriations
    a) Changes in accelerated debreciations
    b) Changes in voluntary provisions
15. Income taxes
16. Other direct taxes
17. PROFIT OR LOSS FOR THE
    FINANCIAL YEAR

Profit and Loss Account (KPA 1:2 §)

1. LIIKEVAIHTO
2. Hankinnan ja valmistuksen kulut
3. Bruttokate
4. Myynnin ja markkinoinnin kulut
5. Hallinnon kulut
6. Liiketoiminnan muut tuotot
7. Liiketoiminnan muut kulut
8. LIIKEVOITTO (- TAPPIO)
9. Rahoitustuotot ja -kulut
    a) Tuotot osuuksista saman konsernin
       yrityksissä
    b) Tuotot osuuksista omistusyhteysyrityksissä
    c) Tuotot muista pysyvien vastaavien
       sijoituksista
    d) Muut korko- ja rahoitustuotot
    e) Arvonalentumiset pysyvien vastaavien
       sijoituksista
    f) Arvonalentumiset vaihtuvien vastaavien
       rahoitusarvopapereista
    g) Korkokulut ja muut rahoituskulut
10. VOITTO (TAPPIO) ENNEN SATUN-
    NAISIA ERIÄ
11. Satunnaiset erät
    a) Satunnaiset tuotot
    b) Satunnaiset kulut
12. VOITTO (TAPPIO) ENNEN
    TILINPÄÄTÖSSIIRTOJA JA VEROJA
13. Tilinpäätössiirrot
    a) Poistoeron muutos
    b) Vapaaehtoisten varausten muutos

1. NET TURNOVER
2. Cost of sales
3. Gross profit or loss
4. Distribution costs
5. Adminstration expenses
6. Other operating income
7. Other operating charges
8. OPERATING PROFIT (LOSS)
9. Financial income and expenses
    a) Income from affiliated
       undertakings
    b) Income from participating interests
    c) Income from other investments
       forming part of the fixed assets
    d) Other interest and financial incom
    e) Value adjustments in respect of
       financial assets held as fixed assets
    f) Value adjustments in respect of financial
       assets held as current assets
    g) Interest and other financial expenses
10. PROFIT (LOSS) BEFORE
    EXTRAORDINARY ITEMS
11. Extraordinary items
    a) Extraordinary income
    b) Extraordinary charges
12. PROFIT (LOSS) BEFORE
    APPROPRIATIONS AND TAXES
13. Appropriations
    a) Changes in accelerated debreciations
    b) Changes in voluntary provisions

14. Tuloverot	14. Income taxes
15. Muut välittömät verot	15. Other direct taxes
16. TILIKAUDEN VOITTO (TAPPIO)	16. PROFIT (LOSS) FOR THE FINANCIAL YEAR

Balance Sheet (KPA 1:6 §)

VASTAAVAA	ASSETS
A. PYSYVÄT VASTAAVAT	A. FIXED ASSETS
I Aineettomat hyödykkeet	I Intangible assets
1. Perustamis- ja järjestelymenot	1. Formation and organizing expenses
2. Tutkimusmenot	2. Research expenses
3. Kehittämismenot	3. Development expenses
4. Aineettomat oikeudet	4. Intangible rights
5. Liikearvo	5. Goodwill
6. Muut pitkävaikutteiset menot	6. Other capitalized expenditure
7. Ennakkomaksut	7. Advance payments
II Aineelliset hyödykkeet	II Tangible assets
1. Maa-ja vesialueet	1. Land and water
2. Rakennukset ja rakennelmat	2. Buildings
3. Koneet ja kalusto	3. Machinery and equipment
4. Muut aiheelliset hyödykkeet	4. Other tangible assets
5. Ennakkomaksut ja keskeneräiset hankinnat	5. Advance payments and construction in progress
III Sijoitukset	III Financial assets
1. Osuudet saman konsernin yrityksissä	1. Shares in affiliated undertakings
2. Saamiset saman konsernin yrityksiltä	2. Loans to affiliated undertakings
3. Osuudet omistusyhteysyrityksissä	3. Participating interests
4. Saamiset omistusyhteysyrityksiltä	4. Loans to undertakings with which the company is linked by virtue of participating interests
5. Muut osakkeet ja osuudet	5. Investments held as fixed assets
6. Muut saamiset	6. Other loans
7. Omat osakkeet tai osuudet	7. Own shares
B. VAIHTUVAT VASTAAVAT	B. CURRENT ASSETS
I Vaihto-omaisuus	I Stocks
1. Aineet ja tarvikkeet	1. Raw materials and consumables
2. Keskeneräiset tuotteet	2. Work in progress
3. Valmiit tuotteet/ tavarat	3. Finished goods/ goods for resale
4. Muu vaihto-omaisuus	4. Other stocks
5. Ennakkomaksut	5. Payments on account
II Saamiset	II Debtors
1. Myyntisaamiset	1. Trade debtors
2. Saamiset saman konsernin yrityksiltä	2. Amounts owed by affiliated undertakings
3. Saamiset omistusyhteysyrityksiltä	3. Amounts owed by undertakings with

	which the company is linked by vitue of participating interests
4. Lainasaamiset	4. Loan receivables
5. Muut saamiset	5. Other debtors
6. Maksamattomat osakkeet/ osuudet	6. Subscribed capital called but not paid
7. Siirtosaamiset	7. Prepayments and accrued income

III Rahoitusarvopaperit	III Investments
1. Osuudet saman konsernin yrityksissä	1. Shares in affiliated undertakings
2. Omat osakkeet tai osuudet	2. Own shares
3. Muut osakkeet ja osuudet	3. Other shares
4. Muut arvopaperit	4. Other investments
IV Rahat ja pankkisaamiset	IV Cash on hand and at banks

VASTATTAVAA	LIABILITIES
A OMA PÄÄOMA	A. CAPITAL AND RESERVES
I Osake-, osuus- ja muu vastaava pääoma	I Share capital
II Ylikurssirahasto	II Share premium account
III Arvonkorotusrahasto	III Revaluation reserve
IV Muut rahastot	IV Other reserves
1. Omien osakkeiden tai osuuksien rahasto	1. Reserve for own shares
2. Vararahasto	2. Restricted reserve
3. Yhtiöjärjestyksen tai sääntöjen mukaiset rahastot	3. Other legal reserves
4. Muut rahastot	4. Other reserves
V Edellisen tilikauden voitto(tappio)	V Profit/loss for the previous accountung
VI Tilikauden voitto (tappio)	VI Profit/ loss for the accountung period

B. TILINPÄÄTÖSSIIRTOJEN KERTYMÄ	B. ACCUMULATED APPROPRIATIONS
1. Poistoero	1. Accelerated debreciation
2. Vapaaehtoiset varaukset	2. Voluntary provisions
C PAKOLLISET VARAUKSET	C. OBLIGATORY PROVISIONS
1. Eläkevaraukset	1. Provisions for pensions
2. Verovaraukset	2. Provisions for taxation
3. Muut pakolliset varaukset	3. Other obligatory provisions
D VIERAS PÄÄOMA	D. CREDITORS
1. Joukkovelkakirjalainat	1. Debentures
2. Vaihtovelkakirjalainat	2. Convertible debentures
3. Lainat rahoituslaitoksilta	3. Loans from credit institutions
4. Eläkelainat	4. Pension loans
5. Saadut ennakot	5. Advances receivables
6. Ostovelat	6. Trade payables
7. Rahoitusvekselit	7. Notes payable

8. Velat saman konsernin yrityksille	8. Amounts owed to affiliated undertakings
9. Velat omistusyhteysyrityksille which the company is linked by virue of	9. Amounts owed to undertakings with participating interests
10. Muut velat	10. Other creditors
11. Siirtovelat	11. Accrued liabilities and deferred income

Tamfelt Group

Tamfelt is one of the pioneers of Finnish industry. The company was founded 200 years ago in 1797. It was first listed on the Helsinki Stock Exchange in 1942. Tamfelt has four plants: one in the United States, one in Portugal and two in Finland. The company's main products are forming fabrics, press felts and dryer fabrics for the pulp and paper industry. Filter fabrics cover a broad range, including the pulp, mining and chemical industries.

These statements are based on the 1992 Accounting Legislation. At this moment no financial accouts based on the 1997 accounting legislation are available.

Consolidated Statement of Income January 1 - December 31, 1997

(FIM 1 000)

	1997	%	1996	%
NET SALES	607 313	100	531 765	100
Increase (+) or decrease (-) in				
finished goods inventories	17 673	16 657		
Production for own use	2 077	1 259		
Other operating income	8 587	6 974		
Costs and expenses				
Materials, supplies and products				
Purchases during the year	124 362	108 996		
Increase (-) or decrease (+)				
in inventories	-4 630	-630		
External services	8 230	4 152		
Personnel expenses	238 691	216 271		
Rents	2 630	3 463		
Other costs and expenses	112 832	103 182		
	-482 115	-435 434		
OPERATING INCOME BEFORE				
DEPRECIATION	153 535	25	121 221	23
Depreciation on fixed assets and other				
long-term expenditure	-29 887	-37 645		
OPERATING INCOME	123 648	20	83 576	16
Financial income and expenses				
Interest income	6 550	10 638		
Other financial income	12 504	11 478		
Interest expenses	-600	-3 700		
Other financial expenses	-4 961	-3 480		
	13 493	14 936		
INCOME BEFORE EXTRAORDINARY				
ITEMS, TAXES AND MINORITY INTEREST/				
INCOME BEFORE TAXES AND				
MINORITY INTEREST	137 141	23	98 512	19
Income taxes	-38 379	-24 319		
Minority interest	-63	-38		
NET INCOME FOR THE YEAR	98 699	16	74 155	14

Consolidated Balance Sheet December 31, 1997
(FIM 1 000)

ASSETS	1997	%	1996	%
FIXED ASSETS AND OTHER				
LONG-TERM INVESTMENT				
Intangible assets				
Intangible rights	3 360		3 084	
Consolidated goodwill	808	1 617		
Other long-term expenditure	2 733		3 011	
	6 901	1	7 712	1
Tangible assets				
Land and water	5 686		8 166	
Buildings	55 683		53 303	
Machinery, equipment and furniture	150 358		115 590	
Other tangible assets	458		473	
Advance payments and construction				
in progress	6 178		15 306	
	218 363	32	192 838	32
Financial assets				
Shares and holdings	1 519		1 501	
Loans receivable	4 049		4 827	
	5 568	1	6 328	1
CURRENT ASSETS				
Inventories				
Raw materials and consumables	28 431		23 676	
Work in progress	68 805		54 037	
Finished products	75 039		68 846	
	172 275	25	146 559	24
Receivables				
Sales receivable	85 790		71 809	
Loans receivable	788		707	
Prepaid expenses and accrued income	20 062		16 679	
Other receivables	1 063		684	
	107 703	15	89 879	14
Securities				
Shares and holdings	6 816	1 823		
Other securities	81 073		92 964	
	87 889	13	94 787	16
Cash in hand and at bank	90 107	13	75 052	12
	688 806	100	613 155	100

LIABILITIES	1997	%	1996	%

STOCKHOLDERS' EQUITY

Restricted equity

Capital stock	66 450		66 450	
General reserve	15 522		15 522	

Non-restricted equity

Contingency reserve	19 806		19 806	
Other non-restricted equity	322 508		274 867	
Net income for the year	98 699		80 754	
	522 985	76	457 399	75

MINORITY INTEREST	377	0	314	0
CREDITORS				

Long-term liabilities

Other long-term liabilities	1 948		2 459	
Deferred tax liability	39 924		41 341	
	41 872	6	43 800	7

Current liabilities

Loans from financial institutions	504		13 795	
Advance received	5 905		6 280	
Accounts payable	26 525		22 013	
Accrued liabilities and deferred income	88 021		68 576	
Other current liabilities	2 617		978	
	123 572	18	111 642	18
	688 806	100	613 155	10

Consolidated Statement of Cash Flows

(FIM 1 000)	1997	1996
OPERATING ACTIVITIES		
Internal financing		
Operating income	123 648	83 576
Depreciation	29 887	37 645
Financial income and expenses	13 493	14 936
Taxes	-38 379	-24 319
	128 649	111 838
CHANGE IN WORKING CAPITAL		
Increase (-) or decrease (+) in inventories	-25 716	-18 145
Increase (-) or decrease (+)		
in short-term receivables	-17 824	18 430
Increase (+) or decrease (-) in		
interest-free short-term debt	24 715	-417
	-18 825	-132
Cash flow from operations	109 824	111 706
INVESTMENT		
Capital expenditure in fixed assets	-60 053	-53 039
Sales of fixed assets	8 922	3 596
Translation adjustments of fixed assets	-3 488	-2 288
	-54 619	-51 731
Cash flow before financing	55 205	59 975
FINANCING		
Increase (-) or decrease (+)		
in long-term receivables	778	588
Increase (+) or decrease (-)		
in long-term loans	-511	-32 081
Increase (+) or decrease (-)		
in deferred tax liability	-1 417	-2 566
Increase (+) or decrease (-)		
in short-term loans	-14 847	-34 095
Dividends	-38 021	-21 920
Share subscription	2 227	
Exchange rate differences on long-term loans	1 983	
Exchange rate differences on short-term loans	2 062	2 195
	-51 956	-83 669
Calculated increase in liquid assets		
increase (+) or decrease (-)	3 249	-23 694
Adjustments 1)	4 908	570
Balance-sheet increase (+) or decrease (-)		
in liquid assets	8 157	-23 124

The items of this Statement are not directly deducible from the Balance Sheet on account of changes in the Balance Sheet items.
1) including translation adjustments.

Statement of Income January 1—December 31, 1997 Parent company
(FIM 1 000)

	1997	%	1996	%
NET SALES	526 216	100	455 928	100
Increase (+) or decrease (-) in finished				
goods inventories	17 411		17 160	
Production for own use	2 077		1 259	
Other operating income	7 257		5 226	
Costs and expenses				
Materials, supplies and products				
Purchases during the year	106 778		103 906	
Increase (-) or decrease (+)				
in inventories	-4 405		-1 781	
External services	7 891		3 731	
Personnel expenses	200 565		175 627	
Rents	19 790		19 986	
Other costs and expenses	92 177		80 235	
	– 422 796		– 381 704	
OPERATING INCOME BEFORE				
DEPRECIATION	130 165	25	97 869	21
Depreciation on fixed assets and other				
long-term expenditure	– 24 270		– 23 144	
OPERATING INCOME	105 895	20	74 725	16
Financial income and expenses				
Interest income	2 837		5 396	
Other financial income	16 550		10 569	
Interest expenses	– 1 691		– 272	
Other financial expenses	– 3 671		– 2 627	
	14 025		13 066	
INCOME BEFORE EXTRAORDINARY				
ITEMS, RESERVES AND TAXES	119 920	23	87 791	19
Extraordinary income and expenses				
Extraordinary income	15 600		16 700	
Extraordinary expenses			– 21 912	
	15 600		– 5 212	
INCOME BEFORE RESERVES AND TAXES	135 520	26	82 579	18
Increase (-) or decrease (+) in				
accelerated depreciation	– 45 199		– 17 939	
Increase (-) or decrease (+) in				
voluntary reserve	51 379		27 437	
Income taxes	– 39 726		– 26 669	
NET INCOME FOR THE YEAR	101 974	19	65 408	14

Balance Sheet December 31, 1997 Parent company
(FIM 1 000)

ASSETS	1997	%	1996	%
FIXED ASSETS AND OTHER LONG-TERM INVESTMENT				
Intangible assets				
Intangible rights	3 766		3 897	
Other long-term expenditure	2 521		2 867	
	6 287	1	6 764	1
Tangible assets				
Land and water	4 294		4 294	
Buildings	13 315		6 335	
Machinery, equipment and furniture	132 181		95 347	
Other tangible assets	458		473	
Advance payments and construction				
in progress	5 500		15 236	
	155 748	21	121 685	18
Financial assets				
Shares and holdings	205 104		205 086	
Loans receivable	54 781		51 200	
	259 885	33	256 286	39
CURRENT ASSETS				
Inventories				
Raw materials and consumables	24 273		19 868	
Work in progress	58 729		46 327	
Finished products	59 345		54 335	
	142 347	19	120 530	18
Receivables				
Sales receivable	66 775		54 961	
Loans receivable	695		3 852	
Prepaid expenses and accrued income	28 847		28 671	
	96 317	13	87 484	13
Securities				
Shares and holdings	2 053		1 823	
Other securities	27 370		39 000	
	29 423	4	40 823	6
Cash in hand and at bank	66 669	9	32 200	5
	756 676	100	665 772	100

LIABILITIES	1997	%	1996	%
STOCKHOLDERS' EQUITY				
Restricted equity				
Capital stock	66 450		66 450	
General reserve	15 522		15 522	
Non-restricted equity				
Contingency reserve	19 806		19 806	
Other non-restricted equity	268 538		241 151	
Net income for the year	101 974		65 408	
	472 290	63	408 337	61
RESERVES				
Total accelerated depreciation	137 444	18	92 245	14
Voluntary reserve				
Other reserves	51 379	8		
CREDITORS				
Long-term liabilities				
Other long-term liabilities	1 862	0	2 223	0
Current liabilities				
Advance received	5 904		6 279	
Accounts payable	21 355		25 468	
Accrued liabilities and deferred income	77 459		59 387	
Other current liabilities	40 362		20 454	
	145 080	19	111 588	17
	756 676	100	665 772	100

Statement of Cash Flows Parent company

(FIM 1 000)	1997	1996
OPERATING ACTIVITIES		
Internal financing		
Operating income	105 895	74 725
Depreciation	24 270	23 144
Financial income and expenses	14 025	13 066
Extraordinary items	15 600	– 5 212
Taxes	– 39 726	– 26 669
	120 064	79 054
CHANGE IN WORKING CAPITAL		
Increase (–) or decrease (+)		
in inventories	– 21 817	– 18 941
Increase (–) or decrease (+)		
in short-term receivables	2 567	2 139
Increase (+) or decrease (–)		
in interest-free short-term debt	13 584	5 776
	– 5 666	– 11 026
Cash flow from operations	114 398	68 028
INVESTMENT		
Capital expenditure in fixed assets	– 58 000	– 52 797
Sales of fixed assets	126	2 474
	– 57 874	– 50 323
Cash flow before financing	56 524	17 705
FINANCING		
Increase (–) or decrease (+) in		
long-term receivables	3 372	– 31 969
Increase (+) or decrease (–)		
in long-term loans	–361	1 138
Increase (+) or decrease (–)		
in short-term loans	19 908	18 910
Dividends	– 38 021	– 21 920
Stock subscription		2 227
Exchange differences on long-term receivables	– 6 953	– 1 225
	– 22 055	– 32 839
Calculated increase in liquid assets		
increase (+) or decrease (–)	34 469	– 15 134
Balance-sheet increase (+) or decrease (–)		
in liquid assets	34 469	– 15 134

Significant Accounting Policies

Principles of consolidation

The consolidated accounts cover the parent company and those companies in which Tamfelt Corp., directly or indirectly, holds over 50 % of the voting stock. A 50 % share has been consolidated according to instructions governing joint companies. Other associated undertakings have been consolidated according to their capital contribution.

The acquisition method has been adopted for consolidation.

A surplus of the purchase price of the shares in subsidiary company over their underlying net worth at the date of acquisition is shown in the consolidated accounts as goodwill, to be amortized over five years using the straight line method.

All inter-group transactions, pending margins, internal balances, and internal profits have been eliminated. Minority interests are deducted in the statement of income as an item of net income, and in the balance sheet as an item of stockholders' equity.

The income statements of the foreign group companies have been translated into markka at the average exchange rate for the year. Their balance sheets have been translated at the average rate quoted by the Bank of Finland on the balance sheet date. The resulting two-rate differences, together with the conversion adjustments resulting from the application of the acquisition method, and the exchange rate differences of equity-ranked inter-group loans are dealt with as translation adjustment in the non-restricted equity.

Change in accelerated depreciation and voluntary reserve has been split between change in deferred tax liability and income for the year. Total accelerated depreciation and voluntary reserve have been divided between equity and the deferred tax liability included in creditors.

Net sales

For the computation of net sales, indirect taxes, discounts, and exchange rate differences have been deducted from the sales revenue.

Foreign currencies

The parent company receivables and liabilities are booked at the average exchange rate quoted by the Bank of Finland on the balance sheet date. Current hedging instruments for foreign denominated items are entered at the value of the date, including the effect of interest.

Fixed assets and depreciation

Fixed assets are stated in the balance sheet at acquisition cost less annual depreciation according to plan. Total accelerated depreciation is recorded as a separate item in reserves.

Planned depreciation is computed using the straight line method over the useful economic life of the asset. The most common periods are:

Intangible rights	3 to 10 years
Consolidated goodwill	5 years
Other long-term expenditure	10 years
Buildings	25 to 50 years
Machinery and equipment	4 to 15 years
Other tangible assets	10 years

Inventories

Inventories are valued at lower of cost or market, at either the purchase price, or estimated net realizable value, whichever is lower. The purchase price is defined using the direct cost of acquisition or manufacture on the FiFo principle.

For foreign subsidiaries, inventories are valued in accordance with local practice and also include indirect costs of production.

Securities

Bonds are entered in assets at acquisition cost, allocating the difference between acquisition cost and nominal value as an increase or decrease of acquisition cost, according to maturity. In the final accounts, however, they are not valued higher than the market price. Shares and holdings are stated at the acquisition cost or market price, whichever is lower.

Nominal interest income from bonds is booked in interest income. The difference between acquisition cost and nominal value is allocated as an increase or decrease of interest income. If bonds are sold in advance of maturity date, a gain is entered in other financial income and a loss in other financial expenses.

Research and development

The R&D expenditure is booked as expenses of the financial period during which they arose, with the exception of equipment purchases, which are depreciated according to plan over five years by the straight line method.

Taxes

Computed estimates of taxes are entered in the statement of income of the domestic group companies. Foreign subsidiary taxes are presented in the consolidated statements as booked in their respective original accounts.

Pension liability in Finland

Liability for working employees is covered by pension insurance corporations. The parent company is responsible for voluntary, unregistered old age pensions. Corresponding figures are shown in the pledged assets included in Financial Data.

Tamfelt Group's financial accounts contain the income statement and balance sheet specifications (financial and other data) which has been eliminated here only to save space.

Board of Directors' Proposal to Annual General Meeting

Consolidated distributable earnings total: FIM 338,351,000.00.

Parent company distributable earnings total: FIM 390,318,533.77, of which

• retained earnings from previous years	268,538,045.68
• net income for the year	101,974,061.90
	370,512,107.58

The Board proposes that this sum be appropriated as follows:

• a dividend of FIM 6.20 a share paid on 2,599,272 common shares	16,115,486.40
• a dividend of FIM 6.40 a share paid on 4,045,728 preferred shares	25,892,659.20
• to be retained	328,503,961.98
	370,512,107.58

Helsinki, February 23, 1998

Mikael von Frenckell
Axel Cedercreutz
Martin Lilius
Vesa Kainu
Jouko Oksanen
Risto Hautamäki
President

Auditors' report

To the shareholders of Tamfelt Corp.

We have audited the accounting records and the accounts, as well as the administation by the Board of Directors and the President of Tamfelt Corp. for the year ended December 31, 1997. The accounts prepared by the Board of Directors and the President include the report of the Board of Directors, consolidated and parent company income statements, balance sheets, cash flow statements and notes to the accounts. Based on our audit we express our opinion on these accounts and the parent company's administration.

We have conducted the audit in accordance with Finnish Generally Accepted Auditing Standards. Those standards require that we plan and perform the audit in order to obtain reasonable assurance about whether the accounts are free of material misstatement. An audit includes examining, on a test basis, evidence supporting the amounts and disclosures in the financial statements, assessing the accounting principles used and significant estimates made by the management, as well as evaluating the overall financial statement presentation. The purpose of our audit of the administration has been to examine that the Board of Directors and the President have complied with the rules of the Finnish Companies Act.

In our opinion, the accounts have been prepared in accordance with the Finnish Accounting Act and other rules and regulations governing the preparation of financial statements in Finland. The accounts give a true and fair view, as defined in the Accounting Act, of both the consolidated and parent company result of operations for the year 1997 as well as of the financial position at the year end. The accounts can be adopted and the members of the Board of Directors and the President of the parent company can be discharged from liability for the period audited by us. The proposal by the Board of Directors on how to deal with the retained earnings is in compliance with the Finnish Companies Act.

We have reviewed the interim reports made public by the company during the year. It is our understanding

that the interim reports have been prepared in accordance with the rules and regulations governing the preparation of such reports in Finland.

Tampere, March 5, 1998

Eric Haglund	Jari Paloniemi
Authorized Public Accountant	Authorized Public Accountant

Country Highlights
FRANCE

Common Legal Forms of Company
Société anonyme (SA)
Société à responsabilité limitée (Sarl)

Sources of Financial Reporting Requirements
Code de Commerce
Plan Comptable Général

Corporate Taxation
France has an extremely complex taxation system. Companies are taxed on profits, but social security charges, based on payroll, are also a substantial cost. Companies also pay various taxes to municipalities.

Auditing Requirements
All SA and those Sarl that exceed EU small company limites are subject to audit. The audit appointment for an SA is for six years, and two auditors must be named.

Organization of the Accounting and Auditing Professions
Membership in professional bodies is restricted to practitioners. There are separate bodies for accountants (*Ordre des Experts Comptables*) and auditors (*Compagnie Nationale des Commissaires aux Comptes*). In reality most professionals are members of both bodies, but may not provide both audit and other services to the same client.

Constitution and Legal System
France is a republic. Politically the president has executive authority for foreign relations, but domestic matters are the responsibilitey of the prime minister. The legal system is based on Roman law.

Currency
The French franc, but France is due to switch to the euro.

Official Languages
French

FRANCE

Jean-Claude Scheid
*Institut National des Techniques Economiques et Commerciales
(INTEC), Conservatoire Nationale des Arts et Métiers, France*
Peter Walton
University of Geneva, Switzerland

1. Background

1.1 Introduction

The pace of change in French accounting has been relatively fast in the 1980s and 1990s, with the result that Anglo-Saxon perceptions of French accounting are frequently out of step with reality. This lag is sometimes further compounded by a failure to recognize that the existence of a detailed set of regulations does not necessarily mean that (a) all those regulations are complied with in the normal course of business or (b) that accountants do not think to go beyond these official requirements.

A modern capital market with an active supervisory body, a thriving and competitive multinational business, and a willingness by the state to support evolution of regulation provide an environment in which accounting has progressed rapidly, and standards of reporting and disclosure are high. The days of profit-smoothing, lack of consistency of accounting policies, and minimal disclosures are largely a thing of the past, even if France did pass through that stage of development historically later than did Great Britain or the United States.

Inevitably the development of reporting in a jurisdiction is one of incremental change, sometimes evolving slowly, sometimes taking sudden leaps. Accounting meets new challenges and finds new solutions, but usually the process involves grafting onto or modifying what has already been established, rather than scrapping the existing rules and starting again. A consequence is that an outsider taking an overview at any given moment will see a set of rules and regulations that may well be inconsistent and may appear convoluted and even illogical. A further complication is that accepted practice and existing regulations do not necessarily match exactly.

This chapter provides a guide through the French version of the regulatory labyrinth, and it seems useful to approach the subject with a brief analysis of the historical development of both accounting and business, in order to demonstrate the evolution of reporting.

1.2 Accountants and Auditors

Whereas accounting as a regulated feature of business activity first made its appearance in anglophone countries in the nineteenth century, in response to the needs of the industrial revolution, in France accounting was introduced as a compulsory feature of business in 1673 by a law (known as the Savary law) that required traders to maintain daybooks of their business transactions and prepare an annual list of assets, as well as to keep copies of all letters.

In 1807 the Savary Law was incorporated into a Commercial Code, as French law was reorganized into Napoleonic codes. In fact, the Savary statute, either directly or through the Napoleonic Commercial Code, was widely borrowed or imitated throughout continental Europe and is the original building block of the continental European family of legally based accounting systems.

The next major reform of company law was in 1867, which was part of the Europe-wide pattern of introducing corporate vehicles and reporting in response to the industrial revolution. The 1867 act introduced the *Société Anonyme* (share-issuing company) and with it the profession of auditor (*Commissaire aux Comptes*).

It is a particular feature of the French professional accounting scene that the profession of auditor has historically been separate from that of accountant. Indeed, it is an apposite example of the complexity of France that there are today two quite distinct professional organizations, one for accountants and one for auditors, giving the impression of two separate professions. Nearly all auditors are also members of the accounting body, however.

In fact, diversity of organization has been a feature of the development of the profession, and no dominant professional organization emerged until the Second World War. The first reasonably successful professional body, the *Société de Comptabilité de France* (SCF) was formed in 1881 and embraced everyone involved in accounting activity, classifying members as *teneurs de livres*, *comptables*, and *expert-comptables*, titles that have no exact English equivalent. The term *expert-comptable* has since become established as meaning the top tier of accounting professionals who offer accounting and related tax and legal advice to business.

No private sector professional association managed to establish itself, and it was only in the late 1930s that the government intervened in a number of professions to create regulatory structures. The war intervened, and some work done during the Vichy government subsequently gave rise to a 1945 government order that created the *Ordre des Experts Comptables et des Comptables Agréés*, which is now known as the *Ordre des Experts Comptables* (OEC).

Only members of the OEC are allowed to call themselves *expert comptable* and provide specialist accounting services (OEC pursues a policy of actively protecting this, bringing about a hundred cases a year before the courts against people who offer the same services). Furthermore, only partners in an accounting practice or employees of a practice are eligible to be members. This means that someone leaving a firm to work in industry automatically loses his or her membership in the professional body (which is one reason why international statistical comparisons of the accounting profession are of dubious value). There is a body, the *Association des Directeurs de Comptabilité* (APDC), that brings together senior accounting executives from industry, but this organization has more the characteristics of a pressure group than a professional body. Some also belong to the French chapter of the Institute of Management Accountants. However, the bulk of accountants in commerce and industry have no formal professional representation.

Several different training routes exist, for *experts comptables*, reflecting the diversity of qualifications offered by the public and private educational institutions in France. A student must, though, spend 3 years with a professional firm (a *cabinet*) and take the OEC professional examinations. The final part of the process consists of writing a dissertation on which the candidate is also given an oral examination. Currently about a thousand students a year gain their *diplôme d'expertise comptable*, and there are approximately three thousand students on training contracts with firms.

Accounting firms have seen a rapid expansion in the past 30 years, and there has been a major concentration of activity in the hands of large firms. As elsewhere, market pressures have encouraged the larger national firms to join the major international networks, and only two or three major national firms have so far resisted. However, the importance of accounting services as well as audit means that national firms can be quite large, without necessarily having a large slice of the audit market.

The development of auditing has taken a rather different line, as may be symbolized by the fact that accounting comes within the remit of the Ministry of the Economy, while auditing is under the Ministry of Justice. The statutory auditor, as envisaged by French company law in 1867, was required to make a report to the annual general meeting on the company's situation and on the balance sheet presented by the company's directors. The function, though, could be carried out by anyone.

A major reform took place in 1935. The task of the auditor was extended to one of verifying the books and assets of the company (at any time in the year) and the information given by the directors as well as making the report to shareholders. The appointment of auditor was always for a 3-year period. At the same time the equivalent of the County Courts were given the duty of establishing a list of official auditors, membership of which was achieved by passing a state examination. From this point on, auditors had a strongly regional base, and although they formed professional associations, these associations tended to parallel the regional basis of the courts.

The next major reform in auditing took place in the late 1960s, when the role of auditors was widened (1966) and their fees fixed in relation to the size of clients, and finally a new professional organization, the *Compagnie Nationale des Commissaires aux Comptes* (CNCC) was formed (1969). In particular, they were required from 1966 to make a report giving their opinion on the individual accounts of SAs and SARLs. They were required to certify (or not) the *regularité* of the accounts (conforming with legal requirements) and their *sincerité* (application of accepted valuation methods in good faith). At that time, many auditors feared that their role would become quasi-judicial, being required to assess other people's accounts, but as events turned out, the CNCC has progressively developed the audit function along the lines of Anglo-American practice and issues regular auditing guidelines on much the same basis.

Nonetheless, the role of the auditor has not in the past been exactly the same as in anglophone countries. Checking compliance with the law was the main function, and in particular there was no requirement to think in terms of the quality of economic information for shareholders. What is understood by "sincerity" and "regularity" in the accounts has been open to question. It was felt that the auditor was obliged to give a positive certificate if individually all the transactions were sanctioned by law or conformed with established practice, even if taken altogether the effect might be to give a misleading picture of the company as a whole.

Since 1984, when the EC Fourth Directive was implemented in France, French companies have also been obliged to give a true and fair view of the state of affairs of the company, and this has led to auditors approaching matters differently. One should, however, be wary of assuming that the French auditor now automatically has the same reaction as an Anglo-Saxon auditor. For example, where a company normally charges accelerated depreciation for tax purposes in its individual accounts (see Section 2.2) and in a poor year decides only to charge economic depreciation, this would not be regarded as worthy of mention.

The role of the auditor differs also in that the French auditor has a stutory duty to report to the state prosecutor any breaches of law discovered during the course of the audit and also has a hand in helping to revive failing companies. This latter system, introduced in 1984, requires that auditors, if they think that the company is approaching failure, should so advise the management and insist that a rescue plan be drawn up. The auditor can appeal to the courts to force this action through.

1.3 Accounting, Business, and the State

A popular misconception appears often in the anglophone literature that French accounting is heavily controlled by the state (this is often paralleled by another misconception, that the state does not intervene in accounting in the Anglo-American world). This idea probably derives from misunderstanding a long tradition of centralization in France and one of seeking state endorsement to lend authority. This is compounded by the idea that French enterprise accounting is designed to create inputs for a national accounting system through which the government controls the economy. In fact, the enterprise accounting arrangements predate the national accounting arrangements, and attempts to reconcile the two have largely failed. It should be made clear, however, that INSEE, the state statistical office, does collect and aggregate the financial statements of enterprises, thereby producing useful statistics about industry sectors, margins, and so on, even if they do not fit neatly into the national accounting system used for economic measurement. The major state impact on accounting rather has been through the impact of taxation and the requirement that all expenses claimed for tax purposes should appear in the shareholder accounts.

Insofar as it is acceptable to generalize, the French state, since the Second World War, has taken an interventionist stance with industry, but this has usually been with a view to promoting or protecting industry, providing grants for research and development, accelerated tax allowances for investment, and so on, although also with a view to protecting employment and raising taxes.

In the period between the World Wars, successive French governments took a *laissez-faire* attitude to industry, and the economy was stagnant during that period. Industry was polarized between a small number of quite large concerns and a multitude of small, family-owned businesses. In a reaction to the invasion of France during the Second World War, military failure was blamed on economic weakness, and economic weakness was blamed on the lack of initiative of French industry. It was resolved that after the war the economy would be revitalized, but through the leadership of the state.

France, influenced by Jean Monnet, a prominent political figure who was also influential in the creation of the European Community, started on a succession of 5-year economic plans designed to rebuild the economy in partnership with the private sector, to create an *économie concertée*, where public and private investment worked together. At the same time, the state nationalized a large slice of the economy. It was decided that a uniform accounting system should be installed in the nationalized industries to make management control easier, and such a system would also be compulsory for all bodies receiving grant aid from the state (a draft system had been prepared during the War under the Vichy government but had been abandoned). A commission was established (*Commission de Normalisation de la Comptabilité*, 1946) to prepare the new system. The Commission consisted of civil servants, senior accountants, auditors, business people, lawyers, academics, and others, a grouping typical of the many committees set up under Monnet's influence to deal with particular issues of rebuilding the economy.

This Commission produced in 1947 its *Plan Comptable Général* (PCG), a chart of accounts that provided a system of ledger codes and annual statements that should emerge from the records kept in this way. What then happened was that, over a period of many years, private industry gradually adopted the PCG voluntarily, until the tax authorities (the *Fisc*) adopted it as the basis for tax returns in 1965, after which it was used by practically all enterprises.

There have been many further developments. The Commission changed its name to the *Conseil National de la Comptabilité* (CNC, National Accounting Council). The PCG was revised in 1957, largely to go some way toward meeting the needs of the national accounting system, which had been introduced progressively since 1952. From 1959 the CNC was given the task of preparing industry-specific variants of the basic 1957 plan, and from that time it can be judged as spreading eventually to all French industry.

In fact, a key period of change for French industry occurred in the late 1960s. Company law underwent a major revision in 1966, including the revision of the audit function and the introduction into law of definitions of the form and content of the balance sheet and profit and loss account (albeit without any direct reference to the PCG1957) and more precise details of what other information should be included in annual reports to shareholders.

This was accompanied by reform in the capital markets, including in 1967 the creation of a stock exchange regulatory authority, the *Commission des Opérations de Bourse* (COB), which has since been quite influential in pressing for better accounting and disclosure. At the same time, management attitudes were also changing: the first contested takeover bid was made, and there were the strikes of 1968. The old attitudes of secrecy started to change, and managers began to perceive that it was necessary to inform both workers and shareholders about what was going on.

Since 1945 companies that have more than 50 workers have been obliged to have a *Comité d'Entreprise*, a workers' council. Workers' rights were extended at this time to include receiving management reports.

From 1965 the CNC started to issue guidance on numerous points of interpretation and amplification of the PCG1957, by way of notes or recommendations. At the same time, the OEC also started to issue technical guidance, although neither the CNC interpretations nor the OEC had any statutory force, and there was a low rate of compliance.

Starting in 1968, the COB asked quoted companies to give more information either in prospectuses issued when raising funds or in the annual reports sent to shareholders. Such information concerned primarily further detail of elements of the balance sheet and profit and loss account and was asked for in the form of notes to the accounts.

It was also in the late 1960s and early 1970s that companies themselves began to prepare and publish consolidated accounts on a voluntary basis and using a wide range of accounting policies. An important development from a user perspective was the appearance of "secondary" reports, voluntary disclosures often framed in English and giving consolidated figures that were intended as public relations documents both for the international capital markets and for international business generally.

The COB made it a requirement in 1971 to produce consolidated accounts as part of the prospectus when raising funds, and from 1973 it was required that such accounts be audited.

1.4 European Harmonization

The 1980s were a period of substantial change for French accounting, seeing the introduction of both the Fourth and Seventh Directives. Plans to revise the PCG had been held back by a desire to introduce a new version in line with European Union harmonization initiatives, and the new plan was first exposed in 1979, after final approval of the Fourth Directive by the Council of Ministers. The new plan (PCG1982) was published in its final form in 1982, to be followed by the Accounting Act of April 1983 (Act 83 353 of April 30, 1983) and the Decree of November 29, 1983, providing for implementation of the Fourth European Directive for the accounting year 1984.

Part of the particularity of the system is that the Accounting Act and implementing decree make barely any mention of the PCG1982, although much of the detailed accounting implementation, standard ledger codes, and their relationship with the annual statements, and so on, are contained in the PCG1982. The accounting law and decree introduced into the legal framework the requirements of the Fourth Directive: standard formats for the profit and loss account and balance sheet, explanatory notes to the accounts (*annexe*), and overall an obligation to give a true and fair view (*image fidèle*). An Act of March 1, 1984 extended the audit requirement to all enterprises classified as medium or large and introduced a requirement that the auditor be presented with forecasts, which were not submitted to shareholders but were shown to the Comité d'*Entreprise*. Company law required that managers provide accounts that give a true and fair view— and provided penal sanctions in the event that they failed to do this.

The Seventh Directive was implemented through an Act of January 3, 1985 and a Decree of February 17, 1986, requiring listed companies to produce consolidated accounts from 1986 and unlisted companies to do so from the accounting year 1990. The PCG82 was modified (December 9, 1986) to include rules for consolidated statements.

A number of particularities about the way in which the Directives were implemented in France will be considered in detail below. However, two main points need to be borne in mind. First, the requirements to show all deductions to be claimed for tax purposes remained in force for individual company accounts, but consolidated accounts do not have to be in line with tax regulations, and companies are free to restate the individual figures for inclusion in group accounts.

Second, group accounts do not necessarily have to comply with French generally accepted accounting principles (GAAP). French law sees individual company accounts as playing a long-established role in relation to regulation of dividends, taxation, and disclosure, while consolidated accounts are "just" supplementary information of a more economic nature.

Companies that operate in other markets are free to produce group accounts using the GAAP of the appropriate market (Act of January 3, 1985). In effect this means that where, for example, a French multinational was already producing two sets of accounts, one set of individual accounts complying with tax regulations and submitted formally to shareholders for approval and the other based on U.S. GAAP for international business purposes, the U.S. GAAP accounts could become the official group accounts: no French GAAP group accounts need be prepared. Consequently, a number of French companies (e.g., Peugeot) publish group accounts based on U.S. GAAP, and a number of companies use International Accounting Standards (e.g., Thomson).

This situation has been seen to lead to some abuses and a perceived lack of reliability in French reporting, so the government stepped in during the 1990s to tighten up the rules for consolidated accounts. It is in the process of carrying out reforms, which at the time of writing have not been completed. The structure of the CNC has been modified (1996), and the accounting profession has been given more influence. In particular, the president of the CNC is no longer a government official but rather a former senior partner of an accounting firm who has also been chairman of the Board of the IASC. In addition, the CNC now has a *comité d'urgence*, which provides short-term guidance on emerging issues.

A second phase of reform, expected to be implemented from late 1998, is the creation of a new, supreme, rule-endorsing body, the *Comité de Réglementation Comptable* (CRC). This will be a small committee consisting of the president of the CNC, the OEC, and the CNCC as well as representatives of the ministries of justice, finance and the economy, and business and trade unions. The CRC will not issue standards but will give endorsement with the authority of a ministerial order to standards issued by the CNC and others. This body will in particular regulate the principles used by listed companies in preparing consolidated accounts and is likely to insist that only IASC rules may be followed as an alternative to French rules. However, it is expected that those companies that currently use other principles, such as U.S. GAAP, will be able to do so until the year 2003.

1.5 Business Finance

France has a tradition of an economy with a high proportion of small and medium-sized family businesses, and although this image is changing, notably with the enormous growth of businesses such as Peugeot, Bouygues, and Bic, companies often seek to finance themselves through debt rather than equity funding. It is not, therefore, unusual to see companies that have only bonds quoted on the Bourse. This tendency is further reinforced by nationalized industries that make major borrowings on the public market. The State prefers generally not to inject new share capital as such, and companies such as Electricité de France and the SNCF are frequent and major issuers of bonds.

Further, the State itself is a regular borrower on the capital markets for its own financing needs. It holds a weekly auction of Treasury bonds with the banks, as well as making large public issues from time to time with varying conditions attached, and these government securities are very actively traded. All of this goes to explain why turnover in bonds on the stock exchanges is 10 times that of shares.

Since the beginning of the 1980s, however, the French financial markets have undergone a number of important changes. First, the nationalized industries (whose number increased significantly in 1982 with the nationalizations carried out after the election of President Mitterand in 1981) wished to increase their equity without issuing any new shares, leading to the creation of new equity instruments:

- The *titre participatif* (certificate of participation), which gives a dividend payout that varies with the success of the company, albeit with a minimum dividend, is not repaid except if the issuer wishes to redeem it and carries no voting rights.

- The *certificat d'investissement* (investment certificate) is a straightforward ordinary share except that it does not carry any voting rights.

These are bound up in voting certificates (*certificat de droit de vote*), which are themselves separately quoted on the Bourse.

There are also new financial instruments, such as floating rate bonds, redeemable bonds, renewable bonds, and convertible bonds with various types of warrant attached. A considerable variety of instruments now exist, situated on a spectrum between debt and equity.

A second development is the creation of new markets to deal in new types of financial instruments:

- Share options (*marché d'options négociables de Paris*, or MONEP)
- Financial futures: interest rates, fixed term contracts, options, future rate agreements (*marché à terme des instruments financiers*, or MATIF)
- Index funds: options on the CAC40 index of the 40 top listed shares (part of MONEP)

France has seven provincial stock exchanges (Nantes, Nancy, Lille, Bordeaux, Toulouse, Lyon, and Marseille), as well as the Paris Bourse, but the last is by far the most active and has both a senior market and a junior market. The French financial markets have become the most active in Europe after London.

A particular phenomenon of the late 1980s was the arrival of medium-sized family-owned enterprises on the market, looking either for a quotation on the *Second Marché,* as the junior market was then known, or to be taken over because of the absence of a management successor within the family. There is an active market in such businesses, which, although not obvious, has as much economic significance as the few large public takeover bids that receive substantial press coverage in France and abroad.

The banking sector has undergone a number of changes during the 1980s, with nationalization in 1982, followed by some privatization in 1987, as well as large scale changes in banking regulation in 1984 and 1986. The commercial banking scene is a mixture of retail banks and smaller specialist banks. The retail banks include some that started as mutual banks (e.g., Crédit Agricole, Banque Populaire) and some that have always been commercial (Société Générale, Banque Nationale de Paris, Crédit Lyonnais), though some have been under state control for many years. The private banks, which may, like Indosuez or Paribas, have substantial international connections, often specialize in loans to industry without offering any clearing or similar retail services. The banks are an important source of financing, particularly to small and medium-sized companies, and some have strong regional and industry bases (particularly the mutual organizations). Large companies typically maintain banking ties with a number of different banks at the same time.

Since 1993 successive governments have set about reducing the state's holdings in commercial businesses. In a major privatization program, stakes have been sold in Banque Nationale de Paris, Elf Aquitaine, Rhône Poulenc insurance group UAP, Renault, Usinor, and France Télécom. The privatization program has generated a great deal of interest from private buyers who previously preferred to invest primarily in the bond market, usually through collective investment vehicles such as unit trusts (SICAV). It has, in effect, introduced a number of large companies to the stock exchange, building the overall capitalization and turnover of the equities market.

1.6 State of Play before the Millennium

We have given an idea of the development of accounting in France and in this section will pull together a number of strands and present a sketch of the overall accounting environment as it exists toward the end of the century.

The first point to make is that the law is the paramount authority, and that different sources of law (act of parliament, decree, government order) have different priorities in relation to each other, so not all incorporated entities are necessarily subject to exactly the same legal requirements (for example, banks are theoretically subject to the Accounting Act and Decree but do not have to comply because there are specific laws concerning banks). Equally, there are statutes that apply to accounting, to company management, and to taxation, all of which may have an impact on reporting.

Looking first at legal types of business entity, five legal forms are considered to be "commercial" to which the Commercial Code applies: *Société Anonyme* (SA, a public, share-issuing company), *Société à Responsibilité Limitée* (SARL, normally described as a private company but by contrast with American or British private companies does not issue shares as such; modeled on the German *Gesellschaft mit beschrankter Haftung*, GmbH), *Société en Commandite par actions* (SCA, a sort of limited partnership and not much used now, although this was the earliest form of incorporation to exist in France—Michelin is incorporated in this form), *Société en nom collectif*, and *Société en commandite simple*. There are also corporate forms outside the Commercial Code, the most important being the *Société Civile* (SC, which is in Anglo-Saxon terms a cross between a partnership and a limited company, members' liabilities for the company's obligations are limited only in proportion to the individual member's interest) and the *Etablissement Public à activité Industrielle et Commerciale* (EPIC, a business with profit-making objectives but 100% state control, e.g., Renault, SNCF, EDF).

Government statistics show that at the beginning of 1992 there were the following entities:

Form	Total (in thousands)
Unincorporated	1,674
SARL	631
SA	169
1901 Associations	192
Sociétés Civiles	297
Others	335
	3,298

Source: INSEE, *Annuaire Statistique*, 1993

It should be said that the system for compiling the above figures is thought to be accurate for recording new entities becoming active but suspect in identifying those that have ceased to exist: it probably over-states the number of entities, perhaps by as much as 10%.

Starting in 1983, the following legal instruments affecting accounting were passed:

- Act 83-353 of April 30, 1983 to harmonize the accounting requirements for "commercial" entities and some other corporate bodies with the Fourth Directive
- Decree 83-1020 of November 29, 1983, which set out the details of how the Accounting Act 83-353 should be applied
- Decree 84-184 of March 14, 1984, which recognized the previous instruments as providing accounting definitions that were to be applied in tax law
- Act 84-148 of March 1, 1984, on the prevention and regulation of business difficulties (which extended the accounting obligations to all legal bodies constituted under private law, as opposed to public law, which have a business activity but are not classified as "commercial")
- Decree 85-295 of March 1, 1985, which set out the method of application of Act 84-148

- Act 85-11 of January 3, 1985, to harmonize requirements for consolidated accounts for certain commercial companies and public enterprises with the Seventh Directive
- Decree 86-221 of February 17, 1986, which applied Act 85-11

It is likely that users will most frequently be concerned with the accounts of an SA or SARL, but it is possible that they will meet an SC (frequently used as a vehicle for professional firms and also for property companies) or even an EPIC. Generally, the Fourth Directive accounting requirements and the statutory audit requirement apply to all "commercial" entities (incorporated or not but subject to the different levels of disclosure provided in the Directive) and noncommercial entities that exceed two of three size criteria (balance sheet 10 million francs (Fr), Turnover 20 million francs, Employees 50). They also apply to banks and insurance companies, but these are subject to other specific legislation in addition, which may override some of the more general requirements.

A decree of August 26, 1996 provided for the reorganization of the *Conseil National de la Comptabilité* and the creation of its *Comité d'Urgence*, which provides short-term guidance on issues that are just coming to the surface.

In addition to statutory requirements of one sort or another, the main sources of accounting regulation are the CNC (PCG1982 and guidance notes and recommendations on particular issues), COB (regulations for listed companies), OEC, and CNCC (professional guidance). The accounts preparer in fact has a maze of potential regulations to wade through and assess to determine whether or not the regulations apply to a particular business. This may help make more understandable the notion of a specialist accounting body. At the same time, there are a number of professional guides, notably *Memento Comptable Francis Lefebvre*, which publishes annual GAAP handbooks detailing the regulations and their sources on an issue-by-issue basis. These handbooks are a convenient and useful tool for anyone wanting to look at some point in detail.

In general, accounting harmonization has been taken seriously, and the attitudes behind harmonization of greater disclosure and more reliable information for the capital markets have coincided with changes in the French business environment. In some ways (for example, the extension of reporting requirements beyond the SA and SARL specified by the Fourth Directive) France has gone well beyond the minimum requirements. Nonetheless, the revised requirements have been part of a period of enormous change in the capital markets, and there is still a relatively wide diversity of attitude and, indeed, measurement technique, which may well disappear as accountants become accustomed to the new approaches and a new consensus emerges on various issues.

A particular feature of the French scene is that there is a complex web of legislation or quasi-legislation, but the existence of the regulation does not necessarily mean that companies comply with it. Sometimes there are no penalties for nonobservance, sometimes there is no machinery to police compliance, and sometimes there appears to be a tacit agreement that some regulations will simply be ignored.

For example, the 1983 Accounting Act and Decree specifies in considerable detail what information is to be given in the notes to the accounts. The CNC, however, under pressure from the auditing body, subsequently took the position that all this information needed to be disclosed only if it was material. This position was confirmed by an Order of December 9, 1986 (the main focus of which was consolidated accounts), even though there is no established concept of materiality in French accounting.

Similarly, the statutes require disclosure in the notes of the remuneration of the directors, but the CNCC took the position (Bulletin Trimestriel, December 1986, p. 446) that "information on remuneration is by nature not material" and left it to the individual auditor to decide if the information might be material to the reader in any particular case.

2. The Form and Content of Published Accounts

An analyst approaching a set of French financial statements will need to check thoroughly the basis on which the accounts have been prepared— the first port of call must be the accounting policies because of the choices that are open to preparers. Broadly, an analyst could expect to have available in the annual report of a French group (a) the parent company ("individual") accounts, framed according to the Fourth Directive and the 1983 Accounting Act and Decree, and (b) group accounts, which might have been prepared on one of three bases. These bases are (a) same measurement rules as the individual accounts, therefore including, for instance, tax depreciation; (b) options available within the French GAAP group rules to restate the figures disregarding tax rules; and (c) U.S. GAAP, or those of some other financial market (as noted above, this position is likely to change by 2003 to one where compliance with IASC rules is the only alternative to French rules).

Majority practice is that French groups use version (b), French GAAP without the tax distortion—a recent survey of published accounts,[1] which reviewed the published accounts of 100 listed companies (for fiscal 1992) found that 36 referred to non-French GAAP, of which 19 cited IASC standards, 10 U.S. GAAP, and 5 "international" GAAP.

We will present below two sets of accounts, group accounts based on option (*b*) and individual accounts so that readers have the opportunity to review both. We will deal with the French GAAP measurement rules used in group accounts in the next section but point out where individual accounts diverge significantly from these. We do not believe that it would serve any purpose to review measurement rules based on U.S. GAAP, since users may well be familiar with U.S. GAAP, but in any event there is plenty of literature available on the subject.

2.1 Group Accounts

The accounts used are those of Pernod Ricard, the drinks group, ranked within the top 50 in France. It has operations not only in Western Europe but also in the United States and Australia. Its major non-French companies are Austin Nichols in the United States, Orlando Wyndham in Australia, and Irish Distillers. Its major brands include, apart from Pernod and Ricard, Cinzano, Cognac Bisquit, Jameson Irish Whisky, Bushmills, Wild Turkey Bourbon, and Jacob's Creek wine. Fifty-seven percent of its 1996 turnover was from outside France. The company was notable in 1997 for selling its Orangina (carbonated orange drink) brand to Coca-Cola.

Following our own advice, we will look first at the note on accounting policies, which is reproduced at the end of this chapter. The first statement confirms that the group accounts conform with the group accounting legislation, and although the note does not specify that the accounts are framed in accordance with French GAAP (as opposed to IASC or U.S. standards), this would be the normal assumption.

Looking at specific details, it seems that the company uses 50% ownership of voting shares or "effective control" as the criteria for inclusion of a company as a subsidiary. Joint ventures are accounted for by using proportional consolidation. Foreign currency translation has been done on the net investment basis (balance sheets translated at closing rate, exchange differences taken to reserves), with the average rate used for the income statements.

Taking the intangible asset note with the goodwill note, goodwill arising on consolidation before 1987 has been written off against reserves, while goodwill arising on subsequent acquisitions is being amortized over a period "appropriate to the acquisition but not exceeding forty years." The amortization expense is disclosed as a separate item after tax in the consolidated income statement, which complies with a COB recommendation (October 1988) that goodwill expense be separately disclosed in this way. The intangibles in the balance sheet (excluding goodwill, which is disclosed separately on the balance sheet, and after tangible fixed assets) amount to Fr 2600 million in 1996. According to the note, they consist mostly of trademarks and are held at "original cost" and depreciated only if market value drops below cost. Their value at balance sheet date is "estimated based on future profits which may be generated by the brand in question."

The notes indicate that tangible fixed assets are carried at historical cost or valuation where that is in accordance with legal dispositions. The effect of the latter is likely to be minimal because the last "legal" revaluation in France was in 1976. The note points out that real estate assets held under finance leases have been capitalized. This is a possibility under French group accounting rules but not a requirement as such. The company does not, however, disclose in its notes whether other leased assets have been capitalized, and one must assume not, which seems rather inconsistent. There is no disclosure of what value of real estate is held under finance leases, nor what proportion of the company's debt is in the form of leasing. The only additional information given is the commitment to rental payments (note 13).

The note analyzing the tangible fixed assets (note 6) gives relatively little information, confining itself to a breakdown of gross cost and accumulated depreciation with the previous two years' net figures for comparison (only one year is necessary). There is no reconciliation between opening and closing fixed assets, no detail of acquisitions and disposals, and no indication of the depreciation charge for the year. The income statement presentation approximates to a disclosure of expenses by function, and there is therefore no disclosure of depreciation expense for the year.

The consolidated statements themselves comprise:

1. Income statement
2. Balance sheet
3. Changes in shareholders' equity (voluntary disclosure)

4. Cash flow statement (not required for shareholders; however, many French companies publish it voluntarily: The 1996 survey found that 92% of the sample included a cash flow statement of some kind, with 52% providing one based on the IAS or U.S. format).

The income statement is set out in vertical format, based loosely on the functional approach. The 1983 Accounting Act and Decree allows only a horizontal format and expenses disclosed by nature (personnel, materials, depreciation), but the full Fourth Directive range of vertical or horizontal formats and expenses either by function (cost of sales, marketing, administration) or by nature are available for group accounts. Another particularity is that the interest expense is shown net, although the European Directives, and indeed French custom, do not allow offset of revenues and expenses. There is no note to amplify the interest expense figure. The group's share of the profits of associated companies should normally also be included in this section of the income statement, but instead it appears after deduction of taxes.

There is a legal requirement that any French company (this applies to individual companies, not the group as such) having more than 100 employees should have a profit-sharing scheme for employees, and the deduction for employees' share of profits is usually shown as an appropriation; however, Pernod Ricard (note 15) includes this in employment costs.

In France, gains and losses on disposals of fixed assets are normally treated as being outside the ordinary operating result, regardless of the nature of the disposal. The note on extraordinary items (note 3) confirms that gains on asset sales have been treated in this way, as have provisions for restructuring, legal claims, and asset impairment. The note does not provide an exact analysis of the net extraordinary charge of FF49 million, only remarking that a gain of FF40 million was realized on asset sales and that no individual provision was greater than FF15 million. Here again, the presentation of a net charge in the income statement after offset of revenue and expense runs contrary to European tradition.

The English language balance sheet and income statement include two years' comparative figures (only the previous year is required), as well as an extra column that gives the 1996 figures converted to U.S. dollars. This is a "convenience translation," which simply converts all the French franc numbers to dollars at the average rate for 1996 (income statement) and closing rate (balance sheet) and is intended presumably for the use of those more accustomed to thinking in terms of dollars—it does not imply the use of U.S. GAAP, even though some other French companies do restate to U.S. GAAP and the provision of three years' data and the use of a functional presentation in the income statement might suggest this.

The balance sheet follows broadly the standard PCG82/Fourth Directive format of a horizontal presentation, with assets on the left, set out in reverse order of liquidity. At the same time, goodwill is presented after tangible fixed assets and not with other intangibles, as noted above, and the final asset entries (prepaid expense, currency translation adjustment) are specific to the French adaptation of the Fourth Directive. Prepaid expenses, deferred charges, and accrued income are normally shown in this part of the balance sheet in the hoizontal format specified by the Fourth Directive. The currency translation adjustment is discussed below. These are usually set out in more detail in the parent company accounts. There is a corresponding account in the liabilities and equity side of the balance sheet for deferred credits and accruals.

The Pernod Ricard accounts show the heading "Adjustments liabilities," which might raise a few eyebrows among Anglo-Saxon analysts but presumably indicates accruals and deferred credits. The right-hand side of the balance sheet shows equity before deduction of the final dividend *(avant répartition)*, which is the correct procedure in terms of legal requirements. Many companies also show the situation after attribution of dividend *(après répartition)*, but this is a voluntary disclosure and Pernod Ricard discusses the dividend in its management report, thereby providing the information if an analyst wished to make an adjustment.

Pernod Ricard has translated *provisions pour risques et charges* as "provisions for contingencies" and includes a breakdown between pensions and other contingencies in the notes. The note says that the "other risks" total of FF325 million includes "contingency reserves" of FF115 million for tax, a reserve for disputes with third parties for FF40 million, with the rest being for restructuring and promotional activities. This probably seems a little difficult to understand for an Anglo-American analyst: there is a separate provision for deferred tax of FF57 million, so one wonders what is the nature of the taxation provision shown in provisions for other risks. It is reasonably sure that this represents unpaid current tax liabilities that are in the nature of an accrued expense, but classification of that as a provision is more common in Switzerland than elsewhere. The reference within this general provisions category to "reserves for advertising and promotional expenses" also seems quite curious. Of course, there is the linguistic error of confusing provision (deducted from profits before tax and classified in the balance sheet as a liability) with reserve (an appropriation of profit after tax and classified as equity). Leaving that aside, French practice generally considers that provisions must be triggered by an event that has already taken place at balance sheet date, and it is difficult to see how promotional expenses would fit into this framework.

The information given on debt is minimal—note 12 breaks this down by repayment term, which is all the French requirements call for and gives no indication of the split among leasing, bank loans, and market securities. There is no breakdown at all of short-term liabilities: the balance sheet gives trade and other accounts payable of FF3,968 million and other liabilities FF733 million.

The company also has undated subordinated notes (TSDI, *titres subordinés à durée indeterminée*), a form of hybrid capital instrument that is not clearly debt or equity but which have been classified in the group balance sheet as debt.

The notes provide some information on financial commitments in relation to leasing contracts, bank guarantees, and general purchasing commitments. There is an analysis of the group's forward contracts in foreign currencies and its rate guarantee contracts.

2.1.1 Voluntary Disclosures

The group provides a statement of changes in shareholders'equity, showing the progression over the three years. However, there is no information in the notes or on the face of the balance sheet to give details of how equity is made up—shares in issue, share premium. For more information, one is obliged to look in the parent company accounts.

The consolidated cash flow statement follows broadly the U.S. cash flow statement. This provides an operating cash flow derived by using the indirect method (reported profit with add backs of noncash items), followed by details of investing activities, financing activities, and net change in cash.

Precise details are given of the name and location of all subsidiaries (legal requirement), but segment information is limited in French regulations to turnover by major product and geographic area, in line with the Fourth Directive. The 1996 survey found that 89% of its sample published segment information, but there was wide diversity as to its location, between the management commentary and the notes and summaries of key figures. Similarly, the nature of the information was also highly variable.

Pernod Ricard gives a breakdown that goes through to net profit, split four ways between wines and spirits in France and sold outside France, and nonalcoholic beverages in France and sold outside France. In some ways, this is useful in that it allows a matrix analysis (usually companies provide product breakdown and geographic breakdown separately so that it is not possible to identify sales of one product line in one geographic area), but it is also limited in that it lumps everything outside France into one segment, whereas it is likely that if one applied IAS14 rules, there would be several more geographic segments, including Ireland, the United States, and Australia, in each of which the group has major subsidiaries. The company does, though, identify the main manufacturing locations and trademarks used around the world. No information is given on net assets used, so no computation of comparative return on capital employed is possible.

2.2 Individual Accounts

Whereas there is little of interest in terms of evaluating the group to be found in the individual accounts, in general these statements comply with the Accounting Act and Decree of 1983 and the Fourth Directive and are therefore an illustration of the different presentation used for single companies. The Pernod Ricard parent company accounts are a good example of a classic set of French accounts prepared for the domestic market.

The balance sheet is more detailed than the version used for the consolidated accounts and sticks strictly to the legally required format. It gives an analysis of assets among land, buildings, plant, and other items, with both gross cost and accumulated depreciation shown on the face of the accounts, although the analyst would have to do a little work to reintegrate the information given in note 2 (acquisitions and disposals) with that in note 3 (depreciation). Accumulated depreciation and write-offs are shown for current as well as fixed assets. The *comptes de régularisation* (after current assets) are spelled out in more detail, giving a split among prepayments, deferred expenses, and translation differences.

The equity section is given in much more detail than in the group accounts, and a note gives details of shares in issue and nominal value. The detailed components of equity are explained in Section 3, below, but analysts should note that in the parent company accounts the undated subordinated notes appear in the balance sheet as "other equity" and not as debt.

2.3 Income Statement

The income statement is presented in vertical form (both vertical and horizontal are permitted) but gives expenses by nature (the French have not implemented the option of giving expenses by function for individual accounts, the majority British practice). This contrasts with the new presentation used for the group accounts. The income statement can be broken down, as the Fourth Directive requires, into (*a*) operating income and expense, (*b*) financial income and expense, (*c*) extraordinary items, and (*d*) taxation.

The extraordinary items section represents some difficulties for analysis. Depreciation that is in excess of economic depreciation but that is charged to reduce taxation is expensed here. In addition, French tax law permits the establishment of some special reserves (which are basically tax incentives); they too appear in this section, as do profits and losses on sales of nonfinancial assets, regardless of the nature of the underlying transaction.

A peculiarity of the Pernod Ricard accounts is that only one figure is given for extraordinary income and one for extraordinary expense, with no breakdown. This would make life quite difficult if the analyst were using these accounts rather than the group accounts.

In the balance sheet the company's undated subordinated notes are shown as a separate line item between equity and debt.

In general terms, the Pernod Ricard accounts are typical of what an analyst might expect to find—detailed disclosures in some areas (e.g., financial investments, subsidiary companies, accruals and prepayments) and very little in others (movements on tangible fixed assets, borrowings). It should be pointed out that there are a significant number of companies whose disclosures go well beyond this.

A curiosity of the accounts is that French law requires large listed companies to name two auditors, and recent practice has been to insist that they be two different firms. Pernod Ricard use two smaller firms and one very large one. The main auditors are the firm of Mazars et Guérard—one of the largest national firms, but which does not belong to one of the Anglo-American international networks. This is unusual for a company that has major activities in Anglophone countries, and may be seen as a kind of policy statement.

3. Measurement Policies: Implications for the Analyst

3.1 Group Accounts

The history of group accounting in France has been one of diversity, in the absence of any formal group accounting requirement. Companies preparing group accounts have largely done so on a voluntary basis and have therefore adopted accounting principles that seemed useful to them. The 1986 consolidation requirements specified rules for consolidation but at the same time gave companies the freedom to use rules acceptable in other financial markets. Research evidence so far suggests that the majority of companies that have published group accounts since 1986 are converging on the 1986 rules. Analysts should check the accounting policy notes of any company they are reviewing for clarification on the approach used by the company.

The 1986 rules specify that all companies over which the parent company has exclusive control should be included as subsidiaries. Exclusive control may be determined by (a) direct or indirect majority voting power; (b) direct or indirect voting power of 40% of the votes if no other partner or shareholder holds a higher percentage; or (c) controlling influence as a result of a management or other agreement (provided that the parent has a share of the capital). Subsidiaries whose activities are significantly different from those of the parent may be accounted for by the equity method.

Associates, where the parent has significant influence (normally deemed to occur with a holding of 20% or more) should be accounted for by the equity method. Joint ventures, however, are accounted for by using proportional consolidation. A joint venture is defined as a business run by a limited number of associates in such a way that decisions are taken in common.

Subsidiaries are accounted for on an acquisition basis, and any excess of purchase consideration over book value of the acquired subsidiary should be allocated in the first instance to the individual assets and liabilities acquired. Any unallocated balance is capitalized as goodwill and should be amortized on a regular basis.

Actual practice on the treatment of goodwill is becoming quite uniform. The 1996 survey of the published accounts of 100 listed companies showed that all 95 companies that mentioned goodwill in their accounts had capitalized it. However, while 32 showed goodwill within intangible fixed assets in the balance sheet, 47 showed it in a separate category included between intangible and tangible fixed assets, 6 showed it ahead of intangible assets, and the remaining 10 found even more alternatives within the asset side of the balance sheet.

Of the 90 companies that gave details of amortization, the useful life was:

No. of Companies	Life (years)
8	0–10
42	11–20
40	21–40

In recent years there has emerged a tendency to write off goodwill over the 11–20 year category, and also to allocate a larger amount to specific intangible assets such as trademarks, market share, and brands and treat these as nondepreciable.

3.2 Foreign Currency Translation

Translation of the statements of foreign subsidiaries, since it only arises from group accounting, has not been an issue in France, and many different variants are to be found. The 1986 rules do not specify any particular methodology. Some researchers suggest that majority practice is to use closing rate for translating the balance sheet, with differences taken into equity, and average rate for the income statement. Analysts should check the policy note carefully on this point.

There are, however, detailed rules for the treatment of individual transactions, and these rules give rise to the currency translation adjustments seen in the Pernod Ricard balance sheet. Unsettled monetary assets and liabilities denominated in a foreign currency must be restated to their closing value at each balance sheet date. Where this results in an exchange gain, the gain is posted as a long-term deferred credit (the last part of the liabilities side of the balance sheet in the Fourth Directive horizontal format) and released when the account is settled. Where translation results in an exchange loss, there are four entries to be made: the original account is adjusted and the equal and opposite entry is as a deferred charge in the balance sheet (last section of assets); at the same time a balance sheet provision is created, with a corresponding debit to the income statement (but there are five exceptions to creating a provision in that case). Analysts should adjust the balance sheet by offsetting the deferred charge against provisions.

There are no rules for the conversion of individual sale or purchase transactions and the *Memento Comptable Francis Lefebvre* takes the view that items may be translated at one of the following rates: the rate used as the basis for negotiations, the rate ruling on the day the order was passed, the rate ruling at the time of invoice, or the rate ruling when the invoice was accounted for.

3.3 Capital and Reserves

The definition of equity (*capitaux propres*) includes some elements that would be classified differently in other jurisdictions, and within equity the

PCG82 distinguishes a figure (*situation nette*), which excludes these items. The plan calls for disclosure of equity in the following way:

> Nominal share capital
> Share premium
> Revaluation reserve
> Other reserves:
>> Legal
>> Contractual
>> Regulated capital gains
>> Others
>
> Retained profits
> Profit and loss for the year
> Subtotal = Net position
> Investment grants
> Special tax allowances
> Total = Equity

French limited companies are obliged to have a minimum legal reserve of 10% of their share capital. The contractual reserves are those that may be called for by the company's articles of association or similar voluntary reserves. The revaluation reserve arises because revaluation of assets normally gives rise to a tax liability, but from time to time the government has allowed companies to revalue fixed assets free of tax liability. The last such occasion was in 1976, and so the incidence of this normally should be slight.

There is also the regulated capital gains reserve. This arises from a tax concession: where a company realizes a capital gain by disposing of an asset, it may claim a special tax rate of 18% on the gain, and this is given on the condition that the gain remains in reserves. If the company wishes to distribute the gain, then it becomes liable to full taxation.

A gain of 100 will have suffered tax at 18%, so appearing as a reserve of 82; if distributed the tax rate would move up to $33^1/_3\%$, so giving rise to an additional tax charge of $15^2/_3$ and leaving $66^2/_3$ available for distribution. Analysts could allocate therefore $15^1/_3/82$ to deferred tax and $66^2/_3/82$ as permanent equity.

Government grants appear within equity and are subsequently released to the income statement in line with the depreciation of the asset for which the grant was given. Special tax allowances (*provisions réglementées*) consist largely of accelerated depreciation, but there are also other concessions that provide tax incentives for export activities and similar objectives and are included here. For analytical purposes, it would be reasonable to treat both these items as being part equity and part deferred taxation.

French companies may buy and sell their own shares but only in specific circumstances, such as to give to employees, to reduce the share capital overall, or to steady the market if the company is listed (in which case it may deal in no more than 10% of its shares). When a company owns its own shares they appear in the balance sheet as an asset, compared with the U.S. practice of netting them against equity.

After equity there is a special category in individual company accounts called *autres fonds propres*. This is a French adaptation of the Fourth Directive and was created to allow state-owned companies to raise near-equity funding from the markets without diluting the state's holdings. This is sometimes used for hybrid capital instruments by commercial companies.

3.4 Liabilities and Provisions

French accounting distinguishes among three major classes of provision: (a) provision for depreciation: a nondefinitive diminution of the value of an asset, where the balance sheet credit is offset against the asset (e.g. a provision for doubtful debts); (b) special tax provision: a provision that, in effect, is a special tax allowance and not concerned with the economic valuation of the company (this appears within equity, as described above); and (c) provision for contingencies and expenses (*provisions pour risques et charges*), which are disclosed in a separate component of the liabilities side of the balance sheet, usually split into the two types. The provision for contingencies might include amounts for pending litigation, foreign exchange risk, guarantees, and so on. The provision for expenses would include provisions for deferred expenses, pension obligations, and similar items. It may include items that would be considered as creditors in other jurisdictions, such as the provision for Corporation Tax.

The question of pension obligations is potentially a delicate one for the analyst. Whereas many companies rely first on participation in the state pension scheme and second on special industry schemes, there are often top-up or other arrangements that are not necessarily funded. Companies are permitted to recognize a pension liability in the balance sheet for these items and take an expense, but for the present only disclosure in the notes is required.

As far as liabilities are concerned, different categories of liability (convertible debt, bank overdraft, trade creditors, tax and social security creditors, etc.) are distinguished separately on the face of the accounts, with details in the notes dividing debt into that falling due within 1 year, from 2 to 5 years, and in more than 5 years. Contingent liabilities, such as debt guarantees, are disclosed in the notes.

3.5 Property, Plant, and Equipment

French law permits tangible fixed assets and investments to be held at valuation, but recognition of a gain in value normally involves a liability to capital gains tax (except in the special case of fiscal revaluation discussed above). Consequently, companies do not revalue assets in their individual accounts. Given that companies are freed from this constraint in their consolidated accounts, it may be that in due course revaluation of some assets may become the norm, but so far this is not the case. Where a revaluation takes place, it should give rise to a revaluation reserve as part of equity. Depreciable revalued assets would subsequently be depreciated on the new carrying value.

As previously discussed, the individual accounts show commercial depreciation within the ordinary result and extra tax-driven depreciation in the extraordinary result. For group accounts, only commercial depreciation normally should be charged. Commercial depreciation is usually allocated on a straight line basis over the useful life of the asset but generally without reference to a residual value.

Interest costs incurred during the construction of assets may be capitalized, but this is not widespread practice. The interest is available as an immediate tax deduction regardless of capitalization.

Property companies (*sociétés civiles de placements immobiliers*) are entitled to revalue their property folio, building by building, at each balance sheet date (decree of February 27, 1985). Gains arising are credited to a revaluation reserve as part of equity (and exceptionally do not give rise to a tax liability); losses are provided for with an expense to the income statement.

3.6 Leased Assets

The French consolidation regulations leave the question of capitalization of finance leases to the discretion of the preparer, and analysts should check the notes to the accounts to confirm whether or not such leases have been capitalized. Early evidence suggests that majority practice is to follow IAS17. For individual accounts, assets acquired under a finance lease may be capitalized only where the lease includes a purchase option and the lessee has exercised that option—so effectively finance leases are not capitalized in such accounts. Rental obligations are disclosed in the notes to the accounts, however, so analysts may make some adjustment to capitalize on the basis of an assumed interest rate.

3.7 Oil, Gas, and Other Mineral Resources

There is no special requirement for the disclosure of oil, gas, or other mineral reserves. The regulations for mining companies (which extend to oil companies) allow some concessions in terms of research and development. In general the regular research and development rules apply: pure research must be expensed, but applied research and development may be capitalized and amortized over a maximum of 5 years. However, the costs of successful exploration may be capitalized and amortization deferred until the asset is exploited commercially; the amortization period may be the whole economic life of the asset. Unsuccessful exploration costs must be taken directly to the income statement, however, and companies that have unamortized research and development costs may not pay a dividend unless they have reserves greater than the outstanding asset, or a parent company guarantees the absorption of unamortized research and development in a subsidiary.

Oil companies benefit from a particular tax concession in that they can create tax-free reserves to rebuild their mineral reserves as existing resources are consumed.

3.8 Intangible Assets

Purchased intangibles may be capitalized, and where one company acquires another, any excess of purchase price over book value of the acquired company should in the first instance be attributed to the assets, including intangibles, acquired. The CNC ruling on this specifically mentions allocating purchase cost to such intangibles as brands, trademarks, and even market share. Intangible assets should then be amortized over their useful life. It is not possible to revalue intangibles nor recognize internally developed intangibles.

3.9 Participations

A "participation" in a company, according to French law, starts when the investor holds 10% or more in the investee and has to be listed in the notes to the individual company accounts. Once the holding reaches 20%, the investor is deemed to have significant influence, and the investment should then be accounted for by using either proportional consolidation or the equity method. Proportional consolidation is required where the investment is in a joint venture, which is defined by the 1985 law as where there is joint control, that is, the company is managed jointly by a limited number of associates in such a way that decisions are made by common agreement.

Where a minority holding involves significant influence but is not a joint venture, however, this will be accounted for under the equity method. The notes to the accounts are required to specify whether any participations are accounted for under these methods.

3.10 Inventories

The basic rule for inventory is lower of cost or market value. For individual accounts only FIFO and average cost are allowed, with average cost as majority practice. LIFO can be used for consolidated accounts. Where market value is applied, a provision is expensed and the stock is carried at the written-down value.

For long-term contracts profit may be recognized either on the percentage of completion basis (majority practice) or on final completion of the contract. Analysts should check the disclosure in the accounting policies note.

3.11 Taxation

The basic corporate tax rate in 1997 was 42.15%. As far as individual accounts are concerned, taxable profit is the same as that reported to shareholders, and no deferred taxation provisions arise in the accounts. As indicated above, the *provisions réglementées* included in equity should be split between deferred taxation (say 40%) and equity.

In consolidated accounts the special tax effects should in theory have been adjusted out and appropriate deferred tax provisions created. The

1996 survey takes the view that compliance by large groups is now routine but notes that there has been a substantial move toward the liability method of calculation. The vast majority of its sample (93%) provided for deferred taxation on the liability basis, while the remaining 7% simply did not specify on what basis they had provided for deferred taxation.

3.12 Pensions

As a general rule the main provision for pensions is made through the state pension scheme applying to that industry sector, with both employer and employee making a regular contribution. It is not uncommon, however, for large companies to have supplementary schemes, often with insurance companies. Where these are funded, they will probably be defined contribution schemes, but there is some evidence that many companies have unfunded pension obligations. For the moment, the COB requires listed companies to disclose in a note to the accounts any unfunded liability, with a view to creating a balance sheet provision. Many companies already have some provision in the balance sheet. Self-invested schemes as such are not a feature of French pension accounting.

3.13 Other Matters

A general point that should be made is that analysts who have been trained in an Anglo-Saxon environment are probably accustomed to operating with relatively few regulations, but these are carefully followed. In a code law environment in which there is a proliferation of detailed regulation, noncompliance is quite common, and the relevant question is not so much "Is there a rule?" but "Does anyone observe the rule?"

In French accounting this has always been a relevant point, and it is even more so after a period of some years of rapid change during which different companies, particularly those with wide international interests, have been subject to different pressures. Whereas the regulations have changed a great deal, the people responsible for preparing and auditing accounts are largely the same. Although the current spirit that is abroad is one of moving to international standards by large companies, these standards are applied in a wide variety of ways, and analysts must expect in the short term to find the notes to the accounts occasionally silent on matters that patently should be there.

4. Expected Future Developments

The main expected development is that the practices of accountants will catch up with the legislative developments and a more uniform approach will be used in the preparation of consolidated accounts. The market has been critical of the idiosyncratic way in which consolidated accounts have been prepared in the 1990s, and the Pernod Ricard accounts are a good example of the kind of hybrid reporting that is frequently encountered—clearly showing their roots in traditional French practices but not sticking absolutely to them, and throwing in nods in the direction of U.S. and IASC practice without clearly complying with any one complete set of generally accepted accounting practices.

The government has responded with the creation of its *Comité de Reglementation Comptable* and the statutory status that its endorsement will provide for accounting regulation. The intention is to provide clear authority for specific accounting rules, and as a consequence to reduce the degree of choice that may be exercised by companies in the principles used in consolidated accounts.

In theory this should lead to a situation in which companies are no longer allowed to use U.S. principles but must opt unequivocally for IASC rules or French rules, and then must apply the full range of rules without exception. This would lead to accounts that were consistent and comparable.

We are a long way from that position at the time of writing. The legislation has nearly completed its passage through the parliamentary process, and insiders are predicting that the statute will be in place before the end of 1998. It then remains for the new body to meet, to work out its strategy, and then to start implementation. The more responsive companies may well move to standardize their position in their 1998 accounts, but it is probable that those companies that currently use U.S. GAAP will not move to change their accounting principles until it becomes absolutely necessary, and that those listed in the United States will lobby hard for some relaxation if the SEC has not by then agreed to the use of IASC rules by foreign issuers.

Notes

1. *L'Information financière: 100 groupes industriel et commerciaux,* Cauvin Angleys Saint Pierre, Deloitte Touche Tohmatsu, Ernst & Young, Groupe Chaussumier Conseil, Mazars & Guérard accounts, published by CPC, 1996, Meylan, France.

Useful Addresses

Ordre des Experts Comptables
153 rue de Courcelles
75817 Paris Cedex
Tel 01.44.15.60.00

Compagnie Nationale des Commissaires aux Comptes
8 rue de l'Amiral de Coligny
75001 Paris
Tel: 01.44.77.82.82

Compte de résultat consolidé

En millions de francs	1996	1995	1994	1996 / 1995
Chiffre d'affaires H.D.T.	16 814	15 934	15 832	+5,5%
Achats consommés	(7 513)	(7 263)	(7 095)	+3,4%
Marge brute	**9 301**	**8 671**	**8 737**	**+7,3%**
Frais de commercialisation et de distribution	(4 286)	(3 884)	(3 870)	+10,4%
Frais de production et frais généraux	(3 080)	(2 915)	(3 003)	+5,7%
Résultat opérationnel	**1 935**	**1 872**	**1 864**	**+3,4%**
Résultat financier	(208)	(271)	(252)	-23,2%
Résultat courant	**1 727**	**1 601**	**1 612**	**+7,9%**
Résultat Exceptionnel	(49)	(43)	(66)	+14,0%
Impôts sur les sociétés	(465)	(424)	(373)	+9,7%
Résultat des sociétés mises en équivalence	60	39	43	+53,8%
Résultat net avant amortissement des survaleurs	1 273	1 173	1 216	+8,5%
Amortissement des survaleurs	(51)	(51)	(47)	+0,0%
Résultat net	1 222	1 122	1 169	+8,9%
Droit des Tiers dans le résultat	32	19	22	+68,4%
Droit du Groupe dans le résultat	**1 190**	**1 103**	**1 147**	**+7,9%**
Résultat par action (en francs)				
Résultat courant	30,63	28,40	28,59	+7,9%
Résultat net part du Groupe	21,10	19,56	20,34	+7,9%
Résultat net avant impôt				
Global (en millions de francs)	1 687	1 546	1 542	+9,1%
Par action (en francs)	29,92	27,42	27,35	+9,1%

Consolidated Statement of Income

FF millions	million US$* 1996	1996	1995	1994	1996 / 1995
Net sales excluding taxes and duties	3,284	16,814	15,934	15,832	+5.5%
Cost of goods sold	(1,467)	(7,513)	(7,263)	(7,095)	+3.4%
Gross margin	**1,817**	**9,301**	**8,671**	**8,737**	**+7.3%**
Marketing and distribution costs	(837)	(4,286)	(3,884)	(3,870)	+10.4%
Production costs and overhead	(602)	(3,080)	(2,915)	(3,003)	+5.7%
Operating profit	**378**	**1,935**	**1,872**	**1,864**	**+3.4%**
Net interest expense	(41)	(208)	(271)	(252)	-23.2%
Pretax profit before exceptional items	**337**	**1,727**	**1,601**	**1,612**	**+7.9%**
Exceptional items	(10)	(49)	(43)	(66)	+14.0%
Income taxes	(91)	(465)	(424)	(373)	+9.7%
Interest in earnings of equity companies	12	60	39	43	+53.8%
Net income before amortization of goodwill	**248**	**1,273**	**1,173**	**1,216**	**+8.5%**
Amortization of goodwill	(10)	(51)	(51)	(47)	+0.0%
Net income	**238**	**1,222**	**1,122**	**1,169**	**+8.9%**
Minority interests	6	32	19	22	+68.4%
Net income after minority interests	**232**	**1,190**	**1,103**	**1,147**	**+7.9%**

Earnings per share (FF and US$)

Pretax profit	5.98	30.63	28.40	28.59	+7.9%
Net earnings, adjusted	4.11	21.10	19.56	20.34	+7.9%

Net pre-tax earnings

Total	329	1,687	1,546	1,542	+9.1%
Per share (in FF and US$)	5.83	29.92	27.42	27.35	+9.1%

* Average 1996 Exchange rate: US$ 1 = FF 5.12.

Bilan consolidé

Actif

En millions de francs	31/12/1996 Valeur brute	31/12/1996 Amortissements et Provisions	31/12/1996 Valeur nette	31/12/1995 Valeur nette	31/12/1994 Valeur nette
Actif immobilisé					
Immobilisations Incorporelles	2 983	(383)	2 600	2 500	2 219
Immobilisations Corporelles	7 171	(3 704)	3 467	3 214	3 220
Survaleurs	1 891	(505)	1 386	1 295	1 319
Immobilisations Financières	2 103	(60)	2 043	1 840	2 028
Total de l'actif immobilisé	**14 148**	**(4 652)**	**9 496**	**8 849**	**8 786**
Actif circulant					
Stocks	5 179	(59)	5 120	4 499	4 559
Créances d'exploitation	4 889	(230)	4 659	4 215	4 106
Valeurs mobilières de placement	739	(29)	710	482	506
Disponibilités	1 064		1 064	752	1 133
Total de l'actif circulant	**11 871**	**(318)**	**11 553**	**9 948**	**10 304**
Comptes de régularisation Actif	**193**	**(11)**	**182**	**158**	**147**
Ecart de conversion Actif	**6**		**6**	**17**	**38**
Total actif	**26 218**	**(4 981)**	**21 237**	**18 972**	**19 275**

Consolidated Balance Sheet

Assets

FF millions	US$ 1996* Net value	12/31/1996 Gross	12/31/1996 Amortization and provisions	12/31/1996 Net value	12/31/1995 Net value	12/31/1994 Net value
Fixed assets						
Intangible assets	496	2,983	(383)	2,600	2,500	2,219
Property, plant and equipment	662	7,171	(3,704)	3,467	3,214	3,220
Goodwill	264	1,891	(505)	1,386	1,295	1,319
Investments	390	2,103	(60)	2,043	1,840	2,028
Total fixed assets	**1,812**	**14,148**	**(4,652)**	**9,496**	**8,849**	**8,786**
Current assets						
Inventories	977	5,179	(59)	5,120	4,499	4,559
Current receivables	889	4,889	(230)	4,659	4,215	4,106
Marketable securities	136	739	(29)	710	482	506
Cash	203	1,064	-	1,064	752	1,133
Total current assets	**2,205**	**11,871**	**(318)**	**11,553**	**9,948**	**10,304**
Prepaid expenses	**35**	**193**	**(11)**	**182**	**158**	**147**
Currency translation adjustment	**1**	**6**	**-**	**6**	**17**	**38**
Total assets	**4,053**	**26,218**	**(4,981)**	**21,237**	**18,972**	**19,275**

* Exchange rate at December 31, 1996 : US$ 1 = FF 5.24.

Passif

En millions de francs	31/12/1996	31/12/1995	31/12/1994
Capitaux propres Groupe	**10 476**	**9 278**	**8 994**
dont Résultat Net part Groupe	1 190	1 103	1 147
Intérêts minoritaires	**332**	**325**	**341**
dont Résultat Tiers	32	19	22
Provisions pour Risques & Charges	462	436	511
Impôt différé passif	57	68	77
Dettes			
Dettes financières	5 098	4 537	5 053
Emballages consignés	86	102	95
Dettes d'exploitation	3 968	3 584	3 515
Dettes diverses	733	618	684
Total des dettes	**9 885**	**8 841**	**9 347**
Comptes de régularisation Passif	**25**	**24**	**4**
Total passif	**21 237**	**18 972**	**19 275**

Capital and liabilities

FF millions	US$ 1996*	12/31/1996	12/31/1995	12/31/1994
Shareholders' Equity	**1,999**	**10,476**	**9,278**	**8,994**
including Group share Net Income	232	1,190	1,103	1,147
Minority Interest	**63**	**332**	**325**	**341**
including Third Party Income	6	32	19	22
Provisions for contingencies	88	462	436	511
Deferred income taxes	11	57	68	77
Liabilities				
Long-term debt	973	5,098	4,537	5,053
Returnable containers	16	86	102	95
Trade and other accounts payable	758	3,968	3,584	3,515
Other liabilities	140	733	618	684
Total Liabilities	**1,887**	**9,885**	**8,841**	**9,347**
Adjustments Liabilities	**5**	**25**	**24**	**4**
Total Capital and Liabilities	**4,053**	**21,237**	**18,972**	**19,275**

* Exchange rate at December 31, 1996: US$ 1 = FF 5.24.

Tableau de variation
des capitaux propres du Groupe

En millions de francs	Capitaux propres du Groupe
AU 31 DÉCEMBRE 1993	**8 418**
Dividendes payés aux actionnaires	(417)
Variation des réserves	55
Variation de l'écart de conversion	(209)
Résultat net consolidé 1994 - part du groupe	1 147
AU 31 DÉCEMBRE 1994	**8 994**
Dividendes payés aux actionnaires	(443)
Variation des réserves	(20)
Variation de l'écart de conversion	(356)
Résultat net consolidé 1995 - part du groupe	1 103
AU 31 DÉCEMBRE 1995	**9 278**
Dividendes payés aux actionnaires	(444)
Variation de l'écart de conversion	452
Résultat net consolidé 1996 - part du groupe	1 190
AU 31 DÉCEMBRE 1996	**10 476**

Consolidated statement
of changes in shareholders' equity

FF millions	Group shareholders' equity
SHAREHOLDERS' EQUITY AT DECEMBER 31, 1993	**8,418**
Dividends paid	(417)
Net change in reserves	55
Change in currency translation adjustment	(209)
Consolidated net income after minority interests for 1994	1,147
SHAREHOLDERS' EQUITY AT DECEMBER 31, 1994	**8,994**
Dividends paid	(443)
Net change in reserves	(20)
Change in currency translation adjustment	(356)
Consolidated net income after minority interests for 1995	1,103
SHAREHOLDERS' EQUITY AT DECEMBER 31, 1995	**9,278**
Dividends paid	(444)
Change in currency translation adjustment	452
Consolidated net income after minority interests for 1996	1,190
SHAREHOLDERS' EQUITY AT DECEMBER 31, 1996	**10,476**

Tableau de financement consolidé

En millions de francs	1996	1995	1994
Résultat net consolidé part du Groupe	1 190	1 103	1 147
Résultat net consolidé part des minoritaires	32	19	22
Résultat des sociétés mises en équivalence (net des dividendes reçus)	(45)	(11)	(41)
Dotation aux amortissements sur immobilisations	406	417	405
Dotation aux amortissements des survaleurs	51	51	47
Variation des provisions et de l'impôt différé	21	(84)	150
Plus-value sur cession d'immobilisations et autres éléments	(42)	(54)	(127)
Capacité d'autofinancement	**1 613**	**1 441**	**1 603**
Diminution (augmentation) du besoin en fonds de roulement	(209)	(320)	(423)
Variation de la trésorerie issue des opérations d'exploitation	**1 404**	**1 121**	**1 180**
Acquisition d'immobilisations non financières (nette des cessions)	(440)	(548)	(404)
Acquisition d'immobilisations financières (nette des cessions)	(154)	(68)	(25)
Incidence des variations du périmètre de consolidation	(159)	(29)	(236)
Variation des créances et des dettes sur immobilisations	7	(36)	76
Variation de la trésorerie issue des opérations d'investissement	**(747)**	**(681)**	**(589)**
Augmentation de capital	-	-	-
Augmentation (diminution) des emprunts et dettes financières	(29)	26	(168)
Dividendes versés	(459)	(449)	(424)
Variation de la trésorerie issue des opérations de financement	**(488)**	**(423)**	**(592)**
Incidence des écarts de conversion	(24)	26	34
Variation nette de la trésorerie	**145**	**43**	**33**
Trésorerie à l'ouverture de l'exercice	(726)	(769)	(802)
Trésorerie à la clôture de l'exercice	(581)	(726)	(769)

Consolidated Cash-Flow Statement

FF millions	1996	1995	1994
Consolidated net income after minority interests	1,190	1,103	1,147
Minority interests	32	19	22
Interest in earnings of equity companies (net of dividends)	(45)	(11)	(41)
Depreciation of fixed assets	406	417	405
Amortization of goodwill	51	51	47
Change in provisions and deferred taxes	21	(84)	150
Gains on disposals of fixed assets (net of taxes)	(42)	(54)	(127)
Cash flow	**1,613**	**1,441**	**1,603**
Change in working capital need	(209)	(320)	(423)
Cash provided by operating activities	**1,404**	**1,121**	**1,180**
Acquisition of property, plant and equipment (net of disposals)	(440)	(548)	(404)
Acquisition of investments (net of disposals)	(154)	(68)	(25)
Effect of change in scope of consolidation	(159)	(29)	(236)
Net change in long-term liabilities	7	(36)	76
Cash used in investment activities	**(747)**	**(681)**	**(589)**
Increase in capital			
Increase (decrease) in borrowings and long-term debt	(29)	26	(168)
Dividends paid	(459)	(449)	(424)
Cash used in financing activities	**(488)**	**(423)**	**(592)**
Currency translation adjustment	(24)	26	34
Increase in cash	**145**	**43**	**33**
Cash position, beginning of year	(726)	(769)	(802)
Cash position, end of year	(581)	(726)	(769)

ANNEXE
Aux comptes consolidés

NOTE 1 - PRINCIPES ET MÉTHODES COMPTABLES

1.1. Principes de consolidation

Les comptes consolidés du Groupe ont été établis conformément aux dispositions de la Loi n° 85-11 du 3 janvier 1985 et du décret d'application n° 86-221 du 17 février 1986.

Les états financiers consolidés regroupent, par intégration globale, les filiales d'importance significative dans lesquelles le Groupe PERNOD RICARD contrôle, directement ou indirectement, plus de 50 % du capital ou exerce un contrôle de fait.

Les sociétés dans lesquelles le Groupe exerce une influence notable sont mises en équivalence.

Toutes les transactions d'importance significative entre les sociétés intégrées ainsi que les résultats internes au Groupe sont éliminés.

La liste des sociétés consolidées figure à la note 17. Par mesure de simplification ou en raison du préjudice grave qui pourrait en résulter, seuls les noms et coordonnées des principales sociétés faisant partie du périmètre de consolidation y sont indiqués.

1.2. Méthodes de conversion

La conversion des comptes établis en devises étrangères est effectuée selon les principes suivants :

• les comptes de bilan sont convertis en utilisant les cours officiels de change à la fin de l'exercice ;

• les comptes de résultat sont convertis en utilisant pour chaque devise le cours moyen de l'exercice ;

• l'écart de conversion, résultant d'une part de l'impact de la variation du taux de change entre le 31 décembre 1995 et le 31 décembre 1996 sur les capitaux propres d'ouverture et, d'autre part, de l'utilisation de taux différents pour le compte de résultat et le bilan, est inclus dans les réserves consolidées.

Les transactions réalisées en devises étrangères sont converties au cours des devises à la date des transactions. Les pertes et profits, résultant de la conversion des soldes concernés aux cours du 31 décembre 1996, sont portés au compte de résultat.

1.3. Immobilisations incorporelles

Les immobilisations incorporelles sont évaluées à leur coût d'entrée. Elles sont dépréciées lorsque leur valeur d'inventaire devient inférieure à leur valeur brute.

En application de la Loi du 3 janvier 1985, les fonds de commerce dégagés à l'occasion de fusions anté-

rieures à l'exercice 1987, ont été amortis en 1987 par imputation de leur valeur nette sur les capitaux propres.

1.4. Immobilisations corporelles

Les immobilisations corporelles sont évaluées à leur coût d'acquisition ou, s'il y a lieu, à une valeur réévaluée en application des dispositions légales.

L'amortissement est calculé selon le mode linéaire ou, le cas échéant, dégressif, appliqué à la durée d'utilisation estimée.

Les durées moyennes d'amortissement retenues pour les principaux types d'immobilisations sont les suivantes :

Constructions	15 à 50 ans
Installations, matériel et outillage	5 à 15 ans
Autres immobilisations	3 à 5 ans

Les biens immobiliers d'un montant significatif qui sont acquis au moyen d'un contrat de crédit-bail sont capitalisés et amortis selon la durée de vie économique du bien.

Les immeubles ayant fait l'objet de cession-bail font l'objet d'un retraitement similaire. La plus-value dégagée lors de ces opérations est éliminée des résultats de l'exercice de cession.

Les emballages consignés sont évalués au prix de revient. Sur la base des statistiques de chaque entreprise, un retraitement est effectué pour, d'une part, ajuster la valeur d'actif des emballages en fonction des pertes découlant de la casse, d'autre part, comptabiliser le profit éventuel résultant de la freinte en clientèle. Lors de tout changement des taux de consignation, la dette correspondant aux emballages en clientèle est évaluée aux nouveaux taux et la perte éventuelle constatée en résultat.

L'obsolescence est prise en compte par voie d'amortissement.

1.5. Immobilisations financières

Les titres de participation non consolidés sont évalués à leur coût d'acquisition. S'il y a lieu, une provision pour dépréciation est constituée lorsque la valeur d'inventaire est inférieure à la valeur brute.

Cette valeur d'inventaire est égale à la valeur actuelle, qui, d'une façon générale peut être estimée à partir du cours de bourse, ou correspondre à la quote-part des capitaux propres de la société que ces titres représentent.

to the Consolidated Financial Statements

NOTE 1 - ACCOUNTING PRINCIPLES

1.1. Principles of consolidation

The Group's consolidated financial statements have been prepared in compliance with French legal requirements as set forth in Law No. 85-11 of January 3, 1985 and the related Application Decree No. 86-221 of February 17, 1986.

The financial statements of significant subsidiaries which are over 50%-owned or effectively controlled are included in the consolidated financial statements.

Companies over which the Group exercises joint control with another partner are consolidated using the proportional method.

All intercompany and intra-Group transactions have been eliminated.

A list of the consolidated companies is provided in Note 17. For purposes of simplification and to avoid any serious prejudice to the Group, only the names and addresses of the main companies included in the scope of consolidation are listed.

1.2. Foreign currency translation

Financial statements prepared in foreign currencies have been translated according to the following principles:

• Balance sheets have been translated at official year-end rates.

• Statements of income have been translated using the average yearly rate for each currency.

• Differences in currency translation resulting from the effect of fluctuations in the year-end to year-end exchange rate on opening shareholders' equity and from the use of different rates in translating the balance sheet and the statement of income have been included in consolidated reserves.

Foreign currency transactions are translated at the exchange rate prevailing at the transaction date. Gains and losses resulting from foreign currency translation up until December 31, 1996 are recorded in the statement of income.

1.3. Intangible assets

Intangible assets are valued at original cost; they are amortized when their market value falls below cost.

In compliance with the Law of January 3, 1985 concerning French companies' consolidated financial statements, goodwill arising from mergers prior to 1987 was fully amortized that year by a direct charge to shareholders' equity.

1.4. Property, plant and equipment

Property, plant and equipment are valued at cost or when applicable, at a revalued cost in compliance with legal requirements.

Depreciation is calculated according to the straight-line method or, when applicable, according to the declining-balance method over the estimated useful life of the underlying asset.

Average periods of depreciation for these assets are as follows:

Buildings	15 to 50 years
Machinery and equipment	5 to 15 years
Other fixed assets	3 to 5 years

Real estate of significant value which is acquired through leasing contracts is capitalized and depreciated over the estimated useful life of the asset.

Buildings under sale and leaseback agreements are subject to a similar restatement. Any resulting capital gains are eliminated from the year's income.

Returnable containers are valued at cost. Based on statistics provided by each company, this item is restated to adjust the asset value of the containers to reflect losses from breakages and to recognize unrealized income from non-returns. In the case of changes in deposit rates, the debt corresponding to non-returned containers is valued at the new rates, with possible losses charged to expenses.

Obsolescence is reflected in the depreciation calculations.

1.5. Investments

Equity investments in non-consolidated companies are valued at acquisition cost. A provision for depreciation is made if the market value falls below cost.

1.6. Écarts d'acquisition

Depuis le 1er janvier 1986, les écarts d'évaluation sont affectés aux actifs et en particulier aux marques s'il y a lieu.

L'écart d'acquisition (survaleur) est amorti selon le mode linéaire sur une durée n'excédant pas 40 ans et appropriée à la nature de l'acquisition effectuée. Pour les investissements stratégiques et notamment les acquisitions d'IRISH DISTILLERS Group et d'ORLANDO WYNDHAM, les écarts d'acquisition sont amortis sur une durée de 40 ans. Ceux-ci représentent environ 70 % du montant net des survaleurs au 31 décembre 1996.

Les écarts d'acquisition font l'objet d'une analyse à chaque arrêté en fonction de l'évolution de la filiale et peuvent, le cas échéant, faire l'objet d'une dépréciation.

1.7. Stocks

Les stocks sont évalués au prix de revient ou au prix de marché, si ce dernier est inférieur. Une provision pour dépréciation est constituée lorsque la valeur d'inventaire est inférieure à la valeur nette comptable.

La majeure partie des stocks est évaluée selon la méthode des coûts moyens pondérés.

Le prix de revient des stocks à cycle long est calculé, de façon uniforme, en incluant les coûts de distillation et de vieillissement hors frais financiers ; ces stocks sont classés en actif circulant selon les usages de la profession, bien qu'une part substantielle de ceux-ci ne soit destinée à la vente qu'après un délai de stockage supérieur à 1 an.

1.8. Valeurs mobilières de placement

Les valeurs mobilières de placement sont inscrites au bilan, pour leur valeur d'origine. Lorsque la valeur de marché de ces titres à la clôture de l'exercice est inférieure à leur valeur d'origine, une provision pour dépréciation est constituée.

1.9. Emprunts en livres irlandaises

Les effets de la variation du cours de change sur les remboursements à l'échéance des emprunts en livres irlandaises, contractés pour l'acquisition du Groupe IRISH DISTILLERS, ont été éliminés par la constitution d'un dépôt, dans la même devise, d'un montant identique à celui de la dette.

1.10. Provisions pour risques et charges

Le poste enregistre l'ensemble des provisions pour risques et charges comptabilisées par les sociétés du Groupe, et en particulier la provision pour indemnités de départ à la retraite hors charges sociales.

Les sociétés étrangères du Groupe provisionnent dans leurs comptes les engagements de retraite en fonction des dispositions nationales en vigueur. Les sociétés françaises du Groupe enregistrent dans leurs comptes les indemnités de départ à la retraite acquises à la clôture de l'exercice pour l'ensemble des personnes ayant 45 ans et plus et dont l'ancienneté est supérieure à 10 ans.

1.11. Impôt sur les bénéfices

Depuis le 1er janvier 1977, le Groupe PERNOD RICARD bénéficie du régime de l'intégration fiscale pour les sociétés françaises détenues à plus de 95 %.

Les écarts temporaires entre résultat fiscal et résultat comptable donnent lieu à la comptabilisation des impôts différés actifs ou passifs qui en résultent selon la méthode du report variable ; il s'agit principalement des décalages temporaires, des annulations de provisions réglementées et des retraitements de consolidation.

Les impôts différés actifs au titre de déficits fiscaux et moins-values à long terme n'ont été enregistrés que dans la mesure où la probabilité de leur imputation à court terme sur des bénéfices fiscaux futurs est élevée.

Le poste Impôt Différé Passif enregistre la charge latente nette d'impôt tant à long terme qu'à court terme.

Les impôts différés en France ont été réévalués pour tenir compte de la contribution supplémentaire de 10 % en fonction de leur échéance. Une réévaluation de l'ensemble des impôts différés en France aurait généré un impôt différé passif net supplémentaire de 2 MF.

1.12. Gestion des risques financiers et comptabilisation des instruments de couverture du risque de taux d'intérêt

En 1996, la politique de gestion des risques financiers s'est poursuivie en respect des règles de prudence antérieures : le Groupe PERNOD RICARD s'est attaché à couvrir ses expositions de taux, de change et de liquidités par des positions fermes fondées sur la stricte anticipation de son activité. En particulier, la pratique d'une gestion centralisée du risque de change et la réalisation d'une compensation multilatérale des flux inter-compagnies (netting) ont eu pour effet de réduire de façon significative l'exposition au risque de change.

La comptabilisation des résultats liés aux contrats de garantie de taux souscrits sont rapportés les résultats du Groupe PERNOD RICARD prorata temporis tout au long de la durée de vie de ces opérations :

• les primes payées sont étalées comptablement sur la durée de vie du contrat ;

This inventory value is equal to the current value, which can generally be estimated based on the market price, or which may correspond to the company's portion of shareholders' equity represented by these securities.

1.6. Goodwill

Since January 1, 1986, goodwill on acquisition has been reflected in assets and assigned by brand name if appropriate.

Goodwill is amortized on a straight-line basis over a period appropriate to the acquisition but not exceeding 40 years. Regarding strategic investments, notably the acquisitions of IRISH DISTILLERS Group and ORLANDO WYNDHAM, goodwill on acquisition is amortized over a 40year period and represents about 70% of the net amount of the goodwill at december 31, 1996.

At the end of every accounting period, the acquisition variances are analyzed in terms of the development of the company and may be depreciated if necessary.

1.7. Inventories

Inventories are valued at the lower of cost or market value, mainly using average weighted costs. A depreciation reserve is set up when the inventory value is less than the net book value.

The cost of long-term inventories is uniformly determined to include distilling and aging costs but excludes interest expense. These inventories are classified in current assets according to prevailing business practices, although a large part remains in inventory for over one year before being sold.

1.8. Investment securities

Investment securities are recorded on the balance sheet at their original value. When the market value of these securities at the close of the fiscal period is less than their original value, a depreciation reserve is set up.

1.9. Borrowings denominated in Irish Pounds

The effects of variations in exchange rates on repayments on the maturity dates of borrowings in Irish pounds contracted for the acquisition of the Irish Distillers Group have been eliminated by the constitution of a deposit in the same currency and of an amount identical to that of the debt.

1.10. Provisions for contingencies

This item records all provisions for contingencies made by Group companies, notably provisions for retirement benefits, excluding related social charges.

The Group's foreign companies provide for their retirement-related commitments in compliance with local practice and legislation. The Group's French companies record retirement benefits accrued at year-end for those employees 45 years of age and older, and who have been employed by the company for more than ten years.

1.11. Income taxes

Since January 1, 1977, Groupe PERNOD RICARD's tax liability has been determined according to the regulations governing tax consolidation of French companies more than 95% owned.

Deferred tax credits or liabilities resulting from timing differences between taxable income and accounting income are accounted for by the accrual method. These concern primarily timing differences, cancellations of regulated provisions and restatements on consolidation. Deferred income taxes as tax liabilities and long-term capital losses have been recorded only if there is a high probability of charging them in the short term to tax credits. The resulting long-term and short-term tax liability is recorded as deferred income taxes.

Deferred taxes in France have been revalued to reflect the additional 10% contribution based on the due date.

A reassessment of all deferred taxes in France would have generated an additional net deferred tax liability of FF 2 million.

1.12. Management of financial risks and interest rate hedging instruments

In 1996, the policy of managing financial risks continued to respect the previously introduced rules of prudence. The PERNOD RICARD Group has deemed it essential to hedge its exposure to risks of interest rates, exchange rates and liquidity strictly based on its own anticipated operations. In particular, the practice of centralized management of exchange rate risks and the realization of multilateral clearing of intercompany flows (netting) has had the effect of significantly reducing the Company's exposure to exchange rate risks.

Income and expenses relating to contractual guarantees entered into are recorded in the PERNOD RICARD Group income statement on a prorata basis over the life of the contract:

•les différentiels d'intérêts perçus ou payés périodiquement, sont comptabilisés dans l'exercice de référence .

NOTE 2 - PÉRIMÈTRE DE CONSOLIDATION

Le seul changement notable dans le périmètre de consolidation est l'intégration globale de la Société NIHCO (société de distribution de vin et spiritueux au Canada).

NOTE 3 - CHARGES ET PRODUITS EXCEPTIONNELS NETS

En millions de Francs	1996	1995	1994
Charges et produits exceptionnels nets	(49)	(43)	(66)

En 1994, le Groupe a enregistré diverses plus-values sur cessions d'actifs, notamment de la marque Tullamore Dew et d'une partie de la participation qu'il détient dans la Compagnie de Suez, compensées par d'importantes provisions pour charges de restructuration en France et à l'étranger ayant pour objectif une rationalisation industrielle et des gains de productivité administrative.

En 1995 et 1996, les opérations de rationalisation ont généré un certain nombre de plus-values sur des cessions de titres et d'actifs pour un montant de l'ordre de 40 MF. Ces produits n'ont pu compenser diverses charges exceptionnelles (provisions sur divers éléments d'actifs immobilisés, litiges, coût de rationalisation, etc...) dont aucune n'excède 15 MF individuellement.

NOTE 4 - AMORTISSEMENTS DE SURVALEURS

En millions de Francs	1996	1995	1994
Amortissements de survaleurs	(51)	(51)	(47)

NOTE 5 - IMMOBILISATIONS INCORPORELLES

Les immobilisations incorporelles qui figurent à l'actif du bilan en fin d'exercice sont principalement constituées de marques.

La valeur des marques acquises est déterminée en fonction du secteur d'activité de la société et de l'importance de leur diffusion internationale.

La valeur d'inventaire est estimée à partir des profits futurs que peut générer la marque concernée.

NOTE 6 - IMMOBILISATIONS CORPORELLES

En millions de Francs	1996 Valeur brute	Amort. provisions	Valeur nette	1995 Valeur nette	1994 Valeur nette
Terrains	368	(12)	356	363	382
Constructions	2 375	(1 026)	1 349	1 260	1 301
Installations techniques, matériel et outillage	3 197	(2 014)	1 183	1 050	1 063
Autres immobilisations corporelles	1 092	(652)	440	422	388
Immobilisations corporelles en cours	136	-	136	118	77
Avances et acomptes	3	-	3	1	9
Total	**7 171**	**(3 704)**	**3 467**	**3 214**	**3 220**

Les investissements industriels annuels sont stables, autour de 520 millions de francs, avec la répartition suivante par secteur d'activité en 1996 :

Vins et spiritueux France	14 %
Vins et spiritueux Etranger	35 %
Boissons et produits sans alcool France	19 %
Boissons et produits sans alcool Etranger	32 %

NOTE 7 - IMMOBILISATIONS FINANCIÈRES

En millions de Francs	1996 Valeur brute	Provisions	Valeur nette	1995 Valeur nette	1994 Valeur nette
Titres mis en équivalence	282	-	282	231	190
Autres titres de participations	1 564	(53)	1 511	1 380	1 371
Créances sur participations	124	(3)	121	105	407
Autres	133	(4)	129	124	60
Total	**2 103**	**(60)**	**2 043**	**1 840**	**2 028**

Les titres mis en équivalence représentent les sociétés suivantes : Heublein do Brazil, L'Igloo, Beijing Pernod Ricard Winery, Dragon Seal, Simeon Wines, Eight to Twelve.

Les autres titres de participation comprennent les titres Société Générale (2,06 % du capital), Financière Saresco (35 % du capital) et Compagnie de Suez (0,51 % du capital).

Les titres Société Générale et Compagnie de Suez sont valorisés au coût historique.

NOTE 8 - VARIATIONS DE RÉSERVES

Les variations de réserves constatées en 1995 correspondent principalement aux subventions d'investissement reclassées en compte de régularisation passif.

• Premiums paid are spread, for accounting purposes, over the duration of the contract.

• Interest rate differentials received or paid from time to time are accounted for in the year earned or incurred.

NOTE 2 - SCOPE OF CONSOLIDATION

The only notable change in the scope of consolidation is the global integration of the NIHCO Company (a wine and spirits distribution company in Canada).

NOTE 3 - NET EXTRAORDINARY ITEMS

FF millions	1996	1995	1994
Net extraordinary charges and income	(49)	(43)	(66)

In 1994, the Group recognized various capital gains realized on the divestment of assets, particularly of the Tullamore Dew brand and a portion of the interest it holds in the Compagnie de Suez, which were more than offset by substantial provisions for restructuring charges in France and abroad for purposes of industrial streamlining and administrative productivity gains.

In 1995 and 1996, streamlining operations generated a certain amount of capital gains on the sale of securities and assets for a total of approximately FF 40 million. These earnings were not sufficient to offset various exceptional expenses (reserves for various fixed assets, legal disputes, streamlining costs, etc.), none of which individually exceeds FF 15 million.

NOTE 4 - AMORTIZATION OF GOODWILL

FF millions	1996	1995	1994
Amortization of goodwill	(51)	(51)	(47)

NOTE 5 - INTANGIBLE ASSETS

The intangible assets recorded at year-end mainly consist of trademarks.

The value of acquired trademarks is determined according to the Company's sector of activity and the importance of their international distribution.

The inventory value is estimated based on future profits which may be generated by the brand in question.

NOTE 6 - PROPERTY, PLANT AND EQUIPMENT

FF millions	Gross value	1996 Depreciations and provisions	Net value	1995 Net value	1994 Net value
Land	368	(12)	356	363	382
Buildings	2,375	(1,026)	1,349	1,260	1,301
Machinery and, equipment	3,197	(2,014)	1,183	1,050	1,063
Other	1,092	(652)	440	422	388
Work in progress	136	-	136	118	77
Advances	3	-	3	1	9
Total	**7,171**	**(3,704)**	**3,467**	**3,214**	**3,220**

Annual industrial investments are stable, totaling approximately FF 520 million, with following breakdown by activity sector in 1996:

Wines and spirits, France	14 %
Wines and spirits abroad	35 %
Nonalcoholic beverages and products, France	19 %
Nonalcoholic beverages and products abroad	32%

NOTE 7 - INVESTMENTS

FF millions	Gross value	1996 Provisions	Net value	1995 Net value	1994 Net value
Shareholdings accounted for by the equity method	282	-	282	231	190
Other equity investments	1,564	(53)	1,511	1,380	1,371
Receivables on investments	124	(3)	121	105	407
Other	133	(4)	129	124	60
Total	**2,103**	**(60)**	**2,043**	**1,840**	**2,028**

Companies accounted for by the equity method include Heublein do Brazil, L'Igloo, Beijing Pernod Ricard Winery, Dragon Seal, Simeon Wines, Eight to Twelve.

Other equity investments include Société Générale shares (2.06% of capital), Financière Saresco (35% of capital) and Compagnie de Suez shares (0.51% of capital).

Société Générale and Compagnie de Suez are valued at the historic cost.

NOTE 8 - VARIATIONS IN RESERVES

Variations in reserves recorded in 1995 correspond mainly to investment subsidies reclassified in adjustments liabilities.

NOTE 9 - STOCKS ET EN-COURS

La répartition des stocks et en-cours à la clôture des exercices 1996, 1995 et 1994 est la suivante :

En millions de Francs	1996	1995	1994
Matières premières	944	772	958
En-cours de biens	2 880	2 591	2 460
Stocks de marchandises	617	502	570
Produits finis	679	634	571
Total	**5 120**	**4 499**	**4 559**

NOTE 10 - PROVISIONS POUR RISQUES ET CHARGES

En millions de Francs	1996	1995	1994
Provisions pour indemnités de départ à la retraite	137	135	128
Provisions pour risques divers	325	301	383
Total	**462**	**436**	**511**

Les provisions pour risques divers correspondent principalement à des provisions pour risques fiscaux et sociaux à hauteur de 115 MF, des provisions pour litiges avec tiers à hauteur de 40 MF, le solde étant constitué de provisions pour rationalisation et restructurations ainsi que de provisions pour charges publi-promotionnelles à encourir.

Il n'existe pas à notre connaissance de fait ou de litige qui pourrait affecter de façon significative les résultats, la situation financière ou le patrimoine du groupe.

NOTE 11 - IMPÔT SUR LES BÉNÉFICES

En millions de Francs	1996	1995	1994
Impôt exigible	(476)	(433)	(408)
Impôt différé	11	9	35
Total	**(465)**	**(424)**	**(373)**

Les impôts différés sont calculés selon la méthode du report variable. Au bilan, ils se décomposent de la manière suivante :

En millions de Francs	1996	1995	1994
Impôt différé actif	(289)	(266)	(242)
Impôt différé passif	346	334	319
Impôt différé passif net au bilan	**57**	**68**	**77**

Les impôts différés actifs constatés au 31.12.1996 sur des déficits fiscaux (qui ne sont constatés que si la probabilité d'imputer des bénéfices fiscaux futurs apparaît importante) s'élèvent à 9 MF.

La société CECO en France bénéficie d'un statut fiscal particulier.

NOTE 12 - DETTES FINANCIÈRES

La répartition des dettes financières par date d'exigibilité est la suivante :

En millions de Francs	1996	1995	1994
Court terme (moins de 1 an)	3 163	3 479	2 201
dont concours bancaires	*2 355*	*2 042*	*2 073*
Moyen terme (de 1 à 5 ans)	1 318	471	2 403
Long terme (plus de 5 ans)	618	587	449
Total	**5 098**	**4 537**	**5 053**

• Au 31 décembre 1996, le Groupe PERNOD RICARD dispose de lignes de crédits confirmés pour un montant de 476 millions de francs pour une durée comprise entre 6 mois et 4 ans.

• Le 20 Mars 1992, PERNOD RICARD a procédé à l'émission, hors de France, d'un emprunt obligataire sous forme de Titres Subordonnés à Durée Indéterminée pour un montant nominal de 400 millions de Francs.

Les TSDI sont qualifiés de " reconditionnés ", par suite de la conclusion avec une société tierce d'une convention concomitante à l'émission.

Le montant net disponible au 31 décembre 1996 (soit 249 millions de francs) a été inclus dans le poste " Dettes Financières ".

Les emprunts n'ont donné lieu à constitution d'aucune sûreté ou hypothèque autre que les garanties données par PERNOD RICARD SA et détaillées dans la note 13.

NOTE 13 - ENGAGEMENTS FINANCIERS

En millions de Francs	1996	1995	1994
ENGAGEMENTS DONNÉS			
Crédit-bail	77	87	80
Cautions et garanties	673	581	987
Engagements d'achat aux fournisseurs	110	109	46

La caution donnée à la Société Générale par PERNOD RICARD afin de contre-garantir les obligations (loan notes) émises pour financer en partie l'acquisition du Groupe IRISH DISTILLERS et garanties en principal par la Société Générale, a été réduite à 56 millions de Francs au 31 décembre 1996 contre respectivement 553 et 72 millions de Francs aux 31 décembre 1994 et 1995 (suite au remboursement d'une partie des loan notes.)

En 1994, PERNOD RICARD s'est porté garant à hauteur de 40 millions de Livres Sterling des sommes pouvant être dues par les sociétés BWG Foods et BWG NI au titre d'un emprunt et contrats de swap souscrits par ces sociétés.

Au 31 décembre 1996, le solde restant dû et pour lequel PERNOD RICARD s'est porté garant s'élève à 36,1 millions de Livres Sterling.

NOTE 9 - INVENTORIES AND WORK IN PROCESS

Inventories and work in process at 1996, 1995 and 1994 yearends were as follows:

FF millions	1996	1995	1994
Raw materials	944	772	958
Work in process	2,880	2,591	2,460
Goods in inventory	617	502	570
Finished products	679	634	571
Total	**5,120**	**4,499**	**4,559**

NOTE 10 - PROVISIONS FOR CONTINGENCIES

FF millions	1996	1995	1994
Provisions for retirement benefits	137	135	128
Provisions for other risks	325	301	383
Total	**462**	**436**	**511**

Contingency reserves correspond mainly to reserves for taxes and benefits in the amount of FF 115 million, reserves for disputes with third parties, in the amount of FF 40 million, with the remainder consisting mainly of reserves for restructuring activities and reserves for advertising and promotional expenses to be incurred.

To our knowledge, there are no facts or disputes which could significantly affect the results, financial position, or assets of the Group.

NOTE 11 - INCOME TAXES

FF millions	1996	1995	1994
Taxes payable	(476)	(433)	(408)
Deferred taxes	11	9	35
Total	**(465)**	**(424)**	**(373)**

Deferred taxes are calculated according to the accrual method. They are broken down as follows on the balance sheet:

FF millions	1996	1995	1994
Deferred tax credit	(289)	(266)	(242)
Deferred tax liability	346	334	319
Net deferred tax	**57**	**68**	**77**

Deferred tax assets recorded on 12/31/96 on tax losses (which are recorded only if there appears to be a high probability of applying future tax credits) total FF 9 million.

The CECO company in France enjoys a special tax status.

NOTE 12 - LONG-TERM DEBT

The breakdown of long-term debt by maturity date is as follows:

FF millions	1996	1995	1994
Short term (less than one year)	3,163	3,479	2,201
including bank loans	*2,355*	*2,042*	*2,073*
Medium term (from one to five years)	1,318	471	2,403
Long term (over five years	618	587	449
Total	**5,098**	**4,537**	**5,053**

- As of December 31, 1996, the PERNOD RICARD Group had available confirmed credit lines totaling FF 476 million for a period of six months to four years.

- On March 20, 1992, PERNOD RICARD issued, outside of France, bonds in the form of Perpetual Subordinated Notes for a total nominal amount of FF 400 million.

The Perpetual Subordinated Notes are qualified as "repackaged" following the conclusion of an agreement at the time of the issue with a third party.

The net amount available as of December 31, 1996 (FF 249 million) has been included in the "Financial Debts" account.

Borrowings resulted in no guarantees or mortgages other than the guarantees provided by Pernod Ricard SA, listed in Note 13.

NOTE 13 - FINANCIAL COMMITMENTS

FF millions	1996	1995	1994
COMMITMENTS GIVEN			
Leasing	77	87	80
Bank guarantees	673	581	987
Purchasing commitments	110	109	46

The guarantee given to Société Générale by PERNOD RICARD in order to reguarantee the loan notes issued for the partial financing of the Irish Distillers Group was reduced to FF 56 million as of December 31, 1996 compared with FF 553 and 72 million respectively as of December 31, 1994 and 1995.

In 1994, PERNOD RICARD provided guarantees of up to £ 40 million for amounts which may be owed by the BWG Foods and the BWG NI companies in the form of a loan and swap contracts taken out by these companies. As of December 31, 1996, the balance remaining due and which is guaranteed by Pernod Ricard totals £ 36.1 million.

Comme mentionné dans la Note 1.12, dans le cadre de la politique de couverture du risque de change du Groupe PERNOD RICARD, PR Finance dispose d'un portefeuille de couverture devises qui représente au 31 décembre 1996 un montant total de 173 MF se décomposant comme suit :

Contrat	Echéance	Montant	Taux
Achat à terme	3/2/97	22 M AUD	3,9715 - 4,0090
Achat à treme	27/3/97	2 M AUD	3,9860
Vente à terme	10/1/97	2 M GBP	8,3295
Option de vente	26/3/97	1 500 M ESP	0,040175

NOTE 14 - CONTRATS DE GARANTIE DE TAUX

Comme mentionné dans la Note 1.12, le Groupe PERNOD RICARD dispose d'un portefeuille de contrats de garantie de taux qui représente au 31 décembre 1996 un montant total de 1 294 MF se décomposant comme suit :

Société	Contrat	Echéance	Assiette	Garanties
Pernod Ricard	Collar	Sept. 1997	300 MF	5,20% - 6,25%
PR Finance	Options de taux fixe	Déc. 1998	200 MF	5,55%
PR Finance	Swap taux fixe	Janv. 1999	300 MF	3,5%
House of Campbell	Collar	Janv. 1998	160 MF	4% - 6,4%
Orlando	Swap taux fixe	Nov. 2000	80 M AUD	6,58%

NOTE 15 - EFFECTIFS MOYENS ET FRAIS DE PERSONNEL

Les effectifs moyens de l'exercice 1996 s'élèvent à 11 233 personnes contre 11 150 personnes en 1995 et 10 839 en 1994. Ces effectifs sont calculés en moyenne annuelle et tiennent compte de personnels intérimaires.

Les frais de personnel se sont élevés à 2 736 millions de francs contre 2 632 millions de Francs en 1995 et 2 658 millions de Francs en 1994. Ces chiffres incluent outre les charges de personnel intérimaire, l'intéressement et les taxes sur les salaires.

NOTE 16 - INFORMATIONS PAR SECTEUR D'ACTIVITÉ

VINS ET SPIRITUEUX FRANCE

	1996	1995	1994
Volumes commercialisés en millions de litres	111	104	106
Effectifs moyens	2 262	2 253	2 863

13 centres de production en France

Marques principales :

- Ricard, Pastis 51, Pernod.
- Suze.
- Ambassadeur, Dubonnet, Cinzano, Byrrh, Vabé, Bartissol.
- Scotch Whiskies Clan Campbell, White Heather, Aberlour, Cutty Sark (*).
- Irish Whiskeys Jameson, Bushmills, Power, Paddy.
- Whisky canadien Royal Canadian.
- Bourbon Wild Turkey.
- Vodkas Karinskaya, Altaï, Stolichnaya (*).
- Calvados Busnel, Anée.
- Cognacs Bisquit, Renault, Armagnac Marquis de Montesquiou.
- Rhum Havana Club.
- Portos Cintra, Warre.
- Liqueurs Soho, Alaska, Cusenier, eaux de vie la Duchesse.
- Gins Black Jack, Hastings.
- Café de Paris, Blancs de fruits.

(*) concession
(Ces marques concédées, représentent une part peu significative de l'activité du groupe).

Sociétés dont l'activité contribue au secteur :

- Ricard et ses filiales : Renault Bisquit, Galibert & Varon.
- Pernod et sa filiale : Cusenier.
- CSR Pampryl.

Les principaux clients du secteur sont les groupes de grande distribution en France, les grossistes et les cafés-hôtels-restaurants.

Vins et spiritueux France

En millions de Francs	1996	1995	1994	Variation 1996/1995
Chiffre d'affaires HDT	3 523	3 351	3 326	+ 5,1 %
Achats consommés	(615)	(691)	(675)	- 10,9 %
Marge brute	2 908	2 660	2 651	+ 9,3 %
Frais de commercialisation et de distribution	(1 455)	(1 281)	(1 231)	+ 13,6 %
Frais de production et frais généraux	(686)	(641)	(694)	+ 7,0 %
Résultat opérationnel	767	738	726	+ 4,0 %

As mentioned in Note 1.12, as part of the PERNOD RICARD policy of hedging against exchange risks, PR Finance has a currency hedging portfolio which, at December 31, 1996, totales FF 173 million, broken down as follows:

Contract	Maturity	Amount	Rate
Forward buying	2/3/97	22 M AUD	3.9715 - 4.0090
Forward buying	3/27/97	2 M AUD	3.9860
Forward sale	1/10/97	2 M GBP	8.3295
Put option	3/26/97	1 500 M ESP	0.040175

NOTE 14 - GUARANTEED RATE CONTRACTS

As mentioned in Note 1.12, the PERNOD RICARD Group has a portfolio of rate guarantee contracts which represented, on December 31, 1996, a total sum of FF 1,294 million, as follows:

Company	Contract	Maturity	Basis	Guarantees
Pernod Ricard	Collar	Sept. 1997	FF 300 million	5.20% - 6.25%
PR Finance	Fixed rate options	Dec. 1998	FF 200 million	5.55%
PR Finance	Fixed rate swap	Jan. 1999	FF 300 million	3.5%
House of Campbell	Collar	Jan. 1998	FF 160 million	4% - 6.4%
Orlando	Fixed rate swap	Nov. 2000	AUD 80 million	6.58%

NOTE 15 - AVERAGE NUMBER OF EMPLOYEES AND PAYROLL EXPENSES

The average number of employees in 1996 was 11,233, compared with 11,150 in 1995 and 10,839 in 1994. These figures are calculated on an average annual basis and include temporary personnel.

Payroll expenses totaled FF 2,736 million in 1996 compared with FF 2,632 million in 1995, and FF 2,658 million in 1994. These figures include employee profit-sharing and payroll taxes in addition to temporary personnel costs.

NOTE 16 - BUSINESS SEGMENT INFORMATION

WINES AND SPIRITS FRANCE

	1996	1995	1994
Volumes sold millions of liters	111	104	106
Employees	2,262	2,253	2,863

13 production facilities in France

Major trademarks:

- Ricard, Pastis 51, Pernod.
- Suze.
- Ambassadeur, Dubonnet, Cinzano, Byrrh, Vabé, Bartissol.
- Scotch Whiskies Clan Campbell, White Heather, Aberlour, Cutty Sark (*).
- Irish Whiskeys Jameson, Bushmills, Power, Paddy.
- Canadian Whiskey: Royal Canadian.
- Bourbon Wild Turkey.
- Vodkas Karinskaya, Altaï, Stolichnaya (*).
- Calvados Busnel and Anée.
- Cognac Bisquit Renault and Armagnac Marquis de Montesquiou.
- Rums Havana Club.
- Portos Cintra, Warre.
- Liqueurs Soho, Alaska, Cusenier, eaux de vie La Duchesse.
- Gins Black Jack, Hastings.
- Café de Paris, Blancs de fruits

(*) licensed
(These franchised brands account for a negligible portion of the group's activity.)

Companies operating in the segment:

- Ricard and its subsidiaries: Renault Bisquit, Galibert & Varon,
- Pernod and its subsidiary: Cusenier.
- CSR Pampryl.

The principal clients in this sector are mass distribution companies in France and wholesalers as well as cafés, hotels and restaurants.

Wines and Spirits, France

(FF millions)	1996	1995	1994	Change 1996/1995
Net sales excluding taxes and duties	3,523	3,351	3,326	+ 5.1 %
Cost of goods sold	(615)	(691)	(675)	- 10.9 %
Gross margin	2,908	2,660	2,651	+ 9.3 %
Production and overheads expenses	(1,455)	(1,281)	(1,231)	+ 13.6 %
Marketing and distribution expenses	(686)	(641)	(694)	+ 7.0 %
Operating profit	767	738	726	+4.0 %

VINS ET SPIRITUEUX EXPORT ET ÉTRANGER

	1996	1995	1994
Volumes commercialisés **en millions de litres**	242	228	230
Effectifs moyens	3 794	3 709	3 375

21 centres de production et d'embouteillage :

- USA : Lawrenceburg.
- Royaume Uni : Aberlour, Kilwinning, Glenallachie.
- Irlande : Bushmills, Fox and Geese, Cork, Midleton.
- Australie : Rowland Flat, Griffith, Hunter Estate.
- Espagne : Dicastillo.
- Suisse : Genève.
- Argentine : Capilla, Mendoza, Cafayatte.
- Italie : Canelli.
- Pays-Bas : Almelo, Tilburg.
- Grèce : Palini.
- Autriche : Vienne.

Marques principales :

- Ricard, Pastis 51, Pernod.
- Suze.
- Dubonnet.
- Scotch Whiskies Clan Campbell, Aberlour, White Heather, House of Lords, Glenforres.
- Irish Whiskeys Jameson, Bushmills, Paddy, Power.
- Bourbon Wild Turkey.
- Whisky canadien Royal Canadian.
- Cognacs Bisquit, Renault.
- Armagnac Marquis de Montesquiou, Calvados Busnel, Brandies Dorville.
- Rhum Havana Club.
- Liqueurs Zoco, Amaro, Sambuca, Fior di Vite, Mariposa, Ocho Hermanos, Millwood, Eoliki.
- Cork Dry Gin, vodkas Huzzar, Altaï, Petroff, genièvre Legner Light.
- Vins Cruse, Alexis Lichine, Victor Bérard, Pasquier Desvignes.

- Jacob's Creek, Orlando, Wyndham, Etchart, Palacio de la Vega, Long Mountain, Dragon Seal, Terra Andina.
- Canei, Carrington, Café de Paris, Carlton.

Sociétés dont l'activité contribue au secteur :

- SEGM et ses filiales : Prac SA (Espagne) et sa filiale Palacio de la Vega, Perisem (Suisse), Ramazzotti (Italie), IGM Deutschland (Allemagne) et sa filiale Polacek (Autriche), PR Nederland BV et sa filiale Kerstens (Pays-Bas), Lizas & Lizas (Grèce), Somagnum (Portugal), Casella Far East (Hong Kong), Cusenier Saic (Argentine) et sa filiale Etchart (Argentine), Perising (Singapour), Pernod Ricard Japan (Japon), Casella Taiwan (Taiwan), Perithaï (Thaïlande), PRC Diffusion (Caraïbes), PRK Distribution Ltd (Corée).
- Irish Distillers Group Plc et ses filiales Irish Distillers Ltd (Irlande), Old Bushmills Distillery Ltd (Irlande du Nord), Fitzgerald (Irlande), PR South Africa (Afrique du Sud).
- Campbell Distillers et sa filiale Caxton Tower.
- Austin Nichols et sa filiale Boulevard Distillers.
- Nihco (Canada)
- Orlando Wyndham.
- Ricard et ses filiales.
- Pernod et ses filiales : Cusenier, Crus et Domaines de France.
- CSR Pampryl.
- World Brands Duty Free et ses filiales World Brands Duty Free Inc (USA), Perau Associates (Suède), Brand Partners (Norvège), World Brands Denmark, World Brands Finland.

Les principaux clients du secteur sont les groupes de grande distribution, les grossistes, les cafés-hôtels-restaurants et les magasins spécialisés.

Vins et spiritueux export et étranger

En millions de Francs	1996	1995	1994	Variation 1996/1995	Hors effet devise
Chiffre d'affaires HDT	4 843	4 358	4 450	+ 11,1 %	+ 8,9 %
Achats consommés	(1 748)	(1 579)	(1 650)	+ 10,7 %	
Marge brute	3 095	2 779	2 800	+ 11,4 %	
Frais de commercialisation et de distribution	(1 394)	(1 205)	(1 210)	+ 15,7 %	
Frais de production et frais généraux	(977)	(912)	(951)	+ 7,1 %	
Résultat opérationnel	724	662	639	+ 9,4 %	+ 6,1 %

Note : L'effet devise correspond à l'impact des variations de devise sur la conversion des comptes des filiales étrangères.

WINES AND SPIRITS, EXPORT AND INTERNATIONAL

	1996	1995	1994
Volumes sold			
millions of liters	242	228	230
Employees	3,794	3,709	3,375

21 production and bottling facilities:

- United States: Lawrenceburg.
- Great Britain: Aberlour, Kilwinning, Glenalachie.
- Ireland: Bushmills, Fox and Geese, Cork, Midleton.
- Australia: Rowland Flat, Griffith, Hunter Estate.
- Spain: Dicastillo.
- Switzerland: Geneva.
- Argentina: Capilla, Mendoza, Cafayate.
- Italy: Canelli.
- Netherlands: Almelo, Tilburg.
- Greece: Palini.
- Austria: Vienna.

Major trademarks:

- Ricard, Pastis 51, Pernod.
- Suze.
- Dubonnet.
- Scotch Whiskies Clan Campbell, Aberlour, White Heather, House of Lords, Glenforres.
- Irish Whiskeys Jameson, Bushmills, Paddy, Power.
- Bourbon Wild Turkey.
- Canadian Whiskey: Royal Canadian.
- Cognacs Bisquit, Renault.
- Armagnac Marquis de Montesquiou, Calvados Busnel, Brandies Dorville.
- Rums Havana Club
- Liqueurs Zoco, Amaro, Sambuca, Fior di Vite, Mariposa, Ocho Hermanos, Millwood, Eoliki.
- Cork Dry Gin, vodkas Huzzar, Altaï, Petroff, genièvre Legner Light.

- Vins Cruse, Alexis Lichine, Victor Bérard, Pasquier Desvignes.
- Jacob's Creek, Orlando, Wyndham, Etchart, Palacio de la Vega, Long Mountain, Dragon Seal, Terra Andina.
- Canei, Carrington, Café de Paris, Carlton.

Companies operating in the segment:

- SEGM and its subsidiaries: Prac SA (Spain) and its subsidiary Palacio de la Vega, Périsem (Switzerland), Ramazzoti (Italy), IGM Deutschland (Germany) and its subsidiary Polacek (Austria), PR Nederland BV and its subsidiary Kerstens (Netherlands), Lizas & Lizas (Greece), Somagnum (Portugal) Casella Far East (Hong Kong), Cusenier Saic (Argentina) and its subsidiary Etchart (Argentina), Perising (Singapore), Pernod Ricard Japan (Japan), Casella Taiwan (Taiwan), Perithaï (Thaïland), PRC Diffusion (Caribbean), PRK Distribution Ltd (Korea).
- Irish Distillers Group Plc and its subsidiaries Irish Distillers Ltd (Ireland), Old Bushmills Distillery Ltd (Northern Ireland), Fitzgerald (Ireland), PR South Africa (South Africa).
- Campbell Distillers and its subsidiary Caxton Tower.
- Austin Nichols and its subsidiary Boulevard Distillers.
- Nihco (Canada)
- Orlando Wyndham.
- Ricard and its subsidiaries.
- Pernod and its subsidiaries : Cusenier, Crus et Domaines de France
- CSR Pampryl.
- World Brands Duty Free and its subsidiaries, World Brands Duty Free Inc (USA), Perau Associates (Sweden), Brand Partners (Norway), World Brands Denmark, World Brands Finland.

The major clients of this division are mass distribution companies, wholesalers, bars, hotels and restaurants and specialty stores.

Wines and Spirits, Export and International

FF millions	1996	1995	1994	Change 1996/1995	Excluding currency effect
Net sales excluding taxes and duties	4,843	4,358	4,450	+ 11.1 %	+8.9 %
Cost of goods sold	(1,748)	(1,579)	(1,650)	+ 10,7 %	
Gross margin	3,095	2,779	2,800	+ 11.4 %	
Marketing and distribution expenses	(1,394)	(1 205)	(1 210)	+ 15.7 %	
Production and overheads expenses	(977)	(912)	(951)	+ 7.1 %	
Operating profit	724	662	639	+ 9.4 %	+ 6.1 %

The currency effect corresponds to the effect of currency variations on the conversion of foreign subsidiary accounts.

BOISSONS ET PRODUITS SANS ALCOOL FRANCE

	1996	1995	1994
Volumes commercialisés			
en millions de litres *	418	441	539
Effectifs moyens	1 818	1 919	2 138

(*) *Hors activités aromatiques et préparations aux fruits.*

13 centres de production et d'embouteillage :

Marques principales :

- Orangina.
- Banga.
- Cidres La Cidraie, Loïc Raison, Duché de Longueville,
  Flagger.
- Brut de Pomme.
- Champomy.
- Pacific.

- Pampryl, Pam-Pam.
- Agruma.
- Sirops Cusenier.
- Pepsi-Cola (1).

(1) Accord de distribution en CHR.

Sociétés dont l'activité contribue au secteur :

- SIAS-MPA et sa filiale SIAS France.
- Cusenier.
- CSR Pampryl.
- Ricard.
- CFPO et ses filiales Orangina France, CECO,
  New Drinks Company

Les principaux clients du secteur sont les groupes de grande distribution, les grossistes et les cafés-hôtels-restaurants. Pour l'activité Préparations aux Fruits, il s'agit des principaux groupes de l'industrie agro-alimentaire.

Boissons et produits sans alcool France

En millions de Francs	1996	1995	1994	Variation 1996/1995
Chiffre d'affaires HDT	2 789	2 857	3 398	- 2,4 %
Achats consommés	(1 168)	(1 226)	(1 643)	- 4,7 %
Marge brute	1 621	1 631	1 755	- 0,6 %
Frais de commercialisation et de distribution	(781)	(782)	(862)	- 0,2 %
Frais de production et frais généraux	(647)	(625)	(655)	+ 3,5 %
Résultat opérationnel	193	224	238	- 13,8 %

Note : Les chiffres de l'exercice 1994 comprenaient l'activité Ventes à Emporter, rétrocédée par Orangina à Pepsico à compter du 1er janvier 1995.

BOISSONS ET PRODUITS SANS ALCOOL EXPORT ET ÉTRANGER

	1996	1995	1994
Volumes commercialisés			
en millions de litres*	327	350	323
Effectifs moyens	3 359	3 269	2 463

(*) *Hors activités aromatiques et préparations aux fruits.*

20 centres de production à l'étranger

- Allemagne : Constance, Nauen.
- Royaume Uni : Corby.
- Australie : Mangrove Mountain.
- USA : Anna Botkins (Ohio), Winter Haven (Floride),
  Fort Worth (Texas), Carlstadt (New Jersey), Hialeah
  (Floride), Opelousas (Louisiane).
- Mexique : Zamora, Jacuna.
- Italie : Turin.
- Grèce : Le Pirée.

- République Tchèque : Kaplice.
- Corée : Séoul.
- Autriche : Kröllendorf.
- Pologne : Ostrolenka.
- Argentine : Arroyo-Seco.
- Fidji : Fidji.

Marques principales :

- Orangina.
- Yoo-Hoo.
- Minerva.
- Pampryl.
- La Cidraie, E33

NONALCOHOLIC BEVERAGES AND PRODUCTS, FRANCE

	1996	1995	1994
Volumes sold **millions of liters ***	418	441	539
Employees	1,818	1,919	2,138

(*) Excluding flavors and fruit preparations.

13 production facilities in France

Major trademarks:

- Orangina.
- Banga.
- Ciders La Cidraie. Loïc Raison. Duché de Longue-ville. Flagger.
- Brut de Pomme.
- Champony.
- Pacific.

- Pampryl. Pam-Pam.
- Agruma.
- Sirops Cusenier.
- Pepsi-Cola (1).

(1) Distribution agreement.

Companies operating in the segment:

- SIAS-MPA and its subsidiary SIAS France.
- Cusenier.
- CSR Pampryl.
- Ricard.
- CFPO and its subsidiaries Orangina France, CECO, New Drinks Company.

The principal clients in this sector are mass distribution companies in France and wholesalers as well as cafés, hotels and restaurants. In the fruit preparation sector, the main clients are the large food processing companies.

Nonalcoholic Beverages and Products, France

FF millions	1996	1995	1994	Change 1996/1995
Net sales excluding taxes and duties	2,789	2,857	3,398	- 2.4 %
Cost of goods sold	(1,168)	(1,226)	(1,643)	- 4.7 %
Gross margin	1,621	1,631	1,755	- 0.6 %
Marketing and distribution expenses	(781)	(782)	(862)	- 0.2 %
Production and overheads expenses	(647)	(625)	(655)	+ 3.5 %
Operating profit	193	224	238	- 13.8 %

Figures for the year 1994 included the Carry-out Sales activity resold to Pepsico by Orangina as of January 1, 1995.

NONALCOHOLIC BEVERAGES AND PRODUCTS, EXPORT AND INTERNATIONAL

	1996	1995	1994
Volumes sold **millions of liters***	327	350	323
Employees	3,359	3,269	2,463

(*) Excluding flavors and fruit preparations.

20 production facilities abroad

- Germany: Constance. Nauen.
- Great Britain: Corby.
- Australia: Mangrove Mountain.
- United States: Anna Botkins (Ohio). Winter Haven (Florida). Fort Worth (Texas). Carlstadt (New Jersey). Hialeah (Florida). Opelousas (Louisiana).

- Mexico: Zamora. Jacuna.
- Italy: Turin.
- Greece: Le Piraeus.
- Czech Republic : Kaplice
- Korea: Seoul.
- Austria: Kröllendorf.
- Poland: Ostrolenka.
- Argentina: Arroyo-Seco.
- Fiji: Fiji.

Major trademarks:

- Orangina.
- Yoo-Hoo.
- Minerva.
- Pampryl.
- La Cidraie. E33

Sociétés dont l'activité contribue au secteur :

- SEGM et ses filiales, dont notamment Cusenier SAIC.

- SIAS-MPA et ses filiales : SIAS France, DSF (Allemagne), Ramsey et Flavors from Florida (Etats-Unis), SIAS Foods UK (Royaume-Uni), San Giorgio Flavors (Italie), MMF SIAS (Australie), SIAS Mex et SIAS Port (Mexique), SIAS Korea, YB SIAS (Autriche), SIAS Polska (Pologne), SIAS Fruit Argentina (Argentine), SIAS Bohemia (République Tchèque).

- CSR Pampryl.
- CFPO.
- Yoo-Hoo Industries.
- Orlando Wyndham.
- B.W.G. et sa filiale J&J Haslett.

Les principaux clients du secteur sont les groupes de grande distribution, les grossistes et les cafés-hôtels-restaurants. Pour l'activité Préparations aux Fruits, il s'agit des principaux groupes de l'industrie agro-alimentaire

Boissons et produits sans alcool export et étranger

En millions de Francs	1996	1995	1994	Variation 1996/1995	Hors effet devise
Chiffre d'affaires HDT	**5 659**	**5 368**	**4 659**	**+ 5,4 %**	**+ 4,0 %**
Achats consommés	(3 982)	(3 767)	(3 127)	+ 5,7 %	
Marge brute	**1 677**	**1 601**	**1 532**	**+ 4,7 %**	
Frais de commercialisation et de distribution	(656)	(616)	(566)	+ 6,5 %	
Frais de production et frais généraux	(770)	(736)	(704)	+ 4,6 %	
Résultat opérationnel	**251**	**249**	**262**	**+ 0,8 %**	**+ 0 %**

Note : L'effet devise correspond à l'impact des variations de devise sur la conversion des comptes des filiales étrangères.

NOTE 17 - LISTE DES PRINCIPALES SOCIÉTÉS CONSOLIDÉES

Sociétés	Siège	% d'intérêt 1996	% d'intérêt 1995	Méthode de consolidation	Numéro Siren
Pernod Ricard	142, boulevard Haussmann, 75379 Paris Cedex 08	Société mère			582 041 943
PR Finance	142, boulevard Haussmann, 75379 Paris Cedex 08	100	100	I.G.	349 785 238
Ricard	4 et 6, rue Berthelot, 13014 Marseille	100	100	I.G.	303 656 375
- Renault Bisquit	Domaine de Lignères, 16170 Rouillac	100	100	I.G.	905 420 170
- Galibert & Varon	Lignères, 16170 Rouillac	99,3	99,3	I.G.	457 208 437
Pernod	120, avenue du Maréchal Foch, 94105 Créteil	100	100	I.G.	302 208 301
- Cusenier	142, boulevard Haussmann, 75008 Paris	100	100	I.G.	308 198 670
- Crus et Domaines de France	109, rue Achard - 33000 Bordeaux	100	100	I.G.	384 093 290
SEGM	2, rue de Solférino, 75007 Paris	100	100	I.G.	302 453 592
PR Europe					
- Prac SA (Espagne)	Avenida Diagonal 477, Planta 14, Barcelone 36	100	100	I.G.	
- Palacio de la Vega (Espagne)	31263 Di Castello, Navarre	100	100	I.G.	
- Perisem (Suisse)	44, route de St-Julien, 1227 Carouge, Genève	100	100	I.G.	
- Ramazzotti (Italie)	Corso Buenos Aires, 54, 20124 Milan	100	100	I.G.	
- Somagnum (Portugal)	Rua Antonia Maia n∞6, Quinta do Borel, 2720 Amadora	60,0	60,0	I.G.	
- IGM Deutschland (Allemagne)	Schloss Strasse 18-20, 56068 Koblenz	100	100	I.G.	
- Polacek (Autriche)	Resselgasse 1, 2201 Gerasdorf	100	100	I.G.	
- PR Nederland (Pays-Bas)	De Kroonstraat 1, 5048 AP Tilburg	100	100	I.G.	
- Lizas & Lizas (Grèce)	L. Anthousas, 15344 Palini Attiki	100	100	I.G.	
- PR Belux (Belgique)	104/106 rue Emile Delva B1020 Bruxelles	66,7	-	I.G.	
PR Asia					
- Pernod Ricard Japan K.K. (Japon)	Tamaya Building, 3rd Floor, 14-12 Shinjuku 1 Chome Shinjuku-Ku, Tokyo 160	100	100	I.G.	
- Casella Far East Ltd. (Hong Kong)	1007-8 New Kowloon Plaza - 38 Tai Kok Tsui Road, Kowloon, Hong Kong	100	100	I.G.	
- Beijing Pernod Ricard Winery (Chine)	N∞2 Yu Quan Road, Western Suburb, Beijing 100039	65,0	65,0	M.E.E.	
- Dragon Seal (Chine)	N∞2 Yu Quan Road, Western Suburb, Beijing 100039	53,0	53,0	M.E.E.	
- Casella Taïwan (République de Chine)	Pao Fu Commercial Center 15/F.2, 420 Fu Hsin N. Road - Taipei	80,0	80,0	I.G.	
- Perithaï (Thaïlande)	2533 Sukhumvit Rd, Bangchack Praekhanong, Bangkok 10250	100	100	I.G.	
- PRK Distribution Ltd (Corée)	941-26 Daechi-Dong-Kangnam-Ku, 135-081 Séoul	95,6	95,6	I.G.	
- Perising Pte Ltd. (Singapour)	60B, Martin Road, # 05-07/08 Trade Mart, Singapour	100	100	I.G.	

Companies operating in the segment:

- SEGM and its subsidiary. especially Cusenier SAIC.
- SIAS-MPA and its subsidiary: SIAS France. DSF (Germany). Ramsey and Flavors from Florida (United States). SIAS Foods UK (Great Britain). San Giorgio Flavors (Italy). MMF SIAS (Australia). SIAS Mex and SIAS Port (Mexico). SIAS Korea. YB SIAS (Austria). SIAS Polska (Poland). SIAS Fruit Argentina (Argentina). SIAS Bohemia (Czech Republic).

- CSR Pampryl.
- CFPO.
- Yoo-Hoo Industries.
- Orlando Wyndham.
- B.W.G. and its subsidiary J&J Haslett.

The principal clients in this sector are mass distribution companies and wholesalers as well as cafés, hotels and restaurants. In the fruit preparation sector, the main clients are the large food processing companies.

Nonalcoholic Beverages and Products, Export and International

FF millions	1996	1995	1994	Change 1996/1995	Excluding currency effect
Net sales excluding taxes and duties	**5,659**	**5,368**	**4,659**	**+ 5.4 %**	**+ 4.0 %**
Cost of goods sold	(3,982)	(3,767)	(3,127)	+ 5.7 %	
Gross margin	**1,677**	**1,601**	**1,532**	**+ 4.7 %**	
Marketing and distribution expenses	(656)	(616)	(566)	+ 6.5 %	
Production and overheads expenses	(770)	(736)	(704)	+ 4.6 %	
Operating profit	**251**	**249**	**262**	**+ 0.8 %**	**+ 0 %**

The currency effect corresponds to the effect of currency variations on the conversion of foreign subsidiary accounts.

NOTE 18 - PRINCIPAL CONSOLIDATED COMPANIES

Company	Head Office	% Interest 1996	% Interest 1995	Consolidation method	Register
Pernod Ricard	142, boulevard Haussmann, 75379 Paris Cedex 08	Parent company			582 041 943
PR Finance	142, boulevard Haussmann, 75379 Paris Cedex 08	100	100	Full	349 785 238
Ricard	4 et 6, rue Berthelot, 13014 Marseille	100	100	Full	303 656 375
- Renault Bisquit	Domaine de Lignères, 16170 Rouillac	100	100	Full	905 420 170
- Galibert & Varon	Lignères, 16170 Rouillac	99.3	99.3	Full	457 208 437
Pernod	120, avenue du Maréchal Foch, 94105 Créteil	100	100	Full	302 208 301
- Cusenier	142, boulevard Haussmann, 75008 Paris	100	100	Full	308 198 670
- Crus et Domaines de France	109, rue Achard - 33000 Bordeaux	100	100	Full	384 093 290
SEGM	2, rue de Solférino, 75007 Paris	100	100	Full	302 453 592
PR Europe					
- Prac SA (Spain)	Avenida Diagonal 477, Planta 14, Barcelona 36	100	100	Full	
- Palacio de la Vega (Spain)	31263 Di Castello, Navarre	100	100	Full	
- Perisem (Switzerland)	44, route de St-Julien, 1227 Carouge, Geneva	100	100	Full	
- Ramazzotti (Italy)	9, via San Petro All Orto, 20121 Milan	100	100	Full	
- Somagnum (Portugal)	Rua Antonia Maia nº 6, Quinta do Borel, 2720 Amadora	60.0	60.0	Full	
- IGM Deutschland (Germany)	Schloss Srasse 18-20, 56068 Koblenz	100	100	Full	
- Polacek (Austria)	Resselgasse 1, 2201 Gerasdorf	100	100	Full	
- PR Nederland (Netherlands)	De Kroonstraat 1, 5048 AP Tilburg	100	100	Full	
- Lizas & Lizas (Greece)	L. Anthousas, 15344 Palini Attiki	100	100	Full	
- PR Belux (Belgium)	104/106 rue Emile Delva B 1020 Bruxelles	66.7	-	Full	
PR Asia					
- Pernod Ricard Japan K.K. (Japan)	Tamaya Building, 3rd Floor, 14-12 Shinjuku 1 Chome Shinjuku-Ku, Tokyo 160	100	100	Full	
- Casella Far East Ltd. (Hong Kong)	1007-8 New Kowloon Plaza - 38 Tai Kok Tsui Road, Kowloon, Hong Kong	100	100	Full	
- Beijing Pernod Ricard Winery (China)	Nº 2 Yu Quan Road, Western Suburb, Beijing 100039	65.0	65.0	Equity	
- Dragon Seal (China)	Nº 2 Yu Quan Road, Western Suburb, Beijing 100039	53.0	53.0	Equity	
- Casella Taïwan (The People's Republic of China)	Pao Fu Commercial Center 15/F.2, 420 Fu Hsin N. Road - Taipei	80.0	80.0	Full	

Sociétés	Siège	% d'intérêt 1996	% d'intérêt 1995	Méthode de consolidation	Numéro Siren
PR Americas					
- Cusenier Saic (Argentine)	Lima 229 - 4e - 1073 Buenos Aires	100	100	I.G.	
- Etchart (Argentine)	Lima 229, 4e, 1073 Buenos Aires	100	50,0	I.G.	
- PRC Diffusion (Caraïbes)	Z.I. Californie, Immeuble Synergie, Centre d'affaires, 97232 Le Lamentin	100	100	I.G.	390 984 912
Nihco (Canada)	2155 Cagnon, Lachine, Québec H8T3M7	100	-	I.G.	
Austin Nichols (USA)	156, East, 46th Street, New York N.Y. 10017	100	100	I.G.	
- Boulevard Distillers (USA)	156, East, 46th Street, New York N.Y. 10017	70,0	70,0	I.G.	
- Yoo-Hoo Industries (USA)	156, East, 46th Street, New York N.Y. 10017	100	100	I.G.	
World Brands Duty Free (Grande-Bretagne)	924, Great West Road, Brentford, Middlesex TW8-9DY	100	100	I.G.	
- World Brands Duty Free Inc (USA)	1200 Bayhill Drive, Suite 302, San Bruno, California 94056 USA	100	100	I.G.	
- Perau Associates AS (Suède)	Box 6703, Yxkullsgatan 18, 11385 Stockholm	100	100	I.G.	
- Brand Partners A/S (Norvège)	PO Box 2752 Solli, N0204 Oslo	50,0	50,0	I.G.	
- World Brands Denmark A/S (Danemark)	Homemansgate 36/A, PO Box 861, 2100 Copenhagen 0	100	100	I.G.	
- World Brands Finland O/Y (Finland)	Salomonkatu 17a, 00100 Helsinki	100	-	I.G.	
CSR*	160 avenue Paul Vaillant Couturier, 93126 La Courneuve Cedex	99,2	99,2	I.G.	552 024 275
JFA Pampryl	160 avenue Paul Vaillant Couturier, 93126 La Courneuve Cedex	99,2	99,2	I.G.	035 680 016
CSR Pampryl	12 rue François Mignotte, 21700 Nuits Saint George	99,2	99,2	I.G.	321 875 007
Campbell Distillers (Grande-Bretagne)	West Byrehill, Kilwinning, Ayrshire KA 136 LE	100	100	I.G.	
- White Heather Distillers (G.B.)	West Byrehill, Kilwinning, Ayrshire KA 136 LE	100	100	I.G.	
- Aberlour Glenlivet Distillery (G.B.)	West Byrehill, Kilwinning, Ayrshire KA 136 LE	100	100	I.G.	
- Caxton Tower (G.B.)	4 Harlequin Ave., Brentford, Middlesex TW8 9EW	100	100	I.G.	
Santa Lina	2, rue de Solférino, 75007 Paris	100	100	I.G.	045 920 105
SIAS-MPA	142, boulevard Haussmann, 75379 Paris Cedex 08	100	100	I.G.	436 380 521
- SIAS-France	17, avenue du 8-mai-1945, 77295 Mitry-Mory	100	100	I.G.	341 826 006
- Ramsey SIAS (USA)	6850 Southpointe Parteway, Brecksville, Ohio 44141	100	100	I.G.	
- Flavors From Florida (USA)	203 Bartow Municipal Airport, Bartow, Florida 33830-9599	100	100	I.G.	
- DSF GmbH (Allemagne)	Lilienthalstrasse 1, D.78467 Konstanz	60,0	60,0	I.G.	
- SIAS Port (Mexique)	Martinez de Navarrete 83B, Col. Franscico Villa, 59845 Jacona, Michoacan	100	100	I.G.	
- SIAS Mex (Mexique)	Martinez de Navarrete 83B, Col. Franscico Villa, 59845 Jacona, Michoacan	100	100	I.G.	
- MMF SIAS (Australie)	CNR George Downs Drive & Wisemans Ferry Road, Central Mangrove, NSW 2250	100	100	I.G.	
- SIAS Korea (Corée)	77-1 Kanak-Dong, Songpa-Ku - Séoul	95,6	95,6	I.G.	
- SIAS Foods UK Ltd (Grande-Bretagne)	Oakley Hay Lodge, Great Fold Road, Corby NN 189 AS	100	100	I.G.	
- YB SIAS GmbH (Autriche)	A-3363 Kröllendorf	50,0	50,0	I.G.	
- SIAS Polska (Pologne)	UL. Lawska 2, 07-410 Ostroeka	93,0	90,0	I.G.	
- SIAS Fruit Argentina (Argentine)	456, avenue Cordoba, 1054 Cap. Fed., Buenos Aires	100	74,0	I.G.	
- SIAS Bohemia (République Tchèque)	Pohorska 290, Kaplice, République Tchèque	100	100	I.G.	
- South Pacific Foods (Fidji)	POB 80, Nayama Road, Sigatoka, Fidji Islands	100	100	I.G.	
- San Giorgio Flavors (Italie)	Via Fossata 114, 1047 Torino	100	100	I.G.	
Compagnie Financière des Produits Orangina	595, rue Pierre Berthier, Domaine de St Hilaire, 13855 Aix en Provence Cedex 3	100	100	I.G.	56 801 254
- Centre d'Elaboration des Concentrés Orangina	Parc d'activités du plateau de Signes, 83870 Signes	100	100	I.G.	382 255 016
- Orangina France	595, rue Pierre Berthier, Domaine de St Hilaire, 13855 Aix en Provence Cedex 3	95,4	95,1	I.G.	056 807 076
- L'Igloo	7, Première Avenue, 13127 Vitrolles	47,7	47,6	M.E.E.	085 720 217
- The New Drinks Company	595, rue Pierre Berthier, Domaine de St Hilaire, 13855 Aix en Provence Cedex 3	100	-	I.G.	
Comrie Plc (Irlande)	61 Fitzwilliam Square, Dublin 2 (siège statutaire)	100	-	I.G.	
Irish Distillers Group Plc (Irlande)	Bow Street Distillery, Smithfield, Dublin 7	100	100	I.G.	
- Irish Distillers Limited (Irlande)	Bow Street Distillery, Smithfield, Dublin 7	100	100	I.G.	
- Old Bushmills Distillery Ltd (Irlande du Nord)	Distillery Road, Bushmills, Co Antrim BT57 BXH	100	100	I.G.	
- Fitzgerald & Co. Ltd (Irlande)	11-12 Bow Street, Dublin 7	100	100	I.G.	
- Dillon Bass Limited (Irlande du Nord)	Distillery Road, Bushmills, Co Antrim BT57 BXH	42,5	42,5	M.E.E.	
- BWG Limited (Irlande)	Greenhills Road, Walkinstown, Dublin 12	100	100	I.G.	
- J&J Haslett (Irlande du Nord)	20, The Cutts, Derriaghy, Dunmurry, Belfast, BT 17 9HR	100	100	I.G.	
- PR South Africa (Afrique du Sud)	Van der Bijl House, 37 Market Street, Stellenbosch, 7600 South Africa	100	100	I.G.	
Pernod Ricard Australia (Australie)	Grosvenor Place, 225 George Street, Sydney NSW 2000 Australia	100	100	I.G.	
- Orlando Wyndham Group Pty Limited	33 Exeter Terrace, Devon Park SA 5008, Australia	88,4	80,7	I.G.	
- Simeon Wines**	170 Greenhill Road Parkside SA 5063, Australia	33,0	30,0	M.E.E.	
Heublein do Brazil (Brésil)	655, rue Araporé, Sao Paulo	30,0	30,0	M.E.E.	

I.G. : *Intégration globale* - M.E.E. : *Mise en équivalence*
* *La société CSR est cotée sur le marché hors cote de la bourse de Paris* - ** *La société Simeon Wines est cotée à la Bourse de Sidney*

Le pourcentage de contrôle est égal au pourcentage d'intérêt sauf pour L'Igloo (50 %) et Simeon Wines (38 %).

Company	Head Office	% interest 1996	% interest 1995	Consolidation method	Register
- Perithaï (Thailand)	2533 Sukhumvit Rd, Bangchack Praekhanong, Bangkok 10250	100	100	Full	
- PRK Distribution Ltd (Korea)	941-26,Daechi-Dong-Kangnam-Ku, 135-081 Séoul	95.6	95.6	Full	
- Perising Pte Ltd. (Singapore)	60B, Martin Rd,# 05-07/08 Trade Mart, Singapore	100	100	Full	
PR Americas					
- Cusenier Saic (Argentina)	Lima 229 - 4e - 1073 Buenos Aires	100	100	Full	
- Etchart (Argentina)	Lima 229, 4e, 1073 Buenos Aires	100	50.0	Full	
- PRC Diffusion (Caribbean)	Z.I. Californie, Immeuble Synergie, Centre d'affaires, 97232 Le Lamentin	100	100	Full	390 984 912
Nihco (Canada)	2155 Cagnon, Lachine, Québec H8T3M7	100	--	Full	
Austin Nichols (USA)	156, East, 46th Street, New York N.Y. 10017	100	100	Full	
- Boulevard Distillers (USA)	156, East, 46th Street, New York N.Y. 10017	70.0	70.0	Full	
- Yoo-Hoo Industries (USA)	156, East, 46th Street, New York N.Y. 10017	100	100	Full	
World Brands Duty Free (United Kingdom)	924, Great West Road, Brentford, Middlesex TW8-9DY	100	100	Full	
- World Brands Duty Free Inc (USA)	1200 Bayhill Drive, Suite 302, San Bruno, California 94056 USA	100	100	Full	
- Perau Associates AS (Sweden)	Box 6703, Yxkullsgatan 18, 11385 Stockholm	100	100	Full	
- Brand Partners A/S (Norway)	PO Box 2752 Solli, N0204 Oslo	50.0	50.0	Full	
- World Brands Denmark A/S (Denmark)	Homemansgate 36/A, PO Box 861, 2100 Copenhagen 0	100	100	Full	
- World Brands Finland O/Y (Finland)	Salomonkatu 17a, 00100 Helsinki	100	-	Full	
CSR*	160 avenue Paul Vaillant Couturier, 93126 La Courneuve Cedex	99.2	99.2	Full	552 024 275
JFA Pampryl	160 avenue Paul Vaillant Couturier, 93126 La Courneuve Cedex	99.2	99.2	Full	035 680 016
CSR Pampryl	12 rue François Mignotte, 21700 Nuits Saint George	99.2	99.2	Full	321 875 007
Campbell Distillers (United Kingdom)	West Byrehill, Kilwinning, Ayrshire KA 136 LE	100	100	Full	
- White Heather Distillers (U.K.)	West Byrehill, Kilwinning, Ayrshire KA 136 LE	100	100	Full	
- Aberlour Glenlivet Distillery (U.K.)	West Byrehill, Kilwinning, Ayrshire KA 136 LE	100	100	Full	
- Caxton Tower (U.K.)	4 Harlequin Ave., Brentford, Middlesex TW8 9EW	100	100	Full	
Santa Lina	2, rue de Solférino 75007 Paris	100	100	Full	045 920 105
SIAS-MPA	142, boulevard Haussmann, 75379 Paris Cedex 08	100	100	Full	436 380 521
- SIAS-France	17, avenue du 8-mai-1945, 77295 Mitry-Mory	100	100	Full	341 826 006
- Ramsey SIAS (USA)	6850 Southpointe Parteway, Brecksville, Ohio 44141	100	100	Full	
- Flavors From Florida (USA)	203 Bartow Municipal Airport, Bartow, Florida 33830-9599	100	100	Full	
- DSF GmbH (Germany)	Lilienthalstrasse 1, D.78467 Konstanz	60.0	60.0	Full	
- SIAS Port (Mexico)	Martinez de Nazarrete 83B, Col. Franscico Villa 59845 Jacona, Michoacan	100	100	Full	
- SIAS Mex (Mexico)	Martinez de Nazarrete 83B, Col. Franscico Villa 59845 Jacona, Michoacan	100	100	Full	
- MMF SIAS (Australia)	CNR George Downs Drive & Wisemans Ferry Road, Central Mangrove, NSW 2250	100	100	Full	
- SIAS Korea (Korea)	77-1 Kanak -Dong, Songpra-ku - Séoul	95.6	95.6	Full	
- SIAS Foods UK Ltd (United Kingdom)	Oakley Hay Lodge, Great Fold Road, Corby NN 189 AS	100	100	Full	
- YB SIAS GmbH (Austria)	A-3363 Kröllendorf	50.0	50.0	Full	
- SIAS Polska (Poland)	UL. Lawska 2, 07-410 Ostroeka	93.0	90.0	Full	
- SIAS Fruit Argentina (Argentina)	456, avenue Cordoba, 1054 Cap. Fed., Buenos Aires	100	74.0	Full	
- SIAS Bohemia (The Czeck Republic)	Pohorska 290, Kaplice, The Czeck Republic	100	100	Full	
- South Pacific Foods (Fidji)	POB 80, Nayama Road, Sigatoka, Fidji Islands	100	100	Full	
- San Giorgio Flavors (Italy)	Via Fossata 114, 1047 Torino	100	100	Full	
Compagnie Financière des Produits Orangina	595, rue Pierre Berthier, Domaine de St Hilaire, 13855 Aix en Provence Cedex 3	100	100	Full	56 801 254
- Centre d'Elaboration des Concentrés Orangina	Parc d'activités du plateau de Signes, 83870 Signes	100	100	Full	382 255 016
- Orangina France	595, rue Pierre Berthier, Domaine de St Hilaire, 13855 Aix en Provence Cedex 3	95.4	95.1	Full	056 807 076
- L'Igloo	7, Première Avenue, 13127 Vitrolles	47.7	47.6	Equity	085 720 217
- The New Drinks Compagny	595, Rue Pierre Berthier, Domaine de St Hilaire, 13855 Aix en Provence Cedex 3	100		Full	
Comrie Plc (Ireland)	61 Fitzwilliam Square, Dublin 2 (Statutory head office)	100	100	Full	
Irish Distillers Group Plc (Ireland)	Bow Street Distillery, Smithfield, Dublin 7	100	100	Full	
- Irish Distillers Limited (Ireland)	Bow Street Distillery, Smithfield, Dublin 7	100	100	Full	
- Old Bushmills Distillery Ltd (Northern Ireland)	Distillery Road, Bushmills, Co Antrim BT57 BXH	100	100	Full	
- Fitzgerald & Co. Ltd (Ireland)	11-12 Bow Street, Dublin 7	100	100	Full	
- Dillon Bass Limited (Northern Ireland)	Distillery Road, Bushmills, Co Antrim BT57 BXH	42.5	42.5	Equity	
- BWG Limited (Ireland)	Greenhills Road, Walkinstown, Dublin 12	100	100	Full	
- J&J Haslett (Northern Ireland)	20, The Cutts, Derriaghy, Dunmurry, Belfast, BT 17 9HR	100	100	Full	
- PR South Africa (South Africa)	Van der Bijl House, 37 Market Street, Stellenbosch, 7600 South Africa	100	100	Full	
Pernod Ricard Australia (Australia)	Grosvenor Place, 225 George Street, Sydney NSW 2000 Australia	100	100	Full	
- Orlando Wyndham Group Pty Limited	33 Exeter Terrace, Devon Park SA 5008, Australia	88.4	80.7	Full	
- Simeon Wines**	170 Greenhill Road Parkside SA 5063, Australia	33.0	30.0	Equity	
Heublein do Brazil (Brazil)	655, rue Araporé, Sao Paulo	30.0	30.0	Equity	

* *The CSR company is listed on the over-the-counter market of the Paris Stock Exchange.* ** *The Simeon Wines company is listed on the Sydney Stock Exchange*

The percentage of control is equal to the amount of interest owned except for Igloo (50%) and Simeon Wines (38 %).

Rapport des
Commissaires aux Comptes

Comptes consolidés - Exercice clos le 31 décembre 1996

Mesdames, Messieurs,

En exécution de la mission qui nous a été confiée par vos Assemblées Générales, nous avons procédé au contrôle des comptes consolidés de la société Pernod Ricard relatifs à l'exercice clos le 31 décembre 1996, présentés aux pages 39 à 52.

Les comptes consolidés ont été arrêtés par le Conseil d'Administration. Il nous appartient, sur la base de notre audit, d'exprimer une opinion sur ces comptes.

Nous avons effectué notre audit selon les normes de la profession ; ces normes requièrent la mise en oeuvre de diligences permettant d'obtenir l'assurance raisonnable que les comptes consolidés ne comportent pas d'anomalies significatives. Un audit consiste à examiner, par sondages, les éléments probants justifiant les données contenues dans ces comptes. Il consiste également à apprécier les principes comptables suivis et les estimations significatives retenues pour l'arrêté des comptes et à apprécier leur présentation d'ensemble. Nous estimons que nos contrôles fournissent une base raisonnable à l'opinion exprimée ci-après.

Nous certifions que les comptes consolidés sont réguliers et sincères et donnent une image fidèle du patrimoine, de la situation financière, ainsi que du résultat de l'ensemble constitué par les entreprises comprises dans la consolidation.

Par ailleurs, nous avons également procédé à la vérification des informations relatives au Groupe, données dans le rapport de gestion. Nous n'avons pas d'observation à formuler sur leur sincérité et leur concordance avec les comptes consolidés.

Fait à Paris, le 25 mars 1997

Les Commissaires aux Comptes

CCC-JD	Société d'Expertise	Cabinet MAZARS & GUERARD
Jean DELQUIÉ	Comptable A & L GENOT	Frédéric ALLILAIRE
	Alain GENOT - Louis GENOT	Xavier CHARTON

Report of the Auditors

Consolidated Statements for the Year Ended December 31, 1996

Ladies and Gentlemen

In conformity with the mission assigned to us by your General Shareholders Meetings, we have conducted an audit of the consolidated statements of the Pernod Ricard company for the fiscal year ended December 31, 1996, which is presented on pages 39 to 52.

The consolidated statements were approved by the Board of Directors. Based on our audit, we hereby express our opinion regarding these statements.

Our audit was conducted in accordance with professional standards. These standards require the utmost diligence in order to ensure that the consolidated statements do not include any significant errors or inconsistencies. An audit involves the use of sampling to examine the underlying information justifying the data contained in these statements. It also involves an assessment of the accounting principles followed as well as the resulting calculations and the overall presentation. We believe that our audit provides a reasonable basis for the opinion expressed below.

We hereby certify that the consolidated statements are in order and present an accurate picture of the assets and the financial position, as well as the overall results of Pernod Ricard and its consolidated companies.

Furthermore, we have also audited the data pertaining to the Group provided in the Management Report. We have no comment to make on the sincerity of the information given in the Management Report or on the consistency of this information with the consolidated financial statements.

Paris, March 25, 1997

The Statutory Auditors

CCC-JD	**Société d'Expertise**	**Cabinet MAZARS & GUERARD**
M. Jean DELQUIÉ	Comptable A & L GENOT	Frédéric ALLILAIRE
	Alain et Louis GENOT	Xavier CHARTON

Bilan Pernod Ricard

Actif

En milliers de francs	Brut	31.12.1996 Amortissements et provisions	Net	31.12.1995 Net	31.12.1994 Net
Immobilisations incorporelles	**225 226**	**(9 197)**	**216 029**	**215 105**	**214 953**
Licences, marques	225 226	(9 197)	216 029	215 105	214 953
Immobilisations corporelles	**45 750**	**(23 576)**	**22 174**	**21 507**	**17 713**
Terrains	6 733	0	6 733	6 812	6 010
Constructions	17 207	(7 695)	9 512	9 793	6 709
Matériel et outillage	986	(975)	11	16	16
Autres	20 824	(14 906)	5 918	4 886	4 978
Immobilisations financières	**6 638 458**	**(16 950)**	**6 621 508**	**6 472 610**	**7 409 351**
Participations	4 219 324	(14 632)	4 204 692	4 021 676	4 081 996
Créances rattachées à des participations	2 352 801	(2 318)	2 350 483	2 391 246	3 326 432
Prêts	689	0	689	689	689
Autres	65 644	0	65 644	58 999	234
Total actif immobilisé	**6 909 434**	**(49 723)**	**6 859 711**	**6 709 222**	**7 642 017**
Avances et acomptes versés sur commandes	**1 205**	**0**	**1 205**	**1 086**	**1 253**
Créances d'exploitation	**125 219**	**0**	**125 219**	**85 387**	**86 833**
Créances clients et comptes rattachés	102 521	0	102 521	69 537	69 683
Autres	22 698	0	22 698	15 850	17 150
Créances diverses	**124 745**	**(1 680)**	**123 065**	**117 305**	**572 415**
Valeurs mobilières de placement	**509 757**	**(28 382)**	**481 375**	**262 390**	**304 836**
Disponibilités	**34 320**	**0**	**34 320**	**2 178**	**17 057**
Total actif circulant	**795 246**	**(30 062)**	**765 184**	**468 346**	**982 394**
Charges constatées d'avance	**1 007**	**0**	**1 007**	**954**	**3 558**
Charges à répartir sur plusieurs exercices	**4 956**	**0**	**4 956**	**5 668**	**5 805**
Écart de conversion - Actif	**32 462**	**0**	**32 462**	**51 567**	**28 229**
Total comptes de régularisation	**38 425**	**0**	**38 425**	**58 189**	**37 592**
Total général	**7 743 105**	**(79 785)**	**7 663 320**	**7 235 757**	**8 662 003**

Passif

En milliers de francs	31.12.1996	31.12.1995	31.12.1994
Capital	1 127 733	1 127 733	1 127 733
Primes d'émission, de fusion, d'apport	248 967	248 967	248 967
Réserves	2 095 542	2 095 542	2 076 747
Réserve légale	112 773	112 773	93 978
Réserves réglementées	1 982 769	1 982 769	1 982 769
Report à nouveau	1 022 310	1 140 035	974 201
Résultat de l'exercice	1 002 202	326 094	627 154
Provisions réglementées	5 770	8 339	8 407
Total des capitaux propres	5 502 524	4 946 710	5 063 209
Autres fonds propres (TSDI)	257 763	267 429	277 095
Provisions pour risques et charges	67 892	72 168	50 579
Dettes financières	663 359	831 919	1 922 491
Emprunts obligataires non convertibles	400 000	400 000	400 000
Emprunts et dettes auprès des établissements de crédit	15 474	190 419	1 184 853
Emprunts et dettes financières diverses	247 885	241 500	337 638
Dettes d'exploitation	68 930	57 556	54 483
Dettes fournisseurs et comptes rattachés	40 615	35 499	33 722
Dettes fiscales et sociales	28 315	22 057	20 761
Dettes diverses	1 101 819	1 059 975	1 294 146
Dettes fiscales (impôts sur les bénéfices)	51 218	54 964	-
Autres	1 050 601	1 005 011	1 294 146
Total des dettes	1 834 108	1 949 450	3 271 120
Produits constatés d'avance	401		
Écart de conversion - Passif	632		
Total comptes de régularisation	1 033		
Total général	7 663 320	7 235 757	8 662 003

Compte de résultat
Pernod Ricard

En milliers de francs	1996	1995	1994
Redevances	264 764	220 467	218 128
Autres produits	151 403	140 865	134 104
Reprises sur provisions			46
Total des produits d'exploitation	**416 167**	**361 332**	**352 278**
Services extérieurs	(293 397)	(269 488)	(270 136)
Impôts, taxes et versements assimilés	(5 628)	(5 902)	(5 613)
Charges de personnel	(39 818)	(38 939)	(40 957)
Dotations aux amortissements et aux provisions	(3 611)	(2 961)	(3 469)
Autres charges	(1 918)	(2 003)	(1 970)
Total des charges d'exploitation	**(344 372)**	**(319 293)**	**(322 145)**
Résultat d'exploitation avant opérations financières	**71 795**	**42 039**	**30 133**
Produits de participations	850 514	418 537	539 384
Autres intérêts et produits assimilés	29 996	109 724	105 954
Reprises sur provisions	51 567	29 586	1 359
Différences positives de change	209	13 402	37 351
Produits nets sur cessions de valeurs mobilières de placement		545	1 264
Total des produits financiers	**932 286**	**571 794**	**685 312**
Dotations aux provisions	(32 271)	(51 567)	(29 586)
Intérêts et charges assimilés	(111 949)	(228 828)	(216 024)
Différences négatives de change	(1 955)	(20 434)	(9 804)
Total des charges financières	**(146 175)**	**(300 829)**	**(255 414)**
Résultat financier	**786 111**	**270 965**	**429 898**
Résultat courant	**857 906**	**313 004**	**460 031**
Produits exceptionnels	120 092	72 176	510 724
Charges exceptionnelles	(22 643)	(139 678)	(397 123)
Résultat exceptionnel	**97 449**	**(67 502)**	**113 601**
Résultat avant impôt	**955 355**	**245 502**	**573 632**
Impôt sur les bénéfices	46 847	80 592	53 522
Bénéfice de l'exercice	**1 002 202**	**326 094**	**627 154**

Country Highlights
GERMANY

Common Legal Forms of Companies
- Limited liability companies and limited partnerships are the dominating legal forms. The importance of stock corporations has been increasing considerably during the past 10 years.

Sources of Financial Reporting Requirements
- The German Commercial Code is of supreme importance. In addition, seperate laws exist for specific legal forms, for specific industries, and large noncorporations falling under the so-called Publicity Law.

Corporate Taxation
- There are two types of income taxes, the trade tax on income and the corporation income tax. Whereas the first one is a municipal tax applicable to all companies, the second type is subject to corporations only and is a federal tax. Temporarily, a surtax (the so-called solidarity charge) in order to finance the German reunification process has been levied also. As of January 1, 1998, the last type of net asset tax (trade tax on capital) has been abolished.

Auditing Requirements
- German law differentiates auditing requirements according to a company's legal form and size. Subject to statutory audits are the single entity financial statements of medium-sized and large corporations as well as of large noncorporations. Furthermore, there is a need for the audit of group financial statements, in case corporations or large noncorporations are obliged to set up such accounts.

Organization of the Accounting and Auditing Profession
- The profession is headed by the Chamber of Auditors, an independent organization responsible for the supervision of its members and for the representation of the profession to other parties. A second important organization is the Institute of Certified Auditors. The first main task of the Institute of Certified Auditors is to generate generally accepted accounting and auditing standards. In the future, acounting standards will be set by a committee, which also comprises representatives from outside the profession.

Constitution and Legal System

- Germany is a federal republic with sixteen states, or *Länder*. The system of government is parliamentary at both federal and state levels. The head of the federal government is the Chancellor (*Kanzler*), while the government of each *Land* is headed by a Chief Minister (*Minister präsident*). The Federal President is a nonexecutive head of state.

- The federal parliament consists of a lower house, the *Bundestag*, and an upper house, the *Bundestrat*. Germany operates under a system of codified law, which includes the Commercial Code. Various laws govern the activities of different types of corpoations, including the *Aktiengesetz* with respect to AGs, the *Börsengesetz* on quoted companies and the *Publizitätsgesetz* for large unincorporated enterprises. The tax courts, and expecially the Federal Fiscal Court (*Bundesfinanzhof*), are also important in providing interpretations of the law with regard to accounting requirements

Currency

The financial statements must be prepared in DEM. From 1999 on German companies can switch to the euro.

Official Languages

The German language is mandatory for financial statements.

GERMANY

Günter Seckler
Partner of Arthur Andersen & Co. GmbH
Frankfurt am Main

1. Background

1.1 History of German Accounting Regulations

German accounting regulations and, especially, German accounting law have only a relatively brief history compared with those of some other European countries. In 1937 general accounting standards and principles were codified for the first time in the Stock Corporation Law. This came about as a reaction to the large number of companies going bankrupt during the worldwide economic crisis of the late 1920s and early 1930s. Existing accounting practice failed to protect adequateley the creditors of German companies in cases of bankruptcy. Consequently, the dominating principle incorporated in the Stock Corporation Law of 1937 was that of prudence in order best to protect the interests of creditors.

A significant modification of the Stock Corporation Law of 1937 took place in 1965. Under the revised law the interests of the shareholders were given more consideration than under the previous law. In particular, the opportunities for asset underevaluations were limited. The principle of prudence and the idea of creditor protection remained important, however, if no longer dominant.

Until 1985 the Stock Corporation Law of 1965 was more or less the sole source of accounting law in Germany, codifying accounting principles and standards. No other specific regulations existed, either for other corporations like limited liability companies or for noncorporations such as partnerships. There was, however, a broad understanding that the standards incorporated in the Stock Corporation Law represented to a large extent generally accepted accounting principles. This applied especially to the rules regarding the format and content of the balance sheet and the income statement. Furthermore, certain evaluation rules were broadly accepted as applicable for companies of other legal forms. Nevertheless, there were no binding rules for nonstock corporations, and therefore, those companies could be highly flexible in their accounting approaches.

In 1985, however, the Fourth, Seventh, and Eighth EC Directives were embodied in German law, thereby completely changing the existing regulatory systems with regard to preparation, publication, and auditing of single and group financial statements.

Technically, the modification of German law was achieved by incorporating the three EC Directives into the Accounting Directives Law, which is a pure modification law covering a total of 39 separate laws. Of supreme importance was the revision of the Commercial Code and, especially, the insertion of a third book (last amended in May 1998) with accounting and auditing rules applicable to all businesses.

Second, supplementary rules were retained or codified in separate laws for specific legal forms (e.g., in Stock Corporation Law and Limited Liability Company Law) as well as for specific industries (e.g., in Banking Law and the Insurance Supervisory Law). Third, specific provisions for large noncorporations included in the Publicity Law of 1969 were modified.

With the adoption of the three EC Directives, the most important "Anglo-Saxon" accounting principles were implemented into German accounting law. The reader of German financial statements should always remember, however, that to a large extent, new and old accounting standards still can be applied in parallel.

The Accounting Directives Law itself became effective on January 1, 1986. For single company financial statements it had to be applied not later than for fiscal years commencing after December 31, 1986. The latest application for group financial statements was for fiscal years beginning after December 31, 1989.

1.2 The German Auditing Profession

As with German accounting law, the German auditing profession has a rather short tradition compared with those of some other European countries. The first auditing firms were formed at the turn of the twentieth century. Their main purpose was to audit and to provide consultancy services for large businesses on a voluntary basis. The first official professional organization was established in 1931, when the consequences of the worldwide economic crisis demonstrated the need for audited financial statements.

A decree of the *Reichspräsident* dated September 19, 1931, announcing statutory audits by independent auditors, can be regarded as the birth of the German auditing profession. Further milestones in its development are represented by the statutory audit requirements established for stock corporations in 1937, for large nonstock corporations in 1969, and for (at least medium-sized) limited liability companies in 1985.

The growing demands of stockholders, banks, and other creditors for audited financial statements, as well as a dramatic expansion of the range of services provided by audit firms, has led to considerable growth of the profession during the past 30–40 years. Today the German auditing profession is headed by the Chamber of Auditors (*Wirtschaftsprüferkammer*), an independent professional organization supervised by the Federal Minister of Economics. The tasks of the Chamber of Auditors range from the supervision of its members to the representation of the profession to other parties.

Members of the *Wirtschaftsprüferkammer* are both certified auditors (*Wirtschaftsprüfer*, or WP) as well as certified accountants (*vereidigte Buchprüfer*, or vBP). The difference between the two types of professional is that certified accountants benefit from simplified admission and examination procedures, while on the other hand, they are allowed to perform only voluntary audits, as well as statutory audits of medium-sized limited liability companies, or *Gesellschaften mit beschränkter Haftung* (GmbHs). All other statutory audits must be performed by certified auditors.

Before one may be appointed as a certified auditor, one must surmount many hurdles. This requires passing an examination that covers in depth the subjects of accounting, auditing, business administration, law, taxation, general economics, and taxation. Furthermore, candidates must usually have 4 years of practical experience in auditing or audit-related activities.

Because of stringent admission, examination, and supervisory regulations, the German Professional Law (*Wirtschaftsprüferordnung*) is widely regarded as one of the strictest worldwide.

Besides the Chamber of Auditors, the Institute of Certified Auditors (*Institut der Wirtschaftsprüfer*, IdW) is the other important organization of the profession. Its main task is to publish statements on principal accounting and auditing questions that then usually serve as generally accepted standards and principles within the profession. Unlike the Chamber of Auditors, membership in the Institute of Certified Auditors is voluntary.

Auditing financial statements and rendering opinions thereon are the exclusive right of certified auditors and certified accountants.

1.3 General Accounting Rules in Germany

As a general rule, applicable for all businesses, financial statements are to be drawn up in accordance with generally accepted accounting principles (§243 (1) HGB).

For corporations only, the general rule has been expanded. Their financial statements must, in compliance with generally accepted accounting principles (GAAP), present a true and fair view of the net worth, the financial position, and the results of the company (§264 (2) HGB).

Both general rules require that the financial statements comply with German GAAP, which mostly were incorporated into the German Commercial Code in connection with the adoption of the Fourth Directive. They can be briefly summarized as follows:

- The financial statements must be clear and understandable.
- They must be complete.
- Offsetting of assets against liabilities and income against expenses is prohibited.
- The amounts included in the opening balance sheet must agree with the closing balance sheet of the preceding year.
- To the extent not disproved by facts or action of law, a going concern must be assumed.
- Valuation must be made on an item-by-item basis.
- Accounting must be done prudently; that is, all anticipated risks and losses that arise up to the balance sheet date are to be recognized, even if they become known only after the balance sheet date but before the date of preparation of the financial statements; profits may be recognized only if they are realized (realization and imparity principle).
- Accounting must be made on an accrual basis and with due consideration of the matching principle.

- Valuation principles must be applied consistently over the years.
- Valuation is based on historical cost.

Deviations from the above principles are allowed only to the extent that exceptional circumstances exist. It should also be noted that in accordance with the prudence principle, provisions and allowances can be set up if it is possible, but not necessarily probable, that an asset has been impaired or a liability has been incurred.

As mentioned earlier, the general rule for corporations requires not only that their financial statements comply with GAAP, but also that they provide a true and fair view. This latter principle has been taken over from Anglo-Saxon countries. In Germany, however, its interpretation may be different. It still seems to be the dominant opinion in Germany that compliance with legal requirements ensures a true and fair presentation, even if the law allows exceptions from GAAP, for instance, the creation of hidden reserves. It is broadly understood that the form and content of financial statements are derived first from the specific rules of laws and ordinances. The general rule needs to be referred to only if doubts arise in the interpretation and application of individual rules or if uncertainties in the legal provisions need to be resolved.

With regard to the transformation of significant option rights established by the Fourth and Seventh EC Directive into the German Commercial Code and the comparison of material differences between German GAAP and U.S. GAAP as well as International Accounting Standards (IAS), reference is made to Exhibits I through IV at the end of the chapter.

1.4 The Relationship Between Commercial and Tax Accounting

It is of the utmost practical importance to recognize that commercial accounts in Germany are linked directly with tax accounts. According to the so-called authoritative principle (*Maßgeblichkeitsprinzip*), which is incorporated in §5 EStG (German Income Tax Law) and which is almost unknown in the accounting rules of most other countries, commercial financial statements form an authoritative basis for tax accounts. Tax accounts do not represent an independent set of accounts but are derived from the commercial accounts.

As a consequence, the accounting treatment in the commercial financial statements in general directly affects the tax position of a company. In addition, most of the tax incentives can be claimed only if the same treatment is applied to the items in question in the commercial financial statements. In practice this often leads to a reversal of the authoritative nature of commercial financial statements for the tax accounts.

As a result, German companies are compelled to evaluate their assets at the lowest amount possible and their liabilities at their highest amount possible under GAAP in their commercial financial statements in order to minimize their tax liability. Furthermore, in order to benefit from tax incentives, they may be led to record in their commercial accounts special tax-allowed depreciations and reserves, or to not reverse write-downs even though the reasons for them no longer exist. To avoid the possibly misleading effects resulting from the departure from the true and fair view, such accounting practices must be explained in the Notes..

1.5 Financing of German Industry

Financing of German industry is characterized by a relatively low number of companies traded on the stock exchange, a relatively low equity ratio, and typically high financing by banks. Another important source of financing is through pension accruals.

Of about 440,000 corporations, only around 550 were listed on the stock exchange at the end of 1990. Traditionally, these were very large stock corporations (*Aktiengesellschaft*, AG). This picture has changed to a certain extent, since a considerable number of medium-sized corporations have decided to go public since then. The main reasons for this development were considered to be:

- The inability or unwillingness of the old shareholders to provide additional equity funds
- The relative reduction of disadvantages (e.g., publication requirements) attributed to AGs, compared with other legal forms
- Fund raising partially because of the long lasting bull market in the 1990s
- Positive publicity from stock markets becoming more popular

For a number of years the average equity ratio of German companies has been only 20%, or even lower. This rather low ratio is often attributed to the fact that from a tax point of view, loan debt financing is preferable compared with equity financing, since unlike equity financing, debt financing reduces the tax basis for net wealth tax at least partially for trade tax on capital and—via interest expense—also for income taxes. This also explains the tendency for shareholders to try to classify a high portion of their investments in firms as loans and not as equity.

The high degree of funding via pension accruals is mainly due to the fact that from a tax, administrative, and financial point of view, this form of funding is often preferable to external funding.

2. The Form and Content of Published Financial Statements

2.1 Introductiory Notes

As described in Section 1.1 above, the German accounting and disclosure rules are codified in various laws, although the majority of the regulations are now incorporated in the third book of the Commercial Code (last revised in May 1998). Nevertheless, within the framework of this accounting guide, it would be impossible to cover every particular rule. Accordingly, all rules and regulations specifically relating to registered cooperatives, as well as to companies of particular industries like banks and insurance companies, are not further commented on. This limits the range of entities taken into account to the following:

- Corporations, for example, stock corporations (AGs), partnerships limited by shares (*Kommanditgesellschaft auf Aktien*, KGaAs) and limited liability companies (GmbHs).
- Small noncorporations, for example, sole proprietorships, partnerships (*Offene Handelsgesellschaft*, OHG; and *Kommanditgesellschaft*, KG) and partnerships with at least one limited liability company as general partner (e.g., GmbH & Co.'s).
- Large noncorporations, with the same legal form as above but exceeding certain size criteria (see Section 2.3)

Whereas the first two types of company are governed by the Commercial Code, the accounting, auditing, and disclosure rules for noncorporations are included in the Publicity Law.

As a particular point, it should be mentioned that GmbH & Co.'s and AG & Co.'s are partnerships that, until December 31, 1994, had to follow only the less strict requirements for noncorporations (e.g., the absence of net worth taxes on company level, comparatively low accounting, audit, and publication requirements), although they contain strong corporation elements from an economic point of view. This regulation has been greatly discussed in the EC in past years. As a result, it can be expected that such partnerships will have to meet the requirements set up for corporations soon.

2.2 Components of Single and Group Financial Statements

The financial statements must include at least the following components:

| | | Noncorporations | |
	Corporations	Small	Large
Balance sheet	X	X	X
Income statement	X	X	X
Notes	X		X
Management report	X*a*		X

a Except for small corporations (since 8/94)

In the terminology of German law, financial statements consist of the first three components; the management report is a separate element of year-end reporting. For the purpose of this guide, however, this stringent interpretation is not followed, and the management report is regarded as an integral part of the financial statements. It should be noted, however, that the auditors' opinion must state whether the management report is consistent with the financial statements.

2.3 Differentiation of Financial Statements According to Legal Form and Size

In order to establish different levels of requirements for the preparation, audit, and disclosure of single entity and group financial statements, certain size criteria were incorporated into the Commercial Code and the Publicity Law, in addition to the differentiation according to legal form (see Table 1).

TABLE 1 *Size Criteria for Disclosure of Single Entity and Group Financial Statements*

	Balance Sheet Total (thousands DEM)	Sales (thousands DEM)	Number of Employees
A. Corporations			
I. Single entity financial statements (§267 HGB)			
1. Small	≤ 5,310	≤ 10,620	≤ 50
2. Medium-sized	> 5,310 ≤ 21,240	> 10,620 ≤ 42,480	> 50 ≤ 250
3. Large	> 21,240	> 42,480	> 250
II. Consolidated financial statements (§293 HGB)			
1. Consolidated	> 53,100	> 106,200	> 500
2. Combined	> 63,720	> 127,440	> 500
B. Noncorporations			
I. Single entity financial statements (§1 PublG)			
1. Small	≤ 125,000	≤ 250,000	≤ 5,000
2. Large	> 125,000	> 250,000	> 5,000
II. Consolidated financial statements (§11 PublG)			
Consolidated	> 125,000	> 250,000	> 5,000

DEM, Deutsche marks.

The requirements set out in the following paragraphs and sections apply only if at least two of the three size criteria are met by corporations in *two* consecutive years and by noncorporations in *three* consecutive years. It should be noted that quoted stock corporations, or those that are traded over the counter, are always deemed to be "large" corporations.

2.4 Overview of Preparation, Audit, and Disclosure Requirements

Table 2 provides an overview of the minimum legal requirements concerning financial statements. Companies are free to establish stricter requirements in their statutes.

TABLE 2   *Minimum Legal Requirements for Financial Statements*

	Single Entity Financial Statements					Group Financial Statements	
	Corporations			Noncorporations		Corporations	Noncorporations
	Small	Medium-sized	Large	Small	Large		
Balance sheet							
Preparation	yes	yes	yes	yes	yes	yes	yes
Disclosure	CR	CR	FG	—	FG	FG	FG
Income statement							
Preparation	yes	yes	yes	yes	yes	yes	yes
Disclosure	—	CR	FG	—	FG	FG	FG
Notes							
Preparation	yes	yes	yes	—	—*	yes	yes
Disclosure	CR	CR	FG	—	—*	FG	FG
Management report							
Preparation	—	yes	yes	—	—*	yes	yes
Disclosure	—	CR	FG	—	—*	FG	FG
Statutory audit	—	yes	yes	—	yes	yes	yes
Maximum preparation period (months)	6	3	3	"Adequate period"	3	5	5
Maximum disclosure period (months)	12	9	9	—	9	9	9

* Very few exceptions

Abbreviations: CR, Commercial Register; FG, Federal Gazette

Notes: Except for small corporations, all other companies must prepare a full set of financial statements.

Except for small corporations and small noncorporations, statutory audits are required.

Except for small noncorporations, all other companies must publish a full set or at least part of their financial statements.

Large companies must publish their single entity and group financial statements in the Federal Gazette before filing them with the Commercial Register; the disclosure requirement for small and medium-sized corporations is limited to the Commercial Register; however, small and medium-sized corporations must announce in the Federal Gazette that the financial statements have been filed with the Commercial Register.

Large noncorporations do not have to publish their income statement, provided they disclose limited information (sales, investment income, payroll expenses, number of employees, depreciation/evaluation methods) in an annex to the balance sheet (§9 (2) PublG).

In addition to the requirements shown in Table 2, corporations must publish the proposal for the appropriation of the result and the report of the supervisory board, if applicable. The latter also applies to noncorporations. Furthermore, the auditor's opinion or disclaimer, but not the full auditor's report, which usually is a long-form report, must be disclosed in the case of statutory audits.

The company's management must forward a full auditor's report to the members of the supervisory board only. On a voluntary basis, this is usually also made available to selected other addressees (e.g., banks and other important creditors).

It should be recognized that despite the legal requirements, the quota of firms that publish financial statements is currently estimated to be far below 20%. Small and medium-sized companies in particular still prefer to make their financial statements available only to selected outside addressees (e.g., banks), in order not to disclose any information that might be of interest to competitors. The Commercial Code does not adequately prevent such practice, since no serious penalties are incorporated for nonpublication.

2.5 Published Financial Statements and the Management Report

2.5.1 General Remarks

Detailed legal regulations concerning the form and content of financial statements exist for corporations only. Large noncorporations must also follow them. No such detailed rules exist for small noncorporations. It is common practice, however, for these companies to prepare their financial statements similarly to those of corporations but mostly to a less detailed extent. Because of the lack of regulations and the absence of disclosure requirements for these companies, the following paragraphs deal only with corporations and large noncorporations.

2.5.2 Balance Sheet

The basic format of the balance sheet to be applied by corporations and large noncorporations in their single and group financial statements is presented in §266 HGB. The main captions within the prescribed accounts format are:

Assets	Equity and Liabilities
A. Fixed assets	A. Equity
I. Intangible assets	I. Subscribed capital
II. Tangible assets	II. Capital reserves
III. Financial assets	III. Revenue reserves
	IV. Retained profits/accumulated
	losses brought forward
	V. Result for the year
B. Current assets	B. Accruals
I. Inventories	
II. Receivables and other	
current assets	
III. Securities	
IV. Liquid funds	
C. Prepaid expenses	C. Liabilities
	D. Deferred income

Whereas small corporations are allowed to present and disclose their balance sheet in the above format, all other companies must break down the subheadings into various prescribed items.

In addition to the general principles, which require a clear, understandable, and complete presentation and forbid the netting of items, the following presentation and disclosure rules are incorporated in §265 HGB:

- Continuity of disclosure and classification

- Presentation of comparative figures

- Notes, where items belong to more than one heading

- Extension of the basic classification, if required because of different industries included in one legal entity

- Change of classification/description, if appropriate

- Option to add new items, if appropriate

- Option to eliminate items with no current and prior year amount

- Combination of headings in case of immaterial amounts or to improve the clarity of presentation

Other important rules are the options to present

- The fixed assets movements analysis
- The remaining terms of liabilities (less than 1 year, over 5 years) and of receivables (over 1 year)
- The type and amounts of contingent liabilities

in the notes to the financial statements instead of on the face of the balance sheet.

In order to avoid overloading the balance sheet and to improve the clarity of presentation, there is a strong tendency to put as many disclosures as possible into the notes, where optional, and also to use the legal opportunities to combine headings in the balance sheet with supplementary analyses in the notes.

2.5.3 Income Statement

The basic formats of the income statement for corporations and noncorporations are incorporated in §275 HGB. They apply to the single entity as well as to the group financial statements.

The income statement must be presented in a vertical form following either the "type-of-expenditure" or the "functional" format. The general presentation principles as described earlier also apply to the profit and loss account.

The traditional format in Germany, the type-of-expenditure format, is a production-oriented presentation. According to the underlying philosophy, the measurement for the performance of a company is not only sales but also inventories produced on or taken from stock, as well as the value of internal resources used to create or improve fixed assets.

Accordingly, the change in work-in-progress and finished goods as well as own work capitalized are disclosed separately. Together with sales, they make up the "gross performance" for the year. As a further typical characteristic, income and expense items are disclosed according to their type, disregarding where they were incurred.

The type-of-expenditure format as defined in §275 (2) HGB shows the following structure:

	Item no.
Sales	1
± Change in work in progress/finished goods	2
+ Own work capitalized	3
Gross performance	1 – 3
+ Other operating income	4
– Cost of materials	5
– Personnel expenses	6
– Depreciation	7
– Other operating expenses	8
Operating result	1 – 8
± Financial result	9 – 13
Result from ordinary operations	14
± Extraordinary result	15 – 17
– Taxation	18 – 19
Result for the year	20

The traditional format for the income statement in Anglo-Saxon countries is the "functional" format. Although that format was allowed to German non-AGs before 1987, it achieved some importance only after incorporation into the Commercial Code.

According to its underlying philosophy, the measurement for the performance of a company is primarily sales. Consequently, the change in inventories and own cost capitalized are not disclosed separately. Instead, expenses are mainly structured according to the "cost centers" or functions where they are incurred.

The "functional" format as prescribed in §275 (3) HGB shows the following structure:

	Item no.
Sales	1
– Cost of sales	2
Gross profit	3
– Selling expenses	4
– Administrtive expenses	5
+ Other operating income	6
– Other operating expense	7

Operating result	1 – 7
+ Financial result	8 – 12
Result from ordinary operations	13
+ Extraordinary result	14 – 16
– Taxation	17 – 18
Result for the year	19

It should be noted that the subheadings used above for the most part are not official line descriptions according to §275 HGB and, therefore, are mostly not disclosed separately. However, they are frequently used by financial analysts in order to structure the income statement.

It should further be noted that the contents of subheadings and single lines are not identical in both formats, even if the same descriptions are used. This makes the comparison of companies more difficult and is mainly a result of the following:

- Companies applying the functional format partly allocate nonincome taxes and interest expenses to cost of sales, selling, or general and administrative (G&A) expenses. Accordingly, there may be differences with regard to taxation, financial, and operating results, since under the type-of-expenditure approach such allocations are not known.

- "Other operating expenses" in the cost-of-sales format are usually lower, since only those amounts not allocable to cost of sales, selling, or G&A are classified under this line. On the other hand, "other operating expenses" in the cost-of-sales format may also show a higher amount. As a German peculiarity, and deviating from international practice, it is regarded as acceptable to classify the difference between direct and full cost valuation of inventories as other operating expense, if the company has decided to price its inventories at direct cost only (reference is also made to this in Section 3.2.4).

- Small and medium-sized corporations are allowed to combine lines 1–5 (type-of-expenditure format), or lines 1–3 and 6 (functional format) into a heading described "gross results" (§276 HGB) and need not split up this heading for disclosure purposes; it should be borne in mind that the contents of this heading may be completely different, depending on the format used.

Apart from these particulars, the contents of the single lines in the German cost-of-sales income statement comply with international standards and do not need further comment. On the other hand, the internationally less well-known type-of-expenditure format requires some additional explanations:

- The "change in work in progress and finished goods" line represents the difference in values compared with the previous year. Thus, the amount disclosed includes changes in units, in prices, and in allowances. With respect to the background of this line as well as of "own cost capitalized," reference is made to the previous explanations.

- Material costs must be broken down into cost of raw material, consumables, supplies, and purchased merchandise, as well as cost of purchased services. It is broadly accepted that the latter should include only costs of the same character as for material, for instance, expenses for having goods manufactured by other parties.

- Personnel expenses must be split into wages and salaries, social security, and old-age pensions.

- Depreciation must be split into usual and unusual portions, if any. The latter refers only to depreciation on current assets to the extent that it exceeds a level, for example, a percentage or absolute amount, that is deemed to be usual for the company. Because it remains doubtful what exactly is to be understood by the term usual, particular attention should be given to the explanations in the notes.

- Separate disclosure of income from participations, particularly from those in affiliated companies, is required within the financial results caption. Although not required by law, it is common practice to disclose income or losses resulting from income and loss pooling contracts separately.

  Such contracts are mostly concluded in order to arrive at taxation on a group basis. A second, usually less important, reason for such contracts is that funds for dividend payments are available at the parent company level in the same year in which they are incurred in the group companies.

- The amounts to be classified as extraordinary income or expense are defined as those incurring outside the regular activities of a company (§277 (4) HGB).

Although a common interpretation and practice of what exactly is to be understood by "extraordinary" has not yet been achieved, there seems to be a strong trend toward the Anglo-American understanding. More and more, *extraordinary* is characterized by nonrecurring events resulting in significant amounts. On the other hand, typical results of a recurring nature, such as gains/losses from the disposal of fixed assets or from the release of excess accruals, are regarded as contributing to the results of ordinary activities, unless of very high amounts.

- Taxation must be split into income taxes and other taxes. Deferred tax expenses need not be disclosed separately.

  Although a netting of income and expenses is not allowed in general, some important commentaries consider it to be acceptable or even preferable to net income from reversal of tax accruals or tax refunds with the tax expense of the year, since it is regarded as misleading to classify that income as "other operating income," as is still common practice.

It is to be noted that common practice for many classification issues, particularly with regard to the cost-of-sales format income statement and "unusual" or "exceptional" items, has not yet been finally developed. Therefore, particular attention should be given to the corresponding explanations in the notes to financial statements.

2.5.4 Notes to Financial Statements

The notes form an integral part of financial statements. Before 1987, notes had to be prepared and disclosed only by stock corporations and large companies falling within the ambit of the Publicity Law (but with less quantity of information); they are frequently regarded as representing the most important change brought about by the Accounting Directives Law.

As with Anglo-Saxon disclosure practice, notes provide additional information for the interpretation of the balance sheet and income statement. Furthermore, they fulfill a replacement function, since they contain information that otherwise would need to be incorporated in the balance sheet or income statement.

The form and structure of the notes are not prescribed by law. Accordingly, various presentation formats can be found in practice. The most common basic structure used is:

I. General information to financial statements
  1. Significant accounting principles
  2. Other
 II. Specific information to financial statements
  1. Disclosures to balance sheet
  2. Disclosures to income statement
III. Sundry disclosures

The provisions concerning individual disclosures to be included in the single and group notes are spread over a large number of paragraphs in the Commercial Code and other specific laws. Therefore, completeness of disclosure usually can be achieved only by using checklists, although §§284–288 (single entity financial statements) and §§313–314 HGB (group financial statements) can be regarded as key provisions. Using the above basic format, the most important disclosures are:

General information:

- Accounting principles applied to single entity balance sheet and income statement items
- Method of foreign currency translation
- Departures from consistency
- Note, if contents or amounts of items are not comparable
- Disclosure of hidden reserves in inventories, if values are significantly below market
- Disclosure of the extent to which the results were affected by claiming tax benefits
- Method of goodwill amortization

Specific information, balance sheet:

- Fixed assets movement analysis, if not on the face of the balance sheet
- Amounts due to or due from shareholders (GmbHs only)
- Receivables with a term of more than 1 year; payables with a term of less than 1 year or more than 5 years, if not disclosed in the balance sheet

- Amount and type of collaterals on payables
- Disclosures to capitalized start-up/expansion costs and to deferred taxes
- Pension obligations not accrued for
- Details to sundry accruals, if significant
- Details of equity investment of at least a 20% interest (information can also be given in a separate listing, not to be published in the Federal Gazette but only in the Commercial Register)

Specific information, income statement:

- Details of extraordinary and prior period items, if material
- If a functional format is adopted, disclosure of materials and personnel costs as in the type-of-expenditure format
- Analysis of depreciation by balance sheet item
- Breakdown of sales by areas of activity and geographically defined markets
- Breakdown of tax expense relating to ordinary and extraordinary activities

Sundry disclosures:

- Type and amounts of contingent liabilities, if not set out in the balance sheet
- Total amount of other financial commitments
- Average number of employees
- The names of and financial relations with current and previous members the management and supervisory boards
- Total remuneration of the current and previous management and supervisory boards (separately for each group), unless the remuneration for single board members can be determined by such a disclosure

It should be noted that small and medium-sized corporations are granted certain simplifications for preparation and/or publication. For instance, small corporations neither have to provide details on extraordinary items and a fixed assets movement analysis, nor do they have to publish any disclosures relating to the income statement. Medium-sized corporations do not have to disclose the breakdown of sales by product lines and geographic markets. It is to be noted that apart from the analysis of sales (to be disclosed only by large corporations), no segment reporting is required by German law.

To a large extent, the above-described disclosures are also to be made in the notes to group financial statements. Important further disclosures in the group notes are:

- Uniform accounting and valuation principles applied
- Consolidation principles applied
- Details of consolidated and nonconsolidated group companies
- Translation of foreign currency financial statements

2.5.5 *Management Report*

The provisions (§§289 and 315 HGB) relating to the contents of the single entity and group management report are quite limited.

At a minimum, the management report must include a true and fair description of the company's/group's position and the business development during the fiscal year. In addition, the management report should include:

- Past balance sheet date events of great importance
- Anticipated future developments and a statement regarding future business policies
- Management's assessment of potential risks in anticipated future developments
- Disclosures regarding research and development
- Existing branches of the company

It should be noted that the management reports of smaller companies or groups usually reflect only the minimum requirements, are very brief, and do not contribute further important information.

On the other hand, large and, especially, public companies use their management report as a promotional tool by adding analyses of accounts, by commenting on variations from previous years, by giving details of new products and markets, as well as by including a social report or a funds or cash flow statement. Unlike Anglo-Saxon countries, the cash flow statement is not a compulsory component of financial statements, and if it is included, several different formats may be used, including those based on "net working capital" or "cash and equivalents" or variations thereof.

2.6 Auditor's Opinion

As previously mentioned, certified auditors/audit firms have the exclusive right to perform statutory audits and to issue opinions thereon. As an exception, certified accountants are allowed to perform statutory audits of medium-sized corporations.

The auditor must report on the audit. In particular, the auditor must confirm that the financial statements reflect a true and fair view of the company's situation. In addition, mention must be made of all material negative changes in net worth, financial position, and results, as well as of material losses that could jeopardize the going-concern assumption.

Unlike some other European countries, it is professional practice to prepare long-form audit reports only. The auditor's opinion included in the report (but not the rest of the report) must be published by the companies along with their financial statements. Before the recent amendment of the HGB, the standard audit opinion provided in §322 HGB reads as follows:

> Based on my/our audit performed in accordance with my/our professional duties, the accounting records and the (consolidated) financial statements comply with the legal regulations. The (consolidated) financial statements present, in compliance with generally accepted accounting principles, a true and fair view of the net worth, financial position and results of the company (group). The (group) management report is in agreement with the (consolidated) financial statements.

With the last amendment of the HGB in May 1998, the form of opinion was changed. Instead of the standard short form as above, the auditor now must render an opinion the in form of a report, which has to include at least the following:

- A description of the audit subject and scope as well as the type and extent of audit work performed.
- Mention of scope qualifications and exceptions (if there are non this must be explicitly stated).

- A statement whether the audited (consolidated) financial statements comply with generally accepted accounting principles and give a true and fair view of the net worth, financial position, and results of the company (group)
- Mention of any risks that could affect the company´s going-concern
- A statement whether the management report truly and fairly reflects the company´s (group´s) situation and also a statement whether management´s assessment of potential risks in anticipated future developments is reasonable.

The auditor's opinion must be modified, if additional comments appear necessary in order to avoid creating a misleading impression regarding the scope of the audit and the scope of the opinion, or if single entity and consolidated financial statements are combined in one set (see Section 2.7 below). Reference to the company's statutes is to be made, if they contain accounting-related regulations.

If there are objections, the auditor must qualify or disclaim his opinion. The objections must be explained in the opinion. Additions to the opinion like those described above do not represent qualifications.

According to statistics provided by the professional organizations, additions, qualifications, or disclaimers usually occur in less than 5% of cases.

It should be noted that the auditor's opinion refers to the financial statements as prepared. The auditor is not responsible for the publication of these financial statements.

2.7 Combination of Single Entity and Group Financial Statements

According to §298 and §315 HGB, parent companies are allowed to combine their single and consolidated financial statements and management reports. It is to be expected that in future an increasing number of companies will make use of this provision.

2.8 Sample Set of Financial Statements

As a sample, excerpts of the 1996 annual report of SAP AG are presented at the end of this chapter. We regard the statements of Friedrich Grohe AG as typical insofar as:

- They combine single entity and consolidated accounts.
- The balance sheet and income statements are presented in a simplified manner with supplementary analyses included in the notes.

On the other hand, we believe that the content of the management report might be typical only for publicly listed stock corporations; the majority of German companies tend to publish less information.

3. Accounting Policies and Practices: Implications for the Analyst

3.1 Consolidated Financial Statements

3.1.1 Overview

Consolidated financial statements are not the basis for either taxation or profit distributions but are of growing importance because of increasing national and international economic integration.

Regulations and principles for consolidated financial statements are largely the same for corporations and noncorporations. Important differences are described at the end of this section.

The basic consolidation provisions are incorporated in §§290–315 HGB. These are:

- Parent companies with a domestic head office are obliged to prepare and to publish consolidated financial statements, either:

  —if they exercise *de facto* control over one or more companies in which they own a participation of usually more than 20% (traditional German concept); or

  —if in principle they are able to exercise control by having the majority of voting rights, by being able to appoint or dismiss the members of the subsidiary boards, or because of a contract of domination or a domination clause incorporated in the bylaws of the subsidiary (Anglo-Saxon control concept).

There are exemptions for groups not exceeding certain size criteria (see Section 2.3 above), or if an ultimate parent having its head office in the EC or in certain countries (e.g. United States) with similar legal requirements and auditing standards, reports on the group including the German sub-group on a statutory or voluntary basis.

- The group financial statements must include the parent and all do-mestic and foreign subsidiaries. Enterprises must be excluded from full consolidation if their inclusion would conflict with the require-ment of a true and fair view (e.g., as a result of extremely divergent activities). Subsidiaries can be excluded, for instance, if they are immaterial or if the shares are held solely for the purpose of resale. Furthermore, exclusion of subsidiaries is allowed if the parent company's rights with regard to the subsidiary's assets are limited significantly or if the required information cannot be obtained from the subsidiary within a reasonable period of time or only at excessive costs.

- According to the one entity theory, the fiscal year-end and the accounting and valuation principles of all group companies must be identical. (As an important exception, however, German law allows consolidation of single entity financial statements if their closing date is earlier than the group's closing date but by not more than 3 months).

- Three forms of consolidation are permitted by law:
  —Full consolidation for subsidiaries under control (e.g., over 50% of the voting rights)
  —Equity accounting for associated enterprises on which a signifi-cant influence is exerted (e.g., 20%–50% of the voting rights).
  —Proportional consolidation for joint ventures with uniform man-agement by equal partners

As mentioned previously, only a few important deviations are allowed to noncorporations. These are:

- Group financial statements must be prepared only if control over subsidiaries actually is exercised (traditional German concept); the ability alone to exercise such control is not sufficient.

• The less strict valuation principles for noncorporations (§253 HGB) can be applied (mainly retention of written-down values, even if the reasons for them no longer exist; write-downs of fixed and intangible assets also in case of a nonpermanent impairment in value; opportunity to create hidden reserves via "excess" depreciation within the framework of sound business judgment).

3.1.2 Capital Consolidation

Full Consolidation   The primary method of capital consolidation is the Anglo-Saxon purchase or acquisition method (§301 HGB). Under exceptional circumstances (e.g., exchange of shares), the pooling of interests or merger method may be applied, although this method is quite rare and not expected to become important. Therefore, the following comments focus on the purchase method, two sub-forms of which are permitted by law for the first consolidation:

• According to the book value method, the book values in the individual balance sheets (as adjusted because of the application of identical valuation principles) are compared with the cost of the investment. If a debit balance arises (e.g., because hidden reserves have been paid for in the purchase price), this must be allocated to the relevant balance sheet headings in the proportion of shares held. Any amount remaining is to be recorded as goodwill. Any credit balance arising must be recorded as a consolidation difference on the liability side of the balance sheet (negative goodwill, or "badwill") or as equity ("lucky buy").

• According to the current value method, the subsidiaries' book values are replaced by market values so that hidden reserves are fully reflected. After the revaluation, however, the proportional net equity of the subsidiary is not allowed to exceed the cost of the investment.

Any debit or credit balances between proportional net equity and acquisition cost of the shares are classified as goodwill or badwill (or "lucky buy"). Disclosed hidden reserves relating to other shareholders are dealt with by inclusion in the minority interest. As a result, differences from applying either method can only arise where minority interests exist.

Under the book value method hidden reserves are only allocated proportionally to the share quota held, and therefore minority interests remain unchanged. Using the current value method also affects minority interest value, because hidden reserves are also allocated to these.

Because there is no specific regulation as to how upward revaluations must be allocated, future income can be manipulated to a certain and often not insignificant extent. This is because revaluations reverse quickly, slowly, or not at all, depending on whether inventories, fixed assets, or other items are revalued.

It is broadly understood that there are only classification differences between the book value and the current value method.

Goodwill arising at the time of the first consolidation can be handled very flexibly, as it can either be offset against equity reserves or be amortized systematically over the years that are likely to benefit (§ 309 (1) HGB). Although a 4-year period is mentioned by law as the regular amortization period, a range of 0–40 years is widely regarded as acceptable.

"Badwill" (or "lucky buy") has to be shown as a consolidation difference on the liability side of the balance sheet and in principle should remain unchanged in future consolidations. Depending on its character, a reclassification to capital reserves or to accrued liabilities may be acceptable, if not even preferred. A release to income is allowed only if it becomes clear that it corresponds to a realized profit or if the unfavorable developments anticipated in a reduced purchase price actually occur (§ 309 (2) HGB).

Determination of goodwill or "badwill" (or "lucky buy") can be made on the basis of the values at the time of the acquisition of shares, at the time of the first consolidation, at the time the new consolidation regulations are first applied, or, in the case of a successive purchase of shares, at the time the enterprise becomes a subsidiary.

As described in the preceeding paragraphs, there are several options with regard to capital consolidation. Common practice has not been finally developed. However, surveys performed by German Institute of Certified Public Accountants (IdW) revealed the following indications:

- The clearly preferred capital consolidation method is the book value method.

- A clear majority of groups offset goodwill arising at the time of the first consolidation against equity reserves; this may be spread over 2 or more years.

- Of the remainder, most groups use an amortization period of more than 4 years. There is a tendency toward a 15-year period, which corresponds to the regular amortization period prescribed by the German Income Tax Law for goodwill arising in the single equity financial statements (see the section "Fixed Asset Movement Analysis" below).

Proportional and Equity Consolidation   As far as it can be foreseen currently, proportional consolidation will not become important in Germany. If it is applied, the same principles as for full consolidations (see preceeding section) are to be followed (§310 (2) HGB).

The time and method of goodwill determination as described above are basically also applicable to equity consolidation (§311 HGB). Classification can follow two methods: Either the full equity value of the investment can be disclosed on the balance sheet, with separate disclosure of the goodwill portion in the notes, or the equity value can be split between a participation value and goodwill already on the balance sheet.

3.1.3 Debt and Income Consolidation

Elimination of intercompany debt, of intercompany income and expenses, as well as of intercompany profits and losses in principle follow international standards. It should be noted, however, that in the first year of including subsidiaries in a consolidation, consolidation impacts may be directly offset against reserves, instead of affecting profit and loss (Article 27 EGHGB).

3.1.4 Deferred Taxation

According to §306 HGB, timing differences incurred in connection with consolidation measures (e.g., intercompany profit elimination) must be addressed by accounting for deferred taxes. This applies to deferred tax liabilities as well as to deferred tax assets.

At the same time, the deferred taxation provision for single entity financial statements (§274 HGB) applies, and this requires accounting for deferred tax liabilities but offers an option to account for a deferred tax asset.

Thus, timing differences resulting from the (revalued) single entity financial statements and from consolidation entries may be handled differently. Furthermore, there is no general understanding with regard to the tax rules and/or tax rates to be applied. Consequently, there is a broad range of choice for deferred tax accounting policies.

3.1.5 Foreign Currency Translation

Neither the Commercial Code nor the Seventh Directive defines a method of translating foreign currency financial statements. Furthermore, common practice has not yet been established in Germany in that regard, so that the IdW has not yet issued a statement on this subject, although a draft version has been available since 1986. Consequently, a broad variety of methods like the current/noncurrent, the monetary/nonmonetary, the temporal, the closing, and the current rate method (FAS-52/IAS 21) and variants thereof are used.

Translation differences are dealt with in very different ways. Whereas some companies neutralize the differences in the balance sheet via cumulative translation adjustments, others let them affect profit and loss. A third group charges profit and loss in cases of translation losses and neutralizes translation gains via corresponding accruals.

Special attention must be given to the explanations in the notes to group financial statements, since the translation of foreign currency statements often materially affects the financial position and results of a group.

3.1.6 Summary

In Germany there is great scope for affecting consolidated financial statements by the choice of accounting policies. When analyzing financial statements, particular attention should be given to notes regarding capital consolidation, foreign currency translation, and deferred taxation.

3.2 Single Entity Financial Statements

3.2.1 Capital and Reserves

The minimum subscribed capital is DEM 100,000 for AGs and DEM 50,000 for GmbHs. The subscribed capital usually represents the maximum liability of the shareholders for liabilities of the company and is divided into single shares. Nevertheless, in certain situations of this capitalization, shareholder's loans can be considered equity-substitute, putting severe restrictions on pay-backs by the company. Whereas GmbHs are allowed to acquire their own shares without restriction, if certain provisions, as described in §33 GmbHG, are met, the purchase of own shares by stock corporations is limited to 10% and to specific purposes (§71 AktG).

Sole proprietorships and partnerships cannot have a subscribed capital by nature. Nevertheless, the so-called fixed capital accounts are sometimes described as subscribed capital, since those accounts have a similar function.

Regulations concerning reserves exist only for corporations. Reserves can be split into capital and revenue reserves. Capital reserves need not be broken down on the balance sheet and can include funds provided from outside. Revenue reserves must be split on the balance sheet by type and are created by transfers from retained earnings.

Capital reserves consist of:

1. The premiums paid in connection with the issuance of new shares
2. Amounts received on the issuance of debentures with convertible rights and share options
3. Contributions from shareholders as consideration for preferential rights of their shares
4. Other shareholders' contributions to the capital

Revenue reserves are composed of:

5. Legal revenue reserves
6. Statutory reserves
7. Reserves for own shares
8. Other reserves

Provisions for reserves 1–7 are prescribed by law. Provisions for "other reserves" out of retained earnings are usually subject to the management board's decision. The reserve for own shares must be set up in an amount corresponding to the value of own shares capitalized. It must be established by transfer from free reserves or retained earnings. A legal revenue reserve is compulsory for AGs and KGaAs only. According to §150 AktG, the annual provision is 5% of the annual net income until the reserves 1–3 and 5 reach 10% (or a higher amount if required by the bylaws) of the corporation's subscribed capital. No such regulations exist for GmbHs.

Whereas the reversal of reserves for GmbHs is only restricted to types 6 and 7, AGs and KGaAs are also restricted regarding types 1–3 and 5. These reserves may be reversed only in order to compensate accumulated losses or to serve as funds for the increase of the subscribed capital. Special reference is made to §150 AktG.

3.2.2 Liabilities, Accruals, and Special Tax Items

Definitions

- *Liabilities* are obligations that are certain regarding existence, value, and maturity.
- *Accruals* are provisons for uncertain obligations, anticipated losses, and certain expenses incurred before the balance sheet date.
- *Special tax items* represent one element of the influence of the German tax law on commercial financial statements. They can include items with an equity portion, as well as items having a contra asset character.

The following comments focus on accruals and special tax items, which are of special importance to the analyst of German financial statements.

Special Tax Items Special tax items are usually classified under a heading placed between equity and accruals on the face of the balance sheet. Such items can contain items with an equity portion or differences between commercially required and tax-allowed depreciation.

The first type represents untaxed reserves and includes a liability portion (for deferred taxation) as well as an equity portion (for retained net income). The item may be accounted for only if it would otherwise not be tax deductible, as is usually the case for corporations.

Mainly capital gains from the disposal of fixed and financial assets (§6b EStG reserve) are "parked" here. Taxes on such capital gains are postponed if and to the extent that the capital gains are reinvested in qualifying assets.

The second type is a contra asset by nature. It includes the accumulated difference between depreciation allowed for tax purposes and that which is commercially justified. Special tax depreciation in particular is allowed in the area of the former German Democratic Republic as well as for research and development (R&D) assets. Alternatively, the special tax depreciation can also be accounted for as a reduction of assets (see Section 3.4 below). The Commercial Code requires that the rules for setting up special tax items be disclosed. Since analysis by types and single items is not required, future income implications, in particular the timing of the reversal of these items, cannot be adequately determined by external analysts. This is partly addressed by the requirement to disclose in the notes the amounts by which the current year's income as well as subsequent years' income will be affected by setting up items with an equity portion or by applying special tax depreciation.

Accruals   German accounting legislation requires pension, tax, and other accruals to be separately disclosed on the balance sheet. Whereas pension and tax accruals represent provisions for uncertain liabilities, other accruals also include amounts to reflect loss contingencies and expense equalization accruals.

Accrued Pensions. German pension plans are mostly of a defined benefit type and generally are funded via:

- Pension accruals (internal funding) (the most common instrument)
- Companies' welfare funds (a common instrument)
- Independent pension funds (preferred by very large companies)
- Direct insurance policies (preferred by small companies)

Accrued pensions are one of the most critical issues in analyzing German financial statements, since there are significant exceptions from the need to accrue for pensions, and the accruals may be understated because of the calculation method usually applied.

The exceptions from setting up pension accruals are defined in Article 28 EGHGB. They refer to:

1. Pensions based on direct promises granted before 1987 (this also applies to claims increased thereafter but obtained before 1987)
2. Pensions based on indirect promises (mostly via companies' welfare funds)

Exception 1 must be interpreted as a transitional compromise (a so-called biological solution) with respect to companies that before the implementation of the Accounting Directives Law did not or did not fully account for pensions.

No such explanation is available for exception 2, which is important for companies financing their pensions via welfare funds. Because of certain labor court decisions, companies remain liable for the pension claims although the promises (formally) were granted by the welfare fund. In case of underfunding, therefore, from an economic point of view (but not by law), additional accruals for those indirect obligations are required. (It should be noted that such obligations do not occur if indirect promises are funded via pension funds or direct insurance policies.)

In order to compensate for the lack of accounting duties for certain direct and indirect claims, the amounts not accrued for must be disclosed in the notes. Overfunding of welfare funds, however, need not be disclosed.

As previously mentioned, the second significant problem in connection with pension accounting in Germany is the actuarial method normally used to determine the present value of the pension liabilities. This is a method prescribed in §6a of the German Income Tax Law, which works with a fixed discount rate of 6% but disregards future payroll increases and forbids the establishment of accruals for employees less than 30 years old. The latter may be regarded as an indirect consideration of the staff turnover factor, which is also not taken directly into account.

Because of the above weaknesses, the present values determined according to the tax method are mostly below the amounts determined according to more reasonable methods, for instance, below the projected benefit obligation as calculated according to the provisions of FAS-87. Although German companies may choose other methods to determine their pension obligations, the majority apply the tax method since only expenses incurred in accordance with this method are tax deductible. This must be seen in connection with the close relationship between commercial and tax accounting (see Section 1.4 above) in Germany.

Other Accruals. Other accruals contain provisions for uncertain liabilities, anticipated losses, and for expense equalizations.

The legal requirements and common practice for the first two categories mostly comply with international standards. As an exception, it may be recognized that provisions for anniversary grants (cash payments or other benefits offered to employees if they stay, for instance, 5, 10, 15 years with the firm) often are not accounted for, since they will become tax deductible only to the extent that claims occur after 1992.

Expense equalization accruals mainly include repair and maintenance measures as well as other specific expenses to be allocated to past periods, if probable but uncertain with regard to amount or time.

Repairs and maintenance must be accrued for if carried out within 3 months of the balance sheet date. They may be provided for if carried out within 12 months.

Provisions for other specific expenses are optional, too. These provisions can include amounts for major repairs, for advertising campaigns and R&D projects not yet executed, or similar items. However, because of the lack of precision of the rule, adequate discretion is left to the preparers.

In this connection it should be noted that the external reader may be unable to determine to what extent various accounting options have been used, since this is not subject to a separate disclosure. Furthermore, it is becoming increasingly common practice not to break down other accruals by amounts but to comply with the disclosure requirements in the notes by mentioning only the type of significant other accruals.

In addition, it should be noted that accruals for anticipated losses (since January 1, 1997) and optional accruals are not tax deductible and that, according to the prudence principle, the amounts accrued for need not be probable (except for expense equalization accruals) but only possible. This leaves considerable scope for conservative accounting.

3.2.3 Fixed Assets

Property, Plant, and Equipment: Overview   As a part of fixed assets, property, plant, and equipment (PPE) include only items that are supposed to remain in the business for a long period of time. Corporations must disclose separately land, land rights, and buildings, machinery, factory and office equipment, and advanced payments and construction in progress.

As a general rule, PPE should be evaluated at acquisition or manufacturing cost, less regular depreciation. Acquisition cost includes the purchase price (after price reductions) plus incidental cost and expenses incurred to render the asset ready for use. Details of the definition of manufacturing cost are given in Section 3.2.4 below.

No specific methods are prescribed by law as to how to determine regular depreciation. The most common methods are the straight-line and the declining balance methods. Estimated useful lives are taken mostly from the tax tables available for various industries. The assumptions used in these tables are in general conservative.

Provisions for extraordinary depreciation are required if a permanent impairment of value is anticipated. It should be noted, however, that noncorporations are also allowed to write down PPE, if the impairment is only of a temporary nature. For corporations this option is applicable for financial assets only.

Furthermore, noncorporations are permitted to write down PPE within the framework of "sound business judgment." This rule has been incorporated explicitly into the Commercial Code in order to further allow noncorporations to create hidden reserves. Because small noncorporations are not obliged to prepare notes, and large noncorporations do not have to include a specific disclosure regarding the use of "sound business judgment," external analysts are hardly able to determine to what extent net worth and results are affected by extremely conservative accounting.

Another important simplification for noncorporations is that a written-down value may be retained, even if the reasons for the write-down no longer apply. Principally, corporations are obliged to reverse write-downs accounted for in the past if the reasons that had caused an extraordinary depreciation have become void. This ruling becomes optional if the retention of the lower carrying value is accepted for tax purposes and necessary for being accepted taxwise (i.e., the "authoritative principle," see also Section 1.4).

As a result, there are only two situations for corporations that make a reversal of a previously performed write-down mandatory:

- The write-down was recognized in the commercial books only but disregarded for tax purposes.
- Reasons for a write-down permissible only for tax purposes have become void.

It should be noted that the retention option for corporations has been implemented in the Commercial Code in order not to force such companies to create taxable income by making the write-ups.

Special Tax Depreciation   Valuation of PPE is highly influenced by tax regulations. This applies not only to the use of tax tables or the retention option as described earlier but also to special tax depreciation, which is accepted as a tax-deductible item only if accounted for in the commercial financial statements, too. In this case, however, the effect of special tax depreciation on the current and future years' results (but not the cumulative effect from previous years) needs to be disclosed in the notes.

The limit for capitilization (DEM 800) commonly used for low value items, as well as the common practice of depreciating moveable fixed assets acquired in the first half of the year with the full annual rate and those acquired in the second half with half of the annual rate, are taken from German Income Tax Law.

Treatment of Government Grants   There is still no generally accepted practice in Germany with respect to accounting for government grants. Whereas some German companies immediately take those grants into income when received, others prefer to amortize the grants over the period that benefits therefrom. The latter method is becoming dominant, and it complies with a corresponding statement of the main technical committee of the IdW issued in 1984. The main provisions of that statement are as follows:

- Government grants must be accounted for at the time the claim is made, not just at the time cash payments are received.
- Investment grants are to be amortized according to the useful lives of the assets for which they are received.
- Grants to compensate expenses must be taken into profit and loss in the periods when the respective expenses are incurred.
- Unamortized portions of government grants preferably should be shown as a special item on the liability side of the balance sheet.
- Alternatively, investment grants may also reduce the "at cost" values of the corresponding assets.

Although it is broadly accepted that corporations and large noncorporations should disclose the accounting method applied for government grants in their notes, the relating impact on the income statement is in general hardly recognizable to external analysts. In addition, misinterpretations of the fixed asset movement analysis may occur if companies directly reduce the "at cost" values instead of presenting the unamortized portion of the grants in a separate item.

Intangible Assets   Intangible fixed assets are to be capitalized, if purchased. They may not be capitalized if created by the use of internal resources. Intangible current assets, however, are to be recognized even if not purchased from third parties.

The Commercial Code differs with regard to concessions, industrial rights, patents, licences, and similar rights on the one hand and goodwill and advances on intangibles on the other.

Accounting for Leases   As for many other issues, accounting for leases is in practice dominated by tax regulations, which are incorporated in various statements of the fiscal authorities.

The basic principles applicable to real estate as well as to other fixed assets leases are as follows:

* The leased asset must be accounted for by the lessor unless the lease is considered a financial or capital lease.

* Financial leases are assumed to exist if the basic lease term is less than 40% or more than 90% of the useful life of the lease asset, and/or if bargain purchase or lease prolongation options have been agreed on.

* Special leased assets only usable by the lessee always must be accounted for by the lessee.

It should be noted that standard lease contracts are mostly structured in such a manner that the leased assets are to be capitalized by the lessor.

The IdW recommends that lessors show the leased assets separately on the balance sheet, but this cannot yet be regarded as a general accounting practice.

Lessees do not need to disclose details about the amounts of their financial or operating leases. Although corporations and large noncorporations must disclose future financial commitments in their notes, they need not distinguish between lease and other commitments, and they also do not have to give an analysis of the obligations by year.

Participations   Participations are defined as holdings in other enterprises that are designed to serve a business through a long-term relationship with the other business (§271 HGB).

According to the Commercial Code, two types of participation, namely, shares in affiliated companies and investments, must be differentiated. Whereas investments need comply only with the general definition provided above, shares in affiliated companies are only shown if the other company should in principle be included in the consolidated statements of the ultimate parent, according to the provisions for full consolidation.

For the application of this rule, it is irrelevant whether or not group financial statements are actually prepared or if the other company must be or can be excluded from consolidation in agreement with the legal provisions.

Bearing in mind the above, participations usually qualify as investments if 20%–50% of the other entity's nominal share capital is held. They normally qualify as shares in affiliated companies if the interest exceeds 50%.

It should be noted that there is a second definition of affiliated companies included in the Stock Corporation Law, which is not applicable to accounting questions but to other issues like the duty of AGs to prepare a dependency report. Such a dependency report is supposed to include all transactions between the dominated subsidiary, its parent, and its affiliates, as well as measures imposed on the subsidiary and how disadvantages to it, if any, are compensated. It is only required in case of a dominating influence of a parent without a domination agreement. If such an agreement exists, the subsidiaries and their minority shareholders are protected by the parent's legal obligation to carry all of its losses incurred. Another important definition in the Stock Corporation Law is the question of how many members of the supervisory board must be representatives of employees.

Like other financial assets, participations are to be carried at cost, unless exceptional depreciation is required. Participations in partnerships are an exception from historical cost accounting, being partly accounted for on an equity basis, as is usual for tax purposes.

Provisions for exceptional depreciation must be made in cases of a permanent impairment of capitalized value. They can be also made in cases of a temporary impairment. Unlike for property, plant, and equipment, the latter is applicable to corporations, too.

As a further special point, it should be mentioned that exceptional write-downs of participations can be retained, if once accepted by the tax authorities, even if their *raison d'être* no longer applies.

Fixed Asset Movement Analysis   Corporations and large noncorporations must provide a fixed asset movement analysis, either on the balance sheet or in the notes, which must include tangible, intangible, and financial assets as well as capitalized start-up/business expansion costs. Small noncorporations usually provide such an analysis on a voluntary basis in the balance sheet.

The format used by SAP AG in its 1996 notes to financial statements (see the financial statements at the end of this chapter) is the most commonly used format in Germany. As a particular point, it should be noted that German accounting legislation does not require the development of accumulated depreciation from the opening to the closing balance but only the disclosure of the closing balance and the depreciation expense of the year on an item-by-item basis.

The amounts classified as acquisition or manufacturing cost may include a mixture of historical cost and net book values as presented in the last financial statements prepared according to the old accounting legislation (mostly fiscal year 1986). This is because of a transitional simplification permitted by the Accounting Directives Law, making it difficult for external analysts to analyze the real aging of the fixed assets. Special attention therefore should be given to any reference to Article 24 (6) EGHGB in the notes.

It should be added that as an accounting convenience, start-up and business expansion costs may be capitalized. If so, annual amortization must be at least 25%—a specific depreciation method is not required. Furthermore, the amounts capitalized are unavailable for profit distribution. This rule also applies to deferred tax assets, if capitalized (see Section 3.2.6 below).

The valuation principles to be applied are the same as for PPE. Specific provisions exist for the depreciation of goodwill. Such provisions define a regular annual amortization rate of at least 25% but also allow a longer or faster amortization, if justifiable.

In this connection the 15-year depreciation period, as defined in the German Income Tax Law, plays a special role. Because of the common practice of differentiating between the commercial and tax accounts only where unavoidable, this 15-year period is often applied in commercial financial statements, too. The maximum period recognized by most commentators is 40 years.

Goodwill in the single entity financial statements must be differentiated from that incurred through consolidation. It arises, for example, if a business is bought at a price exceeding the fair market value of the acquired assets. It can also occur when a partnership is merged at a net asset value that is below the book value of the participation. It cannot occur when shares are acquired, since all costs incurred in this connection are to be reflected as acquisition cost of the investment. With respect to the goodwill arising from consolidation, reference is made to Section 3.1.2 above.

3.2.4 Inventories

Inventories are usually divided into raw materials, work-in-progress, and finished goods and merchandise. Advance payments received on orders of material may be openly deducted from inventories or, alternatively, shown as liabilities.

Inventories must be stated at the lower of historical cost or market value. Historical cost can be derived by applying simplifying assumptions with regard to the usage of inventories like FIFO, LIFO, or average cost. It is to be expected that the LIFO method will become more important in the future, since starting in 1990 it has been accepted for tax purposes. Currently, average cost followed by FIFO are the most common methods.

Acquisition cost, which represents the basic values for raw material and merchandise, has been defined under Section 3.2.3 above.

Manufacturing cost, which is the basic value for work-in-progress and finished goods, comprises expenditures that are incurred through the consumption of goods and services in order to manufacture, enlarge, or improve an asset significantly beyond its original state. Table 3 identifies those cost components that need to or may be included in valuation.

As Table 3 shows, German companies have a wide range of options for valuation of inventories. In practice, most companies comply with the tax regulations that require the capitalization of components 1–6. Only a minority of companies capitalize fewer or more components in their commercial accounts.

Interest expenses may be included in manufacturing cost only under exceptional conditions. They may be capitalized if incurred directly for the production of an asset but only to the extent that they are incurred during the production period. Idle capacity costs must be excluded from manufacturing costs.

Write-downs of inventories must be made if market values fall below historical cost (lower of cost or market principle). The applicable market for raw materials and supplies is usually the purchase market (replacement value). The market for finished goods is the sales market (net realizable

TABLE 3 *Components of Inventory Cost That Should Be or May Be Included in Inventory Valuation*

	Commercial Accounts		Tax Accounts	
	Compulsory	*Optional*	*Compulsory*	*Optional*
1. Direct material cost	x		x	
2. Direct labor cost	x		x	
3. Special production costs	x		x	
4. Material overhead costs		x	x	
5. Labor overhead cost		x	x	
6. Depreciation of fixed assets		x	x	
7. General administration costs		x		x
8. Pensions and other social benefits		x		x
9. Interest expense		(x)		(x)
10. Selling expenses		–		–

value). For work-in-progress and merchandise, either market may apply. In any case, the lowest amount reasonably applicable must be used. This also means, for instance, that unlike the rule in some other countries, the replacement value is to be used if lower than historical cost, even if the net realizable value is above historical cost.

As a second peculiarity, the net realizable value in Germany is often determined by considering a mark-down to the sales price for an adequate entrepreneur's profit, since this is allowed for tax purposes.

A third point is the opportunity to anticipate expected future price reductions ("future" often being defined as up to 2 years) via inventory reserves, and the option for noncorporations to set up reserves within the framework of "sound business judgment."

Fourth, §80 of the Income Tax Execution Regulation (EStDV) allows the setting up of special allowances on imported goods like tobacco, coffee, and tea of up to 10% of the replacement cost at the balance sheet date, if also reflected in the commercial accounts.

Whereas the latter may be of importance for specific industries only, the definition of manufacturing cost and the option to set up allowances for future price reductions in particular provide great latitude for valuation. In addition, there remain judgmental areas with respect to the definition and evaluation of obsolete and excess items even though restricted by tax laws.

External analysts may find it difficult to estimate to what extent these options have been used, because the explanations in the notes are mostly limited to general remarks concerning accounting policy.

Deferred Income and Expenses   As a special feature of German accounting regulations, certain qualifying cash receipts and expenditures, respectively, must be recognized as deferral items shown seperately on the balance sheet. These captions are not to be qualified as assets or liabilities but only as mere deferral positions set up for proper allocation of income and expenses.

This ruling mainly applies to

- Expenditures made before the balance sheet date insofar as they must be reflected as expense within a distinct and identifiable period after year-end; as a result, these expenditures must be capitalized as deferred expense.
- Cash collected before the balance sheet date insofar as this must be reflected as income within a distinct and identifiable period after year-end; these cash receipts must be set up separately on the liability side as deferred income.

In practice, the main components of these captions are cash receipts or expenditures, respectively, with regard to services that will be rendered or claimed after year-end only (e.g., prepaid leases and insurance premiums) or prepaid rental income and deferred revenues.

Long-term Production Projects   As a general rule, income may be recognized only if the agreed-upon product or service has been (almost) completely rendered. Exceptions to this basic principle are accepted for long-term production projects in order to avoid high fluctuations of income. Thus, besides the still dominant completed-contract-method, under specific and restrictive circumstances, the percentage-of-completion method optionally can be applied.

Because of the absence of specific provisions, the income recognition principles as outlined in IAS 11 are widely accepted by German accounting practice. In either case, the income recognition method must be described in the notes, if material amounts are concerned.

3.2.5 Receivables

Accounting for receivables and other current assets in Germany is quite similar to practice in other European countries and, therefore, will not be commented on in detail. It should be noted, however, that, differing from practice in other countries, receivables denominated in foreign currencies are mostly not translated at the closing date rate but at the lower of the closing date or historical rates. For payables, the opposite rule is applied, which leads to the result that translation losses are considered but translation gains are not.

Whereas this practice might comply with the so-called imparity principle, departures from a true and fair presentation may well occur, particularly if there are corresponding foreign currency receivables and payables. Therefore, exceptions to the stringent imparity principle are widely accepted, at least in the case of corresponding assets and liabilities denominated in foreign currencies, as well as in the case of forward contracts.

According to a new statement published by the law, current foreign currency receivables and payables can both be translated at the closing date rate.

The translation method applied must be disclosed in the notes.

3.2.6 Taxation

The following comments are confined to income taxes, two types of which are levied in Germany.

The *trade tax on income* (TTI) is a municipal tax set at between 10% and 20% of the taxable income, depending on the rates fixed locally. Except for timing differences, the main deviation between taxable and commercial income is usually that 50% of interest expenses on long-term loans must be added back to the commercial income. Corporations and noncorporations are subject to TTI.

Only corporations are subject to the *corporation income tax* (CIT), which is a federal tax. There is a split tax rate, amounting to 30% if profits are fully distributed, and to 45% if profits are fully retained. Because of the imputation system, from a German shareholder's point of view, the CIT qualifies as a prepayment of personal income taxes. For foreign investors the CIT typically results in a definite tax charge. Except for timing differences, the taxable income for CIT purposes can be determined roughly as equal to commercial income after deducting TTI and adding back property taxes and certain nondeductible expenses as 20% of entertainment expense or 50% of the supervisory board's compensation. Depending on the local TTI rate and the decision whether to retain or distribute profits, the total income tax burden for corporations may range between approximately 38% and 59% of pretax income, including a 5.5% surtax (rate for 1998) that will be imposed on CIT resulting from the additional fiscal needs due to the ongoing reunification process in Germany.

Although the majority of German companies tend to prepare only one set of financial statements, there can be many differences between commercial and taxable income, due to technical reasons. In addition, those differences may occur because of accounting measures that are not acceptable for tax purposes. For instance:

- If start-up or business expansion cost is capitalized
- If gross inventories are priced below the minimum amounts accepted for tax purposes
- If inventory reserves are established at amounts exceeding the amounts allowed for tax purposes (e.g., anticipation of future price reductions, reserves based on "sound business judgment")
- If accruals are not accepted for tax purposes (e.g., provision for anticipated losses, expense equalization accruals, repair and maintenance accruals for accruals not spent within 3 months of the balance sheet date, retrieval of pension reserves not accrued in the past)

Although the above deviations are in principle subject to deferred taxation, accounting for deferred taxation does not play an important role in Germany, since in most cases a deferred tax asset arises that does not need to be capitalized according to §274 HGB and usually is not capitalized by German companies. Thus, analysts may still find discrepancies between the tax expense and the pretax income reported in the commercial financial statements.

It should be added that the Commercial Code mainly follows the liability method of deferred tax accounting as presented in IAS 12.

As a side point, the substantially higher CIT rate on retained profits has been established in order to persuade German companies to distribute their profits rather than retain them. The shareholders in this case must decide whether to reinvest the dividends in the company or in an alternative investment. It is commonly understood that this decision process contributes to a better allocation of funds within the whole economy.

4. Recent and Expected Future Developments

As mentioned in the introductory part of this chapter, the implementation of the Fourth and Seventh EC Directives into German law in the late 1980s represented an important step in German accounting history. At present there are no further indications that its significance will change in the short to medium term.

In April and May of 1998 two new laws—"Law for Control and Transparence in Companies" (KonTraG) and "Law for improved Equity Raising Capabilities" (KAEG) were passed by the legislature. Through these laws several changes especially affecting stock corporations and their auditors were introduced. The most important are the following:

- The management of a stock corporation must implement a risk-management and control system to sufficiently monitor business and fraud risks, and the auditor will have to assess the sufficiency and adequacy of this system;

- The management report will have to include management's assessment of potential risks in anticipated future developments and a statement regarding future business policies

- In the future the supervisory board will be responsible for assigning the auditor and will be the adressee of the audit report (in the past that was the responsibility of management)

- The auditor will have to attend supervisory board meetings regarding financial statements.

- For publicly listed stock corporations preparation of cash-flow statements and segment reporting will become mandatory (for fiscal years beginning after December 31, 1998)

- Publicly listed stock corporations can choose to either prepare their consolidated financial statements according to German GAAP or according to equally suited and internationally accepted accounting standards, as for example, IAS, U.S. GAAP, U.K. GAAP, French GAAP etc.)

- Under specific circumstances subsidiaries whose parent companies are contractually bound to cover any losses incurred by the subsidiary are no longer subject to a mandatory audit

A change to be faced in the near future is the extension of the strict accounting, auditing, and disclosure requirements for corporations to GmbH & Co.'s, which formally represent partnerships but contain strong elements of corporations. The exclusion of GmbH & Co.'s from the regulations applicable to corporations never was accepted by the majority of the other European countries and the above extension decision recently passed by the Cabinet Council of the EC will be applicable for all partnerships whose only general partner is a corporation in the near future.

Useful Addresses

Institut der Wirtschaftsprufer
Tersteegenstrasse 14
4000 Dusseldorf 30
Germany
Tel: +(211) 45610
Fax: +(211) 454 1097

Wirtschaftspruferkammer
Tersteegenstrasse 14
4000 Dusseldorf 30
Germany
Tel: +(211) 45610
Fax: +(211) 4561 193

Exhibit I Survey of Transfer of Significant Option Rights Established by the 4th EC Directive into German Commercial Code (GCC)

Article 4th Dir.	Description of Option	Codification §§ GCC	Remarks
2 VI	Optional codification of the statements, i.e., in particular to attach a cash-flow statement as an integral part of the annual statements	n/a	No transfer of this option into GCC
6	Optional disclosure of disposition of earnings as part of the income statement	268 I	Option has been fully transferred to the reporting entity
17,2	Qualification of investments as participations optional up to a capital share of 20% (from a share > 20% disclosure as participation is compulsory)	271 I	Application of the 20% (=max.) limit
20 II	Option for setting up certain identified accruals for future expenses	249 II	Option has been fully transferred to the reporting entity
30	Optional aggregation of tax expense due from both ordinary and extraordinary results within income statement	275	Option has been exerted by GCC
33	Option for deviating from the purchase cost method with regard to the presentation of certain balance sheet items, i.e., inflation accounting, valuation at replacement value and face value, respectively	253	No transfer of this option into GCC
35 I, 39 I	Option for extraordinary depreciation of PP&E, financial assets, and current assets under certain identified conditions	253, 255	Option has been fully transferred to the reporting entity

Article 4th Dir.	Description of Option	Codification §§ GCC	Remarks
37 I	Optional capitalization of R&D expenses	n/a	No transfer of this option into GCC; handling of R&D related expenses is covered by general GAAP not codified by German commercial law
37 II	Option with respect to the extension of the amortization period applicable to goodwill beyond the standard period of 5 years	255 IV	Option has been fully transferred to the reporting entity, i.e., the amortization period can be extended to the estimated period of benefit from the goodwill
38, 40 I	Optional valuation of movable PP&E and Inventories by application of the weighted average method, LIFO- and FIFO-method, or minimum-balance method	240, 256	Option has been fully transferred to the reporting entity
45 I	Application of a protection clause optional re disclosure of participation details such as name of the respective entity, investor's capital share, and entity's results for the year ended; previous authorization can be demanded by each member country	286 III, 287	Option has been transferred to the reporting entity with the exception that no previous authorization is required
47	Optional facilities with regard to identified footnote disclosure requirements dependent upon size of the respective company	288	Option has been fully transferred to the reporting entity
51	Optional exemption from audit requirements dependent on company's size	316 I	Option has been exerted by GCC

(Exhibit continues)

Exhibit I (continued)

Article 4th Dir.	Description of Option	Codif- ication §§ GCC	Remarks
59	Optional accounting for investments in affiliated subsidiaries under the equity method	253 II, 271 II	No transfer of this option into GCC; interests in affiliated entities must be recorded at cost

Exhibit II Survey of Transfer of Significant Option Rights Established by the 7th EC Directive into German Commercial Code (GCC)

Article 7th Dir.	*Description of Option*	*Codif- ication §§ GCC*	*Remarks*
1. Composition of companies to be included into consolidation:			
1 c)	Compulsory inclusion of an entity into consolidation can be combined with the requirement of a 20% interest in the subsidiary in the case that the parent company has direct control over the formation of the entity's management and/or supervisory board	290 II Nr.2	No transfer of this option into GCC
1 d) aa)	Compulsory inclusion of an entity into consolidation can be combined with the requirement of a minimum 20% interest in the subsidiary in the case that the parent company has direct control over the formation of the entity's management and/or supervisory board	290 II Nr.3	No transfer of this option into GCC
2. Exemption rules:			
6	Optional exemption from consolidation requirements dependent on entity's size	293	Option has been exerted by GCC
7 III	Option for nonapplication of Article 7 (general exemption rules) for companies quoted at an EC stock exchange	291 I, II	No transfer of this option into GCC
8	Option for application of Article 7 only under the condition that shareholders of the parent company owning a determined minimum share have not claimed for the presentation of consolidated financial statements within a period of 6 months prior to year-end	291 III	Option has been exerted by GCC

(Exhibit continues)

Exhibit I (continued)

Article 7th Dir.	Description of Option	Codif-ication §§ GCC	Remarks
9	Option for application of Articles 7 and 8 only under the condition that additional disclosure requirements determinable by each member country have been considered by the reporting entity	n/a	No transfer of this option into GCC
11	Option for exemption of an EC parent company from presenting consolidated financial statements in the case that this company and all its subsidiaries are included in the con-solidated statements of a non-EC parent company that meets the requirements of consolidated statements set up under the 7th EC Directive	292	Option has been exerted by GCC
15	Option to exempt a parent company from consolidation in the case that this company —is not active in the commercial or trade area and —is shareholder of a subsidiary owing to an agreement with one or more companies not included in the consolidated financial statements	n/a	No transfer of this option into GCC

3. Techniques of capital consolidation:

19	Option to offset the investment in the subsidiary against its proportional equity at the time of purchase of shares or, in the case that shares have been acquired subsequently, at the moment when the entity has become a subsidiary company (i e., the par-ent's investment equals or exceeds 20% of the subsidiary's share capital)	301 II	Option has been exerted by GCC

Article 7th Dir.	Description of Option	Codif- ication §§ GCC	Remarks
20	Option for application of Article 19 only in the case that a minimum capital share of 90% is owned by the parent company	n/a	No transfer of this option into GCC
30	Option to offset goodwill from consolidation within the equity section against earned or capital surplus; the offsetting entry has to be shown separately	309 I	Option has been fully transferred to the reporting entity

4. Other consolidation items:

27	Option for deviation of balance sheet dates between parent company's single financial statements and consolidated statements, i.e., presentation of consolidated financial statements as of a cut-off date applied by the most significant entities or the majority of entities included in consolidation, respectively	299 I	Option has been exerted by GCC
28	Option for adjustment of a subsequent year's opening balance sheet in case of significant changes with respect to the composition of the consolidated companies	n/a	No transfer of this option into GCC
29	Optional adoption of allowances from single financial statements that had been set up for tax purposes only under the condition that appropriate disclosure concerning these impacts is made in the footnotes	308 I	Option has been exerted by GCC

(Exhibit continues)

Exhibit II (continued)

Article 7th Dir.	Description of Option	Codification §§ GCC	Remarks
5. Other consolidation methods:			
32	Optional application of the proportional consolidation method in the case of an investment in an entity together with nonconsolidated companies	310	Option has been fully transferred to the reporting entity
33 II	Option for applying the equity method either by presenting the carrying amount of the respective investment or by disclosing the investment at an amount equal to the proportional share in the subsidiary's equity	312 I	No transfer of this option into GCC; by application of the equity method both alternatives are available
33 III	Under the equity method application of valuation methods used for consolidation purposes can be prescribed in the case that the investment shall be recorded at an amount equal to the pro-rata portion of the subsidiary's equity	312 V	No transfer of this option into GCC, application of valuation method used for consolidation purposes is optional
6. Specific disclosure requirements			
34 Nr. 12	Option to demand disclosure of compensation received by management or supervisory board members regarding activities at companies consolidated under the proportional method or the equity method	314 I Nr. 6	No transfer of this option into GCC
35 I a)	Option for separate presentation of specific details with regard to the parent company's investments in subsidiaries in order to avoid public	313 IV	Option has been fully transferred to the reporting entity

Article 7th Dir.	Description of Option	Codification §§ GCC	Remarks
	disclosure (i.e., name and place of registration of the respective subsidiary as well as capital share of the parent company or the subsidiary's equity and its net income, if available)		
35 I b)	Option to omit disclosure of details mentioned under Article 35 I a) in the case that disclosure would prove a significant handicap to the respective subsidiaries; omittance can be made dependent on prior approval by administration authorities or court decision	313	No transfer of this option into GCC

Exhibit III Comparison of Significant Differences between German GAAP and U.S. GAAP

Caption	Source HGB	German GAAP	U.S. GAAP	Source FAS, APB, ARB
ASSETS				
Current Assets				
Deferred charges/ prepaid expenses	§269	Optional capitalization of start-up costs as an accounting convenience, disclosed under a separate caption and amortized over a period up to 5 years	Current and noncurrent portion of prepaid expenses are disclosed separately as prepaid expenses or other assets, respectively	ARB 43
Deferred tax asset	§§274 II, 306	Optional for individual financial statements; compulsory for tax assets resulting from consolidation entries; no recognition of a future tax benefit resulting from a loss carryforward in the year the loss has been incurred; only the reversal of deferred tax liabilities is possible to an extent that future tax expenses are compensation for by the loss carryforward	Compulsory both for individual and consolidated financial statements; future tax benefits due to loss carryforwards have to be recognized if future realization is "more likely than not" (i.e., likelihood >50%), the tax asset is subject to a valuation allowance in case the asset becomes impaired	FAS-109
Marketable securities	§§252 I, 240 IV	Basically separate valuation of each single item, group valuation possible for homogeneous kinds of securities	Portfolio approach for securities representing ownership rights, i.e., allowances are calculated on the basis of the portfolio balance as of balance sheet date	FAS-12
Accounts receivable, trade	§253 III	Simultaneous recognition of bad debt allowances and lump sum allowance for general risk of collection permissible	Recognition of lump sum allowances not approved	APB 12

	§			
Inventories	§255	Wide range of options for capitalization of manufacturing costs between direct and full costs; capitalization of interest only in case of direct relation of interest expense incurred by identified projects, in addition to determination of net realizable value as of balance sheet date allowance due to anticipation of expected future price reductions are optional; for noncorporations additional volume of write-downs is available within the range of "sound business judgment"	Capitalization of full costs	ARB 43
			Capitalization of interest for qualifying assets	FAS-34
	§253 III	Application of the lower of cost or market principle; no devaluation down to lower replacement costs in the case that net realizable value less mark-down still exceeds replacement costs: then inventory write-down is limited to NRV less an allowance for a normal profit margin	Application of the lower of cost or market principle; no devaluation down to lower replacement costs in the case that net realizable value still exceeds replacement costs: then inventory write-down is limited to NRV less an allowance for a normal profit margin	ARB 43
Noncurrent assets				
Investments	§255	Application of the cost method; if decrease of value is —nontemporary: write-down is compulsory —temporary: write-down is optional For investments in noncorporations additional volume of write-downs is optional within the range of "sound business judgment"	In general application of	APB 18
	§§253 II, 279	Reversal of previous extraordinary write-downs when reasons for write-down have become void:	—the equity method for investments of 20% or more of the voting stock	
	§253 IV	• for corporations only compulsory when —write-down was performed in trade books only but disregarded for tax purposes —reasons for write-down permissible for tax purposes only have become void	—the cost method for investments of less than 20% of the voting stock Nontemporary losses in value of the investment:	
	§280	• for noncorporations generally optional	—reversal of previous extraordinary write-downs is generally mandatory in case reasons for extraordinary write-downs have become void For noncurrent marketable equity securities accumulated changes in the valuation allowance for decline in market value assessed to be temporary shall not be included in the determination of net income but reflected within the equity section and shown separately.	
	§253V			

(Exhibit continues)

(Exhibit III, cont.)

Caption	German GAAP	Source HGB	U.S. GAAP	Source FAS, APB, ARB
Property, plant, & equipment	As a general rule: valuation at cost	§255	As a general rule: valuation at cost	APB 6
	Wide range of options for recognition of manufacturing costs Re capitalization of interest, see inventories		Re capitalization of interest, see inventories	
	Extraordinary depreciation required —for corporations if permanent impairment in case of premature wear and tear ment of value is anticipated	§§253 II 279 I	Extraordinary depreciation required	APB 20 + 30
	—for noncorporations: even permissible if impairment is only of temporary nature and within a range of "sound business judgment"	§253 II, IV	—in case of restricted usage	
	Re reversal of write-downs in case that related reasons have become void: see Investments		Re reversal of write-downs in case that related reasons have become void: see Investments	
Intangibles	Only to be recorded as assets by applying the cost method when acquired from third	§248 II	If acquired: recognition as assets by applying the cost method	APB 17
	Amortization over the estimated period of benefit	§253 II	If incurred internally only recognition of assets if they —can be specifically identified —have determinable lives —are not an inherent part in a continuing business and not related to an enterprise as a whole	
			Amortization over the estimated period of benefit up to a maximum of 40 years	
	With regard to business combinations: disclosure of acquired goodwill as an asset is optional, if capitalized goodwill has to be amortized over a period of up to 15 years	§255 IV §7 I EStG	With regard to business combinations: disclosure of acquired goodwill as an asset is compulsory if the purchase method is applied; maximum amortization period: 40 years	APB 16
			In the case that pooling-of-interests method is applied, no goodwill will be recognized since all related assets and liabilities are recorded at historical carrying values	

LIABILITIES

Current Liabilities

Accrued liabilities	In trade books presentation of qualifying accruals for future expenses are optional but not permissible for tax purposes. Principle of prudence is established as the basic principle, i.e., valuation and estimates are subject to management's "sound business judgment," basically resulting in the opportunity to set up hidden reserves more easily than under U.S. GAAP	§249 II §252 I	Only obligations to third parties resulting from transactions of the past can be accrued; presentation of a true & fair view is the basic principle, i.e., the likelihood of occurrence has to be identified as probable, reasonably possible, or remote; in the case that only a certain range can be applied to an identified probably contingency amount, the amount at the lower edge of the respective range has to be recorded.	FAS-5, s. 70
Long-term debt (noninterest bearing)	General rule: disclosure at face value	§253 I	General rule: disclosure at present value	APB 21

Other Liabilities

Pension reserves	In most cases application of tax rules (i.e., s. 6a EStG) also for trade books: —discount rate fixed at 6% —no consideration expected future compensation levels influenced by future wage and inflation rates Application of the "claimed when claimable" rule	§249 I §6a EStG	Computation of net periodic pension cost under consideration of estimated future compensation levels and assumed discount rates which shall reflect the rates at which the pension benefits could be settled in the future; retroactive plan amendments have to be included at the time they have been contractually agreed, i.e., no application of the "claimed when claimable" rule	FAS-87

(Exhibit continues)

(Exhibit III, cont.)

Caption	German GAAP	Source HGB	U.S. GAAP	Source FAS, APB, ARB
PROFIT & LOSS STATEMENT	Option between cost-of-sales method and cost-summary method	§275 I	Cost-of-sales method is compulsory	APB 9
OTHER ISSUES				
Translation of foreign currencies	No legal codification with regard to foreign currency translation methods; according to the principle of prudence no recognition of unrealized gains from translation is possible		Application of the functional currency concept, both gains and losses from translation of foreign currencies have to be recorded	FAS-52
Cash flow statement	Disclosure is optional.		The cash flow statement is an integral part of the financial statements.	FAS-95
CONSOLIDATED ITEMS				
General consolidation policy	Subsidiaries have to be included if —parent owns more than 20% of shares and exercises de facto control, or —parent owns more than 50% of voting shares or has direct control of the composition of the entity's board or via a domination contract Wider range of optional application of the equity method as a substitute for full consolidation; for corporate joint ventures alternative application of both equity or proportional consolidation is possible	§§290 I, 271 I §290 II §§311, 295, 296	Generally the condition for a controlling financial interest is ownership of a majority voting interest; exclusion from consolidation only applies in the case that control is only temporary or control does not rest with the majority owner (i.e., for instance, the entity is in legal reorganization, bankruptcy, or operates under public restrictions). Application of the equity method for —Corporate joint ventures and —Investments within a range from 20% to 50% of the voting stock if the investor is able to exercise significant influence	FAS-94 ARB 51
Accounting for goodwill resulting from consolidation	Option for offsetting goodwill from consolidation within the equity section (to be shown separately, if applied)	§309 I	Goodwill from consolidation has to be capitalized and amortized over a maximum period of 40 years	APB 16 + 17

Exhibit IV Comparison of Significant Differences between German GAAP and International Accounting Standards (IAS)

Caption	German GAAP	Source HGB	IAS	Source IAS
ASSETS				
Current Assets				
Deferred charges/ prepaid expenses	Optional capitalization of start-up costs as an accounting convenience, disclosed under a separate caption and amortized over period up to 5 years	§269	Prepaid expenses and deferred income shall be included in other assets and other liabilities, respectively	IAS 5
Deferred tax asset	Effects have to be accounted for under the liability method; recognition of a tax asset is optional for individual financial statements but compulsory for tax assets resulting from consolidation entries; no recognition of a future tax benefit resulting from a loss carryforward in the year the loss has been incurred; only the reversal of deferred tax liabilities is possible to an extent that future tax expenses will be compensated for by the loss carryforward	§§274 II, 306	Option for either applying the deferral method or the liability method; exceptions can be made for timing differences that will not reverse for at least 3 years. Recognition of a future tax benefit resulting from a loss carryforward is permissible in the case that realization of the tax asset is "beyond any reasonable doubt."	IAS 12
Marketable securities	Basically separate valuation of each single item at the lower of cost or market; group valuation possible for homogeneous kinds of securities	§§252 I, 240 IV	Valuation at either market value or the lower of cost or market value, whereby the carrying amount should be determined either on a portfolio basis, in total, or by category of investment, or on an individual investment basis	IAS 25
Accounts receivable, trade	Simultaneous recognition of bad debt allowances and lump sum allowances for general risk of collection permissible	§253 III	Recognition of lump sum allowances not mentioned	

(Exhibit continues)

(*Exhibit IV, cont.*)

Caption	German GAAP	Source HGB	IAS	Source IAS
Inventories	Wide range of options for capitalization of manufacturing costs between direct and full costs	§255	For manufactured inventories, systematic allocation of those production overhead costs is required that "relate to putting the inventories in their present location and condition."	IAS 2
	Capitalization of interest only in cases of direct relation of interest expense incurred by identified projects, in addition to determination of net realizable value as of balance sheet date allowances due to anticipation of expected future price reductions are optional; for noncorporations, additonal volume of write-downs is available within the range of "sound business judgment."	§253 III	Application of the lower or cost or market principle; net realizable value is determined as the estimated selling price in the ordinary course of business less costs of completion and less costs necessarily to be incurred in order to make the sale	
Noncurrent Assets				
Investments	Application of the cost method; if decrease of value is —nontemporary: write-down is compulsory —temporary: write-down is optional For investments in noncorporations, additional volume of write-downs is optional within the range of "sound business judgment." Reversal of previous extraordinary write-downs when reasons for write-down have become void: • For corporations only compulsory when —write-down was performed in trade books only but disregarded for tax purposes —reasons for write-down permissible for tax purposes only have become void • For noncorporations generally optional	§255 §§253 II, 279 §253 IV §280 §253 V	Long-term investments should be carried at cost or revalued amounts (i.e., at fair value) or in the case of marketable equity securities, the lower of cost and market value determined on a portfolio basis; reversal of previous extraordinary write-down is compulsory when reasons for write-down have become void; an increase in book value resulting from revaluation should be credited to owner's equity except for write-ups arising from the reversal of a previous decrease in the same investment which was charged to income; for investments in subsidiaries the equity method should be applied if the investor holds 20% or more of the voting stock (if <20%: valuation at cost)	IAS 25 IAS 28

Property, plant, & equipment	As a general rule: valuation at cost Wide range of options for recognition of manufacturing costs Re capitalization of interest, see inventories Extraordinary depreciation required —for corporations if permanent impairment of value is anticipated —for noncorporations even permissible if impairment is of only temporary nature and within a range of "sound business judgment" Re reversal of write-downs in case that related reasons have become void: see Investments	§255 §§253 II, 279 I 253 II, IV	Valuation at either historical cost or at a revaluation amount (both upwards and downwards). An increase in book value resulting from revaluation should be credited to owner's equity and shown separately as revaluation surplus, except that such increase is related to and not greater than a decrease arising on devaluation recorded as charged to income; borrowing costs should be capitalized as part of the cost of assets that take a substantial period of time to get them ready for use; amount capitalized should not exceed total borrowing costs of that period. No restrictions with regard to the use of various kinds of depreciation methods as long as they are applied consistently from period to period; extraordinary depreciation required in case of premature wear and tear, restricted usage and obsolescence not explicitly covered by IAS	IAS 16 IAS 23 IAS 4
Intangibles	Only to be recorded as assets by applying the cost method when acquired from third parties Amortization over the estimated period of benefit With regard to business combinations: disclosure of acquired goodwill as an asset is optional; if capitalized, goodwill has to be amortized over a period of up to 15 years	§248 II §253 II §255 IV §7 I EStG	With regard to business combinations: An acquired goodwill should be recognized as an asset, straight-line amortization over its useful life (i.e., generally not longer than 5 years unless a longer period	IAS 22

(Exhibit continues)

(*Exhibit IV, cont.*)

Caption	German GAAP	Source HGB	IAS	Source IAS
			can be justified—>max. 20 years); write-down of unamortized balance according to results from annual recovery check; in the case that the pooling-of-interests method is applied, no goodwill will be recognized since all related assets and liabilities are recorded at historical carrying values.	
LIABILITIES				
Current Liabilities				
Accrued liabilities	In trade books presentation of qualifying accruals for future expenses are optional but not permissible for tax purposes. Principle of prudence is established as the basic principle, i.e., valuation and estimates are subject to management's "sound business judgment," basically resulting in the opportunity to set up hidden reserves more easily than under IAS	§249 II §252 I	No coverage for accruals set up for determined future expenses under IAS, i.e., the likelihood of occurrence has to be probable and a reasonable estimate of the loss can be made; in case only a certain range can be applied to an identified probable contingency amount, the amount at the lower edge of the respective range has to be recorded	IAS 10
Other Liabilities				
Pension reserves	In most cases application of tax rules (i.e., s. 6a EStG) also for trade books: —discount rate fixed at 6% —no consideration of expected future compensation levels influenced by future wage and inflation rates Application of the "claimed when claimable" rule	§249 I §6a EStG	Accounting for retirement benefit plans is covered by IAS 26 by an overall approach only, i.e., the actuarial present value of promised retirement benefits should be recorded under the terms of the plan using either current or projected salary levels; plan assets shall be carried at fair value; the relationship between the actuarial present value and the net plan assets available for benefits shall be disclosed	IAS 26

PROFIT & LOSS STATEMENT	Option between cost-of-sales method and cost-summary method	§275 I
	No prescription of a certain method under IAS, IAS 5 only provides a listing of basic P&L-captions that should be disclosed, e.g., depreciation, unusual charges/credits and significant intercompany transactions	IAS 5
OTHER ISSUES		
Translation of foreign currencies	No legal codification with regard to foreign currency translation methods. According to the principle of prudence, no recognition of unrealized gains from translation is possible.	
	At each balance sheet date foreign currency monetary items should generally be reported at the closing rate and gains and losses should be recognized; exchange differences on long-term monetary assets may be deferred, except that exchange losses should not be deferred in the case that recurring exchange losses will arise on that item in the future, any cumulative deferred exchange differences must be disclosed	IAS 21
Cash flow statement	Disclosure is optional	
	The cash flow statement is an integral part of the financial statements	IAS 7

(Exhibit continues)

(Exhibit IV, cont.)

CONSOLIDATION ITEMS

Caption	German GAAP	Source HGB	IAS	Source IAS
General scope of consolidation	Subsidiaries have to be included if —parent owns more than 20% of shares and exercises de facto control, or —parent owns more than 50% of voting shares or has direct control of the composition of the entity's board or via a domination contract	§§290 I, 271 I §290 II	Generally the condition for a controlling financial interest is ownership of a majority voting interest, exclusion from consolidation applies only in the case that control is only temporary or control does not rest with the majority owner (for instance, the entity is in legal reorganization, bankruptcy, or operates under public restrictions)	IAS 27
	Wider range of optional application of the equity method as a substitute for full consolidation; for corporate joint ventures alternative application of both consolidation at equity or proportional consolidation is possible	§§311, 295, 296 §310	For joint ventures alternative application of both consolidation at equity or proportional consolidation is available; joint ventures should be accounted for in accordance with IAS 25 (see Investments) if the interest is acquired and held exclusively with a view to its subsequent disposal in the near future or if it operates under long-term restrictions	
Accounting for goodwill resulting from consolidation	Option for offsetting goodwill from consolidation within the equity section (to be shown separately, if applied)	§309 I	Goodwill resulting from consolidation should be recognized as an asset; straight-line amortization over its useful life (i.e., generally not longer than 5 years unless a longer period can be justified—>max. 20 years); write-down of unamortized balance according to results from annual recovery check	IAS 22

Financial Statements

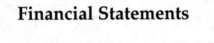

BILANZ DES SAP-KONZERNS

(in Tausend DM)

AKTIVA

	Anhang	31.12.1996		31.12.1995
Immaterielle Vermögensgegenstände	(7)	5.742		7.473
Sachanlagen	(8)	621.903		575.014
Finanzanlagen	(10)	161.429		169.464
ANLAGEVERMÖGEN		**789.074**		**751.951**
Vorräte	(11)	7.799		5.556
Forderungen aus Lieferungen und Leistungen	(12)	1.555.869	1.000.864	
Sonstige Vermögensgegenstände	(14)	55.895	46.934	
Forderungen und sonstige Vermögensgegenstände		1.611.764		1.047.798
Wertpapiere	(15)	164.891		69.992
Flüssige Mittel	(16)	737.394		327.763
UMLAUFVERMÖGEN		**2.521.848**		**1.451.109**
AKTIVPOSTEN LATENTE STEUERN	(17)	37.462		0
RECHNUNGSABGRENZUNGSPOSTEN		18.720		15.102
SUMME		**3.367.104**		**2.218.162**

CONSOLIDATED BALANCE SHEET

(in thousands of DM)

ASSETS

	Note	12/31/1996		12/31/1995	
Intangible assets	(7)		5,742		7,473
Tangible fixed assets	(8)		621,903		575,014
Other financial assets	(10)		161,429		169,464
FIXED ASSETS			**789,074**		**751,951**
Inventories	(11)		7,799		5,556
Accounts receivable	(12)	1,555,869		1,000,864	
Other assets	(14)	55,895		46,934	
Accounts receivable and other assets			1,611,764		1,047,798
Marketable securities	(15)		164,891		69,992
Cash and cash equivalents	(16)		737,394		327,763
CURRENT ASSETS			**2,521,848**		**1,451,109**
ASSET ITEM FOR DEFERRED TAXES	(17)		**37,462**		**0**
PREPAID EXPENSES AND DEFERRED CHARGES			**18,720**		**15,102**
TOTAL			3,367,104		2,218,162

PASSIVA

	Anhang	31.12.1996		31.12.1995
Gezeichnetes Kapital *)	(18)	517.537		506.163
Kapitalrücklage	(19)	353.344		137.851
Gewinnrücklagen	(20)	1.095.516	750.098	
./. Geschäftswert aus Erstkonsolidierung		25	1.428	
		1.095.491		748.670
Konzerngewinn (Bilanzgewinn der SAP AG)		240.698		133.784
Anteile anderer Gesellschafter		4.242		3.052
EIGENKAPITAL		2.211.312		1.529.520
SONDERPOSTEN FÜR INVESTITIONSZULAGEN ZUM ANLAGEVERMÖGEN	(22)	66		73
Rückstellungen für Pensionen und ähnliche Verpflichtungen		29.526	10.526	
Übrige Rückstellungen	(23)	604.860	322.871	
RÜCKSTELLUNGEN		634.386		333.397
Anleihen	(24)	8.669	20.014	
Übrige Verbindlichkeiten	(25)	494.382	329.856	
VERBINDLICHKEITEN		503.051		349.870
RECHNUNGSABGRENZUNGSPOSTEN		18.289		5.302
SUMME		3.367.104		2.218.162

*) bedingtes Kapital TDM 8.713

SHAREHOLDERS' EQUITY AND LIABILITIES

	Note	12/31/1996		12/31/1995	
Subscribed capital*	(18)		517,537		506,163
Capital reserve	(19)		353,344		137,851
Revenue reserves	(20)	1,095,516		750,098	
Less: goodwill		25		1,428	
			1,095,491		748,670
Group retained earnings (retained earnings of SAP AG)			240,698		133,784
Minority interests			4,242		3,052
SHAREHOLDERS' EQUITY			2,211,312		1,529,520
SPECIAL RESERVES FOR CAPITAL INVESTMENT SUBSIDIES	(22)		66		73
Pension reserves and similar obligations			29,526		10,526
Other reserves and accrued liabilities	(23)		604,860		322,871
RESERVES AND ACCRUED LIABILITIES			634,386		333,397
Bonds	(24)		8,669		20,014
Other liabilities	(25)		494,382		329,856
OTHER LIABILITIES			503,051		349,870
DEFERRED INCOME			18,289		5,302
TOTAL			3,367,104		2,218,162

* Contingent capital DM 8,713,000

GEWINN- UND VERLUSTRECHNUNG
SAP-KONZERN

(in Tausend DM)

	Anhang	1996	1995
Umsatzerlöse	(29)	**3.722.150**	**2.696.381**
Erhöhung des Bestands an fertigen und unfertigen Erzeugnissen		961	628
Sonstige betriebliche Erträge	(30)	73.712	54.161
		3.796.823	2.751.170
Aufwendungen für Hilfs- und Betriebsstoffe und für bezogene Waren		-13.967	-11.475
Aufwendungen für bezogene Leistungen		-380.417	-289.172
Materialaufwand		**-394.384**	**-300.647**
Personalaufwand	(31)	-1.338.473	-956.744
Abschreibungen auf immaterielle Vermögensgegenstände und Sachanlagen	(32)	-164.591	-144.456
Sonstige betriebliche Aufwendungen	(33)	-955.746	-697.455
Betriebsaufwand		**-2.458.810**	**-1.798.655**
Betriebsergebnis		**943.629**	**651.868**
Beteiligungsergebnis	(34)	1.745	0
Erträge aus anderen Wertpapieren und Ausleihungen des Finanzanlagevermögens		2.188	2.109
Abschreibungen auf Finanzanlagen	(35)	-8.192	-2.124
Zinsergebnis	(36)	27.843	22.213
Ergebnis der gewöhnlichen Geschäftstätigkeit		**967.213**	**674.066**
Steuern vom Einkommen und vom Ertrag	(37)	-382.414	-258.665
Sonstige Steuern		-17.263	-10.573
Steuern		**-399.677**	**-269.238**
Jahresüberschuß		**567.536**	**404.828**
Anteile anderer Gesellschafter am Jahresüberschuß		-1.317	-1.504
Gewinnvortrag		133.784	88.081
Ausschüttung bei der SAP AG		-133.615	-88.058
Einstellung in die Gewinnrücklagen		-325.690	-269.563
Konzerngewinn (Bilanzgewinn der SAP AG)		**240.698**	**133.784**

CONSOLIDATED INCOME STATEMENT

(in thousands of DM)

	Note	1996	1995
Sales revenues	(29)	**3,722,150**	**2,696,381**
Increase in inventories of finished goods and work-in-process		961	628
Other operating income	(30)	73,712	54,161
		3,796,823	2,751,170
Supplies and purchased goods		-13,967	-11,475
Purchased services		-380,417	-289,172
Cost of materials		**-394,384**	**-300,647**
Personnel expenses	(31)	-1,338,473	-956,744
Depreciation and amortization	(32)	-164,591	-144,456
Other operating expenses	(33)	-955,746	-697,455
Operating expenses		**-2,458,810**	**-1,798,655**
Operating result		**943,629**	**651,868**
Income from investments	(34)	1,745	0
Income from marketable securities and loans of financial assets		2,188	2,109
Write-down of financial assets	(35)	-8,192	-2,124
Net interest income	(36)	27,843	22,213
Result from ordinary operations		**967,213**	**674,066**
Taxes on income	(37)	-382,414	-258,665
Other taxes		-17,263	-10,573
Total taxes		**-399,677**	**-269,238**
Net income		**567,536**	**404,828**
Minority interests		-1,317	-1,504
Net income from prior periods		133,784	88,081
Distribution of dividends to SAP AG shareholders		-133,615	-88,058
Transfer to revenue reserves		-325,690	-269,563
Group retained earnings (retained earnings of SAP AG)		**240,698**	**133,784**

GEWINN- UND VERLUSTRECHNUNG
SAP AKTIENGESELLSCHAFT

(in Tausend DM)

	Anhang	1996	1995
Umsatzerlöse	(29)	1.699.340	1.250.476
Sonstige betriebliche Erträge	(30)	36.754	31.222
		1.736.094	1.281.698
Aufwendungen für Hilfs- und Betriebsstoffe und für bezogene Waren		-7.220	-7.148
Aufwendungen für bezogene Leistungen		-352.149	-257.676
Materialaufwand		-359.369	-264.824
Personalaufwand	(31)	-538.486	-427.399
Abschreibungen auf immaterielle Vermögensgegenstände und Sachanlagen	(32)	-90.768	-93.773
Sonstige betriebliche Aufwendungen	(33)	-285.225	-281.405
Betriebsaufwand		**-914.479**	**-802.577**
Betriebsergebnis		462.246	214.297
Beteiligungsergebnis	(34)	41.493	64.545
Erträge aus Ausleihungen des Finanzanlagevermögens		2.150	2.218
Abschreibungen auf Finanzanlagen	(35)	-2.123	-3.082
Zinsergebnis	(36)	15.239	13.299
Ergebnis der gewöhnlichen Geschäftstätigkeit		519.005	291.277
Steuern vom Einkommen und vom Ertrag	(37)	-207.090	-94.915
Sonstige Steuern		-7.386	-6.601
Steuern		**-214.476**	**-101.516**
Jahresüberschuß		304.529	189.761
Gewinnvortrag		133.784	88.081
Ausschüttung		-133.615	-88.058
Einstellung in andere Gewinnrücklagen		-64.000	-56.000
Bilanzgewinn		240.698	133.784

INCOME STATEMENT FOR
SAP AKTIENGESELLSCHAFT

(in thousands of DM)

	Note	1996	1995
Sales revenues	(29)	**1,699,340**	**1,250,476**
Other operating income	(30)	36,754	31,222
		1,736,094	1,281,698
Supplies and purchased goods		-7,220	-7,148
Purchased services		-352,149	-257,676
Cost of materials		**-359,369**	**-264,824**
Personnel expenses	(31)	-538,486	-427,399
Depreciation and amortization	(32)	-90,768	-93,773
Other operating expenses	(33)	-285,225	-281,405
Operating expenses		**-914,479**	**-802,577**
Operating result		**462,246**	**214,297**
Income from investments	(34)	41,493	64,545
Interest from loans of financial assets		2,150	2,218
Write-down of financial assets	(35)	-2,123	-3,082
Net interest income	(36)	15,239	13,299
Result from ordinary operations		**519,005**	**291,277**
Taxes on income	(37)	-207,090	-94,915
Other taxes		-7,386	-6,601
Total taxes		**-214,476**	**-101,516**
Net income		**304,529**	**189,761**
Net income from prior periods		133,784	88,081
Dividend distribution		-133,615	-88,058
Transfer to revenue reserves		-64,000	-56,000
Retained earnings		**240,698**	**133,784**

BILANZ DER SAP AKTIENGESELLSCHAFT

(in Tausend DM)

AKTIVA

	Anhang	31.12.1996		31.12.1995
Immaterielle Vermögensgegenstände	(7)	3.806		4.761
Sachanlagen	(8)	335.773		310.588
Anteile an verbundenen Unternehmen	(9)	355.938	324.436	
Beteiligungen		14.018	4.252	
Wertpapiere des Anlagevermögens		100.000	100.000	
Übrige Finanzanlagen	(10)	38.642	49.267	
Finanzanlagen		508.598		477.955
ANLAGEVERMÖGEN		848.177		793.304
Roh-, Hilfs- und Betriebsstoffe		2.496	2.185	
Geleistete Anzahlungen		3.071	1.921	
Vorräte	(11)	5.567		4.106
Forderungen aus Lieferungen und Leistungen	(12)	256.339	191.446	
Forderungen gegen verbundene Unternehmen	(13)	176.691	123.371	
Forderungen gegen Unternehmen, mit denen ein Beteiligungsverhältnis besteht		1.998	0	
Sonstige Vermögensgegenstände	(14)	20.278	17.321	
Forderungen und sonstige Vermögensgegenstände		455.306		332.138
Wertpapiere	(15)	139.264		43.824
Flüssige Mittel	(16)	453.967		131.003
UMLAUFVERMÖGEN		1.054.104		511.071
AKTIVPOSTEN LATENTE STEUERN	(17)	84		0
RECHNUNGSABGRENZUNGSPOSTEN		6.023		7.996
SUMME		1.908.388		1.312.371

BALANCE SHEET FOR SAP AKTIENGESELLSCHAFT

(in thousonds of DM)

ASSETS

	Note	12/31/1996		12/31/1995	
Intangible assets	(7)		3,806		4,761
Tangible fixed assets	(8)		335,773		310,588
Investments in affilliated companies	(9)	355,938		324,436	
Other investments		14,018		4,252	
Long-term portfolio investments		100,000		100,000	
Other financial assets	(10)	38,642		49,267	
Financial assets			508,598		477,955
FIXED ASSETS			848,177		793,304
Raw materials and operating supplies		2,496		2,185	
Advance payments received		3,071		1,921	
Inventories	(11)		5,567		4,106
Accounts receivable, trade	(12)	256,339		191,446	
Accounts due from affiliated companies	(13)	176,691		123,371	
Accounts due from other Group companies		1,998		0	
Other assets	(14)	20,278		17,321	
Accounts receivable and other assets			455,306		332,138
Marketable securities	(15)		139,264		43,824
Cash and cash equivalents	(16)		453,967		131,003
CURRENT ASSETS			1,054,104		511,071
ASSET ITEM FOR DEFERRED TAXES	(17)		84		0
PREPAID EXPENSES AND DEFERRED CHARGES			6,023		7,996
TOTAL			1,908,388		1,312,371

PASSIVA

	Anhang	31.12.1996	31.12.1995
Gezeichnetes Kapital *)	(18)	517.537	506.163
Kapitalrücklage	(19)	353.344	137.851
Gewinnrücklagen	(20)	320.252	256.254
Bilanzgewinn		240.698	133.784
EIGENKAPITAL		1.431.831	1.034.052
SONDERPOSTEN MIT RÜCKLAGEANTEIL	(21)	2.945	0
Rückstellungen für Pensionen und ähnliche Verpflichtungen		27.575	8.814
Übrige Rückstellungen	(23)	242.953	120.355
RÜCKSTELLUNGEN		270.528	129.169
Anleihen	(24)	8.669	20.014
Übrige Verbindlichkeiten	(25)	193.851	128.385
VERBINDLICHKEITEN		202.520	148.399
RECHNUNGSABGRENZUNGSPOSTEN		564	751
SUMME		1.908.388	1.312.371

*) bedingtes Kapital TDM 8.713

SHAREHOLDERS' EQUITY AND LIABILITIES

	Note	12/31/1996	12/31/1995
Subscribed capital*	(18)	517,537	506,163
Capital reserve	(19)	353,344	137,851
Revenue reserves	(20)	320,252	256,254
Retained earnings		240,698	133,784
SHAREHOLDERS' EQUITY		1,431,831	1,034,052
SPECIAL RESERVE WITH ACCRUAL CHARACTER	(21)	2,945	0
Pension reserves and similar obligations		27,575	8,814
Other reserves and accrued liabilities	(23)	242,953	120,355
RESERVES AND ACCRUED LIABILITIES		270,528	129,169
Bonds	(24)	8,669	20,014
Other liabilities	(25)	193,851	128,385
OTHER LIABILITIES		202,520	148,399
DEFERRED INCOME		564	751
TOTAL		1,908,388	1,312,371

* Contingent capital DM 8,713,000

ENTWICKLUNG DES ANLAGEVERMÖGENS
SAP-KONZERN

(in Tausend DM)

	Anschaffungs- oder Herstellungskosten					
	1.1.1996	Veränderung Konsolidierungskreis	Zugänge	Abgänge	Umbuchungen	31.12.1996
I. Immaterielle Vermögensgegenstände						
1. Gewerbliche Schutzrechte und ähnliche Rechte und Werte	25.894	-78	4.414	327	-477	29.426
	25.894	**-78**	**4.414**	**327**	**-477**	**29.426**
II. Sachanlagen						
1. Grundstücke, grundstücksgleiche Rechte und Bauten einschließlich Bauten auf fremden Grundstücken	411.309	-41	33.000	2.755	1.459	442.972
2. Andere Anlagen, Betriebs- und Geschäftsausstattung	539.409	-2.866	153.223	69.179	961	621.548
3. Geleistete Anzahlungen und Anlagen im Bau	850		30.001	256	-1.943	28.652
	951.568	**-2.907**	**216.224**	**72.190**	**477**	**1.093.172**
III. Finanzanlagen						
1. Anteile an verbundenen Unternehmen	15.379		288	3.555		12.112
2. Ausleihungen an verbundene Unternehmen	228					228
3. Beteiligungen	2.500		9.795			12.295
4. Genossenschaftsanteile	1					1
5. Wertpapiere	100.499		205			100.704
6. Sonstige Ausleihungen	58.755		6.020	16.246		48.529
	177.362		**16.308**	**19.801**		**173.869**
ANLAGEVERMÖGEN	**1.154.824**	**-2.985**	**236.946**	**92.318**		**1.296.467**

CONSOLIDATED STATEMENT OF FIXED ASSETS

(in thousands of DM)

	Purchase or manufacturing cost					
	1/1/1996	Changes in consolidated companies	Additions	Retirements	Transfers	12/31/1996
I. Intangible assets						
1. Trademarks, similar rights and assets	25,894	-78	4,414	327	-477	29,426
	25,894	**-78**	**4,414**	**327**	**-477**	**29,426**
II. Property, plant and equipment						
1. Land, leasehold rights and buildings, including buildings on third-party land	411,309	-41	33,000	2,755	1,459	442,972
2. Other property, plant and equipment	539,409	-2,866	153,223	69,179	961	621,548
3. Advance payments and construction in progress	850		30,001	256	-1,943	28,652
	951,568	**-2,907**	**216,224**	**72,190**	**477**	**1,093,172**
III. Financial assets						
1. Shares in affiliated companies	15,379		288	3,555		12,112
2. Loans due from affiliated companies	228					228
3. Other investments	2,500		9,795			12,295
4. Shares in cooperatives	1					1
5. Long-term investments	100,499		205			100,704
6. Other loans	58,755		6,020	16,246		48,529
	177,362		**16,308**	**19,801**		**173,869**
FIXED ASSETS	**1,154,824**	**-2,985**	**236,946**	**92,318**		**1,296,467**

Kumulierte Abschreibungen							Buchwert	
1.1.1996	Veränderung Konsolidie- rungskreis	Zugänge	Abgänge	Umbu- chungen	Zuschrei- bungen	31.12.1996	31.12.1996	31.12.1995
18.421	-57	5.472	225	73		23.684	**5.742**	7.473
18.421	**-57**	**5.472**	**225**	**73**		**23.684**	**5.742**	**7.473**
57.195	-28	26.200	3.133	12	2.137	78.109	**364.863**	354.114
319.359	-2.206	132.919	56.827	-85		393.160	**228.388**	220.050
							28.652	850
376.554	**-2.234**	**159.119**	**59.960**	**-73**	**2.137**	**471.269**	**621.903**	**575.014**
351		6.591	2.140			4.802	**7.310**	15.028
228						228		
							12.295	2.500
							1	1
							100.704	100.499
7.319		1.601	721		789	7.410	**41.119**	51.436
7.898		**8.192**	**2.861**		**789**	**12.440**	**161.429**	**169.464**
402.873	**-2.291**	**172.783**	**63.046**		**2.926**	**507.393**	**789.074**	**751.951**

Accumulated depreciation and amortization							Book value	
1/1/1996	Changes in consolidated companies	Additions	Retirements	Transfers	Write-ups	12/31/1996	12/31/1996	12/31/1995
18,421	-57	5,472	225	73		23,684	5,742	7,473
18,421	-57	5,472	225	73		23,684	5,742	7,473
57,195	-28	26,200	3,133	12	2,137	78,109	364,863	354,114
319,359	-2,206	132,919	56,827	-85		393,160	228,388	220,050
							28,652	850
376,554	-2,234	159,119	59,960	-73	2,137	471,269	621,903	575,014
351		6,591	2,140			4,802	7,310	15,028
228						228		
							12,295	2,500
							1	1
							100,704	100,499
7,319		1,601	721		789	7,410	41,119	51,436
7,898		8,192	2,861		789	12,440	161,429	169,464
402,873	-2,291	172,783	63,046		2,926	507,393	789,074	751,951

ENTWICKLUNG DES ANLAGEVERMÖGENS
SAP AKTIENGESELLSCHAFT

(in Tausend DM)

	Anschaffungs- oder Herstellungskosten				
	1.1.1996	Zugänge	Abgänge	Umbu-chungen	31.12.1996
I. Immaterielle Vermögensgegenstände					
1. Gewerbliche Schutzrechte und ähnliche Rechte und Werte	18.701	3.631	1		22.331
	18.701	**3.631**	**1**		**22.331**
II. Sachanlagen					
1. Grundstücke, grundstücksgleiche Rechte und Bauten einschließlich Bauten auf fremden Grundstücken	280.784	13.847	200	307	294.738
2. Andere Anlagen, Betriebs- und Geschäftsausstattung	314.004	81.483	34.774	16	360.729
3. Geleistete Anzahlungen und Anlagen im Bau	323	22.373		-323	22.373
	595.111	**117.703**	**34.974**	**0**	**677.840**
III. Finanzanlagen					
1. Anteile an verbundenen Unternehmen	354.573	37.891	7.789		384.675
2. Beteiligungen	4.252	9.766			14.018
3. Genossenschaftsanteile	1				1
4. Wertpapiere	100.000				100.000
5. Sonstige Ausleihungen	56.041	5.069	15.630		45.480
	514.867	**52.726**	**23.419**		**544.174**
ANLAGEVERMÖGEN	**1.128.679**	**174.060**	**58.394**		**1.244.345**

STATEMENT OF FIXED ASSETS
FOR SAP AKTIENGESELLSCHAFT

(in thousands of DM)

	Purchase or manufacturing cost				
	1/1/1996	Additions	Retirements	Transfers	12/31/1996
I. Intangible assets					
1. Trademarks, similar rights and assets	18,701	3,631	1		22,331
	18,701	3,631	1		22,331
II. Property, plant and equipment					
1. Land, leasehold rights and buildings, including buildings on third-party land	280,784	13,847	200	307	294,738
2. Other property, plant and equipment	314,004	81,483	34,774	16	360,729
3. Advance payments and construction in progress	323	22,373		-323	22,373
	595,111	117,703	34,974	0	677,840
III. Financial assets					
1. Shares in affiliated companies	354,573	37,891	7,789		384,675
2. Other investments	4,252	9,766			14,018
3. Shares in cooperatives	1				1
4. Long-term investments	100,000				100,000
5. Other loans	56,041	5,069	15,630		45,480
	514,867	52,726	23,419		544,174
FIXED ASSETS	1,128,679	174,060	58,394		1,244,345

Kumulierte Abschreibungen						Buchwert	
1.1.1996	Zugänge	Abgänge	Umbu-chungen	Zuschrei-bungen	31.12.1996	31.12.1996	31.12.1995
13.940	4.585				18.525	**3.806**	**4.761**
13.940	4.585				18.525	**3.806**	**4.761**
71.466	14.658	200			85.924	**208.814**	**209.318**
213.057	71.525	28.439			256.143	**104.586**	**100.947**
						22.373	**323**
284.523	**86.183**	**28.639**			342.067	**335.773**	**310.588**
30.137	608	2.008			28.737	**355.938**	**324.436**
						14.018	**4.252**
						1	**1**
						100.000	**100.000**
6.775	1.515	682	769		6.839	**38.641**	**49.266**
36.912	**2.123**	**2.690**	**769**		35.576	**508.598**	**477.955**
335.375	**92.891**	**31.329**	**769**		396.168	**848.177**	**793.304**

Accumulated depreciation and amortization						Book value	
1/1/1996	Additions	Retirements	Transfers	Write-ups	12/31/1996	12/31/1996	12/31/1995
13,940	4,585				18,525	3,806	4,761
13,940	4,585				18,525	3,806	4,761
71,466	14,658	200			85,924	208,814	209,318
213,057	71,525	28,439			256,143	104,586	100,947
						22,373	323
284,523	86,183	28,639			342,067	335,773	310,588
30,137	608	2,008			28,737	355,938	324,436
						14,018	4,252
						1	1
						100,000	100,000
6,775	1,515	682		769	6,839	38,641	49,266
36,912	2,123	2,690		769	35,576	508,598	477,955
335,375	92,891	31,329		769	396,168	848,177	793,304

INVESTMENTS OF SAP AKTIENGESELLSCHAFT AND THE GROUP

As of December 31, 1996, figures in thousands of DM

Name and location of company	% held	Company equity 12/31/1996[1]	Company sales in 1996[1]	Net income/ loss (–) for 1996[1]	Number of employees as of 12/31/1996[2]
GERMANY					
DACOS Beteiligungsgesellschaft mbH, Walldorf	100	52	0	-1	0
Steeb Anwendungssysteme GmbH, Abstatt	100	3,529	27,356	1,457	103
STEEB-CAS Informationstechnik GmbH i.L., Abstatt	100	768	0	579	0
AsseT GmbH Assessment & Training Technologies, Friedrichshafen	75	723	2,223	223	9
DACOS Software GmbH, St. Ingbert	52	8,460	44,100	2,627	256
SRS Software- und Systemhaus Dresden GmbH, Dresden	50	5,660	57,562	1,783	324
SAP Solutions GmbH, Freiberg a.N.	40	7,370	34,734	4,365	139
REST OF EUROPE					
SAP (Schweiz) AG, Biel/Switzerland	100	161,641	126,617	19,968	153
SAP (UK) Limited, Feltham/UK	100	44,078	138,881	12,428	226
SAP Ireland Ltd., Dublin/Ireland	100	79,797	0	3,092	6
SAP France S.A., Fontenay-sous-Bois/France	100	22,512	108,298	7,505	173
SAP Danmark A/S, Brøndby/Denmark	100	20,492	54,470	13,181	80
SAP Svenska Aktiebolag, Stockholm/Sweden	100	5,771	33,150	-18	71
SAP Nederland B.V., DG 's Hertogenbosch/Netherlands	100	30,139	86,301	17,941	119
SAP ESPANA Y PORTUGAL, SISTEMAS APLICACIONES Y PRODUCTOS EN LA INFORMATICA S.A., Madrid/Spain	100	14,452	44,409	2,827	82
SAP Italia S.p.A., Milan/Italy	100	13,601	54,534	6,201	86
SAP Österreich, Systeme, Anwendungen und Produkte in der Datenverarbeitung Gesellschaft m.b.H., Vienna/Austria	100	20,336	89,492	12,736	110
N.V. SAP BELGIUM S.A., Brussels/Belgium	100	22,207	68,777	11,228	78
SAP CR, s.r.o., Prague/Czech Republic	100	6,364	39,723	1,950	120
SAP Consult C.I.S., Moscow/Russia	100	1,370	4,697	737	81
SAP Polska Sp. z.o.o., Warsaw/Poland	100	860	9,292	-824	34
STEEB-CAS Informationstechnik AG in Liq., Pieterlen/Switzerland	100	6	0	373	0
DACOS Software S.A., Vaumarcus (NE)/Switzerland[3]	52	175	604	335	1
AMERICAS					
SAP America, Inc., Wayne, PA/USA	100	435,058	1,200,620	127,041	1,730
SAP International, Inc., Miami, FL/USA	100	215	288	7	6
SAP Technology, Inc., Foster City, CA/USA	100	5,599	22,125	1,336	170
SAP Canada Inc., North York, ONT/Canada	100	35,289	117,272	11,067	200
SAP MEXICO S.A. DE C.V., Mexico City/Mexico	100	10,075	31,989	4,744	65
SAP ARGENTINA S.A., Buenos Aires/Argentina	100	5,676	16,179	-36	39
SAP BRASIL COMERCIO E REPRESENTACOES LTDA., São Paulo/Brazil	100	7,945	36,878	2,824	63
SAP Andina y del Caribe C.A., Caracas/Venezuela	100	9,713	26,943	6,344	29
WS Investment Holdings, L.P., Wilmington, DE/USA[3]	99	12,934	1,740	314	0
ASIA/AUSTRALIA					
SAP Asia Pte. Ltd., Singapore	100	12,974	62,699	-3,205	201
SAP AUSTRALIA PTY LTD, Sydney/Australia	100	28,652	116,638	10,407	180
SAP New Zealand Limited, Auckland/New Zealand	100	7,024	13,276	2,550	19
SAP Japan Co., Ltd., Tokyo/Japan	100	72,782	274,089	16,727	424
SAP Data Processing (Malaysia) Sdn Bhd, Kuala Lumpur/Malaysia	100	1,992	9,819	14	55
SAP SYSTEMS, APPLICATIONS AND PRODUCTS IN DATA PROCESSING (THAILAND) LTD., Bangkok/Thailand	100	3,638	12,219	1,483	28
SAP PHILIPPINES SYSTEMS, APPLICATIONS AND PRODUCTS IN DATA PROCESSING, INC., Makati City/Philippines	100	1,142	4,265	-388	19
SAP (Beijing) Software System Co., Ltd., Beijing/China	100	3,003	4,091	-4,340	48
SAP Korea Limited, Seoul/Korea	100	-1,206	16,424	-3,626	32
SAP India Systems, Applications and Products in Data Processing Private Limited, Bangalore/India	100	2,634	10,814	1,043	33
SAP India (Holding) Pte. Ltd., Singapore	100	805	0	-23	0
AFRICA					
SYSTEMS APPLICATIONS PRODUCTS (SOUTHERN AFRICA) (PTY) LTD, Dunkeld West/South Africa	100	12,832	58,771	8,839	97

1) These figures are not consolidated and therefore do not reflect the contributions of these companies to the consolidated financial statements
2) As of 12/31/1996, including managing directors
3) Not included according to Article 296 (2) of the German Commercial Code

A. General Information

(1) Application of the German legal regulations

The consolidated financial statements and the financial statements of SAP Aktiengesellschaft (SAP AG) are prepared in accordance with the German Commercial Code and Stock Corporation Act.

In the interests of clarity, the notes to the financial statements include both the notes required by law on the individual items of the balance sheet and income statement, and the information which may optionally be included either on the balance sheet and income statement or in the notes to the financial statements.

Unless otherwise stated, the notes apply to both the consolidated financial statements and the financial statements of SAP AG.

B. Accounting and Valuation Policies

(2) Consolidated companies

The consolidated financial statements include, in addition to SAP AG, six domestic and 36 foreign subsidiaries in which SAP AG holds, directly or indirectly, a majority of the voting rights. One joint venture, SRS Software-und Systemhaus Dresden GmbH, Dresden/Germany, in which SAP AG holds a 50% interest, is consolidated on a proportional basis. SAP Solutions GmbH, Freiberg/Germany, which had previously been consolidated in full, is now included in the consolidated financial statements as an associated company, applying the equity method, due to the sale of stock in this company. This change does not have a significant impact on the accounts of the Group.

The following seven newly established companies are included in the consolidated financial statements for the first time:

– AsseT GmbH Assessment & Training Technologies, Friedrichshafen/Germany
– DACOS Beteiligungsgesellschaft mbH, Walldorf/Germany
– SAP Andina y del Caribe C.A., Caracas/Venezuela
– SAP India (Holding) Pte. Ltd., Singapore
– SAP India Systems, Applications and Products in Data Processing Private Limited, Bangalore/India
– SAP International, Inc., Miami, FL/USA
– SAP Technology, Inc., Foster City, CA/USA

All of these new companies were consolidated in full. The increase in the number of companies included in the consolidated financial statements did not give rise to effects that would limit comparability of the annual financial statements with those of the previous year.

Two subsidiaries have not been consolidated, since their impact on the Group's net worth, financial position and results of operations is immaterial (their balance sheet totals amount to about 1% of the consolidated balance sheet total). They have been excluded according to the option available under Article 296 (2) of the German Commercial Code. Please refer to the information on the Group's investments.

(3) Consolidation policies

The book value method of consolidation has been used unless otherwise noted. This method entails setting off the acquisition cost against the share of capital attributable to each company as of the date of acquisition. Any remaining goodwill is offset against the reserves, pursuant to Article 309 (1) sentence 3 of the German Commercial Code.

Intercompany receivables, payables, revenues, expenses and profits among the consolidated companies are eliminated. Deferred taxes are calculated after consolidation entries affecting income, when it is expected that the difference in the tax expense will be reversed in a future year. Minority interest is identified for subsidiaries not wholly owned by the parent company.

The investment consolidated by the equity method is shown at the book value of the equity held.

The retained earnings of the Group, as shown in the consolidated financial statements, are the retained earnings of SAP AG. The retained earnings of the subsidiaries are included in the Group's revenue reserves.

(4) Accounting and valuation policies

The accounting and valuation policies of SAP AG also apply to the consolidated financial statements. The financial statements of consolidated subsidiaries whose accounting policies differ from those of the parent company have been adjusted. Such adjustments are waived only where the effect is immaterial.

Fixed assets

Purchased intangible assets are shown at cost and amortized on a straight-line basis over a maximum of five years.

Tangible fixed assets are shown at cost less scheduled depreciation, based on their estimated useful lives.

Buildings are depreciated using the straight-line method over useful lives of 25 to 50 years. Leasehold improvements are depreciated using the straight-line method over the period of the lease. The useful lives of movable fixed assets range between two and 20 years. In most cases, the declining-balance method of depreciation is applied, where permissible, with a scheduled transfer to the straight-line method at a subsequent date. The company applies the rules regarding elective valuation set forth in Article 6 (2) of the German Income Tax Act.

In the financial statements of SAP AG, buildings acquired up through 1991 are depreciated by the straight-line method over useful lives of 25 to 50 years. Additions from 1992 onward are depreciated by the declining-balance method pursuant to Article 7 (5) sentence 1 no. 1 of the German Income Tax Act.

Investments in affiliated companies and other shareholdings are shown at the lower of cost or market value. Long-term investments are shown at cost. Interest-bearing loans to employees and to third parties are shown at their nominal value. Interest-free loans to employees are discounted to their present value.

Current assets

Inventories are shown at purchase or production cost, or at the lower market value.

Accounts receivable from software sales are posted on the basis of the number of authorized users, provided that the customer has signed an irrevocable contract with the company, and the software has been delivered in full. Accounts receivable are stated at their nominal value. Foreseeable individual risks are written down on a case-by-case basis. General credit risk is reflected by means of a lump-sum allowance for doubtful accounts. Interest-free loans with a remaining term exceeding one year are discounted to their present value. Other assets in the form of reinsurance claims under life insurance policies are capitalized at the value of the insurance company's premium reserve, as shown in its general operational plan.

Marketable securities are valued at purchase cost or the lower market value as of the balance sheet closing date.

Other assets are shown at their nominal value. Cash and cash equivalents in Postbank accounts and in banks are stated at their nominal amounts.

Prepaid expenses and deferred charges

Prepaid expenses and deferred charges are determined by allocating expenses to the periods to which they are attributable.

Reserves and accrued liabilities

Pension reserves for companies in Germany are stated at the highest amounts allowable for tax purposes, in accordance with Article 6a of the German Income Tax Act. An interest rate of 6% p.a. has been applied. Foreign subsidiaries record their pension reserves in accordance with similar principles.

The relief fund of SAP Altersvorsorge e.V. has assumed indirect pension commitments towards employees of SAP AG. SAP AG, as the sponsor of the relief fund, has established a reserve for indirect pension obligations, exercising its option to establish accruals under Article 28 (1) sentence 2 of the Introductory Act to the German Commercial Code.

The amount of DM 16,500,000 contained in this item corresponds to the difference between the value of the obligations determined in accordance with Article 6a of the German Income Tax Act, admissible under commercial law, and the value of the assets held by the relief fund.

Accrued taxes are calculated on the basis of the planned distribution of income. The other reserves and accrued liabilities take into account all foreseeable risks and contingent obligations.

Liabilities

Liabilities are shown at the amounts payable.

(5) Currency translation The financial statements of the individual companies include accounts receivable in foreign currencies, which are translated at the lower of the exchange rate on the transaction date or the buying rate on the balance sheet closing date. Losses arising from movements in exchange rates are recorded. Accounts payable in foreign currencies are valued at the highest applicable rates.

In the consolidated financial statements, the financial statements of foreign subsidiaries are translated to DM using the historical exchange rate. Fixed assets (excluding loans), shareholders' equity, depreciation and amortization are translated at the applicable rate at the time of acquisition or first consolidation. The remaining assets and liabilities are translated at the mid-market rates on the balance sheet date (closing rate).

Differences arising from the translation of balance sheet items are charged directly to the revenue reserves, without affecting income for the year.

With the exception of depreciation and amortization, which are translated at historical rates, expense and income items are translated at the average rate for the year. The resultant differences on translation are reflected in the income statement.

The net income for the year is translated at the closing rate. The translation difference from the income statement is charged to income.

The exchange rates of key currencies changed as follows:

		Exchange rate as of December 31		Average exchange rate	
		1996	1995	1996	1995
1	US dollar	1.5548	1.4335	1.5083	1.4211
100	Japanese yen	1.3408	1.3908	1.3811	1.5243
1	pound sterling	2.6267	2.2135	2.3689	2.2476
1	Swiss franc	1.1500	1.2454	1.2159	1.2153

C. Notes to the Balance Sheets

(6) Fixed assets

Fixed assets movements for the Group and SAP AG during the year under review are shown on pages 76 through 79.

(7) Intangible assets

The additions to trademarks, similar rights and assets relate to software programs.

(8) Tangible fixed assets

The additions consist primarily of the construction of office buildings, the acquisition of land and the purchase of hardware, automobiles and other business equipment.

Region	Additions 1996 DM (1,000s)	Book value 12/31/1996 DM (1,000s)
Germany	130,012	389,186
Rest of Europe	36,630	132,150
America	25,854	64,961
Asia/Australia	22,887	34,165
Africa	841	1,441
	216,224	621,903

(9) Investments in affiliated companies

Of the additions for SAP AG, the amount of DM 37,891,000 relates to the following newly established, wholly-owned subsidiaries:

– DACOS Beteiligungsgesellschaft mbH, Walldorf/Germany
– SAP Andina y del Caribe C.A., Caracas/Venezuela
– SAP India (Holding) Pte. Ltd., Singapore
– SAP India Systems, Applications and Products in Data Processing Private Limited, Bangalore/India

Furthermore, the additions include a 75% share of the newly established AsseT GmbH Assessment & Training Technologies, Friedrichshafen/Germany.

In addition, the following companies recorded increases in capital:

– SAP ESPANA Y PORTUGAL SISTEMAS APLICACIONES Y PRODUCTOS EN LA INFORMATICA, S.A., Madrid/Spain
– SAP (UK) Limited, Feltham/UK
– SAP CR, s.r.o., Prague/Czech Republic
– SAP Consult C.I.S., Moscow/Russia
– SAP BRASIL COMERCIO E REPRESENTACOES LTDA., São Paulo/Brazil
– SAP ARGENTINA S.A., Buenos Aires/Argentina
– SAP Asia Pte. Ltd., Singapore
– SAP (Beijing) Software System Co., Ltd., Beijing/China
– SAP Korea Limited, Seoul/Korea

The disposals, amounting to DM 7,789,000, relate to the liquidation of SAP-M GmbH i.L. and SAP Finance Ireland Ltd. Dublin/Ireland, as well as the sale of a 35% share in the stock of SAP Solutions GmbH, Freiberg/Germany.

The investments of the SAP Group are shown on page 80.

(10) Other financial assets

The other financial assets of SAP AG consist of loans to employees and to third parties. On the consolidated balance sheet, the other financial assets also include investments in affiliated companies not included in consolidation, as well as other investments.

(11) Inventories

Inventories are primarily office supplies and documentation, as well as advance payments received on orders.

(12) Accounts receivable

Of the accounts receivable shown as of December 31, 1996, DM 90,837,000 for the Group and DM 2,584,000 for SAP AG have a remaining term greater than one year.

(13) Accounts due from affiliated companies

As in the previous year, all receivables shown on the balance sheet of SAP AG are due within one year.

(14) Other assets

	Group		SAP AG	
	1996 DM (1,000s)	1995 DM (1,000s)	1996 DM (1,000s)	1995 DM (1,000s)
Other assets	55,895	46,934	20,278	17,321
– thereof with a remaining term greater than one year	(30,378)	(23,794)	(10,978)	(8,898)

Other assets include interest receivable for the period, repayment claims, reinsurance claims under life insurance policies and rental deposits.

(15) Marketable securities

This item consists primarily of fixed-income securities. During the fiscal year, SAP AG acquired 68,197 of its own shares with a par value of DM 5, representing 0.07% of the capital stock, at market prices close to DM 212, for the purpose of offering them to its employees (Article 71 (1) no. 2 of the German Stock Corporation Act). They were transferred to employees during the year at a price of DM 169 per share. The company did not hold any of its own shares as of the balance sheet closing date.

(16) Cash and cash equivalents

As in the previous year, this balance sheet item includes cash and cash equivalents in Postbank accounts and in banks.

(17) Asset item for deferred taxes

The asset item for deferred taxes for SAP AG mainly results from the set-off of deferred tax liabilities recorded as a liability, arising from the differences between the depreciation of buildings shown on the commercial and tax balance sheets until and including 1991 (DM 9,794,000), against deferred tax assets arising from the discounting of interest-free loans to employees, as required under commercial law, and the accrual for indirect pension obligations and employee anniversary gifts (DM 9,878,000), which are not deductible for tax purposes.

The corresponding item in the consolidated financial statements results primarily from the amounts shown in the individual financial statements, and only to a lesser degree from consolidation measures.

(18) Subscribed capital

The subscribed capital of SAP AG as of December 31, 1996, totaled DM 517,537,000, comprising 5,393,170 shares of common stock with a par value of DM 50 per share, and 7,060,000 shares of common stock with a par value of DM 5 per share, as well as 2,074,792 shares of non-voting preferred stock with a par value of DM 50 per share, and 21,767,815 shares of non-voting preferred stock with a par value of DM 5 per share.

As conversion rights for the 1988/1998 convertible bond issue were exercised, DM 35,000 of contingent capital, corresponding to 555 shares of common stock with a par value of DM 50 each, and 139 shares of preferred stock with a par value of DM 50 each, was converted into capital stock. As conversion rights for the 1994/2004 convertible bond issue were exercised, DM 11,339,000 of contingent capital, corresponding to 2,267,815 shares of preferred stock with a par value of DM 5 each, was converted into capital stock.

As a result, contingent capital decreased by DM 11,374,000, amounting to DM 8,713,000 as of December 31, 1996.

(19) Capital reserve   Of the increase in the capital reserve, DM 50,000 resulted from the premium necessary to cover the exercise of conversion rights for the 1988/1998 convertible bonds, and DM 215,443,000 from the premium necessary to cover the exercise of conversion rights for the 1994/2004 convertible bonds.

(20) Revenue reserves   The other revenue reserves shown on the balance sheet of SAP AG are as follows:

	1996 DM (1,000s)	1995 DM (1,000s)
Balance as of January 1	256,250	200,250
Allocation from net income for the year	64,000	56,000
Balance as of December 31	**320,250**	**256,250**

Following a DM 2,000 reversal effected during the course of the fiscal year, the special-purpose reserve pursuant to Article 218 (sentence 2) of the German Stock Corporation Act now amounts to DM 2,000.

Group revenue reserves are as follows:

	1996 DM (1,000s)	1995 DM (1,000s)
Balance as of January 1	748,670	501,725
Amounts allocated to revenue reserves in financial statements of subsidiaries	6,006	5,415
Amount allocated to revenue reserve of SAP AG from net income	64,000	56,000
Adjustment to retained earnings of SAP AG	257,493	210,458
Netting of goodwill	-25	-1,428
Effect of exclusion of companies from consolidation	-1,053	–
Balance sheet currency translation difference	20,400	-23,500
Balance as of December 31	**1,095,491**	**748,670**

(21) Special reserve with accrual character   A reserve pursuant to Article 6b of the German Income Tax Act was established on the balance sheet of SAP AG.

(22) Special reserves for capital investment subsidies   Special reserves for capital investment subsidies were established on the consolidated balance sheet, pursuant to Article 1 of the German Capital Investment Subsidy Act.

(23) Other reserves and accrued liabilities		Group		SAP AG	
		1996 DM (1,000s)	1995 DM (1,000s)	1996 DM (1,000s)	1995 DM (1,000s)
Accrued taxes		273,933	165,247	143,347	64,207
Deferred taxes		–	683	–	7,095
Other reserves and accrued liabilities		330,927	156,941	99,606	49,053
		604,860	**322,871**	**242,953**	**120,355**

Accrued taxes primarily include amounts set aside for the current fiscal year and for prior years.

Other reserves and accrued liabilities are made up as follows:

	Group		SAP AG	
	1996 DM (1,000s)	1995 DM (1,000s)	1996 DM (1,000s)	1995 DM (1,000s)
Obligations to employees	183,642	61,657	32,913	7,774
Vacation entitlement	54,533	39,124	29,319	23,299
Obligations to customers and suppliers	48,122	25,633	14,869	4,904
Warranty risks	20,380	8,531	11,155	1,887
Financial statements	1,975	1,321	490	515
Other	22,275	20,675	10,860	10,674
	330,927	**156,941**	**99,606**	**49,053**

Obligations to employees relate primarily to bonus payments tied to earnings performance. "Other" mainly comprises contributions to the employees' accident insurance association and other obligations.

(24) Bonds This item comprises the outstanding portion of the 6% 1994/2004 convertible bond, which amounts to DM 8,661,000 (DM 20,000,000 as of December 31, 1995), and the outstanding portion of the 1988/1998 floating-rate convertible bond, issued by SAP AG, which amounts to DM 8,000 (DM 14,000 as of December 31, 1995). The 1988/1998 convertible bond issue is divided into DM 50 registered bonds, and carries a right to convert to SAP common stock at a ratio of 1:6.25 of the share's par value. The conversion right can be exercised up until October 20, 1998. The 1994/2004 convertible bond issue is divided into 400,000 registered convertible bonds with a par value of DM 50. This convertible bond carries the right to convert to shares at a ratio of 1:1 of the share's par value. The conversion right can be exercised on June 30, September 30, and November 30 of every year up until June 30, 2004.

(25) Other liabilities The information on liabilities required by German law is included in the following summary. The liabilities are unsecured, excluding retention of title and similar rights as is customary in the industry.

Other liabilities

	Group			
	Balance on 12/31/1996	Remaining term less than 1 year	Remaining term more than 5 years	Balance on 12/31/1995
	DM (1,000s)	DM (1,000s)	DM (1,000s)	DM (1,000s)
Bank loans and overdrafts	90,428	90,272	156	60,218
Advance payments received	5,361	5,361	–	3,143
Accounts payable	198,862	198,862	–	150,952
Payables due to unconsolidated affiliates	5,514	5,514	–	66
Taxes	112,507	112,507	–	49,712
Social security	35,431	35,431	–	24,293
Other liabilities	46,279	43,973	2,270	41,472
	494,382	**491,920**	**2,426**	**329,856**

In the previous year, liabilities with a remaining term not exceeding one year amounted to DM 327,183,000, and those with a remaining term exceeding five years amounted to DM 2,673,000.

	SAP AG			
	Balance on 12/31/1996	Remaining term less than 1 year	Remaining term more than 5 years	Balance on 12/31/1995
	DM (1,000s)	DM (1,000s)	DM (1,000s)	DM (1,000s)
Advance payments received	862	862		300
Accounts payable	86,452	86,452	–	75,283
Intercompany payables	34,289	34,289		2,174
Payables due to unconsolidated affiliates	4,899	4,899	–	33
Taxes	33,371	33,371	–	22,735
Social security	14,742	14,742	–	11,787
Other liabilities	19,236	16,966	2,270	16,073
	193,851	**191,581**	**2,270**	**128,385**

In the previous year, liabilities with a remaining term not exceeding one year amounted to DM 126,244,000, and those with a remaining term exceeding five years amounted to DM 2,141,000.

(26) Contingent liabilities

	Group		SAP AG	
	1996 DM (1,000s)	1995 DM (1,000s)	1996 DM (1,000s)	1995 DM (1,000s)
Guarantees and endorsements	1,019	1,149	–	–
Warranty obligations	105,090	62,235	102,727	59,000
	106,109	**63,384**	**102,727**	**59,000**

(27) Other financial commitments

Commitments under rental and leasing contracts:

	Group DM (1,000s)	SAP AG DM (1,000s)
Due in 1997	102,995	22,597
Due 1998 – 2001	199,561	24,204
Due after 2001	49,726	9,409

Order commitments extended within the limit of the authorized capital expenditure of SAP AG amount to DM 17,705,000.

(28) Derivative financial instruments

SAP AG uses derivative financial instruments in its ordinary operations to hedge against currency and interest-rate risk.

For this purpose, SAP AG works only with banks that have the highest credit rating. The use of derivative financial instruments is subject to clear, consistent guidelines and strict internal controls, and is limited to hedging against risks in ordinary operations, including financial investments and financing transactions.

Currency-hedging transactions are effected exclusively with the currencies of the major industrialized countries.

At year-end, the notional value of outstanding contracts was DM 59,000,000 for currency-related derivative instruments, and DM 60,000,000 for interest-rate derivatives.

D. Notes to the Income Statements

(29) Sales revenues Sales revenues by types of activity were as follows:

	Group		SAP AG	
	1996 DM (1,000s)	1995 DM (1,000s)	1996 DM (1,000s)	1995 DM (1,000s)
Product revenues	2,630,512	1,933,811	1,327,479	936,758
Consulting and training	1,041,404	724,134	333,834	281,291
Other	50,234	38,436	38,027	32,427
Total	**3,722,150**	**2,696,381**	**1,699,340**	**1,250,476**

The geographical breakdown of sales revenues, based on the location of the registered offices of customers, is as follows:

	Group		SAP AG	
	1996 DM (1,000s)	1995 DM (1,000s)	1996 DM (1,000s)	1995 DM (1,000s)
Germany	914,281	798,538	876,450	728,152
Rest of Europe	885,369	624,040	304,171	223,185
America	1,385,654	947,926	343,760	198,990
Asia/Australia	464,489	280,866	149,377	84,643
Africa	72,357	45,011	25,582	15,506
Total	**3,722,150**	**2,696,381**	**1,699,340**	**1,250,476**

(30) Other operating income Other operating income comprises:

	Group		SAP AG	
	1996 DM (1,000s)	1995 DM (1,000s)	1996 DM (1,000s)	1995 DM (1,000s)
Exchange gains	27,962	20,436	13,534	9,484
Employee contributions for company cars	7,324	8,281	7,080	8,023
Sale of company stock	6,748	–	6,748	–
Rental income	2,944	3,134	515	167
Gain on sale of marketable securities	1,826	6,431	555	1,357
Income from increase in premium reserve of reinsurance policy	1,794	2,061	1,635	1,871
Income from prior periods	104	51	–	40
Reversal of special reserve for capital investment premiums	59	161	–	–
Write-ups of marketable securities	5	2,861	5	1,832
Other income	24,946	10,745	6,682	8,448
Total	**73,712**	**54,161**	**36,754**	**31,222**

Other income mainly comprises gains on the disposal of fixed assets and income from insurance claims.

(31) Personnel expenses/number of employees

Personnel expenses comprise:

	Group		SAP AG	
	1996 DM (1,000s)	1995 DM (1,000s)	1996 DM (1,000s)	1995 DM (1,000s)
Salaries	1,138,518	825,931	447,714	367,004
Social security	143,630	102,691	58,667	46,631
Expenses for pension plan contributions	56,325	28,122	32,105	13,764
Total	**1,338,473**	**956,744**	**538,486**	**427,399**

A reserve was established during the fiscal year in the amount of the difference between the obligations determined in accordance with Article 6a of the German Income Tax Act and the premium reserve of the relief fund of SAP Altersvorsorge e.V. for the indirect pension commitments towards employees of SAP AG.

Applying the calculation method prescribed by Article 267 (5) of the German Commercial Code, the average number of employees was as follows:

	Group		SAP AG	
	1996	1995	1996	1995
Employees	8,177	6,443	3,501	3,028

The average number of employees of the joint venture company consolidated on a proportional basis, in accordance with Article 310 of the German Commercial Code, was 322 in 1996, compared with 296 in the previous year.

(32) Depreciation and amortization

In accordance with the Development Areas Act, additional depreciation of DM 1,587,000, applied in accordance with the German tax rules, has been charged to income with respect to the companies included within the consolidated financial statements. In the current financial statements, special depreciation taken in earlier years for German tax purposes has resulted in a lower depreciation charge and a correspondingly higher tax charge. The net effect was a small increase in net income for the year.

(33) Other operating expenses

Other operating expenses comprise the following:

	Group		SAP AG	
	1996 DM (1,000s)	1995 DM (1,000s)	1996 DM (1,000s)	1995 DM (1,000s)
Travel and entertainment expenses	191,973	139,998	55,796	48,313
Marketing	162,786	102,264	31,994	30,878
Rent	118,553	79,529	24,774	16,782
Licenses and commissions	104,819	95,887	51,590	95,139
Additional personnel expenses	58,038	52,195	15,175	10,845
Telecommunications/postage	51,423	40,312	12,919	14,632
Repairs and maintenance	42,642	35,241	23,155	20,344
Accounts receivable valuation adjustments	31,739	17,557	8,096	224
Documentation	20,633	17,391	7,628	7,559
Exchange rate differences	18,225	20,541	12,962	10,993
Translation differences from consolidation of income statements	10,371	2,793	–	–
Allocation to special reserve with accrual character	–	–	2,945	–
Other	144,544	93,747	38,191	25,696
Total	**955,746**	**697,455**	**285,225**	**281,405**

(34) Income from investments

	Group		SAP AG	
	1996 DM (1,000s)	1995 DM (1,000s)	1996 DM (1,000s)	1995 DM (1,000s)
Income from investments	–	–	41,493	64,545
– thereof from affiliated companies	–	–	(41,493)	(61,831)
Result from associated companies	1,745	–	–	–

(35) Write-down of financial assets

The amount for SAP AG mainly comprises the extraordinary write-down of the value of the shares held in SAP-M GmbH i.L., Walldorf/Germany, and the discounting of the interest-free loans to employees to their present values.

(36) Net interest income

	Group		SAP AG	
	1996 DM (1,000s)	1995 DM (1,000s)	1996 DM (1,000s)	1995 DM (1,000s)
Other interest and similar income	30,461	27,450	17,314	14,758
– thereof from affiliated companies	–	–	(130)	(144)
Interest and similar expenses	2,618	5,237	2,075	1,459
– thereof to affiliated companies	–	–	(1,313)	–
	27,843	**22,213**	**15,239**	**13,299**

(37) Taxes on income

Taxes on income for SAP AG are imposed exclusively on the net income from ordinary operations.

E. Additional Information

(38) Members of the Supervisory Board and Executive Board

The members of the Supervisory Board and Executive Board of SAP AG are listed on page 98.

(39) Total remuneration of members of the Supervisory Board and Executive Board, loans granted

Subject to the adoption of the dividend resolution by the shareholders at the Annual General Meeting, the total remuneration of the Supervisory Board will amount to DM 1,086,750. The total remuneration of the Executive Board will amount to DM 7,510,005. In addition, members of the Executive Board were granted interest-free loans in the amount of DM 274,000 (repayments of DM 406,000 were made in 1996), with a remaining term to maturity of four to five years. Loans bearing interest at an annual rate of 6% were extended in the amount of DM 75,000, with a remaining term to maturity of eight years (repayments of DM 125,000 were made in 1996).

(40) Proposed appropriation of retained earnings

After the transfer of DM 64,000,000 from 1996 net income to the revenue reserves of SAP AG, retained earnings amount to DM 240,698,000.

We will propose at the Annual General Meeting that this amount be appropriated as follows:

DM 1.80 dividend, plus a DM 0.50 bonus dividend (anniversary bonus), per share of common stock with a par value of DM 5.00 carrying dividend rights   DM 140,281,000

DM 1.85 dividend, plus DM 0.50 bonus dividend (anniversary bonus), per share of preferred stock with a par value of DM 5.00 carrying dividend rights   DM 99,912,000

To be carried forward   DM 505,000

The dividend qualifies for a tax credit in the amount of 3/7 of the dividend value.

Walldorf, February 24, 1997

SAP Aktiengesellschaft
Systems, Applications, Products in Data Processing
Walldorf, Germany

The Executive Board

Hopp   Plattner   Heinrich   Kagermann   Oswald   Tschira   Wahl   Zencke

CASH-FLOW

	Konzern		SAP AG	
	1996 TDM	1995 TDM	1996 TDM	1995 TDM
I. Cash-flow aus betrieblicher Tätigkeit				
Jahresüberschuß	567.536	404.828	304.529	189.761
Abschreibungen auf immaterielle Vermögensgegenstände und Sachanlagen	164.591	144.456	90.768	93.773
Zuschreibungen auf Sachanlagen	-2.137	-	-	-
Abschreibungen auf Finanzanlagen	8.192	2.124	2.123	3.082
Zuschreibungen auf Finanzanlagen	-789	-635	-770	-609
Erhöhung der Pensionsrückstellungen	19.000	723	18.761	438
Erhöhung/Verminderung der mittel- und langfristigen Forderungen und sonstigen Vermögensgegenstände	-71.377	-33.569	-475	4.284
Erhöhung/Verminderung der mittel- und langfristigen Rückstellungen und Verbindlichkeiten	24.909	-8.746	-11.742	2.136
Erhöhung der kurzfristigen Aktiva	-630.811	-252.629	-217.706	-96.801
Erhöhung der kurzfristigen Passiva	404.383	172.150	199.619	60.528
	483.497	**428.702**	**385.107**	**256.592**
II. Cash-flow aus dem Investitionsbereich				
Zugänge von immateriellen Vermögensgegenständen und Sachanlagen	-220.638	-255.619	-121.334	-121.749
Zugänge zum Finanzanlagevermögen	-16.308	-11.829	-52.726	-82.200
Zugänge durch Veränderungen des Konsolidierungskreises	694	-74	-	-
Abgänge vom Anlagevermögen, netto	29.272	58.977	27.065	79.364
Veränderung des Sonderpostens mit Rücklageanteil	-	-	2.945	
Veränderung des Sonderpostens für Investitionszulagen	-7	-105	-	-
	-206.987	**-208.650**	**-144.050**	**-124.585**

CASH FLOW		Group		SAP AG	
		1996	1995	1996	1995
		DM (1,000s)	DM (1,000s)	DM (1,000s)	DM (1,000s)
I.	**Cash flow from operating activities**				
	Net income for the year	567,536	404,828	304,529	189,761
	Depreciation and amortization	164,591	144,456	90,768	93,773
	Write-ups of plant and equipment	-2,137	–	–	–
	Write-downs of financial assets	8,192	2,124	2,123	3,082
	Write-ups of financial assets	-789	-635	-770	-609
	Increase in pension reserves	19,000	723	18,761	438
	Increase/decrease in medium- and long-term accounts receivable and other assets	-71,377	-33,569	-475	4,284
	Increase/decrease in medium- and long-term reserves and liabilities	24,909	-8,746	-11,742	2,136
	Increase in short-term assets	-630,811	-252,629	-217,706	-96,801
	Increase in short-term liabilities	404,383	172,150	199,619	60,528
		483,497	**428,702**	**385,107**	**256,592**
II.	**Cash flow from investment activities**				
	Additions to intangible assets and tangible fixed assets	-220,638	-255,619	-121,334	-121,749
	Additions to financial assets	-16,308	-11,829	-52,726	-82,200
	Change in companies subject to consolidation	694	-74	–	–
	Disposal of fixed assets, net	29,272	58,977	27,065	79,364
	Change in the special reserve with accrual character	–	–	2,945	–
	Changes in special reserves for capital investment subsidies	-7	-105	–	–
		-206,987	**-208,650**	**-144,050**	**-124,585**

CASH-FLOW	Konzern		SAP AG	
	1996 **TDM**	**1995** **TDM**	**1996** **TDM**	**1995** **TDM**
III. Cash-flow aus dem **Finanzierungsbereich**				
Dividendenausschüttung	-133.615	-88.921	-133.615	-88.058
Agio aus Wandelschuldverschreibung	215.493	14	215.493	14
Erhöhung Grundkapital aus Wandlungen	11.374	10	11.374	10
Wandlung von Wandelanleihen	-11.345	-2	-11.345	-2
Erhöhung/Verminderung mittelfristiger Bankkredite	-376	-1.399	-	-
Nicht liquiditätsmäßige Veränderung des Eigenkapitals	21.004	-22.617	-	-
	102.535	**-112.915**	**81.907**	**-88.036**
IV. Veränderung des **Nettofinanzvermögens**	**379.045**	**107.137**	**322.964**	**43.971**
V. Nettofinanzvermögen **zum 1. Januar**	268.077	160.940	131.003	87.032
VI. Nettofinanzvermögen **zum 31. Dezember**	647.122	268.077	453.967	131.003
	379.045	**107.137**	**322.964**	**43.971**

CASH FLOW		Group		SAP AG	
		1996 DM (1,000s)	1995 DM (1,000s)	1996 DM (1,000s)	1995 DM (1,000s)
III. Cash flow from financing activities					
	Dividends	-133,615	-88,921	-133,615	-88,058
	Premium on convertible bonds	215,493	14	215,493	14
	Increase in capital stock resulting from exercise of conversion rights	11,374	10	11,374	10
	Conversion of convertible bonds into common stock	-11,345	-2	-11,345	-2
	Increase/decrease in long-term bank debt	-376	-1,399	–	–
	Changes in shareholders' equity not affecting liquidity	21,004	-22,617	–	–
		102,535	**-112,915**	**81,907**	**-88,036**
IV. Change in net financial assets		**379,045**	**107,137**	**322,964**	**43,971**
V. Net financial assets as of January 1		268,077	160,940	131,003	87,032
VI. Net financial assets as of December 31		647,122	268,077	453,967	131,003
		379,045	**107,137**	**322,964**	**43,971**

Bestätigungsvermerk

Nach dem Ergebnis unserer Prüfung erteilen wir dem Jahresabschluß und dem Konzernabschluß zum 31. Dezember 1996 sowie dem zusammengefaßten Lagebericht der

SAP Aktiengesellschaft
Systeme, Anwendungen, Produkte in der Datenverarbeitung

den folgenden uneingeschränkten Bestätigungsvermerk:

"Die Buchführung, der Jahresabschluß und der Konzernabschluß entsprechen nach unserer pflichtgemäßen Prüfung den gesetzlichen Vorschriften. Der Jahresabschluß und der Konzernabschluß vermitteln unter Beachtung der Grundsätze ordnungsmäßiger Buchführung ein den tatsächlichen Verhältnissen entsprechendes Bild der Vermögens-, Finanz- und Ertragslage der Aktiengesellschaft und des Konzerns. Der Bericht über die Lage der Aktiengesellschaft und des Konzerns steht im Einklang mit dem Jahresabschluß und dem Konzernabschluß."

Eschborn/Frankfurt am Main, 27. Februar 1997

ARTHUR ANDERSEN
Wirtschaftsprüfungsgesellschaft
Steuerberatungsgesellschaft mbH

Prof. Dr. Weber   Klein
Wirtschaftsprüfer   Wirtschaftsprüfer

Independent Auditors' Report

Following our audit of the financial statements and the consolidated financial statements at December 31, 1996 and the combined annual report of

SAP Aktiengesellschaft
Systems, Applications, Products in Data Processing

we are issuing the following unqualified auditors' certificate.

"The accounting records, the financial statements and the consolidated financial statements, which we have audited in accordance with professional standards, comply with the German legal regulations. The financial statements and the consolidated financial statements present a true and fair view of the net worth, financial position and operating results of the company and the Group in compliance with accounting principles generally accepted in Germany. The annual report on the company and the Group is consistent with the financial statements and the consolidated financial statements."

Frankfurt am Main, Germany, February 27, 1997

ARTHUR ANDERSEN
Wirtschaftsprüfungsgesellschaft
Steuerberatungsgesellschaft mbH

Prof. Dr Weber   Klein
Auditor   Auditor

Country Highlights
GREECE

Common Legal Forms of Companies

Corporation - Ανώνυμος Εταιρεία (AE) also known as Société Anonyme (SA)

Limited liability company - Εταιρεία Περιορισμένης Ευθύνης (ΕΠΕ)

Branch of foreign corporation -Υποκατάστημα ξένης εταιρείαςΚοινοπραξία

Joint Venture - Κοινοπραξία

Offshore branch of foreign corporation - established under Law 89/1967

General or limited partnerships - Ομόρρυθμος ή Ετερόρρυθμος εταιρεία

Sources of Financial Reporting Requirements

Company law 2190/1920 and 3190/1955, Code of Book and Records P.D. 186/1992, Greek General Chart of Accounts P.D. 1123/1980 (Special Chart of Accounts for Banks and for Insurance Companies).

Corporate Taxation

Codified law 2238/1994 - Income Tax Code for Individuals and Legal Entities.

Auditing Requirements

All corporations and limited liability companies meeting certain size criteria as well as banks, insurance, petroleum and investment companies and mutual funds are subject to audit by Certified Auditors, members of the Institute of Certified Auditors (SOE).

Organization of the Accounting and Auditing Professions

Institute of Certified Auditors (SOE).

Contitution and Legal System

Constitutional democracy. Independent Judiciary branch, with various levels of courts and special courts for taxation and organized labor matters. Supreme Judicial Council. European Union Court of Justice takes precedence over national law.

CURRENCY

Greek Drachmae.

OFFICIAL LANGUAGES

Greek.

GREECE

Richard H. Caseley
Price Waterhouse, Athens

1. Background

1.1 Company Law

Before 1920, when Law 2190/1920 was issued, Greek company law was not codified and had not followed developments elsewhere during the twentieth century. Law 2190/1920 was based more or less on foreign legislation of the past century. Requirements for the publication of annual financial statements dated back to 1872, whereas the appointment of auditors had been optional.

Since 1962 there has been a requirement for the formal presentation of financial statements. The provisions of Law 2190/1920 and subsequent amendments were codified into a single text in 1963. This text was amended slightly between 1967 and 1980, and to a greater extent with presidential decrees 409/1986, 498/1987, 325/1994, 326/1994, 367/1994, and Law 2339/1995 by means of which the law was harmonized with the provisions of the EU Directives.

1.2 Tax Law

Income tax in its modern form was introduced to Greece in 1919. The related Law 1640/1919 was based on French standards, modified according to the local economic and social situation. This law was repealed by Law 3323/1955, relating to taxation of individuals, and by Law 3843/1958, relating to taxation of corporations. These two laws have been amended several times and were codified in 1989. Law 3843/1958 relating to taxation of corporations has been incorporated in the Income Tax Code (Law 2238/94), Articles 98–116. In addition, bookkeeping requirements were established by a special law in effect from 1952. This special law constitutes the Code of Books and Documents and was last extensively amended with presidential decree 186/1992. The Code of Books and Documents specifies the accounting records and relevant documents to be maintained. It also provides rules for the updating of accounting records, balance sheet preparation, certain basic accounting principles, retention of records, and periodic information returns.

1.3 The General Accounting Plan

Companies are obliged to prepare financial statements according to the provisions of the General Accounting Plan (GAP), which took effect in 1987. The GAP is fully harmonized with the Fourth and Seventh EU Directives and certain International Accounting Standards. However, implementation of the GAP, relating to rules other than those referring to the preparation of the financial statements, is obligatory only for companies that are subject to audit by members of the Institute of Certified Auditors (SOE). All corporations and limited liability companies that fulfill any two of the following three criteria are subject to audit by Certified Auditors:

1. Total assets of at least Dr 500 million
2. Annual turnover of at least Dr 1,000 million
3. Average of at least 50 persons employed during the financial year

1.4 Conflict of Regulations

In certain instances there are conflicts between the requirements of the tax legislation and those of company law or the General Accounting Plan. To some extent there is a trend not to record provisions until they materialize since they are not deductible for tax purposes (see also Section 3).

1.5 Accounting and Auditing Professions

The Greek Institute of Certified Auditors—"Soma Orkoton Elekton" (SOE)—is the official body of the auditing profession and consists of about 420 full members. SOE is under the supervision of the Ministry of National Economy. SOE is governed by a seven-member Supervisory Council, which is elected from the general assembly of certified auditors. In effect this Supervisory Council has the authority to regulate the profession within the framework of the law and to monitor the activities of the registered members. It specifies professional and ethical standards and has the power to strike members from the Register. Steps are underway for a thorough review of all existing legislation relating to the operation of SOE.

At present the auditing standards that apply are those established many years ago by the predecessor public body of accountants (SOL). There is no direct linkage between those standards and the International Standards on Auditing (ISAs). Such supplementary statements that have been issued relate mainly to reporting approved by the Supervisory Council.

Ethical standards are set by regulations included in presidential decrees. There is a Disciplinary Council to which related matters are referred. According to a decree passed in November 1997, this comprises three persons, but no appointments have yet been made. An auditor who violates the rules can be prohibited from practicing, following a decision of the Supervisory Council.

There are no other significant regulations affecting the conduct of auditors.

The accounting profession in Greece has not yet achieved the level of development found in the United States and most European countries. As described above, the institute designed to provide qualifications similar to those of a CPA, ACA, WP, or *Expert Comptable* was established in May 1993. For this reason, little or no attention has been given to the setting and application of accounting standards, or to dealing officially with current accounting issues such as the EMU.

1.6 Securities Market

At present a stock exchange operates only in Athens; it deals largely in shares and bonds of local corporations (*anonymos eteria*, AE, or *société anonyme*, SA). The shares of 182 such corporations and the bonds of numerous government loans are currently listed on the Athens Stock Exchange. The main registration requirements for shares are as follows:

1. Minimum equity must equal the drachma equivalent of 3.5 million European Currency Units (ECU).

2. Existing share capital is to be increased by at least 25%; all new shares are to be sold through a public subscription.

3. At least one underwriter is required who will guarantee that the issue will be fully subscribed.

4. At least five annual balance sheets must have been published.

5. Operating profits for the past 5 financial years must be satisfactory.

The obligation in item 2 does not apply to companies whose shares are listed on the stock exchange or exchanges in one or more EU member countries. This obligation also does not apply to companies that have resulted from a merger or absorption of companies, on the condition that at least one of the companies involved is already listed on the stock exchange.

The principal registration requirements for bonds issued by a corporation are as follows.

1. The issuing corporation must have an equity of at least Dr 1 billion on the basis of the last financial statements.

2. The value of the bonded loan together with any balance unpaid of past loans must not exceed half of the net equity.

3. The minimum amount of the issued bonded loan required for obtaining registration in the Athens Stock Exchange is Dr 20 million.

4. The application for registration of the bonded loan should represent the full amount of the issue.

5. The total subscription must be guaranteed by at least one underwriter.

6. Bonds that have been issued by a corporation with its head office in another EU member country must be in accordance with the valid regulations of that country. When these regulations are different from those prevailing in Greece, the difference is made known to the public by the Athens Stock Exchange.

The principal requirements for registration of shares in the Parallel Market are as follows.

1. Net equity over Dr 250 million increased for registration purposes by at least 15%.

2. The full issue must be guaranteed by at least one underwriter.

3. Corporations satisfying the requirements of the main Stock Exchange may enter into the Parallel Market, depending on their decision.

Listing on the stock exchange is compulsory for companies raising capital or loans through public subscription. Public subscription of shares and bonds can be made only through banks, the Loans and Consignment Fund, the Postal Savings Bank, and the Athens Stock Exchange.

Legislation enacted for the purpose of upgrading and strengthening the capital market has introduced the following elements:

- Establishment and operation of depositories of securities for the safekeeping of certificates.
- Provisions for the establishment of stock exchange (brokerage) companies. Such companies are established as SAs with special permission from the Capital Market Committee. A foreign brokerage company is required to be a member of the stock exchange in its country of origin in order to be established and operate as a stock exchange company. The share capital of a stock exchange company must be at least Dr 100 million fully paid at formation and must consist only of cash. A foreign stock exchange company must import capital of at least Dr 200 million.

1.7 Banking System

1.7.1 Central Bank

The Bank of Greece, the Central Bank, issues banknotes and exercises control over monetary circulation and foreign exchange. There are no current account dealings with the public, and deposits are accepted only from banks and the government. The Bank of Greece acts as the central clearinghouse and finances government expenditure. In addition, it enforces credit and monetary policy measures concerning banking and credit facilities in general and exercises direct control over foreign exchange transactions and indirect determination of foreign exchange rates through its participation in the market. These measures cover compulsory deposits with the Bank of Greece, the general framework of bank financing, the total amount of financing available to the manufacturing, commercial, and tourist sectors, and related matters. However, in view of Greece's obligation toward the EU to liberalize the banking system gradually, some very important steps toward relaxation of controls have been made in recent years concerning interest rates charged by commercial banks, bank financing terms in both drachmae and foreign currency, and extension of forward transactions in foreign currency. As a result, there are now no exchange control restrictions.

1.7.2 Commercial Banks

There are many commercial banks in Greece, some of which have branches throughout the country. In conjunction with the development of new banking products as a result of gradual liberalization, innovations in the management decision-making process currently underway are expected to enhance the role of the banking system and to improve its effectiveness in the future.

Commercial banks extend overdraft facilities and short-term loans for working capital. Medium- and long-term loans are granted for acquisition of plant and equipment (in the sense of machinery, equipment, and the buildings in which they are installed) and, to some extent, for acquisition of shares or parts of companies. Subject to the regulations of the Bank of Greece, loans are extended to both local and foreign companies established in Greece. Commercial banks are also allowed to extend housing loans at negotiable interest rates. Forward transactions in foreign currencies against the drachma, transactions for exchanging foreign currencies against drachmae (swaps), and certain other transactions have also been liberalized.

In March 1994 the first interest rate of reference for the drachma interbank market was put into practice, based on an agreement of 13 banks (both state-owned and private). This interest rate is called ATHIBOR (Athens Interbank Offered Rate). It is similar to the British LIBOR, and it concerns rates for one, two, three, and six months. The purpose of this agreement is the widening of the interbank market, costing of new financial products, and the development of a positive climate for both banks and businesses.

2. The Form and Content of Published Financial Statements

2.1 Disclosure Requirements

Following amendments to corporate legislation, beginning in 1987 the form and content of financial statements were changed to comply with related EU Directives. The annual financial statements include:

- Balance sheet
- Profit and loss account (income statement)
- Profit distribution table
- Attachment (notes to the financial statements)

At the end of this chapter is a specimen set of published financial statements and an auditor's report, in Greek and translated into English. Publishing consolidated financial statements became a legal requirement in 1991.

2.2 Publication

The annual financial statements, as well as the report of the Board of Directors and the audit report, must be filed with the register of *sociétés anonymes* in the district where the company has its seat and be published in the *Government Gazette*. Furthermore, all of these items except for the attachment and the board of directors' report must be published in two daily newspapers (one political and one financial). The register of *sociétés anonymes* files are open for public inspection.

2.3 Layout

Regarding the specimen set of financial statements, it is worth noting the following:

- The layout is in accordance with the General Accounting Plan (see Section 1.3). The alphanumeric references in the various captions are set out in this plan.
- The audit report contains a clean opinion. This is mainly because the company has disclosed on the face of the balance sheet certain additional information about doubtful accounts receivable, revaluation of fixed assets and related depreciation charges, severance pay provision, and so on, which otherwise could amount to fairly typical findings (equivalent to qualification) by the auditor.

2.4 Notes to the Accounts

According to corporate legislation, the disclosures required to be made in the attachment, or notes, are as follows:

- The methods of asset valuation, depreciation, and provisions (see details in Section 3)
- Changes in accounting principles or valuation methods, including their effects on the financial statements insofar as these may be quantified
- The basis of translation of transactions and balances in foreign currency (see details in Section 3)
- Analysis of investments exceeding 10% of the share capital of investees
- The number and value of shares issued in the year to cover increase of share capital
- The number of any titles issued per category (e.g., preferred shares, convertible bonds)
- Amounts of liabilities due 5 years after the balance sheet date, as well as amounts of liabilities that are secured, mentioning the details of security
- The total amounts of commitments, guarantees, and contingent liabilities not disclosed in the memo accounts, as long as this information is useful for the evaluation of the financial position of the company
- Analysis of sales by activity and geographic area, as long as such activities and areas present essential differences from a sales organization point of view. The Minister of Development (formerly Minister of Commerce) may approve the nonpublication of this information if the Minister is satisfied that such disclosure might cause damage to the company. This deviation should be mentioned in the attachment.
- The average number of staff employed during the year by category (e.g., administrative staff, workers). The amounts of salaries, wages, and social security contributions should also be disclosed by category of staff.
- The effect on the results for the year resulting from inappropriate evaluation of current assets for the purpose of saving taxes. If it is anticipated that significant additional taxes will result in following years, detailed explanations should be given.
- Explanatory comments on the amount and nature of nonrecurring income and expense.

- Amounts of taxes payable plus any unrecorded significant amounts that are expected to be paid
- Remuneration to members of the board of directors and administrators, as well as any liability to such members who have retired. Advances and loans given to members of the board of directors and administrators. The above information may be omitted in the cases where the identity and the income of related persons may become known.
- The name and the head office of the companies that issue consolidated financial statements in which the company's annual financial statements are or will be included, as well as the location at which the consolidated financial statements are available
- If the company has purchased its own shares, the following should be disclosed:

  —The reason for the purchase

  —The number and nominal value of own shares purchased or transferred during the year, as well as the represented share capital

  —Any amount paid for the acquisition of such shares or collected in case of transfer
- Fees paid in respect of the audit of the financial statements
- Any other information aiming at a more complete understanding of the financial statements

3. Accounting Policies and Practices in Valuation and Income Measurement: Implications for the Analyst

3.1 Group Accounts

3.1.1 Background

For financial years beginning on or after July 1, 1990, parent companies are required to prepare consolidated financial statements. Subject to certain conditions and exemptions, the parent company and its subsidiaries, as well as the subsidiaries of its subsidiaries, must prepare consolidated financial statements. More specifically, companies subject to consolidation are parent undertakings with one or more subsidiary undertakings where the parent or one or more of its subsidiary undertakings is one of the following:

1. A company limited by shares, AE
2. A company with limited liability, E.P.E
3. A company limited by shares partnership, E.E

A parent company is exempt from the obligation to prepare consolidated financial statements if all the companies that are subject to consolidation on the basis of their latest financial statements do not fulfill any two of the following three criteria.

1. Total assets of Dr 500 million.
2. Annual net turnover of Dr 1000 million.
3. Average of 250 persons employed.

3.1.2 Method of Consolidation

The purchase or acquisition accounting method of consolidation is to be adopted, in accordance with local regulations. Asset and liability items of undertakings whose accounts are consolidated are incorporated in full in the consolidated balance sheet. Income and expenditure of undertakings whose accounts are consolidated are incorporated in full in the consolidated profit and loss statement. Shares in subsidiaries must be set off against the book values of the capital and reserves of those subsidiaries; differences that arise from the set-off must be allocated as far as possible to the relevant items in the consolidated balance sheet. Differences remaining after all set-offs mentioned above must be shown as a separate item in the consolidated balance sheet. If the difference is positive, it should be shown under the heading "Other intangible assets" and can be treated as follows:

1. Carried in the balance sheet as an intangible asset and amortized in equal amounts over a period not exceeding 5 years
2. Written off immediately on acquisition

It is also permissible to eliminate this positive consolidation difference directly against reserves.

If the difference arising on consolidation is a credit balance, it may be shown as a reserve arising on consolidation. It may be written off partly or wholly to the consolidated profit and loss only if:

1. It corresponds to an expectation, at the date of acquisition, of unfavorable future results in the undertaking, or to the expectation of costs which that undertaking would incur, insofar as this expectation materializes.
2. The difference corresponds to a realized profit.

3.1.3 Proportional Consolidation

Proportional consolidation is not provided for in law.

3.1.4 Equity Accounting

In accordance with local regulations, equity accounting is to be used on consolidation for participating interests in associated companies following the criteria in the Seventh EU Directive. When applied for the first time, the participating interest shall be shown in the consolidated balance sheet at its book value, which is to be the lower of cost or market value.

Any difference that arises between the cost of the investment and the proportion of the equity of the associated company may be shown either in the consolidated balance sheet or in the notes to the consolidated financial statements. In the case in which an associated company's assets or liabilities have been valued by methods other than those used for consolidation, they may, for the purpose of calculating the difference mentioned above, be revalued by the methods used for consolidation.

The book value referred to above is to be increased or reduced by the amount of any variation that has taken place during the financial year in the proportion of the associated company's capital and reserves represented by the participating interest, and it will be reduced by the amount of the dividends relating to that participating interest.

3.2 Foreign Currency Translation

3.2.1 Translation of the Financial Statements of Foreign Subsidiaries

Translation to drachmas is performed by using the so-called monetary-nonmonetary method, as follows:

1. Inventories, fixed assets, and marketable securities at historical rates

2. All receivables, cash balances, and payables at closing rates

3. Income and expenses at the year's average rate

Differences arising from the translation of inventories, fixed assets, marketable securities, cash balances, and income and expenses are taken to the income statement currently. For receivables and payables see Section 3.2.2.

3.2.2 Translation of Foreign Currency-Denominated Assets and Liabilities

Exchange differences on cash balances are taken to the income statement currently.

Exchange differences on receivables and payables are recorded in separate accounts by currency and nature (short or long term) and are treated as follows:

1. Short- and long-term exchange losses are taken to the income statement currently.

2. Short-term exchange gains are deferred and are taken to the income statement in the following year.

3. Long-term exchange gains are deferred, and after offsetting with any losses in the following year, are taken to the income statement to the extent corresponding to the collection or payment of the receivable or the payable.

Exchange differences on loans or credits for purchases of fixed assets are recorded in separate accounts by loan. After offsetting exchange losses and gains of the same loan, remaining debit balances are recorded as deferred charges and amortized over the period of the loan. Credit balances are also deferred and are taken to the income statement, to the extent corresponding to the loan repaid in each year.

Realized Exchange Differences   Exchange differences arising on transactions upon receipt or payment of a receivable or a payable are taken directly to income, except for those arising on the repayment of loans for the purchase of fixed assets, which are matched with unrealized exchange differences and treated as mentioned above.

3.3 Capital and Reserves

Capital must be shown at par value; any premiums thereon should be disclosed separately. Companies may purchase their own shares only under exceptional circumstances (e.g., reduction of share capital, distribution of shares to employees).

Corporate legislation requires that not less than 5% of the annual profits of corporations and limited liability companies be appropriated to a legal reserve until it reaches one-third of the share capital. This reserve may not be distributed. General reserves can be formed freely; their distribution requires approval at annual shareholders' meetings. Both legal and general reserves are taxable.

Companies that carry out productive investments are entitled to tax-deferred reserves.

3.4 Liabilities and Provisions

The presentation of liabilities and provisions in the balance sheet complies with the requirements of the EU Directive for financial statement presentation. Corporate legislation requires that provisions be made for all losses concerning current or prior financial years.

In this connection, companies should make adequate provisions for employee severance pay, bad debts, and so on. In practice, provision for severance pay is not often made, because it is not deductible for tax purposes until it materializes. On the other hand, provision for bad debts is calculated as a percentage of sales. The fact that this provision is deductible for tax purposes may lead to unnecessary provisioning. Users of financial statements need to exercise particular caution in this respect.

3.5. Property, Plant, and Equipment

3.5.1 Valuation

Tangible fixed assets should be valued at historic cost plus improvements; only two departures are allowed:

1. Revaluation according to special legislation: in practice such laws are passed occasionally and provide for obligatory revaluation of land and buildings according to specific indices. There was also one

instance of revaluation for machinery, but it was not obligatory. Revaluation applies to both cost and accumulated depreciation. The surplus is transferred to reserves and then capitalized or offset against losses.

2. Devaluation to arrive at the current value of an asset if this devaluation is considered of a permanent nature

3.5.2 Depreciation

Depreciation according to Law 2190 should be based on estimated economic life. Economic rates may be used according to the company's management. However, maximum depreciation rates are prescribed by the law. Accelerated depreciation is also provided under various incentive laws. This depreciation is shown separately in the profit and loss in nonoperating expenses. Any depreciation in excess of that calculated with the maximum tax depreciation rates is not recognized as an allowable expense. Deferred taxation as mentioned in Section 3.11 is not accounted for.

3.5.3 Government Grants

According to the General Accounting Plan, government grants relating to the purchase of fixed assets should be credited to a deferred account (reserve) and taken to other income in proportion to the depreciation expense of the fixed assets purchased with the grant.

3.5.4 Interest Charges

Interest charges relating to borrowings for the construction of fixed assets may be written off to income or deferred (capitalized) and amortized over a period of 5 years.

3.6 Assets Whose Services Are Acquired by Means of Leases

According to law, with the lease agreement the lessor is obliged to grant (a) the usage of a movable asset to the lessee against a determined rental, and (b) the purchase option at the conclusion of the agreement or at a previous stage. The leasing period cannot be less than 3 years.

The accounting treatment is still the one provided by law, according to which:

1. The lessee records the rentals in operating expenses. Also, an appropriate value for the asset is recorded in both assets and liabilities in memo accounts as third-party property, which are offset upon termination of the lease agreement.

2. The lessor depreciates the value of the asset and takes to income-related expenses such as commissions and legal fees. Also, the value of the asset is recorded in memo accounts as property in the hands of third parties.

In the case of operating leases, no specific disclosures are required.

3.7 Oil, Gas, and Other Mineral Resources

Oil exploration rights belong to the Greek state and may be transferred to private companies only through special government permits.

The rights and the obligations of the Greek state and of private companies that enter into a leasing and/or distribution agreement for the exploration and distribution of the resources are specifically dealt with in Law 2289/1995. The law defines the bookkeeping requirements and the tax obligations of the lessor/distributor company.

The company should keep special accounting records and issue annual income statement and balance sheet accounts in connection with the specific agreement activities. These accounting records should be kept in accordance with the Code of Books and Documents regulations and may be kept in Greek drachmae or in another foreign currency.

The only exception to the applicable accounting policies and practices as described in this section is that depreciation of the company's fixed assets and of initial installation and of research expenses is calculated on the basis of fixed rates or fixed maximum amounts per year, depending on the total annual production. The depreciation method is defined in a decision of the Ministries of Finance, Industry, Energy and Technology and is published in the *Government Gazette*.

3.8 Intangible Assets

Legally protected intellectual property rights, such as patents and trademarks, are recorded at cost and amortized over the period of their productive use. Deferred charges such as preoperating expenses and research and development costs are either written off as incurred or amortized over 5 years.

3.9 Participations (Equity Investments in Other Companies)

Participations in corporations (*Sociétés Anonymes*) or unincorporated enterprises are valued at the lower of cost or market value, determined on an individual basis. Differences arising are taken to the income statement currently.

Market price is determined as follows. For quoted shares, market price is the average price of the year's final month. For nonquoted shares of companies that prepare financial statements under the provisions of Law 2190, market price is the book value of these shares, based on the latest published financial statements.

3.10 Inventories

3.10.1 Valuation

Inventories are valued at the lower of cost or market (replacement) price. The net realizable value is used when the market value is below the historic cost but in excess of the net realizable value.

Acceptable methods for the determination of the cost are FIFO, LIFO, average, individual, and base stock. In practice, FIFO and average cost are the most usual methods.

3.10.2 Overhead Expenses—Interest Charges

Overhead expenses are allocated to cost to the extent relating to the production (general production expenses, direct distribution cost, etc.). Interest charges are not allocated to cost.

3.10.3 Construction Contracts—Percentage of Completion Method

Although the law does not specifically address this matter, it specifies that only profit made at the balance sheet date may be included. On the basis of the interpretation of the law, incomplete constructions should be accounted for according to the stage of completion (i.e., invoices, including profit, should be issued on the basis of an engineer's certificate of completion).

3.11 Taxation

Financial statements are prepared under the provisions of Law 2190. However, accounting is still affected by income tax regulations, although there is a trend toward accounting on an economic basis.

The reported income in the financial statements might differ materially from the taxable income mainly because of the following:

1. Tax-deferred reserves provided under various incentive laws

2. Income taxed in a special way (as provided by law) (mainly interest income)

3. Nonallowable expenses (mainly provisions)

4. Tax losses carried forward

5. Additional taxes and penalties

However, the corporate tax expense of the year is shown separately in the profit distribution table, which also includes any additional taxes assessed by the tax authorities for prior years and item 1, above. Moreover, deferred taxation is not provided for by the local regulations and therefore is not reflected in the financial statements.

3.12 Pensions

Few pension schemes have been implemented in Greece. However, the law provides that all employees and any lawyers on retainer who retire are entitled to a retirement indemnity determined by their status and length of service. Law 2190 provides that this liability be accrued.

Nevertheless, many companies, on the basis of an opinion issued by the Legal Counsel of the State, record an accrual only for the severance pay due to those employees retiring in the following year. Therefore, users of financial statements should be aware of the policy adopted, since the unrecorded liability can be significant.

In the cases of companies providing for the full liability, best estimates based on present data are used instead of actuarial studies. The related expense in either case is not deductible.

3.13 Other

3.13.1 Memo Accounts

Memo accounts are a separate category of accounts that operate dually (as assets and liabilities) in an autonomous accounting system. Memo accounts should include details of the following:

- Third-party property
- Guarantees given and received as security
- Contracts in progress (incomplete portion)
- Various accounts including statistics (untaxed surplus on mergers, tax-free reserve rights, leased assets, etc.)

4. Expected Future Developments

The regulations of the SOE provide that International Standards on Auditing and International Accounting Standards are to be applied. In practice, this is a substantial task, particularly regarding accounting standards in light of prevailing practice described earlier. Considering only the changes in legislation required, it is something that will take several years to achieve.

Company law has been amended, with the aim of removing outdated requirements and introducing provisions to reflect present conditions.

As more and more companies seek a listing on the Athens Stock Exchange, reporting and other requirements have become stricter. With the relaxation of exchange controls, there is increasing interest by foreign investors in the Athens Stock Exchange.

The banking system has gradually been liberalized as the Bank of Greece has delegated more responsibility to commercial banks, and several significant changes were effected toward the relaxation of regulations and internationalization of the monetary system, within the context of the Maastricht treaty requirements. Competition has become more intense, and several private banks operate, targeting at specific sectors and planning their short-term strategic movements and alliances.

Starting from a position somewhat behind most other European countries, Greece is experiencing significant changes in order to be able to join the EMU at a second stage in the year 2001, one year before the implementation of the common currency.

Acknowledgment

The author would like to express his appreciation for the valuable assistance and contributions by Antonis Dousmanopoulos, Sotiris Christou, and Stefanos Arvanitakis, managers with Price Waterhouse.

Useful Address

Institute of Certified Auditors (SOE)
28 Kapodistriou street
106 82 Athens

ΟΜΙΛΟΣ ΕΤΑΙΡΙΩΝ "ΗΡΑΚΛΗΣ"
16ος ΕΝΟΠΟΙΗΜΕΝΟΣ ΙΣΟΛΟΓΙΣΜΟΣ ΤΗΣ 31ης ΔΕΚΕΜΒΡΙΟΥ 1996
(ΣΕ ΧΙΛ. ΔΡΧ.)

ΕΝΕΡΓΗΤΙΚΟ

	ΧΡΗΣΕΩΣ 1996			ΧΡΗΣΕΩΣ 1995		
	ΑΞΙΑ ΚΤΗΣΕΩΣ	ΑΠΟΣΒΕΣΕΙΣ	ΑΝΑΠΟΣΒΕΣΤΗ ΑΞΙΑ	ΑΞΙΑ ΚΤΗΣΕΩΣ	ΑΠΟΣΒΕΣΕΙΣ	ΑΝΑΠΟΣΒΕΣΤΗ ΑΞΙΑ
Β. ΕΞΟΔΑ ΕΓΚΑΤΑΣΤΑΣΗΣ						
1 Έξοδα ίδρυσης & πρώτης εγκατ/σης	117.787	106.988	10.799	143.374	122.374	21.000
2. Συν/κές διαφορές για κτήσεις παγίων	356.312	350.821	5.491	369.307	350.821	18.486
3. Τόκοι δανείων κατασκ/κής περιόδου	1.996.790	1.996.790	-	-	-	-
4. Λοιπά έξοδα πολυετούς απόσβεσης	630.329	359.384	270.945	294.008	138.735	155.273
ΣΥΝΟΛΟ ΕΞΟΔΩΝ ΕΓΚΑΤΑΣΤΑΣΗΣ (Β)	3.101.218	2.813.983	287.235	806.689	611.930	194.759
Γ. ΠΑΓΙΟ ΕΝΕΡΓΗΤΙΚΟ						
Ι. Ασώματες ακινητοποιήσεις						
1. Έξοδα ερευνών & ανάπτυξης	154.100	69.877	84.223	129.070	106.146	22.924
5. Διαφορά ενοποίησης	2.379.166	-	2.379.166	-	-	-
	2.533.266	69.877	2.463.389	129.070	106.146	22.924
ΙΙ. Ενσώματες ακινητοποιήσεις						
1. Γήπεδα-Οικόπεδα	17.386.254	-	17.386.254	9.243.270	-	9.243.270
2. Ορυχεία-μεταλλεία. λατομεία κτλ.	11.532.818	1.465.110	10.067.708	8.843.907	565.129	8.278.778
3. Κτίρια & τεχνικά έργα	61.860.089	51.931.607	9.928.482	34.848.150	29.643.540	5.204.610
4. Μηχανήματα-τεχν.εγκατ.& λοιπ.μηχ.εξοπλ.	59.741.159	35.438.210	24.302.949	31.903.747	21.526.932	10.376.815
5. Μεταφορικά μέσα	14.124.445	7.028.864	7.095.581	12.491.329	5.046.707	7.444.622
6. Έπιπλα & λοιπός εξοπλισμός	2.150.643	1.110.417	1.040.226	1.043.982	651.699	392.283
7. Ακινητοποιήσεις υπο εκτέλ. & προκ/λές	3.192.292	-	3.192.292	1.036.565	-	1.036.565
	169.987.700	96.974.208	73.013.492	99.410.950	57.434.007	41.976.943
ΣΥΝΟΛΟ ΑΚΙΝΗΤΟΠΟΙΗΣΕΩΝ(Γ1+ΓΙΙ)	172.520.966	97.044.085	75.476.881	99.540.020	57.540.153	41.999.867
ΙΙΙ Συμμετοχές & άλλες μακροπρόθεσμες χρηματοοικονομικές απαιτήσεις						
2. Συμμετοχές σε εταιρίες εκτός Ομίλου & ίδια μερίδια Ομίλου		751.051			281.370	
Μείον : Οφειλόμενες δόσεις		31.960	719.091		-	281.370
5. Γραμμάτια εισπρακτέα μακρ. λήξης			4.621			
7. Λοιπές μακροπρόθεσμες απαιτήσεις			898.105			628.926
			1.621.817			910.296
ΣΥΝΟΛΟ ΠΑΓΙΟΥ ΕΝΕΡΓΗΤΙΚΟΥ (Γ)			77.098.698			42.910.163
Δ. ΚΥΚΛΟΦΟΡΟΥΝ ΕΝΕΡΓΗΤΙΚΟ						
Ι. Αποθέματα						
1. Εμπορεύματα		200.054			126.192	
2. Προϊόντα έτοιμα & ημιτελή		3.730.652			2.476.123	
3. Παραγωγή σε εξέλιξη		41.880			44.226	
4. Πρώτες & βοηθ. ύλες - Αναλώσιμα						
υλικά -ανταλλ/κά. υλικά συσκευασίας	11.919.367			8.567.895		
Μείον: Προβλέψεις υποτιμήσεως αποθ.	5.796	11.913.571		-	8.567.895	
5. Προκαταβολές για αγορές αποθεμάτων		348.055	16.234.212		248.573	11.463.009
ΙΙ. Απαιτήσεις						
1. Πελάτες		14.826.961			11.110.261	
2. Γραμμάτια Εισπρακτέα						
- Χαρτοφυλακίου	228.531			129.882		
- Στις τράπεζες για είσπραξη	446.082			779.144		
- Στις τράπεζες για εγγύηση	-	674.613		-	909.026	
3. Γραμμάτια σε καθυστέρηση		509.744			380.753	
3α. Επιταγές εισπρακτέες	20.147.104			17.087.195		
3β. Επιταγές σε καθυστέρηση	17.099	20.164.203		-		
8. Δεσμευμένοι λ/σμοί καταθέσεων		2.274.137			5.600	
10. Επισφαλείς-επίδικοι πελάτες & χρεώστες	2.802.592			6.811.252		
Προβλέψεις επισφαλών απαιτήσεων	301.413	2.501.179		(4.009.612)	2.801.640	
11. Χρεώστες διάφοροι	7.411.098			6.800.566		
11α. Χρεώστες Ελληνικό Δημόσιο	1.508.707	8.919.805		-	6.800.566	
12. Λογ/σμοί διαχειρίσεως προκαταβολών		70.988	49.941.630		38.606	39.133.647
IV. Διαθέσιμα						
1. Ταμείο		93.737			60.245	
3. Καταθέσεις όψεως & προθεσμίας		3.204.353			1.764.052	
Λοιπά		2.159	3.300.249		-	1.824.297
ΣΥΝΟΛΟ ΚΥΚΛΟΦΟΡΟΥΝΤΟΣ ΕΝΕΡΓΗΤΙΚΟΥ (Δ)			69.476.091			52.420.953
Ε. ΜΕΤΑΒΑΤΙΚΟΙ Λ/ΣΜΟΙ ΕΝΕΡΓΗΤΙΚΟΥ						
1. Έξοδα επομένων χρήσεων		544.617			475.173	
2. Έσοδα χρήσεως εισπρακτέα		22.353			34.380	
3. Λοιποί μεταβ. λ/σμοί ενεργητικού		98.180	665.150		53.384	562.937
ΓΕΝΙΚΟ ΣΥΝΟΛΟ ΕΝΕΡΓΗΤΙΚΟΥ (Β+Γ+Δ+Ε)			147.527.174			96.088.812
ΛΟΓΑΡΙΑΣΜΟΙ ΤΑΞΕΩΣ ΧΡΕΩΣΤΙΚΟΙ			11.704.550			8.868.105

ΣΗΜΕΙΩΣΕΙΣ : 1. Οι εταιρίες του Ομίλου με τις διευθύνσεις τους που περιλαμβάνονται στην ενοποίηση είναι : α. Εσωτερικού : ΑΓΕΤ ΗΡΑΚΛΗΣ, ΕΒΙΕΣΚ Α.Ε., ΑΝΕ ΗΡΑΚΛΗΣ, ΗΡΑΚΛΗΣ ΔΙΕΘΝΗΣ Α.Ε., ΗΡΑΚΛΗΣ ΣΥΣΚΕΥΑΣΙΑ Α.Ε., ΛΑΒΑ Α.Ε., ΑΜΠΕΡ Α.Ε., ΕΠΕΝΔΥΣΗ ΣΙΛΟ ΠΟΡΤ ΣΑΪΔ Α.Ε., ΗΡΑΚΛΗΣ ΝΑΥΤΙΚΕΣ ΠΡΑΚΤΟΡΕΥΣΕΙΣ Ε.Π.Ε., Γ. ΧΑΤΖΗΚΥΡΙΑΚΟΣ Ν.Ε., Α. ΧΑΤΖΗΚΥΡΙΑΚΟΣ Ν.Ε., ΔΥΣΤΟΣ Ν.Ε. ΠΡΩΤΟΠΟΡΟΣ Ν.Ε., ΘΑΛΑΣΣΟΠΟΡΟΣ Ν.Ε., ΠΟΝΤΟΠΟΡΟΣ Ν.Ε., ΒΟΛΟΣ Ι Ν.Ε., ΦΑΕΘΩΝ Ι Ν.Ε., ΙΟΚΑΣΤΗ Ν.Ε., ΝΑΥΣΙΚΑ Ν.Ε., ΗΡΑΚΛΗΣ ΓΚΛΟΡΥ Ν.Ε., ΗΡΑΚΛΗΣ ΑΣΦΑΛΙΣΤΙΚΕΣ ΕΠΙΧΕΙΡΗΣΕΙΣ Ε.Π.Ε., (Σόφ. Βενιζέλου 49-51. Λυκόβρυση) Ε.Κ.Ε.Τ. Ε.Π.Ε. (Κ. Πατέλη 15. Λυκόβρυση). ΕΜΜΥ ΚΤΙΡΙΑΚΑ ΣΤΟΙΧΕΙΑ ΑΒΕΕ. ΑΙΓΙΣ Α.Ε. (Βενιζέλου & Ανδρούτσου 29. Λυκόβρυση). ΑΣΤΗΡ - ΛΑΤΟ ΑΒΕΕ (Τέρμα οδού Ηρας. Γαλάτσι). ΣΚΥΡΟΔΕΜΑ ΕΒΑΕ (Νεοχωρούδα. Θεσσαλονίκη). ΤΣΙΜΕΝΤΑ ΧΑΛΚΙΔΟΣ Α.Ε. ΤΣΙΜΕΝΤΑ ΧΑΛΚΙΔΟΣ ΕΜΠΟΡΙΚΗ Α.Ε. ΤΣΙΜΕΝΤΑ ΧΑΛΚΙΔΟΣ ΔΙΕΘΝΗΣ Α.Ε., ΜΕΤΑΦΟΡΑΙ ΗΝΙΟΧΟΣ ΕΠΕ. ΜΕΤΑΦΟΡΙΚΑΙ ΕΠΙΧΕΙΡΗΣΕΙΣ FINDA Α.Ε. (Ηρ/γνος Αθηνών) β. Εξωτερικού : ALEXANDRIA SILO INVESTMENT COMPANY S.A. HERMES COMPANIA NAVIERA S.A., PORT SAID SILO INVESTMENT COMPANY S.A., LOYDIAS COMPANIA NAVIERA S.A., MARITIME COMPANY ESPERIDES S.A., DEPOT AND COORDINATION CO S.A.(Panama). INTERNATIONAL MEDITTERANEAN SHIPPING S.A.(Luxemburg). INTERNATIONAL FLAG (Egypt). Διευκρίνηση ότι η ΑΓΕΤ ΗΡΑΚΛΗΣ αγόρασε στις 27.11.1996 το 51% των μετοχών της Α.Ε. ΤΣΙΜΕΝΤΑ ΧΑΛΚΙΔΟΣ στην οποία περιλαμβάνονται και τέσσερις θυγατρικές της με ποσοστό συμμετοχής 100% 2. Με βάση τις διατάξεις του Ν.2065/1992 έγινε στη χρήση 1996 αναπροσαρμογή της αξίας κτήσεως των γηπέδων. των κτιρίων και των συσσωρευμένων αποσβέσεων των κτιρίων εξαιτίας της οποίας αυξήθηκαν οι αξίες κτήσεως των γηπέδων και κτιρίων κατά δρχ. 16.112 εκατ. και προκύπτει διαφορά αναπροσαρμογής ποσού δρχ. 8.747 εκατ. που ποσό δρχ. 6.929 εκατ. κατοχυρώθηκε στο Λογαριασμό των ιδίων κεφαλαίων Α ΙΙΙ-2 "διαφορές από αναπροσαρμογή αξίας λοιπών περιουσιακών στοιχείων" ενώ με ποσό δρχ. 1.818 εκατ. καλύφθηκε απόσβεση του συνόλου του υπολοίπου (ζημία) προηγουμένων χρήσεων. Οι αποσβέσεις της χρήσεως 1996 υπολογίσθηκαν επί της νέας αναπροσαρμοσμένης αξίας και είναι μεγαλύτερες από εκείνες που θα προέκυπταν εάν είχαν υπολογισθεί στην αξία των προσαρμογή κατά δρχ. 537 εκατ. περίπου. 3. Η αποτίμηση ορισμένων συμμετοχών έγινε στην αξία κτήσεως τους σύμφωνα με τις διατάξεις του άρθρου 20 παρ.5 του Π.Δ. 186/1992. Εάν γινόταν με βάση τις Διατάξεις του άρθρου 43 Ν.2190/1920 που προβλέπει διαφορετικό τρόπο αποτιμήσεως, η εσωτερική λογιστική αξία των συμμετοχών αυτών θα ήταν μικρότερη κατά δρχ. 206 εκ. περίπου. 4. Μεταξύ

"HERACLES" GROUP OF COMPANIES
16th CONSOLIDATED BALANCE SHEET AS AT DECEMBER 31ST 1996
(AMOUNTS IN DRS. THOUS.)

ASSETS

	1996 COST	1996 ACCUMULATED DEPRECIATION	1996 NET BOOK VALUE	1995 COST	1995 ACCUMULATED DEPRECIATION	1995 NET BOOK VALUE
B. ESTABLISHMENT EXPENSES						
1. Preliminary expenses	117.787	106.988	10.799	143.374	122.374	21.000
2. Exchange diff. from fix. assets acquis.	356.312	350.821	5.491	369.307	350.821	18.486
3. Interest during constr. period	1.996.790	1.996.790	-	-	-	-
4. Other deferred expenses	630.329	359.384	270.945	294.008	138.735	155.273
TOTAL ESTABLISHMENT EXPENSES (B)	3.101.218	2.813.983	287.235	806.689	611.930	194.759
C. FIXED ASSETS						
I. Intangible assets						
1. Research & development costs	154.100	69.877	84.223	129.070	106.146	22.924
5. Consolidation difference	2.379.166	-	2.379.166	-	-	-
	2.533.266	69.877	2.463.389	129.070	106.146	22.924
II. Tangible assets						
1. Land	17.386.254	-	17.386.254	9.243.270	-	9.243.270
2. Mines, quarries etc.	11.532.818	1.465.110	10.067.708	8.843.907	565.129	8.278.778
3. Buildings & technical works	61.860.089	51.931.607	9.928.482	34.848.150	29.643.540	5.204.610
4. Machinery, tech. install & other equip.	59.741.159	35.438.210	24.302.949	31.903.747	21.526.932	10.376.815
5. Transportation equipment	14.124.445	7.028.864	7.095.581	12.491.329	5.046.707	7.444.622
6. Furniture & other equip.	2.150.643	1.110.417	1.040.226	1.043.982	651.699	392.283
7. Paym. on acc. & work in progress	3.192.292	-	3.192.292	1.036.565	-	1.036.565
	169.987.700	96.974.208	73.013.492	99.410.950	57.434.007	41.976.943
TOTAL TANG. & INTANG. ASSETS (CI+CII)	172.520.966	97.044.085	75.476.881	99.540.020	57.540.153	41.999.867
III Investments						
2. Participating interest in other undertakings and Group own shares		751.051			281.370	
Less : Amounts due		31.960	719.091		-	281.370
5. Notes receivable after more than one year			4.621			
7. Other long-term receivables			898.105			628.926
			1.621.817			910.296
TOTAL FIXED ASSETS (C)			77.098.698			42.910.163
D. CURRENT ASSETS						
I. Inventories						
1. Merchandise		200.054			126.192	
2. Finished & semi-finished products		3.730.652			2.476.123	
3. Work in progress		41.880			44.226	
4. Raw & auxiliary materials, consumables spares parts & packing materials	11.919.367			8.567.895		
Less: Provision for obsolescence	5.796	11.913.571		-	8.567.895	
5. Advance payments for stock purchases		348.055	16.234.212		248.573	11.463.009
II. DEBTORS						
1. Trade debtors		14.826.961			11.110.261	
2. Notes receivable						
- In portfolio	228.531			129.882		
- At banks for collection	446.082			779.144		
- At banks as pledge	-	674.613		-	909.026	
3. Notes overdue		509.744			380.753	
3a. Cheques receivable	20.147.104				17.087.195	
3b. Cheques overdue	17.099	20.164.203				
8. Blocked deposits		2.274.137			5.600	
10. Doubtful trade & other debtors	2.802.592			6.811.252		
Less: provision	301.413	2.501.179		(4.009.612)	2.801.640	
11. Sundry debtors	7.411.098			6.800.566		
11a. Greek State	1.508.707	8.919.805		-	6.800.566	
12. Advances		70.988	49.941.630		38.606	39.133.647
IV. Cash at bank and in hand						
1. Cash		93.737			60.245	
3. Sight & term deposits		3.204.353			1.764.052	
Other		2.159	3.300.249		-	1.824.297
TOTAL CURRENT ASSETS (D)			69.476.091			52.420.953
E. PREPAYMENTS & ACCRUED INCOME						
1. Deferred charges		544.617			475.173	
2. Accrued income		22.353			34.380	
3. Other prepayments & accrued income		98.180	665.150		53.384	562.937
GRAND TOTAL ASSETS (B+C+D+E)			147.527.174			96.088.812
MEMO ACCOUNTS			11.704.550			8.868.105

NOTES : 1. Companies included in the consolidation are listed below : a.Domestic: HERACLES GENERAL CEMENT CO. S.A., EVIESK S.A., HERACLES SHIPPING CO. S.A., HERACLES INTERNATIONAL S.A.,HERACLES PACKAGING S.A., LAVA S.A., AMPER S.A., PORT SAID SILO INVESTMENT CO.S.A., HERACLES MARITIME AGENCY LTD., G. HADJIKYRIAKOS SHIPPING CO., A. HADJIKYRIAKOS SHIPPING CO., DYSTOS SHIPPING CO., PROTOPOROS SHIPPING CO.,THALASSOPOROS SHIPPING CO.,PONTOPOROS SHIPPING CO., POSEIDON SHIPPING CO., VOLOS SHIPPING CO., PHAETHON SHIPPING CO., IOKASTI SHIPPING CO., NAFSIKA SHIPPING CO., HERACLES GLORY SHIPPING CO., HERACLES INSURANCE ENTERPRISES LTD.(Soph.Venizelou 49-51 Lycovrissi), HELLENIC CEMENT RESEARCH CENTRE LTD.(K.Pateli 15 Lykovrissi) EMMY BUILDING MATERIALS S.A.,AIGIS SA (E.Venizelou & Androutsou Lycovrissi),ASTIR-LATO SA (Iras Str Galatsi),SKYRODEMA SA (Neochorouda (Thessaloniki), CHALKIS CEMENT C.A.,CHALKIS CEMENT TRADING S.A., CHALKIS CEMENT INTERNATIONAL S.A. INIOHOS TRANSPORTATION LTD, FINDA TRANSPORTATION ENTERPRISES S.A. (Tower of Athens), b.Foreign : ALEXANDRIA SILO INVESTMENT COMPANY S.A., HERMES COMPANIA NAVIERA S.A., PORT SAID SILO INVESTMENT COMPANY S.A., LOYDIAS COMPANIA NAVIERA S.A., MARITIME COMPANY ESPERIDES S.A., DEPOT AND COORDINATION CO S.A.(Panama), INTERNATIONAL MEDITERRANEAN SHIPPING S.A.(Luxemburg), INTERNATIONAL FLAG (Egypt). HERACLES General Cement Co on 27-11-96, acquired 51% of CEMENT CHALKIS SA which fully owns four subsidaries. 2. Land and buildings were revalued in 1996 in accordance with L.2065/92 provisions. As a rusult the cost of land and buildings revalued by drs. 16,112 million, and the respective accumulated depreciation by drs 7,365 million. The revaluation surplus, amounting to drs 8,747, was posted to the equity account A-III-2 "Other Fixed Assets' Revaluation Reserve" by an amount of Drs 6,929 million, while the rest, amounting to Drs 1,818 million set-off prior years' losses carried forward. Depreciation " charge for the year was calculated on the revalued amounts and is higher than the respective charge before revaluation, by approximately drs 537 million. 3. Some of the participations are valued at cost, according to Art 28 para.5 of P.D. 186/1992. If the relevant provisions of Art 43,

484　European Accounting Guide

ΠΑΘΗΤΙΚΟ

	ΧΡΗΣΕΩΣ 1996		ΧΡΗΣΕΩΣ 1995	

Α. ΙΔΙΑ ΚΕΦΑΛΑΙΑ
Ι. Κεφάλαιο Μετοχικό
(50.490.957 μετοχές των 808 δρχ.)
1. Καταβλημένο　40.796.693　　40.796.693

ΙΙ. Διαφορά από έκδοση μετοχών υπέρ το άρτιο　401.642　　401.642

ΙΙΙ. Διαφορές αναπροσαρμογής-Επιχορηγήσεις επενδύσεων
1. Διαφορές από αναπροσαρμογή αξίας συμμετ.& χρεογράφων　556.170　　556.167
2. Διαφορές από αναπροσ. αξίας λοιπών περιουσ. στοιχείων　6.654.174　　16.520
3. Διαφ.από αναπρ.αξίας Ετ. Ομίλου　441.736　7.652.080　　-　572.687

IV. Αποθεματικά κεφάλαια
1. Τακτικό αποθεματικό　2.276.010　　1.881.262
2. Εκτακτο αποθεματικό　5.397.386　　5.679.386
3. Ειδικά φορ.αποθ.Ν.1892/90 άρ.23α　1.133.000　　-
4. Αφορολόγητα αποθεματικά
ειδικών διατάξεων νόμων　13.073.820　21.880.216　11.765.928　19.326.576
Μείον : Διαφορά ενοποίησης　　(85.504)　　(210.023)

V. Υπόλοιπο κερδών (ζημιών) εις νέο　　2.992.925　　969.355

VI. Δικαιώματα μειοψηφίας
1. Στο Κεφάλαιο　64.235　　103.937
2. Στα αποθεματικά & κέρδη　569.549　633.784　401.769　505.706
ΣΥΝΟΛΟ ΙΔΙΩΝ ΚΕΦΑΛΑΙΩΝ (Α)　　74.271.836　　62.362.636

Β. ΠΡΟΒΛΕΨΕΙΣ ΓΙΑ ΚΙΝΔΥΝΟΥΣ & ΕΞΟΔΑ
1. Προβλέψεις για αποζημ. προσωπ. λόγω εξόδου από την υπηρεσία　9.096.005　　2.018.545
2. Λοιπές προβλέψεις　2.008.329　11.104.334　709.335　2.727.880

Γ. ΥΠΟΧΡΕΩΣΕΙΣ
Ι. Μακροπρόθεσμες υποχρεώσεις
2. Δάνεια τραπεζών　20.871.021　　892.658
8. Λοιπές μακροπρ. υποχρεώσεις　1.182.365　22.053.386　　892.658

ΙΙ. Βραχυπρόθεσμες υποχρεώσεις
1. Προμηθευτές　4.609.314　　2.760.272
2. Γραμμάτια πληρωτέα　1.682.948　　1.595.124
2α. Επιταγές πληρωτέες　440.771　　-
3. Τράπεζες λ/Βραχυπροθ. υποχρ.　12.177.897　　11.416.793
4. Προκαταβολές πελατών　161.951　　101.996
5. Υποχρεώσεις από φόρους-τέλη　5.998.463　　4.264.782
6. Ασφαλιστικοί Οργανισμοί　1.835.658　　1.225.114
7. Μακροπρόθεσμες υποχρεώσεις πληρωτέες στην επόμ. χρήση　2.611.092　　979.049
10. Μερίσματα πληρωτέα εκτός Ομίλου　5.377.958　　4.379.928
11. Πιστωτές διάφοροι　3.957.362　38.853.414　3.033.861　29.756.919
ΣΥΝΟΛΟ ΥΠΟΧΡΕΩΣΕΩΝ (Γ)　　60.906.800　　30.649.577

Δ. ΜΕΤΑΒΑΤΙΚΟΙ ΛΟΓ/ΣΜΟΙ ΠΑΘΗΤΙΚΟΥ
1. Εσοδα επομένων χρήσεων　-　　-
2. Εξοδα χρήσεως δουλευμένα　1.234.627　　347.619
3. Λοιποί μεταβ.λ/σμοί παθητικού　9.577　1.244.204　1.100　348.719
ΓΕΝΙΚΟ ΣΥΝΟΛΟ ΠΑΘΗΤΙΚΟΥ (Α+Β+Γ+Δ)　　147.527.174　　96.088.812
ΛΟΓΑΡΙΑΣΜΟΙ ΤΑΞΕΩΣ ΠΙΣΤΩΤΙΚΟΙ　　11.704.550　　8.868.105

των απαιτήσεων περιλαμβάνονται : α) Λοιπές απαιτήσεις ύψους δρχ. 1.664 εκατ. που βρίσκονται σε καθυστέρηση. Το εν λόγω κονδύλι αντικρύζεται με μέρος από τον λογαριασμό του Παθητικού του Ισολογισμού (Λήψος Β-2) "Λοιπές Προβλέψεις" κατά δρχ. 2.008 εκατ. β) "Επισφαλείς - επίδικοι πελάτες και χρεώστες" (Λήψος Δ/ΙΙ-10) ύψους δρχ. 2.501 εκατ. Ο Όμιλος για κάλυψη πιτακίων κινδύνων και
απροβλέπτων έξόδων έχει σχηματίσει "Εκτακτο Αποθεματικό" (Λήψος Α/IV-2) δρχ. 5.397 εκατ. Σημειώνεται ότι ο Όμιλος για κάλυψη των κινδύνων από επισφαλείς δανειγχρήσεις πρόσθετη πρόβλεψη στα
αποτελέσματά του. εκείνης που προβλέπει το άρθρο 10 παράγρ. 12 του Ν.2065/92 ύψους δρχ. 1.000 εκατ. ενώ κατά την προηγούμενη χρήση το αντίστοιχο ποσό ήταν 750 εκατ. δρχ. γ) Στο Λογαριασμό
Χρεώστες Διάφοροι (Δ/ΙΙ-11) περιλαμβάνεται και το κονδύλι δρχ. 2.144 εκατ. περίπου, το οποίο αφορά σε καταβολή επιλήψιμων από την Τράπεζα της Ελλάδος ποινικών μητρών στην ΑΓΕΤ ΗΡΑΚΛΗΣ
λόγω παραδόσεων συναλλαγματικών κανόνων της, ετών 1981-1991. Η ΑΓΕΤ ΗΡΑΚΛΗΣ έχει προσφύγει κατά των αποφάσεων της Τραπέζης της Ελλάδος, ενώπιον των αρμοδίων δικαστηρίων και έχει
βάσιμες ελπίδες ότι τελικά θα δικαιωθεί. δ) Στο Λογαριασμό του Ενεργητικού του Ισολογισμού (Λήψος Δ/ΙΙ-8) "Δεσμευμένοι λ/σμοι καταθέσεων" περιλαμβάνεται κατάθεση ύψους δρχ. 207.2 εκατ. υπό αμ-
φισβήτηση. 5. Η "πρόβλεψη αποζημιώσεως προσωπικου λόγω εξόδου από την υπηρεσία" έγινε σύμφωνα με τις διατάξεις του άρθρου 10 παρ.13 του Ν.2065/92 και την 205/1988 γνωμοδότηση της Ολομέλειας των Νομικών Συμβούλων Διοικήσεως με συνέπεια να αποτελέσματα της χρήσεως με δρχ. 47 εκ. Επί πλέον ο Όμιλος σχημάτισε έκτακτη πρόβλεψη αποζημιώσεως προσωπικού ύ-
ψους δρχ. 1.350 με την οποία επιβάρυνε τα αποτελέσματα χρήσεως(βλέπε παρούσσημια). 6. Σε εταιρεία του Ομίλου (θυγατρική της ΤΣΙΜΕΝΤΑ ΧΑΛΚΙΔΟΣ ΑΕ) δεν διενεργήθηκε πρόβλεψη σε βάρος
των αποτελεσμάτων για προσθέτους φόρους αποδήματος και προσωρίσεις ύψους δρχ. 245.000.000 για τις χρήσεις 1990-1993, που καταλογίστηκαν μετά από προσωρινό φορολογικό έλεγχο. Η Διοίκη-
ση της Εταιρίας εκτιμά ότι το τελικό ύψος των προσθέτων φόρων που θα καταλογιστούν μετά από συμβιβασμό θα ανέλθει σε δρχ. 130 εκατ. Η σχετική πράξη συμβιβασμού υπεγράφη. 7. Η Ευρωπαϊκή Επιτροπή με την από 30.11.1994 απόφασή της επέβαλε στην ΑΓΕΤ ΗΡΑΚΛΗΣ πρόστιμο ύψους 5.748.000 ECU και στα ΤΣΙΜΕΝΤΑ ΧΑΛΚΙΔΟΣ ΑΕ πρόστιμο ύψους 1.856.000 ECU θεωρώντας ότι υπήρξε παρα-
βαση του άρθρου 85 της συνθήκης της Ε.Ο.Κ. Κατά της αποφάσεως της Επιτροπής έχει γίνει προσφυγή στο Πρωτοδικείο του δικαστηρίου της Κοινότητος με τη βάσιμη προσδοκία ότι ο Όμιλος θα δικαιωθεί και ως εκ τούτου δεν σχημάτισε σχετική πρόβλεψη στον Ισολογισμό.

LIABILITIES

		1996		1995
A. SHAREHOLDERS' EQUITY				
I. Share Capital				
(50.490.957 shares at par value Drs. 808)				
1.Paid-up		40.796.693		40.796.693
II. Share premium		401.642		401.642
III. Revaluation reserves and grants				
1. Investments' Revaluation Reserve	556.170		556.167	
2. Other Fixed Assets' Revaluation Reserve	6.654.174		16.520	
3. Other Fixed Assets' Revaluation Reserves-Other Group Companies	441.736	7.652.080	-	572.687
IV. Other Reserves				
1. Legal reserve	2.276.010		1.881.262	
2. Exrtraordinary reserve	5.397.386		5.679.386	
3. Special reserve of L. 1892/90 art 23A	1.133.000			
4. Tax-free reserves under special laws	13.073.820	21.880.216	11.765.928	19.326.576
Less : Consolidation difference		(85.504)		(210.023)
V. Profit carried f/ward		2.992.925		969.355
VI. Minority interests				
1. Share capital	64.235		103.937	
2. Profits & reserves	569.549	633.784	401.769	505.706
TOTAL SHAREHOLDERS' EQUITY (A)		74.271.836		62.362.636
B. PROVISIONS				
1. Provisions for staff termination indemnities	9.096.005		2.018.545	
2. Other provisions	2.008.329	11.104.334	709.335	2.727.880
C. CREDITORS				
I. Long term debt				
2. Bank loans	20.871.021		892.658	
8. Other long-term debts	1.182.365	22.053.386	-	892.658
II. Current liabilities				
1. Suppliers	4.609.314		2.760.272	
2. Notes payable	1.682.948		1.595.124	
2a. Cheques payable	440.771		-	
3. Bank overdrafts	12.177.897		11.416.793	
4. Customers' advances	161.951		101.996	
5. Taxes and duties	5.998.463		4.264.782	
6. Social Security	1.835.658		1.225.114	
7. Long-term debt falling due within next year	2.611.092		979.049	
10. Dividends payable to third parties	5.377.958		4.379.928	
11. Sundry creditors	3.957.362	38.853.414	3.033.861	29.756.919
TOTAL CREDITORS (C)		60.906.800		30.649.577
D. ACCRUALS AND DEFERRED INCOME				
1. Deferred income	-		-	
2. Accrued expenses	1.234.627		347.619	
3. Other accruals	9.577	1.244.204	1.100	348.719
GRAND TOTAL LIABILITIES (A+B+C+D)		147.527.174		96.088.812
MEMO ACCOUNTS		11.704.550		8.868.105

L.2190/1920, were used instead, then their valuation would be lower by approximately Drs 206 million. 4. Included in receivables are the following : a) Other overdue receivables amounting to Drs 1,664 million. A provision has been made for these overdue debts, included in Liabilities' account B-2 "Other Provisions" which amounts to Drs 2,008 million. b) Doubtful trade receivables and overdue trade receivables at Court amounting to Drs 2,502 million. (Account D/II-10). The Company provided for an "Extraordinary Reserve"-(A/IV-2) amounted to Drs 5,397 million, for special risks and unforecasted expenditure. The company,besides provision for doubtful debts in accordance with L.2065/1992, provided for an additional amount of drs 1.000 million (the respective amount for 1995 was Drs 750 million) c) "Sundry Debtors (D/II-11) include "penalties imposed by Bank of Greece and amouting to approximately Drs 2,144 million, concerning violations of foreign exchange regulations for the years 1981-1991. The Company has filed lawsuits against Bank of Greece resolutions and there is "reasonable expectation for its vindication. d) "Blocked deposits" (D/II-8) include an amount of Drs 207,2 million under dispute. 5. In accordance with Law 2065/92 and opinion No 205/1988 of the Legal Advisory Board, the Group provided Drs 47 million for staff termination indemnities. Furthermore the Group provided for an extra amount of Drs 1,350 million for the same purpose. (see Notes to the Consolidated Accounts). 6. No provision has been made to the accounts of one of the subsidiaries of Chalkis Cement Co the books of which have been audited by the tax authorities for the years 1990-1993. The tax assesment amounted to Drs 245 million but Company's management believe that the final charge,after settlement with the tax Authorities, will not exceed Drs 130 million. The settlement action is still pending. 7. With its resolution of 30-11-94, the E.U. Commission has imposed the HERACLES General Cement Co a fine of ECU 5,748,000 and Chalkis Cement SA a fine of ECU 1,856,000 for violating provisions of Art 85 of EU Pact. The Group have filed appeal to the EU Court. Based on sound expectation for its vindication the Group has not made a relevant provision.

ΚΑΤΑΣΤΑΣΗ ΛΟΓΑΡΙΑΣΜΟΥ ΑΠΟΤΕΛΕΣΜΑΤΩΝ ΧΡΗΣΕΩΣ ΟΜΙΛΟΥ
31ης ΔΕΚΕΜΒΡΙΟΥ 1996 (1 ΙΑΝΟΥΑΡΙΟΥ - 31 ΔΕΚΕΜΒΡΙΟΥ 1996)
(ΣΕ ΧΙΛ. ΔΡΧ.)

	ΠΟΣΑ ΚΛΕΙΟΜΕΝΗΣ ΧΡΗΣΕΩΣ 1996		ΠΟΣΑ ΠΡΟΗΓΟΥΜΕΝΗΣ ΧΡΗΣΕΩΣ 1995	
Συνολικός κύκλος εργασιών Ομίλου		131.650.076		116.256.227
Μείον : Ενδοεταιρικός κύκλος εργασιών		19.967.053		16.658.511
ΜΕΙΟΝ: Κόστος πωλήσεων		111.683.023		99.597.716
		82.611.497		75.377.879
Μικτά αποτελέσματα εκμετάλλευσης (κέρδη)		29.071.526		24.219.837
ΠΛΕΟΝ: Αλλα έσοδα εκμετάλλευσης		331.508		302.026
ΣΥΝΟΛΟ		29.403.034		24.521.863
ΜΕΙΟΝ: Εξοδα διοικ. λειτουργίας		7.190.293		5.815.104
Εξοδα λειτ.ερευνών-ανάπτυξης		38.588		42.155
Εξοδα λειτουργίας διάθεσης		2.392.120 9.621.001		2.219.537 8.076.796
Μερικά αποτελέσματα εκμετάλλευσης (κέρδη)		19.782.033		16.445.067
ΜΕΙΟΝ: Χρεωστ. τόκοι & συναφή έξοδα		2.854.389		2.648.879
ΜΕΙΟΝ: Εσοδα συμμετοχών	15.652		25.580	
Πιστωτικοί τόκοι	161.373	177.025 2.677.364	241.527	267.107 2.381.772
Ολικά αποτελέσματα εκμετάλλευσης (κέρδη)		17.104.669		14.063.295
ΜΕΙΟΝ: Εκτακτα αποτελέσματα				
Εκτακτα & ανόργανα έξοδα	1.784.507		1.830.930	
Αποσβέσεις συν/κών διαφορών	-			
Εξοδα προηγούμενων χρήσεων	584.474		433.589	
Προβλέψεις για έκτ. κινδύνους	2.548.648	4.917.629	1.296.692	3.561.211
ΜΕΙΟΝ: Εκτακτα & ανόργανα έσοδα	748.548		1.769.433	
Εσοδα προηγούμενων χρήσεων	429.033		293.814	
Εσοδα από προβλ.προηγ.χρήσ.	152.055	1.329.636 3.587.993	90.050	2.153.297 1.407.914
		13.516.676		12.655.381
ΜΕΙΟΝ: Συνολικές αποσβέσεις		4.653.640		3.960.772
Μείον: Οι ενσωματωμένες στο				
λειτουργικό κόστος		4.402.930 250.710		3.840.219 120.553
ΚΑΘΑΡΑ (ΚΕΡΔΗ) ΧΡΗΣΕΩΣ προ φόρων		13.265.966		12.534.828
ΜΕΙΟΝ: Φόρος εισοδήματος		4.759.976		3.447.499
Καθαρά κέρδη χρήσεως		8.505.990		9.087.329
ΜΕΙΟΝ: Δικαιώματα μειοψηφίας		(138.764)		214.150
Καθαρά κέρδη χρήσεως Ομίλου		8.644.754		8.873.179

Λυκόβρυση, 4 Απριλίου 1997

Ο ΠΡΟΕΔΡΟΣ ΤΟΥ ΔΙΟΙΚΗΤΙΚΟΥ ΣΥΜΒΟΥΛΙΟΥ
MASSIMO GIUDICI
22399089/92

Ο ΔΙΕΥΘΥΝΩΝ ΣΥΜΒΟΥΛΟΣ
UGO ALESSI
33662398/93

Ο ΓΕΝΙΚΟΣ ΔΙΕΥΘΥΝΤΗΣ ΟΙΚΟΝΟΜΙΚΟΥ
ΣΩΤ. Ι. ΠΑΠΑΣΠΗΛΙΩΤΟΠΟΥΛΟΣ
Ρ.149102/93

Ο ΠΡΟΙΣΤΑΜΕΝΟΣ ΤΟΥ ΛΟΓΙΣΤΗΡΙΟΥ
ΙΩΑΝΝΗΣ ΑΘ. ΚΑΠΝΟΠΟΥΛΟΣ
Λ.214432/81

GROUP PROFIT AND LOSS ACCOUNT
FOR THE YEAR ENDED DECEMBER 31, 1996
(AMOUNTS IN DRS. THOUS.)

		1996			1995
Turnover		131.650.076		116.256.227	
Less : Inter-company turnover		19.967.053	111.683.023	16.658.511	99.597.716
LESS: Cost of sales			82.611.497		75.377.879
Gross margin			29.071.526		24.219.837
PLUS: Other operating income			331.508		302.026
TOTAL			29.403.034		24.521.863
LESS: Administrative expenses		7.190.293		5.815.104	
Research & development expenses		38.588		42.155	
Selling & Distribution expenses		2.392.120	9.621.001	2.219.537	8.076.796
Operat. income before investing & financial activities			19.782.033		16.445.067
LESS: Interest expense and financial charges		2.854.389		2.648.879	
LESS: Income from participations	15.652			25.580	
Interest income	161.373	177.025	2.677.364	241.527	267.107	2.381.772
Total operating income			17.104.669		14.063.295
LESS: Extrordinary and					
non-operating exps.	1.784.507			1.830.930	
Amortisation of exchange diff.	-			-	
Prior years' expenses	584.474			433.589	
Provisions	2.548.648	4.917.629		1.296.692	3.561.211
LESS : Extraordin. & non-operating income	748.548			1.769.433	
Prior year's income	429.033			293.814	
Unrealised provisons	152.055	1.329.636	3.587.993	90.050	2.153.297	1.407.914
			13.516.676		12.655.381
LESS: Total depreciation		4.653.640		3.960.772	
Less: Charged to the					
operating cost		4.402.930	250.710	3.840.219	120.553
NET INCOME FOR THE YEAR before tax			13.265.966		12.534.828
LESS : Income tax			4.759.976		3.447.499
Net Income after tax			8.505.990		9.087.329
LESS : Minority interest			(138.764)		214.150
Group after - tax income for the year			8.644.754		8.873.179

Lycovrissi, 4th April 1997

CHAIRMAN OF THE BOARD OF DIRECTORS
MASSIMO GIUDICI
22399089/92

MANAGING DIRECTOR
UGO ALESSI
33662398/93

THE GROUP GENERAL FINANCIAL DIRECTOR
SOT. I. PAPASPILIOTOPOULOS
P.149102/93

CHIEF ACCOUNTANT
IOANNIS A. KAPNOPOULOS
L. 214432/81

ΠΙΣΤΟΠΟΙΗΤΙΚΟ ΕΛΕΓΧΟΥ ΟΡΚΩΤΟΥ ΛΟΓΙΣΤΗ - ΕΛΕΓΚΤΗ

Ελέγξαμε τον ανωτέρω ενοποιημένο ισολογισμό. τα αποτελέσματα χρήσεως και το σχετικό προσάρτημα του Ομίλου Εταιριών "ΗΡΑΚΛΗΣ", κατά τη χρήση που έληξε την 31η Δεκεμβρίου 1996. Κατά τον έλεγχό μας εφαρμόσαμε τις ελεγκτικές διαδικασίες, τις οποίες κρίναμε κατάλληλες, βάσει των αρχών και κανόνων ελεγκτικής που ακολουθεί το Σώμα Ορκωτών Ελεγκτών. Ο ανωτέρω ι-σολογισμός και ο λογαριασμός αποτελεσμάτων χρήσης προέκυψαν από την ενοποίηση των κονδυλίων ενεργητικού, παθητικού και αποτελεσμάτων χρήσης των επί μέρους οικονομικών καταστάσεων των εταιρειών του Ομίλου, που περιλαμβάνονται στη σημείωση Νο 1, η οποία παρατίθεται κάτω από τον ισολογισμό. Για την ενοποίηση αυτή εφαρμόστηκε η μέθοδος της ολικής ενοποίησης, οι δε ανωτέρω σημειώσεις του Ομίλου αναφέρονται τόσο στον από εμάς έλεγχο της ΑΓΕΤ ΗΡΑΚΛΗΣ όσο και τον έλεγχο των λοιπών ε-ταιρειών του Ομίλου που έγινε από άλλους συναδέλφους του Σώματος Ορκωτών Ελεγκτών. Το προσάρτημα περιλαμβάνει τις πλη-ροφορίες που προβλέπονται από το άρθρο 107 του κωδ. Ν. 2190/1920. Ο ανωτέρω ενοποιημένος ισολογισμός και η κατάσταση των ενοποιημένων αποτελεσμάτων χρήσης απεικονίζουν μαζί με το προσάρτημα, με την επιφύλαξη των ανωτέρω σημειώσεων του Ομίλου, βάσει των σχετικών διατάξεων που ισχύουν και λογιστικών αρχών, οι οποίες έχουν γίνει γενικά παραδεκτές και δεν διαφέ-ρουν από εκείνες που ο Όμιλος είχε εφαρμόσει στην προηγούμενη χρήση, την περιουσιακή διάρθρωση και την Οικονομική θέση του Ομίλου κατά την 31η Δεκεμβρίου 1996 καθώς και τα αποτελέσματα της χρήσης που έληξε αυτή την ημερομηνία.

Αθήνα. 8 Απριλίου 1997

Ο ΟΡΚΩΤΟΣ ΛΟΓΙΣΤΗΣ - ΕΛΕΓΚΤΗΣ

ΙΩΑΝΝΗΣ Ν. ΛΑΜΠΡΟΥ
Κ. 227220/77
Σ.Ο.Λ. α.ε.ο.ε.

CERTIFIED AUDITOR'S REPORT

We have audited the accompanying consolidated financial statements and the related Notes thereto of the HERACLES Group of Companies for the year ended 31 December 1996. Our audit was performed in acordance with the auditing procedures which we considered necessary based on the principles followed by the Institure of Certified Auditors in Greece. The consolidated financial statements referred to above, derived from the consolidation of the items of Assets, Liabilities and Profit and Loss Accounts of the Group companies included in Note 1 above. The accounts of the Group companies are included in full in the consolidated financial statements. Regarding the notes mentioned above, reference is made both by us in the audit report for HERACLES General Cement Co as well as by the other auditors who audited the financial statements of the other Group Companies. The Notes to the Accounts include all the information required by Art.107 of L. 2190/1920. In our opinion the consolidated financial statements referred to above, together with the Notes to the Consolidated Accounts, present fairly, except for the notes made above by the Group, the financial structure and position of Group at 31 December 1996 and the results of its operations for the year then ended, in accordance with the prevailing legislation and the accounting principles which are generally accepted and are consistent with those applied in the previous year.

Athens 8 April 1997

THE CERTIFIED AUDITOR

IOANNIS N. LAMPROU
K 227220/77

Key Data for Subsidiaries
(Amounts in drs million.)

	TURNOVER		COST OF SALES		GROSS MARGIN		OPERATIONAL EXPENSES	
	1995	1996	1995	1996	1995	1996	1995	1996
1. AIGIS S.A. Packaging Materials Manufacturing Co.	4.057,8	4.319,7	3.012,0	3.630,6	1.045,8	689,1	266,6	197,2
2. AMPÉR S.A. Computer Services	548,2	549,0	324,7	351,1	223,5	197,9	144,4	135,4
3. STAR LATO S.A. Ready-Mix Concrete Co.	2.083,6	3.051,0	1.986,5	2.992,9	97,1	58,0	369,5	418,4
4. EVIESK S.A. General Industrial Enteprises	5.979,5	6.047,6	5.553,5	5.512,0	426,0	535,6	197,4	212,1
5 EMMY - BULDING MATERIALS S.A. Transportation Service- ALFABLOK	1.374,7	1.448,2	887,9	738,7	486,8	709,5	223,8	290,3
6. HELLENIC CEMENT RESEARCH CENTER LTD Research & Development Co.	205,6	256,2	141,7	164,6	63,9	91,6	15,3	18,9
7. HERACLES PACKAGING Co S.A. Shipping Company	1.448,8	1.453,5	1.103,8	1.133,3	345,0	320,2	367,2	386,3
8. HERACLES PACKAGING Co. S.A. Manufacturing & Trading Co.	387,6	488,9	263,1	327,9	124,5	160,9	67,0	69,0
9. LAVA S.A. Mining & Quarring Co.	2.812,9	2.805,4	1.130,8	1.166,7	1.682,2	1.638,7	851,2	840,1
10. SKYRODEMA S.A. Ready-Mix Concrete Co.	1.758,7	2.450,5	1.390,7	1.878,6	368,0	571,9	425,5	488,2
11. CHALKIS CEMENT GROUP *	25.291,9	28.153,9	24.444,6	27.108,5	847,3	1045,4	4.203,9	5.175,1

* Yearly figures are included.

The smooth recovery in 1996, in the markets of Thessaloniki and Kavala contributed to the comeback of the Company into profits which amounted to drs 56,3 million (as compared to losses amounting to drs 111 million in 1995). Turnover amounted to drs 2.451 million in 1996 as compared to drs 1.759 million in 1995.

The improvement in market conditions, which is expected to continue in 1997, will result in the prosperous performance of the Company for the current year.

HELLENIC CEMENT RESEARCH CENTER LTD

The Company operates in the following fields:

It provides technical and technology support on clinker and cement production process as well as on ready-mix concrete production.

H.C.R.C. submits proposal files and undertakes the realisation and administration of subsidised, by the Research and Technology Secreteriat or by the EU, research programs. It also cooperates on this field with other firms and research centres.

The Company provides expert reports on the resistance and corrosion of concrete structures as well as studies on the properties, the microstructure and the chemical composition of various materials, solid fuels and rocks, issuing approved certificates.

Furthermore H.C.R.C. provides consulting services to Group companies namely AIGIS SA, ASTIR - LATO SA, SKYRODEMA SA and LAVA SA in order to be qualified by ISO 9000.

Finally the Company has developed the building materials sector based on its experience and infrastructure. The involvement in this area includes new products' design, production quality control and introduction to the building systems. Primarily these products will arise from the activities of EMMY-BUILDING MATERIALS SA and LAVA SA.

Pre-tax profits for 1996 amounted to drs 76 million and turnover to drs 256 million. The respective figures for 1995 were drs 49 million and drs 206 million.

It should be finally noted that since 1997 a new Marketing and Sales department was brought into operation in order to achieve a more effective penetration of the Company into the services area.

Board of Directors' Report on the consolidated financial statements as at December 31st, 1996

Dear Shareholders,

Herebelow is reported useful information regarding the true view of the financial condition and the state of operations of the Companies included in the consolidation. For more detailed information refer to the respective Board of Directors' or Partners' Reports to the Annual General Meetings of those Companies.

Consolidated results showed a significant improvement. Specifically:

— Turnover increased by 12,1%
— Operational profit margin increased from 24,3% in 1995 to 26% in 1996.
— The increase in net profit before tax didn't exceed 5,8% mainly due to the increased depreciation and provisions.

Below is listed, in general terms, information required by Art 107, para. 3 of Companies Act L.2190/ 1920 concerning the report on consolidated operations.

    a. No significant post balance sheet events have occurred which would adversely affect the financial position of the Group, taken as a whole.

    b. The business of the companies included in the consolidation is developing and is expected to continue to develop within normal business conditions around the main activities of HERACLES General Cement Co.

    c. None of the companies included in the consolidation own shares or parts belonging to those companies.

Other information on the 1996 consolidated financial statements.

1. Group companies included in consolidation are listed below:

a. Domestic: HERACLES GENERAL CEMENT CO. S.A., EVIESK S.A., HERACLES SHIPPING CO. S.A., HERACLES INTERNATIONAL S.A., HERACLES PACKAGING S.A., LAVA S.A., AMPER S.A., PORT SAID SILO INVESTMENT CO. S.A., HERACLES MARITIME AGENCY LTD., G. HADJIKYRIAKOS SHIPPING CO. S.A., A. HADJIKYRIAKOS SHIPPING CO., DYSTOS SHIPPING CO., PROTOPOROS SHIPPING CO., THALASSOPOROS SHIPPING CO., PONTOPOROS SHIPPING CO., POSEIDON II SHIPPING CO., VOLOS I SHIPPING CO., PHAETHON SHIPPING CO., IOKASTI SHIPPING CO., NAFSIKA SHIPPING CO., HERACLES GLORY SHIPPING CO., HERACLES INSURANCE ENTERPRISES LTD., (Sof. Venizelou 49-51, Lycovrissi) HELLENIC CEMENT RESEARCH CENTER LTD., (15 K. Pateli, Lycovrissi), EMMY BUILDING MATERIALS S.A., AIGIS S.A. (El. Venizelou & 29 Androutsou, Lycovrissi), ASTIR-LATO S.A. (Iras Street, Galatsi), SKYRODEMA S.A. (Neochorouda Thessaloniki), CHALKIS CEMENT S.A., CHALKIS CEMENT TRADING S.A., CHALKIS CEMENT INTERNATIONAL S.A., INIOHOS TRANSPORTATION LTD, FINDA TRANSPORTATION ENTERPRISES S.A. (Tower of Athens).

b. Foreign : ALEXANDRIA SILO INVESTMENT COMPANY S.A., HERMES COMPANIA NAVIERA S.A., PORT SAID SILO INVESTMENT COMPANY S.A., LOUDIAS COMPANIA NAVIERA S.A., MARITIME COMPANY ESPERIDES S.A., DEPOT AND COORDINATION CO. S.A.(Panama), INTERNATIONAL MEDITERRANEAN SHIPPING S.A. (Luxemburg), INTERNATIONAL FLAG (Egypt).

2. Fixed assets denominated in foreign currencies are translated into drachmas using the exchange rates ruling at the Balance Sheet date.

3. Group participations:

a. Other Participations	NUMBER OF SHARES	TOTAL INVESTMENT
NATIONAL BANK OF GREECE	5.606	29.718.971
MACEDONIA-THRACE BANK	16.760	40.511.640
KARMOR HELLAS	420	4.450.000
EKEP	–	100.000
CEMENT MARKET ASSOCIATION	1	1.248.973
HOME OF INDUSTRY	–	308.620
AXIOS SHIPPING	19	51.550.354
ALFIOS COMPANIA NAVIERA	10	40.993.145
ARMSTOCK CO SA	–	40.264.260
EQUITABLE MARINE TRANS. SA	–	8.892.720
HERACLES OVERSEAS	–	15.170
ROBOCA & VAFOPOULOS S.A.	1.220	100.000.000
LAMA S.A.	94.000	94.000.000
METROPOLITAN AUTOMOTIVE ENTERPRISES	33.100	299.041.524
MIDLE EAST SHIPPING & HANDLINE	10.000	9.800
ERECO	10	500.000
b. In own shares :		
HERACLES GENERAL CEMENT CO.	44.640	39.445.050
Total		751.050.232

4. Loan balances amounting to Drs. 130.360 thousand have been secured by mortgages and securities, amounting to Drs. 1.112.309 thousand, on fixed assets of HERACLES Group companies. Furthermore, loans amounting to Drs. 971.223 thousand have been secured by mortgages on vessels amounting to Drs. 6.027.288 thousand.

5. HERACLES Group Companies provided for Staff Termination Indemnities for personnel who are eligible for retirement in 1997, as it is provided by Art. 10, Law 2065/1992. In contrast, CHALKIS CEMENT Group Companies provided for Staff Termination Indemnities for the entire personnel, as it is provided by L.2190/1920.

6. Group provided for doubtful debts with an amount of Drs. 1,775 million.

Lycovrissi, 4 April 1997

THE BOARD OF DIRECTORS

We certify that this Board of Directors' report is that referred in our Audit Report of 8th April 1997.

Athens, 8 April 1997

THE CERTIFIED PUBLIC ACCOUNTANT

JOHN N. LAMBROU

K 227220/77

Notes to the Consolidated Accounts for the year ended on 31st December 1996

The following notes to the Consolidated Balance Sheet as at 31st December 1996 and the Consolidated Profit and Loss account for the year then ended, have been prepared in accordance with the provisions of the Greek Companies Act, Law 2190/1920 and the Group's accounting policies.

Basis of Consolidation

According to the provisions of Art 90-99 of Companies Act Law 2190/1920, the consolidated financial statements incorporate the accounts of HERACLES General Cement Co, the Holding Company, and its Subsidiaries.

Method of Consolidation

The accounts of the Group companies are included in full in the consolidated financial statements, a method which is consistently followed. The consolidated financial statements include the companies listed in Note (1) of the consolidated Balance Sheet, in which HERACLES General Cement Co owns directly or indirectly over 51% of their shares. Minority interests are separately disclosed under para. 7.4 («Minority Interests»).

1. Intangible Fixed Assets.

1.1. Analysis of movement in the year in drs million.

Establishment Expenses	Cost 31.12.95	Deletions of fully amort. items	Additions in 1996	Group CHALKIS	Cost 31.12.96	amortisation 31.12.95	Deletions of fully amort. items	Amortisaation for 1996	Group CHALKIS	Accumulated amortisation 31.12.96	Net book value 31.12.96
1. Preliminary expenses	143	(49)	24	–	118	(123)	49	(33)	–	(107)	11
2. Exchange differenc. for F.A. acquisition	369	(19)	6	–	356	(351)	–	–	–	(351)	5
3. Interest incurred during the constr. per.	–	–	–	1.997	1.997	–	–	–	(1.997)	(1.997)	0
4. Other establishment expenses	294	(37)	187	186	630	(139)	37	(98)	(159)	(359)	271
Total Establishment Expenses	806	(105)	217	2.183	3.101	(613)	86	(131)	(2.156)	(2.814)	287

1.2. The consolidation difference disclosed as an asset in the Consolidated Balance Sheet (CI-5), represents the excess of the acquisition cost over the Group's share of CHALKIS CEMENT Co SA's net equity, reduced by the amount allocated to the fixed assets of CHALKIS Group, in accordance with the provisions of art.103 para.2 of Law 2190/1920.

The cost of acquisition has been adjusted for accumulated depreciation for each Group Company. The cost of tangible fixed assets of the companies situated in Greece is the historical cost as adjusted by statutory revaluations, plus additions and improvements. Depreciation has been calculated according to Presidential Decree 88/73. No additional depreciation provided by investment incentives laws was calculated. Finally no provision for the impairment in value of tangible fixed assets has been made, as none is anticipated.

2.3. The fixed assets of CHALKIS CEMENT Co SA and its subsidiaries have been valued by an independent and reputable firm of valuers at drs 39.724 million, compared to the net book value of drs 5.114 million. For consolidation purposes, the excess value, was allocated to the tangible fixed assets according to the provisions of Art 103 para.2 of Law 2190/1920. The resulting consolidation difference is shown as an asset in the consolidated Balance Sheet (CI-5).

3. **Unconsolidated companies and investments in own Group shares.**

Account «Participating Interests in other Undertakings and Group own shares includes:

a. The cost of acquisition of shares and parts in companies not controlled by the Group.

b. The cost of acquisition or current value, if lower, of HERACLES General Cement Co. SA owned by Group companies.

4. **Inventories**

4.1. Stocks of raw materials, supplies, spare parts, auxiliary materials semi - finished products, finished products and other goods are stated at the values which are included in the individual Balance Sheets of Group companies. Intercompany profits are eliminated upon consolidation. Stocks have been individually valued at the lower of cost and current value at the Balance Sheet date.

4.2. The stock valuation method is consistent with that of the previous year.

4.3. The value of stocks in the Balance Sheet is in line with their market value at 31st December 1996.

5. **Receivables**

5.1. No loans or advances have been paid to members of the Board of Directors (Companies Act Law 2190/1920 art. 43a para. 1/id).

5.2. Receivables and payables in foreign currency.

Receivables and payables denominated in foreign currencies have been translated into drachmas at the official exchange rates ruling at the Balance Sheet date. Exchange differences arising therefrom were recorded and monitored in separate accounts by currency. Thus their accounting treatment complies with the provisions of para. 8/b, Art 43-Companies Act Law 2190/1920.

5.3. Criteria for the classification of receivables and liabilities as long-term (Companies Act Law 2190/1920, art. 42/e para.6).

Receivables and liabilities falling due after one year from the Balance Sheet date are considered long-term.

6. Prepayments and Accrued Income

These are analysed as follows :

6.1. Prepaid expenses drs thous :

a. Repairs of vessels	281.052
b. Insurance premia	133.289
c. Other expenses	130.267
Total	544.617

7. Capital and Reserves

7.1. The total equity of the parent company has been included in the consolidated Balance Sheet.

7.2. Consolidation difference

Consolidation differences shown in the consolidated Balance Sheet under shareholders' equity, represent the difference between the cost of acquisition and the net assets of the consolidated subsidiaries, except for CHALKIS CEMENT Group which have been allocated to fixed assets as explained in para. 1.2 and 2.3.

7.3. Provisions of Art 47 and 48 para. 1c of Companies Act Law 2190/1920 are applicable for some companies of CHALKIS CEMENT Group, according to the respective Auditors' Reports.

7.4. Minority Interests

This account, shown under Shareholders' equity, includes the third parties' participating interests in the equity of consolidated companies. Such interests are listed below.

Company	% of Participation 31-12-96	Total shareholders' equity (in drs.thous)	Minority Interests (in drs.thous)
AIGIS SA	40,00	1.577.278	630.911
CHALKIS CEMENT SA	49,00	5.864	2.873
Total			633.784

The fixed assets of CHALKIS CEMENT Group have been valued by an independent and reputable firm of valuers at drs 39.724 million, compared to the net book value of drs 5.114 million.

Intangible Assets	Cost 31.12.95	Changes Deletions & disposals	Additions in 1966	Revaluation	Group CHALKIS	Fixed Assets Valuation CHALKIS	Cost 31.12.96	Accumulated amortisation 31.12.95	Changes Deletions & disposals	Amortisation for 1996	Revaluation	Group CHALKIS	Amortisation (Valuation)	Accumulated amortisation 31.12.96	Net book value 31.12.96
1. Research and Development	129	(58)	40	–	43	–	154	(106)	59	(23)	–	–	–	(70)	84
5. Consolidation Difference			2.379	–		–	2.379	–	–	–	–	–	–	–	2.379
Total Intagible Assets	**129**	**(58)**	**2.419**	**–**	**43**	**–**	**2.533**	**(106)**	**59**	**(23)**	**–**	**–**	**0**	**(70)**	**2.463**

2 Tangible Fixed Assets

2.1. Analysis of movement made in the year in drs million:

	Cost 31.12.95	Changes Deletions & disposals	Additions in 1966	Revaluation	Group CHALKIS	Fixed Assets Valuation CHALKIS	Cost 31.12.96	Accumulated depreciation 31.12.95	Changes Deletions & disposals	Charge for the year	Revaluation	Group CHALKIS	Depreciation (Valuation)	Accumulated Depreciation 31.12.96	Net book value 31.12.96
1. Land	9.243	(148)	973	4.396	2.597	325	17.386	–	–	–	–	–	–	–	17.386
2. Mines-Quarries	8.844		2	1.677	964	48	11.533	(565)	–	(300)	–	(600)	–	(1.465)	10.068
3. Buildings-Tech. wor.	34.848	(1)	630	8.625	14.745	3.013	61.860	(29.643)	–	(1.471)	(7.295)	(13.511)	(12)	(51.932)	9.928
4. Machinery	31.904	(70)	1.998	–	12.186	13.723	59.741	(21.527)	69	(2.123)	–	(11.685)	(172)	35.438	24.303
5. Transportation equip.	12.491	(655)	574	–	1.428	286	14.124	(5.047)	204	(909)	–	(1.275)	(2)	(7.029)	7.095
6. Furniture etc.	1.044	(3)	237	–	586	287	2.151	(652)	1	(56)	–	(400)	(3)	(1.110)	1.041
7. Under construction	1.037	(2.092)	4.229	–	18	–	3.192	–	–	–	–	–	–	–	3.192
Total II	**99.411**	**(2.969)**	**8.643**	**14.698**	**32.524**	**17.680**	**169.987**	**(57.434)**	**274**	**(4.859)**	**(7.295)**	**(27.471)**	**(189)**	**(96.974)**	**73.013**

2.2. Tangible fixed assets have been consolidated at their acquisition cost as stated in the respective Balance Sheets of the Group companies. Tangible fixed assets of foreign subsidiaries, denominated in US Dollars, were translated at the interbank fixing rate of exchange ruling at the balance sheet date.

8. Provisions

Provisions at the Balance Sheet date are analysed as follows:

8.1. Provision for Staff Termination Indemnities.

Regarding HERACLES Group companies, (i.e. CHALKIS CEMENT Group companies exempted), provisions for staff termination indemnities were made in compliance with Law 2065/92 and the opinion No 205/1988 of the Legal Advisory Board, for those employees who will become eligible for retirement in 1997. This provision amounted to drs 47 million. CHALKIS CEMENT Group companies provided for drs 1.412 million , which accounts for 80% of the staff termination indemnity liabilities payable in case of dismissal of their entire personnel at 31-12-96. This method complies with Law 2190/1920 and is followed consistently by CHALKIS CEMENT Group companies. Furthermore the Group made an additional provision for staff termination indemnities amounting to Drs 1.350 million.

Had the Group provided for 40% of the indemnity liabilities payable in case of dismissal of its entire personnel at 31-12-96, the provision would amount to drs 9.454 million. Had the Group provided for 100% of the indemnity liabilities, the provision would amount to drs 22.166 million. Instead the Group, at 31-12-96, has made a provision for Staff Termination Indemnities amounting to drs 9.096 million.

8.2. Other provisions:

a. Deferred exchange gains arising from the translation of receivables and payables denominated in foreign currency.	Drs.thous	922.240
b. Deferred exchange gains accumulated through 31-12-96 on foreign currency translation of overdue claims	» »	576.150
c. Other provisions	» »	509.939
Total other provisions	Drs.thous	2.008.329

The Group companies provided for doubtful debts in accordance with L.2065/1992. HERACLES General Cement Co has made an additional provision for doubtful debts amounting to drs 1.000 million (the respective additional provision for 1995 amounted to drs 750 million).

9. Liabilities - Mortgages and Charges

9.1. There are no liabilities falling due after five years from the Balance Sheet date.

9.2. Liabilities for the security of which mortgages and charges have been granted by the Group are analysed as follows:

Liability account	Loan balance 31-12-96 (Drs thous.)	Mortgages' and charges' value in Drs thous.	Type of security
– C/I/2 Long-term bank loans	1.112.309	130.360	Mortgages and prenotices.
– C/II/3 Bank overdrafts	971.223	6.027.288	Preliminary agreement for mortgages
Total	2.083.532	6.157.648	

10. Accruals and Deferred Income

These are analysed as follows:

a. Accrued interest expense 1996	Drs.thous	522.654
b. Accrued expenses (Plants, Distribution Centres and Headoffices)	»	721.550
	Drs.thous	1.244.204

11. Memo Accounts

Memo accounts are analysed as follows:

a. Third parties' assets	Drs.thous	1.342
b. Debit accounts for guarantees and securities	»	11.101.787
c. Other memo accounts	»	601.421
	Drs.thous	11.704.550

12. Turnover

Group turnover, after eliminating intercompany transactions, amounted to drs 111,683,023 thousand.

13. The average number of personnel employed by the Group, per employment category, and the Group's cost for the year for wages, salaries, social benefits and allowances are analysed as follows:

Staff remuneration and expenses (in drs.thous)

	Number of personnel	Salaries and employer's contribution	Wages and employer's contribution	Total
Employees	3.278	22.364.847	–	22.364.847
Workers	418	–	1.683.456	1.683.456
Total	3.696	22.364.847	1.683.456	24.048.303
Social benefits and allowances	–	1.491.720	55.202	1.546.922
Total	3.696	23.856.567	1.738.658	25.595.225

14. Management and Directors' emoluments are analysed as follows:

a. Directors' fees	Drs.thous	90.886
b. Remuneration of members of the Board of Directors for services rendered under special service contracts	»	69.933
Total	Drs.thous	160.819

There are no liabilities or commitments for allowances or other benefits to retired members of the Board or Management.

15. «**Extraordinary and non-operating Expenses**», «**Prior Years' Expenses**», «**Extraordinary and non-operating Income**» and «**Prior years' Income** » are analysed as follows:

15.1. Extraordinary and Non-Operating Expenses   Drs.thous

a. Exchange differences	865.848
b. Staff termination indemnities	158.927
c. Loss on Disposal of «Tsimentoklis» vessel	64.845
d. Tax on revaluation surplus	383.032
e. Other expenses	311.855
Total	1.784.507

15.2. Extraordinary and Non-Operating Income   Drs.thous

a. Exchange differences	109.569
b. Profit on disposal of fixed assets	119.723
c. Grants	30.590
d. Sales of raw materials	11.737
e. Various income from vessels	108.519
f. Other income	368.410
Total	748.548

15.3. Prior Years' Expenses   Drs.thous

a. Prior Years' Staff Termination Indemnities	163.753
b. Prior years' taxes and duties	1.391
c. Leases for quarries	17.143
d. Expenses for Quality Certifications	16.042
e. Other prior years' expenses	386.145
Total	584.474

15.4. Prior Years' Income   Drs.thous

a. Recovery of bad debts	50.822
b. Insurance premia refunds	94.082
c. Various subsidies	92.100
d. Other prior years' income	192.029
Total	429.033

16. Other Information

16.1.   The Group valuation methods in 1996 were consistent to those of the previous year.

16.2.   No calculations for Inflation Accounting were made by the Group since no such legal requirement exists.

16.3.   Group turnover and cost of sales have been reduced by the value of inter - company sales during the year. Inventories from inter- company transactions as well as fixed assets purchased or constructed by Group companies have been valued at cost to the Group.

16.4.   Inter - company dividends received have been eliminated.

16.5.   Other Group profit and loss accounts resulted from the consolidation of the respective accounts of individual Group companies after eliminating inter-company transactions.

16.6.   Group net income is stated on an after-tax basis. Tax charge comprises the consolidation of income tax charges of individual Group Companies.

16.7.   Group net income is stated before any appropriation of profits of individual Group Companies which has been reflected to the «Profit Carried Forward» and to the «Minority Interests» (Reserves and Profit and Loss Statement) accounts. Dividends payable to third parties have been accounted for as Group liabilities (account C/II/10).

17. The EU Commission is re-examining the capitalisation of debts of HERACLES General Cement Co in 1986 following the rescindment of the previous approval.

In theory it is possible that the EU Commission may rule that the above mentioned capitalisation was contrary to E.U. legislation either in part or in full. However the Company believes that there are adequate defences based on sound legal and substantial reasons which the Commission shall have to take into account in order to support its decision which will lead to a new approval of capitalisation.

18. Group has filed a lawsuit against the Industry Reconstruction Organisation (IRO, in Greek OAE) claiming the amount of drs 560.814.572 million, in respect of taxes paid to the State, which, according to Art.49 of Law 1892/90, as revised by Art. 2 para.9 of Law 2302/95, should be borne by OAE (IRO).

Lycovrissi, 4th April 1997

THE CHAIRMAN OF THE BOARD
OF DIRECTORS

THE MANAGING DIRECTOR

MASSIMO GIUDICI
22399089/92

UGO ALESSI
33662398/93

THE GROUP
GENERAL FINANCIAL DIRECTOR

THE CHIEF ACCOUNTANT

SOTIRIS I. PAPASPILIOTOPOULOS
R. 149102/93

IOANNIS A. KAPNOPOULOS
L.214432/81

It is certified that the above Notes to the Accounts consist of 10 pages and refer to our audit report of 8th April 1997.

Athens, 8th April 1997

THE CERTIFIED PUBLIC ACCOUNTANT

JOHN N. LAMBROU
K 227220/77

ΑΝΩΝΥΜΟΣ ΓΕΝΙΚΗ ΕΤΑΙΡΙΑ ΤΣΙΜΕΝΤΩΝ ΗΡΑΚΛΗΣ
ΑΡ. ΜΗΤΡ. Α.Ε. : 13576/06/B/86/096

ΓΕΝΙΚΟΣ ΙΣΟΛΟΓΙΣΜΟΣ ΤΗΣ 31ης ΔΕΚΕΜΒΡΙΟΥ 1996
86η ΕΤΑΙΡΙΚΗ ΧΡΗΣΗ (1 ΙΑΝΟΥΑΡΙΟΥ - 31 ΔΕΚΕΜΒΡΙΟΥ 1996) (ΣΕ ΧΙΛ. ΔΡΧ.)

ΕΝΕΡΓΗΤΙΚΟ

	ΧΡΗΣΕΩΣ 1996			ΧΡΗΣΕΩΣ 1995		
	ΑΞΙΑ ΚΤΗΣΕΩΣ	ΑΠΟΣΒΕΣΕΙΣ	ΑΝΑΠΟΣΒΕΣΤΗ ΑΞΙΑ	ΑΞΙΑ ΚΤΗΣΕΩΣ	ΑΠΟΣΒΕΣΕΙΣ	ΑΝΑΠΟΣΒΕΣΤΗ ΑΞΙΑ
Β. ΕΞΟΔΑ ΕΓΚΑΤΑΣΤΑΣΗΣ						
1. Εξοδα ιδρυσης & πρώτης εγκατ/σης	13.499	2.700	10.799	21.943	21.943	-
3. Λοιπά έξοδα πολυετούς απόσβεσης	128.421	92.799	35.622	145.208	103.773	41.435
ΣΥΝΟΛΟ ΕΞΟΔΩΝ ΕΓΚΑΤ/ΣΗΣ (Β)	141.920	95.499	46.421	167.151	125.716	41.435
Γ. ΠΑΓΙΟ ΕΝΕΡΓΗΤΙΚΟ						
I. Ασώματες ακινητοποιήσεις						
1. Εξοδα ερευνών & ανάπτυξης	42.497	40.054	2.443	101.144	90.975	10.169
II. Ενσώματες ακινητοποιήσεις						
1. Γήπεδα-Οικόπεδα	11.587.326	-	11.587.326	7.724.838	-	7.724.838
2. Ορυχεία-μεταλλεία. λατομεία κτλ.	10.523.614	865.202	9.658.412	8.843.907	565.129	8.278.778
3 Κτίρια & τεχνικά έργα	39.375.399	34.552.841	4.822.558	30.680.084	26.096.853	4.583.231
4 Μηχανήματα-τεχν.εγκατ.& λοιπ.μηχ.εξοπλ.	28.823.787	20.055.506	8.768.281	27.331.381	18.322.593	9.008.788
5 Μεταφορικά μέσα	3.049.572	805.090	2.244.482	3.031.943	690.982	2.340.961
6. Επιπλα & λοιπός εξοπλισμός	772.065	425.518	346.547	571.871	326.008	245.863
7. Ακινητ/σεις υπο εκτέλ. & προκ/λές	2.941.446	-	2.941.446	947.589	-	947.589
	97.073.209	56.704.157	40.369.052	79.131.613	46.001.565	33.130.048
ΣΥΝΟΛΟ ΑΚΙΝΗΤ/ΣΕΩΝ (ΓΙ+ΓΙΙ)	97.115.706	56.744.211	40.371.495	79.232.757	46.092.540	33.140.217
III. Συμμετοχές & άλλες μακροπρόθεσμες χρηματοοικονομικές απαιτήσεις						
1. Συμμετοχές σε συνδεμένες επιχειρήσεις			27.212.150			6.896.316
2. Συμμετοχές σε λοιπές επιχειρήσεις			42.169			42.169
7. Λοιπές μακροπρόθεσμες απαιτήσεις			602.352			617.107
			27.856.671			7.555.592
ΣΥΝΟΛΟ ΠΑΓΙΟΥ ΕΝΕΡΓΗΤΙΚΟΥ (Γ)			68.228.166			40.695.809
Δ. ΚΥΚΛΟΦΟΡΟΥΝ ΕΝΕΡΓΗΤΙΚΟ						
I. Αποθέματα						
1. Εμπορεύματα		80.121			119.079	
2. Προϊόντα έτοιμα & ημιτελή		2.230.450			1.995.144	
4. Πρώτες & βοηθ. ύλες - Αναλώσιμα υλικά -ανταλλ/κά. υλικά συσκευασίας		8.073.374			6.679.766	
5. Προκαταβολές για αγορές αποθεμάτων		173.777	10.557.722		245.804	9.039.793
II. Απαιτήσεις						
1. Πελάτες		11.911.808			10.281.623	
2. Γραμμάτια Εισπρακτέα						
- Χαρτοφυλακίου	118.052			76.454		
- Στις τράπεζες για είσπραξη	446.082	564.134		779.144	855.598	
3. Γραμμάτια σε καθυστέρηση		483.741			349.372	
3α. Επιταγές εισπρακτέες		15.663.830			15.106.630	
5 Βραχυπρ.απαιτ.κατά συνδεμ.επιχειρήσεων		1.881.580			1.841.647	
10. Επισφαλείς-επίδικοι πελάτες & χρεώστες	2.515.961			4.490.680		
Μείον : Προβλέψεις	-	2.515.961		750.000	3.740.680	
11. Χρεώστες διάφοροι		5.232.796			4.460.441	
12. Λογ/σμοί διαχειρ. προκατ. & πιστώσεων		15.472	38.269.322		10.384	36.646.375
IV. Διαθέσιμα						
1. Ταμείο		28.423			44.257	
3. Καταθέσεις όψεως & προθεσμίας		1.489.391	1.517.814		408.741	452.998
ΣΥΝΟΛΟ ΚΥΚΛΟΦΟΡΟΥΝΤΟΣ ΕΝΕΡΓΗΤΙΚΟΥ (Δ)			50.344.858			46.139.166
Ε. ΜΕΤΑΒΑΤΙΚΟΙ Λ/ΣΜΟΙ ΕΝΕΡΓΗΤΙΚΟΥ						
1. Εξοδα επομένων χρήσεων		49.310			13.843	
3. Λοιποί μεταβ. Λ/σμοι ενεργητικού		62.152	111.462		38.660	52.503
ΓΕΝΙΚΟ ΣΥΝΟΛΟ ΕΝΕΡΓΗΤΙΚΟΥ (Β+Γ+Δ+Ε)			118.730.907			86.928.913
ΛΟΓΑΡΙΑΣΜΟΙ ΤΑΞΕΩΣ ΧΡΕΩΣΤΙΚΟΙ						
1. Αλλότρια περιουσιακά στοιχεία			1.325			1.344
2. Χρεωστ. Λ/σμοί εγγυήσεων και εμπράγματων ασφαλειών			7.171.067			8.498.718
4. Λοιποί λογαριασμοί τάξεως			227.155			423.887
			7.399.547			8.923.949

ΣΗΜΕΙΩΣΕΙΣ : 1. Με βάση τις διατάξεις του Ν.2065/1992 έγινε στη χρήση 1996 αναπροσαρμογή της αξίας κτήσεως των γηπέδων, των κτιρίων και των ουσσωμειωμένων αποσβέσεων των κτιρίων εξαιτίας της οποίας αυξήθηκε η αξία κτήσεως των γηπέδων και κτιρίων κατά δρχ. 13.836 εκατ. και η αξία των ουσσωμειωμένων αποσβέσεων των κτιρίων κατά δρχ. 7.198 εκατ. και προέκυψε διαφορά αναπροσαρμογής ποσού δρχ. 6.638 εκατ. που καταχωρήθηκε στο λογαριασμό των ιδίων κεφαλαίων Α ΙΙΙ-2 "Διαφορές από αναπροσαρμογή αξίας λοιπών περιουσιακών στοιχείων". Οι αποσβέσεις της χρήσεως 1996 υπολογίσθηκαν επι της νέας αναπροσαρμοσμένης αξίας και είναι με γαλύτερες από εκείνες που θα είχαν υπολογισθεί στην αξία πριν την αναπροσαρμογή κατά δρχ. 500 εκατ. περίπου. Η Εταιρία στη χρήση 1996 αγόρασε το 51% των μετοχών της Α.Ε. "ΤΣΙΜΕΝΤΑ ΧΑΛΚΙΔΟΣ" αντί του ποσού των δρχ. 20.316 εκατ. το οποίο (ποσό) εμφανίζεται στο λογαριασμό Γ.ΙΙΙ.1. "Συμμετοχές σε συνδεμένες επιχειρήσεις". 3. Η αποτίμηση των συμμετοχών σε συνδεδεμένες επιχειρήσεις έγινε στην αξία κτήσεως τους συμφωνα με τις διατάξεις του άρθρου 20 παρ.5 του Π.Δ. 186/1992 και του άρθρου 42α παραγρ.3 του κωδ. Ν.2190/1920 (βλέπε προσάρτημα) η οποία είναι μεγαλύτερη από την τρέχουσα κατά δρχ. 3.700 εκ. περίπου. 4. Μεταξύ των απαιτήσεων περιλαμβάνονται : α) Λοιπες απαιτήσεις ύψους δρχ. 2.650 εκατ. που βρίσκονται σε καθυστέρηση, εκ των οποίων ποσό δρχ. 1.390 εκατ. αφορά απαιτήσεις κατά συνδεμένων επιχειρήσεων σε "αριστική λογιστική καθαρή θέση. Το εν λόγω κονδύλι αντικρίζεται με τον λογαριασμό του Παθητικού του Ισολογισμού (Λ/σμος Β-2) "Λοιπές Προβλέψεις" κατά δρχ. 561 εκατ. β) "Επισφαλείς - επίδικοι πελάτες και χρεώστες" (ΔΙΙ-10) ύψους

HERACLES GENERAL CEMENT COMPANY S.A.
Reg. No.: 13576/06/B/86/096
BALANCE SHEET AS AT DECEMBER 31, 1996 (86TH)
(AMOUNTS IN DRS. THOUS.)

ASSETS

	1996 COST	1996 ACCUMULATED DEPRECIATION	1996 NET BOOK VALUE	1995 COST	1995 ACCUMULATED DEPRECIATION	1995 NET BOOK VALUE
B. ESTABLISHMENT EXPENSES						
1 Preliminary expenses	13.499	2.700	10.799	21.943	21.943	-
3 Other deferrred expenses	128.421	92.799	35.622	145.208	103.773	41.435
TOTAL ESTABLISHMENT EXPENSES (B)	141.920	95.499	46.421	167.151	125.716	41.435
C. FIXED ASSETS						
I. Intangible assets						
1. Research & develop. costs	42.497	40.054	2.443	101.144	90.975	10.169
II. Tangible assets						
1. Land	11.587.326	-	11.587.326	7.724.838	-	7.724.838
2. Mines, quarries etc.	10.523.614	865.202	9.658.412	8.843.907	565.129	8.278.778
3 Buildings & tech. works	39.375.399	34.552.841	4.822.558	30.680.084	26.096.853	4.583.231
4 Machinery, tech. instal. & other equip.	28.823.787	20.055.506	8.768.281	27.331.381	18.322.593	9.008.788
5 Transportation equipment	3.049.572	805.090	2.244.482	3.031.943	690.982	2.340.961
6. Furniture & other equip.	772.065	425.518	346.547	571.871	326.008	245.863
7. Payments on acc.and work in progress	2.941.446	-	2.941.446	947.589	-	947.589
	97.073.209	56.704.157	40.369.052	79.131.613	46.001.565	33.130.048
TOTAL TANGIBLE & INTANGIBLE ASSETS (CI+CI)	97.115.706	56.744.211	40.371.495	79.232.757	46.092.540	33.140.217
III Investments						
1. Participating interests in subsidiary undertakings			27.212.150			6.896.316
2. Participating interests in other undertakings			42.169			42.169
7. Other long - term receivables			602.352			617.107
			27.856.671			7.555.592
TOTAL FIXED ASSETS (C)			68.228.166			40.695.809
D. CURRENT ASSETS						
I. Inventories						
1. Merchandise		80.121			119.079	
2. Finished & semi - finished products		2.230.450			1.995.144	
4. Raw & auxiliary materials - consumables spare parts and packing materials		8.073.374			6.679.766	
5. Advances for stock purchases		173.777	10.557.722		245.804	9.039.793
II. Debtors						
1. Trade debtors		11.911.808			10.281.623	
2. Notes receivable						
- In portfolio	118.052			76.454		
- At banks for collection	446.082	564.134		779.144	855.598	
3. Notes overdue		483.741			349.372	
3a. Cheques receivable		15.663.830			15.106.630	
5 Amounts due by affiliated companies		1.881.580			1.841.647	
10. Overdue Debts	2.515.961			4.490.680		
Less : Provisions	-	2.515.961		750.000	3.740.680	
11. Sundry debtors		5.232.796			4.460.441	
12. Advances		15.472	38.269.322		10.384	36.646.375
IV. Cash at bank and in hand						
1. Cash		28.423			44.257	
3. Current and term deposits		1.489.391	1.517.814		408.741	452.998
TOTAL CURRENT ASSETS (D)			50.344.858			46.139.166
E. PREPAYMENTS AND ACCRUED INCOME						
1. Deferred charges		49.310			13.843	
3. Other prepayments and accrued income		62.152	111.462		38.660	52.503
GRAND TOTAL ASSETS (B+C+D+E)			118.730.907			86.928.913
MEMO ACCOUNTS						
1. Third parties' assets			1.325			1.344
2. Guarantees and other securities (debit balances)			7.171.067			8.498.718
4. Other memo accounts			227.155			423.887
			7.399.547			8.923.949

NOTES : 1. Land and buildings were revalued in 1996 in accordance with L.2065/1992 provisions. As a result the cost of land and buildings revalued by drs 13,836 million while the respective accumulated depreciation by drs 7,198.The revaluation surplus, amounting to drs 6,638 million was posted to the "Other fixed assets' Revaluation Reserve" account. Depreciation charge for the year was calculated on the revalued amounts and is higher than the respective charge before revaluation, by approximately drs 500 million. 2. The Company, in 1996, acquired 51% of "Chalkis Cement SA" at drs 20,316 million. This investment is included in the account C.III.1 "Participating interests in subsidiary undertakings 3. Participations in subsidiary and other undertakings were valued at cost, in accordance with the provisions of Art 28, para. 5 of Presidential Decree 186/1992 and Art. 42a, para.3 of L.2190/1920 (See also the Notes to the Accounts). The acquisition "cost is higher than the current value of the investments by drs 3,700 million. 4. Included in receivables are the following : a) Other overdue receivables amounting to drs 2,650 million,out of which drs 1,390 million concern receivables from affiliated companies having a negative equity. A provision has been made for these debts "amounting to drs 561 million and included in account B-2 "Other provisions" b) Doubtful trade receivables and overdue trade receivables at

ΠΑΘΗΤΙΚΟ

		ΧΡΗΣΕΩΣ 1996		ΧΡΗΣΕΩΣ 1995
Α. ΙΔΙΑ ΚΕΦΑΛΑΙΑ				
I. Κεφάλαιο Μετοχικό				
(50.490.957 μετοχές των 808 δρχ.)				
1. Καταβλημένο		40.796.693		40.796.693
II. Διαφορά από έκδοση μετοχών υπέρ το άρτιο		401.642		401.642
III. Διαφορές αναπροσαρμογής-Επιχορηγήσεις επενδύσεων				
1. Διαφορές από αναπροσαρμογή αξίας συμμετ.& χρεογράφων	556.170		556.167	
2. Διαφορές από αναπροσ. αξίας λοιπών περιουσ. στοιχείων	6.654.174	7.210.344	16.520	572.687
IV. Αποθεματικά κεφάλαια				
1. Τακτικό αποθεματικό	2.276.010		1.881.262	
2. Εκτακτο αποθεματικό	5.397.386		5.679.386	
3. Ειδ.φορ.αποθ.Ν.1892/90 άρθρ.23α	1.133.000		-	
5. Αφορολόγητα αποθεματικά ειδικών διατάξεων νόμων	13.073.820	21.880.216	11.765.928	19.326.576
ΣΥΝΟΛΟ ΙΔΙΩΝ ΚΕΦΑΛΑΙΩΝ (Α)		70.288.895		61.097.598
B. ΠΡΟΒΛΕΨΕΙΣ ΓΙΑ ΚΙΝΔΥΝΟΥΣ & ΕΞΟΔΑ				
1. Προβλέψεις για αποζημ. προσωπ. λόγω εξόδου από την υπηρεσία	2.646.727		1.812.869	
2. Λοιπές προβλέψεις	560.594	3.207.321	490.441	2.303.310
Γ. ΥΠΟΧΡΕΩΣΕΙΣ				
I. Μακροπρόθεσμες υποχρεώσεις				
2. Δάνεια τραπεζών	18.058.400			
8. Λοιπές μακροπροθ. υποχρεώσεις	184.141	18.242.541		
II. Βραχυπρόθεσμες υποχρεώσεις				
1. Προμηθευτές	3.026.123		2.698.971	
2. Γραμμάτια πληρωτέα	621.993		325.035	
3. Τράπεζες λ/βραχυπροθεσ. υποχρ.	7.071.685		9.524.251	
5. Υποχρεώσεις από φόρους-τέλη	4.901.252		2.942.035	
6. Ασφαλιστικοί Οργανισμοί	788.453		838.016	
7. Μακροπρόθεσμες υποχρεώσεις πληρωτέες στην επόμ. χρήση	2.257.627		729.658	
8. Υποχρ. προς συνδεμ. επιχειρήσεις	690.431		85.999	
10. Μερίσματα πληρωτέα	5.153.422		4.166.810	
11. Πιστωτές διάφοροι	1.842.007	26.352.993	1.944.260	23.255.035
ΣΥΝΟΛΟ ΥΠΟΧΡΕΩΣΕΩΝ (Γ)		44.595.534		23.255.035

Δ. ΜΕΤΑΒΑΤΙΚΟΙ ΛΟΓ/ΣΜΟΙ ΠΑΘΗΤΙΚΟΥ				
2. Εξοδα χρήσεως δουλευμένα		639.157		272.970
ΓΕΝΙΚΟ ΣΥΝΟΛΟ ΠΑΘΗΤΙΚΟΥ (Α+Β+Γ+Δ)		118.730.907		86.928.913
ΛΟΓΑΡΙΑΣΜΟΙ ΤΑΞΕΩΣ ΠΙΣΤΩΤΙΚΟΙ				
1. Δικαιούχοι αλλότρ. περιουσ. στοιχείων		1.325		1.344
2. Πιστωτ. λ/σμοί εγγυήσεων & εμπράγματων ασφαλειών		7.171.067		8.498.718
4. Λοιποί λογαριασμοί τάξεως		227.155		423.887
		7.399.547		8.923.949

δρχ. 2.516 εκατ. Η Εταιρία για κάλυψη εκτάκτων κινδύνων και απρόβλεπτων εξόδων έχει σχηματίσει Έκτακτο Αποθεματικό (Α/IV-2) ύψους δρχ. 5.397 εκατ. Σημειώνεται ότι η Εταιρία για κάλυψη των κινδύνων από επισφάλειες διενήργησε πρόσθετη πρόβλεψη στα αποτελέσματά της, εκείνης που προβλέπει το άρθρο 10 παράγρ. 12 του Ν.2065/92 ύψους δρχ. 1.000 εκατ. ενώ κα κατά την προηγούμενη χρήση το αντίστοιχο ποσό ήταν 750 εκατ. δρχ. νj στο λογαριασμό "Χρεώστες Διάφοροι" (Δ/II-11) περιλαμβάνεται και κονδύλι δρχ.2.144 εκατ. περίπου το οποίο αφορά σε καταβολή επιβληθέντων από την Τράπεζα της Ελλάδος ποινικών ρητρών λόγω παραβάσεων συναλλαγματικών κανόνων τις ετών 1981-1991. Η Εταιρία έχει προσφύγει κατά των αποφάσεων της Τραπέζης της Ελλάδος ενώπιον των αρμοδίων δικαστηρίων και έχει βάσιμες ελπίδες ότι τελικά θα δικαιωθεί.5. Η "πρόβλεψη αποζημιώσεως προσωπικού λόγω εξόδου από την υπηρεσία" (Β.I) έγινε σύμφωνα με τις διατάξεις του άρθρου 10 παρ. 13 του Ν.2065/92 και την 205/1988 γνωμοδότηση της Ολομέλειας των Νομικών Συμβούλων Διοικήσεως με συνέπεια να επιβαρυνθούν τα αποτελέσματα της χρήσεως με δρχ. 47 εκ. Επί πλέον η Εταιρία σχημάτισε έκτακτη πρόβλεψη αποζημιώσεως προσωπικού ύψους δρχ. 1.000 εκατ. με την οποία επιβάρυνε τα αποτελέσματα της χρήσεως (Β.I. Προσαρτημα). 6. Η Ευρωπαϊκή Επιτροπή με την από 30.11.1994 απόφαση επέβαλε στην Εταιρία πρόστιμο ύψους 5.748.000 ECU θεωρώντας ότι υπήρξε παράβαση του άρθρου 85 της Συνθήκης της Ε.Ο.Κ. Κατά της αποφάσεως της Επιτροπής έχει γίνει προσφυγή στο Πρωτοδικείο του δικαστηρίου της Κοινότητος με τη βάσιμη προσδοκία ότι η Εταιρία θα δικαιωθεί και ως εκ τούτου δεν σχημάτισε σχετική πρόβλεψη στον ισολογισμό.

LIABILITIES

	1996		1995

A. SHAREHOLDERS' EQUITY
I. Share capital
(50.490.957 shares at par value of Drs. 808)
  1. Paid-up — **40.796.693** — 40.796.693

II. Share premium — **401.642** — 401.642

III. Revaluation reserves - Investment grants
  1. Investments' revaluation reserve — **556.170** — 556.167
  2. Other fixed assets' revaluation reserve — **6.654.174** **7.210.344** — 16.520 — 572.687

IV. Other Reserves
  1. Legal reserve — **2.276.010** — 1.881.262
  2. Extraordinary reserve — **5.397.386** — 5.679.386
  3. Special res. of L. 1892, Art. 23a — **1.133.000** — -
  5. Tax-free reserves under special laws — **13.073.820** **21.880.216** — 11.765.928 — 19.326.576
TOTAL SHAREHOLDERS' EQUITY (A) — **70.288.895** — 61.097.598

B. PROVISIONS
  1. Provisions for staff termination indemnities — **2.646.727** — 1.812.869
  2. Other provisions — **560.594** **3.207.321** — 490.441 — 2.303.310

C. CREDITORS
I. Long-term debts
  2. Bank loans — **18.058.400** —
  8. Other long - term liabilities — **184.141** **18.242.541** —

II. Current liabilities
  1. Suppliers — **3.026.123** — 2.698.971
  2. Notes payable — **621.993** — 325.035
  3. Bank overdrafts — **7.071.685** — 9.524.251
  5. Taxes & duties — **4.901.252** — 2.942.035
  6. Social Security — **788.453** — 838.016
  7. Long-term debt falling due within next year — **2.257.627** — 729.658
  8. Payables to affiliated companies — **690.431** — 85.999
  10. Dividends payable — **5.153.422** — 4.166.810
  11. Sundry creditors — **1.842.007** **26.352.993** — 1.944.260 — 23.255.035
TOTAL CREDITORS (C) — **44.595.534** — 23.255.035

D. ACCRUALS AND DEFERRED INCOME
  2. Accrued expenses — **639.157** — 272.970

GRAND TOTAL LIABILITIES (A+B+C+D) — **118.730.907** — 86.928.913
MEMO ACCOUNTS
  1. Beneficiaries of third parties' assets — **1.325** — 1.344
  2. Guarantees & other securities (credit balances) — **7.171.067** — 8.498.718
  4. Other memo accounts — **227.155** — 423.887
   — **7.399.547** — 8.923.949

Court amounting to Drs 2.516 million (Account D/II-10). The Company provided for an "Extraordinary Reserve" (A/IV-2) amounted to Drs 5,397 million, for special risks and unforecasted expenditures. The Company, besides provision for doubtful debts,in accordance with L.2065/92, provided for an additional amount of drs 1,000 million (the respective amount for 1995 was Drs 750 million). c) "Sundry Debtors" (D/II-11) include penalties imposed by Bank of Greece and amounting to Drs 2,144 million, concerning violations of foreign exchange regulation for the years 1981-1991. The Company has filed lawsuits against Bank of Greece resolutions and there is reasonable expectation for its vindication. 5. In accordance with Law 2065/92 and opinion No205/1988 of the Legal Advisory Board, the Company provided drs 47 million for staff termination indemnities.Furthermore the Company provided for an extra amount of Drs 1.000 million the same purpose. 6. With its resolution of 30-11-94, the EU Commission has imposed the Company a fine amounting to ECU 5,748,000 for violating Art 85 of EU Pact. The Company has filed an appeal to the EU Court. Based on sound expectation for its vindication, the Company has not made a relevant provision.

ΚΑΤΑΣΤΑΣΗ ΛΟΓΑΡΙΑΣΜΟΥ ΑΠΟΤΕΛΕΣΜΑΤΩΝ ΧΡΗΣΕΩΣ
31ης ΔΕΚΕΜΒΡΙΟΥ 1996 (1 ΙΑΝΟΥΑΡΙΟΥ - 31 ΔΕΚΕΜΒΡΙΟΥ 1996)
(ΣΕ ΧΙΛ. ΔΡΧ.)

	ΠΟΣΑ ΚΛΕΙΟΜΕΝΗΣ ΧΡΗΣΕΩΣ 1996		ΠΟΣΑ ΠΡΟΗΓΟΥΜΕΝΗΣ ΧΡΗΣΕΩΣ 1995	
I. Αποτελέσματα εκμεταλλεύσεως				
Κύκλος εργασιών (πωλήσεις)		92.885.581		83.971.244
ΜΕΙΟΝ : Κόστος πωλήσεων		70.930.470		66.399.421
Μικτά αποτελέσματα εκμετάλλευσης		21.955.111		17.571.823
ΠΛΕΟΝ: Αλλα έσοδα εκμετάλλευσης		96.045		91.486
ΣΥΝΟΛΟ		22.051.156		17.663.309
ΜΕΙΟΝ: Έξοδα διοικ. λειτουργίας	4.408.686		4.137.037	
Έξοδα λειτουργίας διάθεσης	899.859	5.308.545	839.132	4.976.169
Μερικά αποτελέσματα εκμετάλλευσης		16.742.611		12.687.140
ΜΕΙΟΝ: Χρεωστ. τόκοι & συναφή έξοδα		2.331.582		2.164.765
ΜΕΙΟΝ: Εσοδα συμμετοχών	906.697		550.238	
Πιστωτικοί τόκοι	122.206	1.028.903	72.859	623.097
Ολικά αποτελέσματα εκμετάλλευσης (κέρδη)		1.302.679		1.541.668
ΜΕΙΟΝ: Εκτακτα αποτελέσματα		15.439.932		11.145.472
Εκτακτα & ανόργανα έξοδα	1.178.254		863.012	
Εξοδα προηγούμενων χρήσεων	304.903		257.161	
Προβλέψεις για έκτακτ.κινδύνους	2.445.638	3.928.795	1.159.885	2.280.058
ΜΕΙΟΝ: Εκτακτα & ανόργανα εσοδα	197.007		171.969	
Εσοδα προηγούμενων χρήσεων	294.083		141.647	
Εσοδα απο προβλέψεις				
προηγούμενων χρήσεων	143.864	634.954	88.894	402.510
Οργανικά & έκτακτα αποτελέσματα (κέρδη)		3.293.841		1.877.548
		12.146.091		9.267.924
ΜΕΙΟΝ: Συνολικές αποσβέσεις		3.631.446		3.190.948
Μείον: Οι ενσωματωμένες στο				
λειτουργικό κόστος		3.631.446		3.190.948
ΚΑΘΑΡΑ ΑΠΟΤΕΛΕΣΜΑΤΑ (ΚΕΡΔΗ) ΧΡΗΣΕΩΣ προ φόρων		12.146.091		9.267.924

ΠΙΝΑΚΑΣ ΔΙΑΘΕΣΗΣ ΑΠΟΤΕΛΕΣΜΑΤΩΝ

	ΧΡΗΣΕΩΣ 1996	ΧΡΗΣΕΩΣ 1995
Καθαρά κέρδη χρήσεως	12.146.091	9.267.924
ΜΕΙΟΝ : Φόρος εισοδήματος	4.323.355	2.590.135
Κέρδη προς διάθεση	**7.822.736**	**6.677.789**

Η διάθεση κερδών γίνεται ως εξής:		
Τακτικό αποθεματικό	394.748	301.207
Μερίσματα	5.049.096	4.039.277
Διάθεση κερδών στο προσωπικό	220.000	200.000
Αφορολόγητη έκπτωση Νο. 1892/90	1.307.892	1.541.945
Αφορολόγητη έκπτωση Νο. 1828/89	-	595.360
Ειδικό φορολ. αποθεματικό		
Ν. 1892/90 άρθρ. 23α	851.000	-
	7.822.736	6.677.789

Η πληρωμή του ανωτέρω μερίσματος δρχ.100 (εκατό) κατά μετοχή, θα αρχίσει μετά την έγκριση του παρόντος Ισολογισμού από την Τακτική Γενική Συνέλευση των Μετόχων. και σε ημερομηνία που θα ορισθεί από το Διοικητικό Συμβούλιο.

Λυκόβρυση 4 Απριλίου 1997

Ο ΠΡΟΕΔΡΟΣ ΤΟΥ ΔΙΟΙΚΗΤΙΚΟΥ ΣΥΜΒΟΥΛΙΟΥ
MASSIMO GIUDICI
22399086/92

Ο ΔΙΕΥΘΥΝΩΝ ΣΥΜΒΟΥΛΟΣ
UGO ALESSI
33662398/93

Ο ΓΕΝΙΚΟΣ ΔΙΕΥΘΥΝΤΗΣ ΟΙΚΟΝΟΜΙΚΟΥ
ΣΩΤ. Ι. ΠΑΠΑΣΠΗΛΙΩΤΟΠΟΥΛΟΣ
P.149102/93

Ο ΠΡΟΪΣΤΑΜΕΝΟΣ ΤΟΥ ΛΟΓΙΣΤΗΡΙΟΥ
ΙΩΑΝΝΗΣ ΑΘ. ΚΑΠΙΝΟΠΟΥΛΟΣ
Λ.214432/81

PROFIT AND LOSS ACCOUNT
FOR THE YEAR ENDED DECEMBER 31, 1996
(AMOUNTS IN DRS. THOUS.)

		1996			1995	
Turnover			92.885.581			83.971.244
LESS : Cost of sales			70.930.470			66.399.421
Gross Margin			21.955.111			17.571.823
PLUS: Other operating income			96.045			91.486
TOTAL			22.051.156			17.663.309
LESS: Administrative expenses		4.408.686			4.137.037	
Selling & Distribution expenses		899.859	5.308.545		839.132	4.976.169
Operat. income before financial and investing activities			16.742.611			12.687.140
LESS: Interest expenses & financial charges		2.331.582			2.164.765	
LESS: Income from participations	906.697			550.238		
Interest income	122.206	1.028.903	1.302.679	72.859	623.097	1.541.668
Total operating income			15.439.932			11.145.472
LESS: Extraordinary & non-operating						
expenses	1.178.254			863.012		
Prior years' expenses	304.903			257.161		
Provisions	2.445.638	3.928.795		1.159.885	2.280.058	
LESS : Extraordinary & non-operating income	197.007			171.969		
Prior years' income	294.083			141.647		
Income from unrealised						
provisions	143.864	634.954	3.293.841	88.894	402.510	1.877.548
			12.146.091			9.267.924
LESS: Total depreciation		3.631.446			3.190.948	
Less: Depreciation charged to						
the operating cost		3.631.446	-		3.190.948	-
NET INCOME FOR THE YEAR BEFORE TAX			12.146.091			9.267.924

APPROPRIATIONS ACCOUNT

	1996	1995
Net income for the year	12.146.091	9.267.924
LESS : Income Tax	4.323.355	2.590.135
Profits for Appropriation	7.822.736	6.677.789
Appropriated to:		
Legal reserves	394.748	301.207
Dividends	5.049.096	4.039.277
Appropriation to personnel	220.000	200.000
Tax free reserves of L. 1892/90	1.307.892	1.541.945
Tax free reserves of L. 1828/89	-	595.360
Special res. of L. 1892, Art. 23a	851.000	
	7.822.736	6.677.789

The payment of the above dividend of drs 100 (hundred) per share shall commence after approval of the Financial Statements at the Annual General Meeting of Shareholders, at a date to be fixed by the Board of Directors.

Lycovrissi 4th April 1997

CHAIRMAN OF THE BOARD OF DIRECTORS
MASSIMO GIUDICI
22399089/92

GENERAL FINANCIAL DIRECTOR
SOTIRIOS I. PAPASPILIOTOPOULOS
P.149102/93

MANAGING DIRECTOR
UGO ALESSI
33662398/93

CHIEF ACCOUNTANT
IOANNIS A. KAPNOPOULOS
L.214432/81

ΠΙΣΤΟΠΟΙΗΤΙΚΟ ΕΛΕΓΧΟΥ ΟΡΚΩΤΟΥ ΛΟΓΙΣΤΗ - ΕΛΕΓΚΤΗ

Προς τους κ.κ. Μετόχους της Ανώνυμης Γενικής Εταιρίας Τσιμέντων ΗΡΑΚΛΗΣ

Ελέγξαμε τις ανωτέρω Οικονομικές Καταστάσεις καθώς και το σχετικό Προσάρτημα της Ανώνυμης Γενικής Εταιρίας Τσιμέντων ΗΡΑΚΛΗΣ της εταιρικής χρήσεως που έληξε την 31η Δεκεμβρίου 1996. Ο έλεγχός μας, στα πλαίσια του οποίου λάβαμε και γνώση πλήρους λογιστικού απολογισμού των εργασιών των υποκαταστημάτων της Εταιρείας, έγινε σύμφωνα με τις διατάξεις του άρθρου 37 του κωδ. Ν.2190/1920 περί Ανωνύμων Εταιρειών και τις ελεγκτικές διαδικασίες που κρίναμε κατάλληλες, με βάση τις αρχές και κανόνες ελεγκτικής που ακολουθεί το Σώμα Ορκωτών Ελεγκτών. Τέθηκαν στη διάθεσή μας τα βιβλία και στοιχεία που τήρησε η Εταιρία και μας δόθηκαν οι αναγκαίες για τον έλεγχο πληροφορίες και επεξηγήσεις που ζητήσαμε. Η Εταιρία εφάρμοσε ορθά το Γενικό Λογιστικό Σχέδιο.

Το κόστος παραγωγής που προκύπτει από τα λογιστικά βιβλία προσδιορίσθηκε σύμφωνα με τις παραδεγμένες αρχές λογισμού του κόστους και δεν τροποποιήθηκε η μέθοδος απογραφής σε σχέση με την προηγούμενη χρήση. Επαληθεύσαμε τη συμφωνία του περιεχομένου της Εκθέσεως Διαχειρίσεως του Διοικητικού Συμβουλίου προς την Τακτική Γενική Συνέλευση των μετόχων με τις σχετικές Οικονομικές Καταστάσεις. Το Προσάρτημα περιλαμβάνει τις πληροφορίες που προβλέπονται από την παράγραφο 1 του άρθρου 43α του κωδ. Ν.2190/1920.

Κατά τη γνώμη μας οι ανωτέρω Οικονομικές Καταστάσεις προκύπτουν από τα βιβλία και στοιχεία της Εταιρίας και, απεικονίζουν μαζί με το προσάρτημα, αφού ληφθούν υπόψη οι παραπάνω σημειώσεις της Εταιρίας, την περιουσιακή διάρθρωση και την οικονομική θέση της Εταιρίας κατά την 31η Δεκεμβρίου 1996, καθώς και τα αποτελέσματα της χρήσεως που έληξε αυτή την ημερομηνία, βάσει των σχετικών διατάξεων που ισχύουν και λογιστικών αρχών, οι οποίες έχουν γίνει γενικά παραδεκτές και δεν διαφέρουν από εκείνες που η Εταιρία εφάρμοσε στην προηγούμενη χρήση.

Αθήνα. 8 Απριλίου 1997

Ο ΟΡΚΩΤΟΣ ΛΟΓΙΣΤΗΣ - ΕΛΕΓΚΤΗΣ
ΙΩΑΝΝΗΣ Ν. ΛΑΜΠΡΟΥ
Κ. 227220/77
Σ.Ο.Λ. α.ε.ο.ε.

CERTIFIED AUDITOR'S REPORT

To the shareholders of HERACLES General Cement Co Societe Anonyme

We have audited the accompanying financial statements and related Notes thereto of the Societe Anonyme HERACLES General Cement Co for the year ended 31 December 1996. Our audit was performed in accordance with the provisions of article 37 of L.2190/1920 for societe anonymes and the auditing procedures which we considered necessary based on the principles followed by the Institute of Certified Auditors in Greece.

The Company made available to us all its books and records and provided all the necessary information and other explanations that we requested. The Company has complied with the provisions of the Greek Chart of Accounts. There has been no change in the accounting policies followed in the previous year and the cost of production has been determined in accordance with generally accepted costing standards. We agreed the contents of the Directors's Report to the General Assembly of the shareholders with the underlying financial statements. The Notes to the Accounts include all the information required by paragraph 1 of article 43a of L. 2190/1920.

In our opinion the financial statements referred to above, derive from the books and records of the Company and together with the Notes to the Accounts present fairly, except for the notes made above by the Company, the financial structure and position of the Company at 31 December 1996 and the results of its operation for the year then ended, in accordance with the prevailing legislation and the accounting principles which are generally accepted and are consistent with those applied in the previous year.

Athens, 8th April 1997

THE CERTIFIED AUDITOR

IOANNIS N. LAMBROU
K 227220/77

Notes to the Accounts for the year ended 31st December 1996

The following notes to the Balance Sheet as at 31st December 1996 and the Profit and Loss Account for the year then ended, have been prepared in accordance with the provisions of the Greek Companies Act, Law 2190/1920 and the Company's accounting policies.

1.   Intangible Fixed Assets (Companies Act art. 42e para. 8 and art. 43 para. 3a,3c,3e,4a and 4b Law 2190/1920).

Analysis of movement made in the year in drs million :

Category	Cost 31.12.95	Deletions of fully amort. items	Additions in 1996	Cost 31.12.96	Accumulated amortisation 31.12.95	Deletions of fully amort. items	Amortisation for 1996	Accumulated amortisation 31.12.96	Net book value 31.12.96
Preliminary expenses	22	(22)	13	13	(22)	22	(3)	(3)	10
Other establishment expenses	145	(37)	21	129	(104)	37	(26)	(93)	36
Sub total	167	(59)	34	142	(126)	59	(29)	(96)	46
Research & development	101	(59)	–	42	(91)	59	(8)	(40)	2
GRAND TOTAL	268	(118)	34	184	(217)	118	(37)	(136)	48

2.   Tangible Fixed Assets (Companies Act art. 42e par 8, art. 43 para. 5d, 5e, 9 and art 43a para. 1a Law 2190/1920).

2.1.   Analysis of movement made in the year in drs million :

	Cost 31.12.95	Changes			Cost 31.12.96	Accumulated depreciation 31.12.95	Charge for the year	Changes		Accumulated depreciation 31.12.96	Net book value 31.12.96
		Additions	Revaluation	Disposals				Revaluation	Disposals		
Land	7.725	115	3.747	–	11.587	–	–	–	–	–	11.587
Mines - Quarries	8.844	3	1.676	–	10.523	565	300	–	–	865	9.658
Buildings - Tech.works	30.680	284	8.412	–	39.376	26.097	1.258	7.198	–	34.553	4.823
Machinery	27.331	1.556	–	(63)	28.824	18.323	1.796	–	(63)	20.056	8.768
Transportation equip.	3.032	48	–	(30)	3.050	691	141	–	(27)	805	2.245
Furniture etc.	572	202	–	(2)	772	326	100	–	(1)	425	347
Under construction	948	3.979	–	(1.986)	2.941	–	–	–	–	–	2.941
TOTAL	79.132	6.187	13.835	(2.081)	97.073	46.002	3.595	7.198	(91)	56.704	40.369

2.2.   Tangible fixed assets are stated at cost (historical cost), as adjusted by subsequent statutory revaluations, plus additions and improvements, less disposals and depreciation. Depreciation has been calculated in accordance with the provisions of Presidential Decree 88/73.

No provision for impairment in the value of tangible fixed assets has been made, as none is anticipated.

2.3.   In 1996 the Company's land and buildings were revalued according to Law 2065/1992 as described in Note 1 to the Balance Sheet.

3. **Participations (Companies Act Law 2190/1920, art. 43 para. 7c and art. 43a para. 1b).**

The Company's participations are analysed as follows:

Name		% Participation in the equity	Equity 31.12.1996 (drs. thous.)	Profit or loss for 1996 (drs. thous.)
CHALKIS CEMENT	Tower of Athens, Athens	51%	4.200.117	(5.009.039)
AIGIS S.A.	Lycovrissi, Attica	60%	1.577.278	400.213
HERACLES SHIPPING CO. S.A.	" "	99,99%	5.248.537	933.141
SKYRODEMA S.A.	Neohoroúda, Thessaloniki	34,81%	892.953	56.362
EMMY-BUILDING MATERIALS S.A.	Lycovrissi, Attica	85,71%	1.133.888	637.642
CARMOR HELLAS LTD.	31, N. Phalirou str. Ag. Ioannis, Rentis	40%	53.222	7.730
EVIESK S.A.	Lycovrissi, Attica	87%	981.930	130.413
HERACLES PACKAGING CO. S.A.	Lycovrissi, Attica	83,98%	512.714	80.209
HELLENIC CEMENT RESEARCH CENTER LTD.	" "	90%	22.057	75.995
HERMES COMPANIA NAVIERA S.A.	Panama	100%	747.214	(225.670)
ASTIR - LATO S.A.	11, Iras st. Galatsi	85,71%	1.656.614	(360.750)
Under liquidation :				
HERACLES INTERNATIONAL S.A.	Lycovrissi, Attica	90%	264.697	(16)
PORT SAID SILO INVESTMENT CO S.A.	Lycovrissi, Attica	99%	(333.249)	27.973
HERACLES MARITIME AGENCY LTD.	Lycovrissi, Attica	40%	687	(8.095)
ALEXANDRIA SILO INVEST. CO SA	Panama	100%	(865.952)	146.447
HERACLES INSURANCE ENTERPRISES LTD.	Lycovrissi, Attica	5%	(46.824)	(3.238)

Total results for 1996 represent net profits or losses before taxes for the year. The table of investments includes also companies in which the direct interest of the Company is less than 10% but are indirectly controlled through subsidiary companies.

With regard to Note 3 of the Balance Sheet, concerning the valuation of participations it should be noted that:

Included in affiliated companies is ASTIR - LATO SA which resulted from the merger of ASTIR SA and LATO SA during 1996. The cost of acquisition of this company exceeds its net worth by drs 1.000 million. However the current market value of the merged company is substantially different from its net book value (net worth) because of the high value of its fixed assets. Furthermore, as the ready - mix concrete industry is anticipated to stabilise, the profitability of the company is expected to improve significantly in the future.

Therefore the valuation of the participation at the lower of cost and net equity pursuant to the provisions of article 43 para 6 of the Companies Act, L2190/20, would result in a misleading view of the financial position and results of operations of the company.

The fixed assets of CHALKIS CEMENT Co. SA and its subsidiaries have been valued by an independent and reputable firm of valuers at drs 39.724 million, compared to the net book value of drs 5.114 million and, consequently, the group's current net equity is increased by drs 34.666 million. Therefore the current net worth of these companies is substantially different from the book value of their equity.

Hence the difference between the cost of acquisition and the current net equity of the group is Drs 2.700 million.

D–ue to the reasons mentioned above, the Company stated its participations at cost which is in accordance with the provisions of art. 42a of L2190/1920.

4.   Inventories (Companies Act Law 2190/1920, art. 43 para. 7/a,7b, 7/c and art. 43a para. l/a, 1/i, 1/ia).

4.1. Valuation of inventories and cost of production.

Stocks of finished and semi-finished products have been valued at the lower of historical production cost and their net realizable value. Other stocks have been valued on an individual basis at the lower of cost and current value at the Balance Sheet date.

The production or acquisition cost (historical cost) of finished goods, materials, spare parts and bags has been computed using the monthly weighted average method.

Production cost includes the depreciation charge of fixed assets used in the production process. The depreciation rates used are those stipulated by P.D. 88/1973 (see paragraph 2.2 above).

4.2. The inventories' valuation method is consistent with that of the previous year.

4.3. The value of inventories in the Balance Sheet is in line with their market value at 31st December 1996.

5.   Receivables

5.1. No loans or advances have been made to members of the Board of Directors (Companies Act Law 2190/1920, art. 43a para. 1/id).

5.2. Receivables and payables denominated in foreign currencies have been trans-lated into drachmas at the official exchange rates ruling at the Balance Sheet date (Companies Act Law 2190/1920 art. 43a par l/a).

Exchange differences arising therefrom were recorded and monitored in separate accounts by currency. Thus accounting treatment complies with the provisions of para 8/b, Art 43 - Companies Act Law 2190/1920.

5.3. Criteria for the classification of receivables and liabilities as long-term (Companies Act Law 2190/1920 art. 42/e para. 6).

Receivables and liabilities falling due after one year from the Balance Sheet date are considered long-term.

6.   Prepayments and Accrued Income

These are analysed as follows (Companies Act Law 2190/1920 art.42e para. 12):

6.1. Prepaid expenses

a. Insurance premia	3.019
b. Repairs of «Persefs» vessel	41.720
c. Other expenses	4.571
Total	49.310

6.2. Analysis of «Other Prepayments»

a. Consignment duties	46.000
b. Goods in transit	2.884
c. Defective spare parts returned to the supplier for replacement	13.174
d. Other	94
Total	62.152

7. Capital and Reserves

7.1. a. There was no increase in share capital in 1996. (Companies Act Law 2190/1920, art. 43a. para. 1/c.)

7.2. The Company's share capital consists of 50.490.957 ordinary registered shares of par value of drs. 808 each (Companies Act Law 2190/1920 art. 42e par. 10 and art. 43a para 1/d, 1/e).

7.3. There was no redemption of Company's shares during the year (Companies Act Law 2190/1920 art. 43a para. 1/f)

7.4. The appropriation of the 1996 after tax profits to the legal reserves of drs. 394.748 thous. and the declaration of dividends of drs.5.049.096 thous. were made in accordance with the provisions of Law 2065/1992, as for 1995, hence the income tax was borne by the Company.

8. Provisions (Companies Act Law 2190/1920 art. 42e, para. 14 and art. 43a para. 1/a).

Provisions at the Balance Sheet date are analysed as follows:

8.1. Provision for Staff Termination Indemnities.

In accordance with Law 2065/92 and opinion No 205/1988 of the Legal Advisory Board, the Company provided drs 47 million for staff termination indemnities for those employees who will become eligible for retirement in 1997.

Had the Company made a provision for 40% of the indemnity payable in case of dismissal of its entire personnel at 31-12-1996, the provision would amount to drs 5.092 million as opposed to the amount of drs 2.647 million provided for as at 31-12-1996.

As a standard policy, the Company indemnifies in full (100%) all employees who retire. Had the Company made a provision for 100% of the staff termination indemnities for all personnel at 31-12-1996, the provision would amount to drs. 12.730 million as opposed to the amount of Drs 2.647 million actually provided for as at 31-12-1996.

The S.T.I. provision at the Balance Sheet date is analysed as follows:

	drs.thous.
— Accumulated provision for indemnities up to 31-12-91 for employees still employed on 31-12-96	1.599.764
— Provisions for compensation of personnel retiring in 1997	46.963
— Extra STI provision	1.000.000
Total	2.646.727

8.2. Other provisions:

	drs.thous
a. Deferred exchange gains arising from the translation of receivables and payables denominated in foreign currencies	987
b. Deferred exchange gains accumulated through 31-12-1996 on foreign currency translation of overdue claims	559.607
Total other provisions	560.594

8.3 Provision for doubtful debts

The Company made a provision for doubtful debts amounting to drs 1.446 million out of which drs. 446 million was calculated in accordance with Law 2065/1992 provisions. The respective provision for the previous year was drs 1.160 million out of which drs 410 million was calculated as per Law 2065/1992. The balance of the account «Provision for Doubtful Debts» at 31-12-1995 of drs 750 million together with that of the current year of drs. 1.446 million (totalling drs 2.196 million) were used to write-off equivalent amounts of doubtful debts.

9. Liabilities - Mortgages and Charges

9.1. There are no liabilities falling due after five years from the Balance Sheet date (Companies Act Law 2190/1920, art. 43a para. 1/f).

9.2. There are no secured liabilities other than those detailed in note 11.2 below. (Companies Act Law 2190/1920 art. 42e, para 14 and art. 43a para 1/f).

9.3. Amounts in respect of other securities or other guarantees provided by the Company in favour of affiliated companies and/or other third parties are analyzed below in note 11.2 (Companies Act Law 2190/1920, art. 42e para. 9).

9.4. Tax liabilities (Companies Act Law 2190/1920, art. 43a para. 1/ib).

The Company's books have been audited by the tax authorities through 1985. The audit of 1985 was completed in 1996. The tax assessment will be assumed by OAE, the Greek Reconstruction Organisation.

10. Accruals and Deferred Income

These are analysed as follows (Companies Act Law 2190/1920, art. 42e para. 12):   drs.thous.

Accrued expenses	
a. Provisions for accrued loan interest	497.575
b. Accrued expenses (Plants Distribution Terminals and Head Office)	141.582
Total	639.157

11. Memo Accounts

Memo accounts are analysed as follows (Companies Act Law 2190/1920, art. 42e para.9 and 11):

11.1. Third party assets	
a. Unclaimed share depository receipts	45.803
b. Company shares for delivery	16.780
c. Third parties raw materials	3.718
d. Dividends payable (year 1990) at the Savings and Loans Funds	1.258.000
Total	1.324.301

11.2. Guarantees and other securities:

No mortgages granted by the Company as security for its liabilities (see also note 9.2). The table below lists amounts of other guarantees granted in favour of or provided by the Company as security for (a) claims by the Company (b) Company liabilities and (c) liabilities of Affiliated companies. (Companies Act Law 2190/1920, art. 42e, para. 9):

		drs.thous	drs.thous
a.	Guarantees provided by third parties to secure claims of HERACLES General Cement Co		3.098.998
b.	Guarantees provided by third parties as security for HERACLES General Cement Co. liabilities		2.550.306
c.	Guarantees provided by HERACLES General Cement Co, to secure liabilities in favour of the following related companies :		
	SKYRODEMA S.A.	360.000	
	EMMI-BUILDING MATERIALS SA	490.000	
	EVIESK S.A.	329.746	
	HERACLES SHIPPING CO S.A.	1.000	
	LAVA S.A.	149.000	
	AMPER S.A.	142.017	
	HERACLES PACKAGING S.A.	50.000	1.521.763
	Total		7.171.067

11.3. Other Memo Accounts:

Various bilateral agreements   drs.thous   227.155

11.4. There are no commitments, guarantees or other contingent liabilities arising from agreements or legislation which do not appear in the above memo accounts. Similarly there are no liabilities arising from payment of special monthly allowances (i.e. monthly benefits) or commitments to affiliated enterprises (Companies Act Law 2190/1920, art. 43a para. 1/g).

12. Turnover (Sales)

Turnover is analysed as follows (Companies Act Law 2190/1920, art. 43a. para. 1/h):

Turnover in drs. Million

Category of activity	Domestic	Foreign	Total
a. Sales of products	53.806	27.760	81.566
b. Sales of other stocks	10.028	94	10.122
c. Provision of services	1.197	–	1.197
Total	65.031	27.854	92.885

Income from services rendered mainly represents management fees charged to Subsidiaries.

13. **The average number of staff employed by the Company per job category, and the Company's cost for the year, for salaries, wages, social benefits and allowances are analyzed as follows (Companies Act Law 2190/1920, art. 43a. para. 1i):**

Staff remuneration and expenses in drs. thous.

Job Category	Number of personnel	Salaries and employer's contribution	Wages and employer's contribution	Total
Employees	1.596	15.346.606	–	15.346.606
Workers	159	–	1.291.317	1.291.317
Total	1.755	15.346.606	1.291.317	16.637.923
Total Social benefits & allowances	–	–	–	272.296
Total	1.755	15.346.606	1.291.317	16.910.219

14. **Management and Director's emoluments are analyzed as follows (Companies Act Law 2190/1920, art. 43a para. 1/ic):**

	drs. thous.
a. Directors' fees	55.297
b. Remuneration of members of the Board of Directors for services rendered under service contracts.	65.550
Total	120.847

There are no liabilities or commitments for allowances or other benefits to retired members of the Board or Management

15. **"Extraordinary and Non-Operating Expenses", "Prior Years' Expenses", "Extraordinary and Non-Operating Income" "Prior Years' Income" and "Income from Prior Years' Unrealised Provisions" are analyzed as follows (Companies Act Law 2190/1920, art. 42e para. 15/b):**

15.1. Extraordinary and Non-Operating Expenses — drs. thous.

a. Exchange differences	731.228
b. Real estate expenses	9.007
c. Tax on revaluation of fixed assets as per L. 2065/92	368.281
d. Other expenses	69.738
Total	1.178.254

15.2. Extraordinary and Non-Operating Income   drs. thous.

a. Sales of fixed assets	95.183
b. Sales of raw materials	11.737
c. Other income	90.087
Total	197.007

15.3 Prior Years' Expenses   drs. thous.

a. Prior Years' Staff Termination Indemnities	149.556
b. Leases for quarries	15.179
c. Expenses for Quality Certifications	16.042
d. Other prior years' expenses	124.126
Total	304.903

15.4. Prior Years' Income   drs. thous.

a. Recovery of bad debts previously written off	50.822
b. Subsidies	81.031
c. Insurance premia refunds	68.937
d. Other	93.293
Total	294.083

15.5. Income from prior years' unrealised provisions:
Unrealised prior years' provision for
personnel indemnities in drs thousand   143.864

16. Other Information.

16.1. The disclosure of information under the following provisions of the Companies Act
Law 2190/1920 is not applicable:

a. Article 42a. Para 3 of L 2190/1920 (Departure from the provisions for the
preparation of financial statements which is considered necessary in order to
show a true and fair view as required by para. 2 of this Article).

b. Article 42b para 1 of L 2190/1920 (Departure from consistency concept)

c. Article 42b para 2 of L 2190/1920 (Assets or liabilities which are related to more
than one account compulsorily disclosed).

d. Article 42b para. 3 of L 2190/1920 (Adjustment of the structure and titles of
accounts required by the special nature of the business).

e. Article 42b para. 4 of L 2190/1920 (amalgamations of balance sheet accounts
which correspond to arabic numbers).

16.2.Some amounts in the profit and loss statements were re-classified in order to be comparable with the respective amounts of the previous year. These amounts were considered immaterial to be disclosed. (Art 42b para. 5 L.2190/1920).

16.3.No departure from accounting policies consistently followed concerning valuation methods as well as from the relevant legal provisions was made in 1996.

16.4.No calculations for Inflation Accounting made since no such legal requirement exists.

16.5.The Company, being a holding company, prepared for 1996 consolidated financial statements (Balance-Sheet and Profit and Loss Account) of Group companies.

16.6.Audit fees for the audit of the 1996 Financial Statements amounted to drs. 21.000.000

16.7.The EU Commission is re-examining capitalisation of debts of HERACLES General Cement Co in 1986 following the rescindment of the previous approval.

In theory it is possible, that the E.U. Commission may rule that the abovementioned capitalization was contrary to E.U. Legislation either in part or in full. However, the Company believes that there are adequate defences based on sound legal and substantial reasons which the Commision shall have to take into account in order to support its decision will lead to a new approval of the capitalization.

16.7.HERACLES General Cement Co. has filed a lawsuit against the Industry Reconstruction Organization (IRO, in Greek O.A.E) claiming the amount of Drs 418.202.157, in respect of taxes paid to the State which, according to Art. 49 of Law 1892/90 as revised by Art. 2 para. 9 of Law 2302/95, should be borne by O.A.E (IRO).

Lycovrissi, 4th April 1997

THE CHAIRMAN OF THE BOARD OF DIRECTORS	THE MANAGING DIRECTOR
MASSIMO GIUDICI	**UGO ALESSI**
22399089/92	33662398/93
THE GROUP GENERAL FINANCIAL DIRECTOR	THE CHIEF ACCOUNTANT
SOTIRIS I. PAPASPILIOTOPOULOS	**IOANNIS A. KAPNOPOULOS**
R. 149102/93	L.214432/81

It is certified that the above Notes to the Accounts consist of 13 pages and refer to our audit report of 8th April 1997.

Athens, 8th April 1997

THE CERTIFIED PUBLIC ACCOUNTANT
IOANNIS N. LAMBROY
K 227220/77

Country Highlights
ITALY

Common Legal Forms of Companies
- *società per azioni* (s.p.a.)—public limited company
- *società a responsabilità limitata* (s.r.l.)—private limited company
- *società in nome collettivo* (s.n.c.)—quasi-partnership

Sources of Financial Reporting Requirements
- Civil Code
- Statutory laws (e.g. legislative decree no. 127/1991)
- Consolidated Act on Income Taxes
- Italian accounting standards
- CONSOB deliberations

Corporate Taxation
- I.R.P.E.G. on income (dual income tax)
- I.R.A.P. on a value added figure

Auditing Requirements
- External audit
  - Listed companies
  - A few categories of companies (e.g. publishers, banks, newspapers, insurance companies)
- "Institutional" audit (*sindaci*)
  - All limited companies with a share capital exceeding 200 million lire

Organization of the Accounting and Auditing Professions
- *Dottori commercialisti*
- *Ragionieri*
- *Revisori contabili* ("Register")

Constitution and Legal System
- Civil law–based system

Currency
- Italian lira

Official Language
- Italian

Stefano Zambon
University of Padua

1. The Historical and Economic Background of Accounting in Italy

1.1 The Evolution of Accounting Theory: An Introduction

1.1.1 The Origins of Italian Accounting

The Italian tradition of accounting presents some distinctive, but also contradictory, features. In this respect, it is certainly true that accounting in this country has a long-lived tradition, starting from the late Middle Ages, if not from ancient Rome. It is also true, however, that it is not very well known outside Italy, and one could probably say that its Medieval period is by and large more renowned than its recent developments in both theory and practice. In a similar vein, even though Italy is commonly held as the country where the double-entry method of keeping books was first applied, accounting theorizing has been incorporated from the beginning of this century into a wider conceptual body, called *Economia Aziendale*, so that accounting studies in today's Italy are perceived as belonging academically to a much larger discipline, which is concerned with the economic profile of organizations.

It must be noted that the lack of attention in the international literature to the Italian tradition is, of course, linked to the language barrier, but also to subtle conceptual differences underlying terms and expressions that make Italian accounting theory exceedingly difficult to noninitiates. As extreme examples of this, consider that an appropriate translation in English of *Economia Aziendale* is virtually impossible (the same problem exists, though, with the Dutch *Bedrijfseconomie* and the German *Betriebswirtschaftslehre*), and that *accounting* is used here to translate the Italian word *ragioneria*, even if the former is perhaps wider in terms of concept and content.

Strictly speaking, it would not be fully correct to talk about Italian accounting until 1861, because Italy did not attain political unity until then, hitherto being divided into a number of independent city states (Florence and Tuscany, Milan and Lombardy, Venice, the Papal States, and so on). It is nevertheless reasonable to consider this geographic area from the Middle Ages onward as constituting a single nation having a cultural, linguistic, and artistic identity of its own, this being valid also for accounting.

The emergence and spread of the double-entry bookkeeping technique occurred in Italy between the 13th and 15th centuries. This method of keeping accounting records was first used, in fact, by Italian merchants (it is still not clear if for the first time in Florence, Genoa, or Venice) and for public accounting purposes (see the accounting registers of the Commune of Genoa dating from the first half of the 14th century). However, no books describing such a technique can be found until the end of the 15th century. Double entry was, in other words, a technique without systematically stated principles.

In 1494 a Franciscan friar named Luca Pacioli, a mathematician, pupil of Piero della Francesca and Leon Battista Alberti, and close friend of Leonardo da Vinci, published in Venice a book called *Summa de Arithmetica Geometria Proportioni et Proportionalita*, which contains a long section devoted to a description of the principles and functioning of double-entry bookkeeping. Although Luca Pacioli was not the inventor, he is considered the first systematizer and popularizer of this bookkeeping method, which he saw applied in Venice in a mercantile environment.

In fact, a quick and unclear reference to this method seems to have also been made by a 13th century mathematician named Leonardo Fibonacci in his work *Liber Abaci*. Another mathematician, Benedetto Cotrugli, is said to have written in 1458—before Pacioli's work— a short book on double-entry technique titled *Della mercatura e del mercante perfetto*. However, this book was published in Venice (by Giovanni Giuseppi di Ragusa) only in 1573, well after Pacioli's *Tractatus*, which thus appears to be the first comprehensive printed book on the subject matter.

Pacioli's description of double-entry bookkeeping spread through Italy and Europe as a result of several translations and elaborations of the *Tractatus*, which were made throughout the 16th century and, with some improvements and extensions, the 17th century.

In particular, from the beginning of 16th century, many works were published in Italy on the double-entry technique, but many Italian authors think that no substantial advances in the concept were achieved until around the 1840s. During this period of perceived theoretical decay, double entry could hence be labeled a method in search of conceptual foundations, and the writings thereon a literature without a theory.

1.1.2 Fabio Besta and the Nineteenth Century Theoretical Approaches

From about the first half of the 18th century, three main schools of thought developed in Italy in a partially overlapping sequence: the Lombard, the Tuscan, and the Venetian. The Venetian school of thought commonly includes Fabio Besta, originator of modern accounting in Italy, and Gino Zappa, founder of a new discipline into which accounting has been systematically included in Italy. From this point of view, Zappa could hardly be defined as an accounting scholar according to an Anglo-Saxon perspective, being the initiator and perhaps the main representative of the new disciplinary discourse of *Economia Aziendale*.

It is interesting to note that, in parallel to the development of the mentioned schools, the first Chairs of accounting in Italy (in particular, public accounting) were established in Pavia and Padua in 1839.

Some brief notes on the authors that characterized each of these schools of thought will be given in the following sections, while a somewhat more extensive—though by necessity incomplete—description of Besta's and Zappa's ideas will be provided later in consideration of their profound impact on Italian accounting theory and, to a large extent, practice.

The Lombard School   The beginning of the Lombard School is generally fixed by Italian accounting historians in 1838 with the publication of Lodovico Crippa's work "The Science of the Accounts" (*La Scienza dei conti*), where the author, for the first time in Italy, discussed the nature and the domain of accounting, stating that the science of accounts belongs to the realm of functions linked to business activity.

The second scholar, Francesco Villa, is perceived by Italian historiography as the most important of this school. His main work, published in 1840–1841, is "Accountancy applied to private and public administrative bodies" (*La contabilità applicata alle amministrazioni private e pubbliche*), followed in 1850, by "Elements of administration and accountancy" (*Elementi di amministrazione e contabilità*). Often referred to as the father of Italian accounting, Villa develops the view of accounting as part of a wider administrative process. In fact, in his approach accounting deals with the *azienda* (the basic unit of economic activity), regarding in particular (a) the investigation of organizational issues, (b) the administration of the economic effects of operations on *azienda*'s overall wealth, and (c) the recording of economic transactions. He proposed a theory of accounts based partly on personalist (i.e., on the personification of accounts) and partly on materialist (i.e., on values) theories. He was appointed Chair of Accounting (of "Science of Governmental Accounting") in 1843 at the University of Pavia.

A further relevant author of this school is Antonio Tonzig, who published "Treatise on the science of state accountancy" (*Trattato della scienza di contabilità di Stato*) in 1847.

The Tuscan School The Tuscan school has been comparatively more influenced by the French tradition, especially by the theoretical approaches of the so-called five accountists (*cinquecontisti*) put forth by the two Degranges. In this sense, the first author of this school, Francesco Marchi— in his 1867 work *I Cinquecontisti, ovvero la ingannevole teorica che viene insegnata negli Istituti Tecnici del Regno e fuori del Regno, intorno al sistema della scrittura a partita doppia, e nuovo saggio per la facile intelligenza e applicazione di quel sistema* ("The Cinquecontisti, or the deceptive theory taught in the Technical Accounting High Schools inside and outside the [Italian] Kingdom, with respect to the system of double entry records, and a new essay aimed at the easy understanding and application of that system")—aimed on the one hand to disprove the *cinquecontisti* theory and on the other hand to draw up a rational theory in order to replace it. Marchi's new theory was the "theory of all personal accounts," which is based on a strong reliance on the personification of accounts, such that to address them always and only as *persons*, no matter whether physical or legal. In this respect, Marchi is to be seen as a developer of previous approaches, especially French ones (Degranges and Vannier).

Giuseppe Cerboni continued and developed Marchi's work by rationalizing the latter's concepts and proposing a new method of double-entry recording, which he called *logismografia*, a word combining the cognate Greek terms *logismos*, computation, and *logikos*, logical reasoning (see his 1873 book *Primi saggi di logismografia* ["First essays of logismography"]). *Logismografia*, as a scientific proposal, reflects the author's need to investigate the foundations of accounting using a highly interdisciplinary approach. The accounting discipline is, in fact, divided into a new partitioning, involving (a) the study of the economic administration of the unit, (b) the study of the organization of the firm, (c) the process of computational analysis, and (d) the *logismografia* as the method of representing administrative phenomena. *Logismografia* is then part of the accounting discipline broadly conceived, the aim of which is to search for the "eternal law of administrative mechanics." This search leads Cerboni to single out some administrative functions (e.g., start-up, executive, conclusive functions) as procedures or laws generally applicable to all kinds of businesses. Over the years he tried to enlarge and deepen his approach in order to arrive at a comprehensive, self-contained theory of the firm. The classical positivistic intonation of Cerboni's theoretical construction is clear.

From a narrower accounting theory point of view, this author pushed even further the personification of accounts approach, grounding it in legal roots, wherein the wealth of the firm itself is seen as the "general and specific sum of rights and duties" of this economic entity. In his opinion, all the obligations and rights in existence between the various stakeholders of a business (i.e., proprietor, directors, agents, correspondent firms) are to be registered in the two classes of general accounts: the owner's (rights and duties of the owner and individual elements of the firm's wealth) and the agency's (consignees and correspondents who are debtors or creditors of owner's assets and liabilities). An idiosyncratic "quadruple entry" system for keeping accounts is then proposed.

Cerboni's most important work, "Scientific Accountancy and its relations with the administrative and social disciplines" (*La Ragioneria Scientifica e le sue relazioni con le discipline amministrative e sociali*), was published in 1886, and the acceptance of his theories was such that they were applied to the entire Italian public administration during the period (1876–1892) in which he remained in office as the State General Accountant (*Ragioniere Generale dello Stato*).

Giovanni Rossi was the third main author of the Tuscan School and supporter of the *logismografia*. In his 1882 work "The economic administrative entity" (*L'ente economico amministrativo*), adopting a unitary and wide approach to accounting (similarly to Cerboni), Rossi addressed his interest toward both the construction of a theory of social entities, which give rise to several classes of economic organizations, and the identification of common vital functions therein, which are—in this scholar's approach—the economic, legal, and administrative ones.

Strictly from the standpoint of accounting theory, Rossi remains within the paradigm of the personification of accounts, according to which each element is treated as a person or personality, of which it represents rights and/or obligations. A particular contribution of this author is his "mathematical theory of accounts," expounded in his "Treatise on the theoretical unitarity of double entry methods" (*Trattato sull' unità teoretica dei metodi di scrittura doppia*), published in 1895, which is based once again on personification theory, and which formulates the basic equation Assets – Liabilities = Equity.

In the 20th century, the Tuscan School has produced significant scholars, such as Alberto Ceccherelli, Egidio Giannessi, and Gluido Ponzanelli, who kept alive and strengthened a distinctive approach to accounting and *economia aziendale* thought within the wider Italian theoretical tradtion.

The Venetian School and Fabio Besta (1845–1922)   Fabio Besta took the Chair of Accountancy at the Royal High School of Commerce in Ca' Foscari, Venice, in 1872, and held it until 1918. He is universally considered the initiator of modern accounting theory in Italy. He strenuously opposed Giuseppe Cerboni and his followers (the so-called *logismografi*), and proposed new theoretical ideas, which look, interestingly enough, quite similar in many respects to current Anglo-American theoretical approaches to accounting.

Besta's main work, "Accountancy" (*La Ragioneria*), was initially published in 1882–1883 in the form of lecture notes based on his teaching. Its first publication in book form dates from 1909–1910, and the final version, the one usually quoted, was published in 1922.

Besta considers "economic administration" a new discipline, whose subject of interest is the activity of the *azienda*, or the economic unit, which is not a physical or legal subject but is described as "the sum of phenomena, businesses and relationships concerning a given set of capital goods" belonging to a person, a family, or to any other subject, from the individual firm to the state. This new discipline can then be defined as "the governance of phenomena, businesses, and relationships linked with the evolution of an *azienda*'s wealth."

Economic administration consists of three distinct, logical elements, or functions: operations (*gestione*), management (*direzione*), and control (*controllo*). However, the first two functions are so different from one kind of firm to another that, in Besta's opinion, they cannot be studied in a unitary and standardized way. Thus, economic administration remains a sort of general idea, the implementation of which is made impossible by the variety and variability of economic units (industrial, commercial, financial, and so on).

Only the third function, economic control, that is, accounting, reveals features that are similar, if not identical, in any firm. Therefore, accounting is conceived by Besta as the science of economic control and is placed at the center of his theoretical construction.

The object of this new science should be the element best expressing the firm's value: its current wealth or, perhaps better, the (a) value, (b) composition, and (c) change of firm's assets and equities, which are all assumed to be perfectly measurable. Thus, accounting studies become the "science of the economic control" of assets and net wealth. Note that the legal concept of wealth, on which Cerboni's approach was based, is here replaced by an economic concept of wealth, which relies on the valuation of a firm's resources: wealth is nothing but a set of net assets.

Within this theoretical framework, income is a mere sum of gains and losses deriving from the management of the individual elements of the firm's wealth. The valuation nexus hence goes from wealth to income and, as a consequence, from balance sheet to profit and loss account. In fact, a major emphasis is placed on the former statement, which exposes the central phenomenon of the firm's economy (asset and liability values and composition), while the profit and loss account has only a residual, illustrative function (asset-centered accounting system).

In accordance with this framework, Besta proposes an accounting system based on two main characteristics: (a) recognition in the accounts of all the values pertinent to the firm, even if they are not objects of legal rights and duties; and (b) reporting of all the modifications (of internal and external origin) of the elements from which the wealth measurement derives, by recording in the accounts their value during all the process of their transformation from input value into output value (works-in-progress). This way, one can calculate the value of a firm's wealth at any moment in time by aggregating its individual values. Besta's atomistic-reductionist perspective emerges clearly, according to which each phenomenon can be measured singularly, the income statement being nothing but an aggregation of "partial results" (i.e., changes) associated with specific individual assets.

Characteristic (a) implies a "revolutionary" passage from an account personification (Tuscan school) to a "value-based" theory of accounts (that is, an impersonal or materialist approach, as opposed to the personalist one), according to which accounts refer to objects, to determinable, measurable quantities, in order to keep track of their modifications of value.

Characteristic (b) involves the juxtaposition of partial costs and revenues related to a particular production or commercial process. Margins and specialized profit and loss accounts concerning "distinct" firm activities are considered theoretically sound and economically meaningful. Consistent with the objective of wealth measurement assigned to accounting, the general valuation principle should be the "reproduction cost" (*costo di riproduzione*).

Interestingly, Besta's proposal shows some similarities with today's Anglo-Saxon accounting systems, which in fact allow conceptually both the calculation of partial cost figures via allocation and, thus, the preparation of a "progressive format" income statement.

Besta felt the positivistic climate that was widespread in Italy during the last 30 years of the 19th century. Accordingly, he proposed a careful study of a firm's facts, as well as the empirical method as the method of his new "science of economic control." He had many pupils, who became in their turn professors of accounting, such as Vittorio Alfieri, Vincenzo Vianello, Francesco De Gobbis, Pietro D'Alvise, Pietro Rigobon, and Carlo Ghidiglia. His youngest pupil was Gino Zappa, who was to originate what has been somewhat emphatically called in the Italian literature the *Economia Aziendale* revolution.

1.1.3 Gino Zappa and the Twentieth Century Theoretical Approaches

Gino Zappa (1879–1960)   Gino Zappa achieved a major breakthrough in Italian accounting theory, even if some of his conceptual roots lie in the Tuscan and Lombard Schools and in Besta's work. Zappa's thought brought about a large body of doctrine and many of his pupils followed and developed his ideas, so that Zappa's school is still considered the dominant one in Italy in conceptual terms.

Only some aspects of Zappa's highly abstract theory can be presented here. Further, it should be borne in mind that these aspects belong to different periods of Zappa's conceptual elaboration, and thus, the present reconstruction could be regarded to some extent as inaccurate from a temporal viewpoint. In fact, Zappa's work extends over a period of nearly 40 years. The main works are the following:

1. "The firm's income. Double entry, accounts and financial statements of commercial firms" (*Il reddito d'impresa. Scritture doppie, conti e bilanci di aziende commerciali*), published in its first edition in two

volumes, the first appearing in 1920 and the second in 1929, while an extensively rewritten second edition was published in 1937

2. "New trends in accounting studies" (*Tendenze nuove negli studi di ragioneria*). Inaugural lecture of the 1926–1927 academic year at the Royal High School of Commerce of Venice

3. "The productions in the economy of the firms" (*Le produzioni nell'economia delle imprese*), a three-volume work (consisting of more than 2,000 pages), which was published in 1957.

Central to Zappa's conceptual construction is the notion of *azienda*. According to Zappa, the economic profile of any organized human entity (where economic activities take place) could be abstracted from others and be the subject of a new discipline, the *Economia Aziendale*. An *azienda* can be a state, a family, a firm, a charity, and so on; in more general terms, it is the basic unit of production or consumption in its specific space-time context. In this respect, a possible translation of *Economia Aziendale*—but still a problematic one—might be "economics of basic economic units." For simplicity, in the following we will consider only the category of firms (i.e., the economic units of production).

Zappa conceives of a firm as "an economic coordination in process" (1920–1929). Later he expanded this notion, defining a firm as an "economic institution apt to last through time" (1957). Within this framework, the firm (or, if you like, the *azienda*) is conceived as *decoupled* from all the constituencies having an interest in it (shareholders, workers, creditors, state, managers) and has as its main objective that of its own survival through time. Some of the main characteristics that derive from this conceptual approach are:

- A unitary conception of the firm through time and across space

- A stress on a processual view of the firm in its continuous change ("becoming")

- A strong systemic view of the firm, which in the evolution of Zappa's thought has been increasingly transforming itself into "a radical holistic position." As a consequence, all the activities within the firm are bound together in a specific "economic combination," within which each element (of the human, technical, economic, and financial kind, including assets and liabilities) loses its individuality to merge into the wider economic coordination.

All this implies an economic unity of all different activities taking place within a firm and, in logical sequence, also of the disciplines that study them. Therefore, *Economia Aziendale* is a unitary knowledge-discipline and consists of the joint, synthetic study of operations (*gestione*), organization (*organizzazione*), and accounting (*rilevazione*).

Within this theoretical framework, income assumes a predominant role, since it represents the result of the entire economic-systemic coordination. It is the emerging property of the system as a whole. If income is the result of the whole firm's co-ordination, then it can be produced only by transactions with external agents. In this respect, the firm is to be seen as a set of coordinated, contracted prices with external parties, from which revenues and costs (i.e., income) originate. On the contrary, internal operations (works-in-progress) could not in principle generate income, as was possible for Besta, since, once again, it is the whole system in its transactions with the environment that produces increases in wealth. Therefore, wealth is generated by, and does not generate, income, and it is not—as for Besta—a set of goods/assets but an abstract fund of values from which income flows and to which it is continuously accrued. An inversion in the valuation nexus therefore takes place (no longer wealth leads to income as for Besta, but income leads to wealth).

In narrower accounting system terms, the profit and loss account thus becomes central within Zappa's theoretical construction, which is called in this respect *sistema del reddito* (income-based accounting system), it being in fact a transaction-rooted approach to income and wealth calculation. Logically, the values of the balance sheet (except for monetary items) are costs and revenues whose underlying operations did not come to an economic end within the reporting period.

Some other accounting implications of this broad theory should be stressed:

1. If income is produced by the continuous and unitary flow of operations, then to interrupt this flow for periodic income calculation is logically, let alone economically, impossible. Thus, the implied income allocations between financial years are only acceptable for practical reasons. The same applies *a fortiori* for *interim* reporting. The only theoretically meaningful measurement of income would be the so-called firm's total life income.

    Financial statements are then a consequence of practical needs, but they are logically flawed and economically indeterminate in their results, owing to the break in the economic continuity of a firm's operations that they imply. In this sense, it is logically possible to draw up different annual reports, as long as valuations may be subjectively calculated according to different practical needs.

2. The accounting system is centered on the profit and loss account, but the latter should assume an *en tableau* and *par nature* format (so-called *a costi, ricavi e rimanenze*) in order to better express the general coordination among the firm's elements and thus the juxtaposition of all costs to all revenues.

   In fact, if the periodic income is to have a possible meaning from the economic standpoint, no partial juxtaposition between some costs and revenues is theoretically sound (e.g., operating income, pre-tax income) nor are any margin determinations (e.g., cost of sales) because of the unity of the whole firm-system. Costs should then be shown by their nature and for their total amount (e.g., salaries, materials costs, financial charges, depreciation allowances) and not be imputed to the processes in which they participated, so to obtain partial cost figures (e.g., cost of sales, administrative costs, manufacturing costs). Incidentally, in terms of Schedule 4 of the British Companies Act 1985, this suggests the use of Format 4 rather than Format 1.

   Formats *en liste* and *par destination* of the profit and loss account are instead considered—in Zappa's thought—as overlooking the economic linkages of all the firm's factors and operations. In this respect, the "T format" of the profit and loss account is not primitive in the sense of being double-entry-dependent, but it is the unique, consistent outcome of a radically holistic position in income determination.

3. Within this unitary conception of the firm, skepticism and circumspection surround unit and partial cost determination, since the allocation of overheads is shown to be logical and economic nonsense and, hence, theoretically impossible. As a consequence, full costs are judged misleading and, above all, cost calculation should be made outside the accounting system, which is aimed only at calculating a transaction-based type of income.

Zappa was in a sense a child of his times. He felt many influences of contemporaneous cultural, social, economic, and philosophical developments. However, he was able to amalgamate them and to apply them to an interdisciplinary object of study, the *azienda*. In particular, from a philosophical perspective, Zappa seems to have derived some of his ideas both from "critical positivism," that is, the extreme phase of the trajectory of the positivistic approach in sciences, and from the "neo-idealism," which dominated by and large the Italian cultural atmosphere from the second decade of the century onward. In the latter respect, the use of unifying concepts, the idea of continuous becoming, and the notion of the partiality of abstractions are likely in fact to be drawn from the Italian neo-idealist philosopher Benedetto Croce.

After Gino Zappa: The Second Part of the Twentieth Century   Gino Zappa had many direct and indirect followers. The vast majority of today's accounting professors in Italy are, to different degrees, Zappian or at least have to come to terms with Zappa's theories or influence.

The disciples extended and specialized the fields of investigations, although maintaining in the main Zappa's "imprinting." Among the direct disciples of Zappa are Pietro Onida (the institutionalizer of Zappa's thought), Ugo Caprara (banks and financial institutions), Teodoro D'Ippolito (cost accounting), Giordano Dell'Amore (banks and international trade), Giorgio Pivato (manufacturing firms), Carlo Masini (a developer of Zappa's ideas), Lino Azzini (income dynamics and firm's intertemporal equilibria), Luigi Guatri (marketing and economic value of capital), and Tancredi Bianchi (banks and finance).

All the above-mentioned scholars have been and still are quite influential in the formation pattern of today's young Italian scholars of *Economia Aziendale*. As to accounting, though, the practical relevance of Zappa's ideas—also in respect to the legislation on company annual reports—has probably been fading away, so that at present accounting theory and accounting practice in Italy can be effectively described as two loosely coupled markets.

1.2 Accounting Regulations

In general terms, it must first be pointed out that Italy has a civil law-based legal system, of Roman derivation, and therefore statutes are expected to play a dominant role in regulating commercial subjects, including accounting and related matters. Hence, a concise history of accounting regulation in Italy becomes largely a history of the laws dealing with such a subject. The most significant steps in the evolution of accounting regulation in Italy—before the 1991 reform—can be briefly summarized as follows.

In 1808, during the period of Napoleon's domination, the French Commercial Code of 1807 was introduced to the Italian Kingdom. (Napoleon himself was the King of Italy.) After Napoleon's fall in 1815 and the restoration of the previous States in Italy (namely, the Kingdom of Piedmont, the Kingdom of Lombardy and Venice—under Austrian domination—the Duchy of Parma, the Duchy of Ferrara, the Papal States, the Grand Duchy of Tuscany, the Kingdom of Etruria, and the Kingdom of the Two Sicilies), the influence of the French codification was largely preserved, since commercial laws issued by these preunitary states were heavily drawn from the Napoleonic code. Thus, even before the attainment of political unity in 1861, one could say that in Italy there was substantially uniform commercial legislation.

In particular, there were requirements for state authorization to set up a public limited company (*società anonima*), and public surveillance over this category of companies. As to accounting, every merchant was to keep a journal that had been previously numbered, signed, and stamped by commercial courts or the mayor, and to draw up each year a stock-taking to be transcribed in an *ad hoc* book. Accounting books, if regularly kept, could be used as proof in litigations between merchants. The obligation of drawing up financial statements emerged implicitly by the requirement of distributing dividends only from actually realized profits. No rules were given concerning accounting general principles, formats, and year-end valuations, however. These rules were substantially confirmed by the Italian Commercial Code of 1865, which was promulgated after unification.

It is noteworthy that the mandatory filing of financial statements with the commercial courts and the publication of excerpts from these statements have been required by the *società anonime* since 1865.

The second Italian Commercial Code of 1882 changed some of the previous regulations, abolishing the need for public authorization to set up a *società anonima*, and stating, in Article 176, the general principle that the accounts should give with "straightforwardness and truth" (*evidenza e verità*) the financial situation and the performance results of a company. No detailed rules on formats and valuations were given, though. A legal reserve had to be provided for by transferring to it at least 5% of the net profit for the year, until this reserve reached at least 20% of the share capital (Article 182). As in the 1865 code, dividends could be paid out only from actually realized profits. The 1882 code confirmed the cancellation of public surveillance on *società anonima* (it had already been reduced in scope in 1869). In its place was introduced (by Article 183) a new body in the governance structure of this kind of company, that is, the so-called *Collegio sindacale* composed of *sindaci* (see Section 2.2), to be elected by the members of the company, and whose principal duty was the surveillance of the directors' actions and of respect for the law and the articles of association. Note that since 1882 the concept of a company in Italy automatically embraces the existence of the *collegio sindacale*, which is thus an essential component part thereof.

The 1942 Civil Code (C.C.) took the place of the previous Commercial Code. It regulated company accounts in a more comprehensive way, adding another general principle—with a similar function to the "true and fair view" formula in the United Kingdom—to that of *evidenza e verità* (which was maintained in this 1942 Civil Code from the 1882 Commercial Code but referred to individual firms), as well as presentation and valuation requirements. According to the then new basic principle of Article 2423 C.C., the balance sheet and the profit and loss account should present with "clearness and precision" (*chiarezza e precisione*) a company's financial position and results. The formula was intended as a guideline in relation to which specific rules had to be interpreted. It was generally accepted that both *clearness* and *straightforwardness* referred to form and content, while both *precision* and *truth* referred to valuations.

The next article (2424 C.C.) related to "clearness," since it dealt with the balance sheet *minimum* content, indicating the assets and liabilities required to be included therein. The account format was that implicitly indicated by the law for the balance sheet. The 1942 Civil Code did not mention any compulsory contents of the income statement, so that companies were allowed to present quite condensed and unsatisfactory information regarding their performance results.

Valuation rules were given in Article 2425: the historical cost principle was the fundamental one and marked the maximum amount at which fixed assets, both tangible and intangible, were to be stated; inventory was to be valued at the lower of cost and net realizable value. The historical cost basis was usually required in accounting for associates, even when the investor had a substantial interest. No rules were set for liability valuation.

Departures from legal rules were permitted by the last section of Article 2425 Civil Code, only for "special reasons" (*speciali ragioni*) relating to the company or to a specific asset. Much debate took place on the content and limits of this overriding principle: the simplicity of its form contrasted with its problematic application on practical grounds (see Section 3.1).

Several revaluation laws, permitting the restatement of assets at a higher value than their historical cost, were issued in a nonsystematic way after the 1942 promulgation of the Civil Code. These laws were different in aims, scope, and revaluation mechanisms. Some examples are law-decree no. 436/1946; law-decree no. 49/1948; law no. 74/1952; law no. 576/1975 (the so-called Visentini law); law no. 72/1983 (the so-called Visentini-*bis* law); law no. 408/1990; and law no. 413/1991. The latter two revaluation laws will be discussed in Section 4.1.

A further step in the evolution of financial statement regulation in Italy came with law no. 216 of 1974. This so-called mini-reform of the public limited companies stemmed from both the academic and jurisprudential need to establish that the purpose of financial statements is to give objective information, since this purpose had been severely compromised during the 1960s by secrecy and creative approaches. Hence, the *format* and *minimum* content of the income statement were legally defined and the directors' report with its minimal information to be disclosed introduced. Moreover, a 6-monthly report was required to be produced by listed companies. Some important gaps in Italian accounting legislation, especially related to "clearness" requirements, were thus eventually filled in.

With the same law the National Commission for Companies and the Stock Exchange (*Commissione Nazionale per le Società e la Borsa*, or CONSOB) was set up to monitor quoted companies, and during the ensuing years its power and scope increased (law no. 281 of 1985).

The 1974 law also included the fundamental innovation of the introduction of compulsory external audit for listed companies, which was afterwards regulated in a detailed way by presidential decree no. 136 of 1975. This change may be explained to a great extent by the general unreliability of internal audit performed by *sindaci*, which had been introduced by the 1885 Commercial Code (a *sindaco* is a sort of company institutional auditor, peculiar to the Italian company law tradition—see Section 2.2). This new obligation was welcomed as a significant step toward increasing the legally required information content of the company accounts. Independent auditors had to expressly verify whether the company's financial statements complied with *both* legal rules and *corretti principi contabili* (correct accounting principles—Article 4, section 2, decree no. 136). Confirmation of the equivocal relationship between legal regulation and accounting standards is found in the official "Guidelines for the Auditors'

Figure 1   *Changes in the Italian Regulatory Framework of Accounting*

Decree no. 127/1991	Implementation of the 4th and 7th EC Directives
Decree no. 87/1992	Implementation of the 11th EC Directive and of EC Act no. 1986/633 (financial reporting for banks and financial institutions)
Decrees no. 408/1990 and no. 413/1991	Revaluation laws
Decrees no. 183/1992 and no. 206/1992	Access to the accounting profession
Decree no. 115/1992	Implementation of EC Act no. 1989/48 (mutual recognition of European professional qualifications)
Decree no. 88/1992	Implementation of the 8th EC Directive: qualification of "institutional" auditors (*sindaci*) and new Register (*Registro*) of the *revisori contabili*
Decree no. 115/1992	Implementation of EC Act. no. 1989/48 (mutual recognition of European professional qualifications)
Decrees no. 183/1992 and no. 206/1992	Access to the accounting profession
Law-Decree no. 416/1994 (converted into law no. 503/1994)	Amendments to the income statement format and the accounts notes (as in Decree no. 27/1991), and to the income tax law where it deals with accounting valuations
Decree no. 173/1997	Implementation of the EC Directive 91/674 (financial reporting for insurance companies)
Decree no. 446/1997	Recognition of Italian accounting standards (no. 12) for fiscal purposes (classification basis for the IRAP tax)
Decree no. 58/1998	Reform of external audit and *collegio sindacale* for listed companies. Possibility of referring to "standards of international recognition" by Italian inter-listed companies for preparing consolidated accounts

Report" issued by CONSOB in 1983 and updated in 1987. These guidelines do not even tackle the problem. The ambiguity of the requirement for the compulsory audit report to verify compliance with both the legal rules and the correct accounting principles was thus perpetuated at least until 1991 (for more depth see Section 2.3).

Mandatory audit was subsequently extended to other categories of firms, such as newspaper publishers, insurers, and state-owned companies, among a few others.

Progress in ruling consolidated accounts has been much slower. Consolidated financial statements have not, in fact, been traditionally prepared in Italy. Despite the issue in 1983 of standard no. 8, hardly any Italian groups prepared these accounts, apart from the few categories of firms for which consolidated reporting was compulsory. Until 1991, in fact, no *general* legal requirement for group accounts was established in law. Before the Seventh Directive's implementation, group accounts were legally required only for certain categories of firms (newspaper publishers, state-owned groups, and so on). Further, the stock exchange regulatory body (CONSOB) could command consolidated reporting for listed companies whenever it was deemed necessary. CONSOB has been using this power since 1983, but in absolute terms only a few Italian groups could possibly be required to file consolidated statements because of the small proportion of the Italian industrial system represented by listed companies. Conversely, some large groups present consolidated accounts on a voluntary basis, especially for supporting bank lending decisions.

Tax legislation strongly affects financial reporting in Italy. Since the 1970s tax distortions of commercial accounts have been common in order to obtain fiscal benefits. At the same time, tax rules, being comparatively more exhaustive, were regarded *de facto* as providing the detail to superimpose on the very general 1942 commercial legislation. This view, which is traditionally referred to as the "single track approach" (*teoria del binario unico*), argues in favor of the tax influence on the annual accounts, so that a sort of dependence of the commercial rules on the fiscal ones occurs (reverse dependence). Accordingly, taxation in Italy affects income measurement in the profit and loss account, with some explanations given (but not necessarily until 1993) in the notes. This situation of reverse dependence found a legislative basis from 1973 with the income tax reform (called Visentini reform from the surname of the then Minister of Finance), which linked the tax burden to accounting numbers in a similar way to that in Germany. This link was confirmed in 1986 by the Consolidated Act on Income Tax (*Testo*

Unico sulle Imposte sui Redditi—Presidential Decree no. 917/1986), which includes also a section on Corporation Tax (see Section 3.1).

In the 1990s accounting regulation in Italy has been undergoing a period of major change. In a short time, relevant aspects of company financial reporting and professional life have been profoundly reshaped, and the process is still going on. The rapidity and magnitude of such a revolution are quite impressive, especially when compared with the relatively unchanging situation that characterized accounting regulation in Italy during the past 20 years or so.

The main contents of this—at least formal—discontinuity concern the formats and principles of the annual accounts of companies and financial institutions (including banks and insurance companies), the generalized introduction of consolidated financial statements, the promulgation of two revaluation laws, the relationship between commercial and tax accounts, and the role of accounting standards. The accounting profession, too, has been affected by these regulatory changes with regard to access, as well as the qualification of companies' institutional auditors (*sindaci*). Clearly, most of these innovations derive from the close implementation of many of the EU Directives concerning company law (in particular, the Third, Fourth, Sixth, Seventh, Eighth, and Eleventh Directives, and Act no. 86/635 regarding financial reporting for banks, and no. 86/674 regarding financial reporting for insurance companies). However, other innovations find their origin in the autonomous trajectory of Italian accounting. (For a comprehensive overview of the recent regulatory innovations in Italian accounting and profession see Figure 1).

The wide scope and importance of the above-mentioned changes seem largely self-evident. In a few years virtually all previous regulation dealing with the technical and professional side of accounting were swept away and replaced. The detailed contents of this revolution will be described in the following sections.

1.3 The Accounting Profession

The accounting profession has a long history in Italy. In fact, the first accounting professionals were probably found in Venice at the beginning of the 16th century (the *rasonati*, the accountants), with the function of auditing the Doge's expenses. Later in that century (December 11, 1581), the "Council of Ten" issued a decree setting up the College of Auditors (*Collegio dei Rasonati*), whose members had to check and control the accounts of Venetian state bodies. In order to gain access to this *collegio,* some family and personal requirements, as well as an apprenticeship period of 6 years, were needed (the criteria were laid down by a decree dated June 29, 1596 issued by the Senate), and a professional examination had to be passed. These examinations took place until the fall of the Venice Republic in 1797.

In Milan a College of Accountants (*Collegio dei Ragionieri*) was set up in 1742 by decree of Maria Teresa of Austria. A list of agreed fees (*tariffa*) was also sanctioned.

The first Italian statute regarding the profession of accountant (*ragioniere*) was the regulation published on November 3, 1805 by Prince Eugenio, Viceroy of Italy, in the name of Napoleon I. This regulation set the requirements of sitting for the professional examination and the procedure thereof, the rights and duties of the *Ragioniere*, and the obligation by the local Prefectures to publish a list of the *Ragionieri* who obtained the professional qualification to practice in all the territory of the Italian Kingdom.

The conservative Papal States also recognized the profession of public accountant with the ordinance issued on July 6, 1836 by the Vatican *Congregazione degli Studi* and approved by Pope Gregory XVI.

The *ragionieri* grouped spontaneously in territorially determined bodies called *collegi.* However, in order to study and analyze the various conceptual and technical problems facing the accounting profession ("to research the theories and practical cognitions concerning the accounting profession"), some academies were also founded. In particular, it is worth mentioning the Accademia dei Logismofili (Academy of Logismophiles) set up in Bologna in 1813, and the Accademia dei Ragionieri (Academy of Accountants) established in 1868 in Milan. The former, after several transformations, became in the second half of this century the Accademia Italiana di Economia Aziendale (Italian Academy of Economia Aziendale, AIDEA), which gathers all the Italian university (full) professors dealing with such a subject area.

The first Italian law after unification concerning the accounting profession was issued on June 25, 1865 and was closely followed by a number of decrees regarding access, professional fees, and the required pattern of studies. In 1879 the first National Congress of Italian Accountants was held in Rome, followed by a series of biennial Congresses.

Around the same period many professional journals were launched—especially by members of the Tuscan School—such as *Rivista di Contabilità* (1874), *Il Logismografo* (1877), *Il Ragioniere* (1879), *Il Monitore dei*

Ragionieri (1880), *Rivista di Amministrazione e Contabilità* (1881). It is clear that between 1870 and 1890 Italian accountants, together with accounting scholars, were in the process of institutionalizing their competences and knowledge, building on an autonomous and distinct professional discourse.

Law no. 327 of July 15, 1906 set up legally (or legally recognized) the *Collegi dei Ragionieri* on a national scale and established a roll to be kept by each *collegio*. New requirements for membership were laid down, and the right to act as public accountants was exclusively attributed to *Ragionieri* belonging to the *collegi*.

Until 1929, the accounting profession in Italy was staffed exclusively by the *Ragionieri*. In that year, law no. 588 set up a second accounting profession, the *Dottori Commercialisti*, with duties similar to those of *Ragionieri* but with a separate roll. This development was a result of the creation of the Higher Institutes of Economic and Commercial Sciences (*Istituti Superiori di Scienze Economiche e Commerciali*), which subsequently became Faculties of Economics and Commerce, where subjects such as accountancy (general and applied), business management, and mercantile, banking, and industrial procedures acquired the status of university subjects, whereas previously they had been taught only in the technical high schools for accountants *(Istituti Tecnici per Ragionieri*).

In 1953 two different laws, still enforced, put some order in the accounting profession, definitively recognizing two bodies, the *Dottori Commercialisti* and the *Ragionieri*, with their own autonomous roll, and organized on a territorial scale respectively in *Ordini* and *Collegi*.

In conclusion, the two professional figures dealing with accounting in today's Italy seem to be the result of a historical (and not fully governed) legal and institutional stratification, rather than the outcome of a deliberate governmental plan of attributing different competences and responsibilities to distinct branches of the accounting profession.

1.4 The General Economic Context and the "Accounting Value System"

At a general level, Italian accounting practice is internationally regarded as civil law-based, tax-driven, and conservative-oriented. In addition, textbooks indicate that in Italy listed companies represent a class apart since they must satisfy supplementary accounting rules and requirements (such as a 6-month interim accounting report and the drawing up of consolidated financial statements); that the tradition of the *Economia*

Aziendale has exerted a significant influence on accounting practice; and that today a major impetus to change has an exogenous origin (the European Union). All these features have some validity, but they must be located in the context of the Italian economic and social environment; otherwise they risk being simplistic and misleading to a certain extent. In order to approach Italian accounting, further elements must be considered, which are context-specific and sometimes contradictory in character.

In this respect, it should be remembered that the Italian industrial system is, comparatively speaking, small and medium sized (in 1997 only 13 Italian companies were in the Fortune 500). Generally their ownership system is of a closed nature. The two factors are of course interrelated.

On the former factor, it is enough to point out that the largest Italian group in 1996 was Fiat (a privately owned conglomerate with a strong presence in the car industry), with consolidated revenues of US$50,509 million, followed by I.R.I., which is state owned and in the process of being privatized, with a turnover of $49,055 million, and by E.N.I. ($38,843 million, state owned). Of the remaining 10 companies, 8 are either banks or insurance companies. Despite the fact that Italy is the fifth most industrialized country of the world by GNP, only 24 Italian companies were included in the 1997 Fortune top 500 European companies by market capitalization. In a nutshell, Italian capitalism is poor of capital, made up mostly of economic dwarfs.

In addition, none of the major privately owned groups are substantially public companies, since they belong to well-known families. Thus, what we face in Italy is a family capitalism that is not generally open to share ownership and to external takeovers. Another characteristic of this closed ownership system is small and medium-sized firms, which are mostly family-based, and where an entrepreneur makes the most important decisions. This class of firms is generally recognized as the most innovative driving force of Italian industrial capitalism.

In terms of business finance, self-financing and credit financing are traditionally the main sources of funds for Italian firms. As a specific feature of the Italian system, self-financing is carried out largely through the unfunded provisions for the employee severance indemnity. Fiscal advantages, too, are attached to the choice of keeping a low debt/equity ratio, in that debt financing—unlike equity financing—reduces via interest expense the basis for income taxes.

In correlation with this business finance situation, a relatively small number of companies is traded on the Milan Stock Exchange (only 213 as of December 31, 1997), and the largest eight groups capitalize on average (as of April 30, 1998) 68%-70% of the total market value. As of April 30, 1998, the total market capitalization of the Milan Stock Exchange was 818,195 billion Lire. There are also a junior market (*Mercato Ristretto*) and an over-the-counter market (*terzo mercato*) based in Milan. Today, as in many other international financial markets, negotiations take place on a continuous basis through computer network devices. In 1974 a stock exchange supervisory body, the CONSOB, was set up. As a self-regulating and autonomous body, the CONSOB is today authorized to control the functioning of Italian stock exchanges, to identify the type and content of information to be publicly provided by listed companies (e.g., consolidated financial statements), and to check on the fulfilment of stated requirements. Nevertheless, the role played by the *Borsa* in the Italian economic system is not particularly relevant, and its trends are not always good indicators of the true economic situation.

From this specific capitalistic structure and business financing situation, a series of consequences derive with implications for accounting.

If in this economic context, the firm size tends to be bounded, the number of company members is in principle limited, and entrepreneurs frequently run their own firm, then the external demand for detailed and reliable accounting information is expected to be relatively low; this demand will derive mainly from tax authorities and banks, and often exclusively from the former, since for bank lending decisions either financial statements are not seriously considered or, frequently, ad hoc accounts are prepared. Multiple accounting statements are hence likely to be quite customary in practice.

The demand for independent auditing is also reduced. None or very few shareholders are really outside the company, waiting for financial information thereon. They generally have direct access to the data they need. Accordingly, the general level of disclosure is comparatively quite low and complies essentially only with legal requirements (which increased dramatically after decree no. 127/1991 came into force). Conservatism and information secrecy are recognized as important values in business activity.

As mentioned earlier, Italian accounting regulation has largely been influenced by fiscal rules, due also to the lack of detail, so far, of the Civil Code on the subject. Therefore, as one would expect, the objective of keeping taxable income at the lowest possible amount is, by and large, the leading one for accounting professionals and for the financial directors of companies, especially in the case of small and medium-sized enterprises.

In more general socioeconomic terms, accounting—at least in its official dimension—seems to be perceived by many Italian entrepreneurs more as an unavoidable evil than as a potentially fruitful tool for governing a firm's operations. Consistently, from a socioeconomic point of view, accounting practice appears to be perceived in Italy as a sort of Cinderella, being considered a craft that is almost exclusively related to tax purposes and not useful for offering a meaningful view of the economic and financial situation of a firm. Therefore, one might also say that in Italy the ritual dimension of the annual accounts is stressed in comparison with their economic function. In this respect, there is an apparent contradiction between the large spread and volume of accounting practice and the skepticism toward it and the economic significance of its results. It should be borne in mind that Italy has the second largest number of accounting professionals in Europe after the United Kingdom, currently more than 80,000 (without implying, of course, any value judgment on the quality of Italian accounting). In addition, the huge proportion of small and medium-sized firms within the Italian industrial system obviously means that many accounting actions must be performed daily. In contrast, the low confidence in "official" accounting in Italy may be witnessed by the well-known frequent existence of multiple accounts, the substantial disregard for accounting data on the part of banks and even entrepreneurs, and the common inattention paid to financial statements in bankruptcy judgments.

On the whole, then, Italy cannot be considered a valid example of the relationship (if any) between the degree of sophistication and the diffusion of accounting techniques, and a country's socioeconomic development, given that Italy went through two economic booms (in the 1960s and 1980s) without financial information being regarded as significant. Curiously enough (without suggesting any acceptance of the following statement), the 1991 FEE "Survey on Published Accounts" pointed out that Italian annual accounts were not inferior as to quality and level of disclosure than those of other EU member states that had already implemented the Fourth and Seventh Directives.

On the other hand, it is also notable that management accounting techniques appear not to be systematically used in many firms, this probably being related to the scarce appreciation that accounting data have from Italian entrepreneurs and the often practical (rather than university-based) education of the latter.

The ongoing privatization processes of large state-owned firms (such as the National Institute of Insurance, I.N.A.; Italian Telecommunication

Company, Telecom Italia; Central Electricity Generating Board, Enel; and National Body for Hydrocarburs, ENI), with the expected vast increase in the number of shareholders and in the demand for accounting information, may bring about a change as to the socioeconomic role and perception of accounting in Italy, even if it is too early to appreciate and to formulate any judgment on any economic and accounting consequences of this process.

2.   The Accounting Profession, Audit, and Standards in Today's Italy

2.1 The Accounting Profession

2.1.1 Introductory Aspects

Accounting professionals are an increasingly important phenomenon in Italy from a socioeconomic point of view. Their total number is rapidly increasing, and is now more than 80,000, around 94% of whom are in practice. Those not in practice preserve their professional qualification anyway. The average age is less than 45 years (for *Dottori Commercialisti* 56.9% are less than 40 years old). Their rate of growth has been beyond 6–7% per year in the 1990s. *Dottori Commercialisti* are 0.7 per 1,000 inhabitants, and 8.9 per 1,000 firms (third quarter 1997).

The growing importance and social prestige of accounting practitioners have been linked to the complexity of the tax legislation, and to their fundamental role in helping the huge number of small to medium-sized firms carry out their accounting actions and tax obligations. It is, in fact, customary in Italy for such a firm to have an external professional to look after these aspects, and, in turn, small to medium-sized enterprises are the primary source of business for Italian accountants.

The Italian accounting profession shows a certain number of distinctive features relating to its institutional setting, operational organization, and legal roles.

A clear characteristic of the accounting profession in Italy is that, as mentioned earlier, it is organized into two bodies, the *Dottori Commercialisti* (the more prestigious one) and the *Ragionieri*. The former now has 7,000 members more than the latter. This division is mostly historical (see Section 1.3) rather than deriving from a functional differentiation of professional competences. In fact, the difference between these two categories does not relate to their legally permitted roles, which are quite wide and *de facto* overlapping (accounting, tax and commercial law counseling, *sindaco* activity, management consultancy, judicial expert, bankruptcy trustee, etc.). Moreover, all accounting practitioners have the right to refuse to testify before civil and penal courts (so-called professional secrecy recognized by law no. 507 of 1987). The two bodies are also together in the struggle against the so-called abusivism, that is, the delivery of accounting services by people who do not have the legally required professional qualification. This problem seems to be quite serious, and may damage the image of the accounting profession.

The main *de facto* differentiation between the two accountancy bodies relies today upon the dissimilar paths to qualification (see Figure 2). Once the prescribed admission conditions to the bodies have been met, however, the two categories of accountants follow a similar pattern: they may apply for official registration with the respective body and thereafter begin to practice as independent professionals.

Figure 2 *Access to the Accounting Profession in Italy*

Dottori Commercialisti

Before 1996	*Laurea* degree in economics and commerce (4 years) + state exam
From 1996 (Law no. 206/1992)	*Laurea* degree in economics and commerce (4 years) + apprenticeship (3 years) + state exam

Ragionieri

Before 1994	Secondary school degree in accounting (5 years) + apprenticeship (2 years) + qualification exam (run by the local unit of the accountancy body)
From 1994 (Law no. 183/1992)	Secondary school degree in accounting (5 years) + "short" university degree in business administration or in management of public administration (3 years) + apprenticeship (3 years)* + state exam run by the universities where the short degrees are offered

---

*For those who hold a full university degree (*laurea*) in economics and business administration, economics and banking, or law, the apprenticeship period is reduced to 2 years.

Further distinctions between *Dottori Commercialisti* and *Ragionieri* can be summarized as follows. Each body has a specific membership roll (*albo*), which is independently run under the supervision of the Ministry of Justice, the latter exerting control of a general nature over the two professional bodies. Moreover, these are organized in distinct local units called *Ordini* for the *Dottori Commercialisti* and *Collegi* for the *Ragionieri*.

Each body has legally determined fee ranges, chargeable to clients for any of the different roles that it is expected to play (e.g., Presidential decree no. 645/1994 regarding *Dottori Commercialisti*, and Presidential decree no. 100/1997 regarding *Ragionieri*). The *Dottori Commercialisti*'s fees are *in practice* expected to be slightly higher than those of *Ragionieri*'s because more education is required of the former, even if there are not significant differences in the legal fee rates laid down by the two presidential decrees. The application of these fees is looked upon carefully, with particular reference to the stated minimum levels in order to avoid dumping policies among professionals. The two sets of fees are put together, approved, and from time to time, updated by the Ministry of Justice.

Another feature of Italian accounting practice is that it is operationally organized in a "studio," that is, the professional's firm for which he or she has single personal liability. Italian studios are in general quite small, and in this respect quite different from typical Anglo-Saxon accounting firms. One of the reasons for this is that an old law has for a long time hampered professionals in setting up companies or partnerships (in whatever form) aimed at exercising professional activity (Article 2, law no. 1815 of 1939), the only exception allowed being audit (law no. 1966 of 1939). In particular, a further decree states that a legally compulsory audit must be performed through a company or a partnership (Presidential decree no. 136/1975). The rationale for law no. 1815/1939 was that professional performance must remain individually delivered to any client (Article 2232 Civil Code). Clearly, legislators reasoned that the individual nature of the performance would be lost if this were to be provided from within a company or a partnership. As a consequence, Italian accounting professionals are not permitted to exert their activity under any of the latter legal forms. In 1997, however, article 2 of the old 1939 law was cancelled, and professionals will now be granted permission to set up companies and partnerships for running their activity.

A further distinguishing element of the Italian accounting profession is that there is quite a sharp division between commercial accounting and related legal services such as tax requirements and declarations—which are provided by *Dottori Commercialisti* and *Ragionieri*—and external auditing—which is provided by audit firms. This dichotomy was imposed by the 1975 law dealing with legal audit, since any professionals entering an audit firm registered in a special roll with the CONSOB (as all the major ones are) were not allowed to carry out professional activity of their own (penultimate section, Article 8, Presidential decree no. 136 of 1975). This rule, though, was changed in 1995 (see below). In turn, a *Dottore Commercialista* or a *Ragioniere* cannot perform a compulsory external audit on his or her own. This work must be carried out by an audit firm included in a special roll held by the CONSOB, with the majority of its directors and members being a *Revisore contabile* (new article 8, decree no. 136/1975) (see below).

Thus, Italian accountants customarily choose between an individual career in a "studio" and a career in an audit firm generally registered with the CONSOB, the two paths being exclusive on practical and, at one time, legal grounds. *Dottore commercialista* and *Ragioniere* are not therefore synonymous with auditors, as in many other countries, but they are accountants carrying out roles other than legal audit. If they have the qualification *Revisore contabile* (as the vast majority of them do), then they can perform the so-called voluntary audit as well as the institutional audit as *sindaco*.

In the 1990s, the Italian accounting profession has experienced a period of intense change. This is not only because practitioners must cope with the recent innovations in the rules referring to annual accounts (see below), but also because of the current restructuring of some fundamental aspects of the profession. Such modifications deal with (a) access to this career, (b) the implementation of EU Directive no. 89/48 on the mutual recognition of professional qualifications and the related 3-year academic degrees, (c) the implementation of the EU Eighth Directive regarding the qualification of statutory auditors, and (d) the abolition of the impossibility of setting up a company or a partnership for dilivering professional services.

The above-mentioned difference in the paths to qualification as *Dottore commercialista* and *Ragioniere* applied until 1992. Two recent laws made the two paths more similar, while preserving some differences between them (see Figure 2).

At any rate, one may say that in either case there has been an upgrading of the qualification in terms both of the number of years of apprenticeship, and (for the *Ragionieri*) of the minimum educational level. It is fair to say, however, that before the introduction of the new rules the apprenticeship period was *de facto* already in place for the *Dottori Commercialisti* and frequently longer than the then required 2 years for the *Ragionieri*. In the context of the new legal framework, it is likely that the number of *Ragionieri* will progressively decrease in relative terms (they are already marginally the minority of accounting professionals), since the difference between access to their membership roll and to that of *Dottori Commercialisti* (the more prestigious body) has been significantly reduced.

A particular modification of access to the accounting profession comes from the recent implementation in Italy of EU Directive no. 89/48 dealing with the mutual recognition of European professional qualifications (legislative decree no. 115/1992). According to this decree, in order to get recognition of his or her qualification by Italian law, a professional from another EU state needs to pass an *ad hoc* state exam (Article 6). The transfer exam is periodically run under the superivision of the Ministry of Justice (office no. VII). Even though it does not seem at present that there will be a massive influx of EU accountants to Italy in the near future, it is clear that in the long term the new legal framework might bring about some changes in the composition and qualification of the professionals operating in this country.

The third recent legislative innovation concerning the Italian accounting profession, the one concerning the qualification of statutory auditors, will be illustrated below in the context of the analysis of audit activity (Section 2.2.2).

The fourth ongoing change that could have a large impact on the structure of the Italian accounting profession is that regarding the possibility—as a consequence of the 1997 cancellation of an article of law no. 1815/1939—of setting up partnerships and companies among professionals. At the moment it is not yet clear whether they will be also allowed to establish limited liability companies, and whether nonprofessionals will also be authorized to be members of these professional partnerships and companies. This change is part of a wider reform program of the professions pushed by the government with the aim of revising their (exclusive) roles and the controlling function of the related bodies. Also the prohibition against advertising professional activities should be abolished.

In the following the most relevant features of the two accountancy bodies will be more closely examined.

2.1.2 Dottori Commercialisti

The first step toward entering the *Dottori Commercialisti* is to graduate in economics (in general this happens when one is between 23 and 25 years old) with a Faculty of Economics from either a public or a private state-recognized university, after having completed 5 years of primary school, 3 years of junior high school, 5 years of any (Italian) high school, and a 4-year university course covering a minimum of 23 subjects including accounting, banking, economics, law (public, civil, commercial, and tax), statistics, and foreign languages. Graduation from the university is attained after an oral presentation, before a Board of Professors formally appointed by the Rector of the Faculty, of a dissertation regarding a specific subject included in the candidate's study program.

Until 1995, those who graduated as Doctors in Economics could, if they so wished, without any practical apprenticeship, sit for a professional state examination, consisting of written and oral portions, offered twice a year at any university where a Faculty of Economics exists. Having successfully passed both parts, such an applicant could apply for membership in the *Ordine dei Dottori Commercialisti* in their geographic area. Since 1996, an apprenticeship period of 3 years after graduation has been required before one may sit for the professional examination (see Figure 2). On December 31, 1997 the *Ordine dei Dottori Commercialisti,* generally recognized as the most prestigious of the organizations, had around 44,000 members (up from 24,000 in 1990). The following offers a brief look at the way the *Dottori Commercialisti* are institutionally structured and at their detailed legal roles.

Ordine dei Dottori Commercialisti The *Ordine dei Dottori Commercialisti* is a recognized legal body that gathers all the *Dottori Commercialisti* of a geographic area and supervises, in a general sense, their professional activity. At present, 125 local *Ordini* are established, virtually in any town where a Tribunal is in existence.

The most important activities of the *Ordine*, apart from that mentioned earlier of keeping the professional roll, are the following:

1. Accept new applicants after having ascertained the existence of the required prerequisites
2. Supervise respect of the professional law and on members' activity
3. Report on infringements by nonqualified people practicing
4. Resolve disputes that might arise in connection with fees charged by members to their clients
5. Select members for appointment to the body's National Council
6. Impose disciplinary sanctions on members

As to the first activity, in order to register with the *Ordine*, an applicant—in addition to having passed the examination referred to above—must fulfil certain requirements, such as having (a) Italian citizenship (now one may hold citizenship in one of the European Union member states, see decree no. 115/1992), (b) a *laurea* degree (graduation) in Economics and Commerce from an Italian University, and now (c) a minimum 3 years' practical experience in a *Dottore Commercialista*'s studio.

Each *Ordine* maintains two different registers of memberships: (a) the roll (*albo*) of practicing *Dottori Commercialisti*; and (b) the roll of (temporary) nonpracticing members. Only those in the first *albo* are authorized to practice as public accountants. There is no particular requirement for transferring from one register to the other.

The professional roles that each *Dottore Commercialista* can perform are set by law no. 1067/1953, which recognized a general competence in commercial, economic, financial, tax, and accounting matters. In particular, the following activities are included among such competencies:

- The administration and liquidation of business concerns, estates, and single assets
- Appraisals, surveys, and advice thereon
- Auditing of account books of enterprises and any other inquiry into the reliability of financial statements, accounts, entries, and any other accounting document
- Settlement and liquidation of losses
- Institutional audit as *sindaco* of limited liability companies
- Assistance to judges with respect to the evaluation of assets, liabilities, and so on, in connection with judicial cases
- Bankruptcy trustee

One may observe that the *Dottori Commercialisti* can perform external audit activity on their own or with a firm, but—as will be pointed out below—audit must be of only a voluntary type, that is, an audit that is voluntarily undertaken by a company (without being legally obligated to do so).

National Council of *Dottori Commercialisti*   Based in Rome, under the auspices of the Ministry of Justice, the National Council of *Dottori Commercialisti* is the highest authority governing the *Dottori Commercialisti* accountancy body. It is composed of eleven members (*consiglieri nazionali*), who are elected by the local *Ordini* and remain in office for a period of 3 years; they may be re-elected subsequently. The activity of *consigliere nazionale* is not a full-time job, to the extent that it requires generally a two- or three-day trip to Rome twice a month to attend Council meetings and various committee meetings.

In the 1970s this National Council promoted the setting up of committees for the preparation of Italian accounting and auditing standards. As mentioned earlier, in 1982 the second accountancy body also joined these committees.

As far as professional ethics is concerned, in 1987 the National Council issued a booklet called "Rules of professional deontology," and in 1996— together with the national council of the other professional body—a second booklet titled "Principles of conduct of the *collegio sindacale*" (i.e., company institutional auditor body). Noteworthy in particular is the 1987 rule according to which any form of advertisement of his or her *studio* is forbidden to *Dottori Commercialisti* (which will be abolished as a consequence of the current professions reform). Moreover, it is stated that a *Dottore Commercialista* may not (a) carry out industrial or commercial activities; (b) act as a managing director of business enterprises; (c) serve simultaneously as consultant and *sindaco*; (d) reveal the affairs of his or her clients. It must be said that not all these ethical rules are consistently followed in practice.

Further rules of professional conduct are laid down in the Civil Code— in connection with the independence of *sindaci*—and in the decree governing the legally compulsory audit.

2.1.3 Accountants and Commercial Experts (Ragionieri e Periti Commerciali)

A school diploma as *Ragioniere e Perito Commerciale* is attained (generally when one is 19 years old) after having attended a business high school and passed a state-run examination. A student's career at that point will have included 5 years of primary school, followed by 3 years of junior high school and 5 years of the above-mentioned high school. The subjects studied in high school will have included accounting, mathematics, and business and company law, but not auditing. Until 1994, after the Diploma, in order to obtain the professional qualification of *Ragioniere* (that of *Perito commerciale* is no longer in use), a candidate had to go through two years of apprenticeship and pass a state examination organized by the local *collegi*. Now he or she must have at least a so-called short university degree (3 years of study) and carry out generally a 3-year apprenticeship before sitting for the professional state examination (see Figure 2).

This body has around 37,000 members at present (it had 24,200 in 1990). The following section offers a brief look at the way in which Ragionieri are institutionally structured.

Collegio dei Ragionieri e dei Periti Commerciali   In a similar way to the *Ordine* for the *Dottori Commercialisti*, the *collegio* is a recognized legal body that gathers all the *Ragionieri* and *Periti commerciali* of a geographic area and supervises in a broad sense their professional activity. It is responsible for keeping and updating the professional roll. At present, 118 *collegi* are established.

The activities of a *collegio* are much the same as those of an *ordine*. As for *Dottori Commercialisti*, the state exam for qualifying as *Ragionieri* is offered twice a year by all universities where a relevant short degree is awarded (see Figure 2). It is interesting to note that before 1994 each *collegio* ran its own professional qualifying examination. A new applicant must fulfill the same required prerequisites as the *Dottori Commercialisti*.

The professional roles that each *Ragioniere* can perform are set by law no. 1068/1953 and are *de facto* overlapping with those of *Dottori Commercialisti*.

National Council of Accountants and Commercial Experts (*Consiglio Nazionale dei Ragionieri e dei Periti Commerciali*)   The National Council of Accountants and Commercial Experts is the highest authority of the *Ragionieri e Periti Commerciali* accountancy body and is based in Rome, officially under the auspices of the Ministry of Justice. It is composed of eleven members (*consiglieri nazionali*), who are elected by the *collegi* and remain in office for 3 years; they may be re-elected subsequently.

With regard to ethics, in 1983 a "Code of deontological conduct" was issued by the National Council. In essence, these rules are quite similar to those applying to *Dottori Commercialisti*.

2.2   Auditing

2.2.1 General Background

Auditing in Italy is a complex issue because of the legislative maze produced by the different laws that have been ruling this subject for about the past 60 years. At first sight, it can be said that Italian audit is characterized by an evident anomaly. Since 1974–1975 there have been two competing approaches to audit: an institutional-internal one, and an external one. On the one hand, there are the old, established *sindaci*, who make up one of the limited liability company bodies, the *collegio sindacale*, and who are most often accounting professionals (*Dottori Commercialisti* and *Ragionieri*) working on their own.

On the other hand, there is an Anglo-American type of audit, which is performed by companies and professional partnerships. The most important of these are registered with CONSOB (e.g., the Big Five), and as such they are the only ones that can deal with legally compulsory audit.

The two audits involve carrying out tasks that are in part mutually overlapping and not thoroughly clarified by law. Even though the law requires that the audit firm inform the *sindaci* of a company about the existence of censurable facts, that is, irregularities that have had a material impact on financial statements, one may assume that the relationships between the two bodies and the two processes aimed at verifying accounts appear in the vast majority of cases as ambiguous and inconsistent or, more likely, nonexistent.

In this respect, those who were expecting the implementation of the Fourth Directive in Italy (decree no. 127/1991) to extend external audit to medium and large unlisted companies have been proved wrong. On the eve of the implementation of the Fourth Directive, there arose a sharp disagreement between the *Dottori Commercialisti* and *Ragionieri* on the one side—who were much in favor of preserving the role and activity of *sindaci*—and the accountancy firms (mainly the Big Six) on the other side—pressing for an enlargement of independent external audit to all limited liability companies. Each category was, of course, trying to ensure that its form of audit was the one required by the decree. In any event, the two accountancy bodies were successful. In fact, the final text of the decree commands that only the audit by *sindaci* must be performed for all limited liability companies whose share capital exceeds 200 million lire, while external audit is a requirement only for listed companies, state-owned companies, insurance companies, and a few others. Therefore, the *status quo ante* on the matter has been essentially maintained.

Another important interpretative dimension of audit in Italy is the distinction between voluntary and legally required audit. These are addressed to different companies and performed by auditors on different rolls. Also, the firms authorized to carry out the two types of audits differ.

It should be pointed out that within a wider reform of financial markets a recent regulatory change (legislative decree no. 58/1998) has brought some clarification as to the respective competencies of the two audits, at least for listed companies: in fact, from July 1998 the audit responsibilities of the *collegio sindacale* of these companies have been entirely transferred to the external accountancy firms, while its supervisory powers on the company compliance with the law and on the adequacy of its administrative and organizational structure have been strengthened (this change makes the *collegio sindacale* of listed companies look more like a German-type supervisory board). Notwithstanding this significative legal clarification, the contradictions between the functions of the *collegio sindacale* and those played by the audit firm remain for nonlisted companies that are subject (voluntarily and compulsorily) to external audit.

In the following a description of the audit context in Italy will be sketched out.

2.2.2 Sindaci and the Collegio Sindacale (Institutional-Internal Audit)

The *collegio sindacale* (the body composed of *sindaci*) is a body of the company that has defined responsibilities toward the company itself, the business community, and society in general (Article 2397–2409 Civil Code for nonlisted companies; Article 148–154 decree no. 58/1998 for listed companies). Its presence, when legally required, is a condition of existence of the company itself as a legal person, very much the same as the annual general meeting (*assemblea dei soci*) and the board of directors (*consiglio di amministrazione*). In this sense, the *sindaci* exert a sort of institutional-internal audit in nonlisted companies, or an institutional supervisory function in listed companies.

As already mentioned, the Civil Code requires that all limited liability companies (*società per azioni* and *società a responsabilità limitata*) with a share capital exceeding 200 million lire must appoint, at the annual general meeting, a *collegio sindacale* consisting of three to five members, that is, a president of the body and two to four effective members. At least two substitute members are also appointed. In principle, the *sindaci* are appointed for 3 years, but they can be reappointed indefinitely.

Its duties can be summarized as follows (Article 2403 Civil Code):

1. Control the administration of the company
2. Verify general compliance with law and articles of association of the company's operations and the legality of the accounting records

3. Check the correspondence of the balance sheet and income statement with the results of the company's account books
4. Ensure the conformity to legal rules of the financial statement valuations
5. Ascertain every 3 months the amount of petty cash and the existence of the company's documents of credit and of the receipts of pledge, custody, or caution from third parties in the company's favor
6. Participate, if the *sindaci* so wish, in the meetings of the board of directors

For quoted companies (Article 149, decree no. 58/1998) the duties under 3, 4, and 5 are not to be carried out by the *collegio sindacale*, which has instead to supervise on the adequacy of the company's organizational structure and the internal control and administrative system, as well as on the latter's reliability. As to the duty under 6, the *collegio sindacale* of a listed company has to attend the meetings of the shareholders, the board of directors, and the executive committee (if in existence). As a further special duty, the *collegio sindacale* in these companies has to report immediately any irregularities found to the CONSOB.

Only since 1995 (thanks to decree no. 88/1992) has a *sindaco* been allowed to employ an assistant to help perform these activities. This assistant will operate under the *sindaco*'s direction and will be paid by the *sindaco* (Article 2403-*bis* Civil Code). This also applies to listed companies (Article 151, Section 3, decree no. 58/1998).

The regulations do not set a minimum number of hours to be spent in audit and controls (unlike in France). The fees are determined by the law in relation to the company's net worth, and in 1995 they were limited in any case to 140 million lire for the president and 80 million lire for the other full members of the *collegio sindacale* (law no. 336/1995).

The audit activity of the *collegio sindacale* results in an annual report (*Relazione del Collegio Sindacale*), which is included in the financial statements and in which this body points out its observations and proposals regarding the regularity of the books, the annual accounts, and their approval by the general meeting. There is no legally prescribed format of the *Relazione del Collegio Sindacale*. In the vast majority of cases, though, this report merely confirms the stated figures and proposes the latter's approval by the general meeting. It is to be noted that financial statements must be signed not only by the members of the board of directors but also by each of the *sindaci*. Since 1994 the *sindaci* have also been required to verify and control the group accounts, if the company for which they are carrying out this function is a parent undertaking (Article 41, decree 127/1991).

For listed companies the report by the *collegio sindacale* addresses the supervisory activity it carried out over the financial year, and it proposes approval of the annual accounts. If the parent company is listed on one of the E.U. markets, then the control of group as well as subsidiary accounts is attributed to an external audit firm, while the *collegio sindacale*'s report has to deal only with its supervisory activity and related findings (Article 165, decree no. 58/1998).

Until 1992 officially, but *de facto* until 1995 (i.e., the date of the complete coming into force of legislative decree no. 88/1992), virtually anybody could be eligible for a *sindaco* position, with the consequence that not all the persons carrying out such a function had the appropriate qualification. In most cases *sindaci* are accounting professionals.

Since 1995 all *sindaci* must belong to a special register under the auspices of the Ministry of Justice. In fact, as a consequence of the implementation of the Eighth EU Directive in Italy through legislative decree no. 88/1992, from 1995 *only* those who have the functional qualification of *revisore contabile* (auditor) can carry out auditing activity with legal relevance, and then be appointed *sindaci* of a company.

The professional qualification of *revisore ufficiale dei conti* has quite a long history. In fact, according to a regulation of 1936 (Royal law-decree no. 1548/1936 converted into law no. 517/1937), the *sindaci* who have served for some years (e.g., 5 years for lawyers and engineers; 3 years for *Dottori Commercialisti*) and have an indisputable morality could enter— after an undemanding examination by a national committee—the membership (*ruolo*) of theofficial statutory auditor (*revisori ufficiali dei conti*) (Article 12). The 1992 decree has now also slightly modified the professional label of *revisore ufficiale dei conti*, which has now become *revisore contabile* (auditor).

In order to join the register (*registro*) of the *revisori contabili* it is necessary to have at least a "short" university degree in economics, business administration, or law (3 years), to serve an apprenticeship period of 3 years under the guidance of a *revisore contabile*, and to pass a state-run exam (three written papers and an oral examination).

As a transitional *régime*, however, those who were previous members of the *Revisori Ufficiali dei Conti*, as well as the *Dottori Commercialisti* and the *Ragionieri* (who have served as a *sindaco* of a company for at least one year), have been allowed to be inserted *de jure* in the new register. There-fore, the level of qualification of the *sindaci* is likely to be higher than beforehand, but it may also be negatively influenced by the presence of inadequately trained members who belonged to the previous membership.

It should also be noted that in this new register there can be inscribed partnerships and limited liability companies between accounting profes-sionals, who hold the qualification of *revisore contabile*, aimed at provid-ing companies with voluntary audit (see below).

The *sindaci* are highly peculiar to the tradition of Italian company law. They are perceived as carrying out functions in the public interest, thus helping to legitimize the company's activity. In addition to the *sindaci*'s not always adequate professional audit qualifications, however, some weaknesses can be pointed out of both the *collegio sindacale* as a company's body and the *sindaco*'s role, which lessen its capability of carrying out an effective audit:

1. Its subordinate position toward company's owners, since the latter elect the *sindaci* via their control over the annual general meeting (in this respect, it is a clear case of who controls the controllers)

2. The further reduction of *sindaci*'s independence due to their consultancy activity, often rendered for the same company in which they participate in the *collegio sindacale*

3. The limited powers of the *sindaci vis-à-vis* the company's directors

4. The breadth of the *sindaci*'s duties in relation to their scarce re-sources, which are essentially based on a single person's commit-ment

5. The poor remuneration granted by law to the *sindaci* role

6. The potentially unlimited number of participations in different *collegi sindacali* that a professional may have, with a negative impact on the time, length, and qualitative level of the audit that can be devoted to each of them

Therefore, one might wonder about the significance and incisiveness of the control and role exerted by the *collegio sindacale* in the past and, if no changes occur, in the future (for example, see some of the recent episodes linked to bribery scandals, where the financial statements of big enterprises, which have been found irregular, had been signed by the company's *sindaci*).

It is clear that for nonlisted companies the type of audit exerted by the *collegio sindicale* is larger in scope than the accounting-centered one characterizing the Anglo-Saxon tradition, and as such it may be labeled an administrative audit. At the same time, however, it is clear that the *collegio sindacale* does not give rise to an arm's length audit in the sense of the EU Fourth Directive. It essentially represents a formal confirmation of the legitimacy of the company directors' actions. In this respect, the general assumption in ordinary circumstances is to regard the duties of the *collegio sindacale* as legalistic rather than requiring any value judgment. As to listed companies, some of the above reservations on the incisiveness of the role of *collegio sindacale* appear relatively less appropriate, since its duties are more focused and demanding.

Notwithstanding those longstanding concerns, a seeming contradiction referring to this type of audit should be noted—that a body similar to the *collegio sindacale* —called *collegio dei revisori* (auditor committee)—has been legally extended in 1982 to utilities controlled by the communes and provinces, and in 1990 to the latter bodies themselves, as well as in 1995 to national health system units. In particular, it is interesting to note that as to these *collegi*, which are a component part of several relevant bodies of the Italian public administration, a maximum number has been set for a professional of eight different participations (decree no. 77/1995), with a maximum remuneration of 36 million lire per each of them (decree of the Ministry for Internal Affairs no. 475/1997).

2.2.3   The External Independent Audit and the Società di Revisione (Audit Firms)

The activity of external independent audit, similar to the Anglo-Saxon one, can be carried out in Italy under three different legal-institutional forms, which only partially overlap. These forms are:

1. *Revisore contabile* (auditor) (legislative decree no. 88/1992)
2. *Società fiduciaria e di revisione* (fiduciary and auditing company) (law no. 1966 of November 23, 1939)
3. *Società di revisione* (audit company) (legislative decree no. 58/1998, which has superseded Presidential decree no. 136 of 1975)

We have already described the evolution of the *revisore contabile* from 1936 to the implementation of the Eighth EU Directive in Italy. In particular, the *revisore contabile* can perform the voluntary audit, that is, an audit that is freely undertaken by companies (which are not bound to do so), and be *sindaco* of a limited liability company. This professional qualification may be attributed to a physical person, a partnership (*società in nome collettivo* or *società in accomandita semplice*) or a limited liability company. In the latter two cases, in order to get the inscription in the *Register*, all the partners signing the audit reports must be be *revisori contabili*, as well as most of the directors, the majority of voting rights must belong to persons having such a qualification, and the objects of the partnership/company (according to their memorandum) must be limited to auditing and company accounting organization. The register is kept under the general supervision of the Ministry of Justice. The appointment as *sindaco* of a company is restricted to physical persons. For audit firms already included in the special roll of decree no. 58/1998 (formerly Presidential decree no. 136/1975), inclusion in the register of the *revisori contabili* is not required—even though 22 of the 24 audit firms of the special roll also belong to this register—while audit firms authorized on the basis of law no. 1966/1939 can be inscribed in the roll of *revisori contabili* if they apply for it.

It is important to observe that decree no. 99/1998, which has set the operational details of the qualification pattern and the activity of the *revisore contabile*, has established that his or her activity is incompatible with: (a) a consultancy relationship with the company or its subsidiaries at the time of the audit appointment or in the two previous years, (b) an employee or a professional work relationship with the company or its parent at the time of the audit appointment or in the 3 previous years, and (c) the role of director in the audited company or its parents at the time of the audit appointment or in the three previous years (Article 39).

Second, the *società fiduciaria e di revisione* are authorized—according to a law of 1939 that is still in force—by the Ministry of Industry and Commerce to perform the following roles: (a) fiduciary administration of third parties' properties; (b) company audit and accounting organization; (c) shareholder's and bondholder's representation at general meetings.

This kind of firm can take the legal form of partnership or limited liability company (*società per azioni* or *società a responsabilità limitata*), where, in the latter case, one member at least of the board of directors must be a professional (not necessarily an accounting one), the chairman, the managing director, and the majority of the board of directors and of the management are to be Italian (note that in 1939 Italy was still in the fascist era), and the *collegio sindacale* has to be composed of professionals, at least two taken from the accounting professional rolls. The *società fiduciaria e di revisione* can undertake only a voluntary type of audit, as the members of the register of *revisori contabili*.

In a historical perspective, this type of audit firm is important since, after the Second World War, all major international accounting firms opened branches in Italy to carry out their services in accordance with the provisions of the legislation regarding voluntary audit, that is law no. 1966/1939.

As an important part of the so-called mini-reform of the *società per azioni* in 1974 (enacted by law no. 216 of June 7, 1974, which established, *inter alia*, also the CONSOB), Presidential decree no. 136 of March 31, 1975, introduced into Italian company law the requirement for quoted companies to submit their annual accounts to independent audit. The same requirement was later introduced for newspaper publishing companies (now excluded), state-owned groups, insurance companies, and a few other categories of firms.

As mentioned earlier, from financial year 1994 there must be submitted to legal audit not only company accounts—when this is so required—but also group accounts, if those companies for which external audit is compulsory (e.g., listed companies) play also the role of parent undertakings (Article 41, decree 127/1991).

As to their tasks, audit firms must check and verify: (a) along the financial year, the regularity of company bookkeeping, and the correctness of the representation of administrative facts in the accounting records, and (b) the correspondence of the balance sheet and income statement with the results of the company's account books, as well as the conformity of the financial statement valuations to norms. It seems also useful to remember that from July 1998, as a result of recent reform of financial intermediaries (decree no. 58/1998), all audit activity that used to be run by the *collegio sindacale* has been attributed for listed companies to the external audit firm, probably contributing to a clarification of the relationships between these two bodies of the company institutional life.

In order to accomplish this delicate publicly relevant function, it has been deemed appropriate to create a new "special roll" under the supervision and control of CONSOB, which only audit firms with the particular characteristics of professional competence and financial soundness could enter. From July 1998 the legal basis of this special roll is Article 161 of legislative decree no. 58/1998 (beforehand, this basis was given by Article 8 of the above-mentioned Presidential decree no. 136/1975).

Audit firms may be set up as partnerships or limited liability companies: in this respect, the most common legal structure of Italian audit firms was traditionally that of *società in accomandita semplice* (similar to the

U.K. quasi-partnership), but the form of public limited company (*società per axioni*) is becoming more and more frequent.

Admission to this special roll is granted when (Article 161, section 2, decree no. 58/1998, which refers to the conditions for admission to the register of *revisori contabili* —Article 6 of legislative decreee no. 88/1992 implementing in Italy the EU Eighth Directive):

1. Their objects—according to the audit firm memorandum—are limited to the auditing and accounting organization of a company, and specifically exclude any other professional activity (e.g., consulting).

2. The partners underwriting audit reports, as well as the majority of directors, should belong to the register of *revisori contabili* (before 1995 they had to be members of one of the Italian accountancy bodies or be a *Revisore Ufficiale dei Conti*, and have at least 5 years' auditing experience or alternatively to have passed a special examination organized by and under the auspices of CONSOB).

3. The majority of the partnership or company members are *revisori contabili* as well as the individuals owning the majority of the capital.

4. The company or partnership must be "technically suitable (i.e. capable)" (this is to be assessed by the CONSOB).

Also an insurance guarantee that is judged adequate by CONSOB should be available to the audit firm. Italian subsidiaries of foreign auditing firms may also be registered in the CONSOB special roll, provided that they respect the same requisites set for other Italian firms.

Before 1995, there could be inscribed in this special roll only firms previously authorized by the Ministry of Industry and Commerce to exert (voluntary) audit activity on the basis of law no. 1966/1939. Moreover, if a firm was a branch of an international audit company, it had to have carried out such activity for at least 10 years. These limitations were removed in 1992 by the revised version of Article 8 of decree no. 136/1975.

The narrowing of the firm's objects to audit and *accounting organization* was stretching itself, until the coming into force of decree no. 88/1992 (which occurred in April 1995), also to all professionals while working for this type of audit firm, in that one cannot render any professional service on an autonomous basis. Decree no. 88/1992 currently allows this individual delivery of accounting services, thus canceling one of the most acute formal points of separation between an individual career as an accounting professional in a studio and a career with a *società di revisione* (see Section 2.1.1). Of course, this double activity is possible for these professionals only to the extent that this is allowed by their contract with the audit firm.

In order to get around the prohibition for a *società di revisione* recorded in the CONSOB special roll to perform any activity other than audit, many firms set up a legally distinct company to deliver consultancy services. Thus, parallel companies did and do come into existence, with no formal linkages with the audit firm, but both having the same name and, in most cases, both related to the same parent company abroad (examples include the Big Five).

The audit appointment is given to a firm by the annual general meeting of the company asking to be audited. The appointment lasts for 3 years and can be renewed not more than twice (i.e., in total 9 years). It can be revoked only for just cause (*giusta causa*) and after receiving an opinion on this from the *collegio sindacale*. The appointment can be assigned again to the same audit firm only after at least one 3-year appointment of another audit firm has been made. In 1994 most of the major Italian groups reshuffled audit appointments.

With regard to the independence of the *società di revisione*, the appointment of an audit firm is incompatible when there are contractual arrangements or participating interests between the latter and the company to be audited, or when partners, directors, *sindaci*, or directors general of an audit firm are related by blood or marriage to their equivalents of the company asking to be audited, or have had connections with the latter in the recently preceeding years by means of a service agreement of any kind, including employee work, or they have served during the same period as director or *sindaco* thereof (Article 3, decree no. 136/1975). Furthermore, partners, directors, *sindaci*, and employees of an audit firm cannot take up, for a period of 3 years after the termination of the audit appointment or of their work relation therewith, any occupation whatsoever with the company that has been audited by their firm. It is relevant to note that the "incompatible activities" set for the *revisore contabile* (Article 39, Presidential decree no. 99/1998) apply also to the *società di revisione* and their members (partners, directors, employees) to the extent they are included in the register of the *revisori contabili* (as aforementioned, 22 out of 24 of the CONSOB "Special Roll"). In particular, this implies that a *revisore* working for an audit firm cannot carry out its activity in a firm for which he or she is currently *sindaco* or has been *sindaco* in the past 3 years. At present the CONSOB is revising the incompatibilities of the *società di revisione* as a consequence of the issuance of decree no. 58/1998.

The outcome of the legally compulsory auditing process is the audit report, which states an opinion on the accounts examined in accordance with certain accounting and auditing standards, not differently from international practice. Before July 1998 this outcome was the so-called *relazione di certificazione*, whose translation to English as "audit report" is to some extent problematic, since this *relazione* had to certify the quality of the accounts audited, and not be simply a professional judgment thereon.

In 1983 the CONSOB imposed a mandatory model of the *relazione di certificazione* (which was slightly modified in 1987 and made shorter and more succinct in 1994) to the *società di revisione* when carrying out a legal audit. Beyond the fact of not being easily reconcilable with the standard Anglo-American auditor's reports, this model has been highly criticized because of its rigidity, its relative lack of clarity, its excessive length (criticism now overcome by the 1994 version), and the contradiction between section 3, which is devoted to auditor's comments and remarks, and section 4, where the audit firm expresses its judgment and releases its "certification" of the annual accounts audited, or alternatively does not release the certification and points out the reasons for doing so. In this respect, it should be remembered that before July 1998 there was a legal impossibility in Italy of delivering an auditors' report with any form of qualified opinion on the examined financial statements: in fact it was only possible for Italian auditors to state either a fully positive or a fully negative judgment thereon. Now, as an effect of the reform imported by decree no. 58/1998, the CONSOB is revising its audit report model, substituting the expression "professional opinion" for the term *certificazione* (certification), and allowing the possibility of delivering qualified opinions (according to the provisions of Article 156, decree no. 58/1998). The new audit report will be more similar to that proposed by auditing standard no. 18, which previously used to be different from that of CONSOB and much more in conformity with that familiar in the Anglo-Saxon environment.

Until 1991 audit firms were asked by law to state, in their legal audit report, the compliance of financial statements with the civil rules and the accounting standards *at the same time*. However, the two sets of regulations were not mutually compatible in all cases. As a consequence, some auditors' reports in Italy stressed the conformity of the audited annual accounts to commercial regulation, but some others to the professional standards, despite the explicit request by CONSOB for stating the required double compliance in those reports. With the introduction in 1991 of decree no. 127, this problem has been at least formally solved by asking audit firms to state compliance only with the "rules that discipline financial statements." This approach has been confirmed in the main also by the recent decree no. 58/1998 (Article 156) for the new audit report: now audit firms are required to express an opinion on the compliance of the company and group accounts with the "norms which discipline the drawing up criteria of these statements." The term *norms* seems to refer primarily to legal rules (Civil code and decree no. 127/1991), but also to specified accounting standards (see Section 2.3).

As a legal effect of a non-negative audit report delivered in relation to compulsory audit, the approval of the company annual accounts by the ordinary general meeting can be judicially contested for their lack of compliance with the relevant norms only by as many members as represent at least 5% of the share capital. A similar rule applies to the consolidated accounts drawn up by a quoted parent company. Within 6 months from their deposit in the company registrar, CONSOB too can contest a company or a group financial report.

The legal responsibilities of the audit firm and of its employees, directors, and partners are quite extensive and have a civil, penal, and professional-deontological nature. The sanctions may be heavy and include the cancellation of the guilty audit firm from the CONSOB special roll.

As to the fees of audit firms, there are not at present, as for the *Dottori Commercialisti* and *Ragionieri*, legally determined fees. Audit firms tried to agree among themselves on self-regulation of their fees, but this attempt was opposed by the Authority for Market and Competition, which saw it as going against the rules of free competition. Consequently, Italian *Società di revisione* find themselves without any framework for setting their fees, and a price war among them is said to have begun recently, with a possible risk to the quality of the auditing process given the lack of any required minimum number of hours for performing both legal and voluntary audit. Despite the lack of any regulation on the subject matter, CONSOB fixed some criteria for offering guidance and transparency in price setting by audit firms in its proposals to potential clients (CONSOB communication no. 3556/1996). These proposals must clearly show prices and include a mix of working hours by responsibility levels that should be respected as a minimum requirement (4% of the hours carried out by partners, 14% by managers, 25% by seniors, the rest by juniors). The average cost for a working hour to be paid by clients is around 160,000 lire.

The total turnover of the Italian audit business can be estimated around 750 billion lire a year. However, it is remarkable that the number of companies that voluntarily undergo an auditing process (for image and bank financing purposes) is much larger than that of companies for which it is legally required. In fact, the market for voluntary auditing seems to represent in Italy about 75–80% of the total auditing market (estimate by the Italian Association of Auditors). This could also explain why many audit firms, such as those authorized to operate only according to law no. 1966/1939, can nonetheless survive while remaining outside the business of the legal audit.

Audit firms are grouped into two national associations, which are to some extent rivals: the larger and politically more influential is the *Associazione Italiana Revisori Contabili* (ASSIREVI), the Italian Association of Auditors, which includes the most important 16 Italian audit firms (including the Big Five), which are members of the CONSOB special roll for a total turnover as of 1997 year end of 722 billion lire (490 billion in 1993), and with more than 300 partners (244 in 1993) and 4000 professionals (3,500 in 1993). The other association is the *Associazione Italiana Società di Revisione* (AIRE), the Italian Association of Audit Firms, which represents 8 audit firms (4 belonging to the CONSOB special roll), for a yearly global turnover of around 25 billion lire and 150 employees (for contact numbers see the section "Useful Addresses" at the end of this chapter). In Italy this business shows a strong turnover in professional personnel (e.g., in the past 5 years more than 2,500 employees left audit firms associated with ASSIREVI).

In independent external auditing, the international crisis of legitimation and significance hitting auditors and their work has emerged in Italy, leaving room for uncertainty and contradictions. In the 1990s some events clearly revealed the potential weakness of the auditors' report in assessing the soundness of the accounts, seriously shaking public confidence therein. At the beginning of the 1990s an audit firm was sued for the first time in Italy. A Milan bank had bought a leasing company with audited financial statements. After purchase, however, a remarkable loss, which had not been indicated in the auditors' report, was discovered. The case was settled out of court. Moreover, at the beginning of 1993 the CONSOB forbade a listed company from renewing its auditing contract with a well-known international firm, since the latter was not able, according to CONSOB, to give enough assurance on the quality of the auditing process. The same position was taken by CONSOB in 1994 with reference to another international audit firm. Furthermore, as a by-product of the 1992 bribery scandal and in the related judicial inquiry, it was revealed that a primary audit firm was being sued and penally investigated in connection with its inability to find any traces of the bribes paid by a large company with audited annual accounts. Once again the case was settled out of court. There have been other cases in which firms with audited financial reports and seemingly in a healthy financial situation revealed instead a very difficult one, because of the illegalities and irregular actions that were operated by the company's board of directors. Neither the audit firms nor the *collegio sindacale* of these companies were able to discover those actions or the bribes paid and signed the financial statements and issued their respective reports thereon. CONSOB tried to face this difficult and delegitimizing situation for Italian audit by inviting audit firms and *sindaci* in two 1993 communications to accomplish extra inquiries and checks in order to identify and report any possible censurable facts linked to bribery payments.

2.3   Accounting Standards (*Principi Contabili*) and Auditing Standards (*Principi di Revisione*)

For many decades no need was felt in Italy for accounting standards. This was due to the civil law–based legal system, which did and does oblige companies to follow legal rules, and to the strong and lasting resistence of Italian academics to any standardization process of company financial reporting and accounting year-end valuations.

However, law no. 216/1974 imposed compulsory external audit on listed companies, and the following decree (no. 136/1975, Article 4, section 2) required that this legal audit also be performed according to "correct accounting principles." Curiously enough, at the time neither such standards nor any legally or professionally recognized standard-setting body existed. Therefore, the new legal requirements accelerated the preparation of Italian "GAAP."

In fact, auditors began to feel the need for a set of statements that provided the necessary reference for their work. Further, according to some authors, standards were needed in order to contribute to the interpretation and completion of the legal rules, because these latter obviously could not deal with every specific problem concerning accounts.

Some institutions and associations, such as the Ministry for State-owned groups (*Ministero per le Partecipazioni Statali*) and the Association of Italian Public Limited Companies (*Assonime*), started issuing their own accounting standards, trying to legitimize them in their territory of competence. For some years, different sets of standards competed in Italy, until CONSOB made a choice in 1982 in favor of the standards prepared by the accounting professionals, with the backing of the audit firms (see below).

In fact, the National Council of the most authoritative professional body (*Consiglio Nazionale dei Dottori Commercialisti*, CNDC) set up an *ad hoc* committee in 1975 to cope with issues arising from the introduction of compulsory audit. This committee started its activity as a standard setter producing accounting principles (*principi contabili*) related to valuation and presentation criteria. The aim is to offer guidelines for annual accounts and a benchmark for auditing, taking into account authoritative literature, best practice (both national and international), and the EU accounting directives. In 1982, the National Council of the other Italian professional body (*Consiglio Nazionale dei Ragionieri*) joined the standard-setting venture (so the standard setting committee has become appointed by both accountancy bodies—in short CNDCR). Today, this committee is composed of 21 members, of whom 11 are *Dottori Commercialisti* and 10 *Ragionieri*. The chairman is a *Dottore Commercialista*. The majority of members work in their own studio, but some of them come from audit firms. Some academics are also included.

To date, 23 statements have been published (see Figure 3). As a consequence of the criticisms about the slowness with which standards were prepared or updated, a major revision of them has been carried out in order to take into consideration the new legal framework for accounting originating from decree no. 127/1991 coming into force. The main aim of the revision process was to make standards as close as possible to legal rules and to play an interpretative role of the latter.

Although the accounting standards represented a preliminary step to a rigorous audit, they were perceived as not sufficient since they were partially divergent from the auditors' aims and operating needs. In this respect, in 1975 a second committee was also appointed by the CNDC, which the National Council of *Ragionieri*, as for the accounting standards, joined later. The objective of this second committee was to issue auditing standards (*principi di revisione*) concerning professional ethics, audit planning and procedures, and implications of electronic data processing. To date, 21 audit standards have been issued, dealing with all aspects of the auditing process. Among them, standard no. 18, which has been mentioned earlier, deals with the audit report (*relazione di certificazione*). This standard serves as a reference for auditor's reports in all voluntary audit activity. At present many auditing standards are undergoing a revi-

Figure 3   *List of the Italian Accounting Standards*

Jointly issued by the *Consiglio Nazionale dei Dottori Commercialisti* and *Consiglio Nazionale dei Ragionieri*

1. Financial statements: objectives and postulates (1977, but approved in 1975) (Revised in 1994: now Standard no. 11)
2. Formats (1977; revised in 1994: now Standard no. 12)
2. *bis* Interpretations of and clarifications to Accounting Standard no. 2 (1982)
3. Stock valuation (1978; revised in 1994: now Standard no. 13)
4. Tangible assets (1979)
5. Liquid funds and bank overdrafts (1980; revised in 1994: now Standard no. 14)
6. Debtors (1980)
7. Creditors and other liabilities (1981)
8. Investments, participating interests and consolidated accounts (1983)
9. Translation of items in foreign currency (1988)
10. Long-term contracts (1991; superseded by standard no. 23)
11. Financial statements: objectives and postulates (1994)
12. Formats (1994)
13. Stocks (1994)
14. Liquid funds (1994)
15. Debtors (1996)
16. Tangible fixed assets (1996)
17. Consolidated financial statements (1996)
18. Prepayments, accrued income, accruals and deferred income (1996)
19. Creditors and other liabilities (statutory provisions for severance indemnities, provisions for risks and future costs) (1996)
20. Securities and participating interests (1996)
21. Equity method (1996)
22. Memorandum accounts (1997)
23. Long-term contracts (1997)

Exposure drafts
- Intangible fixed assets
- Accounting for income tax and fiscal-derived values
- Shareholder's funds
- Translation of items expressed in foreign currency (revision of standard no. 9)

sion process: international auditing standards issued by IFAC have been taken as guidance, and their Italian version is currently under examination by the CONSOB. At any rate, it is fair to say that, on the whole, Italian audit standards are not expected to materially part from those commonly used in Anglo-Saxon countries.

Regarding accounting standards, an important feature is that they are not compulsory either in legal or professional terms. They have never been awarded full legal authority: only a short reference to them was made, as already pointed out, in Article 4, section 2, of decree no. 136/1975, according to which the external auditor's report should ensure compliance *at the same time* with correct accounting principles and legal rules.

This requirement, which was a source of ambiguity and practical problems, was canceled by a new version of Article 4 of decree no. 136/1975, put forth by decree no. 127 of 1991 (Article 23). As mentioned earlier, according to this innovated legal text, audit had to verify the conformity of the accounts *exclusively* to the "norms that discipline financial statements," this expression referring to commercial regulation. Even though this legislative intervention might sound like a formal dismissal of accounting standards from any legal relevance, the Ministerial Commentary to decree no. 127/1991 confirmed their technical role of interpretation and integration of the legal rules, especially where obscure points persist in the new legal provisions: in other words, they cannot be "creative" with respect to the latter since they are not normative sources and have to be subordinated to, and compatible with, the legal requirements. It is in this perspective, in fact, that the above-mentioned revision process of accounting standards has been carried out. As mentioned earlier, the recent Article 156, section 2, of decree no. 58/1998 superseded Article 4 of decree no. 136/1975, confirming, though, the need for annual accounts to comply with the "norms which discipline the drawing up criteria of these statements"—a formula that appears similar to that of the former Article 4. Notwithstanding that, some feel that there is still some room for accounting standards to play an autonomous role in the identification and treatment of the so-called *casi eccezionali* (exceptional circumstances, new Article 2423, section 4, Civil Code), that is, when it is mandatory to depart from legal rules (see Section 3).

On the other hand, their practical acceptance has often been a matter of discretion and discussion, although CONSOB in 1982 indicated that they must be considered a reference (*punto di riferimento*) for listed companies, and suggested, but did not require, their application "where not in contrast with extant law" (CONSOB Ordinance no. 1079 dated April 8, 1982). The same ordinance stated that for accounting issues not covered by the CNDCR's principles, the IASC standards are relevant for consideration. The low profile taken by CONSOB was probably due to the then expected imminent implementation of the Fourth Directive.

As for CNDCR's auditing standards, they were also sanctioned by CONSOB in the 1982 ordinance, but—as opposed to accounting standards—their use was overtly recommended to auditing firms.

In more general terms, however, the significance and effectiveness of these standards within a civil law–based legal system remain problematic. Accounting and commercial law literatures did, and to some extent still do, show an ambivalent attitude toward those statements. It must be remembered that one of the central doctrines of Italian legal scholars is that what really matters is not what practice is (as in the Anglo-Saxon countries), but what practice should be (as in some German legal approaches to accounting). This attitude, of course, opposes the very idea and role of generally accepted accounting standards, since generalized acceptance is not a relevant element in legal terms in Italy.

As a result, Italian accounting standards have always had an uncertain status *vis-à-vis* legal rules, since the latter have been considered preeminent over the former, and they did not clearly specify the standards' role. Also, a legally clear and unequivocal identification of a standard-setting body has always been missing. The contradictory and ambiguous nature of accounting standards in Italy did, and does, influence their scarce application and recognition by professionals and companies. These statements seem in fact very little known and used in economic entities other than large ones. The latter are small in number and not representative of average Italian firms.

However, two recent events may produce some rapid changes in the general attitude toward accounting standards. From December 1997 (legislative decree no. 446/1997) a newly introduced tax called IRAP (Regional Tax on Production Activities), which hits a value added-like figure, again gives legal recognition to Italian accounting standards, and in particular to standard no. 12, assigning it a role for correctly classifying revenues and costs within the income statement in order to determine the new tax basis. Incidentally, it is curious to observe that fiscal law, which represents an approach to accounting opposed to that of professional standards (form over substance), is playing a role to legitimize once again accounting standards in Italy from a legal point of view.

The second event relates to the possibility set by Article 117, section 2, of legislative decree no. 58/1998 that from July 1998 Italian companies listed on both an EU market and a non-EU market can depart from national rules (decree no. 127/1991) and refer to "accounting standards of international recognition," which are compatible with EU Directives in order to prepare consolidated financial statements, provided that these standards are acceptable to the non-EU market. These alternative standards are to be identified by an *ad hoc* decree of the Ministry of Justice and are likely to correspond to those issued by the International Accounting Standards Committee (IASC). Therefore, the IAS is facing a probable radical change in its role within the Italian regulatory system for financial reporting: from a residual source of reference—as they are intended in the CONSOB Ordinance of 1982—to a primary legislative source for preparing consolidated accounts, even though it should be noted that this modification in its legal status is likely to create interpretative problems and issues.

2.4 Expected Future Developments Regarding the Accounting Profession and Audit

The future of the accounting profession in Italy will largely depend on the outcome of six challenges, which are highly interrelated:

1. The development of a unitary accounting profession between *Dottori Commercialisti* and *Ragionieri*
2. The legal granting of competencies exclusive to the accounting profession, in particular in relation to the struggle against the so-called *abusivismo;*
3. Definition of the strategic areas for development of the accounting profession
4. The possibility of setting up professional companies and partnerships
5. Definitive clarification of the *sindaci* roles, also *vis-à-vis* the external independent audit
6. Transformation of the *revisori contabili* into a full accountancy body, and the relationships between the accounting profession and audit firms.

As to the first challenge, the upgrading of the qualification of accounting professionals in Italy, which is imposed by the extant rules, seems to find a correspondance in the growth of their socioeconomic importance.

However, the accounting profession remains divided in two competing bodies, with a relative loss of contractual strength and a certain lack of coordination. Since 1929 various attempts have been made to merge the two bodies, without much result. It is most likely that the urgency of this issue will emerge strongly in the near future and that the two bodies will find eventually a compromise in order to reinforce the overall Italian accounting profession.

As to the second challenge, the question is whether in the framework of reform of liberal professions, currently taking place in Italy, accountants will be incisive institutional actors in order to impose in clearer terms than today their expertise and socio-political relevance, in order to legitimize the granting by law of exclusive competencies in certain areas. On the other hand, this would be decisive to help Italian *Dottori Commercialisti* and *Ragionieri* in their battle for defending their professional territory from the attack of nonqualified practitioners who abusively render accountancy services. The outcome of this struggle is crucial for the very survival and growth of the professional identity of Italian qualified accountants.

As to the third challenge, in recent years the *Dottore Commercialista* and *Ragioniere* have achieved increased socioeconomic relevance, especially because of the staggering complexity of tax regulations. Nowadays one might say that the Italian accountant is not, as the Marxists used to say, the slave of the capitalist, but rather a sort of slave of the state since he or she must cope, on behalf of clients, with the new fiscal requirements that are continually introduced by the government. However, the introduction of the *Centri Autorizzati di Assistenza Fiscale* (CAAF, Authorized Agencies for Fiscal Assistance) (Article 78 of law 413/1991) is taking some of the "heavy" fiscal work away from accounting professionals, such as the keeping of account books and the filing of tax declarations of employees and other private citizens (such as pensioners). This might be an opportunity for Italian accountants to expand in the future their presence in different segments of the professional market such as business consultancy.

As to the fourth challenge, it will be interesting to observe whether the Italian profession will be able to reinforce its service supply capacity by aggregating small "studios" in larger structures under the legal umbrella (recently introduced) of professional partnerships or companies.

As to the fifth challenge, Italians agree that the *collegio sindacale* must be profoundly reformed, but there is no clear consensus so far in what direction (e.g., to increase its administrative control role—to make it similar to a supervisory board—or, alternatively, to increase its internal audit responsibilities. Further, who has to elect it? The company owners or the minorities?). A first clarifying step for listed companies has been the introduction of decree no. 58/1998, which attributed all audit responsibility to the audit firm, while leaving the *collegio sindacale* —one member of which is elected by minorities—an incisive supervisory function. What is now to be addressed is the role of this body in the nonlisted companies, which are the vast majority of the Italian industrial system.

As to the sixth challenge, it may well be that in the near future the *revisori contabili* could be transformed into a proper accountancy body and today's "register" into a "roll" such as that of *Dottori commercialisti* and *Ragionieri*. This would mean that in Italy we could arrive in the medium term at having a structure of the accounting profession similar to that in France, with a body that gathers the *experts comptables* (the *Dottori commercialisti* and *Ragionieri*) and another body collecting the *commissaires aux comptes* (the *revisori contabili*), who correspond in the main to the *experts comptables* when they play an audit function within companies. If this is the path ahead for the structuring of the Italian accountancy profession, the new institutional actor could also imply a reconsideration of the relationships between accounting professionals and audit firms. The current *de facto* and to some extent legal dichotomy has in fact produced a situation of tension and competition between auditors and professionals, so that *Dottori Commercialisti* and *Ragionieri* of audit firms, though formally included in the same rolls (*albi*) run by the professional local units, were in the main disregarded by the other collegues and perceived by the latter as not belonging to the same profession. The possible development of a new accountancy body could then contribute to a new phase of the above relationship, which appears nonetheless uneasy, and due to change at a low pace, in parallel to the evolution of the country's industrial and legal structure.

3. The Form and Content of Financial Reporting in Italy

3.1 The Current Legal Framework and the Implementation of European Accounting Directives

Several EU Directives have recently been implemented in Italian accounting legislation in order to harmonize it with that of other European countries. In 1991 the Fourth and Seventh Directives on annual and consolidated accounts were together implemented by legislative decree no. 127/1991. One year later, the directives on financial reporting of banks and other financial institutions (Directive no. 1986/633 and the Eleventh Directive) and in 1997 the Directive on financial reporting of insurance companies were implemented (see Figure 1). For one of those (the Fourth Directive), Italy was seriously late in its implementation, but for the others, relatively quick progress was made in spite of the surrounding general skepticism.

As a result of these legal changes, accounting regulation in Italy has been largely reshaped in the 1990s. In particular, the rules of decree no. 127/1991 dealing with company accounts have been introduced directly into the Civil Code, Book V, in place of the existing ones, while on the contrary, the rules dealing with consolidated reporting have not been included in the Civil Code and remain external to it. In this case, reference will be made to the relevant articles of decree no. 127/1991.

Today, an Italian (company and group) annual report may be expected to be composed of the following documents:

1. Balance sheet (*stato patrimoniale*)
2. Income statement (*conto economico*)
3. Notes to the accounts (*nota integrativa*)
4. Report on operations (*relazione sulla gestione*)
5. Report by the *collegio sindacale* (*relazione del collegio sindacale*)
6. Changes in shareholders' funds statement (*prospetto delle variazioni di capitale netto*)
7. Cash flow statement (*rendiconto finanziario di liquidità*);
8. Chairman's statement (*relazione del Presidente*)
9. Directors' report (*relazione del Consiglio di amministrazione*)
10. Auditor's report (*relazione di certificazione*)

Only the first five statements are legally required to be produced by all limited liability companies in Italy (primarily *Società per azioni*, or *S.p.A.*— comparable to an English public limited company by shares; *Società a responsabilità limitata*, or *S.r.l.*—comparable to an English private limited company; *Società in accomandita per azioni*, or *S.a.p.a.*—a sort of English quasi-partnership by shares, not much in use now). Of course, the auditor's report is also mandatory, where appropriate (e.g., quoted companies, insurance companies, newspaper publishers; see Section 2.2).

A major innovation relates to the composition of the annual accounts, since the notes (*nota integrativa*) to the latter have become an integral part of the legal concept of financial statements and, hence, are no longer included in the directors' report (now called *relazione sulla gestione*, "report on operations"). Thus, the first three of the above statements are to be considered a single whole from a legal point of view, giving content to the *bilancio d'esercizio* (annual financial statements) (Article 2423, section 1, Civil Code).

Documents from no. 6 to no. 9 are presented on a voluntary basis and generally prepared only by medium to large companies (quoted or not). However, note that statement no. 6 is required by accounting standard no. 12 as part of the notes. A further relevant aspect is that neither the European Directive nor Italian law have required a flow of funds statement in any form, even though the latter's importance is clearly pointed out by CNDCR's accounting standard no. 12 (see Figure 3), which explicitly asks for this statement to be included in the notes. At any rate, this document is customarily produced by all listed companies and many of the medium to large Italian enterprises.

Moreover, it must be considered that listed companies must also produce a 6-month report on operating trends (the so-called *relazione semestrale*). This report is to be drawn up by company directors according to the criteria established by CONSOB and must be made public (Article 2427 Civil Code, section 3).

The figures of the previous accounting period must be shown for each item of the balance sheet and income statement, for both company and group financial reports.

Annual accounts (including consolidated statements) are to be prepared either in lire or in lire and ECU, according to EU Directive no. 90/604, which was implemented in Italy through legislative decree no. 526/1992. From 1999 the figures can also be stated in euro, the new single European currency unit.

On group acccounting, it should be noted that virtually all Italian large (nonlisted) groups have voluntarily presented consolidated accounts since the second half of the 1980s, while only quoted companies and a few other categories (newspaper publishers, insurance companies, banks, and so on) are legally bound to do so. Sometimes consolidated reports are also published in English (see the 1996 Merloni Consolidated Accounts at the end of this chapter), and this version could be the preeminent one. There are cases—occurring recently in Italy, and expected to expand to some extent in the near future—when Italian companies are listed only on foreign Stock Exchanges, especially New York (e.g., Luxottica, Natuzzi, De Rigo, Fila).

As to unlimited liability firms (*Impresa individuale*, sole proprietorship; *Società in nome collettivo*, or *S.n.c.*, comparable to an English conventional partnership; *Società in accomandita semplice*, or *S.a.s.*, a sort of English quasi-partnership), they must prepare only a balance sheet (as a by-product of the annual stock-taking) and an income statement, but they do not have to comply with the formats and rules set for limited companies, except for the year-end valuation criteria that are the same. The general principle to be followed by these firms in the preparation of their accounts is that these shall give with "straightforwardness and truth" the firm's financial situation and year's performance (Article 2217, section 2, Civil Code). Unlimited liability firms are not required to make their annual accounts public, but they are obliged to enclose them with their annual tax declaration.

A peculiar aspect of the 1990s practice of financial reporting in Italy has been the accounting treatment of bribes (*tangenti*) paid by firms to public officials in order to gain access to public works. Mention of these "black" monetary outflows started to appear in the notes and directors' reports of some companies in the 1993 accounts.

Another recent—and still much limited—accounting phenomenon in Italy is the publication by some groups (e.g., Fiat, IBM Italy, Ferruzzi, Enichem, Ciba Geigy Italy) of an environmental report (*bilancio ambientale*), where environmental inputs and outputs (say, consumption of electricity and methane, issuance of polluting substances) of the already existing production activities are accounted for, and plans to improve this relationship are put forth. It is probably too soon to talk about a *greening* of Italian accounting, even though such environmental reports are an interesting development in this direction.

In procedural terms for limited liability entities, the company's annual general meeting (*assemblea dei soci*) must be called within 4 months (or within 6 months, if the memorandum so specifies) from the end of the financial year. At least 30 days (45 days, if a quoted company) before the general meeting, a copy of the company's annual accounts (*bilancio d'esercizio*), together with the report on operations and the consolidated accounts (if a parent company of a group), are communicated from the company's directors to the *collegio sindacale* and, if relevant, to the external audit firm. At least 15 days before the general meeting a copy of all the above statements, accompanied by the report of the *collegio sindacale* and the auditor's report, are made available to members in the company's registered office. Within 30 days after approval of company's accounts (group accounts need not be formally approved) by the general meeting, directors are required to deposit a copy of all the above documents and a copy of the minutes of the meeting in the register of undertakings (*registro delle imprese*), which was set up by Article 8 of law no. 580/1993 at the Chambers of Commerce; before 1993 *ad hoc* registers at the Chancery of Tribunals were used) and to mention the occurrence of this deposit in the Official Bulletin of Public and Private Limited Companies (*Bollettino Ufficiale delle Società per Azioni e a Responsabilità Limitata*, BUSARL).

There are two further issues that affect in a relevant way the general form and content of annual accounts in Italy, and hence they must be described somewhat more in depth: (a) the Italian approach to the "true and fair view" principle, and (b) the relationship between accounting and taxation.

An Italian View of "True and Fair View"   The fundamental principle of the new legislation, which drives in principle the whole preparation of *both company and group annual accounts* comes, according to the Ministerial Commentary that accompanies decree no. 127/1991, from the British "true and fair view" formula. Accounts are now required to "represent in a true and correct manner" a company's economic and financial situation and the annual results (*rappresentare in modo veritiero e corretto*) (Article 2423 Civil Code, section 2). The Ministerial Commentary on this point states only that this newly phrased principle "seems to be the most exact translation of the expression 'true and fair view' from which the directive norm derives." No definition is given by this official commentary, however, nor by the law, of the actual meaning of this British-derived formula.

In addition to this principle, accounts must also be drawn up with clearness (*chiarezza*).

Additional disclosures and departures from legal rules, when needed to comply with the new fundamental formula of the true and correct representation (*rappresentazione veritiera e corretta*) are *compulsory,* and any relevant explanations thereof must be included in the notes (Article 2423 Civil Code, sections 3 and 4). Any gains from departures from legal rules must not be taken to the income statement but must be "sterilized" from any income effect by being imputed in an *ad hoc* reserve.

It is important to remember that the principles of *rappresentazione veritiera e corretta* and of *chiarezza*, as well as the compulsory additional disclosures and departures from law, apply also to the accounts of groups and financial institutions and of insurance companies (Article 29, decree no. 127/1991; Article 2, decree no. 87/1992; Article 65, decree no. 173/ 1997).

Since it came into force in 1993, there has been great concern in Italy about how to interpret the true and correct representation formula and about its actual consequences. The transfer of such a context-specific concept from one jurisdiction to another is deemed to be problematic, especially in a legal system, such as the Italian, where a general principle guiding the drawing up of accounts has virtually always existed (see Section 1.2) and when it is not clear what the new general principle adds *vis-à-vis* the previous ones. Because of its importance, and in order to fully appreciate its concrete role in Italian accounting, the evolution of this principle needs to be further analyzed.

In a historical perspective, the original 1942 version of the Civil Code presented two expressions acting as general principles in preparing annual accounts: these must give with straightforwardness and truth (*evidenza e verità*) (Article 2217) and with clarity and precision (*chiarezza e precisione*) (Article 2423, section 2) the financial situation of a firm and its economic results. Despite these general principles, however, there were a number of legal rules set in the Civil Code dealing with specific year-end valuation criteria, so that the role of those formulas has always been ambiguous and not very incisive on the whole.

As to departures from legal rules—inherent in the British "true and fair view" formula—they were allowed in Italy by the last section of the original version of Article 2425 Civil Code, only for special reasons (*speciali ragioni*). Thus, while the meaning of the above-mentioned general legal formulas was sufficiently agreed upon in the literature, this overriding principle has always represented a controversial matter, not least because it introduced a sort of deviance within a legal system that is otherwise strictly civil-law based. The several contrasting opinions about the correct interpretation of *speciali ragioni* may be summarized under two main theoretical headings. One approach interpreted special reasons as specific circumstances regarding the company as a whole, so that, for example, a particular situation of the company could justify exceeding the maximum value prescribed by law. Avoiding a loss either bringing disrepute to the firm or implying a substantial capital reduction (when it is possible to cover it by revaluing an asset) was indicated as an example of special reasons (but a 1983 decision of the Venice Courts was explicitly against the latter interpretation). A second more prevalent approach in the literature deemed that special reasons were to be related to a firm's individual assets. Events changing an asset's economic nature could permit the abandonment of its historical cost and the adoption of a higher and more appropriate value. This was the case for an agricultural site turned into a building site, or that of grazing land transformed into a camping site, or that of land converted into an oil field. It was common opinion that the above formula did not refer to monetary inflation, since it was argued that the question of the impact of this phenomenon on company accounts was periodically addressed by *ad hoc* legislation (the so-called revaluation laws).

In 1983, after a 40-year debate on the role and significance of the special reasons formula, the time was ripe for legal clarification. Article 9 of the revaluation law called *Visentini-bis* (no. 72/1983) stated that special reasons were intended as those requiring departures from legal rules in order to give a faithful picture (*quadro fedele*) of the company's economic and financial situation. The 1983 law drew this formula from the Fourth Directive: *quadro fedele* was in fact the official translation of "true and fair view" in the Italian version of the EU Directive. Therefore, on that occasion, the "true and fair view" concept entered Italian legislation for the first time, almost 10 years before the introduction of decree no. 127/1991. The primary intention of the Italian government was probably to state an authoritative interpretation—legally sanctioned—of the special reasons formula in order to clarify its correct application. In this respect, it was probably decided to anticipate in part the Fourth Directive implementation, which at the time was believed to be imminent.

However, this statutory intervention did not solve the problem. "Special reasons" were explained through the use of a new concept, unknown to Italian law, which in turn required clarification. Thus, during the 1980s the dispute on the overriding principle was revived because of the different scholarly reactions to the *quadro fedele* formula. This legal interpretation of "special reasons" was variously considered an innovation or nothing new, a step toward inflation accounting or a barrier in that direction, and so on. Some emphasized that the *quadro fedele* concept, drawn from the Fourth Directive, was incompatible with the Italian civil law tradition, and that this was the reason for misunderstanding. According to one opinion, the *quadro fedele* formula did not differ essentially from the fundamental principle of "clearness and precision" (Article 2423 of the 1942 version of the Civil Code): it would be achieved, in fact, when legal rules were respected. By contrast, it appeared to some that accounting standards could prevail over the legal principles. In this respect, the risk perceived by some legal scholars was that practitioners could be granted too great a flexibility in deciding departures from stated rules, if an interpretation of the *quadro fedele* expression in terms of complete freedom in overcoming valuation limits was to prevail.

In order to avoid the risk of allowing too much flexibility, and not to create confusion with past accounting rules, decree no. 127/1991—in implementing the Fourth Directive—abandoned the *quadro fedele* phrase and enforced the above-mentioned formula *rappresentare in modo veritiero e corretto*. In addition, as already pointed out, the latter was perceived (rightly or wrongly) as closer to the Anglo-Saxon "true and fair view" actual meaning, according to the Ministerial Commentary. Besides, the above formula was intended to prevent the general legal principle of "true and correct representation" being a device to loosen the accounting regulation, as some interpretations of the *quadro fedele* tried to support in earlier times. The clearly persued aim would be now to guarantee information objectivity.

A minimal degree of flexibility is preserved in particular situations. In fact, the overriding principle, which was implied by the special reasons expression in 1942, is maintained and newly phrased in the 1991 legal provisions: departures from civil rules are now *mandatory* in "exceptional cases," which must be intended as *very* rare circumstances concerning primarily the valuation of firm's identified assets (e.g., a change in their economic nature). Further, it is generally agreed that inflation is not an exceptional case and, hence, once again, no Civil Code rule provides for the accounting treatment of this phenomenon.

Paradoxically, the early insertion of the *quadro fedele* concept in 1983 seems then to have determined its rejection and substitution with a more precisely defined and strictly bounded formula, which is consistent with a rigid interpretation of the civil law nature of the Italian legal system.

Despite some optimistic expectations linked to the introduction in Italian accounting of a principle allegedly similar to "true and fair view," however, it appears that the role of any general legal principle (such as "clearness and precision" or "true and correct representation") within the Italian civil law framework will probably remain limited in practice, because, where specific rules are given, these must be followed (exceptional cases apart). Their application leads then quite automatically—by a sort of legal presumption—

to the respect of the stated general principle. From this perspective, the role and scope of application of any general legal principle in Italy are restricted by the existence of *ad hoc* regulations dealing with accounts formats and valuations. As a consequence, this general formula is likely to have some effect only where no detailed legal rule—either of a civil or fiscal nature—is provided (broadly similar to Germany).

To these general considerations must be added, on more specific grounds, the conceptually and legally problematic relationship between the recently implemented principle of "true and correct representation" (Article 2423, section 2, Civil Code) and the old (1882) but still enforced principle of "straightforwardness and truth" (*evidenza e verità*—Article 2217, section 2, Civil Code), which continues to apply to annual accounts of unlimited liability entities. In fact, it seems that the two principles cannot be different in their essence, because of the need for a systematically coherent interpretation of the legal codified framework. As an ironic result of this situation, the 1882 principle must necessarily have the same meaning and role as the fresh, European-derived formula.

Accounting and Taxation   Taxation is a factor that influences strongly the preparation of company accounts in Italy, given that consolidated accounts are tax-neutral for the time being in Italy (as in other countries).

Commercial and tax regulations progressively moved closer in the years after 1974 (reform of the income tax, including corporation tax), and they are now probably inextricably intertwined.

Therefore, the scholarly view, which is conventionally identified as the "double track approach" (*teoria del doppio binario*), and according to which there should be a clear independence of the commercial rules from fiscal provisions, has been defeated in practice, even before it was defeated in legal terms. As a consequence of this approach, in fact, tax valuations would be taken into account only for the filing of the annual tax return, and no items of a merely fiscal nature would appear in published accounts. It is instead rather clear that a second view more and more prevailed in Italy from the 1970s, the so-called single track approach (*teoria del binario unico*), which establishes an influence of tax rules on commercial accounts, giving rise to a sort of reverse dependence of the latter from the former (see also Section 1.2).

In detail, this result has been caused mainly by the combined effect of two fiscal rules. The first requires that company taxable income is in principle that resulting from the accounting records kept for commercial purposes (Article 52, 1986 Consolidated Act on Income Taxes, T.U.I.R.), while the second rule makes it compulsory for Italian companies to include certain expenses in their profit and loss account in order to deduct them from tax (Article 75, section 4, T.U.I.R.). These provisions give rise to a system of relationships between tax and commercial legislation in accounting that is somewhat similar to that induced by the German *Maßgeblichkeitsprinzip*, that is, the "authoritative principle."

An attempt to overcome the problematic relationship between commercial law and fiscal rules has been made by the original version of decree no. 127/1991, which adopted an odd middle way between the above-mentioned two extreme positions, requiring that the final section of the income statement include adjustments of valuations and provisions both resulting purely from the application of the tax legislation (former items no. 24 and 25 of the income statement format), with a clear attempt to separate the influence of taxation from accounting profit calculation. In this way, however, the intrusion of the tax rules into the Italian commercial accounts was definitively stated and recognized by the Civil Code itself. In other words, there had taken place an institutionalization of the linkage between commercial and tax accounting, which was previously supported only by the joint effect of articles 52 and 74 of the 1986 Consolidated Act on Income Taxes, and which was commonly applied in practice but never overtly set in the Civil Code. As an example, accelerated depreciation exceeding the "correct" amount under the Civil Code's rule had to be shown in the "corrections to valuations that resulted purely from the application of fiscal law" (item no. 24 of the original income statement format). This treatment of accelerated depreciation was similar to that of the French system (*amortissement dérogatoire*). The two lines of fiscal corrections led to a final result that was similar but does not fully overlap with taxable income. This was because, according to most authors and the Ministerial Commentary, only additional charges caused by tax allowances being greater than commercial accounting ones could be entered in these adjustment lines. Where the difference was the other way, that is, the tax allowance was less than the accounting one, the difference could not be included in these two lines, and therefore the reconciliation between the tax profit and the commercial profit was one-sided and partial.

This fiscal section of the income statement format became a source of interpretative problems, its exact use being unclear. Although the intention in the original approach of the 1991 decree to clarify the relationship between commercial and tax laws was in principle commendable, technical problems and cultural resistences arose considering the above-described explicit recognition of the fiscal influence on commercial accounts on the one hand and the stated formal autonomy of commercial accounts from taxation on the other hand (see Article 1 of Parliamentary law no. 69/ 1990 empowering the Italian government to implement the Fourth Directive). In particular, many firms complained that, given the then new treatment required for accelerated depreciation in the income statement (item no. 24), they could not any longer deduct it—as they did traditionally—from relevant tangible fixed assets, but they had to take this fiscal-derived value to a shareholder funds' provision (a sort of special reserve) titled "accelerated depreciation," and in parallel to account for deferred tax, which is quite uncommon for company accounts in Italy.

As a consequence of this perceived problem, a new rule was issued in August 1994 (Article 2-*bis*, law no. 503/1994), which cancelled the fiscal section in the income statement format (items no. 24 and 25), as well as the "result of the financial year" (item no. 23), which was basically the accounting result before fiscal corrections. The same article stated that it is permitted to operate fiscal corrections to accounting values in company accounts, and that the reasons and amounts of these corrections have to be disclosed in the notes on point no. 14. Incidentally, Article 2-*bis* of law no. 503/1994 cancelled the requirement that consolidation accounts be freed from fiscal interferences existing in company accounts and imposed the requirement that in the notes there should be disclosed the reasons and amounts of these tax-originated values in the group accounts (point 0-*bis* of the notes to consolidated accounts).

The effect of these regulatory changes on the relationship between commercial accounts and tax rules is that companies are allowed to apply the latter in the preparation of the former, and virtually no value nor result in their income statement is now free from fiscal influences, while beforehand the "result of the financial year" (former item no. 23) was relatively unbiased by tax interferences. The "principle of reverse dependence" is thus confirmed, that is, of the dependence of commercial accounting rules on tax rules, so that one could say—ironically—that the former are now completely harmonized with the latter. In a nutshell, the evolution of this relationship went full circle, and Italy went back to the situation existing before decree no. 127/1991.

It must be pointed out once again, though, that the "profit for the year" line does not correspond to taxable income, since a number of fiscal allowances and variations of accounting numbers are carried out by companies directly in their annual tax return (*dichiarazione dei redditi*). In particular, for income tax purposes a 5-year carry-forward of an accounting loss for the financial period is allowed to any limited or unlimited entity (Articles. 5 and 102, Consolidated Act on Income Tax).

It is also noteworthy that the fiscal section of the income statement was in use for the 1993 financial year, and some companies started to treat the fiscal corrections as a sort of reserves in the shareholder funds. Hence, interpretative and technical adjustment problems arose in company accounts relating to year 1994.

On the other hand, it is possible to give a further example of the existing close relationship between fiscal and civil legislation in Italy. In order to make accounts legal from the commercial point of view, the Civil Code requires companies to comply with a great deal of formal requirements, such as the stamping and numbering of the account books (Article 2215 Civil Code). These requirements can also be carried out by the tax authorities and are necessary to legalize accounts from the fiscal standpoint, too.

Presented on pages 633-669 are two sets of 1996 accounts, group accounts and parent company (individual company) accounts, of the Merloni, so that readers have the opportunity to review both.

In the following the main Italian format and disclosure rules in company and group accounts will be dealt with, although it would be impossible within the framework of this book to cover all the detailed regulations regarding financial reporting of different industries (e.g., mining, oil) and/or types of companies (e.g., co-operatives).

3.2 The Form and Content of Company Accounts

As already pointed out, the Fourth EU Directive of 1978 on annual accounts was eventually implemented in the Italian Civil Code, with the first part of legislative decree no. 127 dated April 9, 1991. For financial years ending after April 17, 1993, all limited companies are required to produce financial statements that comply with the new legislation. Its *de facto* relevance extended also to 1992 accounts, however, given the already mentioned need for comparative figures.

The company financial statements (*bilancio d'esercizio*) are legally composed, as indicated above, of a balance sheet, an income statement, and notes to the account, accompanied by a report on operations. The detailed contents of each of these documents will be illustrated below.

Table 1	*Size Thresholds for Abridged Financial Statements*
	(Article 2435-bis Civil Code)

Assets (net of depreciation funds)	3.09 billion Italian lira
Sales (net of discounts)	6.18 billion Italian lira
Employees (financial year average)	50

In order to benefit from the special (balance sheet) format and abridged notes and report on operations, the above limits must not be exceeded for two consecutive financial years (or for the first year of life of an undertaking).

However, there exists an abridged form of company financial statements (*bilancio in forma abbreviata*), which is allowed for small companies not exceeding—for two consecutive financial years or in the first year of their existence—two of the three size thresholds indicated in Table 1 (Article 2435-*bis* Civil Code).

It is worth observing that since their introduction these thresholds have been updated twice by decree no. 526/1992 implementing in Italy EU Directive no. 90/604 and most recently by law no. 52/1996 (Article 19).

These abridged annual accounts consist of a simplified balance sheet format (where only items marked by capital letters and roman numbers must be shown, see Figure 4), a standard income statement, and a reduced number of compulsory notes (seven out of the ordinarily required eighteen disclosures). The report on operations (*relazione sulla gestione*) may be omitted, if some of its information (namely, nos. 3 and 4) are included in the notes. However, decree no. 526/1992 requires small enterprises to *explicitly* show both the depreciation and amortization provisions as deductions from the fixed assets on the face of the balance sheet, and debtors and creditors due beyond next financial year. Note that, on the contrary, for companies that are not small, the net fixed asset figure alone can be shown on the face of the balance sheet, while detail about related depreciation and amortization provisions can be disclosed in the notes.

As discussed earlier, the general principle guiding the drawing up of the annual accounts in Italy is now that of "representing in a true and correct manner" the financial situation of a company and its economic results (Article 2423, section 2, Civil Code).

Other general, well-known accounting postulates are specified in the new provisions in order to develop the above fundamental principle:

prudence, accrual, consistency in valuation criteria, and *going concern* (Article 2423-*bis*, Civil Code). However, these were already applied as common practice and in the main already implicit in the previous law. No particular differences exist with the Anglo-American interpretation of the same postulates.

In the following sections the compulsory legal formats of company accounts and their contents will be analyzed more in detail.

3.2.1 Legal Formats and Contents

The minimum contents of financial statements, which had previously been defined by the Civil Code, have now been extended, and *highly rigid formats* (also in the *sequence of items*) prescribed, applying in principle to all companies and groups prevalently performing industrial activity (banks and financial institutions as well as insurance companies have their own formats, see Section 3.4).

Some flexibility is allowed for modifying the name and the degree of details only of the items that are preceded by Arabic numbers in the balance sheet format, and by small letters in the income statement one (Article 2423-*ter*, Civil Code, see Figures 4 and 5).

Clearly, these formats do not always provide information in a manner suitable for financial analysis and need the analyst's quite complex elaborations to pursue successfully this end.

Balance Sheet (Stato Patrimoniale, Article 2424 Civil Code)   From the options available in the Fourth Directive, Italy has chosen the traditional, horizontal balance sheet format (Article 9 of the directive), with assets on the left and set out apparently in reverse order of liquidity (see Figure 4). In fact, the balance sheet is organized according to the German-based destination principle, which leads to an inappropriate classification according to the American approach, which is based on the items' liquidity, since it implies putting items having the same economic nature together. For example, all trade debtors go in the Current Assets section (item C.II. of Assets), independent of their maturity time (that may be beyond the next financial year). This is on the basis that they spring from the same economic process, that is, the trade of the company's (and group's) products. The same applies to debtors having a financial nature that are all to be imputed to Investments (item no. B.III.2. of Assets). Furthermore, the items' liquidity principle of classification is clearly not

---

Figure 4   *Mandatory Balance Sheet Format*
(Article 2424 Civil Code)

1997   1996

ASSETS:

A. Called-up share capital not paid, with a specific note of the amounts already called in

B. Fixed assets:
   I. *Intangible assets:*
      1. start-up costs
      2. research, development, and advertising costs capitalized
      3. patent rights and royalties
      4. brands and licences
      5. goodwill
      6. intangible assets under construction and prepayments [difference on consolidation]*
      7. others

   Total

   II. *Tangible assets:*
      1. land and buildings
      2. plant and machinery
      3. fixtures and fittings
      4. other tangible assets
      5. tangible assets under construction and prepayments

   Total

   III. *Investments, with a specific note, for each item of debtors,* of amounts receivable within the next financial year:
      1. participating interests in:
         a. subsidiary undertakings
         b. associated undertakings
         c. parent undertakings
         d. other undertakings
      2. debtors:
         a. amounts owed by subsidiary undertakings
         b. amounts owed by associated undertakings
         c. amounts owed by parent undertakings
         d. amounts owed by other undertakings

(Figure continues)

(Figure 4, continued)

1997   1996

    3. other securities
    4. own shares, with a note on their total nominal value

                        Total

Total fixed assets (B)

C. Current assets:
    I. *Stocks:*
        1. raw materials and consumables
        2. work-in-progress
        3. long-term contract stocks
        4. finished goods and merchandise
        5. prepayments

                        Total

    II. *Debtors, with a specific note for each item of amounts* due beyond the next financial year:
        1. trade debtors
        2. amounts owed by subsidiary undertakings
        3. amounts owed by associated undertakings
        4. amounts owed by parent undertakings
        5. amounts owed by other undertakings

                        Total

    III. *Financial assets other than long term:*
        1. participating interests in subsidiary undertakings
        2. participating interests in associated undertakings
        3. participating interests in parent undertakings
        4. participating interests in other undertakings
        5. own shares, with a note also of their total nominal value
        6. other securities

                        Total

    IV. *Liquid funds:*
        1. cash at bank and in post office accounts
        2. cheques
        3. cash in hand

                        Total

Total current assets (C)

D. Accrued income and prepayments, with a specific note of discounts on loans

1997   1996

LIABILITIES:

A. Shareholders' capital:
  I.   Called-up share capital
  II. Share premium account
  III. Revaluation reserve
  IV. Legal reserve
  V.   Reserve for own shares
  VI. Reserves provided for by the articles
       [Consolidation reserve]*
  VII. Other reserves
       [Capital and reserves of third parties
       (i.e., minority interests)]*
  VIII. Profits (losses) of previous years
  IX. Profit (loss) for the year
                                        Total

B. Provisions for risks and liabilities:
  1. provisions for pensions
  2. provisions for taxes
      [consolidation provision for risks
      and future expenses]*
  3. others
                                        Total

C. Statutory provisions for severance indemnities

D. Creditors, with a specific note for each item of amounts due beyond the
    next financial year:
  1. debentures
  2. redeemable debentures
  3. bank overdrafts and loans
  4. other loans
  5. prepayments
  6. trade creditors
  7. bills of exchange
  8. amounts owed to subsidiary undertakings
  9. amounts owed to associated undertakings
  10. amounts owed to parent undertakings
  11. taxes
  12. social security
  13. others
                                        Total

(Figure continues)

(Figure 4, continued)

1997   1996

E.   Accruals and deferred income, with a specific note of premiums on loans

Memorandum Accounts
1.   List of direct and indirect guarantees, with a specific indication of:
  a.   fiduciary garantees in favor of subsidiary, associated, parent, and group undertakings
  b.   endorsement garantees in favor of subsidiary, associated, parent, and group undertakings
  c.   personal guarantees in favor of subsidiary, associated, parent, and group undertakings
  d.   real property guarantees in favor of subsidiary, associated, parent, and group undertakings
2.   Other memorandum accounts

---

* This item is to be included—where relevant—only in the consolidated balance sheet.

respected as to liabilities, since, for instance, all creditors must be classified in the same section, without taking into consideration any of their time length to maturity. As a consequence, balance sheet items may be easily misleading to an analyst fully adopting a mere financial approach.

In the following, a closer look at the sections composing asset and liability sides will be given.

Assets (*Attivo*)   Moving on to the analysis of the individual sections, there appears to be nothing relevant in Section (A) (*Crediti verso soci per versamenti ancora dovuti, con separata indicazione della parte già richiamata*), apart from the facts that (*a*) the amounts of this section are both those that have already been called up and those that are not yet so, and that (*b*) this item should probably be deducted from shareholder funds when carrying out a financial analysis, or put in Current Assets' debtors.

Section (B) (*Immobilizzazioni*) deals with all kinds of fixed assets (B.I: *Immobilizzazioni materiali*; B.II: *Immobilizzazioni immateriali*; B.III: *Immobilizzazioni finanziarie*). As already stated, tangible assets and intangible assets and trade debtors must be shown at their net value (i.e., their respective provisions being deducted). In contrast to some other European countries, it is possible to capitalize research and development costs, as well as advertisement expenses, where relevant. The capitalization of these items hinders the distribution of dividends, however, if the amounts of

---

Figure 5   *Mandatory Income Statement Format*
(Article 2425 Civil Code)

1997   1996

A. Value of production:
1. turnover
2. change in stocks of finished goods and in work-in-progress
3. change in long-term contract stocks
4. own work capitalized
5. other income, with a specific note of the public "ordinary grants"

Total

B. Production costs:
6. raw materials and consumables
7. external services
8. rents
9. staff costs:
    a. wages and salaries
    b. social security costs
    c. statutory severance costs
    d. other pension costs
    e. other staff costs
10. depreciation and write-offs:
    a. depreciation of intangible assets
    b. depreciation of tangible assets
    c. other amounts written off from fixed assets
    d. amounts written off from current debtors and from liquid funds
11. change in stock of raw materials, consumables, and merchandise;
12. provisions for risks
13. other provisions
14. other operating charges

Total

Difference between production value and costs (A – B).

(Figure continues)

(Figure 5, continued)

1997   1996

C. Income and charges from financial assets:
    15. income from participating interests, with a separate note of that from subsidiary and associated undertakings
    16. other income from financial assets:
        a. income from debtors under fixed assets, with a separate note of that from subsidiary and associated undertakings, and that from parent undertakings
        b. income from fixed asset investments other than participating interests
        c. income from current asset investments other than participating interests
        d. other income from financial assets, with a separate note of that from subsidiary and associated undertakings, and that from parent undertakings
    17. interest and similar charges, with a separate note of those to subsidiary, associated and parent undertakings

Total (15 + 16 – 17)

D. Changes in value of financial assets:
    18. revaluations:
        a. of participating interests
        b. of fixed asset investments other than participating interests
        c. of current asset investments other than participating interests
    19. write-offs:
        a. of participating interests
        b. of fixed asset investments other than participating interests
        c. of current asset investments other than participating interests

Total of changes in value (18 – 19)

E. Extraordinary income and charges:
    20. extraordinary income, with a separate note of gains from disposals which cannot be recorded under no. 5
    21. extraordinary charges, with a separate note of losses from disposals which cannot be recorded under no.

1997   1996

14, and of taxes relating to previous financial years
    Total of extraordinary items (20 – 21)
    Profit or loss before taxation (A – B ± C ± D ± E)
22. taxes on profit
    [profit (loss) for the financial year to third parties
    (i.e., minority interests)]*
23. profit (loss) for the financial year

---

* This item is to be included—where relevant—only in the consolidated income statement.

intangibles capitalized are not counterbalanced by at least an identical amount of available reserves in the shareholder funds. Goodwill (*avviamento*) can be shown in item B.I.5. only if a cost has been incurred by the company and it has been "purchased" to the latter from operations of merger and acquisition. No self-valuation of company brands (*marchi*) is permitted. Equity investments (*partecipazioni*) in other companies are considered fixed assets on the basis of a legal presumption, according to which, if these investments are in associated undertakings (or *a fortiori* in subsidiary undertakings), that is, they exceed at least the 20% of the share capital of the participated company (10% if this is quoted), then these values should be included in section B.III.1. of the balance sheet (since a "significant influence" is attached to them). Note that section B.III.1. was amended in May 1994 by decree no. 315/1994 (Article 6), implementing in Italy EU Directive no. 92/101 regarding the purchase of both own and controlling entities' shares. As a consequence of this regulatory change, item B.III.1.c. has been introduced requiring disclosure of the value of equity investments in parent undertakings. If a company owns an equity investment in another company through a fiduciary firm, then it may write this value under the heading (financial) "debtors" (one of the items in B.III.2.) instead of under the caption "investments" (one of the items in B.III.1).

All fixed assets must mandatorily be devalued if the loss occurring to them is of a lasting nature; otherwise, they must be maintained at historic cost. When the reason for which a fixed asset has been devalued ceases, this must be written up again at its original (historic) cost. In Italy, lease capitalization is not permitted, and consequently, operating and financial leasing are treated in the same way, that is, taking the lease rentals to income statement in accordance with the accrual principle.

Section (C) (*Attivo circolante*) includes the values to be used in, and originating from, the ordinary course of business, such as inventory, trade debtors, short-term securities, and cash (C.I: *Rimanenze*; C.II: *Crediti*; C.III: *Attività finanziarie*; C.IV: *Disponibilità liquide*). A small change in section C.III. was brought about by decree no. 315/1994, which added a new line disclosing the value of current investments in parent undertakings (now item C.III.3.).

In Section (D) (*Ratei e risconti attivi*) note the inclusion of discounts on loans (*disaggio su prestiti*) in "prepayments and accrued income" is noteworthy, following the French influence. Discounts on loans should generally be taken to intangible assets for the purposes of financial analysis.

Liabilities (*Passivo*)   Section (A) (*Patrimonio netto*) deals with Shareholders' Capital and Reserves. It is divided into many subsections indicated by a Roman number. They are the following:

I. Called-up share capital	I. *Capitale*
II. Share premium account	II. *Riserva da sovraprezzo azioni*
III. Revaluation reserve	III. *Riserve di rivalutazione*
IV. Legal reserve	IV. *Riserva legale*
V. Reserve for own shares	V. *Riserva per azioni proprie in portafoglio*
VI. Reserves provided for by the articles [Consolidation reserve]	VI. *Riserve statutarie* [*Riserva di consolidamento*]
VII. Other reserves [Capital and reserves of third parties]	VII. *Altre riserve* [*Capitale e riserve di terzi*]
VIII. Profits (losses) of previous years	VIII. *Utili (perdite) portati a nuovo*
IX. Profit (loss) for the year	IX. *Utile (perdita) dell' esercizio*

The items in brackets are to appear only in consolidated accounts. The law does not attribute to them any specific number or identification.

On the individual items, it should be noted that:

- "Called-up share capital" is the amount of capital in issue (paid or not paid) at the end of a financial year.

- "Share premium account" is the reserve where the amount of the issue price over share face value is taken (in Italy shares cannot be issued at a price lower than their nominal value). The amounts of this reserve cannot be distributed before the legal reserve has reached the level indicated below (Article 2431 Civil Code).

- "Revaluation reserve" is the account in which the credit surpluses of the revaluation processes enacted in accordance with the different revaluation laws (see Section 4.1) are written.
- "Legal reserve" is made up of a mandatory annual allowance of 5% from the profit for the year, until this reserve reaches the amount of 20% of the share capital in issue (Article 2430 Civil Code).
- "Reserve for own shares" is a reserve to be mandatorily provided for when a company buys back own shares: these must be included either in section B.III.4 or in section C.III.5 of Assets, while a nondistributable reserve of the same amount is to be set up with profits of previous years or distributable reserves in the shareholder funds (Article 2357-*ter*, section 3, Civil Code). This reserve has to be maintained as long as the company remains in possession of the shares.
- "Reserves provided for by the articles" are reserves that may be changed only by an *ad hoc* decision of an extraordinary-type of shareholders' general meeting.
- "Consolidation reserve" is an account in which a negative difference between the purchase price of a company and the fair value of its net assets is written to, unless this difference depends on the anticipation of unfavorable trends in the acquired company's future economic results (Article 33, decree no. 127/1991). In the latter case, this difference has to be taken to a "consolidation provision for risks and future expenses" (see below).
- "Other reserves" must be specified one by one; typical examples of reserves falling in this category are "Reserve for credit balances from departures from legal rules according to the true and correct representation principle"; "Reserve for accelerated depreciation" (virtually eliminated as a consequence of the August 1994 change in the relationship between commercial and tax rules; see Section 3.1); "Reserve for public grants"; and "Reserve for gains from the equity method of investment valuation" (see Section 4.1).
- "Capital and reserves of third parties" is an item that in the Anglo-American environment is better known under the label "minority interests" (Article 32, decree no. 127/1991).
- "Profits (losses) of previous years" comprises the amounts of income not yet decided upon by the annual general meeting (note that,

with reference to losses, until these are covered, the distribution of dividends is not allowed; Article 2433, section 3, Civil Code).

* "Profit (loss) for the year" corresponds to the amount calculated in the income statement, that is, it includes the dividends to be distributed to shareholders. This implies that shareholder funds in Italian balance sheets are overestimated by the amount of dividends, which is on the contrary usually disclosed as a current liability in British accounts. This derives from a legal approach in Italy to financial statements, according to which they come into existence legally only after the annual general meeting approved them; before that, they are a mere proposal by company directors. Consistently, dividends are accounted for as a reserve movement in the financial year subsequent to that to which they refer, and not as a decrease in profit like in Britain (they would then be, in British terms, a prior-year adjustment).

Section (B) (*Fondi per rischi e oneri*) displays the provisions for risks and future expenses, which must have, though, a concrete possibility of coming into existence in order to be provided for. In other words, these accounts should not be used with a conservative orientation according to law (Article 2424-*bis*, section 3, Civil Code) but only when there are definite, identifiable contingencies potentially impairing the value of company capital. If a provision refers clearly to a specific asset, however, it has to be directly deducted from the latter. Among the provisions of this section should be mentioned (a) the "provision for pensions," which copes with additional pension schemes when they exist at the company or at the industry level; (b) "provisions for taxes," which comprises both a provision for tax debits in litigation with tax authorities and a provision for deferred taxes, which is not common in Italian company accounts and anyway not legally required to be disclosed; (c) other provision funds, such as the "provision for exchange rate differences," "provision for future manufacturing maintenance," and any other provision for protecting company value from future potential liabilities. As mentioned previously, in consolidated accounts the negative difference between a company purchase price and its net assets—when reasonably relatable to negative future economic events potentially affecting company value—is to be taken to a "consolidation provision for risks and future expenses" to appear in this section of the consolidated balance sheet.

Section (C) (*Trattamento di fine rapporto di lavoro subordinato*) is a one-item section dealing with a characteristic legal arrangement of the

Italian (and Japanese) employment system, which is the employee severance indemnity to be paid to each employee when leaving the firm (Article
2120 Civil Code). The amount of the indemnity is linked to the number of
years for which the employee worked for that firm and to his or her
position within the organization. In general, it corresponds to the average
monthly salary times the number of years worked for the company. In this
respect, it must be pointed out that this indemnity is an unfunded provision
and tends to assume a large number in Italian balance sheets, thus being an
important context-specific element of the self-financing process of firms
(i.e., increase in cash flow from operating activity). It is expected, though,
that from 1998–1999 this provision will be partially funded, thus reducing
its self-financing role for Italian companies (some of its amounts will be
transferred to an external fund).

Section (D) (*Debiti*) shows all kinds of company creditors: from debenture holders to banks, from trade suppliers to tax authorities and other
group undertakings. It is specifically required to disclose the creditor
amounts falling due beyond the next financial year. In contrast to the
amounts under section (B) of Liabilities, those in this section are certain
and acknowledged (e.g., tax debtors in D.11 are due to be paid, while tax
amounts included in provision for taxes in C.2 are not definitive or clearly
determined).

Section (E) (*Ratei e risconti passivi*) discloses company accruals and
deferred income. A specific note on "premiums on loans" is required, but
these are not commonly found in practice.

At the foot of the balance sheet memorandum accounts (the so-called
conti d'ordine) must be disclosed. Their role is to point out off-balance-
sheet future risks and obligations, such as guarantees given or received, or
commitments to buy and sell. It is noteworthy that in this kind of accounts
there can be, and generally there is, exposed the *residual debts for lease
operations*.

Income Statement (*Conto Economico*, Article 2425 Civil Code) From
the options available in the Fourth Directive, Italy has chosen the vertical
income statement format (Article 23 of the directive). This format is of the
progressive type (*en liste*) and is based on the cost classification by *nature*
(*par nature*) rather than by destination (*par destination*) (see Figure 5).

This German-derived model starts with the "Value of production" and
shows some intermediate results, but unfortunately none of them can be
easily interpreted as operating income. It is divided into five sections

identified by capital letters. In the following a brief description of each section will be given.

Section (A) (*Valore della produzione*, items no. 1–5) is made up of income values deriving from ordinary operations, such as sale and service revenues (*ricavi delle vendite e delle prestazioni*, item no. 1), change in stocks of finished goods and in work-in-progress (*variazioni delle rimanenze di prodotti in corso di lavorazione, semilavorati e finiti*, item no. 2), change in long-term contract stocks (*variazioni dei lavori in corso su ordinazione*, item no. 3), own work capitalized, including financial charges capitalized (*incrementi di immobilizzazioni per lavori interni*, item no. 4), and other income (*altri ricavi e proventi*, item no. 5). In the latter caption must be included a quite wide (and confusing) array of values, such as research and development and advertisement costs capitalized, public grants for "ordinary operations" (to be specifically disclosed), "revaluations" to historic cost of tangible and intangible fixed assets (see Section B) Assets and Section 4.1), gains from disposals of an "ordinary" nature (which might or might not be exceptional in British terms).

It is noteworthy that sale and service revenues, as well as costs and expenses, must be disclosed net of any discounts or premiums, respectively, made or received, and from VAT and duties (Article 2425-*bis* Civil Code).

In Section (B) (*Costi della produzione*, items no. 6–14) all "ordinary" costs incurred for the production activity (to be broadly interpreted) are shown (purchases, services, rentals, staff, depreciation and write-offs, change in stocks of raw materials, consumables and merchandise, allowances for risks, other provisions, and other operating charges). In particular, bad trade debtors allowance is to be put in item no. 10.d., while provisions for risks and other provisions find a correspondence with provisions under section (B) of Liabilities. The last, residual item of this section (*oneri diversi di gestione*) collects a large number of other operating costs, such as taxes other than income tax, realized losses on debtors and on foreign exchange differences, and losses on "ordinary" disposals (which again might or might not have an exceptional nature according to the British definition).

The difference between the total of section (A) and that of section (B) represents a value close to operating income but not identical to it, considering that interest receivable has not been taken into account and that gains from and losses on "ordinary" disposals are ambiguous items, which have not been defined by law.

Section (C) (*Proventi e oneri finanziari*, items no. 15–17) discloses any kind of revenues and expenses from financial activity, such as dividends (item no. 15), interest receivable (item no. 16), and interest payable (item no. 17). It is clear, though, that the balance of this section is rather equivocal and unhelpful, because of the different management logics underlying the financial investment policy on the one hand (items no. 15–16), and the company leveraging choices on the other hand (item no. 17).

Section (D) (*Rettifiche di valore di attività finanziarie*, items no. 18–19) has a quite limited use in practice. Both items refer only to values linked to financial activity: in particular, item no. 18 is the revaluations (*rivalutazioni*) to historic cost of these assets that had undergone a previous devaluation; item no. 19 is the write-offs (*svalutazioni*), which are to be accomplished in any relevant case as to financial values included in current asset section, and only when facing a lasting loss in their value as to the financial values in fixed assets. It is interesting to note that, while item no. 19.a. is due to disclose losses deriving from the equity method in *both* company and group financial statements (in accordance with the conservatism principle), item no. 18.a. is used *only* in the *consolidated* profit and loss account to show income from the equity method of valuing associate undertakings. In fact, as mentioned previously, in company accounts gains arising from this method, when applied to both associate and subsidiary investment valuation, are to be "sterilized" in *ad hoc* equity reserve.

Section (E) (*Proventi e oneri straordinari*, items no. 20–21) deals with extraordinary values, but no legal definition or list is provided. From the legal text one can infer only that, in item no. 20, extrordinary gains on disposals and, in item no. 21, extraordinary losses on disposals and taxes relating to previous financial years must be included. In accordance with the Ministerial Commentary (which in turn just replicates what is ambiguously stated by Article 29 of the Fourth Directive), extraordinary items consist of income and charges not related to ordinary operations. However, this interpretation clearly does not appear satisfactory and is contrary to both theoretical opinions and practice, which tend to link extraordinary items to their temporal exceptionality or nonrecurrence. Divergent practical applications have therefore taken place, complicating the process of reinterpreting Italian company (and group) income statements for financial analysis purposes. An emerging scholarly interpretation and the current trend in company accounts seem, however, to lean toward a restriction of the meaning and scope of application of extraordinary items, in parallel with theoretical and practical stances that are already widely adopted in some other European countries (such as Germany and the United Kingdom).

After the five above-illustrated sections, the result before taxation is to be calculated, followed by income taxes in item no. 22. No distinction between taxes on ordinary and extraordinary profit is asked for (Italy chose to adopt the option permitted by Article 30 of the Fourth Directive). As pointed out (see Section 3.1), the original version of the income statement format required that items resulting purely from the application of fiscal rules were to be shown. This has been cancelled in the new version of the last lines of the format, according to law no. 503/1994. More simply now, right after income taxes, profit (or loss) for the financial year is to be stated (item no. 23).

In the consolidated income statement, before the last amount representing the holding share of group profit (or loss), a further item must be added dealing with the minority interests in group profit or loss (Article 32, section 4, decree no. 127/1991).

Notes to the Accounts (*Nota Integrativa*, Article 2427 Civil Code)   Most of the dislosure in Italian company financial statements is now concentrated on the so-called *nota integrativa* (literally, integrating note). Many new disclosures are required in the notes, including details of any departures from legal rules, and the presence of, and quantification of the effects of, valuations induced merely by tax law. Some are doubtful about the benefits of the increased amount of information because quantity seems to have been given preference over quality. But the new requirements seem to represent a step forward in the level of disclosure in company accounts.

The notes to the accounts have a legally determined minimum content,which is listed in the following (Article 2427 Civil Code). Note that the order of this list should be in principle respected.

1. Valuation criteria applied to financial statement items and conversion methods of the foreign currency items

2. Fixed asset (tangible, intangible, and financial) variation analysis referred to the financial year, with a specific indication for each of them of their historic cost, previous revaluation amounts, depreciation (or amortization) provisions, write-downs, acquisitions, movement from one category to another, disposals in the financial year, and any appropriate similar information

3. Composition and amortization criteria of start-up costs, of research and development costs and of advertisement costs capitalized, and reasons for their capitalization

4. Variations in other assets and liabilities, with particular reference to provisions and employee severance indemnity and the amounts taken to and from them

5. List of participations (equity investments) directly or indirectly (i.e., through a fiduciary firm or intermediary) owned by the company, with an indication for each of the name of the participated company, its registered office, its share capital and shareholder's funds, the profit or loss for the last financial year, the percentage owned, and the book value attributed to this investment;

6. For each relevant item, the amount of debtors and creditors of a residual maturity exceeding 5 years, and the amount of creditors supported by security on the company's own assets (with specific indication of the nature of these securities)

7. Composition of the balance sheet items "prepayments and accrued income," "accruals and deferred income," "other provisions," as well as "other reserves"

8. For each relevant item, the amount of financial charges capitalized in assets

9. Disclosure on the composition and nature of off-balance-sheet financial commitments and of memorandum accounts, where relevant to appreciate the financial situation of the company and with an indication of those relating to subsidiary, associated, parent, and group undertakings

10. If relevant, the breakdown of sales revenues according to categories of activities and geographic areas

11. Gains from equity investments, indicated in item no. 15 of the income statement format, which are different from dividends received

12. Partitioning of financial interest and similar items, indicated in item no.17 of the income statement format, relating to debentures, bank debts, and others

13. Composition of income statement extraordinary items (items no. 20 and 21 of the income statement format)

14. Reasons for the corrections to valuations and allowances resulting purely from the application of fiscal law, and the amounts thereof compared with the overall corrections to valuations and allowances operted on the appropriate items of the income statement (requirement changed by law no. 503/1994)

15. Annual average number of employees, divided by categories

16. Amount of fees due to directors and *sindaci* (internal-institutional auditors), expressed in an aggregate way for each category

17. Number and nominal value of each category of company shares, and number and face value of the new underwritten shares issued during the financial year

18. Special shares (*azioni di godimento*), convertible debentures, and similar securities issued by the company, with a specific indication of their number and the rights they grant.

It is easy to observe that the above information can be usefully grouped in four general headings: (a) illustration of accounting valuation criteria (point no.1); (b) asset and liability variations (points no. 2 and 4, (c) detailed disclosure on particular balance sheet and income statement items (points no. 3, 5–14, 17–18); (d) miscellaneous disclosure (points no. 15–16).

It should be recalled that the above list is not exhaustive, since other articles of the Civil Code refer to the need for disclosing in the notes further information, as well as the impact of, and the reasons for, the company adopting a legally allowed option (say, for example, departures from legal rules in "exceptional cases," modifications to mandatory formats, changes in valuation criteria, current cost valuation of stocks, and reasons for exemption from group accounts).

Nevertheless, any other disclosure, which would be appropriate in order to represent in a true and correct way the company's financial position and economic performance, must be *mandatorily* included in the *Nota integrativa* (Article 2423, section 3; see also Section 3.1). Therefore, a generic legal obligation is imposed on companies to provide any additional disclosure in the notes that is relevant to pursue that general objective.

Within the framework of the new Italian accounting legislation, disclosure in the notes has rapidly assumed a meaningful role, especially after the 1994 change in commercial rules, according to which income statement values deriving merely from the application of tax law must be disclosed in the notes and no longer in the income statement.

Report on Operations (*Relazione sulla Gestione*, Article 2428 Civil Code) The Report on Operations does not belong to the legal concept of financial statements (*bilancio*), but it must accompany them. *De facto* the *Relazione sulla gestione* is a necessary component of the company's annual report.

According to Article 2428 of the Civil Code, this report should (a) be prepared by the directors, (b) deal with the general situation of the company and the trends of its operations, considered both globally and in the various sectors in which it has operated, including through its subsidiaries; and (c) report especially on company costs, revenues, and investments. At any rate, the following information must be derived from this report:

1. Research and development activities

2. Relationships with subsidiary, associate, parent, and group undertakings

3. Number and nominal value of both company own shares and parent's shares owned at the end of the financial year, including through either a fiduciary undertaking or intermediary, with an indication of the percentage of share capital to which these shares correspond

4. Number and nominal value of both company own shares and parent's shares purchased or disposed of during the financial year, including through either a fiduciary undertaking or intermediary, with an indication of the percentage of share capital that these shares correspond to, of the relative prices, and of the reasons explaining the purchases and disposals

5. Contingencies occurring after the close of the financial year

6. Foreseeable evolution of operations

It must be remembered that the Report on Operations may be omitted if a company is allowed to prepare the abridged form of annual accounts (see Section 3.1). In this case, though, the company must provide items 3 and 4 in the notes to the accounts.

Merloni Elettrodomestici S.p.A. 1996 Annual Accounts   At the end of this chapter, after the consolidated financial statements and notes, may be found the 1996 annual accounts of the individual company Merloni Elettrodomestici S.p.A., both in Italian and in English (translation by the author).

Merloni Elettrodomestici is family owned but quoted on the Milan and Rome Stock Exchanges. It is the holding company of the Merloni Elettrodomestici group, whose core business is household appliances (refrigerators and freezers, dishwashers and washing machines, ovens and cookers). The group is one of the European market leaders, and its products are marketed under three major brand names Ariston, Indesit, and Scholtès. Foreign sales account for a high percentage of group total revenues.

As can be noted, the structure and sequence of the balance sheet and income statement follow those set by law and illustrated in the preceding sections. A few items have been omitted from the compulsory formats, presumably because their value was nil.

Together with these statements, the Merloni Elettrodomestici company provided also the *nota integrativa* (notes), the *Relazione sulla gestione* (report on operations), the *Relazione del Consiglio di Amministrazione* (report of Board of Directors), and the *Relazione del Collegio Sindacale* (internal-insitutional auditors report). However, these documents have not been reproduced here for reasons of space.

3.3 The Form and Content of Group Accounts

As pointed out earlier (see Sections 1.2 and 3.1), before decree no. 127/1991 group accounts were required to be presented *only* by groups including listed companies (since the beginning of the 1980s), and by a few other special categories, such as newpaper publishers, insurance companies, public utilities, and in general entities receiving public support on an ordinary basis.

Because of the lack of any specific legislation, the accounting criteria used were to some extent various: in particular, for quoted companies, CONSOB indicated as a reference point the Italian accounting standards prepared by *Dottori commercialisti* and *Ragionieri* (but interestingly enough did not indicate standard no. 8 dealing with consolidated accounts), and when national standards were silent, those issued by the International Accounting Standards Committee (IASC). However, for other categories of groups required to prepare consolidated accounts, no clear and consistent regulatory source existed, so that accounting criteria and methods deriving from Italian professionals, IAS and group policies were mixed together in different proportions. In this respect, it was always necessary to check carefully which were the sources followed in the preparation of these accounts.

The implementation of the Seventh Directive through decree no. 127/1991 introduced in Italy for the first time the *generalized* obligation for any group of companies to prepare consolidated accounts, starting from the 1994 financial year. The new legal rules dealing with consolidated reports—differently from those regarding company accounts—have not been introduced into the Civil Code. Thus, reference will be made here, if not differently stated, to articles of decree no. 127/1991 (in particular Article 25–43).

In general, all limited liability companies (i.e., *società per azioni, società a responsabilità limitata,* and *società in accomandita per azioni*) that have control over one or more undertakings must prepare group accounts according to stated legal rules (Article 25, section 1). Further, this obligation applies also to cooperatives and public entities running a commercial activity (Article 25, section 2). It does not apply, though, to sole traders or partnerships, nor to associations or foundations that do not carry out commercial operations.

As to *exemptions* from consolidated accounts, these will be mandatory only for groups that exceed, for two consecutive financial years or in the first year of their existence, two of the following three size thresholds (Article 27, as amended in 1996):

1. Total assets 19 billion lire—US$10.5 million (gross of consolidation adjustments)
2. Turnover 38 billion lire—US$21 million (gross of consolidation adjustments)
3. 250 employees

The limits are transitionally *doubled* until the 1998 financial year included (Article 46, section 2), with the obvious consequence that only rather large groups will need to comply with this requirement. However, in contrast to company accounts, no abridged form of group accounts is provided by the law. The exemption does not apply if one of the group companies is listed.

A nonlisted parent, which is itself controlled by another company, is exempted from preparing group accounts as long as the parent's parent (a) owns at least 95% of the former's shares (or, if not, there is not a specific request to prepare these accounts at least 6 months before the financial year end—from the owners of at least 5% of share capital), (b) is in an EU member state, and (c) produces consolidated accounts according to Seventh Directive–derived legal rules. It is interesting to note that in France and the Netherlands an opposite approach has been taken on points (b) and (c). In those countries the parent's parent may be located outside the EU and prepare group accounts equivalent to those prepared under the Seventh Directive, that is, adopting I.A.S.C. standards.

As to *scope of consolidation*, the general principle states that a company must be consolidated when it is a subsidiary (*società controllata*) of a parent undertaking. This qualification is determined by the parent's capability to *control* or *exert a dominant influence* (*influenza dominante*) over the subsidiary, through either (a) direct or indirect (e.g., a fiduciary company or an intermediary person) possession of voting rights in the ordinary annual general meeting, or (b) a "domination" contract or an Article of Association producing a similar effect, or (c) agreements with other shareholders (Article 26). Domestic and foreign subsidiaries must be included, irrespective of the legal form and geographic location of the subsidiary. The decree did not take up the option to extend consolidation to companies in which the parent exercises a *de facto* dominant influence thanks only to particular contractual arrangements (e.g., control through market domination). Subsidiaries must be fully consolidated by using the acquisition (purchase) method. No mention is made by law of the merger accounting method (known in the United States as the pooling-of-interests method).

As to *exclusions* from the above general principle, subsidiaries must be excluded from consolidation if they run activities that are so divergent that their inclusion would compromise the "true and correct representation" (Article 28, section 1). In this case, subsidiaries must be accounted for in group financial statements by the equity method as internationally known (Article 36, section 1). In fact, these investments may be already valued by using this method in the parent company accounts: the relevant difference in consolidated financial statements is that the group's proportion of subsidiary profit can be taken to the income statement (item no. 18.a.), which is not permitted in individual company accounts (as mentioned, it must be written in an *ad hoc* equity reserve). It is noteworthy that CONSOB—in a 1996 opinion directed at listed companies—has declared its preference for enlarging the scope of consolidation, encompassing in it the undertakings that run dissimilar activities. On this it should also be remembered that IAS, which will have an impact in the near future on group accounts of Italian companies transnationally quoted (see Section 2.3), are in favor of a global consolidation, regardless of the types of activities performed by group companies.

According to decree no. 127/1991, subsidiaries may also be *excluded* if they are immaterial, if the parent's actual control is restricted, if they are only temporarily under the control of the parent, or if there is difficulty in obtaining on time or without a disproportionate expense the necessary accounting information (Article 28, section 2).

A company is considered an associate (*società collegata*) if it is under a significant influence (*influenza notevole*) of another company (Article 2357 Civil Code). A significant influence is presumed to exist whether a company controls—directly or indirectly—at least 20% (10% if listed) or more of another company's voting rights. Associates should be accounted for (as for subsidiaries excluded from consolidation on the basis of their strong difference with the rest of the group) by the international version of the equity method (Article 36, section 3). Of course, if the participating percentage goes up to 50%, then the legal presumption is that the undertaking becomes a subsidiary.

As to joint ventures, they may be included in the scope of consolidated when (a) one of the group companies has a joint control on it together with other members and on the basis of *ad hoc* agreements with them, and (b) the participating investment reaches at least 20% (10% if the joint venture is listed) of the share capital of this enterprise. Joint ventures having such characteristics should be accounted for by the proportional consolidation method (Article 37), or if excluded from the scope of consolidation, by the equity method (since they exceed the threshold for being treated as associates). If they do not exceed such a threshold, they must be stated at cost in consolidated financial statements.

As for individual company accounts, group accounts must comply with the general principle according to which they must represent in a true and correct manner (*rappresentare in modo veritiero e corretto*) the financial situation and the economic results of the whole group (Article 29, section 2). Additional disclosures in the notes are mandatory if this is necessary to give a "true and correct representation" of the group state of affairs. Departures from legal rules are compulsory but to be enacted only in "exceptional" cases (for an illustration of these rules see Sections 3.1 and 3.2). The well-known accounting postulates, such as prudence, consistency through time, uniform accounting policies, and going concern apply also to consolidated accounts.

The date of the group accounts is to be in principle the closing date of the parent company's financial year, yet it is also possible to adopt the date on which the majority of subsidiaries or the most important of them close the financial year. If the closing date of a subsidiary is different from that for group accounts, then this undertaking is required—with no exceptions allowed—to prepare *ad hoc* interim financial statements (Article 30).

The consolidated formats are those used for individual company accounts (Article 32), of course, suitably amended for minority interests, difference on consolidation, consolidation provision for risks and future expenses, and consolidation reserve, as described above (see Section 3.2).

The disclosures legally required to appear in the notes to the group accounts (*nota integrativa*) are quite similar to those already illustrated with reference to the company annual report. Some adjustments are introduced to take into consideration the nature and the technical preparation of the consolidated accounts (Articles 38 and 39). Examples of these specific indications are principles and criteria of consolidation, and in particular determination and treatment of the difference arising on this process; foreign currency translation methods; closing date of group accounts (if different from the parent's); special adaptations of the formats; list of subsidiaries included in consolidation and of undertakings excluded from it, and their variations through time; when relevant, information needed to keep on ensuring comparability of the figures from one financial year to another.

The report on operations (*relazione sulla gestione*) to be presented together with consolidated financial statements is virtually identical to that described with respect to company accounts.

Further statements and reports (such as, for instance, consolidated flow of funds, Chairman's statement, and changes in shareholders' funds) are voluntary, but they are generally provided by most medium to large groups. What will happen in this area remains to be seen after 1998, when the doubling of the exemption criteria will cease.

Consolidated accounts must be audited by the same body legally due to audit the parent's accounts. Therefore, this can be either its *collegio sindacale* or, if the company is subject to an external-independent audit by a *società di revisione*, it will be the latter to audit also group financial statements (Article 41, section 3). The control activity and its outcomes must result in an *ad hoc* report that can be either a *Relazione del Collegio Sindacale* (*sindaci* report) in the former case, or a *relazione della società di revisione* (auditors' report) in the latter.

In procedural terms, group accounts follow the same pattern and timing in preparation and presentation to the annual general meeting as the parent company individual accounts (see Section 3.2). However, a fundamental difference is that consolidated financial statements are not to be approved by the parent's shareholders, who can only look over them and not ask for a change or revision of these statements. In fact, only the parent's individual accounts would need the shareholders' endorsement, since on their basis dividend distribution is decided. In addition to the parent's approved accounts, a copy of the consolidated financial statements, together with the report on operations and the audit report, must be deposited in the Register of Undertakings at the local Chamber of Commerce. Mention of the deposit must be made in the Official Bulletin of Public and Private Limited Companies (BUSARL, Article 42).

As to their technical preparation, group accounts must include all values (assets and liabilities, revenues and costs) relating to subsidiary undertakings (full consolidation method), while intra-group items (debits and credits, revenues and expenses) and unrealized profits must be eliminated (Article 31). These eliminations can be overlooked if they are immaterial. Intra-group profits can also be maintained in consolidated accounts, provided that a three-fold condition is complied with: if these profits derive from a company's ordinary operations, from an arm's length transaction, and if the elimination of these profits would imply disproportionate costs.

A point of major importance in the drawing up and interpretation of group accounts is their relationship with fiscal-based values. As in other European countries, consolidated financial statements are tax-neutral in Italy, since income taxes are levied on company account figures. Therefore, the EU Seventh Directive required that, where tax-based values have been used in individual company accounts, these shall either be disclosed in the notes or corrected in consolidated financial statements. The original version of Article 31, section 5, of decree no. 127/1991 was clearly moving toward the correction solution, requiring that all company account values resulting purely from the application of fiscal law were to be eliminated in group accounts (a similar approach was taken in France). However, in law no. 503/1994, which was commented upon earlier (see Section 3.1), Article 2-*bis*, section 4, cancelled section 5 of Article 31 and imposed the obligation on groups to disclose in the notes "the reasons of corrections to valuations and allowances resulting purely from the application of fiscal law, as well as the amounts thereof compared with the overall corrections to valuations and allowances drawn from the appropriate income statement items." As a consequence, now it is no longer required in Italy to "purify" consolidated financial statements of fiscal interferences, since it is only necessary to give appropriate disclosure on this point in the notes (a similar approach has been taken in Germany).

Nevertheless, some commentators noted that the law does not *impose* the nonelimination of the tax-based values in group accounts, and thus, according to the option granted by Article 29, section 5, of the Seventh Directive, the elimination of these values was permitted, leaving companies free to choose.

The Merloni Elettrodomestici 1996 Group Accounts The Merloni Elettrodomestici 1996 group accounts are provided at the end of this chapter. They comprise the consolidated balance sheet (in Italian and English), the consolidated income statement (in Italian and English), the consolidated statement of changes in shareholders' equity, the consolidated statement of changes in financial position, the notes to the consolidated financial statements, and the auditors' report.

As can be seen, the form and contents of consolidated financial statements are slightly different from those prescribed by law. This is because the accounts reproduced here are an international version of the Italian accounts, which of course conform fully with the legal rules of Italy.

In terms of subsidiary consolidation, Merloni Elettrodomestici followed international and Italian practice to include only companies where the group has a direct or indirect control through the majority possession of voting rights (point no. 1 of the notes). Majority holdings that were "inactive or insignificant" have been excluded. Changes in the scope of consolidation are described in detail.

Accounting policies applied are illustrated in point no. 1 of the notes, and they are in line with both those applied in the parent's individual accounts and those indicated by the CONSOB.

Tax-based values have been eliminated. The auditors' report confirms that "consolidated accounts have been prepared with clearness and represent in a true and correct manner" the group financial and economic situation "in conformity with the norms which discipline consolidated financial reporting."

3.4 The Accounts of Banks and Financial Institutions

Until 1992 Italian accounting regulation of financial companies and banking firms consisted of the 1942 Civil Code and some special provisions related to their particular activity. Legislative decree no. 87 dated January 27, 1992 implemented both the 1986 EU Directive on the annual and consolidated accounts of banks and other financial institutions and the 1989 EU Eleventh Directive on the publication of annual accounts of branches established in a member state but with headquarters outside that state. This double implementation came into force in 1993.

Decree no. 87/1992 provides a special set of rules for the above entities, whereas for the general principles it refers to decree no. 127/1991. The new provisions delegated to the Italian Central Bank, among other things, the authority to precisely define the account contents and formats and to modify them in the future, putting special emphasis on comparability. With particular reference to formats, the decree states two innovative rules for the Italian context: when possible, substance has to be preferred over form in drawing up company accounts, and the time of settlement has to be given precedence over that of negotiation (Article 7, section 4). These provisions should be particularly meaningful for the presentation of a bank's financial situation and for the accounting treatment of such innovative financial instruments as interest rate swaps, forward rate agreements, currency swaps, and futures.

The Bank of Italy has chosen a two-sided format for the balance sheet, with assets on the left, set out in order of increasing liquidity. No net worth total is required to be disclosed. A progressive income statement format (*en liste*) has been imposed for credit institutions and a horizontal one for financial companies. As for industrial company accounts, the influence of taxation on accounts is *not* shown in an *ad hoc* section of the income statement, but it is pointed out in the notes. It therefore seems that the relationship between commercial rules and taxation has been treated since the beginning in a clearer, but not necessarily more satisfactory, way by decree no. 87/1992 than by decree no. 127/1991 described in Section 3.1.

As to valuation rules, loans must be presented at their net realizable value. Historical cost is to be used for other assets. In particular, marketable securities, when listed, are valued either at the lower of cost and market value or at market value, the chosen policy being used consistently. Participating interests are valued at historical cost or by the equity method. Provisions for general risks from banking operations, that is, credit interest and exchange risks, are allowed; net adjustments deriving from variations in those provisions are shown on the credit or debit side of the income statement. Only the final outcome of all the transactions in marketable securities, currencies, and other financial instruments is to be taken to the profit and loss account, and no distinction should be made between realized and unrealized results.

Rules for consolidated accounts comply with the Seventh Directive provisions. As for industrial groups, value adjustments that have been made exclusively in application of fiscal law in the individual accounts, can be either eliminated or maintained in consolidated statements (Article 39, decree no. 87/1992).

Branches of banks and financial institutions established in a member state, which are controlled by companies inside the EU, are required to integrate their accounts with those of their parents drawn up in accordance with the accounting regulation of the latter's country. Branches with headquarters outside the EU are allowed to act in the same way only if mutual recognition between the accounting regulation of their parent's country and that of Italy exists. When this is not the case, branches must present, in addition to their own accounts, the balance sheet and income statement of their parent restated according to Italian rules.

Legislative decree no. 173 dated May 26, 1997, has implemented in Italy the EU Directive on individual company and consolidated accounts for insurances (91/674/CEE). The new rules will come into force beginning with financial year 1998 (the first financial statements according to the new provisions will then be available in the Spring of 1999). Some of the major points that deserve attention are: (a) there are compulsory legal formats for both types of accounts; (b) the current value of land, buildings, and investments is to be stated in the notes; (c) as to the requirement to prepare consolidated accounts, this is imposed also when two or more insurance companies that do not have any parent-subsidiary relationship operate under a unified management by virtue of a contract or a claus of their Articles of Association, or when the majority of the respective boards are composed of the same directors (principle of the *direzione unitaria*); (d) the treatment of fiscal-derived values in group accounts is in line with that of industrial companies (these values and the related provisions, and their impact on the company's financial and economic situation, are identified and exposed in the notes).

As a final effect of EU pressure, it is interesting to observe that the regulation on mergers and demergers (i.e., Third and Sixth Directives) have been changed in Italy (in 1991).

4. Rules, Policies, and Practices of Accounting Valuations in Italy

4.1 Valuations in Company Accounts

In addition to Civil Code and other legal requirements discussed earlier, some more detailed valuation rules were introduced by legislative decree no. 127/1991 (Article 2426 Civil Code).

Of extreme relevance in the Italian environment are the valuation criteria set by fiscal law, which quite often are used in practice as the *actual* legal reference source when individual company accounts are prepared (in particular, Presidential decree no. 917/1986, the so-called Consolidated Act on Income Taxes, T.U.I.R., which came into force in 1988 and includes a section on corporation tax; since then the decree has been subject to many amendments).

A further normative source on valuations is the accounting standards issued by Italian professionals. These statements are not as authoritative, however, and they are in general considered only when neither tax legislation, nor commercial rules are detailed enough in a given area. These standards can only play a role of interpreting legal rules.

In the following some of the most relevant year-end valuations in company accounts will be presented in order to give a comprehensive picture of the contents of the different regulatory sources (Civil Code, tax law, accounting standards) thereon. If the reference to a source is omitted in the description of a given valuation, this implies that either it does not have significantly dissimilar contents from the others or it does not deal with that valuation at all.

Incidentally, it should be noted that the decision—when legally and technically possible—of including a value under a heading rather than under another competing one in the balance sheet (e.g., shares can be taken either to "investments" in section B.III.1. or to "securities" in section C.III. of Assets; if their nature is uncertain between trade or finance, debtors can be included either in section B.III.2. or in section C.II. of Assets) is not just a formal one, but it does have implications in valuation terms. In fact, to stick with the examples provided above, only shares in investment section can be valued by using the equity method; items included in fixed assets have to be devalued when an *enduring* loss in value takes place: the remaining assets have to be devalued simply when a loss in their value (of either a lasting or a temporary nature) occurs.

The Legal Definition of Historic Cost   The general principle imposed by Article 2426 Civil Code for asset valuation is the historic cost, which is divided into purchase cost (*costo di acquisto*) and production cost (*costo di produzione*). The same rule specifies also the methods of the respective calculation.

As to purchase cost, assets should be valued   at the acquisition cost increased by all other relevant expenses that have been incurred in order to put the asset in the condition of operating (e.g., tax duties, notary expenses, transport costs, installation and running expenses, various fees, nondeductible VAT). To this amount can be added a "reasonable" share of interest payable, but only during the period in which the asset is being (externally) fabricated.

As to production cost, the basis is made up of direct costs, plus a "reasonably" attributable portion of overheads. Also in this case, part of interest payable can be capitalized. The addition of overheads and interest payable to an asset's internal production cost is allowed only during its production period and ceases when it can be utilized by the firm.

Interestingly enough, fiscal law sets a definition of historic cost that is slightly more limiting in scope than that of the Civil Code (Article 76, section 1, T.U.I.R., as recently amended by law-decree no. 416/1994 converted into law no. 503/1994). It permits, in fact, the capitalization of overheads and interests only with reference to tangible and intangible fixed assets. This aspect apart, fiscal rule follows the commercial legislation. A related point, but in this case showing a divergence between the two sets of regulations, is given by the possibility implicitly granted by the tax rules to revaluate above the historic cost—the gain being nontaxable (change in Article 54, T.U.I.R.), which is not permitted by the Civil Code.

Accounting standard no. 16 provides some technical details useful for implementing the legal indications for calculating historic (purchase and production) costs. In particular, it poses the requirements (which in general are followed in practice) of capitalizing interest on assets only if (a) the time period necessary for their production, either internal to the firm or external by the selling entity, is relevant, (b) interest payable is traceable in a clear way to the acquisition or own production of the asset (e.g., loans that have been taken on just for the purpose of financing either the purchase of the asset or its internal construction), and (c) the loan has actually been used for the acquisition of the asset. The capitalization of interest is limited by the standard to the period during which the asset is produced.

Tangible Fixed Assets   Tangible assets must be valued at historic cost, according to the described rules. As mentioned previously, they must be devalued only if an *enduring* loss in value occurs, but their (historic) cost must be restored when the cause justifying the revaluation ceases.

Tangible assets, whose utilization is temporally limited (e.g., buildings but not land), must be depreciated systematically over their useful (economic) life "in relation to their residual possibility of use." This means that the net value of these assets in the balance sheet should always be "recoverable" through the profitability of the future financial years during which that asset will be providing its economic contribution. The rule also suggests implicitly the preparation of a depreciation plan for each depreciable tangible asset, and the application of the straight line depreciation method. Any change in depreciation method and/or rate must be illustrated and justified in the notes.

It must be remembered that a statement on "tangible (and intangible) asset variations" is to be compulsorily included in point no. 2 of the notes, unless a company is permitted to produce the so-called abridged accounts (*bilancio in forma abbreviata*).

A further aspect of tangible asset valuation according to commercial rules is given by the legal revaluation allowed from time to time by special statutory laws. Considering the peculiarity and the relative frequency, compared with other European countries of this approach to asset revaluation, it seems appropriate to devote a short section to this topic in order to exemplify the functioning of the last two revaluation laws, whose effects can still be traced in Italian accounts.

Revaluation Laws In addition to the aforementioned changes in accounting rules, two revaluation laws were passed in 1990 and 1991 (law no. 408/1990 and law no. 413/1991). Such a short time lag between the acts is unusual. In the past 40 years only three similar laws were promulgated in Italy (in 1952, 1975, and 1983).

Relating in principle to inflationary periods, an *ad hoc* revaluation law is occasionally issued in Italy in order to allow companies to legitimately overcome the valuation limit of historical cost, without being obliged to justify the new value with reference to "special reasons" (now called "exceptional cases"). In this event, however, the actual reason underlying the promulgation of two revaluation laws of the 1990s is probably to be traced back to the persistent and pressing problem of public debt financing rather than to the inflationary process, which affected the Italian economy in the second half of the 1980s at an average yearly rate of 7–8%. This interpretation is supported by the short time lag between the two acts: the failure of the first voluntary law to meet its objectives in terms of tax inflows may explain the need, after only one year, for a second revaluation law, this time of compulsory application to all firms.

The two laws resembled each other as to the legal entities involved (all limited liability companies, as well as partnerships and individual businesses) and the taxable nature of the revaluation gains (unlike the laws of 1952, 1975, and 1983). The two laws were dissimilar with reference to the degree of compulsion, scope of application in terms of balance sheet values, revaluation criteria, calculation of the tax burden, and depreciation procedures for tax purposes.

As to the first aspect of differentiation, it has already been noted that the 1990 law could be applied on a voluntary basis, whereas the 1991 law was compulsory. Moreover, the former permitted the revaluation of tangible assets, intangibles legally recognized (such as patents, brands, and licensing rights), and investments in associates and subsidiaries. Conversely, the 1991 law dealt only with buildings and land.

There were differences also in the revaluation methods adopted by the two laws. In the 1990 law the revaluation principle (and limit) was the current value of the asset with regard especially to its value in use to the company, thereby leaving it largely free to choose the most appropriate figure. The resulting credit (revaluation gain) was taxed, if relating to buildings and land, at 16%, and, if relating to other assets, at 20%. The remaining credit had to be allocated to a special revaluation reserve.

The 1991 law imposed a more complex and restrictive revaluation method based on the determination of a maximum amount and a minimum one. Thus, buildings could be revalued up to an amount deriving from the multiplication of their nominal rents by legally defined indices (e.g., 100 for housing estates). The same applied also to land, even though it could be revalued only up to 80% of its "value" calculated according to the described procedure; 38% of the resulting increase, reduced by 1 billion lire, was the minimum amount of the revaluation. The revaluation actually carried out was taxed (at 16%), and the residual credit went to an *ad hoc* reserve. In the 1991 case, companies were thus restricted to a great extent in determining the "fair value" of the assets, given the highly mechanical procedure for establishing both the maximum and the minimum amount of the revaluation.

For the 1991 law, increased depreciation provisions are immediately tax and commercially deductible. For the 1990 law they are instead tax deductible only from the third financial year after that of the revaluation (but they have been deductible since 1990 for commercial regulation purposes).

As a result of the two laws, financial statements of Italian companies clearly cannot be said to be drawn up in accordance either with the current value principle or with the historical cost principle. On the contrary, instead of leading to some amelioration in the consistency and quality of the published accounting data, the two revaluation laws are likely to have produced further distortions by stressing once again the use of the accounts as a tool for collecting financial resources to help with the state's deficit problem.

As to tax rules dealing with tangible fixed assets, they are quite influencial in practice and *de facto* substitute for commercial law rules. The T.U.I.R. requires the application of a specific "ordinary tax depreciation rate" (*ammortamento ordinario*, "ordinary depreciation") to each (large) category of tangible assets used in different industries (Article 67). The ordinary rate must be reduced by half in the first year of useful life of an asset. In the following years it can be reduced by the same percentage every year without a negative tax implication (i.e., it is possible to recover the difference between the ordinary tax depreciation rate for that category of assets and the actual depreciation rate used in a given year).

If the intensity of an asset utilization exceeds that normal in an industry, then the "ordinary rate" can be increased (*ammortamento accelerato*). This rate can be doubled in the first 3 years of use of an asset for accelerated depreciation (*ammortamento anticipato*). The amount of tax depreciation exceeding commercial depreciation can be put either in the same provision fund together with the latter or in an autonomous equity reserve (item no. A.VII. of Liabilities). In order to be deductible, tax depreciation charges must be taken to the income statement ("single track approach," see Section 3.1).

A further tax rule relevant to tangible fixed assets is that requiring their immediate expense to the income statement when being of an amount lower than one million lire. It is also noteworthy that ordinary repairing and maintenance are tax deductible up to 5% of the historic cost of depreciable tangible assets as of at the beginning of the financial year.

Intangible Assets   The valuation of intangible assets follows in principle the same rules established for tangible assets (historic cost, compulsory restoration of historic cost, depreciation principle and method, statement of "intangible asset valuations").

Some legal provisions deal specifically with intangibles, however. In particular, the capitalization of research and development, advertising, and business start-up costs is allowed. They must be amortized within 5 years. It is also required that companies having capitalized these categories of intangibles can distribute dividends only when available reserves exist in excess of the unamortized amount of these assets.

Goodwill can be recognized only if a cost has been incurred for its acquisition and with the consent of the *collegio sindacale*. It must be amortized over 5 years, but this period can be extended for a limited number of years when goodwill's useful life is estimated to be longer.

Own brand capitalization is not permitted. In order to be tax deductible, fiscal rules state that (a) the amortization allowances of royalties, patents, and similar items cannot exceed one-third of their book value, (b) brands are to be amortized for fiscal purposes in 10 years at least, (c) amortization period of licences is the same as their contractual or legal length, (d) amortization allowances of purchased goodwill cannot exceed one-tenth of its book value (different from the Civil Code rule) (Article 68, T.U.I.R.), (e) research and development costs can be either expensed immediately to the income statement or amortized by the straight line method within 5 years, (f) advertising and promotion costs can be either expensed immediately to the income statement or amortized by straight line method over 5 years (Article 74, T.U.I.R.). No detailed tax rule is set for start-up cost amortization: it is considered acceptable for fiscal purposes to use the period fixed by the Civil Code (5 years).

Equity Investments   Equity investments can be valued either at *cost* or by the *equity method*. In the following these approaches will be examined separately.

If the first option is taken, then *historic cost* represents the upper possible limit of valuation. Like tangible and intangible assets, investments must be devalued only when facing an enduring loss in value. Their historic cost must be restored as soon as the reason for which they have been devalued ceases to exist.

For tax purposes, investments (apart from those valued by the equity method) have to be considered at a "minimum value" corresponding to the application of LIFO on an annual basis to such investments. Any other valuation method, such as FIFO or weighted average, is acceptable, provided that it leads to a value higher than that according to LIFO. In other words, the same criteria for tax valuing stocks must be applied (see below). Losses in value are tax deductible if, and to the extent that, the resulting value of the investment is not lower than the proportion of the investee's shareholder capital emerging from the last approved annual accounts (or not lower than the last 6-month average share price, if the investee company is listed) (Article 66, section 1-*bis*, T.U.I.R.).

Certainly, a major innovation imported by decree no. 127/1991 is the option to use the *equity method* for valuation of investments in an individual company's accounts where the investor has a dominant or significant influence (i.e., it can be applied only to investments included in section B.III.1.a. or B.III.1.b. of Assets). As mentioned in Section 3.3, associates are defined as those over which a company has a significant influence, which is presumed to be the case where 20% or more (10% if the investee company is listed) of the annual general meeting ordinary votes can be controlled. If a parent controls the majority of voting rights in, or exerts a dominant influence on, the investee annual general meeting, then this company is to be considered a subsidiary.

Nevertheless, the enforcement of the equity method takes place in a somewhat Italian way. In fact, income from associates must be credited to an undistributable equity reserve in the investor's individual balance sheet and not to the profit and loss statement, insofar as that income corresponds to unrealized gains (realized dividends are instead to be recorded in the income statement). It must be recalled that, according to the Italian interpretation of the realization principle, dividends are realized when already cashed or at least cashable, that is, when the annual general meeting of the investee has given its formal approval.

The adoption of the equity method in individual company accounts is generally limited in practice. In 1994 the previously mentioned law-decree no. 416/1994 changed the fiscal attitude toward this valuation method, considering income from subsidiaries and associates—exceeding any previously deducted loss in value—as nontaxable (new Article 54, section 2-*bis*, T.U.I.R.). This legal innovation should somewhat favor the adoption of the equity method, which is not expected to be very extensive anyway.

Any loss in value of investments valued by this method is tax deductible within the limits set with reference to investments valued at cost (Article 66, 1-*ter*, T.U.I.R.).

Stocks (Inventories)   The rule of lower of cost (calculated according to the previously discussed guidelines) and net realizable value applies to the valuation of stocks. For valuation at cost, the LIFO method is permitted, as well as the FIFO and weighted average methods. Of interest is the required indication in the notes of the current cost of the individual categories of stocks, when this is materially different from that stated in the accounts.

Tax rules are once again quite influencial, stating that stock valuation can be made either at the stock's specific cost or (more frequently in practice) at a "minimum value" that corresponds to the use of either LIFO or FIFO or weighted average methods. The LIFO version suggested by the tax rule is the one applied on an annual basis (so-called *LIFO a scatti*, Article 59, T.U.I.R.). If at the closing of a financial year the average unit value of stocks is higher than their average current market value in the last month, then their tax "minimum value" is determined by multiplying stock physical quantities by their market value.

Noteworthy is the indication by accounting standard no.13 concerning the possible capitalization of interest payable on stocks, when the latter are necessarily subject to a quite long maturity process before being marketable (e.g., some liqueurs such as brandy, or Parmesan cheese, or Parma ham).

Securities   Securities in the Current Asset section (C.III. of Assets) are to be valued at cost, but this has to be decreased when the asset is subject to any kind of loss. Correspondingly, the asset value has to be brought back to historic cost if its (market) value goes up again.

In fiscal terms, securities have to be valued by adopting the same criteria stated for stocks (either at specific cost or by using the LIFO, FIFO, or weighted average method) (Article 61, T.U.I.R.).

Own (or Treasury) Shares   According to legislative decree no. 315/ 1994 (implementing in Italy EU Directive no. 92/101), own shares in the balance sheet cannot exceed the tenth part of the company's share capital, taking into account any company shares owned by subsidiaries. Own shares are excluded from dividend distribution, and the voting right linked to them is temporarily suspended (Articles 2357 and 2357-*ter* Civil Code).

Own shares must be recorded separately in the balance sheet (items no. B.III.4. and C.III.5. of Assets) and valued at historic cost. While they remain in the possession of the company, a non-available equity reserve of an equal amount must be provided for out of profits (item no. A.V. of Liabilities).

Leased Assets   Accounting for financial leasing of assets is a point deliberately not addressed in the new valuation rules. As a result of favorable tax treatment, the practice of taking rents to the income statement and of writing the amount of the residual debt only in the memorandum accounts will probably continue.

Operative leasing must be expensed directly, as in the Anglo-American practice.

Trade Debtors   According to the Civil Code rule, trade debtors must be valued at their net realizable value.

Very influential on practice is the tax deductibility limit set with reference to the provision for bad debts. This allowance is in fact deductible in any year only up to 0.5% of the nominal value of debtors as of the end of a financial year. This tax deduction is no longer permitted when the overall provision for bad debt has reached 5% of the face value of debtors as of at the financial year end.

At any rate, once proven, bad debts are tax deductible (Article 71, T.U.I.R.). Similar fiscal rules also apply to banks and financial institutions, but if the allowance exceeds the 0.5% limit, the exceeding amount is tax deductible on a straight line basis in the following 7 years. For the above tax calculation, banks must also consider as part of debtors the revaluations of the off-balance sheet operation values.

Pensions and Employee Severance (or Termination) Indemnity   In Italy pensions are generally paid by the state or by public entities, from payments made both by companies (in the more relevant part) and by employees, throughout their work life. Thus, no provisions for this are necessary, and the Civil Code requires only that the amounts paid by the company are recorded in accordance with the accrual principle in item no. B.9.b. of the income statement.

Sometimes additional company or group pension schemes exist. In this case, pension costs are provided for in the income statement (item no. B.9.d.) and balance sheet (item no. B.1. of Liabilities).

When employees leave a company, however, for whatever reason, a severance (or termination) indemnity must be paid, and this has to be accrued in the accounts.The annual allowance for each company employee is to be calculated according to legally determined parameters and written in item B.9.c. of the income statement. This allowance has then to be taken to an *ad hoc* non-funded provision, called *fondo di trattamento di fine rapporto*, in section C of Liabilities. This fund is built up year by year in relation to an employee's salary for the year (see also Section 3.2).

From 1998 part of this annual provision (but all of it for the new employees) will be paid by companies to a pension fund in order to complement employee pension treatment.

Long-Term Contracts   According to the Civil Code, the percentage of completion method may be used for valuing long-term contracts, but the completed contract method is not excluded either. Technical guidelines for implementation of the two valuation methods can be found in Italian accounting standard no. 23. The percentage of completion method—according to this standard—does not differ In most material aspects from Anglo-Saxon common practice.

It is important to mention the tax rule on this topic, since it is followed most of the time in practice. T.U.I.R. requires as a general principle the application of the percentage of completion method, with some minor adjustments in favor of the taxpayer, such as the 50% recognition of price increases until they are approved, and an allowance of 2% for unforeseeable contractual risks (Article 60, T.U.I.R.). However, as an alternative, the fiscal rule permits also the application of the completed contract method, if requested by the company.

Italian practice appears to lean toward the use of the percentage of completion method rather than the alternative completed contract method.

Foreign Currency Transactions   There is no rule in the Civil Code on how to translate values in foreign currency for individual company accounts. There is only the requirement to indicate in the notes which criteria were used (point no. 1).

Conversely, fiscal law deals with such a topic, permitting the use of the year-end exchange rate method. In particular, negative translation differences are to be provided for through an annual tax-deductible allowance in the income statement, which is accrued to an *ad hoc* fund (*fondo rischi su cambi*, provision for foreign exchange risks) to be decreased when an actual loss or an unexpected gain on foreign exchange occurs (Article 72, T.U.I.R.).

Accounting standard no. 9 is concerned with this topic as well. It states that, if (trade and finance) debtors and creditors expressed in foreign currency are short-term, then they have to be translated using the year-end exchange rate, and the negative and positive translation differences taken to the income statement. It is permitted, though, to defer the recognition of a positive translation difference. If debtors and creditors are long-term, the same rules apply, but when a positive translation difference emerges there is no option granted, since it must not be recorded in the accounts. The conservative attitude taken by the Italian profession in this subject area seems clear.

Accounting for Tax   The generally applied method of accounting for taxes is the "flow-through" method. Accounting for deferred tax in company accounts is very rare.

The income tax burden on limited companies is today 37% of taxable income (corporation income tax, IRPEG). From 1998 a dual income tax rate system has been introduced: a 19% rate hits a share of profit corresponding to the amount of the "ordinary" increase of the shareholders' equity variation due to both the reinvestment of the previous year's profit (i.e., nondistributed profit), and the contribution of new share capital by company members. The ordinary increase is defined as a percentage of that variation, which is fixed every year by the Ministry of Finance with reference to the average government bond rate plus a 3% risk premium. The above more favorable corporation tax rate has been designed to strengthen the capitalization of Italian firms.

A tax that complements the corporation tax is the Regional Tax on Production Activities (IRAP, legislative decree no. 446/1997). Its basis is a value added figure (net of depreciation and amortization allowances) deriving from the income statement. As mentioned in Section 2.3., the items to be included in the basis of calculation are to be identified by using accounting standard no. 12, this giving again a legal recognition to the documents issued by Italian professionals. The ordinary rate is 4.25%.

A further relevant aspect is the tax credit recognized on company dividends paid to shareholders, which is equal to 58.73% of the amount distributed, that is, the state income tax levied upon the company's profit.

A 5-year carry forward of accounting losses is allowed to all limited and unlimited entities.

The accounting effects of tax amnesties, which are from time to time granted to Italian taxpayers, should also to be mentioned. The last tax amnesty with accounting implications took place in 1991: in this case law no. 413/1991 granted a taxpayer (e.g., a company) either a fiscal amnesty, where it declared spontaneously income amounts that did not appear from accounting records, or a significant discount on the incumbent taxes and fines if it paid them before the definitive sentence of the fiscal court was pronounced. In the former case, companies were allowed to add assets to their balance sheet that previously had been omitted and cross out assets and liabilities that were invented. This way, the fiscal amnesty also had an accounting impact. The amended financial statements resulting from such a process, though, are likely to be a little more realistic but not necessarily more internally consistent in valuation terms.

Public Grants The Civil Code does not provide any detailed valuation rule as to public grants. The only mention on this point made by the Code is that requiring the inclusion of "ordinary grants" (*contributi in conto esercizio*) in item no. A.5. (as revenue within the value of production) of the income statement. In the main they are contributions given by public authorities, that is, state, regions, provinces, and communes, on a recurrent basis to support the operations of certain kinds of businesses with a general relevance (such as public transportation, newspapers, and utilities). Also, tax law recognizes the "ordinary grants" as revenue (Article 53, T.U.I.R.).

Less clear is the treatment of "capital grants" (*contributi in conto capitale*), that is, of grants given by public authorities in order to assist companies in the expansion and/or strengthening of their production structure (purchase/construction of tangible fixed assets). No mention whatsoever of this kind of grant is made in the Civil Code. Accounting standard no. 16 permits two alternative approaches to accounting for capital grants:

1. To take them directly to an *ad hoc* equity reserve (A.VII. of the Liabilities)

2. To gradually credit them to the income statement in relation to the residual economic life of the relative asset. This approach can be carried out acording to two alternative methods: (a) offsetting the grants against the value of the asset whose acquisition they have

facilitated, or (b) recording them as deferred income in the profit and loss account and in the balance sheet (on the liability side) to be progressively decreased in parallel with the asset depreciation process.

This latter method (2b) is indicated as the preferable one by standard no. 12.

Fiscal legislation permits a company to choose if the taxation of capital grants must be done either in just one go when they are cashed or in several years (up to 5) on a straight line basis (Article 55, section 3, T.U.I.R.).

Oil, Gas, and Other Mineral Resources   No specific legal provision (neither of commercial nor of fiscal nature) is stated on this point. Also, Italian accounting standards do not mention explicitly such an issue.

4.2 Valuations in Group Accounts

As previously indicated (see Section 3.3), subsidiaries must be fully consolidated by using the accounts of the date when they are consolidated for the first time; moreover, intragroup items and unrealized profits must be completely eliminated (apart from particular cases), and minority interests shown as a part of consolidated shareholders' fund and income. Accounting policies must be uniformly applied to all subsidiary accounts included in the consolidation. Nonconsolidated subsidiaries and associates are to be accounted for by the equity method (however, unlike in the individual company accounts, income from associates must be taken into the income statement). Joint ventures are to be treated by the same method, or by the proportional one if the participating interest in them exceeds 20% (10% if the joint venture is listed). If this interest accounts for less than that percentage, they have to be valued at cost.

As elsewhere in Europe, group accounts are tax-neutral in Italy (apart from some cases for VAT purposes), and thus income tax rules disregard such statements.

It should also be remembered that a recent law (legislative decree no. 58/ 1998) introduced the possibility from July 1998 for Italian companies listed on both an EU market and a non-E.U. market to depart from national rules (decree no. 1271991) and to refer to "accounting standards of international recognition," which are compatible with EU Directives for the preparation of their consolidated accounts, provided that these standards are acceptable to the non-EU market. These "alternative" standards are to be identified by an *ad hoc* decree of the Ministry of Justice and are likely to correspond to those issued by the International Accounting Standards Committee (IASC).

In principle, the valuation criteria used in subsidiary and parent company individual accounts are transferred to group financial statements via the consolidation process; thus, the foregoing analysis (Section 4.1) preserves much of its validity for consolidated accounts. This also implies that some of the Anglo-Saxon oriented group accounting choices, which were widely used before decree no. 127/1991 fully came into force, are now probably adopted to a lesser extent in favor of a more German-like model of consolidated reporting (treatment of tax items, no capitalization of financial leasing, minorities interests as a component part of shareholders' funds and of profit for the year, account formats, and so on).

Notwithstanding the similarity of the valuation policies with those of the individual company accounts, there are some valuation issues that could be considered specific to these statements. They are briefly discussed in the following.

4.2.1 Difference on Consolidation

The acquisition (or purchase) method must be applied. "Merger accounting" (in the United States, the pooling-of-interests method) is not allowed (and not even mentioned by decree no. 127/1991).

In this respect, the difference between the cost of acquisition of a subsidiary and the corresponding book equity value of the subsidiary should be first allocated over the latter's individual assets and liabilities probably up to their current value (this benchmark is not specified, though, by the law).

Any residual difference is to be treated according to its sign. If negative, its treatment varies according to the cause. In fact, a negative difference (subsidiary value exceeding the cost of acquisition) must be allocated to an *ad hoc* reserve when deriving from a perceived bargain but classified as a provision on the liability side representing negative goodwill when caused by unfavorable trading prospects (*fondo di consolidamento per rischi ed oneri futuri*, consolidation provision for future risks and expenses).

A positive difference (acquisition cost exceeding the value of the subsidiary) has to be treated as goodwill (but called *differenza di consolidamento*, difference on consolidation) or, alternatively, written off immediately against group reserves. As mentioned earlier (see Section

4.1), goodwill arising from consolidation, when capitalized, should be amortized over 5 years, but the period may be extended for a limited number of years if its useful life is reckoned to be longer. Anyway, the consensus of the parent company's *collegio sindacale* (board of internal-institutional auditors) on the recognition of goodwill among group intangible assets, is required.

Currency Translation of Foreign Subsidiaries   No specific rule is given on this point by decree no. 127/1991 or in the Civil Code. There is only a requirement to indicate in the notes the criteria adopted. Nor do Italian accounting standards deal with this topic. Because of the lack of domestic regulatory guidelines, the most authoritative source is probably IAS 21.

Leased Assets   No legal rule permitting financial lease capitalization is provided. Before decree no. 127/1991 came into force, and because of the lack of a general legal framework, some Italian groups used to capitalize leasing in their consolidated accounts. Since financial year 1994, this does not seem to be allowed, even though—given the lack of an explicit prohibition—many Italian groups decided to continue this capitalization (see the Merloni financial statements at the end of the chapter).

Accounting for Taxes   The original version of Article 31, section 5, of decree no. 127/1991 *required* the full elimination in group accounts of all tax-based values written in the individual company statements, tacitly implying the need to provide for deferred taxation. All major Italian groups used to account for deferred tax in their consolidated statements. The cancellation of section 5 of Article 31 by law no. 503/1994 seemed to have had as a consequence that of *only permitting* the elimination of fiscal interferences in group accounts. In this respect, contradictory treatments of deferred taxes are followed in the application of the legal rules on consolidated statements imported by decree no. 127/1991. Law no. 503/1994 has also introduced the point *o-bis* in the notes to consolidated financial statements, where the same information as that in point 14 of the notes to individual company accounts has to be disclosed (see Section 3.2.1.).

It is interesting to observe that a subsequent law-decree (no. 1/1995, Article 12) changed once again the treatment of taxes in consolidated financial reporting, getting back to the original approach: according to this 1995 law-decree, it was *mandatory* to eliminate all fiscal influences and to provide for deferred taxes (no specific method for that is indicated, though).

Consequently, the point *0-bis* of the notes introduced by law no. 503/1994 was no longer needed, and hence it has been cancelled.

However, the 1995 law-decree was never converted into a full law and ceased to have effect two months after its publication. Therefore, we are now back to the situation determined by the previous decree no. 504/1994, with the possibility for Italian groups to decide whether to eliminate or preserve fiscal-related values in their consolidated accounts. The reader is advised to look into the group accounting policies in the notes (point o-*bis* of the *Nota integrativa*).

4.2.2 Merloni Elettrodomestici Valuation Policies

Merloni valuation policies in group accounts (but the same would hold also for individual company accounts) reflect in general the regulatory principles and methods discussed above (see point no. 1 in the notes to the Merloni consolidated financial statements).

In particular, it seems interesting to observe that Merloni capitalizes consolidation goodwill (in 1993—before decree no. 127/1991 came into force—this item was written off against group reserves), and exposes minority interests within shareholders' equity and as a part of the profit for the year (in 1993 this item was in a sort of limbo between liabilities and shareholders' funds in the balance sheet and outside the profit for the year in the income statement.

Foreign currency translation follows the closing rate method as to assets and liabilities, the average rate method as to costs and revenues, and the temporal method as to equity items. Stock valuation is made—unlike the UK practice—by using the LIFO method applied on an annual basis. Depreciation is calculated according to rates that are said to be in line with the tax-imposed ones.

Among intangible assets, the Merloni parent company has included, in compliance with particular statutory regulations, costs deriving from early retirements in 1992 (i.e., employees leaving the company before the legally determined age by virtue of a special decree with the aim to sustain the group in times of recession), structuring costs, and costs relating to the 1991 tax amnesty mentioned above. All these kinds of costs ended their amortization process in 1996.

Deferred taxes are provided for in group accounts with reference to temporary differences arising especially on selling gains, and to consolidation adjustments.

"Capital grants" are taken to an equity reserve (net of deferred taxes), while "operating grants" (here referred to as ordinary grants) are taken directly to the income statement.

Foreign currency transactions are originally recorded at the exchange rate ruling at the day when the transaction took place and their amounts are updated by using the closing rate. Any negative differences, which could stem from the comparison between these two amounts, are provided for in an *ad hoc* fund.

5. Expected Future Developments

In conclusion, it must be pointed out that the formal revolution that has been previously highlighted is certainly producing a positive effect, but it is also impacting on a context that has particular characteristics and its own accounting tradition. Change, then, is not likely to be linear or painless, since it is probably influenced by the dynamics of a context that seems resistent to change and tends to show quite a strong accounting inertia.

In this respect, whether the series of innovations in the Italian accounting regulatory framework implies a new era in this country's financial reporting is a matter largely still to be discovered. One could say that Italian accounting has surely ended up formally changed and probably improved in certain areas such as disclosure and group accounts, but, on the other hand, the actual depth of the innovations may be questioned. The described discontinuities do not seem in fact likely to have led to a radical change in the socioeconomic foundations of Italian accounting, which will probably continue to be inspired for a certain period by the same issues of fiscal consequences, conservatism, and secrecy.

However, three events of a more general nature might be having a substantial impact not just on accounting practices, but also on their socioeconomic role and perception. These are (a) the current privatization process of large state-owned firms—leading to a substantial increase in the number of shareholders—and in the demand for accounting information; (b) the creation of small secondary interconnected stock exchanges (*Borse regionali*) to be run in a decentralized way at a regional level and hopefully to be entered in due course by many of the small and medium-sized, entrepreneurial-based firms characterizing the Italian economic system, and (c) the ongoing reform of company law and financial markets, which has already changed some of the most relevant aspects of accounting and audit regulations dealing with listed companies..

Useful Addresses

Borsa Italiana S.p.A.
(Italian Stock Exchange)
Piazza Affari
20100 Milan
Tel. +39-02724261
Fax +39-72004333

CONSOB
Via Isonzo, 19/E
00198 Rome
Tel. +39-0684771
Fax +39-068417707

Consiglio Nazionale dei Dottori Commercialisti
Via Poli, 29
00187 Rome
Tel. +39-6-675861
Fax +39-6-67586349/67586348

Consiglio Nazionale dei Ragionieri e Periti Commerciali
Via Paisiello, 24
00198 Rome
Italy
Tel. +39-6-8415123/8541354
Fax +39-6-8417829
Tel. +39-068523613
Fax +39-068417829

Associazione Italiana Revisori Contabili (ASSIREVI)
Via Vincenzo Monti, 16
20123 Milane
Italy
Tel. +39-02436950
Fax +39-02437326

Associazione Italiana Società di Revisione (AIRE)
Via Ugo Foscolo, 4,
20121 Milan
Tel. +39-0272002191
Fax +39-0272001322

Ministero di Grazia e Giustizia (Ministry of Justice)
Ufficio VII: Libere Professioni
Via Arenula
00100 Rome
Tel. +39-0668851
Fax +39-066833611 (Ufficio VII)

Accademia Italiana di Economia Aziendale (AIDEA)
Via Garibaldi, 3
40124 Bologna
Tel. +39-051227683/227684
Fax +39-051226012

Financial Statements

Stato patrimoniale consolidato al 31 dicembre 1996

Attivo

(milioni di lire)	1996	1995
Crediti verso soci per versamenti ancora dovuti	–	–
Immobilizzazioni		
Immobilizzazioni immateriali:		
Costi di impianto e di ampliamento	1.822	973
Costi di ricerca, di sviluppo e di pubblicità	2.594	4.800
Diritti di brevetto industriale e diritti di utilizzazione delle opere dell'ingegno	19.516	14.650
Concessioni, licenze, marchi e diritti simili	14.660	16.090
Avviamento	15.534	17.005
Altre	922	2.073
	55.048	**55.591**
Immobilizzazioni materiali:		
Terreni e fabbricati	219.418	223.556
Impianti e macchinario	215.898	202.052
Attrezzature industriali e commerciali	64.384	58.483
Altri beni	29.627	34.257
Immobilizzazioni in corso e acconti	13.668	24.694
	542.995	**543.042**
Immobilizzazioni finanziarie:		
Partecipazioni in:		
- imprese controllate	249	359
- imprese collegate	18.811	19.631
- altre imprese	9.504	7.765
Crediti:		
- verso imprese collegate	11.094	-
- verso altri	842	1.054
Altri titoli	3.719	3.719
Azioni proprie	11.181	-
	55.400	**32.528**
Totale immobilizzazioni	**653.443**	**631.161**
Attivo circolante		
Rimanenze:		
Materie prime, sussidiarie e di consumo	74.260	108.828
Prodotti in corso di lavorazione e semilavorati	12.598	16.319
Prodotti finiti e merci	190.412	251.954
Acconti	3.980	8.126
	281.250	**385.227**
Crediti:		
Verso clienti (di cui esigibili oltre l'esercizio succ. lire 2.657)	721.898	686.073
Verso imprese controllate	1.493	2.317
Verso imprese collegate	13.101	12.912
Verso controllanti	45	-
Verso altri (di cui esigibili oltre l'esercizio succ. lire 711)	116.453	110.074
	852.990	**811.376**
Attività finanziarie che non costituiscono immobilizzazioni:		
Crediti finanziari non immobilizzati	218.456	193.895
	218.456	**193.895**
Disponibilità liquide:		
Depositi bancari e postali	134.762	211.136
Danaro e valori in cassa	451	443
	135.213	**211.579**
Totale attivo circolante	**1.487.909**	**1.602.077**
Ratei e risconti	**10.239**	**5.137**
Totale attività	**2.151.591**	**2.238.375**

Passivo

(milioni di lire)	1996	1995
Patrimonio netto		
Capitale	112.548	112.548
Riserva da sovrapprezzo delle azioni	43.058	54.239
Riserve di rivalutazione	5.284	5.284
Riserva legale	5.481	4.989
Riserva per azioni proprie in portafoglio	11.181	-
Altre riserve, distintamente indicate nella nota	66.949	85.532
Utili (perdite) portati a nuovo	102.025	81.379
Utile (perdita) dell'esercizio di pertinenza del gruppo	13.330	22.904
Patrimonio netto del Gruppo	**359.856**	**366.875**
Capitale e riserve di terzi	19.017	20.346
Utile (perdita) dell'esercizio di pertinenza di terzi	228	(193)
Patrimonio netto di terzi	**19.245**	**20.153**
	379.101	**387.028**
Fondi per rischi e oneri		
Per trattamento di quiescenza e obblighi simili	3.779	4.684
Per imposte	9.272	10.408
Altri	32.427	26.235
	45.478	**41.327**
Trattamento di fine rapporto di lavoro subordinato	**105.669**	**99.476**
Debiti		
Obbligazioni convertibili	-	-
Debiti verso banche	635.670	671.059
(di cui esigibili oltre l'esercizio succ. lire 259.370)		
Debiti verso altri finanziatori	111.214	80.811
(di cui esigibili oltre l'esercizio succ. lire 101.114)		
Acconti	14.738	11.310
Debiti verso fornitori	· 712.908	796.069
Debiti rappresentati da titoli di credito	11.354	21.670
(di cui esigibili oltre l'esercizio succ. lire 248)		
Debiti verso imprese controllate	1.211	2.002
Debiti verso imprese collegate	2.286	2.729
Debiti verso controllanti	4.469	206
Debiti tributari	26.695	25.057
Debiti verso istituti di previdenza e sicurezza sociale	22.119	21.914
Altri debiti	68.809	70.487
	1.611.473	**1.703.314**
Ratei e risconti	**9.870**	**7.230**
Totale passività	**2.151.591**	**2.238.375**

Conti d'ordine	1996	1995
Elenco garanzie dirette e indirette:		
Fidejussioni:		
- a favore di terzi	21.307	9.597
- a favore di imprese controllate	5.805	6.303
Garanzie reali a favore di terzi	172.215	148.525
Altri conti d'ordine	387.250	169.463
Totale	**586.577**	**333.888**

Consolidated balance sheets as of 31 December 1996 and 1995

Assets

(million lire)	1996	1995
Amounts due from shareholders	–	–
Fixed assets		
Intangible fixed assets:		
Start-up and expansion costs	1,822	973
Research, development and advertising costs	2,594	4,800
Industrial patents and intellectual property rights	19,516	14,650
Concessions, licences and trademarks and similar rights	14,660	16,090
Goodwill	15,534	17,005
Other intangible fixed assets	922	2,073
	55,048	**55,591**
Tangible fixed assets:		
Land and buildings	219,418	223,556
Plant and machinery	215,898	202,052
Industrial and commercial equipment	64,384	58,483
Other assets	29,627	34,257
Assets under construction and advance payments	13,668	24,694
	542,995	**543,042**
Financial fixed assets:		
Equity investments:		
- subsidiary companies	249	359
- associated companies	18,811	19,631
- other companies	9,504	7,765
Financial receivables		
- associated companies	11,094	-
- third parties	842	1,054
Other securities	3,719	3,719
Own shares	11,181	-
	55,400	**32,528**
Total fixed assets	**653,443**	**631,161**
Current assets		
Inventoires:		
Raw, ancillary and consumable materials	74,260	108,828
Work in progress and semi-finished products	12,598	16,319
Finished products and goods for resale	190,412	251,954
Advance payments	3,980	8,126
	281,250	**385,227**
Receivables:		
Customers (due beyond 12 months - 2,657 lire)	721,898	686,073
Subsidiary companies	1,493	2,317
Associated companies	13,101	12,912
Parent companies	45	-
Third parties (due beyond 12 months - 711 lire)	116,453	110,074
	852,990	**811,376**
Financial assets not held as fixed assets:		
Other securities	-	-
Financial receivables not held as fixed assets	218,456	193,895
	218,456	**193,895**
Liquid funds:		
Bank and postal deposits	134,762	211,136
Cash and cash equivalents	451	443
	135,213	**211,579**
Total current assets	**1,487,909**	**1,602,077**
Accrued income and prepaid expenses	**10,239**	**5,137**
Total assets	**2,151,591**	**2,238,375**

Liabilities and shareholders' equity

(million lire)	1996	1995
Shareholders' equity		
Share capital	112,548	112,548
Share premium account	43,058	54,239
Revaluation reserve	5,284	5,284
Legal reserve	5,481	4,989
Reserve for own shares	11,181	-
Other reserves	66,949	85,532
Retained earnings	102,025	81,379
Net income for the year	13,330	22,904
Group interest in shareholders' equity	**359,856**	**366,875**
Minority interest in capital and reserves	19,017	20,346
Income (loss) attributable to minority shareholders	228	(193)
Minority interests	**19,245**	**20,153**
	379,101	**387,028**
Reserves for risks and charges		
Pensions and similar commitments	3,779	4,684
Taxation	9,272	10,408
Other	32,427	26,235
	45,478	**41,327**
Reserve for employee termination indemnities	**105,669**	**99,476**
Payables		
Convertibles bonds	-	-
Due to banks (due beyond 12 months - 259,370 lire)	635,670	671,059
Due to other providers of finance (due beyond 12 months - 101,114 lire)	111,214	80,811
Advances from customers	14,738	11,310
Due to suppliers	712,908	796,069
Securities issued (due beyond 12 months - 248 lire)	11,354	21,670
Due to subsidiary companies	1,211	2,002
Due to associated companies	2,286	2,729
Due to parent companies	4,469	206
Due to tax authorities	26,695	25,057
Due to social security institutions	22,119	21,914
Other payables	68,809	70,487
	1,611,473	**1,703,314**
Accrued expenses and deferred income	**9,870**	**7,230**
Total liabilities and shareholders' equity	**2,151,591**	**2,238,375**

Memorandum accounts	1996	1995
Direct and indirect guarantees given:		
Guarantees:		
- in favour of third parties	21,307	9,597
- in favour of subsidiary companies	5,805	6,303
Secured guarantees in favour of third parties	172,215	148,525
Other memorandum accounts	387,250	169,463
Total	**586,577**	**333,888**

Conto economico consolidato al 31 dicembre 1996

(milioni di lire)	1996	%	1995	%
Valore della produzione				
Ricavi delle vendite e delle prestazioni	2.507.830	100,0	2.526.364	100,0
Variazioni delle rimanenze di prodotti in corso di lavorazione, semilavorati e finiti	(42.380)	(1,7)	76.860	3,0
Incrementi di immobilizzazioni per lavori interni	4.775	0,2	2.301	0,1
Altri ricavi e proventi (di cui contributi in conto esercizio lire 1.076)	37.014	1,5	30.598	1,2
	2.507.239	100,0	**2.636.123**	104,3
Costi della produzione				
Per materie prime, sussidiarie, di consumo e di merci	1.322.706	52,7	1.531.220	60,6
Per servizi	434.185	17,3	437.541	17,3
Per godimento di beni di terzi	24.920	1,0	21.786	0,9
Per il personale:				
- salari e stipendi	291.960	11,6	300.121	11,9
- oneri sociali	98.301	3,9	92.415	3,7
- trattamento di fine rapporto	15.321	0,6	16.174	0,6
- trattamento di quiescenza e simili	8.842	0,4	7.440	0,3
- altri costi	13.580	0,5	15.776	0,6
Ammortamenti e svalutazioni:				
- ammortamento delle immobilizzazioni immateriali	18.160	0,7	23.570	0,9
- ammortamento delle immobilizzazioni materiali	86.282	3,4	84.114	3,3
- svalutazione dei crediti compresi nell'attivo circolante e delle disponibilità liquide	17.994	0,7	18.176	0,7
Variazioni delle rimanenze di materie prime, sussidiarie, di consumo e merci	35.988	1,4	(38.578)	(1,5)
Accantonamenti per rischi	12.035	0,5	10.711	0,4
Altri accantonamenti	336	0,0	558	0,0
Oneri diversi di gestione	39.169	1,6	47.991	1,9
	2.419.779	96,5	**2.569.015**	101,7
Differenza tra valore e costo della produzione	**87.460**	3,5	**67.108**	2,7
Proventi e oneri finanziari				
Proventi da partecipazioni	-	-	226	0,0
Altri proventi finanziari:				
- da crediti iscritti nelle immobilizzazioni	49	0,0	-	0,0
- da titoli iscritti nelle immobilizzazioni che non costituiscono partecipazioni	381	0,0	412	0,0
- proventi diversi dai precedenti	69.461	2,8	79.121	3,1
Interessi e altri oneri finanziari	135.975	5,4	117.686	4,7
	(66.084)	(2,6)	**(37.927)**	(1,5)
Rettifiche di valore di attività finanziarie				
Rivalutazioni:				
- di partecipazioni	1.174	0,0	1.779	0,1
Svalutazioni:				
- di partecipazioni	1.239	0,0	5.289	0,2
	(65)	(0,0)	**(3.510)**	(0,1)
Proventi e oneri straordinari				
Proventi (di cui plusvalenze da alienazioni lire 175)	3.387	0,1	4.641	0,2
Oneri (di cui minusvalenze da alienazioni lire 52)	6.792	0,3	6.113	0,2
	(3.405)	(0,1)	**(1.472)**	(0,1)
Risultato prima delle imposte	**17.906**	0,7	**24.199**	1,0
Imposte sul reddito dell'esercizio	4.348	0,2	1.488	0,1
Utile (perdita) dell'esercizio	**13.558**	0,5	**22.711**	0,9
Utile (perdita) dell'esercizio di pertinenza di terzi	228	0,0	(193)	(0,0)
Utile (perdita) dell'esercizio di pertinenza del Gruppo	**13.330**	0,5	**22.904**	0,9

Il presente bilancio è conforme alle scritture contabili

Consolidated statement of income for the years ended 31 December 1996 and 1995

(million lire)	1996	%	1995	%
Value of production				
Revenues from sales and services	2,507,830	100,0	2,526,364	100,0
Changes in work in progress, semi-finished and finished products inventoires	(42,380)	(1,7)	76,860	3,0
Capitalisation of internal work	4,775	0,2	2,301	0,1
Other income and revenues (including operating grants 1,076 lire)	37,014	1,5	30,598	1,2
	2,507,239	100,0	**2,636,123**	104,3
Production costs				
Raw, ancillary and consumable materials and goods for resale	1,322,706	52,7	1,531,220	60,6
Services received	434,185	17,3	437,541	17,3
Leases and rentals	24,920	1,0	21,786	0,9
Payroll costs:				
- wages and salaires	291,960	11,6	300,121	11,9
- social security charges	98,301	3,9	92,415	3,7
- employee termination indemnities	15,321	0,6	16,174	0,6
- pensions and similar commitments	8,842	0,4	7,440	0,3
- other costs	13,580	0,5	15,776	0,6
Amortisation, depreciation and writedowns:				
- amortisation of intangible fixed assets	18,160	0,7	23,570	0,9
- depreciation of tangible fixed assets	86,282	3,4	84,114	3,3
- writedown of receivables included in current assets and of liquid funds	17,994	0,7	18,176	0,7
Changes in inventories of raw, ancillaryand consumable materials and goods for resale	35,988	1,4	(38,578)	(1,5)
Provisions for risks and charges	12,035	0,5	10,711	0,4
Other provisions	336	0,0	558	0,0
Other operating expenses	39,169	1,6	47,991	1,9
	2,419,779	96,5	**2,569,015**	101,7
Difference between value and cost of production	**87,460**	3,5	**67,108**	2,7
Financial income and expenses				
Income from equity investments	-	0,0	226	0,0
Other financial income:				
- receivables held as fixed assets	49	0,0	-	0,0
- securities held as fixed assets, notrepresenting equity investments	381	0,0	412	0,0
- income other than the above:	69,461	2,8	79,121	3,1
Interest and other financial charges	135,975	5,4	117,686	4,7
	(66,084)	(2,6)	**(37,927)**	(1,5)
Adjustments to financial assets:				
Revaluations of:				
- equity investments	1,174	0,0	1,779	0,1
Writedown of:				
- equity investments	1,239	0,0	5,289	0,2
	(65)	0,0	**(3,510)**	(0,1)
Extraordinary income and charges				
Income (of which: gains on disposal of assets, 175 lire)	3,387	0,1	4.641	0,2
Charges (of which: losses on disposal of assets, 52 lire)	6,792	0,3	6,113	0,2
	(3,405)	(0,1)	**(1,472)**	(0,1)
Results before taxes	**17,906**	0,7	**24,199**	1,0
Income taxes for the year	4,348	0,2	1,488	0,1
Net income for the year	**13,558**	0,5	**22.711**	0,9
Income (loss) attributable to minority shareholders	228	0,0	(193)	(0,0)
Group share of net income for the year	**13,330**	**0,5**	**22,904**	0,9

These financial statements are consistent with the accounting records

⦂ Prospetti allegati al bilancio consolidato

Analisi delle variazioni nel patrimonio netto consolidato avvenute negli esercizi chiusi al 31 dicembre 1995 e 1996

(milioni di lire)	Capitale sociale	Riserva da sovrapprezzo delle azioni	Riserve di rivalutazione	Riserva legale	Riserva azioni proprie	Altre riserve	Utili (perdite) portati a nuovo	Utile dell'esercizio	Totale patrimonio netto
Saldi al 31 dicembre 1994	**112.548**	**54.239**	**5.183**	**3.265**	**0**	**80.491**	**45.803**	**52.811**	**354.340**
Riparto utile consolidato 1994				1.198		3.734	36.203	(41.135)	**0**
Distribuzione dividendi								(11.676)	**(11.676)**
Utilizzo riserve per il pagamento dell'imposta patrimoniale della capogruppo per l'anno 1994							(2.126)		**(2.126)**
Contributi per investimenti							718		**718**
Variazione dell'effetto cumulativo della conversione dei bilanci in valuta							2.715		**2.715**
Variazione dell'area di consolidamento			101	526			(627)		**0**
Utile dell'esercizio								22.904	**22.904**
Saldi al 31 dicembre 1995	**112.548**	**54.239**	**5.284**	**4.989**	**0**	**85.532**	**81.379**	**22.904**	**366.875**
Riparto utile consolidato 1995				479		280	22.145	(22.904)	**0**
Distribuzione dividendi							(7.815)	(1.610)	**(9.425)**
Riclassifica a Riserva azioni proprie		(11.181)			11.181				
Utilizzo riserve per il pagamento dell'imposta patrimoniale della capogruppo per l'anno 1995							(1.871)		**(1.871)**
Contributi per investimenti							5.346		**5.346**
Variazione dell'effetto cumulativo della conversione dei bilanci in valuta							(14.523)		**(14.523)**
Valutazione ad equity							158		**158**
Variazione dell'area di consolidamento					13		(47)		**(34)**
Utile dell'esercizio								13.330	**13.330**
Saldi al 31 dicembre 1996	**112.548**	**43.058**	**5.284**	**5.481**	**11.181**	**66.949**	**102.158**	**13.330**	**359.158**

Schedules attached to the consolidated financial statements

Statement of changes in consolidated shareholders' equity for the years ended 31 December 1996 and 1995

(million lire)	Share capital	Share premium account	Revaluation reserves	Legal reserve	Reserve for own shares	Other reserves	Retained earnings	Net income for the year	Total shareholders' equity
Balance as of 31 December 1994	112,548	54,239	5,183	3,265	0	80,491	45,803	52,811	354,340
Allocation of 1994 consolidated net income				1,198		3,734	36,203	(41,135)	0
Dividends paid								(11,676)	(11,676)
Utilisation of reserves to cover the Parent Company's 1994 capital taxes						(2,126)			(2,126)
Capital grants received						718			718
Change in cumulative translation adjustment arising from the translation of foreign currency financial statements						2,715			2,715
Changes in the scope of the consolidation			101	526			(627)		0
Net income for the year								22,904	22,904
Balance as of 31 December 1995	112,548	54,239	5,284	4,989	0	85,532	81,379	22,904	366,875
Allocation of 1995 consolidated net income				479		280	22,145	(22,904)	0
Dividends paid						(7,815)	(1,610)		(9,425)
Reclassification to reserve for own shares		(11,181)			11,181				
Utilisation of reserves to cover the Parent Company's 1995 capital taxes						(1,871)			(1,871)
Capital grants received						5,346			5,346
Change in cumulative translation adjustment arising from the translation of foreign currency financial statements						(14,523)			(14,523)
Valutations applying the equity method						158			158
Changes in the scope of the consolidation				13			(47)		(34)
Net income for the year								13,330	13,330
Balance as of 31 December 1996	112,548	43,058	5,284	5,481	11,181	66,949	102,158	13,330	359,158

⋮ **Prospetti allegati al bilancio consolidato**

Rendiconto finanziario consolidato

(milioni di lire)	1996	1995
A. Disponibilità monetarie nette iniziali [1]	**(208.346)**	**(56.310)**
B. Flusso monetario da (per) attività di esercizio		
Utile (perdita) del periodo	13.330	22.904
Ammortamenti	104.442	107.684
(Rivalutazioni) o svalutazioni di immobilizzazioni	65	3.510
Variazione del capitale di esercizio:		
- crediti del circolante	(41.279)	(120.963)
- rimanenze	103.977	(117.542)
- debiti verso fornitori ed altri debiti	(87.270)	237.132
- ratei e risconti	(2.462)	5.041
Variazione netta del "trattamento di fine rapporto"	6.193	10.483
Variazione fondo rischi per imposte	(1.136)	(4.508)
Variazione altri fondi rischi	5.287	(4.361)
	101.147	**139.380**
C. Flusso monetario da (per) attività di investimento		
Disinvestimenti (investimenti) netti in immobilizzazioni:		
- immateriali (esclusi goodwill)	(13.423)	(19.072)
- immateriali (goodwill)	(4.206)	(19.348)
- materiali	(92.885)	(147.581)
- finanziarie:		
partecipazioni	(874)	(6.808)
crediti	(10.882)	36.702
azioni proprie	(11.181)	-
	(133.451)	**(156.107)**
D. Flusso monetario da (per) attività finanziarie		
Incremento (decremento) di attività finanziarie non immobilizzate	(24.561)	(185.339)
Debiti finanziari a m/l termine ricevuti al netto dei rimborsi	38.639	103.340
Valutazioni ad equity	158	-
Contributi in conto capitale ricevuti	5.346	718
Dividendi	(9.425)	(11.676)
Utilizzo riserve per imposta patrimoniale	(1.871)	(2.126)
Variazione patrimonio netto di terzi	(908)	13.762
	7.378	**(81.321)**
E. Effetto cambio su poste a medio e lungo termine	**(7.733)**	**(4.628)**
F. Variazione area di consolidamento		
Capitale di esercizio netto	79	(23.024)
Immobilizzazioni immateriali	(2)	(12)
Immobilizzazioni materiali	(125)	(46.770)
Immobilizzazioni finanziarie	-	550
Fondi per rischi ed oneri	-	14.890
Finanziamenti a m/l termine	-	5.006
Riserva di consolidamento	(34)	-
	(82)	**(49.360)**
G. Flusso monetario del periodo	**(32.741)**	**(152.036)**
H. Disponibilità monetarie nette finali [1]	**(241.087)**	**(208.346)**

[1] Ovvero indebitamento finanziario netto a breve

⋮ Schedules attached to the consolidated financial statements

Statement of consolidated cash flows for the years ended 31 December 1996 and 1995

(million lire)	1996	1995
A. Net short-term financial indebtedness, beginning of the year	**(208,346)**	**(56,310)**
B. Cash flows from (used in) operating activities		
Net income (loss) for the year	13,330	22,904
Amortisation and depreciation	104,442	107,684
(Revalutation)/writedown of fixed assets	65	3,510
Changes in operating capital:		
- current receivables	(41,279)	(120,963)
- inventoires	103,977	(117,542)
- payables to suppliers and other liabilities	(87,270)	237,132
- accruals and deferrals	(2,462)	5,041
Net change in reserve for employee termination indemnities	6,193	10,483
Change in taxation reserve	(1,136)	(4,508)
Change in other risk reserves	5,287	(4,361)
	101,147	**139,380**
C. Cash flows from (used in) investment activities		
Disposal of (investment in) fixed assets, net		
- intangible fixed assets (excluding goodwill)	(13,423)	(19,072)
- (goodwill)	(4,206)	(19,348)
- tangible fixed assets	(92,885)	(147,581)
- financial fixed assets:		
equity investments	(874)	(6,808)
receivables	(10,882)	36,702
own shares	(11,181)	-
	(133,451)	**(156,107)**
D. Cash flows from (used in) financing activities		
Increase (decrease) in financial assets not held as fixed assets	(24,561)	(185,339)
Long-term loans received, net of repayments	38,639	103,340
Valuations applying equity method	158	-
Capital grants received	5,346	718
Dividends paid	(9,425)	(11,676)
Utilisation of reserves to cover capital taxes	(1,871)	(2,126)
Change in minority interests	(908)	13,762
	7,378	**(81,321)**
E. Effect of exchange fluctuations on long-term positions	**(7,733)**	**(4,628)**
F. Changes in the scope of consolidation		
Operating capital, net	79	(23,024)
Intangible fixed assets	(2)	(12)
Tangible fixed assets	(125)	(46,770)
Financial fixed assets	-	550
Reserve for risk and charges	-	14,890
Long-term loans	-	5,006
Consolidation (differences) reserves	(34)	-
	(82)	**(49,360)**
G. Cash flow for the year (B+C+D+E+F)	**(32,741)**	**(152,036)**
H. Net short-term financial indebtedness, end of the year (A+G)	**(241,087)**	**(208,346)**

⁞ Explanatory notes

Form and content of the consolidated financial statements

The consolidated financial statements as of 31 December 1996 have been prepared in conformity with Decree 127/1991, making reference, for matters not covered by such Decree, to the accounting principles established by the Italian Accounting Profession and, in the absence thereof, those laid down by the International Accounting Standards Committee (I.A.S.C.).

These financial statements consolidate on a line-by-line basis the financial statements of Merloni Elettrodomestici Spa and its subsidiaries, except those which are inactive or insignificant.

The companies included within the scope of the consolidation as of 31 December 1996 are listed below:

Companies consolidated on a line-by-line basis	Registrered offices	Share capital	Percentage Group ownership	
			direct	indirect
Merloni Ariston International Sa	Luxembourg	USD 94,169,000	100	–
Merloni Electrodomésticos Sa	Spain	ESP 1,200,000,000	–	100
Merloni Domestic Appliances Ltd	United Kingdom	GBP 21,501,000	46.5	53.5
Merloni Electrodomésticos Sa	Portugal	PTE 3.365,000,000	–	99.4
Merloni International Trading Bv	Netherlands	NLG 600,000	–	100
Merloni Huishoudapparaten Bv	Netherlands	NLG 1,000,000	–	100
Indesit Pts Ltd	United Kingdom	GBP 1,000	–	100
Merloni Electroménager Sa	France	FRF 100,000,000	–	100
Merloni Electromenager Suisse Sa	Switzerland	CHF 280,000	–	100
Scholtès Nederland Bv	Netherlands	NLG 175,000	–	100
Scholtès Warenhandelsgesmbh	Austria	ATS 250,000	–	100
Scholtes Ireland Ltd	Ireland	IEP 5,000	–	100
Fabrica Portugal Sa	Portugal	PTE 2,250,000,000	–	96.4
Merloni Elettrodomestici Beyaz Esya Sanayi Ve Ticaret As	Turkey	TUL 3,000,000,000,000	90*	–
Merloni Elettrodomestici Beyaz Esya Pazarlama As	Turkey	TUL 17,000,000,000	100	–
Belimovel Construcoes Lda	Portugal	PTE 2,400,000	–	80
Hevdove Ltd	Ireland	IEP 102	–	99
Merloni Financial Services Sa	Luxembourg	ITL 10,000,000,000	100	–
Faber Factor Spa	Italy	ITL 8,000,000,000	60	40
Merloni Hausgeräte Gmbh	Germany	DEM 200,000	–	100
New World Holdings Ltd	United Kingdom	GBP 2,758,322	–	100
New World (Group) Ltd	United Kingdom	GBP 16,043,381	–	100
Merloni Investment Ltd	Cayman Isl.	USD 3,000,000	95	5
Merloni South America Investment Ltd	Cayman Isl.	USD 3,000,000	–	100
Merloni Reinsurance Company Ltd	Ireland	USD 750,000	–	100
Philco Italia Spa	Italy	ITL 15,000,000,000	51.7	–
Merloni Indesit Polska Spzoo	Poland	PLN 1,178,000	100	–

Companies carried at equity	Registred offices	Share capital	Percentage Group ownership	
			direct	indirect
Merloni Progetti Spa	Italy	ITL 5,000,000,000	33	–
Merloni Progetti International Sa	Luxembourg	ITL 25,000,000,000	–	33
Protecno Sa	Switzerland	CHF 500,000	–	33
Progelease Spa	Italy	ITL 1,000,000,000	–	33
Star Spa	Italy	ITL 6,500,000,000	30	–
Factor Industriale Spa	Italy	ITL 10,000,000,000	–	22.1
Argentron Sa	Argentina	USD 22,000,000	–	31.2

* This percentage includes the 4.12% interest held by SIMEST Spa, over which the Parent Company retains the voting rights

Annual
Report 1996

Other investments in subsidiary and associated companies	Registred offices	Share capital	Percentage Group ownership direct	indirect
M&B Marchi e Brevetti Srl	Italy	ITL 20,000,000	50	–
Sofarem Sarl	La Rèunion	FRF 2,500,000	–	20
Merloni Appliance Asia Pacific Pte Ltd	Singapore	SGD 2	–	100
Merloni Indesit Háztartástechnikai kft	Hungary	HUF 10,000,000	99	–
Merloni Indesit Bulgaria Srlu	Bulgaria	BGL 650,000	100	–
Merloni Indesit Domácí Elektrospotrebice Sro	Czech Republic	CZK 1,200,000	100	–

The changes in the scope of the consolidation during the year reflect the following events:
- Merloni Ariston International Sa purchased an additional 14.8% interest in Fabrica Portugal Sa;
- The Parent Company increased its holding in Merloni Elettrodomestici Beyaz Esaya Sanayi Ve Ticaret As from 69.3% to 90%;
- The Parent Company's holding in Merloni Elettrodomestici Beyaz Esaya Pazarlama As was increased from 54% to 100%;
- Merloni Financial Services Sa took over the activities of its subsidiary Merloni Overseas Ltd which was put into voluntary liquidation;
- The sale of the holding in Sodamec Sa;
- The consolidation on a line-by-line basis of Merloni Indesit Polska Spzoo, whose activities became significant to the Group from July 1996; the company has been consolidated for the whole year.

The financial statements used for the consolidation as of 31 December 1996 were those approved at the Shareholders' Meetings of the Parent Company or the individual companies concerned, or prepared for such approval by the respective Boards of Directors.

All companies prepare financial statements as of the accounting reference date, regardless of their financial year-end.

The Group is controlled by Fineldo Spa, a holding company, which uses these consolidated financial statements it prepare its own consolidated financial statements.

The financial statements of companies included in the consolidation were prepared on the basis of the accounting principles laid down by articles 2423 et seq. of the Italian Civil Code. In accordance with Consob recommendations, such principles were supplemented by those established by the Italian Accounting Profession and, where necessary, by the International Accounting Standards Committee (IASC).

Exceptions allowed by Decree 127/1991
There have been no deviations from the established accounting principles, as would be allowed under paras. 4 and 5 of article 29, Decree 127/1991.

Accounting policies
The accounting policies adopted for the preparation of the consolidated financial statements are essentially consistent with those applied by the Parent Company and conform with Consob recommendations.

Consolidation principles and translation to Italian lire
- The assets and liabilities of consolidated companies are combined on a line-by-line basis. The carrying value of the related investments is eliminated against the equity interests in the companies concerned, determined with reference to the date such investments were consolidated for the first time.
- The difference between purchase cost and the share of equity acquired at the time of purchase (goodwill), is recorded among intangible fixed assets and amortised over five years.
- The "Legal reserves" and the "Reserves for capital grants" of subsidiaries are not eliminated when the related equity interests are consolidated.
- The minority shareholders' interests in the capital and reserves of consolidated subsidiaries are classified separately as "Minority interests" among the equity accounts in the consolidated balance sheet and as "Income (losses) attributable to minority shareholders" in both the consolidated balance sheet and statement of income.
- All unrealised profits on intercompany transactions are eliminated, as are receivables, payables and all transactions between consolidated companies.
- The financial statements of foreign subsidiaries are translated into Italian lire as follows:
– balance sheet items, using year-end exchange rates;
– statement of income items, using average exchange rates for the year;
– equity accounts, using historical exchange rates.
Exchange differences deriving from the translation of shareholders' equity using historical rather than the year-end exchange rates are reflected in the "Cumulative translation adjustment" classified among "Other reserves" within consolidated shareholders' equity, as are the differences arising by translating the results for the year using average rather than the year-end exchange rates.
The table below presents the exchange rates applied:

⋮ **Explanatory notes**

Currency	Opening exchange rates	Average exchange rates	Closing exchange rates	Prior year average exchange rates
US dollar	1,584.72	1,542.95	1,530.57	1,628.36
Deutsche mark	1,105.49	1,028.25	982.71	1,140.48
French franc	323.41	300.45	291.32	326.44
Netherlands guilder	987.73	914.48	875.56	1,017.45
Turkish lira	0.027	0.014	0.014	0.027
Portuguese escudo	10.60	10.00	9.76	10.91
English sterling	2,458.22	2,411.40	2,583.91	2,566.60
Spanish peseta	13.05	12.17	11.66	13.10
Swiss franc	1,376.70	1,250.28	1,131.58	1,380.51
Polish zloty	–	532.96	532.96	–

• Investments in foreign subsidiary and associated companies operating in hyper-inflationary economies are adjusted by applying internationally-recognised inflation accounting procedures (I.A.S. 29).

Intangible fixed assets
These are recorded at purchase or production cost, including related charges, and amortised on a systematic basis over the period they are expected to benefit.
• Start-up and expansion costs are amortised over five years.
• Research, development and advertising costs are amortised over three years.
• Industrial patents and intellectual property rights are recorded at purchase or production cost, including any purchase-related costs. This caption also comprises costs for the development and integration of EDP systems. These costs are amortised over the period they are expected to benefit, which is generally five years.
• Licences and trademarks are stated at purchase cost, including any directly-related costs, and amortised over the period they are expected to benefit.
• Goodwill is amortised over five years.
Other intangible fixed assets mainly include:
a) costs deriving from early retirements and tax amnesty payments, which are deferred in accordance with specific legislation, amortised over five financial periods (amortisation completed 1996);
b) factory building costs, amortised over five financial periods (amortisation completed in 1996);
c) other deferred charges (charges for loan acquisition, expenditures made for third-party properties) amortised in function of the length of the respective contracts.

Tangible fixed assets
Tangible fixed assets are stated at purchase or production cost, including directly-related charges, net of accumulated depreciation. The cost of certain assets has been restated on the basis of specific revaluation laws. Certain tangible fixed assets, acquired at the time of spin-offs or mergers, are stated at their appraised market value at that time.
Ordinary maintenance costs are expensed as incurred.

Improvement costs are allocated to the related assets and depreciated over their residual useful lives.
Depreciation is computed on a straight-line basis using rates that reflect the estimated useful lives of tangible fixed assets which, for Italian companies, correspond to the ordinary fiscally-admissible rates. Such rates are halved in the year of addition. The depreciation rates applied to the individual asset categories are as follows:

Buildings and temporary constructions	3%	10%
Plant and machinery	10%	20%
Industrial and commercial equipment	10%	33%
Other tangible fixed assets:		
Vehicles and internal transport	15%	30%
Office furniture, machines and EDP system	12%	30%

Tangible fixed assets are written down in cases where, regardless of the depreciation accumulated, there is a permanent loss in value. The value of such assets is reinstated in future accounting periods should the reasons for the writedowns no longer apply. Assets under construction and advances to suppliers are stated on the basis of costs incurred, including any directly-related expenses.

Financial fixed assets
Investments in associated companies are carried at equity. Other equity investments over which the Group does not exercise significant influence, or whose operations are limited, are carried at cost. The book value of such investments is prudently written down in cases where there is a permanent loss in value.
– Receivables held as financial fixed assets are stated at their estimated realisable value.
– Securities are recorded at purchase cost and written down where there is a permanent loss in value, taking account of market trends.
– Own shares, purchased in accordance with a mandate from the shareholders, as required by and within the limits allowed by Italian law, are stated at cost; they are written down should there be a permanent loss in value.

Inventoires
Inventories are stated at the lowest of current purchase or production cost, or their estimated realisable value, taking account of market trends. The Parent Company values closing inventories on a LIFO basis with annual layers; in the circumstances, these values are not significantly different to those determined using the current cost method. The components of cost are the same as those described in relation to tangible fixed assets. The calculation of estimated realisable value takes account of direct selling expenses. Obsolete and slow-moving inventories are written down to their useful or realisable value.

Receivables
Receivables are stated at their estimated realisable value by

Annual
Report 1996

deducting the allowance for doubtful accounts from their nominal value.

Liquid assets
Liquid assets are stated at their nominal value at the balance sheet date.

Accruals and deferrals
Accruals and deferrals are recorded in accordance with the matching principle.

Capital grants
Capital grants are reflected in the equity account, "Other reserves", at the time their collection becomes certain. Due to changes in tax law, grants received after 1993 are stated net of the related deferred taxation, which is reflected in the taxation reserve.
Operating grants are credited to the statement of income.

Reserves for risks and charges
These reserves cover specific known or likely losses, the timing and amount of which cannot be determined at year-end. Provisions reflect the best estimate of losses to be incurred based on the information available.
Contingent liabilities are described in the notes, but no specific reserves are provided.

Reserve for employee termination indemnities
This reserve represents the Group's liability to employees of Italian companies for indemnities that will be payable, net of advances, upon termination of their employment. Such indemnities are accrued in accordance with the national collective labour contract and current labour legislation.

Payables
Payables are stated at their face value.

Revenue recognition
Revenue from the sale of products is recognised at the time ownership passes, which is generally upon shipment to the customer.

Current income taxes
Current taxes are provided in accordance with fiscal legislation with reference to a realistic estimate of the taxable income for the current and other open fiscal years, taking account of any available exemptions and tax credits. Such provisions are stated, net of advance payments and tax withholdings, as "Due to tax authorities".
Deferred taxes are also provided on timing differences between reported and taxable income (mainly in relation to gains on the disposal of tangible fixed assets), and on consolidation adjustments.
Any equalisation taxes payable upon the distribution of dividends are paid out of reserves at the time of distribution.

Leased assets
The economic effects of sale and leaseback contracts arranged in prior years by a subsidiary company that merged with the Parent Company in 1990 are reflected in the consolidated financial statements in accordance with the lease accounting methodology established in I.A.S. 17, since this treatment more closely reflects the economic substance of the underlying transactions.
Charges incurred in relation to operating leases are expensed on an accruals basis.

Foreign currency translactions
Trade and financial receivables and payables originally expressed in foreign currency are recorded using the exchange rates in effect at the transaction dates. An exchange fluctuation reserve is provided only if an overall net loss emerges from their adjustment using year-end rates. An exception is made in the case of receivables and payables covered by hedging contracts, which are recorded using the contractual exchange rates.

Commitments, guarantees and contingencies
Commitments and guarantees are reflected among the memorandum accounts at their contractual value.
The reserve for risks and charges is provided to cover known or likely losses.
Contingent liabilities are described in the notes, but no specific reserves are provided.

Other information

Reclassification of the financial statements of a consolidated company with dissimilar activities
For greater clarity, the operating costs of Faber Factor Spa (a factoring company) have been reclassified as "Interest and other financial expense" within the consolidated statement of income.

Comments on the principal balance sheet captions

Assets

Fixed assets

Intangible fixed assets
Intangible fixed assets as of 31 December 1996 comprise the following:

⋮ **Explanatory notes**

Description (million lire)	Opening balance	Increase	Decr.	Translation differences	Closing balance
Start-up and expansion costs	973	1.165	406	90	**1,822**
Research, development and advertising expenses	**4,800**	110	2,151	(165)	**2,594**
Industrial patents and intellectual propriety rights	**14,650**	10,790	5,912	(12)	**19,516**
Concessions, licenses, trademarks and similar rights	**16,090**	934	2,352	(12)	**14,660**
Goodwill	**17,005**	4,206	5,677	-	**15,534**
Other	**2,073**	638	1,874	85	**922**
Total	**55,591**	**17,843**	**18,372**	**(14)**	**55,048**

Start-up and expansion costs benefit future years and include formation expenses, the cost of capital increases and the merger-related expenses of Group companies.
This caption is analysed as follows:

Historical cost (million lire)	1996	1995
Formation	2,314	2,372
Capital increases	1,090	1,158
Merger-related expenses	98	115
Start-up of new production	1,060	-
Total	4,562	3,645
Accumulated amortisation	2,740	2,672
Balance as of 31 December 1996	1,822	973

Research, development and advertising expenses mainly include the costs incurred in 1995 to launch the Ariston brand in Turkey for a residual value of 949 million (historical cost of 1,444 million lire) and for the production of the Ariston commercial, for a residual value of 981 million lire (historical cost of 2,943 million lire).
The increase in *Industrial patents and intellectual property rights* of 10,790 million lire principally reflects costs incurred by the Parent Company to implement the new integrated platforms (10,684 million lire). No amortisation has been charged in relation to certain projects (5,218 million lire) since they are not yet completed.

Concessions, trademarks, licences and similar rights include:
– licences to use the Ariston trademark owned by M&B Marchi e Brevetti Spa, an associated company. These costs increased by 692 million lire in 1996 following the extension of usage rights. Amortisation charges, 185 million lire in 1996, reflect the duration of the concession, which was extended to 2050 in 1994;
– the residual value of the Indesit trademark (1,400 million lire), acquired on the merger of Indesit Srl Amortisation, 1,400 million lire in 1996, is provided over the ten-year period the trademark is expected to benefit;
– the licence to use the three-dimensional CAD/CAM software, which is amortised over five years. The amortisation charge for the year was 309 million lire.

The increase in *Goodwill* by Lire 4,206 million reflects the difference between purchase cost and the Group's equity interest in Fabrica Portugal Sa (1,082 million lire) and Merloni Elettrodomestici Beyaz Sanayi Ve Ticaret As (3,124 million lire).
The closing balance therefore includes the unamortised goodwill of: Merloni Progetti Spa (4,680 million lire), which arose in 1994 on the acquisition of a 33% interest in the company; Philco Italia Spa (7,489 million lire), which arose in 1995 on the acquisition of a further 3.3% interest in the company; Fabrica Portugal Sa (866 million lire), which arose in 1996 on the acquisition of a further 14.8% interest in the company; and Merloni Elettrodomestici Beyaz Sanayi Ve Ticaret (2,499 million lire), which also arose in 1996 on the acquisition of a further 20.7% interest in the company.

Other intangible fixed assets include:
– the cost of opening offices in the C.I.S. (432 million lire);
– leasehold improvements incurred by the Turkish subsidiary (203 million lire).

Tangible fixed assets
The changes in tangible fixed assets are summarised in the following table:

Changes (million lire)	Land and buildings	Plant and machinery	Industrial and commercial equipment	Other assets	Assets under construction and advantage payments	Total
Opening balances						
Historical cost (*)	242,069	450,589	226,674	85,475	24,694	1,029,501
Revaluations	39,046	10,390	329	1,808	–	51,573
Accumulated depreciation	(57,559)	(258,927)	(168,520)	(53,026)	–	(538,032)
Writedowns	–	–	–	–	–	–
Total	**223,556**	**202,052**	**58,483**	**34,257**	**24,694**	**543,042**
Changes						
Purchases	8,061	42,947	27,588	10,182	12,286	101,064
Revaluations	(959)	–	–	–	–	(959)
Disposals	(1,325)	(6,349)	(934)	(15,348)	–	(23,956)
Release of accumulated depreciation	719	5,356	880	9,918	–	16,873
Depreciation charge for the year	(8,117)	(43,263)	(24,769)	(10,195)	–	(86,344)

Annual
Report 1996

Changes (million lire)	Land and buildings	Plant and machinery	Industrial and commercial equipment	Other assets	Assets under construction and advantage payments	Total
Writedowns	–	–	–	–	–	–
Changes in the scope of consolidation	–	–	–	128	–	128
Translation differences	(2,919)	(2,662)	(245)	(148)	(801)	(6,775)
Other changes	401	17,817	3,381	834	(22,511)	(78)
Total	**(4,139)**	**13,846**	**5,901**	**(4,629)**	**(11,026)**	**(47)**
Closing balances						
Historical cost	248,804	487,188	253,328	80,436	36,980	1,106,736
Revaluations	38,088	10,390	329	1,808	–	50,615
Accumulated depreciation	(64,957)	(296,834)	(192,409)	(53,303)	–	(607,503)
Writedowns	–	–	–	–	–	–
Translation differences	(2,919)	(2,662)	(245)	(148)	(801)	(6,775)
Other changes	401	17,817	3,381	834	(22,511)	(78)
Total	**219,418**	**215,898**	**64,384**	**29,627**	**13,668**	**542,995**

(*) Historical cost includes the effect of exchange rate fluctuations on tangible fixed assets denominated in foreign currency since 1987, the first year of line-by-line consolidation

Investment during the year mainly related to the renewal and completion of the product range, as well as the consolidation of production facilities and logistics.

Disposals included the sale of a warehouse in the Bologna area, not used by the Parent Company; this transaction involved the elimination of earlier revaluations. The Parent Company has also sold its EDP facilities and data transmission systems, which are now outsourced. Other disposals reflect the routine replacement of assets.

The depreciation charge includes the re-entry of accelerated depreciation reversed in prior years, 3,981 million lire, and the reversal of accelerated depreciation recorded by Philco Italia Spa, 1,899 million lire. Provision has been made for the related deferred tax.

The depreciation charges of the Portuguese subsidiary according to local law have been reduced. This change benefited net income by around 536 million lire.

The tangible fixed assets of the two Turkish subsidiaries have been revalued in accordance with inflation accounting principles (IAS 29). These revaluations are classified together with the translation differences in the above table.

Certain tangible fixed assets are mortgaged and otherwise pledged to guarantee long-term loans, as discussed in the memorandum accounts.

Financial fixed assets

Equity investments

The principal equity investments not consolidated on a line-by-line basis as of 31 December 1996 are as follows:

(million lire)	1996		1995	
Investments in subsidiary companies	% owned	Book value	% owned	Book value
Merloni Indesit Háztartástechnikai Kft	99.00	149	99.00	149
Merloni Indesit Polska Spzoo	–	–	100.00	110
Merloni Indesit Bulgaria Srlu	100.00	40	100.00	40

Merloni Indesit Domácí				
Elektrospotrebice Sro	100.00	60	100.00	60
Total		**249**		**359**

With the exception of Merloni Indesit Polska Spzoo these controlling interests, carried at cost, have not been consolidated since their activities are insignificant in the context of the Group.

(million lire)	1996		1995	
Investments in associated companies	% owned	Book value	% owned	Book value
M&B Marchi e Brevetti Srl	50.00	10	50.00	10
Necchi Compressori Spa	–	–	15.00	791
Argentron Sa	31.18	5,193	31.18	6,271
Merloni Progetti Spa	33.00	9,369	33.00	8,136
Star Spa	30.00	1,669	30.00	1,697
Factor Industriale Spa	22.08	2,442	22.08	2,516
Other minor investments	–	128	–	210
Total		**18,811**		**19,631**

The change reflects the reclassification of Necchi Compressori Spa from investments in associated companies to investments in other companies. This follows a reduction in ownership from 15% to 8.75%, given that the holder of the investment, Merloni Ariston International Sa, did not participate in the last capital increase. In prior years, the investment in Necchi Compressori Spa was carried at equity. Prudently, this method was not applied in 1996 and no other revaluations were recorded. The change is also due to equity adjustments recorded by Merloni Ariston International Sa in relation to its investment in Bakmil Jv, a small company.

The key combined financial information of associated companies carried at equity is summarised below:

⋮ **Explanatory notes**

(million lire)	1996	1995
Net income (loss) for the year	562	(17,475)
Total stockholders equity:	61,660	80,536
including Merloni Group	18,670	19,411

This combined information has been extracted from financial statements that have not yet been approved by the Boards of Directors concerned.

(million lire) Equity investments in other companies	% owned	1996 Book value	% owned	1995 Book value
Haier Merloni (Qingdao) Washing Machine Co. Ltd	16.62	4,860	16.62	4,860
Meurice Ets	10.00	1,870	10.00	1,936
Istituto Mobiliare Italiano	0.00	1,204	–	–
Necchi Compressori Spa	8.75	791	–	–
Akros Spa	0.18	587	0.18	701
Other minor investments	–	192	–	268
Total		**9,504**		**7,765**

Apart from Necchi Compressori Spa (discussed above), the increase in investments in other companies was due to the acquisition by the Parent Company of 100,000 shares in IMI, in connection with the privatisation of this agency. The Parent Company also wrote down its investment in Akros Spa by 269 million lire, and subscribed 155 million lire to a new capital increase in that company. The decrease in other minor investments reflects the sale of the Parent Company's interest in Centergross Srl (77 million lire).

Financial receivables
Associated companies
This balance, 11,094 million lire, reflects the loan granted by Merloni Ariston International Sa to Proglease Spa, an associated company. This loan, repayable in 1997, earns interest at market rates.
Own shares
Following a resolution adopted at the extraordinary shareholders' meeting held on January 16, 1996, the Parent Company purchased 3,551,500 own ordinary shares, par value 1,000 lire each, for 11,181 million lire. The purpose of this transaction was to stabilise share prices and make a profitable investment, considering the growth potential of the Company.

Current assets

Inventoires
The substantial decrease, 103,977 million lire, is due to the policy of reducing inventory levels.

Receivables
This balance, 852,990 million lire (811,376 million lire in 1995), includes:
Customers
This balance, 721,898 million lire, is stated net of the allowance for doubtful accounts totalling 39,822 million lire, and derives from commercial transactions and services rendered.
The Parent Company and some of its subsidiaries have obtained insurance cover for collection risks.
Among the Parent Company's receivables there are payments for 1,352 million lire due beyond five years.
Receivables are written down to cover the risk of loss inherent in disputed balances and other doubtful accounts. The net increase of 35,825 million lire is due to the extension of payment terms in order to maintain market share.

Subsidiary and associated companies:
These balances are analysed as follows:

Subsidiary companies (million lire)	1996	1995
Merloni Indesit Bulgaria Srlu	271	624
Merloni Indesit Domácí Sro	691	831
Merloni Indesit Háztartástechnikai Kft	131	823
Merloni Appliance Asia Pacific Pte Ltd	400	–
Merloni Indesit Polska Spzoo	–	39
Total	**1,493**	**2,317**

Associated companies (million lire)	1996	1995
Argentron Sa	6,440	3,498
Merloni Progetti Spa	4,677	6,034
Protecno Sa	880	1,503
Sofarem Sarl	993	1,671
Nasr Ltd	–	78
Star Spa	–	3
Factor Industriale Spa	–	125
M&B Marchi e Brevetti Srl	111	–
Total	**13,101**	**12,912**

Transactions of a commercial and financial nature between Group companies are conducted on an arm's-length basis.

Parent Company
This caption represents amounts due to the group parent company, 45 million lire, in relation to guarantees given to Fineldo Spa, the ultimate parent.

Third parties
This caption is analysed as follows:

Annual
Report 1996

Description (million lire)	1996	1995
Social security institutions	1,556	879
Advantages to employees	1,288	2,541
Tax authorities	29,280	35,500
Grants receivable	435	435
Advances to suppliers	15,946	11,657
Factoring advances to customers	42,765	39,516
Related companies	72	14
Other amounts due	25,111	19,532
Total	**116,453**	**110,074**

These receivables, which include 711 million lire due beyond 12 months, have not been written down since their recovery is certain.

Advances to employees mainly relate to 1997 wages and salaries.

The amount relating to the deferral of invoices for goods and services not supplied has been reclassified to Advances to suppliers. The amount reclassified for 1995 was 4,575 million lire, while the 1996 amount was 11,142 million lire. Other amounts due from related companies comprise R.T.C. International (63 million lire) and Aermarche Spa (9 million lire). Other amounts due include 910 million lire for insurance refunds on receivables, as well as 10,402 million lire due by third parties to Merloni South America Investment Ltd following the sale of 40% of the investment in Argentron Sa, and 7,710 million lire due to Merloni Elettrodomestici Spa by the new shareholders of Merloni Elettrodomestici Beyaz Esya Sanayi Ve Ticaret As.

Financial assets not held as fixed assets
This caption is analysed as follows:

Description (million lire)	1996	1995
Factoring advances to suppliers	196,732	180,899
Factoring advances to associated companies	643	56
Factoring advances to related companies	10,063	7,226
Factoring advances to Parent companies	4,254	–
Receivable from Barclays Finanziaria Spa	6,764	5,714
Total	**218,456**	**193,895**

Factoring advances to associated companies relate to Factor Industriale Spa, 600 million lire, and Merloni Progetti Spa, 43 million lire; while factoring advances to related companies include 5,409 million lire to Aermarche Spa, 3,001 million lire to Rtc International Spa and 1,653 million lire to Merloni Partecipazioni e Servizi Spa.

Factoring advances to Parent Companies, 4,254 million lire, include 4,233 million lire advanced against the future repayment of tax credits transferred to Fineldo Spa.

These advances by Faber Factor Spa to the associated, related and parent companies indicated above are remunerated at

the rates applied to other lending.

The increase in the receivable from Barclays Finanziaria Spa reflects interest earned on the deposit with that company.

Liquid funds
Liquid funds, 135,213 million lire, reflect bank and postal deposits, together with cash and cash equivalents held at year-end. The decrease of 76,366 million lire reflects the improved management of liquidity, achieved through a centralized system of control of the treasury, passed from the Parent Company to Merloni Ariston International Sa.

The caption also includes 10,043 million lire deposited to secure loans from the banking system to subsidiary companies. Interest earned on such deposits is consistent with that earned on other deposits.

Accrued income and prepaid expenses
This balance, 10,239 million lire, has increased by 5,102 million lire with respect to 1995.

The change principally reflects accrued exchange gains on export advances financing the Parent Company's transactions with foreign subsidiaries, 3,236 million lire, and the deferred cost of exchange hedges, 1,590 million lire, which became significant in 1996.

The caption also includes accrued interest income (1,094 million lire) and deferred interest expense (332 million lire), as well as prepaid insurance premiums (380 million lire), advertising (574 million lire), rentals (759 million lire), and consultancy fees (648 million lire).

Liabilities and shareholders' equity

Shareholders' equity

Share capital
The Parent Company's issued and fully-paid share capital is analysed below as of 31 December 1996:

Description	As of 31 December 1996	
(million lire)	Number	Value
Ordinary shares	91,508,268	91,508,268,000
Savings shares	21,039,668	21,039,668,000

Legal reserve
The increase of 492 million lire reflects the allocation of 1995 net income, 479 million lire, and the increase in investment in Fabrica Portugal Sa, 13 million lire.

Other reserves
These reserves are analysed below :

⋮ Explanatory notes

Description (million lire)	1996	1995
Capital grants	54,191	58,530
Cumulative translation adjustment	8,495	23,019
Extraordinary reserve	4,060	3,780
Consolidation adjustments	203	203
Totale	**66,949**	**85,532**

The cumulative translation adjustment includes exchange differences arising from the translation to Italian lire of financial statements denominated in foreign currencies. In conformity with I.A.S. 21, this amount is classified among consolidated shareholders' equity. The balance also includes the exchange effect on the equity value of foreign investments (31 December 1996: negative for 1,213 million lire).

Retained earnings
This caption includes accumulated losses of 16,457 million lire relating to associated companies carried at equity and to Necchi Compressori Spa.
It also includes 16,839 million lire which would be subject to taxation upon distribution, or if utilised for purposes other than to cover losses.
The capital tax levied on the Parent Company, being the balance due in respect of 1996 and the advance for 1997, around 1,500 million lire, will be recorded at the time of payment. This accounting treatment is permitted under special legislation as an alternative to charging the capital tax to the statement of income, as would be required under generally accepted accounting principles. Had the latter accounting treatment been applied, net income for the year and shareholders' equity would have been lower by around 1,500 million lire and 700 million lire respectively. Faber Factor Spa and Philco Italia Spa have, conversely, recognised their capital taxes for 1996, 44 million lire and 192 million lire respectively, on an accruals basis.

Reconciliation with the Parent Company's financial statements
The shareholders' equity as of 31 December 1996 and 1995, and net income for the years then ended, reported in the statutory financial statements of Merloni Elettrodomestici Spa are reconciled with the related consolidated amounts as follows:

(million lire)	1996		1995	
	Shereholders' equity	Net income	Shareholders' equity	Net income
Per Merloni Elettrodomestici Spa financial statements	**246,073**	**3,806**	**248,678**	**1,695**
Effect of consolidating subsidiary and associated companies	108,056	6,656	115,246	26,309
Elimination of intragroup profit included in inventory	(3,512)	3,578	(7,049)	(3,000)

Adjustments anbd provisions recorder by the Parent Company solely for tax purposes:				
Reversal of depreciacion in excess of that computed over the useful economic lives of the related assets, net of tax effest	1,139	(710)	1,900	(2,100)
Writedown of equity investments	8,100	–	8,100	–
Per consolidated financial statements	**359,856**	**13,330**	**366,875**	**22,904**

Reserves for risk and charges

This caption, totalling 45,478 million lire (41,327 million lire in 1995), comprises:

Pensions and similar commitments
This caption, 3,779 million lire (4,684 million lire in 1995), includes the estimated pension costs to be incurred by a number of foreign subsidiaries.

Taxation
The reserve for taxation includes provisions for deferred taxation, 9,145 million lire (10,408 million lire in 1995), to cover the residual tax due on gains arising from the disposal of fixed assets in prior years and the tax effect of consolidation adjustments. Such adjustments primarily reverse accelerated depreciation and adjust the financial statements of subsidiary companies for consistency with the accounting policies applied throughout the Group. The decrease with respect to 1995 is mainly due to the utilisation of provisions recorded in prior years for income subject to the deferral of taxation. In addition, this caption includes a contingency reserve of 127 million lire that mainly comprises 89 million lire provided by the Parent Company to cover a VAT dispute.
The Parent Company has closed its fiscal years from 1985 to 1990 pursuant to Law 413/91. In agreement with its tax consultants, Management considers that the settlement of open fiscal years, including disputed matters, will not substantially change the taxable income reported in the related annual tax declarations, which was used as the basis for provisions to the taxation reserve.
The financial statements of the Parent Company and certain foreign subsidiaries have been subjected to review by the competent tax authorities. Based on the information available, Group Management believes that the provisions made for taxation are adequate.
A number of subsidiary companies have tax losses as of 31 December 1996 totalling about 103,009 million lire.
In 1996, as in prior years, the Group benefited from the offset of accumulated tax losses and tax exemptions.
No taxes have been provided on consolidation in relation to the undistributed earnings of foreign subsidiaries, since the

Annual
Report 1996

Parent Company considers these amounts to be permanently invested.

Other

This caption mainly comprises:

Early retirement expenses
This reserve, 260 million lire, was established in prior years by the Parent Company to cover liabilities deriving from early retirement arrangements made with 220 employees. Utilisations during the year totalled 873 million lire.
Product warranty reserve
This represents an estimate of the costs to be incurred in connection with the repair under warranty of products sold under guarantee. The reserve totals 24,382 million lire (23,082 million lire in 1995) and is considered adequate to cover the specific risk to which it relates.
Restructuring reserve
This reserve amounts to 5,754 million lire and relates to the future reorganisation of several foreign subsidiaries.
Exchange fluctuation reserve
No provisions have been made to this reserve, since no unrealised losses were identified from a year-end review of the foreign currency balances deriving from commercial and financial transactions.
Agents' leaving indemnity reserve
This reserve amounts to 1,227 million lire, of which 845 million lire was allocated by the Parent Company, which established the reserve in 1995.

Reserve for employee termination lindemnities

The movements in this reserve during the year were as follows:

Balance as of 31 December 1995 (million lire)	**99,476**
Provision for the year	15,342
Indemnities and advances paid during the year	(9,149)
Closing balance	**105,669**

The number of employees is analysed below, by category:

Category	Employee as 31/12/1996	Employee as 31/12/1995	Average during 1996
Managers	95	95	95
Clerical personnel	2,375	2,230	2,300
Factory personnel	5,417	5,909	5,530
Total	**7,887**	**8,234**	**7,925**

Of the above, 396 people (370 factory personnel and 26 clerical personnel) were employed on fixed-term contracts during 1996, against 810 people (728 factory personnel and 82 clerical personnel) in 1995.

The decrease with respect to 1995 is attributable to the restructuring of production.

Payables

Due to banks
The changes in this caption are summarised below:

Description (million lire)	1996	1995
Bank current account	376,300	419,925
Long-term bank loans	259,370	251,134
Total	**635,670**	**671,059**

Credit lines granted by the banking system, for the most part unsecured, total 1,486,150 million lire.
Medium-long term bank loans outstanding as of 31 December 1996 amount to 635,670 million lire, of which 376,300 million lire due within 12 months while the remainder are broken down by maturity dates:

Maturities (million lire)	Amount
Between 2 and 5 years	238,136
Beyond 5 years	21,234
Total	**259,370**

The Group obtained new bank loans during the year totalling 424,517 million lire, the greater part of which replaced repayments made by the Parent Company.
Loans are generally repayable in six-monthly instalments. Some of these loans are secured by mortgages on tangible fixed assets totalling 73,924 million lire.
The risk of exchange fluctuations in relation to foreign currency loans was considered when determining the related reserve; no provisions were needed in 1996.
Due to other providers of finance
Loans outstanding as of 31 December 1996 amount to 111,214 million lire, including 10,100 million lire due within 12 months. The remaining loans are analysed below by maturity:

Maturities (million lire)	Amount
Between 2 and 5 years	78,713
Beyond 5years	22,401
Total	**101,114**

The Group obtained loans amounting to 48,810 million lire during 1996.
Loans are generally repayable in six-monthly instalments; some are secured by mortgages on tangible fixed assets totalling 87,577 million lire.
In connection with capital investment through 1996, the Parent Company has applied for, but not yet received, assisted loans and capital grants totalling about 94,000 million lire.
Amounts due to other providers of finance between two and five years include the liability to Simest Spa (which provides

⋮ **Explanatory notes**

technical assistance and administrative, organisational and financial services in foreign markets), following renewal of the contract by which the Parent Company sold its holding in Merloni Elettrodomestici Beyaz Esya Sanayi Ve Ticaret As (share capital: 124 billion Turkish lira) to Simest for 7,400 million lire, excluding the premium payable for control of the company.

Under the sale contract, the Parent Company is committed (backed by guarantees) to repurchase this holding by 30 September 1999 for the original sale price or the equity value of the holding, whichever is the greater.

During the contract period, Simest Spa has undertaken to exercise the related voting rights on the basis indicated by Merloni Elettrodomestici Spa.

As a result, the 90% interest in this company is reflected in the consolidated financial statements, while the 7,400 million lire due to Simest Spa is classified among long-term payables.

Advances from customers
This balance, 14,738 million lire, mainly relates to the Parent Company and includes around 10,967 million lire of year-end volume rebates which will be settled in 1997.

In 1996, 3,737 million lire has been reclassified to this caption in relation to the quantity rebates of Philco Italia Spa which, in 1995, were classified as accrued expenses totalling 2,874 million lire.

Payables to suppliers
This balance has decreased by 83,162 million lire due to a significant drop in the price of raw materials, principally in the second half of the year, and to a reduction in purchasing designed to lower the level of inventories.

Securities issued
This caption comprises notes issued to suppliers by certain foreign subsidiaries and, in relation to the Parent Company, notes issued to Mediocredito in relation to assisted loans for the purchase of machinery under the Sabatini Law. These purchases totalled 1,596 million lire, of which 248 million lire is due beyond 12 months.

Net financial indebtedness emerging from an analysis of payables and financial assets is illustrated below:

(million lire)	1996	1995
Receivables from associated companies	11,094	–
Receivables from other companies	842	1,054
Other securities	3,719	3,719
Own shares	11,181	–
Total financial fixed assets	**26,836**	**4,773**
Financial receivables not held as fixed assets	218,456	193,895
Bank and post office deposits	134,762	211,136
Cash and cash equivalents	451	443
Total current assets	**353,669**	**405,474**
Due to banks	635,670	671,059

Due to other providers of finance	111,214	80,811
Notes payable (assisted loans under Sabatini Law)	1,596	3,600
Total payables	**748,480**	**755,470**
Total	**367,975**	**345,223**

Due to subsidiary and associated companies
This caption comprises:

Subsidiary companies (million lire)	1996	1995
Merloni Indesit Bulgaria Srlu	165	600
Merloni Indesit Domaci Sro	1,021	816
Merloni Indesit Haztartastechnikai Kft	25	508
Merloni Indesit Polska Spzoo	–	78
Total	**1,211**	**2,002**

Associated companies (million lire)	1996	1995
M&B Marchi e Brevetti Srl	–	62
Merloni Progetti Spa	330	533
Argentron Sa	936	1,017
Factor Industriale Spa	891	1,117
Star Spa	129	–
Total	**2,286**	**2,729**

The above payables mostly derive from services received.

Due to parent companies
This balance, 4,469 million lire, reflects the transfer to Faber Factor Spa by Fineldo Spa of tax credits totalling 4,315 million lire, as well as commission due, 154 million lire, on guarantees given by the ultimate parent company, Fineldo Spa, on behalf of the Parent Company.

Due to tax authorities
This caption includes: VAT payable, 12,061 million lire; taxes withheld from employees, freelance workers and professionals, 10,196 million lire; and current income taxes, 4,252 million lire, determined on the basis of a reasonable estimate of the tax charge, taking account of any exemptions, fiscal legislation and the tax rates in force locally.

Other payables
This balance includes the following:

(million lire)	1996	1995
Due to employees	27,783	26,576
Due to factoring customers	30,306	29,955
Due to related companies	2,406	2,342
Residuability on purchase of New World Ltd	–	6,093
Residuability on purchase of Fabrica Portugal Sa	3,510	–
Residuability on purchase of Star Spa	1,175	1,175
Other	3,629	4,346
Total	**68,809**	**70,487**

Annual
Report 1996

Amounts due to employees comprise wages, salaries and accrued holiday entitlement as of 31 December 1996.

Amounts due to related companies include 1,000 million lire received from Centro Energia Spa as a deposit for the purchase of land; 341 million lire due to Aermarche Spa for aircraft services provided to the Parent Company; 1,041 million lire due to Aermarche SpA by Faber Factor Spa in relation to factoring transactions, and 24 million lire due to Rtc International Spa.

Accrued expenses and deferred income
This caption is analysed as follows:

(million lire)	1996	1995
Interest expense	3,104	4,293
Commission expense	554	424
Other	1,929	277
Total accrued expense	**5,587**	**4,994**
Interest income	2,693	1,754
Other	1,590	482
Total deferred income	**4,283**	**2,236**
Total	**9,870**	**7,230**

Memorandum accounts
A guarantee amounting to 5,805 million lire has been given to Banque Paribas in favour of Banco Portuguese do Atlantico and other Portuguese banks to secure the commitments of the subsidiary company, Fabrica Portugal Sa Philco Italia Spa has given guarantees amounting to 354 million lire to the tax authorities. Merloni Electroménager Sa has given guarantees totalling 2,061 million lire to French banks. Merloni Indesit Polska Spzoo has given a guarantee amounting to 69 million lire to the tax authorities. The Turkish affiliated company has given guarantees totalling 3,973 million lire to the tax authorities. In addition, the Parent Company has given a guarantee totalling 14,850 million lire to Fineldo Spa, to counterguarantee the ultimate parent company's commitments to Centro Energia Spa. This commitment was given pro rata by the Parent Company, since it holds 33% of Merloni Progetti Spa which, in turn, holds an interest in Centro Energia Spa. Commission earned on this guarantee, determined at market rates, is charged to the ultimate parent company.
Secured guarantees consist of mortgages amounting to 172,215 million lire given to third parties to cover loans received from the agencies listed below:

Issuing agency (million lire)	
Mediocredito Regionale Marche	2,632
ISVEIMER	10,034
IMI	64,483
Efibanca	50,392
Banca Nazionale del Lavoro	15,245

Istituto Bancario San Paolo di Torino	7,992
Cassa di Risparmio di Fabriano e Cupramontana	295
Mediocredito Lombardo	21,142
Total	**172,215**

The other memorandum accounts totalling 387,250 million lire are analysed below :

Caption (million lire)	
Notes in circulation	1,814
Customers subject to bankruptcy proceedings	6,141
Lease and rental commitments	11,430
Helding commitments	211,238
Guarantees received from the ultimate Parent Companies	13,514
Guarantees received from the third parties	99,945
Incomesubject to the deferral of taxation	15,752
Expense that will be tax-deducible in future periods	(14,196)
Commitments to purchase fixed assets	41,612
Total	**387,250**

Lease commitments relate to Factory No.3 at None, where a purchase option can be exercised in 2003.
Hedging commitments relate to forward contracts which mature in 1997.
In addition, the Parent Company has arranged financial derivative contracts to hedge foreign currency receivables falling due to in 1997.
The guarantee given from the Parent Company to Fineldo Spa relates to loans obtained.
Guarantees received from third parties are analysed as follows:
• Assicurazioni Generali, 3,614 million lire, and Credito Italiano, 8,669 million lire, regarding grants received under Law 219/81 for factories in Southern Italy;
• Banca Commerciale Italiana, 5,408 million lire, including 5,000 million lire to guarantee a loan from the EIB; the balance relates to guarantees given to public agencies;
• Banco Ambroveneto, 7,400 million lire, to guarantee the commitment to repurchase shares in Merloni Elettrodomestici Beyaz Esya Sanayi Ve Ticaret As from Simest Spa;
• Istituto Bancario San Paolo di Torino, 605 million lire, to guarantee payments to Government Administration and local authorities;
• Banca Nazionale di Lavoro, 16,354 million lire, mainly in favour of Mediocredito Centrale to purchase the investment in Merloni Elettrodomestici Beyaz Esya Sanayi Ve Ticaret As;
• Monte dei Paschi di Siena, 8,756 million lire, to secure the ECSC loan issued by IMI;
• Cassa di Risparmio di Fabriano e Cupramontana, 1,085 million lire, in favour of Mediocredito Centrale;
• Credito Italiano, 964 million lire, including 954 million lire in favour of Customs and Excise to guarantee lotteries and prize competitions;
• Banque National de Paris, 3,407 million lire, including

⋮ **Explanatory notes**

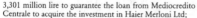

3,301 million lire to guarantee the loan from Mediocredito Centrale to acquire the investment in Haier Merloni Ltd;
- Banca di Roma, 35,000 million lire, to secure loans granted by the EIB;
- Midland Bank, 684 million lire, to secure a loan for the purchase of New World Ltd;
- 7,999 million lire received by the Turkish affiliate from its customers.

Commitments to purchase fixed assets, other than tangible fixed assets, include options to acquire equity investments totalling 20,134 million lire.

Comments on the principal statement of income captions

Value of production
This balance, 2,507,239 million lire, has decreased by 128,884 million lire.
Revenues from the sale of products and services are analysed as follows:

Revenues from sales and services (million lire)	1996	1995
Revenue from the sale of finished product and raw materials	2,435,027	2,459,178
Revenue from the sale of services	72,803	67,186
Total	**2,507,830**	**2,526,364**

Revenues from sales and services are analysed as follows:

Geographic area (million lire)	1996	1995
Italy	614,528	656,332
EU	1,185,306	1,420,130
Countries outside the EU	707.996	449,902
Total	**2,507,830**	**2,526,364**

The slowdown in consumption and the strengthening of the lira with respect to other leading currencies caused a reduction in EU sales, while the volume of sales to countries outside the EU increased.
Capitalised internal production comprises 2,616 million lire capitalised by the Parent Company, mainly representing overheads and payroll costs specifically attributable to the development of software for integrated logistics, consumer services, planning and control.
In addition, the balance includes 1,060 million lire capitalised by Philco Italia Spa in relation to the start-up of new production. The residual amount, 1,099 million lire, represents internal construction by Merloni Electroménager Sa.
Other income and revenues principally comprise the release of provisions recorded in prior years, 14,021 million lire; out-of-period income, 4,423 million lire; customs duties recovered on the export of finished products, 2,715 million lire; insurance reimbursements, 2,712 million lire; gains on

the routine disposal of assets, 1,664 million lire; operating grants, 1,076 million lire; recovery of expenses, 1,700 million lire; export grants to the Turkish subsidiary, 1,479 million lire; and royalties, 326 million lire.

Production costs
This balance, 2,419,780 million lire, has fallen by 149,235 million lire.
- *Raw, ancillary and consumable materials and goods for resale* have decreased by 208,514 million lire, mainly due to the significant drop in raw material prices and the reduction in purchasing in order to contain inventory levels.

Services received are analysed below:

Service received (million lire)	1996	1995
Advertising and promotion	110,265	108,810
Distribution	138,139	127,099
Subcontracted work	13,263	10,482
Maintenance	16,443	20,588
Consultancies	19,406	18,516
Utilities and electric power	16,838	19,183
General expenses	119,831	132,863
Total	**434,185**	**437,541**

General expenses include 35,851 million lire incurred for technical assistance.
The rise in distribution costs is due to the introduction of home deliveries and the growth in exports to countries outside the EU.
- *Other operating costs* amount to 39,169 million lire. As of 31 December 1996, they mainly include losses on receivables (8,842 million lire), insurance premiums (9,176 million lire), duties and taxes (5,680 million lire), out-of-period expenses (3,347 million lire) and printing and stationery (1,816 million lire); this balance also includes losses on disposals, 2,382 million lire, of which 1,410 million lire incurred on the disposal by Merloni Elettrodomestici Spa, of its data processing facilities and data transmission system; and losses of 394 million lire on the sale of the Parent Company's Bologna warehouse.
- Directors of the ultimate Parent Company who also serve as Directors in other companies included within the scope of consolidation receive fees from the Parent Company amounting to 60 million lire and 100 million lire from other companies.
- The statutory auditors, who perform these same duties in other companies included within the scope of consolidation, receive fees amounting to Parent Company and 10 million lire from the other companies.

Financial income and expenses

Income from long-term receivables from associated companies
The balance reflects interest on loans granted by Merloni

Financial Services Sa to Progelease Spa, which are repayable in 1997 and regulated on market terms.

Other financial income
• *from securities held as financial fixed assets, not representing equity investments:* this caption consists of interest on the Parent Company's fixed-income securities.
• *other income:* this caption comprises:

(million lire)	1996	1995
Interest from associated companies	597	–
Interest from Parent Companies	235	–
Interest from customers	22,010	19,894
Interest on bank deposits	11,057	4,663
Exchange gains	28,352	30,246
Effect of applying inflation accounting procedures	–	14,367
Miscellaneous interest and financial revenues	7,210	9,951
Total	**69,461**	**79,121**

Interest from associated companies, 597 million lire, represents interest charged by Faber Factor Spa to Factor Industriale Spa (558 million lire) and Merloni Progetti Spa (39 million lire). Interest from Parent Companies, 235 million lire, represents interest paid by Fineldo Spa to Faber Factor Spa (190 million lire) and Merloni Elettrodomestici Spa (45 million lire). Miscellaneous interest and financial revenues include interest charged by Faber Factor Spa to Aermarche Spa (793 million lire) and RTC International Spa (548 million lire).

Interest and other financial charges
This balance comprises:

(million lire)	1996	1995
Interest charged the Parent Company	91	–
Bank interest expense	62,825	52,236
Interest charged by other providers of finance	6,437	9,433
Exchange losses	49,333	39,034
Effect of applying inflation accountig procedures	1,954	–
Settlement discount	9,469	11,407
Miscellaneous interest and financial charges	5,866	5,576
Total	**135,975**	**117,686**

Interest charged by the Parent Company of 91 million lire reflects the commission payable by Merloni Elettrodomestici Spa on guarantees received from Fineldo Spa.
Miscellaneous interest expense includes 1,901 million lire representing the operating expenses of Faber Factor Spa (2,723 million lire in 1995).
The effect of applying inflation accounting procedures reflects the application of international inflation accounting principles (I.A.S. 29) to the financial statements of Merloni Elettrodomestici Beyaz Esya Sanayi Ve Ticaret As, which operates in a hyper-inflationary economy.

Adjustments to financial assets

Revaluation of equity investments
This balance, 1,174 million lire, reflects the Group's share of the 1996 net income earned by Merloni Progetti Spa, which is carried at equity.
Writedown of equity investments
This balance, 1,239 million lire, reflects the Group's share of losses incurred in 1996 by the following companies carried at equity: Argentron Sa, 868 million lire (3,044 million lire in 1995), Star Spa, 28 million lire (232 million lire in 1995), and Factor Industriale Spa, 74 million lire (income of 123 million lire in 1995). In addition, the Parent Company has written down its investment in Akros Finanziaria Spa by 269 million lire.

Extraordinary income and charges

Extraordinary income
This caption includes 2,469 million lire released from the reserve for deferred taxes, disposal gains of 175 million lire realised by New World Ltd (139 million lire), in relation to the restructuring of the Warrington factory, and by Merloni Elettrodomestici Beyaz Esya Sanayi Ve Ticaret As (36 million lire). The balance also comprises out-of-period income of 565 million lire, earned by the Parent Company, deriving from the settlement of a dispute with a supplier of services, and other out-of-period income, 1,556 million lire.

Extraordinary charges
This balance includes the cost of redundancy incentives, 2,262 million lire (5,251 million lire in 1995); losses on disposals, 52 million lire, and 4,265 million lire (3,903 million lire in 1995) incurred in relation to the reorganisation of New World Ltd, which began in 1995.
The Parent Company is currently involved in disputes with the Italian social security institutions and with the tax authorities. Management, having taken legal advice, has made no provisions in this regard.

Current income taxes
This account reflects the provisions for both current and deferred taxation.

The difference between the tax liability reported in the statement of income and the theoretical tax liability, resulting from applying the standard rate of taxation to income before taxes, mainly reflects the offset of tax losses accumulated in prior years by a number of subsidiary companies.
The Board of Directors of the Parent Company has proposed a dividend of 40 lire per ordinary share and 60 lire per savings share, totalling 4,923 million lire.

These financial statements provide a true and fair view of the consolidated financial position and results of operations for the year.

Relazione di certificazione

Coopers & Lybrand

organizzazione
e revisione contabile

Via S. Stefano 97
40125 Bologna
tel. (051) 345762 - 346736
fax (051) 345781

sedi in Italia
Bologna Bari Brescia
Firenze Genova Milano
Napoli Padova Palermo
Roma Torino Treviso
Udine Verona

RELAZIONE DI CERTIFICAZIONE SUL BILANCIO CONSOLIDATO AI SENSI DELL'ART. 1 DEL D.P.R. 31 MARZO 1975, N. 136

Agli Azionisti della
MERLONI ELETTRODOMESTICI S.p.A.

1   Abbiamo assoggettato a revisione contabile il bilancio consolidato della MERLONI ELETTRODOMESTICI S.p.A. e sue controllate per l'esercizio chiuso al 31 dicembre 1996. Abbiamo inoltre controllato la concordanza della relazione sulla gestione con il bilancio consolidato.

2   Il nostro esame è stato svolto secondo i principi e criteri per il controllo contabile raccomandati dalla Consob ed effettuando i controlli che abbiamo ritenuto necessari per le finalità dell'incarico conferitoci. Per il giudizio relativo al bilancio consolidato dell'esercizio precedente, i cui dati sono presentati ai fini comparativi, si fa riferimento alla relazione di certificazione emessa in data 5 aprile 1996. I bilanci di alcune società controllate e collegate che rappresentano il 7% dell'attivo consolidato ed il 7% dei ricavi consolidati, sono stati esaminati da altri revisori che ci hanno fornito le loro relazioni. Il nostro giudizio, espresso in questa relazione, per quanto riguarda i valori relativi a tali società inclusi nel consolidamento, è basato anche sulla revisione svolta da altri revisori.

3   A nostro giudizio, il bilancio consolidato nel suo complesso è stato redatto con chiarezza e rappresenta in modo veritiero e corretto la situazione patrimoniale e finanziaria ed il risultato economico della società e delle sue controllate, in conformità alle norme che disciplinano il bilancio consolidato. Pertanto, rilasciamo certificazione al bilancio consolidato della MERLONI ELETTRODOMESTICI S.p.A. e sue controllate al 31 dicembre 1996.

4   Per una migliore comprensione del bilancio d'esercizio si richiama l'attenzione sulle seguenti informazioni:

*   la società ha adottato le opzioni previste da norme civilistiche speciali per la rilevazione della imposta patrimoniale. L'effetto netto di tale impostazione rispetto all'addebito diretto al conto economico, ha comportato l'esposizione in bilancio di un maggior utile dell'esercizio e di un maggior patrimonio netto al 31 dicembre 1996 rispettivamente di lire 1.500 milioni e di lire 700 milioni.

Bologna, 4 aprile 1997

COOPERS & LYBRAND S.p.A.

Giovanni Fanizza
(Socio)

Report of the Independent Auditors

Coopers &Lybrand	organizzazione e revisione contabile	Via S. Stefano 97 40125 Bologna tel. (051) 345762 - 346736 fax (051) 345781	sedi in Italia Bologna Bari Brescia Firenze Genova Milano Napoli Padova Palermo Roma Torino Treviso Udine Verona ·

**Report of the Independent Auditors on the Consolidated Financial Statements
pursuant to art. 1 of Presidential Decree no. 136 of March 31, 1975**
(Translation from the original issued in Italian)

To the Shareholders of
MERLONI ELETTRODOMESTICI S.p.A.

1   We have audited the consolidated financial statements of MERLONI
ELETTRODOMESTICI S.p.A. and subsidiaries as of and for the year ended December 31,
1996. We have also checked the consistency of the Board of Directors' report on operations
with the consolidated financial statements.

2   Our examination was made in accordance with the auditing standards and procedures
recommended by the Italian Regulatory Commission for Companies and the Stock Exchange
("Consob") and included such tests as we considered necessary for the purposes of our
engagement. For our opinion on the prior year's consolidated financial statements, which are
presented for comparative purposes, references should be made to our report dated April 5,
1996. The financial statements of certain subsidiaries, the total assets and revenues of which
represent 7% and 7% respectively of the consolidated amounts, have been examined by other
auditing firms. Our opinion expressed in this report insofar as it relates to the amounts included
for those companies, is based also upon the audits of the other auditing firms.

3   In our opinion, the consolidated financial statements, taken as a whole, have been
prepared clearly and give a true and fair view of the financial position and results of operations
of the Company and its subsidiaries, in accordance with the law related to consolidated
financial statements. Therefore, we certify the consolidated financial statements of MERLONI
ELETTRODOMESTICI S.p.A. and its subsidiaries as of December 31, 1996.

4   For a better understanding of the financial statements, attention should be focused on
the following:

- the Company has adopted the special options foreseen by the civil law for the
  accounting of the tax on the shareholders' equity. The net effect of such a treatment
  compared to charge the statement of income, has resulted in a higher net income for
  the year and shareholders' equity as at December 31, 1996 of Lit. 1.500 million and Lit.
  700 million respectively.

Bologna, April 4, 1997

COOPERS & LYBRAND S.p.A.

Giovanni Fanizza
(Partner)

Coopers & Lybrand S.p.A. è membro della Coopers & Lybrand International, un'associazione svizzera a responsabilità limitata.

Coopers & Lybrand S.p.A. · capitale sociale 4.600.000.000 interamente versato · autorizzata ai sensi della legge 23/11/1939 n. 1966 e del R.D. 22/4/1940 n. 531 · iscritta nell'albo speciale delle società di revisione con delibera Consob n. 694 e nel registro dei revisori contabili D.M. 12/4/1995 · C.C.I.A.A. Bologna n. 276215 · C.F. / P.IVA 00714780152 · registro imprese Bologna n. 54587

MERLONI ELETTRODOMESTICI SPA

Sede legale: V.le A. Merloni, 47, 60044 Fabriano
Capitale sociale: Lire 112.547.936.000
Codice Fiscale/Partita Iva 00693740425
Iscritta al Registro delle Imprese del Tribunale di
Ancona N. 9677

Bilancio dell'esercizio
(importi in Lire italiane)

STATO PATRIMONIALE   31 dicembre 1996   31 dicembre 1995

ATTIVO

A) Crediti verso soci per versamenti ancora dovuti   -   -

B) Immobilizzazioni:

I *Immobilizzazioni immateriali*:

1) costi di impianto e di ampliamento	83.332.000	135.731.680
2) costi di ricerca, di sviluppo e di pubblicità	1.043.383.019	1.961.742.534
3) diritti di brevetto industriale e diritti di utilizzazione delle opere dell'ingegno	19.239.304.890	14.229.817.821
4) concessioni. licenze. marchi e diritti simili	14.774.764.423	14.018.549.544
7) altre	831.239.948	1.677.024.943
Totale	35.972.024.280	32.022.866.522

II *Immobilizzazioni materiali*:

1) terreni e fabbricati	109.156.497.055	110.319.379.297
2) impianti e macchinario	127.309.163.962	109.518.820.101
3) attrezzature industriali e commerciali	52.713.613.713	49.401.458.870
4) altri beni	16.582.192.318	19.272.936.927
5) immobilizzazioni in corso e acconti	3.674.727.690	14.242.361.325
Totale	309.436.194.738	302.754.956.520

III *Immobilizzazioni finanziarie*

1) partecipazioni in:		
a) imprese controllate	202.771.982.137	153.561.431.026
b) imprese collegate	21.747.000.400	21.747.000.400
d)altre imprese	6.716.560.000	5.699.085.000
2) crediti:		
a) verso imprese controllate	549.800.000	549.800.000
3) altri titoli	3.718.700.000	3.718.700.000
4) azioni proprie	11.180.772.715	-
(valore nominale Lire 3.551.500.000)		
Totale	246.684.815.252	185.276.016.426

Totale immobilizzazioni (B)	**592.093.034.270**	**520.053.839.468**

MERLONI ELETTRODOMESTICI S.p.A.
Registered office: V.le A. Merloni - 47, 60044 Fabriano
Authorised capital: Lire 112.547.936.000 (fully paid)
Fiscal Code/VAT no. 00693740425
Registered at the Tribunal of Ancona
Company Register no. 9677

FINANCIAL STATEMENTS AS OF 31 DECEMBER   1996   1995
(amounts in Italian Lira)

BALANCE SHEET

ASSETS

A.   Called up share capital not paid

B.   Fixed assets

    I-   *Intangible assets:*
       1) start-up costs
       2) research, development and advertisement costs
       3) patent rights and royalties
       4) brands and licences
       7) others

          Total

    II-   *Tangible assets:*
       1) land and buildings
       2) plant and machinery
       3) fixtures and fittings
       4) others
       5) tangible assets under construction and prepayments

          Total

    III-   *Investments:*
       1) participating interests in:
         a) subsidiary undertakings
         b) associate undertakings
         c) other companies
       2) debtors:
         a) amounts owed by associate undertakings
       3) other participating interests
       4) own shares (face value Lire 3.551.500.000)

          Total

          Total fixed assets (B)

C) Attivo circolante:

I *Rimanenze*:

1) materie prime, sussidiarie e di consumo	43.778.956.074	59.926.382.771
2) prodotti in corso di lavorazione e semilavorati	6.507.524.364	8.793.058.076
4) prodotti finiti e merci	73.666.507.807	91.181.777.256
5) acconti	311.032.155	28.640.730
Totale	124.264.020.400	159.929.858.833

II *Crediti*

1) verso clienti	267.559.378.560	274.857.605.541
(di cui esigibili oltre l'esercizio succ. Lire 2.657.481.969)		
2) verso imprese controllate	417.536.634.627	437.771.000.988
3) verso imprese collegate	10.686.814.882	8.983.631.417
4) verso imprese controllanti	44.850.000	-
5) verso altri	40.915.727.763	34.882.019.998
(di cui esigibili oltre l'esercizio succ. Lire 671.679.825)		
Totale	736.743.405.832	756.494.257.944

III *Attività finanziarie che non costituiscono immobilizzazioni*:

7) crediti finanziari non immobilizzati	6.764.373.115	5.714.000.000
Totale	6.764.373.115	5.714.000.000

IV *Disponibilità liquide*:

1) depositi bancari e postali	27.287.495.730	42.669.604.151
3) danaro e valori in cassa	292.569.623	301.400.970
Totale	27.580.065.353	42.971.005.121
Totale attivo circolante (C)	**895.351.864.700**	**965.109.121.898**
D) Ratei e risconti	**2.657.762.789**	**770.404.944**
TOTALE	**1.490.102.661.759**	**1.485.933.366.310**

PASSIVO	31 dicembre 1996	31 dicembre 1995

A) Patrimonio netto:

I Capitale	112.547.936.000	112.547.936.000
II Riserva da soprapprezzo delle azioni	43.058.391.285	54.239.164.000
III Riserve di rivalutazione	-	-
IV Riserva legale	2.203.305.468	2.118.550.842
V Riserva per azioni proprie in portafoglio	11.180.772.715	-
VI Riserve statutarie	-	-
VII Altre riserve	73.276.958.693	78.076.968.408
VIII Utile (perdite) portati a nuovo	-	-
IX Utile (perdita) dell'esercizio.	3.805.785.904	1.695.092.515
Totale patrimonio netto (A)	**246.073.150.065**	**248.677.711.765**

C.   **Current assets**

I-   *Stocks:*
1) raw materials and consumables
2) work in process
3) finished goods and merchandise
5) prepayments

Total

II-   *Debtors:*
1) trade debtors
(of which L. 2,657,481,969 fall due beyond next financial year)
2) amounts owed by subsidiary undertakings
3) amounts owed by associate undertakings
4) amounts owed by parent undertakings
5) amounts owed by other undertakings
(of which L. 671,679,825 fall due beyond next financial year)

Total

III-   *Financial assets other than long term:*
7) financial debtors other than long term

Total

IV-   *Liquid funds:*
1) cash at bank and in the post accounts
3) cash in hand

Total
Total current assets (C)

D.   **Accrued income and prepayments**

TOTAL

BALANCE SHEET

LIABILITIES

A.   **Shareholders' capital**

I-   Called up share capital
II-   Share premium account
III-   Revaluation reserve
IV-   Legal reserve
V-   Reserve for own shares
VI-   Reserves provided for by the articles
VII-   Other reserves
VIII-   Profits (losses) of previous years
IX-   Profit (loss) for the year

Total

B.   **Provisions for risks and liabilities**

B) Fondi per rischi e oneri:

2) per imposte	8.260.429.768	9.774.604.686
3) altri	11.576.175.823	11.027.263.094
Totale fondi per rischi e oneri (B)	**19.836.605.591**	**20.801.867.780**

C) Trattamento di fine rapporto di lavoro subordinato   **92.393.807.010**   **85.217.023.733**

D) Debiti

3) debiti verso banche	386.804.911.637	356.177.673.995
(di cui esigibili oltre l'esercizio succ. Lire 242.022.135.626)		
4) debiti verso altri finanziatori	84.326.358.162	56.475.253.095
(di cui esigibili oltre l'esercizio succ. Lire 76.694.428.028)		
5) acconti	10.966.691.388	11.114.147.010
6) debiti verso fornitori	253.437.942.112	324.249.277.456
7) debiti rappresentati da titoli di credito	1.596.341.100	3.599.733.550
(di cui esigibili oltre l'esercizio succ. Lire 248.144.700)		
8) debiti verso imprese controllate	345.617.477.435	335.500.360.637
9) debiti verso imprese collegate	579.910.098	1.621.248.055
10) debiti verso controllanti	154.029.040	206.040.498
11) debiti tributari	7.737.345.604	7.129.486.083
12) debiti verso istituti di previdenza e sicurezza sociale	14.720.056.998	14.113.667.713
13) altri debiti	20.996.434.398	19.094.447.071
Totale debiti (D)	**1.126.937.497.972**	**1.129.281.335.163**

E) Ratei e risconti	**4.861.601.121**	**1.955.427.869**
TOTALE	**1.490.102.661.759**	**1.485.933.366.310**

CONTI D'ORDINE

Elenco garanzie dirette e indirette:
fideiussioni:

a favore di imprese controllate	5.804.749.929	6.303.098.504
a favore di imprese controllanti	14.850.000.000	-
garanzie reali:		
a favore di terzi	151.072.621.777	109.817.662.036
altri conti d'ordine	378.380.973.009	150.398.304.619
TOTALE	**550.108.344.715**	**266.519.065.159**

2) provisions for taxes
3) others

Total

C. **Statutory provisions for severance indemnities**

D. **Creditors**

3) bank overdrafts and loans
(of which L. 242,022,135,626 fall due beyond next financial year)
4) other loans
(of which L. 76,694,428,028 fall due beyond next financial year)
5) prepayments
6) trade creditors
7) bills of exchange
(of which L. 248,144,700 fall due beyond next financial year))
8) amounts owed to subsidiary undertakings
9) amounts owed to associate undertakings
10) amounts owed to parent undertakings
11) taxes
12) social security
13) others

Total

E. **Accruals and deferred income**

TOTAL

MEMORANDUM ACCOUNTS

List of direct and indirect guarantees:
fiduciary garantees:
in favor of subsidiary undertakings
in favor of parent undertakings
real property guarantees:
in favor of third persons
other memorandum accounts

TOTAL

CONTO ECONOMICO   31 dicembre 1996   31 dicembre 1995

A) Valore della produzione:

1) ricavi delle vendite e delle prestazioni	1.664.594.551.377	1.548.605.054.975
2) variazioni delle rimanenze di prodotti in corso di		
lavorazione, semilavorati e finiti	(19.800.803.161)	30.281.184.677
4) incrementi di immobilizzazioni per lavori interni	2.615.707.463	697.337.690
5) altri ricavi e proventi	11.793.037.915	7.736.781.543
Totale valore della produzione (A)	**1.659.202.493.594**	**1.587.320.358.885**

B) Costi della produzione:

6) per materie prime, sussidiarie, di consumo e di merci	989.844.709.899	1.052.159.944.649
7) per servizi	224.459.020.491	204.161.553.827
8) per godimento di beni di terzi	10.871.777.296	9.195.169.356
9) per il personale:		
a) salari e stipendi	172.269.129.815	163.822.199.394
b) oneri sociali	67.461.629.152	58.191.456.061
c) trattamento di fine rapporto	13.482.751.045	14.278.574.194
e) altri costi	6.202.940.714	7.120.725.610
10) ammortamenti e svalutazioni:		
a) ammortamento delle immobilizzazioni immateriali	10.486.370.647	9.925.760.527
b) ammortamento delle immobilizzazioni materiali	55.100.533.407	47.439.755.934
d) svalutazione dei crediti compresi nell'attivo		
circolante e delle disponibilità liquide	5.400.000.000	3.000.000.000
11) variazioni delle rimanenze di materie prime,		
sussidiarie, di consumo e merci	16.147.426.697	(23.014.504.533)
12) accantonamenti per rischi	167.500.000	2.150.000.000
14) oneri diversi di gestione	16.440.285.137	17.277.223.838
Totale costi della produzione (B)	**1.588.334.074.300**	**1.565.707.858.857**
Differenza tra valore e costo della produzione	*70.868.419.294*	*21.612.500.028*

C) Proventi e oneri finanziari:

15) proventi da partecipazioni	962.282.250	597.668.750
(di cui da controllate Lire 807.343.750)		
(di cui da collegate Lire 154.687.500)		
16) altri proventi finanziari:		
a) da crediti iscritti nelle immobilizzazioni	65.976.000	65.976.000
(di cui da controllate Lire 65.976.000)		
b) da titoli iscritti nelle immobilizzazioni che non		
costituiscono partecipazioni	380.663.327	411.642.077
d) proventi diversi dai precedenti	26.498.218.864	28.489.408.913
(di cui da controllate Lire 6.527.570.629)		
(di cui da controllanti Lire 44.550.000)		
17) interessi e altri oneri finanziari	70.725.798.772	50.619.989.675
(di cui da controllate Lire 4.455.297.104)		
(di cui da controllanti Lire 91.329.040)		
Totale proventi e oneri finanziari (C)	**(42.818.658.331)**	**(21.055.293.935)**

PROFIT AND LOSS ACCOUNT   **1996**   **1995**

A)   **Value of production**

      1)   turnover
      2)   change in stocks of finished goods and in work in progress
      4)   own work capitalised
      5)   other income

                  Total value of production

B)   **Production costs**

      6)   raw materials and consumables
      7)   external services
      8)   rents
      9)   staff costs:
             a) wages and salaries
             b) social security costs
             c) statutory severance costs
             d) other staff costs
     10)   depreciation and write-offs:
             a) depreciation of intangible assets
             b) depreciation of tangible assets
             c) amounts written off from current debtors and from liquid funds
     11)   change in stock of raw materials, consumables and merchandise
     12)   provisions for risks
     14)   other operating charges

                  Total production costs

                  Difference between production value and costs (A-B)

C)   **Income and charges from financial assets**

     15)   income from participating interests
           (of which L. 807,343,750 from subsidiary undertakings)
           (of which L. 154,687,500 from associate undertakings)
     16)   other income from financial assets:
             a) income from debtors under fixed assets
               (of which L. 65,976,000 from subsidiary undertakings)
             b) income from fixed asset investments other than participating interests
             d) other income from financial assets
               (of which L. 6,527,570,629 from subsidiary undertakings)
               (of which L. 44,550,000 from parent undertakings)
     17)   interest and similar charges
           (of which L. 4,455,297,104 from subsidiary undertakings)
           (of which L. 91,329,040 from parent undertakings)

                  Total income and charges from financial assets

D) Rettifiche di valore di attività finanziarie:

19) svalutazioni:		
a) di partecipazioni	25.007.774.617	2.013.131.000
Totale delle rettifiche (D)	(25.007.774.617)	(2.013.131.000)

E) Proventi e oneri straordinari:

20) proventi	1.201.876.551	4.499.038.492
21) oneri	438.076.993	1.348.021.070
Totale delle partite straordinarie (E)	763.799.558	3.151.017.422
Risultato prima delle imposte	*3.805.785.904*	*1.695.092.515*
22) Imposte sul reddito dell'esercizio	-	-
23) Utile (perdita) dell'esercizio	*3.805.785.904*	*1.695.092.515*

Il presente bilancio è conforme alle scritture contabili

D)   Changes in value of financial assets

19)   write-offs:
a) of participating interests

Total of changes in value

E)   Extraordinary income and charges

20)   extraordinary income
21)   extraordinary charges

Total of extraordinary items (20-21)

Profit before taxation (A-B+C+D+E)

22)   Taxes on profit

23)   *Profit (loss) for the financial year*

These financial statements are in conformity with the accounting records of the company.

26 March 1997

The Chairman of the Board of Directors

Vittorio Merloni

The Board of Statutory Auditors

Dr. Giorgio Venturini

Rag. Mario Ninno

Prof. Valeriano Balloni

Country Highlights
LUXEMBOURG

Common Legal Forms of Companies

The *société anonyme* (public limited company) is the most common form, particularly for international investors, whereas the *société à responsabilité limitée* (private limited company) or the various unlimited companies are mostly used by smaller local businesses; of particular relevance is the *société anonyme* as a holding company, which limits its activities to the holding and the management of investments and is exempt from corporate income taxation.

Sources of Financial Reporting Requirements

The law of August 15, 1915, as amended, determines the rules for financial reporting and accounting applicable to all businesses; the rules are in line with the Fourth and Seventh EU directives.

Corporate Taxation

Corporate income taxation is based on the German model, which takes as a basis of taxation of businesses the opening and closing fiscal balance sheets and thus effectively subjects income and capital gains to taxation, subject to exemptions and assessment rules. The capital stock of companies is subject to a combination of German-style taxation on net assets (at 0.5% per annum) for commercial companies and/or a French-style capital transfer tax (at 1% on formation/capital increase for all companies and an annual charge of 0.2% per annum on equity for holding companies).

Auditing Requirements

Large and medium-sized companies (per Fourth EU directive) are required to have their accounts audited on an annual basis by a qualified auditor (*Réviseur d'Entreprises*, see below); small companies and thus most holding companies are exempt from this requirement.

Organization of the Accounting and Legal Professions

The accounting profession is organized into two groups: The *Institut des Réviseurs d'Entreprises* (IRE) comprises all persons and firms authorized as auditors, *Réviseurs d'Entreprises*; this is the qualification in the context of the Eighth EU Directive, which is obtained after a 3-year training period and successful completion of the prescribed exams. The *Ordre des Experts Comptable* regroups most qualified accountants (*Ex-*

pert *Comptable*), but it does not have the statutory role of the IRE; the qualification of *Expert Comptable* is accorded after completion of the necessary academic and practical training, but without a formal examination. Only those working in public practice may be members of the two bodies.

Constitution and Legal System

The Grand-Duchy of Luxembourg is a constitutional monarchy; head of state is the Grand-Duke; the parliament is elected every 5 years, which then elects the government; second chamber is the state council, whose members are formally appointed by the Grand-Duke; the state council also acts as the ultimate court of appeal, for cases not settled before the (usually) two first instances.

Currency

Luxembourg Franc (LUF); currency union with Belgium since 1921, with parity between LUF and BEF; introduction of the euro expected with effect from January 1, 1999.

Official Languages

French, German, and Luxembourgish; new legislation and most administrative regulation is issued in French.

LUXEMBOURG

Gerd H. Gebhard
Chartered Accountant, Luxembourg

1. Background

1.1 Introduction

The Grand Duchy of Luxembourg lies at the very heart of Europe, nestled between Belgium, Germany, and France. It covers 2,586 square kilometers and has 418,300 inhabitants, of whom 34% (142,800) are foreigners.[1]

Luxembourg is a constitutional monarchy and a member of the European Union. A number of EU institutions are located in Luxembourg, including the Court of Justice, Court of Auditors, European Investment Bank, and Secretariat of the European Parliament. French, German, and Luxembourgish are the official languages, French being most widely used in administration.

Between 1952 and 1996 the composition of the gross domestic product changed dramatically, as can be seen in the following table:

	1952 (%)	1996 (%)
Agriculture and mining	13.5	2.5
Industry and construction	52.1	20.3
Trade and services	34.4	77.2

Although ARBED, Luxembourg's large steel manufacturer, remains the largest private-sector employer, it is the growth of banking and financial services that has marked the economic development and the international reputation of the Grand Duchy.

There are about 220 banks, 1400 investment funds, and 13,000 holding companies registered in Luxembourg. The majority are owned by foreign companies or individuals. Legally, the administration of such banks and investment funds must be situated in Luxembourg, ensuring near full employment in the Grand Duchy. The government encourages and supports all investment from abroad. Government aid is available for investment in manufacturing and for certain services. No particular restrictions affect foreign investment, in respect to the type of investment, its ownership, or the flow of funds.

Luxembourg has had close economic and political links with its neighbors for a long time, and this is reflected in the development of its accounting conventions and practices.

1.2 Legal and Regulatory Framework

1.2.1 Historical Background

The Commercial Code of 1807 determines the contents of the basic accounting records that must be kept by each business. These are a journal for day-to-day transactions and such registers of assets and liabilities as will enable annual accounts to be drawn up.

Another legacy is the system of registration of commercial transactions and the capital taxation of companies. In fact, the annual taxation of the capital of a company (*taxe d'abonnement*) remains the only periodic charge to taxation for investment funds (at 0.06% of net assets) and holding companies (at 0.20% of capital). The taxation of income is otherwise based on the German tax system, which was introduced during the occupation in the 1940s and has evolved separately since.

The Company Law of 1915 is based on Belgium's Company Law of 1913. Belgian case law and academic doctrine is referred to if a question of interpretation arises. Luxembourg's Company Law was modified in 1933 to introduce private limited companies and, in the 1980s, to adopt the EU Directives.

Before the adoption of the Fourth Directive on company accounts, there were no specific regulations relating to the form or content of annual financial statements, other than that they had to consist of a balance sheet and a profit and loss account. Financial information produced was shaped by the requirements of the tax authorities. The resultant accounts consisted of "some lines of vague and imprecise headings with numbers against them."[2]

1.2.2 Business Entities

The public limited company (*société anonyme*) is the most common form of business entity and the focus of this chapter. Other types include the private limited company (*société à responsabilité limitée*), limited and unlimited partnerships, co-operatives and branches of foreign businesses.

The public limited company is a separate legal entity, and the liability of its shareholders for losses of the company is limited to the amount of capital subscribed for. It requires at least two shareholders and three directors, who need not be Luxembourg residents. Companies are incorporated before a notary public, the articles of incorporation and certain other information must be filed with the District Court and be published in the Official Gazette (*Mémorial*). The minimum subscribed capital is LUF 1,250,000, which may be denominated in any currency. An annual meeting must be held in Luxembourg, which appoints directors and auditors, approves the accounts, and decides upon the distribution of profits.

1.2.3 Implementation of EU Directives

Rules on the preparation of accounts entered the statute book with the implementation of the EU Directives on the harmonization of accounting information:

- Law of May 4, 1984: Fourth Directive on company accounts, their contents, format, and valuation of balances
- Law of June 28, 1984: Introduction of audits by independent professional accountants
- Law of July 11, 1988: Seventh Directive on consolidated accounts

The new section 13 to the Law of August 10, 1915 relating to commercial companies closely follows the structure and text of the Fourth Directive, with subsequent amendments for the implementation of the Seventh Directive.

Most of the options given to member states in the Directives have been maintained, for the benefit of preparers of accounts in Luxembourg. This is in line with government policy to provide businesses with the most liberal environment possible.

The law applies to the following types of companies:

- *Société anonyme* (S.A.) (public limited company)
- *Société à responsiblité limitée* (S.à.r.l) (private limited company)
- *Société en commandite par actions* (partnership limited by shares).

Special rules apply to banks, investment funds and insurance companies. The *Institut Monétaire Luxembourgeois* (IML) supervises banks and investment funds. Luxembourg has implemented the rules of the Bank Accounts Directive. The financial statements of investment funds are set out in the Law of March 30, 1988, which provides the framework of this important industry for the Grand Duchy. The *Commissariat des Assurances* regulates the insurance sector. The provisions of the third generation insurance Directives as well as the Insurance Accounts Directive have been implemented.

1.2.4 Accounting Standards

The Luxembourg Institute of Auditors (*Institut des Réviseurs d'Entreprises*, or IRE) has legal authority to issue accounting standards by itself. It has, in fact, not used this mandate but is seeking to set up a body of parties concerned with accounting and audit regulation to develop standards. In practice, international accounting standards are generally followed, except where they contradict Luxembourg law.

1.3 Holding Companies

1.3.1 1929 Holding Companies

Holding companies are an important feature of the financial services sector in Luxembourg. There were nearly 13,000 holding companies registered in Luxembourg at the end of 1995. It should be noted that a holding company is subject to the same rules and regulations as all other companies, except for its liability to taxation and the restrictions on its activities related to the tax benefits it enjoys.

This section deals only with the classic Luxembourg holding company, based on the law of July 31, 1929.

Definition A holding company may have as its object only the acquisition and management of investments in other enterprises. Such investments include shares, bonds, loans to companies in which a significant interest is held, the holding of patents, and the granting of licenses. Holding companies may not engage in industrial or commercial activities. There are, however, no specified minimum or maximum amounts that must be invested. There is no specific authorization requirement for a new holding company. It may commence its activities as soon as it is formed.

Taxation   Holding companies are exempt from taxation of their income and capital in Luxembourg, except for the two registry taxes indicated below. They do not have to deduct withholding taxes from dividends or interest paid but cannot obtain relief for withholding taxes suffered. Double taxation treaties concluded by the Grand Duchy generally do not apply to holding companies.

Holding companies are subject to the following taxes:

- Capital duty at the rate of 1% on the capital contributed to the company on formation or when the capital is increased.
- Registry tax at the rate of 0.2% per annum on the value of the shares of the company. The value is one of the following:

   —the stock exchange price (if shares are quoted)

   —the paid-in capital and share premium

   —ten times the dividend paid for the previous year, if such dividend exceeded 10% of the paid-in capital

Capital Requirements   The capital requirements of a holding company are as follows:

- Minimum subscribed capital LUF 1,250,000.
- All shares must be at least 25% paid.
- Paid-in capital must be at least LUF 1,000,000.
- Creditors, excluding bonds, may not exceed three times subscribed capital.
- Bonds issued may not exceed ten times paid-in capital.

Accounting Requirements   Holding companies are generally classified as small companies because:

- They are not allowed to pursue any industrial or commercial activity, and therefore have no turnover.
- Few if any Luxembourg holding companies are known to have more than fifty employees.

The Fourth Directive gave member states the option to implement special accounts formats for holding companies and similar institutions. The grand ducal regulation of June 29, 1984 introduced the simplified format of balance sheet and profit and loss account for holding companies as shown on pages 691–692.

1.3.2 SOPARFI

A second type of holding company was created by the implementation of the EU Directive of July 23, 1990 on the taxation and distribution within groups of companies, referred to as SOPARFI. SOPARFI are fully taxable and may thus benefit from double tax agreements.

Dividend payments within the same group of companies and certain capital gains on the sale of shares are exempt from tax in the hands of the receiving company, subject to certain conditions (*Schachtelprivileg*). The exemptions are available to all fully taxable companies, whether they are trading companies or just perform the function of holding company. Legally, SOPARFI are treated as normal companies, and they are subject to the normal audit and reporting requirements.

2. Audit and Publication

2.1 Statutory Auditor

According to the Company Law of 1915, every company must appoint a *commissaire aux comptes* (usually translated as a statutory auditor). The statutory auditor is charged with the ongoing supervision and management of the audit of the annual accounts. The results of the audit must be presented in a report to the shareholders at the annual general meeting.

The statutory auditor, whether person or legal entity, need not be professionally qualified nor independent of the company. He or she is an officer of the company, elected at the annual general meeting for up to 6 years. He or she has unlimited rights of access to company records and to information from the directors.

The law prescribes that the statutory auditor must receive a statement of affairs every 6 months and the annual accounts 1 month before the annual general meeting, in order to report on them at least 2 weeks before the meeting.

The Law of May 4, 1984 introduced the requirement for an independent professional audit of large and medium-sized companies and also abolished the office of the statutory auditor for such companies. In practice, many subsidiaries of international companies are audited by professional accountants acting as their statutory auditors.

2.2 *Réviseur d'Entreprises*

The law of June 28, 1984 established the profession of *réviseurs d'entreprises* (independent auditor). The audit of large and medium-sized companies, banks, insurance companies, and investment funds must be carried out by a *réviseur d'entreprises*.

A number of other assignments are also reserved for this profession:

- Audit of consolidated accounts
- Audit of certain financial intermediaries and insurance companies
- Report on issue of shares for consideration other than cash by a public company
- Report on merger and demerger proposals

The *réviseur d'entreprises* must be professionally qualified. A university degree, 3 years' practical training, and two sets of examinations are required. Authorized auditors from other EC countries may be admitted after taking conversion examinations in Luxembourg.

Upon authorization by the Ministry of Justice, each *réviseur* becomes a member of the *Institut des Réviseurs d'Entreprises*. The Institute represents the profession externally and exercises disciplinary control over the conduct of its members.

The *réviseur d'entreprises* carries out his or her work for a company under a contract for services and is elected at the AGM, usually for a term of 1 year.

The auditor of a bank is appointed by the board of directors, and for investment funds the law stipulates appointment "by the fund." For banks, investment funds, and insurance companies, the appointment of the auditor is in practice subject to approval by the relevant supervisory authority.

2.3 Publication

A full set of accounts (balance sheet, profit and loss account, notes, and directors' report) and the report of the auditors must be filed with the registrar of the commercial court within 1 month of the AGM approving the accounts. The fact of their filing will then be published in the official gazette, the *Mémorial*.

By law the shareholders are entitled to receive only the balance sheet, profit and loss account, and the report of the statutory auditor. They need not be furnished with the notes, the directors' report, or the report of the *réviseur d'entreprises*. This anomaly is the result of the old publication requirements of 1915 not having been updated for the new definition of annual accounts in the law of May 4, 1984.

2.4 Small/Medium-sized Companies

Audit and publication requirements have been reduced for small and medium-sized companies. In order to qualify as small or medium-sized, a company must remain below at least two of the following three criteria (amounts in Luxembourg francs, LUF):

	Medium-sized	*Small*
Total assets	LUF 372 million	LUF 93 million
Turnover	LUF 745 million	LUF 186 million
Number of employees	250 employees	50 employees

If the criteria are exceeded for two consecutive years, then the company will change its classification. Exemptions available for small and medium-sized companies are summarized in Table 1. Small companies do not have to be audited by a *Réviseur d'Entreprises*.

3. Accounting Principles and Practices

3.1 Basic Principles

The basic principles governing the annual financial statements of companies are those laid down by the Fourth Directive. They are summarized below in the order in which they appear in the law.

3.1.1 Inventory

Every business must prepare an annual inventory (*l'inventaire*), which must include all assets and amounts receivable and payable. The rules of

TABLE 1   *Publication Exemptions for Small and Medium-sized Companies*

	Information to Shareholders		Information to Outsiders—Publication	
	Medium-sized	*Small*	*Medium-sized*	*Small*
Balance sheet	In full	Abbreviated	Some detail omitted	Abbreviated
Profit and loss account	Abbreviated	Abbreviated	Abbreviated	Not published
Notes to the accounts	In full	Abbreviated	Some detail omitted	Abbreviated
Directors' report	In full	In full	Published in full	Not published
Auditors' report	*Réviseur d'entreprises*	Statutory auditor	Published	Not published

the Commercial Code of 1807 were amplified in 1986 to include the requirement that double-entry bookkeeping be used and financial statements be prepared.

3.1.2 Annual Accounts

The annual accounts are made up of:

- Balance sheet
- Profit and loss account
- Notes

Directors' and auditor's reports are also required. With the exception of the auditor's report, the directors are responsible for the preparation of all these documents.

3.1.3 True and Fair View

The accounts must be prepared in such a way as to give a true and fair view of the state of affairs of the company. The information given in the accounts must be free from ambiguities and must be consistent from year to year. Assets and liabilities, expenses and revenues, respectively, may not be netted. All items must be evaluated separately. Consistency means that items in the accounts are described and presented in the same manner and are valued by using the same principles from one year to the next. Any material changes of description or in valuation method must be justified and explained in the notes.

3.1.4 Accounting Concepts

The accounts must be prepared according to the following concepts:

- Going concern assumption
- Accruals/matching concept
- Prudence concept

Of significance is the "inequality" principle derived from the prudence concept, particularly in the context of the conversion to the euro (see Section 4). This prescribes the immediate recognition of unrealized losses as soon as they become known but prohibits the recognition of gains until they are realized.

3.1.5 Reporting Basis

The accounts are to be expressed in nominal monetary terms. At present, inflation accounting is not permitted, even though the government is empowered by law to introduce it. It is thought unlikely that this option will be exercised in the near future.

3.1.6 Valuation Basis

Historical cost accounting is the basic method of valuation. The historical cost of an asset represents its maximum value in the balance sheet. Revaluations (upward) are not permitted.

3.1.7 Formats

The balance sheet and the profit and loss account must be drawn up in one of the formats prescribed by law. See pages 688–690 for an example of a balance sheet and profit and loss account.

3.2 Foreign Currencies

The accounts of a company must be in the currency of the share capital, which may be any freely convertible currency. There is no requirement to use the national currency, the Luxembourg franc. Any statutory amounts (e.g., size criteria) are calculated by reference to the Luxembourg franc, as is the liability to taxation. There are no specific rules relating to foreign currency translation in the Fourth Directive or in Luxembourg law.

3.3 Financial and Tax Accounts

3.3.1 Maßgeblichkeitsprinzip

The valuation of assets in the financial accounts is binding for the tax accounts. This principle is the same as the one established in German tax law (*Maßgeblichkeitsprinzip*). Thus, allowable depreciation for tax purposes is limited to the depreciation charged in the financial accounts. If the depreciation charged is in fact in excess of the economic rate of amortization (in order to reduce the tax liability), then this must be explained in the notes to the accounts.

3.3.2 Tax Accounts

The tax liability of a company is always calculated by reference to the opening and closing balance sheet, expressed in LUF. If the accounts of a company are maintained in another currency, then the balance sheets must be converted and net assets restated in LUF, using tax accounting rules. This conversion will give rise to differences arising from the restatement of equity at historical rates and from the recalculation of depreciation based in LUF.

Net gains arising from the conversion may be deferred by banks and certain other entities, and net cumulative losses are immediately deductible for tax purposes; the latter provision may then result in deferred tax balances being created in the financial accounts of the company.

3.4 Valuation

The basic principles of valuation are those commonly followed throughout the EU.

3.4.1 Fixed Assets

Fixed assets are depreciated over their useful lives on a systematic basis. All assets must be shown net of their related depreciation. Depreciation need not be charged on assets with an indefinite useful life.

Fixed assets must be written down if the value to be attributed to them is lower than the current book value and the reduction in value is expected to be long-term. Investments must be written down in all cases. If the reason for the write-off ceases to apply, the amount written off must be reinstated via the profit and loss account to the level at which it would have been recorded in the books under normal depreciation policy

3.4.2 Current Assets

Current assets are valued at the lower of cost or market value, equivalent to net realizable value. Actual cost, average cost, LIFO, and FIFO may be used to determine cost. The use of net realizable value, LIFO, and FIFO may not be accepted by the tax authorities, however, and thus may generate deferred tax balances.

3.4.3 Liabilities

Loans are normally stated at the amount due for repayment. If the amount originally received is lower, the difference may be capitalized and written off over the term of the loan.

Provisions are defined as known or probable liabilities that are known as to their nature but not as to their precise amount or due date.

3.5 Specific Accounting Practices

3.5.1 Format

The law leaves the choice of the format of the accounts open to each company. The balance sheet is usually in account form, showing gross assets and liabilities.

The profit and loss account may be shown by using the analysis of operating profit by function (i.e., the traditional Anglo-Saxon method, showing gross profit, distribution costs, and administrative expenses) or by type of income and expenses (e.g., raw materials, staff costs)

The first note to the accounts will normally give general information about the company and its principal activities. The second note relates to accounting policies, and the remainder follow the order in which items appear in the accounts.

3.5.2 Share Capital

Share capital not paid in must be shown, whether or not it has been called up, and be stated in the notes. At the same time, the capital subscribed must be shown in full on the liabilities side of the balance sheet.

3.5.3 Formation Expenses

Expenses arising relating to the incorporation or development of the company may be capitalized as formation expenses. Professional fees and taxes on capital issued are the most common items under this heading. Formation expenses must be written off within 5 years. Dividends may be distributed only to the extent that distributable reserves and available profits exceed unamortized formation expenses.

3.5.4 Research and Development Costs

Research and development costs may be capitalized and normally must be written off over 5 years. Their nature and reasons for adopting a longer period of amortization must be explained in the notes to the accounts. Dividend distributions are subject to the same restrictions as formation expenses.

3.5.5 Goodwill

Purchased goodwill is determined after the allocation of fair values to the assets of the business acquired or in the first consolidation. It should be written off over 5 years. Longer periods of amortization must be explained in the notes to the accounts.

3.5.6 Accruals and Prepayments

Prepayments and deferred income are shown separately in the balance sheet, but accrued income and accrued expenses are to be included in debtors and creditors, respectively.

3.5.7 Legal Reserve

A legal reserve must be accumulated by public companies. Five percent of the annual profit must be allocated to this reserve, until it reaches 10% of the subscribed capital. The legal reserve may not be distributed.

3.5.8 Profit for the Year

The profit (or loss) for the year is to be shown in the balance sheet before appropriations. The annual general meeting votes on the appropriation proposed in the directors' report. Proposed dividends are not charged to the profit and loss account and are not included in liabilities.

3.6 Consolidation

The implementation of the Seventh Directive introduced the requirement to produce consolidated accounts. These were previously only required of banks under the regulations of the IML.

In principle, every company owned at least 50% by another company must be consolidated into group accounts. Some exemptions are available, however. Consolidations are normally by the acquisition method, but in certain circumstances merger accounting is permitted.

Associated companies and joint ventures (with a participation of at least 20% and up to 50%, respectively) may be consolidated on a proportional basis under certain conditions. Otherwise, equity accounting must be used.

4. Future Developments

4.1 Introduction of the Euro

4.1.1 Overview

The euro is expected to be introduced on January 1, 1999, and the existing participating currencies will disappear after the end of the transitional phase in 2002. Accordingly, the financial records and statements of each company based in or trading with a participating country must be amended to reflect this change.

The introduction of the euro as an expression of its participating currencies is based on three principles:

- Conversion to the euro does not represent a rupture of existing contracts or agreement and is therefore not a realization of assets or liabilities.
- No prohibition, no compulsion: In the transitional phase, all economic agents are free to use the euro or the old currency for their activities. Settlement of claims in participating currencies can be made in euro and vice versa.
- All conversion to and from participating currencies and from and into euro must be made using the prescribed conversion rules.

Luxembourg has maintained a monetary union and currency parity with Belgium since 1921, and it already allows accounts to be maintained in any currency. It is therefore well prepared for issues arising in the conversion to the euro and the transitory phase, when the old participating currencies and the euro will co-exist. The government sees a smooth and tax-neutral changeover as a priority and is seeking to ensure that the public sector will accept financial information and payments in euro from January 1, 1999. The banking sector is encouraged to do the same.

4.1.2 Accounting and Tax Issues

Conversion Differences   In principle, realized losses on the conversion to the euro must be recognized immediately, and unrealized gains may not be so recognized. In practice, the criteria for realization of assets and liabilities have been interpreted flexibly, provided that they are applied consistently. Accordingly, the *Institut des Réviseurs d'Entreprises* proposes to allow companies the choice of both options in respect of the exchange gains arising from the conversion to the euro. It is expected that the tax treatment of unrealized gains will follow the rules for neutralization of such gains for banks (see Section 3.3.2).

Conversion Costs   Specific provisions for covering the costs of conversion to the euro may be made. Capitalization of such expenditure is possible only in respect of a substantial improvement or extension of the useful life of tangible fixed assets. All provisions must be used or written back by the end of the year 2002. It is expected that the tax treatment will follow the accounting approach described. Alternatively, banks are allowed to create general provisions in respect of the transition to the euro, which also must be written back in full by 2002.

Notes

1. Statistical data taken from *Luxembourg in figures*, published by STATEC, the government statistical office. All data as of December 31, 1997, unless otherwise indicated.
2. Berna/Leclerc (1984), *Les nouveaux comptes sociaux des societes de capitaux luxembourgeoises,* p. 9, Luxembourg (translated from the French original).

Useful Addresses

Institut des Réviseurs d'Entreprises
7 rue Alcide de Gasperi
BP 1362, Kirchberg
Luxembourg 1615
Tel: +437 484

Ordre des Experts Comptables
Luxembourgeois
7 rue Alcide de Gasperi
BP 1362, Kirchberg
Luxembourg 1615
Tel: +437 484

Financial Statements

Standard Accounts Format

BILAN ACTIF	*BALANCE SHEET ASSETS*

Capital souscrit non versé dont appelé
Frais d'établissement
Actif immobilisé
   Immobilisations incorporelles
   Frais de recherche et de développement
   Concessions, brevets, licences, marques, ansi que droits et valeurs similaires
   Fonds de commerce
   Acomptes versés
   Immobilisations corporelles
      Terrains et constructions
      Installations techniques et machines
      Autres installations, outillage et mobilier

      Acomptes versés et immobilisations en cours
Immobilisations financières
   Parts dans des entreprises liées
   Créances sur des entreprises liées
   Participations
   Créances sur des entreprises avec lesquelles la société a un lien de participation

   Titres ayant le caractère d'immobilisations
   Autres prêts
   Actions propres
Actif circulant
   Stocks
      Matières premières et consommables
      Produits en cours de fabrication
      Produits finis et marchandises
      Acomptes versés
   Créances
      Créances résultant de ventes et prestations de services
      Créances sur des entreprises liées

      Créances sur des entreprises avec lesquelles la société a un lien de participation

---

Capital subscribed, unpaid of which called up
Formation expenses
Fixed assets
   Intangible assets
   Research and development costs
   Concessions, patents, licences, trademarks and similar rights and assets
Goodwill
Payments on account
Tangible assets
   Land and buildings
   Plant and machinery
   Other fixtures and fittings, tools and equipment
   Payments on account and assets under construction
Financial assets
   Shares in affiliated undertakings
   Amounts due from affiliated undertakings
   Participating interests
   Amounts due from undertakings with which the company is linked by virtue of participating interests
   Other fixed asset investments
   Other loans
   Own shares
Current assets
   Stocks
      Raw materials and consumables
      Work-in-progress
      Finished goods
      Payments on account
   Debtors
      Trade debtors

      Amounts due from affiliated undertakings
      Amounts due from undertakings with which the company is linked by virtue of participating interests

Autres créances	Other debtors
Valeurs mobilières	Securities
Parts dans des entreprises liées	Shares in affiliated undertakings
Actions propres	Own shares
Autres valeurs mobilières	Other securities
Avoirs en banques, avoirs en compte de chèques posteaux, chèques et encaisse	Cash at bank and in hand
Comptes de régularisation	Prepayments
Perte de l'exercice	Loss for the period

PASSIF   LIABILITIES

Capitaux propres	Shareholders' funds
Capital souscrit	Subscribed capital
Primes d'émission	Share premium
Réserve de réévaluation	Revaluation reserve
Réserves	Reserves
Réserve légale	Legal reserve
Réserve pour actions propres	Capital redemption reserve
Réserve statutaires	Reserves provided for by the articles of the company
Autres réserves	Other reserves
Résultats reportés	Profit brought forward
Provisions pour risques et charges	Provisions for liabilities and charges
Provisions pour pensions et obligations similaires	Pension provisions
Provisions pour impôts	Provision for taxation
Autres provisions	Other provisions
Dettes	Creditors
Emprunts obligataires	Debenture loans
Dettes envers des établissements de crédits	Amounts due to banks
Acomptes récus	
Dettes sur achats et prestations de services	Payments on account received
Dettes représentées par des effets de commerce	Trade creditors
Dettes envers des entreprises liées	Bills of exchange
Dettes envers des entreprises avec lesquelles la société a un lien de participation	Amounts due to affiliated undertakings Amounts due to undertakings with which the company is linked by virtue of participating interests
Autres dettes	Other creditors
Comptes de régularisation	Deferred income
Bénéfice de l'exercice	Profit for the period

COMPTE DE PROFITS ET PERTES	*PROFIT AND LOSS ACCOUNT*
Montant net du chiffre d'affaires	Turnover
Variation du stock de produits finis et en cours de fabrication	Change in stocks of finished goods and work-in-progress
Travaux effectués par l'entreprise pour ellemême et portés à l'actif	Own work capitalized
Autres produits d'exploitation	Other operating income
Charges de matières premières et consommables	Raw materials and consumables
Autres charges externes	Other external charges
Frais de personnel	Staff costs
Salaires et traitements	Wages and salaries
Charges sociales avec mention séparée de celles couvrant les pensions	Social security, with indication as to amounts in respect of pensions
Corrections de valeur sur frais d'établissement et sur immobilisations corporelles et incorporelles	Depreciation and amortization of formation expenses, tangible and intangible assets
Corrections de valeur sur éléments de l'actif circulant dans la mesure où elles dépassent les corrections de valeur normales au sein de l'entreprise	Exceptional value adjustments to current assets
Autres charges d'exploitation	Other operating charges
Produits provenant de participations avec mention séparée de ceux provenant d'entreprises liées	Income from investments, with indication of income from affiliated undertakings
Produits provenant d'autres valeurs mobilières et de créances de l'actif immobilisé avec mention séparée de ceux provenant d'entreprises liées	Income from other securities and other fixed assets, with indication of income from affiliated undertakings
Autres intérêts et produits assimilés avec mention séparée de ceux provenant d'entreprises liées	Other interest and similar income, with indication of income from affiliated undertakings
Corrections de valeur sur immobilisations financières et sur valeurs mobilières faisant partie de l'actif circulant	Value adjustments of investments and securities included in current assets
Intérêts et charges assimilées avec mention séparée de ceux concernant des entreprises liées	Interest and similar charges, with indication of amounts paid to affiliated undertakings
Impôts sur le résultat provenant des activités ordinaires	Tax on profit from ordinary activities
Résultat provenant des activités ordinaires après impôts	Profit/loss from ordinary activities after taxation
Produits exceptionnels	Extraordinary income
Charges exceptionnelles	Extraordinary charges
Résultat exceptionnel	Profit/loss from extraordinary items
Impôts sur le résultat exceptionnel	Tax on profit/loss from extraordinary items
Autres impôts ne figurant pas sous les postes ci-dessus	Other taxes
Résultat de l'exercice	Profit/loss for the period

Holding Company Accounts

BILAN ACTIF	*BALANCE SHEET ASSETS*
Capital souscrit non versé, dont appelé	Subscribed capital not paid up of which called up
Frais d'établissement	Formation expenses
Actif immobilisé	Fixed assets
Immobilisations incorporelles	Intangible assets
Immobilisations corporelles	Tangible assets
Immobilisations financières	Financial assets
Actif circulant	Current assets
Créances	Debtors
Valeurs mobilières	Investments
Avoirs en banque, compte chèques postaux, chèque et encaisse	Cash at bank, on postal cheque accounts and in hand
Comptes de regularisation	Prepayments
Perte de l'exercice	Loss for the period

BILAN PASSIF	*LIABILITIES*
Capitaux propres	Capital and reserves
Capital souscrit	Subscribed capital
Primes d'émission	Share premium
Réserve de réévaluation	Revaluation reserve
Réserves:	Reserves:
Réserve légale	Legal reserve
Réserve pour actions propres ou parts propres	Capital redemption reserve
Réserves statutaires	Reserve provided for by the statute of the company
Autres réserves	Other reserves
Résultat reportés	Profit/loss brought forward
Provisions pour risques et charges	Provisions for liabilities and charges
Dettes	Creditors
Emprunts obligataires	Debenture loans (bonds)
Autres dettes	Other creditors
Comptes de régularisation	Deferred income
Bénéfice de l'exercice	Profit for the period

COMPTE DE PROFIT ET PERTES	PROFIT AND LOSS ACCOUNT

Charges

Corrections de valeur sur éléments d'actifs
Intérêts et charges assimilées
Autres charges
Bénéfice de l'exercice

Produits

Produits de l'actifs immobilisé
Produits provenant de l'actif circulant
Produits exceptionnels
Perte de l'exercice

Expenses

Value adjustments on assets
Interest and similar charges
Other charges
Profit for the period

Income

Income from fixed assets
Income from current assets
Extraordinary income
Loss for the period

Country Highlights
THE NETHERLANDS

Common Legal Forms of Companies
Naamloze vennootschap (NV)—public limited company
Besloten vennootschap (BV)—private limited company
Coöperatie—cooperative association
Onderlinge waarborgmaatschappij—mutual guarantee association
Verenigingen—association
Stichtingen—foundation

Sources of Financial Reporting Requirements
Civil code: Book 2, Title 9
Raad voor de Jaarverslaggeving (Council for Annual Reporting):
Guidelines for Annual Reporting
Company division of the Court of Appeal

Corporate Taxation
Incorporated businesses are subject to corporate income tax
(*vennootschapsbelasting*). General rate: 35%.

Auditing Requirements
NIVRA: Code of Conduct and Auditing Guidelines

Organization of the Accounting and Auditing Professions
The Dutch Institute is the NIVRA *Nederlands Instituut voor
Registeraccountants* (Dutch Institute of Chartered Accountants).

Constitution and Legal System
Constitutional monarchy with parliamentary system of government
Codified Roman Law

Currency
Dutch Guilder (NLG) or Florin (Fl)

Official Language
Dutch

THE NETHERLANDS

Martin N. Hoogendoorn
Moret Ernst & Young and University of Amsterdam
Amsterdam

1. Background

1.1 The Accounting and Auditing Profession

The Dutch accounting and auditing profession began to develop in the last decades of the nineteenth century. Early accountants were primarily bookkeepers, but soon the function of independent auditor of financial accounts became a necessity, as the separation between ownership and management of limited liability companies, which gained importance in the years 1890–1910, created the need for the independent and professional judgment of an auditor. In the course of time, accountants started to perform other duties, like internal auditing, governmental auditing, and advising management on internal control and accounting matters.

In 1895 the Netherlands Institute of Accountants (NIVA) was founded. One of its purposes was to create statutory rules for the accounting profession. A bill was drawn up in 1900, but it did not receive a parliamentary reading.

In 1918, the Minister of Education, Arts and Sciences established a committee to prepare a new bill, which was published in 1920. The accounting profession was unenthusiastic, mainly because the degree of government interference embodied in the bill was considered too drastic. The belief that the new law would involve high governmental expenditure in a period of economic crisis was the main reason that this bill also did not receive a parliamentary reading.

Further bills were drawn up in 1930 and again in 1939. The 1939 bill was discussed in Parliament but not accepted. Finally, a committee established in 1956 produced a bill that led to the Chartered Accountants Act (*Wet op de Registeraccountants*) in 1962. This law became partially effective in 1963 and fully effective in 1967.

The Chartered Accountants Act reserved the auditing of financial statements for what are known as *registeraccountants* (RA, chartered accountants whose names are entered in a register). An RA is automatically a member of the public professional body, created by this law, the Dutch Institute of Chartered Accountants (NIVRA, *Nederlands Instituut van Registeraccountants*).

Another related group of accountants was created in 1974, when the *Accountants-Administratieconsulenten* Act came into effect: the *accountant-administratieconsulent* (AA). Comparable to the NIVRA, but with a lower official status, is the NOVAA, *Nederlands Instituut van Accountants-Administratieconsulenten*. The AA was not authorized to certify accounts but provided only other services, for example, implementing and maintaining accounting records, reviewing the manner in which records are kept, preparing financial statements, analyzing and interpreting (in explanatory reports) the data extracted from a company's records, and providing data and advice in connection with such data. The RA provides for such services as well, but the main function of the RA has always been the audit of financial statements and providing specific audit-related services. The traditional field of the AA is the small and medium-sized company; the traditional field of the RA is the large and medium-sized company.

The adaptation of Dutch law to the EC Eighth Directive, regulating the accounting profession, was used to reorganize the division of labor between RAs and AAs. The new Act of 1993 accepted both RAs and AAs as statutory auditors. Both categories will have the right to audit financial statements regardless the size of the company. However, the level of education will remain different, resulting in a continued difference in level of knowledge. Therefore, although officially entitled to do so, an AA will normally not audit the financial statements of a large company.

The education and examination of AAs will be on the minimum level required by the Eighth Directive. This will result in more education than the current level of education. In particular, AAs currently do not need to know the audit process.

The education and examination of RAs will remain on the currently high academic level, which goes beyond the requirements of the Eighth Directive. Traditionally, the education and examination of RAs can be obtained by way of a university course or by courses organized by the NIVRA.

The university-based course is offered at universities with an economics faculty. The first step is to obtain a business economics degree by completing a full-time course that takes about 5 years. The final step is a part-time postgraduate course taking 2 or 3 years, during which candidates are usually employed by public accounting firms.

The NIVRA courses are available only on a part-time basis. Students start these courses after finishing normal high school or the higher economic and administration schools. They attend evening and day classes. It normally takes between 8 and 12 years to complete the full program of courses leading to RA qualification. Since 1994 the NIVRA has cooperated with Nijenrode University. The RA education program is under the Faculty of Information Management and will lead not only to an RA qualification but also to the *doctorandus* degree, as does full-time business economics study at universities.

Currently, there is no practical training requirement. However, following the Eighth Directive, beginning in 1999 all RAs and AAs should have received 3 years of practical training.

1.2 Statutory Accounting Rules

1.2.1 Historical Development

The first statutory accounting rule was published in 1928 (Article 42 of the Commercial Code): the rule contained some requirements for limited liability companies for preparing the assets side of the balance sheet. There were no requirements for the liabilities side, nor for the income statement.

This situation lasted for more than 40 years, during which time, however, there were several discussions about the desirability of introducing further rules, especially in view of developments in the United States and the United Kingdom. Employers published working papers (in 1955 and 1962), as did the scientific committees of political parties (in 1959 and 1962). All these working papers recommended additional rules be promulgated.

Many companies, primarily large companies listed on the Amsterdam Stock Exchange, voluntarily followed the specific recommendations. In the period from 1928 to 1970, however, it was management itself that primarily decided whether or not to follow the suggestions for improving financial reporting. Some companies used the freedom provided by the law and confined themselves to minimal reporting.

A radical change took place in 1970. In that year, the first Act on Financial Reporting was published, becoming effective on May 1, 1971. The bill was prepared by a committee of the Ministry of Justice, which had been working on it from 1960 to 1965. Preparation of the bill and subsequent parliamentary debates took a further 5 years. The act embodied some general rules for preparing financial statements. It applied to limited liability companies (*naamloze venootschap*, NV), private companies (*besloten vennootschap*, BV), cooperative associations (*coöperatie*), and mutual guarantee associations (*onderlinge waarborgmaatschappij*)

The main consideration that governed accounting policies in the formulation of the act was that they should be generally acceptable, and that financial statements should give a true and fair view (i.e., a view that makes possible a sound judgment by users of the financial statements). The act also contained provisions for the publication of financial statements and the administration of justice. The provision relating to the administration of justice offered interested parties the opportunity to complain about financial statements to the Company Division of the Court of Appeal, with the possibility of further appeal to the Supreme Court. These rules were created as an alternative to creating a supervisory authority like the U.S. Securities and Exchange Commission. Departures from statutory rules should be referred to in the auditor's report.

The Act on Financial Reporting was incorporated into the Dutch civil code in 1976 (Book 2, Title 6), with only minor changes in the requirements. More important was the transition from Title 6 to Title 8 because of the adaptation of the Dutch accounting requirements to the Fourth EC Directive. This transition became effective on January 1, 1984. The main differences between Title 6 and Title 8 were:

- Title 8 had more detailed rules, especially concerning the format of the balance sheet and the income statement and concerning the information to be given in the notes to the accounts.

- Title 8 required an indication of the basic valuation rules of historical cost and current value, although the general rule still was that of using generally acceptable accounting policies.

- Title 8 introduced what are known as legal reserves (or statutory reserves).

- There were stricter rules on the publication of the financial statements.

- The mandatory audit requirements were extended. (Because of a transitional arrangement, this rule did not become effective for 5 years.)

Two government orders were published in connection with Title 8: one on the formats of the balance sheet and the income statement, and the other on the application of the current value concept. Title 8 became Title 9 on January 1, 1989.

The statutory accounting rules had to be adapted once again because of the Seventh EC Directive on consolidated accounts. The amendment was published in November 1988 and became effective on January 1, 1990. Preparing consolidated accounts had been mandatory since the 1970 Act on Financial Reporting so the practical consequences of adaptation to the Seventh Directive were only minimal.

Important additions were made as a result of the adaptation to the EC Bank Directive and the EC Insurance Companies Directive: Title 9 was extended in 1993 by new sections on accounting by banks and on accounting by insurance companies, effective for all statutory years beginning on or after January 1, 1993, respectively January 1, 1995. In 1997 the scope of Title 9 was extended to commercial foundations and associations with net sales equal to or exceeding NLG 6 million and to Dutch entities that maintain their head office abroad but are in reality operating mainly in the Netherlands. These extensions are effective from January 1, 1998.

1.2.2 The Use of the Current Value Concept

One of the elements requiring special attention is the use of the current value concept in the Netherlands. The theory of current values (replacement values) was developed by Theodore Limperg in the 1930s, a period of rapid inflation. This theory had great impact on accounting thought in the Netherlands. The first company adopting the current value system in its primary accounts was Philips, in 1953. Current value accounting has always been considered a generally acceptable accounting principle in the Netherlands, and it is explicitly mentioned in the current statutory accounting rules.

Recently, however, almost all companies that had adopted the current value accounting system returned to the historical cost system, including Philips in 1992. The main reason for this development is international harmonization: in most other countries the historical cost system is the only acceptable system for the primary accounts. Notwithstanding this development, many companies still value part of their fixed assets at current value (for instance, property), and many companies provide supplementary information on current values.

The practical application of the current value concept is discussed in more detail in Section 3.5 below.

1.2.3 Accounting and Taxation

The financial statements for tax purposes are based on tax law. The general requirement is that taxable income should be calculated on the basis of sound business practice (*goed koopmanschap*). Although sound business practice is equivalent to generally accepted accounting principles in the commercial financial statements (except for certain specific tax rules), there is no direct relationship between the two sets of financial statements. In this way, it is possible to use a certain accounting policy in the commercial statements and to use another policy in the statements for tax purposes. The practical implications are discussed in more detail in Section 3.11 below.

1.2.4 Stock Exchange Regulations

Companies listed on the Amsterdam Stock Exchange are required to disclose information in accordance with the Stock Exchange Regulations (*Fondsenreglement*), in addition to other requirements discussed here. For stock exchange flotations and new issues, a prospectus should be published that fairly presents the state of affairs of the issuing organization as of the balance sheet date of the last financial year for which annual accounts have been published. The prospectus should also contain information on events of special significance that have taken place after the balance sheet date. Other information, for instance, 3 years of comparative figures and certain forecasts, should be included. Listed companies should make available to the public their biannual and annual accounts and their directors' report, prepared in accordance with generally acceptable accounting principles and giving a true and fair view. As a rule, consolidated and unconsolidated data should be provided. The annual accounts must be audited, the biannual accounts need not. Listed companies are obliged to keep the public informed of any major developments that may have a significant effect on the price of their securities.

1.3 Accounting Standards

In the explanatory statement to the 1970 Act on Financial Reporting, the Ministry of Justice expressed its expectation that the business community and auditors, because of the main statutory rule that accounting policies should be generally acceptable, would survey the accounting policies used and examine the general acceptability of those accounting polices. The Dutch Institute of Chartered Accountants (NIVRA), the joint employers' organizations (*Raad van Nederlandse Werkgeversverbonden*), and the Trade Union Federation (*Overleorgaan Vakcentrales*) fulfilled this expectation by setting up the Tripartite Accounting Standards Committee (*Tripartiete Overleg*) in 1971. This committee published opinions on the Act of Financial Reporting (*Beschouwingen naar aanleiding van de Wet op de Jaarrekening van Ondernemingen*). As the title "opinions" suggests, these "standards" were nonmandatory and therefore not very effective.

This may be the main reason for replacing the *Tripartiete Overleg* by the *Raad voor de Jaarverslaggering* (Council for Annual Reporting; hereafter referred to as RJ) in 1980. The tripartite structure was maintained and adapted: the RJ consisted of representatives of the providers of information (the employers), representatives of the auditors of information (the accounting profession, NIVRA), and representatives of the users of information (employees and financial analysts). The government is not represented in the RJ. The RJ replaced the opinions by Guidelines for Annual Reporting (*Richtlijnen voor de Jaarverslaggeving*).

These guidelines have a more formal character and should be regarded as authoritative pronouncements to be taken into consideration by producers of financial statements in choosing generally acceptable accounting policies and in presenting a true and fair view. The guidelines have no legislative status but may be considered an important frame of reference by the auditor in evaluating financial statements and by the Company Division of the Court of Appeal in arriving at its decisions.

Departures from the guidelines are, however, not referred to in the auditor's report. The guidelines incorporate as far as possible the accounting standards of the International Accounting Standards Committee (IASC) and those opinions of the Company Division of the Court of Appeal (and the Supreme Court) that have a general application. In general, the Dutch accounting guidelines are of an Anglo-Saxon nature (emphasizing the true and fair view, and with a dominant emphasis on "economic substance" rather than "legal form"), but they have generally developed independently of accounting standards in the United States and the United Kingdom.

Recently, a process of revising the guidelines has begun with the objective of coming closer to IASC. As a start, IAS 32 on Financial

Instruments has been literally translated into Dutch and is issued as a Dutch Guideline, with only a few deviations.

Summarizing, the current frames of reference for accounting (concerning commercial financial statements) in the Netherlands are (in decreasing order of importance):

1. Civil Code (Title 9) and related government orders
2. Case Law (Company Division of the Court of Appeal, Supreme Court)
3. Guidelines of the RJ
4. International Accounting Standards
5. Other authoritative sources, such as literature and generally accepted practice

Wherever article numbers are used throughout this chapter, they refer to the latest version of Title 9. Reference is also made to the guidelines of the RJ (for instance, "RJ 4.20. 103" means that the requirement or recommendation is included in the guidelines of the RJ chapter 4.20, paragraph 103). References to the RJ guidelines are updated to issue no. 19 (December 1997).

1.4 Auditing Standards and the Auditor's Report

The Dutch auditing profession is fully autonomous in setting the standards required to meet legal audit requirements. Historically, the profession has avoided detailed guidance to public accountants on auditing principles and procedures. Dutch audit philosophy was mainly to be found in literature.

In 1973, a Code of Conduct for RAs was published by the NIVRA. This code set standards for ethical behavior, impartiality, secrecy, independence, the auditor's report, accepting engagements, and so on.

In the 1970s, the NIVRA started issuing ad hoc opinions on various topical subjects and interpretations of its Code of Conduct, but it was not until 1985 that the NIVRA started working on a comprehensive set of auditing guidelines (*Richtlijnen voor de Accountantscontrole*). The contents of these guidelines were highly influenced by the Union des Experts Comptables (UEC) Auditing Statements and the International Federation of Accountants (IFAC) International Auditing Guidelines.

In 1996, a radical step was taken to abolish all existing auditing guidelines and to replace them with a Dutch translation of the (renewed)

International Standards on Auditing (ISAs) of the IFAC. Specifically Dutch matters (for instance resulting from legal requirements) have been added to the existing texts.

The structure and the wording of the auditor's report follow international developments in this respect. An auditor who has audited financial statements in accordance with generally accepted auditing standards can express the following opinions.

1. An unqualified opinion. This opinion is given when an auditor is convinced that the financial statements give a true and fair view of the financial position and financial results.

2. An opinion with limitation (a qualified opinion). This opinion is given in two situations:

   —In the case of uncertainties of material importance in the audit

   —In the case of objections of material importance to the annual accounts

3. A disclaimer of opinion. This opinion should be given in the situation of uncertainties of fundamental importance in the audit.

4. An adverse opinion. This opinion is used in the situation of objections of fundamental importance to the annual accounts.

As can be inferred from the various alternatives, the distinction between *material* and *fundamental* is important. There are, however, no strict criteria for differentiating between the two. So, in practice, this is an important element of professional judgment.

The standard wording of the unqualified opinion is:

Introduction

We have audited the financial statements of xxx (company name), xxx (registered office) for the year xxx. These financial statements are the responsibility of the company's management. Our responsibility is to express an opinion on these financial statements based on our audit.

Scope

We conducted our audit in accordance with auditing standards generally accepted in the Netherlands. Those standards require that we plan and perform the audit to obtain reasonable assurance about whether the financial statements are free of material misstatement. An audit includes examining, on a test basis, evidence supporting the amounts and disclosures in the financial statements. An audit also includes assessing the accounting principles used and significant estimates made by management, as well as evaluating the overall financial statement presentation. We believe that our audit provides a reasonable basis for our opinion.

Opinion

In our opinion, the financial statements give a true and fair view of the financial position of the company as at xxx (balance sheet date) and of the result for the year then ended in accordance with accounting principles generally accepted in the Netherlands and comply with the financial reporting requirements included in Part 9, Book 2 of the Netherlands Civil Code.

As can be seen, the standard wording includes a reference to compliance with Dutch legal requirements for financial statements as included in Part 9 (or Title 9), Book 2 of the Netherlands Civil Code (see Section 1.2). When other legal requirements apply (for instance for specific not-for-profit entities), reference should be made to these requirements. No reference is made to the guidelines of the RJ (see Section 1.3).

When financial statements are not in compliance with legal requirements, the departure should be mentioned in the auditor's report. A departure can be compatible with giving a true and fair view and, therefore, with an unqualified opinion. If the departure leads to financial statements not giving a true and fair view, an opinion with limitation or an adverse opinion should be given, depending on whether the objection is of a material or a fundamental nature.

In addition to the standard wording given above, additional information in the form of an emphasis of matter can or should be given. An emphasis of matter is mandatory in the case of a serious uncertainty as to the going concern status of the company. In this case, an additional paragraph is added at the end of the report, of which the standard wording is:

Without qualifying our opinion above, we draw attention to note xxx, which refers to the uncertainty as to the company's ability to continue as a going concern. It is not impossible, however, that in the long term the company will be able to continue operating as a going concern. The financial statements have therefore been prepared on a going concern basis.

An emphasis of matter is nonmandatory in other cases. It is used to draw the reader's attention to an important matter, for instance, to a possible claim for which no provision is made in the balance sheet.

There are also standard wordings for the other opinions, which will not be fully reproduced here. For the opinion with limitation it is essential that the words "subject to" are used when the cause of the limitation is the uncertainty in the audit, and that the words "except for" are used when the cause of the limitation is the objection to the annual accounts. For the disclaimer of opinion, it is essential to use the words "unable to form an opinion as to whether the financial statements give a true and fair view." The disclaimer might include a negative assurance, stating that the audit did not reveal any errors or omissions in the financial statements. For the adverse opinion, the words "these financial statements do not give a true and fair view" should be used.

The auditors' report need not be addressed, the assumption being that the report is meant for any potentially interested party. The report can be signed by either an individual in his or her name or in the firm's name, or both, if applicable. The report is dated to indicate that the effect on the financial statements of post-balance sheet events until that date is included in the opinion. Preferably, the date of the audit report is the same as the date of the annual accounts.

2. The Form and Content of Published Financial Statements

2.1 Content of the Annual Report

The annual report includes the executive directors' report on the financial statements and certain other information

2.1.1 Executive Directors' Report

The executive directors' report gives a fair review of the position at balance sheet date and of the development of the business during the financial year. In addition, this report contains information in respect of:

- Significant post-balance sheet events
- Likely future developments, with particular attention to capital expenditure, financing and employment, and to the circumstances on which future net turnover and profitability depend
- Activities in the field of research and development.

The executive directors' report may not be at variance with the financial statements.

2.1.2 Financial Statements

The financial statements comprise the balance sheet, the income statement, the notes, and other prescribed information. There are two different sorts of financial statements: the legal entity's own financial statements and the consolidated financial statements. Specific information concerning the content of the legal entity's own financial statements is given in Section 2.2 below, and information concerning the content of consolidated financial statements is given in Section 2.3 below. The requirements for preparing and publishing the legal entity's and consolidated financial statements are discussed in Section 2.4 below.

As part of the notes, many companies publish a cash flow statement. It is not obligatory to include such a statement, with the exception that the Stock Exchange Regulations require it for new companies to be listed. The new guideline of the RJ of February 1996 (RJ 4.20) requires large companies to include a cash flow statement, based on the principles of IAS 7 (revised).

2.1.3 Other Data

Certain other information must be included in the annual report (in a separate section, normally called "other data"). Included with this supplementary information (Article 392) is:

- The auditor's report
- The profit appropriation clauses of the articles of association
- The appropriation of the profit or the treatment of the loss or, if these have not yet been adopted, the relevant proposal
- The names of holders of special controlling rights arising from the articles of association, as well as the nature of these rights
- The number of profit-sharing certificates including similar rights
- Post-balance sheet events having material financial consequences, and their significance
- The existence of branches, the names of the countries in which these branches are established, and their trading name (when this name differs from that of the reporting entity)

2.2 The Content of the Legal Entity's Own Financial Statements

The provision regarding the objective of the financial statements (Article 362 (1)) reads:

> The financial statements shall in accordance with generally acceptable accounting principles furnish such information as to enable a responsible opinion to be formed regarding the financial position and the profit and loss and, to the extent that the nature of financial statements permits, regarding the solvency and liquidity of the corporate body.

We summarize this objective as follows: the financial statements shall give a true and fair view.

The balance sheet shall present the financial position and the income statement shall present the profit or loss in a fair, consistent and clear manner (Articles 362 (2) and (3)).

Should the true and fair view so demand, it is the company's duty to include information in addition to that which is legally required. Should this be necessary for presenting a true and fair view, the company is obliged to depart from the special requirements laid down in or pursuant to the law. The reasons shall then be stated as far as necessary, with mention of the impact on the financial position and on the profit or loss (Article 362 (4)). This so-called true and fair override is invoked by the RJ in two situations: measuring current marketable securities at market value and recognizing all changes in the profit and loss account (whereas Title 9 requires measurement at the lower of cost or market) and application of the percentage of completion method (whereas Title 9 does not allow inventories to be measured at an amount higher than cost).

In preparing the financial statements, the general principles of going concern, consistency, accrual, prudence, substance over form, and materiality apply (Articles 362 (5), 363 (3), 384 (2), 384 (3)). Substance over form is a relatively dominant criterion (RJ 1.05.1). Significant accounting policies should always be disclosed (Article 384 (5)). Furthermore, corresponding figures for the preceding period should be shown in the balance sheet and the income statement (Article 363 (5)). Where necessary in the interest of comparability, that figure must be adjusted and the change resulting from the adjustment must be explained. These general principles are in line with IAS 1. The revenue recognition rules of IAS 18 are covered by these general principles as well.

The foregoing general principles are part of the statutory accounting rules. From a general point of view, it is important to mention also the publication by the RJ in September 1996 of the Dutch translation of the International Accounting Standards Committee (IASC) Framework for the Preparation and Presentation of Financial Statements as the conceptual framework underlying Dutch accounting.

In preparing the balance sheet and income statement, a company should follow one of the standard formats for the layout of accounts, prescribed by governmental decree as a consequence of the EC's Fourth Directive.

For the balance sheet, two standard formats are available: a horizontal format (with assets on the left and liabilities on the right), and a vertical format (with assets at the top and liabilities at the bottom, with a separate reference to working capital).

For the income statement, there are four standard formats, differing from each other in the horizontal layout (seldom used) versus the vertical layout, and in the functional classification of costs (cost of sales, distribution expenses, general administrative expenses) versus the classification of costs by category (wages and salaries, social security expenses, raw materials and consumables, amortization and depreciation).

Examples of some formats are given in Section 2.5 below. Further requirements concerning the classification of items are discussed in Section 3.

Important disclosure items, specified in the statutory accounting rules, not relating to the classification of items, include the following (if applicable):

1. General

    —Any (additional) information required for giving a true and fair view (Article 362 (4))

    —The principles underlying the valuation of the assets and liabilities and the determination of the financial results in relation to each item (Article 384 (5)), including the methods of calculating depreciation and amortization (Article 386 (2)); furthermore, if applicable, the information that interest is included in the asset value (Article 388 (2)) and whether and in what way, in connection with revaluation, allowance has been made for the effect of taxation on the financial position and results (Article 390 (5))

    —Changes in accounting policies and in the layout of the balance sheet and income statement, the well-founded reasons for the change, and the significance for the financial position and results (Article 363 (4) and 384 (6))

—A reconciling statement of movements in each of the fixed asset items (tangible, intangible, and financial) during the financial year (including acquisitions, disposals, revaluations, depreciation, downward value adjustments, and rectifications thereof) (Article 368 (1))

—Relating to each fixed asset item held at the balance sheet date, the cumulative total of any revaluation and the cumulative total of amounts written off and the downward value adjustments (Article 368 (2))

—Any major financial commitments entered into by the legal entity for a number of years to come and not shown in the balance sheet, with separate disclosure of commitments to group companies (Article 381);

—The average number of employees of the legal entity during the financial year, broken down in a manner compatible with the way the business is organized (Article 382)

—The aggregate amount of remuneration, including retirement benefit costs, and other payments, of the present and former executive board members and, separately, of the present and former supervisory board members, except when this amount is attributable to one natural person (Article 383 (1))

—The amount of loans, advances, and guarantees granted by the legal entity, its subsidiaries, or its consolidated companies for the benefit of the executive and supervisory board members of the legal entity, with specific disclosure of the amounts receivable, the rate of interest, the most important other terms, and the repayments during the financial year (Article 383 (2))

2. Intangible assets:

—Explanatory notes to capitalized incorporation and share expenses and research and development costs (Article 365 (2))

—If goodwill is amortized over a period longer than 5 years, the period of amortization together with the reasons why it is in excess of 5 years (Article 386 (3))

3. Tangible assets:

—A limited right (*in rem* or *in personam*) of permanent enjoyment in or in respect of tangible fixed assets (Article 366 (2))

4. Financial fixed assets:

—The name, principal place of business, and proportion of the issued capital of any company to which it, alone or together with subsidiaries, has furnished or has caused to be furnished at least 20% of the issued capital, on its own account, and of any company in which it is fully liable as a partner for its debts to creditors (Article 379 (1))

—Relating to the same companies as mentioned above, the amount of shareholders' equity and the result for the latest financial year for which financial statements are available (unless certain conditions are met) (Article 379 (2))

—The name and principal place of business of the company managing the group to which it belongs and of any company consolidating the financial statements of the legal entity in its published consolidated financial statements, as well as the name and place of office where copies may be obtained (at no more than cost) (Article 379 (3))

5. Current assets:

—For each group of receivables classified under current assets: the amount becoming due and payable after more than one year (Article 370 (2))

—The extent to which securities are not at the legal entity's free disposal (Article 371 (2))

—The extent to which bank and postal giro (bank) balances are not at the legal entity's free disposal (Article 372 (2))

6. Shareholders' equity:

—A statement showing the movements in the shareholders' equity during the financial year, stating additions and disposals subdivided by item according to their nature (Article 378 (1))

—The issued share capital and the paid-in capital or paid-in and called-up capital (Article 373 (2)), broken down into classes of shares (Article 378 (2))

—The book value of and the movements in a legal entity's own shares or depositary receipts thereof (treasury shares)

—As treasury shares may not be capitalized but should be deducted from the shareholders' equity (see Section 3.3 below), the item of the shareholders' equity from which the acquisition cost or book value thereof has been deducted (Article 378 (2))

—For a public limited liability company: every acquisition and disposal for its own account of treasury shares (and depositary receipts thereof), with reasons for the acquisition, the number, par value, and agreed price of the shares involved in each transaction, and the proportion of the capital that they represent (Article 378 (3))

— The way in which payment for shares, demandable or voluntarily deposited during the financial year, has been effected, and the substance of contracts, underlying payments on shares otherwise than in cash (Article 378 (3))

7. Provisions:

—A precise definition of the provisions and an indication, as far as possible, to what extent the provisions are regarded as long term (Article 374 (3))

—If the legal entity has accepted liability for the debts of others, or is still at risk in respect of discounted bills of exchange or checks: obligations arising from these commitments in accordance with the form of security furnished, insofar as no provisions have been made for them in the balance sheet; commitments entered into for the benefit of group companies must be disclosed separately (Article 376)

8. Liabilities

—For each category of debt, the amount becoming due and payable after more than 1 year, with an indication of the interest rate and with separate disclosure of the amount becoming due and payable after more than 5 years (Article 375 (2))

—The amount that must be repaid within 1 year on loans classified under liabilities with a term of more than 1 year (Article 375 (6))

—For each category of debt, the amount and nature of any collateral and, to the extent necessary for giving a true and fair view, those liabilities for which the company (conditionally or unconditionally) has committed itself to encumber or not to encumber its assets to provide collateral (Article 375 (3))

—The amount of debts that have been subordinated to all other debts and an explanation of the nature of any such subordination (Article 375 (1))

—For convertible loans, the terms of conversion (Article 375 (7)); any major commitments entered into for a number of years to come and not shown in the balance sheet, such as those arising out of long-term contracts (Article 381)

9. Turnover:

—If the legal entity is divided into various industry sectors, the extent to which each type of activity has contributed to net turnover (Article 380 (1))

—The breakdown of net turnover by the various geographic areas in which the legal entity supplies goods and services (Article 380 (2)). A breakdown of results and assets employed is not required in the Netherlands, although the RJ recommends that large companies provide a breakdown of operational results (RJ 2.71. 616)

10. Earnings per share:

—It is recommended, but not required, to disclose a basic earnings per share figure (RJ 4.24)

Many more disclosure requirements are formulated by the RJ. We will summarize some of them in Section 3, but to give a complete description of them would exceed the scope of this chapter.

2.3 The Content of Consolidated Financial Statements

Consolidated financial statements are the financial statements integrating assets, liabilities, income, and expenses of legal entities and partnerships constituting a group or a part of a group. A group is defined as those companies that form an economic unity under common control; a group company is any company in the group.

In accordance with Article 362 (1), consolidated financial statements should give a true and fair view of the (part of the) group (Article 405). In IAS 27 the term *group company* is not used. The equivalent term is *subsidiary*. In the Netherlands a subsidiary has a specific meaning, which is somewhat different from a (subordinate) group company. A subsidiary is not a group company unless it is under the control of the holding company; but in practice both terms are normally equivalent. When prepared, the consolidated financial statements are officially included in the notes to the legal entity's (i.e., the holding company's) own financial statements (Article 406 (1)). In practice, the consolidated financial statements are considered to be of primary importance, and they are normally presented before the legal entity's own statements.

Included in the consolidated statements are the legal entity (holding company) itself and its (sub)group companies (Article 406 (1,2)) . Subsidiaries not belonging to the group (see above) as well as some group companies (see below) are not included in the consolidated accounts; in that case they are normally valued at net asset value (which is a variant of the equity method, see Section 3.1 below).

If, because of a major difference in its activities, consolidation of a group company would conflict with the true and fair view, its financial statements or, when applicable, its consolidated financial statements, must be disclosed separately in the notes. Important but invisible consequences of this separate disclosure must be elucidated (Article 406 (3)). Furthermore, consolidation is not required for data (Article 407 (1)):

- Of group companies whose total significance is negligible
- Of group companies whose financial data can be obtained only at disproportionate costs, or with great delay
- Of group companies that are held to be sold

In comparison with IAS 27 there is one important point of difference concerning the scope of consolidation: IAS 27 does not allow exclusion from consolidation of group companies with dissimilar business activities.

The legal entity may itself be excluded from consolidation when it has no activities other than managing and financing group companies and participations, and when the management of group companies takes place under the terms of a joint operating agreement with another legal entity not included in the consolidated statements (Article 407 (3)).

In the case of joint ventures, the financial data may be included in the consolidated financial statements in proportion to the interest held in it, if this meets the legal requirement of a true and fair view (Article 409, RJ 2.03). Proportional consolidation is not acceptable in other cases. If joint ventures are not consolidated, they are normally accounted for using the equity method. This is in line with IAS 31, although IAS 31 prefers proportional consolidation. In 1996 DSM changed its method of accounting for joint ventures from equity accounting to proportional consolidation (see the first part of the notes to the consolidated statements).

The requirements mentioned in Section 2.2 above regarding the content of the legal entity's own financial statements apply to the consolidated financial statements as well, with a few exceptions (Article 410 (1)). The most important exceptions are:

- Shareholders' equity is not specified, and the specific disclosures concerning this item are not given; however, disclosure of the interest of third parties in the consolidated equity and result is required, and differences between equity and result in the legal entity's own and in the consolidated statements should be elucidated (Article 411)
- The information mentioned above concerning financial fixed assets is not disclosed; however, specific information must be given concerning the group companies, including disclosure of the companies for which the reporting legal entity has accepted liability for their debts (Article 414)
- The information concerning remuneration of board members and loans, advances and guarantees granted by the legal entity to board members is not given (Article 401(1))
- Inventories need not be specified if this would require disproportionate costs due to special circumstances (Article 410(2)).

Accounting policies are normally the same as those used in the legal entity's own financial statements; different principles may be used only for valid reasons, which are to be disclosed in the notes (Article 410(3)).

The balance sheet date of the consolidated financial statements must correspond with the balance sheet date of the legal entity's own financial statements. On no account may consolidated statements be drawn up by using information determined more than three months before or after the group's balance sheet date (Article 412).

Specific consolidation procedures such as the elimination of intragroup balances and transactions and the application of uniform accounting policies are not elaborated upon in law, but on this point practice is equivalent to IAS 27.

2.4 Obligations to Prepare and Publish the Annual Report

As indicated above, the annual report includes (in its most extended form) the executive directors' report, the legal entity's own financial statements, the consolidated financial statements, and certain other information. In this section we will identify the obligations concerning the preparation and publication of the annual report. These requirements apply to the companies mentioned in Section 1.2 above.

A public limited company (NV) and private limited company (BV) are required to prepare their annual reports within 5 months of the balance sheet date (cooperative associations and mutual guarantee associations, including commercial foundations and associations, have 6 months). The annual report must be approved within 6 months of the balance sheet date (cooperative associations and mutual guarantee associations have 7 months) and must be published within 8 days of approval. The annual general meeting can extend the time limit for preparing/approving the annual report, by a maximum of 6 months (cooperative associations and mutual guarantee associations: 5 months). If the accounts are not approved within 2 months of the latest possible (extended) date of preparing the annual report, the board of directors must file a draft set of accounts with the annotation that the accounts have not yet been approved. In all cases the annual report must be published not later than 13 months after the balance sheet date; if they are not, the company commits an economic offense.

Publication of the annual report is realized by filing the annual report at the Company Registry. The accounts must be signed by all executive and supervisory directors. Certain parts of the report may be excluded from filing, provided they are available for inspection at the office of the company and a copy is provided on request; this fact must then be reported to the Company Registry.

In principle, every NV and BV is obliged to prepare, as a part of the annual report, its own financial statements, subject to the exceptions mentioned below. In addition, a legal entity managing a group of companies, alone or together with another group company, must include consolidated financial statements in the notes to its own financial statements, combining the financial statements of its group companies together with its own financial statements. If the legal entity is not managing the whole group, but only part of the group, it must present consolidated financial statements as well, which are to include group companies of which it exercises dominant control (Article 406).

Consolidated statements need not be prepared if all of the following apply (Article 407 (2)):

- The company is small (see below).
- None of the companies involved is listed.
- The company is not a credit institution.

- No notices of objection have been lodged with the legal entity within 6 months of commencement of the financial year by at least 10% of the members or by holders of at least 10% of the issued share capital.

A legal entity that is considered to be the head of a part of a group is exempted from preparing consolidated accounts if all of certain conditions are met. The most important conditions (Article 408) are that the shareholders are in agreement; that the accounts of the company and of the companies to be consolidated are included in the consolidated statements of a larger part of the group; and that these consolidated statements are prepared in accordance with the EU Seventh Directive, or, when this Directive does not apply, in a similar way. The legal entity must disclose in its own financial statements that the exemption is applied. This regulation is equivalent to that in IAS 27.

A legal entity is exempted from preparing full own accounts if all of certain conditions are met. The most important conditions (Article 403) are that simplified statements are prepared; that the shareholders are in agreement; that the accounts are included in the consolidated accounts of an EC-based group (prepared in accordance with the Seventh Directive); and that the company preparing the consolidated accounts has guaranteed the liabilities of the company being exempted.

For any entity, if the financial data of a legal entity have been included in its consolidated financial statements, the legal entity's own profit and loss account need disclose as a separate item only the income from participating interests after taxes (Article 402). The application of this provision must be disclosed in the notes to the consolidated financial statements.

The obligations to prepare and publish the annual report differ according to the size of the company (as does the question of whether the accounts need to be audited). There are three size categories: small companies, medium-sized companies, and large companies.

A small company is a company, not engaged in insurance or banking, that satisfies at least two of the following three criteria:

1. The value of the assets on the basis of historical cost accounting does not exceed 6 million Dutch guilder (NLG)
2. The net turnover (sales) for the year does not exceed NLG 12 million.
3. The average number of employees during the year is less than 50.

A medium-sized company is a company not engaged in insurance or banking and not being a small company that satisfies at least two of the following three criteria:

1. The value of the assets on the basis of historical cost accounting does not exceed NLG 24 million.
2. The net turnover (sales) for the year does not exceed NLG 48 million.
3. The average number of employees during the year is less than 250.

A large company is a company that is neither a small company nor a medium-sized company.

The above criteria are based on consolidated amounts, including all group companies that would have been consolidated if consolidated statements had been prepared. The criteria are subject to periodic adjustment. A company moving up or down from one category to another continues to be subject to the legal requirements for its previous category during the year in which its status changes.

A large company is required to prepare and publish:

- An executive directors' report
- A full balance sheet and notes thereto
- A full income statement and notes thereto
- Full other information, including the auditor's report

A medium-sized company is required to prepare:

- An executive directors' report
- A full balance sheet and notes thereto
- A condensed income statement and notes thereto
- Full other information, including the auditor's report

A medium-sized company is required to publish the same information, with the following exceptions:

- Only a condensed and not a full balance sheet need be published.
- Not full but only limited other information need be published, including the auditor's report.

A small company is obliged to prepare:

- An executive directors' report
- A condensed balance sheet and notes thereto
- A condensed income statement and notes thereto
- Limited other information (no auditor's report)

A small company is required to publish only a condensed balance sheet and notes thereto. An executive directors' report, an income statement, and other information need not be published. Furthermore, a small company is never required to prepare consolidated accounts.

Only large and medium-sized companies are required to have their accounts audited.

2.5 An Example of Published Financial Statements

An example of a published set of financial statements is shown on pages 768-795. We reproduce parts of the annual report for the year 1996, published by DSM, a large chemical company in the Netherlands. We reproduce from the official English language version as well as from the original Dutch version.

Reproduced at the end of this chapter are:

1. Consolidated balance sheet at December 31, 1996 (after profit appropriation) in the original Dutch version
2. Consolidated balance sheet at December 31, 1996 (after profit appropriation) in the English version
3. Consolidated 1996 statement of income in the Dutch version
4. Consolidated 1996 statement of income in the English version
5. Consolidated 1996 statement of cash flows in the Dutch version
6. Consolidated 1996 statement of cash flows in the English version
7. Accounting policies, in the English version
8. Notes to the consolidated financial statements, in the English version
9. The legal entity's own balance sheet at December 31, 1996, and its own 1996 statement of income, in the Dutch and English versions

10. Notes to the legal entity's own balance sheet, in the English version

11. Other information, including the auditor's report, in the English version

12. Quarterly financial data, ten-year summary, and some key data in ECUs and U.S. dollars, in the English version.

The excerpts from the DSM annual report should be studied in light of the following short clarifications and comments.

2.5.1 Consolidated Balance Sheet

DSM has adopted a horizontal layout, with separate balance sheet totals for assets on the one hand and group equity and liabilities on the other hand. The numbers in brackets refer to the notes.

If the vertical layout had been used, the current liabilities would have been deducted from the current assets, presenting a separate working capital amount. The long-term liabilities, provisions, equalization account (for an explanation: see Section 3.5.3 on government grants) and group equity would then have been presented at the bottom of the balance sheet, in that order and without a total amount.

2.5.2 Consolidated Income Statement

DSM applies the vertical layout, with a classification of costs by category. The majority of cost elements are identified not in the income statement but in the notes (included in "other operating costs," note 15).

2.5.3 Classification

The classification of assets, liabilities, revenues and expenses in the consolidated balance sheet and income statement is in conformity with Dutch law and can be found in the financial statements of other companies as well. A difference between companies might be that some subclassifications (for instance inventories, provisions) are given either in the balance sheet or in the notes to the balance sheet (as in the DSM financial statements).

2.5.4 Statement of Cash Flows

The changes in cash are subdivided into operating activities, investing activities, and financing activities. The indirect method is applied, adjusting the net result by changes in balance sheet amounts to arrive at the net cash provided by operating activities. In note 19 a reconciliation is made of certain balance sheet movements and items in the statement of cash flows.

2.5.5 Legal Entity's Balance Sheet

The layout of the legal entity's balance sheet does not differ from the consolidated one. However, the layouts of the two income statements do differ. As indicated in Section 2.4 above, the legal entity whose financial data are included in the consolidated statements is allowed to prepare a simplified own income statement, showing only as a separate item the income from participating interests after taxes. The application of this provision (Article 402) is disclosed in the general note to the consolidated statements.

As indicated in Section 2.3 and further explained in Section 3.1 below, the accounting policies in the consolidated financial statements and in the legal entity's own financial statements are normally the same. This can be illustrated in the annual report of DSM by comparing stockholders' equity and net result in both statements: the amounts in both statements are equal.

2.5.6 Accounting Policies

Accounting policies regarding the scope of consolidation show that status as a group company is decisive for being included in the consolidated financial statements. Other accounting policies will be discussed in more detail in Section 3.

2.5.7 Notes

The notes to the consolidated financial statements and to the legal entity's own balance sheet show several of the disclosure items mentioned in Sections 2.2 and 2.3.

In notes 1, 2 and 3, the reconciling statements of movements in each of the fixed asset items during the financial year are given. The classification and statement of movements of shareholders' equity is partially given in the notes to the consolidated accounts (note 7) and fully in the notes to the legal entity's own balance sheet (note 5).

The obligatory breakdown of net sales by division and by region is given in note 12 of the consolidated statements. The geographic breakdown is presented by origin as well as by destination. Note 16 shows the breakdown of the operating profit by division, and note 2 of the consolidated statements shows a geographic breakdown of capital expenditure and the book value of tangible assets at year end. These breakdowns are not obligatory.

The commitments not shown in the balance sheet are disclosed in note 11 of the consolidated statements and in note 8 of the legal entity's own balance sheet. In Section 3 reference will be made to some more notes.

2.5.8 Other Information

Other information includes, among other things, the auditor's report. The auditor's report covers the parent company and group accounts of DSM for the year 1996, following the standard form and wording laid down by the NIVRA (see Section 1.4 above). The auditors, Moret Ernst & Young, attest that the financial statements give "a true and fair view" (in Dutch, *"een getrouw beeld"*) of the financial position and the result.

3. Accounting Policies and Practices in Valuation and Income Measurement: Implications for the Analyst

3.1 Group Accounts

3.1.1 Group Accounts and Legal Entity's Accounts

The general content of group accounts is discussed in Section 2.3 above. As indicated in Section 2.3, the group accounting policies are normally the same as those in the legal entity's own financial statements. This normally means that equity accounting is used in the legal entity's own financial statements in the same way as in the consolidated statements. As a consequence, in the Netherlands, equity and income in the legal entity's own financial statements are normally the same as those in the consolidated statements, as is the case with DSM. A notable exception is Unilever, the large Dutch-British company. Unilever does not use equity accounting in its own legal entity financial statements. This is without doubt a consequence of applying British accounting rules, in which equity accounting is used only in group accounts.

3.1.2 Equity Accounting

The use of equity accounting in the legal entity's financial statement is obligatory for all enterprises in which the investor exercises significant influence on business and financial policy. These investments comprise subsidiaries (group companies), associated companies, and joint ventures. It is irrelevant whether or not the investments are consolidated. In the consolidated statements the same principle applies, with the difference, of course, that group companies are consolidated.

For participations with significant influence, Dutch law allows equity accounting not to be used in the legal entity financial statements only when there are well-founded reasons (Article 389 (9)). International entanglement, such as with Unilever, is considered to be such a well-founded reason, as is the use of Article 408 in not preparing consolidated accounts (see Section 2.4).

The method of equity accounting has several variants (Article 389; RJ 2.03.2):

1. The *net asset value* method: the investor must determine the net asset value of its investment by valuing assets, provisions, and liabilities of the company in which it participates and by calculating its financial results by means of the same method as that applied to its own assets, provisions, liabilities, and financial results.

2. The *visible equity* method: the investor does not use its own method of valuing assets, provisions, liabilities, and financial results, but uses the method that is used by the company itself, as shown in its own financial statements.

3. The *equity method on the basis of cost*: the investor values its investment at cost and adjusts this value by the amount of its share in the retained profits and other reserve movements of the company

in which it participates. Usually, no adjustment is made to the investor's share in the financial results for amortization of goodwill.

In all variants, the income statement reflects the investor's share in the results of operations of the investee.

The *net asset value* method is the principal method. The *visible equity* method is allowed when insufficient information is available to the legal entity to determine the net asset value. The *equity method on the basis of cost* normally should not be used.

Except for the last variant, application of the equity method leads to a separate identification of goodwill. Because of the equivalence between the legal entity's financial statements and the consolidated statements, goodwill is shown in both statements in the same way.

In IAS 27 and 28, the term *equity accounting* has a specific meaning, namely, what is called above "the equity method on the basis of cost," with the difference that adjustments are made for amortizing goodwill. An important difference with IAS 27 and 28 is that in the Netherlands the investments in which the investor has a significant influence may not be accounted for by using the cost method. According to the cost method the investment is recorded at cost and the income statement reflects the dividends received from profits distributed. The cost method can be acceptable in other cases, however (see Section 3.9 below).

The DSM accounting policy for financial fixed assets is the *net asset value* method (the share in equity is determined in accordance with DSM Group policies).

3.1.3 Goodwill

Positive goodwill, paid on the acquisition of a participation, can be accounted for in the following ways:

- It can be capitalized under intangible fixed assets and amortized (Articles 365, 386 (3), 389 (7))
- It can be charged directly to the income statement (shown separately) (Article 389 (7))
- It can be charged directly to the reserves (shown separately) (Article 389 (7)

If goodwill is capitalized and amortized, the amortization will have to be charged to the income statement. The period of amortization is the estimated useful life. If amortization takes place over a period greater than 5 years, that longer period should be disclosed, together with an explanation of why the period is longer. A periodic evaluation of the future economic benefits of goodwill in relation to its capitalized amount is required. In case of a permanent decline in value, an additional write-off will be required (RJ 2.03.225).

In practice, most companies charge the goodwill direct to the reserves, as does DSM. This practice is no longer allowed in IAS 22 (revised 1993), which contains the requirement to capitalize goodwill and amortize it and not to take it directly to the reserves (immediate write-off to income would be acceptable, but only in the case where goodwill is not offset by future economic benefits).

For negative goodwill, the only legal requirement is to add the goodwill to the revaluation reserve as long as there are no disadvantages connected with the acquired company, that is, in the case of a lucky buy (Article 389 (8)). According to the RJ, negative goodwill should be reduced as much as possible by making fair value adjustments to assets (impairments) and liabilities (provisions for reorganization). Remaining negative goodwill, not attributable to a lucky buy, should be credited to equity when positive goodwill is written off from equity, and should be recognized as a deferred liability when positive goodwill is capitalized. The deferred liability is systematically released over time to the profit and loss account.

This treatment is not fully in line with IAS 22. Proportional reduction on nonmonetary assets to amounts below the fair value (the benchmark treatment) is not allowed in the Netherlands. On the other hand, direct recognition of negative goodwill in shareholders' equity is not allowed by IAS 22.

3.1.4 Pooling-of-Interests Accounting

Until recently, there were no definite rules for opting between purchase accounting (or acquisition accounting) and pooling-of-interests accounting (or merger accounting). Pooling-of-interests accounting should be applied, and may only be applied, in the case of a uniting of interests, where the shareholders of the combining enterprises combine control over the whole, or effectively the whole, of their net assets and operations to achieve a continuing mutual sharing in the risks and benefits attaching to the combined entity such that neither party can be identified as the acquirer. This requires that the substantial majority of the voting common shares of the combining enterprises be exchanged or pooled, that the fair value of one enterprise be not significantly different from that of the other, and that the shareholders of each enterprise maintain substantially the same voting rights and interests in the combined entity, relative to each other, after the combination as before. These criteria are equivalent to those in IAS 22.

3.2 Foreign Currency Translation

In dealing with foreign subsidiaries and associated companies, a distinction is made between foreign entities and direct foreign operations. (RJ 1.03.913). In drawing up their financial statements, for each of their foreign participating interests investors should classify their operations either as foreign entities or as direct foreign operations. Nonconsolidated foreign investments should always be regarded as foreign entities. For practical reasons, it is acceptable to group all foreign-based operations in one of the two categories, on the basis of the nature of the more important of those foreign operations (RJ 1.03.914).

In IAS 21 (revised 1993), a similar distinction is made, and "direct foreign operations" are defined as "foreign operations that are integral to the operations of the reporting enterprise." A difference with IAS 21 is that the option to group all foreign-based operations into one category for practical reasons is not available.

Foreign currency translation can also play a role in foreign currency transactions of the reporting entity itself. While the translation of foreign entities and direct foreign operations is discussed in Sections 3.2.1 and 3.2.2, respectively, the treatment of foreign currency transactions is discussed in Section 3.2.3.

3.2.1 Foreign Entities

A foreign entity is a type of foreign operation in which the foreign-based activities take place independently and where there are few or no connections between the cash flows arising from those activities and those of the investor (RJ 1.03.913).

In translating the assets and liabilities of foreign entities, the closing rate should be used, that is, the rate of exchange ruling at the balance sheet date. The resulting translation difference in relation to the shareholders' equity of (the net investment in) the foreign entity at the beginning of the accounting period should be taken directly to the investor's reserves (RJ 1.03.916/7), either to a separate foreign exchange equalization reserve or to the general reserves (other reserves). DSM accounts for the translation differences in its "other reserves" (note 5 to the legal entity's own balance sheet).

Income statement accounts should be translated at transaction rates or average rates for the period (RJ 1.03.919).

To the extent that the intragroup receivables and liabilities are in effect an expansion or contraction of the net investment in a foreign entity, the exchange differences arising on those receivables and liabilities should be taken directly to the reserves as well (RJ 1.03.921).

Furthermore, if a loan has been contracted in a foreign currency in order to finance or provide a hedge against the net investment, the exchange differences arising on the loan should also be taken directly to the reserves, to the extent that they are effective as a hedge against the exchange differences arising from the net investment (RJ 1.03.922). In its accounting policies, DSM mentions the situation of loans for hedging purposes.

These requirements are equivalent to those set by IAS 21, with the exception that the RJ does not require the cumulative exchange differences that have been deferred to be recognized as income or as expenses on disposal of the foreign entity (as does IAS 21).

3.2.2 Direct Foreign Operations

A direct foreign operation is defined as a foreign-based activity that is not a foreign entity. In such cases, the investor will look at the foreign activities primarily from its own currency point of view, because the investor regards the foreign subsidiary's assets and liabilities as its own (RJ 1.03.913). In the case of translating direct foreign operations, the temporal method is prescribed.

When current values are applied, the assets and liabilities of a direct foreign operation should be translated at the closing rate. The difference arising from this translation should be regarded as part of the revaluation, insofar as it relates to items for which a revaluation reserve has been created. The translation difference should be regarded as part of the income from ordinary operations, insofar as it relates to other items (RJ 1.03.923).

When historical cost accounting is applied, the assets, liabilities, income, and expenditure of direct foreign operations should be translated as if they directly form part of the financial statements of the investor. This means that fixed assets and stocks are to be translated at the rates ruling on the dates on which the valuation of the relevant item is based (historical rates) and other assets and liabilities at closing rates. Translation differences should be shown in the income statement as part of the result on ordinary operations (RJ 1.03.924/6).

In the income statement, items related to balance sheet items that have been translated at historical rates should likewise be translated at historical rates. The other income statement items should be translated at settlement rates or at average rates (RJ 1.03.925). These requirements are equivalent to those of IAS 21.

3.2.3 Foreign Currency Transactions

Transactions in foreign currencies that have been settled during the accounting period should be reported in the financial statements at the settlement rate (RJ 1.03.906). Where transactions have not been settled by the balance sheet date, assets and liabilities arising from those transactions should be carried in the balance sheet at the closing rate. Where the exchange risk has been hedged, this shall be taken into account in determining the results (RJ 1.03.907). DSM translates the assets and receivables that have been hedged at the forward rates.

The exchange gains and losses on short-term transactions and the exchange losses on long-term transactions should be taken to income in the period in which they arise. Exchange gains on long-term transactions are preferably accounted for in the same way, but it is also acceptable to allocate the gains over the period remaining to maturity. In that case the unallocated portion of such differences is shown in the balance sheet as a deferred gain. Subsequent exchange losses on long-term transactions in the same currency are deducted from this deferred gain (RJ 1.03.908/10). In the case of forward transactions that have been concluded as a hedge, the difference between the spot rate and the forward rate should be allocated over the duration of the forward transaction (RJ 1.03.911).

There is one important difference between the Dutch rules and IAS 21: IAS 21 does not allow any deferment of losses or gains, which is more restrictive than the Dutch rules.

3.3 Capital and Reserves

Shareholders' equity is specified only in the legal entity's financial statements, not in the consolidated statements, as can be illustrated in the DSM annual report. The legal specification (Article 373 (1)) is:

1. Issued share capital
2. Share premium (paid-in surplus)
3. Revaluation reserves
4. Other legally required reserves (subdivided according to their nature)
5. Statutory reserves
6. Other reserves
7. Retained profits

Some of these elements of shareholders' equity will be discussed in the following paragraphs.

3.3.1 Issued Share Capital

If the issued share capital has not been paid up, the legal specification starts with the paid-in capital or, if payments have been called, the capital paid in and called up. In these cases, the issued share capital is mentioned in the notes (Article 373 (2)).

It is possible for an NV or BV to purchase its own paid-up shares (or depositary receipts thereof), provided that the following four cumulative conditions are met (presented here in simplified form):

- The capital and reserves after purchase amount to no less than the called-up portion of the company's issued share capital, plus legal and statutory reserves;
- The nominal amount of the shares to be acquired does not exceed 10% (NV) or 50% (BV) of the issued capital.
- The articles of association allow the acquisition.
- The annual general meeting has authorized the executive directors to make the acquisition.

Article 373 (3) stipulates that the company's share capital may not be reduced by the amount of its own shares purchased. Furthermore, according to Article 385 (5), own shares may not be shown as assets. Therefore, the purchase price of the acquired own shares normally must be deducted from the other reserves (RJ 2.41.107). If the shares of the company are held by a subsidiary, the value attributed to the interest in the subsidiary should be reduced by the acquisition price of the shares (Article 385 (5)). If that subsidiary is a group company, the reduction normally should be made in full, irrespective of the interest in the subsidiary (RJ 2.03.220).

Information on share capital is disclosed in the DSM annual report in note 5 to the legal entity's own financial statements. In this note, information is also given on outstanding options on shares granted to employees.

3.3.2 *Revaluation Reserve*

A revaluation reserve is formed if assets and liabilities are valued at current value. When a company revalues an asset (at a higher amount), the company must carry in the balance sheet a revaluation reserve equal to the difference between the book value before and after the revaluation (Article 390 (1)). The revaluation reserve may be converted into share capital (Article 390 (2)).

Downward value adjustments reduce the revaluation reserve. Where the revaluation reserve is insufficient, the reduction in value is charged to the income statement and shown separately (Article 387(5)). The revaluation reserve may not be reduced below the sum of the revaluations included in the reserve in respect of assets that are still held by the company at the balance sheet date (Article 390 (3)). This is called the minimum position of the revaluation reserve (the unrealized revaluation).

The revaluation reserve must be reduced to the extent that the amounts transferred thereto are no longer necessary for the implementation of the valuation method adopted and for the object of the revaluation (Article 390(3)). This can be the case, for instance, when the financial structure is considered to be an integral part of the valuation system (gearing adjustment), so that the changes in value financed by capital other than equity are recognized in the income statement when realized (RJ 2.41.225).

Any reductions of the revaluation reserve that are taken to the income statement (for instance upon realization of the revaluation), are to be shown separately (Article 390 (4)). Realization of the revaluation can also lead to a transfer from the revaluation reserve to the other reserves.

The notes must disclose whether and in what way allowance has been made for the effect of taxation on revaluations (Article 390 (5)).

3.3.3 Legally Required Reserves

The aforementioned minimum position of the revaluation reserve is a legally required reserve. Other legal reserves include, among others:

- A reserve for capitalized incorporation and share issue expenses and the capitalized research and development costs (Article 365 (2));
- A reserve for undistributed profits of subsidiaries and associated companies accounted for under the equity method, unless the profits can be distributed on the authority of the company and received without limitations (Article 389 (4)). DSM has indicated that no legal reserve for retained profits is required (see note 5 to the own balance sheet).

The reserves may be created on an item-by-item basis or collectively for similar items (RJ 2.41.217), and they may be created as a charge against the profit appropriation account or against the free reserves (other reserves, retained profits). Reductions of the legal reserves (for instance, because of amortization of the capitalized costs or the distribution of profits) can also be credited to the free reserves or included in profit distribution (RJ 2.41.215). Legal reserves are mandatory, and they are intended to protect creditors against excessive profit distributions to shareholders.

3.3.4 Other Reserves and Retained Profits

Other reserves and retained profits are what are known as free reserves, and are normally disclosed together. A point at issue is whether direct movements in other reserves (bypassing the income statement) are allowed. The basic principle in the Netherlands is that of an all-inclusive income statement, with the only acceptable direct movements in shareholders' equity being the result of share issues, share reductions, dividend payments charged to the free reserves, and revaluations based on the current value method. However, several exceptions to this general rule prevail. As described in Section 3.2 above, a direct movement is required in the case of some foreign exchange translations. A direct movement in the other reserves is allowed for the following items (RJ 2.41.211):

- Goodwill (see Section 3.1)
- Adjustments to the provision for deferred tax liabilities resulting from changes in tax rates but only as far as related to deferred tax on revaluation
- The consequences of a financial reorganization under which creditors and shareholders surrender some or all of their rights, accompanied by the writing off of a loan
- Losses resulting from the destruction of assets (e.g., owing to a disaster), which it would have been impossible or unusual to insure against
- Losses resulting from nationalization, unexpected capital levies, or similar forms of expropriation
- The cumulative effect of changes in accounting policies (see Section 3.13.1)

The direct movements should be made net of tax.

In general, the IASC follows a stricter all-inclusive income statement approach. Insofar as IAS 8 (revised 1993) is interpreted in a way that all unusual items should be included in net income, the foregoing rules of the RJ are in conflict with IAS 8.

3.3.5 Financial Instruments: Classification as Equity or Liability

IAS 32, "Financial Instruments: Disclosure and Presentation," has been translated literally as a Dutch accounting standard (RJ 1.10). As a result, financial instruments are classified as a liability when there is a contractual obligation to deliver cash (or other financial assets) or to exchange financial instruments under potentially unfavorable conditions. If such a contractual obligation does not exist, the financial instrument is classified as equity. The substance of the contractual arrangements on initial recognition is decisive in this respect. However, there are two important differences between the Dutch standard and IAS 32. The first is that, according to IAS 32, the classification as equity or liability should be made on initial recognition. This classification may not be changed until derecognition applies. In the Netherlands, a change in classification is allowed in some restricted situations. Furthermore, IAS 32 requires the component parts of a financial instrument that contains both a liability and an equity element to be classified separately. This is the preferred method in the Netherlands, but classifying the financial instrument in one category is also permitted.

The disclosure requirements with respect to interest rate risk, credit risk, and fair values also apply in the Netherlands. An example of such disclosures can be found in note 17 to the consolidated statements of DSM.

3.4 Liabilities and Provisions

In the balance sheet, a distinction is made between provisions, long-term debts, and short-term debts. The term *liabilities* refers to all three elements. Furthermore, part of the liabilities are the accruals and deferred income, normally classified as a part of short-term debts. One element of deferred income, however, the equalization account for investment grants, is normally classified separately between shareholders' equity and provisions (see Section 3.5 below), as is the case in the DSM financial statements.

Some commitments are not shown in the balance sheet. In this respect a distinction is made between:

- Guarantee commitments: commitments to pay to a counter-party if a third party fails to honor its commitments, and commitments to bear the losses of third parties (RJ 2.65.1)
- Long-term financial commitments, including commitments in connection with operational leases (RJ 2.65.2)
- Other commitments not shown in the balance sheet, like commitments regarding payments on fixed assets and commitments in respect of purchase and sales contracts (RJ 2.65.3)

These commitments should normally be disclosed, partly because of Articles 376 and 381 (see Section 2.2, above).

DSM has shown these commitments in note 11 to the consolidated balance sheet and in note 8 to the legal entity's own balance sheet.

3.4.1 Debts

Debts should be carried under liabilities and may not be offset against assets for the financing of which debt has been contracted (RJ 2.51.104).

A debt that has to be paid or that will become due and payable not more than one year after it has come into existence is to be considered a short-term debt. If the agreed period for payment is longer, the debt will be of a long-term nature (RJ 2.51.105).

Debts are normally valued at face value.

3.4.2 Accruals and Deferred Income

Accruals and deferred income are normally classified under short-term debts. These items are a consequence of using the matching principle, and may be (RJ 2.62.102):

- Amounts received in advance for income to be recognized in subsequent periods, for instance, subscriptions and membership fees
- Amounts still to be paid after the balance sheet date relating to expenses imputed to a period that has elapsed, such as telephone costs, energy costs, and current interest on debts.

3.4.3 Provisions

According to Article 374 (1) the balance sheet shall show provisions against:

1. Liabilities and losses, the amount of which is uncertain at the balance sheet date but which can be reasonably estimated
2. Risks existing at the balance sheet date in respect of expected liabilities or losses, whose size can be reasonably estimated
3. Costs that will lead to an expense in a subsequent financial year, provided that a part of these costs originated before the balance sheet date and that the provision is intended to allocate costs evenly over a number of years

The provision under item 3 is a cost-smoothing provision. Regarding items 1 and 2, it is clear that not every uncertainty will provide grounds for making a provision.

Such grounds will exist only when two conditions are satisfied (RJ 2.53.105):

- There are concrete, specific risks, that is, risks attaching to particular assets or liabilities, or attaching to particular business activities. No provision is to be made for the general risk inherent in entrepreneurial activity.

- The risks must exist on the balance sheet date. They must arise from events that took place before the balance sheet date, from acts performed before that date or from commitments entered into before that date.

The general criteria for recognizing provisions under items 1 and 2 are the same as those for recognizing contingent losses in IAS 10.

A reduction in the value of an asset may not be expressed by creating a provision (Article 374 (2)). Provisions related to specific assets, for instance, provisions for stock obsolescence and bad debts, should be accounted for in the balance sheet as a deduction from the assets concerned (RJ 2.53. l03). Other provisions should be shown separately in the balance sheet on the liabilities side. The use of the term *reserve* for provisions is not acceptable; reserves are part of equity (RJ 2.53.107).

The notes must indicate, where possible, to what extent the provisions are regarded as long term (Article 374 (3)). A provision is regarded as long term when settlement is expected to take place after one year (RJ 2.53.110).

Provisions should be valued at face value, except for pension and similar provisions and provisions for deferred taxation (see Section 3.11 and 3.12 below) (RJ 2.53.111). The amount of a provision can be determined by using the static method or the dynamic method.

In applying the static method, the best possible estimate is made of the cash value of current liabilities and risks. When the company is running a (large) number of similar risks, the estimate may be made collectively. Otherwise, the estimate is made on an item-by-item basis (RJ 2.53.115).

In applying the dynamic method, the addition to the provision is calculated on the basis of a percentage of the amount of a related item. An example is the addition to the provision of bad debts as a percentage of sales effected in the period under review. A periodic examination of the validity of the underlying assumptions (for instance, the percentage used) will be essential (RJ 2.53.113/114).

Provisions must be subdivided (in the balance sheet or in the notes) according to the nature of the liabilities, losses, and costs for which they are made, and they must be precisely defined in accordance with their nature (Article 374 (3)). Article 374 (4) states that in any case, separate disclosure must be made of:

- Provisions for tax liabilities (hereafter called provisions for deferred taxation) that may arise after the financial year but which are chargeable to that financial year or to a preceding financial year, including a provision for taxation that may arise from a valuation at above purchase price or production costs
- Provisions for pension commitments

In addition to the legal distinction, the RJ identifies (RJ 2.53.9):

- Provisions related to early retirement of personnel and other release schemes (RJ 2.53.4)
- Provisions for specific assets
- Guarantee provisions
- Provisions for contract risks
- Provisions for risks from disputes and legal actions
- Provisions for cleaning environmental pollution
- Provisions for major maintenance
- Provisions for uninsured risks
- Provisions for costs related to the discontinuation of operations
- Provisions for redundancy payments
- Provisions for disability payments
- Provisions for site restoration costs

Several of these provisions are shown in the DSM annual report (note 9 to the consolidated financial statements).

We will not elaborate on these individual provisions, except for the provisions for deferred taxation and the provisions for pension commitments, which are discussed in Sections 3.11 and 3.12 below.

3.5 Property, Plant, and Equipment

Article 366 (1) identifies the following separate categories of tangible fixed assets:

1. Land and buildings

2. Plant and machinery
3. Other operating fixed assets, such as technical and office equipment
4. Fixed assets under construction, and payments on account
5. Tangible fixed assets not used in the production process (for instance dwellings for management and personnel and tangible fixed assets held as investments)

3.5.1 Valuation

The general principle of valuation is stated in Article 384 (1): in choosing a principle for the valuation of an asset and for the determination of the financial results, the company should be guided by the rules of Article 362. The general rule of Article 362 (1) is discussed in Section 2.2 above: financial statements should give a true and fair view. Article 384 (1) identifies two suitable bases for tangible fixed assets: historical cost (i.e., purchase price or production cost) and current value.

The purchase price of an asset is the price at which it was acquired. The term *production cost* is applicable to assets produced by the company, and it comprises the purchase price of the raw materials and consumables used and the other expenses attributable to the production of those assets. The production cost may include a reasonable proportion of the indirect costs and the interests on debts over the period attributable to the production of the asset (Article 388 (2)). If interest is included in the valuation of the assets, this must be stated in the notes. The foregoing is in line with IAS 16 (revised 1993) and IAS 23 (revised 1993), although specific rules on the capitalization of borrowing costs are lacking.

The current value of an asset is arrived at by means of the Asset Valuation Decree, which contains rules on the content, limits, and method of application in financial statements of the valuation of assets at current value. The current value of an asset can be the replacement value, the recoverable amount, or the net realizable value (RJ 103.203).

The replacement value is defined as the amount required to acquire or produce as a replacement for the existing asset another asset of equal significance economically for the operation of the business.

The recoverable amount is defined as the value, at the time of valuation, of net turnover attributable to the asset that may be generated by operating the business in which the asset is employed or for which it is intended.

The net realizable value is defined as the amount for which the asset can be sold to best advantage, net of the costs still to be incurred.

If replacement of the tangible fixed asset may reasonably be assumed, the relevant current value is the replacement value. Otherwise, the relevant current value is the recoverable amount if the asset will still be employed for the operation of the business, and the net realizable value if the asset will no longer be employed.

The choice between the valuation principles of historical cost (purchase price or production cost) and current value is in principle a free one. However, if the balance sheet and the income statement have been drawn up on the basis of historical cost, it should be considered whether the information on the basis of current value must be given in the notes per item (or heading) of the balance sheet and the income statement in order to give the true and fair view required (RJ 1.03.403). The information to be provided resembles that mentioned in IAS 15. DSM applies the principle of historical cost but provides limited supplementary data based on current value (see note 2 to the consolidated statements).

If the balance sheet has been drawn up on the basis of current value, the income statement should be based on current value as well (RJ 1.03.408). It is recommended (but not required) that there be the same uniformity between balance sheet and income statement in the case when the balance sheet has been drawn up on the basis of historical cost (RJ 1.03.408).

In IAS 16, property, plant, and equipment should be valued at either historical cost or at a revalued amount, with a preference for the first basis. Valuation in the context of a comprehensive system reflecting the effects of changing prices is allowed according to IAS 15. In the Netherlands there is only the basic choice between valuation at historical cost and at current value. When current value accounting is applied, revaluation should take place on a consistent basis. Incidental revaluation is not normally allowed. However, although the RJ suggests application of current value either to all tangible fixed assets and stocks or to none, in practice some companies carry part of the fixed assets at current value and part at historical costs. When the current value system is applied to a specific asset, however, revaluation takes place systematically.

When the current value principle is applied, changes in the current value are recognized in the revaluation reserve. The rules governing the revaluation reserve are discussed in Section 3.3 above.

Article 401 (2) states that investments, including investment properties, held by an investment company may be valued at market value. The market value of investment properties is considered to be equal to the net realizable value. The investment company may also apply the general rules of Article 384, including valuation at historical cost.

3.5.2 Depreciation

Depreciation and amortization must be applied irrespective of the results for the financial year. The methods of calculating depreciation and amortization must be stated in the notes (Article 386 (1,2)). Depreciation should take place on a consistent basis, taking into account the expected useful life, the estimated residual value, and the decline in value of the performance potential of the asset (Article 386 (4); RJ 2.02.216).

The depreciation method for tax purposes can be different from that for commercial purposes, for instance, accelerated depreciation for tax purposes and straight-line depreciation for commercial purposes. Differences are taken to the provision for deferred taxation (see Section 3.11 below).

The valuation basis for depreciation for tax purposes is historical cost. Depreciation on the basis of current value is not allowed. These differences may or may not be taken to the provision for deferred taxation (see also Section 3.11).

The depreciation guidelines are in line with IAS 16.

In addition to consistent depreciation, when valuing the tangible fixed assets at historical costs, it may be necessary to recognize other reductions in the value of the asset. Pursuant to Article 387 (4), it is mandatory to recognize a reduction in the value where this reduction is expected to be permanent. The lower value to be taken into account is either the net realizable value or the recoverable amount, but not the replacement value (RJ 2.02.224). The value adjustments must be charged to the income statement and shown separately. The charge must be reversed as soon as the value ceases to be reduced (Article 387 (5)).

Special write-downs for tax purposes in excess of what would be justifiable for commercial purposes may not be included in commercial financial statements.

3.5.3 Grants

Government grants related to tangible fixed assets (investment grants) may not be credited direct to shareholders' equity but should be either included separately as an equalization account under liabilities or deducted from the invested amount itself (RJ 3.01.110). The equalization account is normally classified between shareholders' equity and provisions (see the DSM balance sheet).

Each year, a part of the equalization account should be released to the income statement. This part should be calculated consistently with due regard to the way in which the expenditure for which the subsidy has been granted is itself accounted for in the financial statements (RJ 3.01.112).

If the subsidy is deducted from the invested amount, the yearly depreciation amounts are automatically lowered.

Account should be taken of any grant to be reimbursed.

Although the investment grant facility was abolished in 1988, the financial statements are still affected by grants received in the past. The accounting for government grants is in line with IAS 20.

3.6 Assets Whose Services Are Acquired by Means of Leases

In accounting for leases, a distinction is made between finance leases and operating leases. A finance lease is a form of financing in which the legal ownership of the asset generally remains with the lender (lessor), while the economic risks are borne entirely or almost entirely by the borrower (lessee). In the case of an operating lease, the economic risks are borne by the lessor. In practice, there are a number of hybrid forms. The terms of the contract as a whole determine whether the accounting method for finance leases or the accounting method for operating leases should be used (RJ 1.05.127). Some general guidelines for determining the existence of economic ownership are given in RJ 1.05.127, which states that economic ownership in principle exists where:

- The lessee has the right to buy the leased goods for an amount well below the expected fair value, or
- The lessor has the right to sell the leased goods to the lessee for an amount well above the expected fair value, or
- At any time during or immediately after expiration of the contract period entered into by the lessor, the lessee has the right to rent the goods for a rent that is substantially lower than expected market rentals, or
- The lease period amounts to 75% or more of the useful life of the leased assets, or

- The lessee is committed to the contract for a shorter period than the useful life but has an option to continue leasing the asset at a substantially lower rate for the ensuing period up to approximately the end of the useful life, or
- The discounted value of all payments to be made by the lessee in connection with the lease is 90% or more of the value of the leased asset at the commencement of the lease.

The quantitative criteria of 75% and 90% are taken from U.S. GAAP (FAS-13) and are not included in IAS 17 (revised 1997).

The accounting method for finance leases is for the lessee to capitalize the leased asset and to show the lease commitments as liabilities. Valuation should take place at the price that would have been paid in the event of a cash payment. If the cash price is not known, it is assumed to be the present value of the installments, excluding service charges. The interest rate to be applied should include a factor for credit risk. A proportion of the installment is accounted for as repayment of the lease commitment. The capitalized lease asset should be depreciated in line with the other tangible assets (RJ 2.02.220). It should be stated in the balance sheet or in the notes that the company is the economic but not the legal owner. In note 2 to the consolidated financial statements of DSM, the amount of capitalized leased assets is disclosed.

The accounting method for operating leases is for the lessor to capitalize the leased asset. An operating lease can never give rise to the leased items being carried as an asset in the balance sheet of the lessee. Where the legal entity has entered into commitments involving substantial sums of money for rather long periods, however, this should be disclosed in the notes (RJ 1.05.128). In note 11 to the DSM consolidated financial statements, the amount of long-term commitments concerning, among others, operating leases is disclosed.

The requirements for both operating and finance leases are in line with IAS 17, although in the Netherlands there are no specific requirements for lessor accounting.

3.7 Oil, Gas, and Other Mineral Resources

In the Netherlands, there are no specific requirements for oil and gas accounting. Therefore, in principle, there is a free choice between the full cost method and the successful-efforts method in accounting for exploration costs. According to the accounting policies for tangible fixed assets, DSM uses the successful-efforts method for investments relating to oil and gas recovery.

3.8 Intangible Assets

Article 365 distinguishes the following categories of intangible fixed assets:

1. Incorporation and share issue expenses
2. Research and development costs
3. Expenses related to concessions, licenses, and intellectual property rights
4. Cost of goodwill, acquired from third parties
5. Prepayments on intangible fixed assets

In addition to the intangible assets referred to in the law, there may be others such as brand names, publishing rights, and computer software. These assets are also included separately under intangible fixed assets (RJ 2.01.l03). DSM identifies "pre-operating and start-up expenses" as a special category.

The problem of accounting for goodwill was discussed in Section 3.1. If expenses referred to under items 1 and 2 above are capitalized, explanatory notes should be furnished and a legal reserve should be formed for the amounts at which these costs are capitalized (see Section 3.3 above) (Article 365(2)).

Intangible fixed assets are only shown in the balance sheet if there is a well-founded expectation that the future yields from these assets allow sufficient scope for amortization (RJ 2.01.108). Intangible assets cannot be valued at a price higher than the amount of expenditure or the price paid, with allowance being made for amortization (RJ 2.01.109).

Research and development costs meet the criteria for capitalization only if (RJ 2.01.111):

- The product or process is (accurately) defined and the costs to be allocated can be determined separately
- The technical feasibility of the product or process is proven
- The management has decided to introduce the new product or process and bring it on to the market or to start using it

- There is a clear indication of a future market for the product or process, or— if it is to be used internally instead of being sold—its usefulness to the company can be proved
- Sufficient funds are available or can reasonably be expected to become available for completion of the process and for the marketing (or the internal use) of the product or process.

Costs of research (basic research work) will very often not qualify for capitalization. In IAS 9 (revised 1993) research costs may never be capitalized, which is a stricter rule. The general criteria for capitalization of development costs in IAS 9 are similar to the above-mentioned criteria.

The total amount of the costs of research and development charged to the results for the financial year should be disclosed (RJ 2.01.123).

Intangible assets should be amortized consistently. Amortization in proportion to the sale or the use of the product or process also meets this requirement. When the future yields do not allow sufficient scope for consistent amortization, the intangible asset must be written down to its recoverable amount by means of exceptional amortization (RJ 2.01.113).

Incorporation and share issue expenses, and cost of research and development should be amortized over a maximum period of five years from their date of origin (Article 386 (3)).

There clearly is a need for revision of RJ Guideline 2.01, taking into account developments in practice. Several companies now capitalize publishing rights, brands, copyrights on music, and databases, sometimes without systematic amortization. The RJ has published a Consideration in this regard but is now waiting for IASC developments before turning this Consideration into a revised Guideline.

3.9 Participating Interests

Equity investments in other companies can be divided into three categories:

1. Participations in companies in which the investor exercises significant influence on business and financial policy
2. Participations in companies in which the investor does not exercise the significant influence indicated above
3. Equity investments that are not considered to be participations

An equity investment is considered to be a participation if there is a durable link between both companies and if the investment is undertaken for the purpose of the company's own activities (Article 24c (l)). To make it easier to ascertain whether a relationship of participation exists or not, the law has introduced a statutory assumption of participation. If the company or a subsidiary, alone or together with a subsidiary or group company, provides at least 20% of the issued capital, the existence of a participation is assumed. This statutory assumption may be refuted.

There is also a statutory assumption related to the question as to whether significant influence is exercised on the invested company. Significant influence is assumed if the company or one or more of its subsidiaries, alone or together, are authorized to cast 20% or more of the votes of members, partners, or shareholders at their own discretion. The statutory assumption in the foregoing paragraph was 20% of the issued capital; this statutory assumption is 20% of the voting rights. Normally, a significant influence will be assumed for all or most of the participations.

The applicable accounting method differs for the three types of equity investments.

Participations in which the investor exercises significant influence are accounted for by using the equity method, as described in Section 3.1 above (Article 389(1)). Recall that in legal entity accounts, investments in subsidiaries are accounted for by using the equity method (see Section 3.1 above). DSM uses the equity method for all its participations.

Participations in which the investor does not exercise significant influence are accounted for by using the cost method or the current value method (Article 384 (1)). In both cases, only the dividends declared are reflected in the income statement. The cost method implies valuation of the investment at purchase price, without making adjustments for amortization of goodwill. The current value method implies valuation at current value, but it is unclear how the current value of a participation should be measured.

Equity investments which are not considered to be participations can be classified as long-term investments (an element of the financial fixed assets in the balance sheet, as with DSM) or as short-term investments (an element of the investment category under current assets). The long-term investments may be valued at historical cost or at current value, while the short-term investments must be valued at the lower of historical cost and market value (net realizable value) (Article 384 (1)). If, in the case of the short-term investments, the market value is higher than the balance sheet value, the market value should be disclosed in the notes (RJ 2.13.108)

Notwithstanding the specific statutory rules, the RJ allows the possibility of marketable securities to be valued at higher market value, including the unrealized gains in the income statement (RJ 2.13.107/110). However, valuation at higher market value requires the use of Article 362 (4) (see Section 2.2), according to which the company is obliged to depart from the special requirements laid down in the law, should this be necessary for presenting a true and fair view. The reasons for applying Article 362 (4) should be disclosed, as well as the impact on the financial position and the profit or loss.

The above mentioned Dutch rules are generally in line with IAS 25, which allows current investments to be carried at either market value or the lower of cost or market value. A difference is that current investments that are not marketable securities may not be carried at market value.

3.10 Inventories

Article 369 distinguishes four categories of inventory:

1. Raw material and consumables
2. Work in progress
3. Finished goods and goods for resale
4. Payments on account of inventories

The valuation of inventories is similar to that of tangible fixed assets: Article 384 (1) allows the choice between historical cost and current value. The following specific rules for inventories apply:

- Similar components of inventories may be valued on the basis of weighted average prices or by the FIFO method, the LIFO method, or some similar method, such as the base stock method (Article 385 (2))
- If the LIFO method, or a similar method is used, the current value of the inventory should either be shown in the balance sheet or disclosed in the notes (RJ 2.11.212).
- If the inventories are valued at historical cost and the market value (net realizable value) is lower, a downward value adjustment to the lower market value should be made (Article 387 (2)); where an exceptional reduction in the value of inventories in the near future is foreseeable, this may be taken into account (Article 387 (3)).

- The recoverable amount may not be used in determining the current value of inventories; the only alternative to the replacement value is the net realizable value, to be used when replacement is not anticipated, or when the net realizable value is lower than the replacement value (RJ 1.03.2; Asset Valuation Decree).

The valuation for tax purposes does not affect the valuation for accounting purposes.

The historical cost rules for inventories are in line with IAS 2 (revised 1993), although the base stock method is not explicitly forbidden in the Netherlands.

DSM values raw materials and consumables at the historical purchase prices plus additional costs or, if lower, at the current price on the purchase market plus additional costs. Work in progress and finished products are valued at manufacturing cost (excluding internal storage costs, selling expenses, and interest charges) or at the lower net realizable value. Products for which the manufacturing cost cannot be calculated because of shared cost components are stated at net realizable price after deduction of a margin.

Accounting for work in progress under long-term contracts (construction contracts) depends on the possibility of making a reliable estimate of the outcome of the contract (RJ 2.11.406). When a reliable estimate can be made, the percentage of completion method should be applied. The percentage of completion method requires revenue (including allocated profit) and costs incurred to be recognized by reference to the stage of completion of the contract activity at the balance sheet date.

When no reliable estimate can be made, profit should be recognized at the completion of the contract. For recognition of revenue and costs, two alternatives exist:

- Revenues may be recognized to the extent of costs incurred that are recoverable, while at the same time costs are recognized when incurred

- Revenues and costs are recognized at the completion of the contract (completed contract method).

Expected losses should always be taken into account.
IAS 11 (revised 1993) does not allow the completed contract method.

3.11 Taxation

In the Netherlands there is a distinction between calculating reported income and taxable income. The calculation of reported income is based on the principles outlined so far and is directed at presenting a true and fair view.

Taxable income is calculated on the basis of rules identified in tax law and is directed at determining a fair tax charge.

One basic rule in tax law is that in calculating taxable income the principles of accounting for reporting purposes should be used, except when different specific rules are given. One of these specific rules is that tangible fixed assets should always be depreciated on the basis of historical cost; depreciation on the basis of current value is not allowed. With the exception of these specific rules, it is possible for reported income and taxable income to be the same, and this will often be the case with smaller companies. However, it is also possible to choose one acceptable policy for determining reported income and another acceptable policy for determining taxable income. Larger companies normally choose that option. The general situation is that in those cases, the prudence concept plays a much more important role in calculating taxable income than it does in calculating reported income. Therefore, taxable income will normally be lower than reported income, and a provision for deferred taxation is included on the liabilities side of the balance sheet.

3.11.1 Deferred Tax Liabilities

The provision for deferred taxes should be presented separately, either in the balance sheet or in the notes, as in the DSM financial statements (Article 374 (4)). Valuation of deferred taxes at either nominal value or present value is acceptable (RJ 2.53.510). DSM applies valuation at nominal value.

Tax allocation should be made on the basis of the fully comprehensive method (full provision). Partial tax allocation (partial provision) is not allowed (RJ 2.53.509). The liability method should be used to calculate the deferred tax liability (RJ 2.53.515).

A tax liability can be accrued for taxes payable on the distribution of retained earnings of subsidiaries and associated companies. However, there is no obligation to do so (RJ 2.03.504) .

In general, the above rules are in line with IAS 12 (revised 1996), with the exception that valuation of deferred taxes at present value is not allowed in IAS 12.

3.11.2 Deferred Tax Assets

The general rule is that deferred tax assets should be recognized to the extent that it is reasonable to expect future profits for tax purposes to be sufficient to offset the deferred tax debits (RJ 2.53.512). Deferred tax assets are always recognized if there are deferred tax credits (provisions) that can be set off against the debits. However, deferred tax credits either arising from revaluations to current cost or disputed by tax authorities may not be taken into account for this purpose.

The general rule also applies to deferred tax debits attributable to a tax loss carryforward (RJ 2.53.520). The carryforward period in the Netherlands is not limited. There is a carryback period of 3 years. Carryback does not give rise to a deferred tax asset, but to a tax receivable.

When deferred tax debits and credits are of the same duration, the net figure may be shown in the balance sheet when they relate to the same tax group (RJ 2.53.512). The amount of deferred tax assets not accounted for in the balance sheet should be disclosed separately (RJ 2.53.513).

The requirements concerning the recognition of deferred tax assets are in line with IAS 12.

3.11.3 Deferred Taxes and Current Value Accounting

The deferred tax resulting from the application of current value accounting is not normally a timing difference but a permanent difference, as tax law does not allow depreciation on the basis of current value. This means that part of the depreciation costs in the financial statements is not accepted in calculating taxable income. This extra tax charge may be accounted for by charging it to equity (revaluation reserve) or to the income statement (RJ 2.53.533).

Apart from accounting for this extra tax charge, there is the option to present in the balance sheet at the moment of revaluation a deferred tax provision charged to the revaluation reserve, but there is no obligation to do so (Article 390 (5)). IAS 12 requires the recognition of a deferred tax liability. Upon realization of the deferred tax (by depreciation), the deferred tax provision, if identified, is either added to the revaluation reserve again (when the extra tax is charged to the income statement) or reduced against the extra tax payment (in which case the extra tax charge is charged to equity) (RJ 2.53.533). IAS 12 requires the extra tax be charged to equity.

3.12 Pensions

3.12.1 Pension Systems

In the Netherlands the usual systems of accruing pension entitlements are (RJ 2.53.301):

- Defined contribution plan: the amounts to be paid as retirement benefits are determined by reference to contributions to a fund with investment earnings thereon
- Defined benefit plan: the amounts to be paid as retirement benefits are determined by reference to a formula, usually based on employees' remuneration and/or years of service; typical alternatives are the average pay system (related to the wages in the individual years of service) and the final pay system (related to the wage at the time of retirement).

When a pension scheme is being introduced or improved, pension entitlements are sometimes granted in respect of past service as if the new scheme had been applicable from the commencement of the service. The ensuing liability is called back-service (or past-service) liability (RJ 2.53.306).

If a legal entity operating in the Netherlands makes legally enforceable commitments towards its employees in the matter of retirement benefits, under the Pension Funds and Savings Funds Act those commitments are in general required to be covered by a life insurance company, a company pension fund, or an industry-wide pension fund (RJ 2.53.303).

There are only a number of cases in which the Pension Funds and Savings Funds Act permits the legal entity to provide funds to cover pension entitlements itself. One example is the case of retirement benefits for directors who are also major shareholders.

Funding must take place by means of the advance funding system, which implies that the funds are provided during the employee's active working life (RJ 2.53.307).

3.12.2 Accounting for Pension Liabilities

In valuing the provisions for pension commitments, a choice may be made between the static method and the dynamic method (see Section 3.4 above) (RJ 2.53.310). In either case, valuation should be at present value (or discounted value). There are no requirements regarding the interest rate to be used in discounting. There is only the recommendation to give an indication of the interest rate used (RJ 2.53.324).

Retirement benefits are normally determined by using an accrued benefit valuation method as required by IAS 19 (revised 1998).

A provision for pension liabilities is to be made in the following situations:

- For pension costs (for instance, back-service) to be paid by way of future premiums (RJ 2.53.313)
- For deficits in the company's pension fund (RJ 2.53.314)
- For conditional entitlements, even if they are not legally enforceable (RJ 2.53.318)
- For entitlements to be granted on the basis of a company's firm intention to make legally enforceable pension arrangements (RJ 2.53.319)

A recommendation for a provision is made for the share in the deficits of an industry-wide pension fund.

Surpluses in a company's pension fund should be taken into account when they are considered to be of a permanent nature.

Dutch accounting for pensions is normally of a static nature, not taking into account future salaries and other future developments (as in the projected benefit valuation method), and on the other hand not allocating unconditional back-service costs to future periods. The RJ has recently explicitly accepted foreign pension accounting standards (indicating IAS 19, FAS-87, and SSAP-24), however, taking into account that the minimum liability for all vested benefits should at the least always be recognized, even if this would not be required by the foreign standards.

3.12.3 Early Retirement Schemes

In the case of an early retirement scheme, a provision should be made for the liability that arises (RJ 2.53.405). The provision should be made for all employees who have already opted for the scheme for the entire period, for employees who under the existing scheme are entitled to opt for early retirement but have not yet done so, and for other employees who are not yet entitled to exercise that option but who will be able to do so while the existing scheme is in operation.

3.13 Some Other Topics

In this section we will discuss four other important topics:

1. Changes in accounting policies
2. Extraordinary items
3. Post-balance sheet events
4. Specific industry rules

3.13.1 Changes in Accounting Policy

One of the basic principles in preparing financial statements is that of consistency. The consistency principle means that changes in accounting policies normally should not be made. Changes, relating to the presentation of financial statements and to the principles of valuation and income determination, however, may be made when there are justified reasons for doing so (Articles 363 (4), 384 (6)). A basic justified reason is to present a better true and fair view by using the new accounting policy.

Changes should, if possible, be accounted for retrospectively, that is, as if the new policy had always been in use. The resulting cumulative effect may be accounted for either as an immediate adjustment of shareholders' equity or as an extraordinary item in the income statement (RJ 1.06.113/ 117). There is a preference for the first method. The effect of the change on shareholders' equity and on net income should be disclosed (RJ 1.06.121). The comparative figures for the year before should be adjusted to the new policy, irrespective of the method in accounting for the cumulative effect (RJ 1.06.118). The adjustment of the comparative figures is made only to retain comparability, and it does not formally adjust the previous year's financial statements. Adjustment of historical summaries is recommended but not required (RJ 1.06. 119).

Comparable requirements exist for accounting for fundamental errors (RJ 1.07). In general, there is agreement between these Dutch requirements and IAS 8 (revised 1993).

3.13.2 Extraordinary Items

Article 377 (1) requires that, among other things, income and expense arising from ordinary activities, and extraordinary income and expense be shown separately in the income statement. In Article 377 (7), extraordinary income and expense are defined as income and expense arising otherwise than in the ordinary course of the company's business. According to the RJ (2.71.205), the frequency of occurrence is important in this respect. Possible examples are:

- Insurance payments, to the extent that they differ from the book value of the assets lost
- Gains/losses on the disposal of participating interests
- Changes arising from reorganizations or related to discontinuity
- Special provisions, such as those for litigation

Examples of extraordinary items are given in note 18 to the consolidated statements of DSM. Income and expenses that are substantially larger in volume than is usual for the enterprise, but that nevertheless arise from its ordinary operations, should not be regarded as extraordinary income and expense (RJ 2.71.213).

The cumulative effect of a change in accounting principle, when accounted for in the income statement, is always an extraordinary item.

The concept of extraordinary items in IAS 8 differs substantially from that in the Netherlands. Although the definition of an extraordinary item according to IAS 8 resembles that of Article 377, the interpretation is different. The examples mentioned above would probably never be an extraordinary item according to IAS 8. Examples IAS 8 mentions are gains and losses from the expropriation of assets and from an earthquake.

3.13.3 Post-Balance Sheet Events

For post-balance sheet events a distinction can be made between (RJ 4.03.103):

- Information that becomes known after the balance sheet date and provides further details of the actual position at the balance sheet date; this information should be accounted for when the annual accounts are drawn up (changing the balance sheet and income statement, when necessary); and

- Particulars that become known after the balance sheet date and that give no further information on the actual situation at the balance sheet date; these particulars should not be accounted for in the financial statements, unless they raise doubt about the going-concern assumption; if these particulars have important financial consequences, they should be disclosed in the section on other data (see Section 2.1 above).

These requirements are in line with IAS 10.

3.13.4 Specific Industry Rules

The Dutch civil code contains specific industry rules for insurance companies, credit institutions, and investment companies. Those companies normally must use the general principles of Title 9, with some specific additions.

Insurance Companies For insurance companies, new regulation came in force in 1995. The regulation is included in Articles 427–446. Generally speaking, all options in the EC Insurance Directive have been included in Dutch law. The RJ has published Guideline 3.23 on accounting by insurance companies to interpret and extend the legal requirements. It would be beyond the scope of this chapter to go into detail in this respect. However, one interesting feature should be elucidated: accounting for investment. All investments may be measured at historical cost or at market value (for fixed-rate investments amortized value is an additional alternative). When measured at market value, changes in market value may be accounted for in the following ways (RJ 3.23.217):

- Unrealized and realized changes are recognized in the revaluation reserve
- Unrealized changes are recognized in the revaluation reserve; upon realization the cumulative changes are recognized in income
- All changes, realized and unrealized, are recognized in income
- Unrealized and realized changes are recognized in the revaluation reserve and an amount is transferred yearly to income, following a

system that takes into account the long-term yield on investments (specifically for shares).

For fixed rate investments, like bonds, carried at cost or amortized value, gains and losses on sale before maturity may be amortized until original maturity date, but only when the sold investments have been replaced by new investments in the same category.

Besides the rules for financial reporting to shareholders, policyholders, and the general public, there are separate rules for giving detailed financial information to the Insurance Supervisory Authority (*Verzekeringskamer*).

Banks　For banks, the new regulation, in force from 1993 on, is included in Articles 415–426 and in the Bank Accounting Decree. For banks the same holds as for insurance companies: generally speaking, all options in the EC Bank Directive have been included in Dutch law. Again, we will not go into detail, with the exception of accounting for investments and for general banking risks.

For banks, investments are either part of the investment portfolio (long-term) or of the trading portfolio. The measurement principles are equivalent to those for insurance companies, with the dominant practice being that shares are measured at market value and that fixed-rate investments are measured at amortized value when they are part of the investment portfolio and at market value when they are part of the trading portfolio. Changes in market value in the trading portfolio, realized and unrealized, are included in the profit and loss account. Changes in market value of shares in the investment portfolio are recognized in the revaluation reserve and are transferred to income upon realization.

Regarding general banking risks it has always been possible to understate certain assets by at most 4% of book value. However, beginning with financial statements of 1997, all banks have abolished the secret reserves and most have replaced them by a Fund for General Banking Risks. This fund is disclosed in the balance sheet and all additions and deductions are separately disclosed in the profit and loss account. However, the fund is not part of group equity, and all movements in the fund are taken into account when determining net income.

Banks are also required to give detailed information to the Dutch Central Bank. The Dutch Central Bank will publish additional detailed accounting and disclosure rules in this respect, which go beyond the general rules in Dutch law. In their reporting to the Central Bank, banks are required to follow these detailed rules. In their reporting to shareholders, clients, and the general public, however, they are only restricted by the requirements in the law.

Investment Companies   Financial reporting rules for investment companies are of a general nature and are included in Article 401. The RJ has published Guideline 3.22 on accounting by investment companies. In general, the RJ prefers measurement of all investments at market value and recognizing all changes, realized and unrealized, in income. However, on the basis of legal regulation, it is also allowed to include only realized gains in income or even to recognize all realized and unrealized changes in market value in a separate reserve as part of shareholders' equity.

Other Industry Rules   The RJ has also published guidelines on pension funds (RJ 3.26), cooperative associations (RJ 3.31), housing associations (RJ 3.61), and charity institutions (RJ 3.81).

4. Expected Future Developments

As described in the foregoing sections, the Netherlands has a tradition of financial reporting aimed at presenting a true and fair view—a good insight into financial position and results. The impact of tax law on financial reporting is minimal. This tradition resembles that of the IASC and of practice in the United Kingdom and the United States. The basic idea of presenting a true and fair view is deep-seated and will certainly not change in the near future.

One of the important differences with practice in the United Kingdom and the United States is the less powerful role of the accounting standard-setting body. Companies may deviate from published accounting standards when they consider it to be acceptable for presenting a true and fair view, and they need not disclose the deviation as part of the notes to their financial statements. This is one of the reasons why Nobes and Parker (Comparative International Accounting, 1998) consider Dutch accounting to be "extremely judgmental" and state: "International and EC harmonization notwithstanding, Dutch accounting is still *sui generis*" (p. 164). The *sui generis* aspect has also to do with the traditional impact of current value accounting as an element of presenting a true and fair view. The isolated position of Dutch accounting is vividly described in Zeff, Camfferman, and Van der Wel (*Company Financial Reporting*, North-Holland, 1992)

There are, however, indications that in the future Dutch accounting will be gradually more influenced by international harmonization. Some of these indications are the following:

1. The call for less flexibility in applying accounting standards and the call for adoption of IASC standards as much as possible (see Zeff, Camfferman and Van der Wel (1992), as well as the proceedings of the conference on the future of financial reporting in the Netherlands: *Financial Reporting in the Nineties, Regulation and Innovation at a Crossroads*, Kluwer Bedrijfswetenschappen, 1992).

2. The near abolition of the use of the current value accounting system in the primary statements, as a consequence of the worldwide use of historical cost accounting

3. The use of some FASB accounting standards by multinationals, like Royal Dutch/Shell and Philips; examples are the use of FAS-87 on pensions and FAS 95 on cash flow statements.

4. The literal translation of the IASC Conceptual Framework, with the intention of considering this to be the Dutch Conceptual Framework as well

5. The fact that the most recent Dutch accounting standards are explicitly based on or adapted from IASC standards: examples are those on cash flow statements, long-term construction contracts, pooling-of-interests accounting, and accounting for joint ventures. IAS 32 on financial instruments has even been translated literally as a Dutch standard.

These indications might be the forerunners of Dutch accounting adapting to the international community.

Useful Address

Nederlands Institut van Registeraccountants
AJ Ernststraat 55 (1083 GR)
Postbus 7984
1008 AD Amsterdam
Netherlands
Tel: +(20) 3010301
Fax: +(20) 3010302

Appendix A: Comparisons with IASC Standards and U.S. GAAP

1. International Accounting Standards

The following International Accounting Standards correspond in all material respects with the requirements in the Netherlands (updated until 1997):

- IAS 1 Disclosure of Accounting Policies (to be replaced)
- IAS 1 Presentation of Financial Statements
- IAS 4 Depreciation Accounting
- IAS 5 Information to be Disclosed in Financial Statements
- IAS 7 Cash Flow Statements (revised 1992)
- IAS 10 Contingencies and Events Occurring after the Balance Sheet Date
- IAS 13 Presentation of Current Assets and Current Liabilities
- IAS 15 Information Reflecting the Effects of Changing Prices
- IAS 18 Revenue (revised 1993)
- IAS 20 Accounting for Government Grants and Disclosure of Government Assistance
- IAS 23 Borrowing Costs (revised 1993)
- IAS 24 Related Party Disclosures
- IAS 31 Financial Reporting of Interests in Joint Ventures

The following International Accounting Standards do not fully correspond with the requirements in the Netherlands (only the most important differences between the IASC regulations and the Dutch requirements are explained):

- IAS 2 Inventories (revised 1993)

  IAS 2 forbids the use of the base stock method. This method is not explicitly forbidden in the Netherlands.

- IAS 8 Net Profit or Loss for the Period, Fundamental Errors and Changes in Accounting Policies (revised 1993)

  Insofar as IAS 8 is interpreted in a way that all unusual items should be included in net income, IAS 8 is in conflict with the Guidelines of the RJ which allow certain items to be directly recognized in a shareholders' equity.

Furthermore, the concept of extraordinary items in IAS 8 is substantially more restrictive than in the Netherlands.

- IAS 9 Research and Development Costs (revised 1993)

  IAS 9 never allows research costs to be capitalized. In the Netherlands capitalization is allowed, but only when the general conditions for capitalization are met, which will seldom be the case for research costs.

- IAS 11 Construction Contracts (revised 1993)

  In case no reliable estimate can be made of the outcome of the contract, IAS 11 requires the recognition of revenue to the extent of costs incurred that are recoverable and the recognition of costs as an expense in the period when incurred. This method is allowed in the Netherlands, but as an alternative the completed contract method may be applied, which method is not allowed according to IAS 11.

- IAS 12 Accounting for Taxes on Income (revised 1996)

  In the Netherlands, valuation at present value is allowed, which is not in line with IAS 12.

- IAS 14 Reporting Financial Information by Segment (revised 1997)

  A breakdown of profit/loss and assets employed (among others), comparable to the breakdown of net turnover as discussed above, is not required in the Netherlands, contrary to IAS 14.

- IAS 16 Property, Plant and Equipment (revised 1993)

  Changes in useful life may be applied retrospectively in the Netherlands for gains and should be applied retrospectively for losses. Retrospective application implies that the cumulative effect is recognized in income. IAS 16 allows only prospective application.

- IAS 17 Accounting for Leases (revised 1997)

  In the Netherlands, there are no specific requirements concerning lessor accounting.

- IAS 19 Retirement Benefit Costs (revised 1993)

  In IAS 19, it is required to allocate back-service costs systematically over a period not exceeding the expected remaining working lives of the participating employees. This method is not allowed in the Netherlands: in the case of unconditional back service entitlements, immediate recognition is required.

- IAS 21 The Effects of Changes in Foreign Exchange Rates (revised 1993)

  The RJ allows all foreign-based operations to be grouped in one category for practical reasons, which is not allowed by IAS 21. In the Netherlands, exchange gains on long-term transactions may be deferred, which is not allowed by IAS 21. Finally, the RJ does not require the cumulative exchange differences that have been deferred to be recognized as income or as expenses on disposal of the foreign entity.

- IAS 22 Business Combinations (revised 1993)

  IAS 22 requires positive goodwill to be capitalized and amortized, while Dutch law allows goodwill to be written off direct to reserves. For negative goodwill, proportional reduction of nonmonetary assets to amounts below the fair value (the benchmark treatment in IAS 22) is not allowed in the Netherlands. On the other hand, direct recognition of negative goodwill in shareholders' equity is not allowed by IAS 22.

- IAS 25 Accounting for Investments

  IAS 25 allows current investments to be carried at either market value or the lower of cost or market value. In the Netherlands, current investments that are not marketable securities must be carried at the lower of cost or market value.

- IAS 26 Accounting and Reporting by Retirement Benefit Plans

  The RJ has recently published a Guideline (3.26) on accounting by pension funds. An important difference is that, while IAS 26 requires investments to be carried at fair value, this is only an option in the Netherlands.

- IAS 27 Consolidated Financial Statements and Accounting for Investments in Subsidiaries

  IAS 27 does not allow exclusion from consolidation of group companies with dissimilar business activities, but Dutch law does allow exclusion when consolidation of the group company would conflict with the true and fair view. According to IAS 27, investments in subsidiaries may be accounted for in the legal entity's own financial statements by using the cost method. In the Netherlands, valuation according to the equity method is required.

- IAS 28 Accounting for Investments in Associates

  According to IAS 28, investments in associates may be accounted for in the legal entity's own financial statements by using the cost method. In the Netherlands, valuation according to the equity method is required.

- IAS 29 Financial Reporting in Hyperinflationary Economies

  No specific rules exist in the Netherlands.

- IAS 30 Disclosures in the Financial Statement of Banks and Similar Financial Institutions

  The Fund for General Banking Risks is fully disclosed but is not part of shareholders' equity (as required by IAS 30). Furthermore, all movements in the Fund are included in determining net income.

- IAS 32 Financial Instruments: Disclosure and Presentation

  According to IAS 32 the classification as equity or liability should be made on initial recognition. This classification may not be changed until derecognition applies. In the Netherlands, a change in classification is allowed in some restricted situations.

  IAS 32 requires the component parts of a financial instrument that contains both a liability and an equity element to be classified separately. This is the preferred method in the Netherlands, but it is also permitted to classify the financial instrument in one category.

- IAS 33 Earnings Per Share

  In the Netherlands it is not required to publish earnings per share figures.

The following International Accounting Standards are no longer operative:

- IAS 3 Consolidated Financial Statements (superseded by IAS 27 and IAS 28)
- IAS 6 Accounting Responses to Changing Prices (superseded by IAS 15)

2. U. S. GAAP

An in-depth comparison between the requirements in the Netherlands and U. S. Generally Accepted Accounting Principles (U.S. GAAP) would be too lengthy. A general difference is the level of detail of the requirements: the U.S. requirements are far more detailed than those in the Netherlands. In this section we limit ourselves to a short description of some of the most important differences.

Most requirements in the United States are laid down in:

- The Statements of Financial Accounting Standards (FAS) of the Financial Accounting Standards Board (FASB)
- The Opinions of the Accounting Principles Board (APB), the predecessor of the FASB
- The Accounting Research Bulletins (ARB) of the Committee on Accounting Procedure (CAP), the predecessor of the APB.

  1. The companies to be included in the consolidated statements

     U.S. GAAP (FAS-94) requires consolidation of all majority-owned subsidiaries. In the Netherlands, group companies must be excluded from consolidation when this would conflict with the true and fair view.

  2. Research and development costs

     In the Netherlands, research and development expenses may be capitalized when certain conditions are met. In the United States (FAS-2), these expenses should always be charged to income when incurred, except for expenses related to computer software (FAS-86).

3. Valuation of tangible fixed assets

   U.S. GAAP (APB Opinion No. 6) requires valuation on the basis of historical costs. In the Netherlands, valuation at current value is acceptable as well.

4. Goodwill

   U.S. GAAP (APB Opinion No. 17) requires goodwill to be capitalized and amortized over the expected useful economic life. The maximum period of amortization is 40 years.

   In the Netherlands, capitalization and amortization is an acceptable policy. Amortization should take place on the basis of the expected useful life. A maximum period of amortization is not defined. However, goodwill may also be charged directly to shareholders' equity and this policy is the dominant policy in practice. A direct charge to shareholders' equity is not allowed in the US.

5. Valuation of inventories

   U.S. GAAP (ARB No. 43) requires valuation on the basis of historical costs. In the Netherlands, valuation at current value is acceptable as well.

6. The provision for pensions

   Dutch accounting for pensions is normally of a static nature, not taking into account future salaries and other future developments, and on the other hand not allocating unconditional back-service costs to future periods. The RJ has recently explicitly accepted foreign pension accounting standards (among them FAS-87), however, taking into account that the minimum liability for all vested benefits should at least always be recognized, even if this would not be required by the foreign standards.

7. Changes in accounting policy

   In most cases, U.S. GAAP (APB Opinion No. 20) requires recognition of the cumulative effect of the accounting change in net income. This is allowed in the Netherlands as well, although a preference exists for immediate recognition in shareholders' equity and adjustment of the comparative figures.

Appendix B: EU Directives and Dutch Legislation

1. The Fourth Directive and Dutch Legislation

In this section an overview is given of the options of the Fourth Directive and of the choices that are made in the Netherlands. First, the option will be stated, then the choice made, including the related article numbers in Title 9 or the governmental decrees (article numbers mentioned as such in the "choice" section relate to Title 9; article numbers stated in the "option" section relate to the Fourth Directive). The phrase "option adopted" means that the free choice in the Fourth Directive is a free choice in Dutch law as well.

Option 1. The balance-sheet and profit and loss account items that are preceded by arabic numerals may be combined in the interests of clarity. However, items so combined must be dealt with separately in the notes on the accounts (Article 4(3)(b)).

Choice. Option adopted (combination is allowed) (Governmental Decree on the Standard Chart of Accounts, Article 8).

Option 2. Where the figures and items in the balance sheet and in the profit and loss account are not comparable with the corresponding figures for the preceding financial year, the later figures may be adjusted. Any adjustment of the figures must be disclosed in the notes on the accounts, with relevant comments (Article 4(4)).

Choice. Adjustment is required (Article 363(5)).

Option 3. Member states may authorize or require the layout of the balance sheet and the profit and loss account to be adapted to include the appropriation of profit or the treatment of loss (Article 6). Where the appropriation of profit or the treatment of loss appears in the annual accounts, it need not be disclosed separately (Article 50).

Choice. Option adopted (Governmental Decree on the Standard Chart of Accounts, Article 11).

Option 4. For the presentation of the balance sheet, Member states may prescribe a layout in account form (Article 9) or in vertical form (Article 10) or they may allow companies to choose between the two forms (Article 8).

Choice. Companies are allowed to choose between the two forms (Governmental Decree on the Standard Chart of Accounts, Article 1).

Option 5. The following options are available for showing capital (Article 9, Assets A and D II 5, Liabilities A l; Article 10 A, D 115 and L 1):

(a) Subscribed capital to be shown on the liabilities side under A I or L 1.

The subscribed capital unpaid must then be shown under A on the assets side. The portion of subscribed capital called must be disclosed.

(b) The part of the capital called is to be shown on the liabilities side under A I or L 1, with the amounts of subscribed and paid-up capital being shown separately. Under those circumstances, the part of the capital called but not yet paid is to be shown on the assets side, either under A or under D II ("Debtors") 5.

Choice. Alternative (b) is required (Article 373 (2)).

Option 6. Formation expenses (Article 9, Assets B; Article 10 B):

(a) These expenses may be shown as an asset. They must be written off within a maximum period of 5 years. If such expenses have not been completely written off, there are restrictions on the distribution of profits. The amounts entered under "formation expenses" must be explained in the notes on the accounts (Article 34).

(b) In the event of such expenses appearing as an asset, they may be shown either under B or as the first item under "Intangible assets" (CI).

Choice. The option under (a) is adopted, with the expenses to be indicated as "incorporation and share issue expenses" (Article 365 (1, 2) and 386 (3)). Concerning (b) the item is required to be shown as the first item of intangible assets (Article 365 and the formats included in the Governmental Decree on the Standard Chart of Accounts).

Option 7. Concessions, patents, licenses, trademarks, and similar rights and assets may be shown as assets even if they were created by the undertaking itself (Article 9, Assets C12(b);Article 10 C I 2(b)).

Choice. They may only be shown as assets as far as expenditures to third parties are made (Article 365 (2)).

Option 8. Research and developments costs.

(a) These costs may be shown as assets (Article 9, Assets C I 1; Article 10 C 1 1). The amounts entered must be explained in the notes on the accounts (Article 37 (1) and Article 34).

(b) Where they are shown as an asset they may either be written off within a maximum period of 5 years or in exceptional cases (the reasons for which must be disclosed in the notes on the accounts) within a longer period (Article 37 (1)) EC Directives and Dutch legislation 223

(c) In exceptional cases (the reasons for which must be disclosed in the notes on the accounts), derogations from the restrictions on the distribution of profits during the depreciation period may be allowed (Article 37 (1)).

Choice. The option under (a) is adopted (Article 365 (1)). Concerning (b) the maximum period is always 5 years (Article 386 (3)). The option under (c) is not adopted: derogations from the restrictions on the distribution of profits are never allowed (Article 36S (2)).

Option 9. Goodwill may be systematically written off over a limited period exceeding 5 years, provided that this period does not exceed the useful economic life of the asset and is disclosed in the notes on the accounts together with the reasons for so doing (Article 37 (2)).

Choice. Option adopted (Article 386 (3)).

Option 10. Own shares may be shown as an asset. If they represent fixed assets, they are to be shown on the assets side under C III 7 or, if they represent current assets, under D III 2. It is specifically prohibited for them to be shown in items other than those prescribed (Article 13 (2)). Furthermore, in the case of public limited companies a transfer to reserve must be made on the liabilities side (Article 9, Liabilities A IV 2 or Article 10 L IV 2).

Choice. Option not adopted. Own shares should be subtracted from shareholders' equity (Article 378 (2)).

Option 11. Prepayments and accrued income.

(a)   These are to be shown either under E or under "Debtors" in D 116.

(b)   Income which is not due until after the expiration of the financial year in question may be included in "Debtors" (Article 18).

Choice. Both options adopted (Governmental Decree on the Standard Chart of Accounts, Article 12 (1)).

Option 12. Accruals and deferred income.

(a)   These are to be shown either under D or K or are to be included in "Debtors" under C 9 and I 9.

(b)   Where they represent charges that will be paid only in the course of a subsequent financial year, they may be included in "Creditors" (Article 21).

Choice. Both options adopted (Governmental Decree on the Standard Chart of Accounts, Article 12 (2)).

Option 13. A loss for the financial year may be shown either on the assets side under or on the liabilities side in "Capital and reserves" under A VI or L VI (profit or loss for the financial year).

Choice. Loss to be shown on the liabilities side in "Capital and reserves" (Article 373 (1), formats in the Governmental Decree on the Standard Chart of Accounts).

Option 14. A profit for the financial year may be shown on the liabilities side either under E or in "Capital and reserves" under A VI or L VI (Profit or loss for the financial year).

Choice. Profit to be shown on the liabilities side in "Capital and reserves" (Article 373 (1), formats in the Governmental Decree on the Standard Chart of Accounts).

Option 15. Provisions for pensions and similar obligations are to be shown either on the liabilities side in the balance sheet under B 1 or J 1 or are to be disclosed in the notes on the accounts (Article 43 (1) (7)).

Choice. Companies may choose either alternative (Article 374 (4)), Governmental Decree on the Standard Chart of Accounts, Article 8 (1)).

Option 16. Commitments by way of guarantee that are not to be shown as liabilities must be shown either at the foot of the balance sheet or in the notes on the accounts (Article 14).

Choice. Option adopted (Article 376; no specific requirement; disclosure in the notes is the regular case).

Option 17. Movements in the various fixed asset items and, if necessary, formation expenses (see Option No. 6) are to be shown in the balance sheet or in the notes on the accounts (Article 15 (3) (A)).

Choice. A reconciliation statement is required and is automatically shown in the notes (Article 368).

Option 18. The percentage required for the presumption of a participating interest may be set lower than a share of 20% of the capital of another undertaking (Article 17). Such an option also exists for the obligation to disclose details of such undertakings in the notes on the accounts (Article 43 (1) (2)).

Choice. Presumption is set at 20% or more (Article 24c); 20% is also the criterion in disclosing details of undertakings (Article 379).

Option 19. Provisions may be created to cover certain charges (Article 20 (2)).

Choice. Option adopted (Article 374).

Option 20. For the presentation of the profit and loss account, member states may prescribe the total costs procedure or the turnover costs procedure (both in account or vertical form), or may permit companies to choose between all or part of the layouts in question (Articles 22–26).

Choice. All options adopted; all presentations are allowed (Governmental Decree on the Standard Chart of Accounts, Article 1 (1)).

Option 21. For the disclosure of taxes on the profit or loss, the following option is available regarding the prescription of separate items (Article 30):

First solution:

Taxes on the profit or loss on ordinary activities; profit or loss on ordinary activities after taxation; extraordinary profit or loss; taxes on the extraordinary profit or loss; other taxes not shown under the above items; profit or loss for the financial year.

Second solution:

Profit or loss on ordinary activities; extraordinary profit or loss; taxes on the profit or loss; taxes not included under the above items; profit or loss for the financial year.

In the event of the second solution being adopted, the notes on the accounts must disclose the extent to which the taxes on the profit or loss affect the profit or loss on ordinary activities and the extraordinary profit or loss.

Choice. First solution is required (formats in the Governmental Decree on the Standard Chart of Accounts).

Option 22. Valuation other than on the basis of purchase price or production cost (Article 33)

(a) valuation by the replacement value method for tangible fixed assets with limited useful economic lives and for stocks, or

(b) valuation by methods designed to take account of inflation, or

(c) revaluation of tangible fixed assets and financial fixed assets

(d) valuation by the equity method for holdings on the basis of which a dominant influence is exercised (Article 59).

In cases (a), (b), and (c), the method used must be disclosed in the notes on the accounts, a revaluation reserve must be created, and a comparison must be provided with valuations based on the purchase price and production cost methods.

Choice. Choice (a) is allowed (Article 384 (1)) but not (b) and (c), (c) being interpreted as occasional revaluation; systematic revaluation takes place in the context of the replacement value (or current cost) system. Concerning (d), the equity method is required for holdings in which a significant influence (which is less influential than having dominant influence) is exercised (Article 389 (1)).

Option 23. Value adjustment may be made to financial fixed assets so that they are valued at a lower figure on the balance sheet date (Article 35 (1) (c) (aa)). These value adjustment must be charged to the profit and loss account or disclosed in the notes on the accounts.

Choice. Option adopted (Article 387 (4)).

Option 24. Exceptional value adjustments may be made in respect of fixed and current assets for taxation purposes. The amounts of such adjustments and the reasons for making them must be indicated in the notes on the accounts (Article 35 (1)(d), Article 39 (1)(e)).

Choice. Option not adopted (exceptional value adjustments for taxation purposes not allowed, although this is not stated directly in the statutory regulations; as stated in Chapter 5 (see Section 3.4), income for tax purposes is independent of income for reporting purposes).

Option 25. A reasonable proportion of the costs that are only indirectly attributable to the product in question may be added into the production costs to the extent that they relate to the period of production (Article 35 (3) (b) and Article 39 (2)).

Choice. Option adopted (Article 388 (2)).

Option 26. Interest on capital borrowed to finance the production of fixed assets may be included in the production costs. The inclusion of such interest under "Assets" must be disclosed in the notes on the accounts (Article 35 (4)).

Choice. Option adopted (Article 388 (2)).

Option 27. Interest on capital borrowed to finance the production of current assets may be included in the production costs. The inclusion of such interest under "Assets" must be disclosed in the notes on the accounts (Article 39 (2)).

Choice. Option adopted (Article 388 (2)) 74 (4), Governmental Decree on the Standard Chart of Accounts, Article 8 (1)).

Option 28. Exceptional value adjustments may be made in respect of current assets to take account of future fluctuations in value. The amount of such adjustments must be disclosed separately in the profit and loss account or in the notes on the accounts. (Article 39 (1)(c)).

Choice. Option adopted (Article 387 (3)).

Option 29. The purchase price or production cost of goods of the same category may be calculated on the basis of weighted average prices according to various methods (Article 40 (1)). The method used must be disclosed in the notes on the accounts (Article 43 (1) (l)). Where such a valuation differs materially from that based on the market value, the amount of that differences must likewise be disclosed in the notes on the accounts (Article 40 (2)).

Choice. Option adopted (Article 385 (2)); method to be disclosed in the notes (Article 384 (5)). There is no separate requirement in law to disclose material differences between book value and market value of inventory.

However, such a requirement is included in the Guidelines for Annual Reporting of the RJ (2.11.505).

Option 30. Where the amount repayable on account of any debt is greater than the amount received, the difference may be shown as an asset. It must be shown separately in the balance sheet or in the notes on the accounts and must be written off no later than the time of repayment of the debt (Article 41).

Choice. Option adopted (Article 375 (S)).

2. The Seventh Directive and Dutch Legislation

Seventh Directive Article	*Choice of the Netherlands*
1(1) (d) (aa)	Required if necessary to give a true and fair view
1(1) (d) (bb)	Not introduced
1(2)	Required only if necessary to give a true and fair view
4(2)	Only NVs, BVs, Cooperative Associations and Mutual Guarantee Companies are required to prepare consolidated accounts.
5	Exempt if no group exists (i.e., in the case of a passive holding company)
6	Not exempt; not permitted to ignore consolidation adjustments; size criteria not increased
7(2) (b)	Exempt subject to conditions. The intermediate parent must not: (1) have any of its securities listed; (2) have any bearer securities outstanding; (3) be a bank, financial institution, or insurance company. (4) Its shareholders must all have formally agreed to the exemption. (5) Its obligations must be guaranteed by the entity preparing the consolidated accounts for the group to which it belongs.
9(1)	Not required
9(2)	Not required
11(1)	Exemption depends on parent outside Community preparing audited consolidated accounts in a manner equivalent to that required by the Directive.
11(3)	As above
12(1)	Required if necessary for a true and fair view
15(1)	Not permitted
16(5)	None defined
16(6)	No additional information required; any may be given
17(2)	Permitted; circumstances not defined
19(1) (b)	Date not defined, but goodwill must be calculated at date of acquisition

Seventh Directive *Article*	*Choice of the Netherlands*
20(1)	Permitted but not required (mergers normally take the form of "fusions" in which one legal entity disappears).
26(1) (c)	Proportional eliminations permitted only under conditions of joint venture relations
26(2)	Not permitted
27(2)	Closing date of parent should be within 3 months (earlier or later) of the date of the date of the consolidated accounts
28	Permitted, not required
29(2) (a)	Not required but not forbidden
29(5)	Not applicable
30(2)	Permitted
32(1)	Permitted, subject to a true and fair view being given, and powers over the jointly owned subsidiary being jointly exercised
33(2) (c)	Method described in Article 33(2) (b) required, that is, at an amount equivalent to the proportion of the associated undertaking's capital and reserves represented by the participating interest, with the difference between that amount and the book value (normally cost) being disclosed separately.
33(2) (d)	Not required; no specific rules
33(3)	Required
34(5)	Allowed for holding of less than 20%
34(12)&(13)	Aggregate remuneration of executive directors and aggregate remuneration of supervisory board members, loans to executive directors and aggregate loans to supervisory board members must be disclosed.
35(1)	Permitted. Reference to separate information must be made in the notes.
36(2) (d)	Required
39(1)&(2)	Not required or permitted
39(3)	Permitted
40(1)	Excluded (banks and other financial institutions are covered by Directive 86/635/EEC)
40(2)	Not excluded
41(3)	Not adopted
41(5)	Not excluded
49(2)	Not adopted

Accounting policies

Consolidation

The consolidated financial statements include DSM N.V. and the Group companies in which DSM holds, directly or indirectly, more than 50% of the voting capital or in which DSM, owing to supplementary regulations, has a decisive say in matters of management and financial policy. The assets, liabilities and results of these companies are wholly consolidated. Minority interests in the Group's equity and income are stated separately.

In addition, the financial data of 50% participations important to DSM, in which policy decisions are made jointly by DSM N.V. and third parties, are included in the consolidated financial statements according to the proportional-consolidation method. A '50% participation which is important to DSM' is a participation in a company which is directly involved in DSM's core activities and which is of sufficient size.

Companies whose activities bear no relation to those of the Group are not included in the consolidated statements.

Goodwill, which is determined at the time of acquisition as the amount paid in excess of DSM's share in the net asset value of the company acquired, is charged direct to shareholders' equity.

The results of companies acquired in the course of the year are incorporated into the consolidated statement of income as from the takeover date. Results of companies sold are included in the accounts up to the date of sale.

A list of affiliated companies, drawn up in conformity with Book 2 of the Dutch Civil Code, articles 379 and 414, has been filed at the Trade Registry in Heerlen.

Translation of foreign currencies

Commercial transactions expressed in foreign currencies are stated in the accounts of the local companies at the relevant day rates or at forward rates if forward contracts have been concluded in connection with those commercial transactions.

Balance-sheet items in foreign currencies are translated at spot rates as at the balance-sheet date or at the original forward rate if the exchange risks attaching to the relevant receivables and liabilities have been hedged through forward transactions. As a rule, exchange-rate differences are taken to the statement of income.

Assets and liabilities of foreign participations are translated at the spot rates prevailing at balance-sheet date, while the items of the statements of income of foreign participations are translated at the average exchange rates of the period under review. Exchange-rate differences arising from translation of the equity invested in these companies are taken to Other reserves. The same applies to exchange-rate differences arising from foreign currency loans in so far as such loans hedge the currency-exchange risk associated with foreign Group companies.

Intangible fixed assets

Intangible fixed assets are stated at cost less amortization calculated on a straight-line basis. Concessions and permits are amortized in 10 years, licences and patents in 4 years, pre-operating and start-up expenses in 6 years. Pre-operating and start-up expenses included under this heading relate exclusively to large projects.

Tangible fixed assets

Tangible fixed assets are carried at cost less depreciation calculated on a straight-line basis or at recoverable value, if this is permanently lower. Office buildings are generally depreciated in 30 years, other buildings in 20 years, plant and machinery in 10 years. For large projects, interest expense during construction is capitalized.

Investments relating to oil and gas recovery are grouped under tangible fixed assets. Costs of proven oil and gas reserves are capitalized from the moment development is decided upon. Costs which in the past were charged to the statement of income but which afterwards appear to relate to items that will be used as production tools in a project to be developed are then capitalized. Depreciation is determined on the basis of the production quantities in relation to proven reserves.

Financial fixed assets

Consolidated participations are valued according to DSM Group policies.

Valuation of non-consolidated companies is based on DSM's share in these companies' equity, in principle determined in accordance with DSM Group policies. Results are determined on the same basis.

Long-term receivables are shown at face value, where necessary after deduction of a value adjustment. Other securities are valued at cost or at recoverable value or market value, if this value is lower.

Inventories

Raw materials and consumables are valued at cost, i.e. historical purchase prices plus additional costs. If the price on the purchase market at balance-sheet date or during the time of consumption of existing inventories is lower, valuation is effected at the lower market value plus additional costs. If necessary, an allowance for obsolete inventories is made.

Work in progress and finished products are valued at manufacturing cost, where necessary less an allowance for obsolescence. Internal storage costs, selling expenses and interest charges are not taken into account in determining manufacturing cost. Where the market selling price at balance-sheet date or during the time of sale of existing inventories is lower than manufacturing cost, valuation is based on the net realizable price. Products for which the manufacturing cost cannot be calculated because of shared cost components are stated at net realizable price after deduction of a margin.

Unrealized intercompany results are eliminated in the valuation of inventories.

Receivables

Receivables are stated at face value less an allowance for doubtful debts. Also included is the portion of receivables forming part of the financial fixed assets that falls due within one year.

Cash

Items hereunder are stated at face value.

Provisions

Provisions are shown at face value, except the provision for pension obligations, which is determined on the basis of present cash value by actuarial methods.

Liabilities

These are stated at face value. Amounts payable within one year on long-term liabilities are included under Current liabilities.

Operating income

Net sales comprises the income from the supply of goods and services to third parties less discounts and sales taxes.

Change in inventories of finished products and work in progress relates to the difference in value between opening and closing inventories.

Own work capitalized relates to internally generated fixed assets included under Operating costs.

Other operating income includes DSM's share in the net result of Energie Beheer Nederland BV.

Operating costs

Operating costs are calculated on a historical cost basis. Intra-group supplies are allocated at competitive prices.

Investment grants are credited to the operating result (Other operating costs) in proportion to the depreciable life of the assets concerned. Premiums and grants not yet credited to the operating result are carried in the Equalization account.

Corporate tax

This item covers taxes currently payable or receivable for the year under review, as well as deferred tax liabilities. Matured tax liabilities of loss-making Group units are withdrawn from the Provision for deferred taxes.

Result of non-consolidated companies

The share in the result of non-consolidated companies is determined in proportion to the respective holdings owned by the Group in the year under review, after deduction of applicable taxes.

Geconsolideerde balans (na winstbestemming)

ACTIVA

in NLG miljoen	ultimo 1996		ultimo 1995	
vaste activa				
immateriële vaste activa (1)	96		54	
materiële vaste activa (2)	5 306		4 503	
financiële vaste activa (3)	576		630	
		5 978		5 187
vlottende activa				
voorraden (4)	1 661		1 349	
vorderingen (5)	2 395		1 951	
liquide middelen (6)	417		1 561	
		4 473		4 861
totaal		10 451		10 048

PASSIVA

in NLG miljoen	ultimo 1996		ultimo 1995	
groepsvermogen (7)				
eigen vermogen	4 940		5 164	
belang van derden	175		52	
		5 115		5 216
egalisatierekening investeringspremies (8)		83		105
voorzieningen (9)		1 577		1 523
langlopende schulden (10)		1 444		1 142
kortlopende schulden (11)		2 232		2 062
totaal		10 451		10 048

Consolidated balance sheet as at December 31 (after profit appropriation)

ASSETS

NLG million	1996		1995
fixed assets			
intangible fixed assets (1)	96		54
tangible fixed assets (2)	5 306		4 503
financial fixed assets (3)	576		630
		5 978	5 187
current assets			
inventories (4)	1 661		1 349
receivables (5)	2 395		1 951
cash (6)	417		1 561
		4 473	4 861
total		10 451	10 048

GROUP EQUITY AND LIABILITIES

NLG million	1996		1995
group equity (7)			
shareholders' equity	4 940		5 164
minority interests' share	175		52
		5 115	5 216
equalization account (8)		83	105
provisions (9)		1 577	1 523
long-term liabilities (10)		1 444	1 142
current liabilities (11)		2 232	2 062
total		10 451	10 048

Geconsolideerde winst- en verliesrekening

in NLG miljoen	1996		1995
netto-omzet (12)	10 263	9 822	
andere bedrijfsopbrengsten (13)	327	383	
som der bedrijfsopbrengsten		10 590	10 205
afschrijvingen (14)	-752	-704	
andere bedrijfslasten (15)	-8 840	-7 979	
som der bedrijfslasten		-9 592	-8 683
bedrijfsresultaat (16)		998	1 522
financiële baten en lasten (17)		-60	-58
resultaat uit gewone bedrijfsuitoefening voor belastingen		938	1 464
belastingen resultaat uit gewone bedrijfsuitoefening		-263	-469
resultaat niet-geconsolideerde deelnemingen		54	79
resultaat uit gewone bedrijfsuitoefening na belastingen		729	1 074
buitengewoon resultaat na belastingen (18)		-5	-2
groepsresultaat na belastingen		724	1 072
belang van derden		-4	-1
nettoresultaat		720	1 071
nettoresultaat		720	1 071
dividend op cumulatief preferente aandelen		-28	-
nettoresultaat toekomend aan de houders van gewone aandelen		692	1 071

Consolidated statement of income

NLG million	1996		1995
net sales (12)	**10 263**	9 822	
other operating income (13)	**327**	383	
total operating income	**10 590**		10 205
amortization and depreciation (14)	**-752**	-704	
other operating costs(15)	**-8 840**	-7 979	
total operating costs	**-9 592**		-8 683
operating result (16)	**998**		1 522
balance of financial income and expense (17)	**-60**		-58
result from ordinary activities before taxation	**938**		1 464
tax on result from ordinary activities	**-263**		-469
result of non-consolidated companies	**54**		79
result from ordinary activities after taxation	**729**		1 074
extraordinary result after taxation (18)	**-5**		-2
group result after taxation	**724**		1 072
minority interests' share in result	**-4**		-1
net result	**720**		1 071
net result	**720**		1 071
dividend on cumulative preference shares	**-28**		-
net result available to holders of ordinary shares	**692**		1 071

Overzicht van kasstromen

in NLG miljoen	1996	1995
BEDRIJFSACTIVITEITEN		
nettoresultaat	**720**	1 071
herleiding naar middelen uit bedrijfsactiviteiten:		
- afschrijvingen	**752**	704
- resultaat op desinvesteringen	**-46**	-53
- winstinhouding bij niet-geconsolideerde		
deelnemingen	**12**	85
- mutatie bedrijfskapitaal [1]	**-192**	92
- mutatie egalisatierekening	**-36**	-36
- mutatie voorzieningen	**-36**	24
- overige mutaties	**155**	104
middelen uit bedrijfsactiviteiten	**1 329**	1 991
INVESTERINGSACTIVITEITEN		
investeringen in:		
- immateriële vaste activa	**-26**	-23
- materiële vaste activa	**-1 041**	-737
verwerving van geconsolideerde deelnemingen	**-462**	-1
opbrengst verkochte materiële vaste activa	**17**	47
verkoop van geconsolideerde deelnemingen	**88**	116
financiële vaste activa:		
- verwervingen en kapitaalstortingen	**-10**	-47
- opbrengst verkochte deelnemingen	**7**	35
- mutatie leningen u/g.	**-13**	-71
middelen aangewend voor investeringsactiviteiten	**-1 440**	-681
UITGEKEERD DIVIDEND	**-260**	-272
FINANCIERINGSACTIVITEITEN		
opname leningen	**319**	25
aflossing leningen o/g.	**-494**	-167
mutatie schulden aan kredietinstellingen	**-31**	-4
betaling aan de Staat in verband met		
conversie van aandelen	**-602**	-
uitgifte nieuwe aandelen	**25**	1
mutatie belang van derden	**10**	11
middelen uit financieringsactiviteiten	**-773**	-134
mutatie liquide middelen	**-1 144**	904
[1] mutatie bedrijfskapitaal:		
- voorraden	**-133**	-136
- vorderingen	**-194**	205
- kortlopende schulden (excl. leningen,		
schulden aan kredietinstellingen en dividend)	**135**	23
	-192	92

Zie toelichting 19 op pagina 57

Statement of cash flows

NLG million	1996		1995
OPERATING ACTIVITIES			
net result	720		1 071
adjustments to reconcile net result with			
net cash provided by operating activities:			
- amortization and depreciation	752		704
- revenue from divestments	-46		-53
- profit retention at non-consolidated companies	12		85
- change in working capital[1]	-192		92
- change in equalization account	-36		-36
- change in provisions	-36		24
- other changes	155		104
net cash provided by operating activities		1 329	1 991
INVESTING ACTIVITIES			
investments in:			
- intangible fixed assets	-26		-23
- tangible fixed assets	-1 041		-737
acquisitions of consolidated companies	-462		-1
proceeds from sale of tangible fixed assets	17		47
sale of consolidated companies	88		116
financial fixed assets:			
- acquisitions and capital payments	-10		-47
- proceeds from sale of participations	7		35
- change in loans granted	-13		-71
net cash used in investing activities		-1 440	-681
DIVIDENDS PAID		-260	-272
FINANCING ACTIVITIES			
loans taken up	319		25
redemption of loans taken up	-494		-167
changes in liabilities to credit institutions	-31		-4
payment to the Dutch State in connection			
with conversion of shares	-602		-
share issue	25		1
changes in minority interests	10		11
net cash provided by financing activities		-773	-134
change in cash		-1 144	904
[1] specification of change in working capital:			
- inventories	-133		-136
- receivables	-194		205
- current liabilities (excl. loans, liabilities to			
credit institutions and dividend payable)	135		23
	-192		92

See note 19 on page 57.

Notes to the consolidated financial statements

General

Unless stated otherwise, all amounts are in millions of guilders.

In conformity with Book 2 of the Dutch Civil Code, article 402, a condensed statement of income has been included in the DSM N.V. accounts.

As a consequence of the acquisitions made in 1996, the financial data of the fine-chemicals producers DSM Chemie Linz GmbH (DSM interest 70%) and Derivados del Etilo, SA (DSM interest 83%) and of the EPDM producer Nitriflex do Sul Ltda are included in the consolidated statements for the first time.

In 1996 DSM and Exxon Chemical set up a joint venture in the field of plastomers to which DSM contributed production facilities. DSM holds a 50% interest in this joint venture. The financial data of this joint venture are proportionally consolidated

Changes in consolidation policies with effect from 1996

A number of DSM's core activities have been organized into joint ventures in which policy decisions are made jointly by DSM N.V. and third parties. The proportion of DSM activities organized into such partnerships is expected to increase.

To provide a better insight into the significance for DSM of the activities of these joint ventures, we have decided - as announced in the 1995 Annual Report - to include the financial data of 50% participations which are important to DSM in the consolidated financial statements according to the proportional-consolidation method, from the financial year 1996 onwards. A '50% participation which is important to DSM' is a participation in a company which is directly involved in DSM's core activities and which is of sufficient size.

As from 1 January 1996 the following 50% participations are proportionally consolidated: Holland Sweetener Company VoF, DSM Idemitsu Company Ltd., Chemferm VoF and Chemferm SA. The 50/50 DEX-Plastomers joint venture is included in the consolidated financial statements as from 1 January 1996 and is also proportionally consolidated.

The change in our consolidation policies will have no consequences for the net result and the shareholders' equity, but it will affect the composition of the result and the equity. If in 1996 we had still applied the previous consolidation policies, net sales would have been more than NLG 200 million lower. The influence on the operating result and the result of non-consolidated participations is very limited. In the statements of changes the effects of the change in consolidation policies on the major balance-sheet items are shown under 'Introduction of proportional consolidation'.

(1) INTANGIBLE FIXED ASSETS

	total	concessions and permits	licences and patents	pre-operating and start-up expenses
balance at January 1, 1996				
cost	108	3	26	79
amortization	54	1	19	34
book value	54	2	7	45
changes in book value:				
- introduction of proportional consolidation	21	-	14	7
- capital expenditure	26	-	5	21
- acquisitions	6	-	6	-
- amortization	-18	-	-9	-9
- other changes	7	-	18	-11
	42	-	34	8
balance at December 31, 1996				
cost	166	3	71	92
amortization	70	1	30	39
book value	96	2	41	53

(2) TANGIBLE FIXED ASSETS

	total	land and buildings	plant and machinery	other fixed assets	in course of realization or prepaid	not used for operational purposes
balance at January 1, 1996						
cost	13 501	1 972	9 997	799	637	96
depreciation	8 998	900	7 425	606	6	61
book value	4 503	1 072	2 572	193	631	35
changes in book value:						
- introduction of proportional consolidation	189	13	175	1	-	-
- capital expenditure	1 041	18	180	25	818	-
- acquisitions	380	82	281	8	9	-
- put into operation	-	38	303	68	-411	2
- depreciation	-734	-84	-585	-61	-3	-1
- deconsolidations	-28	-	-25	-	-3	-
- disposals	-13	-2	-7	-2	-	-2
- exchange-rate differences	55	18	23	1	12	1
- other	-87	77	-102	-67	4	1
	803	160	243	-27	426	1
balance at December 31,1996						
cost	15 594	2 246	11 399	797	1 066	86
depreciation	10 288	1 014	8 584	631	9	50
book value	5 306	1 232	2 815	166	1 057	36

Included is an amount of NLG 13 million (31 December 1995: NLG 14 million) for assets acquired under financial lease agreements. The related commitments are included under Other liabilities.

A geographic breakdown of capital expenditure on tangible fixed assets and their book value is given below:

	capital expenditure		book value of tangible fixed assets at December 31	
	1996	1995	**1996**	1995
Netherlands	**737**	535	**3 724**	3 505
other EU countries	**179**	98	**864**	491
	916	633	**4 588**	3 996
rest of Europe	**7**	5	**25**	24
North America	**72**	47	**331**	282
rest of the world	**46**	52	**362**	201
total	**1 041**	737	**5 306**	4 503

Approximate current value
The book value of the tangible fixed assets on the basis of current value is approximated at NLG 6.2 billion (31 December 1995: NLG 5.1 billion). The depreciation charge on this basis amounts to NLG 0.9 billion (1995: NLG 0.8 billion).

(3) FINANCIAL FIXED ASSETS

	total	non-consolidated companies		other securities	other receivables
		share in equity	loans		
balance at January 1, 1996	630	488	15	16	111
changes:					
- introduction of proportional consolidation ...	-66	-62	-11	-	7
- share in result.............................	54	54	-	-	-
- dividends.................................	-66	-66	-	-	-
- acquisitions and capital payments	21	6	2	13	-
- advances	17	-	4	-	13
- disposals.................................	-1	-1	-	-	-
- redemptions..............................	-5	-	-	-	-5
- transfer to current receivables..............	-15	-	-	-	-15
- exchange-rate differences	13	5	-	1	7
- other.....................................	-6	5	-3	-4	-4
balance at December 31, 1996	**576**	**429**	**7**	**26**	**114**

(4) INVENTORIES

	1996	1995
raw materials and consumables	406	321
work in progress	74	55
finished products..	1 181	973
total	**1 661**	1 349

(5) RECEIVABLES

	1996	1995
trade accounts receivable	1 796	1 450
receivable from non-consolidated companies	61	93
investment grants	5	14
other receivables	451	331
deferred items	82	63
total	**2 395**	1 951

(6) CASH

	1996	1995
deposits..	168	1 408
cash, bank, giro	249	153
total	**417**	1 561

(7) GROUP EQUITY

	total	shareholders' equity	minority interests' share
balance at January 1, 1996	5 216	5 164	52
changes:			
- net result 1996	724	720	4
- dividend	-289	-289	-
- acquisitions	108	-	108
- financing of minority interests	7	-	7
- exchange-rate differences	112	108	4
- goodwill	-184	-184	-
- payment to the Dutch State in connection with conversion of shares	-602	-602	-
- share issue	25	25	-
- other	-2	-2	-
balance at December 31, 1996	**5 115**	**4 940**	**175**

Over the past ten years a total of NLG 1,451 million in goodwill paid has been charged against shareholders' equity.

For a breakdown of shareholders' equity, the reader is referred to the DSM N.V. financial statements.

(8) EQUALIZATION ACCOUNT

balance at January 1, 1996	105
changes:	
- introduction of proportional consolidation	12
- new claims	8
- released to the statement of income	-33
- other	-9
balance at December 31, 1996	**83**

(9) PROVISIONS

	1996	1995
pensions	**50**	41
deferred taxes	**420**	376
self-insurance fund	**154**	195
restructuring and reorganization costs	**337**	315
other provisions	**616**	596
total	**1 577**	1 523

The provisions can largely be regarded as long term.

The major portion of the pension liabilities is covered by independent pension funds. The Provision for pensions concerns the pension commitments and past service commitments which the company has kept under its own control.

The Provision for deferred taxes reflects the balance of future fiscal liabilities resulting from, among other things, timing differences between equity calculated on the basis of DSM accounting principles and equity determined for tax purposes.

An annual allocation is carried to the Self-insurance fund provision for internal insurance of objects. This allocation roughly equals the amount of the premiums which would be owing in the case of external insurance. Damage cases, if and in so far as covered by the internal insurance, are charged against this provision.

The Provision for restructuring and reorganization costs concerns reorganization of industrial operations and renovation of assets.

Included in Other provisions are some items relating to, among other things, cost equalization, guarantee obligations, redundancy payments and early retirement of personnel.

The item Provisions on balance increased by NLG 54 million. The change can be broken down as follows:

balance at January 1, 1996	1 523
changes:	
- additions charged against the result	179
- withdrawals for intended purposes	-215
- transfer from tax liabilities	24
- exchange-rate differences	9
- acquisitions	60
- other.	-3
balance at December 31, 1996.	**1 577**

The withdrawals mainly concern the financing of the early retirement scheme (NLG 63 million), reorganization costs (NLG 32 million) and equalization of costs such as plant maintenance shutdown costs (NLG 102 million).

(10) LONG-TERM LIABILITIES

	1996	1995
debenture loans.	**600**	412
private loans	**831**	716
other liabilities.	**13**	14
total	**1 444**	1 142

This item includes an amount of NLG 5 million (31 December 1995: NLG 3 million) in subordinated loans contracted by subsidiaries of DSM N.V. and subordinated to all liabilities owing to third parties by these subsidiaries.

For private loans, an amount of NLG 20 million (31 December 1995: NLG 11 million) has been furnished in mortgage collateral. Moreover, agreements governing loans with a residual amount at 31 December 1996 of NLG 1,319 million, of which NLG 112 million of a short-term nature (31 December 1995: NLG 1,391 million, of which NLG 366 million short-term), contain clauses restricting the provision of securities.

Of the total long-term liabilities as at 31 December 1996, NLG 569 million had a remaining term of more than five years. Of this amount, NLG 300 million relates to debenture loans, NLG 261 million to private loans and NLG 8 million to other liabilities.

The schedule of repayment of long-term liabilities is as follows:

- 1998.	200
- 1999.	385
- 2000 and 2001	290
- 2002 through 2006	564
- after 2006	5
	1 444

The repayments scheduled for 1996, totalling NLG 168 million, are included under Current liabilities.

Breakdown of long-term liabilities by currency:

	1996	1995
NLG.	**1 282**	1 039
USD	**47**	30
JPY	**43**	-
ESB.	**22**	-
DEM	**7**	29
other currencies	**43**	44
total	**1 444**	1 142

On balance, Long-term liabilities rose by NLG 302 million owing to the following changes:

balance at January 1, 1996	1 142
changes:	
- introduction of proportional consolidation	184
- acquisitions	38
- loans taken up	319
- transfer to current liabilities	-168
- extra redemptions	-73
- exchange-rate differences	5
- other	-3
balance at December 31, 1996	**1 444**

Debenture loans

			1996	1995
2%	SEK loan	1991-1997	-	46
1.5%	ITL loan	1991-1997	-	66
9%	NLG loan	1992-1999	**300**	300
6.25%	NLG loan	1996-2006	**300**	-
total			**600**	412

A number of the above-mentioned loans were converted into loans in different currencies or with different interest types by means of swaps.

The average effective interest rate on long-term liabilities in 1996 amounted to 6.8% (1995: 7.3%).

The total confirmed credit facilities open to DSM N.V. in the long term amounted to $ 400 million as at 31 December 1996 (31 December 1995: $ 300 million).

(11) CURRENT LIABILITIES

	1996	1995
debenture loans and private loans	167	392
credit institutions	55	27
received in advance on orders	7	7
suppliers and trade credits	984	787
notes and cheques due	24	15
owing to non-consolidated companies	36	25
taxes and social security	165	133
pensions	9	11
dividend payable	203	173
other liabilities	385	346
deferred items	197	146
total	**2 232**	2 062
of which interest-bearing	223	421

COMMITMENTS NOT APPEARING FROM THE BALANCE SHEET

	1996	1995
rents and operational lease	180	118
guarantee obligations on behalf of non-consolidated companies and third parties	112	108
outstanding orders for projects under construction	80	126
amount of negotiated bills of exchange still at risk	16	16
other	186	43
total	**574**	411

Most of the outstanding orders for projects under construction will be completed in 1997.

The increase in other commitments not appearing from the balance sheet mainly relates to the capacity drawing rights acquired for polycarbonate.

The commitments as regards rents and operational lease are spread as follows:

- 1997	37
- 1998	31
- 1999	23
- 2000 and 2001	28
- after 2001	61
	180

(12) NET SALES

Net sales, showing an increase of 4.5% relative to 1995, can be broken down as follows by business segment:

	1996	%	1995	%
Polymers & Performance Materials.........................	4 479	43.6	4 702	47.9
Industrial Chemicals & Fine Chemicals	3 686	35.9	3 060	31.2
Resins & Plastic Products...............................	2 247	21.9	2 360	24.0
Energy & other activities................................	370	3.6	276	2.8
total supplies...	10 782	105.0	10 398	105.9
intra-group supplies	519	5.0	576	5.9
total	10 263	100.0	9 822	100.0

The following is a geographical breakdown of net sales:

By origin

	1996	%	1995	%
Netherlands...	6 168	60.1	6 401	65.2
other EU countries......................................	2 238	21.8	1 840	18.7
	8 406	81.9	8 241	83.9
rest of Europe..	80	0.8	37	0.4
North America	1 610	15.7	1 448	14.7
rest of the world.......................................	167	1.6	96	1.0
total	10 263	100.0	9 822	100.0

By destination

	1996	%	1995	%
Netherlands...	1 289	12.6	1 254	12.8
other EU countries......................................	5 575	54.3	5 747	58.5
	6 864	66.9	7 001	71.3
rest of Europe..	469	4.6	316	3.2
North America	1 617	15.7	1 242	12.6
rest of the world.......................................	1 313	12.8	1 263	12.9
total	10 263	100.0	9 822	100.0

(13) OTHER OPERATING INCOME

	1996	1995
change in inventories of finished products and work in progress	73	158
own work capitalized	52	17
sundry	202	208
total	327	383

(14) AMORTIZATION AND DEPRECIATION

	1996	1995
amortization and depreciation of intangible and tangible fixed assets	737	683
other changes in value of intangible and tangible fixed assets	15	21
total	752	704

(15) OTHER OPERATING COSTS

	1996	1995
raw materials and consumables	4 767	4 386
work subcontracted and other external expenses	2 285	1 926
wages and salaries	1 406	1 317
pension charges	100	77
other social charges	309	283
sundry	-27	-10
total	8 840	7 979

Wages and salaries relate to the following average workforce totals by business segment:

	1996	1995
Polymers & Performance Materials	4 608	4 445
Industrial Chemicals & Fine Chemicals	4 516	3 292
Resins & Plastic Products	5 359	6 030
Energy & other activities	3 542	4 016
total	18 025	17 783

(16) SEGMENTATION OF OPERATING RESULT

The table below shows a breakdown by business segment of the operating result:

	1996	1995
Polymers & Performance Materials	243	799
Industrial Chemicals & Fine Chemicals	467	476
Resins & Plastic Products	97	79
Energy & other activities	191	168
total	998	1 522

(17) FINANCIAL INCOME AND EXPENSE

interest income	51	60
interest expense	-107	-125
other	-4	7
total	-60	-58

An amount of NLG 20 million was deducted from interest expense (1995: NLG 10 million) on account of capitalized interest expense during construction.

Financial instruments
In managing its financial assets and liabilities DSM makes use of so-called derivative instruments to manage the currency-exchange and interest-rate risks relating to the cash flows resulting from normal business operation and from financing activities. The use of these instruments is subject to strict internal procedures so as to prevent speculative use.

Foreign currency risks
DSM's policy is aimed at hedging the risks of exchange-rate movements affecting the cash flows from business activities as well as financing activities in foreign currencies, the so-called transaction exposure. The instruments used to achieve this are forward exchange contracts, foreign-currency swaps and, to a limited extent, the purchase of currency options.

At the balance-sheet date the contract value and the market value of the currency instruments were NLG 1,685 million and NLG -42 million, respectively. The market value is the value that would be received or paid on termination of these contracts at the balance-sheet date.

The risks that arise from the translation of the assets and liabilities and the result of foreign participations due to exchange-rate movements, which risks together form the so-called translation exposure, are as a rule not hedged.

Interest-rate risks
Interest instruments are used to obtain the desired risk profile in fixed and variable interest positions. These instruments are applied only on the basis of underlying positions. For interest-rate risk management use is made of interest-rate swaps and, to a limited extent, the purchase of interest rate options. The contract value and the market value of the interest instruments at the balance-sheet date were NLG 2,648 million and NLG 94 million, respectively.

Credit risk
The credit risk to which DSM is exposed due to the use of financial instruments does not amount to the principal sum but to at most the market value of the contract, this being the difference between the current market-interest rate and/ or the current market-exchange rate on the one hand and the contract rates on the other. DSM limits this credit risk by spreading such contracts among several parties and by concluding the contracts with parties having a high credit rating.

(18) EXTRAORDINARY RESULT AFTER TAXATION

	1996		1995
extraordinary income			
- book profits on the sale of activities	**40**	78	
- other income	**47**	3	
	87		81
extraordinary expense			
- additions to provisions for restructuring and reorganization .	**-29**	-33	
- write-down of assets	**-80**	-88	
- additions to other provisions	**-**	-19	
- other expenses	**-2**	-	
	-111		-140
taxes	**19**	57	
total	**-5**		-2

Other expenses relates primarily to an adjustment of the Self-insurance fund provision to reflect new insights. The write-down of assets relates to value corrections applied to fixed assets in connection with planned restructuring operations.

(19) NOTES TO THE STATEMENT OF CASH FLOWS

The Statement of cash flows is drawn up on the basis of a comparison of the balance sheets as at 1 January and 31 December. Changes that do not involve cash flows, such as currency-exchange-rate changes, revaluations and transfers to other balance-sheet items, are eliminated.

Changes in working capital due to the acquisition or sale of consolidated companies are included under Investing activities. Most of the changes in the Statement of cash flows can be traced back to the detailed statements of changes for the balance-sheet items concerned.

For those balance-sheet items for which no detailed statement of changes is included, the table below shows the link between the change according to the balance sheet and the change according to the Statement of cash flows:

	working capital[1]	provisions	interest-bearing debt[2]
balance at year-end 1995	1 832	1 523	1 563
balance at year-end 1996	2 251	1 577	1 667
balance-sheet change	419	54	104
adjustments:			
exchange-rate changes	-52	-9	-13
acquisition/divestment of consolidated companies	-113	-60	-86
introduction of proportional consolidation	-25	-	-213
transfers, etc.	-37	-21	2
adjusted balance-sheet change	192	-36	-206
change in cash flow	-192	-36	-206

[1] Inventories and receivables less interest-free current liabilities, the latter except dividend payable.
[2] Long-term liabilities and interest-bearing current liabilities.

Quarterly financial data

NLG million 1996	quarter 1st	2nd	3rd	4th	year
net sales	2 604	2 589	2 481	2 589	10 263
operating result	294	288	239	177	998
financial income and expense	-14	-14	-14	-18	-60
result from ordinary activities before taxation	280	274	225	159	938
tax on result from ordinary activities	-83	-80	-62	-38	-263
result of non-consolidated companies	19	15	15	5	54
result from ordinary activities after taxation	216	209	178	126	729
extraordinary result after taxation	-10	0	0	5	-5
result after taxation	206	209	178	131	724
minority interests' share in result	-1	-1	0	-2	-4
net result	205	208	178	129	720
per ordinary share outstanding at year-end in NLG:					
result from ordinary activities after taxation	7.40	6.88	5.81	4.06	24.13*
net result	7.03	6.85	5.82	4.16	23.83*
cash flow	13.39	13.44	12.25	10.69	49.72*

NLG million 1995	quarter 1st	2nd	3rd	4th	year
net sales	2 708	2 571	2 255	2 288	9 822
operating result	502	504	342	174	1 522
financial income and expense	-27	-12	-10	-9	-58
result from ordinary activities before taxation	475	492	332	165	1 464
tax on result from ordinary activities	-153	-161	-114	-41	-469
result of non-consolidated companies	34	6	17	22	79
result from ordinary activities after taxation	356	337	235	146	1 074
extraordinary result after taxation	0	0	0	-2	-2
result after taxation	356	337	235	144	1 072
minority interests' share in result	0	0	-1	0	-1
net result	356	337	234	144	1 071
per ordinary share in NLG:					
result from ordinary activities after taxation	9.84	9.33	6.49	4.04	29.68
net result	9.84	9.33	6.44	4.00	29.60
cash flow	14.72	14.06	11.21	9.07	49.07

* Contrary to what was stated in the quarterly reports and the report for the first half, the figures per ordinary share have been calculated on the number of ordinary shares outstanding at year-end. Based on the year-average number of ordinary shares these figures would be NLG 23.05, NLG 22.75 and NLG 47.48, respectively.

Balans van DSM N.V. (na winstbestemming)

ACTIVA

in NLG miljoen	ultimo 1996		ultimo 1995
vaste activa			
materiële vaste activa (1)	57		61
financiële vaste activa (2)	6 726		5 690
		6 783	5 751
vlottende activa			
vorderingen (3)	3 607		2 285
liquide middelen (4)	147		1 181
		3 754	3 466
totaal		10 537	9 217

PASSIVA

in NLG miljoen	ultimo 1996		ultimo 1995
eigen vermogen (5)			
- aandelenkapitaal	728		724
- agio	236		215
- overige reserves	3 976		4 225
		4 940	5 164
egalisatierekening investeringspremies		0	0
voorzieningen (6)		1 014	1 042
langlopende schulden (7)		1 218	1 040
kortlopende schulden (8)		3 365	1 971
totaal		10 537	9 217

Winst- en verliesrekening van DSM N.V.

in NLG miljoen	1996	1995
resultaat deelnemingen (na belastingen)	517	913
overige resultaten	203	158
nettoresultaat	720	1 071

in NLG miljoen	1996	1995
nettoresultaat	720	1 071
dividend op cumulatief preferente aandelen	-28	-
nettoresultaat toekomend aan de houders van gewone aandelen	692	1 071

DSM N.V. balance sheet as at December 31 (after profit appropriation)

ASSETS

NLG million	1996		1995	
fixed assets				
tangible fixed assets (1)	57		61	
financial fixed assets (2)	6 726		5 690	
		6 783		5 751
current assets				
receivables (3)	3 607		2 285	
cash (4)	147		1 181	
		3 754		3 466
total		10 537		9 217

SHAREHOLDERS' EQUITY AND LIABILITIES

NLG million	1996		1995	
shareholders' equity (5)				
- share capital	728		724	
- share premium account	236		215	
- other reserves	3 976		4 225	
		4 940		5 164
equalization account		0		0
provisions (6)		1 014		1 042
long-term liabilities (7)		1 218		1 040
current liabilities (8)		3 365		1 971
total		10 537		9 217

DSM N.V. statement of income

NLG million	1996	1995
result of consolidated and non-consolidated companies (after taxation)	517	913
other results	203	158
net result	720	1 071

	1996	1995
net result	720	1 071
dividend on cumulative preference shares	-28	-
net result available to holders of ordinary shares	692	1 071

Notes to the balance sheet

General

Unless stated otherwise, all amounts are in NLG million.

For the accounting policies, please refer to pages 42 - 43.

(1) TANGIBLE FIXED ASSETS

This item mainly relates to land and buildings. Capital expenditure amounted to NLG 1 million, while the depreciation charge was NLG 5 million. Cost of tangible fixed assets as at 31 December 1996 was NLG 92 million; accumulated depreciation amounted to NLG 35 million.

(2) FINANCIAL FIXED ASSETS

	total	consolidated companies		non-consolidated companies		other securities	other receivables
		share in equity	loans	share in equity	loans		
balance at January 1, 1996	5 690	3 609	1 735	288	5	1	52
changes:							
- share in result	517	517	-	-	-	-	-
- dividends	-1 075	-1 075	-	-	-	-	-
- acquisitions and capital payments	2 010	2 010	-	-	-	-	-
- goodwill	-184	-184	-	-	-	-	-
- advances	906	-	896	-	-	-	10
- disposals	-95	-95	-	-	-	-	-
- redemptions	-601	-	-598	-	-	-	-3
- transfer to receivables.	-561	-	-556	-	-	-	-5
- exchange-rate differences	121	80	41	-	-	-	-
- other	-2	3	-3	-	-5	-	3
balance at December 31, 1996	**6 726**	**4 865**	**1 515**	**288**	-	**1**	**57**

(3) RECEIVABLES

	1996	1995
receivables from consolidated companies	3 331	1 989
receivables from non-consolidated companies.	47	55
other receivables	229	241
total	**3 607**	2 285

(4) CASH

	1996	1995
deposits.	130	1 171
cash, bank, giro	17	10
total	**147**	1 181

(5) SHAREHOLDERS' EQUITY

	total	share capital	share premium account	other reserves
balance at January 1, 1996	5 164	724	215	4 225
changes:				
- net result 1996..	720	-	-	720
- dividend...	-289	-	-	-289
- exchange-rate differences	108	-	-	108
- goodwill..	-184	-	-	-184
- payment to the Dutch State in connection with conversion of shares	-602	-	-	-602
- share issue	25	4	21	-
- other...	-2	-	-	-2
balance at December 31, 1996.........................	4 940	728	236	3 976

Share capital
The share capital of DSM N.V. at 31 December 1996 amounted to NLG 2.5 billion, divided into 55,160 000 ordinary shares, 7,340,000 cumulative preference shares A and 62,500,000 cumulative preference shares B, having a nominal value of NLG 20 each. At the end of 1995, 36,195,820 ordinary shares and five priority shares, having a nominal value of NLG 20 each, were in issue and fully paid. In the course of 1996 the five priority shares were converted into ordinary shares and 7,340,000 ordinary shares were converted into cumulative preference shares A. In addition, 196,900 new shares were issued in connection with options being exercised. At the end of 1996, 29,052,725 ordinary shares and 7,340,000 cumulative preference shares A, having a nominal value of NLG 20 each, were in issue and fully paid.

Options
Certain groups of employees have been granted options on DSM N.V. shares. Each option entitles the holder to one ordinary share having a nominal value of NLG 20. These options expire after five years.

	issued	outstanding as at Dec. 31, 1996	exercise price (in guilders)	exercise period up to and incl.
1993.....................................	93 400	1 500	76.00	15 January 1998
1994.....................................	120 100	18 700	113.00	14 January 1999
1995	124 900	47 400	135.20	12 January 2000
1996	117 650	51 150	132.70	12 January 2001
total		118 750		

Share premium account
The Share premium account can be regarded as wholly free of tax.

Legal reserve for retained profits
Since the profits retained in DSM N.V.'s consolidated and non-consolidated companies can be distributed, and received in the Netherlands, without restriction, no Legal reserve for retained profits is required.

(6) PROVISIONS

This item can be broken down as follows:

	1996	1995
deferred taxes	354	329
self-insurance fund	116	154
restructuring and renovation costs	270	232
other provisions	274	327
total	**1 014**	1 042

(7) LONG-TERM LIABILITIES

This item relates entirely to debenture loans and private loans. Of the total amount of long-term liabilities outstanding at 31 December 1996, NLG 545 million had a remaining term of more than five years.

The repayment schedule for long-term liabilities is as follows:

- 1998	138
- 1999	329
- 2000 and 2001	206
- 2002 through 2006	545
	1 218

The repayments scheduled for 1997 are included under Current liabilities.

In agreements governing loans with a residual amount of NLG 1,319 million, of which NLG 112 million of a short-term nature (31 December 1995: NLG 1,391 million, of which NLG 366 million short term) clauses have been included which restrict the provision of securities.

(8) CURRENT LIABILITIES

	1996	1995
debenture loans and private loans	112	366
credit institutions	53	82
owing to consolidated companies	2 872	1 118
taxes and social security	1	14
dividend payable	203	173
other liabilities	122	191
deferred items	2	27
total	**3 365**	1 971

Commitments not appearing from the balance sheet
Guarantee obligations on behalf of non-consolidated companies and third parties amounted to NLG 72 million
(31 December 1995: NLG 104 million). DSM N.V. has declared in writing that it accepts several liability for debts arising
from acts-in-law of a number of consolidated companies. These debts are included in the consolidated balance sheet.

Workforce
DSM N.V. employed on average 14 people (1995: 17).

Remuneration for Members of the Managing Board and the Supervisory Board of DSM N.V.
In the financial year under review, remuneration (including pension costs and other commitments) and pension
benefits for members and former members of the Managing Board of DSM N.V. amounted to NLG 4.9 million
(1995: NLG 4.7 million). Members of the Supervisory Board received a fixed remuneration totalling NLG 0.5 million
(1995: also NLG 0.5 million).

Heerlen, 24 February, 1997

Managing Board

S.D. de Bree
R.E. Selman
L.J.A.M. Ligthart
P.A.F.W. Elverding

Supervisory Board

H.H.F. Wijffels
A.C. Helfrich
H. Bodt
M. Epema-Brugman
L.A. Geelhoed
M.G. Kikken
G. Metz
O. Müller
F.W. Rutten

Overige gegevens

Winstbestemming

Ingevolge artikel 32 van de Statuten van de Vennootschap wordt jaarlijks door de Raad van Bestuur onder goedkeuring van de Raad van Commissarissen vastgesteld welk deel van de winst wordt gereserveerd. Uit de winst na deze reservering wordt eerst een dividend uitgekeerd op de cumulatief preferente aandelen B. Ultimo 1996 waren geen cumulatief preferente aandelen B geplaatst.

Vervolgens wordt voorzover mogelijk op de cumulatief preferente aandelen A een dividend uitgekeerd waarvan het percentage gelijk is aan het rekenkundige gemiddelde van het gemiddelde effectieve rendement op staatsleningen met een (resterende) looptijd van 9 tot 10 jaar, zoals opgemaakt door het Centraal Bureau voor de Statistiek en gepubliceerd in de Officiële Prijscourant over de laatste 20 beursdagen voorafgaand aan 8 maart 1996, verhoogd met een door de Raad van Bestuur vast te stellen opslag van maximaal 50 basispunten. Het dividendpercentage van de cumulatief preferente aandelen A zal voor het eerst per 1 januari 2006 en telkenmale 10 jaar nadien opnieuw worden vastgesteld. Het dividendpercentage van de cumulatief preferente aandelen A is voor de jaren tot en met 2005 vastgesteld op 6,78%. De grondslag voor de berekening bedraagt NLG 70 per cumulatief preferent aandeel A. Het dividend over 1996 is berekend naar tijdsgelang. Het daarna overblijvende wordt als dividend op de gewone aandelen uitgekeerd.

Besloten is om aan het nettoresultaat de volgende bestemming te geven:

	1996	1995
ten gunste van de reserves	431	826
uitkering dividend op cumulatief		
preferente aandelen A................	28	-
uitkering dividend op gewone aandelen	261	245
	720	1 071

Accountantsverklaring

Opdracht
Wij hebben de Jaarrekening 1996 van DSM N.V. te Heerlen gecontroleerd. De Jaarrekening is opgesteld onder verantwoordelijkheid van de leiding van de onderneming. Het is onze verantwoordelijkheid een accountantsverklaring inzake de Jaarrekening te verstrekken.

Werkzaamheden
Onze controle is verricht overeenkomstig algemeen aanvaarde richtlijnen met betrekking tot controle-opdrachten. Volgens deze richtlijnen dient onze controle zodanig te worden gepland en uitgevoerd, dat een

Jaarrekening geen onjuistheden van materieel belang bevat. Een controle omvat onder meer een onderzoek door middel van deelwaarnemingen van informatie ter onderbouwing van de bedragen en de toelichtingen in de Jaarrekening. Tevens omvat een controle een beoordeling van de grondslagen voor financiële verslaggeving die bij het opmaken van de Jaarrekening zijn toegepast en van belangrijke schattingen die de leiding van de onderneming daarbij heeft gemaakt, alsmede een evaluatie van het algehele beeld van de Jaarrekening. Wij zijn van mening, dat onze controle een deugdelijke grondslag vormt voor ons oordeel.

Oordeel
Wij zijn van oordeel, dat de Jaarrekening een getrouw beeld geeft van de grootte en de samenstelling van het vermogen op 31 december 1996 en van het resultaat over 1996 in overeenstemming met algemeen aanvaarde grondslagen voor financiële verslaggeving en voldoet aan de wettelijke bepalingen inzake de Jaarrekening zoals opgenomen in Titel 9 BW2.

Heerlen, 24 februari 1997
Moret Ernst & Young Accountants

Bijzondere statutaire rechten

Stichting Preferente Aandelen DSM
In 1989 is de Stichting Preferente Aandelen DSM opgericht. Krachtens de statuten van DSM kunnen 62 500 000 stuks cumulatief preferente aandelen B worden uitgegeven. De uit te geven aandelen kunnen bij de Stichting worden geplaatst teneinde bescherming te bieden tegen een overval.

Het Bestuur is per 31 december 1996 als volgt samengesteld:

Drs. F.A. Maljers, voorzitter
Prof. mr. S.C.J.J. Kortmann
Ir. M.C. van Veen.

De Stichting is onafhankelijk van de vennootschap.

Stichting Prioriteitsaandelen DSM

Met het vervreemden door de Staat van de resterende aandelen DSM was de reden voor het bestaan van de Stichting vervallen. De Stichting is inmiddels opgeheven.

Other information

Profit appropriation According to Article 32 of the DSM N.V. Articles of Association and with the approval of the Supervisory Board of Directors, every year the Managing Board of Directors determines the portion of the net result to be appropriated to the reserves. From the subsequent balance of the net result, dividend is first distributed on the cumulative preference shares B. At the end of 1996 no cumulative preference shares B were in issue. Subsequently, to the extent that this is possible dividend is distributed on the cumulative preference shares A, the dividend percentage being equal to the arithmetic mean of the average effective yield on government bonds with a (remaining) term of 9 to 10 years - as calculated by the Dutch Central Bureau of Statistics and published in the Daily Official List of the Dutch Stock Exchange Association - over the last 20 trading days preceding 8 March 1996, increased by a number of basis points to be determined by the Managing Board of Directors, with a maximum of 50. On 1 January 2006 a new dividend percentage for the cumulative preference shares A will be fixed, and this will be repeated after every ten years. The dividend percentage for the cumulative preference shares A for the years up to and including 2005 has been fixed at 6.78%, based on a share price of NLG 70 per cumulative preference share A. The dividend for 1996 has been calculated on the basis of the number of months these shares were in issue. The remainder will be distributed as dividend on the ordinary shares.

It has been decided to appropriate the net result as follows:

	1996	1995
appropriated to the reserves	431	826
dividend on cumulative preference shares A	28	-
dividend on ordinary shares	261	245
	720	1 071

Auditor's report

Introduction
We have audited the 1996 financial statements of DSM N.V, Heerlen. These financial statements are the responsibility of the company's management. Our responsibility is to express an opinion on these financial statements based on our audit.

Scope
We conducted our audit in accordance with auditing standards generally accepted in the Netherlands. Those standards require that we plan and perform the audit to obtain reasonable assurance about whether the financial statements are free of material misstatement. An audit includes examining, on a test basis, evidence supporting the amounts and disclosures in the financial statements. An audit also includes assessing the accounting principles used and significant estimates made by management, as well as evaluating the overall financial statement presentation, We believe that our audit provides a reasonable basis for our opinion.

Opinion
In our opinion, the financial statements give a true and fair view of the financial position of the company as of. 31 December 1996 and of the result for the year then ended in accordance with accounting principles generally accepted in the Netherlands and comply with the financial reporting requirements included in Part 9, Book 2 of the Netherlands Civil Code.

Heerlen, February 24, 1997
Moret Ernst & Young Accountants

Special statutory rights
DSM Preference Shares Foundation The DSM Preference Shares Foundation was established in October 1989. By virtue of DSM's Articles of Association, 62,500,000 preference shares B can be issued. Shares thus issued can be placed with the Foundation in order to provide protection against a hostile bid.

The Committee members are:

F.A. Maljers, chairman
S.C.J.J. Kortmann
M.C. van Veen

The Foundation is independent of DSM N.V

DSM Priority Shares Foundation
With the Dutch State having disposed of its remaining DSM shares, the raison d'etre for the DSM Priority Shares Foundation ceased to exist. The Foundation was dissolved in 1996.

Country Highlights
PORTUGAL

Common Legal Forms of Companies

Most business in Portugal is conducted by sole proprietorships or limited companies, either private *(sociedades por quotas,* or *Lda*) or public *(sociedades anónimas,* or *S.A.*); some of the latter have a stock exchange listing.

Sources of Financial Reporting Requirements

The content and layout of financial statements are prescribed by the official accounting plan (*Plano Oficial de Contabilidade,* or POC). As issued and revised by the Accounting Standards Commission (*Comissão de Normalização Contabilística,* or CNC). CNC also issues opinions (*normas interpretativas* and, more recently, *directrizes contabilísticas*), which are intended to round out the POC.

For listed companies, special additional disclosure requirements apply.

Corporate Taxation

Corporate income tax is levied on companies' worldwide earnings. Taxable income *(imposto sobre o rendimento das pessoas colectivas,* or IRC) is defined as comprehensive income and calculated by reference to the Companies Income Tax Code (*Código do IRC*) and regulations issued by the tax authority. IRC is assessed at a standard rate of 34%. On top of this local authorities levy a local tax (*derrama*) of up to 10%.

On the mainland value-added tax (*imposto sobre o valor acrescentado,* or IVA) is levied at a standard rate of 17%, with a lower rate (5%) on certain goods and services. Lower rates apply in the archipelagos of Madeira and the Azores.

Auditing Requirements

The Companies Law requires all public companies and those private companies over a certain size to be subject to an annual audit. At least one auditor (*revisor oficial de contas*) must have qualified as a member of the professional auditing body. Listed companies are required to present an additional audit report by an auditor registered under the stock market authority (*auditor externo*).

Organization of the Accounting and Auditing Professions

In Portugal accounting and auditing are separate professions and have separate bodies.

The official body of the auditing profession (*Câmara dos Revisores Oficiais de Contas,* or CROC) was established in 1974. Auditors in Portugal must be registered in the CROC in order to practice.

Constitution and Legal System

The institutions of sovereignty in the Portuguese Republic are the president, Parliament, and the government. The government is led by the prime minister, who is appointed by the president and whose program must be approved by the Parliament (a unicameral *Assembleia da República* of 230 members elected for a maximum term of four years).

Currency

The monetary unit is the *escudo,* made up of 100 *centavos.* In everyday usage 1000 *escudos* are commonly referred to as a *conto* (average exchange rate in 1996 was 1US$ = Es 154$21). There is general agreement that Portugal will join the *Euro* in January 1999.

Official Languages

Portuguese is the official language of Portugal.

PORTUGAL

Leonor Fernandes Ferreira
Universidade Técnica de Lisbõn

1. Background

1.1 General

1.1.1 Political Institutions

Portugal may be described as a form of parliamentary democracy. The present constitution dates from 1976, with major revisions made in 1982, 1988, 1992, and 1997. The constitution was substantially revised in June 1989 to permit, among other things, full privatization of those firms nationalized in the 1970s. The institutions of sovereignty are the presidency, the assembly (Parliament), and the government, headed by the prime minister, who is appointed by the president. The role of the presidency has been a matter of debate. Under the original 1976 constitution there was a strong presidency, so that the country was not a pure parliamentary democracy but was described as "semi-presidential." The powers of the president were substantially reduced in subsequent constitutional revisions, which resulted in the present parliamentary democracy. The national legislature is a unicameral *Assembleia da República* (parliament) of 230 members elected for a maximum term of four years.

Portugal is a member of the United Nations, the International Monetary Fund, the World Bank, the Organization of Economic Cooperation and Development, and the North Atlantic Treaty Organization, as well as being a party to the General Agreement on Tariffs and Trade. Last but not least, Portugal became a member of the European Community in 1986.

1.1.2 The Economy

The Portuguese economy is that of an industrialized country, in which the tertiary sector (services and distribution) produces the largest contribution to the gross national product, followed by the secondary sector (manufacturing). The primary sector (agriculture, fisheries, extraction, etc.) contributes the lowest share of the GNP, and this situation has tended to become more marked in recent years.

The importance of the public sector in the economy has been toward a sustained reduction following the process of privatization that began in 1988. Privatization revenue has contributed to lower public debt and has been an incentive to the stock market.

The pattern of the economically active population of the country, as far as the sectors of the economy are concerned, is much the same as in other European countries, namely a marked reduction in the percentage of people employed in the primary sector, and a shift to the secondary and tertiary sectors, with the latter receiving the major share. The percentage of people employed has risen, especially among women.

The average wage in Portugal is currently the lowest in the European Union. The rate of inflation, as measured by the consumer price index, is 2% to 3% in excess of the EU average, and this makes it one of the government's main preoccupations.

In recent years, the Portuguese economy has been growing faster than the EU average. Growth is sustained by investment, job prospects are improving, and real wages are rising along with productivity. Portugal is an open economy, carrying out more than 75% of all its trade with other EU members. Exchange stability was fixed as a priority objective, and the escudo has stayed within a narrow range against other currencies of the European monetary system since 1993. Portugal's economic growth is forecasted to remain above the European Union average for 2 or 3 years at an annual rate of more than 3.5%. Low inflation, expected to drop to 2% in 1998, helps the government's aim to meet the criteria for joining the Euro and reduces the risks associated with a fast-expanding economy. Inflation, which started the 1990s in double digits, is now at its lowest level since the 1960s, with the average rate for 1998 expected to be around 2.2%. The budget deficit, which stood at 5.8% in 1995, is expected to meet the objective of 2.9%, bringing the deficit within the European Monetary Union requirement. Portugal appears to be one of the countries likely to qualify.

Most businesses in Portugal are conducted as sole proprietorships or limited companies, either private (*limitadas* or *sociedades por quotas*) or public (*sociedades anónimas*), some of the latter having a stock exchange listing.

1.1.3 The Financial System

The Portuguese financial system, with the opening of the banking sector to private enterprise in 1984 and the entry into the EC in 1986, has undergone a major liberalization and a deregulation of capital, financial, and money markets and has become much more dynamic. Since 1987, the central bank (Bank of Portugal) has introduced a number of financial instruments in order to increase liquidity. These include various types of term deposits, medium-term treasury bonds with maturities of between 18 months and 10 years, and interest rates fixed by tender. There has also been legislation authorizing mortgage bonds and asset management companies (which are authorized to manage both real estate and financial assets), among other things.

Changes have occurred in the legal framework of the financial markets, with government approval of the *Regime Geral das Instituições de Crédito e Sociedades Financeiras* (General Regime of Credit Institutions and Finance Companies), due to the effort of integration of Portugal into the EU.

Financial institutions in Portugal may be classified into two large groups (according to the *Regime Geral das Instituições de Crédito e Sociedades Financeiras*):

1. Credit institutions (*instituições de crédito*), those legally authorized to create means of payment, including the central bank, the commercial banks, and the special credit institutions, such as leasing companies, factoring companies, investment companies, and stock exchange companies.

2. Other financial institutions (*sociedades financeiras*), which, although having no credit function, attract savings to be applied in financial activities, such as investment funds, pension funds management companies, and asset management companies. The latter manage both real estate and financial assets on behalf of individuals and corporate entities and are incorporated under a specific legal form that authorizes them to do so (similar to the *Sociétés Civiles Financières et Immobilières* in France).

In 1991 the Stock Exchange Regulation (*Código do Mercado de Valores Mobiliários*) was created in order to develop and supervise both the Lisbon and the Oporto Stock Exchanges. Its functions also include the supervision of the primary market (new issues, disclosures, etc.), as well as authorization for the introduction of new products, such as options, and derivatives, and in general, supervision of all financial intermediaries.

Until 1995 the two stock exchanges operated as separate floors of the national spot market. Globalization of financial markets, however, required simplification and harmonization of regulations. In response, the two national stock exchanges have recently specialized so that since 1996 spot trading is based in Lisbon (*Bolsa de Valores de Lisboa*), while the recently created national derivatives market operates in Oporto (*Bolsa de Derivados do Porto*). It is now possible to trade repos, forward rate agreements, forward contracts, future contracts and equity indexes, such as PSI-20 (a contract on an equity index of 20 leading shares) and OT-10 (a contract based on 10-year Treasury bonds). Options will be available during 1998. The derivative market is similar to the one in Barcelona, having no more than 20 market makers.

Lisbon's main share price index (The BVL 30) has gained almost 95% since the beginning of 1996, ranking as the best performance in western Europe. The Lisbon market has partly been driven by sustained falls in interest rates, and on December 2, 1997, Portugal officially joined Morgan Stanley Europe index and appeared as a developed market.

Absorbing smaller Portuguese banks and foreign subsidiaries into larger groups followed the consolidation of bigger institutions, because banks could no longer sustain increases in their market shares. Accordingly, they tried to expand via acquisitions and move beyond traditional deposit-taking. This trend also involved strategies for rationalization, and diversifying into such businesses as insurance, brokerage, leasing, factoring, and fund management, among others. Growth implies the creation of large groups offering greater potential and making use of cost-cutting, cross-selling of financial products and better information technology (economies of scale and scope).

1.1.4 The Legal Environment

The legal system is a structured hierarchy of laws, with the most important, the constitution (*Constituição da República Portuguesa*) as the basis. In descending order of priority, the other sources of law are *leis* passed by Parliament (the *Assembleia da República*), *decretos-lei* of the government, *decretos-regulamentares*, and *portarias* issued by ministries, and *despachos normativos* and *despachos* signed by secretaries of state.

The legal environment that is relevant to accounting in Portugal comprises the commercial code, the body of tax law, stock market regulations, and the Official Accounting Plan, which has legal backing (see Section 3, below). In general, Portugal is a country in which accounting principles require legal expression or backing in order to be valid. There is no tradition of accounting principles gaining general acceptance through recognition by the accounting profession. The past 20 years have had a particular significance, not only for Portugal's economic and political life, but also for accounting.

The Official Accounting Plan currently in force was established by Decree-Law No. 410/89, dated November 21, 1989 and Decree-Law No. 238/91, dated July 2, 1991. The form and content of financial statements are also regulated by the Companies Law (*Código das Sociedades Comerciais*), under Decree-Law No. 262/86, dated September 2, 1986. Public filing requirements generally are stated in the Companies Law and specifically in the Commercial Register Law (*Código do Registo Comercial*), Decree-Law No. 403/86, dated December 3, 1986, and by the Stock Exchange Regulation *(Lei Sapateiro)*, Decree-Law No. 142-A/91, dated April 10, 1991. Statutory audit requirements are established in the Companies Law and in the Decree-Law No. 422-A/93, dated December 30, 1993. The latter also regulates the auditing profession. Regulation of the accounting profession, which is very recent, is stated under Decree-Law No. 265/95, dated October 17, 1995.

The first eight EU directives had already been enacted into law by early 1994, and it is now possible to assess their impact on the business community.

1.2 The Accounting Background

1.2.1 Early Portuguese Accounting History

According to the noted scholar Fernando Gonçalves da Silva, Portuguese accounting history may be divided into four periods. The first period lasted from the foundation of the Portuguese nation in 1143 to the end of the fifteenth century. Portugal became a leading maritime and trading country in the fifteenth century, so this first period saw the beginning of Portugal's maritime greatness. In spite of Portugal's trading links with the Italian republics, however, it would seem that accounting techniques used in Portugal remained at a primitive level.

The second period included the sixteenth and seventeenth centuries and the first half of the eighteenth century. The sixteenth century saw Lisbon become the center of a vast empire, one of the world's leading ports and commercial centers. Portugal's role as an imperial power received a setback in 1680, however, when the country was invaded by Philip II of Spain, and Portugal remained under Spanish domination for 60 years.

Portugal lost much of its empire, including almost all its Asian possessions, to the Spanish and the Dutch, although it retained enormous territories in Brazil and Africa, as well as some outposts in Asia. It was during this period that the use of Venetian-style double-entry bookkeeping in Portugal became apparent. Surviving examples can be seen in the records of the India Company (*Casa da India*) and the Monastery of Alcobaça (*Mosteiro de Alcobaça*). Little is known, however, regarding the extent to which such methods were used at the time. There are no books on accounting in Portuguese, either original works or translations, dating from this period, nor were any legal requirements for accounting introduced in Portugal.

The third period started with the ministry of Sebastião José de Carvalho e Melo (Minister of Finance and the future Marquis of Pombal) in 1750 and lasted until the early twentieth century. Under Pombal's ministry, efforts were made to lay down a legal structure for trade and commerce, including accounting. In 1755, a Royal Decree created a trade association (*Junta de Comércio*), and in 1756, there followed ordinances concerning mercantile books and the statutes of the Hall of Commerce (*Aula de Comércio*), which were to play a lasting role in the teaching of accounting and business methods. The first accounting texts in Portuguese appeared in 1758 and 1764. However, Gonçalves da Silva comments that the lack of education and the inertia of the businessmen of the period were such that reforms introduced by Pombal were neither as rapid, nor as profound, nor as durable as the Marquis had intended.

In the following century, commercial codes were introduced by Ferreira Borges (1786–1838) in 1833 and by Veiga Beirão (1841–1916) in 1888, under the influence of contemporary French commercial codes. These included requirements for the keeping of books of account and other records. Some of the provisions of the 1888 code are still in force today. Such provisions include the obligation to keep a journal, a ledger, and a balance sheet book (inventory), which must be written up within 90 days and retained for 10 years. The pages of these books must bear the official stamp of the authorities.

The fourth period began in the late 1920s. At this time, accounting was recognized in Portugal as a body of knowledge having a relationship with business economics and the theory of the firm. Several influential books on accounting were published by Portuguese authors, as well as translations of foreign classics by such authors as Schmalenbach, Zappa, and Dumarchey and the appearance of a journal, *Revista de Contabilidade e Comércio* (*Review of Accounting and Commerce*), which began publishing in 1933 and continues today. A scientific and cultural association as well as professional body, the *Sociedade Portuguesa de Contabilidade*, was founded in 1945 and later became a member of the *Union Européenne des Experts Comptables Economiques et Financiers*. Specialized accounting courses began to be taught in high schools. The inclusion of accounting in university curricula was slower to gain acceptance, but in due course it began to make its appearance in economics faculties and in some law faculties.

For much of this time, Portugal's economic development, perhaps even more than that of Spain, lagged behind that of her northern neighbors in Europe. For the first third of the nineteenth century, dynastic wars involving the Spanish, French, and British took place on Portuguese soil, with disastrous consequences for Portugal's economy. Brazil became independent in 1822, but the maintenance and administration of the vast African territories remained a dominant consideration, which in the 20th century became more and more burdensome, impeding the modernization of the country's economy and political institutions.

Almost until the end of the third quarter of the 20th century, while Western Europe in general enjoyed a crucial period of economic growth and modernization, the economic and political fate of Portugal was under the control of an authoritarian regime dating back to the 1930s. This regime lacked the political will to face up to the inevitable issues of decolonization abroad and democratization at home and remained locked in an increasingly vain attempt to retain African territories whose size was quite disproportionate to the resources of the nation. Resources that could otherwise have been applied to the development of Portugal's economy were thus absorbed in colonial administration and, increasingly, in wasteful colonial wars. This was associated with the persistence of archaic structures and methods in the industrial sector, cushioned by privileged positions in colonial markets.

Nevertheless, in the decade before the oil price crisis of 1973, Portugal achieved rapid growth in GDP, averaging more than 7%. As it turned out, however, the postponement of decolonization in Africa and of democratization at home meant that the Portuguese economy had, to some extent, been living on borrowed time.

1.2.2 Recent History and the Present Situation

To Gonçalves da Silva's four periods, one is tempted to add a fifth, since certain developments during the past 25 years have had a particular significance, not only for Portugal's economic and political life, but also for Portuguese accounting. During this time, accounting in Portugal entered in a phase of regulation and has experienced the following important changes:

1. Recognition of the need for accounting standardization by the accounting profession
2. National standardization of accounting via the legal system
3. International harmonization of accounting.

During this period, Portugal relinquished its overseas territories in Africa, notably those in Angola and Mozambique, thus ending the colonial administration and wars that had taken such a heavy toll on its resources. Turning toward Europe, Portugal has become established among the western European democracies and, since January 1986, has been a member state of the European Community (and now of the EU), with all that such membership entails for the country's economic orientation and its accounting and financial reporting practices. In particular, the influences of French ideas and practices, already important in the commercial codes of the nineteenth century, have been especially significant in the field of accounting.

Before joining the EU, Portugal had already embarked on the modernization of its financial accounting practices under the influence of French ideas. In fact, during the period 1970–1973, that is to say, before the 1974 revolution, a study had been undertaken under the aegis of the Directorate General of Taxes in the Ministry of Finance, with the objective of producing proposals for accounting modernizations with a view to achieving greater equity in the taxation of company profits. This study identified the French 1957 *Plan Comptable Général* as a suitable model.

To the impact of the 1973 oil price crisis were added those of the political revolution of 1974 and the negative short-term effects of decolonization. The change in political regime was followed by a period of political instability and doctrinaire socialist measures of a nature unpropitious for economic development. Decolonization resulted in the loss of privileged markets and the repatriation of about 700,000 settlers, which entailed a sudden 7% increase in population.

In spite of these difficulties, Portugal's rate of GDP growth averaged 3.3% from 1973 to 1980. The economy, however, was plagued by inflation of more than 20% per annum, budget deficits, and unemployment. It was therefore ill-equipped to confront the second oil price crisis in the early 1980s. In particular, this resulted in current account deficits on the order of 10.5% of GDP during 1980–1982, which in turn led to unacceptable levels of foreign debt. In order to contain these problems, the government was forced to sacrifice economic growth, which fell to zero in 1983 and –2% in 1984.

The political and economic history of Portugal since the 1950s has not been without its implications for accounting development. Whereas the need for improvements in accounting was recognized in the early 1970s, various endeavors to introduce reforms were constantly overtaken by political events until the early 1980s. Thus, on the one hand, the state of accounting development indicated by Portugal's 1977 Official Accounting Plan may be considered comparable to that in France 20 years earlier, when the *Plan Comptable 1957* made its appearance. On the other hand, the pursuit of the proposed accounting reforms was effectively delayed for about 6 years.

The process of modernizing Portuguese accounting regulation took a step forward in 1976 with the law establishing the Accounting Standards Commission (*Comissão de Normalização Contabilística*, or CNC), and with the issuing of the first Official Accounting Plan (*Plano Oficial de Contabilidade*, POC) in the Decree-Law of February 7, 1977. This signified the official adoption of the institutional model for accounting regulation suggested by the Finance Ministry study group, namely the French model. This model involves a standard-setting body attached administratively to the Ministry of Finance, with powers to lay down a national accounting plan, the provisions of which are given legal force in the form of decrees or decree-laws.

At the same time, although the law creating the CNC was issued in 1976, the decree specifying its structure and powers did not appear until October 1980, and the members of the Commission were not appointed until March 1983. Thus, the political and economic vicissitudes of the 1970s and early 1980s have made the creation of a modern institution for accounting regulation in Portugal a protected affair, spread over some 12 or 13 years. They also resulted in the temporary demise of industrial and financial groups, so that consolidated accounts were hardly called for until new industrial groups emerged. This helps to explain the delay in implementing the Seventh Directive.

In November 1989, a revised version of the POC was issued to give effect to the EU Fourth Directive. Sometime later, in July 1991, a revised version of the POC was issued to give effect to the EU Seventh Directive. This latter has been applied to the annual and group accounts for financial years beginning in 1991. French influence is beginning to lose its importance, as the international standards, mainly from Anglo-Saxon countries, are gaining more and more followers and began having backing in the *directrizes contabilísticas* issued by the CNC (see Section 3.5, below).

The required annual accounts are the balance sheet, the profit and loss account, and the annex (notes). Companies below certain size criteria may present abridged financial statements. These annual accounts, together with the management's report and, if appropriate, the cash flow statement and the auditor's report, must be made public by being deposited with the Commercial Registry (*Registo Comercial*).

The layout of the accounts of certain kinds of companies differs from those in the POC. This happens with banks and other financial institutions for which accounting rules are issued by the Bank of Portugal (*Banco de Portugal*) and also with insurance companies, whose accounting principles, procedures, and financial reports depend on the Insurance Institute of Portugal (*Instituto de Seguros de Portugal*).

Table 1 summarizes the major events in the development of Portuguese accounting regulation during the past 25 years.

1.2.1 The Structure, Membership, and Powers of the CNC

The Ministry of Finance regulation dated April 3, 1987 set out the current powers, structure, and functions of the CNC.

Powers of the CNC The CNC is empowered to ensure the process and improvement of national accounting standardization, and specifically:

1. To promote studies necessary to establish accounting principles, concepts, and procedures to be considered generally accepted
2. To carry out projects concerned with updating, amending, and interpreting the POC
3. To steer the development of sectorial accounting plans or to comment on and approve those developed by other bodies
4. To comment on draft laws with repercussions on company accounting
5. To respond to inquiries made by companies concerning the implementation or interpretation of the POC
6. To participate in international meetings where matters relating to accounting standardization are to be discussed, with the objective of issuing a technical opinion

Structure of the CNC The CNC has a president, a general council, and an executive committee. The president is designated by the minister of

TABLE 1　*Major Events in the Development of Portuguese Accounting Regulation*

Year	Event
1972	Regulation of the auditing profession
1973	Issue of an Accounting Plan Draft by the Ministry of Finance Staff
1976	Creation of the Accounting Standards Commission
1977	Approval of the first Official Accounting Plan
1986	Approval of the Business Companies Code in line with EU Directives
1986	Approval of the Commercial Registry Code in line with EU Directives
1987	Powers given to Accounting Standards Commission
1988	Income Tax Reform
1989	Revision of the Official Accounting Plan to comply with EU Fourth Directive
1989	The Accounting Standards Commission issues its First Opinion
1990	Reform of the Accounting Plan for the Banking System
1991	Reform of the Stock Market Regulation
1991	Creation of the Stock Market Supervisory Body
1991	Amendment of the Official Accounting Plan to comply with EU Seventh Directive
1992	Accounting regulation for group accounts of banks and other financial institutions
1993	The Bank of Portugal approves the accounting plan for banks and other financial institutions in line with the 1986 EU Directive
1993	Cash Flow Disclosures
1993	New regulation of the auditing profession to comply with EU Eighth Directive
1994	Accounting plan for insurance companies in line with the 1991 EU Directive
1995	Group accounts of insurance companies
1995	Regulation of the Accounting Profession
1996	Creation of the official body for the Accounting Profession
1997	Accounting Plan for the Public Sector

finance and must be generally recognized as being professionally and intellectually competent. The chairman of the executive committee may act as vice-president of the CNC.

The president has the power to represent the CNC in its relations with the government and with international bodies and may delegate this power to other CNC members or be accompanied by them. He or she also chairs the general council and attends meetings of the executive committee at the request of the latter or its chairman.

The general council is the deliberative body that represents at national level the various groups interested in accounting standardization. In addition to the president, it consists of 33 members, drawn from government departments, professional associations, the Bank of Portugal, the Insurance Institute of Portugal, and from universities and industry.

The powers of the General Council are:

1. To advise the Minister of Finance on accounting principles, concepts, and procedures as set out in items 1, 2, and 3, above

2. To approve the annual plan of activities and the program of research to be carried out by the executive committee or by working groups

The general council meets normally once a quarter, and a quorum consists of at least 12 members. Decisions are made by a simple majority of those present, with the president also having a vote.

The executive committee has 11 members, chosen from the members of the General Council for a renewable period of 3 years. The chairman of this committee is elected by the general council by secret ballot. The other 10 members are chosen to represent the various constituencies mentioned above.

The executive committee carries out work laid down by the general council. It sets up working groups and coordinates their activities, decides on the submission of draft proposals from the working groups to the General Council, prepares annual activity programs and budgets for submission annually to the General Council, and arranges the publication of periodic reports, the preparation of which will be entrusted to working groups.

The executive committee meets regularly four times a month, and also on the special request of its chairman (or his deputy), who also has a vote.

Working groups are composed of a member of the executive committee, who acts as coordinator, plus other members of the executive committee or of the general council, plus external assessors chosen for their special qualifications in order to ensure the quality or appropriateness of the work. The members of working groups are selected by the executive committee.

The Opinions of the CNC   Since 1987 the CNC has been preparing opinions *(Directrizes Contabilísticas)*. In some cases they include information to amplify and explain items in the POC. In other cases they provide information that is not in the POC. Contrary to what happened with the official accounting plan (POC), however, these opinions are not laws, being only approved by the general council of the CNC and not by any minister. Up to March 1998, 21 opinions have been approved by the general council of the CNC and have already been published in the official journal. Table 2 lists them and their dates of approval. (See Section 3.5 for detailed consideration of the CNC opinions.)

1.2.2   The Accounting and Auditing Professions

In common with certain other European countries (e.g., Belgium), Portugal has separate professions, and not just separate professional bodies, for accounting and auditing. The accounting profession took a step forward with the creation of its official body (*Associação dos Técnicos Oficiais de Contas* or ATOC) in 1995, after the publication of Decree-Law No. 265/95 on October 17, 1995, signed by the Ministry of Finance. This body regulates the profession, as well as undertaking disciplinary measures. Membership in this association is now required in order to practice as a member of the official accounting profession, that is, to be responsible for, and authorized to sign, the financial accounts and income tax returns of a company. To be eligible for registration as a *técnico oficial de contas* (TOC) it is necessary to hold a relevant university degree (in accountancy, business, or economics), or to have gained 5 years' practical experience, before taking the *técnicos de contas* professional examinations. Either route to qualification involves passing theoretical courses in financial accounting, management accounting, and taxation.

The fees of the *técnicos oficiais de contas* in Portugal are calculated in terms of the number and size of an individual TOC's client companies, according to a *points* system, under which each client company is attributed a certain number of points (ranging from 0 to 5) and calculated on the basis of their total turnover. An individual TOC has a maximum allocation of 22 points.

Until 1995, there was no officially recognized professional organization of accountants, but there were several professional associations. The oldest of these is the *Sociedade Portuguesa de Contabilidade*, founded in 1945, but the most influential was and still is the *Associação Portuguesa de Técnicos de Contbilidad* (APOTEC). A third body is the *Associação Portuguesa de Contabilistas*, and a fourth body is the *Câmara dos Técnicos de Contas*. Membership numbers vary among these associations. For example, APOTEC, the largest, has about 8000 members.

Until 1988, according to Portuguese tax law, company accounts prepared for tax purposes had to be signed by an accountant who was also

TABLE 2 *CNC Opinions (Directrizes Contabilísticas)*

Opinion Number	Date Published	Description
1	December 13, 1991	Accounting for business combinations
2	December 13, 1991	Accounting of assets received through donation
3	December 19, 1991	Accounting for long-term contracts
4	December 19, 1991	Accounting for concession contracts
5	December 19, 1991	Accounting for costs and revenues from the bingo game
6	May 6, 1992	Elimination of profits and losses resulting from transactions between undertakings included in a group
7	May 6, 1992	Accounting for research and development expenses
8	November 19, 1992	Clarification on the contents of *Resultados Transitados* account (preceding years' income not appropriated and/or losses carried forward), regarding unusual and very significant adjustments.
9	November 19, 1993	Accounting for investments in subsidiaries and associated companies in the individual accounts of the investing company (revised November 30, 1993)
10	November 19, 1993	Transitional procedures for leasing contracts accounting
11	January 28, 1993	Intracommunitary value added tax accounting
12	January 28, 1993	The accounting concept of goodwill
13	July 7, 1993	The concept of fair value
14	July 7, 1993	Cash-flow statements
15	December 21, 1994	Shares' redemption and amortization
16	January 11, 1995	Revaluation of fixed tangible assets
17	May 29, 1996	Accounting for futures (revised October 11, 1997)
18	December 18, 1996	Objectives of the financial statements and generally accepted accounting principles
19	May 21, 1997	Pension costs (revised October 11, 1997)
20	June 4, 1997	Income statement by functions (revised October 11, 1997)
21		Accounting for the consequences of the adoption of the Euro

responsible for keeping the company's financial records in one centralized location. As a result of the 1989 fiscal reform, it has no longer been necessary for an accountant to be registered with the Ministry of Finance in order to sign a company's tax return, provided he or she is named as the company's official accountant in its statutory declaration of commencement of activities. According to recently approved regulations of the accounting profession, however, annual accounts and tax returns must again be signed by a *técnico oficial de contas* registered with the ATOC for financial years beginning on or after January 1, 1998.

The auditing profession consists of statutory auditors (*revisores oficiais de contas*, or ROCs) registered with the Chamber of Registered Statutory Auditors (*Câmara dos Revisores Oficiais de Contas*, or CROC). The latter is the officially recognized professional body for auditors and is the national representative of Portugal in IASC, IFAC, and FEE. In order to be registered as a statutory auditor, it is necessary to hold a relevant university degree (the same as for registered accountants) or a technical college accounting diploma, followed by a 3-year apprenticeship and passing a written and oral examination. In December 1993 the new legal regime of auditing professionals was approved (Decree-Law 422-A/93, published in the Official Journal on December 30, 1993 and signed by the Ministry of Justice) to regulate the auditing profession in Portugal. This is in line with the Eighth EU Directive and was effective on January 1, 1994.

The auditing profession has been more important than the accounting profession in anticipating the application in Portugal of international accounting rules. Latin countries' influence, however, is becoming less important as Anglo-Saxon standards gain more and more followers.

Auditing standards are specified by the CROC in its periodically updated *Manual*, which embraces international auditing principles. It also includes a set of technical recommendations (*recomendações técnicas*) and opinions (*interpretações técnicas*) issued by the CROC, which guides auditing practice. Tables 3 and 4 list them as of March 1998.

The audit obligation is applicable to all companies that exceed certain size limits, to listed companies, and to financial institutions and insurance companies. Auditors are appointed for a period between 2 and 4 years by the shareholders. In the case of companies not subject to statutory audit, shareholders owning 5% of the capital stock can demand the appointment of auditors. Auditors in Portugal are members of a professional body and must be registered in the Official Auditors Chamber (CROC), which is responsible for issuing standards and undertaking disciplinary measures.

As for auditing, Portuguese corporations (*Sociedade Anónima*, SA) and private limited companies (*sociedade por quotas,* or Ldas) must appoint a statutory board of auditors (*conselho fiscal*), the size and composition of which depend on the size and legal form of the company. All SAs must have a three member audit board, one of whom is the company's *revisor oficial de contas* (ROC), unless the share capital is less than 20 million escudos, in which case a single ROC may act as auditor. For private companies above a certain size as specified in the law implementing the EC Fourth Directive, the same applies as in the case of an SA (50 employees, net assets of 350 million escudos, and sales turnover of 600 million escudos). For smaller Ldas, no statutory audit is required. Although only one member of the statutory board of auditors need be professionally qualified, the following restrictions apply to all members.

No member of the statutory board of auditors may:

- Be a director or employee of the company, or receive any special benefits from it;

- Be a director, employee or audit board member of the company's parent or subsidiary companies or of any company that is in a position to control or be controlled by the company because of any special contractual obligations;

- Be a shareholder, owner or employee of any company carrying out in its own name any of the functions or subject to the restrictions described above;

- Perform any functions in a competitor company;

- Have a close family relationship with persons in any of the preceding categories;

- Be legally incapacitated from carrying out public duties.

In addition to the statutory audit, a number of the largest Portuguese companies employ international accounting firms to carry out an independent audit in accordance with international auditing standards.

Regarding nonstatutory auditing, there has been a significant increase in demand for international auditors in Portugal, both from state-owned companies, especially those undergoing privatization, and from private companies, whether for merger, acquisitions, financing, and stock exchange purposes, or, generally, for greater credibility of their financial statements.

TABLE 3   *Technical Recommendations of the CROC*

CROC Number	Description
1	Auditing of the financial statements and other published reports
2	Influence of initial balances on the final balances to be verified
3	Verification of the application of the principle of consistency
4	Influence of tax rules on the statutory audit
5	Auditing of intermediate financial statements (amended)
6	Annual report on statutory auditing carried out
7	Auditing of nonmonetary paid-up capital (annulled)
8	Auditing of accounts that include comparative figures relating to the previous year
9	Statutory audit of consolidated accounts
10	Information and qualifications in the statutory audit report
11	Auditing of prospective financial information (amended)
12	Annual audit of entities subject to the stock market regulation (amended)
13	Opinion about the information disclosed by companies with listed shares
14	Audit of capital entries in the companies (amended)
15	Audit of companies with fiscal and parafiscal obligations
16	Nondocumented or confidential expenses
17	(Cancelled)
18	Declaration of responsibility
19	Use of others' auditors working papers
20	Information supporting the auditor's opinion

---

2. The Form and Content of Published Financial Statements

Accounts are always published in Portuguese, although some companies—primarily subsidiaries of foreign concerns—present bilingual financial reports.

TABLE 4   *CROC Interpretations*

Number	Description
1	Comparative figures in the consolidated financial statements
2	Leasing
3	Audit of the first consolidated accounts disclosed by certain financial institutions
4	Audit of deferred taxes related to the reinvestment of capital gains obtained in disposals of tangible fixed assets
5	Applicability of the equity method
6	Application of Directriz Contabilística 16 (about revaluation of tangible fixed assets
7	Classification of leasing and rental agreements
8	Items to include under equity capital of financial institutions under the supervision of the Bank of Portugal
9	Declining balance method of depreciation
10	Modification of the legal form of business organization, changing from sole proprietorship to a company form
11	Wording and quantification of qualifications in an audit report.

The requirements of the POC are based on those of the EC Fourth Directive and thus encompass the balance sheet, profit and loss statement, and annex (notes to the financial statements); there is no requirement for a statement of sources and applications of funds. The POC presents, however, a specimen statement of sources and application of funds. Until 1990, companies in Portugal had not been required to publish group accounts, although they have been permitted under certain circumstances to file tax returns on a group basis since 1988. This situation has changed as a result of the extension of the POC in July 1991 to include requirements for consolidated accounts as set out in the Seventh EU Directive. These have applied to financial statements for years beginning on or after January 1, 1991. Details are given in Section 3.4 below.

In 1993, the stock market supervising body pushed the CNC to issue an opinion (*Directriz Contabilística No.14*) concerning the cash flow statements and providing models of presentation. Companies with shares listed on the Portuguese Stock Exchanges must disclose, additionally, a cash flow statement for the year according to the format in that opinion as well as a mid-year balance sheet and profit and loss account, and forecasts for the assets and cash flow for the year. These requirements are stated in the stock markets regulation.

A specimen set of Portuguese financial statements (including consolidated accounts) is included as an appendix to this chapter.

2.2 Balance Sheet Format and Contents

The POC opted for the horizontal format provided in the Fourth Directive. With regard to content, the POC gives a highly detailed version (*Balanço Analítico*), in which most lines of the balance sheet correspond to a single two- or three-digit account code within the national chart of accounts. There is also a summarized version (*Balanço Sintético*), in which most lines correspond to a combination of account codes and that may be used by smaller enterprises, that is, those that during the past two successive years have not exceeded two of the following three size criteria (from the Companies Law): 50 employees; turnover 600 million escudos; total assets 350 million escudos.

The appendix provides the detailed format, with the description of line items in Portuguese and English. It may be noted that three columns are provided for the current year's balance sheet figures: these are for the gross values of assets, provisions for depreciation or amortization, and net values, respectively.

2.3 Profit and Loss Statement Format and Contents

Of the four formats offered by the Fourth Directive, the POC opts for the horizontal format, classified by nature, with expenses and losses on the left-hand side and revenues and income for the year on the right. This is the most traditional of the four, and the one that, generally speaking, discloses least to the financial analyst, omitting the subtotals that are of interest for analytical purposes. However, the Portuguese format provides a number of these in a *résumé* at the bottom of the statement and in some of the notes to the accounts (see the specimen notes in the Appendix).

As with the balance sheet, as far as contents are concerned, the full version (*Demonstração de Resultados Analítica*) is relatively detailed, and smaller enterprises may produce a more succinct version (*Demonstração de Resultados Sintética*). The difference between the level of detail in the two versions is much less than in the case of the balance sheet, however.

The profit and loss account format requires intermediate income balances to be calculated and presented. These balances are calculated in accordance with the step-by-step approach to income calculation.

The POC and the *Directriz Contabilística No.20* also provide a vertical format by function, based on that given in the Fourth Directive. Smaller companies (those that during the past two successive years have not exceeded two out of the three size criteria indicated above) may produce a profit and loss statement by function in addition to the required horizontal format. The former will be obligatory for companies that exceed the said size criteria, in addition to the full version of the statement by nature, but cannot replace it. Noncompliance with this requirement for years after 1997 will give rise to a qualification (*ênfase*) in the auditors' report.

2.4 The Annex

The annex (*Anexo ao Balanço e à Demonstração de Resultados*) required by the POC has been designed to meet the requirements of the Fourth Directive. It includes information intended to amplify and explain items in the financial statements, as well as other information that does not appear in the financial statements but could be useful for the reader or be relevant to the financial position of the enterprise. The POC emphasizes that the quality of the financial information given by companies is dependent on the content of the notes.

The contents of the annex are too numerous to list here in detail. The most significant items contained in it are the following:

1. Any departure from the requirement of the POC in exceptional cases in order to show a true and fair view (*uma imagem verdadeira e apropriada*) and the reasons for such departure
2. Any items in the balance sheet or profit and loss statement that are not comparable with those of the previous year, with an explanation
3. The valuation principles and methods of calculating depreciation and provisions
4. Exchange rates used to translate amounts originally expressed in foreign currency for inclusion in the balance sheet and profit and loss statement
5. Accounting methods used in order to obtain tax benefits:

    a. The use of asset valuation principles different from those referred to above

    b. Depreciation in excess of what is economically justified

    c. Extraordinary provisions (write-downs) against assets

6. Situations having an impact on future taxation

7. Comments on organization costs and research and development costs and on goodwill and other intangibles if amortized over more than 5 years

8. Supplementary schedules on fixed assets, including intangibles, property, plant, and equipment and financial fixed assets

9. Further information on fixed assets, such as interest capitalized during the year, revaluation, breakdown by sector of activity, and other analyses relevant for tax or EU purposes

10. A list of subsidiaries, associated companies, and participations in which the parent company holds at least 10% of the capital. (Associated companies and participations that are not required to publish their financial statements may be omitted.)

11. Information on investments in other companies included in negotiable securities if they have a carrying value amounting to more than 5% of the working capital of the reporting entity

12. Analysis of assets held on account of restricted funds, for example, pension funds

13. For working capital items:

    a. The total difference by category of asset between book value and market value, if material

    b. In the case of items stated at a book value below the lower of cost or market value, the reasons for this

    c. Indication of and reasons for any extraordinary provisions for loss of value

14. The global value of inventories belonging to the entity but not in its possession

15. The overall value of doubtful for each category of receivables

16. Details of advances or loans to members of the board of administration, the executive board, or the audit board of the company

17. Details of the equity capital and changes occurred during the year.

3. Accounting Principles, Policies, and Practices in Valuation and Income Measurement

3.1 Introduction

Portuguese accounting principles are promulgated in the POC (Official Accounting Plan). Given the tax orientation of Portuguese financial accounting, however, tax rules are also influential in certain areas of accounting, such as those for fixed assets and provisions. The basic bookkeeping requirements are laid down in the Commercial Code.

Banks and financial institutions are subject to a separate set of accounting requirements. The POC was drawn up in light of the EU Fourth and Seventh Directives, which do not apply to banks and other financial institutions and to insurance companies. The former are subject to the 1986 Directive on the financial statements of credit and financial institutions. An accounting plan applicable to the financial sector and drawn up in light of the 1986 Directive exists and has been applied informally since January 1, 1990. This accounting plan is the responsibility not of the CNC but of the Bank of Portugal.

The financial statements of insurance companies are also regulated by a sectorial plan that was prepared by the Insurance Institute of Portugal, which was drawn up in light of the 1991 EU Directive.

3.2 The Official Accounting Plan—General

As already noted, the current version of the Official Accounting Plan (POC) was published in October 1989 and was modified and amended in July 1991 to attend to the requirements of the EU Seventh Directive on group accounts. It is perhaps noteworthy that publication took the form of a document annexed to a decree-law approved by the Council of Ministers and not simply by the Finance Ministry, a fact that may indicate the national importance attributed to such a document. The contents are as follows:

1. Introduction
2. General considerations
3. Objectives and qualitative characteristics of financial information
4. Accounting principles
5. Accounting rules for specific classes of items

6. Balance sheet formats and contents
7. Profit and loss statement format and content
8. Notes to the balance sheet and the profit and loss statements
9. Statement of sources and application of funds
10. Overall chart of accounts
11. Detailed code of accounts
12. Explanatory notes on the operation of certain accounts
13. Group accounts methods and procedures
14. Group financial statements format and contents

3.3 Detailed Consideration of the Official Accounting Plan

3.3.1 The Introduction

The introduction to the POC makes clear that the November 1989 POC is a revision of the original 1977 version. The reasons for the revision were as follows: compliance with EU Directives; to take the opportunity to introduce some improvements and clarifications in light of 12 years' experience, for example, titles of accounts; and to remove some minor differences between Portuguese accounting and internationally accepted principles (IASC), for example, accounting for leased assets.

The CNC decided to keep the changes to a minimum in order to facilitate matters for both accountants and users.

3.3.2 General Considerations

The section on general considerations explains the reasons for the changes being introduced and provides justifications for the options exercised under the Fourth Directive. It also provides a number of legal definitions, for example, regarding related companies and provisions.

Portuguese law (POC) makes the following distinctions between different categories of related companies:

- *Group companies*: Those companies that belong to a range that includes the mother company and the subsidiaries (those holding more than 50% the voting capital of another)
- *Associated companies*: When one company holds 20% or more and no more than 50% of the voting capital of another and can not be considered either a mother company or a subsidiary

- *Participations*: When one company does not meet the conditions required to be a group company or an associated company
- A *group* is defined as including subsidiaries but not associated companies and participations.

The Business Companies Code defines totally controlled and simply controlled subsidiaries as follows:

- *Totally controlled subsidiaries*: When one company holds 90% or more of the voting capital of another, either directly or indirectly
- *Simply controlled subsidiaries*: When one company holds a majority of the voting capital of another, either directly or indirectly, or over which it exercises control by other means

3.3.3 Objectives and Qualitative Characteristics of Financial Information

This section of the POC sets out certain general ideas and is mainly a brief summary of those expressed in the FASB's Statements of Financial Accounting Concepts (SFAC) 1 and 2, regarding the objectives and qualitative characteristics of financial statements.

Objectives Financial statements should be suitable for making rational economic decisions and hence contributing to the functioning of efficient capital markets and the accountability of management.

User groups that are specifically cited are investors, lenders, workers, suppliers and other creditors, government and other official authorities, and the public in general. The responsibility for preparing and presenting financial statements is laid on management and, in particular, on the board of directors (these responsibilities are set out in detail in the company law). It is stated that users of financial statements will be better able to analyze the capacity of the firm, in terms of the timing and certainty of the cash flows it may generate, if they are provided with information that focuses on its financial position, results of operations, and changes in financial position.

Qualitative Characteristics The essential quality of financial statement information is understandability by users, and its usefulness depends on three characteristics: relevance, reliability, and comparability. The definitions of these three characteristics given in the POC are derived from those in SFAC 2. The POC states that these characteristics, together with concepts, principles, and accounting rules, make it possible that general purpose financial statements may give a true and fair view of the firm's financial position and results of operations.

3.3.4 Fundamental Accounting Principles

The principles of continuity, consistency, accruals, and prudence included in the POC are similar to those stated in the EC Fourth Directive. This directive also refers to the use of the cost (or entry price) basis of accounting for assets but specifically allows the use of current cost as a member state option. The wording of the POC is somewhat different: it requires the use of "costs of acquisition or production, either in nominal or in constant escudos." (See under "Fixed Assets," below.)

The principle of substance over form requires operations to be accounted for with regard to their substance and financial reality and not merely their legal form. With regard to the treatment of finance leases, in the beginning, finance leases were accounted for in the assets of the lessor company. The latest version of the POC was adapted to the Anglo-Saxon model, in which leased assets under finance leases are accounted for in the assets of the lessee company.

The principle of materiality requires financial statements to show all the items that are relevant and that may affect evaluations or decisions by interested users.

3.3.5 Accounting Rules for Specific Classes of Items

Financial accounting in Portugal has traditionally been tax-oriented, so that an important influence of accounting practice in the sphere of valuation and income measurement is the body of decree-laws and decrees dealing with the calculation of taxable profit and with tax treatments that are mandatory if certain tax allowances are to be obtained. Notwithstanding the fundamental principles enunciated in the POC, if the accounting treatment required to obtain a tax benefit differs from that which is consistent with the POC, it is the former that will prevail (although the POC requires the difference to be disclosed in the notes to the financial statements—see Section 2, above, and Section 3.6.4, below). On the other hand, Portuguese tax law does not set out to provide anything approaching a comprehensive set of accounting guidelines.

The main task of the POC has been to promote the standardization of accounting terminology and classification. Its contribution to valuation and income measurement has been much slighter. In all fairness, it should be said that much the same is true of its model, the French *Plan Comptable Générale* (PCG). However, the latter has been supplemented by a body of accounting principles enunciated by the French *Conseil National de la Comptabilité* (CNC), as well as by technical recommendations by the official French professional accounting body, while the counterpart in Portugal through the *Directrizes Contabilísticas* issued by the CNC appeared later. These facts need to be borne in mind when considering the rules for valuation and income measurement set out in the 1989 POC, which are described below.

Liquid Assets Liquid assets in foreign currencies should be accounted for at closing rates, and unrealized exchanges gains and losses are taken to profit and loss and reported in the section "Financial Expenses and Income."

Negotiable securities are to be treated according to the criteria set out for inventories, as far as these are applicable.

Amounts Due from Third Parties In the case of amounts in foreign currencies, unrealized exchange gains or losses are generally to be dealt with in the same way as those on liquid assets. There are exceptions, however. In the case of medium- and long-term loans, unrealized exchange gains should be deferred if there are reasonable expectations that the gain may be reversed. In the case of exchange differences on financing for fixed assets, it is permitted to impute the exchange differences to the cost of the fixed assets only during the period in which the fixed assets are acquired or in the course of construction.

When the amount of loans payable exceeds that of corresponding loans receivable, the net unrealized difference on exchange may be treated as a deferred charge.

As in the case of other provisions, those for risks and charges (losses) should not exceed what is necessary.

Inventories The valuation basis for inventories is the cost of acquisition or production except if this exceeds the market price, in which case the latter is to be used (the principle of the lower of cost or market value). The cost of acquisition includes the purchase price and any expenditure incurred directly or indirectly to place the item in its present state and location. The cost of production includes that of raw materials, direct labor, variable manufacturing costs plus fixed manufacturing costs necessarily incurred to produce the item and place it in its present state and location. Fixed manufacturing costs can be imputed to cost of production, taking account of the normal capacity of the means of production. Costs of distribution or of general administration and financial costs are not to be incorporated in cost of production.

Obsolescence, physical deterioration, a fall in price, or analogous factors are to be dealt with according to the principle of the lower of cost or market value.

By-products, scrap, and other such items are valued, in the absence of better criteria, at their net realizable value.

Market price is to be understood as replacement cost for goods acquired for production, and as net realizable value for goods acquired for sale.

The following cost-flow conventions are permitted: specific cost, weighted average, FIFO, LIFO, and standard cost. Standard cost may be used if it is checked and, if necessary, adjusted in accordance with accepted accounting principles. Adjustments should be made to take account of confirmed variances.

In the case of agricultural, livestock, and forestry operations, if the determination of production cost is too difficult, the following criterion may be used in valuing inventory: net relizable value less the normal profit margin. The same criterion may also be used in the extractive and fishing industries.

Merchandise inventories in retail sales establishments, when the variety of such items is great, may also be valued at net selling price less the profit margins included in such prices. Cash and carry establishments that predominantly sell small quantities of each type of merchandise to small retailers may also be considered retail sales establishments for the present purpose.

In the case of work-in-process under long-term contracts, either the percentage of completion method or the completed contract method may be used.

Raw materials and consumables may be accounted for by using the base stock method at a fixed quantity and value, provided the following conditions are satisfied: they turn over frequently; they represent an overall value of relatively little importance for the business; and there are no significant variations in quantity, value, or composition.

Fixed Assets   Fixed assets are to be valued at cost of acquisition or production. Such cost is to be determined by using the same principles as those for inventories. However, it may include financial costs associated with the financing of fixed assets, insofar as these are incurred during the period in which the fixed asset was in the course of purchase or production. In the case in which parts of an asset in the course of construction come into service at different dates, financial costs should cease to be imputed to each part as soon as it comes into service.

Fixed assets having a limited useful life must be written off systematically over that life.

The POC refers to the capitalization of finance leases, in the detailed comments on Class 4 of the Chart of Accounts. Finance leases are now capitalized by using the approach of the IAS 17/FAS-13, but the implementation of this was delayed pending the revision of the accounting plan applicable to financial institutions until January 1994. CNC issued an opinion (*Directriz Contabilística No. 10*) containing transitional accounting procedures for capitalization of finance leases.

In the case of financial fixed assets, if at the balance sheet date the market value of such an asset is less than its book value, the latter may be reduced accordingly by using the appropriate account. This provision should be reversed as soon as the loss of value ceases to be confirmed.

The item investments include holdings in group companies, associated companies, and others, as well as bonds and other securities held for more than one year. It also includes land and property (real estate) held as a financial investment.

It is important to note that this item does not include own shares (which are recorded as a contra item on the liabilities side of the balance sheet, in the equity).

The equity method is also valid, as an option, for the valuation of group and associated companies undertakings in the financial statements of the investor company, according to the most recent version of POC, dated July 1991. (*Directriz Contabilística No. 9* states, however, that the equity method is compulsory and not optional).

Also, in a few cases, the increase of the nominal capital of the investee company through the incorporation of reserves is recorded in the asset of the investor company up to the nominal value of the percentage of capital held.

In the case of tangible or intangible fixed assets, whether or not they have a limited useful life, if at the balance sheet date their value is less than the corresponding book value, and it is expected that this loss of value will be permanent, a write-off equal to the loss of value should be made. This exceptional depreciation should be reversed if the reason for its being made no longer applies.

Organization costs and research and development costs may be capitalized but must normally be written off over a maximum of 5 years. Departures from this must be disclosed in the notes.

Goodwill and short-term lease premiums should be written off over a maximum period of 5 years, but this period may be prolonged, provided it does not exceed the asset's useful life.

Although the fundamental accounting principles described in Section 4 of the POC envisage the use of cost in terms of "constant escudos," nothing further is said about this in the POC's rules for fixed assets, so one may suppose that the reference to the use of constant escudos in Section 4 of the POC is intended to bring this within the ambit of accounting principles. The tax law, however, permits the revaluation of fixed assets by using coefficients based on the consumer price index (see Section 3.6.3, below), but the use of the revaluation reserve is limited both by the Companies Law and the tax law to offset future losses and incorporation in the capital. The latter depends on the write-off or disposal of the revalued asset (see Section 3.5.4 and Section 3.6.3. below).

Accruals and Deferrals   The POC uses the deferred accounts to record revenues and expenses that arise in one accounting period but that will be allocated to the profit and loss account in a different period. They are specific kinds of assets and liabilities (prepayments, deferrals, and accruals) and are not the same as ordinary creditors or debtors.

On the assets side, the deferred item is subdivided into accrued revenues and deferred charges. The POC requires deferred charges to appear after liquid assets, at the foot of the balance sheet. Examples include interest to be received on long-term debts, discounts arising on bond issues, and redemption premiums on bond issues.

On the liabilities side, the deferred item is subdivided into deferred revenues and accrued expenses of the current year that will be paid in the future. The POC requires accrued expenses to appear at the bottom of the liabilities side of the balance sheet. These items include interest to be paid, insurance premiums, and subventions received in advance.

3.4 Group Accounts

With regard to consolidated accounts, the most recent amendment to the Official Accounting Plan, published on July 2, 1991, made it mandatory for all groups controlled by a parent company to consolidate. Some groups are exempted, however, for reasons of size or because they belong to consolidated larger groups with parent companies in EU member countries. In any case, the parent companies of listed groups must always present their consolidated annual accounts.

Provisions implementing the requirements of the Seventh Directive regarding the audit and publication of consolidated accounts, and laying down requirements for an annual management report on group activities, are included in the legislation already published.

Regulations on group accounts were added to the POC, in the revision of July 1991, as Chapter 13, "Methods and Procedures for Group Accounting," and Chapter 14, "Group Financial Statements."

3.4.1 Scope of Application

The scope of application is the same as that laid down in the Seventh Directive. SAs and Ldas must prepare consolidated accounts, subject to criteria stated below. The size criteria below which an entity is exempted from the requirement, provide it has not exceeded two out of the three during two successive financial years, are: total assets: 1,500 million escudos; total turnover: 3,000 million escudos; number of employees: 250. These size exemptions do not apply to groups, however, if one or more of their member companies are listed on any EU stock exchange.

The Seventh Directive's exemption of subgroups, when the ultimate "parent" company prepares consolidated accounts under EU Seventh Directive, also applies, subject to the same conditions. The general rule is that subsidiaries are to be consolidated by using full consolidation and associated companies included by using the equity method. Proportional consolidation may be used for joint ventures as an alternative to the equity method. The method of full consolidation mentioned in the POC is the "acquisition" or "purchase" method described in the Directive.

As required by the Seventh Directive, subsidiaries must be excluded from consolidation if their activities are of such a different nature from those of the rest of the group that their inclusion would militate against a true and fair view. In such cases, the equity method should be used.

An optional exclusion exists on grounds of materiality; however, the materiality of companies excluded under this rule must be considered as a whole, not individually. A further optional exclusion exists in the case of subsidiaries in foreign countries over which the group's control is restricted by the policies of the governments of those countries. A subsidiary may also be excluded from consolidation if it is impossible to obtain any accounts from it without disproportionate expense or undue delays. Subsidiaries may also be excluded if the interest in them is held on a short-term basis only.

3.4.2 Methods and Procedures for Group Accounts

According to Chapter 13 of the POC, the following points are to be considered when preparing consolidated accounts:

Consolidated Financial Statements   Consolidated financial statements should comprise a balance sheet, a profit and loss statement, and notes to the accounts (annex), and these documents should make up a composite whole. The preparation of a statement of sources and applications of funds is also recommended, although the POC does not provide any format for it. The methods and procedures of consolidation must be applied consistently from one financial year to the next.

Objective of Group Accounts   The objective is to give a true and fair view of the assets, liabilities, financial position, and profit or loss of the undertakings included in the consolidation taken as a whole. The annex should be used to disclose information related to this objective.

Date of Group Accounts   The group accounts should be drawn up as of the same date as the annual accounts of the parent undertaking, except that another date may be considered in order to take account of the largest number or the most important of the undertakings included in the consolidation (see note 1 at the end).

Changes in the Scope of the Consolidation   If the composition of the undertakings included in the consolidation has changed significantly in the course of a financial year, additional information must be given (in either the balance sheet or the annex) in order to provide the necessary comparability.

Consolidation Method   The full or global method is the rule in the case of subsidiaries. This is the line-by-line method, with assets, liabilities, income, and expense being included in full and with minority interests being shown where appropriate. (See below for the treatment of associated companies).

Valuation Criteria   Valuation criteria should conform to the criteria laid down by the POC (as described above) and be the same as those used in the annual accounts of the parent undertaking. If necessary, consolidating adjustments should be made to the figures of companies being consolidated in order to meet these criteria.

Differences in Taxes   Account shall be taken in the consolidated financial statements of any difference arising on consolidation between the tax *chargeable* for the financial year and for the preceding financial years and the amount of tax *paid* or *payable* in respect of those years.

Eliminations   The POC follows Article 26 of the Seventh Directive and requires elimination of debts and claims between undertakings included in the consolidation, of income and expense relating to transactions between those undertakings, and of profits and losses from such transactions included in the book values of assets. The "prudence principle" applies; also, derogation from the need to eliminate may be accepted if elimination would involve undue expense or if the transaction giving rise to the profit or loss originated outside the group.

3.4.3 Associated Companies

Associated companies must be consolidated by using the equity method. Proportional consolidation, as in a number of countries, is reserved for joint ventures. According to the POC, the method of proportional consolidation (line-by-line) may be used if an undertaking included in a consolidation manages another undertaking jointly with one or more undertakings not included in that consolidation. In that case, the inclusion of that other undertaking in the consolidated accounts may be in proportion to the rights in its capital held by the undertaking included in the consolidation.

3.4.4 Transitional Provisions

According to the POC, when a participating interest in an undertaking is first included in a consolidation, the amount to be included in the consolidated balance sheet is equal to the capital and reserves of the undertaking, and the difference between that amount and the book value of the participating interest in the parent's accounts (i.e., goodwill) should be disclosed separately within the equity capital in the consolidated balance sheet at the relevant date. The treatment of goodwill according to the POC was given in Section 3.3.5 under Fixed Assets.

3.4.5 *Structure of Group Financial Statements*

As already noted, group financial statements consist of a consolidated balance sheet, consolidated statement of profit and loss, and an annex (together with a funds statement if the recommendation given in the POC is followed). The required formats of these statements are essentially the same as those for the parent company (legal entity or "social") accounts, except that items relating to minority interests may appear in the group accounts.

3.5   Detailed Considerations of Some Items Regulated by CNC Opinions

CNC has been strongly influenced by the IAS when preparing the *directrizes contabilísticas*. In some cases, however, the Portuguese opinions are opposite those of the international standards.

The *directrizes* usually explain and detail the contents of the POC. It is, however, too soon to measure the real impact of the *directrizes contabilísticas* on the accounting methods and financial disclosures made by the Portuguese companies. Some of the topics that are ruled out by the *directrizes* and their consistency with IAS are given below. References are also made to items that are currently a matter of debate in Portugal and that will probably be the object of future opinions from the CNC.

3.5.1 *Cash Flow Disclosures*

Cash flow reporting is regulated in *Directriz Contabilística No. 14* This opinion contains the disclosure formats that are in line with IAS 7 requirements. Cash flow for the year must be classified by operating, investing, and financing activities. Cash flow from operating activities should be reported by using either the direct or the indirect method.

3.5.2 *Construction Contracts*

Accounting procedures to use in construction contracts are set out in *Directriz Contabilística No. 3*, which is, in general, in accordance with IAS 11. The *Directriz* requires that when the outcome of a construction contract can be estimate reliably, the percentage of completion method should be used to measure revenue and expenses. It is worth noting that where it is not possible to determine the profit on completed parts of a project with reasonable certainty, the completed contract method should be applied.

3.5.3 Research and Development Costs

According to *Directriz Contabilística No. 7*, in Portugal, it is not mandatory to recognize research and development costs as an asset. According to the Companies Business Code (article 33a) a special reserve has to be maintained equal to the nonamortized balance of capitalized research and development costs (the same applies to the capitalized formation costs). The Portuguese accounting requirements for research and development costs in Portugal are not in conflict with IAS 9.

3.5.4 Revaluation of Tangible Fixed Assets

Fixed tangible assets should be carried at cost or at revalued amounts. In this case, the revaluated amount less the accumulated depreciation is disclosed. If a revaluation takes place, all the fixed assets belonging to the same group must be revalued together.

Directriz Contabilística No. 16 completes the POC regarding the revaluation of tangible fixed assets and helps to clarify the sense of the expressions in the POC *escudos constantes* and *escudos nominais*. The *Directriz* allows free reevaluation of tangible fixed assets without a legal support, that is, revaluation not based on prescribed coefficients. Free revaluation is based on fair values (current market value for land and buildings and depreciated cost of replacement in the case of other tangible fixed assets; the concept of fair value is defined under *Directriz Contabilística No. 13*). Fair values are subjective and not easily verifiable values. This is something new in Portuguese accounting legislation, which did not contain any reference to free revaluation before, and gives legal backing to the accounting practice of revaluation that an increasing number of Portuguese companies have been adopting on the basis of valuation reports from experts, with no tax effetcs.

The Companies Law states that the revaluation reserve must be accounted for in the balance sheet as an equity reserve and may be used only to offset future losses and may be incorporated into capital but not distributed as dividends. *Directriz Contabilística No. 16* indicates that incorporation of the revaluation surplus into the capital is limited to the amount that can be considered "realized." Realization in this sense includes disposal of the asset (in which case the revaluation surplus is included in profit and loss), and also its writing down by means of depreciation. In the latter case, it is the accumulated depreciation relating to the amount of the revaluation that, according to the *Directriz*, may be incorporated into capital.

3.5.5 Futures Contracts

Disclosures and procedures to account for futures contracts are set in *Directriz Contabilística No. 17*, published in 1997 that was inspired by IAS 32 and the IASC's ED 48. The accounting treatment depends on the classification of contracts as hedged or nonhedged contracts. In the latter (speculation and arbitrage) payments and receipts due to adjustments are included in the profit and loss account. In the former (hedged contracts) gains and losses due to changes in the fair value are only recognized in the profit and loss statement at the same time as recognition is made to the corresponding loss or gain due to the modification of the hedged position; the hedged position is accounted at cost, and gains and losses are carried in the balance sheet as deferrals. Disclosures of financial futures contracts include terms and conditions, accounting policies, fair values, and exposures to interest risk and credit risk and must be made in the annex.

3.5.6 Retirement Benefit Pension Costs

CNC has recently approved *Directriz Contabilística No. 19* which rules out accounting for a retirement benefit plan in accordance with IAS 19. The *Directriz* is in force for accounting years beginning on or after January 1, 1998. There are two types of retirement benefit plans: defined benefit plans and defined contribution plans. Disclosures related to a defined contribution plan include a description of the plan with the groups of employees included and the pension cost charged to the profit and loss statement and other amounts that may affect comparability with past years.

Under a defined benefit plan, disclosures include actuarial present value of promised retirement benefits and the fair values of the plan assets. Past services costs, experience adjustments and the effects of changes in actuarial assumptions and of plan amendments should be recognized as an expense or as income systematically over the expected remaining working lives of existing employees. The cost of retirement benefits should be determined by using an accrued benefit valuation method. This is the cost based on services rendered by employees to the date of the actuarial valuation. However, the alternative projected benefit valuation method in IAS 19 is also allowed in Portugal.

Special transitional rules, however, apply for financial institutions, where past services costs must be fully provided for by 1997.

3.5.7 Disclosure Objectives and General Accepted Accounting Principles

Directriz Contabilística No. 18 stresses that the main objective of accounting disclosures is to give a true and fair view (*uma imagem verdadeira e apropriada*) of the financial position, the performance and movements in the financial position of the entity, its total assets, liabilities, and equity, as well as income for the year in order to be useful to decision makers.

This *Directriz* also indicates the prevalence of the accounting principle of substance over form and names by descending order of importance the set of accounting rules that companies must apply. In this hierarchy, the Official Accounting Plan comes at the top, followed by the *Directrizes Contabilísticas*, and the IAS. This is consistent with the fact that the POC was approved by the Government and was published in an annex to a decree-law, while the *Directrizes Contabilísticas* are approved by the General Council of the Accounting Standardization Commission and signed by its president. The topic has, however, been a matter of debate considering that sometimes the latter may be opposite to the POC and that the auditing profession and to a minor extent some accountants are pushing companies to follow the *Directrizes* where they are not in accordance with the letter of the POC. This is the case in the use of the equity method in individual to investor company accounts for the valuation of subsidiaries and associated companies.

3.5.8 Foreign Currency Transactions and Translations of Foreign Operations and Statements

Portuguese valuation rules and practice for foreign currency translation are based on the view that exchange differences on nonhedged foreign currency monetary items are to be recognized in the income statement in the period they arise. In certain circumstances, however, unrealized exchange gains may be deferred (see Section 3.3.5, above under Amounts Due from Third Parties).

For the translation of financial statements of foreign operations, Portuguese accounting rules did not include any reference to the methods to be applied until *Directriz Contabilística No.21* had been approved (November 1997). In practice, however, companies usually follow the treatment suggested in IAS 21. This is the closing rate for assets and liabilities, the average rate or the closing rate for income and expenses, and the exchange differences classified either as equity (before disposal of the net investment) or recognized in the income statement (after disposal of the said asset).

3.5.9 Other Items

Government Grants   Government grants should be recognized in the income statement over the periods necessary to match them with the related costs that they are intended to compensate, on a systematic basis. Government grants related to assets should be presented in the balance sheet by setting up the grant as deferred income. This is in line with IAS 20. The other treatment foreseen in IAS 20, however, consisting of the deduction of the grant in arriving at the carrying amount of the asset is not permitted in Portugal.

Deferred Taxation   Deferred taxation is not clearly addressed in the accounting regulations. It is implicit in the POC that both in the annual accounts and in the consolidated accounts, companies must disclose deferred taxes in the balance sheet, in the profit and loss statement, and in the annex. Although the POC refers to the need to disclose deferred taxes, it is not specified either there or in any other accounting law or opinion how to calculate those differences in taxes. As a consequence, and also as a result of the traditional relationship between accounting and taxation (see Section 3.6, below), calculation and disclosure of deferred taxes has not been very common among Portuguese companies, which usually apply the liability method. Some companies, however, have begun to calculate and disclose (some) deferred taxes in line with IAS 12. This is the case for those companies belonging to major groups or having their shares listed on the stock exchange. And an increasing number of auditors are beginning to require, although still to a limited extent, the use of the deferral method as a condition to avoid qualifications in their audits, according to *Interpretação*

Técnica No. 4 issued by the CROC. This interpretation requires the disclosure and the calculation of deferred taxes related to unrealized capital gains resulting from sales or disposal of tangible fixed assets under certain future reinvestment conditions and states that noncompliance with this interpretation issued by the CROC justifies a qualification in the audit report.

Segment Reporting Portuguese companies are required to disclose information about sales by industry and geographic segments (separating domestic, imports, and exports of goods and services). Also the costs of goods sold and services rendered are separated into raw materials, work in progress, and finished goods. Disclosure of these must be made in the annex (under notes 41, 42, and 44). Information required in segment reporting by Portuguese companies is not consistent with that required by IAS 14.

Proposed Dividends Contrary to IAS 10, which recommends either the adjustment (accrual) or the disclosure of dividends for the period covered by the financial statements if proposed after the balance sheet date but before approval of the financial statements, in Portugal no such accrual or disclosure is to be made.

3.6 The Impact of Tax Rules on Financial Accounting

3.6.1 Taxable Income

Traditionally, accounting in Portugal has been highly influenced by tax regulations. Indeed, the 1977 POC was quite related to the tax authorities and was designed more to facilitate tax inspections and to justify a company's income tax (because the basis for calculation of the tax is the income/profit from the accounting books) more than to disclose information to shareholders and to the public on the company's financial situation and operations report.

This tax orientation continued with the Companies Income Tax Code of 1988 (*Código do IRC*), which provides a set of rules for the valuation and recording of items in order to assess the taxable income.

In some cases, tax rules do not differ from accounting rules and only give more detail to them. For example, the tax treatment of inventories is the same in all material respects as that laid down in the POC, except for the matter of provisions for obsolescence, where the tax rules are much more detailed.

In other cases, the tax rules are opposite the accounting laws. This is the case for the depreciation of goodwill. The POC requires it to be written off, normally over 5 years but if explained in the notes up to 20 years. However, depreciation and other write-downs of goodwill are not tax deductible.

Portuguese tax rules affect financial accounting in the following areas: inventory valuation, revaluation of fixed assets, depreciation of fixed assets, provisions for loss of value of assets, confidential expenses, pension funds, and donations for cultural purposes.

Taxable income is based broadly on the net equity change during the tax period (comprehensive income). It is the net result for the year shown in the financial statements, excluding capital increases, revaluation reserves, some equity increases, dividends, and capital decreases. For income tax computations, accounting income is subject to adjustments, namely, charges not accepted if above certain limits (including donations for cultural, scientific, and humanitarian purposes, depreciation, and provisions for doubtful debts and obsolete inventories), charges not accepted at all (such as real estate tax, fines related to infringement of laws, confidential expenses), and value adjustments (capital gains adjusted, such as 95% of dividends from investments in subsidiaries and associated companies where the participation represents no less than 25% of the share capital).

The adjusted accounting result is then reduced by the previous 6 years' losses brought forward. Adjustments related to tax incentives and tax credits from international bilateral tax agreements are also taken into consideration.

3.6.2 Inventory Valuation

The tax treatment of inventories is the same in all material respects as that laid down in the POC, except for the matter of provisions for obsolescence, where the tax rules are much more detailed (see Section 3.6.5 below under Inventories).

3.6.3 Revaluation of Fixed Assets

The net book value of tangible operating fixed assets held on December 31, 1978, could be revalued on the basis of a set of prescribed price coefficients. This is optional, but in order to obtain the tax benefit of the additional depreciation, the revaluation and the additional depreciation thereon must be shown in the accounts. The first law permitting this expired in 1979, but since then a number of laws of limited duration have been introduced that allow revaluation of fixed assets by using prescribed price coefficients. The coefficients are based on the consumer price index and are published annually by the Ministry of Finance. However, only 60% of the additional annual depreciation is deductible for tax purposes, although all of the additional depreciation must be shown in the accounts. The most recent law permitting the revaluation of fixed assets was published in 1998. This decree-law limits the use of the revaluation reserves resulting from the process of revaluation so that the reserve may not be incorporated into capital unless it is realized (realization occurs with the write-off or disposal of the revalued fixed asset). This has not been indicated either in the Companies Law or past revaluation legislation.

3.6.4 Depreciation of Fixed Assets

Depreciation may be based on either the straight line or the declining balance method, but not the sum of years' digits method. For many categories of asset, the maximum and minimum straight-line depreciation rates are specified by the tax law, the minimum rates being 50% of the maxima. Some representative rates are given in Table 5. If companies charge less than the minimum rate, the difference is not allowable for tax purposes.

TABLE 5 *Selected Percentage Depreciation Rates*

Buildings	
Commercial and administrative	2
Industrial	5
Hotels, restaurants, etc.	5
Fixtures	
Water, electrical, compressed air, refrigeration, and telephones	10
Machinery	
Electronic machines	20
Typewriters and other office machinery	20
Machine tools	
Light	20
Heavy	12.5
Vehicles	
Light	25
Heavy	20

The rates are generic for the assets indicated. In addition, there are a large number of rates for assets specific to particular industries.

If the declining balance method is used, the corresponding straight-line rates are increased by the following coefficients: for useful lives of less than 5 years, 1.5; for useful lives of 5 or 6 years, 2.0; for useful lives of more than 6 years, 2.5.

Under some circumstances, companies may charge additional depreciation in respect of intensive use of assets. "Intensive use" is defined as using the assets for two or more shifts per day. Article 9 of the regulatory decree of January 12, 1990 allows the normal maximum rates to be increased by 25% in the case of two shifts, and 50% for more than two shifts. There are restrictions on allowable depreciation for light vehicles (cars), the maximum depreciable value being 4 million escudos. For fixed assets of small value (less than 20,000 escudos); on the other hand, 100% write-off in the year of acquisition is allowable.

3.6.5 Provisions for Loss of Value of Assets

Financial Fixed Assets and Negotiable Securities   The treatment of financial fixed assets and negotiable securities required by the POC is not acceptable for tax purposes, as provisions for amortization or loss of value in respect of them are not tax-deductible, even though they may be required in order to give a true and fair view. For financial sector enterprises, such as banks and insurance companies, there are special tax rules, and in any case the accounting rules are not those in the POC.

Bad Debts   The tax law lays down the maximum allowable provisions for bad debts, on the basis of the age of the debts, varying from 25% for debts between 6 months and 1 year old to 100% for debts over 2 years old. To take full advantage of the tax deductions, it must be demonstrated that all reasonable efforts have been made to collect the items and the bad debt must have been previously isolated in an appropriate bad debt account.

If a debtor is declared bankrupt during the year, amounts owed by that debtor are treated as losses for tax purposes and do not need to be provided for via the provisions account.

If a debtor holds 10% or more of the creditor company's share capital or is a company in which the creditor holds 10% or more of the share capital, then no bad debts provision is tax deductible. No bad debts provisions are tax deductible on accounts of amounts owed by government agencies.

Inventories   Deductible provisions for inventories are limited to the difference between the cost of acquisition or production and market value at the balance sheet date if lower. Market value is replacement cost for raw materials and (net) selling price for finished goods. A special case is the possibility of increasing the fiscal deductible cost by up to 30% of the cost in the accounts when companies adopt a permanent inventory valuation method.

Goodwill   The POC requires goodwill to be written off, normally over 5 years, but over up to 20 years if this is explained in the notes. Amortization or other write-downs of goodwill are not tax deductible, however.

3.6.6 Pension Funds

For pensions, tax deduction is only allowed if the pension fund is not managed by the contributing company.

Costs of employers' contributions to employee pension funds, voluntary insurance of employees, and similar expenses are tax deductible up to a maximum of 15% or 25% of salary costs, depending on the particular circumstances.

3.6.7 Confidential Expenses

Confidential expenses (those authorized by management but not supported by business documents such as invoices) are subject to a 10% income tax in addition to normal taxation; this tax is payable even if the company pays no normal income tax or reports losses.

3.6.8 Donations for Cultural Purposes

Tax deductions of donations for cultural purposes are limited to 0.4% of the turnover for the financial year, unless the recipient is the government or one of its agencies or branches, in which case the limit does not apply; under special circumstances, the allowed fiscal deduction is 105% of the total amount of the donation. This is a kind of fiscal incentive to cultural activities.

4. Expected Future Developments

The developments in Portuguese financial accounting and reporting that have been described in this chapter are related to the economic and political development of the country itself during the past 25 years. They also include a number of major changes resulting from Portugal's membership in the European Union and its implementation of the Fourth, Seventh, and Eighth Directives. These recent changes are being digested, and further significant developments can be expected. In general, the distinction between tax accounting and financial reporting has now been made, and one may anticipate the further development of financial reporting as an aid to financial analysis.

It is likely that while for the moment most people still associate annual accounts with taxation, perceptions will change in the longer term, and group accounts will take on a much higher profile.

Portugal has influenced taxation and accountancy concepts (and tax and accounting income concepts) adopted by the African Portuguese speaking countries, such as Angola, Mozambique, Guinea-Bissau, and Cabo Verde. Accounting and tax regulation in force in those African countries were inspired by Portuguese versions of the POC and income tax codes. The interchange with Brazil also has been quite important.

The main expected development is that the practices of accountants will catch up with legislative developments. According to the CNC plan of activities for the near future, some consensus is expected to emerge on the treatment of items such as options contracts, financial assets and liabilities, environmental disclosures, joint ventures, installment sales, rental agreements, and deferred taxation.

The forces that influence the disclosures of financial information by Portuguese companies have been mainly the legal environment, tax regulation, and stock exchange regulation. The influence of the accounting and auditing professions has not been important. International influence, traditionally from France, is being replaced by influence from the Anglo-Saxon countries and IAS, which are gaining more and more followers.

Note

1. Companies incorporated in Portugal, and Portuguese branches of foreign companies, are in general subject to income tax on the results computed on 12 months ending on December 31. The tax year may, however, be a different period if authorized by the tax authorities. In accordance with this facility, the Companies Business Code has also authorized, for years after 1996, companies to adopt a financial year end not coincident with December 31, provided that the financial period used for accounting and disclosures is a period of 12 complete months.

Useful Addresses

Associação dos Técnicos Oficiais de Contas (ATOC)
Rua Nova do Almada, 69 - 4º
1200 LISBOA
Tel.: +351 1 342 99 01
Fax.: +351 1 343 98 95

Câmara dos Revisores Oficiais de Contas (CROC)
Rua do Salitre, 51
1250 LISBOA
Tel.: +351 1 353 60 76
Fax: +351 1 353 61 49

Comissão de Normalização Contabilística (CNC)
Rua Angelina Vidal, 41
1196 LISBOA
Tel.: +351 1 814 78 93
Fax.: +351 1 813 87 42

Comissão do Mercado de Valores Mobiliários (CMVM)
Av. Fontes Pereira de Melo, 21
1050 LISBOA
Tel.: +351 1 353 70 77
Fax: +351 1 353 70 78

Supervisory Board's Report

In accordance with Article 441, paragraphs (f) and (g) and Article 454 paragraph (1) of the Commercial Companies Legal Code and of the Articles of Association of the Company, we have examined the Report and Accounts submitted by the Management Board, the Legal Certification of the Accounts and the Auditor's Report, and have prepared this report for the financial year ended 31 December 1997.

The development of the Sonae Investimentos businesses during the 1997 financial year was overseen by the Supervisory Board by means of the Company's quarterly financial accounts and reports as well as through quarterly meetings with the Management Board.

The Supervisory Board also received additional information from the Directors and Managers of the various business areas of the Company. In 1997, the Supervisory Board initiated a new practice whereby, at each of the quarterly meetings, one of the businesses presented a detailed review of its activities.

In compliance with Article 432 of the Commercial Companies Legal Code, the Supervisory Board was notified, in advance, of any business activities which might significantly affect the Company's situation and was also informed of the strategic business guidelines developed during the financial year. The Supervisory Board gave its opinion on these matters, as it thought fit.

The consolidated financial statements covering the first half of the financial year, as presented to the Lisbon Stock Exchange, were appraised after discussion with the Management Board and the Company's Statutory Auditor.

The company's financial statements for 1997 as well as its consolidated financial statements, presented by the Management Board, together with the Auditor's report, correctly reflect the company's structure and situation as well as the events that took place in the year under review. Nevertheless, the following points merit a special mention:

- The significant growth of profitability of the company's core businesses in Portugal, namely Modelo Continente in the hypermarket and supermarket sector, and Sonae Imobilária in the shopping centre sector, resulting from a strategy of rapid expansion and sustained improvement in operational efficiency.

- The progress made in Brazil, in terms of expansion and of operational profitability, which is particularly remarkable given the adverse business environment in that country.

- The achievement of launching four new specialised retail business formats and Banco Universo in only one year.

The consolidated results reflect a significantly lower contribution from extraordinary profits compared with the previous year. The improving trend of recent years in profits from ordinary activities continued during 1997 and compensated for the inevitable start-up losses of the businesses launched during the year.

Having considered all the information and explanations submitted to it, as well as the contents of the company and consolidated financial statements, and in particular the report and legal certification of the accounts by the Statutory Auditor, the Supervisory Board resolved unanimously:

- To approve the company's report and accounts as submitted by the Management Board and supported by the legal certification of accounts.

- To approve the company's consolidated report and accounts as presented by the Management Board supported by on the legal certification of the accounts.

- To propose to the Annual General Meeting a vote of appreciation and confidence in the Management Board of Sonae Investimentos.

Maia, 5th March 1998

Álvaro Barreto
José Viana Batista
Michel Bon
António Borges
Paul David Orchard-Lisle

Balanço Consolidado em 31 de Dezembro 1997

Milhares de escudos

Activo	Activo Bruto	Amortizações e Provisões Acumuladas	1997 Activo Líquido	1996 Activo Líquido
IMOBILIZADO				
Imobilizações incorpóreas:				
Despesas de instalação	13 262 468	6 982 853	6 279 615	5 979 731
Despesas de investigação e de desenvolvimento	3 062 015	1 589 820	1 472 195	2 221 225
Propriedade industrial e outros direitos	336 591	288 943	47 648	303 739
Trespasses	866 602	282 724	583 878	1 028 963
Imobilizações em curso	829 999		829 999	1 012 419
Diferenças de consolidação	14 772 795	3 741 649	11 031 146	11 235 493
	33 130 470	12 885 989	22 244 481	21 781 570
Imobilizações corpóreas:				
Terrenos e recursos naturais	20 899 623		20 899 623	21 616 643
Edifícios e outras construções	92 135 144	6 136 170	85 998 974	75 220 901
Equipamento básico	54 324 413	17 077 487	37 246 926	62 650 667
Equipamento de transporte	5 109 122	2 208 702	2 900 420	2 391 288
Ferramentas e utensílios	674 372	609 402	64 970	227 854
Equipamento administrativo	6 977 998	2 480 315	4 497 683	8 245 486
Taras e vasilhame	64 062	55 549	8 513	14 155
Outras imobilizações corpóreas	949 750	247 261	702 489	536 178
Imobilizações em curso	23 414 856		23 414 856	28 239 861
Adiantamentos por conta de imobilizações corpóreas	6 743 184		6 743 184	13 947 672
	211 292 524	28 814 886	182 477 638	213 090 705
Investimentos financeiros:				
Partes de capital em empresas associadas	12 371 850		12 371 850	14 616 650
Empréstimos a empresas associadas	3 684 118		3 684 118	8 805 432
Partes de capital em outras empresas participadas	175 079		175 079	545 685
Títulos e outras aplicações financeiras	6 618 547		6 618 547	678 933
Outros empréstimos concedidos	2000		2 000	1 200
Imobilizações em curso				4 731
Adiantamentos por conta de investimentos financeiros	1 864 569		1 864 569	171 000
	24 716 163		24 716 163	24 823 631
CIRCULANTE				
Existências:				
Matérias-primas, subsidiárias e de consumo	224 953		224 953	5 948 113
Produtos e trabalhos em curso	3 568 490		3 568 490	2 570 695
Subprodutos, desperdícios, resíduos e refugos				19
Produtos acabados e intermédios	292 528		292 528	3 402 655
Mercadorias	37 719 852	92 219	37 627 633	34 971 456
Adiantamentos por conta de compras				55 923
	41 805 823	92 219	41 713 604	46 948 861
Dívidas de terceiros – Médio e longo prazo:				
Clientes - Títulos a receber	6 125		6 125	11 214
Empresas associadas				71 073
Estado e outros entes públicos	3 035 654		3 035 654	
Outros devedores	727 951		727 951	235 553
	3 769 730		3 769 730	317 840
Dívidas de terceiros – Curto prazo:				
Clientes c/c	6 173 553	138 078	6 035 475	15 224 134
Clientes - Títulos a receber	103 923		103 923	2 709 848
Clientes de cobrança duvidosa	2 261 154	2 212 744	48 410	229 311
Empresas participadas e participantes	457 883		457 883	
Empresas associadas	70 253		70 253	235 590
Outros accionistas				50 000
Adiantamentos a fornecedores	39 377		39 377	146 506
Adiantamentos a fornecedores de imobilizado	309		309	24 569
Estado e outros entes públicos	10 096 240		10 096 240	5 337 508
Outros devedores	17 118 408	1 345 064	15 773 344	8 641 272
Subscritores de capital				55 300
	36 321 100	3 695 886	32 625 214	32 654 038
Títulos negociáveis:				
Outros títulos negociáveis	26 672 317	802 818	25 869 499	23 490 420
Outras aplicações de tesouraria	4 001 166		4 001 166	768 584
	30 673 483	802 818	29 870 665	24 259 004
Depósitos bancários e caixa:				
Depósitos bancários	21 169 802		21 169 802	8 443 200
Caixa	336 699		336 699	329 503
	21 506 501		21 506 501	8 772 703
ACRÉSCIMOS E DIFERIMENTOS				
Acréscimos de proveitos	2 625 581		2 625 581	2 549 312
Custos diferidos	1 970 852		1 970 852	2 601 055
	4 596 433		4 596 433	5 150 367
Total de amortizações		41 700 875		
Total de provisões		4 590 923		
Total do activo	407 812 227	46 291 798	361 520 429	377 798 719

Consolidated Balance Sheet - *31 December 1997*

	Escudos thousand				Ecus thousand			
	1997			1996	1997			1996
Fixed Assets:	A	DP	NA	NA	A	DP	NA	NA
FIXED ASSETS:								
Intangible assents:								
Start up costs	13 262 468	6 982 853	6 279 615	5 979 731	65 614	34 547	31 068	30 780
Research and development costs	3 062 015	1 589 820	1 472 195	2 221 225	15 149	7 865	7283	11 433
Patents and other similar rights	336 591	288 943	47 648	303 739	1 665	1 430	236	1 563
Premiums paid for property occupation rights	866 602	282 724	583 878	1 028 963	4 287	1 399	2 889	5 296
Projects in course	829 999		829 999	1 012 419	4 106		4 106	5 211
Goodwill arising on consolidation	14 772 795	3 741 649	11 031 146	11 235 493	73 086	18 511	54 575	57 833
	33 130 470	**12 885 989**	**20 244 481**	**21 781 570**	**163 908**	**63 752**	**100 157**	**112 118**
Tangible assets:								
Land	20 899 623		20 899 623	21 616 643	103 398		103 398	111 269
Buildings	92 135 144	6 136 170	85 998 974	75 220 901	455 826	30 358	425 468	387 190
Plant and machinery	54 324 413	17 077 487	37 246 926	62 650 667	268 762	84 488	184 274	322 486
Vehicles	5 109 122	2 208 702	2 900 420	2 391 288	25 277	10 927	14 349	12 309
Tools	674 372	609 402	64 970	227 854	3 336	3 015	321	1 173
Fixtures and fittings	6 977 998	2 480 315	4 497 683	8 245 486	34 523	12 271	22 252	42 443
Containers	64 062	55 549	8 513	14 155	317	275	42	73
Other	949 750	247 261	702 489	536 178	4 699	1 223	3 475	2 760
In construction	23 414 856		23 414 856	28 239 861	115 842		115 842	145 361
Advances	6 743 184		6 743 184	13 947 672	33 361		33 361	71 794
	211 292 524	**28 814 886**	**182 477 638**	**213 090 705**	**1 045 340**	**142 558**	**902 783**	**1 096 857**
Investments:								
Shares in related (including associated) undertakings	12 371 850		12 371 850	14 616 650	61 208		61 208	75 237
Loans to related undertakings	3 684 118		3 684 118	8 805 432	18 227		18 227	45 325
Shares in other undertakings	175 079		175 079	545 685	866		866	2 809
Other investments other than loans	6 618 547		6 618 547	678 933	32 744		32 744	3 495
Loans to other undertakings	2000		2 000	1 200	10		10	6
In construction				4 731				24
Advances	1 864 569		1 864 569	171 000	9 225		9 225	880
	24 716 163		**24 716 163**	**24 823 631**	**122 280**		**122 280**	**127 776**
CURRENT ASSETS:								
Stocks:								
Raw materials and consumables	224 953		224 953	5 948 113	1 113		1 113	30 617
Work in progress	3 568 490		3 568 490	2 570 695	17 655		17 655	13 232
By-products				19				
Finished goods	292 528		292 528	3 402 655	1 447		1 447	17 515
Goods for resale	37 719 852	92 219	37 627 633	34 971 456	186 614	456	186 157	180 011
Payments on account				55 923				288
	41 805 823	**92 219**	**41 713 604**	**46 948 861**	**206 828**	**456**	**206 372**	**241 663**
Debtors: amounts failing due after more than one year:								
Bills receivable	6 125		6 125	11 214	30		30	58
Related undertakings				71 073				366
Taxes recoverable	3 035 654		3 035 654		15 018		15 018	
Other debtors	727 951		727 951	235 553	3 601		3 601	1 212
	3 769 730		**3 769 730**	**317 840**	**18 650**		**18 650**	**1 636**
Debtors: amounts falling due within one year:								
Trade debtors	6 173 553	138 078	6 035 475	15 224 134	30 543	683	29 860	78 364
Bills receivable	103 923		103 923	2 709 848	514		514	13 949
Doubtful debtors	2 261 154	2 212 744	48 410	229 311	11 187	10 947	240	1 180
Related undertakings	457 883		457 883		2 265		2 265	
Other shareholders	70 253		70 253	285 590	348		348	1 470
Advances to trade creditors	39 377		39 377	146 506	195		195	754
Advances to fixed assents suppliers	309		309	24 569	2		2	126
Taxes recoverable	10 096 240		10 096 240	5 337 508	49 950		49 950	27 474
Other debtors	17 118 408	1 345 064	15 773 344	8 641 272	84 691	6 655	78 036	44 480
Subscribers to capital				55 300				285
	36 321 100	**3 695 886**	**32 625 214**	**32 654 038**	**179 694**	**18 285**	**161 409**	**168 082**
Short term investments:								
Other negotiable instruments	26 672 317	802 818	25 869 499	23 490 420	131 958	3 972	127 986	120 914
Others	4 001 166		4 001 166	768 584	19 795		19 795	3 956
	30 673 483	**802 818**	**29 870 665**	**24 259 004**	**151 753**	**3 972**	**147 781**	**124 870**
Cash at bank:								
Bank	21 169 802		21 169 802	8 443 200	104 735		104 735	43 460
Cash	336 699		336 699	329 503	1 666		1 666	1 696
	21 506 501		**21 506 501**	**8 772 703**	**106 400**		**106 400**	**45 156**
ACCRUED INCOME AND PREPAYMENTS								
Accrued income	2 625 581		2 625 581	2 549 312	12 990		12 990	13 122
Prepayments	1 970 852		1 970 852	2 601 055	9 751		9 751	13 389
	4 596 433		**4 596 433**	**5 150 367**	**22 740**		**22 740**	**26 511**
Total depreciation		**41 700 875**				**206 309**		
Total provisions		**4 590 923**				**22 713**		
Total assets	**407 812 227**	**46 291 798**	**361 520 429**	**377 798 719**	**2 017 594**	**229 022**	**1 788 572**	**1 944 669**

A = Assets;
DP = Depreciation and Provisions;
NA = Net assets

50

Balanço Consolidado em 31 de Dezembro 1997

Milhares de escudos

Capital próprio, interesses minoritários e passivo	1997	1996
CAPITAL PRÓPRIO		
Capital	40 000 000	40 000 000
Acções proprias - valor nominal	-1 000 000	-1 000 000
Acções proprias - descontos prémios	-3 241 728	-3 247 728
Prémios de emissão de acções	10 000 000	10 000 000
Diferenças de consolidação	8 530 800	8 268 783
Ajustamentos de partes de capital em filiais e associadas	17 857	320 585
Reservas de reavaliação	4 871 802	8 235 477
Reservas:		
Reservas legais	7 445 301	5 389 301
Outras reservas	-799 630	15 681 540
	65 824 402	**83 647 958**
Resultado líquido do exercício	12 197 374	20 681 606
Total do capital próprio	**78 021 776**	**104 329 564**
INTERESSES MINORITÁRIOS	**42 724 370**	**48 510 290**
PASSIVO		
Provisões para riscos e encargos:		
Provisões para impostos		493 785
Outras provisões para riscos e encargos	638 813	2 867 951
	638 813	**3 361 736**
Dívidas a terceiros – Médio e longo prazo:		
Empréstimos por obrigações		
Não convertiveis	92 217 602	67 342 007
Dívidas a instituições de crédito	7 844 768	11 159 988
Fornecedores de imobilizado - Títulos a pagar		35 007
Empresas participadas e participantes	6 611 751	5 237 500
Outros accionistas		815 800
Outros empréstimos obtidos	4 083 298	6 281 083
Fornecedores de imobilizado c/c	510 820	2 007 584
Estado e outros entes públicos	58 045	106 746
Outros credores	585 461	770 476
	111 911 745	**93 756 191**
Dívidas a terceiros – Curto prazo:		
Empréstimos por obrigações:		
Não convertiveis		3 375 000
Dívidas a instituições de crédito	22 856 554	15 851 459
Adiantamentos por conta de vendas	123 435	129 833
Fornecedores, c/c	64 780 723	65 487 225
Fornecedores - Facturas em recepção e conferência	9 565 284	9 102 374
Fornecedores - Títulos a pagar		15 493
Fornecedores de imobilizado - Títulos a pagar		820 849
Empresas participadas e participantes	5 545	32 045
Outros accionistas (sócios)	34 260	42 617
Adiantamentos de clientes	287 168	1 996 817
Outros empréstimos obtidos		493 180
Fornecedores de imobilizado, c/c	9 551 387	6 718 512
Estado e outros entes públicos	7 390 497	6 622 596
Outros credores	1 650 451	1 699 379
	116 738 484	**111 894 199**
ACRÉSCIMOS E DIFERIMENTOS		
Acréscimos de custos	9 588 948	11 672 673
Proveitos diferidos	1 896 293	4 274 066
	11 485 241	**15 946 739**
Total do passivo	**240 774 283**	**224 958 865**
Total capital próprio, dos interesses minoritários e do passivo	**361 520 429**	**377 798 719**

Consolidated Balance Sheet - *31 December 1997*

	Escudos thousand		Ecus thousand	
Shareholder's funds, minority interests and liabilities	1997	1996	1997	1996
SHAREHOLDER'S FUNDS				
Called up share capital	40 000 000	40 000 000	197 894	205 895
Own shares - nominal value	-1 000 000	-1 000 000	-4 947	-5 147
Own shares - premium	-3 241 728	-3 247 728	-16 038	-16 717
Share premium account	10 000 000	10 000 000	49 474	51 474
Goodwill arising on consolidation	8 530 800	8 268 783	42 205	42 562
Post acq. share of accumulated reserves of assoc. undertakings	17 857	320 585	88	1 650
Revaluation reserve	4 871 802	8 235 477	24 103	42 391
Other reserves:				
Legal reserve	7 445 301	5 389 301	36 835	27 741
Other reserves and retained earnings	-799 630	15 681 540	-3 956	80 719
	65 824 402	**83 647 958**	**325 657**	**430 567**
Profit for the financial year	12 197 374	20 681 606	60 345	106 456
Total shareholders' funds	**78 021 776**	**104 329 564**	**386 002**	**537 023**
MINORITY INTERESTS	**42 724 370**	**48 510 290**	**211 373**	**249 700**
LIABILITIES				
Provisions for liabilities and charges:				
Tax provision		493 785		2 542
Other provisions	638 813	2 867 951	3 160	14 762
	638 813	**3 361 736**	**3 160**	**17 304**
Creditors: amounts falling due after more than one year:				
Bonds				
Non convertible	92 217 602	67 342 007	456 234	346 634
Bank loans	7 844 768	11 159 988	38 811	57 445
Fixed assets suppliers - bills payable		35 007		180
Parent company	6 611 751	6 053 300	32 711	31 159
Other shareholders				
Other loans	4 083 298	6 281 083	20 202	32 311
Fixed assets suppliers	510 820	2 007 584	2 527	10 334
Taxes and contributions payable	58 045	106 746	287	549
Other creditors	585 461	770 476	2 896	3 966
	111 911 745	**93 756 191**	**553 668**	**482 598**
Creditors: amounts falling due within one year:				
Bonds:				
Non convertible		3 375 000		17 372
Bank loans and overdrafts	22 856 554	15 851 459	113 080	81 593
Payments received on account	123 435	129 833	611	668
Trade creditors	64 780 723	65 487 225	320 494	337 087
Accruals - invoices	9 565 284	9 102 374	47 323	46 853
Bills payable		15 493		80
Fixed assets suppliers - bills payable		820 849		4 225
Parent company	5 545	32 045	27	165
Other shareholders	34 260	42 617	169	219
Advances from trade debtors	287 168	1 996 817	1 421	10 278
Other loans	493 180			
Fixed assets suppliers	9 551 387	6 718 512	47 254	34 583
Taxes and contributions payable (including income taxation)	7 390 497	6 622 596	36 563	34 089
Other creditors	1 650 451	1 699 379	8 165	8 747
	116 738 484	**111 894 199**	**575 107**	**575 961**
ACCRUALS AND DEFERRED INCOME				
Accruals	9 588 948	11 672 673	47 440	60 084
Deferred income	1 896 293	4 274 066	9 382	22 000
	11 485 241	**15 946 739**	**56 822**	**82 084**
Total liabilities	**240 774 283**	**224 958 865**	**1 188 757**	**1 157 946**
Total shareholders' funds, minority interests and liabilities	**361 520 429**	**377 798 719**	**1 786 132**	**1 944 669**

Balanço Consolidado em 31 de Dezembro 1997

Milhares de escudos

	1997		1996	
Custos e Perdas				
Custo das mercadorias vendidas e das matérias consumidas:				
Mercadorias	324 010 830		302 584 031	
Matérias–Primas	1 398 059	325 408 889	31 601 895	334 185 926
Fornecimentos e serviços externos		43 151 777		52 457 150
Custos com o pessoal:				
Remunerações	28 408 529		35 049 723	
Encargos sociais:				
Pensões	4 522		73 881	
Outros	9 036 323	37 449 374	10 919 197	46 042 801
Amortizações do imobilizado corpóreo e incorpóreo	10 568 417		15 088 279	
Provisões	1 081 994	11 650 411	1 074 430	16 162 709
Impostos	759 746		967 473	
Outros custos operacionais	1 319 159	2 078 905	1 282 737	2 250 210
(A)		419 739 356		451 098 796
Amortizações e provisões de aplicações e investimentos financeiros	654 969		2 087 403	
Juros e custos similares:				
Relativos a empresas associadas	78 729		2 901	
Outros	10 059 366	10 793 064	13 843 538	15 933 842
(C)		430 532 420		467 032 638
Perdas relativas a empresas associadas		3 108 169		154 268
Custos e perdas extraordinárias		2 323 333		3 750 627
(E)		435 963 922		470 937 533
Imposto sobre o rendimento do exercício		5 996 148		4 616 614
(G)		441 960 070		475 554 147
Interesses minoritários		4 842 131		3 774 941
Resultado consolidado líquido do exercício		12 197 374		20 681 606
		458 999 575		**500 010 694**
Proveitos e Ganhos				
Vendas:				
Mercadorias	396 579 050		362 387 766	
Produtos			68 954 536	
Prestação de serviços	15 763 352	412 342 402	19 608 653	450 950 955
Variação da produção		1 060 263		1 498 228
Trabalhos para a própria empresa		2 615 663		1 597 780
Proveitos suplementares	22 817 867		18 570 740	
Subsídios à exploração	4 710		156 749	
Outros proveitos e ganhos operacionais	1 617 019	24 439 596	943 860	19 671 349
(B)		440 457 924		473 718 312
Ganhos de participações de capital:				
Relativos a outras empresas	100 001		104 767	
Rendimentos de títulos negociáveis e de outras aplicações financeiras:				
Relativos a empresas associadas	786 664		4 775	
Outros	3 553 868		2 786 999	
Outros juros e proveitos similares:				
Relativos a empresas associadas	124 834		1 051 304	
Outros	4 355 667	8 921 034	5 888 860	9 836 705
(D)		449 378 958		483 555 017
Ganhos relativos a empresas associadas		115 178		509 343
Proveitos e ganhos extraordinários		9 505 439		15 946 334
(F)		**458 999 575**		**500 010 694**

Resumo:

	1997	1996
Resultados operacionais:(B) – (A) =	20 718 568	22 619 516
Resultados financeiros: [(D) – (B)] – [(C) – (A)] =	-1 872 030	-6 097 137
Resultados correntes: (D) – (C) =	18 846 538	16 522 379
Resultados antes de impostos: (F) – (E) =	23 035 653	29 073 161
Resultado consolidado com os interesses minoritários do exercício: (F) – (G) =	17 039 505	24 456 547

Consolidated Profit and Loss Account 31 December 1997

	Escudos thousand				Ecus thousand			
	1997		1996		1997		1996	
Charges								
Cost of goods sold and materials consumed:								
Goods	324 010 830		302 584 031		1 602 998		1 557 512	
Materials	1 398 059	325 408 889	31 601 895	334 185 926	6 917	1 609 915	162 667	1 720 178
External supplies and services		43 151 777		52 457 150		213 487		270 016
Staff costs:								
Wages and salaries	28 408 529		35 049 723		140 547		180 414	
Social costs:								
Pensions	4 522		73 881		22		380	
Others	9 036 323	37 449 374	10 919 197	46 042 801	44 706	185 276	56 205	236 999
Depreciation of tangible and intangible fixed assets	10 568 417		15 088 279		52 286		77 665	
Provisions	1 081 994	11 650 411	1 074 430	16 162 709	5 353	57 639	5 530	83 195
Taxes, excluding income taxes	759 746		967 473		3 759		4 980	
Other operating charges	1 319 159	2 078 905	1 282 737	2 250 210	6 526	10 285	6 603	11 583
(A)		419 739 356		451 098 796		2 076 602		2 321 972
Depreciation and provisions for investments	654 969		2 087 403		3 240		10 745	
Interest payable and similar charges:								
Related undertakings	78 729		2 901		390		15	
Others	10 059 366	10 793 064	13 843 538	15 933 842	49 767	53 397	71 258	82 017
(C)		430 532 420		467 032 638		2 129 999		2 403 989
Share of losses of associated undertakings		3 108 169		154 268		15 377		794
Extraordinary charges		2 323 333		3 750 627		11 494		19 306
(E)		435 963 922		470 937 533		2 156 871		2 424 089
Income taxation		5 996 148		4 616 614		29 665		23 763
(G)		441 960 070		475 554 147		2 186 536		2 447 853
Profit attributable to minority interests		4 842 131		3 774 941		23 956		19 431
Profit for the financial year		12 197 374		20 681 606		60 345		106 456
		458 999 575		**500 010 694**		**2 270 836**		**2 573 740**
Income								
Sales:								
Goods	396 579 050		362 387 766		1 962 019		1 865 344	
Products			68 954 536				354 934	
Services rendered	15 763 352	412 342 402	19 608 653	450 950 955	77 987	2 040 006	100 933	2 321 211
Change in stocks of finished goods and in work in progress		1 060 263		1 498 228		5 246		7 712
Own work capitalised		2 615 663		1 597 780		12 941		8 224
Supplementary income	22 817 867		18 570 740		112 888		95 590	
Trading subsidies	4 710		156 749		23		807	
Other operating income	1 617 019	24 439 596	943 860	19 671 349	8 000	120 911	4 858	101 256
(B)		440 457 924		473 718 312		2 179 104		2 438 403
Dividend income:								
Other undertakings	100 001		104 767		495		539	
Investment income:								
Related undertakings	786 664		4 775		3 892		25	
Others	3 553 868		2 786 999		17 582		14 346	
Other interest received and similar income:								
Related undertakings	124 834		1 051 304		618		5 411	
Others	4 355 667	8 921 034	5 888 860	9 836 705	21 549	44 136	30 312	50 633
(D)		449 378 958		483 555 017		2 223 240		2 489 036
Share of profits of associated undertakings		115 178		509 343		570		2 622
Extraordinary income		9 505 439		15 946 334		47 027		82 082
(F)		**458 999 575**		**500 010 694**		**2 270 836**		**2 573 740**

Summary:

	Escudos 1997	Escudos 1996	Ecus 1997	Ecus 1996
Operating profit:(B) – (A) =	20 718 568	22 619 516	102 502	116 431
Net financial charges: [(D) – (B)] – [(C) – (A)] =	-1 872 030	-6 097 137	-9 262	-31 384
Profit on ordinary activities: (D) – (C) =	18 846 538	16 522 379	93 241	85 047
Profit before taxation: (F) – (E) =	23 035 653	29 073 161	113 966	149 650
Profit for the financial year before minority interests: (F) – (G) =	17 039 505	24 456 547	84 301	125 887

Anexo ao Balanço e à Demonstração de Resultados Consolidados

Nota prévia:
São apresentadas apenas as notas aplicáveis, mantendo-se, no entanto a ordenação numérica do Plano Oficial de Contabilidade.

Nota 0: Políticas contabilísticas adoptadas
As contas consolidadas foram elaboradas de acordo com os princípios contabilísticos e normas de consolidação do Plano Oficial de Contabilidade, com a alteração introduzida pelo Decreto-Lei n° 238/91, de 2 de Julho de 1991.

As políticas contabilísticas mais significativas utilizadas na elaboração das contas consolidadas foram as seguintes:

(a) Custo histórico
As contas consolidadas foram preparadas em observância da convenção do custo histórico com excepção das imobilizações corpóreas que incluem as sucessivas reavaliações legais, bem como as reavaliações livres referidas na nota n.° 9.

(b) Bases de consolidação
As contas consolidadas incluem a sociedade mãe e todas as suas filiais. Os resultados das filiais adquiridas ou vendidas durante o exercício estão incluídos na demonstração de resultados desde a data da sua aquisição ou até à data da sua venda. As transacções e os lucros entre empresas do Grupo foram eliminados.

(c) Investimentos financeiros
Os investimentos financeiros em filiais excluídas de acordo com o art° 4° do Decreto-Lei n° 238/91 e no capital de outras empresas são relevados ao custo de aquisição.

As sociedades em que o Grupo participe em mais de 20% mas em menos de 50% do capital social e nas quais o Grupo pode exercer influência significativa foram incluídas nas contas como empresas associadas. A parte do resultado líquido das associadas atribuível ao Grupo está incluído na demonstração de resultados. A parte de outros movimentos no activo líquido das associadas ocorridos após a aquisição e atribuíveis ao Grupo é considerada no Balanço. São efectuados ajustamentos na consolidação quando necessário para adaptar as políticas contabilísticas das associadas às definidas pelo Grupo. As transacções e os lucros com empresas associadas são eliminados na consolidação, proporcionalmente.

(d) Títulos negociáveis
Os títulos negociáveis e outras aplicações de tesouraria são valorizadas ao custo de aquisição que inclui os gastos adicionais de compra.

(e) Activo imobilizado corpóreo
O activo imobilizado corpóreo é apresentado ao seu custo de aquisição, incluindo as sucessivas reavaliações legais, acrescido das despesas imputáveis à compra.

Os subsídios recebidos ou a receber relativos a activos específicos são apresentados em proveitos diferidos e considerados proveitos ao longo da vida útil dos respectivos bens. Os subsídios não identificáveis com activos específicos são considerados proveitos no período em que são recebidos.

(f) Depreciação
A depreciação é calculada em duodécimos pelo método das quotas constantes em função da vida útil de cada tipo de activo. As taxas de depreciação anual mais importantes são as seguintes:

	%
Edifícios e outras construções	2
Equipamento básico	10
Equipamento de transporte	20
Equipamento administrativo	10
Imobilizações incorpóreas	20

(g) Marcas e patentes
As marcas e patentes são apresentadas ao custo e amortizadas ao longo da vida útil do correspondente activo ou da duração da patente ou marca, dos dois a mais baixa.

Notes to the consolidated
Financial Statements

Notes to the consolidated Financial Statements

These consolidated financial statements have been prepared in accordance with Portuguese accounting principles, consolidation methods and rules, as required by the Official Chart of Accounts and considering the alteration in Decree-Lawnr. 238/91, of 2 July 1991.

Principal Accounting Policies

A summary of the more important group accounting policies, used in the preparation of these consolidated financial statements, is set out below:

(a) Basis accounting

The consolidated financial statements are prepared in accordance with the historical cost convention modified by the revaluation of tangible fixed assets, which include successive legal revaluations as well as market valuations, as explained in note 9.

(b) Basis of consolidation

The consolidated financial statements include the company and its affiliated undertakings. The results of affiliated undertakings acquired or disposed of during the year are included in the consolidated profit and loss account from the date of their acquisition or up to the date of their disposal. Inter-group transactions and profits are eliminated..

(c) Fixed asset investments

Investments in affiliated undertakings not consolidated (in accordance with Decree-Lawnr. 238/91 – see Note 2) and in other undertaking are stated at cost.

Undertaking in which the Group has holdings between 20% and 50% and is able to exercise significant influence are accounted for as associated undertakings.

The group's share of profits less losses of associated undertakings for the year is included in the consolidated profit and loss account and the group's share of their net assets is included in the consolidated balance sheet.

Where the amounts involved are significant, consolidation adjustments are made to conform with the group's accounting policies.

Transactions and profits with associated undertakings are eliminated proportionally on consolidation.

(d) Short term investments

Short term investments are stated at cost including related purchase expenses.

(e) Tangible fixed assets

Tangible fixed assets are stated at purchase cost (including costs of acquisition) or valuation. Valuations are either calculated using general purchasing power indices as allowed by Portuguese fiscal legislation or are based on independent market valuations.

Investment grants received or receivable that relate to specific assets are treated as deferred income which is then credited to the profit and loss account over the useful life of the related asset. Non-specific grants are credited to the profit and loss account when received.

(f) Depreciation

Depreciation is calculated monthly on a straight line basis over the expected useful lives of the related assets. The principal annual rates use are:

	%
Buildings	2
Plant and machinery	10
Vehicles	20
Fixtures and fittings	10
Intangible assets	20

(g) Patents and other similar rights

Patents and other similar rights are stated at cost and depreciated over the lower of the useful life and the legal life of the related asset.

(h) Trespasses e diferenças de consolidação

Os trespasses e as diferenças de consolidação correspondem ao excesso do montante pago ou a pagar sobre o valor atribuível dos activos líquidos adquiridos. As diferenças de consolidação de abertura e as diferenças de consolidação negativas do exercício encontram-se relevadas em rúbrica própria dos capitais próprios; as diferenças de consolidação positivas encontram-se relevadas em rúbrica própria do activo, sendo amortizadas em quotas constantes por duodécimos no prazo máximo de cinco anos, podendo, no entanto, este período ser dilatado, desde que tal se justifique e não exceda o do uso útil.

(i) Capitalização de encargos financeiros

Os encargos financeiros directamente correlacionados com activos específicos, incorridos até ao momento de entrada em funcionamento do respectivo bem são capitalizados.

(j) Despesas de investigação e desenvolvimento

As despesas de investigação e desenvolvimento de projectos específicos com expectativa razoável de sucesso comercial são capitalizadas desde que se considere serem os proveitos futuros estimados superiores aos custos de desenvolvimento já incorridos ou estimados incorrer e aos respectivos custos de produção, distribuição e administrativos. Estas despesas capitalizadas são amortizadas por um período de cinco anos.

(k) Existências

As existências são apresentadas ao mais baixo entre o custo e o valor líquido de realização. O custo é na generalidade calculado utilizando o critério da média ponderada e os seguintes métodos:

Mercadorias e Matérias-primas
– custo médio das existências, incluindo custos de transporte, despacho e manuseamento;

Produtos em Curso de Fabrico e Produtos Acabado
– todos os custos imputáveis às obras.

Produtos de Consumo
– preço de custo médio

Em 1996 foi utilizado o critério do preço de venda normal deduzido da margem média, o efeito da alteração de critério efectuada não é significativo.

(l) Créditos e débitos em moedas estrangeiras

Os activos e passivos denominados em moedas estrangeiras são convertidos em escudos às taxas de câmbio em vigor no final do exercício. Os resultados das filiais estrangeiras são convertidos à taxa de câmbio média no final do exercício. As diferenças ocorridas na conversão dos capitais próprios iniciais das subsidiárias são registadas numa reserva de conversão cambial. Nos casos em que os saldos no fim do exercício estão regulados por contratos de compra a prazo de moeda estrangeira, a taxa de câmbio definida nesses contratos é utilizada para converter as suas componentes em escudos.

As taxas de câmbio utilizadas no exercício para a conversão em moeda portuguesa das contas das filiais estrangeiras foram as constantes na nota n.º 24.

(m) Interesses minoritários

Os montantes dos capitais próprios das empresas filiais consolidadas, atribuíveis às acções ou partes detidas por pessoas estranhas às empresas incluídas na consolidação, são inscritos no balanço consolidado na rubrica "Interesses minoritários".

Os interesses minoritários sobre o resultado líquido das filiais consolidadas são identificados e ajustados por dedução ao resultado do grupo e inscritos na demonstração de resultados consolidados na rúbrica "Interesses minoritários".

(n) Impostos

O imposto sobre o rendimento do exercício é determinado com base no resultado líquido ajustado de acordo com a legislação fiscal, considerando cada uma das filiais isoladamente ou os grupos de consolidação fiscal quando existentes. Foram considerados impostos diferidos nas situações justificáveis.

(o) Locação financeira

Os activos sob contratos de locação financeira, bem como as correspondentes responsabilidades, estão reflectidas no balanço consolidado, de acordo com o disposto na Directriz Contabilística n.º 10.

(p) Provisões

As provisões são constituídas pelos valores efectivamente necessários para fazer face a perdas estimadas.

(h) Goodwill arising on consolidation
Goodwill arising on consolidation represents the excess of the fair value of the consideration given over the fair value of the identifiable net assets acquired.

The initial net goodwill calculated on the introduction of consolidated financial statements in Portugal on 1 January 1991 and negative goodwill arising on the acquisition of affiliated and associated undertakings since that date are included in shareholder's funds as a separate item.

Positive goodwill arising after 1 January 1991 is included as an intangible asset. This is depreciated through the profit and loss account over five years or more if a longer life is considered more appropriate, always provived that this does not exceed the expected useful life of the respective undertaking.

(i) Capitalisation of interest payable
Interest payable directly related to specific assets is capitalised until the respective assets become operational.

(j) Start-up, research and development costs
Start-up, research and development costs directly related to specific commercial projects are capitalised provided that estimated future income exceeds costs already incurred or still to be incured including future production, distribution and administrative costs. The costs capitalised are written off over a period of 5 years.

(k) Stocks
Stocks are stated at the lower of cost and net realisable value. In general, cost is determined on a moving average basis using the following methods:

Raw materials and consumables:
Purchase cost including transport and handling;

Work in progress and finished goods:
All direct expenditure and an allocation of production overheads based on normal levels of activity;

Goods for resale:
Average purchase cost.

In 1996 normal retail sales prices less average margins achieved was used to value Goods for resale. The effect of the change in the valuation method is immaterial.

(l) Foreign currencies
Assets and liabilities denominated in foreign currencies are translated to escudos at the middle market rates of exchange at 31 December. The financial statements of foreign affiliated undertakings are also translated at the year end middle market rates. Exchange differences arising on the opening net investments in foreign affiliated undertakings are taken to reserves.

Where foreign currency balances are covered by forward exchange contracts the contract rate is used for currency conversion.

The exchange rates used to convert the financial statements of foreign affiliated undertakings are set out in note 24.

(m) Minority interests
The proportion of shareholders' funds held by third parties in affiliated undertakings included on consolidation is shown as Minority Interests in the consolidated balance sheet.

The share of the results for the year that relate to third party participations are shown as Profit attributable to minority interests and are deducted from Group results.

(n) Income taxation
The charge for taxation is based on the adjusted taxable profit for the year for each of the individual companies or groups of companies which are consolidated for tax purposes.

Provision is made for deferred taxation, using the liability method, on all material timing differences to the extent that it is probable that a liability will crystallise.

(o) Leasing
As from 1 January 1995, leased assets and their corresponding liabilities are included in the balance sheet in accordance with Portuguese accounting principles.

(p) Provisions
Provisions are made whenever an estimated loss is expected to arise.

I – INFORMATION IN RESPECT OF COMPANIES INCLUDED IN OR EXCLUDED FROM THE CONSOLIDATED FINANCIAL STATEMENTS

Note 1. Companies included in the consolidated financial statements

	Company	Registered Office	% Capital Held	Legal Reason for Inclusion
	Agloma-Sociedade Industrial de Madeira Aglomerada, S.A.	Oliveira do Hospital	100,00%	a)
	Boxbright Limited	Surrey (U.K.)	100,00%	a)
7)	Casca - Sociedade de Revestimentos, S.A.	Águeda	100,00%	a)
1)	Celdata - Informática, S.A.	Maia	100,00%	a)
3)	Chão Verde - Sociedade Gestora Imobiliária, S.A.	Maia	100,00%	a)
	Citorres - Sociedade Imobiliária, S.A.	Maia	100,00%	a)
	Clinica Miradouro, S.A.	Porto	100,00%	a)
1)	Colombo Gest & Gestão de Centros Comerciais, S.A.	Lisboa	100,00%	a)
	Companhia Real de Distribuição	Portalegre (Brasil)	100,00%	a)
	Contimobe - Imobiliária de Castelo de Paiva, S.A.	Castelo de Paiva	100,00%	a)
	Crediuniverso - Serviços de Marketing, S.A.	Maia	100,00%	a)
	Difusão - Sociedade Imobiliária, S.A.	Maia	100,00%	a)
	Divultec - Informática, S.A.	Maia	100,00%	a)
	Empreendimentos Imobiliários Quinta da Azenha, S.A.	Maia	100,00%	a)
	Espimaia - Sociedade Imobiliária, S.A.	Maia	100,00%	a)
	Fimaia - Serviços na Área Económica e Gestão de Investimentos, S.A.	Maia	100,00%	a)
	Finlog - Aluguer e Comércio de Automóveis, S.A.	Lisboa	100,00%	a)
9)	Grama Grandes Armazéns, S.A.	Matosinhos	100,00%	a)
1)11)	GuimarãesShopping - Empreendimentos Imobiliários, S.A.	Maia	100,00%	a)
4)	Harpa, Beheer, BV	Amsterdam (Holanda)	100,00%	a)
	IGI - Investimento Imobiliário, S.A.	Porto	100,00%	a)
	Igimo - Sociedade Imobiliária, S.A.	Maia	100,00%	a)
	Iginveste- Serviços na Área Económica e Gestão de Investimentos, S.A.	Maia	100,00%	a)
	Imoestrutura - Sociedade Imobiliária, S.A.	Maia	100,00%	a)
	Imoferro - Sociedade Imobiliária, S.A.	Maia	100,00%	a)
	Imolégua - Sociedade Imobiliária, S.A.	Maia	100,00%	a)
	Imomuro - Sociedade Imobiliária, S.A.	Matosinhos	100,00%	a)
	Imosistema - Sociedade Imobiliária, S.A.	Maia	100,00%	a)
	Imo R - Sociedade Imobiliária, S.A.	Porto	62,50%	a)
6)	Interlog - Informática, S.A.	Lisboa	100,00%	a)
4)	Inventory - Acessórios de Casa, S.A.	Maia	100,00%	a)
	Linha - Imobiliária e Planeamento Urbanístico, S.A.	Maia	100,00%	a)
1)	Lisedi - Urbanização e Edifícios, S.A.	Maia	100,00%	a)
1) 10)	LouresShopping - Empreendimentos Imobiliários, S.A.	Maia	100,00%	a)
1) 12)	MaiaShopping - Empreendimentos Imobiliários, S.A.	Maia	100,00%	a)
4)	Max Office - Artigos e Serviços para Escritórios, S.A.	Maia	100,00%	a)
	Modalfa - Comércio e Serviços, S.A.	Maia	100,00%	a)
	Modelo - Sociedade Gestora de Participações Sociais, S.A.	Maia	100,00%	a)
	Modelo Continente Hipermercados, S.A.	Matosinhos	100,00%	a)
	Modelo Continente, S.G.P.S, S.A.	Matosinhos	68,77%	a)
	Modelo Hiper - Exploração de Centros Comerciais, S.A.	Maia	100,00%	a)
	Modelo Investimentos (Brasil), Ltda	Brasil	80,00%	a)
	Modis Distribuição Centralizada, S.A.	Matosinhos	100,00%	a)
	Modis, S.G.P.S., S.A.	Matosinhos	60,00%	a)
	Omala - Imobiliária e Gestão, S.A.	Porto	100,00%	a)
	Parque de Famalicão - Empreendimentos Imobiliários, S.A.	Maia	100,00%	a)
1)	PCU - Planeamento, Construção e Urbanismo, S.A.	Maia	100,00%	a)
	Polivértice - Serviços a Grossistas e Retalhistas, S.A.	Matosinhos	100,00%	a)
	Porturbe - Edifícios e Urbanizações, S.A.	Maia	100,00%	a)
	Praedium - Desenvolvimento Imobiliário, S.A.	Porto	56,00%	a)
	Predicomercial - Promoção Imobiliária, S.A.	Maia	100,00%	a)
	Prediguarda - Sociedade Imobiliária, S.A.	Maia	100,00%	a)
1)	Prédios Consolidados Imobiliária, S.A.	Matosinhos	100,00%	a)
	Prédios Privados Imobiliária, S.A.	Matosinhos	100,00%	a)
	Pridelease Investments, Ltd	Cascais	50,00%	b)
	Quinta da Covilhã - Empreendimentos Imobiliários, S.A.	Maia	100,00%	a)
	RPU - Realizações e Planeamento Urbanístico, S.A.	Maia	100,00%	a)
	Sesagest - Projectos e Gestão Imobiliária, S.A.	Porto	100,00%	a)
1)	Sociloures - Sociedade Imobiliária, S.A.	Matosinhos	100,00%	a)
	Sodiscol - Distribuição de Produtos à Hotelaria, S.A.	Maia	100,00%	a)
	Soira - Sociedade Imobiliária de Ramalde, S.A.	Porto	100,00%	a)
	Sonae Comércio e Serviços, S.A.	Matosinhos	100,00%	a)
	Sonae Distribuição - Sociedade Gestora de Participações Sociais, S.A.	Maia	100,00%	a)
	Sonae Imobiliária - S.G.P.S, S.A.	Maia	50,99%	a)
	Sonae Investimentos - Sociedade Gestora de Participações Sociais, S.A.	Maia	HOLDING	HOLDING
	Sonae Participações Financeiras, Sociedade Gestora de Participações Sociais, S.A.	Porto	100,00%	a)
	Sonae Retalho Especializado - Sociedade Gestora de Participações Sociais, S.A.	Matosinhos	100,00%	a)

Company	Register Offfice Held	% Capital Inclusão	Legal Reason for Inclusion
Sondis Imobiliária, S.A.	Maia	100,00%	a)
Sondis B.V.	Linne (Holanda)	100,00%	a)
SPCC - Sociedade Portuguesa de Centros Comerciais, S.A.	Lisboa	100,00%	a)
SPEL - Sociedade de Parques de Estacionamento, S.A.	Porto	50,00%	b)
8) Sport Zone - Comércio de Artigos de Desporto, S.A.	Vila Nova Famalicão	100,00%	a)
4) Stayfair Ltd	Liverpool (U.K.)	100,00%	a)
Teleporto - Empreendimentos Imobiliários, S.A.	Maia	100,00%	a)
5) The Source (Retail) Ltd	London (U.K.)	100,00%	a)
Top100 - Sociedade Gestora de Participações Sociais, S.A.	Porto	100,00%	a)
UCG - Urbanismo, Construção e Gestão, S.A.	Maia	100,00%	a)
4) Urano, Beheer, BV	Amsterdam (Holanda)	100,00%	a)
2) Vasco da Gama - Promoção de Centros Comerciais, S.A.	Maia	50,00%	a)
Venda Aluga - Sociedade Imobiliária, S.A.	Maia	100,00%	a)
Viacatarinagest - Gestão de Centros Comerciais, S.A.	Maia	100,00%	a)
Viacentro - Engenharia e Serviços Imobiliários, S.A.	Porto	100,00%	a)
Vilalambert - Sociedade Imobiliária, S.A.	Maia	100,00%	a)
Worten - Equipamentos para o Lar, S.A.	Matosinhos	100,00%	a)

a) paragraph a), n.° 1, art.° 1.° of Decree-Law nr. 238/91 – majority holding
b) paragraph d), n.° 1, art.° 1.° of Decree-Law nr. 238/91 – management control exercised

1) Companies excluded in 1996 as not considered significant;
2) Company included up to 7 March 1997, date when it has been sold;
3) Ex-MV – Imobiliária, SA;
4) Companies formed in 1997;
5) Company acquired in May 1997;
6) Company acquired on 31 December 1997;
7) Company sold in November 1997;
8) Ex-Cabaz – Comércio Retalhista, S.A.;
9) Company sold in December 1997;
10) Esforço – Realizações e Planeamento Urbanístico, S.A.;
11) Remaia – Realizações Imobiliárias, S.A.;
12) UCP – Urbanismo, Construção e Planeamento, S.A..

Note 2. Companies excluded from the consolidated financial statements

Company	Register Office	% Capital Held	Legal Reason for Inclusion
Abisus & Gestão de Centros Comerciais, S.A.	Maia	100,00%	a)
Andar - Sociedade Imobiliária, S.A.	Maia	100,00%	a)
2) Autorictas - Empreendimentos Imobiliários, S.A.	Porto	100,00%	a)
Beloc - Urbanizações e Construções, S.A.	Maia	100,00%	a)
2) Choice Car - Comércio de Automóveis, S.A.	Maia	100,00%	a)
2) Datavenia - Gestão de Centros Comerciais, S.A.	Maia	100,00%	a)
2) Igita - Sociadade Imobiliária, S.A.	Maia	100,00%	a)
Imoclub - Serviços Imobiliários, S.A.	Matosinhos	100,00%	a)
2) Imoconti - Sociedade Imobiliária, S.A.	Matosinhos	100,00%	a)
Imohotel - Empreendimentos Turísticos Imobiliários, S.A.	Matosinhos	100,00%	a)
Imoponte - Sociedade Imobiliária, S.A.	Maia	100,00%	a)
Imoresultado - Sociedade Imobiliária, S.A.	Maia	100,00%	a)
Imosedas - Imobiliária e Serviços, S.A.	Matosinhos	100,00%	a)
2) Infofield - Informática, S.A.	Maia	100,00%	a)
Liquidimo - Sociedade Imobiliária, S.A.	Maia	100,00%	a)
Martimope - Sociedade Imobiliária, S.A.	Maia	100,00%	a)
3) Mclane Portugal - Comércio e Serviços, S.A.	Lisboa	100,00%	a)
MDS - Sociedade Mediadora de Seguros, S.A.	Porto	100,00%	a)
1) Mercadis - Gestão de Mercado de Distribuição, S.A.	Amadora	99,89%	a)
Modelo Bricolage Materiais para o Lar, Lda	Matosinhos	100,00%	a)
2) Pincelim Projectos e Consultoria, S.A.	Maia	100,00%	a)
Predisedas - Predial das Sedas, S.A.	Matosinhos	100,00%	a)
Promessa - Sociedade Imobiliária, S.A.	Maia	100,00%	a)
Promosedas - Promoção Imobiliária, S.A.	Matosinhos	100,00%	a)
2) Sempre à Mão - Comércio Retalhista, S.A.	Matosinhos	100,00%	a)
Solução - Apoio à Gestão, S.A.	Maia	100,00%	a)
Sonae Imobiliária Brasil, Ltda	São Paulo (Brasil)	100,00%	a)
2) Sonae Retalho Espana - Servicios Generales, S.A.	Madrid (Espanha)	100,00%	a)
Sonaegest - Sociedade Gestora de Fundos de Investimentos, S.A.	Maia	80,00%	a)
Sontária - Empreendimentos Imobiliários, S.A.	Maia	62,50%	a)
2) Sport Zone Espana - Servicios Generales, S.A.	Madrid (Espanha)	100,00%	a)
Urbisedas - Imobiliária das Sedas, S.A.	Matosinhos	100,00%	a)
2) 24x24 - Produtos Alimentares e Utilidades Domésticas, Lda	Estoril	100,00%	a)

‚a) n.° 1 of art.° 4.° of Decree-Law nr. 238/91 – not significant

1) Company included in 1996, but excluded in 1997 because it is immaterial;
2) Companies formed in 1997;
3) Company acquired in 1997.

Nota 3. Empresas associadas contabilizadas pelo método da equivalência patromonial

Firma	Sede Social	% de Capital Detido
Aveiria - Sociedade Imobiliária, S.A.	Porto	27,74%
Empreendimentos Imobiliários Colombo, S.A.	Lisboa	50,00%
Escolha Directa - Vendas por Correspondência, S.A.	Maia	50,00%
2) Locamo - Controle de Crédito, S.A.	Porto	100,00%
Modelo - Distribuição de Materiais de Construção, S.A.	Maia	50,00%
3) OMNE - Sociedade Gestora de Participações Sociais, S.A.	Maia	25,00%
2) Peninsular - Sociedade Financeira para Aquisições a Crédito, S.A.	Porto	100,00%
2) Peninsular Investimentos, S.G.P.S., S.A.	Porto	100,00%
2) PNS - Sociedade de Gestão Imobiliária, S.A.	Porto	100,00%
3) Potestas - Empreendimentos Imobiliários, S.A.	Maia	25,00%
SM - Empreendimentos Imobiliários, S.A.	Lisboa	25,00%
2) Universo Banco Directo, S.A.	Porto	100,00%
1) Vasco da Gama - Promoção de Centros Comerciais, S.A.	Maia	50,00%
Viacatarina – Empreendimentos Imobiliários, S.A.	Maia	50,00%

1) Filial consolidada pelo método integral até 7 de Março de 1997, data em que ocorreu a alienação de parte da participação;
2) Filiais incluídas pelo método da equivalência patromonial devido à utilização do Plano de Contas Bancário;
3) Empresas constituídas em 1997.

Nota 4. Empresas associadas não contabilizadas pelo método da equivalência patromonial

Firma	Sede Social	% de Capital Detido	Motivos de Exclusão
Integrum - Serviços Partilhados, S.A.	Matosinhos	30,00%	a)
Spel - Serviços Auto, S.A.	Porto	26,00%	a)
Paracentro - Plan.Comerc.e Gestão de Centros Comerciais, S.A.	Maia	50,00%	a)

a) n.º1 do art. 4.º do Decreto-Lei n.º 238/91 (exclusão por imaterialidade).

Nota 6. Empresas participadas

Firma	Sede Social	% de Capital Detido
Insco – Insular de Hipermercados, S.A.	Ponta Delgada	10,00%
Fozimo - Sociedade Imobiliária, S.A.	Maia	10,00%
Imodivor - Sociedade Imobiliária, S.A.	Maia	10,00%

Nota 7. Trabalhadores ao serviço

O número médio de trabalhadores ao serviço, durante o exercício, das empresas incluídas na consolidação pode ser analisado como segue:

Por Actividade:	
Distribuição	17,737
Imobiliária	260
Outras Empresas	112
Total	**18,109**

Por categoria:	
Quadros	1,887
Técnicos	531
Pessoal Administrativo	1,353
Directos	14,338
Total	**18,109**

II – Informações Relativas à Imagem Verdadeira e Apropriada

Nota 9. Afastamento às normas de consolidação

Para se obter a necessária imagem verdadeira e apropriada da situação financeira e dos resultados das empresas incluídas na consolidação, foram efectuadas, em exercícios anteriores, avaliações dos activos imobiliários de uma filial (projecto GAIASHOPING) e de uma associada (projecto COLOMBO) de acordo com os relatórios apresentados por uma sociedade de avaliadores independentes. Essa avaliação foi efectuada em consequência da significativa diferença entre o custo de aquisição e os valores atribuíveis aos terrenos considerando os projectos aprovados.

Note 3. Companies accounted for as associated undertakings (using the equity method)

Company	Registered Office	% Capital Held
Aveiria - Sociedade Imobiliária, S.A.	Porto	27,74%
Empreendimentos Imobiliários Colombo, S.A.	Lisboa	50,00%
Escolha Directa - Vendas por Correspondência, S.A.	Maia	50,00%
2) Locamo - Controle de Crédito, S.A.	Porto	100,00%
Modelo - Distribuição de Materiais de Construção, S.A.	Maia	50,00%
3) OMNE - Sociedade Gestora de Participações Sociais, S.A.	Maia	25,00%
2) Peninsular - Sociedade Financeira para Aquisições a Crédito, S.A.	Porto	100,00%
2) Peninsular Investimentos, S.G.P.S., S.A.	Porto	100,00%
2) PNS - Sociedade de Gestão Imobiliária, S.A.	Porto	100,00%
3) Potestas - Empreendimentos Imobiliários, S.A.	Maia	25,00%
SM - Empreendimentos Imobiliários, S.A.	Lisboa	25,00%
2) Universo Banco Directo, S.A.	Porto	100,00%
1) Vasco da Gama - Promoção de Centros Comerciais, S.A.	Maia	50,00%
Viacatarina – Empreendimentos Imobiliários, S.A.	Maia	50,00%

1)Fully consolidated company until 7 March 1997, when part of it's share capital was sold;
2) Companies included using the Equity method because of diversity of operations (financial concerns);
3) Company formed in 1997

Note 4. Companies not accounted for as associated undertakings

Company	Registered Office	% Capital Held	Legal Reason for Exclusion
Integrum - Serviços Partilhados, S.A.	Matosinhos	30,00%	a)
Spel - Serviços Auto, S.A.	Porto	26,00%	a)
Paracentro - Plan.Comerc.e Gestão de Centros Comerciais, S.A.	Maia	50,00%	a)

a) n.° 1 of art.° 4.° of Decree-Law nr. 238/91 – not significant.

Note 6. Other related undertakings

Company	Registered Office	% Capital Held
Insco – Insular de Hipermercados, S.A.	Ponta Delgada	10,00%
Fozimo - Sociedade Imobiliária, S.A.	Maia	10,00%
Imodivor - Sociedade Imobiliária, S.A.	Maia	10,00%

Note 7. Employee information

The average number of employees of the companies included in the consolidated financial statements was:

By activity:	
Retailing	17,737
Real estate	260
Other activities	112
Total	**18,109**

By categories:	
Directors and managers	1,887
Technical	531
Administrative	1,353
Staff	14,338
Total	**18,109**

II - Information Required to Report a True and Fair View

Note 9. Exceptions to normal accounting principles applied to consolidation financial statements
In order to obtain a true and fair view of the financial position and results of the companies included in the consolidated financial statements independent valuations of real estate assets of an affiliated undertaking (GAIASHOPPING project) and of an associated undertaking (COLOMBO project) were made in prior years.
These valuations were included in the financial statements due to the significant differences between the costs of acquisition and the value of the assets as a result of development authorisations obtained.
The effects on the consolidated financial statements are as follows:

Consolidated balances sheet:	*Escudos thousand*	*Ecus thousand*
Assets:		
Fixed assets – tangible		
Land	1 580 312	7 818
Fixed assets – investments		
Shares in related (including associates) undertakings	3 610 216	17 861
Shareholders funds:		
Goodwill arising on consolidation	5 267 156	26 059
Retained earnings	-1 669 053	-8 257
Minority interests	1 592 425	7 878

At 31 December 1997 these amounts are supported by independent valuations made in 1997.

Os efeitos nas demonstrações consolidadas são os seguintes:

Balanço Consolidado: *milhares de escudos*

Activo
Imobilizado corpóreo   1 580 312
Partes de capital em empresas associadas   3 610 216

Capitais Próprios
Diferença de consolidação de abertura   5 267 156
Resultados transitados   -1 669 053

Interesses Minoritários   1 592 425

A 31 de Dezembro de 1997, estes valores estão suportados por avaliações independentes efectuadas no exercício.

III – Informações Relativas aos Procedimentos de Consolidação

Nota 10. Diferenças de consolidação

a) Descriminação   *milhares de escudos*

	1997	1996	Variação
De Abertura	-7 765 330	-5 669 668	2 095 662
Positivas	14 772 795	14 697 646	75 149
Negativas	765 470	2 599 115	-1 833 645

b) Método de cálculo
Ver Nota 0 (h).

c) Variações mais significativas:

c1) Diferenças de abertura   *milhares de escudos*

	Diminuições
Efeitos da Cisão	2 110 472
Outras	–14 810
	2 095 662

c2) Diferenças positivas   *milhares de escudos*

		Aumentos	Diminuições	Vida útil
	Efeitos da Cisão		1 734 741	
1)	Companhia Real de Distribuição, S.A.	2 094 169		20
2)	Modelo Investimentos Brasil, Lda.		122 193	
3)	Sport Zone - Comércio de Artigos de Desporto, S.A.	192 918		10
	Outros	187 344	542 348	
		2 474 431	2 399 282	

1) Aquisição de 50% do capital social;
2) Alienação de 20% do capital social;
3) Filial incluída no exercício.

c2) Diferenças negativas   *milhares de escudos*

		Aumentos	Diminuições
	Efeitos da Cisão		2 271 081
1)	The Source (Retail) Ltd.	437 868	
	Outros		433
		437 868	2 271 514

1) Filial adquirida no exercício.

Nota 14. Comparabilidade das demonstrações financeiras:

Comparabilidade das demonstrações financeiras

As demonstrações financeiras consolidadas de 31 de Dezembro de 1997, não são comparáveis com as do período homologo do ano anterior, tal facto resulta da cisão da sociedade ocorrida a 1 de Janeiro de 1997.

III – Information on consolidation procedures adopted

Note 10. Goodwill arising on consolidation

a) Analysis:

		Escudos thousand			*Ecus thousand*	
	1997	1996	Net variance	1997	1996	Net variance
Initial negative goodwill (at 1 January 1991)	-7 765 330	-5 669 668	2 095 662	- 38 418	- 29 184	9.234
Positive goodwill (since 1 January 1991)	14 772 795	14 697 646	75 149	73.086	75.654	- 2.568
Negative goodwill (since 1 January 1991)	765 470	2 599 115	-1 833 645	3.787	13.379	- 9.592

b) Methods used:
See Principal Accounting Policy (h).

c) Significant variations:

c1) Changes during 1997 to initial negative goodwill (at 1 January 1991)

	Escudos thousand	*Ecus thousand*
	Reductions	Reductions
Demerger effect	2 110 472	10 441
Others	-14 810	-73
	2 095 662	10 368

c2) Changes during 1997 to positive goodwill:

	Escudos thousand		*Ecus thousand*		
	Increases	Reductions	Increases	Reductions	Used life
Demerger effect		1 734 741		8 582	
1) Companhia Real de Distribuicão, S.A.	2 094 169		10 361		20
2) Modelo Investimentos Brasil, Lda.		122 193		605	
3) Sport Zone - Comércio de Artigos de Desporto, S.A.	192 918		954		10
Others	187 344	542 348	927	2 683	
	2 474 431	2 399 282	12 242	11 870	

1) Purchase of 50% of company's share capital;
2) Purchase of 20% of company's share capital;
3) Company included during 1997.

c2) Changes during 1997 to negative goodwill:

	Escudos thousand		*Ecus thousand*	
	Increases	Reductions	Increases	Reductions
Demerger effect		2 271 081		11 236
1) The Source (Retail) Ltd.	437 868		2 166	
Others		433		2
	437 868	2 271 514	2 166	11 238

1) Company acquired in 1997.

Note 14. Comparability of financial statements:

The consolidated financial statement at 31 December 1997 are not comparable with the previous year's financial statements due to the demerger of the company which occurred at 1 January 1997.
The simulation of the effects of the demerger on the consolidated financial statements at 31 December 1997 are as follows:

	Escudos thousand 000		*Ecus thousand000*	
	1997	1996	1997	1996
Sales and services rendered	412 342	371 880	2 040	1 914
Profit for the financial year	12 197	20 180	60	104
Total net assets	361 520	268 204	1 789	1 381
Shareholders funds and minority interests	120 746	93 678	597	482

Changes to the consolidation perimeter

1) As mentioned in the 1996 Management Board's Report, the mother company demerged with effects after 1 January 1997, as a result of which the following companies were withdrawn from the consolidation perimeter:

Cia. de Industrias Y Negocios, S.A.
Cinclus - Planeamento e Gestão de Projectos, S.A.
Cinclus Imobiliária, S.A.
Cornbark Associates Limited
Dollarange Finance LTD
Duolite, S.A.
Euro Decorative Boards Ltd.
Euromegantic Lteé
Euroresinas - Indústrias Quimicas, S.A.
Explotaciones Comerciales, Industriales y de Servicios, S.A.

Considerando a simulação da cisão nas contas referidas a 31 de Dezembro de 1996, as demonstrações financeiras poderão ser analisadas como segue:

milhares de escudos

	1997	1996
Volume de negócios	412 342	371 880
Resultados líquidos após minoritários	12 197	20 180
Total do activo líquido	361 520	268 204
Total dos capitais próprios e interesses minoritários	120 746	93 678

Alterações do perímetro de consolidação

1) Tal como mencionado no Relatório e Contas de 1996, em 1 de Janeiro de 1997 ocorreu a Cisão da sociedade, que originou a saída do perímetro de consolidação das seguintes empresas:

Cia. de Industrias Y Negocios, S.A.
Cinclus - Planeamento e Gestão de Projectos, S.A.
Cinclus Imobiliária, S.A.
Cornbark Associates Limited
Dollarange Finance LTD
Duolite, S.A.
Euro Decorative Boards Ltd.
Euromegantic Lteé
Euroresinas - Indústrias Químicas, S.A.
Explotaciones Comerciales, Industriales y de Servicios, S.A.
Explotaciones Madereras Catalanas, S.A.
Florestal y Maderera, S.A.
Fozimo - Sociedade Imobiliária, S.A.
Ibersande Restauração, S.A.
Ibersol - Hotelaria e Turismo, S.A.
Ibersol - Restauração, S.A.
Ibersol - Sociedade Gestora de Participações Sociais, S.A.
Imocapital - Sociedade Gestora de Participações Sociais, S.A.
Industrias Quimicas del Carbono, S.A.
Informeios - Projectos e Representações, S.A.
Interlog - Informática, S.A.
Interlog - Sociedade Gestora de Participações Sociais, S.A.
Libra Serviços, Lda
Maestro - Serviços de Gestão de Hotelaria, S.A.
Maiequipa - Gestão Florestal, S.A.
Megantic B.V.
Movelpartes - Componentes para a Indústria do Mobiliário, S.A.
Orbitlândia - Equip.Diversão e Ocup. de Tempos Livres, S.A.
Orbitur - Imobiliária, S.A.
Orbitur - Intercâmbio e Turismo, S.A.
Orpin, S.A.
Plamac - Componentes para a Indústria de Mobiliário, S.A.
Poliface - Componentes e Sist.para Mob. e Construção, S.A.
Prosa - Programação Informática, S.A.
Público - Comunicação Social, S.A.
Publimeios - Soc. Gestora de Participações Sociais, S.A.
Racionalización y Manufacturas Florestales, S.A.
Rhodes Investments Ltd.
Rochester Real Estate, Limited
Selvicola del Norte, S.A.
Siaf - Sociedade de Iniciativa e Aproveitamentos Florestais, S.A.
SIRS - Sociedade Independente de Radiodifusão Sonora, S.A.
SMP - Serviços de Manutenção e Planeamento, S.A.
Sociedade de Iniciativa e Aproveitamentos Florestais - Energias, S.A.
Solinca - Investimentos Turísticos, S.A.
Somit - Soc. de Madeiras Industrializadas e Transformadas, S.A.
Sonae (UK) Ltd
Sonae Indústria - Sociedade Gestora de Participações Sociais, S.A.
Sonae Indústria de Revestimentos, S.A.
Sonae International Ltd
Sonae Produtos e Derivados Florestais, S.A.
Sonae Redes de Dados, S.A.
Sonae Tecnologias de Informação, S.A.
Sonae Turismo, S.G.P.S.,S.A.
Sontrade Lines Ltd
Spanboard Products Ltd
Spred - Sociedade Gestora de Participações Sociais, S.A.
Star Viagens e Turismo, S.A.

Explotaciones Madereras Catalanas, S.A.
Florestal y Maderera, S.A.
Fozimo - Sociedade Imobiliária, S.A.
Ibersande Restauração, S.A.
Ibersol - Hotelaria e Turismo, S.A.
Ibersol - Restauração, S.A.
Ibersol - Sociedade Gestora de Participações Sociais, S.A.
Imocapital - Sociedade Gestora de Participações Sociais, S.A.
Industrias Quimicas del Carbono, S.A.
Informeios - Projectos e Representações, S.A.
Interlog - Informática, S.A.
Interlog - Sociedade Gestora de Participações Sociais, S.A.
Libra Serviços, Lda
Maestro - Serviços de Gestão de Hotelaria, S.A.
Maiequipa - Gestão Florestal, S.A.
Megantic B.V.
Movelpartes - Componentes para a Indústria do Mobiliário, S.A.
Orbitlândia - Equip.Diversão e Ocup. de Tempos Livres, S.A.
Orbitur - Imobiliária, S.A.
Orbitur - Intercâmbio e Turismo, S.A.
Orpin, S.A.
Plamac - Componentes para a Indústria de Mobiliário, S.A.
Poliface - Componentes e Sist.para Mob. e Construção, S.A.
Prosa - Programação Informática, S.A.
Público - Comunicação Social, S.A.
Publimeios - Soc. Gestora de Participações Sociais, S.A.
Racionalización y Manufacturas Florestales, S.A.
Rhodes Investments Ltd.
Rochester Real Estate, Limited
Selvicola del Norte, S.A.
Siaf - Sociedade de Iniciativa e Aproveitamentos Florestais, S.A.
SIRS - Sociedade Independente de Radiodifusão Sonora, S.A.
SMP - Serviços de Manutenção e Planeamento, S.A.
Sociedade de Iniciativa e Aproveitamentos Florestais - Energias, S.A.
Solinca - Investimentos Turisticos, S.A.
Somit - Soc. de Madeiras Industrializadas e Transformadas, S.A.
Sonae (UK) Ltd
Sonae Indústria - Sociedade Gestora de Participações Sociais, S.A.
Sonae Indústria de Revestimentos, S.A.
Sonae International Ltd
Sonae Produtos e Derivados Florestais, S.A.
Sonae Redes de Dados, S.A.
Sonae Tecnologias de Informação, S.A.
Sonae Turismo, S.G.P.S.,S.A.
Sontrade Lines Ltd
Spanboard Products Ltd
Spred - Sociedade Gestora de Participações Sociais, S.A.
Star Viagens e Turismo, S.A.
Star Transportes, S.A.
Tableros Tradema, S.L.
Tafiber, Tableros de Fibras Ibéricas, S.L.
Tafibra - Tableros Aglomerados y de Fibras, A.I.E.
Tafisa - Tableros de Fibras, S.A.
Tafisa Boards B.V.
Tafisa Canadá Societé en Commandite
Tafisa Trading, S.A.
Tafisa U.K.Ltd.
Taiber, Tableros Aglomerados Ibéricos, S.L.
Teconlogias del Medio Ambiente, S.A.
Todoforma Elaboración de Componentes de Tablero, S.A.

2) The following companies were included in the consolidated financial statements for the first time during 1997:

    b) Celdata Informática, S.A.
    b) ColomboGest & Gestão de Centros Comerciais, S.A.
    b) GuimarãesShopping - Empreendimentos Imobiliários, S.A.
    a) Harpa, Beheer, BV
    c) Interlog Informática, S.A.
    a) Inventory - Acessórios de Casa, S.A.
    b) Lisedi - Urbanização e Edifícios, S.A.
    b) LouresShopping - Empreendimentos Imobiliários, S.A.
    b) MaiaShopping - Empreendimentos Imobiliários, S.A.
    a) Max Office - Artigos e Serviços para Escritórios, S.A.
    b) PCU - Planeamento, Construção e Urbanismo, S.A.
    b) Prédios Consolidados Imobiliária, S.A.
    b) Sociloures - Sociedade Imobiliária, S.A.
    b) Sport Zone - Comércio de Artigos de Desporto, S.A
    c) Stayfair Ltd
    c) The Source (Retail) Ltd
    a) Urano, Beheer, BV

      a) Companies formed during 1997;
      b) Companies excluded from the 1996 consolidated financial statements as not considered to be significant;
      c) Companies acquired during 1997.

Star Transportes, S.A.
Tableros Tradema, S.L.
Tafiber, Tableros de Fibras Ibéricas, S.L.
Tafibra - Tableros Aglomerados y de Fibras, A.I.E.
Tafisa - Tableros de Fibras, S.A.
Tafisa Boards B.V.
Tafisa Canadá Societé en Commandite
Tafisa Trading, S.A.
Tafisa U.K.Ltd.
Taiber, Tableros Aglomerados Ibéricos, S.L.
Teconlogias del Medio Ambiente, S.A.
Todoforma Elaboración de Componentes de Tablero, S.A.

2) No exercício foram incluídas no perímetro de consolidação as seguintes empresas:

   b) Celdata Informática, S.A.
   b) ColomboGest & Gestão de Centros Comerciais, S.A.
   b) GuimarãesShopping - Empreendimentos Imobiliários, S.A.
   a) Harpa, Beheer, BV
   c) Interlog Informática, S.A.
   a) Inventory - Acessórios de Casa, S.A.
   b) Lisedi - Urbanização e Edifícios, S.A.
   b) LouresShopping - Empreendimentos Imobiliários, S.A.
   b) MaiaShopping - Empreendimentos Imobiliários, S.A.
   a) Max Office - Artigos e Serviços para Escritórios, S.A.
   b) PCU - Planeamento, Construção e Urbanismo, S.A.
   b) Prédios Consolidados Imobiliária, S.A.
   b) Sociloures - Sociedade Imobiliária, S.A.
   b) Sport Zone - Comércio de Artigos de Desporto, S.A
   c) Stayfair Ltd
   c) The Source (Retail) Ltd
   a) Urano, Beheer, BV

   a) Filiais constituídas no exercício;
   b) Filiais excluídas em 1996;
   c) Filiais adquiridas no exercício.

3) No exercício foram excluídas do perímetro de consolidação as seguintes empresas:

   a) Casca - Sociedade de Revestimentos, S.A.
   b) Mercadis - Gestão de Mercado de Distribuição, S.A.

   a) Filial alienada no exercício;
   b) Filial excluída no exercício por imaterialidade.

Nota 15. Utilização de critérios valorimétricos diferentes dos fixados para a consolidação
Ver Nota 9.

Nota 17. Amortização do valor das "diferenças de consolidação" para além de cinco anos
É entendimento da Direcção da Sonae Investimentos - Sociedade Gestora de Participações Sociais, S.A. que a recuperação total do investimento efectuado na aquisição de algumas empresas só será atingido ao fim de 10 anos, pelo que a amortização das respectivas diferenças de consolidação será também efectuada durante 10 anos por duodécimos, segundo o método das quotas constantes.

Na diferença de consolidação positiva apurada na aquisição da SPEL - Sociedade de Parques de Estacionamento, S.A. foi considerada uma vida útil de 18 anos, correspondente ao período de concessão da respectiva actividade. Foi ainda considerada que a recuperação total dos investimentos efectuados nas aquisições dos 22% do Modelo - Sociedade Gestora de Participações Sociais, S.A. e da Companhia Real de Distribuição, S.A. só serão atingidos ao fim de 20 anos, pelo que as amortizações das respectivas diferenças de consolidação serão também efectuadas durante 20 anos.

Nota 18. Contabilização das participações em associadas
O conjunto das empresas incluídas na consolidação contabilizaram as participações em associadas de acordo com a alínea a) do n.º 5.4.3.1. do anexo II do Plano Oficial de Contabilidade (custo de aquisição). No entanto, e nos casos mencionados na Nota 3. foram efectuados ajustamentos de consolidação para a contabilização das participações em associadas pelo método da equivalência patrimonial, de acordo com o nº 13.6.1 das Normas de Consolidação de Contas.

IV – Informações Relativas a Compromissos

Nota 22. Responsabilidades por garantias prestadas
A 31 de Dezembro de 1997, as responsabilidades das empresas incluídas na consolidação por garantias prestadas podem ser apresentadas como segue:

	milhares de escudos
Garantias	10 194 410
Cauções	30 878
Hipotecas	18 584 854
Penhores	4 418 758
Outros	2 128 982

Note 15. Use of accounting policies or valuation methods different from those defined for consolidation
See note 9.

Note 17. Goodwill on consolidation being depreciated over more than five years
The Management Board of SONAE INVESTIMENTOS, SOCIEDADE GESTORA DE PARTICIPAÇÕES SOCIAIS, S.A. considers that the pay back on the investments in some companies acquired will only be achieved after 10 years. As a result, the positive goodwill arising on consolidation of these companies is being written off monthly on a straight line basis over a period of 10 years.

The positive goodwill arising as a result of consolidation of SPEL – Sociedade de Parques de Estacionamento, S.A. is considered to have a useful life of 18 years, based on the period of the underlying concession held.

It was also considered that the total pay back on the purchase of 22% of Modelo – Sociedade Gestora de Participações Sociais, S.A.'s share capital and of Companhia Real de Distribuição' share capital will only be achieved after 20 years. As a result the positive goodwill arising from these purchases will be written off over a period of 20 years.

Note 18. Accounting for associated undertakings
The companies included in the consolidated financial statements have accounted for their holdings in associated undertakings in accordance with paragraph a) of nr. 5.4.3.1 of Appendix 2 to the Portuguese Chart of Accounts (at purchase cost). However in the cases set out in note 3., consolidation adjustments are made to account for these undertakings as associated companies (by the equity method), in accordance with nr. 13.6.1 of the rules for consolitation.

IV – Information in relation to financial commitments

Note 22. Responsibilities for guarantees given
At 31 December 1997, the responsibilities of the companies included in the consolidation can be analysed as follows:

	Escudos thousand	Ecus thousand
Guarantees	10 194 410	50 435
Securities deposited	30 878	6 241
Mortgages and charges	23 003 612	113 807
Others	2 128 982	10 533

V – Information regarding accounting policies

Note 23. Valuation methods
See Principal Accounting Policies

Note 24 – Exchange rates used to convert to escudos (and ecus)
The exchanges rates used to convert the consolidation financial statements of foreign subsidiaries to escudos and ecus were:

	1997	1996
Pound sterling	303,034	265,742
Peseta	1,208	1,194
Dutch guilder	90,757	89,683
Ecu	202 128	194 274
Brasilian Real	160,263	150,5004

VI – Other information on specific items

Note 25. Start-up, research and development costs
The following were the main projects undertaken during 1997 for which costs were capitalised:

		Escudos thousand	Ecus thousand
Company	Project	Costs	Costs
Companhia Real de Distribuição, S.A:	New stores opened	952 145	4 711
Sonae Imobiliária, SGPS, S.A.	Costs of capital increase	297 953	1 474
		1 250 098	6 185

V – Informações Relativas a Políticas Contabilísticas

Nota 23. Critérios valorimétricos
Ver Nota 0.

Nota 24 – Cotações utilizadas para conversão em moeda portuguesa
As cotações utilizadas para conversão em moeda portuguesa das contas das filiais estrangeiras foram as seguintes:

	1997	1996
Libra	303,034	265,742
Peseta	1,208	1,194
Florim Holandês	90,757	89,683
Real	164,263	150,500

VI – Informações Relativas a Determinadas Rubricas

Nota 25. Despesas de instalação e despesas de investigação
As verbas mais significativas dos aumentos ocorridos no exercício nas contas de Despesas de Instalação e Despesas de Investigação e Desenvolvimento podem ser resumidas como segue:

milhares de escudos

Empresa	Projecto	Custos Imobilizados
Companhia Real de Distribuição, S.A:	Despesas com abertura de lojas	952 145
Sonae Imobiliária, SGPS, S.A.	Despesas incorridas no aumento capital	297 953
		1 250 098

Nota 27. Movimentos das rubricas do activo imobilizado
Os movimentos ocorridos durante o exercício, nas rúbricas do activo imobilizado constantes do balanço consolidado e nas respectivas amortizações e provisões podem ser resumidos como segue:

Activo Bruto

milhares de escudos

Rubricas	Saldo Inicial	Cisão	Aumentos	Alienações (b)	Transferências e Abates (a) (c)	Saldo Final
Imobilizações incorpóreas:						
Despesas de instalação	19 813 722	9 880 356	1 906 989	32 959	1 455 072	13 262 468
Despesas de Investigação e desenvolvimento	3 952 997	737 899	13 581	133 326	-33 338	3 062 015
Propriedade industrial e outros direitos	729 833	355 730	17 763	54 004	-1 271	336 591
Trespasses	1 308 900	517 962	181 614		-105 950	866 602
Imobilizações em curso	1 012 419	471 038	2 172 101	131 665	-1 751 818	829 999
Diferenças de consolidação	14 697 646	1 734 741	2 474 431	379 207	-285 334	14 772 795
	41 515 517	13 697 726	6 766 479	731 161	-722 639	33 130 470
Imobilizações corpóreas:						
Terrenos e recursos naturais	21 650 335	4 115 535	1 737 690	392 076	2 019 209	20 899 623
Edifícios e outras construções	84 613 311	20 908 590	7 243 792	1 038 914	22 225 545	92 135 144
Equipamento básico	112 246 164	74 678 549	5 586 043	6 976 065	18 146 820	54 324 413
Equipamento de transporte	5 380 980	1 630 876	1 376 016	486 081	469 083	5 109 122
Ferramentas e utensílios	996 870	297 547	12 567	43 711	6 193	674 372
Equipamento administrativo	13 129 687	3 898 719	3 493 848	691 460	-5 055 358	6 977 998
Taras e vasilhame	66 743	2 681				64 062
Outras imobilizações corpóreas	1 126 600	531 442	451 134	49 484	-47 058	949 750
(f) Imobilizações em curso	28 239 861	3 538 029	31 550 358	5 647 541	-27 189 793	23 414 856
(g) Adiantamentos p/ conta de imob. corpóreas	13 947 672	2 844 473	4 238 040	6 108	-8 591 947	6 743 184
	281 398 223	112 446 441	55 689 488	15 331 440	1 982 694	211 292 524
Investimentos financeiros:						
Partes de capital em empresas associadas	15 230 051	3 452 820	5 486 302	719 170	-4 172 514	12 371 849
Empréstimos a empresas associadas	8 925 443	661 097	3 232 535	41 401	-7 771 362	3 684 118
Partes de capital em empresas participadas	725 685	90 606		460 000		175 079
(d) Títulos e outras aplicações financeiras	857 083	640 224	12	130 842	6 532 519	6 618 548
Outros empréstimos concedidos	1 200	1 200	2 000			2 000
Imobilizações em curso	4 731	3 231			-1 500	
(e) Adiantamentos p/ conta de invest. financeiros	171 000		1 692 069		1 500	1 864 569
	25 915 193	4 849 178	10 412 918	1 351 413	-5 411 357	24 716 163

a) Inclui o saldo da entrada das filiais incluídas no exercício e excluídas no exercício anterior ou incluídas pelo método da equivalência patrimonial no valor de 797.645 milhares de escudos;

b) Inclui o saldo de saídas de filiais por alienação ou alteração do método de consolidação no valor de 11.868.088 milhares de escudos;

c) A rúbrica de partes de capital em empresas associadas inclui (2.588.698) milhares de escudos relativos à aplicação do método da equivalência patrimonial;

d) Inclui 6.545.004 milhares de escudos de obrigações de uma empresa associada;

Note 27. Details of fixed assets
Movements in consolidated fixed assets during the year can be summarised as follows:

Gross cost or valuation

Escudos thousand

Items	At 1 January 1997	Demerger	Expenditure	Disposals (b)	Transfers and Adjustments (a) (c)	At 31 December 1997
Intangible assets:						
Start-up costs	19 813 722	9 880 356	1 906 989	32 959	1 455 072	13 262 468
Research and development costs	3 952 997	737 899	13 581	133 326	−33 338	3 062 015
Patents and other similar rights	729 833	355 730	17 763	54 004	−1 271	336 591
Premiums paid for property occupation rights	1 308 900	517 962	181 614		−105 950	866 602
Projects in course	1 012 419	471 038	2 172 101	131 665	−1 751 818	829 999
Goodwill arising on consolidation	14 697 646	1 734 741	2 474 431	379 207	−285 334	14 772 795
	41 515 517	13 697 726	6 766 479	731 161	−722 639	33 130 470
Tangible assets:						
Land	21 650 335	4 115 535	1 737 690	392 076	2 019 209	20 899 623
Buildings	84 613 311	20 908 590	7 243 792	1 038 914	22 225 545	92 135 144
Plant and machinery	112 246 164	74 678 549	5 586 043	6 976 065	18 146 820	54 324 413
Vehicles	5 380 980	1 630 876	1 376 016	486 081	469 083	5 109 122
Tools	996 870	297 547	12 567	43 711	6 193	674 372
Fixtures and fittings	13 129 687	3 898 719	3 493 848	691 460	−5 055 358	6 977 998
Containers	66 743	2 681				64 062
Others	1 126 600	531 442	451 134	49 484	−47 058	949 750
(f) In construction	28 239 861	3 538 029	31 550 358	5 647 541	−27 189 793	23 414 856
(g) Advances	13 947 672	2 844 473	4 238 040	6 108	−8 591 947	6 743 184
	281 398 223	112 446 441	55 689 488	15 331 440	1 982 694	211 292 524
Investments:						
Shares in related (including associated) undertakings	15 230 051	3 452 820	5 486 302	719 170	−4 172 514	12 371 849
Loans to related (including associated) undertakings	8 925 443	661 097	3 232 535	41 401	−7 771 362	3 684 118
Shares in other undertakings	725 685	90 606		460 000		175 079
(d) Other investments other than loans	857 083	640 224	12	130 842	6 532 519	6 618 548
Loans to other undertakings	1 200	1 200	2 000			2 000
In construction	4 731	3 231			−1 500	
(e) Advances	171 000		1 692 069		1 500	1 864 569
	25 915 193	4 849 178	10 412 918	1 351 413	−5 411 357	24 716 163

Gross cost or valuation

Ecus thousand

Items	At 1 January 1997	Demerger	Expenditure	Disposals (b)	Transfers and Ajustments (a) (c)	At 31 December 1997
Intangible assents:						
Sturt-up costs	98 026	48 882	9 435	163	7 199	65 614
Research and development costs	19 557	3 651	67	660	−165	15 149
Patents and other similar rights	3 611	1 760	88	267	−6	1 665
Premiums paid for property occupation rights	6 476	2 563	899		−524	4 287
Projects in course	5 009	2 330	10 746	651	−8 667	4 106
Goodwill arising on consolidation	72 715	8 582	12 242	1 876	−1 412	73 086
	205 392	67 768	33 476	3 617	−3 575	163 908
Tangible assets:						
Land	107 112	20 361	8 597	1 940	9 990	103 398
Buildings	418 613	103 442	35 838	5 140	109 958	455 826
Plant and machinery	555 322	369 462	27 636	34 513	89 779	268 762
Vehicles	26 622	8 069	6 808	2 405	2 321	25 277
Tools	4 932	1 472	62	216	31	3 336
Fixtures and fittings	64 957	19 288	17 285	3 421	−25 011	34 523
Containers	330	13				317
Others	5 574	2 629	2 232	245	−233	4 699
(f) In construction	139 713	17 504	156 091	27 940	−134 518	115 842
(g) Advances	69 004	14 073	20 967	30	−42 507	33 361
	1 392 178	556 313	275 516	75 850	9 809	1 045 340
Investments:						
Shares in related (including associated) undertakings	75 349	17 082	27 143	3 558	−20 643	61 208
Loans to related (including associated) undertakings	44 157	3 271	15 993	205	−38 448	18 227
Shares in other undertakings	3 590	448		2 276		866
(d) Other investments other than loans	4 240	3 167		647	32 319	32 744
Loans to other undertakings	6	6	10			10
In construction	23	16			−7	
(e) Advances	846		8 371		7	9 225
	128 212	23 991	51 516	6 686	−26 772	122 280

a) Includes 797 645 thousand escudos (3 946 thousand ecus) in relation to companies included during 1997 and excluded or included by the equity method in 1996;

b) Includes 11 868 088 thousand escudos (58 716 thousands ecus) in relation to companies sold or excluded from consolidation during 1997;

c) Shares in related (including associated) undertakings include 2.588.698 thousand escudos (12.807 thousand ecus) as a result of qccounting for associated undertakings using the quality method;

d) Includes bonds of an associated undertaking 6.545.004 thousand escudos (32.380 thousand ecus);

e) IIncludes advances for the acquisition of a company, 1.567.069 thousand escudos (7.753 thousand ecus), which were recovered in 1998 since the acquisition was called off;

e) Inclui 1.567.069 milhares de escudos para aquisição de uma participação financeira, valor recuperado em 1998, dado que a aquisição não se realizou;
f) Os valores mais significativos, incluídos na rúbrica Imobilizações em Curso referem-se aos seguintes projectos:

	milhares de escudos
Projecto de escritórios na Quinta do Lambert	2 328 548
Projecto NorteShopping	13 476 418
Projecto Continente do Seixal	741 813
Projecto de remodelação da Aqualuz	412 743
Projecto Continente de Benfica	852 264
Projecto Continente da Maia	325 358

g) Os valores mais significativos, incluídos na rúbrica Adiantamentos por conta de Imobilizações Corpóreas referem-se aos seguintes projectos:

	milhares de escudos
Projecto Continente da Expo - 98	4 150 000
Projecto Continente de Loures	737 442
Projecto LouresShopping	758 471

Amortizações e provisões

milhares de escudos

Rubricas	Saldo Inicial	Cisão	Reforço	Regularizações (a)	Saldo Final
Imobilizações incorpóreas:					
Despesas de instalação	13 833 991	8 609 655	1 823 231	−64 714	6 982 853
Despesas de investigação e desenvolvimento	1 731 772	585 220	590 652	−147 384	1 589 820
Propriedade industrial e outros direitos	426 094	161 583	60 558	−36 126	288 943
Trespasses	279 937	157 329	160 116		282 724
Diferenças de consolidação	3 462 153	494 811	870 105	−95 798	3 741 649
	19 733 947	10 008 598	3 504 662	− 344 022	12 885 989
Imobilizações corpóreas:					
Terrenos e recursos naturais	33 692	33 692			
Edifícios e outras construções	9 392 410	4 744 375	1 420 659	67 476	6 136 170
Equipamento básico	49 595 497	33 497 116	4 007 518	− 3 028 412	17 077 487
Equipamento de transporte	2 989 692	1 208 670	742 025	−314 345	2 208 702
Ferramentas e utensílios	769 016	223 782	110 120	−45 952	609 402
Equipamento administrativo	4 884 201	1 909 149	956 174	− 1 450 911	2 480 315
Taras e vasilhame	52 588	1 064	4 025		55 549
Outras imobilizações corpóreas	590 422	377 078	78 268	−44 351	247 261
	68 307 518	41 994 926	7 318 789	−4 816 495	28 814 886
Investimentos financeiros:					
Amortização de Investimentos em Imóveis	41 583	41 583			
Partes de capital em empresas associadas	613 395	431 695		−181 700	
Partes de capital em empresas participadas	180 000			− 180 000	
Empréstimos em empresas associadas	120 018	120 018			
Títulos e outras aplicações financeiras	136 566	136 566			
	1 091 562	729 862		− 361 700	

a) Inclui o saldo de saídas de filiais por alienação ou alteração do método de consolidação no valor de 4.926.310 milhares de escudos

Nota 28. Custos financeiros capitalizados no exercício

O valor de custos financeiros suportados no exercício e respeitantes a empréstimos obtidos para financiar imobilizações, durante a construção, capitalizados foi de 1.528.119 milhares de escudos.

Nota 33. Dívidas a terceiros vencíveis a mais de cinco anos
O montante das dívidas a terceiros apresentadas no balanço consolidado e que se vencem para além de cinco anos é de 77.673.373 milhares de escudos.

Nota 34. Dívidas a terceiros cobertas por garantias reais
A 31 de Dezembro de 1997, era o seguinte o montante das dívidas a terceiros apresentadas no balanço consolidado cobertas por garantias reais prestadas pelas empresas incluídas no perímetro de consolidação:

	milhares de escudos
Penhores	14 590 000
Hipotecas	15 304 604

f) The following were the more significant amounts included in tangible assets – in construction:

	Escudos thousand	*Ecus thousand*
Quinta do Lambert Offices Building	2 328 548	11 520
Norteshopping project	13 476 418	66 673
Seixal Continent Store	741 813	3 670
Refurbishing of Aqualuz	412 743	2 042
Benfica Continente Store	852 264	4 216
Maia Continente Store	325 358	1 610

g) The following were the more significant amounts included in tangible assets – advances:

	Escudos thousand	*Ecus thousand*
Expo 98 Continente Store	4 150 000	20 532
Loures Continente Store	737 442	3 648
Loures Shopping project	758 471	3 752

Accumulated depreciation and provisions: *Escudos thousand*

Items	At January 1977	Demerger	Charge for the year	Adjustments (a)	At 31 December 1997
Intangible Assets:					
Start-up costs	13 833 991	8 609 655	1 823 231	–64 714	6 982 853
Research and development costs	1 731 772	585 220	590 652	–147 384	1 589 820
Patents and other similar rights	426 094	161 583	60 558	–36 126	288 943
Premiums paid for property occupation rights	279 937	157 329	160 116		282 724
Goodwill arising on consolidation	3 462 153	494 811	870 105	–95 798	3 741 649
	19 733 947	10 008 598	3 504 662	– 344 022	12 885 989
Tangible assets:					
Land	33 692	33 692			
Buildings	9 392 410	4 744 375	1 420 659	67 476	6 136 170
Plant and Machinery	49 595 497	33 497 116	4 007 518	– 3 028 412	17 077 487
Vehicles	2 989 692	1 208 670	742 025	–314 345	2 208 702
Tools	769 016	223 782	110 120	–45 952	609 402
Fixtures and fittings	4 884 201	1 909 149	956 174	– 1 450 911	2 480 315
Containers	52 588	1 064	4 025		55 549
Others	590 422	377 078	78 268	–44 351	247 261
	68 307 518	41 994 926	7 318 789	–4 816 495	28 814 886
Investments:					
Freehold property	41 583	41 583			
Shares in related (including associated) undertakings	613 395	431 695		–181 700	
Shares in other undertakings	180 000			– 180 000	
Loans to related (including associated) undertakings	120 018	120 018			
Other investments other than loans	136 566	136 566			
	1 091 562	729 862		– 361 700	

Accumulated depreciation and provisions *Ecus thousand*

Items	At January 1977	Demerger	Charge for the year	Adjustments (a)	At 31 December 1997
Intangible Assets:					
Start-up costs	68 442	42 595	9 020	-320	34 547
Research and development costs	8 568	2 895	2 992	-729	7 865
Patents and other similar rights	2 108	799	300	-179	1 430
Premiums paid for property occupation rights	1 385	778	792		1 399
Goodwill arising on consolidation	17 129	2 448	4 305	-474	18 511
	97 631	49 516	17 339	-1 702	63 752
Tangible assets:					
Land	167	167			
Buildings	46 468	23 472	7 029	334	30 358
Plant and Machinery	245 367	165 722	19 827	-14 983	84 488
Vehicles	14 791	5 980	3 671	-1 555	10 927
Tools	3 805	1 107	545	-227	3 015
Fixtures and fittings	24 164	9 445	4 731	-7 178	12 271
Containers	260	5	20		275
Others	2 921	1 866	387	-219	1 223
	337 942	207 764	36 209	-23 829	142 558
Investments:					
Freehold property	206	206			
Shares in related (including associated) undertakings	3 035	2 136		-899	
Shares in other undertakings	891			-891	
Loans to related (including associated) undertakings	594	594			
Other investments other than loans	676	676		–	
	5 400	3 611		-1 789	

a) Includes 4.926.310 thousand escudos (24.372 thousand ecus) in relation to companies sold or excluded in 1997.

Note 28. Interest payable capitalised during the year

Interest payable relating to the financing of fixed assets in construction totalling 1.528.119 thousand escudos (7.560 thousand ecus) was capitalised in the year.

Nota 36. Vendas e prestações de serviços por actividades e mercados geográficos
A repartição do valor líquido consolidado das vendas e das prestações de serviços por categorias de actividades e mercados geográficos é a seguinte:

a) Por actividade: *milhares de escudos*

Distribuição	395 975 274
Imobiliária	15 211 571
Outras empresas	1 155 557
Total	**412 342 402**

b) Por mercado:

Mercado interno	323 039 706
Mercado externo	89 302 696
Total	**412 342 402**

Nota 38. Impostos diferidos
Foram calculados no exercício impostos diferidos no valor de 417.111 milhares de escudos relevados na rúbrica própria da demonstração consolidada dos resultados e na rúbrica de acréscimo de custos do balanço consolidado.

Valores diferidos em exercícios anteriores, no total de 30.340 milhares de escudos, foram constatados em proveitos extraordinários em virtude de, pelo mecanismo da reversão, estarem agora constatados em impostos no exercício.

Nota 39. Remunerações atribuidas aos membros dos órgãos sociais da empresa-mãe

milhares de escudos

Conselho Geral	9 400
Direcção	110 973
Revisor Oficial de Contas	1 650

Nota 41. Diplomas legais em que se baseou a reavaliação de imobilizações corpóreas
O Imobilizado Corpóreo detido pelas várias empresas incluídas na consolidação foi reavaliado ao longo dos vários exercícios decorridos de acordo com as seguintes disposições legais: Decretos-Lei nºs 430/78, de 27 de Dezembro, 219/82, de 2 de Junho, 278/85, de 17 de Julho, 118/86, de 27 de Maio, 111/88, de 2 de Abril, 49/91, de 25 de Janeiro e 264/92 de 24 de Novembro. Exceptuam-se os casos dos activos adquiridos recentemente a preço de mercado.

No exercício de 1990 foram efectuadas reavaliações livres em duas filiais conforme referido na Nota 9. Em 1996 foi adquirida uma filial que efectuou uma reavaliação livre no exercício de 1992, actualizada em principios de 1996, que foi considerada no cálculo da diferença de consolidação no momento da aquisição dessa filial em conformidade com o disposto na alinea a) do parágrafo 13.4.1 do Plano Oficial de Contabilidade (justo valor dos activos líquidos adquiridos).

Nota 42. Reavaliações
O efeito global das reavaliações efectuadas no activo imobilizado pode ser demonstrado como segue:

milhares de escudos

Rubricas	Custo Históricos (a)	Reavaliações (a) (b)	Valores Contabilisticos Reavaliados (a)
Imobilizações corpóreas:			
Terrenos e recursos naturais	12 568 063	8 331 560	20 899 623
Edificios e outras construções	84 363 933	1 635 041	85 998 974
Equipamento básico	36 378 447	868 479	37 246 926
Equipamento de transporte	2 896 977	3 443	2 900 420
Ferramentas e utensilios	64 909	61	64 970
Equipamento administrativo	4 490 748	6 935	4 497 683
Taras e vasilhame	8 513		8 513
Outras imobilizações corpóreas	702 489		702 489
Imobilizações em curso	23 414 856		23 414 856
	164 888 935	10 845 519	175 734 454

(a) Líquidos de amortizações;
(b) Englobam as sucessivas reavaliações.

Note 33. Amounts owing repayable after more than five years
The consolidated balance sheet includes 77.673.373 thousand escudos (384 278 thousand ecus) of amounts owing repayable after more than five years.

Note 34. Amounts owing to third parties covered by guarantees
At 31 December 1997 the amounts covered by guarantees were as follows:

	Escudos thousand	Ecus thousand
Mortgages and charges	29 894 604	147 899

Note 36. Turnover analysis by activity and market
A repartição do valor líquido consolidado das vendas e das prestações de serviços por categorias de actividades e mercados geográficos é a seguinte:

a) **By activity:**

	Escudos thousand	Ecus thousand
Retailing	395 975 274	1 959 032
Real estate	15 211 571	75 257
Other activities	1 155 557	5 717
Total	**412 342 402**	**2 040 006**

b) **By market:**

	Escudos thousand	Ecus thousand
Home market	323 039 706	1 598 194
Export market	89 302 696	441 813
Total	**412 342 402**	**2 040 006**

Note 38. Deferred taxation
Deferred taxation totalling 417.111 thousand escudos (2.064 thousand ecus) arose in 1997. This shown as income taxation in the consolidated profit and loss account and as accruals in the consolidated balance sheet.

Deferred taxation relating to prior years totalling 30.340 thousand escudos (150 thousand ecus) was written back as an extraordinary gain in 1997 as a result of the reversal of timing differences in the year.

Note 39. Salaries of the boards and other officials of the holding company

	Escudos thousand	Ecus thousand
Supervisory Board	9 400	47
Management Board	110 973	549
Statutory Auditors	1 650	8

Note 41. Revaluations of tangible fixed assets
Tangible fixed assets held by the various companies include in the consolidation wererevalued in previous years allowed by Decree Laws nrs 430/78, 27 December, 219/82, 2 June, 278/85, 17 July, 118/86, 27 May, 111/88, 2 April, 49/41, 25 January and 264/92, 24 November. Assets acquired since the last revaluation are stated at cost.

As explained in Note 9 in 1990 independent market valuations were incorporated in relation to two companies. In 1996 the group acquired a company that included in it's financial statements an independent market valuation initially performed in 1992 and fully revised in 1996. This valuation has been considered in the calculation of the acquisition goodwill arising on consolidation as required in paragraph 13.4.1 a) of the Official Chart of Accounts (fair value of the net assets acquired).

Note 42. Revaluations
The effect of the revaluations of tangible fixed assets can be summarised as follows:

	Escudos thousand			Ecus thousand		
Items	Historical cost (a)	Revaluations (a) (b)	Accounts Value (a)	Historical cost (a)	Revaluations (a) (b)	Accounts Value (a)
Tangible assets:						
Land	12 568 063	8 331 560	20 899 623	62 179	41 219	103 398
Buildings	84 363 933	1 635 041	85 998 974	417 379	8 089	425 468
Plant and machinery	36 378 447	868 479	37 246 926	179 977	4 297	184 274
Vehicles	2 896 977	3 443	2 900 420	14 332	17	14 349
Tools	64 909	61	64 970	321		321
Fixtures and fittings	4 490 748	6 935	4 497 683	22 217	34	22 252
Containers	8 513		8 513	42		42
Others	702 489		702 489	3 475		3 475
In construction	23 414 856		23 414 856	115 842		115 842
	164 888 935	10 845 519	175 734 454	815 765	53 656	869 421

(a) Net of depreciation;
(b) Includes all revaluations to date (as set out in note 41).

Note 44. Analysis of net financial charges

	Escudos thousand		Ecus thousand	
Charges	1997	1996	1997	1996
Interest payable	5 668 470	8 622 553	28 044	44 383
Depreciation on investments		7 883		41
a) Provisions for investments	654 969	2 079 520	3 240	10 704
Exchange losses	1 187 597	1 365 983	5 875	7 031
Payment discounts given	8 635	695 840	43	3 582
Loss on disposals of short term investments	368 116	639 027	1 821	3 289
Other financial charges	2 905 277	2 523 036	14 373	12 987
Net financial charges	−1 872 030	−6 097 137	−9 262	−31 385
	8 921 034	9 836 705	44 136	50 632

Nota 44. Demonstração consolidada dos resultados financeiros

milhares de escudos

	Custos e perdas	1997	1996
	Juros suportados	5 668 470	8 622 553
	Amortizações de investimentos em imoveis		7 883
a)	Provisões para aplicações financeiras	654 969	2 079 520
	Diferenças de câmbio desfavoráveis	1 187 597	1 365 983
	Descontos de pronto pagamento concedidos	8 635	695 840
	Perdas na alienação de aplicações de tesouraria	368 116	639 027
	Outros custos e perdas financeiros	2 905 277	2 523 036
	Resultados financeiros	−1 872 030	−6 097 137
		8 921 034	9 836 705

milhares de escudos

	Proveitos e ganhos	1997	1996
b)	Juros obtidos	5 010 870	3 895 552
	Rendimentos de imóveis		279
	Rendimentos de participações de capital	100 001	104 789
	Diferenças de câmbio favoráveis	343 123	861 398
	Descontos de pronto pagamento obtidos	3 242 708	2 750 192
	Ganhos na alienação de aplicações de tesouraria	2 726	1 993 919
	Outros proveitos e ganhos financeiros	221 606	230 576
		8 921 034	9 836 705

(a) Perda potencial de unidades de participação em Fundo Imobiliário;
(b) Inclui 3.231.000 milhares de escudos relativos a rendimentos de unidades de participação em Fundo Imobiliário.

Nota 45. Demonstração consolidada dos resultados extraordinários

milhares de escudos

Custos e perdas	1997	1996
Donativos	56 854	66 149
Dívidas incobráveis	447 387	235 260
Perdas em existências	35 491	55 356
Perdas em imobilizações	691 394	535 080
Multas e penalidades	71 531	623 153
Aumentos de amortizações e provisões	45 997	785 403
Correcções relativas a exercícios anteriores	327 032	676 509
Outros custos e perdas extraordinários	647 647	773 716
Resultados extraordinários	7 182 106	12 195 708
	9 505 439	15 946 334

milhares de escudos

	Proveitos e ganhos	1997	1996
	Restituição de impostos	4 146	16 001
	Recuperação de dívidas	724	3 688
	Ganhos em existências		19 659
a)	Ganhos em imobilizações	5 049 146	12 924 526
	Benefícios de penalidades contratuais		31 553
	Reduções de amortizações e provisões	743 537	1 033 118
	Correcções relativas a exercícios anteriores	250 216	702 581
b)	Outros proveitos e ganhos extraordinários	3 457 670	1 215 208
		9 505 439	15 946 334

(a) Inclui ganhos na alienação de participações financeiras no valor de 4.866.802 milhares de escudos;
(b) Inclui 2.341.292 milhares de escudos relativos ao acerto de preço de venda de uma filial e 216.922 milhares de escudos relativos a excesso de estimativa para impostos.

Nota 46. Desdobramento das contas de provisões e movimentos ocorridos no exercício

As provisões acumuladas a 31 de Dezembro de 1997 e o seu movimento durante o exercício terminado nesta data, são as seguintes:

milhares de escudos

Contas	Saldo Inicial	Cisão	Aumento (a)	Redução (b)	Saldo Final
Provisões para aplicações de tesouraria	257 827		707 886	162 895	802 818
Provisões para cobranças duvidosas	6 148 200	2 630 342	863 751	685 723	3 695 886
Provisões para riscos e encargos	3 361 736	2 898 686	538 928	363 165	638 813
Provisões para depreciação de existências	405 982	353 982	92 219	52 000	92 219
Provisões para investimentos financeiros	1 049 989	688 279		361 710	
	11 223 734	6 571 289	2 202 784	1 625 493	5 229 736

(a) Inclui 192.766 milhares de escudos relativos à entrada de filiais;
(b) Inclui 425.590 milhares de escudos relativos à saída de filiais.

Income	Escudos thousand		Ecus thousand	
	1997	1996	1997	1996
b) Interest receivable	5 010 870	3 895 552	24 791	20 052
Freehold property income		279		1
Dividends received	100 001	104 789	495	539
Exchange gains	343 123	861 398	1 698	4 434
Payment discounts received	3 242 708	2 750 192	16 043	14 156
Gains on disposal of short term investments	2 726	1 993 919	13	10 263
Other financial income	221 606	230 576	1 096	1 187
	8 921 034	9 836 705	44 136	50 632

(a) Potential loss on sale of units in a Property Investment Fund;
(b) Includes 3 231 000 thousand escudos (15 985 thousand ecus) of income from units in a Property Investment Fund.

Note 45. Analysis of extraordinary items

Charges	Escudos thousand		Ecus thousand	
	1997	1996	1997	1996
Donations	56 854	66 149	281	340
Doubtful debts written off	447 387	235 260	2 213	1 211
Abnormal losses on stocks	35 491	55 356	176	285
Losses on sale of fixed assets	691 394	535 080	3 421	2 754
Fines and penalties paid	71 531	623 153	354	3 208
Exceptional depreciation and provisions	45 997	785 403	228	4 043
Charges relating to prior years	327 032	676 509	1 618	3 482
Others	647 647	773 716	3 204	3 983
Net extraordinary gains	7 182 106	12·195 708	35 532	62 776
	9 505 439	15 946 334	47 027	82 082

Income	Escudos thousand		Ecus thousand	
	1997	1996	1997	1996
Taxation refunded	4 146	16 001	21	82
Collection of doubtful debts written off	724	3 688	4	19
Abnormal gains on stocks		19 659		101
a) Gains on sale of fixed assets	5 049 146	12 924 526	24 980	66 527
Conratual penalties received		31 553		162
Writte back of provisions and depreciation	743 537	1 033 118	3 679	5 318
Gains relating to prior years	250 216	702 581	1 238	3 616
b) Others	3 457 670	1 215 208	17 106	6 257
	9 505 439	15 946 334	47 027	82 082

(a) Includes gains on sale of investments of 4 866 802 thousand escudos (24 078 thousand ecus);
(b) Includes 2 341 292 thousand escudos (11 583 thousand ecus) of an adjustment in the sales price of an affiliated undertaking sold in 1996 and 216 922 thousand escudos (1 073 thousand ecus) of income taxation over provided.

Note 46. Analysis of provisions as at 31 December 1997 and movements during the year
Accumulated provisions at 31 December 1997 and movements during the year are as follows:

					Escudos thousand
Provisions	At 1 January 1997	Demerger	Provisions created (a)	Provisions written back (b)	At 31 December 1997
Provisions for short term investments	257 827		707 886	162 895	802 818
Provisions for doubtfull debts	6 148 200	2 630 342	863 751	685 723	3 695 886
Provisions for other risks and charges	3 361 736	2 898 686	538 928	363 165	638 813
Provisions for stock obsolescence	405 982	353 982	92 219	52 000	92 219
Provisions for fixed assets investments	1 049 989	688 279		361 710	
	11 223 734	6 571 289	2 202 784	1 625 493	5 229 736

					Ecus thousand
Provisions	At 1 January 1997	Demerger	Provisions created (a)	Provisions written back (b)	At 31 December 1997
Provisions for short term investments	1 276		3 502	806	3 972
Provisions for doubtfull debts	30 417	13 013	4 273	3 393	18 285
Provisions for other risks and charges	16 632	14 341	2 666	1 797	3 160
Provisions for stock obsolescence	2 009	1 751	456	257	456
Provisions for fixed assets investments	5 195	3 405		1 790	
	55 528	32 511	10 898	8 042	25 873

a) Includes 192 766 thousand escudos (954 thousand ecus) in relation to new affiliated undertakings;;
b) Includes 425 590 thousand escudos (2 106 thousand ecus) in relation to affiliated undertakings sold or excluded during the year.

Nota 50. Outras informações relevantes para a compreensão da situação financeira e dos resultados consolidados

1) INFORMAÇÃO POR ACTIVIDADES

milhares de escudos

Actividade	Custos com o Pessoal	Imobilizado Incorpóreo	Imobilizado Corpóreo	Existências
Distribuição	34 742 840	17 578 902	143 765 284	31 497 377
Imobiliária	1 722 647	2 126 153	36 652 485	10 073 493
Outras empresas	983 887	539 426	20 059 869	142 734
	37 449 374	20 244 481	182 477 638	41 713 604

2) TÍTULOS NEGOCIÁVEIS

Os valores mais significativos referem-se a 2 030 017 Unidades de Participação em Fundos Imobiliários no valor de 23 255 589 milhares de escudos e 3 001 738 milhares de escudos de Obrigações de uma sociedade. Os Fundos Imobiliários detêm imóveis que estão arrendados a sociedades do grupo, essencialmente, no negócio distribuição e que são por essas sociedades utilizados na prossecução da sua actividade.

3) ACRÉSCIMOS E DIFERIMENTOS

a) Acréscimos de Proveitos

Nesta rubrica estão incluídos os seguintes valores:

milhares de escudos

Descontos de quantidade a receber de fornecedores	427 046
Outros descontos a receber de fornecedores	677 278
Cooperação comercial	68 301
Juros de obrigações	786 664
Outras receitas	666 292
	2 625 581

b) Acréscimos de Custos

Nesta rubrica estão incluídos os seguintes valores :

milhares de escudos

Férias, subsídios de férias e prémios	4 809 321
Impostos diferidos	1 669 258
Juros a liquidar	103 723
Juros a liquidar de obrigações	839 972
Contribuição autárquica	716 161
Outros custos	1 450 513
	9 588 948

O valor de Impostos Diferidos inclui 417 111 milhares de escudos relativos ao exercício.

4) OUTROS DEVEDORES - CURTO PRAZO

Nesta rúbrica do balanço consolidado estão incluídos os seguintes valores:

milhares de escudos

Fornecedores, c/c - saldos devedores	5 631 589
Contratos promocionais com fornecedores	1 368 878
IVA - Regularizações em curso	749 947
Alienação de partes de capital	5 754 857

5) ESTADO E OUTROS ENTES PÚBLICOS (ACTIVO)

a) CURTO PRAZO

Esta rúbrica incluí o valor de 4 814 000 milhares de escudos referente ao Imposto sobre o Valor Acrescentado que foi debitado em compras para investimentos imobiliários, este valor poderá ser recuperável no curto prazo se a empresa optar e lhe for concedida a renúncia à isenção.

b) MÉDIO E LONGO PRAZO

Esta rúbrica incluí o valor de 3 035 000 milhares de escudos de créditos fiscais sobre a Administração Fiscal brasileira, relativos a impostos a recuperar no futuro. Atente à incerteza dessa recuperação foi obtida do anterior accionista garantia de substituição dessa Administração Fiscal no caso de a mesma não deferir a recuperação.

Note 50. Other information relevant to the understanding of the consolidated financial statements

1) INFORMATION BY ACTIVITY:

Escudos thousand

ACTIVITY	Staff costs	Intangible fixed assets	Tangible fixed assets	Stocks
Retailing	34 742 840	17 578 902	143 765 284	31 497 377
Real estate	1 722 647	2 126 153	36 652 485	10 073 493
Other activities	983 887	539 426	20 059 869	142 374
	37 449 374	20 244 481	182 477 638	41 713 244

Ecus thousand

ACTIVITY	Staff costs	Intangible fixed assets	Tangible fixed assets	Stocks
Retailing	171 885	86 969	711 259	155 829
Real estate	8 523	10 519	181 333	49 837
OOther activities	4 868	2 669	10 191	704
	185 276	100 157	902 783	206 370

2) SHORT TERM INVESTMENTS

The most significant values relate to 2 030 017 units in Property Investment Funds in the amount of 23 255 589 thousand escudos (115 054 thousand ecus) and bonds of a company in the amount of 3 001 738 thousand escudos (14 851 thousand ecus). The Property Investment Funds possess properties which are rented to affiliated undertakings, mainly, in the retailing business, who use them in the normal course of their business.

3) ACCRUE INCOME AND ACCRUALS

a) Accrued income

Includes:

	Escudos thousand	Ecus thousand
Quantity rebates receivable from suppliers	427 046	2 113
Discounts receivable from suppliers	677 278	3 351
Fees receivable from suppliers	68 301	338
Bond interest receivable	786 664	3 892
Other revenues	666 292	3 296
	2 625 581	12 990

b) Accruals

Includes:

	Escudos thousand	Ecus thousand
Holiday pay and bonuses	4 809 321	23 793
Deferred taxation	1 669 258	8 258
Interest payable	103 723	513
Bond interest payable	839 972	4 156
Municipality rates	716 161	3 543
Other	1 450 513	7 176
	9 588 948	47 440

Deferred taxation includes 417 111 thousand escudos (2 064 thousand ecus) in relation to the year.

4) OTHER DEBTORS - AMOUNTS FALLING DUE WITHIN ONE YEAR

Includes:

	Escudos thousand	Ecus thousand
Suppliers - debit balances	5 631 589	27 861
Promotion contracts with suppliers	1 368 878	6 772
VAT recoverable on property developments	749 947	3 710
Amounts owing from the sale of shareholdings	5 754 857	24 471

5) TAXES RECOVERABLE

a) AMOUNTS FALLING DUE WITHIN ONE YEAR

Includes 4 814 000 thousand escudos (23 817 thousand ecus) relating to VAT which was paid on purchases of land and buildings and will be recovered if and when to company renounces to VAT exemption and this is accepted.

b) AMOUNTS FALLING DUE AFTER MORE THAN ONE YEAR

Includes 3 035 000 thousand escudos (15 015 thousand ecus) of tax credits to be recovered in the future from the Brazilian Tax Authorities. Due to the uncertainty of the recoverability of this amount a grarantee has been received from the previous shareholder who will replace the Tax Authorities in the payment of this amount if the Tax Authorities do not approve its reimbursement.

6) ECONOMIA DE IMPOSTO

Foi reconhecida a economia de imposto resultante dos vários perímetros de consolidação fiscal do grupo pelo valor de 59 473 milhares de escudos, a qual foi deduzida ao valor da rúbrica Imposto sobre o Rendimento do exercício.

7) EMPRÉSTIMOS OBRIGACIONISTAS

Os empréstimos obrigacionistas podem ser resumidos como segue:

a) SONAE 97 no valor de 30 000 000 milhares de escudos, que será rembolsado ao fim de 10 anos, ao par, em 2 prestações iguais no vencimento do 18.º e 20.º cupão. A taxa de juro corresponde à Lisbor acrescida de 0,17% do 1.º ao 14.º cupão e de 0,22% do 15.º ao 20.ºcupão;

b) SONAE 94 no valor de 7.500.000 milhares de escudos, que será reembolsado na sua totalidade ao fim de 5 anos. A taxa de juro corresponde à Lisbor acrescida de 0,25% e arrendondada para 1/16 de ponto percentual superior;

c) MODELO CONTINENTE 94 no valor de 5 000 000 milhares de escudos, que será reembolsado na sua totalidade ao fim de 5 anos. A taxa de juro corresponde à Lisbor acrescida de 0,25% e arrendondada para 1/16 de ponto percentual superior;

d) MODELO CONTINENTE 95 no valor de 30 000 000 milhares de escudos, que será rembolsado ao fim de 8 anos, ao par, em 2 prestações iguais no vencimento do 14.º e 16.º cupão. A taxa de juro corresponde à Lisbor acrescida de 0,25% e arrendondada para 1/16 de ponto percentual superior do 2.º ao 10.º cupão e de 0,35% do 11.º ao 16.º cupão;

e) MODELO 94 no valor de 5 000 000 milhares de escudos, que será reembolsado na sua totalidade ao fim de 5 anos. A taxa de juro corresponde à Lisbor acrescida de 0,25% e arrendondada para 1/16 de ponto percentual superior;

f) MODELO 95 no valor de 8 000 000 milhares de escudos, que será reembolsado na sua totalidade ao fim de 5 anos. A taxa de juro corresponde à Lisbor acrescida de 0,25% e arrendondada para 1/16 de ponto percentual superior;

g) Empréstimo obrigacionista no valor de 4 811 920 milhares de escudos, emitido em 1991. Não possui prazo de reembolso, poderá ser contudo amortizado se ocorrer uma das seguintes situações, não pagamento dos juros vencidos, dissolução da sociedade ou manifestação do detentor das obrigações em receber como forma de pagamento 90% do imóvel da filial;

h) Empréstimo obrigacionista no valor de 1.905.682 milhares de escudos, emitido em 1996, o referido empréstimo será amortizado em 2006.

Não obstante os empréstimos obrigacionistas no valor de 92 217 602 milhares de escudos conterem clausulas de "call option", optou-se por manter nas contas os vencimentos na data mais longinqua no pressuposto de que, ocorrendo qualquer das opções de reembolso antecipado, se poderá proceder ao seu refinanciamento, mantendo-se, assim, a estrutura dos capitais permanentes.

8) CONTINGÊNCIAS FISCAIS

Existem contingências fiscais numa filial no valor de cerca de 530.000 milhares de escudos, no entanto, é entendimento da Direcção e dos consultores fiscais da filial, que é remota a probabilidade de concretização dessas responsabilidades.

9) SALDOS COM O ACCIONISTA MAIORITÁRIO

À data de 31 de Dezembro de 1997, estão apresentados no passivo suprimentos do accionista maioritário Figest - Gestão de Participações Financeiras, Sociedade de Controlo, S.A. a filiais no valor de 6 611 751 milhares de escudos.

A DIRECÇÃO

6) INCOME TAX SAVINGS

Saving airising from taxation of groups of affiliated companies totalling 59 473 thousand escudos (294 thousand ecus) were set off against related income tax charges.

7) BONDS

Loans denominated with bonds may be described as follows:

a) SONAE 97 amounting to 30 000 000 thousand escudos (148 421 thousand ecus), repayable after 10 years, at par value, in two equal instalments on the 18th an 20 th coupons, earning interest at an annual interest rate equal to Lisbor plus 0.17% from the 1st to the 14th coupon and plus 0.22% from the 15th to the 20th coupon;

b) SONAE 94 amounting to 7 500 000 thousandescudos (37 105 thousand ecus), repayable after 5 years, earning interest at an annual interest rate equal to Lisbor plus 0.25% rounded up to 1/16 of one percent;

c) MODELO CONTINENTE 94 amounting to 5 000 000 thousand escudos (24 737 thousand ecus), repayable after 5 years, earning interest at an annnual interest rate equal to Lisbor plus 0.25% rounded up to 1/16 of one percent;

d) MODELO CONTINENTE 95 amounting to 30 000 000 thousand escudos (148 421 thousand ecus), repayable after 8 years, at par value, in two equal instalments on the 14th and 16th coupons, earning interest at an annual interest rate equal to Lisboor plus 0.25% rounded up to 1/16 of one percent between the 2nd and the10th coupons and plus 0.35% between the 11th and the 16th coupons;

e) MODELO 94 amounting to 5 000 000 thousand escudos (24 737 thousand ecus), repayable after 5 years, earning interest at an annual interest rate equal to Lisbor plus 0.25% rounded up to 1/16 of one percent;

f) MODELO 95 amounting to 8 000 000 thousand escudos (39 579 thousand ecus), repayable after 5 years, earning interest at an annual interest rate eqaual to Lisbor plus 0.25% rounded up to 1/16 of one percent;

g) Bonds totalling 4 811 920 thousand escudos (23 806 thousand ecus) issued in 1991 by an affiliated undertaking. These bonds do not establish a maturity date, but may, however, be repayable in the following conditions: delay in the payment of interest, or dissolution of the company or call for payment through the transfer of property of 90% of a building of the affiliated undertaking;

h) Bond issue of 1 905 682 thousand escudos (9 428 thousand ecus), issued by an affiliated undertaking in 1996, repayable in 2006.

Bonds tottaling 92 217 602 thousand escudos (456 234 thousand ecus) are included in the financial statements based on their full lives, although prior call options exist. In the case of early repayment, it is considered that the borrowing could be refinanced on a similar basis and the borrowing structure maintained.

8) TAX CONTINGENCIES

An affiliated undertaking has tax contingencjes amounting to 530 000 thousand escudos (2 622 thousand ecus). In the opinion of the Management Board and of its tax consultants these contingencies are remote.

9) TRANSACTIONS WITH THE PARENT COMPANY

A 31 December 1997 liabiilities include 6 611 751 thousand escudos (32 711 thousand ecus) of loans from the parent company to the mother company.

THE MANAGEMENT BOARD

Certificação Legal de Contas

Introdução

1. Examinámos as Demonstrações Financeiras Consolidadas da SONAE INVESTIMENTOS – SOCIEDADE GESTORA DE PARTICIPAÇÕES SOCIAIS, SA, as quais compreendem o Balanço Consolidado em 31 de Dezembro de 1997, (que evidencia um total de balanço de 361 520 429 contos e um total de capital próprio de 78 021 776 contos, incluindo um resultado líquido de 12 197 374 contos), a Demonstração Consolidada dos Resultados do exercício findo naquela data e o correspondente Anexo.

Responsabilidades

2. É da responsabilidade da Direcção a preparação de Demonstrações Financeiras Consolidadas que apresentem de forma verdadeira e apropriada a posição financeira do conjunto das empresas compreendidas na consolidação da SONAE INVESTIMENTOS – SOCIEDADE GESTORA DE PARTICIPAÇÕES SOCIAIS, SA, o resultado consolidado das suas operações, bem como a adopção de políticas e critérios adequados e a manutenção de sistemas de controlo interno apropriados.

3. A nossa responsabilidade consiste em expressar uma opinião profissional e independente, baseada no nosso exame daquelas Demonstrações Financeiras.

Âmbito

4. O exame a que procedemos foi efectuado de acordo com as Normas e Directrizes Técnicas da Câmara dos Revisores Oficiais de Contas, as quais exigem que o mesmo seja planeado e executado com o objectivo de obter um grau de segurança aceitável sobre se as Demonstrações Financeiras Consolidadas estão isentas de distorções materialmente relevantes. Para tanto o referido exame inclui (i) a verificação de as demonstrações financeiras das empresas englobadas na consolidação terem sido apropriadamente examinadas e, para casos em que o não tenham sido, a verificação, numa base de amostragem, do suporte das quantias e divulgações nelas constantes e a avaliação das estimativas, baseadas em juízos e critérios definidos pela Direcção, utilizadas na sua preparação; (ii) a verificação das operações de consolidação e, quando for o caso, da aplicação do método da equivalência patrimonial; (iii) a apreciação sobre se são adequadas as políticas contabilísticas adoptadas, a sua aplicação uniforme e a sua divulgação, tendo em conta as circunstâncias; (iv) a verificação da aplicabilidade do princípio da continuidade; e (v) a apreciação sobre se é adequada, em termos globais, a apresentação das Demonstrações Financeiras Consolidadas.

5. Entendemos que o exame efectuado proporciona uma base aceitável para a expressão da nossa opinião.

Opinião

6. Em nossa opinião, as Demonstrações Financeiras Consolidadas referidas apresentam de forma verdadeira e apropriada, em todos os aspectos materialmente relevantes, a posição financeira do conjunto das empresas compreendidas na consolidação da SONAE INVESTIMENTOS – SOCIEDADE GESTORA DE PARTICIPAÇÕES SOCIAIS, SA em 31 de Dezembro de 1997 e o resultado das suas operações no exercício findo naquela data, em conformidade com os princípios contabilísticos geralmente aceites.

Ênfases

7. Sem afectar a opinião expressa no parágrafo anterior chamamos a atenção para as seguintes situações:

7.1. Conforme mencionado no Relatório Consolidado da Direcção foi efectuada escritura de cisão em 1 de Janeiro de 1997 que formaliza a alteração da estrutura organizativa do grupo, tendo sido constituída a Inparsa - Indústrias e Participações, S.G.P.S., que será responsável pela gestão dos negócios detidos pela Sonae Indústria, S.G.P.S., S.A. e pela Pargest, S.G.P.S., S.A. Em consequência foram transferidos para essa sociedade activos no valor de 115 356 000 contos e os Capitais Próprios e Interesses Minoritários do grupo foram diminuídos em 59 307 000 contos;

7.2. Tal como mencionado na Nota 45 os resultados do exercício incluem resultados extraordinários de 7 741 861 contos em virtude da alienação de partes de capital em filiais e associadas.

7.3. Conforme mencionado na Nota 50.2.a) estão apresentadas em Títulos Negociáveis unidades de participação em Fundos Imobiliários, no valor de 23 255 620 contos, os quais detêm imóveis que estão a ser utilizados no negócio distribuição. Esta apresentação decorre da intenção da Direcção de proceder à sua alienação logo que considerado adequado face às oportunidades de negócio que venham a surgir. Esta intenção, que já foi manifestada anteriormente, não se concretizou até ao momento.

Porto, 5 de Março de 1998

Boto, Amorim & Associados, S.R.O.C.
representada por:
José Luís dos Santos Lima Amorim,
R.O.C.

Relatório de Auditoria

1. Efectuámos a auditoria ao Balanço Consolidado da Sonae Investimentos – Sociedade Gestora de Participações Sociais, S.A., à data de 31 de Dezembro de 1997, bem como à Demonstração Consolidada dos Resultados do exercício findo naquela data e ao respectivo anexo. Estas Demonstrações Financeiras Consolidadas são da responsabilidade da Direcção da Empresa, competindo-nos como auditores a emissão de uma opinião sobre estas com base nos testes de auditoria que efectuámos.

2. A nossa auditoria foi efectuada de acordo com as normas internacionais de auditoria. Estas normas exigem que planeemos e executemos a auditoria por forma a obtermos convicção razoável sobre se as referidas Demonstrações Financeiras Consolidadas não contêm distorções significativas. Uma auditoria inclui, numa base de teste, o exame das evidências que suportam os valores e informações constantes das Demonstrações Financeiras Consolidadas. Adicionalmente, uma auditoria inclui a apreciação dos princípios contabilísticos adoptados e a avaliação das estimativas significativas efectuadas pela Empresa bem como da forma de apresentação das Demonstrações Financeiras Consolidadas. Em nosso entender a auditoria efectuada constitui base suficiente para a emissão da nossa opinião.

3. Em nossa opinião, as Demonstrações Financeiras Consolidadas referidas apresentam de forma verdadeira e apropriada, em todos os seus aspectos materialmente relevantes, a posição financeira do conjunto das empresas compreendidas na consolidação da Sonae Investimentos – Sociedade Gestora de Participações Sociais, S.A. em 31 de Dezembro de 1997 e o resultado das suas operações no exercício findo naquela data, em conformidade com os princípios contabilísticos geralmente aceites.

4. Sem afectar a opinião expressa no parágrafo anterior chamamos a atenção para as seguintes situações:

4.1. Conforme mencionado no Relatório Consolidado da Direcção foi efectuada escritura de cisão em 1 de Janeiro de 1997 que formaliza a alteração da estrutura organizativa do grupo, tendo sido constituída a Inparsa – Indústrias e Participações, S.G.P.S., S.A., que será responsável pela gestão dos negócios detidos pela Sonae Indústria, S.G.P.S., S.A., que será responsável pela gestão dos negócios detidos pela Sonae Indústria, S.G.P.S., S.A. e pela Pargeste, S.G.P.S., S.A. Em consequência foram transferidos para essa sociedade activos no valor de 115 356 000 contos e os Capitais Próprios e Interesses Minoritários do grupo foram diminuídos em 59 307 000 contos;

4.2. Tal como mencionado na Nota 45 os resultados do exercício incluem resultados extraordinários de 7 741 861 contos em virtude da alienação de partes de capital em filiais e associadas.

4.3. Conforme mencionado na Nota 50.2 a) estão apresentadas em Títulos Negociáveis unidades de participação em Fundos Imobiliários, no valor de 23 255 620 contos, os quais detêm imóveis que estão a ser utilizados no negócio distribuição. Esta apresentação decorre da intenção da Direcção de proceder à sua alienação logo que considerado adequado face às oportunidades de negócio que venham a surgir. Esta intenção, que já foi manifestada anteriormente, não se concretizou até ao momento.

Coopers & Lybrand
Porto, 5 de Março de 1998

Statutory Auditor's Report

Translation of the Portuguese Original
(Values in thousands of escudos)

Introduction

1. We have examined the consolidated financial statements of SONAE INVESTIMENTOS – SOCIEDADE GESTORA DE PARTICIPAÇÕES SOCIAIS, S.A., comprising the consolidated balance sheet as at 31 December 1997, the consolidated statement of income for the year then ended and corresponding notes to the consolidated financial statements wich present a balance sheet total of 361 520 429, a minority interests total of 42 724 370 and a shareholder's equity total of 78 021 776, including a net profit of 12 197 374.

Responsibilities

2. It is the responsibility of Management to prepare consolidated financial statements which give a true and fair view of the financial position of the company and its subsidiaries, and the consolidated results of their operations, as well as the adoption of adequate accounting policies and valuation criteria and the maintenance of an adequate internal control system.

3. Our responsibility is to express an independent and professional opinion on these consolidated financial statements based on our examination.

Stope

4. We conducted our examination in accordance with the Standards and Recommendations approved by the Statutory Auditor's Institute, which require that we plan and perform the examination to obtain reasonable assurance about whether the consolidated financial statements are free of material misstatement. The examination includes (i) verification, on a test basis, of evidence supporting the amounts in the consolidated financial statements and assessment of estimates, which have been based on judgements and criteria defined by Management, used in the preparation of the consolidated financial statements, (ii) assessment of the adequacy of accounting principles adopted and their disclosure, taking into account existing circumstances, and the appropriateness of the going concern principle, as well as (iii) evaluation of the overall presentation of the consolidated financial statements.

5. We believe that our examination provides a reasonable basis for our opinion on the consolidated financial statements.

Opinion

6. In our opinion, the consolidated financial statements referred to above present fairly, in all relevant and material respects, the financial position of SONAE INVESTIMENTOS – SOCIEDADE GESTORA DE PARTICIPAÇÕES SOCIAIS, S.A., and its subsidiaries as at 31 December 1997 and the consolidated results of their operations for the year then ended in conformity with generally accepted accounting principles in Portugal.

Emphasis

7. Without affecting the opinion expressed in the preceding paragraph, we draw your attention to the following matters:

7.1. As explained in the Management Board Report the Group was formally split into two groups on 1 January 1997, as a result of which a new company was formed named Imparsa – Indústrias e Participações, S.A., which will manage the businesses held by Sonae Indústria – SGPS, S.A. and Pargeste – SGPS, S.A. As a result of the split Assets worth 115 536 000 and Equity and Minority worth 59 307 000 were transferred to the new company;

7.2. As stated in Note 45 the profit for the year includes extraordinary gains on sale of investments in affiliated companies of 7 741 861;

7.3. As explained in Note 50.2. a) Short Therm Investments include shares held in Real Estate Funds valued at 23 255 620. These funds own real estate used by the Group in its retail business. These shares are presented under this caption because it is Management's intention to dispose of them as soon as it is considered adequate considering sale opportunities. This intention has already been presented to us before but it has not materialised so far.

Porto, 5 de Março de 1998

Boto, Amorim & Associados, S.R.O.C.
represented by:
José Luís dos Santos Lima Amorim, R.O.C.

Independent Account's Report

To the shareholders of Sonae Investimentos – Sociedade Gestora de Participações Sociais, S.A.

Translation of the Portuguese Version
(Values in thousands of escudos)

1. We have audited the accompanying consolidated balance sheet of SONAE INVESTIMENTOS – SOCIEDADE GESTORA DE PARTICIPAÇÕES SOCIAIS, S.A. and its subsidiaries as of 31 December 1997, and the related consolidated statements of income and notes to the accounts for the year then ended. These consolidated financial statements are the responsibility of the Company's management. Our responsibility is to express an opinion on these consolidated financial statements based on our audit.

2. We conducted our audit in accordance with International Standards on Auditing. Those standards require that we plan and perform the audit to obtain reasonable assurance about whether the financial statements are free of material misstatement. An audit includes examining, on a test basis, evidence supporting the amounts and disclosures in the consolidated financial statements. An audit also includes assessing the accounting principles used and significant estimates made by management, as well as evaluating the overall consolidated financial statement presentation. We believe that our audit provides a reasonable basis for our opinion.

3. In our opinion, the consolidated financial statements present fairly, in all material respects, the consolidated financial position of the Company and its subsidiaries as of 31 December 1997 and the consolidated results of their operations for the year then ended in accordance with generally accepted accounting principles in Portugal.

4. Without affecting the opinion expressed in the preceding paragraph, we draw your attention to the following matters:

4.1. As explained in the Management Board Report the Group was formally split into two groups on 1 January 1997, as a result of which a new company was formed named Imparsa – Indústrias e Participações, S.A., which will manage the businesses held by Sonae Indústria, SGPS, S.A. and Pargeste, SGPS, S.A. As a result of the split Assets worth 115 536 000 and Equity and Minority worth 59 307 000 were transferred to the new company;

4.2. As stated in Note 45 the profit for the year includes Extraordinary gains on sale of investments in affiliated of 7 741 861;

4.3. As explained in Note 50.2.a) Short Term Investments include shares held in Real Estate Funds valued at 23 255 620. These funds own real estate used by the Group in its retail business. These shares are presented under this caption because it is Management's intention to dispose of them as soon as it is considered adequate considering sale opportunities. This intention has already been presented to us before but it has not materialised so far.

Coopers & Lybrand

Porto, 5 March 1998

Country Highlights
REPUBLIC OF IRELAND

Ireland is one of the favored locations for investment in Europe. The rapid pace of development and industrialization in recent decades has been due in large measure to policies designed to make Ireland an attractive location for overseas investment. More than one thousand overseas companies do business successfully from Ireland, not just throughout Europe, but worldwide. Ireland is recognized as a stable economy with consistently high growth allied with low inflation. The country is renowned for its high quality of life, its clean environment, and its open and supportive attitude to inward investors.

Common Legal Forms of Companies

Private limited liability companies are the most common form of Irish business entity. Other forms of companies include public limited companies, companies limited by guarantee, unlimited companies, single member companies, and unincorporated entities such as partnerships, sole traders, and branches of overseas companies. External companies may also register an Irish place of business under Irish company law.

Sources of Financial Reporting Requirements

The Companies Acts of 1963 to 1990, together with various regulations to be construed as one with those acts, form the corpus of company law regarding financial reporting. For quoted companies this law is supplemented by the listing rules of the Irish Stock Exchange. All entities preparing accounts intended to give a true and fair view must comply with the body of accounting standards promulgated in Ireland. These standards are equivalent to those published in the United Kingdom.

Corporate Taxation

Companies are subject to corporation tax at the national level only. The standard rate of tax on a company's profits is 32% (25% on the first IR£50,000 of profits) with a 20% rate applying to capital gains. The rate of corporation tax is to reduce to 12.5% by 2003 in resepct of trading profits. Nontrading profits are likely to be taxed at 25%.

Ireland has long adopted a policy of using tax incentives to encourage inward investment or to stimulate investment in specific sectors of industry. A 10% rate is available to qualifying manufacturing activities including writing software and to operations located in the Dublin-based International Financial Services Centre (IFSC). This rate expires for IFSC companies in 2005, but expires only in 2011 for manufacturing companies.

Ireland has concluded double taxation agreements with 29 countries. Negotiations for the conclusion of new treaties continue. These treaties secure a reduction in, or in some cases a total elimination of, withholding taxes on royalties and interest. There is no withholding tax on dividends. A number of Ireland's treaties contain tax-sparing provisions, whereby income arising to a resident of a treaty country from sources within Ireland will be relieved from tax on repatriation from Ireland to the home country.

Auditing Requirements

All Irish companies are required to be audited annually by an auditor registered under Irish law.

Organization of the Accounting and Auditing Professions

The Institute of Chartered Accountants in Ireland is the largest single body of Irish accountants and is responsible for the promulgation of accounting and auditing standards in Ireland. Associates and Fellows of the Institute who meet the Institute's stringent conditions for practicing as an auditor are also registered auditors for the purposes of Irish company law.

Constitution and Legal System

A parliamentary democracy, Ireland is a member of the European Union (EU). Irish law is based on common law as modified by subsequent legislation and by the Constitution adopted in 1937 and amended on a number of occasions since then by public referendum. The constitution sets out the fundamental rights of the citizen, the form of government, and the powers of the government. It also defines the system of courts and regulates the appointment of the judiciary.

Currency

The majority of companies report in the local currency—the Irish Pound (Punt), which is denoted by the symbol IEP or IR£. There is no bar to preparing accounts in any other currency. On January 1, 1999, Ireland will adopt the euro as its currency.

Official Languages

Ireland has two official languages. The first official language is Irish. Irish is spoken in a number of regions known as Gaeltachts but is otherwise little used. The other and predominant language is English. All commerce is carried out in English.

REPUBLIC OF IRELAND

Niall W. Deasy and Oliver Holt
Coopers & Lybrand, Chartered Accountants
Dublin

1. Background

1.1 Introduction

The development and codification of accounting and financial reporting requirements in the Republic of Ireland has been greatly influenced by the development of Irish company law for two particular reasons. In the first instance Irish company law is the basic body of regulatory requirements for by far the greatest number of incorporated businesses in the Republic of Ireland and, as such, the provisions of this body of law—in particular, its accounting provisions—have the widest application in the Republic of Ireland. Second, the Irish accountancy profession's response to the accounting and financial reporting requirements of this body of law have served to complement and add to the legislation and in doing so have served to provide the basis for further development in Irish company law.

  Whereas other forms of incorporation of business occur in the Republic of Ireland (such as friendly societies, building societies, credit unions, agricultural and other forms of co-operative societies), none of the various bodies of legislation governing those businesses has had as marked an influence on the manner of organization of Irish business activity and on the accounting and financial reporting requirements of Irish business as has been provided by Irish company law.

  For these reasons, this section primarily consists of a short overview of the development of Irish company law, with particular reference to the accounting and financial reporting requirements it imposes on Irish businesses. The section also contains background information on the Irish accountancy profession and the audit requirements imposed on businesses in the Republic of Ireland.

1.2 The Development of Company Law in the Republic of Ireland

The development of Irish company law can be said to have occurred in three distinct phases in recent history, as follows:

- Up to 1921 (Before 1921 all Irish company law, together with other statute law applicable to Ireland, was enacted in Westminster.)
- From 1921 to 1973 (Over the period from 1921 to 1973 many changes occurred in Irish company law that were largely based on changes in company law in Britain.)
- Since 1973 (The Republic of Ireland joined the European Economic Community in 1973, and many of the changes in Irish company law in the interim have arisen from compliance with the requirements of the EU's harmonization of company law Directives.)

1.3 The Companies Act of 1963

The most significant statute in company law in the Republic of Ireland until recent times was the Companies Act of 1963 (the 1963 act), which had its origins in the recommendations of the Cox Committee on the reform of company law. The 1963 act embodied many of the provisions of the English Companies Act of 1948 and certain of the recommendations of the Jenkins Committee, which reported in Britain shortly after the Cox Committee reported in the Republic of Ireland. Whereas the structure and content of the 1963 act and the English 1948 act are quite similar, if not exactly the same for many provisions, there are enough differences between the content of the two acts to suggest that it would not be prudent to assume that a knowledge of the content of one of these acts automatically provides a knowledge of the content of the other act .

1.4 Post-1963 Act Legislation

Since the 1963 act, the following principal laws affecting companies have been enacted in the Republic of Ireland:

1. The European Communities (Companies) Regulations of 1973 implemented certain aspects of the EEC's First Directive, which

were applicable to the Republic of Ireland. The significant matters involved were the protection of third parties in regard to *ultra vires* transactions and the publication of information about the company.

2. The Companies (Amendment) Act of 1983 implemented the EEC's Second Directive, which introduced the designation "public limited company" (or plc) for public companies with limited liability. This Act sets out requirements for the minimum authorized share capital of public companies and for the payment of such share capital. The Act also sets out requirements for the maintenance of capital of companies and requires the company's auditor to report whether or not a financial situation has arisen in the company's balance sheet at its balance sheet date (a financial situation occurs if the balance sheet discloses net assets that are less than the 50% of the company's issued share capital). The Act also defined the nature of distributable profits.

3. The Companies (Amendment) Act of 1986, which implemented the EU's Fourth Directive, was a significant addition to the body of Irish Company Law. The core provisions of this Act were the requirement for prescriptive formats for profit and loss accounts and balance sheets of all companies and the requirement for Irish private companies to file their accounts with the Registrar of Companies, thereby making these available for public inspection. The content of this Act is reviewed in more detail in the paragraphs following.

4. The Companies (Amendment) Act of 1990 was enacted in August 1990 and introduced a new legal mechanism for the rescue or reconstruction of ailing, but potentially viable, companies. The key feature of the Act is the power to appoint an Examiner to a company and the placement of that company under the protection of the Court for a period of 3 months (which may be extended on application to the Court). If the Examiner believes the company can be saved, then he is required to produce a draft rescue plan for submission to shareholders and creditors and, if agreed, to the Court for confirmation. If the Court confirms the plan it becomes binding on those concerned.

5. The Companies Act of 1990 was enacted in December 1990 and sets out a series of significant additional requirements for Irish

companies that in the main are concerned with expanding the responsibilities of directors of companies and include provisions permitting companies to acquire or buy back their own share capital. The content of this Act is also reviewed in the paragraphs following.

6. In 1992 the provisions of two European Union (EU) Council Directives with implications for financial reporting were brought into Irish Law by means of Statutory Instruments. They were:

   - Statutory Instrument No 201 of 1992 (titled "European Communities [Companies: Group Accounts] Regulations, 1992"), which brought into Irish Law the provisions of the EU Council Directive on the preparation of Group Accounts.

   - Statutory Instrument No 294 of 1992 (titled "European Communities [Credit Institutions: Accounts] Regulations, 1992"), which brought into Irish Law the EU Council Directive on the content of annual accounts and on the preparation of consolidated accounts of banks and other financial institutions. This Statutory Instrument also brings into force the Council directive on the publication of accounts of branches of credit institutions that operate in the Republic of Ireland but that are incorporated outside the State.

7. In 1993 the provisions of two further EU Directives with implications for financial reporting were introduced into Irish Law once again by means of Statutory Instrument. These were:

   - Statutory Instrument No 395 of 1993 (entitled "European Communities (Branch Disclosures) Regulations, 1993") which gave effect to the EU's Council Directive dealing with the disclosure requirements of Branches established within the State of certain types of company which are governed by the law of another State.

   - Statutory Instrument No 396 of 1993 (entitled "European Communities (Accounts) Regulations, 1993") which gave effect to the EU's Council Directive which provides for unlimited companies and partnerships (where all the members or partners have limited liability) to produce and file accounts under the same rules as if they were limited companies.

1.5   The Companies (Amendment) Act of 1986 ("the 1986 Act")

The key provisions of this Act, which, as already indicated, implemented the Fourth Directive, may be summarized as follows:

1. The Act specifies the form and content of profit and loss accounts and balance sheets of companies, including footnotes to these financial statements;

2. The Act differentiates among large, medium, and small companies with large and medium-sized companies being required to publish (by means of filing with the Registrar of Companies) both profit and loss account and balance sheet. Disclosures for medium-sized companies are slightly less onerous than for large companies. Small companies are required to publish only their balance sheet;

3. The Act requires that all limited companies incorporated in the Republic of Ireland file their annual accounts (modified as per item 2 above) with their Annual Returns with the Registrar of Companies in Dublin. This requirement applies to dormant companies and to unlimited companies. In the case of branches of non-Irish incorporated companies, the annual accounts of these companies should be filed.

4. If a private company has a parent company registered in another member state of the European Community (the EC), then that parent company's consolidated accounts may be filed in lieu of the subsidiary company's accounts. The principal requirements in this instance include:

    a. The annual accounts of the company must be consolidated in the parent company's consolidated accounts, which in turn should note the fact that the guarantee has been given.

    b. All of the subsidiary company's shareholders must consent to not filing the company's accounts, at the Annual General Meeting (AGM) following the financial year.

    c. The parent company must irrevocably guarantee all the liabilities of the subsidiary for the financial year.

    d. A copy of the parent company's guarantee must be attached to the company's annual return, together with a statement that the company has availed itself of the exemption, a declaration that all members have consented to the exemption and a copy of the parent company's consolidated accounts. (Note, this exemption does not apply to banks or insurance companies).

5. The act requires that accounts filed with the Registrar of Companies give a true and fair view.

The 1986 act applied in respect of a company's accounting periods commencing after December 31, 1986, which in practice meant that the act's requirements were applicable in the first instance for financial years ended December 1987.

1.6 The Companies Act of 1990

The Companies Act of 1990 ("the 1990 act") was enacted in December 1990, and its provisions may be summarized as follows:

1. Investigation of Company's Affairs—The act empowers the court to appoint inspectors to investigate a company's affairs on the application of various interested parties; previously this power lay with the Minister of Industry and Commerce alone. In addition, the Minister is empowered to investigate the ownership of a company, and if there is difficulty finding out the relevant information regarding those shares (or debentures), the Minister is empowered to impose restrictions on those shares (or debentures).

2. Transactions Involving Directors—The act imposes wide-ranging obligations on directors (or shadow directors, that is, a person or persons in accordance with whose instructions the directors are accustomed to act) in respect of certain of their transactions with companies and sets out value thresholds for those transactions. Greater disclosure of details of transactions involving directors is also required than previously (by the 1963 act).

3. Disclosure of Interests in Shares—The act imposes a duty on directors and secretaries of companies to disclose their beneficial interests in the share capital of a company where the beneficial interest exceeds 5% of the issued share capital of the company (including in this context the interest of parties connected with them). The act also addresses the issue of parties acting in concert and imposes separate disclosure obligations on such parties.

4. Insider Dealing—The act makes it illegal to deal in securities where an individual is in possession of inside information; in consequence, the act has implemented the EU Directive on Insider Dealing.

5. Winding Up and Related Matters—The act strengthens the provisions of the 1963 act in regard to winding up and related matters and imposes increased accountability requirements on company officers.

6. Disqualifications and Restrictions for Directors and Other Officers—The act empowers the court to impose the penalty of disqualification from future directorships (or restrictions thereon) for directors of insolvent companies that have been wound up. The restriction, which can run up to 5 years, is that any company with which that individual becomes involved must have a minimum issued share capital of IR£20,000 Irish pounds (IR£100,000 in the case of a public limited company).

7. Receivers—The act contains some important new provisions in the role and duties of receivers, including a new duty on receivers to obtain the best price reasonably obtainable in disposing of assets.

8. Accounts and Audit—The act strengthens the obligation to keep proper books of account and includes provisions to extend the auditor's obligations (regarding forming an opinion on proper books of account) and for strengthening the auditor's hand in dealing with the company (through penalties for misleading auditors). The part of the act dealing with these issues has implemented the requirements of the EU's Eighth Directive, while the remaining requirements of the Directive were implemented by statutory instrument in 1992.

9. Acquisition of Own Shares and Shares in Holding Company—The act empowers companies to acquire their own shares (or shares in their holding company) either by cancellation on redemption or by holding the redeemed shares as treasury shares.

10. Investment Companies—The act provides for the establishment of variable capital companies that must be authorized by the Central Bank.

Commencement orders for the key provisions of the 1990 act were fixed for various dates over 1990 to 1992.

1.7 Statutory Instrument No. 201 of 1992

Statutory Instrument No. 201 of 1992 (European Communities [Companies: Group Accounts] Regulations, 1992) ("the 1992 Group Accounts Regulations") brings into Irish law the EU Council Directive on preparation of consolidated or group accounts. The regulations address such matters as:

1. The format and content of group accounts and the notes to the accounts
2. The definition of a subsidiary undertaking
3. The circumstances and conditions under which companies may be exempted from the requirement to produce group accounts
4. Matters to be included in the directors' report of a parent undertaking and the disclosure of the ultimate parent company in the accounts of subsidiary companies

These regulations apply to financial years beginning on or after September 1, 1992.

1.8 Statutory Instrument No. 294 of 1992

Statutory Instrument No. 294 of 1992 (European Communities [Credit Institutions: Accounts] Regulations, 1992) brings into Irish law the EU Council Directive on the annual accounts and consolidated accounts of banks and other financial institutions and certain other matters. The more significant requirements of these regulations include:

1. The publication within the State of the accounts of branches of credit and financial institutions operating within the State that are incorporated outside the State
2. The format and content of the group accounts of these institutions and the content of the directors' report
3. The accounting treatment and disclosures to be provided in regard to subsidiary and associated undertakings and for joint ventures

These regulations apply to financial years beginning on or after January 1, 1993.

1.9 Statutory Instrument No. 395 of 1993

Statutory Instrument No. 395 of 1993 (European Communities [Branch Disclosures] Regulations, 1993) imposes a similar disclosure of information requirement on branches to that which Irish company law already imposes on subsidiary companies. The requisite information must be returned to the Registrar of Companies in Dublin in (or accompanied by) prescribed forms.

These regulations came into effect on February 1, 1994.

1.10 Statutory Instrument No. 396 of 1993

Statutory Instrument No. 396 of 1993 (European Communities [Accounts] Regulations, 1993) provides that unlimited companies and partnerships, where all the members or partners have limited liability, must produce and file accounts under the same requirements as are laid down for limited companies. This requirement applies for accounting periods beginning on or after January 1, 1994.

These regulations also provide for the following size criteria for companies to come into effect on January 1, 1994:

	Small (Not Exceeding)	Medium (Not Exceeding)
Total assets (fixed & current)	£1.5 million	£6.0 million
Turnover	£3.0 million	£12.0 million
Average number of employees	50	250

1.11 Statutory Instrument No 23 of 1996

Statutory Instrument No 23 of 1996 (European Communities [Insurance Undertakings: Accounts] Regulations, 1996) ("The Insurance Accounts Regulations") brings into Irish Law, the EU Council Directive on Insurance Company Accounts. Essentially it applies the principles encoded in the fourth (company) and Eighth (group) EU Company Law Directives to entities licensed to write insurance. Such entities are now required to prepare their annual financial statements in accordance with the provisions of this Statutory Instrument. The regulations cover the content, format, and valuation of items to be included in entity and group accounts (balance sheet, profit and loss account, and notes) of insurance undertakings.

The regulations are effective for accounting periods beginning on or after 1 January 1995.

1.12 Additional Legislation

A number of other pieces of legislation affect the financial reporting of Irish companies. The following points briefly outline the most important.

1.12.1 *Safety, Health and Welfare at Work Act, 1989 (No. 7 of 1989)*

Section 12(6) of the Safety, Health and Welfare at Work Act, 1989 applies to all companies formed and registered under the companies acts and requires that the director's report contains an evaluation of the extent to which the policy set out in a safety statement was fulfilled during the period covered by the said report.

1.12.2 *Investment Limited Partnerships Act, 1994 (No. 24 of 1994)*

The Investment Limited Partnerships Act provides for the regulations of investment limited partnerships by the Central Bank and allows partnerships of more than twenty members.

1.12.3 *Investment Intermediaries Act, 1995 (No. 11 of 1995)*

The Investment Intermediaries Act extends the definition of "investment company" to include closed-ended investment companies. Closed-ended investment companies are collective investment schemes in the form of a company where the shareholder cannot redeem directly from the company but can trade the shares in the secondary market. The closed period may be permanent or, alternatively, for a fixed period of time after which the company can revert to being open-ended. Closed-ended investment companies are supervised by the Central Bank, as are all investment companies.

The Investment Intermediaries Act, 1995 also provides for the introduction of a system of regulation and supervision for investment business firms dealing in particular products. The Minister for Enterprise, Trade and Employment, and the Central Bank of Ireland are the supervisory authorities under the Act. The Central Bank regulates all other investment intermediaries.

1.12.4   Irish Take-Over Panel Act, 1997 (No. 5 of 1997)

The Irish Take-Over Panel Act, 1997, provides *inter alia* for the establishment of a Takeover Panel in Ireland to regulate the need to monitor and supervise takeovers and certain other related activity with a view to ensuring fair and equal treatment of a all shareholders in such situations and to provide support and credibility for the Irish financial markets.

1.12.5   Electoral Act, 1997

Section 26 of the Electoral Act, 1997, requires that particulars of all donations exceeding IR£4,000 in value made by a company are to be included in the report by the directors of a company and in the company's Annual Return to the Registrar of Companies in Dublin.

1.13   The True and Fair View Requirement

A central feature of the accounting requirements expressed in Irish company law is that companies' accounts must give a true and fair view. This requirement is expressed in the 1963 act (which is viewed as the principal act in the present corpus of Irish company law), in the 1986 act, which effected the requirements of the Fourth Directive, and, more recently, in certain aspects of the 1990 act. In addition to the requirements of Irish company law, the work of the Accounting Standards Committee (ASC) in the development of Statements of Standard Accounting Practice (SSAPs) up to 1990, and the subsequent work of the Accounting Standards Board (ASB) in the development of Financial Reporting Standards (FRSs) has emphasized the relevance and significance of the true and fair view requirement. In consequence, all of the significant forms of business organization in the Republic of Ireland (which would include friendly societies, building societies, credit unions, agricultural, and other co-operative societies, in addition to limited companies) would recognize the true and fair view requirement as being the primary accounting requirement for financial reporting purposes, if that requirement had not already been imposed by their governing statutes.

From a developmental standpoint, the Irish accounting profession has been closely associated with the work of both the ASC and the ASB by virtue of the involvement of the Institute of Chartered Accountants in Ireland (ICAI) in the standard-setting process. ICAI was a founding member of ASC and fully participated in ASC's development program from its inception. After the establishment of the independent Accounting Standards Board (ASB) in 1990, in succession to ASC, ICAI continues to act as the body with responsibility for promulgating accounting standards in the Republic of Ireland.

1.14 Organization of the Accounting Profession in the Republic of Ireland

The largest body of professionally qualified accountants in the Republic of Ireland is the Institute of Chartered Accountants in Ireland (ICAI), which has a total membership of 10,500 (as of May 1998) of which 6,000 are partners or employees in public practices and 4,500 are involved in industry, commerce, and the public sector. ICAI's membership in the Republic of Ireland is 6,700 members (the remainder being outside the Republic, mainly in Northern Ireland), of which 2,500 are members in practicing offices and 4,200 are members in industry, commerce, and the public sector. The other significant bodies of accountants in the Republic of Ireland are:

- The Chartered Institute of Management Accountants (CIMA)—The membership of CIMA's Republic of Ireland Division is 1,800, almost all of whom are involved in industry, commerce, and the public sector, when due account is taken of CIMA members who are also members of the other accounting bodies in the Republic of Ireland.
- The Chartered Association of Certified Accountants (ACCA)—The membership of ACCA's Irish Region (which includes Northern Ireland) is 3,500 members, of which 2,400 are involved in industry, commerce, and the public sector and 1,100 in the auditing profession.
- The Institute of Certified Public Accountants in Ireland—The membership of ICPAI is approximately 1,500 members, of which some 600 are engaged in the auditing profession, with the balance engaged in industry, commerce, and the public sector.

ICAI together with CIMA, ACCA, and ICPAI make up the Consultative Committee of Accounting Bodies—Ireland (CCAB-I) and through this organization promulgate the views of the Irish accounting profession on issues of importance to the profession.

1.15 Entry to the Irish Accountancy Bodies

Accountancy students who wish to become members of ICAI must:

- Be either university graduates or have attained a school leaving standard equivalent to that required for entry to university
- Enter into and complete a training contract that will provide for practical training in a recognized training establishment, which in most instances will be a firm of practicing chartered accountants. The duration of the training contract will depend on whether the student is a business graduate or otherwise.
- Undertake part-time education and take professional examinations during the period of the training contract, culminating in a final admitting examination. The numbers of examinations to be passed before the final admitting examination will depend on the student's third level educational attainments.

The standards of education of members of ICAI are such as permit reciprocity of recognition of membership with the Institutes of Chartered Accountants in England and Wales, and of Scotland.

Accountancy students who wish to become members of CIMA or ACCA follow a training, education, and examination program consistent with that applied by those bodies to their students in the United Kingdom. Students who wish to become members of ICPAI can enter the accountancy profession both through firms of accountants in public practice and through industry, commerce, and the public sector in Ireland.

1.16 Audit Requirements in the Republic of Ireland

The 1963 act requires that the accounts of all companies incorporated under the provisions of the Irish Companies Act be audited annually. This requirement applies to virtually all other forms of business in the Republic of Ireland through various governing statutes, the most significant exception being that of incorporated businesses organized as partnerships (unless, that is, all of the partners in the partnership have limited liability, in which case an annual audit is required).

The working practices and procedures adopted by the auditing profession in the Republic of Ireland are those prescribed by the Auditing Practices Committee (APC) and its successor body (established in 1991), the Auditing Practices Board (APB). Auditors' reports incorporating true and fair view opinions issued in the Republic of Ireland state that the audit has been conducted in accordance with Auditing Standards issued by the Auditing Practices Board. ICAI was a founding member of APC and promulgated APC's Auditing Standards and Guidelines in the Republic of Ireland. It retains its significant involvement in the standard-setting process carried out by APC's successor body, APB, by virtue of its involvement in the selection of members of APB and by its contribution to the standard-setting process and to the promulgation of standards.

Auditors of limited liability companies are appointed under the provisions of the Companies Acts and are, in effect, automatically reappointed annually thereafter, unless the auditors indicate in advance that they do not wish to be reappointed (in which case the notice filed with the Companies Office must contain a statement to the effect that there are no circumstances connected with the resignation that should be brought to the attention of the shareholders or creditors of the company or, alternatively, a statement of the circumstances should be provided) or a resolution for their dismissal is advised to shareholders after giving appropriate notice.

Irish company law requires that auditors be members of a recognized accounting body. This requirement is met by membership of one of the following:

- The Institute of Chartered Accountants in Ireland
- The Institute of Chartered Accountants in England and Wales
- The Institute of Chartered Accountants of Scotland
- The Chartered Association of Certified Accountants
- The Institute of Certified Public Accountants in Ireland
- The Instutute of Incorporated Public Accountants Limited

In addition, an application for recognition by the Association of International Accountants, which is recognized by the United Kingdom, must have been recorded by the Irish authorities.

1.17 Example of an Auditors' Report in the Republic of Ireland

An example of an auditors' report (without qualification) prepared in accordance with the requirements of Irish company law, and incorporating requirements expressed in the Statement of Auditing Standards titled "Auditors' Reports on Financial Statements," is provided in Appendix B and discussed in Section 2. It will be seen from this example that there are three separate sections in the auditors' report dealing with:

1. The respective responsibilities of directors and auditors
2. The basis of the auditor's opinion
3. The auditors' opinion on the financial statements

The statement of the respective responsibilities of the directors and auditors is for the purpose of distinguishing the responsibilities of both of these parties concerning the preparation of the financial statements and the expression of the auditor's opinion on those statements. If the directors' responsibilities are described elsewhere in the financial statements or in the information accompanying those statements (such as in the Directors' Report), then this section of the auditor's report should cross reference to them.

If, however, they are not so included or the description of the directors' responsibilities is not adequate, then the auditors are required to include an appropriate description of these responsibilities in this section of their audit report.

The section dealing with the basis of the auditors' opinion should explain the basis of the opinion and should identify the auditors' compliance with Auditing Standards in the course of their work, briefly explain the audit process, and indicate that the auditors' work was so planned as to give them reasonable assurance that the financial statements are free from material misstatement.

The final section of the auditors' report sets out the auditors' opinion on the financial statements that the auditors have examined. It will be seen from the following example that the key reporting issue for auditors is whether the accounts under examination show a true and fair view of the results and state of affairs (or financial position). The audit report in Appendix B also shows that many of the auditor's reporting requirements in the Republic of Ireland are similar to those required under company law in the United Kingdom, except that the Irish company law requires affirmative comment in respect of each matter for report, in contrast with the exception basis of reporting required in the United Kingdom. It should also be noted (as mentioned earlier) that Irish company law requires auditors to report (in their audit report) whether or not a financial situation existed at the company's balance sheet date (see Section 2.1.1). This requirement applies to all companies in the Republic of Ireland and is in contrast with the obligation imposed by U.K. Company Law, which requires directors to take action when a financial situation occurs in the case of public limited companies (plc's) only.

The key reporting requirement for auditors of other forms of business organization in the Republic of Ireland is, in general, fundamentally the same as for limited companies in that the key issue is whether the accounts being reported on show a true and fair view of results and state of affairs (or financial position).

2. The Form and Content of Published Financial Statements in the Republic of Ireland

2.1 The Form and Content of Published Financial Statements

This section focuses on disclosure (rather than measurement) consider-ations applicable to entities preparing financial statements in the Republic of Ireland. Emphasis is placed on the requirements laid down in the Irish Companies Acts and Financial Reporting Standards (including Statements of Standard Accounting Practice), which are the principal sources of both accounting disclosure (and measurement) requirements in the Republic of Ireland.

In Appendix B to this chapter are the published consolidated financial statements of Bord Telecom Eireann (BTE) for the year ended April 1997. These financial statements have been included to illustrate the issues discussed following. BTE's annual report and financial statements won the Chartered Accountants Annual Award for annual reports of businesses registered in the Republic of Ireland on a number of occasions in the past, and so they may be viewed as an example of the standard of best practice in published Irish financial statements.

The content of the core elements of BTE's 1996/1997 financial state-ments is described in the following paragraphs.

2.1.1 Auditors' Report

The report of the auditors on BTE's 1996/1997 financial statement is set out on page 959 in the specimen financial statements. A feature of the auditors' statutory reporting requirements in the Republic of Ireland is that each of the matters to be reported on under the requirements of the Companies Acts must be expressly stated in the auditors' report. The matters to be reported upon by auditors, all of which are expressed in the opinion segment of the auditors' report, are as follows:

- Whether all required information and explanations required for the purposes of the audit have been obtained
- Where a company has branches, the audit report also refers to whether adequate returns have been received from branches of the company not visited by the auditors
- Whether proper books of accounts have been maintained by the company
- Whether the financial statements are in accordance with the books of account
- Whether the financial statements give a true and fair view of the company's profit or loss and of its state of affairs per its balance sheet (in compliance with Irish company law) and of its total recognized gains and losses and cash flows (in accordance with professional reporting standards)
- Whether the financial statements have been properly prepared in accordance with the Companies Acts and the 1992 Group Accounts Regulations
- Whether the information given in the directors' report is consistent with the financial statements
- Whether the holding company's balance sheet discloses a financial situation that would require the convening of an extraordinary general meeting (a financial situation arises in circumstances in which the company's net assets amount to half or less of the company's called-up share capital).

The respective responsibilities of directors and auditors are addressed at the beginning of the auditors' report, from which it will be seen that directors' responsibilities are described separately in a stand-alone Statement of Directors' Responsibilities. The basis of the auditors' opinion is set out in the middle segment of the auditors' report.

2.1.2 Accounting Policies

The group's accounting policies are set out in the first two pages of the publication (pages 959–961) in the specimen financial statements) and are included in compliance with the requirements of SSAP 2 (Disclosure of Accounting Policies).

Section 5 of the Companies Act 1986 requires that the company's financial statements be prepared in accordance with the fundamental accounting principles, namely the going concern, consistency, prudence, and accruals principles. In addition, the 1986 act prohibits set-offs of amounts of assets and liabilities (unless there is a legal right to do so) and income and expenditure.

Section 6 of the 1986 act permits directors to depart from the fundamental accounting principles required by Section 5 if there are special reasons for doing so. However, if they do so they must provide particulars of the departure, the reasons for the departure, and its effect on the company's profit and loss account and balance sheet in a note to the financial statements.

Paragraph 44 of the schedule to the 1986 act requires that if a change in accounting policy occurs, then the corresponding amounts for the previous year should be adjusted to ensure comparability. In addition, particulars of any such adjustment and of the reasons for it must be provided in the financial statements.

Notable accounting policies in BTE's financial statements are those in respect of:

- Basis of Consolidation
- Foreign Currencies
- Financial Instruments
- Tangible Assets
- Grants
- Leased Assets
- Stocks
- Deferred Taxation

2.1.3 *Group Profit and Loss Account and Group Balance Sheet*

The group profit and loss account and the group balance sheet are consolidated financial statements in both instances (pages 962 and 963 in the specimen financial statements) and are required both by the provisions of the Irish Companies Acts and by Financial Reporting Standard 2 (Accounting for Subsidiary Undertakings) (FRS2). The principles involved in the preparation of consolidated accounts and embodied in FRS2 are described in more detail in Section 3.1.

2.1.4 *Balance Sheet of the Company*

The balance sheet of the holding company (page 963 in the specimen financial statements) must be published as part of the company's annual financial statements.

2.1.5 *Format and Content of Profit and Loss Account and Balance Sheets*

The format and content of the group profit and loss account and of the group balance sheet and the balance sheet of the holding company comply with the detail specified in the 1986 act and the 1992 Group Accounts Regulations (see Section 1.7) for the format and content of these statements.

2.1.6 *Group Cash Flow Statement*

Although the Irish Companies Acts do not require that a company's financial statements include a cash flow statement, Financial Reporting Standard 1 (revised 1996) (Cash Flow Statements) (FRS1) requires that such a statement be prepared for almost all entities. Investment funds meeting certain criteria, pension funds, building societies, life assurance companies, 90% or more owned subsidiaries and entities that are deemed to be small companies for the purposes of filing financial statements with the Registrar of Companies (size criteria for such companies are set out in Section 1.10) are exempt from this requirement. The cash flow statement (page 965 in the specimen financial statements) in BTE's financial statements complies with the disclosure requirements set out in FRS1.

2.1.7 *Notes to the Financial Statements*

The notes to BTE's financial statements (pages 967–984 in the specimen financial statements) illustrate many of the disclosures specified under the information requirements laid down for companies in the 1986 act and the 1992 Group Accounts Regulations.

The notes to BTE's financial statements deal with:

1. Segmental Information—refer to Section 2.3.1.

2. Turnover—turnover is analyzed over the company's various classes of business, in accordance with the provisions of paragraph 41 of the Schedule to the 1986 Act.

3. Operating Costs—this analysis, *inter alia*, provides details of items for which specific disclosures are required, such as staff costs and auditors and directors' remuneration.

4. Interest Payable and Similar Charges—this note analyzes interest payable over the various segments of the company's loan portfolio (in accordance with the provisions of paragraph 39(2) of the Schedule to the 1986 Act) and also discloses exchange differences.

5. Tax on Profit on Ordinary Activities—details are provided in this note of the incidence of taxation on the company's business activities (see Section 3.11) and of required disclosures regarding deferred taxation (see Section 3.12.3).

6. Tangible Assets—movements on fixed assets in terms of cost and depreciation are set out in this note and are separately disclosed over the parent company and the group (see Section 3.5). Disclosure is also provided of details of tangible assets acquired under finance leases (see Section 3.7).

7. Financial Assets—details of the holding company's investment in its subsidiary and related companies, as required under the Irish Companies Acts, are provided in this note (see Section 3.9).

8. Stocks—details of the make-up of stocks (inventories) are provided in this footnote for both the consolidated and holding company balance sheet (see Section 3.11).

9. Debtors—details of the make-up of debtors (receivables) are provided for both the consolidated and holding company balance sheet and also of the amounts of group balances in the case of the holding company.

10. Loans and Other Debt—this note provides an analysis of consolidated and holding company loans and other debt as required by the 1986 Act; the repayment time analysis is also a specific 1986 Act

requirement (see Section 3.4), and of FRS 4 "Capital Instruments." An analysis by currency is also given following one of the nonmandatory practices indicated by Financial Reporting Exposure Draft FRED 13 "Disclosure of Financial Instruments."

11. Other Creditors—this note discloses the amounts of trade and other creditors analyzed by reference to the holding and consolidated balance sheets, and also, of the amounts of group balances for the parent balance sheet (see Section 3.4).

12. Provision for Liabilities and Charges—this note analyses the make-up of the deferred taxation liability and restructuring provisions.

13. Capital Grants—movements in grants, set out separately for the company and group are disclosed (see Section 3.6.2).

14. Share Capital—the disclosure requirements of the 1986 Act referable to the company's share capital are set out in this note (see Section 3.3).

15. Reserves—analysis of share premium, revaluation reserve, and revenue reserves analyzed by company and by group are given.

16. Cash Flow—the notes here give details as required under FRS 1 (revised 1996) concerning the group's cash flows.

17. Principal Subsidiary and Related Companies—details of the company's subsidiary and related companies as required by the 1986 Act are provided in this note.

18. Profits on Ordinary Activities—as the holding company's profit and loss account is not published separately, the 1996 Act requires this note, which discloses the profit on the ordinary activities of the holding company.

19. Employees—this note provides an analysis of the average number of persons employed by the Group by reference to their various categories as required by the 1986 Act.

20. Pensions—this note provides disclosures relative to the company's pension scheme (see Section 3.13).

21. Contingent Liabilities and Capital Commitments—these notes provide details of the group's contingent liabilities and capital commitments (see Sections 3.4.2 and 3.4.3).

22. Comparative Amounts—the 1986 Act requires changes in comparative figures from those previously published to be explained.

23. Approval of Financial Statements—this note identifies the date at which the financial statements were approved by the Board of Directors of the company.

2.1.8 *Financial Reporting Standard 3 (Reporting Financial Performance)*

FRS3 expanded the requirements for reporting financial performance of companies and for the content of companies' financial statements. The requirements of the Standard are applicable for accounting periods ending on or after June 22, 1993.

The principal features of this Standard are:

1. It requires increased disclosures of financial performance by means of changes in the format of the profit and loss account and by means of the presentation of additional financial statements that include summaries and reconciliations of key data.

2. It requires that the results of continuing and discontinued operations be separately identified in the profit and loss account.

3. It requires that any significant profits or losses arising on termination of an operation, or costs arising from a fundamental reorganization or restructuring of profits or losses on the disposal of fixed assets be separately disclosed after operating profit but before interest in the profit and loss account.

4. It requires that all other significant profit or losses are shown as part of the statutory heading to which the income or expense most closely relates.

5. It redefines extraordinary items, albeit in such an extremely restrictive manner that no incidence of an extraordinary item has been noted in any set of accounts receiving wide circulation.

6. It requires that earnings per share (EPS) be calculated on the profits attributable to the ordinary shareholder of the company *after* accounting for minority interests, extraordinary items, preference shares (if any) and other appropriations in respect of preference shares.

FRS3 supersedes SSAP 6 (Extraordinary Items and Prior Year Adjustments) and amends SSAP 3 (Earnings per Share).

Implementation of the requirements of FRS3 in BTE's financial statements has occurred in the following manner:

1. Continuing Operations—there is a statement at the end of the profit and loss account (page 962) to the effect that all of the company's results are in respect of continuing operations.

2. Additional Financial Statements and Reconciliations—new financial statements and data are set out at page 966 of the specimen financial statements dealing with:

    •   The Statement of Total Recognized Gains and Losses—which facilitates users seeing all recognized gains and losses arising in any accounting period being brought together in a single statement;

    •   The Note of Historical Cost Profits or Losses—which is a memorandum   information for the purpose of showing the difference between the reported results and the historic results that would otherwise have arisen if there had not been a revaluation of fixed assets;

    •   The Reconciliation of Movements in Shareholders' Funds— which brings together the results for the period with all other changes in shareholders' funds during the period under review.

3. A restructuring provision not meeting the definition of a fundamental restructuring as referred to above is shown as a component of operating costs in arriving at operating profit.

BTE's group profit and loss account shows a contribution from ordinary activities essentially operating profit before the charge for depreciation. As a public utility encompassing the Irish telephony network, the company is fixed asset intensive. Accordingly, a degree of prominence is required in relation to the burden of depreciation carried by the company. Striking subtotals both before and after the depreciation is designed to help the reader easily see the extent of depreciation on financial performance.

2.2   Segmental Disclosure

The requirements governing segmental disclosures in the Republic of Ireland are contained in the Companies (Amendment) Act 1986 (the 1986

Act), in the Stock Exchange's regulations and in Statement of Standard Accounting Practice 25 (Segmental Reporting).

The 1986 Act requires that a company's turnover be analyzed over:

1. Class of business, where in the directors' opinion the company has carried on two or more classes of business that differ substantially from each other, and

2. Geographic markets, where in the directors' opinion the company has supplied markets that differ substantially from each other.

However, this analysis need not be provided if the directors are of the opinion that the disclosure of such information would be seriously prejudicial to the interests of the Company. However, if this exemption is availed of, the lack of disclosure of such information must be disclosed.

Finally, immaterial amounts of turnover may be included with another class of business or geographic market for the purposes of this analysis. SSAP 25 requires that where an entity has two or more classes of business or operates in two or more geographic segments it should disclose the following information for each class of business and geographic segment:

- Turnover
- Result before taxation, minority interest, and extraordinary items
- Net assets

The standard permits nondisclosure of this information if, in the opinion of the directors, such disclosure would be seriously prejudicial to the interests of the reporting entity. Any such omission must be stated.

3. Accounting Policies and Practices in Valuation and Income Measurement: Implications for the Analyst

3.1 Group Financial Statements

The requirement to produce consolidated financial statements for groups of companies in the Republic of Ireland is expressed in Company Law (principally in the 1992 Group Accounts Regulations, see Section 1.7) and

FRS2. Note that FRS 2 applies to all parent undertakings, whether or not they are incorporated and whether they are public or private companies.

3.1.1 Subsidiary Undertakings

An undertaking is a parent undertaking of another undertaking (a subsidiary undertaking) if any of the five following conditions apply:

1. The parent holds a majority of the voting rights in the undertaking.

2. The parent is a member of the undertaking and has the right to appoint and remove directors holding a majority of the voting rights at board meetings.

3. The parent (whether or not it has a shareholding) has the right to exercise a dominant influence over the undertaking by virtue of the provisions of its Memorandum and Articles of Association or in a control contract.

4. The parent is a member of the undertaking and controls alone (by virtue of an agreement with other shareholders) a majority of voting rights in the undertaking.

5. The parent has a participating interest in the undertaking and

    -   Actually exercises a dominant influence over it, or,
    -   The parent and the undertaking are managed on a unified basis.

The common feature of the criteria set out above is that of control by the parent (or by the parent and its subsidiaries) over the subsidiary undertaking.

3.1.2 Exclusion of Subsidiary Undertakings

The overriding principle is that a parent should not consolidate a subsidiary that it does not control. FRS2 specifically requires that subsidiary undertakings be excluded from consolidation in the following circumstances:

1. If the parent's control over the subsidiary is subject to severe long-term restrictions

2. Where the group's interest is held exclusively with a view to subsequent resale and the subsidiary undertaking has not previously been consolidated in the consolidated financial statements prepared by the parent

3. Where the subsidiary's activities are so different from those of other subsidiary undertakings that its inclusion would be incompatible with the obligation to show a true and fair view. FRS2 notes that it will be exceptional for exclusions to arise under this category, and in particular it emphasizes that this exclusion does not apply merely because the subsidiary undertakings are involved in different businesses or are dealing with different products and services.

Two other considerations are worth noting, namely:

1. FRS2 permits the exclusion of a subsidiary undertaking if its inclusion is not material for a true and fair view. However, two or more subsidiaries may be excluded only if, taken together, they are not material.

2. Unlike Irish company law, FRS2 does not permit exclusion of a subsidiary's undertaking from the consolidated financial statements on the grounds of undue delay or disproportionate expense.

Where a subsidiary is excluded from the consolidation, then certain information about the results and balance sheet of that subsidiary will still be required to be included in the notes to the financial statements.

3.1.3 Exemption from Consolidation Requirement

There are three situations under the provisions of FRS2 and Irish Company Law, where a parent may be exempt from the consolidation requirements, which are:

1. Parents of small or medium sized groups (small or medium in this context being as defined in Irish Company Law)

2. Intermediate parents (where the parents are registered in an EC member state), namely parents that are in turn subsidiaries of another parent

3. Parents, all of whose subsidiaries are permitted or required to be excluded from consolidation.

3.1.4   Consolidated Financial Statements

FRS2 requires parents preparing financial statements that are to show a true and fair view to prepare them in the form of consolidated financial statements in which appropriate adjustments will be made to:

*   The results of subsidiary companies to ensure uniformity of application of accounting policies throughout the group;
*   Eliminate intergroup balances and unrealized intergroup profits and losses.

In addition it will be necessary to ensure that any outside or minority interests in the share capital, reserves, and results of the group are appropriately disclosed.

While Section 149(5) of the Companies Act of 1963 provides that preacquisition reserves of a subsidiary company may not be distributed, the section also goes on to permit that "where the directors and the auditors are satisfied and so certify that it would be fair and reasonable and would not prejudice the rights and interests of any person," then the preacquisition profits of an acquired company may be treated in a manner other than in accordance with this general provision.

3.1.5   Accounting for Mergers and Acquisitions

After the enactment of the 1992 Group Accounts Regulations merger accounting is permissible under Irish company law subject to compliance with a number of conditions, in particular that:

*   At least 90% of the acquired undertakings' shares are held by the investing undertaking or its subsidiaries, and,

*   No more than 10% of the consideration for the acquisition is for cash.

However, section 62 of the Companies Act of 1963 requires the recognition of share premium, where shares are issued for a value in excess of their nominal value. In a merger, the share premium will essentially represent goodwill. Section 62 forces the recognition of this goodwill contrary to established merger accounting principles. In U.K. law, provided a number of conditions are met, relief, known as "'merger relief'' is given from the requirement to recognize share premium. There is no equivalent provision in Irish law. The absence of such a provision makes the application of pure merger accounting in Irish companies difficult.

FRS 6, "Acquisitions and Mergers" applies to business combinations first accounted for in financial statements relating to accounting periods commencing on or after December 23, 1994. Among other things, the FRS limits the use of merger accounting and increases the disclosures required generally in respect of acquisitions.

FRS 6 complements FRS 7, "Fair values in acquisition accounting," which was published at the same time and applied from the same date. While FRS 7 sets down detailed rules for ascribing fair values in acquisition accounting, FRS 6 deals with the general requirements relating to acquisition and merger accounting and the disclosures that need to be made in the financial statements. The FRS:

- Sets out five new criteria that, in addition to the legal requirements, must be satisfied before merger accounting can be adopted
- Makes merger accounting compulsory where all these criteria are satisfied
- Introduces a definition of a group reconstruction to enable an increased number of such combinations to be merger accounted
- Introduces separate and different criteria that need to be satisfied in the case of group reconstructions for merger accounting to be possible and leaves the choice of merger accounting optional for such combinations
- Describes briefly the acquisition and merger methods of accounting
- Includes disclosures in relation to both acquisition and merger accounting with new and increased disclosures, particularly in respect of "substantial acquisitions."

After FRS 6, merger accounting will apply only to those business combinations where no acquirer can be identified and where two or more parties combine in a "substantially equal partnership where no party is dominant."

The FRS defines a group reconstruction to include a wide variety of combinations and imposes less stringent criteria that need to be satisfied for such combinations to be merger accounted.

The criteria that FRS 6 requires for merger accounting are:

- No party to the combination is portrayed as either acquirer or acquired, either by its own board or management or by that of another party to the combination;
- All parties to the combination, as represented by the boards of directors or their appointees, participate in establishing the management structure for the combined entity and in selecting the management personnel, and such decisions are made on the basis of a consensus between the parties to the combination rather than purely by exercise of voting rights
- The relative sizes of the combining entities are not so disparate that one party dominates the combined entity by virtue of its relative size (domination is presumed if one party is more than 50% larger than each of the other parties to the combination, judged by reference to ownership interests in the combined entity)
- No equity shareholders of any of the combining entities retains any material interest in the future performance of only part of the combined entity
- Under the terms of the combination or related arrangements, the consideration received by equity shareholders of each party to the combination, in relation to its equity shareholding, comprises primarily equity shares in the combined entity.

The criteria described above do not apply to combinations that meet the definition of a group reconstruction. Instead much simpler criteria must be met. These are that:

- The use of merger accounting is not prohibited by companies legislation
- The ultimate shareholders remain the same, and the rights of each such shareholder, relative to the others, are unchanged; and
- No minority's interest in the net assets of the group is altered by the transfer.

The definition of a group reconstruction includes not only those reconstructions that take place within a legal group, but also other combinations of companies that are under common control.

Merger accounting is optional for group reconstructions that meet the criteria.

Regardless of the method of accounting used, FRS 6 requires disclosure of

1. The names of the combining entities (other than the reporting entity);
2. Whether the combination has been accounted for as an acquisition or a merger, and
3. The date of the combination.

There are different disclosure requirements for mergers and for acquisitions. The disclosures in respect of mergers, other than a group reconstruction, include:

1. An analysis of the principal components (showing as a minimum the turnover, operating profit and exceptional items, split among continuing operations, discontinued operations, and acquisitions; profit before taxation; taxation and minority interests; and extraordinary items) of the current year's profit and loss account and statement of total recognized gains and losses into;

   (a) amounts relating to the merged entity for the period after the date of the merger, and

   (b) for each party to the merger, amounts relating to that party for the period up to the date of the merger;

2. An analysis between the parties to the merger of the principal components (as item 1 above) of the profit and loss account and statement of total recognized gains and losses for the previous financial year

3. A statement of the adjustments to consolidated reserves resulting from the merger.

The disclosure requirements for business combinations accounted for as acquisitions include:

- The composition and fair value of the consideration given by the acquiring company and its subsidiary undertakings
- The nature of any deferred or contingent purchase consideration, including, for contingent consideration, the range of possible outcomes and the principal factors that affect the outcome
- A table showing, for each class of assets and liabilities of the acquired entity:
  - (a) The book values, as recorded in the acquired entity's books immediately before the acquisition and before any fair value adjustments:
  - (b) The fair value adjustments, analyzed into:
    - (i) Revaluations
    - (ii) Adjustments to achieve consistency of accounting policies
    - (iii) Any other significant adjustments, giving the reasons for the adjustments
  - (c) The fair values at the date of acquisition.
- The table should include a statement of the amount of purchased goodwill or negative goodwill arising on the acquisition.
- Provisions for reorganization and restructuring costs that are included in the liabilities of the acquired entity, and related asset write-downs, made in the 12 months up to the date of acquisition should be identified separately.
- The profit and loss account or notes to the financial statements of periods following the acquisition should show the costs incurred in those periods in reorganizing, restructuring, and integrating the acquisition. Such costs are those that:
  - (a) Would not have been incurred had the acquisition not taken place
  - (b) Relate to a project identified and controlled by management as part of a reorganization or integration program set up at the time of acquisition or as a direct consequence of an immediate post-acquisition review.
- Movements on provisions or accruals for costs related to an acquisition should be disclosed and analyzed between the amounts used for the specific purpose for which they were created and the amounts released unused.

Special disclosures are required in respect of substantial acquisitions. These are defined for listed companies as Class 1 or Super Class 1 transactions and for other entities as those where the net assets or operating profit of the acquired entity exceed 15% of those of the acquirer or the fair value of the consideration exceeds 15% of the net assets of the acquirer. The required disclosures include the summarized profit and loss account and statement of total recognized gains of the acquired entity for the period from the beginning of the year to the acquisition date. This would include the details of turnover, operating profit, nonoperating exceptional items, profit before tax, tax, minority interests, and extraordinary items. The profit after tax and minority interests for the acquired entity's previous financial year also have to be given.

3.1.6 Fair Values in Acquisition Accounting

FRS 7 sets out the principles that, under the acquisition method of accounting, an acquirer should follow to identify and attribute fair values to the assets and liabilities of an acquired company or business and to determine the cost of acquisition. The fair values ascribed to the identifiable assets and liabilities in aggregate directly affect the amount recognized as purchased goodwill or negative goodwill on an acquisition.

Under FRS 7, the assets and liabilities recognized in the allocation of fair values are those of the acquired entity that existed at the date of acquisition and are measured at fair values that reflect the conditions at the date of the acquisition. Adjustments to restate the assets and liabilities of the acquired entity on to a basis consistent with the acquirer's accounting policies are generally appropriate. However, the FRS states specifically that the following should be treated as post-acquisition items, that is, they cannot be incorporated as fair value adjustments but are reported as part of the post-acquisition financial performance of the acquiring group:

- Changes, such as asset write-downs, that result from the acquirer's own intentions or future actions
- Impairments, or other changes in values, resulting from post-acquisition events
- Provisions for future operating losses
- Provisions for reorganization and integration costs expected to be incurred as a result of the acquisition, whether they relate to the acquired entity or to the acquirer

The rules for determining fair values of individual categories of assets and liabilities of the acquired entity include the following:

- Fixed assets should normally be valued at market values or depreciated replacement cost.
- Stocks and work-in-progress should be valued at the lower of replacement cost and net realizable value. Where long-term contracts are accounted for under SSAP 9, no adjustments to the book values are generally required, except for those that would normally result from assessing the outcome of the contracts.
- Monetary assets and liabilities should be attributed values based on the expected amounts and timing of payments. Adjustments may be required, for example by discounting future cash flows to their present values, where the fair values of long-term monetary items are materially different from their book values because they carry nominal interest at rates significantly different from current market rates.
- Pension surpluses or deficiencies in the acquired entity are identifiable assets or liabilities that should be attributed fair values; in the former case, assets should be recognized only to the extent that they are expected to be realized.
- A separate business of the acquired entity that is to be sold by the acquirer within one year of its acquisition should not be consolidated but should be treated as a single current asset, and its fair value should normally be based on the net sale proceeds obtained, or the estimated net proceeds.

The fair value exercise should be completed, if possible, by the date on which the first post-acquisition financial statements are approved by the directors. If it has not been possible to complete the investigation of fair values by that date, provisional allocations should be made; these should be amended if necessary in the next financial statements with a corresponding adjustment to goodwill. Generally, no further goodwill adjustments should be recognized after the first full financial year after the acquisition.

Amounts of future consideration that are recognized in the cost of acquisition should be reported as part of shareholders' funds where the consideration is to be satisfied by the issue of shares. Otherwise, future consideration should be accounted for as a liability.

Under FRS 7 provisions for costs expected to be incurred after completion of an acquisition for reorganizing acquired companies and integrating them into the acquiring group are not allowed as a fair value adjustment. FRS 7 does this by restricting the definition of identifiable liabilities to those that had been incurred by the acquired company before the acquisition.

Examples of liabilities that would be allowed as fair value adjustments, where they have not previously been booked in the acquired company's accounts, are:

- Provisions for environmental clean-up obligations related to past activities of the acquired company
- Provisions for post-retirement healthcare benefits

3.1.7   Accounting for Goodwill

Under the provisions of the 1986 Act, if goodwill is to be carried forward in the balance sheet, then it should be included under intangible fixed assets and disclosure should be made of the following:

- Cost, accumulated depreciation, and net book value amounts at the beginning and end of the accounting period in each instance
- The amount of goodwill amortized through the profit and loss account for the year

The 1986 Act also provides that financial statements disclose the period over which the amount of goodwill will be written off and the reason for selecting this period.

For accounting periods ending on or after December 23, 1998, purchased goodwill arising from acquisitions is to be treated in accordance with FRS 10, "Goodwill and Intangible Assets," as an asset on the balance sheet. The previous standard on the subject, SSAP 23 is superseded by this FRS. The common and accepted practice of writing off goodwill to reserves immediately on acquisition allowed under SSAP 23 is abolished by FRS 10 for all future goodwill.

Intangible assets acquired with the purchase of a business are subsumed within goodwill but are recognized separately from goodwill if their value can be measured reliably. Intangible assets that have been developed internally may be capitalized only if they have a readily ascertainable market value (i.e. are regularly traded in an active market—which is rare). However, FRS 10 specifically excludes oil and gas exploration and development costs and research and development costs from its scope. Goodwill that has been developed internally should not be recognized. Neither purchased goodwill nor recognized intangible assets may be subsequently revalued, except for any intangibles that have a readily ascertainable market value.

Where goodwill and intangibles are regarded as having limited useful economic lives, they should be amortized to the profit and loss account on a systematic basis over those lives. The useful economic life of purchased goodwill is defined as the period over which the value of the underlying business acquired is expected to exceed the values of its identifiable net assets. There is a rebuttable presumption that the useful economic lives of purchased goodwill and intangibles do not exceed 20 years. An amortization period of more than 20 years may be chosen *only* if:

- The durability of the acquired business or intangible asset can be demonstrated and justifies a longer, or indefinite, useful life; and
- The goodwill or intangible asset is capable of continued measurement, because formal impairment reviews have to be carried out annually.

Where goodwill and intangibles are regarded as having indefinite useful lives they should not be amortized. Earnings would then be charged only if, and when, an impairment is subsequently identified. Nonamortization of goodwill can be adopted only in special circumstances by invoking a "true and fair override" of Company Law, when following the amortization rule would not give a true and fair view.

Where the carrying value of goodwill or an intangible asset has previously been written down to reflect an impairment loss, the loss may be reversed only where it can clearly and demonstrably be attributed to the unforeseen reversal of an external event that caused the original write-down.

Goodwill and intangibles amortized over 20 or fewer years should be reviewed for impairment at the end of the first full financial year after the acquisition and, thereafter, only if there are indications that carrying values may not be recoverable.

Goodwill and intangibles amortized over more than 20 years (or not at all) should be reviewed for impairment at the end of each period by using the forthcoming FRS on impairment of fixed assets and goodwill. In the meantime, the proposals in FRED 15 should be used.

Negative goodwill should be shown on the face of the balance sheet immediately below positive goodwill, with a subtotal of the net amount shown. Negative goodwill should be credited in the profit and loss account in the periods in which the nonmonetary assets of the acquired business are depreciated or sold. If negative goodwill exceeds the fair value of those nonmonetary assets (this would rarely occur in practice), the excess should be credited over the periods expected to be benefited.

The disclosures required by the FRS include:

- The method used to value intangible assets
- The amortization methods and periods and the reasons for choosing those periods (including reasons for rebutting the 20-year presumption)
- The reason and effect of changing an amortization method or period
- Particulars, reasons, and effect where the "true and fair override" is used to avoid amortizing goodwill.

The standard does not require capitalization of goodwill previously written off to reserves as previously permitted by SSAP 23, but companies may reinstate goodwill relating to previous acquisitions if they wish (as a prior year adjustment). They can reinstate either all goodwill or goodwill relating to post December 23, 1989 acquisitions (where the information on earlier acquisitions cannot be obtained), or goodwill eliminated since the adoption of FRS 7. Where goodwill relating to previous acquisitions is reinstated, it should be capitalized at cost less amortization or impairment attributed to previous periods. Where goodwill relating to previous acquisitions remains eliminated against reserves, the goodwill should not be shown as a debit balance on a separate goodwill write-off reserve but should be offset against the profit and loss account or another appropriate reserve. Therefore, companies that carry such negative reserves will have to transfer them to another reserve.

Any impairment loss relating to previously capitalized goodwill and intangibles that is recognized on first implementing the FRS should be charged as an expense in the period, not as a prior year adjustment.

Any previously capitalized intangible assets that do not now meet the recognition criteria (e.g. most internally generated intangibles) set out in FRS 10 are to be written off as a prior year adjustment.

Revalued intangibles not having a readily ascertainable market value are to be restated at cost less amortization or impairment as a prior year adjustment on the introduction of the standard.

3.1.8 Equity Accounting

FRS 9, "Associates and Joint Ventures is effective for accounting periods ending on or after June 23, 1998. FRS 9 supersedes the previous standard on the subject, SSAP 1, "Accounting for Associated Companies."

FRS 9 requires associate companies and joint ventures to be equity accounted in the investor's group financial statements. Among other things, this entails recognition of the investor's share of the associate's profit and net assets.

An associate is defined in the FRS as "an entity (other than a subsidiary) in which another entity (the investor) has a participating interest and over whose operating and financial policies the investor exercises a significant influence."

In FRS 9, the presumption that an interest of 20% or more automatically results in significant influence is rebutted in certain circumstances, but where this is so a note must explain the circumstances. Some associates under SSAP 1 will not qualify as such under FRS 9, and a prior year adjustment will be needed on the FRS's implementation.

The definition of an associate still hinges on "significant influence," which, under FRS 9, means that the investor must influence the direction of its investee by *active* involvement in the financial and operating decisions of its investee.

The FRS deals with joint ventures (JVs) that are entities; joint arrangements that are not entities; and contractual arrangements with the form but not the substance of a JV. A JV is defined as an interest in an entity held on a long-term basis and that, as a result of a contractual arrangement, is jointly controlled by the reporting entity and other venturers.

Unincorporated JV entities carrying on a trade or business of their own must be equity accounted under the FRS, and if they were previously proportionally consolidated a prior year adjustment is required to be made on the implementation of the standard.

The standard lays down significant disclosure requirements. For all the disclosures that follow, the investor's share in JVs must be given separately and before that of its share in associates.

Under FRS 9, disclosure in the investor's consolidated profit and loss account should include:

- The investor's share of turnover for JVs (equivalent disclosure for associates is optional). This has to be shown in such a way that the group turnover excluding associates and JVs is also disclosed as required by Company (Amendment) Act of 1986. In the segmental analysis, the JVs' turnover (and associates' where given) should be distinguished from that of the group.
- The share of operating results *immediately* after the group operating result. This is a change on a growing practice of including the results of associates as a component in arriving at operating profit.
- Any amortization or write-down of goodwill arising on the acquisition immediately after operating profit also.
- The share of super exceptional items (FRS 3 paragraph 20 items) and interest shown separately from the amounts of the group.

The investor's consolidated statement of total recognized gains and losses (STRGL) should include the share of results for each heading. These disclosures may be given on the face of the STRGL or in the notes.

The investor's consolidated balance sheet should include as fixed asset investments the investor's share of the investee's net assets. For JVs the share of gross assets and gross liabilities underlying the net equity amount should be given on the face of the balance sheet (gross equity method).

In the cash flow statement, dividends received should be shown separately between operating activities and returns on investments and servicing of finance. Cash received from or paid to associates or JVs should be shown separately.

In the investor's individual accounts, associates, and JVs should be included as fixed asset investments and shown either at cost less amounts written off or at valuation.

A participant in a JV structure, used only as a framework within which each participant carries on its own business (for example, the use of an oil pipeline or other shared facilities) should account directly for its part of the assets, liabilities, and cash flows held within that framework. Participants in joint arrangements should account for their own assets, liabilities, and cash flows in accordance with the terms of the agreement.

In applying the equity method, FRS 9 requires that the FRS 2 principles for consolidation should be used. Where profits or losses arise on transactions between the investor and investee and are included in the carrying amount of assets, the investor's share should be eliminated.

FRS 9 requires investors to continue equity accounting even where this results in an interest in net liabilities, unless the investor is irreversibly committed (e.g. because of a public statement of intent) to withdrawing from its investment. In this regard FRS 9 is stricter than SSAP 1.

Where the investor does not prepare consolidated accounts, FRS 9 requires that it should prepare a separate set of pro forma accounts, including the equity accounted figures, or show the relevant amounts as additional information to its individual accounts. Entities that are exempt from preparing consolidated accounts are not required to give this additional information.

FRS 9 requires investment funds, such as venture capitalists and investment trusts, to include all investments that are held as part of their investment portfolio (whether or not they have significant influence or joint control) at cost or market value.

In addition FRS 9 has a number of other requirements, including:

- Any information material to an understanding of the investor's accounts is to be disclosed, for instance share of contingent liabilities and capital commitments.
- The extent of any restrictions on the ability of the investee to distribute its reserves to the investor must be shown.
- Related party transactions balances disclosed under FRS 8 are to be analyzed between amounts relating to loans and amounts relating to trading balances.

Additional disclosures arise where the investor's share in its associates in aggregate (or in its JVs in aggregate) exceeds more than 15%, or individually more than 25%, of any of the following consolidated figures (excluding associates and JVs): gross assets; gross liabilities; turnover; or operating results (on a three-year average).

3.2 Foreign Currency Translation

Paragraph 44 of Part IV to the Schedule to the Companies Act 1986 requires that the basis on which amounts denominated into foreign currencies have been translated into Irish currency for the purposes of inclusion in a company's financial statements should be disclosed. Paragraph 13 of the Schedule to the 1992 Group Accounts Regulations requires that the basis on which various items are translated is stated in the financial statements.

The provisions of SSAP 20—which sets out the basis of accounting for foreign currency translation—govern the manner in which foreign currency denominated amounts are translated for the purposes of preparing an entity's financial statements. The provisions of this SSAP deal with accounting considerations referable to both consolidated financial statements and financial statements of individual companies.

3.2.1 Consolidated Financial Statements

The provisions of SSAP 20 in regard to preparing consolidated financial statements that include a foreign subsidiary (or an associated company or branch) may be summarized as follows:

- Normally either the closing rate or the net investment method is used for translating the foreign entity's financial statements for consolidation purposes.
- Exchange differences arising on the translation of the opening net investment at the closing exchange rate should be accounted for as a movement on reserves.
- Profit and loss account items should be translated at either the closing rate or at the average rate for the accounting period. If the average rate is used, the difference between the profit and loss account translated at the average rate and at the closing rate should be accounted for as a movement on reserves.
- Balance sheet items should be translated at the closing rate.

The SSAP permits that the temporal rate method may be used where a business's trade is more dependent on the investing companies' economic environment than that of its own reporting currency.

Also, where foreign currency borrowings have been used to finance a group's equity investment in a foreign enterprise, exchange gains or losses on those borrowings may be accounted for through reserves and offset against exchange differences arising on the retranslation of net investment. If this approach is to be applied, however, the relationship between the investing company and the foreign enterprise must justify the use of the closing rate method.

3.2.2 Individual Companies

The SSAP's provisions in regard to preparing the financial statements of individual companies may be summarized as follows:

- All items (assets, liabilities, revenues, or costs) denominated in a foreign currency should be translated at the rate of exchange applicable at the date on which the transaction took place. An average rate is acceptable in lieu of this approach if rates do not fluctuate significantly. If a rate for a transaction is fixed (such as by contracting for a specific rate or by covering the rate by way of a forward contract), then the fixed rate may be used.
- Monetary assets and liabilities denominated in foreign currencies at the balance sheet date should be translated by using the closing rate or, alternatively, at the rate that is fixed contractually for these items. Normally, no subsequent translations should be made once nonmonetary assets have been translated and recorded.
- Exchange differences arising on settled transactions and on unsettled short-term monetary items should be reported as part of the results of the period. If they result from transactions that are deemed to be extraordinary (or exceptional), then they should be reported as part of the extraordinary (or exceptional) item.
- Exchange differences arising on unsettled long-term monetary items should also be recognized in the profit and loss account. In exceptional cases, however, where there are doubts about the convertibility or marketability of the currency in question, then it will be necessary to consider, on the grounds of prudence, whether the amount of the gain (or the amount by which exchange gains exceed past exchange losses on the same items) should be restricted.
- The closing rate method may be used to translate the value of an equity investment where foreign currency amounts have been used to finance or hedge the amount of the investment, provided the following conditions apply:

  —Exchange differences arising from the borrowings may be offset only to the extent of exchange differences arising from the equity investment in any accounting period.

—The foreign currency borrowings used for offset purposes should not exceed the total amount of cash that the equity investment or investments are expected to generate;

—The accounting treatment adopted should be applied consistently

If the above circumstances apply, then the exchange difference on the borrowing should be taken directly to reserves and offset, as a reserve movement, against any exchange difference arising on the translation of the amount of the equity investment.

SSAP 20 requires the following disclosures in financial statements:

- The methods used in translating the financial statements of foreign enterprises and treatment accorded to exchange differences

- The net amount of exchange gains and losses on foreign currency borrowings less deposits identifying separately the amount offset in reserves and the net amount accounted for in the profit and loss account

- The net movement on reserves arising from exchange differences

3.3 Capital and Reserves

The 1986 act requires disclosure of the amounts of a company's authorized and issued share capital in its financial statements, together with supporting details of that share capital. For redeemable shares, the 1986 act requires that details be provided regarding the basis and timing of the redemption process. Financial Reporting Standard 4 (Capital Instruments) [FRS4] specifies additional disclosure requirements regarding shares, in particular regarding the terms and conditions applicable to them.

The 1990 act permits companies to repurchase their own shares, provided the company's articles of association so permit. Any repurchase must be from distributable profits or from the proceeds of an issue of new shares.

The 1963 and 1986 acts, *inter alia*, require that reserves be treated in the following manner:

1. Retained Profits—Retained profits should be accumulated and identified as the balance on the profit and loss account in the company's

balance sheet. These profits are normally available for distribution by way of dividend.

2. Revaluation Reserves—If a surplus (or deficit) arises from a revaluation of the book value of fixed assets, then it should be separately identified in the company's balance sheet as a "revaluation reserve." Such reserves, being unrealized in nature, are not available for distribution by way of dividend.

3. Share Premium Account—If a company issues shares at a premium over their nominal value, then the amount of that premium must be separately identified in the company's balance sheet. It is permitted to write off against this premium:

   —Preliminary expenses incurred in incorporating the company

   —Expenses, commissions, or discounts incurred in connection with the issue of the shares (or debentures)

   —Any premium arising on the redemption of preference shares

All movements on reserves should be separately identified in the company's financial statements over opening and closing balances and transfers to or from other reserves.

As a general rule, realized profits or surpluses (net of unrealized losses) may be distributed by way of dividend, whereas unrealized profits or surpluses may not be so distributed.

3.4 Liabilities and Provisions

The balance sheet formats specified in the 1986 act require that creditors be separately quantified and identified in the balance sheet by reference to:

- Creditors that are in respect of amounts due within one year of the balance sheet date, and
- Creditors that are in respect of amounts due after more than one year from the balance sheet date.

Amounts of creditors under each of the above headings must be analyzed and disclosed in the company's balance sheet or related notes over the following headings:

- Debenture loans

- Bank loans and overdrafts
- Payments received on account
- Trade creditors
- Bills of exchange payable
- Amounts owed to group companies
- Amounts owed to related companies
- Other creditors, including tax and social welfare
- Accruals and deferred income

For all items included under the heading "Creditors" in the balance sheet, the 1986 act requires that the following information be disclosed:

- The aggregate amount of items included in creditors that are repayable other than by installments after 5 years from the balance sheet date
- The aggregate amount of items in creditors repayable by installments after 5 years from the balance sheet date
- The amounts of debts that have been secured and the nature of the security given
- The fact that any charges exist on the company's assets to secure the debts of the other parties

FRS4 requires that the 1986 act's disclosure requirements for analysis of maturity of debt be expanded to disclose (in addition to the above) amounts falling due between 2 and 5 years from the balance sheet date.

3.4.1 Provisions for Liabilities and Charges

In addition to the creditors' amounts listed above, the 1986 act requires separate disclosure in a company's balance sheet (under the heading "Provisions for Liabilities and Charges") of the following items:

- Pensions and similar obligations
- Taxation, including deferred taxation
- Other provisions

3.4.2 Contingent Liabilities

The 1986 act also requires that the nature and amount of any contingent liabilities that have not been provided for be disclosed in a company's balance sheet. If security has been given for such a liability, this should also be disclosed.

3.4.3 Commitments

The 1986 act requires the following disclosures of commitments entered into by a company:

- Capital Commitments—Amounts contracted for but not provided for and the total amount of capital expenditure authorized but not contracted for must be stated.
- Pension Commitments—Particulars of the amounts of pension commitments provided for and not provided for must be disclosed.
- Other Financial Commitments—Particulars of any other financial commitments that have not been provided for and are relevant to assessing a company's state of affairs must be disclosed.

3.5 Off Balance Sheet Finance

FRS 5, "Reporting the Substance of Transactions," which deals with off balance sheet finance was published on April 14, 1994 and effective for accounting periods ending on or after September 22, 1994. Its provisions are complex and concern rules for the recognition, derecognition, and offset of assets and liabilities. The standard contains application notes that give guidance on how the standard applies in the following areas:

- Consignment stock
- Sale and repurchase agreements
- Factoring of debts
- Securitized assets
- Loan transfers

The application notes describe the principal features of the transaction, then discuss how to analyze the transaction under the terms of the FRS, and finally describe the required accounting treatment. Each application note includes a table that summarizes the salient features of the transactions that will determine whether they should stay fully on the balance sheet, whether a linked presentation is appropriate, or whether they can be derecognized or partially derecognized.

While the standard applies to all financial statements intended to give a true and fair view, the following matters are excluded from its scope:

- Forward contracts and futures contracts
- Foreign exchange and interest rate swaps
- Contracts in which a net amount will be paid or received on the basis of the movement in a price or an index (sometimes referred to as "contracts for differences")
- Expenditure commitments (such as purchase commitments) and orders placed, until the earlier of delivery or payment
- Employment contracts

FRS 5 is written in very broad terms and, accordingly, where FRS 5 is being applied to a matter covered by more specific rules or legislation, the more specific rules apply. For example, in a sale and leaseback, the specific accounting rules set out in SSAP 21 apply. However, the rules in FRS 5 are used to determine whether the commercial substance of the transaction taken as a whole is that of a leaseback in the first instance and if it is, whether the nature of the lease is that of an operating lease or a finance lease.

Under FRS 5, the first step in determining the substance of a transaction is to identify whether it gives rise to new assets or liabilities for the entity or whether or not it has increased or decreased the entity's existing assets or liabilities. The FRS defines assets and liabilities as follows:

> Assets: Rights or other access to future economic benefits controlled by an entity as a result of past transactions or events.

> Liabilities: An entity's obligations to transfer economic benefits as a result of past transactions or events.

Although the definitions only mention benefits they encompass also risks, as risk is defined to include both the potential gain and the exposure to loss.

Once it has been established that an asset or liability has been identified, the next step is to determine whether it qualifies for recognition. The FRS sets out the following two general recognition criteria:

- There is sufficient evidence of the item (including, where appropriate, evidence that a future inflow or outflow of benefit will occur), and
- The asset or liability can be measured at a monetary amount with sufficient reliability.

Assets and liabilities should not generally be offset, but they can be aggregated where they do not constitute separate assets and liabilities. In order to do this, the FRS specifies the following conditions:

- The reporting entity and another party owe each other determinable monetary amounts, denominated either in the same currency, or in different but freely convertible currencies.
- The reporting entity has the ability to insist on a net settlement.
- The reporting entity's ability to insist on a net settlement is assured beyond doubt and would survive the insolvency of the other party.

Quasi-subsidiaries are defined as follows:

> A quasi-subsidiary of a reporting entity is a company, trust, partnership or other vehicle that, though not fulfilling the definition of a subsidiary, is directly or indirectly controlled by the reporting entity and gives rise to benefits for that entity that are in substance no different from those that would arise were the vehicle a subsidiary.

Control in this context means the ability to direct the financial and operating policies of the entity with a view to gaining benefit from its activities. The FRS proposes that the assets, liabilities, profits, losses, and cash flows of quasi-subsidiaries should be included in the group financial statements in the same way as if it were a subsidiary. Inclusion of a quasi-subsidiary in a group's consolidated financial statements does not represent a departure from the provisions of the Group Account Regulations, but merely the provision of additional information in order to give a true and fair view.

3.6 Property, Plant, and Equipment

The Companies Act of 1986 requires that fixed assets comprising property, plant, and equipment be disclosed in a company's balance sheet under the heading "Tangible Fixed Assets" at the net book value (which is cost or valuation less accumulated depreciation) of those assets. Details of such assets must be analyzed over the headings:

- Land and buildings
- Plant and machinery
- Fixtures, fittings, tools, and equipment
- Payments on account and assets in the course of construction

All movements in cost or valuation of these assets during the year (opening, closing balances, additions, and disposals) and also the amount of depreciation of these assets must also be disclosed.

3.6.1 Accounting for Fixed Assets

The rules for accounting for cost or valuation or depreciation of the assets may be summarized as follows:

1. Cost may be either the purchase price or the production cost of the fixed asset. The purchase price of an asset will be the actual price paid for the asset, and the amount may be increased by any expenses incurred in acquiring the asset. The production cost of the asset will comprise the cost of the raw materials and consumables used in producing the asset, together with a reasonable proportion of the costs indirectly incurred in the production of the asset. Interest on capital relative to the financing of the production of the asset may be included in the production of the asset, but if it is, the amount included must be disclosed in a note to the accounts.

2. The value of a tangible fixed asset may be the market value of a fixed asset as of the date of its valuation or the current cost of the asset. Any surplus or deficit arising from the revaluation of a fixed asset must be transferred to a revaluation reserve, which must be separately disclosed in the company's balance sheet. (It should be noted that while it is permitted to reduce the balance on the revalu-

ation reserve—if, in the opinion of the directors, the amount is no longer necessary for the accounting policies followed by the company—the amount may be transferred to the profit and loss account only if it represents realized profit). The application of alternative accounting rules to investments is discussed in Section 3.9, and the principles set out there are also applicable where fixed assets are included in a balance sheet at a valuation.

3.   Depreciation of a fixed asset must be calculated on a basis that will write off the purchase price or production cost of the asset, less the amount of any estimated residual value, over the period of the asset's useful economic life. If the fixed asset is included on the basis of a valuation, then the amount of the valuation will form the basis for the depreciation charge rather than the purchase price or production cost of that asset.

3.6.2 Government Grants

In accordance with the provisions of SSAP 4, government grants received in respect of fixed assets acquired by a company must be credited to the profit and loss account over the expected useful life of the asset to which the grant relates. This accounting requirement may be implemented by one of the following methods:

- Carrying the amount of the grant as a deferred credit in the balance sheet and amortizing the amount thereof annually to the profit and loss account. The net book amount of this credit at any time would be the total amount of the grant received less the amount of accumulated amortization amounts transferred to the profit and loss account.
- If the deferred credit approach is adopted, the net credit amount deferred should be disclosed separately in the balance sheet, but it should not be included as part of shareholders' funds.
- Alternatively, the amount of the purchase price or production cost of the fixed asset should be reduced by the amount of the capital grant and the net resulting cost amount depreciated over the asset's useful economic life.

The amended version of SSAP No. 4 (issued in July 1990) states that on the basis of legal advice received, the option to deduct government grants from the purchase price (or production cost) of fixed assets is not available to companies governed by the 1986 act.

Any contingency to repay grants should be disclosed in the company's accounts.

3.6.3 *Investment Properties*

SSAP 19 ("Accounting for Investment Properties") defines an investment property as a completed or developed property that is "held for its investment potential" and whose rental income is negotiated on an arm's-length basis. Exceptions to this definition are owner-occupied properties, with the concept of owner occupied having groupwide application in groups of companies.

The provisions of SSAP 19 for accounting for such properties may be summarized as follows:

- Investment properties should be included in the balance sheet at their open market value and should not be depreciated (leasehold properties with 20 years or less to run are an exception and should be depreciated over the remaining unexpired term of the lease).

- Where investment properties make up a significant part of a company's total assets, the properties should be valued annually, but every 5 years the valuation should be completed by an external valuer.

- Changes in the value of the portfolio of investment properties should be accounted for through an investment revaluation reserve.

- The carrying value of the investment properties and the investment revaluation reserve should be displayed prominently in the accounts, together with either the name of or qualifications of those who completed the valuation of the properties and the basis of the valuation. If the person is an employee of the company, this fact should also be disclosed.

Paragraph 6 of the schedule to the 1986 act requires that any fixed asset that has a useful economic life must be depreciated over the term of that life. However, the act also imposes an overriding requirement that financial statements shall give a true and fair view of results and balance sheet position, and this consideration permits the application of the provisions of

SSAP 19. It should be noted that the 1986 act requires details of this departure from the act and the reasons therefor to be disclosed in the company's financial statements.

3.6.4   *Deferred Taxation*

Writing down the value of fixed assets for tax purposes is calculated by reference to the rates and bases permitted by the Revenue Commissioners for tax computation purposes. The rates used have varied over time, and the basis on which they are calculated is (mainly) the diminishing balance basis. In these circumstances it is extremely unlikely that a company's depreciation rates and bases of calculation will produce a depreciation charge that equates with the amount of capital allowances permitted for tax computation purposes.

In the more likely event of a value difference materializing between the net book value of fixed assets and their corresponding written down value for tax purposes, consideration will have to be given to the need for providing for deferred taxation in respect of the amount of the difference arising.

There is no need to accelerate depreciation write-downs in the financial statements in excess of the normal depreciation charge in order to obtain an entitlement to write-offs for tax purposes.

Other significant timing differences can arise from provisions made in the financial statements that only become deductible for tax purposes when the expenditure (or event) is actually incurred.

3.7 Assets Whose Services Are Acquired by Means of Leases

Accounting for assets acquired by means of leases in the Republic of Ireland—whether they are formal leases or hire purchase contracts—is based on the principles laid down in SSAP 21, "Accounting for Leases and Hire Purchase Contracts." Under the provisions of this SSAP, leases are categorized into finance leases and operating leases, as follows:

- A finance lease is a lease in which the lessee has substantially all the risks and rewards associated with the ownership of the asset but not the legal title (substantial in this context is normally 90% or more of the fair value of the leased asset).

- An operating lease is a lease other than a finance lease but usually involves the lessee paying for the rental of an asset for a period that is substantially less than its useful economic life, while the lessor retains most of the risks and rewards of ownership.

The accounting provisions of SSAP 21 require that assets acquired under finance lease contracts be accounted for in the lessee's financial statements, usually at the cost of the asset acquired with the lessee's financing obligations in respect of that asset being included as a liability in those financial statements. The accounting rules for these leases (in the lessee's books) may be summarized as follows:

- The fixed asset acquired should be included in the lessee's balance sheet at fair value (usually cost), which amount should be depreciated over the shorter of the term of the lease or the asset's useful life. If the financing contract is a hire purchase contract, however, then the asset should be depreciated over its useful life.
- A liability should be recorded for the present value of the minimum lease payments under the terms of the financing lease, which amount is derived by discounting these payments by the interest rate implicit in the lease. Subsequent rental payments should be analyzed between the amount required to reduce the lease obligation (which should be accounted for against that liability) and the amount of the finance charge (which should be charged to the profit and loss account).

For assets acquired under *finance leases* the following disclosures are required:

- The gross value amounts of assets held under finance leases, together with related accumulated depreciation should be disclosed over each major class of asset, together with the amount of the current period depreciation charge applicable to those assets (which should also be analyzed by major class of asset). Alternatively, if owned and leased fixed assets are merged in the financial statements, then the net book value of the leased assets and the current period depreciation charge relevant to them should be disclosed.
- Finance lease obligations (net of finance charges) should be separately disclosed from other obligations and liabilities. The total amount

involved should be analyzed over the amount payable in the year
following the balance sheet date, the amount payable in the 2nd to
5th year following and the amount payable after 5 years from the
balance sheet date.

- The total amount of the finance charges allocated to the period
  covered by the financial statements should be disclosed.
- The amounts of any finance lease commitments entered into at the
  balance sheet date but whose inception occurred after the year end.
- The accounting policy adopted should be disclosed.

For assets acquired under *operating leases* the following disclosures are
required:

- Total operating lease rentals charged to the profit and loss account for
  the period should be disclosed, analyzed over payments related to
  hire of plant and machinery and for other operating leases.
- Payment commitments under the terms of the operating leases should
  be disclosed and analyzed over the following year's payment, the
  amounts to be paid over years 2 to 5 after the balance sheet date and
  amounts payable after 5 years from the balance sheet date. All of
  these amounts should be analyzed between payments applicable to
  land and buildings and payments under other operating leases;
- The accounting policy adopted in regard to such leases.

3.8   Oil, Gas, and Other Mineral Resources

There are no specific provisions in Irish Company Law regarding the
manner of accounting for oil, gas, and other mineral exploration and
development activities. Guidance on the appropriate approach to be adopted
for oil and gas exploration and development activities is set out in two
SORPs published by the Oil Industry Accounting Committee and franked
by ASC. The Accounting Standards Board (ASB) has not as yet issued
guidance on accounting for mineral exploration and development costs.

The recommended practice required by the SORP for accounting for oil
and gas exploration and development activities should either be the full
cost or successful efforts/methods as set out in the SORP. Whichever
method is adopted should be applied consistently by all companies within
a Group.

3.8.1 Full Cost Accounting

Full cost accounting requires that:

- All costs incurred in exploration and development of oil and gas resources should be capitalized
- All such capitalized expenditures should be recorded within geographic cost pools (which should not normally be smaller in size than one country).
- The basis on which cost pools are established should be disclosed as an accounting policy.
- All expenditure carried forward within each pool should be depreciated on a unit-of-production basis by reference to quantities.
- A ceiling test should be carried out at the balance sheet date to determine whether the net book values of the capitalized costs are recoverable against anticipated future net revenues.
- Proceeds from the full or partial disposal of a property should be credited to the relevant cost pool
- Full cost pools expenditures should be classified in the balance sheet as "tangible assets," whereas any expenditures related to exploration activities but held outside full cost pools should be classified as "intangible assets—exploration expenditure."

3.8.2 Successful Efforts Accounting

The successful efforts approach to accounting for such expenditures requires that:

- While exploration expenses should be capitalized in the first instance, pending determination, they should be written off if commercial reserves are not established.
- General expenditures should be capitalized only where they relate to activities for which costs are also being capitalized.
- Capitalized expenditures should be written off on a unit of production basis by reference to quantities.
- Ceiling tests should be carried out at the balance sheet date to assess whether the net book value of the capitalized costs are recoverable against future net revenues.

- Proceeds from the full or partial disposal of a property should be credited either to the relevant cost center or capitalized cost as appropriate.
- Pending evaluation, exploration expenditures should be classified as "intangible assets—exploration expenditure" and reclassified as "tangible assets" when the existence of commercial reserves is established.

The SORP dealing with disclosures about oil and gas exploration and production activities requires the following matters to be disclosed relative to such activity:

- The method of accounting for oil and gas activities, including the accounting policies applied in respect of accounting for preproduction costs, amortization of capitalized costs, ceiling tests, decommissioning costs, deferred taxation, turnover, and royalties
- The aggregate amount of capitalized costs and related depreciation or amortization analyzed by reference to proven and unproven properties and also by geographic areas
- Preproduction costs and the results of operations of exploration and development activities, in total and by geographic area
- The net quantities of a company's interest in proved developed and undeveloped reserves as of the beginning and end of each accounting period and by geographic area

3.9 Intangible Assets

The schedule to the 1986 act requires that intangible assets be included in a company's balance sheet if either they were acquired for valuable consideration (and are not required to be shown as goodwill; see below) or the assets involved were created by the company itself. Intangible assets must be disclosed over the headings as prescribed in the 1986 act:

- Development costs
- Concessions, patents, licenses, trademarks, and similar rights and assets
- Goodwill

- Payments on account

The 1986 act requires that an amount may be included under the heading "Development Costs" only in special circumstances (which are not specified in the act), in which case the period of write-off of these costs, and the reasons for capitalizing them, must be disclosed. It should be noted that research costs are not included in the list of items to be disclosed, although the information that is required to be disclosed to supplement the profit and loss account includes the amount of any expenditure on research and development in the financial year and the amount committed for R&D for future years (Section 43(4) of the schedule to the 1986 act). If the directors conclude that this information would be prejudicial to the interests of the company, however, then it need not be disclosed, but the fact that it has not been disclosed must be stated. It should also be noted that Section 13(d) of the 1986 act requires that the directors' report contain information concerning the company's research and development activities (and those of its subsidiaries, if applicable).

Goodwill amounts may be included only to the extent that the goodwill is acquired for valuable consideration.

Intangible assets must be accounted for and depreciated in the same manner as specified for tangible fixed assets. Hence, these assets may be accounted for at cost (purchase price or production cost less any estimated residual value) or at current cost (with the exception of goodwill), and they must be depreciated in such a manner as to write off the amount of cost over its useful life. All movements on such assets during the year must be disclosed regarding cost or valuation and depreciation over the relevant component headings.

SSAP 13 requires that R&D expenditures meet the following criteria if they are to be capitalized and written off over future accounting periods:

- The R&D project must be a clearly defined project, and the expenditure involved must be separately identifiable.
- The technical feasibility and commercial viability of the project must be reasonably certain.
- Any additional development costs to be incurred must be aggregated with costs incurred to date and production and selling costs, the total of which must reasonably be expected to be covered by related future revenues.

- Adequate resources exist or are reasonably expected to be available to complete the project.

The accounting policy adopted for accounting for R&D costs must be disclosed, together with details of movements on the R&D account.

3.10 Participations (Equity Investments in Other Companies)

The balance sheet formats provided for in the 1986 act require that equity investments in subsidiary or associated companies shall be disclosed in a company's balance sheet under the heading "financial assets" in the fixed assets segment of the balance sheet or under "investments" in current assets, depending on the nature of the investment involved.

Such investments are accounted for as follows:

1. The cost of the investments may be recorded by reference to historical cost accounting rules or by reference to alternative rules provided for under the 1986 act.

2. Cost, in a historical cost context, represents the actual price paid for the investment, together with any expenses incurred incidental to its acquisition.

3. Under the alternative accounting rules, such investments may be included at a market value determined as of the date of the last valuation, or at a value that the directors deem to be appropriate in the circumstances of the company. (If the latter approach is used, then the method of valuation adopted and the reasons for adopting it must be disclosed). The investments may also be included at their current cost.

4. If there has been a diminution in the value of the investment, a provision may be made in respect of the amount of the diminution. If, however, the diminution is expected to be permanent, then a provision must be made in respect of that diminution. Any such provision must be charged to the profit and loss account and disclosed in the company's accounts.

5. Where an investment is held as a current asset, the value of the investment must be written down to its net realizable value if there

has been a reduction in the value of the investment below its acquisition price. On the other hand, if the reasons for which the write-down occurred no longer apply, then the write-down provision may be written back to the extent that it is no longer necessary.

6. If a surplus arises as a result of a valuation of an investment, it must be taken to a revaluation reserve in the company's balance sheet. Amounts may be transferred to the profit and loss account from the revaluation reserve only if they represent realized profit. It will be necessary to charge the profit and loss account with the amount by which a deficit on a revaluation exceeds the amount of any surpluses in the revaluation account.

7. The 1986 act requires disclosures of:

— Any movements in amounts of investments held as fixed assets
— The amounts of investments in listed securities analyzed over investments listed on a recognized stock exchange and other investments
— The market value of the listed investments

3.11 Stocks/Inventories

Paragraphs 10 and 11 of the schedule to the 1986 act require that current assets—and thereby stocks/inventories—be valued at the lower of purchase price (or production cost) or net realizable value. Paragraph 14 of the schedule defines the purchase price of an asset as being the actual price paid for the assets, together with any expenses incidental to its acquisition. The production cost of an asset is defined as the purchase price of the raw materials and consumables used in producing the asset, together with the amount of the costs incurred in producing the asset and a reasonable proportion of indirect overheads and interest on capital to the extent that these items relate to the period of production of the asset. Distribution costs may not be included in these calculations.

The purchase price or production cost of inventories may be determined by reference to any of the following methods:

- First in, first out (FIFO)
- The weighted average price
- Any other method similar to the FIFO and weighted average method

In addition to the above, paragraph 19(5) of the schedule to the Companies Act of 1986 permits stocks to be included in the balance sheet at current cost.

It will be noted that the above listing does not include the last in, first out (LIFO) stock valuation method or the base stock method of valuation.

Stocks must be disclosed on the face of the company's balance sheet and must be analyzed over the following:

- Raw materials and consumables
- Work-in-progress
- Finished goods and goods for resale
- Payments on account

Paragraph 15(4) of the schedule to the 1986 act provides that if the purchase price or production cost of stocks in the company's balance sheet materially differs from the replacement cost of these assets, then the difference will be disclosed in the company's financial statements.

3.11.1 Long-Term Contracts

With regard to the issue of accounting for long-term contracts (which are defined as contracts that usually exceed a period of one year and that are for the design, manufacture, and construction of a single substantial asset or for the provision of a service), SSAP 9 requires that:

- Where the outcome of a contract can be determined with reasonable certainty, the attributable profit should be calculated on a prudent basis and reflected in the company's financial statements, as should the amount of related turnover.
- The amount by which recorded turnover exceeds the amounts of payment on account should be described as "amounts recoverable on contracts" and separately disclosed in the amount of total debtors.
- The balance of payments on account—that is, the excess amount remaining having matched the payments on account with turnover and offset against long-term contract balances—should be described as "payments on account" and separately disclosed within creditors.
- There should be separate disclosure within the amount of stocks/ inventories in the balance sheet of the costs that have been incurred

in long-term contracts, net of amounts transferred to cost of sales and after deducting foreseeable losses and payments on account not matched with turnover. The amount determined on this basis should be described as "long-term contract balances" within the amount of stocks. There should also be separate disclosures of the amounts of net cost less foreseeable losses and applicable payments on account.

- If the provision or accrual for foreseeable losses exceeds the costs incurred (after transfers to cost of sales), the excess amount should be included in the provisions for either liabilities and charges or creditors, as appropriate.

3.11.2 Accounting Policy

The accounting policies that have been used to determine the amounts of cost and net realizable value of stocks should be disclosed. In the case of long-term contracts, the accounting policies disclosed should describe the bases adopted for determining turnover, attributable profit, and foreseeable losses.

3.12 Taxation

3.12.1 Profit and Loss Account Disclosures Required

Paragraph 40 of the schedule to the 1986 act requires that companies disclose the following in regard to taxation charges in their financial statements:

1. The basis on which the tax charge on its profits is computed, whether the tax charge consists of corporation tax, income tax, or any other tax on the company's profits and whether the amount is payable within or outside the State

2. Particulars of any special circumstances that affect the tax liability arising on the company's profits, income, or capital gains, whether for the current year or for succeeding financial years

3. The amount of the charge for corporation tax, income tax, and other taxation on profits or capital gains, so far as charged to revenue, including tax payable outside the State on profits (distinguishing where practicable between corporation tax and other taxation)

4. The tax relative to the profit or loss on ordinary activities and the tax relative to any extraordinary profits or losses earned by the company

In addition to the above, FRS3 requires that the tax applicable to profits or losses arising on sale or termination of an operation, costs of a fundamental restructuring or reorganization, and profits or losses on disposal of fixed assets should be attributed to these items in the note to the financial statements showing the make-up of the tax charge.

The tax charge on the results of the ordinary activities of the business could, among other things, involve disclosure of the following components:

1. Rate of corporation tax
2. Corporation tax charge
3. Capital gains tax
4. Income tax
5. Any other tax on profits
6. Tax attributable to franked investment income
7. Irrecoverable advance corporation tax (ACT)
8. Overseas taxation, relieved and unrelieved (distinguishing corporation tax and other taxes)
9. Deferred taxation (including any adjustments arising from changes in tax rates and allowances)

In the rare circumstances of an extraordinary item, the tax charge arising on any extraordinary profit or loss should be separately disclosed, usually by means of a footnote disclosure having netted off the charge against the amount of the extraordinary item on the face of the profit and loss account.

3.12.2 Balance Sheet Disclosures

The 1986 act requires that any provision for taxation other than deferred taxation be disclosed. Accordingly, the company's balance sheet should disclose details of amounts due at its balance sheet date in respect of corporation tax, income tax, capital gains tax, value added tax, social welfare, and any other tax.

Notwithstanding the comment in paragraph 33 of the schedule to the 1986 act, implying that deferred taxation may not have to be disclosed, it should be remembered that SSAP 15 requires a disclosure of the deferred taxation balance and analysis of its major components. Further, the balance sheet formats required under the 1986 act require that the amount of deferred taxation be included under the heading "Taxation" in the section of the balance sheet dealing with "Provisions for Liabilities and Charges."

3.12.3 *Deferred Taxation*

Deferred taxation—which is the tax attributable to timing differences between the company's reported results and its results as computed for tax purposes—is computed for Irish companies' financial statements under the provisions of SSAP 15 by the liability method, which requires the deferred tax provision to be calculated at the rate at which it is estimated the eventual tax liability will actually be paid (see also Section 3.5.4). SSAP 15 also provides that:

- A deferred tax provision (or asset) should not be accounted for where it is probable that a liability (or asset) will not crystallize.
- The amount of any unprovided deferred taxation should be disclosed in a note to the financial statements, as should the amount of the deferred tax balance and its major components (for both the current period and the cumulative amount) and any transfers to and from the deferred tax balance.

3.13 Pensions

Paragraph 36(4) of the schedule to the 1986 act requires that particulars of a company's pension commitments be disclosed in its balance sheet either by way of analysis of the total provision or by way of separate disclosure if no provision has been made for the commitment. Separate disclosure is also required of a pension commitment that relates wholly or partly to pensions payable to the company's past directors.

In addition to the above, paragraph 36(5) of the schedule requires disclosure of the following information regarding a company's pension scheme:

- The nature of every pension scheme operated by the company, indicating whether or not each scheme is a defined benefit or a defined contribution scheme
- Whether each scheme is externally funded or internally financed
- Whether professional actuarial advice is obtained in respect of pension costs and liabilities and, if so, the date of the most recent relevant actuarial valuation
- Whether (and where) any such actuarial valuation is available for public inspection

The 1986 act also requires that the profit and loss account disclose the amount of pension costs incurred in respect of the company's employees during the financial year. The Companies Act of 1963 requires disclosure of the total amount of directors' and past directors' pensions, other than pensions provided under a scheme in which contributions are substantially adequate for the maintenance of the scheme. In addition, the 1963 act requires disclosure of contributions paid in respect of directors' pension schemes as a separate item within the disclosure of directors ' emoluments.

In addition to the above, Statement of Standard Accounting Practice 24 (Accounting for Pension Costs) (SSAP 24) sets out additional disclosure requirements relative to pension costs and pension schemes.

3.14 Related Party Transactions

Financial Reporting Standard 8, "Related Party Disclosures," was issued in October 1995 and took effect for accounting periods beginning on or after December 23, 1995. Most standards deal with both measurement and disclosure rules. FRS 9 is a rarity in that it deals exclusively with disclosures and is silent on the measurement of related party transactions.

Another feature of FRS 9 that makes it stand out is its definition of materiality. Whereas other standards generally state in their scope paragraphs that they need be applied only to material items, they do not define or describe that materiality. FRS 9 is unusual in that its explanatory material deals with what is meant by that materiality in the context of related party transactions.

Under FRS 9 a transaction is material if its "disclosure might reasonably be expected to influence decisions made by the users of general purpose financial statements." Thus, quantum is not the only factor to be taken into account when judging materiality. The nature of the item and the preparer's subjective estimate of the likelihood of influencing readers' financial decisions are also key to the determination of materiality.

Where the counterparty to a transaction is key management, directors or their families, or businesses controlled by them, FRS 9 goes on to require materiality to be judged not only in the context of the reporting entity but also in the context of what is material to the individual involved in the transaction.

The standard requires two sorts of disclosure:

1. Information on material related party transactions
2. The name of the party controlling the reporting entity.

Disclosure is required irrespective of whether a price is charged. Accordingly, gifts or free use of property to related parties, where material, require disclosure.

Transactions with related parties may be disclosed on an aggregated basis subject to certain restrictions. The main restrictions are that only like items may be aggregated and that aggregation cannot be used to conceal transactions.

No disclosure is required in consolidated financial statements of intra-group transactions and balances eliminated on consolidation. A parent undertaking is not required to provide related party disclosures in its own financial statements when those statements are presented with consolidated financial statements of its group.

Disclosure is not required in the financial statements of subsidiary undertakings, 90% or more of whose voting rights are controlled within the group, of transactions with entities that are part of the group, or investees of the group qualifying as related parties, provided that the consolidated financial statements in which that subsidiary is included are publicly available.

Pension contributions paid to a pension fund and employee emoluments are specifically excluded from the scope of the FRS. This is not much of a concession as information, albeit on a general level, on both these matters is required by SSAP 24 and Companies Legislation respectively.

The definition of a related party is quite widely drawn. This was deliberately done to prevent the artificial construction of related party transactions that would fall outside narrower definitions. As a result of the wide definition, disclosure of transactions with third party financiers, utilities, and government, or with a supplier, customer, franchiser, distributor, or agent accounting for a significant volume of business is generally not required even though they, on the face of it, meet the definition of related party transactions.

The standard specifies the following as related parties of the reporting entity:

1. Its ultimate and intermediate parent undertakings, subsidiary undertakings, and fellow subsidiary undertakings
2. Its associates and joint ventures
3. The investor or venturer in respect of which the reporting entity is an associate or a joint venture
4. Directors and shadow directors of the reporting entity and the directors and shadow of its ultimate and intermediate parent undertakings. Shadow directors are defined in company law as persons in accordance with whose directions or instructions the directors of the company are accustomed to act
5. Pension funds for the benefit of employees of the reporting entity or of any entity that is a related party of the reporting entity

The standard also sets out a number of parties that are presumed to be related to the reporting entity unless it can be demonstrated that neither party has influenced the financial and operating policies of the other in such a way as to inhibit the pursuit of separate interests:

1. The key management of the reporting entity and key management of its parent undertaking or undertakings
2. A person owning or able to exercise control over 20% or more of the voting rights of the reporting entity, whether directly or through nominees
3. Each person acting in concert in such a way as to be able to exercise control or influence over the reporting entity
4. An entity managing or managed by the reporting entity under a management contract

In addition, the standard specifies that, because of their relationship with certain parties that are, or are presumed to be, related parties of the reporting entity, the following are also presumed to be related parties of the reporting entity:

1. Members of the close family (which is broadly defined in terms of a person's household) of any individual mentioned above
2. Partnerships, companies, trusts, or other entities in which any individual or member of the close family mentioned above has a controlling interest

The list of related parties specified in the standard is not intended to be exhaustive.

The standard also requires disclosure of who controls the reporting entity, even where that person has not undertaken any transactions with the entity during the period being reported on. The disclosures required are:

- The related party relationship
- The name of that party and, if different, that of the ultimate controlling party
- If the controlling party or ultimate controlling party of the reporting entity is not known

3.15 Accounting for Share Options

The accounting rules for share options and employee share ownership plans can be found in a number of UITF abstracts:

- Abstract 10   Disclosure of Directors' Share Options
- Abstract 13   Accounting for ESOP Trusts
- Abstract 17   Employee Share Schemes

Abstract 10 is unusual in that it is, for legal reasons, a nonmandatory abstract. Nonetheless, the Irish Stock exchange has adopted compliance with Abstract 10 as a listed rule and accordingly this abstract is mandatory for listed companies. Essentially, the abstract recommends but does not mandate disclosure by individual directors of details of share options held, including:

- The number of shares under option at the end of the year and at the beginning of the year (or date of appointment)
- The number of options granted, exercised, and lapsed unexercised during the year
- The exercise prices
- The dates from which the options may be exercised
- The expiration dates
- The cost of the options (if any)
- For any options exercised during the year, the market price of the shares at the date of exercise

Abstract 13 applies the principles of FRS 5, "Reporting the Substance of Transactions" to the accounting for employee share ownership plans and applies to accounting periods ending on or after June 22, 1995. It deals with accounting for employee share ownership plans (ESOPs) and requires that the sponsoring company's financial statements recognize certain assets (its own shares) and liabilities (which may include bank borrowings guaranteed by the company) of an ESOP trust on its own balance sheet "whenever it has *de facto* control of the shares held by the ESOP trust and bears their benefits or risks." The abstract says that this will generally be the case when the trust is established in order to hold shares for an employee remuneration scheme and may be so in other circumstances.

The abstract requires the shares held by the ESOP trust to be recognized as assets of the sponsoring company until they vest unconditionally in employees. Shares held for the continuing benefit of the sponsoring company's business are classified as "own shares" within fixed assets and any permanent diminution in their value is to be recognized immediately.

The abstract requires sufficient information to be disclosed in the financial statements of the sponsoring company to enable readers to understand the significance of the ESOP trust in the context of the sponsoring company. The disclosures include:

1. A description of the main features of the ESOP trust, including the arrangements for distributing shares to employees
2. The manner in which the costs are dealt with in the profit and loss account
3. The number and market value of shares held by the ESOP trust and whether dividends on those shares have been waived

4. The extent to which these shares are under option to employees, or have been conditionally gifted to them

Where a company satisfies share awards to employees through an ESOP, then the accounting treatment is governed by UITF 13. This requires that the shares purchased by the ESOP be carried as an asset on the sponsoring company's balance sheet and written down to recoverable amount over the period of service of the employees in respect of which the awards are granted. This means that if the ESOP purchases shares in the market at the date of grant of the award and subsequently gifts these to employees, then the purchase price of the shares (that is, the fair value at the date of grant of the award) will be charged in the sponsoring company's profit and loss account.

However, if the employee share scheme is set up so that shares are issued by the company rather than purchased in the market, then, if the strict legal form is followed, any charge in the company's profit and loss account may be significantly lower than the fair value at the date of grant of the award or may even be nil, for instance if the company issues shares to an employee at nominal value. The UITF has addressed this issue by requiring a charge in the profit and loss based on the fair value of the shares at the date an award is granted.

UITF Abstract 17, "Employee Share Schemes," applies to employee remuneration schemes in the form of share awards, either through annual bonuses or long-term incentive plans (LTIPs). This abstract applies for accounting periods ending on or after June 22, 1997.

Among other things the abstract requires that the amount recognized in the profit and loss account in respect of share awards should be charged over the period to which the employee's performance relates. This means:

- For annual bonuses—the year to which the bonus relates
- For LTIPs—the period to which the performance criteria relate

Abstract 17 mandates that the amount to be recognized in respect of share awards is:

- The fair value of the shares at the date an award is granted, reduced by any consideration payable by the employee for the shares; or
- Where shares have been purchased by an ESOP trust at fair value, the difference between the book value of the shares (as recorded in the

company's books under UITF 13) and any consideration payable by
the employee

Where new shares are to be issued under an employee share scheme, the
credit entry for the charge to the profit and loss account should be reported
in the reconciliation of movements in shareholders' funds, reflecting the
fact that it represents the proceeds of an equity instrument. It should not be
reported in the Statement of Total Recognized Gains and Losses.

This abstract need not be applied in accounting for an employees' share
scheme under which participation is offered on similar terms to all or
substantially all employees of the issuer and any of its subsidiary undertakings whose employees are eligible to participate in the scheme (providing that all or substantially all employees are not directors of the issuer).

3.16 Accounting Implications of the Year 2000 Issue and the Introduction of the Euro

UITF Abstract 20, "Year 2000 Issues: Accounting and Disclosures," applies to accounting periods ending on or after March 23, 1998. This
abstract requires that costs incurred in rendering existing software year
2000 compliant be written off to the profit and loss account except in those
cases where an entity already has an accounting policy for capitalizing
software costs and to the extent that the expenditure clearly represents an
enhancement of an asset beyond that originally assessed rather than merely
maintaining its service potential.

FRS 3 requires disclosure of exceptional items and the abstract comments that the UITF believes that in some cases year 2000 software costs
will fall within this requirement.

The directors' report or any operating and financial review or other
statement included in the annual report published by the entity are suggested as appropriate areas in which to make the disclosures.

The requirements of UITF Abstract 21, "Accounting Issues Arising
from the Proposed Introduction of the Euro," are similar but not identical
to the abstract on the year 2000 issue. Like Abstract 20, Abstract 21
applies to accounting periods ending on or after March 23, 1998.

The abstract also concludes that the introduction of the euro should not
alter the deferral and matching treatment adopted for financial instruments
used as anticipatory hedges.

3.17 Miscellaneous Matters

UITF Abstract 11, "Capital Instruments: Issuer Call Options," was issued in September 1994 and applies to accounting periods ending on or after October 23, 1994. It clarifies the requirements of FRS 4 in the situation where the issuer of a capital instrument has the option to redeem the instrument earlier than its stated redemption date, on payment of a premium by the issuer, and where the holder does not have a similar option.

UITF Abstract 12, "Lessee Accounting for Reverse Premiums and Similar Incentives," was issued at the beginning of December 1994 and is effective for accounting periods ending on or after December 23, 1994 in respect of lease arrangements commencing in the current or the preceding accounting period. It requires that benefits received and receivable by a lessee as an incentive to sign a lease (whatever form they may take) are spread on a straight-line basis over the lease term (or period up to the date when the rent is first adjusted to a market rate, if shorter).

The Companies (Amendment) Act 1986 requires that accounting policies be applied consistently within the same accounts and from one financial year to the next. Where this is not so because, for instance, of a change in accounting policy, disclosure of the particulars and reasons and effect of the departure from the principle of consistency are required. The UITF received legal advice that disclosure is required of the effect of a change in accounting policy on the current period (as well as on the preceding period, as required by FRS 3). UITF Abstract 14, "Changes in Accounting Policy," publicises this legal advice.

UITF Abstract 15, "Disclosure of Substantial Acquisitions," clarifies the scope of the disclosure requirements for substantial acquisitions set out in FRS 6, "Acquisitions and Mergers," following the abolition of Class 1 transactions by the Stock Exchange. FRS 6 defines "substantial" by reference to Class 1 or Super Class 1 transactions. UITF 15 states that FRS 6 should be interpreted as meaning those transactions in which any of the specified ratios set out in the Listing Rules for Super Class 1 transactions exceed 15%.

UITF Abstract 16, "Income and Expenses Subject to Non-standard Rates of Tax," abolishes the practice of grossing up transactions that are nontaxable or taxable at a lower than standard rate. The issue mostly affects financial institutions that invest in instruments with a nonstandard tax treatment, such as lending by way of investing in preference shares and certain types of leases. The abstract took effect for all accounting periods ending on or after June 22, 1997.

Following a change to tax legislation so that pension schemes cannot reclaim a tax credit on dividend income, the UITF issued Abstract 18 to the effect that this of itself does not fall outside the normal scope of the actuarial assumptions as set out in paragraph 82 of SSAP 24. It is simply a change in the expected return on assets, similar to those arising from changes in tax rates. Hence, the loss should be spread forward over the expected remaining service lives of current employees in the scheme whatever the financial position of the scheme and regardless of any additional contributions that are made. Abstract 18 took effect for accounting periods ending on or after December 23, 1997.

UITF Abstract 19, "Tax on Foreign Currency Differences Taken to Reserves," is effective for accounting periods ending on or after March 23, 1998. This abstract deals with accounting for the tax charge or credit that can arise on exchange differences on borrowings taken out to hedge overseas assets.

Where exchange differences on foreign currency borrowings have been taken to reserves in accordance with SSAP 20, paragraphs 51 or 57 ("offset procedure") and reported in the statement of total recognized gains and losses, the UITF has agreed that any tax charges or credits on such exchange differences should also be dealt with in the statement of total recognized gains and losses.

3.18 Accounting Standards Currently Operative in the Republic of Ireland

A listing of Accounting Standards currently operative in the Republic of Ireland (both SSAPs and FRSs) is given in Appendix A.

4. Future Developments

4.1 Company Law Review Group

In February 1994, the Irish government set up a company law review group to examine and make recommendations on various aspects of Irish company law, specifically including such topics as the provisions relating to examinerships, investigations, and insider dealing. Other topics include addressing the recommendations of the Ryan Commission (which reported on the expectations of users of published financial statements) and the needs of smaller businesses. The review group also examined the need for a Commercial Court and the possibility of consolidating all Irish company law. The group's recommendations were reported in December 1994. A program of legislation to enact the recommendations is expected. Recommendations directly affecting annual reporting include:

- Accounting standards, while not to be incorporated into law, should be recognized.
- Provision is to be made for a review panel to examine compliance with financial reporting rules
- Provision is to be made for the voluntary revision of defective financial statements

4.2 Accounting Standards

The Institute of Chartered Accountants in Ireland (ICAI) will continue to maintain close liaison with the Accounting Standards Board (ASB) and will promulgate the ASB's financial reporting standards in the Republic of Ireland after incorporating appropriate modifications to reflect legal differences.

At the time of writing (May 1998), the ASB has an extensive work program in hand that will lead to the development of many new standards. Those preparing or interpreting Irish financial statements face a considerable challenge in staying up to date with these developments.

Appendix

ASB Documents Extant as of March 1, 1998

Accounting Standards

SSAPs developed by the former ASC or ASSC and adopted by the ASB

SSAP 1   Accounting for Associated Companies (superseded by FRS 9)
SSAP 2   Disclosure of Accounting Polices
SSAP 3   Earnings per Share
SSAP 4   Accounting for Government Grants
SSAP 5   Accounting for Value Added Tax
SSAP 8   The Treatment of Taxation under the Imputation System in the Accounts of Companies
SSAP 9   Stocks and Long Term Contracts
SSAP 12   Accounting for Depreciation
SSAP 13   Accounting for Research and Development
SSAP 15   Accounting for Deferred Tax
SSAP 17   Accounting for Post Balance Sheet Events
SSAP 18   Accounting for Contingencies
SSAP 19   Accounting for Investment Properties
SSAP 20   Foreign Currency Translation
SSAP 21   Accounting for Leases and Hire Purchase Contracts
SSAP 22   Accounting for Goodwill (superseded by FRS 10)
SSAP 24   Accounting for Pension Costs
SSAP 25   Segmental Reporting

FRSs issued by the ASB

Financial Reporting Standard for Smaller Entities
FRS 1
(Revised) Cash Flow Statements
FRS 2   Accounting for Subsidiary Undertakings
FRS 3   Reporting Financial Performance
FRS 4   Capital Instruments

FRS 5   Reporting the Substance of Transactions

FRS 6   Acquisitions and Mergers

FRS 7   Fair Values in Acquisition Accounting

FRS 8   Related party Disclosures

FRS 9   Associates and Joint Ventures

FRS 10   Goodwill and Intangible Assets

Amendments to accounting standards

Amendment to SSAP 15 Accounting for Deferred Tax

Amendment to FRS 3 Reporting Financial Performance: Insurance companies

Amendment to SSAP 19 Accounting for Investment Properties

Amendment to FRS 5 Reporting the Substance of Transactions: Insurance Broking Transactions and Financial Reinsurance

Amendment to SSAP 21 Accounting for Leases and Hire Purchase Contracts: Tax free grants

Urgent Issues Task Force Pronouncements

The Application of UITF Abstracts

UITF Abstract 3   Treatment of Goodwill on Disposal of a Business

UITF Abstract 4   Presentation of Long Term Debtors in Current Assets

UITF Abstract 5   Transfers from Current Assets to Fixed Assets

UITF Abstract 6   Accounting for Post-Retirement Benefits Other than Pensions

UITF Abstract 7   True and Fair Override Disclosures

UITF Abstract 9   Accounting for Operations in Hyper-Inflationary Economics

UITF Abstract 10   Disclosure of Directors' Share Options

UITF Abstract 11   Capital Instruments: Issuer Call Options

UITF Abstract 12   Lessee Accounting for Reverse Premiums and Similar Incentives

UITF Abstract 13   Accounting for ESOP Trusts

UITF Abstract 14   Disclosure of Changes in Accounting Policy

UITF Abstract 15   Disclosure of Substantial Acquisitions

UITF Abstract 16   Income and Expenses Subject to Non-Standard Rates of Tax

UITF Abstract 17   Employee Share Schemes

UITF Abstract 18   Pension Costs Following the 1997 Tax Changes in Respect of Dividend   Income

UITF Abstract 19   Tax on Gains and Losses on Foreign Currency Loans that Hedge an   investment in a Foreign Enterprise

UITF Abstract 20   Year 2000 issues: accounting and disclosures

UITF Abstract 21   Accounting issues arising from the proposed introduction of the euro.

Financial Statements

The Directors submit their thirteenth annual report, together with the audited financial statements for the year ended 3 April, 1997, which are prepared under the requirements of the Companies Acts, 1963 to 1990, and the European Communities (Companies: Group Accounts) Regulations, 1992.

Financial Year

The financial year comprises the 52 weeks ended 3 April, 1997 (Previous year 53 weeks).

Principal Activity

The Group's principal activity is the supply of telecommunications services in the Republic of Ireland.

Results

The financial results for the year and the appropriation thereof are set out in the Group Profit and Loss Account on page 43.

Review of the Business and Future Developments

During the year negotiations with our Strategic Alliance Partners were successfully concluded. The Minister for Transport, Energy and Communications now holds 80% of the issued share capital of the Company. The remaining 20% is held by a Consortium comprising PTT Telecom BV and Telia AB (publ). The Consortium has an option which entitles it to increase its shareholding to 35%.

A review of the business and future developments of the Group is set out in the Management Review.

Dividends

The Directors propose the payment of a final dividend of IR£12.638m in respect of the year ended 3 April, 1997.

Directors

The Directors of the Company are listed on page 34.

Directors' Interests in Shares in the Company

According to the Register of Directors and Secretaries, neither the Company Secretary nor any Director had any beneficial interest in the Share Capital of the Company or any of its subsidiary or related companies during the year under review.

Directors' Interests in Contracts

There were no contracts or arrangements of any significance in relation to the Company's business or that of its subsidiary or related companies in which the Directors or Secretary of the Company had any beneficial interest as defined in the Companies Act, 1990.

Ronald J. Bolger is a partner in KPMG. Jack Casey is Group Managing Director of New Ireland Assurance Co. plc and a director of BNP Ireland Limited. James Crotty is a director of the MacDonagh Boland Group. During the period under review the Group, in the normal course of business, entered into transactions for services with these organisations.

Corporate Governance

The Directors support the Code of Best Practice published in December 1992 by the Cadbury Committee on the financial aspects of Corporate Governance. The Company has introduced measures since 1992 to comply, in so far as this is judged appropriate, with the main provisions of the Code of Best Practice.

The roles of the Chairman and Chief Executive are separate. The Board includes nine external non-executive Directors who constitute the majority of the Board. Details of Directors' fees and emoluments are disclosed in accordance with Irish law and practice. The Board has an effective committee structure to assist in the discharge of its responsibilities. Further information on Board Committees is given in the Annual Report.

Internal Controls

The Directors have overall responsibility for the Group's system of internal control and have delegated responsibility for the implementation of this system to executive management. This system includes financial controls which enable the Board to meet its responsibilities for the integrity and accuracy of the Group's accounting records. The Audit Committee, a formally constituted committee of the Board, meets on a regular basis with internal and external auditors and satisfies itself as to the adequacy of the Group's internal control systems, including, inter alia, accounting controls, computer system security and the internal audit function. The Group's system of internal control is designed to provide reasonable, though not absolute, assurance that assets are safeguarded, transactions authorised and recorded properly and that material errors or irregularities are either prevented or detected within a timely period.

Going Concern

After making enquiries, the Directors have a reasonable expectation that the Company, and the Group as a whole, have adequate resources to continue in operational existence for the foreseeable future. For this reason, they continue to adopt the going concern basis in preparing the financial statements.

Group and Related Companies

The information required by Section 158 of the Companies Act, 1963 is shown in Note 18 to the financial statements.

Research and Development

The Group's research and development activities are summarised in the Management Review.

Health and Safety

A comprehensive safety statement, which meets the requirements of The Safety, Health and Welfare at Work Act, 1989, has been developed. This area is kept under continuous review and rigorous health and safety standards are applied throughout all companies in the Group.

Auditors

The auditors, Coopers & Lybrand, Chartered Accountants and Registered Auditors, have indicated their willingness to continue in office in accordance with Section 160 of the Companies Act, 1963.

Signed on behalf of the Board

Ronald J. Bolger
James Crotty

Directors.
Date: 28 May 1997

We have audited the financial statements on pages 40 to 65.

Respective Responsibilities of Directors and Auditors

As described on page 39, the Company's Directors are responsible for the preparation of the financial statements. It is our responsibility to form an independent opinion, based on our audit, on those statements and to report our opinion to you.

Basis of Opinion

We conducted our audit in accordance with Auditing Standards issued by the Auditing Practices Board. An audit includes examination, on a test basis, of evidence relevant to the amounts and disclosures in the financial statements. It also includes an assessment of the significant estimates and judgements made by the Directors in the preparation of the financial statements, and of whether the accounting policies are appropriate to the Company's circumstances, consistently applied and adequately disclosed.

We planned and performed our audit so as to obtain all the information and explanations which we considered necessary in order to provide us with sufficient evidence to give reasonable assurance that the financial statements are free from material misstatement, whether caused by fraud or other irregularity or error. In forming our opinion we also evaluated the overall adequacy of the presentation of information in the financial statements.

Opinion

In our opinion, the financial statements give a true and fair view of the state of affairs of the Company and the Group as at 3 April 1997 and of the profit, total recognised gains and cash flows of the Group for the year then ended and have been properly prepared in accordance with the Companies Acts, 1963 to 1990, and the European Communities

(Companies: Group Accounts) Regulations, 1992. We have obtained all the information and explanations we consider necessary for the purposes of our audit. In our opinion, proper books of account have been kept by the Company. The financial statements of the Company are in agreement with the books of account.

In our opinion, the information given in the Directors' report on pages 36 and 37 is consistent with the financial statements.

The net assets of the Company, as stated in the balance sheet on page 45, are more than half the amount of its called up share capital and, in our opinion, on that basis there did not exist at 3 April 1997 a financial situation which, under Section 40 (1) of the Companies (Amendment) Act 1983, would require the convening of an Extraordinary General Meeting of the Company.

Coopers & Lybrand
Chartered Accountants
and Registered Auditors

DUBLIN
DATE: 28 MAY 1997

Authority

Bord Telecom Eireann (The Irish Telecommunications Board) was established by the Postal and Telecommunications Services Act, 1983. The Company re-registered as a Plc during the year. The financial statements of the Company have been prepared to comply with the Companies Acts, 1963 to 1990, the European Communities (Companies: Group Accounts) Regulations, 1992, and with Section 33 (2) of the Postal and Telecommunications Services Act, 1983.

Basis of Consolidation

The Group financial statements comprise a consolidation of the financial statements of the Company and of its subsidiaries. The financial statements are prepared in accordance with the historical cost convention modified by the valuation of land and buildings, excepting those held on a short leasehold basis. Related companies are accounted for under the equity method of accounting.

Turnover

Turnover comprises the value of all services provided and equipment sold to third parties, exclusive of value added tax.

Research and Development

Expenditure on research and development is written off as incurred.

Goodwill

Goodwill represents the excess of the consideration paid for the acquisition of shares in subsidiary companies over the fair value of their separable net assets.

Goodwill on acquisition of subsidiaries is written off against reserves in the year of acquisition.

Foreign Currencies

Transactions designated in foreign currencies are translated into Irish Pounds at the rate of exchange ruling at the transaction date. Assets and liabilities denominated in foreign currencies are translated at the rates ruling at the balance sheet date, or rates of exchange contracted for under various currency management instruments, with the resulting gain or loss being dealt with through the profit and loss account.

Financial Instruments

The Group enters into transactions in the normal course of business using a variety of financial instruments in order to hedge against exposures to fluctuating exchange and interest rates.

Currency swap agreements and forward exchange contracts are used to cover the Group's foreign currency debt position. These are valued at year end exchange rates and the resulting gains and losses are offset against gains and losses on the translation of the related debt. The interest element of the contracts is reflected in interest payable. Forward contracts and related instruments designated to hedge future transactions are accounted for on a consistent basis with the related transactions.

Interest rate swap agreements and forward rate agreements are used to reduce the effect of interest rate fluctuations. Interest differentials, arising on these agreements, are accrued and reflected in interest payable.

Financial Assets

Financial assets are recorded at cost. Income from these assets is amortised to the profit and loss account over the useful life of the assets.

Tangible Assets

Tangible assets are stated at historical cost or valuation less accumulated depreciation. Land and buildings, excepting those held on a short leasehold basis, are stated at a valuation, the basis of which is depreciated replacement cost or open market value as appropriate.

Depreciated replacement cost is the gross replacement cost of fixed assets less depreciation based on that cost and on the age of the assets.

Plant and equipment assets, stated at a valuation, comprise assets taken over on Vesting Day (1 January 1984) which are stated at valuations determined, as at that date, by the Minister for Communications.

Cost in the case of network services comprises expenditure up to and including the last distribution point before customers' premises and includes contractors' charges, materials, direct labour, and related overheads incurred in the construction of tangible assets.

Depreciation is provided on tangible assets (excluding land) on a straight line basis so as to write off their historical costs or valuations over their estimated useful lives. Following a review during the year, the estimated useful lives assigned to tangible assets are as follows:

	Years
Buildings	40
Network Services -	
Transmission Equipment	
Duct	20
Cable	10 - 18
Radio and Repeater Equipment	11 - 35
Transmission Plant	14
Exchanges	4 - 10

Grants

Non-repayable grants are accounted for as deferred income, a portion of which is amortised to the profit and loss account at the same rate as the related assets are depreciated.

Leased Assets

The capital cost of assets acquired under finance leases is included in tangible assets and written off over the shorter of the lease term or the estimated useful life of the asset. The outstanding capital element of the lease obligations is included in loans and other debt, while the interest is charged to the profit and loss account over the primary lease period.

Stocks

Stocks comprise consumable items, stores which may be used in the construction or maintenance of plant and goods held for resale. Stocks are stated at the lower of cost and net realisable value.

Cost includes invoice price, import duties and transportation costs.

Net realisable value is calculated as cost less provision for damaged, deteriorated, obsolete and unusable items.

Deferred Taxation

Deferred taxation is provided, using the liability method, in respect of all timing differences between profits stated in the financial statements and profits computed for taxation purposes except where, in the opinion of the Directors, the timing differences are not expected to reverse in the foreseeable future.

Pension costs

The pension entitlements of employees arising from
their service with the Group, are secured by
contributions from the Group and the employees to
separately administered superannuation schemes.
The contributions are based on the advice of a
professionally qualified actuary and are included as
staff costs in the profit and loss account.

Pension costs in respect of the Group's defined
benefit schemes are charged in the profit and loss
account on a basis which spreads the cost of
pensions over the service lives of employees in
the schemes.

Additional contributions are made to
superannuation schemes in respect of employees who
take early retirement. These contributions are based
on the advice of a professionally qualified actuary
and are included as restructuring costs in the profit
and loss account.

	Notes	1997 IR£'000	1996 IR£'000
Turnover	2	1,219,034	1,094,149
Operating costs	3	673,984	607,166
Restructuring provision		25,000	35,000
Contribution on ordinary activities		520,050	451,983
Depreciation		274,696	268,936
Operating profit		245,354	183,047
Interest payable and similar charges	4	42,941	66,784
Profit after interest and similar charges		202,413	116,263
Share of profits of related companies		1,153	892
Profit on ordinary activities before taxation		203,566	117,155
Tax on profit on ordinary activities	5	76,332	49,944
Profit on ordinary activities after taxation		127,234	67,211
Minority interests		(850)	(838)
Profit attributable to group shareholders		126,384	66,373
Dividend paid and proposed	6	12,638	
Retained profit for the financial year		113,746	66,373

The movements on reserves are shown in note 16 to the financial statements.

All of the Group's turnover and operating profit relate to continuing activities.

Directors.
RONALD J. BOLGER
JAMES CROTTY

THE NOTES ON PAGES 40 TO 42 AND 48 TO 65 FORM PART OF THESE FINANCIAL STATEMENTS.
AUDITORS' REPORT PAGE 38.

	Notes	1997 IR£'000	1996 IR£'000
Assets employed			
Fixed assets			
Tangible assets	7	1,343,848	1,364,576
Financial assets	8	151,331	1,331
		1,495,179	1,365,907
Current assets			
Stocks	9	18,494	17,134
Debtors: amounts falling due within one year	10	267,347	220,863
Debtors: amounts falling due after one year	10	70,000	
Cash at bank and in hand		22,105	45,559
		377,946	283,556
Creditors: Amounts falling due within one year			
Loans and other debt	11	75,433	201,262
Other creditors	12	282,137	246,258
Proposed dividend		12,638	
		370,208	447,520
Net current assets/(liabilities)		7,738	(163,964)
Total assets less current liabilities		1,502,917	1,201,943
Financed by			
Creditors: Amounts falling due after more than one year			
Loans and other debt	11	470,275	547,730
Other creditors			2,915
		470,275	550,645
Provision for liabilities and charges	13	169,339	111,378
Capital grants	14	19,351	30,564
Capital and reserves			
Called up share capital	15	441,565	335,315
Share premium	16	113,750	
Revenue reserves	16	230,485	113,973
Revaluation reserve	16	50,934	53,700
Equity shareholders' funds		836,734	502,988
Equity minority interests		7,218	6,368
		1,502,917	1,201,943

Directors.
RONALD J. BOLGER
JAMES CROTTY

THE NOTES ON PAGES 40 TO 42 AND 48 TO 65 FORM PART OF THESE FINANCIAL STATEMENTS.
AUDITORS' REPORT PAGE 38.

	Notes	1997 IR£'000	1996 IR£'000
Assets employed			
Fixed assets			
Tangible assets	7	1,165,932	971,402
Financial assets	8	287,884	64,334
		1,453,816	1,035,736
Current assets			
Stocks	9	14,582	13,575
Debtors: amounts falling due within one year	10	437,302	216,551
Debtors: amounts falling due after one year	10	70,000	
Cash at bank and in hand		8,201	31,511
		530,085	261,637
Creditors: Amounts falling due within one year			
Loans and other debt	11	23,288	31,584
Other creditors	12	378,333	273,463
Proposed dividend		12,638	
		414,259	305,047
Net current assets/(liabilities)		115,826	(43,410)
Total assets less current liabilities		1,569,642	992,326
Financed by			
Creditors: Amounts falling due after more than one year			
Loans and other debt	11	545,888	356,912
Provision for liabilities and charges	13	166,594	89,321
Capital grants	14	15,934	30,564
Capital and reserves			
Called up share capital	15	441,565	335,315
Share premium	16	113,750	
Revenue reserves	16	249,133	141,416
Revaluation reserve	16	36,778	38,798
Equity shareholders' funds		841,226	515,529
		1,569,642	992,326

Directors.
RONALD J. BOLGER
JAMES CROTTY

THE NOTES ON PAGES 40 TO 42 AND 48 TO 65 FORM PART OF THESE FINANCIAL STATEMENTS.
AUDITORS' REPORT PAGE 38.

	Notes	1997 IR£'000	1996 IR£'000
Net cash inflow from operating activities	17(a)	473,789	437,156
Returns on Investment and Servicing of Finance	17(b)	(49,109)	(65,280)
Taxation paid	17(c)	(3,326)	(7,654)
		421,354	364,222
Capital Expenditure and Financial Investment	17(d)	(265,724)	(188,359)
Acquisition of Securities		(150,000)	
Acquisitions and Disposals of Group Companies			(12,655)
Equity dividends paid			(10,000)
		(415,724)	(211,014)
Management of liquid resources	17(e)	22	7,240
Financing	17(f)	(22,373)	(165,218)
Decrease in cash		(16,721)	(4,770)

Reconciliation of Net Cash Flow to Reduction in Net Debt

	1997 IR£'000	1996 IR£'000
Decrease in cash in the period	(16,721)	(4,770)
Cash outflow from decrease in loans	172,373	165,218
Cash inflow from decrease in liquid resources	(22)	(7,240)
	155,630	153,208
Exchange rate movement	24,200	5,689
Reduction in net debt	179,830	158,897

THE NOTES ON PAGES 40 TO 42 AND 48 TO 65 FORM PART OF THESE FINANCIAL STATEMENTS.
AUDITORS' REPORT PAGE 38.

	1997 IR£'000	1996 IR£'000
Profit attributable to group shareholders	126,384	66,373
Currency translation differences		35
Total recognised gains relating to the year	126,384	66,408

Note of Historical Cost Profits and Losses

There is no material difference between the profit on ordinary activities before taxation and the retained profit for the year stated above, and their historical cost equivalents.

Reconciliation of Movements in Shareholders' Funds

	1997 IR£'000	1996 IR£'000
Profit attributable to group shareholders	126,384	66,373
Dividends	(12,638)	-
Retained profit for the financial year	113,746	66,373
New share capital issued (including share premium)	220,000	-
Goodwill	-	(9,683)
Currency translation differences	-	35
Net addition to shareholders' funds	333,746	56,725
Shareholders' funds at beginning of year	502,988	446,263
Shareholders' funds at end of year	836,734	502,988

THE NOTES ON PAGES 40 TO 42 AND 48 TO 65 FORM PART OF THESE FINANCIAL STATEMENTS.
AUDITORS' REPORT PAGE 38.

1. Segmental Information

There are no significant segments within the Group's operations which would warrant separate disclosure of segmental information.

2. Turnover

	1997 IR£'000	1996 IR£'000
Telephone income		
Rental	237,182	206,196
Traffic	668,736	607,935
Connection fees	29,366	26,000
Income from overseas telecommunications agencies	79,702	82,520
Total telephone income	1,014,986	922,651
Private circuits	58,857	42,353
Switched data and other network services	33,574	20,626
Total telecommunications services	1,107,417	985,630
Other income	111,617	108,519
	1,219,034	1,094,149

3. Operating Costs

	1997 IR£'000	1996 IR£'000
Staff costs		
Wages & salaries	275,627	283,501
Social welfare costs	7,261	7,160
Pension costs	37,900	38,602
	320,788	329,263
Staff costs capitalised	(29,402)	(32,394)
Net staff costs	291,386	296,869
Charges by overseas telecommunications agencies	69,972	67,699
Other operating costs	312,626	242,598
	673,984	607,166

Operating costs include:-	1997 IR£	1996 IR£
Auditors' remuneration	120,000	125,600
Directors' remuneration		
For services as Directors	62,500	57,500
Other emoluments	386,175	365,304
Compensation for loss of office	-	10,357

The Chief Executive, Mr. A. Kane, has a service contract with the company for a term of five years from 11 April, 1994.

The Directors deem the individuals noted at pages 34 and 35 to be officers of the company for the purposes of S.43 of the Companies Act 1990. No transactions took place with these officers during the year.

4. Interest Payable and Similar Charges

	1997 IR£'000	1996 IR£'000
Interest and associated finance costs payable in respect of financing facilities;		
Repayable within 5 years not by instalments	30,511	43,162
Repayable within 5 years by instalments	2,307	3,455
Repayable wholly or partly in more than 5 years	15,535	17,556
Leases	3,033	5,743
Total interest payable	51,386	69,916
Less: Interest receivable	(6,166)	(3,171)
Net interest payable	45,220	66,745
Exchange differences arising on foreign currency borrowings		
Realised gains	(2,523)	(1,455)
Unrealised gains	(24,009)	(4,234)
Hedging Contract losses	24,253	5,728
	42,941	66,784

5. Tax on Profit on Ordinary Activities

	1997 IR£'000	1996 IR£'000
Corporation tax at 38%	83,271	1,052
Advance corporation tax	(50,570)	-
Deferred taxation	42,478	48,000
Share of taxation of related companies	1,153	892
	76,332	49,944

DEFERRED TAXATION IS DEALT WITH AT NOTE 13.

6. Dividends Paid and Proposed

	1997 IR£'000	1996 IR£'000
Ordinary dividends :		
Proposed: final dividend of 2.86p per share (1996: nil)	12,638	-
	12,638	-

7. Tangible Assets

(a) Group

	Land & Buildings IR£'000	Plant & Equipment IR£'000	Total IR£'000
Cost or Valuation			
Cost	21,838	1,710,711	1,732,549
Valuation	230,149	623,888	854,037
At 4 April 1996	251,987	2,334,599	2,586,586
Additions	6,812	261,618	268,430
Disposals / Retirements	(408)	(17,113)	(17,521)
At 3 April 1997	258,391	2,579,104	2,837,495
Cost	28,597	1,963,453	1,992,050
Valuation	229,794	615,651	845,445
Accumulated Depreciation			
At 4 April 1996	31,889	1,190,121	1,222,010
Charge for year	8,666	279,485	288,151
Disposals / Retirements	(9,304)	(7,210)	(16,514)
At 3 April 1997	31,251	1,462,396	1,493,647
Total Net Book Value at 3 April 1997	227,140	1,116,708	1,343,848
Total Net Book Value at 4 April 1996	220,098	1,144,478	1,364,576

7. Tangible Assets   Cont'd.

(b)

The Depreciation charged in the Group profit and loss account is net of capital grants amortised during the year (see note 14) as follows :

	1997 IR£'000	1996 IR£'000
Depreciation	288,151	276,093
Amortisation of capital grants	(13,455)	(7,157)
	274,696	268,936

(c) Company

	Land & Buildings IR£'000	Plant & Equipment IR£'000	Total IR£'000
Cost or Valuation			
Cost	16,092	1,288,496	1,304,588
Valuation	149,683	246,731	396,414
At 4 April 1996	165,775	1,535,227	1,701,002
Additions	77,254	389,628	466,882
Disposals / Retirements	(823)	(150,392)	(151,215)
At 3 April 1997	242,206	1,774,463	2,016,669
Cost	92,822	1,535,969	1,628,791
Valuation	149,384	238,494	387,878
Accumulated Depreciation			
At 4 April 1996	24,978	704,622	729,600
Charge for year	5,779	178,305	184,084
Disposals / Retirements	(4)	(62,943)	(62,947)
At 3 April 1997	30,753	819,984	850,737
Total Net Book Value at 3 April 1997	211,453	954,479	1,165,932
Total Net Book Value at 4 April 1996	140,797	830,605	971,402

ADDITIONS AND DISPOSALS OF PLANT AND EQUIPMENT INCLUDE TRANSFERS TO AND FROM GROUP COMPANIES.

7. Tangible Assets   Cont'd.

(d)
A valuation of properties owned by Bord Telecom Eireann plc, excepting those held on a short leasehold
basis, was carried out by Hamilton Osborne King, Estate Agents, Auctioneers and Valuers, as at 31 March 1993.
This valuation valued those assets on a depreciated replacement cost basis or open market value.

The historical cost of the property assets shown at valuation amounts to:

	Group IR£'000	Company IR£'000
Cost	200,456	120,660
Accumulated Depreciation	45,930	29,620
Net Book Value	154,526	91,040

(e)
Included in tangible assets is plant and equipment acquired under finance leases as follows:

	Group		Company	
	1997 IR£'000	1996 IR£'000	1997 IR£'000	1996 IR£'000
Cost	264,088	195,523	187,557	184,522
Accumulated depreciation	89,638	46,676	65,106	43,669
Depreciation charge for the year	38,079	15,404	30,100	14,405

8. Financial Assets

(a) Group

	Interest in Securities	Investment in Related Companies	Total
Related companies - unlisted	IR£'000	IR£'000	IR£'000
At beginning of year	-	1,331	1,331
Additions	150,000	-	150,000
At end of year	150,000	1,331	151,331

(b) Company

	Interest in Securities	Subsidiaries Shares	Advances	Total
	IR£'000	IR£'000	IR£'000	IR£'000
At beginning of year - unlisted	-	7,986	56,348	64,334
Additions	150,000	76,000	-	226,000
Disposals	-	(2,450)	-	(2,450)
At end of year - unlisted	150,000	81,536	56,348	287,884

(c)

On April 5, 1996 the trade and assets of the mobile business were transferred to Eircell Limited at a value of IR£76m in return for shares in that company.

On July 25, 1996 the trades of INET Limited and Eirtrade Limited were transfered to Minitel Communications Limited. Minitel Communications Limited now trades as Eirtrade Services Limited.

(d)

Eircable Limited, Eircell Limited, Eirtrade Limited, Eirtrade Services Limited, INET Limited,Telecom Eireann Information Systems Limited, Telecom Ireland International Limited and Telecom Phonewatch Limited which are wholly owned subsidiaries of the Company, have availed of the filing exemption available under Section 17 of the Companies (Amendment) Act , 1986, whereby they will annex the financial statements of the Group to their annual returns.

(e)

The proceeds from the Strategic Alliance were invested in interest bearing securities with maturities ranging from 1999 to 2000.

9. Stocks

	Group		Company	
	1997	1996	1997	1996
	IR£'000	IR£'000	IR£'000	IR£'000
Network development and maintenance stocks	6,987	6,962	3,732	3,962
Consumable and other stocks	11,507	10,172	10,850	9,613
	18,494	17,134	14,582	13,575

10. Debtors

		Group		Company	
		1997	1996	1997	1996
		IR£'000	IR£'000	IR£'000	IR£'000
Amounts falling due within one year:					
Trade debtors		199,591	129,377	168,366	127,779
Prepayments and accrued income		64,957	88,627	60,328	85,921
Amounts owed by subsidiary companies			-	206,382	728
Amounts owed by related companies		1,784	1,518	1,784	1,518
Other debtors		1,015	1,264	442	528
Director's loan	(a)	-	77	-	77
		267,347	220,863	437,302	216,551

		Group		Company	
Amounts falling due after more than one year:					
Promissory note	(b)	70,000	-	70,000	-

(a)
The loan to the Company's Chief Executive, Mr. A. Kane, was repaid in full during the year.

(b)
The Minister for Transport, Energy and Communications and the Minister for Finance have issued an interest bearing, non-negotiable promissory note to the Company in consideration for the issue of new shares, in the amount of IR£70m.

The promissory note will mature on 20 December 2000 or earlier, if certain conditions set out in the promissory note agreement occur before the maturity date. Interest on the note is linked to Irish Government treasury stock coupon rates.

11. Loans and Other Debt

Payable	Within 1 Year IR£'000	Between 1 & 2 Years IR£'000	Between 2 & 5 Years IR£'000	After 5 Years IR£'000	Total IR£'000
Group					
Loans	54,586	75,707	204,470	146,977	481,740
Finance leases	15,844	14,813	27,561	747	58,965
Overdrafts	5,003	-	-	-	5,003
At 3 April 1997	75,433	90,520	232,031	147,724	545,708
At 4 April 1996	201,262	59,206	327,754	160,770	748,992
Company					
Loans from Subsidiaries	-	-	456,986		456,986
Finance leases	19,655	19,275	46,808	22,819	108,557
Overdrafts	3,633	-	-	-	3,633
At 3 April 1997	23,288	19,275	503,794	22,819	569,176
At 4 April 1996	31,584	19,483	311,231	26,198	388,496

The presentation of the maturity analysis of loans and other debt above complies with the provisions of FRS 4 "Capital Instruments". The standard requires that the maturity of debt should be determined by reference to the earliest date on which the lender can require repayment. Included in amounts repayable within one year are amounts of IR£16.5m (1996: IR£80.5m) relating to Irish Commercial Paper which are backed by committed medium term facilities which effectively extends the maturity of these instruments.

Included in the above are amounts:

	Group 1997 IR£'000	Group 1996 IR£'000	Company 1997 IR£'000	Company 1996 IR£'000
Wholly repayable within 1 year	54,059	177,809	4,021	18,123
Wholly repayable within 5 years	306,778	376,299	504,114	323,113
Repayable by instalments, not wholly repayable within 5 years :				
within 5 years	43,554	34,115	38,222	21,062
after 5 years	4,284	20,297	22,819	26,198
Repayable, otherwise than by instalments, due after 5 years	137,033	140,472		
	545,708	748,992	569,176	388,496

11. Loans and Other Debt Cont'd.

Group loans and other debt are denominated in the following currencies:

	'000	IR£'000
Irish Punts	341,398	341,398
ECU's	10,601	7,840
Deutsche Marks	180,160	68,477
Dutch Guilders	26,638	8,999
Luxembourg Francs	332,322	6,120
Swiss Francs	124,674	55,117
French Francs	205,300	23,168
Japanese Yen	4,813,711	26,443
Pounds Sterling	7,827	8,146
TOTAL		545,708

At the year end the capital value of the loans and other debt has been fully hedged into Irish Pounds using a variety of financial instruments maturing in the 1997/98 financial year. It is the Group's intention to renew these agreements as they expire.

The Minister for Finance has guaranteed loans included in the above table at 3 April 1997 to the extent of IR£178.3m (1996: IR£302.4m). Bord Telecom Eireann plc has guaranteed loans of its subsidiaries, Irish Telecommunications Investments plc of IR£286.1m (1996: IR£338.4m), and Telecom Phonewatch Limited of IR£1.1m (1996: IR£0.3m).

12. Other Creditors

Amounts falling due within one year	Group		Company	
	1997 IR£'000	1996 IR£'000	1997 IR£'000	1996 IR£'000
Trade creditors	50,368	71,224	43,645	68,933
Amounts owed to Group Companies			173,208	62,317
Accruals and deferred income	175,534	147,531	135,737	118,964
PAYE/PRSI	471	383	122	154
VAT	23,447	22,921	22,204	20,752
Advance corporation tax	(383)	2,343	(383)	2,343
Corporation tax	32,700	1,856	3,800	
	282,137	246,258	378,333	273,463

13. Provision for Liabilities and Charges

Group	Deferred Taxation IR£'000	Restructuring Provision IR£'000	Total IR£'000
At beginning of year	70,057	41,321	111,378
Utilised		(9,517)	(9,517)
Profit and Loss Account	42,478	25,000	67,478
At end of year	112,535	56,804	169,339

Deferred taxation arises from capital allowances and losses forward offset by advance corporation tax.

Company	Deferred Taxation IR£'000	Restructuring Provision IR£'000	Total IR£'000
At beginning of year	48,000	41,321	89,321
Utilised		(9,517)	(9,517)
Profit and Loss Account	61,790	25,000	86,790
At end of year	109,790	56,804	166,594

The full potential liability for deferred taxation is as set out below.

	Group		Company	
	1997 IR£'000	1996 IR£'000	1997 IR£'000	1996 IR£'000
Capital allowances	163,427	193,604	159,592	111,546
Advance corporation tax	-	(48,437)	-	(48,437)
	163,427	145,167	159,592	63,109

Further provision for deferred taxation is not required because, in the opinion of the Directors, unprovided timing differences are unlikely to reverse in the foreseeable future.

14. Capital Grants

Group and Company	Group		Company	
	1997	1996	1997	1996
	IR£'000	IR£'000	IR£'000	IR£'000
Received				
At beginning of year	68,344	63,223	68,344	63,223
Received during year	2,242	5,121	2,163	5,121
Transferred to subsidiary company	-		(14,541)	-
At end of year	70,586	68,344	55,966	68,344
Amortisation				
At beginning of year	37,780	30,623	37,780	30,623
Amortisation to profit and loss account	13,455	7,157	11,699	7,157
Transferred to subsidiary company	-		(9,447)	
At end of year	51,235	37,780	40,032	37,780
Net book value at end of year	19,351	30,564	15,934	30,564

15. Called Up Share Capital

On the formation of the Strategic Alliance, the company issued 106.25m ordinary shares of IR£1 each for a total consideration of IR£220m. The consideration was satisfied by a cash payment of IR£150m and the issue of a non-negotiable promissory note amounting to IR£70m.

	1997	1996
	IR£'000	IR£'000
Authorised Ordinary Shares of IR£1 each	600,000	500,000
Issued and Fully Paid	441,565	335,315

The following dividends attach to the ordinary shares

10% of retained profits in 1996/97
30% of retained profits in 1997/98
Up to a maximum of 50% of retained profits in 1998/99 and subsequent years.

16. Reserves

Group	Share Premium IR£'000	Revaluation Reserve IR£'000	Revenue Reserves IR£'000
At beginning of year	-	53,700	113,973
Retained profit for the financial year	-	-	113,746
Transfers on realisation of revalued assets	-	(2,766)	2,766
Arising on shares issued ·	113,750	-	-
At end of year	113,750	50,934	230,485

Company	Share Premium IR£'000	Revaluation Reserve IR£'000	Revenue Reserves IR£'000
At beginning of year	-	38,798	141,416
Retained profit for the financial year	-	-	105,697
Transfers on realisation of revalued assets	-	(2,020)	2,020
Arising on shares issued	113,750	-	-
At end of year	113,750	36,778	249,133

No provision has been made for any tax liability that would arise if the revalued property assets were disposed of at their revalued amounts.

17. Amounts in Group Cash Flow Statement

Amounts included in the group cash flow statement are reconciled or analysed as follows:

(a) Net Cash Flow from Operating Activities

	1997 IR£'000	1996 IR£'000
Operating profit	245,354	183,047
Depreciation	274,696	268,936
Increase in stock	(1,360)	(994)
Increase in creditors	8,280	12,927
Increase in debtors	(68,664)	(43,116)
Exchange loss on translation of a Group company		35
Increase in restructuring provision	15,483	16,321
Net cash inflow from operating activities	473,789	437,156

(b) Return on Investment and Servicing of Finance

	1997 IR£'000	1996 IR£'000
Interest received	4,788	3,733
Interest paid	(50,538)	(62,950)
Interest element of finance lease payments	(3,359)	(6,063)
Net interest paid	(49,109)	(65,280)

(c) Taxation Paid

	1997 IR£'000	1996 IR£'000
Advance corporation tax	(2,726)	(5,843)
Corporation tax	(600)	(1,811)
	(3,326)	(7,654)

(d) Capital Expenditure and Financial Investment

	1997 IR£'000	1996 IR£'000
Payments to acquire tangible fixed assets	(267,966)	(193,480)
Capital grants received (of which IR£2.16 million has been received from the European Commission)	2,242	5,121
Capital expenditure	(265,724)	(188,359)

17. Amounts in Group Cash Flow Statement Cont'd.

(e) Management of Liquid Resources

	1997 IR£'000	1996 IR£'000
Net withdrawal of short term deposits	420	8,586
Net increase in deposits	(398)	(1,346)
	22	7,240

(f) Financing

	1997 IR£'000	1996 IR£'000
Repayment of loan capital	(477,552)	(549,647)
Additions to loan capital	324,184	403,045
Capital element of finance lease additions		637
Capital element of finance lease payments	(19,005)	(19,253)
Issue of Share Capital	150,000	
Net cash outflow from financing	(22,373)	(165,218)

The net movement on the loans and finance leases during the year is accounted for by the net cash outflow from financing above together with a favourable exchange rate movement of IR£24.234m (1996: IR£5.725m).

18. Principal Subsidiary and Related Companies

	Interest in Ordinary Shares at 3 April 1997	Business	Registered Office and Country of Incorporation
Subsidiary Companies			
Irish Telecommunications Investments plc (ITI plc)	100%	Telecommunications Financing and Treasury Management.	114 St. Stephen's Green West, Dublin 2, Ireland.
Eircell Limited	100%	Provision of Mobile Telecom Services.	Eircell House, 6-8 College Green, Dublin 2, Ireland.
Telecom Ireland (U.S.) Limited	100%	Marketing of Telecom Services in U.S.A..	114 St. Stephen's Green West, Dublin 2, Ireland.
Eirtrade Services Limited	100%	Provision of Electronic Trading Services.	114 St. Stephen's Green West, Dublin 2, Ireland.
Telecom Ireland International Limited	100%	Provision of Treasury Management and Consultancy Services.	4 Harbourmaster Place, IFSC, Dublin 1, Ireland.
Telecom Phonewatch Limited	100%	Installation, Monitoring and Maintenance of Residential Security Systems.	114 St. Stephen's Green West, Dublin 2, Ireland.
Cablelink Limited	75%	Construction and Operation of Cable and MMDS Television Systems.	10 Pembroke Place, Ballsbridge, Dublin 4, Ireland.
Eirpage Limited	51%	Marketing of Radio Paging Service.	Anglesea House, Donnybrook, Dublin 4, Ireland.
Related Companies			
Golden Pages Limited	49%	Directory Publishing.	. St. Martin's House, Waterloo Road, Dublin 4, Ireland.
Broadcom Eireann Research Limited	45%	Broadband Telecommunications Research and Development.	6 Fitzwilliam Square, Dublin 2, Ireland.

19. Profit on Ordinary Activities Attributable to Bord Telecom Eireann plc

An amount of IR£105.7m (1996: IR£59.6m) of the consolidated profit attributable to the shareholders of Bord Telecom Eireann plc has been dealt with in the financial statements of the Company. A separate profit and loss account for the Company has not been prepared because the conditions laid down in Section 3(2) of the Companies (Amendment) Act, 1986 have been satisfied.

20. Employees

The average number of persons employed by the Company and its subsidiaries during the year was as follows:

	Group		Company	
	1997	1996	1997	1996
Managerial	1,298	1,306	1,227	1,257
Clerical	1,788	1,694	1,554	1,557
Technical	7,332	7,534	7,143	7,390
Operator Services	1,281	1,326	1,235	1,319
Other	537	512	509	502
	12,236	12,372	11,668	12,025

During the last two years, a total of 1,076 people left the company under retirement schemes and 350 additional specialists were recruited.

21. Pensions

(a)

The Group's pension commitments are funded through separately administered Superannuation Schemes and are of a defined benefit nature. The Group's contributions of IR£37.9m (1996: IR£38.6m) in respect of the year to 3 April 1997 are at an average rate of 15.9% of pensionable emoluments as advised by the Actuaries to the schemes.

The last Actuarial Valuation of the principal scheme was carried out as at 20 December 1996 by Mercer Fraser Pension and Investment Consultants who are actuaries to the Scheme (but are neither officers nor employees of the Group).

The actuarial method used involved determining an appropriate future Company contribution rate designed to fund the projected liabilities of the Scheme (related to service subsequent to 1 January 1984) over the remaining working lifetime of the current members. The primary financial assumption underlying the actuarial valuation was that the Scheme's investments will earn a real rate of investment return, over and above salary inflation and pension increases, of 2.5% per annum. At the date of the last actuarial valuation the market value of the pension scheme assets was IR£871m and the actuarial valuation of the assets was sufficient to meet 106% of the value of the scheme's accrued liabilities (making due allowance for future increases in salaries and pensions). Contributions by the Company will decrease to 15.4% as a result of this valuation.

The actuarial report is available for inspection by the members of the scheme.

(b)

The payment of pension entitlements in respect of certain persons who were members of the staff of the Department of Posts and Telegraphs and who retired or died before the Vesting Day (1 January 1984) has been delegated to the Company by the Minister for Finance under Section 46 of the Postal and Telecommunications Services Act, 1983. Payments made by the Company in accordance with the delegation are made out of the Superannuation Fund and the costs are the liability of the Minister for Finance who is also liable in respect of the pension entitlements arising from pre-Vesting Day reckonable service of staff who transferred from the Department to the Company on Vesting Day and who subsequently retired or died. The amount of the liability of the Minister for pre-Vesting service at the year end was IR£170.1m and the manner of discharge by him of the liability has been agreed by the Minister for Finance.

22. Contingent Liabilities

At the balance sheet date there were no contingent liabilities or guarantees in respect of which material losses are expected.

In the normal course of business, the Group has entered into contracts involving the exchange or purchase and sale of foreign currencies. No material losses are expected in respect of these transactions other than losses for which provision has been made in the financial statements.

23. Capital Commitments

Capital commitments approved by the Board at the balance sheet date amounted to approximately IR£293m for the Group and IR£216m for the Company, of which IR£32.9m was contracted for by the Group and the Company. Capital commitments at 4 April 1996 amounted to approximately IR£275m.

24. Comparative Amounts

Certain comparative figures have been re-grouped and re-stated where necessary on the same basis as those for the current year.

25. Approval of Financial Statements

The financial statements were approved by the Board of Directors on 28 May 1997.

Country Highlights
SPAIN

Common Legal Form of Companies

The Commercial Code specifies several forms for companies. The most relevant are described below:

- *Sociedad Anónima*, where partners have limited responsibility to their contributions to the share capital, and their rights are represented by the shares. These companies are regulated by the Companies Act.
- *Sociedad de Responsabilidad Limitada*, very similar to *Sociedad Anónima*, but smaller.
- *Sociedad Colectiva*, where partners have full and personal responsibility.
- *Sociedad Comanditaria*, where each partner could have a different position in regard to the company's rights, and therefore, partners' personal responsibility depends on the rights.

The common form for larger companies in Spain is the *Sociedad Anónima*, although a greater number of smaller companies are classified as *Sociedad de Responsabilidad Limitada*.

Sources of Financial Reporting Requirements

Financial reporting requirements are contained in the Commercial Code, the Companies Act of 1989, PGC-90, the Rules for Consolidation of 1991, and the accounting rules and sectorial plans issued by ICAC

Corporation Tax

Corporation tax regulation is contained in the *Ley del Impuesto sobre Sociedaded* 1995. The general corporation tax rate is 35% on a company's profits.

Auditing Requirements

The Auditing Law of 1989 establishes compulsory audits for the following companies:

1. Those having their securities listed on any stock exchange
2. Those making public issues of debentures
3. Those generally involved in financial business
4. Those governed by the Private Insurance Regulation Act

5. Those receiving subsidies or aids, or undertaking work for the state, or providing services or supplies to the state (within limits still pending definition by the government)
6. Any other companies within the limits determined by the government. At present such limits are:
   - Total assets of no more than 395 million pesetas
   - Net annual turnover of less than 790 million pesetas
   - Average number of employees during the accounting period no more than 50

Organization of the Accounting and Auditing Professions

The *Instituto de Contabilidad y Auditoría de Cuentas* (ICAC) is the body responsible for regulating the accounting profession. It issues and explains the accounting rules. An unofficial professional body known as AECA is a nonmandatory reference for accounting practice in Spain.

The ICAC also has the responsibility to regulate and control the auditing profession and the auditors themselves, in addition to quality control of audits performed. Auditors must be registered by the ROAC in order to work in auditing activity. Auditors may be inscribed in three professional bodies: ICJC, REA, and REGA. An auditor may be part of a company or may be an individual professional.

Constitution and Legal System

Spain is a parliamentary democracy with a constitutional monarchy. The Spanish Constitution was approved in 1978. There is some devolution to regional parliaments in Catalonia and the Basque Country. After the Constitution, the main general Laws are the Civil Code, the Mercantile Code, and the Penal Code. In addition, there are a number of mercantile laws, for example, the Companies Act of 1989, the Competence Act of 1989, the Patents Act of 1986, the Cooperative Companies Act of 1987, the Law of Financial Institutions of 1985, the Law of Consumer Protection of 1984, the Law of Disloyal Competence of 1991, the By-law of Mercantile Register of 1989, and the Mortgages Law of 1981.

Currency

Peseta

Official Languages

Spanish is the official language of the entire country. Other languages are spoken in local regions, where they are considered official languages for some purposes, for example, Catalonian in Catalonia, Basque in Basque Country, and Galician in Galicia.

SPAIN

Francisco J. Martinez
Price Waterhouse, Madrid

1. Background

1.1 A Brief History of Accounting Regulation in Spain

The history of accounting practice in Spain can be traced back to the Middle Ages. In the early modern period, the huge volume of trade with Spain's vast overseas empire gave rise to an impressive quantity of accounting records, examples of which may be seen in an archive in the city of Seville. In more modern times, official regulations were established in the early decades of the 19th century, when the Commercial Code of 1829 laid down some rules for the formalities of account-keeping but imposed no obligations in regard to annual financial reporting. Certain changes were introduced during the following decades, and particularly by the Revised Commercial Code of 1885. The rules contained in the latter still mainly concerned the formal aspects of accounting, although some financial reporting requirements were imposed for limited companies.

The Commercial Code of 1885 essentially remains in force as the basis of commercial rules in Spain, although it has been modified in many respects. In addition, the enactment of various laws and bylaws has produced additional developments.

An important mercantile reform was introduced by means of the Companies Act of 1951, which regulated a number of the main aspects of the business affairs of companies. Although this law introduced some accounting rules, they were quite brief and limited.

More complete development in accounting matters had to wait until 1973, when the first General Accounting Plan was published (PGC-73), consisting of a set of accounting rules and procedures and containing some specimen financial statements. It was based on the French Accounting Plan of 1959.

PGC-73 regulations were excessively rigid and more concerned with the content of the accounts from the point of view of taxation than with meaningful reflection of the economic situation of companies. The definitions and the accounting principles were poor, compared with other countries' standards. Nevertheless, the use of the plan was optional and a number of economic situations were either slightly considered or not considered at all, including such important issues as leasing, deferred taxation, pensions, and exchange rate differences. Certain sectorial accounting plans were issued to deal with problems in specific sectors.

In 1979, a private association was set up, known as *Asociación Española de Contabilidad y Administración de Empresas* (AECA, Spanish Association of Accounting and Business Administration), see Section 2.6.2. This body worked to develop certain pronouncements on accounting matters, which were taken in many instances as a guide for authorities and companies.

Because of the lack of regulation, companies continued for years preparing their financial statements in accordance with the accounting principles generally accepted by custom, taking into account some or all of the pronouncements of PGC-73 and those proposed by AECA.

But PGC-73 was not enough to support all the financial reporting needs of companies, and this situation promoted the existence of a number of individual solutions for the many problems companies had, and therefore, over the years, the accounting performance and practice differed in many instances from international standards. Comparability of financial statement was problematic.

In general, the development of financial reporting and auditing in Spain remained slow and patchy until the stimulus provided by the need to comply with European Community Directives and other international pressures. These brought about a comprehensive reform beginning in the late 1980s, which provides the framework for the present commercial and accounting regulation. The need to adapt commercial regulation to those proposed by the European Community produced reform in 1989.

1.2 Present Accounting Rules

The promulgation in 1989 of the *Ley 19/1989 de Reforma Mercantil y Adaptación a las Directivas de la CEE* (Commercial Reform Act 19/1989) was the vehicle that introduced commercial reform into Spanish practice, being in line with those in force in the European Community and enabling Spain to adopt the Directives in accounting matters. Important changes were introduced to the Commercial Code of 1885 to provide the necessary legal environment, leading to a new set of rules, which constitute the framework for current commercial and accounting rules.

The Legislative Royal Decree 1564/1989, which contains the text of the New Companies Act of 1989 (*Texto Refundido de la Ley de Sociedades Anónimas*), coming into force on January 1, 1990, now provides wide and comprehensive control of accounting practices and completes the criteria and regulations for the preparation and presentation of accounting information in the annual financial statements.

In addition to the above-mentioned rules, the commercial reform process had an important foundation, which was the issue in December 1990 of the General Accounting Plan of 1990 (PGC-90) by Royal Decree 1643/1990. The importance of the PGC-90 is that it imposes a new way to understand accounting practice in Spain. the PGC-90 has three main purposes: (i) to give transparency to the companies' annual accounts, (ii) to achieve comparability of the accounts, and (iii) to adapt Spanish accounting practice to international standards.

The PGC-90 introduces new accounting principles, valuation rules and procedures, and requirements for information to be given in the annual reports, in addition to some models of financial statements. All of them are mandatory for financial years commencing from January 1, 1991 for all companies, whatever their size or legal standing.

Although the Companies Act of 1989 establishes a full detail of accounting principles and a number of accounting rules, the PGC-90 is richer in definitions, descriptions, and development, which are in fact proper interpretations of the law. The latter is therefore the real source of standards required to implement the Companies Act of 1989, in the sense of ensuring that the annual accounts fulfil the legal obligation to give a true and fair view (*imagen fiel*) of the net worth and financial position and of the results and of funds obtained and applied by the companies. Full details of both sets of requirements—the legal ones and those included in the PGC-90—are included in the following sections.

An important regulation was the issue of the rules and procedures for the Consolidation of Annual Accounts, in December 1991 by Royal Decree 1815/1991 as a development of the Commercial Reform Act of 1989, which impose the obligation to prepare consolidated accounts for financial years ending after January 1, 1991. These rules were the last big step to bring Spanish accounting practice into line with international standard practice.

The issue of the above-described rules, which contain general text that needs to be interpreted and clarified in many aspects to be properly applied, including the PGC-90, represents the beginning of a new era in Spanish accounting practice. However, many important tasks had to be implemented in the following years. The most important tasks were related to the need to develop accounting rules to accommodate various economic situations, besides the need to adapt the general rules in cases of certain sectors having special operating functions.

To give complete support for the future development of reform, from the accounting point of view, the Auditing Act issued in 1988 (see Section 1.3) created a new regulatory body responsible for, besides the control and regulation of auditing, the development of accounting practice, interpretations of accounting rules, and approval of any new regulation needed for those purposes. This body is known as *Instituto de Contabilidad y Auditoría de Cuentas* (ICAC, Institute of Accounting and Auditing).

For purposes of the development of accounting practice, ICAC has issued since 1990 several additional rules, consisting of two different kinds of approaches: statements of additional accounting rules and sectorial accounting plans.

The additional statements of accounting rules are mandatory for every company, in the preparation of the annual accounts, and for the auditors in their reviews. The most relevant of such documents are listed in Table 1.

The sectorial accounting plans are in fact extensions of the PGC-90, adapted for specific sectors. They are mandatory in all their premises and rules, besides the financial statement models, for every company operating in the related sectors and for auditors in their reviews. The practical way to define such sectorial plans is to identify what should be changed from the general the PGC-90 to adapt the general rules for the specific operations of the related sector, in order to assure that the annual accounts present properly the true and fair view of the company, as well as to provide the best information to understand the accounts.

To carry out those plans, working groups are nominated, composed of individuals representing a number of experts in each sector. Among the experts, representatives of the following are generally included: official regulators, other government authorities, companies in the sector, auditors, academics, and other groups with an interest in the sector. Once the group has produced a draft, a period of public consultation takes place.

Some sectorial plans have already been issued and are in force, and others are under study. A list is shown in Table 2.

TABLE 1 *Additional Accounting Rules, Documents of ICAC*

Description	Issued
Accounting for mergers and acquisitions	January 1991
Valuation of fixed assets	July 1991
Transitory rules for pensions for electricity sector	July 1991
Consolidation rules and procedures	January 1992
Accounting for deferred tax in pensions	October 1991
Valuation of intangible assets	January 1992
Accounting for income tax	April 1992
Accounting for investments in monetary funds	September 1992
Accounting for nonmonetary share capital contributions	July 1992
Accounting for indirect tax IGIC in Canary Islands	December 1992
Valuation of bonds for insurance companies	December 1992
Accounting for options and financial futures	March 1993
Exchange differences for regulated companies	March 1993
Exchange differences for transportation companies	March 1994
Equity definitions for the purposes of capital reduction	December 1996
Accounting for VAT and tax IGIC of Canary Islands	March 1997
Accounting for income tax	October 1997
Accounting treatments for the introduction of the Euro	October 1997

At present, because of the changes introduced by the regulations in force, accounting practice in Spain is completely in line with European practice and with the International Standards.

1.3 The Auditing Profession

Until quite recently, auditing had no specific coverage under Spanish legislation. There was no general obligation to submit accounts to be reviewed by an auditor, except for listed companies on the Stock Exchange, whose annual accounts had to be reviewed by members of the *Instituto de Auditores-Censores Jurados de Cuentas* (ICJC, Institute of Sworn Auditors).

TABLE 2　*Sectorial Plans issue by ICAC*	
Description	*Issued*
Already in force:	
Building and constructions	January 1993
Sports federations	March 1994
Building promoters	March 1995
Sports companies	October 1995
Health assistance companies	March 1997
Insurance companies	December 1997
Electricity companies	March 1998
Under study:	
Motorways concessionaire companies	Draft
Joint venture businesses	Draft
Nonprofit organizations	Draft
Water concessionaire companies	Under study
Wine producing companies	Under study

The ICJC was founded in 1943 and received legal recognition in the Companies Act of 1951. For years its professional audit effectiveness was limited. There were three main reason for this. First, it had limited support from the accounting community. Second, there was no deep public interest in audit practice, hence the weak enforcement by the authorities of such requirements. Finally, the reviews were generally more restricted than those audits developed under international practice.

The issue of the Auditing Act 19/1988, which came into force on July 16, 1988, brought a profound change in auditing practice in Spain. This law created a body responsible for regulation of accounting rules and auditing standards and procedures: the *Instituto de Contabilidad y Auditoría de Cuentas* (ICAC), which is attached to the Ministry of Finance and Treasury. At the same time, the law established an official register of auditors, the *Registro Oficial de Auditores de Cuentas* (ROAC), where all auditors are required by law to be registered.

Auditors may be individuals or auditing companies and must get permission to act from ICAC in order to register with the ROAC. To get such permission, in the case of individuals, a number of conditions must be met related to academic qualifications and personal skills, and a formal test must be passed.

Besides the ROAC, every auditor must register with any one of the three existing professional bodies: the ICJC, the *Colegio de Economistas (REA,* College of Economists), and the *Colegio de Titulados (REGA, College of Graduates in Commerce).*

In March 1990, the ICAC published the Technical Auditing Standards, with which all auditors must comply. They are similar to the International Auditing Standards.

The Auditing Act 19/1988 established compulsory audits for the following companies for any financial year beginning after July 16, 1998:

1. Those having their securities listed on any stock exchange
2. Those making public issues of debentures
3. Those generally involved in financial business
4. Those governed by the Private Insurance Regulation Act
5. Those receiving subsidies or aids, or undertaking work for the state, or providing services or supplies to the state (within limits still pending definition by the government)
6. Any other companies within the limits determined by the government

The scope of Point 6 had already been laid down for limited companies by the Commercial Reform Act of 1989, which states that an audit is compulsory for the accounts of all companies, except those that qualify for an abridged balance sheet. As a result, an audit must be performed for the accounts of every company meeting the requirements and limits set out in Section 2.1.5 (under "Abridged Balance Sheet"). Similar considerations apply to Point 4.

Within the scope of the audit, the auditor will also review whether or not the accounting information contained in the Management Report agrees with the annual accounts and the accounting books.

In addition to normal auditing, auditors are required by the Companies Act of 1989 to carry out special reviews of certain situations with regard to companies' legal operations. Such reviews are regulated by the ICAC, which has issued certain standard rules to be followed by auditors in such cases. The most relevant of such special legal audit reviews are described in Table 3.

TABLE 3   *Special Audits Regulated by ICAC Documents*

Description	Issued
Report on fair value of shares in increases of capital in case of removal of the right to preferential share subscription	June 1990
Issue of convertible bonds	January 1991
Several cases of changes in legal situation of companies	January 1991
Increases in share capital through capitalization of debts	May 1991
Increases in share capital through capitalizations of reserves	July 1991
Reductions of share capital to reflect losses	March 1993
Special report for financial companies accounts	October 1993
Special report for insurance companies accounts	December 1993
Public periodic information for listed companies	July 1994
Special report for co-operatives having credits sections	September 1994
Special report for Exchange agent companies accounts	October 1997

The ICAC has issued several documents to regulate auditing practice, which are mandatory for all auditors. Such documents are in fact standards for auditors. The most relevant of such documents are listed Table 4. (Some have been modified subsequently.)

TABLE 4   *Audit documents issued by ICAC*

Description	Issued
Audit standards rules and procedures	March 1990
Auditing by-law	December 1990
Materiality	July 1991
Subsequent events	January 1992
Relationship between auditors	January 1992
Quality control on audits	April 1992
Going concern principle considerations	September 1992
Internal control auditing standards	March 1993
Information in case of internal control weaknesses	September 1994
Conditions for tuition required to new auditors	August 1995
Use of independent experts for auditors	October 1995

The ICAC is also responsible for the quality control of audit practice, in conjunction with the professional bodies.

When the Auditing Law was issued, it stated that companies had to appoint their auditors for a minimum term of 3 years and a maximum of 9 years. They could not appoint the auditor again after 3 years. This requirement was changed in 1995 so that once the 9-year period has expired, companies can appoint any auditors annually, even the current auditor.

The Auditing Law has since been modified. A new law is being drafted by the government and is currently under discussion.

A recent report of ICAC shows the situation of the auditing profession in Spain (see Table 5).

TABLE 5   *The Auditing Profession in Spain*

Auditors in ROAC	Number	%
Companies	802	
Individuals	15,347	100%
• Acting	4,580	30%
• Acting for others	1,084	7%
• Nonacting	9,683	63%
In Professional Bodies	Individuals acting	Companies
Total	96%	99%
ICJC	46%	50%
REA	31%	36%
REGA	19%	13%
Auditors with Employees	Individuals acting	Companies
Number of auditors	935	541
Number of professional staff employed	2,156	5,846
Total hours worked in 1996	983,690	5,616,600
Jobs Performed in 1996	Number	%
Statutory mandatory audits	22,184	63%
Voluntary audits	6,928	20%
Other mandatory jobs	2,103	6%
Other voluntary jobs	3,276	9%
Other	648	2%
Total	35,139	100%

Source: ICAC Public Bulletin

2. The Form and Content of Annual Accounts

2.1 Presentation of Accounting Information

As generally described above, accounting practice in Spain is regulated by the Commercial Code of 1885, the Companies Act of 1989, the Commercial Reform Act of 1989, the General Plan of Accounting 1990 (PGC-90), and the rules for consolidation of Annual Accounts set out in Royal Decree 1815/1991 of December 1991, as well as the ICAC statements on accounting rules and sectorial plans. General accounting requirements are analyzed in the following paragraphs.

2.1.1 General Requirements

The present legislation contains certain general requirements, most of them introduced for the first time into Spanish practice. A summary is included below:

- The rules for the preparation of the annual accounts are mandatory for all companies.
- Standard valuation rules and presentation requirements are presented.
- A unique model of financial statements for all companies is given.
- Annual accounts must be prepared by the Board of Directors within 3 months after the year end.
- Final approval of the annual accounts corresponds to the shareholders' meeting, within 6 months after the year end.
- A new responsibility scheme for the Board of Directors is established.
- Mandatory audits are set for independent auditors, under certain limits.
- Annual accounts must be filed in the Public Register for general knowledge.

2.1.2 Preparation and Content of Annual Accounts

Annual financial statements are in respect of the accounts at the close of the financial reporting period, which may not exceed 12 months. The year end can be established at any date, although the most common date is December 31. A management report and a proposal for the distribution of results must also be prepared.

The annual accounts consist of the balance sheet, the profit and loss account, and the notes (*la memoria*), all making up one whole document. They must be worded clearly and must truthfully reflect the *imagen fiel* (true and fair view) of the net worth, the financial position, and the profits and losses and the funds obtained and applied by the company. The notes also include a statement of sources and application of funds.

The annual accounts must be signed by all members of the Board of Directors. If any signature is absent, that fact must be indicated on each of the documents, and the reasons must be stated.

Whenever the application of legal provisions is insufficient to give a true and fair view, additional information is to be provided. In exceptional cases, if the application of a legal provision on accounting matters is incompatible with the true and fair view, such provision will not be applicable. In such cases, mention should be made in the notes, stating the causes and the effects on the net worth, the financial situation, and the profit and loss of the company.

2.1.3 Structure of the Annual Accounts

The Companies Act of 1989 requires that the annual accounts show at least the details and structure shown in Appendix A, at the end of this chapter.

More detailed subdivisions may be made, or new entries included, provided that they comply with the established structure. Grouping may also be made under Arabic numbers whenever necessary for the sake of clarity. Additional information can be provided in *la memoria*.

In addition to the figures for the closing financial year, each of the entries in the balance sheet, profit and loss account, and the statement of sources and application of funds must indicate the figures for the immediately preceding financial year. Whenever these amounts are not comparable, the amounts from the earlier financial year should be adjusted. In any event, any problems of comparison and adjustments of the amounts should be indicated in the notes, with explanations as appropriate.

Legal provisions prohibit offsetting between asset and liability headings. Balance sheet and profit and loss entries showing balances in the present financial year and in the preceding year will not be shown in the aforementioned documents.

2.1.4   *The Notes (memoria)—Concept and Content*

La Memoria is a new document within Spanish accounting doctrine, forming an integral part of the annual accounts, which replaces the former "notes to the financial statements," although in fact the concept is similar. Previously, many companies prepared and published another document, called the "commercial report," which contained accounting, commercial, and management information. The present document is much more generous in terms of information and much more detailed in its analysis. However, the previous document contained nonaccounting information, in many cases with respect to future projects, which do not now form part of the annual report. Nevertheless, much of this information is not altogether lost, as it may be given in the Management Report (see *Section 2.1.6* below).

Nowadays, in normal practice, such a "commercial report," containing commercial information, and the accounting information, containing the annual accounts, the Management Report and the Auditors' Report, are published together in the same booklet, but a clear separation exits between accounting and nonaccounting information.

Conceptually, *la memoria* completes, explains, and comments on the balance sheet and profit and loss account. It must contain all information considered necessary for adequate interpretation of the annual accounts.

The information required in *la memoria* according to the PGC-90 is wider in scope than that demanded under the Commercial Reform Act of 1989 and the Companies Act of 1989. The requirements of each set of regulatory texts are given below.

Requirements of the Commercial Reform Act of 1989 and the Companies Act of 1989   In addition to what has been mentioned in the preceding paragraphs, the annual report should contain the following information:

1. Valuation rules applied to the items in the annual accounts
2. Calculation methods used for provisions on assets
3. The procedure used to calculate the exchange rate for items expressed in foreign currency
4. The names and addresses of companies in which an important participation is held, that is, the direct or indirect possession of a

minimum of 3% of the capital of a company. The fraction of the capital held will also be stated, in addition to the amount of capital and reserves and the profit and loss for the previous financial year.

5. The number and nominal value of each type of share of the company

6. The statement of sources and applications of funds

7. The existence of bonds, convertible securities and securities, and other rights, stating the number and extent of the rights so granted

8. The amount of debts having a remaining duration of more than 5 years

9. The amount of debts actually secure, with an indication of the form and type

10. The overall amount of guarantees committed with third parties

11. Separate mention of existing commitments with respect to pensions

12. Analysis of the net turnover by categories of activity and geographic markets

13. The average number of employees in the current financial year according to category, as well as itemized staff expenses

14. The difference between the accounting results and those earmarked for taxation purposes, indicating the future tax charge

15. The difference between the tax charge allocated in respect of the present and previous financial years and that already paid or to be paid

16. The overall amount of salaries, allowances, and all types of remuneration earned during the financial year by directors, as well as the obligations contracted in terms of pensions or life assurance in respect of former or present staff

17. Overall information with respect to advances and credits granted to staff, stating interest rates, essential facts, and amounts eventually repaid, as well as obligations assumed by the company on their behalf in the form of guarantees

18. Movements of items included under fixed assets, as well as establishment costs. Additions, withdrawals and conveyances, corrections of accrued value, and any rectifications made during the year should be shown separately by category of fixed asset.

19. If the payment of a dividend on account is approved, an accounting statement, prepared by directors and showing the existence of sufficient liquidity

20. Justification for the amortization of goodwill over a period of more than 5 years (if applicable)

Mention of items 4 and 12 may be omitted, this being indicated in the annual report, whenever, owing to their nature, serious prejudice might be caused to the company by their disclosure.

In the event that an abridged annual report may be prepared (see the conditions under Section 2.1.5, "Abridged Memoria," below), it is only necessary to include the information contained in items 1–5, 16, and 18–20. The statement of sources and application of funds need not be included.

Requirements of the PGC-90   As mentioned previously, the General Accounting Plan of 1990 is more demanding with respect to the presentation of information in the annual accounts, because in addition to the requirements listed above, it requires the following information to be included in the annual report:

1. The proposed distribution of results for the year

2. The valuation rules applied, including an exhaustive list of the criteria to be applied for each category of assets and liabilities

3. With respect to fixed assets:
   - Assets owned under leasing agreements: cost at source, length of contract, years expired, contributions paid in previous years and in the current year, pending contributions, and value of the purchase option
   - In the case of significant items of intangible fixed assets, information concerning their use, expiration date, and period of depreciation

4. Company commitments with respect to purchases and foreseeable financing sources, as well as company commitments with respect to the sale of any kind of asset

5. Other information concerning leases, insurance, lawsuits, attachments, and other similar situations that might affect of the company

6. Additional information concerning tangible fixed assets:
   - Details of the updating of the value of tangible fixed assets
   - Useful lives of the assets or depreciation ratios used
   - The characteristics, gross value, and accrued depreciation of elements acquired from group companies
   - Investments located outside Spanish territory
   - Capitalized interest and exchange differences
   - Amount and description that are not used in normal operations
   - Amount of totally written-off items
   - Assets that are technically obsolete or not in use
   - Items subject to guarantees and reversion
   - Subsidies and donations received

7. Point 4 relating to the Commercial Reform Act of 1989 and the Companies Act of 1989 is expanded as follows:
   - Separation of group companies and associates, the latter being those in which a significant participation is held (20%, or 3% if listed on the Stock Exchange), without forming part of the group
   - The activities undertaken by each of the group companies
   - Analysis of extraordinary items in the profit and loss account
   - Dividends received during the financial year
   - An indication as to whether or not the shares are listed on the Stock Exchange, and if so, the average quotation for the last quarter and at the close of the financial year
   - The same information for associated companies
   - Securities given in guarantee
   - Fixed income securities maturing in each of the next 5 years and the remainder, separated according to group companies, associates, and others
   - Securities given in foreign currency
   - The amount of interest due and not collected
   - The average rate of the interest paid during the year

8. Nontrade debits and credits, distinguishing between short and long term, foreign currency, exchange difference cover, maturity in each of the next 5 years, guarantees, and other relevant information

9. With respect to inventory, a breakdown of the following:
   - Firm purchase and sale commitments, as well as future contracts
   - Limitations in availability
   - Stocks appearing under assets at a fixed value

10. With respect to equity:
    - Increases and decreases in equity
    - Detail and movement of every reserve
    - Details of Revaluation Reserves
    - Movement of own shares, number held, final destination of same and amount of the related reserve
    - Details concerning capital increases underway, with respect to number of shares, nominal value, issue premium, rights and restrictions, etc.
    - Amounts of capital authorized by the General Meeting of Shareholders to be floated by the company directors and period of authorization
    - Restrictions on the availability of reserves
    - Any part of the capital held by another company, directly or through its affiliates, which is more than 10%

11. Discount lines and policies granted to the company

12. Debentures and bonds outstanding

13. With respect to taxation:
    - Negative assessments (tax losses) pending compensation, with indication of time limits and conditions
    - The nature and type of applicable and pending tax incentives, as well as commitments acquired in connection with same

14. With respect to pensions, detailed information about the movement of provisions for internal funds, in addition to information relating to the kind of liabilities subscribed and the estimates parameters, such as discount rate and other.

15. Relevant subsequent events, after the year end

16. A funds of flow statement (*cuadro de financiación*)

In the event that an abridged annual report may be prepared (see conditions under Section 2.1.5, "Abridged *Memoria* (Notes),") it is only necessary to give the additional information included under items 1, 2, and 8. The funds flow statement need not be included.

2.1.5 Types of Annual Accounts

Companies must prepare their annual accounts according to what can be called the normal pattern. The structures required under the Commercial Reform Act of 1989 and the Companies Act of 1989 are those indicated in Appendix A , at the end of this chapter, in Spanish and English. The PGC-90 requires that annual accounts are prepared according to more detailed models, indicated in Appendix B at the end of this chapter.

Both the Commercial Reform Act of 1989 and the Companies Act of 1989, as well as the PGC-90, allow the preparation of summarized annual accounts, which are known as "abridged accounts," in the case of small companies and under certain conditions.

The necessary conditions for preparing abridged balance sheets also constitute the limits for the companies to be audited, in the sense that a company that may not prepare abridged balance sheets for its annual accounts must have its annual accounts audited.

The limits for both balance sheet and profit and loss accounts have been modified from the first text of the Companies Act. The most recent update was introduced by Royal Decree 572/1997, of April 18, 1997, relating to accounting limits in the Companies Act.

Abridged Balanced Sheet An abridged balance sheet may be prepared if at least two of the circumstances shown in Table 6 prevail on the closing date of the accounting period for two consecutive years.

TABLE 6 *Requirements for Abridged Balance Sheet*

	Initial figures	Present figures
Total assets of no more than (million pesetas)	230	395
Net annual turnover of less than (million pesetas)	480	790
Average number of employees during the accounting period no more than	50	50

TABLE 7 *Requirements for Abridged Profit and Loss Account*		
	Initial figures	*Present figures*
Total assets of no more than (million pesetas)	920	1,580
Net annual turnover of less than (million pesetas)	1,920	3,160
Average number of employees during the accounting period no more than	250	250

Section 2.2.2 below indicates the required content of the abridged balance sheet.

Abridged Profit and Loss Account   An abridged profit and loss account may be prepared if at least two of the circumstances shown in Table 7 prevail on the closing date of the accounting period for 2 consecutive years.

Section 2.2.2 below indicates the required content of the abridged profit and loss account.

Abridged *Memoria* (Notes)   An abridged *memoria* may be prepared by any company qualifying for an abridged balance sheet. The required minimum information was given in Section 2.1.4 above.

2.1.6   *The Management Report*

The Management Report is a new document under Spanish legislation, although owing to its similarity to the old "commercial report" as indicated in Section 2.1.4, it is not entirely new to commercial practice.

Under the new legislation, the Management Report is included as a document separate from the annual accounts, being compulsory for all companies, regardless of size and the type of annual accounts presented, and should be prepared by the directors of the company at the same time as the annual accounts.

The Management Report includes the following:

1. A true indication of the evolution of the business and the position of the company
2. Important events occurring after the close of the financial year

3. Research and development activities carried out by the company
4. Acquisitions and disposals of own shares:
   - Reasons for acquisitions and disposals during the financial year
   - The number and nominal value of shares acquired and disposed of during the financial year, plus the fraction of capital they represent
   - Consideration received for shares acquired or disposed of on a payment basis
   - The number and nominal value of all own shares acquired and held by the company itself or by an intermediary, plus details of the fraction of capital they represent

The Management Report must be reviewed by the auditor under the terms established in Section 1.3. It must be filed, together with the annual accounts, as indicated in the following section.

2.1.7 Publication of Annual Accounts

An important new requirement of the Commercial Reform Act of 1989 concerns the publication of annual accounts. The maximum time for approval by the shareholders' meeting is 6 months from the year end. After approval, the annual accounts, together with the Management Report and the Auditors' Report, must be filed in the Commercial Register of the city in which the company has its registered office, within a maximum period of one month. The Commercial Register may then provide such information to anyone who requests it.

According to information from the Commercial Registers, the number of companies filing their annual accounts is increasing every year.

The new accounting rules have introduced companies into routine accounting practice, and the standardization of rules and models of accounts has resulted in published accounts of good quality. This was one of the main objectives of the reforms, and it can be said that the objective has been attained.

2.2 Model of Financial Statements since 1990

2.2.1 General Model

Models of the balance sheet, profit and loss account, and statement of sources and applications of funds, as laid down by the PGC-90, are shown in Appendix B, in both Spanish and English, at the end of this chapter. Additionally, a specimen set of financial statements is appended, also in Spanish and English.

2.2.2 *Model of Abridged Accounts since 1990*

Both the Companies Act of 1989 and the PGC-90 coincide with respect to the models of the abridged balance sheet and profit and loss account, which consist of presenting the information specified in the full models under roman numerals, without the further detail specified under Arabic numerals.

2.3 Consolidated Annual Accounts

2.3.1 *Overview*

Consolidation of the accounts of groups of companies has been mandatory in Spain since the implementation of the Commercial Reform Act of 1989. Hence, the obligation started for all accounting periods ending after December 31, 1990, and it then became compulsory to prepare annual consolidated accounts. Before this time, only certain types of companies were required to prepare such accounts, for example financial entities.

The Commercial Reform Act did not specify the rules and models to be followed for the annual group accounts, although it did specify general standards in respect of the structure and content of the consolidated annual report. However, in December 1991 the rules for Consolidation of Annual Accounts were issued by Royal Decree 1815/1991.

2.3.2 *General Definitions*

Consolidated accounts are considered to be an accounting tool to present the financial results and position of a group of companies, but they do not have legal implications or tax effects.

Under Spanish legislation, a group of companies exists when a Spanish company (the parent company) has control of the majority of voting rights in the shareholders' meeting of other companies (the subsidiaries).

TABLE 8 *Exemptions to Consolidate*

	Initial figures	*Present figures*
Total assets of no more than (million pesetas)	2,300	3,950
Net annual turnover of less than (million pesetas)	4,800	7,900
Average number of employees during the accounting period no more than	500	500

To calculate the real control held by the parent company, all direct and indirect control must be considered, and own shares held by the parent company and shares without voting rights must be deducted (the Spanish Companies Act allows the issue of shares having only financial rights and no voting rights).

The consolidation rules have provided a transitory exemption that allows small groups not to prepare annual consolidated accounts. The limits defined relate to the figures shown in Table 8 for the group.

Another exemption (as provided in the Seventh Directive) is when the parent company of a group is a subsidiary of a company of another European Union member state, which effectively prepares and publishes its consolidated accounts. In those circumstances, it is not necessary to prepare the consolidated accounts of a Spanish subgroup. To apply this exemption, certain circumstances must occur and some formal requirements must be observed.

There exists a scheme for consolidated corporation tax returns purposes, which can be applied in certain circumstances, but that follows different principles from the consolidation for financial reporting purposes, in that only companies in which 90% or more of the share capital is held by the group can be included.

In general terms, Spanish consolidation principles are now in line with principles generally accepted internationally.

2.3.3 Methods of Consolidation

Three methods have been defined to consolidate different kinds of investment of the parent company:

1. Full consolidation (*Integración global*)
2. Equity method (*Puesta en equivalencia*)
3. Proportional consolidation (*Consolidación proporcional*)

Subsidiaries effectively controlled by the parent company must be consolidated by using the full consolidation method (line-by-line consolidation). Such a treatment implies the integration of all the assets and liabilities, income and expenses of the subsidiaries with the accounts of the parent company, recognizing the minority interest, and recording separately the goodwill arising on first consolidation of each subsidiary.

Investments in which the parent company has a significant influence must be consolidated by the equity method. A significant influence is defined, in the absence of other evidence, when the a company holds a participating interest greater than 20% of the voting rights (or 3% for listed companies).

The proportional consolidation method may be used for investments in which the parent company participates in a joint venture with other groups, and they are managed jointly. This method is not obligatory, and the parent company may choose this method or the equity method.

2.3.4 Accounting Principles and Policies

The accounting principles and policies to be used in consolidated accounts do not differ from general accounting principles and policies. The only differences are those derived from the consolidation process.

When performing the process of consolidation, the following steps should be observed in all three methods:

- Harmonization *(Homogeneización)*, or the application of homogeneous accounting principles and policies and dates of closing, that is, those of the parent company, to the accounts of all group companies. In addition, assets and liabilities of acquired companies are restated at their fair values (*valor de mercado*).
- Addition *(Agregación)*, or addition of the resultant "homogeneous" accounts
- Eliminations *(Eliminaciones)*, or the elimination of the investments of the parent company together with the equity of the subsidiaries, exclusive of any profits or losses, balances, dividends, and so on, existing from intragroup-group operations.

Goodwill (when positive) is accounted for as an intangible asset and amortized against the profit and loss account over a 10-year period. If the period is longer than 5 years, specific disclosure of the justification should be included in the annual accounts. A periodic evaluation of future economic benefits related to the goodwill is required. Negative goodwill is accounted for as a liability, that is, either as a deferred credit to be amortized back to income or as a provision for future reorganization expenses or losses of the acquired company.

Because the other accounting principles and policies used in consolidated accounts are similar to the general rules, references must be made to the relevant paragraphs in Section 3.

2.4 Breakdown: Geographic or by Activity

Both the Commercial Reform Act of 1989 and the Companies Act of 1989, as well as the PGC-90, stipulate that the annual report must include a breakdown of the net turnover figure according to categories of activity and by geographic markets. No further information is given as to the scope of this analysis.

As stated in the regulations, the aforementioned requirements may be omitted when, owing to their nature, they could cause prejudice to the company. No further information or clarification is given regarding the conditions for this exception or for the causes that would be considered acceptable.

As can be seen from many annual reports, this information is generally shown in published accounts. The descriptions included are sufficient to provide a general indication of the activities of companies.

2.5 Legal or Institutional Requirements

2.5.1 Legal Requirements

As previously mentioned, the legal requirements for the preparation and presentation of annual accounts are basically those stipulated by the Commercial Reform Act of 1989 and the Companies Act of 1989. In addition, the PGC-90 provides a precise interpretation of the requirements of the Commercial Reform Act, and thus it is advisable to follow its pronouncements. The Commercial Reform Act states that when the legal provisions are insufficient to ensure a true and fair view (*imagen fiel*), they shall be extended as necessary in order to reach the desired objective.

Furthermore, with the publication of the PGC-90, a set of transitional regulations came into force that affect a considerable number of companies in Spain. (For further details, see Section 3.2.)

2.5.2   *Institutional Requirements: The Accounting Profession and the Stock Exchange*

Until the new regulations came into effect, accounting practice was guided by the pronouncements of the *Asociación Española de Contabilidad y Administración de Empresas (*AECA, Spanish Association of Accounting and Business Administration), a private body composed of professionals and experts in accounting and business administration. Its pronouncements are of an advisory nature and are neither binding nor compulsory but do represent a consensus of opinion on different situations given by leading professionals and are therefore a model to be followed.

To date, AECA has published several the documents adapted to the new legal environment. The documents issued are of a varied nature, but the most relevant for the purpose for this work are those referring to accounting practice, as shown in Table 9.

Companies whose shares are listed on the Stock Exchange must prepare and present their annual accounts according to the requirements of the Commercial Reform Act of 1989 and the Companies Act of 1989.

3. Accounting Principles and Policies in Valuation and Income Measurement

This section presents the most important accounting principles and policies to be observed in the preparation of the annual accounts.

3.1 Transitory Provisions

Before going into the principles and policies, it is relevant to make a general mention of the transitory provisions that came into effect with the publication of the PGC-90. Some of them are no longer in effect, but others are still in force. Following is a summary of those provisions that

TABLE 9 *Documents Published by AECA*

Accounting principles:

1. Principles and policies of accounting in Spain
2. Fixed assets
3. Intangible fixed assets and deferred expenses
4. Treatment of exchange differences in foreign currency
5. Suppliers, creditors, and other accounts payable
6. Customers, debtors, and others accounts receivable
7. Accruals and prepayments and collections and deferred payments
8. Stocks
9. Corporation tax
10. Equity
11. Provisions, contingencies, and subsequent events to year end
12. Accrued income
13. Income
14. Reversion fund (a provision for the return of assets to the state)
15. Investments
16. Pensions
17. Expenses
18. Financial liabilities
19. Future and options on stocks (draft)
20. Cash flow statement (draft)

Management Accounting:

1. Management accounting definitions
2. Management accounting environment
3. Management accounting as a control tool
4. Cost accounting: concepts and methodology
5. Materials: value, allocation, and control
6. Staff
7. Production indirect costing
8. Overheads
9. Management accounting financial institutions
10. Management accounting insurance institutions
11. Cost of quality
12. Standard costs (proposed document)

were very important in understanding the transition process and those that are still in force:

- During the first accounting period in which the PGC-90 was applied, differences in the values of the assets and liabilities against the recorded figures could be adjusted against the voluntary reserves (distributable).

- Losses in respect of exchange differences activated before January 1, 1990 could be written off within a period of 3 years following the accounting period closed after June 30, 1990.

- Companies with deficits on their provisions for pensions, being the funds invested in the employer company, should systematically endow the respective provisions until such deficit is covered, within the following time limits, starting from the commencement of the first accounting period that closes after June 30, 1990:
  a. In the case of provisions for pensions provided for at the beginning of the relevant accounting period in respect of retired employees: 7 years
  b. In the case of provisions for pensions provided for the beginning of the relevant accounting period in respect of active employees: 15 years

- For the first accounting period for which the PGC-90 was applicable, if leasing arrangements existed, the lessee company could choose between:
  a. Recording the outstanding amounts as of that date according to the criterion used in previous accounting periods (i.e., showing the amounts as an expenditure for the financial year and not including the goods under assets or recognizing the related liabilities)
  b. Applying the valuation standards of the PGC-90, and including the goods under assets and recognizing the liability, as retroactive from the commencement of the contract. The difference arising between the effects of the different criteria will be recorded in the reserve accounts after deduction of tax
  Where there are several contracts in force, the same option selected should be used for all of them.

There was another general provision relating to the considerations in the case of differences between accounting and tax valuations for the assets, but it has no effect today, because tax regulation has recently moved to recognize the accounting figures for tax purposes.

3.2 Accounting Principles

The basic concepts of accounting are reflected in the general accounting principles, that in their main aspects coincide with those contained in the EU Directives. These principles must be followed by companies in the preparation of the annual accounts and are as follows:

- Prudence in the process of valuation of assets and liabilities: only realized gains are to be recorded, while losses should be recognized when known.
- Historical costs or acquisition price basis for all assets and rights.
- Going concern basis for businesses: accounting principles have the objective of showing the company in an operating situation. Therefore, they do not intend to show the value of the assets in a liquidation process.
- Accrual basis: income and expenses must be recorded according to the appearance of goods and services, without considering the moment of payment.
- Correlation of expenses and income: the net profit for a year must be arrived at through the income for the period less the corresponding expenses.
- Consistency, which implies that once any principles have been adopted they must be maintained in the future.
- Separate valuation and presentation: it is not permitted to compensate assets with liabilities or expenses with income, and every item from the balance sheet and profit and loss account must be valued separately.
- Materiality, which says that any principle need not be strictly applied if the effects are irrelevant and the annual accounts are not affected from the perspective of providing a true and fair view.

3.3 Accounting Policies and Valuation Rules

The most important accounting policies and valuation rules included in the PGC-90 are described below.

3.3.1 *Tangible Fixed Assets*

Fixed assets must be accounted for according to the historical cost convention, and therefore they must be disclosed at acquisition price or production cost, or market value if lower. Additional or complementary investment will be incorporated into the cost of the fixed asset.

For the purposes of this rule, the following definitions must be observed:

- Acquisition price:
  - —Acquisition price includes the amount invoiced by the supplier and additional expenses involved until it is in working order.
  - —Financial expenses incurred in the asset's acquisition or production (intercalated interest) may be included, with an indication of the amount in the annual report.
  - —Taxes related to the purchase will be considered as costs only if they cannot be recovered from the Public Treasury.

- Production cost:
  - —Acquisition price of raw materials and components and directly imputable cost
  - —Indirect cost that may be reasonably assigned to the period of manufacture
  - —Financial interest may be included, until the moment when the assets are in the condition to start production, indicating the amount in the annual report.

- Value for assets obtained free of charge:
  - —This kind of asset, those received without cost to a company, must be recorded at the value that a third party would pay for it, bearing in mind the condition of the goods.
  - —This concept will be use only for ongoing companies and operations.

- Corrections in the value of fixed assets:
  - —Systematic depreciation must be recorded, according to the useful life of the assets, and considering also the conditions of use and obsolescence.
  - —In the event of the cessation of the relevant circumstances, the provision will reverse.

—In the case of irreversible loss, this must be written off directly against the asset value.

Besides the general rules explained above, the following specific standards apply to tangible fixed assets:

- Land: cost includes preparation expenses, as well as the demolition of buildings and the costs involved in inspections and preparation of plans before acquisition.

- Buildings: cost includes permanent installations and professional taxes and fees. The value of the land should be disclosed separately.

- Technical installations, machinery, and equipment: cost includes all amount invested until start-up.

- Tools and utensils: when they are incorporated into other assets, i.e., installations or machinery, the cost and depreciation criteria will be those of the latter. In general terms the following aspects must be considered:

  —If they do not form part of any machinery and their useful life is estimated at less than a year, they should be charged to expenses.

  —If they will be used for more than a year, year-end estimates are suggested, through a physical inventory.

  —Patterns used for mass production are considered to be fixed assets and should be depreciated according to their useful life. If they are used only for isolated manufacturing operations, they are not considered part of the inventory.

- Work carried out on a fixed asset: the expenses incurred will be capitalized (charged to the asset) and credited to income at the year end under the heading "work carried out by the company for fixed assets."

- Renewal, expansion, or improvement: these items will be capitalized (charged to the assets) if they represent an increase in the capacity, productivity, or a lengthening of the useful life, when it is possible to estimate the net value of the elements that should be written off owing to replacement.

3.3.2   *Revaluation of Fixed Assets*

As previously mentioned, companies in Spain must use the historical cost convention. Nevertheless, revaluation of fixed assets is permitted when established by law, both for tax and accounting purposes and effects.

This kind of revaluation was common until 1983, when the government withdrew approval for it. In 1996 a new fixed assets revaluation process was approved by means of Royal-Decree-Law 7, 1996.

The accounting effects of the revaluation consist of an increase in the asset value according to the limits permitted by the Law, credited against revaluation reserves.

Revaluation reserves are nondistributable for a period of 10 years but are available for increases in share capital after 3 years.

All revaluation reserves constituted up to 1983 may be used, and in fact many companies have already applied them to share capital or free reserves or to compensate losses. The only present restrictions on revaluation reserves are those derived from the last 1996 revaluation.

3.3.3   *Intangible Fixed Assets*

Intangible fixed assets will be valued at acquisition price or production cost. The rules regarding the depreciation and provisions in respect of tangible fixed assets are applicable to the extent that they do not contradict the specific rules described below.

- Research and development expenses: Research and development expenses will be considered expenses of the accounting period in which they occur. Such expenses can be deferred if they comply with the following conditions:
    - They are individualized according to project and with specifically established costs that can be allocated over time.
    - The success and economic and commercial profitability of the project may reasonably be expected.
    - The amounts deferred should be amortized over a period of not more than 5 years.
    - If any doubts arise as to the project's success or its profitability, immediate write-off to the profit and loss should be made.
    - The amounts included under this heading restrict the possibility of

distributing dividends, as they reduce the availability of the free reserves by an amount equal to their net balance.

- Industrial property rights (e.g., patents) include research and development expenses when the patent is obtained, inclusive of registration charges.

- Goodwill: Goodwill may be recorded in the accounts only when it is purchased, both in individual and consolidated accounts. It is not permissible to capitalize self-generated goodwill of any kind.

    In the case of the purchase of goodwill, an intangible asset may arise in the books of the acquiring company. The amount recorded under this heading should be written off systematically to profit and loss account as a current expense for amortization of the intangible asset over the period of contribution to the activity, which should not exceed 10 years. If this period exceeds 5 years, mention and explanations should be provided in the annual report.

- Transfer rights: Transfer rights may be recorded in the accounts only if purchased. Amounts should systematically be written off over the period during which such rights contribute to the flow of income.

- Software: The expenses incurred for software developed by the company itself can be capitalized only in the event that the use is intended for more than one year.

    In general terms, the rules related to research and development expenses are also applicable to software development expenses.

    Under no circumstances may maintenance costs be included under asset value.

- Leased assets in Spain, as in a number of EU member states, are recognized as intangible assets. In Spain the following aspects must be considered:
    —They must be recorded under asset items when, because of economic conditions, there is no reasonable doubt that the purchase option will be exercised.
    —The amount credited, including the value of the purchase option, is recorded under liabilities. The interest should be considered an accrued expense to be distributed over the period of the lease contract by using a financial criterion.

—Depreciation should be calculated over the useful life of the leased asset.

- Sale and lease-back: If the sale of an asset is connected with the subsequent leasing back of the asset sold so that the transactions have the character of a financial operation, the lessee must account for the transaction as a financial lease, as follows:

  —Transfer the net book value of the asset from fixed assets to leased assets (included under intangibles)

  —Recognize under liabilities the total debt, that is, the present value of the lease payments plus the purchase option

  —Any difference will be allocated to profit and loss over the duration of the lease.

3.3.4 Establishment Costs

Establishment costs are to be valued at the acquisition price or production cost of the asset in question.

The following can be considered establishment costs in the context of company formation or an increase in share capital: the fees of lawyers, notaries, and registrars; the printing of annual reports, bulletins, and share certificates; taxes; advertising; and commissions and placement costs

The following can be considered establishment costs in the context of the launching a new activity or product line: external consulting fees; traveling and prior study expenses; advertising; hiring, training, and distribution of personnel.

Establishment costs should be systematically written off to the profit and loss account over a period of not more than 5 years.

Distributable reserves in an amount equal to the net balance of establishment costs must be transferred to nondistributable reserves.

3.3.5 Deferred Expenses to be Distributed over Several Years

Just a few cases have been considered in the PGC-90 as deferrable expenses. They are as follows:

- Expenses involved in the arrangement of debt:
  —Should be valued at acquisition cost or production cost

—Should be treated as expenses of the respective accounting period

—If capitalized exceptionally, should be written off within the same period as the aforementioned debt, in accordance with the financing plan

- Expenses of the nature of deferred interest:

—Discount on issue or premium on redemption of a debt

—To be amortized as provided for over the maturity of the debt

Nevertheless, practice has provided some additional definitions when the needs have arisen. This was the case, for instance, in the special definitions for the electricity sector, where some deferred expenses permitted in the past as a result of the regulated recovery rules included fixed asset depreciation expenses and exchange differences (see Section 3.2.15 for further details on electricity sector rules).

3.3.6 Negotiable Securities

Short-term and long-term securities, both shares or debenture bonds or other kinds of securities, will be valued at their acquisition price upon subscription or purchase. This price will include the expenses inherent to the operation, and the following should be borne in mind:

- The cost of the rights of preferential subscription will be included in the purchase price.
- The dividends due and the interest payable that are not part of the repayment value of the security will not be considered as forming part of the price.

When the rights are sold, their cost will reduce that of the securities. Such costs will be determined by applying generally accepted valuation formulas following a prudent criterion and bearing in mind the valuation adjustments recorded in the accounts.

The system to be applied in the valuation of the investments will be that of the weighted average price or cost.

In order to record the value of the securities, the following rules must be observed:

- In the case of listed securities, the valuation will be the lower of cost or market value.

- If market value is lower, a provision should be made, the amount of which could reduce even more the net book value, if prevailing circumstances made it advisable.

- Market price is the lower of the average quotation for the last quarter and that of the day of the closing of balance sheet. In the event of any interest that distorts the comparison, such interest should be considered for all purposes.

- If the securities are not listed, they should appear at acquisition cost. When the acquisition cost exceeds rational valuation criteria accepted in practice, a provision must be made against this value.

- In the latter case, the net equity value should be considered after being corrected for any potential surplus derived from fixed assets, when this can be demonstrated.

- The same criteria will be applied to investments in the capital of group companies or associates, with provisions being made to reflect the evolution of the equity of the invest company, even though listed securities are involved.

- In the case of purchasing own shares the following rules are applicable:

  —Own shares are to be valued in the same way as other shares.

  —When own shares are amortized, the difference between the acquisition cost and par value, either positive or negative, must be recorded against reserves.

  —Profits or losses from sales of own shares will be credited or charged as extraordinary items of profit or loss, in accounts established for this purpose.

3.3.7 Nontrade Credits and Debts

Nontrade credits allowed are to be valued at the amount to be paid. The difference between this amount and the nominal value, which represents the interest charged, will be entered as financial income over the maturity term.

Balances from the sale of fixed assets will be valued at selling price, discounting the interest included in the nominal value of the credit.

The accrued interest, whether due or not, will be credited taking account of the due date and will be recognized in accordance with the respective accruals.

Nontrade debts should be included at repayment value. The difference between this value and the amount received will be shown in the assets and will be written off in accordance with a financial criterion.

Debts from fixed assets will be shown at nominal value. Any interest included in the nominal value and not included in the fixed asset will be treated as mentioned above.

3.3.8 Stocks

Stocks must be accounted at acquisition price or production cost. The following definitions must be considered:

- Acquisition price: price included on the invoice plus additional costs until the goods are in the warehouse, including taxes imposed on the sale if such taxes are not recoverable from the public treasury.

- Production cost: acquisition price of raw materials and consumables, plus costs directly imputable and a reasonable part of the indirect costs in the period of manufacture.

- Valuation adjustments: a provision will be recorded when reversible depreciation of the acquisition price or production cost arises against the market value. For this purposes the market value is understood as:

  —In the case of raw materials, the lesser of replacement cost and net completion value

  —In the case of commodities and finished products, the completion value, less the respective trade taxes

  —For work in progress, the completion value of the finished product, less costs to complete and marketing costs

Products subject to a definitive future sale will not be the object of valuation correction, if the price obtained is sufficient to cover all the historical costs as well as those still to be incurred during that particular operation.

If the articles cannot be identified, the method of weighted average cost will be applied in general. Other methods, such as FIFO, LIFO, or similar methods, are also acceptable. In exceptional cases, the stocks can be valued at an overall fixed rate, if:

- They are constantly renewed.
- Their overall value and composition do not vary significantly.
- Their overall value is not material for the company.

3.3.9 Foreign Exchange Differences

Generally, items originally denominated in foreign currency should be included in the annual accounts by using the exchange rate at the date of the acquisition, on the date they were included in the net worth, or on the date of the transaction, as applicable.

Other specific rules are as follows:

- Tangible and intangible fixed assets: depreciation should be calculated according to the value obtained as described above.
- Stocks:

  —The rule will be applied individually for each transaction and will be separate from the method of valuation applied.

  —The calculation of the market value for the purpose of the closing provision will be made by applying the quotations and exchange rates in force at that date.

- Securities: the value at closing may not exceed the result of applying the exchange rate at that date to the market quotation.
- Treasury: at close, all items should reflect current exchange rates, the resulting exchange differences being treated as profit or loss for the accounting period.
- Credits and debits:

  —At close, credits and debits should be valued at the exchange rate in force at that moment, exclusively with respect to the part without exchange cover.

  —Any resulting differences will be classified according to maturity and currency, and in the latter case, it is permitted to group together currencies convertible in Spain that show a similar performance on the market.

—The net balance resulting from the above grouping:

- If positive (profit), it should be treated as a deferred credit under "Income to be distributed over several years."

- If negative (loss), it should be charged to the profit and loss account.

—Unrealized positive differences may be credited to the profit and loss account if they are in respect of groups for which losses have been recorded in previous accounting periods, up to the amount of such losses.

—Income deferred in this way will be applied to profit and loss as:

- The items causing them become due

- Negative exchange differences for equal or greater amounts are recognized

• Other special rules:

—Exchange differences should not be considered as a correction of the value of the fixed assets, except in the case of long-term financing for the purchase of a fixed asset (which in this case would be considered part of the cost of the fixed asset, subject to a general ruling in this respect), provided the following are complied with:

- That the debt has been unmistakably incurred to acquire a specific identifiable fixed asset

- That the period of installation is more than 12 months and the exchange rate difference occurs before start up.

- That the resulting amount does not exceed the market or replacement value of the fixed asset

—Special regulations may be issued for specific industries or sectors. This has been the case for the electricity sector and the transportation sector.

3.3.10 Corporation Tax

Existing differences between the accounting net income and the taxable income (taxable base) are considered as follows:

a. Permanent: differences not reverting in subsequent periods, excluding the compensatable losses
b. Temporary differences: based on differences in the temporary criteria of allocation, reversing in subsequent periods
c. Losses compensated for tax purposes

The expense to be recorded will be calculated on the profit or loss before tax, corrected by the permanent differences. The respective tax rate will be applied to this amount, and the allowances and deductions (not payments on account) will be deducted from the resulting quota.

Deductions and allowances from the quota will be considered as a reduction of the tax accrued in the year.

Temporary differences and compensated losses will not be taken into consideration when determining the expense for corporation tax purposes.

The items resulting from the temporary differences will be stated, according to each case, as assets or liabilities (advance or deferred tax) in the balance sheet. For valuation purposes, the rate actually in force during the accounting period should be used, the appropriate corrections being made to the value in the accounting period in which the quota is modified.

Advance taxes by temporary differences or compensatable tax losses (advance tax assets) may be recognized in the accounting sense only when their future realization is reasonably assured, and will be immediately withdrawn should any doubts arise in this respect.

The deductions and allowances from the quota may be considered as deferred income and be subject to a reasonable time apportionment.

3.3.11 Purchases and Other Expenses

Purchases of commodities and goods for resale follow the rules described below:

- The following items will be charged net of deductible VAT:
  —Purchase expenditures
  —Transportation
  —Tax on acquisitions
- Discounts, etc. included in the invoice will be deducted from the amount of the purchase.

- Discounts, etc. for prompt payment, whether or not they are included in the invoice, will not be deducted and will be treated as financial income.
- The following discounts or credit notes will be recorded as shown below:
  —Those that are based on reaching a specific number of transactions, in one account
  —In another, distinct account, the credit notes in respect of quality defects, delivery times, and other similar reasons
- Containers to be returned to suppliers that are charged in invoices by the latter will be recorded by reducing the balance payable and using a separate account, and the amount that the company keeps for its use (deteriorated or lost containers, etc.) will be allocated to expenses.

3.2.12 Sales and Other Income

The sale of goods will be treated in accordance with the following rules:

- The sales figures will not include the related taxes.
- Inherent expenses (i.e. transportation) will be accounted for in separate accounts, never reduced from sales figure.
- Discounts will be accounted for as follows:
  —Those included in the invoice that are not for prompt payment will be deducted from the sales figure.
  —Those granted for prompt payment will be classified as financial expenses.
  —Those based on a volume of activity to be reached will be recorded as expenses.
  —Goods returned for quality defects, delivery times, or other similar reasons will be registered as returns.
- Containers to be returned to suppliers that are charged in invoices by the latter will be recorded by reducing the balance to be collected and using a separate account, and the amount that the customer keeps for its use (deteriorated or lost containers, etc.) will be allocated to income.

- Income from the sale of service will be registered following in the same rules.

3.3.13 Pensions

Pensions are one of the matters currently under regulation by the government. A draft law exists that requires companies to transfer to an external format all the liabilities for pension plans related to both active and retired employees, but a government bylaw is needed finally to define the procedures and dates for the introduction of such requirement.

At present, companies have to deal with two kinds of pension plans, externally funded and internally funded, in addition to defined contribution and defined benefit plans.

The PGC-90 states just a few rules on pensions for internal funds. These accounting rules are described below:

- Provisions must be made for accrued liabilities.
- Estimates should be made according to actuarial calculations.
- The financial interest generated by the fund should be applied as contributions.

The *memoria* must include detailed information about the movements of the provisions for internal funds, in addition to information related to the kind of liabilities subscribed and the estimates of parameters, such as the discount rate and others.

Most companies follow general international standards or U.S. standards in the recognition of accounting treatment of pensions, based on auditors' support.

3.3.14 Capital Subsidies

Capital subsidies will be recorded as deferred income according to the amount granted when they are of a nonrefundable nature.

They will be considered nonrefundable if:

- The conditions established for the granting of such subsidies have been complied with; or
- There are no doubts as to future compliance.

They will be allocated to the profit and loss for the accounting period in proportion to the depreciation of the assets financed by the subsidy.

3.3.15 Electricity Sector

Regulation for the electricity sector is contained in the *Ley del Sector Eléctrico* 54/1997, entering in force in November 1997. The sectorial plan for the electricity sector issued by the ICAC was approved by Royal Decree 437/98. It will enter in force for annual accounts prepared from January 1, 1998.

The main differences in the sectorial plan with respect to the general rules of the PGC-90 are summarized below:

- Incurred expenses can not be deferred except when the government assures recovery through the tariffs. This rule is very important because it supposes that the electricity sector is considered regulated, for accounting purposes, only through price regulation, and this is an important change, because currently no regulations exist in the sector that assure the recovery of any incurred cost.

- Former special accounting rules for deferred costs are superseded

- The *memoria* must display separate accounts for each activity. Liberalized activities (generation, supply, and international business) should be shown separately from regulated activities (transmission, distribution, and system operation). Balance sheet and profit and loss account formats for the activities are included in the sectorial plan.

- Nuclear fuel must be accounted for as a stock item and the annual charges to profit and loss account are considered as consumption, instead of fixed asset and depreciation as they were in the past.

- Much information must be included in the *memoria* relating to the environment.

- Transitory provisions are provided to regulate the treatment of "stranded costs" defined by the Electricity Sector Law. These give solutions for the problem of costs nonrecoverable through the market, the former deferred costs recognized in the accounts, and to the income for additional recovery of "stranded costs" to be received in future for a transitory period of 10 years.

- Thorough information is required to be provided in the *memoria* relating to the actual amounts received every year of additional retribution for "stranded costs," the amount considered to represent the coverage of fixed assets nonrecoverable through the market, and the expected amount receivable in future.

- Another transitory provision states that any costs derived from the reorganization of the companies due to the liberalization process, which are not to be recovered through operating income nor the additional recovery of "stranded costs" can be charged against free reserves in a 2 year period.

The Electricity Sector Law establishes that electricity companies must perform an unbundling of their activities into different companies before December 31, 2000.

4. Expected Future Developments

The process of harmonization with European practice might now be considered complete, because the recent reforms of Spanish commercial and company law have resulted in a highly developed environment for accounting. The commercial and accounting legislation have pointed the way to changes to be introduced into the Spanish practice. Nevertheless, some committees nominated by the *Instituto de Contabilidad y Auditoría de Cuentas* are currently working to issue statements on accounting policies and interpretations, and others are working on sectorial plans to adapt the general rules to the specific requirements of sectors.

Recent issues concern the projects to harmonize and converge European accounting practices into the accounting rules derived from the IASC. But this is still an ambitious project where many changes must be considered in the current legislation of every country in Europe and America. Although some countries have advanced very quickly, other are still in the first stages of the changes, so many years are needed to evaluate properly the final effects.

Useful Addresses

Instituto de Contabilidad y Auditoría de Cuentas (ICAC)
Huertas, 26
Madrid 28014
Spain
Tel.: +(1) 369 42 18
Fax: +(1) 429 94 86

Asociación Española de Contabilidad y Administración de Empresas
(AECA)
Alberto Aguilera, 31
Madrid 28015
Spain
Tel.: +(1) 547 44 65
Fax: +(1) 541 34 84

Instituto de Auditores-Censores Jurados de Cuentas de España
General Arrando, 9
Madrid 28010
Spain
Tel.: +(1) 446 03 54
Fax: +(1) 447 11 62

Appendix A: Required Structures of the Balance Sheet and the Profit and Loss Account, According to the Companies Reform Act of 1989 and the Companies Act of 1989

BALANCE—ACTIVO

A) Accionistas (socios) por desembolsos no exigidos

   Total A . . . .

B) Inmovilizado

   I Gastos de establecimiento

   II Inmovilizaciones inmateriales

   1. Gasos de investigación y desarrollo

   2. Concesiones, patentes, licencias, marcas y similares

   3. Fondo de comercio

   4. Anticipos

   III Inmovilizaciones materiales

   1. Terrenos y constucciones

   2. Instaliaciones técnicas y maquinaria

   3. Otras instalaciones, utillaje y mobiliario

   4. Anticipos e inmovilizaciones materiales en curso

   IV. Inmovilizaciones financieras

   1. Participaciones en empresas del grupo

   2. Créditos a empresas del grupo

   3. Participaciones en empresas asociadas

   4. Créditos a empresas asociadas

   5. Valores que tengan carácter de inmovilizaciones renta fija

   6. Otros créditos

   7. Acciones propias

   Total B . . . .

C) Activo circulante

   I Accionistas por desembolsos exigidos

   II Existencias

   1. Materias primas y consumibles

   2. Productos en curso de fabricación

   3. Productos terminados y mercancias

   4. Anticipos

BALANCE SHEET—ASSETS

A) Shareholders (partners) per non-required disbursements

   Total A . . . .

B) Fixed Assets

   I. Start-up expenses

   II. Intangible fixed assets

   1. Research and development costs

   2. Concessions, patents, licences, trademarks and similar

   3. Goodwill

   4. Advances

   III. Tangible fixed assets

   1. Land and buildings

   2. Technical installations and machinery

   3. Other installations, equipment and furniture

   4. Advances and tangible investments under way

   VI. Financial fixed assets

   1. Participations in companies of the group

   2. Credits to companies of the group

   3. Participations in associated companies

   4. Credits to associated companies

   5. Fixed income securities

   6. Other credits

   7. Own shares

   Total B . . . .

C) Current assets

   I. Shareholders per required disbursements

   II. Stocks

   1. Raw materials and consumer goods

   2. Products being manufactured

   3. Finished products and merchandise

   4. Advances

III Deudores
1. Clientes por ventas y prestaciones de servicios
2. Empresas del grupo, deudores
3. Empresas asociadas, deudores
4. Otros deudores

IV Valore mobiliarios
1. Participaciones en Sociadades del grupoes de empresas del grupo
2. Particpaciones en empresas asociadas
3. Acciones propias

V Tesorería

VI ajustes por periodificación

Total C . . . .

TOTAL GENERAL (A + B+ C) . . .

BALANCE—PASIVO

A) Fondos propios
I Capital suscrito
II Prima de emisión
III Reserva de revalorización
IV Reservas
1. Reserva legal
2. Reservas para acciones propias
3. Reservas estatutarias

4. Otras resevas

V Resultados ejercicios anteriores

VI Resultado del ejercicio (beneficio o pérdida)

Total A . . . .

B) Provisiones para riesgos y gasios
1. Provisiones para pensiones y obligaciones similares
2. Provisiones para impuestos
3. Otras provisiones
4. Fondo de reversión

Total B . . . .

C) Acreedores a largo plazo
1. Emisiones de obligaciones, separando convertibles
2. Deudas con entidades de crédito
3. Anticipos recibiods por pedidos
4. Deudas por compras o prestaciones de servicios

III. Debtors
1. Customers per sales and services rendered
2. Group companies—debtors
3. Associated companies—debtors
4. Other debtors

IV. Securities
1. Participations in companies of the group

2. Participations in associated companies
3. Own shares

V. Treasury

VI. Accruals and pre-payments

Total C . . . .

GENERAL TOTAL (A + B + C) . . .

BALANCE SHEET—LIABILITIES

A) Equity
I. Subscribed capital
II. Share premium
III. Revaluation reserve
IV. Reserves
1. Legal reserve
2. Reserves for own shares
3. Statutory reserves (created in accordance with a company's own bylaws)
4. Other reserves

V. Profit or loss from previous years

VI. Profit or loss for the year

Total A . . . .

B) Provisions for risks and expenses
1. Provisions for pensions and similar obligations
2. Provisions for taxes
3. Other provisions
4. Reversion fund (a provision for the return of assets to the State)

Total B . . . .

C) Long-term creditors
1. Issues of debentures, separating convertible ones
2. Debts with credit entities
3. Advances received by orders
4. Debts by purchases or services rendered

5. Deudas representadas en efectos de comercio
6. Deudas con Sociedades del grupo
7. Deudas con empresas asociadas al grupo
8. Otras deudas
Total C . . . .
D) Acreedores a certo plaza
 1. Emisiones de obligaciones, separando convertibles
 2. Deudas con entidades de crédito
 3. Anticipos recibiods por pedidos
 4. Deudas por compras o prestaciones de servicios
 5. Deudas representadas en efectos de comercio
 6. Deudas con Sociedades del grupo
 7. Deudas con empresas asiciadas al grupo
 8. Otras deudas
Total D . . . .
TOTAL GENERAL (A + B+ C +D) . .
.

5. Debts represented by trade bills
6. Debts with companies of the group
7. Debts with companies associated with the group
8. Other debts
Total C . . . .
D) Short-term creditors
 1. Issues of debentures, separating convertible ones
 2. Debts with credit entities
 3. Advances received by orders
 4. Debts by purchases or services rendered
 5. Debts represented by trade bills
 6. Debts with companies of the group
 7. Debts with companies associated with the group
 8. Other debts
Total D . . . .
GENERAL TOTAL (A + B + C + D) .
. .

CUENTA DE PERDIDAS Y GANACIAS—DEBE
A) GASTOS
 1. Reducción de existencias de productos terminados y en curso de fabricación
 2. Aprovisionamientos
  a) Consumo de materias primas y mercancias
  b) Otros gastos externos
 3. Gasos de personal
  a) Sueldos, salarios y asimilados
  b) Cargas sociales, separando pensiones
 4. Dotaciones para amortizaciones de inmovilizado
 5. Otros gastos de explotación
 6. Dotaciones para provisiones y amortizaciones de valores mobiliarios
 7. Intereses y gastos asimilados
 8. RESULTADO DE LAS ACTIVIDADES ORDINARIAS
 9. Gastos extraordinarios

PROFIT AND LOSS ACCOUNT— DEBIT
A) EXPENDITURES
 1. Reduction of stock of finished products and work in progress
 2. Supplies
  a) Consumption of raw materials and merchandise
  b) Other external expenditure
 3. Personnel expenses
  a) Salaries, wages and similar
  b) Staff welfare expenses, separating pensions
 4. Fixed asset depreciation transfers
 5. Other operating expenses
 6. Transfers to the provision and depreciation of securities
 7. Interest and similar expenses
 8. RESULTS OF NORMAL ACTIVITIES
 9. Extraordinary expenditures

10. Impuesto sobre sociedades	10. Corporations Tax
11. Otros impuestos	11. Other taxes
12. RESULTADO DEL EJERCICIO (BENEFICIOS)	12. RESULTS FOR THE YEAR (PROFITS)

CUENTA DE PERDIDAS Y GANANCIAS—HABER	PROFIT AND LOSS ACCOUNT— CREDIT
B) INGRESOS	B) INCOME
1. Importe neto de la cifra de negocios	1. Net amount of turnover
2. Aumento de las existencias de productos terminados y en curso de fabricación	2. Increase in stocks of finished products and work in progress
3. Trabajos efectuados por la empresa para el invocilizado	3. Work undertaken by the company for fixed assets
4. Otros ingresos de explotición	4. Other income from operations
5. Ingresos de particpaciones	5. Income from participations
a) En empresas del grupo	a) In group companies
b) En empresas asociadas	b) In associate companies
c) En empresas fuera del grupo	c) In companies outside the group
6. Ingresos de otros valores mobiliarios y créditos del activo inmovilzado	6. Income from other securities and fixed asset credits
a) De empresas del grupo	a) From group companies
b) De empresas asociadas	b) From associate companies
c) De empresas fuera del grupo	c) From companies outside the group
7. Otros intereses e ingresos asimilados	7. Other comparable interest and income
a) De empresas del grupo	a) From group companies
b) De empresas asociadas	b) From associated companies
c) Otros intereses	c) Other interest
8. RESULTADO DE LAS ACTIVIDADES ORDINARIAS	8. PROFITS FROM NORMAL ACTIVITIES
9. Ingresos extraordinarios	9. Extraordinary income
10. RESULTADO DEL AJERCICIO (PERDIDAS)	10. PROFIT (LOSS) FOR THE FINANCIAL YEAR

Appendix B: Model of Accounts According to the 1990 General Accounting Plan (in Spanish and English)*

Balance—Activo

A) Accionistas (socios) por desembolsos no exigidos
  Total A . . . .
B) Inmovilizado
  I Gastos de establecimiento
  II Inmovilizaciones inmateriales
    1. Gastos de investigación y desarrollo
    2. Concesiones, patentes, licencias, marcas y similares
      2 a) Adquiridos a título oneroso
      2 b) Creados por la empresa
    3. Fondo de comercio
    4. Derechos de traspaso
    5. Aplicaciones informáticas
    6. Anticipos
    7. Provisiones
    8. Amortizaciones
  III Inmovilizaciones materiales
    1. Terrenos y construcciones
    2. Instalaciones técnicas y maquinaria
    3. Otras instalaciones, utillaje y mobiliario
    4. Anticipos e inmovilizaciones materiales en curso
    5. Otro inmovilizado
    6. Provisiones
    7. Amortizaciones
  IV Inmovilizaciones financieras
    1. Participaciones en empresas del grupo
    2. Créditos a empresas del grupo
      2 a) Valores de empresas del grupo
      2 b) Otros créditos a empresas del grupo
      2 c) Créditos por intereses
    3. Participaciones en empresas asociadas

Balance Sheet—Assets

A) Shareholders (partners) per non-required disbursements
  Total A . . . .
B) Fixed assets
  I. Establishment costs
  II. Intangible fixed assets
    1. Research and development costs
    2. Concessions, patents, licences, trademarks and similar
      2.a) Acquired by consideration
      2.b) Created by the company
    3. Goodwill
    4. Transfer rights
    5. Computer applications
    6. Advances
    7. Provisions
    8. Depreciations
  III Tangible fixed assets
    1. Land and buildings
    2. Technical plant and machinery
    3. Other installations, tools and furniture
    4. Advances and fixed assets in course of construction
    5. Other fixed assets
    6. Provisions
    7. Depreciation
  IV Investments
    1. Participations in group companies
    2. Credits to group companies
      2.a) Securities of group companies
      2.b) Other credits to group companies
      2.c) Credits from interest
    3. Participations in associated companies

---

* Editors' Note. A specimen set of financial statements is shown in Appendix C, which follows the detailed formats required by the new Spanish General Accounting Plan.

4. Créditos a empresas asociadas
    4 a) Valores de empresas
          asociadas
    4 b) Otros créditos a empresas
          asociadas
    4 c) Créditos por intereses
5. Valores que tengan carácter de
   inmovilizaciones
    5 a) Participación en capital
    5 b) Valores de renta fija
    5 c) Intereses de valores de
          renta fija
6. Otros créditos
    6 a) Principal de crédito
    6 b) Créditos por intereses
7. Depósitos y fianzas entregados a
   largo plazo
8. Provisiones
    8 a) De empresas del grupo
    8 b) De empresas asociadas
    8 c) De otros valores
          mobiliarios
    8 d) De insolvencias
V Acciones propias
Total B . . . .

C) Gastos a distribuir en varios ejercicios

Total C . . . .

D) Activo circulante
  I. Accionistas por desembolsos
    exigidos
  II Existencias
    1. Comerciales
    2. Materias primas y otros
       aprovisionamientos
    3. Productos en curso y
       semiterminados
    4. Productos terminados
    5. Subproductos, residuos y
       materiales recuperados
    6. Anticipos
    7. Provisiones
  III Deudores
    1. Clientes por ventas y
       prestaciones de servicios
    2. Empresas del grupo, deudores

4. Credits to associated companies
    4.a) Securities of associated
         companies
    4.b) Other credits to associated
         companies
    4.c) Credits from interest
5. Securities having the nature of
   investments
    5.a) Participations in capital
    5.b) Fixed income securities
    5.c) Interest on fixed income
         securities
6. Other credits
    6.a) Credit principal
    6.b) Credit from interest
7. Long-term deposits and
   guarantees
8. Provisions
    8.a) Of group companies
    8.b) Of associated companies
    8.c) Of other investments

    8.d) For bad debts
V Own shares
Total B . . . .

C) Expenses to be distributed over various
   accounting periods
Total C . . . .

D) Current Assets
  I Shareholders per required disburse-
    ments
  II Inventory
    1. Commercial
    2. Raw materials and other supplies

    3. Work in progress and
       semicompleted
    4. Finished products
    5. By-products, scrap and recov-
       ered materials
    6. Advances
    7. Provisions
  III Debtors
    1. Customers for sales and services
       rendered
    2. Group companies, debtors

3. Empresas asociadas, deudores
4. Deudores varios
5. Personal
6. Administraciones Públicas
7. Provisiones

IV Inversiones financieras temporales
1. Participaciones en empresas del grupo
2. Créditos a empresas del grupo
   2 a) Valores y créditos de empresas del grupo
   2 b) Créditos por intereses de empresas del grupo
3. Participaciones en empresas asociadas
4. Créditos a empresas asociadas
   4 a) Valores y créditos de empresas asociadas
   4 b) Créditos por intereses de empresas asociadas
5. Cartera de valores a corto plazo
   5 a) Participaciones en capital
   5 b) Valores de renta fija
   5 c) Intereses de valores de renta fija
6. Créditos
   6 a) Principal de créditos
   6 b) Créditos por intereses
7. Depósitos y fianzas entregados a corto plazo
8. Provisiones
   8 a) De empresas del grupo
   8 b) De empresas asociadas
   8 c) De valores mobiliarios
   8 d) De insolvencias

V Acciones propas a corto plazo
VI Tesorería
VII Ajustes por periodificación

Total D . . . .
TOTAL GENERAL (A + B + C + D)
. . . .

3. Associate companies, debtors
4. Miscellaneous debtors
5. Personnel
6. Public Administrations
7. Provisions

IV Temporary financial investments
1. Participations in group companies
2. Credits to group companies
   2.a) Securities and credits of group companies
   2.b) Credits from interest from group companies
3. Participations in associated companies
4. Credits to associated companies
   4.a) Securities and credits of associated companies
   4.b) Credits from interest from associated companies
5. Short-term securities portfolio
   5.a) Participations in capital
   5.b) Fixed income securities
   5.c) Interest from fixed income securities
6. Credits
   6.a) Credits principal
   6.b) Interest from credits
7. Short-term deposits and guarantees
8. Provisions
   8.a) Of group companies
   8.b) Of associated companies
   8.c) Of securities
   8.d) For bad debts

V Own shares short-term
Vl Treasury
Vll Accruals and pre-payments

Total D . . . .
GRAND TOTAL (A + B + C + D)
. . . .

Balance—Pasivo

A) Fondos proprios
   I Capital suscrito
   II Prima de emision
   III Reserva de revalorización
   IV Reservas
      1. Reserva legal
      2. Reservas para acciones propias
      3. Reservas para acciones de la sociedad dominante
      4. Reservas estatutarias
      5. Otras reservas
   V Resultados ejercicios anteriores

      1. Remanente
      2. Resultados negativos de ejercicios anteriores
      3. Aportaciones de socios para compensación de pérdidas
   VI Pérdidas y ganancias (beneficio o pérdida)
   Vll Dividendo a cuenta entregado en el ejercicio

   Total A . . . .

B) Ingresos a distribuir en varios ejercicios
      1. Subvenciones de capital
      2. Diferencias positivas en cambio

      3. Otros ingresos a distribuir en varios ejercicios

   Total B . . . .

C) Provisiones para riesgos y gastos
      1. Provisiones para pensiones y obligaciones similares
      2. Provisiones para impuestos
      3. Otras provisiones
      4. Fondo de reversión

   Total C . . . .

D) Acreedores a largo plazo
   I Emisiones de obligaciones
      1. Obligaciones no convertibles
      2. Obligaciones convertibles

Balance Sheet—Liabilities

A) Equity
   I Subscribed capital
   II Share premium
   III Revaluation reserve
   IV Reserves
      1. Legal reserve
      2. Reserves for own shares
      3. Reserves for shares of the dominant company
      4. Legal reserves
      5. Other reserves
   V Results from previous accounting periods
      1. Retained earnings
      2. Loss from previous accounting periods
      3. Contributions from partners to compensate losses
   Vl Profits and/or losses

   Vll Dividend on account paid during the accounting period

   Total A . . . .

B) Income to be distributed over various accounting periods
      1. Capital grants
      2. Positive exchange rate differences

      3. Other incomes to be distributed over various accounting periods

   Total B . . . .

C) Provisions for risks and expenditures
      1. Provisions for pensions and similar liabilities
      2. Tax provisions
      3. Other provisions
      4. Reversion fund (N.B.: a provision for the return of assets to the State)

   Total C . . . .

D) Long-term creditors
   I Issues of debentures
      1. Non-convertible debentures
      2. Convertible debentures

3. Otras deudas representadas en valores negociables
II Deudas con entidades de crédito
III Deudas con empresas del grupo y asociadas
  1. Deudas con empresas del grupo
  2. Deudas con empresas asociadas
IV Otros acreedores
  1. Deudas representadas por efectos a pagar
  2. Otras deudas
    2 a) Deudas transformables en subvenciones
    2 b) Proveedores de inmovilizado
    2 c) Otros
  3. Fianzas y depositos recibidos a largo plazo
V Desembolsos pendientes sobre acciones no exigidos
  1. De empresas del grupo
  2. De empresas asociadas
  3. De otras empresas
Total D . . . .
E) Acreedores a corte plazo
I Emisiones de obligaciones
  1. Obligaciones no convertibles
  2. Obligaciones convertibles
  3. Otras deudas representadas en valores negociables
  4. Intereses de obligaciones y otros valores
II Deudas con entidades de crédito
  1. Préstamos y otras deudas
  2. Deudas por intereses
III Deudas con empresas del grupo y asociadas a corto plazo
  1. Deudas con empresas del grupo
    1 a) Préstamos y otras deudas
    1 b) Intereses de deudas
  2. Deudas con empresas asociadas
    2 a) Préstamos y otras deudas
    2 b) Intereses de deudas
IV Acreedores comerciales
  1. Anticipos recibidos por pedidos
  2. Deudas por compras o prestaciones de servicios

3. Other debts represented by negotiable securities
II Debts with credit entities
III Debts with group companies and associates
  1. Debts with group companies
  2. Debts with associate companies
IV Other creditors
  1. Debts represented by bills payable
  2. Other debts
    2.a) Debts convertible into subsidies
    2.b) Suppliers of fixed assets
    2.c) Others
  3. Guarantee deposits and deposits received long-term
V Disbursements pending on nondemandable shares
  1. From group companies
  2. From associate companies
  3. From other companies
Total D . . . .
E) Short-term creditors
I Issues of debentures
  1. Non-convertible debentures
  2. Convertible debentures
  3. Other debts represented by negotiable securities
  4. Interest on debentures and other securities
II Debts with credit entities
  1. Loans and other debts
  2. Debts from interest
III Short-term debts with group companies and associates
  1. Debts with group companies
    1a) Loans and other debts
    1b) Interest on debts
  2. Debts with associate companies
    2a) Loans and other debts
    2b) Interest on debts
IV Trade creditors
  1. Advances received on orders
  2. Debts in respect of purchases or services rendered

3. Deudas representadas por efectos a pagar

V Otras deudas no comerciales
1. Administraciones Públicas
2. Deudas representadas por efectos a pagar
3. Remuneraciones pendientes de pago
4. Otras deudas
5. Fianzas y depósitos recibidos a corto plazo

VI Provisiones para operaciones de tráfico

VII Ajustes por periodificación

Total E . . . .

TOTAL GRAND
(A + B + C + D + E) . . . .

3. Debts represented by bills payable

V Other non-trade debts
1. Public Administration
2. Debts represented by bills payable
3. Accrued wages and salaries

4. Other debts
5. Short-term guarantees and deposits received

VI Provisions for trading operations

VII Accruals and pre-payments

Total E . . . . . .

GRAND TOTAL
(A+B+C+D+E) . . . .

Cuenta de Pérdidas y Ganancias—Debe	**Profit and Loss Account—Debit**

A) Gastos

1. Reducción de existencias de productos terminados y en curso de fabricación
2. Aprovisionamientos
   a) Consumo de mercancías
      a1) Compras
      a2) Variación de existencias
   b) Consumo de materias primas y otras materias consumibles
      b1) Compras
      b2) Variación de existencias
   c) Otros gastos externos
3. Gastos de personal
   a) Sueldos, salarios y asimilados
   b) Cargas sociales
      b1) Cargas sociales
      b2) Aportaciones y dotaciones para pensiones
4. Dotaciones para amortizaciones de inmovilizado
5. Variación de las provisiones de circulante
   a) Variación de provisiones de existencias
   b) Variación de provisiones y pérdidas de créditos incobrables
      b1) Fallidos
      b2) Variación de provisión para insolvencias
   c) Variación de otras provisiones de tráfico
6. Otros gastos de explotación
   a) Servicios exteriores
   b) Tributos
   c) Otros gastos de gestión corriente.
I. Beneficios de Explotación
   (Bl + B2 + B3 + B4 – Al – A2 – A3 – A4 – A5 – A6)
7. Gastos financieros por deudas a largo plazo
   a) Con empresas del grupo
   b) Con empresas asociadas
   c) Con terceros
8. Otros gastos financieros y gastos asimilados

A) Expenses

1. Reduction of stocks of finished products and work in progress
2. Supplies
   a) Merchandise consumption
      a1) Purchases
      a2) Change in stock
   b) Consumption of raw materials and other consumer materials
      b1) Purchases
      b2) Change in stock
   c) Other external expenses
3. Staff expenses
   a) Salaries, wages and similar
   b) Staff welfare expenses
      b1) Staff welfare expenses
      b2) Pension contributions
4. Contributions towards repayment of fixed assets
5. Changes in provisions for assets
   a) Changes in inventory provisions
   b) Changes in provisions and losses from bad debts
      b1) Bad debts
      b2) Changes in provision for bad debts
   c) Changes in other trade provisions
6. Other operating expenses
   a) Outside services
   b) Taxes
   c) Other normal business expenses
I. Operating Profits
   (Bl + B2 + B3 + B4 – Al – A2 – A3 – A4 – A5 – A6)
7. Financial expenses in respect of long-term debts
   a) With group companies
   b) With associated companies
   c) With third parties
8. Other financial expenses and similar expenses

a) Por deudas con empresas del grupo

b) Por deudas con empresas asociadas

c) Por deudas con terceros y gastos asimilados

d) Pérdidas de inversiones financieras temporales

9. Variación de las provisiones de inversiones financieras

a) De valores mobiliarias y de créditos a largo plazo

b) De valores mobiliarios y de créditos a corto plazo

10. Diferencias negativas de cambio

II. Resultados Financieros Positivos
(B5 + B6 + B7 + B8 − A7 − A8 − A9 − A10)

III. Beneficios de las Actividades Ordinarias
(AI + AII - BI − BII)

11. Variación de las provisiones de inmovilizado inmaterial y material

12. Pérdidas procedentes del inmovilizado

13. Pérdidas por operaciones con acciones y obligaciones propias

14. Gastos extraordinarios

15. Gastos y pérdidas de otros ejercicios

IV. Resultados Extraordinarios Positivos
(B9 + B10 + B11 + B12 + B13 − A11 − A12 − A13 − A14 − A15)

V. Beneficios Antes de Impuestos
(AIII + AIV − BIII − BIV)

16. Impuesto sobre sociedades

17. Otros impuestos

VI. Resultado del Ejercicio (Beneficios)
(AV − A16 − A17)

a) In respect of debts with group companies

b) In respect of debts with associated companies

c) In respect of debts with third parties and similar expenses

d) Losses of temporary financial investments

9. Changes in provisions for financial investments

a) In respect of securities and long-term credits

b) In respect of securities and short-term credits

10. Losses owing to exchange rates

II. Financial Profits
(B5 + B6 + B7 + B8 − A7 − A8 − A9 − A10)

III. Profits from Normal Activities

(AI + AII − BI − BII)

11. Changes in provisions for intangible and tangible fixed assets

12. Losses originating from fixed assets

13. Losses as a result of operations with own shares and debentures

14. Extraordinary expenses

15. Expenses and losses with respect to other accounting periods

IV. Extraordinary Profits
(B9 + B10 + B11 + B12 + B13 − A11 − A12 − A13 − A14 − A15)

V. Pre-Tax Profits
(AIII + AIV − BIII − BIV)

16. Corporation taxes

17. Other taxes

VI. Profits for the Financial Year
(AV − A16 − A17)

Cuenta de Perdidas y Ganancias—Haber

B) Ingresos
1. Importe neto de la cifra de negocios
   a) Ventas
   b) Prestaciones de servicios
   c) Devoluciones y "rapplels" sobre ventas
2. Aumento de las existencias de productos terminados y en curso de fabricación
3. Trabajos efectuados por la empresa para el inmovilizado
4. Otros ingresos de explotación
   a) Ingresos accesorios
   b) Subvenciones
   c) Exceso de provisiones para riesgos y gastos

I. Perdidas de Explotacion
(A1 + A2 + A3 + A4 + A5 + A6 – B1 – B2 – B3 – B4)
5. Ingresos de participaciones en capital
   a) En empresas del grupo
   b) En empresas asociadas
   c) En empresas fuera del grupo
6. Ingresos de otros valores mobiliarios y créditos del activo immovilizado
   a) De empresas del grupo
   b) De empresas asociadas
   c) De empresas fuera del grupo
7. Otros intereses e ingresos asimilados
   a) De empresas del grupo
   b) De empresas asociadas
   c) Otros intereses
   d) Beneficios en inversiones financieras temporales
8. Diferencias positivas de cambio

II. Resultados Financieros Negativos
(A7 + A8 + A9 + A10 – B5 – B6 – B7 – B8)

III. Perdidas de las Actividades Ordinarias

Profit and Loss Account—Credit

B) Income
1. Net amount of turnover
   a) Sales
   b) Services rendered
   c) Returns and recalls on sales
2. Increase in stocks of finished product and work in progress
3. Work carried out by the company for fixed assets
4. Other income from operations
   a) Non-trading income
   b) Subsidies
   c) Excess of provisions for risks and expenses

I. Operating Losses
(A1 + A2 + A3 + A4 + A5 + A6 – B1 – B2 – B3 – B4)
5. Income from participations in capital
   a) In group companies
   b) In associate companies
   c) In groups outside the group
6. Income from other securities and fixed asset credits
   a) From group companies
   b) From associate companies
   c) From companies outside the group
7. Other comparable interest and income
   a) From group companies
   b) From associate companies
   c) Other interests
   d) Profits in temporary investments
8. Positive exchange differences

II. Financial Losses
(A7 + A8 + A9 + A10 – B5 – B6 – B7 – B8)

III. Losses from Normal Activity

(BI + BII – AI – AII)
9. Beneficios en enajenación de inmovilizado
10. Beneficios por operaciones con acciones y obligaciones propias
11. Subvenciones de capital transferidas al resultado del ejercicio
12. Ingresos extraordinarios
13. Ingresos y beneficios de otros ejercicios

IV. Resultados Extraordinarios Negativos
(A11 + A12 + A13 + A14 + A15 – B9 – B10 – B11 – B12 – B13)
V. Perdidas Antes de Impuestos
(BIII + BIV – AIII – AIV)
VI. Resultado del Ejercicio (Perdidas)
(BV + A16 + A17)

CUADRO DE FINANCIACION— APLICACIONES
1. Recursos aplicados en las operaciones
2. Gastos de establecimiento y formalización de deudas
3. Adquisiciones de inmovilizado
   a) Inmovilizaciones inmateriales
   b) Inmovilizaciones materiales
   c) Inmovilizaciones financieras
      c1) Empresas de grupo
      c2) Empresas asociadas
      c3) Otras inversiones financieras
4. Adqusición de acciones propias
5. Reducciones de capital
6. Dividendos
7. Cancelación o traspaso a corto plazo de deuda a largo plazo
   a) Empréstitos y otros pasivos análogos
   b) De empresas del grupo
   c) De empresas asociadas
   d) De otras deudas

(BI + BII – AI – AII)
9. Profits from disposal of fixed assets
10. Profits from operations involving own shares and debentures
11. Capital subsidies transferred to the profits for the year
12. Extraordinary income
13. Income and profits from other years

IV. Extraordinary Losses
(A11 + A12 + A13 + A14 + A15 – B9 – B10 – B11 – B12 – B13)
V. Losses Before Tax
(BIII + BIV – AIII – AIV)
VI. Profits (Losses) for the Financial Year
(BV + A16 + A17)

FUNDS FLOW STATEMENT— APPLICATIONS
1. Resources applied in operations
2. Establishment and debt formalization expenses
3. Acquisitions of fixed assets
   a) Intangible fixed assets
   b) Tangible fixed assets
   c) Investments
      c.a) Group companies
      c.2) Associated companies
      c.3) Other financial investments
4. Acquisition of own shares
5. Capital reductions
6. Dividends
7. Cancellation or short-term conveyance of long-term debt
   a) Borrowings and other similar liabilities
   b) Of group companies
   c) Of associated companies
   d) Of other debts

e) De proveedores de
   inmovilizado y otros
8. Provisiones para riesgos y gastos

TOTAL APLICACIONES

EXCESO DE ORIGENES SOBRE
APLICACIONES

(AUMENTO DE CAPITAL
CIRCULANTE)

CUADRO DE FINANCIACION—
ORIGENES

1. Recursos procedentes de las
   operaciones
2. Aportaciones de accionistas
   a) Ampliación de capital
   b) Compensación para pérdidas
3. Subvenciones de capital
4. Deudas a largo plazo
   a) Empréstitos y otros pasivos
      análogos
   b) De empresas del grupo
   c) De empresas asociadas
   d) De otras empresas
   e) De proveedores de inmovilizado
      y otros
5. Enajenación de inmovilizado
   a) Inmovilizaciones inmateriales
   b) Inmovilizaciones materiales
   c) Inmovilizaciones financieras
      c1) Empresas del grupo
      c2) Empresas asociadas
      c3) Otras inversiones
           financieras
6. Enajenación de acciones propias
7. Cancelación anticipada o traspaso a
   corto plazo de inmovilizaciones
   financieras
   a) Empresas del grupo
   b) Empresas asociadas
   c) Otras inversiones financieras

TOTAL ORIGENES

e) Of suppliers of fixed assets
   and others
8. Provisions for risks and
   expenses

TOTAL APPLICATIONS

EXCESS OF SOURCE OVER
APPLICATION

(INCREASE OF WORKING CAPI-
TAL)

FUNDS FLOW STATEMENT—
SOURCES

1. Resources from operations

2. Contributions by shareholders
   a) Capital increase
   b) Compensation for losses
3. Capital grants
4. Long-term debts
   a) Borrowings and other similar
      liabilities
   b) Of group companies
   c) Of associated companies
   d) Of other companies
   e) Of suppliers of fixed assets and
      others
5. Disposal of fixed assets
   a) Non-tangible fixed assets
   b) Tangible fixed assets
   c) Investments
      c1) Group companies
      c2) Associated companies
      c3) Other financial investments

6. Disposal of own shares
7. Advance cancellation or short-term
   conveyance of investments

   a) Group companies
   b) Associated companies
   c) Other financial investments

TOTAL SOURCES

Appendix C
Financial Statements
of Gas Natural SDG, S.A.

Edifici Caja de Madrid
Avinguda Diagonal, 640
08017 Barcelona

Tel. 253 27 00
Fax 405 90 32

Price Waterhouse

INFORME DE AUDITORIA INDEPENDIENTE DE LAS CUENTAS ANUALES

A los Señores Accionistas de Gas Natural SDG, S.A.

Hemos auditado las cuentas anuales consolidadas de Gas Natural SDG, S.A. y su Grupo de sociedades, que comprenden el balance de situación consolidado al 31 de diciembre de 1997, la cuenta de pérdidas y ganancias consolidada y la memoria consolidada correspondientes al ejercicio anual terminado en dicha fecha, cuya formulación es responsabilidad de los Administradores de Gas Natural SDG, S.A. Nuestra responsabilidad es expresar una opinión sobre las citadas cuentas anuales consolidadas en su conjunto, basada en el trabajo realizado de acuerdo con las normas de auditoría generalmente aceptadas, que requieren el examen, mediante la realización de pruebas selectivas, de la evidencia justificativa de las cuentas anuales consolidadas y la evaluación de su presentación, de los principios contables aplicados y de las estimaciones realizadas.

De acuerdo con la legislación mercantil, los Administradores de Gas Natural SDG, S.A. presentan, a efectos comparativos, con cada una de las partidas del balance consolidado, de la cuenta de pérdidas y ganancias consolidada y del cuadro de financiación consolidado, además de las cifras del ejercicio 1997, las correspondientes al ejercicio anterior. Nuestra opinión se refiere exclusivamente a las cuentas anuales consolidadas del ejercicio 1997. Con fecha 20 de marzo de 1997 emitimos nuestro informe de auditoría acerca de las cuentas anuales consolidadas del ejercicio 1996 en el que expresamos una opinión favorable.

En nuestra opinión, las cuentas anuales consolidadas del ejercicio 1997 adjuntas expresan, en todos los aspectos significativos, la imagen fiel del patrimonio consolidado y de la situación financiera consolidada de Gas Natural SDG, S.A. y su Grupo de sociedades al 31 de diciembre de 1997 y de los resultados consolidados de sus operaciones y de los recursos consolidados obtenidos y aplicados durante el ejercicio anual terminado en dicha fecha y contienen la información necesaria y suficiente para su interpretación y comprensión adecuada, de conformidad con principios y normas contables generalmente aceptados que guardan uniformidad con los aplicados en el ejercicio anterior.

Price Waterhouse Auditores, S.A.
R. M. Madrid, hoja 87.250-1, folio 75, tomo 9.267, libro 8054, sección 3.ª
Inscrita en el R.O.A.C. con el número S0242
CIF: A-79/031290

Edifici Caja de Madrid
Avinguda Diagonal, 640
08017 Barcelona

Tel. 253 27 00
Fax 405 90 32

Price Waterhouse

INDEPENDENT AUDITORS' REPORT ON THE CONSOLIDATED ANNUAL
ACCOUNTS

To the Shareholders of Gas Natural SDG, S.A.

We have audited the consolidated annual accounts of Gas Natural SDG, S.A. and its Group
companies, consisting of the consolidated balance sheet at December 31, 1997, the
consolidated profit and loss account and the consolidated notes for the year then ended,
whose preparation is the responsibility of the Directors of Gas Natural SDG, S.A. Our
responsibility is to express an opinion on the aforementioned consolidated annual accounts
as a whole, based on our audit work carried out in accordance with generally accepted
auditing standards, which require examining, on a test basis, evidence supporting the
consolidated annual accounts, as well as evaluating the overall consolidated annual accounts
presentation and assessing the accounting principles applied and significant estimates made.

In accordance with company legislation, the Directors of Gas Natural SDG, S.A. have
presented, for comparative purposes only, for each of the items of the consolidated balance
sheet, the consolidated profit and loss account and the consolidated statement of source and
application of funds, corresponding amounts for the previous year as well as the amounts
for 1997. Our opinion refers exclusively to the consolidated annual accounts for 1997. On
March 20, 1997, we issued our audit report on the consolidated annual accounts for 1996 in
which we expressed an unqualified opinion.

In our opinion, the accompanying consolidated annual accounts for 1997 present fairly, in
all material respects, the consolidated shareholders' equity and financial position of Gas
Natural SDG, S.A. and its Group companies at December 31, 1997 and the results of its
consolidated operations and the consolidated resources obtained and applied for the year
ended on that date, and they contain the necessary and relevant information in order to
adequately interpret and understand them, in conformity with generally accepted accounting
principles in Spain applied on a basis consistent with that of the preceding year.

Price Waterhouse Auditores, S.A.
R. M. Madrid, hoja 87.250-1, folio 75, tomo 9.267, libro 8054, sección 3.ª
Inscrita en el R.O.A.C. con el número S0242
CIF: A-79/031290

Página 2

El informe de gestión adjunto del ejercicio 1997, contiene las explicaciones que los Administradores de Gas Natural SDG, S.A. consideran oportunas sobre la situación de Gas Natural SDG, S.A. y su Grupo de sociedades, la evolución de sus negocios y sobre otros asuntos y no forma parte integrante de las cuentas anuales consolidadas. Hemos verificado que la información contable que contiene el citado informe de gestión concuerda con la de las cuentas anuales consolidadas del ejercicio 1997. Nuestro trabajo como auditores se limita a la verificación del informe de gestión con el alcance mencionado en este mismo párrafo y no incluye la revisión de información distinta de la obtenida a partir de los registros contables de la Sociedad y su Grupo.

Price Waterhouse Auditores, S.A.

José Luis Fernández Baños
Socio - Auditor de Cuentas

Barcelona, 25 de marzo de 1998

Page 2

The accompanying Directors' Report for 1997 contains the information that the management of Gas Natural SDG, S.A. considers relevant to the financial situation of Gas Natural SDG, S.A. and its Group companies, the evolution of its business and of other matters and does not form an integral part of the consolidated annual accounts. We have verified that the accounting information contained in the aforementioned Directors' Report coincides with that of the consolidated annual accounts for 1997. Our work as auditors is limited to verifying the Directors' Report within the scope already mentioned in this paragraph and does not include the review of information other than that obtained from the accounting records of the Company and its Group companies.

Price Waterhouse Auditores, S.A.

José Luis Fernández Baños
Partner

Barcelona, March 25, 1998

Free translation from the original in Spanish

Balance Consolidado del Grupo Gas Natural (En millones de pesetas)

Activo	31.12.97	31.12.96
Inmovilizado	**875.962**	**790.270**
Gastos de establecimiento	867	340
Inmovilizaciones inmateriales (Nota 3)	94.800	84.381
Bienes y derechos inmateriales	106.439	91.337
Amortizaciones	(11.639)	(6.956)
Inmovilizaciones materiales (Nota 4)	748.391	681.261
Terrenos y construcciones	50.617	46.164
Instalaciones técnicas y maquinaria	865.186	757.216
Otro inmovilizado	18.866	17.777
Anticipos e inmovilizaciones materiales en curso	65.041	59.906
Provisiones y amortizaciones	(251.319)	(199.802)
Inmovilizaciones financieras (Nota 5)	31.904	24.288
Participaciones puestas en equivalencia	7.418	5.719
Cartera de valores a largo plazo	4.701	2.448
Otros créditos	21.924	17.617
Provisiones	(2.139)	(1.496)
Fondo de comercio de consolidación (Nota 6)	**5.654**	—
De sociedades consolidadas por integración proporcional	5.654	—
Gastos a distribuir en varios ejercicios	**1.827**	**236**
Activo Circulante	**134.790**	**115.123**
Accionistas por desembolsos exigidos	142	134
Existencias (Nota 7)	25.111	16.864
Deudores	87.638	72.136
Clientes por ventas y prestaciones de servicios (Nota 8)	77.719	61.531
Empresas puestas en equivalencia (Nota 9)	2.197	1.762
Otros deudores (Nota 10)	13.609	13.304
Provisiones	(5.887)	(4.461)
Inversiones financieras temporales	14.460	19.416
Cartera de valores a corto plazo (Nota 11)	13.516	19.102
Otros créditos	944	314
Tesorería	6.361	5.957
Ajustes por periodificación	1.078	616
Total General	**1.018.233**	**905.629**

Consolidated Balance Sheet of the Gas Natural Group (Shown in millions of pesetas)

Assets	31.12.97	31.12.96
Fixed assets	**875,962**	**790,270**
Start-up costs	867	340
Intangible fixed assets (Note 3)	94,800	84,381
Intangible fixed assets	106,439	91,337
Accumulated amortization	(11,639)	(6,956)
Tangible fixed assets (Note 4)	748,391	681,261
Land and buildings	50,617	46,164
Technical installations and machinery	865,186	757,216
Other fixed assets	18,866	17,777
Payments on account and fixed assets under construction	65,041	59,906
Accumulated depreciation	(251,319)	(199,802)
Investments (Note 5)	31,904	24,288
Investments in companies accounted for using the equity method	7,418	5,719
Long term securities	4,701	2,448
Other loans	21,924	17,617
Provision for loss in value	(2,139)	(1,496)
Consolidation Goodwill (Note 6)	**5,654**	—
Of proportionally consolidated companies	5,654	—
Deferred expenses	**1,827**	**236**
Current assets	**134,790**	**115,123**
Shareholders for calls on share capital	142	134
Inventories (Note 7)	25,111	16,864
Accounts receivable	87,638	72,136
Trade debtors (Note 8)	77,719	61,531
Due from companies accounted for using the equity method (Note 9)	2,197	1,762
Other debtors (Note 10)	13,609	13,304
Provisions for bad debts	(5,887)	(4,461)
Short term investments	14,460	19,416
Short term securities (Note 11)	13,516	19,102
Other loans	944	314
Cash and banks	6,361	5,957
Prepaid expenses	1,078	616
Total Assets	**1,018,233**	**905,629**

Pasivo	31.12.97	31.12.96
Fondos propios (Nota 12)	**371.643**	**324.735**
Capital suscrito	74.629	22.389
Prima de emisión	—	39.270
Otras reservas de la sociedad dominante	105.220	102.654
Reservas distribuibles	74.366	71.800
Reserva de revalorización	20.716	20.716
Reservas no distribuibles	10.138	10.138
Reservas en sociedades consolidadas por integración global y proporcional	134.684	110.361
Reservas en sociedades puestas en equivalencia	1.572	186
Diferencias de conversión	4.911	1.431
Pérdidas y ganancias atribuibles a la sociedad dominante	50.627	· 48.444
Pérdidas y ganancias consolidadas	55.688	52.770
Pérdidas y ganancias atribuidas a socios externos	(5.061)	(4.326)
Socios externos (Nota 13)	**46.560**	**39.814**
Diferencia negativa de consolidación (Nota 14)	**15.512**	**52.168**
De sociedades consolidadas por integración global	15.512	52.168
Ingresos a distribuir en varios ejercicios (Nota 15)	**89.538**	**79.090**
Subvenciones de capital	46.124	41.990
Otros ingresos a distribuir en varios ejercicios	43.414	37.100
Provisiones para riesgos y gastos (Nota 16)	**35.893**	**39.002**
Provisiones para pensiones y obligaciones similares	24.365	24.152
Otras provisiones	11.528	14.850
Acreedores a largo plazo	**362.948**	**263.399**
Emisiones de obligaciones y otros valores negociables (Nota 17)	9.969	9.662
Deudas con entidades de crédito (Nota 18)	331.376	236.637
Otros acreedores (Nota 19)	21.603	17.100
Acreedores a corto plazo	**96.139**	**107.421**
Emisiones de obligaciones y otros valores negociables (Nota 17)	52	50
Deudas con entidades de crédito (Nota 18)	7.388	4.764
Deudas con sociedades puestas en equivalencia (Nota 9)	423	250
Acreedores comerciales	69.742	74.670
Otras deudas no comerciales	18.402	27.450
Ajustes por periodificación	132	237
Total General	**1.018.233**	**905.629**

Liabilities	31.12.97	31.12.96
Equity (Nota 12)	**371,643**	**324,735**
Share capital	74,629	22,389
Share premium	—	39,270
Other reserves of the parent company	105,220	102,654
Distributable reserves	74,366	71,800
Revaluation reserve	20,716	20,716
Non-distributable reserves	10,138	10,138
Reserves of fully and proportionally consolidated companies	134,684	110,361
Reserves of companies accounted for using the equity method	1,572	186
Foreign currency translation adjustments	4,911	1,431
Profit attributed to the parent company	50,627	48,444
Consolidated profit	55,688	52,770
Profit attributed to minority interests	(5,061)	(4,326)
Minority interests (Note 13)	**46,560**	**39,814**
Negative consolidation difference (Note 14)	**15,512**	**52,168**
On fully consolidated companies	15,512	52,168
Deferred income (Note 15)	**89,538**	**79,090**
Capital grants	46,124	41,990
Other deferred income	43,414	37,100
Provision for liabilities and charges (Note 16)	**35,893**	**39,002**
Provisions for pensions and related obligations	24,365	24,152
Other provisions	11,528	14,850
Long term creditors	**362,948**	**263,399**
Debentures and other negotiable securities (Note 17)	9,969	9,662
Due to financial institutions (Note 18)	331,376	236,637
Other creditors (Note 19)	21,603	17,100
Short term creditors	**96,139**	**107,421**
Debentures and other negotiable securities (Note 17)	52	50
Due to financial institutions (Note 18)	7,388	4,764
Due to companies accounted for using the equity method (Note 9)	423	250
Trade creditors	69,742	74,670
Other non-trade creditors	18,402	27,450
Accrued expenses	132	237
Total Liabilities and Equity	**1,018,233**	**905,629**

Cuenta de Pérdidas y Ganancias Consolidada del Grupo Gas Natural
(En millones de pesetas)

Debe	1997	1996
Gastos		
Consumos y otros gastos externos (Nota 23)	229.753	160.374
Gastos de personal (Nota 24)	31.524	29.595
Sueldos, salarios y asimilados	23.626	21.985
Cargas sociales	7.898	7.610
Dotaciones para amortizaciones de inmovilizado	47.310	29.855
Variación de las provisiones de tráfico	1.381	(1.021)
Otros gastos de explotación (Nota 25)	45.835	40.086
Beneficios de explotación	**83.485**	**82.959**
Gastos financieros	22.238	17.309
Pérdidas en inversiones financieras	41	—
Variación de las provisiones de inversiones financieras	(7)	148
Diferencias negativas de cambio	1.240	121
Amortización del fondo de comercio de consolidación (Nota 6)	33.614	643
Beneficios de las actividades ordinarias	**69.006**	**70.045**
Gastos y pérdidas extraordinarios (Nota 26)	293	2.082
Resultados extraordinarios positivos	**4.469**	**1.486**
Beneficios consolidados antes de impuestos	**73.475**	**71.531**
Impuesto sobre Sociedades	17.787	18.761
Resultado consolidado del ejercicio (beneficio)	**55.688**	**52.770**
Resultado atribuido a socios externos	5.061	4.326
Resultado del ejercicio atribuido a la sociedad dominante (beneficio)	**50.627**	**48.444**

Consolidated Profit and Loss Account of the Gas Natural Group
(Shown in millions of pesetas)

Debit	1997	1996
Expenses		
Cost of sales and other external costs (Note 23)	229,753	160,374
Personnel costs (Note 24)	31,524	29,595
Wages, salaries and related expenses	23,626	21,985
Social security and related costs	7,898	7,610
Charge for depreciation and amortization of fixed assets	47,310	29,855
Movement in trading provisions	1,381	(1,021)
Other operating expenses (Note 25)	45,835	40,086
Operating profit	**83,485**	**82,959**
Financial expenses	22,238	17,309
Losses on investments	41	—
Provisions for loss in value of investments	(7)	148
Exchange losses	1,240	121
Goodwill amortization (Note 6)	33,614	643
Profit from ordinary operations	**69,006**	**70,045**
Extraordinary expenses (Note 26)	293	2,082
Net extraordinary income	**4,469**	**1,486**
Consolidated profit before tax	**73,475**	**71,531**
Corporate tax	17,787	18,761
Consolidated profit for the year	**55,688**	**52,770**
Minority interests	5,061	4,326
Profit for the year attributable to the parent company	**50,627**	**48,444**

Haber	1997	1996
Ingresos		
Importe neto de la cifra de negocios (Nota 22)	428.412	333.195
Aumento de existencias de productos terminados y en curso de fabricación	—	—
Trabajos efectuados por el grupo para el inmovilizado	2.612	2.377
Otros ingresos de explotación	8.264	6.276
Ingresos de participaciones en capital	227	281
Otros ingresos financieros	3.931	3.115
Beneficios en inversiones financieras	471	266
Diferencias positivas de cambio	353	95
Resultados financieros negativos	**18.530**	**13.821**
Participación en beneficios de sociedades puestas en equivalencia	1.009	781
Reversión de diferencias negativas de consolidación	36.656	769
Beneficios procedentes del inmovilizado (Nota 26)	187	617
Ingresos y beneficios extraordinarios (Nota 26)	4.575	2.951

43

Credit	**1997**	**1996**
Income		
Net sales (Note 22)	428,412	333,195
Increase in inventories of finished products and work in process	—	—
Own labour and other costs capitalized	2,612	2,377
Other operating income	8,264	6,276
Dividend income	227	281
Other financial income	3,931	3,115
Profit on investments	471	266
Exchange gains	353	95
Net financial cost	**18,530**	**13,821**
Share in profits of companies accounted for using the equity method	1,009	781
Reversion of negative consolidation differences	36,656	769
Profit on disposal of fixed assets (Note 26)	187	617
Extraordinary income (Note 26)	4,575	2,951

43

Notes to the Consolidated Annual Accounts of the Gas Natural Group for the year ended December 31, 1997

Note 1. Activity and bases of presentation and consolidation

The consolidated annual accounts of the Gas Natural Group have been prepared from the consolidation of the accounts of Gas Natural SDG, S.A. and the following Group, Multigroup and Associated companies:

Company	Registered Office
Group companies (fully consolidated)	
Enagás, S.A.	Madrid
Compañía Española de Gas, S.A.	Valencia
Gas Andalucía, S.A.	Seville
Gas Castilla-La Mancha, S.A.	Guadalajara
Gas Galicia Sociedad para el Desarrollo del Gas, S.A.	Santiago de Compostela
Gas Girona, S.A.	Girona
Gas Lleida, S.A.	Lleida
Gas Natural BAN, S.A.	Buenos Aires
Gas Natural Castilla y León, S.A.	Valladolid
Gas Natural Extremadura, S.A.	Mérida
Gas Natural La Coruña, S.A.	La Coruña
Gas Navarra, S.A.	Pamplona
Gas Penedès, S.A.	Vilafranca del Penedès
Gas Rioja, S.A.	Logroño
Gas Tarraconense, S.A.	Tarragona
Gas Vic, S.A.	Vic
Sagane, S.A.	Madrid
La Propagadora del Gas, S.A.	Barcelona
La Energía, S.A.	Barcelona
Equipos y Services, S.A.	Barcelona
Gas Serviconfort, S.A.	Barcelona
Compañía Auxiliar de Industrias Varias, S.A.	Madrid
Agrupación Energética Ciutat Sanitaria Vall d'Hebrón AIE	Barcelona
Gas Natural Informática, S.A.	Barcelona
Gas Natural International, Ltd.	Dublin
Gas Natural SDG Argentina, S.A.	Buenos Aires
Holding Gas Natural, S.A.	Barcelona
Invergas, S.A.	Buenos Aires
Manra, S.A.	Buenos Aires
Gas Natural Internacional SDG, S.A.	Madrid
Iberlink Ibérica, S.A.	Barcelona
Gas Natural Latinoamericana, S.A.	Madrid
Gas Natural Colombia, S.A.	Barcelona
Multigroup companies (consolidated by the proportional consolidation method)	
Europe Maghreb Pipeline Limited	Jersey
Metragaz, S.A.	Tangiers
Gasoducto Al-Andalus, S.A.	Madrid
Gasoducto de Extremadura, S.A.	Madrid
Gas Natural México, S.A. de C.V.	Mexico City
Repsol Gas de Saltillo, S.A. de C.V.	Mexico City
Companhia Estadual de Gas do Rio de Janeiro, S.A.	Rio de Janeiro (Brazil)
Riogas, S.A.	Rio de Janeiro (Brazil)
Gas Natural, S.A., ESP	Bogota (Colombia)
Associated companies (consolidated by the equity method)	
Gas Aragón, S.A.	Zaragoza
Kromschroeder, S.A.	Barcelona
Sociedad de Gas de Euskadi, S.A.	Bilbao

The company has other holdings, both direct and indirect, in other companies, most of which are inactive. These companies have not been consolidated as their inclusion would not have had a material effect on the consolidated accounts.
The total holding in all companies included in the consolidation is Ptas 205,212 million.

| Activity | % Holding | | | Company which owns |
	Direct	Indirect	Total	the indirect holding
Gas supply, trans. and distr.	91.0	—	91.0	
Gas distribution	98.6	—	98.6	
Gas distribution	100.0	—	100.0	
Gas distribution	95.0	—	95.0	
Gas distribution	60.2	4.4	64.6	(4)
Gas distribution	100.0	—	100.0	
Gas distribution	93.7	—	93.7	
Gas distribution	—	50.4	50.4	(2)
Gas distribution	100.0	—	100.0	
Gas distribution	100.0	—	100.0	
Gas distribution	—	58.8	58.8	(5)
Gas distribution	80.0	—	80.0	
Gas distribution	99.7	—	99.7	
Gas distribution	87.5	—	87.5	
Gas distribution	99.3	—	99.3	
Gas distribution	97.4	—	97.4	
Gas supply	—	91.0	91.0	(4)
Investment company	100.0	—	100.0	
Investment company	100.0	—	100.0	
Gas installations	100.0	—	100.0	
Gas installations	—	100.0	100.0	(8)
Gas installations	100.0	—	100.0	
Electricity generation	81.3	—	81.3	
Information Technology	100.0	—	100.0	
Investment company	100.0	—	100.0	
Investment company	100.0	—	100.0	
Investment company	100.0	—	100.0	
Investment company	—	72.0	72.0	(1)
Investment company	—	100.0	100.0	(3)
Investment company	100.0	—	100.0	
Studies and projects	75.1	—	75.1	
Investment company	—	100.0	100.0	(7)
Investment company	—	100.0	100.0	(7)
Gas transmission	—	66.1	66.1	(6)
Gas transmission	—	65.8	65.8	(6)
Gas transmission	—	60.9	60.9	(4)
Gas transmission	—	46.4	46.4	(4)
Gas distribution	—	50.0	50.0	(7)
Services	—	50.0	50.0	(7)
Gas distribution	18.9	—	18.9	
Gas distribution	25.0	—	25.0	
Gas distribution	—	39.2	39.2	(7)
Gas distribution	35.0	—	35.0	
Gas meters	42.5	—	42.5	
Gas distribution	—	18.7	18.7	(4)

(1) Gas Natural International Ltd. and Manra, S.A.
(2) Invergas, S.A.
(3) Gas Natural International Ltd. and Gas Natural Internacional SDG, S.A.
(4) Enagás, S.A.
(5) Gas Galicia Sociedad para el Desarrollo del Gas, S.A.
(6) Sagane, S.A.
(7) Gas Natural Internacional SDG, S.A.
(8) La Energía, S.A.

The consolidated annual accounts were obtained from the accounting records of the companies subject to consolidation and have been prepared in accordance with generally accepted accounting principles in Spain. The necessary adjustments and reclassifications have been made in order to standardize the accounting policies of the various Group companies and to eliminate significant intercompany balances and transactions.

The methods and procedures of consolidation applied in the preparation of the attached consolidated annual accounts are as follows:

- Full consolidation: For group companies over which control is held by means of the possession of the majority of voting rights.

- Proportional consolidation: For multigroup companies controlled jointly with other parties.

- Equity method: For associated companies over which significant control is exercised, but without the majority of voting rights nor jointly controlled with other parties.

In 1997, the following companies were consolidated for the first time: Gas Natural Colombia, S.A., Gas Natural México, S.A. de C.V. and Repsol Gas de Saltillo, S.A. de C.V., all with effect from January 1, 1997, the company Gas Natural, S.A. ESP with effect from July 1, 1997, and the companies Riogas, S.A. and Companhia Estadual de Gas do Rio de Janeiro, S.A with effect from August 1, 1997. The first company has been consolidated by the full consolidation method and the others by the proportional consolidation method.

The company Gas Natural Latinoamericana, S.A. has been consolidated by the full consolidation method. In 1996, the proportional consolidation method was applied.

The scope of consolidation has not included the companies Gasoducto Braga-Tuy, S.A. and Gasoducto Campo Maior-Leira-Braga, S.A. owing to the slight effect of their inclusion on the consolidated annual accounts.

The heading Scope of consolidation used in certain of the Notes to these accounts describes the adjustments to opening consolidated balances which are due to changes in the perimeter of consolidation of the Group, by virtue of acquisitions and exclusions of companies, and changes in Group holdings which give rise to changes in the consolidation method used.

The accounting year of all Group companies runs from January 1 to December 31.

The amounts shown in the consolidated balance sheet, the consolidated profit and loss account, and these consolidated notes are expressed in millions of pesetas.

The consolidated annual accounts for 1997 have been prepared in accordance with current legislation on the preparation of consolidated annual accounts in Spain. Group company assets and liabilities denominated in foreign currencies are shown at the rate of exchange at the year end.

Note 2. Accounting policies

A summary of the most significant accounting policies applied in the preparation of the consolidated annual accounts is as follows:

a) Start-up costs. These correspond to the costs of incorporation, establishment and increases in share capital, and are amortized over a five year period.

b) Intangible fixed assets. The elements of intangible fixed assets are recorded at the cost of acquisition or the cost of production. These costs are amortized over a five year period.

Exclusive rights of use of transmission gas pipelines are shown at the cost of acquisition or the cost of production, and are amortized over the term of such rights of use.

Administrative concessions granted by the State and other public bodies are amortized over the term of the concession.

c) Tangible fixed assets. Tangible fixed assets are recorded at cost of acquisition or cost of production, except for the revaluation of assets conducted during 1996 and on the merger operation in 1991.

The financial costs corresponding to the financing of infrastructure projects are capitalized as additional cost of tangible fixed assets when the period of construction exceeds one year.

The costs of repairs and improvements of assets are capitalized only when these produce an increase in the capacity, productivity or the useful life of the asset. Where applicable, the net book value of replaced assets is deducted.

Non-extractable base gas necessary for the operation of the subterranean storage of natural gas is registered as a tangible fixed asset, and is depreciated over the shorter of the useful life of the subterranean storage and the term of the corresponding lease agreement where applicable.

The cost of works conducted by the Group on tangible fixed assets (own labour and other costs capitalized) corresponds to the direct cost of production.

Provisions are raised against the accounting value of fixed assets no longer used in the Group's productive activities as considered necessary.

Depreciation is calculated systematically using the straight line method, over the estimated useful life of the respective assets. The depreciation rates applied are as follows:

	Rate %
Buildings	2 - 3
Technical installations (pipeline network)	3.33 - 5
Other technical installations and machinery	5 - 12
Tooling and equipment	30
Furniture and fittings	10
Computer equipment	25
Vehicles	16

Assets received by the company without consideration have been recorded at their theoretical value within tangible fixed assets and will be booked to the profit and loss account as income over the depreciation period of the respective assets using the straight line method. During this period, the balance pending release to the profit and loss account is shown as Other deferred income.

d) Investments. Investments in companies accounted for using the equity method are recorded on the basis of the net book value of the annual accounts of such companies at December 31, 1997.

Investments of less than 20% in unlisted companies are recorded at cost less, where applicable, the provisions required to reflect loss in value.

e) Goodwill. The difference between the acquisition cost of the participated companies and the net book value of the Group's holding in those companies as at the date of acquisition adjusted for applicable acquisition adjustments, is recorded in the consolidated financial statements as goodwill, and is amortised over the period during which these investments are expected to be recovered, subject to a maximum of 10 years.

f) Inventories. The raw material, liquid natural gas, is valued at FIFO (first in-first out) acquisition cost representing a value equal to or less than market value.

Finished products are valued at average production cost and other materials at average acquisition cost representing in both cases a value equal to or less than market value.

The requisite provisions are made to cover the obsolescence of materials.

g) Trade and non-trade debtors and creditors. Payables and receivables originating from operations, whether or not arising from the normal course of trade, are recorded at their nominal value and are classified as short term or long term depending on whether or not these become due within one year of the balance sheet date.

Provisions for potential bad debts are made as considered appropriate. Credit lines are shown at the amount actually used.

h) Reserves of fully consolidated companies, proportionally consolidated companies and companies accounted for using the equity method. These reserves reflect the difference between the book value of the investments in consolidated companies and the theoretical book value of such companies.

i) Conversion of financial statements in foreign currency. Financial statements in foreign currency included in the scope of consolidation have been converted to pesetas applying the year end exchange method. Profit and loss account transactions denominated in foreign currency have been translated to pesetas using the monthly average exchange rate. Cumulative foreign currency translation adjustments are included within Shareholders' equity.

j) Minority interests. This account reflects the interest of minority shareholders in the shareholders' equity of fully consolidated companies at December 31, 1997.

k) Negative consolidation difference. This corresponds to the difference between the acquisition price and the value of the group's share of the net assets acquired as at the date of first consolidation, as adjusted in order to reflect certain valuation adjustments to the assets and liabilities of the companies acquired.

The balance of the Negative consolidation difference is applied to results according as the costs giving rise thereto arise.

l) Capital grants. Non-refundable capital grants are applied to the profit and loss account using the straight line method over the same period in which the fixed assets financed by such grants are depreciated. For the purposes of accurate reflection in the annual accounts, the capital grants booked to the profit and loss account for the year are applied to Other operating income in order to provide a correlation of these grants with the depreciation of the grant-assisted fixed assets.

m) Provisions for pensions and related obligations. Company obligations in respect of supplementary pension payments are covered by the establishing of the corresponding pensions provisions and pensions fund.

Pensions provision. The pensions provision has been calculated following actuarial criteria and represents the present value of the contractual future liabilities in respect of active and retired personnel, of Gas Natural SDG, S.A. and the following Group companies: Compañía Española de Gas, S.A., Gas Tarraconense, S.A., Gas Natural Castilla y León, S.A., Gas Andalucía, S.A., Gas Rioja and Gas Lleida, S.A., in relation to payments complementing Social Security retirement, widows' and disability pensions, in accordance with the respective undertakings of each company. Actuarial calculations have been made on the basis of an annual interest rate of 6%.

Pensions fund. The pensions fund is constituted in accordance with the pensions plans agreed in the light of the Pensions Fund Act. These are defined contribution plans, and cover the liabilities recognized in relation to affected personnel. Under the agreements, the companies recognized certain consolidated rights for past service and undertook to make payments averaging between 2% and 6.8% of salaries into these funds. They are mixed plans, designed to cover retirement, disability and death benefits of members.

n) Other provisions. Liability obligations, both probable or definite, are shown within provisions for liabilities and charges. These provisions are made as and when such circumstances arise, on the basis of the total estimated liability.

o) Corporate tax. The corporate tax expense is reflected in the consolidated profit and loss account. This is calculated as the sum of the tax due on the profit for the year, the effect of any differences between taxable income and book income before taxes which reverse in subsequent years, and all allowances and deductions to which the companies are entitled.

It is Group policy to record deferred tax assets only when it is clear that these will be realized in the future. Deferred tax assets relating to the provision for pensions and related obligations are recorded in accordance with the resolution of the Spanish Institute of Accounting and Auditing dated September 25, 1991.

p) Income and expenses. Income and expenses are recorded on an accruals basis.

Sales of gas are recorded on the basis of invoices for gas consumed. For domestic and commercial customers, an estimate of the amount of gas consumed but not yet invoiced is calculated at the year end in order to match income and expenses for the year. Industrial consumption is recorded by fortnightly or monthly meter readings.

Indemnity payments received in respect of compulsory rerouting of pipelines are recorded as income using the straight-line method over the period in which the related fixed assets are depreciated. During this period, the unamortized portion of these amounts is shown as Other deferred income in the balance sheet.

Payments received in respect of new connections and branch lines are recorded as income in the period of depreciation of the related fixed asset, using the straight-line method. During this period the unamortized portion of these amounts are shown as Other deferred income in the balance sheet.

q) Exchange differences. Receivables and payables denominated in foreign currencies are converted to pesetas by applying the rate of exchange in effect at the date of each operation.

At the year end, balances in foreign currency are converted to pesetas at the rate in effect at that date.

Unrealized exchange differences resulting from specific financing operations undertaken to provide cover for the exchange risk on investments in group companies are included in Shareholders equity under the caption Foreign currency translation adjustments in the consolidated balance sheet.

r) Share in profits of companies accounted for using the equity method. This account reflects the interest of the Group in the post tax profits for the year of companies consolidated using the equity method.

Note 3. Intangible fixed assets
The movements in intangible fixed assets during 1997 were as follows:

	Balance at 1.1.97	Scope of consolidation and reclassifications	Additions	Decreases	Balance at 31.12.97
Research and development costs	2,591	15	274	2	2,878
Concessions, patents, licenses, trade marks and similar assets	81,621	13,236	56	609	94,304
Computer software applications	5,817	659	1,483	9	7,950
Other intangible fixed assets	1,308	(290)	289	—	1,307
	91,337	13,620	2,102	620	106,439
Accumulated amortization	6,956	337	4,358	12	11,639
Net value	**84,381**	**13,283**	**(2,256)**	**608**	**94,800**

Concessions, patents, licenses, trade marks and similar assets include the costs for the obtaining of the exclusive rights of use of the Moroccan part of the Maghreb-Europe pipeline up to 2021, and thereafter renewable.

Note 4. Tangible fixed assets
The movements in tangible fixed assets during 1997 were as follows:

	Balance at 1.1.97	Scope of consolidation and reclassifications	Additions	Disposals	Balance at 31.12.97
Land and buildings	46,164	3,461	1,267	275	50,617
Technical installations and machinery	757,216	57,967	52,110	2,107	865,186
Other fixed assets	17,777	(1,072)	2,469	308	18,866
Payments on account and fixed assets under construction	59,906	(23,085)	28,663	443	65,041
	881,063	**37,271**	**84,509**	**3,133**	**999,710**

The revaluation of tangible fixed assets incorporated by virtue of Royal Decree-Law 7/1996 of June 7, 1996 will have an affect of Ptas 7,340 million on the charge for depreciation of fixed assets for 1998.

The movement of the tangible fixed assets incorporated by virtue of the revaluation of fixed assets is as follows:

Balance at January 1, 1997	104,715
Retirements	(95)
Charge to depreciation provision for the year	(7,995)
Balance at December 31, 1997	**96,625**

Technical installations and machinery include Ptas 19,753 million in respect of non-extractable subterranean base natural gas from subterranean storage.

Additions include Ptas 1,718 million in respect of assets acquired without consideration.

Financial costs applied in 1997 to infrastructure projects in the course of construction totalled Ptas 1,060 million. Total tangible fixed assets cost at December 31, 1997 include Ptas 26,978 million of financial costs.

During 1997, tangible fixed assets purchased from associated companies totalled Ptas 1,424 million.

The movements in provisions and accumulated depreciation balances during the year were as follows:

	Balance at 1.1.97	Scope of consolidation and reclassifications	Charge for the year	Disposals	Balance at 31.12.97
Provisions	1,285	(52)	—	—	1,233
Depreciation:					
Buildings	6,490	513	981	53	7,931
Technical installations and machinery	182,030	9,205	39,379	2,049	228,565
Other fixed assets	9,997	1,378	2,441	226	13,590
	199,802	**11,044**	**42,801**	**2,328**	**251,319**

Provisions cover possible contingencies of temporary inactivity of productive assets.

During 1997, the useful life of natural gas transmission and industrial distribution installations have been re-estimated, at an average of 30 years. This operation has resulted in an increase of Ptas 2,612 million in the depreciation charge for the year.

Gross tangible fixed assets include the revaluation conducted during 1991 on the merger and part spin-off of Catalana de Gas, S.A., Gas Madrid, S.A. and Repsol Butano, S.A. at Ptas 10,483 million corresponding to Land and buildings.

It is Group policy to contract all the insurance policies which are considered necessary to cover tangible fixed assets against all possible risks.

Note 5. Investments

The composition of investments and their movement during the year was as follows:

	Balance at 1.1.97	Scope of consolidation and reclassifications	Additions	Decreases	Balance at 31.12.97
Holdings in companies accounted for using the equity method	5,719	—	2,414	715	7,418
Long term investments	2,448	660	1,801	208	4,701
Other loans	17,617	1,216	4,473	1,382	21,924
Provisions	(1,496)	(286)	(373)	16	(2,139)
	24,288	**1,590**	**8,315**	**2,289**	**31,904**

The movements arising during 1997 in Holdings in companies accounted for using the equity method correspond to equity movements and to the results of the companies consolidated by the equity method.

The most significant shareholdings included in Long term investments are as follows:

	Registered office	Total % Group investment	Activity
Cable i Televisió de Catalunya, S.A.	Barcelona	10	Cable television
Gasoducto Braga-Tuy,S.A.	Lisbon	49	Gas transmission
Gasoducto Campo Maior-Leiria-Braga, S.A.	Lisbon	12	Gas transmission
Gas Natural de Alava, S.A.	Vitoria	10	Gas distribution

The increase in long term investments mainly relates to the investment of Ptas 408 million in Cable i Televisió de Catalunya, S.A.

Other loans is composed mainly of long term financing extended to third parties, at market interest rate.

Note 6. Consolidation Goodwill

This corresponds to the differences arising on the first consolidation of the acquisition of shares of Gas Natural, S.A. ESP, Riogas, S.A. and Companhia Estadual de Gas do Rio de Janeiro, S.A.

The movement in this balance during the year has been as follows:

Balance at January 1, 1997	—
Increases	39,268
Amortization	33,614
Balance at December 31, 1997	**5,654**

The amortization has been calculated in accordance with the prudence principle.

Note 7. Inventories

The breakdown of inventories by activity groups is as follows:

Gas companies	24,666
Other companies	445
	25,111

Note 8. Trade debtors

The detail of this account is as follows:

Customers of gas companies	76,194
Customers of companies other than gas companies	1,525
	77,719

Note 9. Amounts due from/to companies accounted for using the equity method

The detail of these accounts is as follows:

Company	Balance at 31.12.97	
	Debtors	Creditors
Kromschroeder, S.A.	60	418
Sociedad de Gas de Euskadi, S.A.	1,984	4
Gas Aragón, S.A.	153	1
	2,197	**423**

Income and expense transactions with companies accounted for using the equity method comprise total charges of Ptas 82 million by these companies to the Group and Ptas 18,611 million charges by the Group to these companies.

Note 10. Other debtors

The most significant component included within this heading relates to deferred tax assets which amount to Ptas 6,849 million. These assets will mainly revert in the long term.

Note 11. Short term securities

This item corresponds primarily to Government stock and other financial investments. The average interest rate earned on these investments during 1997 was 6.53%.

Note 12. Equity

The detail of share capital and reserve accounts at December 31, 1997 and their movement during the year was as follows:

	Balance at 1.1.97	Distribution of results 1996	Share capital increase	Other movements	Balance at 31.12.97
Share capital	22,389	—	52,240	—	74,629
Share premium	39,270	—	(39,270)	—	—
Revaluation reserve	20,716	—	—	—	20,716
Merger reserve	19,051	—	—	—	19,051
Legal reserve	10,138	—	—	—	10,138
Voluntary reserve and other reserves	52,749	15,917	(12,970)	(381)	55,315
Reserves in consolidated companies	110,547	22,639	—	3,070	136,256
Foreign currency translation adjustments	1,431	—	—	3,480	4,911
	276,291	**38,556**	**·**	**6,169**	**321,016**

The share capital of Gas Natural SDG, S.A. is made up of 149,258,676 shares with a nominal value of 500 pesetas each, all subscribed and fully paid up which are recorded as a book entry. All shares have the same voting and distribution rights.

During 1997, by resolution of the Ordinary General Meeting of Shareholders of Gas Natural SDG, S.A. held on June 18, 1997, the Board of Directors conducted a share split, consisting in the division of the nominal value by four, a simultaneous four-fold increase in the number of shares in circulation and a subsequent increase in share capital, fully charged to freely distributable reserves, by an increase in the nominal value of the shares resulting from the previous operation to five hundred pesetas.

By resolution of the Ordinary General Meeting of Shareholders held on June 18, 1997, the Board of Directors was authorized to increase the share capital by up to Ptas 37,315 million within a period of five years, by means of one or more share issues, to be paid in cash, without having to obtain further authorization. In addition, it was authorized to issue company bonds, not convertible into shares, to a maximum of Ptas 90,000 million, in one or more issues, within a period of five years.

All shares in Gas Natural SDG, S.A. are listed on all four of the official Spanish stock exchanges and are traded on the continuous market.

The most significant holdings in the share capital of Gas Natural SDG, S.A. are as follows:

	Shareholding %
Repsol, S.A.	45.3
Caixa d'Estalvis i Pensions de Barcelona	25.5

The Revaluation reserve is not distributable until it has been examined and accepted by the Tax Administration within the period ended December 31, 1999. After such examination or on expiry of the period for the performance of the examination, the balance of the account may be applied to offset book losses, to increasing the Share capital or, after December 31, 2006, to Freely distributable reserves.

Reserves in consolidated companies at December 31, 1997 correspond principally to:

Enagás, S.A.	105,582
Compañía Española de Gas, S.A.	6,088
Gas Natural Castilla y León, S.A.	3,823

Foreign currency translation adjustments correspond to the difference between the total of assets and liabilities of Group companies the accounts of which are denominated in foreign currency, converted at the rate of exchange at the end of the year and the equity of such companies at the historic rate of exchange.

Note 13. Minority interests

The movements in this account during the year were as follows:

Balance at January 1, 1997	39,814
Increases:	
Share in profit for the year	5,061
Foreign currency translation adjustments	2,750
Share capital increases	141
Others	102
Reductions:	
Distribution of 1996 profit	(1,308)
Balance at December 31, 1997	**46,560**

The breakdown of the Minority interest balance at December 31, 1997 is as follows:

	Participation in share capital and reserves	Share of profit for the year	Total
Enagás, S.A.	19,867	2,632	22,499
Gas Natural BAN, S.A.-Invergas, S.A.	19,582	2,465	22,047
Gas Navarra, S.A.	584	136	720
Gas Rioja, S.A.	207	43	250
Compañía Española de Gas, S.A.	155	9	164
Others	1,104	(224)	880
	41,499	**5,061**	**46,560**

Note 14. Negative consolidation difference

The balance at December 31, 1997 corresponds to the differences arising on the first consolidation of the acquisition of shares of Enagás, S.A. and of Sagane, S.A.

The application to results during 1997 has been conducted as the requisites set out in Article 25.3a) of Royal Decree 1815/1991 have been complied with.

The movement in this balance during the year has been as follows:

Balance at January 1, 1997	52,168
Applications	(36,656)
Balance at December 31, 1997	**15,512**

Note 15. Deferred income

The movement of Capital grants during the year has been as follows:

Balance at January 1, 1997	41,990
Received	6,065
Applied to results	(1,931)
Balance at December 31, 1997	**46,124**

Other deferred income consists mainly of deferred income in respect of the exclusive rights of use of transmission gas pipelines, amounting to Ptas 15,263 million; of tangible fixed assets received without consideration, amounting to Ptas 13,986 million (See Note 2.c); deferred income in respect of indemnity payments received for compulsory rerouting of gas pipelines, amounting to Ptas 5,686 million; and payments received in respect of new connections and branch lines, amounting to Ptas 7,597 million.

Note 16. Provision for liabilities and charges

The detail of the provisions for pensions and related obligations at December 31, 1997 and its movement during the year is as follows:

Balance at January 1, 1997	24,152
Ordinary provisions charged	1,448
Extraordinary provisions charged	6
Applications during the year against the provision	(2,177)
Scope of consolidation and reclassifications	936
Balance at December 31, 1997	**24,365**

The pensions provision corresponds to the pensions established for Gas Natural SDG, S.A., Compañía Española de Gas, S.A., Gas Tarraconense, S.A., Gas Natural Castilla y León, S.A., Gas Andalucía, S.A., Gas Rioja, S.A., and Gas Lleida, S.A.

These companies have defined benefit pension plan to cover currently active and retired eligible employees. These pensions are intended in all cases to supplement the Social Security retirement pensions, and are payable only when the payment levels guaranteed by the plan exceed those paid by Social Security.

The annual charges to cover accrued liabilities of the respective Group companies are charged to the profit and loss account each year.

The balance of Other provisions at December 31, 1997 corresponds mainly to provisions constituted for probable liabilities in relation to identified contingencies.

The movement of Other provisions during the year has been as follows:

Balance at January 1, 1997	14,850
Charge in the year	346
Utilized in the year	(4,815)
Other movements	1,147
Balance at December 31, 1997	**11,528**

Note 17. Debentures and other long term negotiable securities
This corresponds to amounts outstanding under the issue of negotiable Eurobonds issued by Invergas, S.A. for US dollars 100 million at market interest rate, maturing in 1999.

Note 18. Amounts due to financial institutions
The composition of this item is as follows:

	Long term	Short term
Bank loans and credits	331,376	4,320
Accrued interest	—	3,068
	331,376	**7,388**

Long term loans from financial institutions include loans in US dollars of Ptas 147,782 million at a market interest rate.

Long term loans and credits are subject to market interest rates and the scheduled repayments are as follows:

1999	56,760
2000	14,772
2001	42,974
2002	79,332
2003	3,909
After five years	133,629
	331,376

Note 19. Other creditors
Other creditors include a loan of US dollars 18.7 million due to the Repsol Group, which matures in 2000, and bears interest at a market rate.

Note 20. Balances with companies consolidated by the proportional consolidation method
Balances receivable and payable with multigroup companies corresponding to third parties total Ptas 7,688 million and Ptas 308 million, respectively.

Note 21. Tax
Corporate tax is assessed on a consolidated basis on the following companies: Gas Natural SDG, S.A., Enagás, S.A., Gas Natural Castilla y León, S.A., Compañía Española de Gas, S.A., Gas Castilla-La Mancha, S.A., Compañía Auxiliar de Industrias Varias, S.A., Gas Natural Informática, S.A., Gas Girona, S.A., Gas Lleida, S.A., Gas Penedés, S.A., Gas Vic, S.A., Equipos y Servicios, S.A., Gas Serviconfort, S.A., Gas Tarraconense, S.A., Gas Andalucía, S.A., Gas Natural Internacional SDG, S.A., Gas Natural Extremadura, S.A., Holding Gas Natural, S.A., La Propagadora del Gas, S.A., La Energía, S.A. and Sagane, S.A. Corporate tax is assessed on the remaining group companies on an individual basis.

The reconciliation between consolidated profit for the year and taxable income is as follows:

Consolidated profit before tax		**73,475**
Permanent differences:		**(12,143)**
Individual companies	(23)	
Pensions provision	(109)	
Other differences	86	
Consolidation adjustments	(12,120)	
Temporary differences:		**(1,886)**
Individual companies	(2,166)	
Provisions	237	
Pensions fund provision	1,636	
1997 pension payments	(2,158)	
Accelerated depreciation	(1,275)	
Other differences	(606)	
Consolidation adjustments	280	
Taxable income		**59,446**

Investment allowances and double taxation relief in 1997 totalled Ptas 4,011 million.

Retentions and on account payments made during the year totalled Ptas 13,661 million.

Movements in deferred Corporate tax assets and liabilities during 1997 are as follows:

	Balance at 1.1.97	Variation	Balance at 31.12.97
Deferred tax assets			
Pensions provision	6,215	(183)	6,032
Imputed income from subsidiaries			
(fiscal transparency imputation system)	50	14	64
Capital grants	342	—	342
Other deferred tax assets	1,771	385	2,156
	8,378	**216**	**8,594**
Deferred tax liabilities			
Accelerated depreciation	1,921	447	2,368
Other deferred tax liabilities	557	1,776	2,333
	2,478	**2,223**	**4,701**

Group companies are open to inspection in respect of all applicable taxes for all periods which have not prescribed, with the exception of Gas Natural SDG, S.A. in which tax inspections are at present being conducted.

Note 22. Net sales

Group activities are undertaken in the Spanish and Latin-American markets, the composition being as follows:

	Spain	Latin-America	Total
Sales of gas	348,968	59,676	408,644
Other sales of Group gas companies	10,928	3,895	14,823
Other sales (installations, gas engineering, etc.)	4,945	—	4,945
	364,841	**63,571**	**428,412**

Note 23. Cost of sales and other external costs

This item is composed as follows:

	Spain	Latin-America	Total
Gas companies	194,303	34,309	228,612
Other companies	1,141	—	1,141
	195,444	**34,309**	**229,753**

Note 24. Personnel costs

The average number of Group employees during the year and their breakdown by category was as follows:

	Spain	Latin-America	Total
Management and technical staff	1,853	1,011	2,864
Administrative and sales staff	819	533	1,352
Other personnel	1,287	662	1,949
	3,959	**2,206**	**6,165**

Note 25. Other operating expenses

This item corresponds primarily to structural costs, the most significant of which are repairs and maintenance; computer and information technology costs; advertising; external services and taxes.

Note 26. Net extraordinary income

Profit on disposal of tangible fixed assets corresponds primarily to the sale of land by Gas Natural SDG, S.A.

Extraordinary income corresponds primarily to the adjustment of Other provisions.

Extraordinary expenses correspond primarily to the premium for attendance at the General Meeting of Shareholders of Gas Natural SDG, S.A. in 1997.

Note 27. Breakdown of consolidated profit

Details are as follows:

	Profit for the year attributed to the parent company	Profit for the year attributed to minority interests
Gas Activity: Transmission and distribution in Spain	48,578	2,596
Gas Activity: Transmission and distribution outside Spain	2,049	2,465
	50,627	**5,061**

Note 28. Other information

During 1997, the members of the Board of Directors of Gas Natural SDG, S.A. received a total of Ptas 180 million and Ptas 28 million in respect of directors' fees and loans, respectively.

Pension and life insurance premium expenses in respect of members of the Board of Directors totalled Ptas 1 million and Ptas 4 million, respectively.

At the year end, unused credit lines available from financial institutions totalled Ptas 62,083 million.

At December 31, 1997, the Group's gas purchase rights total 3,058,758 million thermies, for the period 1998-2030. All these contracts include "take or pay" clauses.

The Group also has contracts with 8 cryogenic vessels for the transport of LNG, all of which are long term.

At December 31, 1997, the Group has contracts with third parties for the transport of natural gas totalling 353,065 million thermies for the period 1998-2021, which contain "ship or pay" clauses for each of the five sections of pipeline between the border with Morocco and the border between Galicia and Portugal at Tuy.

Note 29. Subsequent events

The Board of Directors of Gas Natural, SDG, S.A. on December 19, 1997 agreed to pay a gross interim dividend for 1997 of Ptas 34 per share, payable as from January 9, 1998.

As from 1998, upon meeting the relevant criteria, Gas Natural Latinoamericana, S.A. and Gas Natural Colombia, S.A. will join the Group of companies presenting a consolidated tax return.

Note 30. Consolidated statement of source and application of funds

The consolidated statement of source and application of funds is as follows:

Consolidated source and application of funds of the Gas Natural Group
(Shown in millions of pesetas)

Applications	1997	1996
Start-up expenses and loan creation costs	2,208	504
Acquisition of fixed assets:	137,844	144,791
Intangible fixed assets	2,102	1,964
Tangible fixed assets	84,510	128,957
Investments	51,232	13,870
Dividends:	11,196	9,237
Parent company	9,888	7,463
Paid to minority interests	1,308	1,774
Cancellation or transfer to short term of long term debt	50,505	42,759
Cancellation or transfer to short term of deferred income	17	521
Provision for liabilities and charges	1,984	2,960
Total applications	**203,754**	**200,772**
Excess of sources over applications	**34,050**	**23,073**
(Increase in working capital)		

Sources	1997	1996
Net funds generated from operating activities	94,666	81,722
Deferred income	11,545	34,057
Long term debts	127,464	106,093
Sale of fixed assets:	3,570	1,570
Intangible fixed assets	608	10
Tangible fixed assets	1,389	709
Investments	1,573	851
Early redemption of long term investments or transfer to short term	418	280
Other sources	141	123
Total sources	**237,804**	**223,845**
Excess of applications over sources	—	—
(Reduction in working capital)		

Movement in working capital

	1997		1996	
	Increases	Decreases	Increases	Decreases
Shareholders for calls on share capital	8	—	134	—
Inventories	7,917	—	2,996	—
Debtors	12,720	—	12,809	—
Creditors	19,425	—	5,877	—
Short term investments	—	798	2,515	—
Cash and banks	—	5,684	—	551
Prepaid expenses	462	—	—	707
Total	**40,532**	**6,482**	**24,331**	**1,258**
Movement in working capital	**34,050**		**23,073**	**—**

The reconciliation between consolidated profit and net funds generated from operating activities is as follows:

	1997	1996
Results for the year	55,688	52,770
Increases:		
Depreciation and amortization		
(including deferred expenses)	47,576	30,350
Provision for liabilities and charges	(3,208)	1,384
Provisions against fixed assets and investments	373	—
Companies accounted for using the equity method		
(dividends)	714	580
Goodwill amortization	33,614	643
Decreases:		
Application of provisions for fixed assets	(7)	(833)
Profit on sale of fixed assets	(584)	(531)
Deferred income and expenses	(1,835)	(1,091)
Companies accounted for using the equity method		
(results)	(1,009)	(781)
Write-back of negative consolidation difference	(36,656)	(769)
Total	**94,666**	**81,722**

Country Highlights
SWEDEN

Common Legal Forms of Companies
Limited company (aktiebolag, AB), partnership (handelsbolag, HB).

Sources of Financial Reporting Requirements
The Company's Act, the Annual Accounts Act, based on the requirements of the European 4th and 7th directives. Standards issued by the Swedish Financial Accounting Council (Redovisningsrådet, RR), primarily dealing with accounting issues related to public companies. Increasingly IAS are being implemented in the standards developed by Redovisningsrådet to the extent possible under the Annual Accounts Act. There are also accounting recommendations issued by the Swedish Accounting Standards Board (Bokföringsnämnden, BFN) and by FAR (see below).

Corporate Taxation
Company income tax is currently 28%. Companies in a group are taxed on an individual basis. However, under certain conditions profits and losses within a group of Swedish companies could be offset by intragroup transfers (group contributions). In principle taxable income should equal the amount stated as "net income before tax" in the income statement. There are, however, a number of exceptions. Losses incurred for tax purposes may be carried forward indefinitely but loss carry-backs are not allowed.

Auditing Requirements
Annual Reports of all limited companies are subject to audit. The Audit Report covers the whole annual report, including the administration report and also the administration of the company's affairs during the year by the Board of Directors and the Managing Director.

Organization of the Accounting and Auditing Professions
Most of the 2,300 authorized public accountants in Sweden are members of the Swedish Institute of Authorized Public Accountants (Föreningen Auktoriserade Revisorer, FAR). FAR issued accounting recommendations before the establishment of RR. All members of FAR must comply with the rules of professional ethics agreed to by the members of the Institute.

Constitution and Legal System

There are four constitutional laws, including the Constitution and laws dealing with freedom of the press, freedom of speach, and order of succession. The Constitution dates back to 1634. The head of state is the King of Sweden, who has no power over the change of government. The prime minister is appointed by the parliament, which institutes laws and decides on any change of government.

Currency

Swedish kronor, SEK.

Official Language

Swedish, belonging to the Scandinavian language family together with Danish and Norwegian.

SWEDEN

Sigvard Heurlin
Coopers & Lybrand AB, Stockholm, Sweden
Erling Peterssohn
Upsala University and Coopers & Lybrand AB, Stockholm, Sweden

1. Background

1.1 The Development of Company and Accounting Law

1.1.1 Company Law

The Royal Ordinance on limited companies of October 6, 1848, was the first law on limited companies in Sweden and the Nordic countries. Long before that law came into effect, however, Sweden had enterprises with a structure similar to that of limited companies. The actual predecessors of our present-day limited companies were the trading companies that came into existence during the seventeenth century. The most famous trading company was probably Tjaruhandelskompaniet, chartered in 1648. In an "audit report" from 1652, the "auditors" of this company expressed an opinion on both the accounts of the directors and the matter of discharge from liability. A Swedish law of 1734 contained stipulations concerning companies with joint and several liability of the shareholders. After its inception, limited companies were nevertheless incorporated both with and without royal charter.

The 1848 ordinance was clearly and strongly influenced by the French *code de commerce*. The ordinance was quite brief, containing only fifteen clauses. It prescribed royal sanction of articles of association, if the shareholders were to enjoy freedom from liability for the company's liabilities. The law did not, however, contain any direct prohibition against forming a limited company without the royal sanction.

The ordinance of 1848 was replaced by the Companies Act of June 28, 1895. The act included a number of rules concerning the payment, increase, and reduction of the share capital, legal reserves, distribution of profits, annual returns, audit, discharge from liability, liquidation, and damages payable by directors. According to the wording of the law, the income for the year had to be reported in the management report. It seems, however, that the concept of income was not quite clear, since the law did not include any rules on valuation. Studies of accounting practice toward the end of the nineteenth century indicate that Swedish companies at this time had started to apply the principle of lower of cost and market value in respect of current assets and had started to depreciate fixed assets. Regarding its content and system, this act seems to have been influenced by German rather than French legislation.

The act of 1895 was not long-lived. It was criticized for the insufficient protection it afforded against unsound corporate activities. Consequently, the act of 1910 contained several new features, for example, comprehensive rules regarding the publication of articles of incorporation, the contents of balance sheets, greater civil and criminal liability for the founders, the directors, and the auditors, the right of minority shareholders to appoint their own auditor to participate in the auditors' examination of a company's accounts, and the administration by its board of directors. In many respects the act was clearly influenced by German law. The impact of German legislation is evidenced by the preparatory work, where an account of the German law was given by far the most space.

When the fall of the Kreuger Group was investigated in the 1930s, the accounts of the group were found to be fraudulent. An undermined financial position had been concealed through the complex, international system of group companies. Shortcomings in the Companies Act were revealed, and the experience drawn from the Kreuger case thus played an important role in the preparatory work for a new Companies Act. The preparatory legislative work was initially carried out in consultation with the other Nordic countries. Because of the Second World War, however, this cooperation was interrupted. Thus, only Sweden issued a new Companies Act in 1944. In the act of 1944, the rules regarding the forms of incorporation and publicity on incorporation were made more stringent. In addition, rules on the limitation of distribution of dividends were introduced to protect creditors. The obligation of the board of directors and the managing director to submit annual reports was significantly enhanced. The rules requiring a parent company to prepare consolidated accounts were quite new. The position of the auditors in relation to the board and the majority shareholders was strengthened. The act also stipulated that large companies should be audited by an authorized public accountant. In other companies as well, a minority of the shareholders could demand that at least one auditor should be an authorized public accountant or a registered accountant. The voting rights of shares were restricted so that no share could have more than ten times the voting power of another share. The board's duty of disclosure at general meetings was also enlarged.

The act is characterized by its scope and detail. The Companies Act of 1944 was amended several times during the 30 years it was in force. The so-called law on public control signified considerable extension of public accountability. The new rules were introduced through an amendment to the law in 1950, in response to demands by the trade unions.

The Companies Act of 1944 was replaced by the present Companies Act of 1975. The preparatory work for this act was carried out in close cooperation with the other Nordic countries, which resulted in largely uniform companies acts in these countries during the 1970s.

In 1990 the government appointed a committee to review the Companies Act and propose necessary amendments with regard to the ongoing process of European integration. So far, a few amendments have been integrated into the law. The barriers to foreign acquisitions of shares in Swedish companies have been removed. The requirement of a minimum share capital has been changed to SEK 100,000, that is, approximately 12,000 EURO. There are two types of limited companies in Sweden today, with different requirements regarding, for example, disclosure of financial information. They are called *private limited companies* and *public limited companies*. The committee is still working on, among other things, amendments to the rules on the responsibilities of the board of directors, the managing director, and the auditors, as well as the rules on merges between limited companies.

The committee has made several comprehensive proposals that have not yet been integrated into the law. These proposals include, among other things, amendments to the rules on corporate governance, increases and reductions in share capital, and repurchase and sale of the company's own shares. The most recent proposal deals with the distribution restrictions treated in Section 3.3.5 below. The requirement of allocating a part of the company's net income for the year to the statutory reserve will be removed, and cash loans to related parties will no longer be prohibited, as long as the loan does not exceed the distributable amount.

The committee continues the work with the intention of designing a completely new Companies Act, which will encompass the proposals mentioned above.

1.1.2 Accounting Law

The first Accounting Act became effective in 1855. It introduced the requirement for a book of first entry and an annual accounts book. The annual accounts book was to contain a balance sheet. The act did not, however, contain any rules on valuation. By contrast, the Accounting Act of 1929 did contain valuation rules. It is quite clear from the preparatory work that the purpose of these rules was to measure the profit of the business and not to establish the value of the company. However, rules for the valuation of assets and liabilities had been introduced in the Companies Act of 1910. There is a significant difference between the rules on valuation contained in these two acts regarding the valuation of current assets, where the Accounting Act permits deviation from the principle of lower of cost and market value. Behind the act of 1929 there was also the wish to enable creditors to assess the manner in which insolvent business people had carried on their business. At that time, however, there was no discussion of the accounts as a basis on which to determine a company's tax liability. The situation was quite different during the preparatory work preceding the Accounting Act of 1976.

An essential new feature in this act, as in the Companies Act of 1975, was the demand for increased disclosure in the case of understatement of assets in relation to the rules of the law, which are designed as rules of maximum valuation. As may be seen in Section 2.1, special models for income statements and balance sheets were developed to satisfy this demand for increased disclosure.

As a consequence of the EES agreement and later membership in the European Union, Sweden has introduced the requirements of the European Fourth and Seventh Directives into the Swedish Annual Accounts Act of 1995, operative as of January 1, 1997.

The Swedish Annual Accounts Act of 1995 regulates the annual accounts and reports of incorporated companies, while the Accounting Act of 1976 is still in effect for unregistered firms and partnerships. Bookkeeping issues (recording of transactions, filing, etc) are still regulated by the Accounting Act of 1976.

1.2 The Development of the Accounting and Auditing Professions

For many years, the bylaws of limited companies in Sweden have made provisions for audits of the companies' accounts. The Companies Act of 1895 prescribed that the administration of the board of directors should be reviewed and that the company's accounts should be examined by one or more auditors. In those days, auditors were often people with business experience, but they were seldom skilled in accounting matters. During the early twentieth century, however, an accounting profession began to develop. An important event in the development of the profession was the action by the Stockholm Chamber of Commerce in 1912, when it adopted its first statutes for authorization of public accountants. One of the prerequisites for authorization of auditors was satisfied by the foundation of the Stockholm School of Economics in 1909, which offered a university education in business administration. In Sweden, chambers of commerce are private and regional organizations. Beginning in 1973 the government took over the task of authorizing public accountants. This is today handled by the Supervisory Board of Public Accountants (*Revisorsnämnden, RN*), which also acts as a sanctioning body. The educational qualifications and experience required for a person to become an authorized public accountant are described briefly below.

All authorized public accountants must have a university degree in business administration, of which accounting, company law, and taxation are compulsory elements and a special professional examination is required. To be granted a license, the authorized accountant must also have 5 years' practical experience, mainly with an authorized accounting firm. The license is valid for a 5-year period, after which a new application must be made.

An authorized public accountant is not allowed to carry out any activities that are incompatible with his or her professional duties as an independent auditor. Most authorized public accountants are members of the Swedish Institute of Authorized Public Accountants (*Foreningen Auktoriserade Revisorer*, FAR). All members of the Institute must comply with the Rules of Professional Ethics agreed to by the members of the Institute.

The Swedish Institute of Authorized Public Accountants was founded in 1923, its objects being to promote a high standard within the profession and to promote rational methods in auditing, accounting, and business organization within Swedish companies. The founder of the Institute, Oskar Sillén, acted as chairman for 18 years and, in this capacity, was also an innovator in the fields of auditing and accounting.

One of the FAR's most important tasks since the mid-1960s has been to prepare recommendations on accounting and auditing matters and professional ethics. During the past 20 years, the institute has also carried out an extensive training program, mainly in the form of basic audit training leading to authorization. Auditing is not offered as a subject at Swedish universities or schools of economics.

When the Accounting Act of 1976 came into being, a body of experts known as the Swedish Accounting Standards Board *(Bokföringsnämnden, BFN)* was founded for the purpose of developing generally accepted accounting principles. The board, which is a governmental body, has been working alongside FAR, focusing on accounting issues. In addition, the Federation of Swedish Industries *(Sveriges Industriforbund, SI)* and the Stockholm Chamber of Commerce have issued accounting recommendations relating to listed companies through the Business Community's Stock Exchange Committee *(Näringslivets börskommitté, NBK).* In order to coordinate these activities, the Swedish Accounting Standards Board, the Swedish Institute of Authorized Public Accountants, and the Federation of Swedish Industries together formed in 1989 a foundation and a body of experts, the Swedish Financial Accounting Standards Council *(Redovisningsradet, RR)* to develop and issue recommendations on financial reporting of public companies, replacing the FAR as a standard-setting body.

1.3 International Influence on Accounting and Auditing in Sweden

During the first half of the twentieth century, German accounting theorists such as Eugen Schmalenbach, Fritz Schmidt, and Ernst Walb exercised considerable influence over the subject of accounting at the two Swedish Schools of Economics, in Stockholm and Gothenburg.

Ernst Walb was the first professor of the subject at the Stockholm School of Economics. He was succeeded by Oskar Sillén, who was in an excellent position to carry on the German tradition, because of his earlier studies at the Cologne School of Economics, where Schmalenbach was teaching.

When the Gothenburg School of Economics appointed its first professor of business management and accounting a few decades later, Professor Mahlberg from Germany was chosen. After only a short time he was succeeded by Professor ter Vehn, who had studied in Frankfurt under Professor Schmidt. It may be added that well into the 1960s, the Schools of Economics in Stockholm and Gothenburg were the only ones to offer higher education and research in accounting.

To a limited extent, the American influence manifested itself during the 1940s, becoming increasingly evident during the 1960s. During that period, teaching and research at the Stockholm School of Economics were molded by Professor Sven-Erik Johansson. The influence of leading American accounting theorists, such as William A. Paton, Maurice Moonitz, Robert T. Sprouse, Edgar O. Edwards, and Philip W. Bell became stronger, partly through literature, partly through research exchange. In Gothenburg, and later at the new seats of learning, teaching and research in the subject of accounting were to come under even stronger influence from the United States. Today the German influence on education is nearly nonexistent, if we disregard the heritage in Swedish legislation and doctrine.

However, with the implementation of the EC Directives, the German influence will probably become stronger.

International influence also reaches Swedish accounting practice through the standards that are set by Swedish bodies, especially the Swedish Financial Accounting Standards Council and, previously, FAR. Other channels of influence are the Swedish multinationals and the international accounting firms. Another source of international influence on accounting practice in Sweden is the international financial market. Of relatively recent origin, this influence is growing in importance. Large Swedish companies that turn to U.S. stock markets for funds must adopt, in certain respects, U.S. GAAP in their reporting.

The main sources of international influence on auditing practices in Sweden are the international accounting firms. Most large Swedish accounting firms cooperate with or are members of an international firm. Such cooperation involves exchange of staff, handbooks, manuals, and education programs.

As a member of the International Federation of Accountants (IFAC), the Swedish Institute (FAR) has committed itself to supporting IFAC's endeavors toward high and uniform professional ethical conduct among public accountants and also to work for adherence to the IFAC statements of guidance on ethics in Sweden, as far as they comply with Swedish law. IFAC's International Auditing Guidelines are incorporated (although not completely) into the auditing standards issued by FAR, thereby influencing auditing practice.

1.4 Sources of Accounting Standards in Sweden

Generally accepted accounting principles in Sweden and applicable standards are derived from the following sources:

- The Swedish Annual Accounts Act (*Årsredovisningslagen 1995:1554*), which comprises established accounting principles, forms and content of financial statements, measurement rules and disclosure requirements for the single entity as well as for the group of companies. Interim reporting is also regulated by this act.

- The Swedish Accounting Act (*Bokföringslagen 1976:125*), which still regulates the accounts of unregistered firms and partnerships.

- Financial Accounting Standards adopted by the Swedish Financial Accounting Council (*Redovisningsrådet,* RR). The main objective of the RR is to issue standards and to deal with accounting issues related to public companies. Increasingly IAS are being implemented in the standards developed by RR to the extent possible under the Annual Accounts Act.

- Recommendations on accounting matters issued by the Swedish Accounting Standards Board (*Bokföringsnämnden,* BFN). The BFN is a government body that develops and interprets generally accepted accounting principles for application in corporate accounting and annual reports. The BFN also prepares and issues general advice on accounting matters and the preparation of financial statements.

- Recommendations on accounting matters issued by the Swedish Institute of Authorized Public Accountants (*Föreningen Auktoriserade Revisorer,* FAR), which describe generally accepted accounting practice and interpret certain regulations in the Swedish Annual Accounts Act.

- Recommendations issued by the Business Community's Stock Exchange Committee (*Näringslivets Börskommitté,* NBK) for companies quoted on the Stockholm Stock Exchange. The NBK was formed by the Stockholm Chamber of Commerce (*Stockholms Handelskammare*) and the Swedish Federation of Industries (*Sveriges Industriförbund,* SI) to issue recommendations concerning information provided to the Stockholm Stock Exchange by quoted companies.

Although standards issued by the RR are of increasing importance, generally accepted accounting principles in Sweden could also be described by reference to the accounting and reporting practice actually adopted by high quality public companies. Thus, not only formal sources of accounting standards, but also other current developments and trends give substance to the concept of "Generally Accepted Accounting Principles in Sweden" (Swedish GAAP).

Finally Swedish tax legislation has had a significant impact on the preparation of the single-entity financial statements; special deductions and allowances for tax purposes (tax appropriations) must be included in the income statement to be allowed in computing taxable income. However, such tax-driven allowances are generally not reflected in the group accounts.

2. The Form and Content of Published Financial Statements

2.1 The Form of Financial Statements

The income statement and balance sheet should be set out in the format required by law, as specified in the Swedish Annual Accounts Act, Chapter 3 with appendices. There are two optional formats for the income statment. Departures from the required format called for by the nature and extent of the business are permitted. Assets and liabilities are segregated between noncurrent and current items in the balance sheet. A noncurrent asset is defined as an asset intended for continuous use or possession by the entity. All other assets are current assets.

According to Swedish tax law, all extra deductions or provisions for tax purposes (tax appropriations or year-end provisions) should be reflected in the income statement in order to be allowed in computing taxable income. When this requirement was first implemented, accounting income and asset values became distorted. Therefore, an accounting model was developed in the 1960s, supported by the Business Community's Stock Exchange Committee (NBK). This model was unique for Sweden for many years but today it is also used in other Scandinavian countries. The model, described in the following paragraph, is prescribed in the Swedish Annual Accounts Act for single entities, which is a deviation from the Fourth Directive.

All tax appropriations, many of which imply asset undervaluation, are reported in a certain segment of the income statement under the heading "appropriations" (sometimes called "allocations" or "year-end provisions").

The "true" before tax accounting income in a Swedish income statement for the single entity is "income before appropriations and taxes" (sometimes called "income before allocations and tax(es)" or "income before year-end provisions and tax(es)"). To maintain the integrity of asset values in the balance sheet, assets are not reduced by the extra write-offs appearing under the tax appropriations heading in the income statement. Instead, the appropriations and the extra write-offs are reflected in the balance sheet as increases in untaxed reserves, similarly reported in a certain segment of the balance sheet. These reserves should be considered a mixture of equity and deferred tax. Beginning in 1991, and as an effect of a tax reform, the taxable proportion of these untaxed reserves has been around 30%. The reserves may not be used for dividend distribution until they have been carried back to income and included in taxable income.

2.2 The Content of Published Financial Statements

Under the Swedish Annual Accounts Act, limited companies are required to present to their shareholders an annual report containing a management report, an income statement, a balance sheet, a statement of changes in financial position, and notes to the accounts. Notes to financial statements are considered an integral part of the statements. A parent company shall also prepare the same documents on a consolidated basis.

2.3 The Scope of Consolidated Financial Statements

The Swedish Company Act stipulates that where a company—directly or indirectly—holds more than half the votes attached to the shares of a Swedish or a foreign legal entity, the company is a parent company and the legal entity is a subsidiary. Furthermore, where a company exercises controlling influence over a legal entity, the company is a parent company and the legal entity a subsidiary.

Chapter 7 of the Swedish Annual Accounts Act deals with reporting requirements and in particular those relating to consolidated financial statements. As indicated above, a parent company shall for each financial year prepare, in addition to its annual report, consolidated financial statements. The consolidated financial statements should be prepared to the same date as the balance sheet of the parent company, and group members should have the same financial year, except in cases where the subsidiary's fiscal year ends three months or less before the parent's fiscal year.

The consolidated income statement and the consolidated balance sheet shall be a combination of the parent company's financial statements and those of its subsidiaries, prepared in conformity with generally accepted accounting principles in Sweden. Uniform accounting policies should be used for the transactions and other events in similar circumstances. Intercompany balances, dividends, and profits should be eliminated. The consolidated balance sheet should show the group's nonrestricted equity capital or accumulated loss after deduction of intercompany profits, a requirement that is unique to Sweden.

Minority interests should be presented separately in the consolidated balance sheet and the consolidated income statement.

A subsidiary should be excluded from consolidation when control is intended to be temporary. In this case and in such other rare cases where consolidated financial statements are not prepared because difficulties are encountered, the reasons should be stated in the notes to the accounts.

The methods and valuation principles used in the preparation of the consolidated financial statements should be described in the annual report. In addition, the amount that, according to the annual reports of the companies of the group, should be transferred from the nonrestricted equity capital to the restricted equity capital in the consolidated balance sheet, should be stated.

As described in Section 3.1 below, the purchase method, the pooling of interest method, the proportional consolidation method and equity accounting are used for the preparation of consolidated financial statements.

2.4 Segmental Disclosure

The Swedish Annual Accounts Act stipulates that information should be disclosed about sales for each industry segment and each geographic segment. A recommendation issued by BFN (revised in 1996) provides guidelines on how the requirements of the law should be fulfilled. According to this recommendation, not only sales, but also operating results for each industry segment should be disclosed. For public companies segment assets should also be disclosed. Similarly, segment revenue should be disclosed for each geographic segment. For listed companies the disclosure should also include operating results as well as capital investments and average number of employees.

The above BFN recommendation is inspired by IAS 14 (revised), but is more limited in its disclosure requirements.

2.5 Status of Form and Content

From a regulatory point of view the Swedish standard-setting system is a combination of a system with certain requirements prescribed by law (a basic form and content of financial statements, as well as valuation principles and disclosure requirements) and a self-regulation system (accounting principles and disclosures).

The recommendations and the pronouncements developed under the Swedish self-regulation system have no precise legal status

The interrelationship between law and private sector standard-setters has been debated recently, and a governmental committee suggests that the BFN should get a supervisory and controlling function, whereas standard-setting, especially for listed companies, increasingly should be performed by RR.

3. Accounting Principles and Practices in Valuation and Income Measurement

3.1 Group Accounts—Methods of Consolidation

3.1.1 Purchase Method

The Swedish RR Standard on consolidated financial statements was prepared by using IAS 22 as a model.

Normally a corporate combination is regarded as a true purchase, and the purchase method for consolidation should be applied.

Under the purchase method, the buyer accounts for the cost of an acquisition as an indirect acquisition of the net assets of the subsidiary. Assets and liabilities thus acquired are restated to their fair value at the date of acquisition. Fair value adjustments are made by the end of the first annual accounting period commencing after the acquisition.

A positive difference between the purchase price of the shares and the fair value of the net assets is classified as goodwill arising on acquisition. According to the Standard on Consolidated Financial Statements, goodwill is an asset to be amortized over its useful life, which should not exceed 5 years unless a longer period is justified. If a longer period is applied, disclosure should be made, including the reaons for the period chosen. The amortization period must not, however, exceed 20 years in any case.

When the cost of acquisition is less than the acquirer's interest in the fair values of the assets and liabilities acquired, the fair values of the nonmonetary assets acquired should be reduced proportionally. Any remaining negative difference is classified as a long-term liability to be recognized as income on a systematic basis, reflecting the estimated performance of the subsidiary at the date of acquisition.

Although not generally applicable in Swedish accounting, nor covered (so far) by any specific Swedish Standard, deferred taxes should, when applicable, be provided for in the consolidated financial statements, reflecting temporary differences under the liability method. Discounting is generally not allowed.

The Swedish Standard on consolidated financial statements does not include any opportunity for reverse acquisitions, which are deemed not to be fully in line with the requirements of the law.

Provisions are sometimes made for activities arising as a result of an acquisition, often labeled as provisions for restructuring. In practice, such provisions are sometimes made without proper observance of the definition of a liability ("big bath provisions"). This practice has been developed partly because the Standard on consolidated financial statements, applying the language of IAS 22, is not very specific on the criteria to be met for allowing such provisions. Also, the possibility under generally accepted accounting principles in Sweden to apply practices adopted by other companies has led to aggressive accounting for provisions for restructuring.

3.1.2 Pooling of Interest Method

The pooling of interest method should be applied when the shareholders of previously independent companies decide to unite their interests. The prerequisite is that none of the companies could be defined as an acquirer, or as a dominating party in the transaction.

A number of guidelines must be applied to assess whether the pooling of interests method is justified, relating, for example, to the fair values of the uniting companies, changes in voting rights, and the composition of the Board.

Under the pooling of interests method, the values of the assets and liabilities of the acquired company are not adjusted but are retained at the amounts recorded in the formally acquired company's balance sheet. The difference between the cost of the shares acquired and the subsidiary's underlying equity does not need to be determined; the cost of the shares acquired will be eliminated against the corresponding amount of the subsidiary's equity. Through the Standard on Consolidated Financial Statements, the earlier practice of frequently using the pooling of interest method has been discontinued. However, as Sweden is one of the relatively few countries requiring goodwill on consolidation to be amortized over a period not exceeding 20 years, the guidelines of the Standard on Consolidated Financial Statements are often challenged, resulting in a rather aggressive application of the Standard and its guidelines on pooling of interest methods. As a consequence, the pooling of interest method has been applied in a number of cases in the late 90s.

3.1.3 *Proportional Consolidation Method*

According to the Annual Accounts Act, the proportional consolidation mehod may be aplied to jointly controlled entities.

The FAR recommends the proportional consolidation method of accounting for an investment in a jointly controlled entity as the benchmark treatment, with the equity method as an allowed alternative.

3.1.4 *Equity Accounting*

According to the Annual Accounts Act investments in associated companies should be accounted for in the consolidated financial statements by using equity accounting. As indicated above, investments in a jointly controlled entity could alternatively be accounted for in the consolidated financial statements applying proportional consolidation accounting (the law does not, however, allow the use of equity accounting only in the parent's financial statements).

An entity is defined as an associated company to another company (the investor) if the investor has significant influence over and has the power to govern the operating and financial policies of the enterprise. It is also required that the investment should be of a permanent nature. If the investor holds shares in an enterprise to the extent that it controls 20% or more of the voting power, the enterprise should be defined as an associated company unless there are contradictory circumstances. The FAR has issued an exposure draft (revised in 1997) dealing with investments in associated companies, according to which equity accounting may be used in consolidated financial statements only. The draft has been increasingly applied in practice. An important requirement of the exposure draft deals with the equity in an associated company's undistributed earnings, which must be classified as restricted (nondistributable) consolidated equity. The exposure draft represents, in fact, a departure from a fundamental principle, that is, that the same approach should be applied in the preparation of consolidated financial statements as in the preparation of a single entity's financial statements. Under the new Annual Accounts Act, however, such departure is allowed, if there are special reasons.

Goodwill arising on equity participations is amortized in the same manner as under the purchase method.

3.2 Foreign Currency Translation

3.2.1 Translation of the Financial Statements of Foreign Subsidiaries

The Swedish Companies Act did not specifically regulate how to translate foreign subsidiaries' financial statements for the purpose of consolidation. As a consequence, accounting practice in this area may not have been uniform. In an exposure draft issued by the FAR in the mid-1980s (and revised in 1997), however, a basis for a uniform accounting treatment has been established. This draft has today reached the status of a proposed but not yet definitive recommendation. It introduced into accounting in Sweden the same view as SFAS-52 did in the United States at the beginning of the 1980s, a view that is consistent with IAS 21. The proposed recommendation, accordingly, differentiates between "independent" and "integrated" foreign operations. Where a foreign subsidiary is independent, assets and liabilities of the subsidiary should be translated by using the current rate method (sometimes called the closing rate method). Income statement items should be translated at the exchange rates at the dates of the transactions. If the effects are not material, income statement items may be translated at the current rate according to the FAR. This is a difference in relation to IAS 21. Translation differences should be taken directly to equity, and disclosed separately in a note describing changes in consolidated equity.

When a foreign operation is integrated with the reporting company, its financial statements should be translated by using the temporal method and resulting exchange differences arising from translation of monetary items should be included as other exchange gains and losses in the consolidated income statement.

There is no Swedish equivalent of IAS 29. Subsidiaries in countries with particularly high inflation rates (e.g., greater than 25%) raise special problems. Translation of their financial statements by the current rate method usually results in an incorrect description of their financial position and their result of operations. In such cases, even financial statements of independent subsidiaries should be translated by use of the temporal method (or the monetary-nonmonetary method, which, is another expression of the same method). Alternatively, inflation-adjusted financial statements may be translated by the current rate method.

Exchange differences arising on noncurrent intercompany monetary items that are in effect an extension to or a deduction from a parent's net investment in a foreign subsidiary should be taken to equity. Similarly, if foreign currency loans are designated as, and provide, an effective hedge against a net investment in a foreign subsidiary, exchange differences on the loans may be taken to equity, to the extent that they are covered by exchange differences arising on the net investment.

The Swedish Companies Act requires that the consolidated balance sheet disclose the amount of unrestricted equity or the accumulated deficit of the group after deduction of internal profits. Therefore, it is necessary to split accumulated translation differences between restricted and unrestricted equity or accumulated deficit.

There is a draft Standard by the RR dealing with foreign currency transactions, prepared with IAS 21 as a model. Once adopted, it will supersede the above FAR recommendation.

3.2.2 Translation of Foreign Currency Denominated Assets and Liabilities

According to the Annual Accounts Act receivables and liabilities denominated in foreign currencies may be translated by using the rate prevailing at the balance sheet date, if this is in line with generally accepted accounting principles in Sweden and gives a true and fair view.

In 1989 the BFN issued a recommendation on valuation of receivables and payables denominated in foreign currencies, effective from January 1990.

According to the BFN recommendation, receivables and payables denominated in foreign currency should be reported in the balance sheet at the closing rates. The difference between the historical rates (or the closing rates at the previous balance sheet date) and the closing rates should be recorded as a gain or loss in the period in which the exchange rates change. However, unrealized exchange gains arising from long-term receivables and payables should be taken to an untaxed currency reserve in the balance sheet.

If a receivable or a payable denominated in foreign currency is effectively hedged, a change in the currency rate should have no effect on the value of the item in the balance sheet. A transaction should be classified as a hedge only when the intention to hedge was present at the time of entering into the hedging transaction. If the hedge is a foreign currency forward contract, the spot rate at the date of inception of the forward contract should be used for valuation of the underlying receivable or payable.

The discount or premium on a forward contract should be recognized in income over the life of the contract. Other forms of hedging, which are effective hedges in a similar way as a forward contract, should be treated in the same manner as a forward contract.

The above BFN recommendation will be superseded, partly or in total, by the forthcoming RR Standard on foreign currency transactions, mentioned above.

3.3 Capital and Reserves

3.3.1 General

Equity is accounted for in somewhat different ways in unregistered firms, partnerships, and limited companies. This review concentrates on limited companies. Shareholders' equity is generally divided between two subheadings: restricted equity and nonrestricted equity or accumulated deficit. Restricted equity includes share capital, share premium reserve, revaluation reserve, and legal reserve. Nonrestricted equity includes nonrestricted reserves (each disclosed separately), retained earnings brought forward, and net income for the year.

3.3.2 Share Capital

Where a company's share capital is divided into several classes of shares, the amount of each class should be disclosed. The number of shares of each class should also be reported.

Holdings of the company's own shares are generally not permitted, except for interim periods. Any such holdings should be entered as assets having no value, but their aggregated face value should be disclosed, preferably on the balance sheet.

All changes since the preceding balance sheet in the amounts specified under various equity headings should be specified in a note to the balance sheet.

In accordance with the Swedish Annual Accounts Act, the regulations of the disclosure of a single entity's equity shall also apply to consolidated accounts, where appropriate.

3.3.3 Restricted Reserves

Three kinds of restricted reserves may appear in a limited company's balance sheet: the statutory reserve, the share premium reserve, and the revaluation reserve.

The Statutory Reserve   The following allocations should be made to the statutory reserve:

1. At least 10% of the net income for the year after deduction of any deficit brought forward. Such allocation must continue until the reserve together with the share premium reserve equals 20% of the share capital.
2. Any amount paid by a person whose shares have been declared forfeited
3. Any amount according to the bylaws or approved by the general meeting

The reduction of the statutory reserve requires a decision by the company in general meeting and may be made for only the following purposes:

1. To cover losses that cannot be covered by nonrestricted equity
2. To increase the share capital through a bonus issue
3. For any other purpose, provided that the court has given its consent

The Revaluation Reserve   The revaluation reserve arises as a result of the revaluation of tangible and financial noncurrent assets. It may be used only for a bonus issue or to cover a loss—appearing in a balance sheet adopted by the annual general meeting—provided that the loss cannot be covered by available unrestricted equity.

A decision to use the revaluation reserve to cover a lossrequires consultation with the auditors. Such a decision prevents the company from declaring a dividend for a period of 3 years if the court has not given its consent or if the share capital is not increased by an amount at least equal to the loss covered by the revaluation reserve.

In case of depreciation and write-down of assets or of sale and disposal of assets, the revaluation reserve shall be reduced by a corresponding amount, but as a maximum by the part of the revaluation reserve that corresponds to the asset in question. The reduction of the revaluation reserve just mentioned may be carried out only by means of a bonus issue, covering losses appearing in the adopted balance sheet, or by transferring the amount to nonrestricted equity.

The Share Premium Reserve   If shares have been issued at a price that exceeds the face value, the excess amount must be transferred to a Share Premium Account. This requirement was introduced by the Swedish Annual Accounts Act in accordance with the Fourth Directive.

The reduction of the share premium reserve requires a decision by the company in general meeting and may be made only for purposes corresponding to those of the statutory reserve.

3.3.4 Nonrestricted Equity

Each nonrestricted reserve should be disclosed separately. Such reserves include retained earnings brought forward (losses to be shown as deductions) and net income for the current financial year (a loss to be shown as a deduction).

3.3.5 Distribution Restrictions

Dividends to the shareholders may not exceed the amount that is distributable according to the adopted balance sheet and, regarding a parent company, also according to the consolidated balance sheet. The distributable amount includes the net income for the year, retained earnings brought forward, and nonrestricted reserves less reported losses, less the amount that according to the Companies Act or the company's bylaws shall be allocated to the legal reserve, and finally, less the amount that according to the articles of association shall otherwise be used for a purpose other than dividends to the shareholders.

Dividends may not be distributed to such an extent that—in light of the company's or the group's consolidation needs, cash needs, or financial position in other respects—the distribution would be contrary to good business practice.

The general meeting may not declare a dividend that is higher than the dividend proposed or approved by the board of directors, unless otherwise provided in the articles of association.

A company may not grant cash loans to a person who owns shares in the company or who is a member of the board or managing director of the company or of another entity in the same group. The same rule shall apply to persons who are relatives of or are otherwise closely related to a shareholder, to a member of the board, or to the managing director of the company.

3.3.6 Untaxed Reserves

Untaxed reserves are the result of tax appropriations. All tax appropriations, some of which imply asset undervaluation, are reported in a certain segment of the income statement. These appropriations are taken directly to the credit of the balance sheet as increases in untaxed reserves. These reserves should be considered a mixture of equity and deferred tax. Since 1991 the tax proportion has been around 30%. Untaxed reserves may not be used directly for dividend distribution. In that case, they will have to be carried back to the income statement and included in the taxable income. Examples of untaxed reserves are inventory reserve, investment reserves, accumulated excess depreciation, and, since 1991, the tax equalization reserve. Most of these untaxed reserves will gradually disappear as a result of recent changes in the tax laws. However, accumulated excess depreciation, together with a new tax appropriation, will appear in the accounts in the future.

The practice described above is not used any longer in group accounts as a result of the RR Standard on Consolidated Financial Statements, effective from January 1992.

3.4 Provisions and Liabilities

3.4.1 Provisions

According to the Annual Accounts Act, provision should be made for all obligations relating to the fiscal year or previous fiscal years, provided that these obligations are likely or certain to be incurred and that the amount or timing of the expenditure to settle the obligation is uncertain. The legal definition of a provision is derived from the EC Directives and is not necessarily in line with the definition of a liability and relating recognition criteria according to IASC's framework. This lack of clarity may affect the reporting practice in Sweden. As in previous years general provisions are not permitted, as a provision must relate to a specific existing obligation. Provisions for future expenses are not permitted unless the circumstances giving rise to such an expense have occurred.

Provisions for future expenses relating to warranties may be recognized at the point of sale of the item under warranty.

3.4.2 Current Liabilities

The concept of "normal operating cycle" is not used in Sweden for segregation between current and noncurrent receivables and liabilities. Instead, the one-year rule is the valid criterion for classification purposes. Current liabilities should include amounts payable within one year from the date of the balance sheet. Current liabilities should be segregated among advances from customers, trade credits, bills payable, taxes payable, other liabilities and accrued liabilties. Payables to group companies and associated companies should also be disclosed in the balance sheet.

Commitments such as purchase orders or other kinds of contractual obligations do not qualify as liabilities until the corresponding services have been performed. Contingencies that are highly probably are accounted for as liabilities.

3.4.2 Long-Term Debt

The most common forms of long-term debt in Sweden are debentures, bonds, mortgages, and other long-term bank credit. The general accounting treatment applied to these items is basically the same as for current liabilities, that is, they are carried in the balance sheet at their face value.

As with current liabilities, long-term debt must be segregated on the face of the balance sheet Long-term payables to group companies and associated companies should be disclosed separately in the balance sheet.

If a company has raised loans by issuing convertible bonds or bonds containing an option to subscribe for new shares, the amount not yet converted and the time and conditions for conversion or subscription should be disclosed for each loan. Regarding participating debentures, the amount still outstanding and the interest provisions should be disclosed.

3.4.3 Contingencies

A contingent liability is defined as a possible obligation that is dependent upon one or more future events that have some probability of occurrence. Typical of contingencies is that it is more likely than not that no outflow of resources embodying economic benefits will occur. The accounting treatment of contingencies depends on the probability of occurrence of the future event that will determine the contingency. If the probability is high, the contingencies should be included among liabilities.

Except for the Annual Accounts Act, there are no rules dealing with contingencies in Sweden. The Annual Accounts Act requires that contingent liabilities be disclosed under the headings (a) pension obligations that are not reported as a liability or covered by the assets of a pension fund and (b) other contingent liabilities (e.g. guarantees and discounted bills).

Contingencies are disclosed as memorandum items at the bottom of the balance sheet.

3.4.5 Untaxed Reserves—Deferred Tax

As mentioned in Section 3.3, untaxed reserves should be considered a mixture of equity and deferred tax. The deferred tax portion is not disclosed in the single-entity balance sheet. According to the RR Standard on Consolidated Financial Statements, however, untaxed reserves should be allocated between tax liability and an equity portion in the balance sheet of the group. There is also a requiement in the Annual Accounts Act to disclose deferred taxes not accounted for.

3.5 Property, Plant, and Equipment

Expenditures on capital assets, which result in a lasting improvement of the asset and thereby in an increase in its value, may be capitalized as a part of the cost of the asset. Expenditures to maintain normal operating efficiency should be expensed.

3.5.1 Basis of Valuation

Fixed assets shall be carried at historical cost. For exceptions see Section 3.5.4.

Fixed assets with a limited time of useful economic life should be depreciated on a systematic basis over that period of time. Intangibles, however, are assumed to have a useful life no longer than 5 years, unless a longer period of life could be determined with a reasonable degree of certainty.

Where the value of a fixed asset has permanently declined, a write-down shall be made to an amount in agreement with generally accepted accounting principles. A financial asset may, however, be written down even if the decline in value is not assumed to be permanent.

If the circumstances and events that led to the write-down disappear, the write-down shall be reversed.

3.5.2 Depreciation

As Cost Allocation   The Swedish Annual Accounts Act requires fixed assets to be depreciated in a systematic way over the useful economic life of each asset. According to FAR's recommendation on accounting for tangible fixed assets, this implies that depreciation should be based on the historical cost concept, an estimation of the useful life of the asset, and an allocation method. The most commonly used method is the straight-line method. However, any method consistently applied that produces a reasonable and systematic allocation over the asset's useful life is acceptable.

As Tax Allowances   According to Swedish tax law, companies are allowed to apply a depreciation schedule that implies that machinery and equipment are depreciated over a total period of 5 years. Companies may choose between an accelerated and a straight-line profile. For many kinds of machinery and equipment, this means an accelerated rate of depreciation compared with "an appropriate depreciation plan." The difference—"the excess depreciation over and above depreciation according to plan"—

is disclosed as an appropriation in the single-entity income statement. This tax appropriation will not, however, appear in the income statement of the group.

3.5.3 Disclosure

The accounting policies adopted in relation to valuation and depreciation of fixed assets must be disclosed. Details of cost, acquisitions and disposals, transfers, the depreciation charge for the period, revaluations, and accumulated depreciation must be disclosed. Also the book value of each class of assets must be disclosed in notes to the balance sheet. If any fixed asset is carried at an appraised value, this must be shown. The amount of depreciation charged for the accounting period should be disclosed in one of the optional formats prescribed for the income statement. Details for each class of assets should be presented in notes to the income statement in a way that is consistent with the presentation in the balance sheet.

3.5.4 Revaluation

A fixed asset that has a reliable and enduring value substantially in excess of the amount at which it is carried in the books may be revalued at an amount not in excess of that value, provided that the amount of revaluation is used for issuing bonus shares or for an appropriation to a revaluation reserve (part of the restricted equity).

In unregistered firms and partnerships the amount of revaluation of fixed assets shall be used for a necessary write-down of the value of other fixed assets, provided that there are particular reasons for such a compensating adjustment.

If an entity chooses to revalue its fixed assets upward, the depreciation should then be applied to the basis of the revalued amount.

3.5.5 Tax Appropriation in the Single-Entity Income Statement

Most tax appropriations, many of which imply asset undervaluation, are reported in a certain segment of the income statement. When one is looking for the "true" before-tax accounting income in a Swedish single-entity income statement, one should look for "income before tax appropriations." In order to maintain the information content of the asset values in the balance sheet, these are not reduced by such extra write-offs, classified as tax appropriations in the income statement. Instead, the appropriations and the extra write-offs are taken directly to the credit of the balance sheet as increases in untaxed reserves. This practice is applied to the single-entity accounts only. No tax appropriations are shown in the group accounts (see Section 3.4.5).

3.5.6 Accounting for Government Grants

The BFN has issued a recommendation on accounting for government grants and assistance, effective as of 1989. The BFN recommendation is in line with the principles of IAS No. 20, "Accounting for Government Grants and Disclosure of Government Assistance." Government assistance should be reported in the income statement under the same heading as the expenses that it is supposed to cover and in a consistent manner from period to period.

The cost of the fixed asset should be reduced by the amount of the government grant. The net cost is the basis for depreciation. The gross value of the asset and the amount of the grant should be disclosed, consistently with IAS 20, in a note to the financial statements.

The accounting policy in relation to government grants and assistance shall be disclosed, if material. Benefits or commitments that will remain for several periods in the future should be continually disclosed. The effect on the company's result and financial position from government assistance should be recognized in multiperiod highlights.

3.5.7 Capitalized Interest Costs

According to the Swedish Annual Accounts Act, interest cost during a construction period may be capitalized as a part of the cost of the fixed assets. The capitalized amounts should be disclosed. However, it is only the paid-out interest that can be capitalized. Computed interest on the entity's equity shall not be capitalized at all. According to the RR Standards on Inventories, interest cost shall be capitalized if the storage period constitutes a significant part of the production process (e.g., when producing wine or cheese).

3.6 Leases

Accounting for leases is regulated by the RR Standard No 6, operative as of January 1, 1997. The Standard is with minor exceptions in conformity with IAS 17, "Accounting for Leases." For the single entity there is an option in the Standard to report a finance lease according to the rules prescribed for an operating lease, which is considered to be accepted by the EC Seventh Directive.

3.6.1 Classification of Leases

The classification of leases adopted by the above RR Standard is based on the extent to which risk and rewards incident to ownership of a leased asset lie with the lessor or the lessee. Risks include the possibilities of losses from idle capacity or technological obsolescence and variations in return due to changing economic conditions. Rewards may be represented by the expectation of profitable operation over the asset's useful life and gain from appreciation in value.

Whether a lease is a finance lease or not depends on the substance of the transaction rather than the form of the contract. A lease is classified as a finance lease if it transfers substantially all the risks and rewards incident to ownership. Such a lease is normally noncancellable and secures for the lessor the recovery of the lessor's capital outlay plus return for the funds invested. Examples of situations or conditions where a lease would normally be classified as a finance lease are:

- The present value, at the inception of the lease, of the minimum lease payments is greater than, or equal to substantially all of, the fair value of the leased asset, net of any benefits to the lessor at that time,
- The lease term is for the major part of the useful life of the asset; and
- The lessee has the option to purchase the asset at a price that, at the inception of the lease, is expected to be sufficiently lower than the fair value at the date the option becomes exercisable to make it reasonably certain that the option will be exercised.

3.6.2 Finance Leases

Leases in the Financial Statement of Lessees   A finance lease should be recognized at the inception of the lease as a fixed asset and a liability in the balance sheet of a lessee at amounts equal to the fair value of the leased property, net of any benefits to the lessor or, if lower, at the present value of the minimum lease payments. In calculating the present value the interest rate implicit in the lease contract is used, if it is practical to determine; otherwise the lessee's incremental borrowing rate is used.

The depreciation policy for leased assets should be consistent with that for depreciable assets that are owned. The write-down rules of tangible assets should be applied to leased assets in a consistent manner.

Rentals should be apportioned between the finance charge and the reduction of the outstanding liability. The finance charge should be allocated during the lease term in order to produce a constant, or at least an approximately constant, periodic rate of interest on the remaining balance of the liability for each period.

Leases in the Financial Statements of Lessors   An asset held under a finance lease should be recognized in the balance sheet as a receivable at an amount equal to the net investment in the lease.

The recognition of finance income should be based on a pattern reflecting a constant periodic rate of return on the lessor's net investment of each period. A modification of the pattern of income recognition to reflect uncertainties in connection with long term contracts may be justified by reason of conservatism.

3.6.3   Operating Leases

Leases in the Financial Statements of the Lessees   The charge to income under an operating lease should be the rental expense for the accounting period, recognized on a systematic basis that is representative of the time pattern of the user's benefit.

Leases in the Financial Statements of the Lessors   Rental income should be recognized on a straight line basis over the lease term, unless another systematic basis is more representative of the of the time pattern of the earning process contained in the lease.

The depreciation of leases should be on a basis consistent with the lessor's normal depreciation policy for similar assets.

3.6.4   Disclosure

Disclosure in the Financial Statements of the Lessees   Leased assets should be specified in notes to the balance sheet, with disclosure of cost and accumulated depreciation for each class of asset. Corresponding liabilities should be allocated to current and noncurrent items. Long-term liabilities should be specified further regarding the amounts that mature annually for the next 5 years and then for each 5-year period.

Rentals paid out for operating leases during the year should be disclosed in a note to the income statement. Future rentals should also be disclosed for contracts with a remaining term of more than one year.

Disclosure in the Financial Statements of the Lessors Disclosure should be made in a note to the balance sheet of the gross investment in leases reported as finance leases, and the related unearned finance income.

When a significant part of the lessor's business comprises operating leases, the lessor should disclose the cost of assets and the related accumulated depreciation by each class of asset in a note to the balance sheet.

3.7 Extractive Operations

In order to unify accounting practices in the mining business, the BFN has issued a recommendation according to which the expenditure for the acquisition of the actual deposit and expenditure for underground work on plant/facilities (such as roads, galleries, shafts, and inclined drifts) to be used for a period exceeding one year should be capitalized. Expenditure for plant/facilities to be used for a maximum of one year should be treated as current expenses. The expenses that are capitalized should be included in a depreciation plan and should be the subject of annual depreciation. The amount of depreciation should be based on the value of the extraction made (depletion). It should be kept in mind, however, that there is no alternative use for a mine in the event of a planned or ongoing extraction becoming unprofitable. Because of this circumstance, special attention must be paid to the need for a lump-sum write-down pursuant to Section 5, Chapter 4 of the Swedish Annual Accounts Act.

3.8 Intangible Assets

Where the entity has acquired a business for a consideration that exceeds the value of the acquired assets, the difference may be recognized as a fixed asset to the extent that it represents goodwill. This asset shall be amortized annually by an appropriate amount, at least one-fifth annually, unless a longer period is justified.

Expenditures for technical assistance, research and development, trial runs, market research, and similar activities may be recognized as intangible assets, provided that the expenditures are of material value for the entity during future years. Such assets shall be amortized annually by an appropriate amount, at least one-fifth, unless on account of special circumstances amortization at a lower rate may be considered to be in accordance with generally accepted accounting principles.

Until 1989 there was a lack of uniformity in Sweden regarding reporting practice in the research and development field. Therefore, the BFN issued a recommendation on Accounting for Research and Development, with the aim of harmonizing with international accounting practice. This recommendation is in line with IAS 9. The general rule is that research and development expenditures should be expensed as incurred unless the criteria set out below are satisfied:

1. The R&D project and expenditures attributed to it should be clearly defined.

2. The R&D project should have a certain application as its goal.

3. The product or process resulting from the R&D project should be intended for sale or internal use.

4. The expected revenue or cost savings as a result of the R&D project should be known with a reasonable probability.

5. There should be adequate resources to complete the R&D project.

Once capitalized, research and development cost must be amortized annually according to the rules stated in the Accounting Act, that is, by at least one-fifth annually.

3.8.1 Disclosure

The financial statements—either on the face of the statements or in notes— should disclose:

- The accounting policy concerning accounting for R&D
- The R&D expenditures expensed in the year and the amortization of R&D expenditures capitalized in previous years
- The R&D expenditures capitalized in total and the accumulated amortization applying to this asset

3.9 Investments in Associated Companies

An entity is defined as an associated company of another company (the investor) if the investor holds shares in the entity to the extent that it controls at least 20% but less than 50% of the voting power .

Equity accounting financial information is not to be included in the balance sheet and income statement of the investor—such a treatment would not comply with the Swedish Accounting Act. However, in 1986 FAR issued an exposure draft dealing with investments in associated companies, according to which equity accounting may be applied in consolidated financial statements only. This is also one of the accounting options according to the Annual Accounts Act (see Section 3.1).

In the parent or single company's accounts, the cost method of accounting is compulsory. However, equity accounting information should be disclosed on the face of the financial statements or in notes. The disclosure should include the investor's share of the associated entity's result after financial items and its share of untaxed reserves and equity.

3.10 Inventories and Work in Progress

3.10.1 Basis of Valuation for Inventories

According to the Annual Accounts Act, inventories should be carried at the lower of cost or fair value. Fair value is defined as net realizable value, but replacement cost, less allowance for obsolescence where appropriate, is permissible for raw materials and semifinished products. Net realizable value is the estimated proceeds from the sale of the inventory, less all further costs necessary for marketing, selling, and distribution to customers and an appropriate share of the entity's administration and storage costs, including interest expenses.

The FIFO method for determining cost should be applied according to the RR Standard and is also prescribed by the tax law.

To determine the carrying amount of inventory, each item should be analyzed separately; where this is impracticable, similar items may be dealt with in aggregate.

3.10.2 Overhead and Interest Cost for Manufactured Inventories

When inventories are manufactured, cost should be determined by using absorption costing based on the entity's normal operating capacity. Cost relating to abnormal circumstances, such as idle facilities, should be excluded. Interest expenses during the production period may not be included, except when the storage period is a considerable part of the production process.

3.10.3 Construction Contracts

According to the Annual Accounts Act, construction contracts may be carried at amounts exceeding cost if there are special reasons for such treatment and this could be perceived to be in line with generally accepted accounting principles and give a true and fair view.

Long-term construction and installation contracts are usually accounted for on the completed contract basis, but the percentage of completion method appears to be slowly gaining acceptance in practice. Furthermore, this method is deemed to be acceptable under the Directives.

3.11 Extraordinary or Unusual Items

The RR has issued a Standard on Extraordinary Items, which includes disclosure requirements for comparative purposes, thereby replacing a previous FAR Recommendation on extraordinary items.

The RR standard, which is effective January 1, 1994 has been modeled from IAS 8 and classifies virtually all items of income and expense as part of the ordinary activities of the enterprise. The standard has confirmed the profile of the previous FAR Recommendation, which, however, was not always adhered to in practice.

The disclosure requirements of the standard relate to events and transactions that it is important to observe when the results of operations of an accounting period are compared with other accounting periods or with other entities.

Although the definition of extraordinary items in the Annual Accounts Act ("other than normal activities of the enterprise") seems to allow for some flexibility, the above RR standard has generally been applied in a strict manner.

3.12 Taxation

The Swedish corporate tax system was reformed with effect from 1991. Further changes have been made since. The main goal of reform was to reduce the tax rate and at the same time broaden the tax base, with the intention of diminishing the locking-in effects on capital. The new tax system does not contain tax appropriations in the income statement to the inventory reserve or the investment reserves.

The basic tax depreciation rules for equipment, allowing depreciation of up to 30% of the remaining balance, continued in the reformed tax system. If this depreciation in a certain year is larger or smaller than the "depreciation according to plan," the difference should appear in the appropriation segment of the single-entity income statement.

Previously allowed untaxed reserves for inventory, work-in-progress, and the profit equalization reserve should be reversed and taxed on a gradual basis. The appropriation segment of the single-entity income statement will then be used for the reversal of untaxed reserves.

As reflected in Section 3.4.5, however, deferred tax accounting has been introduced in the consolidated accounts only, thereby creating income and equity concepts that are in line with dominant international practice. The balance sheet liability method is, however, applied by only a few companies. There is no Swedish standard on income taxes yet, but an exposure draft has been prepared by RR, using IAS 12 as a model.

3.13 Pensions

Pension plans in respect of white-collar employees are governed by nationwide trade unions employer organization agreements. Mainly, two systems are used: one in which actuarially computed premiums are currently paid to an independent pension insurance company and another in which an independent organization computes the actual liability that must be provided for. Under this latter system, the liability must be reported in companies' balance sheets as a long-term liability.

The defined benefits provided for are a function of the employee's salary at each date of computation (balance sheet date). Overfunding is unlikely to occur, and in principle, neither should underfunding. Companies' obligations to pay pensions may be secured and represented by a separate but company-related pension foundation.

Pension expenses in respect of blue-collar employees, under state schemes, are financed by direct charges.

The Swedish Annual Accounts Act requires that pension provisions be separately disclosed on the face of the balance sheet as provisions. To the extent to which pension commitments are clearly fixed in terms of amount and due date, they shall be reported as current or long-term liabilities.

However, it is not compulsory to report all pension commitments on the face of the balance sheet. It is an acceptable alternative to disclose the actuarially computed amount of such commitments as a contingent liability. This alternative treatment is used mainly in connection with older commitments, often made for the benefit of former owners. The amounts involved in such alternative treatments are usually relatively insignificant.

FAR's recommendation on accounting for pension liabilities and pension expenses requires companies to charge the actual pension expenses for the year to operating income. The effect of any extraordinary circumstances on the pension expenses should be disclosed

There is no RR standard on Employee Benefits yet, but an exposure draft based on IAS 19 is planned to be issued.

3.14 Earnings per Share

The Swedish Annual Accounts Act does not require companies to disclose earnings per share (EPS). There are requirements regarding disclosure of the number of shares, which makes it possible for analysts to make their own computations. However, the Swedish Society of Financial Analysts (*Sveriges Finansanalytikers Förening, SFF*) has issued a recommendation on the computation of financial ratios containing a definition of earnings per share. The income base to be used in the computation is generally the net income reported in the group income statement. This implies, among other things, that the income is charged with the current tax as well as changes in the deferred tax liability in accordance with the RR standard 1. If income includes items affecting comparability, they should be disclosed in notes together with their tax effects. The recommendation also prescribes how to handle the number of shares in computing EPS when the company has issued or redeemed shares, issued convertible bonds, etc.

4. Expected Future Developments

Until the beginning of the 1980s, financial reporting in Sweden had developed with little influence from the ongoing internationalization and globalization of business in general. Financial accounting standards were based on the requirements of the Accounting Act and Companies Act and were further detailed in accounting recommendations mainly issued by

FAR and by certain business associations, for example, the Swedish Construction Federation (*Byggentreprenörerna*). Gradually the BFN also took an interest in financial reporting. The system so designed was one of self-regulation that worked fairly well in its domestic environments; recommendations issued were principally followed by the business community.

With the increasing globalization of capital markets, international influence has become more significant. Certain differences between Swedish generally accepted accounting principles and standards generally applied on an international scene have become more evident, including disclosure requirements.

Established in 1989, the Swedish Financial Accounting Standards Council (*Redovisningsrådet*, RR) is responsible for the preparation of accounting standards, primarily for listed companies. It is assumed, however, that the standards also will be applied by other companies.

The RR is using IAS as a model for its own standards. The ambition to produce standards in line with IAS might conflict, in certain respects, with the effect of the Fourth, Seventh, and Eleventh EC Directives and the EC Accounting Directives for banks and insurance companies, which have been implemented in Swedish legislation.

Some of the potential areas for future development are discussed below.

- The EC Directives have been implemented in Swedish legislation with certain Swedish concepts and requirements added in an ambition to maintain concepts and requirements included in previous legislation. One example is the concept of Swedish GAAP, which remains in the legislation although the similar, but not identical concept of "true and fair view" has been implemented. Generally the implementation of the EC Directives in Swedish legislation has been a matter for the legislators rather than the accounting profession. The directives are interpreted in a rather strict manner, which in certain instances deviate from corresponding interpretations in other European countries. Sweden has not applied "the true and fair override," which might be one reason why Swedish interpretations and application of the directives come out differently. Whereas some European countries would find the directives flexible enough to fully implement International Accounting Standards (IAS), current Swedish interpretations of the directives would find this objective difficult to achieve. How to interpret the directives in a way that is compatible with Swedish law as well as with corresponding interpretations elsewhere in Europe is one issue to be dealt with in the future.

- Although the Swedish Standard Setter, the RR, has full support in principle in applying IAS as a model for Swedish local accounting standards, there is some resistance in practice to adjusting Swedish GAAP to some of the accounting treatments required by IAS. One example is the Swedish equivalent of IAS 8 and the RR's ambition to more or less get rid of extraordinary items in Swedish financial statements. This attempt has not been quite well received by Swedish listed companies, and in practice there are some deviations from the Swedish Standard on this point. This experience may point at one of the remaining features in Swedish accounting: the reliance on "Swedish GAAP" rather than on standards as the norm for accounting solutions and developments. Those who would rely on the rather unspecified concept of "Swedish GAAP" would find support in legislation, both previous and current. Those who would favour a strict adherence to standards, which are modeled on IAS, would find support in the requirements of an increasingly international capital market. How to move forward in this area is a major point for the future.

- With the implementation of the EC Directives in Swedish legislation, aspects and interpretations of law have become more important in Swedish accounting life. On the other hand, standard setters are given an important role in the new Swedish Annual Accounts Act. However, there are a number of standard setters in Sweden, both a governmental one, the BFN, and a major private sector body, the RR, primarily setting standards for listed companies. There is no general agreement yet how the interrelationship between these and perhaps also other standard setting bodies should be structured. This issue is currently being considered by a governmental committee, which is expected to propose a structure in the near future. The outcome of the work of this committee will be of vital importance for future accounting developments in Sweden.

Currently a number of leading listed companies in Sweden make reference to their application of IAS by the label "comply in all material respects" or similar expressions. Such references are always incomplete regarding disclosure requirements and are often not correct in terms of recognition and measurement. Although the current

Swedish practice in this respect should be banned under IAS 1 and its requirements, it could be excused, since the main norm for Swedish listed companies is Swedish GAAP, which may or may not follow IAS and/or Swedish standards in line with IAS. How Swedish listed companies should adjust properly to the application of IAS and the mentioning thereof without conflicting with existing law and the concept of Swedish GAAP is one of the major issues to be dealt with in the future.

Resultaträkning

KONCERNEN

		1997		1996	
		Mkr	MECU	Mkr	MECU
Nettoomsättning		58.595	6.794	55.405	6.596
Förändring av varulager		334	39	35	4
Aktiverat arbete för egen räkning		65	8	40	5
Övriga rörelseintäkter		430	50	688	82
		59.424	6.891	56.168	6.687
Rörelsens kostnader	Not 1				
Råvaror och förnödenheter		–24.606	–2.853	–24.750	–2.946
Övriga externa kostnader		–11.729	–1.360	–10.259	–1.221
Personalkostnader		–12.371	–1.435	–11.932	–1.421
Avskrivningar av materiella och immateriella tillgångar	Not 2	–3.843	–446	–3.575	–426
Övriga rörelsekostnader		–1.374	–159	–1.103	–132
Summa rörelsens kostnader		–53.923	–6.253	–51.619	–6.146
Intäkter från andelar i intressebolag	Not 3	67	8	32	4
RÖRELSERESULTAT		5.568	646	4.581	545
Finansiella poster					
Intäkter från aktier och andelar	Not 4	70	8	70	8
Ränteintäkter och liknande resultatposter		210	24	249	30
Räntekostnader och liknande resultatposter		–1.391	–161	–1.327	–158
Summa finansiella poster		–1.111	–129	–1.008	–120
RESULTAT EFTER FINANSIELLA POSTER		4.457	517	3.573	425
Skatt på årets resultat	Not 5	–1.337	–155	–1.144	–136
Minoritetens andel i årets resultat	Not 6	–361	–42	–312	–37
ÅRETS NETTORESULTAT		2.759	320	2.117	252

PER AFFÄRSOMRÅDE

	Nettoomsättning		Resultat	
Mkr	1997	1996	1997	1996
Hygienprodukter	26.086	24.131	2.596	2.323
– Fluff- och sjukvårdsprodukter	13.859	12.664	1.090	660
– Tissue	12.227	11.467	1.506	1.663
Förpackningar	14.282	13.697	1.196	939
– Wellpapp inkl. råvaror	11.164	10.419	987	830
– Linerprodukter – externa leveranser	3.118	3.278	209	109
Grafiska Papper	16.562	15.872	884	510
– Trähaltiga tryckpapper	6.390	6.190	458	990
– Finpapper, grossiströrelse, massa	10.172	9.682	426	–480
Skog och Trä	4.158	3.948	812	607
Övrigt	1.598	1.576	384	436
Avyttrade enheter	–	1.061	–	54
Internleveranser	–4.091	–4.880	–	–
Goodwill-avskrivningar	–	–	–304	–288
SUMMA	58.595	55.405	5.568	4.581
Finansiella poster			–1.111	–1.008
Resultat efter finansiella poster			4.457	3.573

Statement of earnings

CONSOLIDATED

		1997		1996	
		SEK M	ECU M	SEK M	ECU M
Net sales		58,595	6,794	55,405	6,596
Change in inventories		334	39	35	4
Work performed and capitalized		65	8	40	5
Other operating revenues		430	50	688	82
		59,424	6,891	56,168	6,687
Operating expenses	Note 1				
Raw materials and consumables		−24,606	−2,853	−24,750	−2,946
Other external costs		−11,729	−1,360	−10,259	−1,221
Personnel costs		−12,371	−1,435	−11,932	−1,421
Depreciation of tangible and intangible assets	Note 2	−3,843	−446	−3,575	−426
Other operating expenses		−1,374	−159	−1,103	−132
Total operating expenses		−53,923	−6,253	−51,619	−6,146
Share in earnings of associated companies	Note 3	67	8	32	4
OPERATING PROFIT		5,568	646	4,581	545
Financial items					
Income from shares and participations	Note 4	70	8	70	8
Interest income and similar profit/loss items		210	24	249	30
Interest expense and similar profit/loss items		−1,391	−161	−1,327	−158
Total financial items		−1,111	−129	−1,008	−120
EARNINGS AFTER FINANCIAL ITEMS		4,457	517	3,573	425
Taxes on profit for the year	Note 5	−1,337	−155	−1,144	−136
Minority interest	Note 6	−361	−42	−312	−37
NET EARNINGS FOR THE YEAR		2,759	320	2,117	252

BY BUSINESS AREA

SEK M	Net sales		Earnings	
	1997	1996	1997	1996
Hygiene Products	26,086	24,131	2,596	2,323
– Fluff and clinical products	13,859	12,664	1,090	660
– Tissue	12,227	11,467	1,506	1,663
Packaging	14,282	13,697	1,196	939
– Corrugated board, incl. raw materials	11,164	10,419	987	830
– Liner products – external deliveries	3,118	3,278	209	109
Graphic Paper	16,562	15,872	884	510
– Wood-containing publication papers	6,390	6,190	458	990
– Fine papers, paper merchanting, market pulp	10,172	9,682	426	−480
Forest and Timber	4,158	3,948	812	607
Other operations	1,598	1,576	384	436
Divested units	–	1,061	–	54
Intra-Group deliveries	−4,091	−4,880	–	–
Goodwill amortization	–	–	−304	−288
TOTAL	58,595	55,405	5,568	4,581
Financial items			−1,111	−1,008
Earnings after financial items			4,457	3,573

Balansräkning

KONCERNEN

		1997-12-31		1996-12-31	
		Mkr	MECU	Mkr	MECU
TILLGÅNGAR					
ANLÄGGNINGSTILLGÅNGAR					
Immateriella anläggningstillgångar	Not 7				
Goodwill		5.083	584	4.678	548
Patent, varumärken och liknande rättigheter		1.095	126	1.210	142
		6.178	710	5.888	690
Materiella anläggningstillgångar	Not 8				
Byggnader och mark		17.693	2.034	17.625	2.066
Maskiner och inventarier		24.916	2.864	23.994	2.813
Pågående nyanläggningar		569	65	306	36
		43.178	4.963	41.925	4.915
Finansiella anläggningstillgångar	Not 9				
Aktier och andelar	Not 10	870	100	604	71
Andra långfristiga fordringar		125	14	182	21
Kapitalplaceringsaktier	Not 11	1.112	128	866	102
Räntebärande fordringar		258	29	206	24
		2.365	271	1.858	218
Summa anläggningstillgångar		51.721	5.944	49.671	5.823
OMSÄTTNINGSTILLGÅNGAR					
Varulager	Not 12	5.780	664	5.570	653
Kundfordringar		9.006	1.035	7.928	929
Övriga kortfristiga fordringar	Not 13	1.940	223	1.963	230
Kortfristiga placeringar		676	78	1.469	172
Kassa och bank		1.582	182	1.393	163
Summa omsättningstillgångar		18.984	2.182	18.323	2.147
SUMMA TILLGÅNGAR		70.705	8.126	67.994	7.970
EGET KAPITAL, AVSÄTTNINGAR OCH SKULDER					
EGET KAPITAL	Not 15				
Bundet eget kapital					
Aktiekapital		1.974	227	1.974	231
Bundna reserver		11.426	1.313	11.050	1.296
		13.400	1.540	13.024	1.527
Fritt eget kapital					
Fria reserver		8.494	973	7.765	910
Årets nettoresultat		2.759	320	2.117	248
		11.253	1.293	9.882	1.158
Summa eget kapital		24.653	2.833	22.906	2.685
MINORITETSINTRESSEN		1.496	172	3.331	390
AVSÄTTNINGAR					
Avsättningar för pensioner	Not 16	3.237	372	3.153	370
Avsättningar för skatter	Not 17	5.450	626	4.710	552
Övriga avsättningar	Not 18	1.765	203	1.578	185
Summa avsättningar		10.452	1.201	9.441	1.107
SKULDER					
Räntebärande skulder	Not 19	22.647	2.603	21.396	2.508
Leverantörsskulder		5.884	676	5.282	619
Övriga ej räntebärande skulder	Not 20	5.573	641	5.638	661
Summa skulder		34.104	3.920	32.316	3.788
SUMMA EGET KAPITAL, AVSÄTTNINGAR OCH SKULDER		70.705	8.126	67.994	7.970
ANSVARSFÖRBINDELSER	Not 21	484		772	
STÄLLDA PANTER	Not 22	1.291		1.902	

Balance sheet

CONSOLIDATED

		31 Dec. 1997		31 Dec. 1996	
		SEK M	ECU M	SEK M	ECU M
ASSETS					
FIXED ASSETS					
Intangible assets	Note 7				
Goodwill		5,083	584	4,678	548
Patents, trademarks and similar rights		1,095	126	1,210	142
		6,178	710	5,888	690
Tangible assets	Note 8				
Buildings and land		17,693	2,034	17,625	2,066
Machinery and equipment		24,916	2,864	23,994	2,813
Construction in progress		569	65	306	36
		43,178	4,963	41,925	4,915
Financial assets	Note 9				
Shares and participations	Note 10	870	100	604	71
Other long-term receivables		125	14	182	21
Capital investment shares	Note 11	1,112	128	866	102
Interest-bearing receivables		258	29	206	24
		2,365	271	1,858	218
Total fixed assets		51,721	5,944	49,671	5,823
CURRENT ASSETS					
Inventories	Note 12	5,780	664	5,570	653
Accounts receivable		9,006	1,035	7,928	929
Other current receivables	Note 13	1,940	223	1,963	230
Short-term investments		676	78	1,469	172
Cash and bank balances		1,582	182	1,393	163
Total current assets		18,984	2,182	18,323	2,147
TOTAL ASSETS		70,705	8,126	67,994	7,970
EQUITY, PROVISIONS AND LIABILITIES					
SHAREHOLDERS' EQUITY	Note 15				
Non distributable equity					
Share capital		1,974	227	1,974	231
Restricted reserves		11,426	1,313	11,050	1,296
		13,400	1,540	13,024	1,527
Distributable equity					
Retained earnings		8,494	973	7,765	910
Net earnings for the year		2,759	320	2,117	248
		11,253	1,293	9,882	1,158
Total shareholders' equity		24,653	2,833	22,906	2,685
MINORITY INTEREST		1,496	172	3,331	390
PROVISIONS					
Provisions for pensions	Note 16	3,237	372	3,153	370
Provisions for taxes	Note 17	5,450	626	4,710	552
Other provisions	Note 18	1,765	203	1,578	185
Total provisions		10,452	1,201	9,441	1,107
LIABILITIES					
Interest-bearing debt	Note 19	22,647	2,603	21,396	2,508
Accounts payable		5,884	676	5,282	619
Other interest-free liabilities	Note 20	5,573	641	5,638	661
Total liabilities		34,104	3,920	32,316	3,788
TOTAL EQUITY, PROVISIONS AND LIABILITIES		70,705	8,126	67,994	7,970
CONTINGENT LIABILITIES	Note 21	484		772	
ASSETS PLEDGED	Note 22	1,291		1,902	

Kassaflödesanalys

KONCERNEN

Mkr	1997	1996
RÖRELSEN		
Nettoomsättning	58.595	55.405
Rörelsens kostnader	–49.251	–47.281
Rörelseöverskott	9.344	8.124
Förändring av		
– Rörelsefordringar	–535	206
– Varulager	–125	749
– Rörelseskulder	127	–287
Förändring av rörelsekapital	–533	668
Löpande investeringar i anläggningar	–2.207	–2.489
Förändring av pensionsskuld	85	139
Strukturkostnader	–123	–249
Övrig operativ kassaflödesförändring	–53	–364
OPERATIVT KASSAFLÖDE [1]	6.513	5.829
Finansiella poster	–1.111	–1.008
Skattebetalning	–731	–659
Övrigt	179	48
RÖRELSENS KASSAFLÖDE	4.850	4.210
STRATEGISKA INVESTERINGAR OCH AVYTTRINGAR		
Anläggningar	–983	–1.126
Företagsförvärv	–3.247	–1.558
Summa strategiska investeringar	–4.230	–2.684
Avyttringar	46	480
Kassaflöde från strategiska investeringar och avyttringar	–4.184	–2.204
KASSAFLÖDE FÖRE UTDELNING	666	2.006
Utdelning till aktieägare	–1.092	–994
NETTOKASSAFLÖDE	–426	1.012

NETTOLÅNESKULD

Mkr	1997	1996	1995	1994	1993
Nettolåneskuld vid årets början	–17.462	–17.566	–10.573	–10.814	–10.799
Nettokassaflöde	–426	1.012	–4.400	–155	3.209
Nyemission genom konvertering	–	–	342	–	28
Nettolåneskuld i förvärvade resp avyttrade verksamheter	–184	–925	–3.763	80	–
Valutaeffekter m.m.	–946	17	828	316	–3.252
Nettolåneskuld vid årets slut	–19.018	–17.462	–17.566	–10.573	–10.814

[1] Jämförande siffror är förändrade på grund av omklassificeringar.

Cash flow statement

CONSOLIDATED

SEK M	1997	1996
OPERATIONS		
Net sales	58,595	55,405
Operating expenses	−49,251	−47,281
Operating surplus	9,344	8,124
Changes in		
– Current receivables	−535	206
– Inventories	−125	749
– Operating liabilities	127	−287
Changes in working capital	−533	668
Current capital expenditures	−2,207	−2,489
Change in pension provisions	85	139
Restructuring expenses	−123	−249
Other operating cash flow changes	−53	−364
OPERATING CASH FLOW[1]	6,513	5,829
Financial items	−1,111	−1,008
Income taxes paid	−731	−659
Other	179	48
CASH FLOW FROM CURRENT OPERATIONS	4,850	4,210
STRATEGIC CAPITAL EXPENDITURES AND DIVESTMENTS		
Plants	−983	−1,126
Company acquisitions	−3,247	−1,558
Total strategic capital expenditures	−4,230	−2,684
Divestments	46	480
Cash flow from strategic capital expenditures and divestments	−4,184	−2,204
CASH FLOW BEFORE DIVIDEND	666	2,006
Dividend to shareholders	−1,092	−994
NET CASH FLOW	−426	1,012

NET DEBT

SEK M	1997	1996	1995	1994	1993
Net debt, 1 January	−17,462	−17,566	−10,573	−10,814	−10,799
Net cash flow	−426	1,012	−4,400	−155	3,209
New issue of shares through bond conversions	–	–	342	–	28
Net debt in acquired and divested operations	−184	−925	−3,763	80	–
Currency effects, etc.	−946	17	828	316	−3,252
Net debt, 31 December	−19,018	−17,462	−17,566	−10,573	−10,814

[1] Comparison figures adjusted to reflect reclassifications.

Moderbolaget

RESULTATRÄKNING

Mkr		1997	1996
Rörelsens intäkter		76	30
Rörelsens kostnader			
Övriga externa kostnader		-90	-89
Personalkostnader		-120	-84
Avskrivningar och nedskrivningar av			
materiella och immateriella tillgångar	Not 2	-34	-33
Övriga rörelsekostnader, netto		38	-84
Summa rörelsens kostnader		-206	-290
RÖRELSERESULTAT		-130	-260
Finansiella poster	Not 4		
Intäkter från aktier och andelar			
i koncernföretag		1.522	1.491
Intäkter från aktier och andelar			
i andra företag		1	59
Ränteintäkter och liknande resultatposter		231	168
Räntekostnader och liknande resultatposter		-490	-552
Summa finansiella poster		1.264	1.166
RESULTAT EFTER FINANSIELLA POSTER		1.134	906
Koncernbidrag		95	-81
Bokslutsdispositioner		163	163
Skatt på årets resultat		1	–
ÅRETS NETTORESULTAT		1.393	988

KASSAFLÖDESANALYS

Mkr	1997	1996
Rörelseöverskott	-96	-227
Övrigt kassaflöde från rörelsen	2.256	1.230
Investeringar och avyttringar	-1.230	-930
Koncernbidrag	-81	268
Utdelning till aktieägare	-1.036	-938
Nettokassaflöde	-187	-597

BALANSRÄKNING

Mkr		1997-12-31	1996-12-31
TILLGÅNGAR			
ANLÄGGNINGSTILLGÅNGAR			
Materiella anläggningstillgångar	Not 8		
Byggnader och mark		3.870	3.858
Maskiner och inventarier		2	3
		3.872	3.861
Finansiella anläggningstillgångar	Not 9		
Aktier och andelar	Not 10	21.805	19.958
Kapitalplaceringsaktier	Not 11	–	617
Räntebärande fordringar		10	9
		21.815	20.584
Summa anläggningstillgångar		25.687	24.445
OMSÄTTNINGSTILLGÅNGAR			
Kortfristiga fordringar på dotterbolag		2.021	2.149
Övriga kortfristiga fordringar	Not 13	31	66
Kortfristiga placeringar		1	81
Kassa och bank		12	12
Summa omsättningstillgångar		2.065	2.308
SUMMA TILLGÅNGAR		27.752	26.753

Mkr		1997-12-31	1996-12-31
EGET KAPITAL, AVSÄTTNINGAR OCH SKULDER			
EGET KAPITAL	Not 15	19.156	18.799
OBESKATTADE RESERVER	Not 14	595	758
AVSÄTTNINGAR	Not 16	165	126
SKULDER			
Räntebärande skulder	Not 19	1.441	1.274
Skulder till dotterbolag		6.270	5.621
Leverantörsskulder		14	15
Övriga ej räntebärande skulder	Not 20	111	160
Summa skulder		7.836	7.070
SUMMA EGET KAPITAL, AVSÄTTNINGAR OCH SKULDER		27.752	26.753
ANSVARSFÖRBINDELSER	Not 21	14.818	15.886
STÄLLDA PANTER	Not 22	482	481

Parent Company

STATEMENT OF EARNINGS

SEK M		1997	1996
Revenues		76	30
Operating expenses			
Other external costs		–90	–89
Personnel costs		–120	–84
Depreciation of tangible assets	Note 2	–34	–33
Other operating expenses, net		38	–84
Total operating expenses		**–206**	**–290**
OPERATING PROFIT		**–130**	**–260**
Financial items	Note 4		
Income from shares and participations,			
Group companies		1,522	1,491
Income from shares and participtations,			
other companies		1	59
Interest income and similar profit/loss items		231	168
Interest expense and similar profit/loss items		–490	–552
Total financial items		**1,264**	**1,166**
EARNINGS AFTER FINANCIAL ITEMS		**1,134**	**906**
Group contribution		95	–81
Appropriations		163	163
Taxes on profit for the year		1	–
NET EARNINGS FOR THE YEAR		**1,393**	**988**

CASH FLOW STATEMENT

SEK M	1997	1996
Operating surplus	–96	–227
Other cash flow from operations	2,256	1,230
Company acquisitions and divestments	–1,230	–930
Group contribution	–81	268
Dividend to shareholders	–1,036	–938
Net cash flow	**–187**	**–597**

BALANCE SHEET

SEK M		31 Dec. 1997	31 Dec. 1996
ASSETS			
FIXED ASSETS			
Tangible assets	Note 8		
Buildings and land		3,870	3,858
Machinery and equipment		2	3
		3,872	3,861
Financial assets	Note 9		
Shares and participations	Note 10	21,805	19,958
Capital investment shares	Note 11	–	617
Interest-bearing receivables		10	9
		21,815	20,584
Total fixed assets		25,687	24,445
CURRENT ASSETS			
Receivables from subsidiaries		2,021	2,149
Other current receivables	Note 13	31	66
Short-term investments		1	81
Cash and bank balances		12	12
Total current assets		2,065	2,308
TOTAL ASSETS		27,752	26,753

SEK M		31 Dec. 1997	31 Dec. 1996
EQUITY, PROVISIONS AND LIABILITIES			
SHAREHOLDERS' EQUITY	Note 15	19,156	18,799
UNTAXED RESERVES	Note 14	595	758
PROVISIONS	Note 16	165	126
LIABILITIES			
Interest-bearing debt	Note 19	1,441	1,274
Liabilities to subsidiaries		6,270	5,621
Accounts payable		14	15
Other interest-free liabilities	Note 20	111	160
Total liabilities		**7,836**	**7,070**
TOTAL EQUITY, PROVISIONS AND LIABILITIES		27,752	26,753
CONTINGENT LIABILITIES	Note 21	14,818	15,886
ASSETS PLEDGED	Note 22	482	481

Accounting principles

The SCA Group financial statements are prepared in accordance with the Swedish Financial Accounting Standards Council's recommendations.

The new Swedish Annual Accounts Act is applied by SCA as of 1997. Accordingly, SCA reports a cost-based statement of earnings.

CONSOLIDATED ACCOUNTS

Group composition
The consolidated financial statements include the accounts of the Parent Company and all subsidiaries, in accordance with the definitions in the Swedish Annual Accounts Act. In addition, SCA's share in joint-venture companies is included (see below). The financial statements have been prepared in accordance with the Swedish Financial Accounting Standards Council's recommendations regarding consolidated accounting.

Purchase method
The consolidated accounts have been prepared in accordance with the purchase method. The shareholders' equity in acquired subsidiaries is determined on the basis of a market or utility valuation of assets and liabilities at the time of acquisition (a so-called purchase analysis). In those instances in which the market or utility valuation of assets and liabilities results in significantly different values than the acquired company's book values, these values constitute the Group's acquisition cost. The difference between the acquisition cost of shares in the subsidiaries and the estimated value of the shareholders' equity at the time of the purchase analysis is reported as goodwill in the consolidation.

If necessary, an allocation to a reserve for future costs of reorganization and staff reductions may be made at the time of the purchase analysis.

Divested subsidiaries are included in the consolidated financial statements up to and including the date of divestment.

Translation of foreign subsidiary accounts
The balance sheets and statement of earnings of foreign subsidiaries are translated in accordance with the current method. The assets and liabilities in foreign subsidiaries are translated at the year-end exchange rates. All items in the statement of earnings are translated at the average exchange rate for the year. Translation differences are not reported in the statements of earnings but are charged directly to consolidated shareholders' equity.

Minority interest
Minority interest in the consolidated statements of earnings is reported as a share in after-tax earnings.

Minority interest in shareholders' equity in the subsidiaries is reported as a separate items in the balance sheet. This item also included minority interest in the shareholders' equity portion of untaxed reserves in subsidiaries.

Taxes
Deferred tax is estimated and reported in accordance with the principles in IAS 12. However, deferred tax liabilities or claims attributable to differences between the reported value of the asset and the tax value of long-term nondepreciable assets is not reported, to the extent that it is not probable that the assets will be realized in the foreseeable future. In the balance sheet, the estimated liability is reported to the tax authorities as current. Deferred tax liabilities are reported as provisions.

The tax expenses reported for the year include the tax that is payable on the taxable income for the year, changes in deferred taxes and the tax on the share of earnings of associated companies.

Associated companies
An associated company is a long-term shareholding representing at least 20% of the voting rights of the shares outstanding. Accounting for associated companies is according to the equity method.

In the consolidated statement of earnings, SCA's share in earnings of associated companies is reported on two levels.
- The Group's share in earnings after financial items is included in the consolidated operating profit.
- The share in income tax expenses at associated companies, in accordance with the full-tax method, is included in the consolidated income tax expenses.

The Group's share of earnings of an associated company is computed on the basis of SCA's equity portion in that particular associated company.

In the consolidated balance sheets, shares in associated companies are reported separately under shares and participations. The book value of the shareholding changes to reflect SCA's share of the after-tax earnings of the respective companies, reduced by dividends received. Non-distributed earnings of associated companies are included under non-distributable equity.

Joint-venture companies
Joint-venture companies are defined as companies in which the shareholding amounts to 50% and in which SCA is liable for its share of the financial risk. Joint-venture companies are reported in accordance with the proportional consolidation method.

In applying the proportional consolidation method, 50% of all statement of earnings and balance sheet items are included in the SCA Group's statement of earnings and balance sheet.

PRINCIPLES OF VALUATION

Receivables and liabilities in foreign currencies
In the consolidated financial statements, receivables and liabilities in foreign currencies are valued using year-end exchange rates. Gains and losses on current receivables and operating liabilities are netted and included in operating profit. To the extent that forward contracts are used to hedge operating receivables, the contract rate is used for valuation of the corresponding receivables. Gains and losses on financial receivables and liabilities are reported as other financial items.

SCA hedges its investments in foreign net assets, including goodwill. Hedging is implemented through loans in foreign currencies and forward exchange contracts. These are valued at the exchange rate prevailing at year-end. Exchange rate differences on hedging operations, after tax, as well as differences that arise when foreign net assets are translated at the exchange rate prevailing at year-end, are carried directly to shareholders' equity in the balance sheet.

Inventories and accounts receivable
Inventories consist of finished and semi-finished goods, raw materials, fuels, warehouse supplies and felling rights. These are valued at the lower of cost or market value in accordance with the first-in, first-out principle. The acquisition costs of inventories of finished and semi-finished goods, raw materials and fuels are based on the average production or acquisition costs for the year. Interest is not included in the inventory values.

Felling rights are calculated at contract prices which, on average, do not exceed market value.

Doubtful accounts receivable are reported in the amount which, after a careful assessment, is deemed likely to be paid.

Property and plant
Property and plant are reported at acquisition cost after deducting accumulated depreciation according to plan.

Unlike acquisition values for other capital expenditures, acquisition costs for property and plant related to major projects shall also include funds appropriated for start-up and commissioning work and for interest expenses during the construction and assembly period.

Depreciation according to plan is based on the historical cost and estimated useful lives of the assets.

The following depreciation rates are used on property and plant:

	%
Forest industry machines	5–10
Converting machinery	7–14
Mobile and other light equipment	20
Buildings	2–6
Land improvements	5

Intangible assets
Goodwill is amortized according to plan. The economic life is normally 20 years. SCA selected this time frame since the company acquisitions represent a long-term strategic value. Other intangible assets (primarily patents and trademarks) are amortized 10–20% per year.

Notes to the financial statements

PARENT COMPANY

The Parent Company's statement of earnings, balance sheet and cash flow statement are shown in condensed form on page 40. The following notes pertain to the financial statements of the Parent Company and the SCA Group.

STATEMENT OF EARNINGS

Note 1   Operating expenses

Operating expenses include capital gains from divestments amounting to SEK 425 M.
   Operating expenses include R&D expenses amounting to SEK 751 M (749) for the Group.

Note 2   Depreciation of tangible and intangible assets

	Group		Parent Company	
SEK M	1997	1996	1997	1996
Buildings	519	476	2	2
Land	65	52	31	30
Machinery and equipment	2,788	2,658	1	1
Subtotal	3,372	3,186	34	33
Goodwill	372	288	–	–
Patents, trademarks and similar rights	99	101	–	–
Total	3,843	3,575	34	33

Depreciation according to plan is based on the historical cost and estimated useful lives of the assets concerned, as specified in the accounting principles on page 41.

Note 3   Share in earnings of associated companies

SCA's interest in associated companies' earnings and shareholders' equity is reported applying the equity method. See accounting principles on page 41.
   Shares in pre-tax earnings are included in consolidated operating profit and amount to SEK 67 M (32).
   Dividends amounting to SEK 4 M (3) were received from associated companies.

Note 4   Financial items

	Group		Parent Company	
SEK M	1997	1996	1997	1996
Income from shares and participations in Group companies				
Dividends from subsidiaries	–	–	1,522	1,491
Income from shares and participations in other companies				
Dividends from other companies	70	70	1	59
Interest income and similar profit/loss items				
Interest income, external	210	249	0	1
Interest income, subsidiaries	–	–	81	132
Other financial income, subsidiaries	–	–	150	35
Interest expense and similar profit/loss items				
Interest expense, external	–1,362	–1,297	–100	–110
Interest expense, subsidiaries	–	–	–217	–395
Other financial expense, external	–29	–30	–173	–46
Other financial expense, subsidiaries	–	–	0	–1
Total	–1,111	–1,008	1,264	1,166

Note 5   Taxes on profit for the year

SEK M	1997	1996
Current taxes – consolidated companies	–688	–476
Deferred taxes – consolidated companies	–619	–659
Taxes attributable to shares in earnings of associated companies	–30	–9
Total income taxes	–1,337	–1,144

Note 6   Minority interest

Interest, %	1997	1996
SCA Laakirchen AG, Austria	24	27
Uni-Charm/Mölnlycke B.V.	60	60
Thai Klinipro Co. Ltd	51	51
Papierwerke Waldhof Aschaffenburg AG (PWA)	6	25
Sodipel SARL	12	12

Minority interest in net earnings from PWA is reported at 25% since the minority owned 25% during most of 1997.
   Minority interest in net earnings is reported in the statement of earnings in an amount of SEK 361 M (312), specified as follows:

SEK M	1997	1996
Minority interest in:		
– earnings after financial items	565	491
– income taxes	–204	–179
Minority interest	361	312

BALANCE SHEET

Note 7   Intangible assets

	Goodwill		Patents, trademarks and similar rights	
Group, SEK M	1997	1996	1997	1996
Acquisition value, 1 Jan.	6,378	6,013	1,879	2,196
Investments	552	360	41	566
Sales and disposals	–9	–	–197	–832
Reclassifications	4	–3	12	9
Translation differences	216	8	55	–60
Accumulated acquisition value, 31 Dec.	7,141	6,378	1,790	1,879
Amortization, 1 Jan.	–1,700	–1,402	–669	–811
Sales and disposals	46	–	78	216
Reclassifications	–5	–25	–4	–7
Amortization during the year	–372	–288	–99	–101
Translation differences	–27	15	–1	34
Accumulated amortization, 31 Dec.	–2,058	–1,700	–695	–669
Residual value according to plan, 31 Dec.	5,083	4,678	1,095	1,210

Note 8   Tangible assets

	Buildings		Land		Machinery and equipment		Construction in progress	
Group, SEK M	1997	1996	1997	1996	1997	1996	1997	1996
Acquisition value, 1 Jan.	12,442	11,421	5,446	5,526	39,410	34,427	306	2,969
Investments	173	1,162	469	136	3,558	3,746	392	73
Sales and disposals	–400	–260	–220	–187	–991	–1,095	–78	–43
Reclassifications	22	359	32	14	24	2,573	–51	–2,707
Translation differences	329	–240	134	–43	403	–241	–	14
Accumulated acquisition value, 31 Dec.	12,566	12,442	5,861	5,446	42,404	39,410	569	306
Depreciation, 1 Jan.	–2,889	–2,304	–474	–453	–15,416	–13,615	–	–
Sales and disposals	94	25	4	26	883	881	–	–
Reclassifications	61	–161	–	3	–65	–59	–	–
Depreciation during the year	–519	–476	–65	–52	–2,788	–2,658	–	–
Translation differences	–46	27	–	2	–102	35	–	–
Accumulated depreciation, 31 Dec.	–3,299	–2,889	–535	–474	–17,488	–15,416	–	–
Write-ups, 1 Jan.	–	–	3,100	3,100	–	–	–	–
Accumulated write-ups, 31 Dec.	–	–	3,100	3,100	–	–	–	–
Residual value according to plan, 31 Dec.	9,267	9,553	8,426	8,072	24,916	23,994	569	306

Note 8 Tangible assets, cont.

Parent Company, SEK M	Buildings		Land		Machinery and equipment	
	1997	1996	1997	1996	1997	1996
Acquisition value, 1 Jan.	57	55	999	971	7	6
Investments	1	3	46	60	0	1
Sales and disposals	–	–1	–2	–32	–	–
Accumulated acquisition value, 31 Dec.	58	57	1,043	999	7	7
Depreciation, 1 Jan.	–27	–26	–271	–264	–4	–3
Sales and disposals		1		23		
Depreciation during the year	–2	–2	–31	–30	–1	–1
Accumulated depreciation, 31 Dec.	–29	–27	–302	–271	–5	–4
Write-ups, 1 Jan.	–	–	3,100	3,100	–	–
Accumulated write-ups, 31 Dec.	–	–	3,100	3,100	–	–
Residual value according to plan, 31 Dec.	29	30	3,841	3,828	2	3

Note 9 Financial assets

SEK M	Shares and participations				Capital investment shares			
	Group		Parent Company		Group		Parent Company	
	1997	1996	1997	1996	1997	1996	1997	1996
Acquisition value, 1 Jan.	604	1,410	19,960	18,993	838	890	589	626
Investments	336	195	2,947	967	1,084	–	102	–
Sales	–26	–2	–	–	–838	–52	–691	–37
Net increase in associated companies during the year	34	21	–	–	–	–	–	–
Reclassifications	–68	–1,013	–	–	–	–	–	–
Translation differences	–10	–7	–	–	–	–	–	–
Accumulated acquisition value, 31 Dec.	870	604	22,907	19,960	1,084	838	0	589
Write-ups, 1 Jan.	–	–	140	140	29	29	29	29
Sales	–	–	–	–	–	–	–29	–
Accumulated write-ups, net, 31 Dec.	–	–	140	140	29	29	0	29
Write-downs, 1 Jan.	–	–	–142	–142	–1	–1	–1	–1
Sales	–	–	–	–	–	–	1	–
Write-downs during the year	–	–	–1,100	–	–	–	–	–
Accumulated write-downs, 31 Dec.	–	–	–1,242	–142	–1	–1	0	–1
Residual value according to plan, 31 Dec.	870	604	21,805	19,958	1,112	866	0	617

Note 10 Shares and participations

Group and Parent Company holdings of shares and participations were as follows:

SEK M	Group		Parent Company	
	1997	1996	1997	1996
Subsidiaries	–	–	21,789	19,942
Associated companies	741	449	–	–
Other companies	129	155	16	16
Total	870	604	21,805	19,958

For specification, see page 50.

Major changes during 1997 in the Parent Company's and Group's holdings were as follows:

Subsidiaries
The Parent Company's book value of shares in subsidiaries increased by SEK 1,847 M. During the year SEK 2,247 M was paid in capital contributions, of which shares in SCA Recycling Holding AB at a value of SEK 742 M, to SCA Group Holding B.V. In addition, SEK 341 M was paid into SCA Holding AB and SEK 1,100 M into SCA Hedging AB.

Associated companies
Among other transactions, Productos Familia S.A. and operations in the packaging field in China and India were acquired during the year.

Note 11 Capital investment shares

SEK M	Number	Book value
AB Industrivärden	3,598,413	1,112
Total		1,112

The Parent Company divested all of its shares in AB Industrivärden during the year to SCA Group Holding B.V. All shares in SAS Sverige AB were sold during the year.

Of the holding in AB Industrivärden, 1,830,000 shares are available for future redemption in accordance with the so-called exchangeable bonds issued during spring 1997. At year-end, the conversion price was SEK 458. The market value of shares in AB Industrivärden exceeds the consolidated book value by SEK 489 M.

Note 12 Inventories

	Group	
SEK M	1997	1996
Raw materials and consumables	1,603	1,160
Work in progress	476	574
Finished goods	2,912	2,809
Spare parts and warehouse supplies	519	736
Felling rights	270	291
Total	5,780	5,570

Note 13 Other current receivables

	Group		Parent Company	
SEK M	1997	1996	1997	1996
Bills receivable	403	536	–	–
Prepaid expenses and accrued income	634	497	23	17
Other receivables	903	930	8	49
Total	1,940	1,963	31	66

Note 14 Untaxed reserves in Parent Company

Untaxed reserves in the Parent Company include an SEK 475 M (633) allocation to the tax equalization reserve and SEK 120 M (125) in accumulated deprecation in excess of plan.

Note 15 Shareholders' equity

Group, SEK M	Share capital	Share premium reserve	Legal reserve	Equity proportion reserve	Translation differences	Other restricted reserves	Distributable equity	Total
Balance, 1 Jan.	1,974	1,870	687	1,308	–1,545	8,730	9,882	22,906
Translation differences	–	–	–	–	607	–	–181	426
Exchange rate differences on hedging instruments	–	–	–	–	–346	–	–	–346
Transfer between distributable and nondistributable shareholders' equity	–	–	50	–	–	28	–78	0
Equity in associated companies	–	–	–	37	–	–	–37	0
Dividend paid	–	–	–	–	–	–	–1,092	–1,092
Net earnings for the year	–	–	–	–	–	–	2,759	2,759
Balance, 31 Dec.	1,974	1,870	737	1,345	–1,284	8,758	11,253	24,653

The Share premium reserve, Legal reserve, Equity proportion reserve, Translation differences and Other restricted reserves amount in total to SEK 11,426 M (11,050) and are reported in the balance sheets as Restricted reserves. Distributable equity includes negative translation differences of SEK 223 M (negative: 42).

Parent Company, SEK M	Share capital	Share premium reserve	Legal reserve	Write-up reserve	Distributable equity	Total
Balance, 1 Jan.	1,974	1,870	395	806	13,754	18,799
Dividend paid	–	–	–	–	–1,036	–1,036
Net earnings for the year	–	–	–	–	1,393	1,393
Balance, 31 Dec.	1,974	1,870	395	806	14,111	19,156

SCA's share capital consists of 197,399,935 shares with a par value of SEK 10 each. The issues, etc., for the period 1990–1997 are presented below. For additional information on the SCA share, see pages 8–9.

Note 15 Shareholders' equity, cont.

Issues, etc. 1990–1997

Since 1990, the share capital and number of shares, has increased through
stock dividends and new issues, conversions and splits as follows

SEK M (except no. of shares)		No. of shares	Increase in share capital	Cash payment
1990	Conversion of debentures and new subscription through Series 1 warrants	1,008,284	10.1	5.9
1991	Conversion of debentures and new subscription through Series 1 warrants	371,118	3.7	10.5
1992	Conversion of debentures and new subscription through Series 1 warrants	777,453	7.8	19.6
1993	Conversion of debentures and new subscription through Series 1 warrants	4,030,286	40.3	119.1
	New issue 1:10	17,633,412	176.3	1,410.7
1994	Conversion of debentures	16,285	0.2	–
1995	Conversion of debentures	3,416,113	34.2	–
1996	–	–	–	–
1997	–	–	–	–

Conversion of debentures pertained to a 1987 loan, 9.5% at SEK 350 M, which fell due for payment in 1995. New subscription of Series 1
warrants pertained to a 1983 debenture loan, 7% at SEK 266 M, with detachable warrants. The subscription right expired in 1993.

Note 16 Provisions for pensions

	Group		Parent Company	
SEK M	1997	1996	1997	1996
PRI pensions	1,036	1,041	29	28
Other pensions	2,201	2,112	136	98
Total	3,237	3,153	165	126

The calculated interest on the amount allocated to pensions is reported
as an operating expense. The interest rate for PRI pensions was 3.7%
(6.0).

Provisions are made in accordance with local law.

Note 17 Provisions for taxes

SEK M	1997	1996
Balance, 1 Jan.	4,710	4,072
Deferred tax charges	619	659
Other changes	121	–21
Total	5,450	4,710

Note 18 Other provisions

This includes a restructuring reserve of SEK 1,582 M (1,311). In conjunction with the further acquisition during the year of PWA shares,
these provisions increased. Provisions were made in the acquisition
analysis for the continued integration work between SCA and PWA. In
addition, provisions were withdrawn for the ongoing integration and
restructuring program in accordance with decisions in prior years.

Note 19 Interest-bearing debt

	Group		Parent Company	
SEK M	1997	1996	1997	1996
Amortization within one year	376	415	3	3
Loans maturing within one year	3,791	4,134	–	–
Total short-term interest-bearing debt	4,167	4,549	3	3
Bond loans	846	29	15	29
Convertible loans	38	38	36	36
Other long-term loans	17,596	16,780	1,387	1,206
Total long-term interest-bearing debt	18,480	16,847	1,438	1,271
Total	22,647	21,396	1,441	1,274

A total of SEK 300 M (300) in short-term debts have been netted
against fund investments secured for the corresponding loans.

Bond loans include a five-year exchangeable bond in a nominal
amount of DEM 200 M which was issued in spring 1997 at SEK 828
M.

Assets have been pledged as security for SEK 1,145 M (1,121) of
these long- and short-term loans.

Redemption structure for interest-bearing debts

Year	SEK M
1998	4,167
1999	2,075
2000	672
2001	3,229
2002	6,555
2003 and later	5,949
Total	22,647

Note 15 *Shareholders' equity, cont.*

Issues, etc. 1990–1997

Since 1990, the share capital and number of shares, has increased through stock dividends and new issues, conversions and splits as follows

SEK M (except no. of shares)	No. of shares	Increase in share capital	Cash payment
1990 Conversion of debentures and new subscription through Series 1 warrants	1,008,284	10.1	5.9
1991 Conversion of debentures and new subscription through Series 1 warrants	371,118	3.7	10.5
1992 Conversion of debentures and new subscription through Series 1 warrants	777,453	7.8	19.6
1993 Conversion of debentures and new subscription through Series 1 warrants	4,030,286	40.3	119.1
New issue 1:10	17,633,412	176.3	1,410.7
1994 Conversion of debentures	16,285	0.2	–
1995 Conversion of debentures	3,416,113	34.2	–
1996 –	–	–	–
1997 –	–	–	–

Conversion of debentures pertained to a 1987 loan, 9.5% at SEK 350 M, which fell due for payment in 1995. New subscription of Series 1 warrants pertained to a 1983 debenture loan, 7% at SEK 266 M, with detachable warrants. The subscription right expired in 1993.

Note 16 Provisions for pensions

SEK M	Group 1997	1996	Parent Company 1997	1996
PRI pensions	1,036	1,041	29	28
Other pensions	2,201	2,112	136	98
Total	3,237	3,153	165	126

The calculated interest on the amount allocated to pensions is reported as an operating expense. The interest rate for PRI pensions was 3.7% (6.0).

Provisions are made in accordance with local law.

Note 17 Provisions for taxes

SEK M	1997	1996
Balance, 1 Jan.	4,710	4,072
Deferred tax charges	619	659
Other changes	121	−21
Total	5,450	4,710

Note 18 Other provisions

This includes a restructuring reserve of SEK 1,582 M (1,311). In conjunction with the further acquisition during the year of PWA shares, these provisions increased. Provisions were made in the acquisition analysis for the continued integration work between SCA and PWA. In addition, provisions were withdrawn for the ongoing integration and restructuring program in accordance with decisions in prior years.

Note 19 Interest-bearing debt

SEK M	Group 1997	1996	Parent Company 1997	1996
Amortization within one year	376	415	3	3
Loans maturing within one year	3,791	4,134	–	–
Total short-term interest-bearing debt	4,167	4,549	3	3
Bond loans	846	29	15	29
Convertible loans	38	38	36	36
Other long-term loans	17,596	16,780	1,387	1,206
Total long-term interest-bearing debt	18,480	16,847	1,438	1,271
Total	22,647	21,396	1,441	1,274

A total of SEK 300 M (300) in short-term debts have been netted against fund investments secured for the corresponding loans.

Bond loans include a five-year exchangeable bond in a nominal amount of DEM 200 M which was issued in spring 1997 at SEK 828 M.

Assets have been pledged as security for SEK 1,145 M (1,121) of these long- and short-term loans.

Redemption structure for interest-bearing debts

Year	SEK M
1998	4,167
1999	2,075
2000	672
2001	3,229
2002	6,555
2003 and later	5,949
Total	22,647

Note 19 *Interest-bearing debt, cont.*

Gross debt by currency

Taking into account currency swaps and other derivatives, SCA's gross debt is distributed among the following currencies:

Currency	Gross debt, SEK M 1997	1996
DEM	2,661	7,502
GBP	4,546	7,441
NLG	2,515	4,417
ATS	1,597	3,171
FRF	831	2,080
BEF	445	1,176
ITL	2,480	1,162
USD	556	851
SEK	6,846	–7,180
Other	170	776
Total	22,647	21,396

Convertible loans

SEK M	1997	1996
1990 GBP 10,516,384 at 10%	36	36

Subordinated bond loan convertible into SCA Series B shares between 1 October 1990 and 31 July 2000. The loan may be called at any time during term, in which case repayment will be made in the nominal amount, plus accrued interest. The conversation price at 31 December 1997 was SEK 159.10.

Total loans issued by Parent Company	36	36

Bond loan issued by SCA Group Holding B.V. 1989 ECU 101 M at 4.25%	2	2

Subordinated bond loan convertible into SCA Series B shares between 25 April 1989 and 10 January 2004. The conversion price at 31 December 1997 was SEK 130.00.

Total loans issued by Group	38	38

Conversion of the 1990 GBP loan means that a maximum of 224,167 Series B shares will be issued. The amount of the loan decreased in 1997 through a repayment that did not involve conversion of debentures into shares.

Note 20 Other interest-free liabilities

SEK M	Group 1997	1996	Parent Company 1997	1996
Accrued expenses and prepaid income	3,072	3,261	92	145
Tax liabilities	447	464	4	–
Other operating liabilities	1,681	1,499	3	3
Total interest-free current liabilities	5,200	5,224	99	148
Interest-free long-term liabilities	373	414	12	12
Total	5,573	5,638	111	160

Accrued expenses and prepaid income

SEK M	Group 1997	1996	Parent Company 1997	1996
Accrued social costs	446	531	5	4
Accrued vacation pay liability	447	446	5	4
Accrued financial expenses	236	199	16	16
Other items	1,943	2,085	66	121
Total	3,072	3,261	92	145

Note 21 Contingent liabilities

SEK M	Group 1997	1996	Parent Company 1997	1996
Discounted bills	143	516	–	–
Guarantees for				
– employees	48	32	3	2
– associated companies	64	38,	–	–
– customers and other	95	91	0	2
– subsidiaries	–	–	14,806	15,874
Other contingent liabilities	134	95	9	8
Total	484	772	14,818	15,886

As stated in the Board of Directors' report (page 32), a so-called Control Agreement was established during 1997 between SCA, through its German holding company SCA Group Holding (Deutschland) GmbH, and PWA, effective 1 January 1998. The agreement is valid until further notice with a mutual cancellation notice period of six months. The Control Agreement entails a liability for the German holding company to carry any losses which arise in PWA during the period of the agreement. SCA has provided a surety for this commitment and to pay an annual dividend of DEM 17.15 per share to the remaining minority shareholders in PWA.

The former owners of 20% of the shares in SCA Laakirchen Holding AG which, as a result of an organization change, was replaced by a holding in a newly formed company, are entitled during the year 2000 to sell their share to SCA for a price of approximately SEK 480 M.

As reported in the 1996 Annual Report, SCA entered into lease-out/lease-in transactions during 1996 with American banks as counterparties pertaining to the two LWC plants in Ortviken, Sweden. The terms of the contracts are 32 and 36 years. However, SCA has the opportunity to cancel the transactions after 18 years without incurring any financial consequences. At the time the transactions were effected, the current value of the leasing amount which SCA has undertaken to pay amounts to about SEK 4 billion. This amount, in accordance with the agreements, is partly deposited in accounts in banks with at least AA rating, and partly in U.S. securities with a AAA rating. SCA carries the credit risk against the depositary banks, but this is considered, as a result of the structure of the agreements, to be insignificant. Should the rating of a depositary bank decline in the future, SCA has the possibility to transfer the deposit to another bank with a better rating. Moreover, SCA is liable to take such action if the depositary bank's rating falls below A. The counterparties have accepted that the deposited funds are applied for the leasing undertakings. The advance payments and deposits were netted during 1996 in the balance sheet. Should SCA as the result of extraordinary events (of a force majeure nature) elect not to fulfill, or cannot fulfill the leasing contracts, SCA is liable to compensate the counterparties for

Note 25 *Number of employees and wages, salaries and remuneration, cont.*

Salaries and other remunerations distributed by country and between Board members, others and employees

	1997		1996	
	Board, Presidents, VPs	Other employees	Board, Presidents, VPs	Other employees
SEK M	(of which, bonus)		(of which, bonus)	
Parent Company				
Sweden	16	27	14	28
	(2)		(2)	
Subsidiaries				
Sweden	29	1,931	32	1,943
	(2)		(3)	
Germany	25	2,101	36	2,319
	(5)		(13)	
Great Britain	11	1,259	5	897
	(1)		(1)	
France	13	649	10	724
	(2)		(0)	
The Netherlands	14	856	8	789
	(1)		(1)	
Belgium	36	376	13	385
	(0)		(1)	
Italy	9	241	6	219
	(1)		(0)	
Austria	9	773	14	885
	(1)		(0)	
U.S.	10	183	7	195
	(3)		(1)	
Norway	1	146	1	144
	(–)			
Finland	2	75	2	54
	(1)			
Denmark	0	59	–	67
	(0)			
Other countries[1]	4	256	6	258
	(0)		(–)	
Total, subsidiaries	163	8,905	140	8,879
	(17)		(20)	
Total, Group	179	8,932	154	8,907
	(19)		(22)	

[1] Spain, Ireland, Greece, Portugal, Switzerland, Poland, Hungary, Czech Republic, Slovakia, Canada, Japan, Thailand.

Note 26 Executive management conditions of employment

The Chairman of the Board of Directors, who previously held the position of Chief Executive Officer (CEO), received a consideration during 1997 of SEK 1,572,656 (4,368,079) in accordance with his employment contract until his retirement on May 1997, and housing benefits. In addition, during 1997 he received a Board fee from PWA of SEK 35,448 (35,688) and, as a member of the Board of PWA, a bonus of SEK 189,000. After retirement in May 1997, the Board Chairman received his retirement pension in accordance with pension agreement and, as Chairman of the Board of SCA, a Board fee of SEK 600,000.

During 1997, the CEO received SEK 5,234,475 (4,788,125), car benefits (fuel excluded) and housing benefits as well as a Board fee from PWA of SEK 35,448 (35,688). As a member of the Board of PWA, he also received a bonus of SEK 189,000. In the case of the CEO, as well as other senior executives in the Group, there is one bonus agreement which is linked to the Group's return on capital employed and one related to the development of the SCA share. The first, including any bonus awarded from PWA, can result in a maximum bonus amounting to 30% of base salary, which for the CEO in 1997 resulted in a bonus corresponding to 23.5 (12)% of base salary. The latter bonus agreement is related to the development of the SCA share during 1997, 1998 and 1999 and can, after 1999, result in a maximum bonus corresponding to 10% of base salary for each of the three years. The latter bonus shall preferentially be paid in the form of options to acquire SCA shares.

The pension agreement for the CEO is formulated so that old age pension (including general pension benefits) is paid from the age of 65 at 70% of salary at retirement. This is contingent upon employment being sustained during at least 20 years from the date he reached 40 years of age. At termination at the request of the Company, the pension age may be reduced to not lower than 55. Upon termination of employment at own request between the ages of 55 and 60, a paid-up policy is received for pension payments from age 60. In the case of the CEO, the company also paid out SEK 104,735 (104,562) in 1997 pertaining to supplementary pension commitments.

Moreover, the agreement with the CEO stipulates that, in the event of termination of employment after age 55, he is entitled to be transferred to a position as expert advisor. Pension benefits are not paid while serving in the position of expert advisor.

The agreement with the CEO stipulates a period of notice of termination of five years if such notice is given prior to age 60. This notice period, which is mutual and accordingly also applies upon termination at the request of the CEO, is reduced to two years after age 60. The agreement does not contain any stipulations with regard to severance pay.

In the case of other senior executives in the Group there is a pension plan which, in the normal case, grants the executive the right at age 65 to receive a pension (including general pension benefits) at up to 70% of the salary. Normally, full pension requires the executive having been employed in the Group for 20 years. Upon termination of employment prior to reaching retirement age, a paid-up policy is received for pension payments from age 65, under the condition that the executive, after reaching the age of 40, has been employed in the Group for at least three years.

Specification to Note 10

Parent Company shareholdings in subsidiaries

Company name	Org. no.	Registered office	No. of shares	Capital %	Book value, SEK M
Swedish subsidiaries:					
SCA Research AB	556146-6300	Sundsvall	500	100	0.1
AB SCA Finans	556108-5688	Stockholm	420,750	100	50.1
SCA Holding AB	556313-1621	Stockholm	10,374,430	100	341.4
SCA Hedging AB	556237-4867	Stockholm	50,000	100	72.0
SCA Kraftfastigheter AB	556449-7237	Stockholm	1,000	100	0.1
Fastighets- och Bostadsaktiebolaget FOBOF	556047-8520	Stockholm	1,000	100	0.1
SCA Försäkrings AB	516401-8540	Stockholm	140,000	100	14.0
SCA Recovered Papers Holding AB	556537-5739	Stockholm	1,000	100	0.1
SCA Konsult AB	556351-6029	Stockholm	1,000	100	0.1
Foreign subsidiaries:					
SCA Group Holding B.V.	181970	Amsterdam	202,347	100	21,311.3
Parent Company shareholdings in subsidiaries					**21,789.3**

Group holdings of shares and participations in associated companies

Company name	Org. no.	Registered office	No. of shares/participations	Capital %	Book value, SEK M
Staper Ltd	1130403	Aylesford	100,000	50	5.7
Centrale Eerbeek		Eerbeek		50	19.8
Kaplamin Ambalaj Sanayi ve Ticaret AS		Izmir		29	38.0
SCA Packaging Ambalaj ve Ticaret AS		Altinova		34	33.8
Ova SCA Packaging Ambalais Ticaret AS		Tarsus		29	32.3
Selkasan Kagit ve Pakerleme Malzemeleri Imalati Sanayi ve Ticaret AS		Manisa		16	21.1
Nordliner IL Returpapper		Stockholm	14,000	15	2.7
ASCA Holding AG		Oftringen	49,900	50	116.1
SCA Weyerhaeuser Packaging Holding Co Asia Ltd		Hong Kong		50	66.9
Rank SCA Packaging India Ltd		India	7,731,882	50	35.6
Les Bois de la Baltique SA		Rochefort	75,000	38	18.0
AB Sladen	556094-8001	Östersund	25,000	25	6.1
GAE Smith		Leicester	44,300	50	35.9
Atkasan		Izmir	44,625	35	4.7
Paredes	B955 509 609	Genas	43,747	35	61.3
Productos Familia SA		Medellin	15,700,416	20	190.4
Other associated companies					52.7
Group holdings of shares and participations in associated companies					**741.1**

The difference between the book value in the Group and the Group's share in the associated companies' shareholders' equity amounts to SEK 89.4 M.

Group holdings of shares and participations in other major companies

Company name	Org. no.	Registered office	Capital %	Company name	Org. no.	Registered office	Capital %
SCA GROUP HOLDING B.V.	181970	Amsterdam	100	SCA Packaging Holding BV	196416	Amsterdam	100
SCA Reinsurance Ltd	168575	Dublin	100	*SCA Packaging International B V*		Amsterdam	100
SCA Coordination Center NV	547534	Brussels	100	*– SCA Packaging Obbola AB*	556147-1003	Umeå	100
SCA Graphic Holding AB	556479-2058	Stockholm	100	*– SCA Packaging Munksund A B*	556237-4859	Piteå	100
SCA Graphic Paper AB	556379-3586	Sundsvall	100	*– SCA Packaging Belgium NV*		Gent	100
– SCA Graphic Sundsvall AB	556093-6733	Sundsvall	100	*– SCA Packaging Italia Spa*		Arcore	100
– SCA Transforest AB	556431-6965	Sundsvall	100	*– SCA Packaging Sweden AB*	556036-8507	Värnamo	100
– SCA Laakirchen AG		Laakirchen	95	*– Zewawell GmbH*		Mannheim	100
– Aylesford Newsprint Holdings Ltd		Aylesford	50	*– SCA Packaging France SA*		Eragny	100
				– SCA Corporate UK Ltd	2263948	Aylesford	100
SCA Hygiene Holding AB	556479-2181	Stockholm	100				
SCA Mölnlycke AB	556007-2356	Härryda	100	*SCA Finance BV*		Eerbeek	100
– SCA Mölnlycke Clinical Products AB	556239-3701	Härryda	100	*– SCA Packaging Nederland BV*	9062936	Barneveld	100
– SCA Mölnlycke Consumer Products AB	556412-1035	Härryda	100	*– SCA Packaging Benelux BV*		Eerbeek	100
– SCA Mölnlycke Incontinence Care AB	556239-3719	Härryda	100	*– SCA Packaging DeHoop BV*		Eerbeek	100
– SCA Mölnlycke Inc	421987	Canada	100				
– SCA Mölnlycke A/S	30877	Alleröd	100	PWA Holding AB	556204-5434	Stockholm	100
– SCA Mölnlycke GmbH	HRB934	Hilden	100	*SCA Group Holding Deutschland GmbH*	HRB4014	Mettmann	100
– SCA Mölnlycke Kft	13-09-063186	Budapest	100	*– SCA Capital Corporation Inc*	52-1383747	New York	100
– SCA Mölnlycke Ltd	47636	Dunmanway	100	*– SCA Packaging Deutschland Holding GmbH*	HRB61506	Berlin	100
– SCA Mölnlycke Holding B.V	185911	Ar Zeist	100	*– Papierwerke Waldhof Aschaffenburg AG*	HRB42709	Munich	94
– SCA Mölnlycke A/S	915620019	Tönsberg	100	*SCA Hygiene Paper Holding GmbH*	HRB 10455	Raubling	100
– SCA Mölnlycke Lda	PT 503237612	Linda-a-Velha	100	*SCA FINE PAPER GmbH*	HRB 3098	Raubling	100
– SCA Mölnlycke o.o.o.		Moscow	100	*ECCO Paper Trade GmbH*	HRB 10326	Raubling	100
– SCA Mölnlycke s.r.o.	31723837	Gemerská-Hôrka	100	*SCA Packaging Industriepapier GmbH*	HRB 3097	Raubling	100
– SCA Mölnlycke Holdings Inc	A-28451383	Madrid	100				
– SCA Mölnlycke SA	58-2011277	Philadelphia	100	SCA Recycling Holding AB	556513-8590	Stockholm	100
– SCA Mölnlycke SA		Linselles	100	*SCA Recycling Holding B V*		Amsterdam	100
– Productos Sanitarios Sancela SA	890937981-1	Medellin	49	*– SCA Recycling Belgium NV*		St Stevens Woluwe	100
– Uni-Charm KK	660779	Tokyo	50	*– SCA Recycling France SA*		Courbevoie	100
– Comercializadora Sancela SA de CV	CSA-880531-EX3	Ecatepec De Morelos	49	*– SCA RML Europe NV*		Zaventem	100
– Sancela de CV	SAN-790424-8K1	Ecatepec De Morelos	49	*– SCA Recycling UK Ltd*		Aylesford	100
– Uni-Charm Mölnlycke BV	330631	Hoogezand	40	*– Italmaceri Srl*		Torino	50
– Taiwan Sancella Enterpris	16093200	Taiwan	50				
– Thai Klinipro Co Ltd		Thailand	49				
				The complete statutory specifications are included in the Annual Report submitted			
SCA Forest Holding AB	556479-1100	Stockholm	100	to the National Swedish Patent and Registration Office. This specification is avail-			
SCA Forest and Timber AB	556379-3594	Sundsvall	100	able from SCA, Corporate Communications, Box 7827, SE-103 97 Stockholm.			
– Svanö AB	556056-7694	Kramfors	100				

Förslag till vinstdisposition

Fritt eget kapital enligt koncernens balansräkning uppgår till 11.253 Mkr.

Fritt eget kapital i moderbolaget är:

balanserade vinstmedel	12.717.633.731
årets nettoresultat	1.392.876.434
Kronor	14.110.510.165

Styrelsen och verkställande direktören föreslår:

att till aktieägarna utdelas 5:75 kr per aktie	1.135.049.626
samt att återstående belopp balanseras	12.975.460.539
Kronor	14.110.510.165

Stockholm den 19 februari 1998

Bo Rydin	Christer Gardell	Gerhard Gustavsson	Sören Gyll	Tom Hedelius
Ordförande				
Tjell-Åke Hägglund	Lars Ramqvist	Clas Reuterskiöld	Alf Söderlund	Sverker Martin-Löf
				Verkställande direktör

Revisionsberättelse

TILL BOLAGSSTÄMMAN I SCA   Org.nr: 556012-6293

Vi har granskat årsredovisningen, koncernredovisningen och räkenskaperna samt styrelsens och verkställande direktörens förvaltning i SCA för år 1997. Det är styrelsen och verkställande direktören som har ansvaret för räkenskapshandlingarna och förvaltningen. Vårt ansvar är att uttala oss om årsredovisningen, koncernredovisningen och förvaltningen på grundval av vår revision.

Revisionen har utförts i enlighet med god revisionssed. Det innebär att vi planerat och genomfört revisionen för att i rimlig grad försäkra oss om att årsredovisningen och koncernredovisningen inte innehåller väsentliga fel. En revision innefattar att granska ett urval av underlagen för belopp och annan information i räkenskapshandlingarna. I en revision ingår också att pröva redovisningsprinciperna och styrelsens och verkställande direktörens tillämpning av dem samt att bedöma den samlade informationen i årsredovisningen och koncernredovisningen. Vi har granskat väsentliga beslut, åtgärder och förhållanden i bolaget för att kunna bedöma om någon styrelseledamot eller verkställande direktören är ersättningsskyldig mot bolaget eller på annat sätt har handlat i strid mot aktiebolagslagen, årsredovisningslagen eller bolagsordningen. Vi anser att vår revision ger oss en rimlig grund för våra uttalanden nedan.

Årsredovisningen och koncernredovisningen har upprättats i enlighet med årsredovisningslagen, varför vi tillstyrker

att resultaträkningen och balansräkningen för moderbolaget och för koncernen fastställs och

att vinsten i moderbolaget disponeras enligt förslaget i förvaltningsberättelsen.

Styrelseledamöterna och verkställande direktören har inte vidtagit någon åtgärd eller gjort sig skyldiga till någon försummelse som enligt vår bedömning kan föranleda ersättningsskyldighet mot bolaget varför vi tillstyrker

att styrelsens ledamöter och verkställande direktören beviljas ansvarsfrihet för räkenskapsåret.

Stockholm den 19 februari 1998

Öhrlings Coopers & Lybrand AB
Bertil Edlund

Proposed disposition of earnings

As shown in the consolidated Balance Sheets, distributable shareholders' equity
amount to SEK 11,253 M.
Distributable shareholders' equity at the parent company:

retained earnings	12,717,633,731
net earnings for the year	1,392,876,434
Total	14,110,510,165

The Board of Directors and the President recommend:

to the shareholders, a dividend of SEK 5.75 per share	1,135,049,626
retained earnings to be carried forward	12,975,460,539
Total	14,110,510,165

Stockholm, 19 February 1998

Bo Rydin
Chairman

Christer Gardell

Gerhard Gustavsson

Sören Gyll

Tom Hedelius

Tjell-Åke Hägglund

Lars Ramqvist

Clas Reuterskiöld

Alf Söderlund

Sverker Martin-Löf
President

Auditor's report

TO THE GENERAL MEETING OF THE SHAREHOLDERS OF SCA   Reg.No: 556012-6293

We have audited the parent company and the consolidated financial statements, the accounts and the administration of the Board of Directors and the President of SCA for 1997. These accounts and the administration of the Company are the responsibility of the Board of Directors and the President. Our responsibility is to express an opinion on the financial statements and the administration based on our audit.

We conducted our audit in accordance with Generally Accepted Auditing Standards in Sweden. Those Standards require that we plan and perform the audit to obtain reasonable assurance that the financial statements are free of material misstatement. An audit includes examining, on a test basis, evidence supporting the amounts and disclosures in the financial statements. An audit also includes assessing the accounting principles used and their application by the Board of Directors and the President, as well as evaluating the overall presentation of information in the financial statements. We examined significant decisions, actions taken and circumstances of the Company in order to be able to determine the possible liability to the Company of any Board member or the President or whether they have in some other way acted in contravention of the Companies Act, the Annual Accounts Act or the Articles of Association. We believe that our audit provides a reasonable basis for our opinion set out below.

In our opinion, the parent company and the consolidated financial statements have been prepared in accordance with the Annual Accounts Act and consequently we recommend

that the income statements and the balance sheets of the Parent Company and the Group be adopted, and

that the profit of the Parent Company be dealt with in accordance with the proposal in the Board of Directors' Report.

In our opinion, the Board members and the President have not committed any act or been guilty of any omission, which could give rise to any liability to the Company. We therefore recommend

that the members of the Board of Directors and the President be discharged from liability for the financial year.

Stockholm, 19 February 1998

Öhrlings Coopers & Lybrand AB
Bertil Edlund

Country Highlights
UNITED KINGDOM

Common Legal Forms of Companies

Most companies are formed by registration, and may be public or private. Banks and insurance companies have special provisions. Co-operatives (mainly in retailing, but becoming rarer), like trade unions, are formed under the Friendly Societies Acts.

Financial Reporting Requirements

Annual accounts are required by the 1985 Companies Act. Listed companies must also comply with the Stock Exchange Agreement for Listing (the "Yellow Book") and publish half-yearly accounts. Accounting standards ("Financial Reporting Standards" and earlier "Statements of Standard Accounting Practice") are set by the private sector Accounting Standards Board with statutory backing.

Corporate Taxation

Corporation Tax has for 25 years taken the form of "Advanced Corporation Tax" (ACT), paid at the time of dividend payments and deducted from the "Mainstream Corporation Tax" (MCT), assessed on annual profits (using a tax base that differs from the published profit figures). MCT has been paid in the year after assessment. ACT will end in 1999, and MCT will then be assessed on profits and paid in quarterly installments during the course of the accounting year.

Auditing Requirements

All except small companies must be audited annually. Audit reports are "short form" rather than commenting on every policy issue. Registered Auditors alone can sign audit reports and are specially qualified members of one of five professional bodies: the Institute of Chartered Accountants in England and Wales, the Association of Chartered Certified Accountants, the Institute of Chartered Accountants of Scotland, the Institute of Chartered Accountants in Ireland, and the Association of Authorized Practitioners in Accounting.

Organization of the Accounting and Auditing Professions

Each of the five accounting bodies admits members on the basis of its own professional examinations, but none requires entrants to hold a university degree in accounting. Each requires specified professional experience as well as passing examinations. The AAPA represents auditors who qualified under earlier legislation: it no longer admits members. Currently, each auditing body runs its own disciplinary processes; a Joint Disciplinary Board, which investigates cases with high levels of public interest, is under review.

Constitution and Legal System

Common law jurisdiction, with no written constitution but statute, case, and common law components. Company law for the United Kingdom is the responsibility of the central government (Department of Trade and Industry), but newly reconstituted regional governments in Scotland, Wales, and Northern Ireland may acquire some powers to administer companies within their boundaries.

Currency

The pound sterling. The U.K. is not in the "first wave" of European Union countries adopting the common currency, the Euro, after January 2002.

Official Languages

English, and Welsh (within Wales)

UNITED KINGDOM

Michael J. Mumford
Lancaster University Management School
Lancaster, United Kingdom

1. Background

1.1. History: Development of Company Law from 1844

The use of companies in Britain grew substantially after the 1844 Companies Act made it easy to form a company by a simple process of registration. After the 1855 Joint Stock Companies Act, it became possible for the first time to form a company in which the stockholders enjoyed limited liability for the debts of the company. Major legislation was passed over subsequent years, so that by the early 1980s there were five major companies acts all in force, together with numerous other provisions.

In 1985 a new Companies Act consolidated current company law. This act is now the basic statute in the area, amended in significant ways by the 1989 Companies Act and by lesser provisions elsewhere. In the rest of this chapter, the 1985 and 1989 Companies Acts are usually referred to simply as "the 1985 act" and "the 1989 act," respectively. It is important to note that in Britain it is usual to refer to compliance as being in accordance with "the 1985 Companies Act," to include reference to subsequent amendments to that act, both in the form of statutes ("primary legislation") and also statutory instruments ("secondary legislation") that do not have to be fully debated by parliament. Several of these statutory instruments are referred to later in the chapter.

1.2 Explanatory Background to the Legal Authority of Standards

Britain has no written constitution. It is a common law jurisdiction, in which legal authority is based on (1) statutes (and statutory instruments), (2) decisions taken in the courts, and (3) a body of "common law," deemed to exist and be capable of recognition by the courts, even though it has not yet been stated authoritatively either orally or in writing.

To a large extent the regulations governing registered companies are framed in the Companies Acts (described further below).

On a number of questions affecting accountants, however, the law is not clear. The nature and authority of "generally accepted accounting principles" is a good example. The existence of accounting standards is recognized in Section 256 of the 1985 act, as amended by Section 19 of the 1989 act, which also empowers the relevant minister to prescribe regulations (by way of statutory instrument) to recognize standard-setting bodies. (The Department of Trade and Industry is the branch of government responsible for company policy.) It is reasonable to assume that accounting standards (analyzed in more detail in Section 1.4.2) constitute strong authority, but there has been no case law to test the matter. There is a further complication in that the courts concerned might differ in their views, depending on whether any legal action that might arise is brought within Britain or before the European Court of Justice. Different legal traditions of interpretation arise in each case.

This is all in contrast with the state of the law in the United States, where the Securities and Exchange Commission has the authority to lay down detailed rules for drawing up published accounts for listed companies. In Britain no such formal legal powers to lay down detailed accounting rules have been defined. Neither the Department of Trade and Industry nor the accounting profession sets accounting standards enforceable directly through the courts, even though departure from standards needs to be defended by the company concerned (see Section 1.4). Thus, the American term *Generally Accepted Accounting Principles* has a meaning that is more clearly defined than it is in Britain. Although the term *accounting principles* appears in the 1985 Companies Act, the expression *GAAP* has not been generally used in Britain until recently; the London office of Ernst and Young has published comprehensive surveys under the title "UK GAAP" since 1989—a 5th edition was published in 1997—and use of the term has grown among practitioners since then. Whereas certain provisions are laid down by law and by established practice, a great deal is left to the discretion of company directors to decide, usually on the advice of professional accountants.

In the mid-1990s, of the 1.3 million companies registered in Britain, the overwhelming majority are "private" companies (including some 600,000 that are "dormant"). There are only about 12,000 "public" companies, out of which about 3,000 are listed on the International Stock Exchange (as the London Stock Exchange is now known).

There is also a small number of companies formed by Royal Charter or by statute, but few of these are listed, and it is generally safe to treat them as being the same as registered public companies when it comes to accounting rules.

Registered companies are automatically "private" unless they meet the specific requirements that make them public. These are, basically, that the company's memorandum of association (the document that defines the existence of the company) states that it is to be a public company and that it has a share capital of not less than £50,000 (of which not less than £12,500 is to be paid up). Only public companies may have their securities listed; the minimum paid-up share capital of listed companies under current rules of the International Stock Exchange is £250,000.

Most of the material in this chapter is devoted to public companies, since these include all the companies whose securities are traded on the financial markets.

1.3 Accounting Standards: The Present Backing

The major accounting provisions of the 1985 Companies Act appear in Part VII of the act, in Sections 221–262. It is possible to read the original 1985 Companies Act without being aware of the changes made by the 1989 act.

The revised Section 262 (3), inserted into the 1985 act by Section 22 of the 1989 act (and expanded by paragraph 91 of Schedule 4) describes how "realized" profits and losses are to be defined in Part VII of the act and refers to "principles generally accepted," although it leaves this latter phrase undefined. The matter is significant for two reasons. One is that realized profits might well be regarded as more certain and hence more meaningful than conjectural unrealized profits; the other is that the law on distributable profits is defined in terms of what has been realized, and it excludes profits that have not been realized. This matter is alluded to again in Section 1.4.6, in the context of identifying the meaning of the phrase "true and fair view."

The 1989 act was the background for a new Financial Reporting Council with the duty of overseeing the work of its three offshoots: the Accounting Standards Board (ASB), which replaced the former ASC from June 1990, an Urgent Issues Task Force (UITF), and a Review Panel to consider departures from accounting standards and secure compliance (see Section 1.4 below). (The FRC was not actually stipulated in the 1989 act.)

The new Section 256(1), inserted by Section 19 of the 1989 act, contains the following provision in interpreting Part VII of the act (see Section 2.1 below):

> In this part "accounting standards" means statements of standard accounting practice issued by such body or bodies as may be prescribed by regulations.

Regulations laid down under the act have given the ASB this formal recognition, although in fact the ASB chose to use the name Financial Reporting Standards (FRS) in place of the former term Statements of Standard Accounting Practice (SSAP). It remains possible for the Secretary of State to increase the formal authority of the ASB, its UITF, and the Review Panel still further in the future, by way of Statutory Instruments (which, unlike Acts of Parliament, do not require full debate by both Houses of Parliament).

It is unclear from the statutes just what status is enjoyed by the set of SSAPs and FRSs (listed below), and how the status of SSAPs has been altered under the 1989 Companies Act (see Section 1.4.1 below). There are certainly cases in which the provisions of existing SSAPs seem to conflict with practices permitted by the Companies Acts, for example, in the valuation of inventories (see Section 3.10.1) where the act permits the use of methods that SSAP 9 forbids. Current standards also require far more disclosure than the act does (see, for example, the list in the second paragraph of Section 2.1.2).

1.4 The Accounting Standards Board, Urgent Issues Task Force, and Financial Reporting Review Panel

The former Accounting Standards Committee enjoyed a status that was loosely defined in company law. Created in 1970 as a result of financial scandals in the late 1960s, its major source of authority arose from its implicit recognition by law and from its position as a subcommittee of the Consultative Committee of Accountancy Bodies (the CCAB), comprising the six major U.K. professional accounting bodies. Its method of operation reflected this. The councils of each of the CCAB bodies had to adopt each SSAP before it could be issued in final form by the CCAB. It was up to the six bodies individually to enforce standards on their own members.

After the Dearing Report was issued in 1988, the government made major changes to the standard-setting process. An independent Financial Reporting Council was set up, consisting of about 30 members, each appointed in an individual capacity, of whom roughly half are from the accountancy profession and half from elsewhere, including government. Its members serve on a part-time basis, full meetings of the Council usually taking place twice a year. The executive functions are discharged by the ASB, the UITF, and the Review Panel.

The chairman and technical director of the ASB serve full time, together with a technical staff mainly on short-term contracts, and a further eight part-time members of the Board. The ASB has the authority to publish standards in its own name. Its due process includes publishing exposure drafts and standards for comment, often after a discussion paper. Although the CCAB bodies are invited to comment, they now have no veto. Enforcement is no longer left to the CCAB bodies.

The UITF is, constitutionally, a committee of the ASB. Its main role is "to assist the ASB in areas where an accounting standard or a Companies Act provision exists (including the requirement to give a true and fair view), but where unsatisfactory or conflicting interpretations have developed or seem likely to develop." The UITF forms a view within the framework of the law and existing ASB statements, and the stated views of the UITF are normally accepted by the ASB as having similar authority to its own. In case of any conflict, the ASB's views prevail.

The Financial Reporting Review Panel was set up one year later than the FRC and ASB with a view to strengthening the enforcement of standards. Its duties are outlined briefly at the end of the next section (Section 1.4.1).

Three features of the ASB's policies are worth particular note.

1. It has specifically stressed the need for accounting standards to lay down matters of principle rather than detailed legal prescriptions. It has also stated its wish to reduce the emphasis placed by analysts on a single "bottom line" accounting profit figure. (See also Section 1.4.6 on "Substance over Form"). One consequence of this is that it is more difficult to find exhaustive treatment of any individual reporting issue by reference to any single standard.

2. It has been working to develop an explicit "conceptual framework," unlike its predecessor the ASC, in the form of a "Statement of Principles" published in 1994. This has proved controversial, and it is discussed further in Section 4.1.8.

3. Greater distinction has come to be made, both in statute law and accounting standards, between larger and smaller companies. The old ASC held to the principle that disclosure standards might

reasonably distinguish between large and small companies on the basis of size criteria, but recognition and valuation principles were universal. The ASB has not accepted the latter principle, and it has always been more concerned with public, particularly listed, companies. It is possible that separate accounting principles will eventually develop for large and small companies, and a separate Financial Reporting Standard for Smaller Entities (FRSSE), and came into effect in 1997. Smaller entities might regard the FRSSE as a complete set of reporting requirements when in fact authoritative reference must still usually be made to the full standards for larger entities. (In fact, smaller entities must still comply with SSAP1 rather than FRS 9 for associates and joint ventures). This chapter is concerned almost entirely with larger companies, so the issue is not pursued further here.

1.4.1 The True and Fair View

It is considered important by the British accounting profession that Section 226(2) of the 1985 act specifies:

> The balance sheet shall give a true and fair view of the state of affairs of the company as at the end of the financial year; and the profit and loss account shall give a true and fair view of the profit or loss of the company for the financial year.

This implies that applying the generally accepted principles laid down in accounting standards may not be sufficient to provide the "true and fair view" as required by law. There clearly exists an overriding concept of the "true and fair view" which can be recognized and shown by the accounts quite distinctly from the result that arises when accepted accounting principles are applied, as laid down in Schedule 4 of the 1985 act. Section 226(4) reinforces this point:

> Where compliance with the provisions of that Schedule, and the other provisions of this Act as to the matters to be included in a company's individual accounts or in notes to those accounts, would not be sufficient to give a true and fair view, the necessary additional information shall be given in the accounts or in a note to them.

(Section 227 similarly requires group accounts to show a true and fair view of the affairs of the group.) Abstract 7 of the Urgent Issues Task

Force (1992) sets out the information that must be disclosed when a company invokes this provision of the 1985 act. What is lacking is guidance as to the criteria for defining such a "true and fair view," and for recognizing when it is lacking. Given that accepted accounting principles must be used in any case, why does the act anticipate that such principles might be insufficient, particularly when augmented by the "other matters" required by the Act, referred to in Section 226(4)?

In 1993 the ASB published its "Foreword to Accounting Standards," which contains the statement (paragraph 16):

> Accounting standards are authoritative statements of how particular types of transaction and other events should be reflected in financial statements and accordingly compliance with accounting standards will normally be necessary for financial statements to give a true and fair view.

In an appendix to this foreword, an opinion of leading counsel (Hon. Mrs. Justice Arden) sets out her support for this statement, although it is made plain that the final arbiter must still be the court. There has still been no case to test the court's view since the 1989 Companies Act established the FRC and its satellite bodies. But as Judge Arden points out in her opinion, there is an increasingly strong presumption that since 1989 all accounts that comply with standards present a true and fair view, and any departure requires specific justification. She quotes Schedule 4 paragraph 36A of the 1985 act (as amended by the 1989 act):

> It shall be stated whether the accounts have been prepared in accordance with applicable accounting standards and particulars of any material departure from those standards and the reasons for it shall be given.

Clearly the Review Panel reviews cases of noncompliance that come before it. It is specifically authorized to do so by the Secretary of State under the (revised) 1985 act. Some of these cases it identifies for itself (usually as a result of qualified audit reports or reported nondisclosure in company statements themselves), but more often they are referred to the Review Panel by individual or corporate third parties (including press commentators). Before the FRRP was established, pressure on accountants to conform with standards came from the possibility of a court action, say against the auditor for negligence following insolvency of the company. Setting up the Review Panel in 1992 added a powerful new force for compliance, but it only reviews the accounts of listed companies. The Review Panel has powers to act as a form of quasi-judicial tribunal. In most cases it discusses matters privately with the company concerned rather than calling upon its formal powers to refer the matter to the Secretary of State or to the courts with a request that the court should order the defective accounts to be corrected (under Section 245 of the 1985 act). On the minority of occasions when the Review Panel has made a public statement on a concluded case, the company concerned has always complied with the panel's suggested treatment, and reference to the court has not been necessary (although it has been threatened more than once). Since 1993, the panel has been more explicit in its public statements about the precise section of the 1985 Companies Act or the accounting standard at issue. Half a dozen of the FRRP Press Notices (now approximately 50 in number) describe procedural issues, but the great majority present a summary of a contentious accounting issue, and they name the company concerned.

1.4.2 Statements of Standard Accounting Practice (SSAPs) and Financial Reporting Standards (FRSs)

Accounting principles evolve over time, and there is always the likelihood that new financial conditions and problems will arise in the future for which existing accounting principles present no satisfactory treatment. The need for SSAPs 4, 5, 8, 11, 20, 21, and 24 (listed below) all arose from changes in the business environment. Moreover, current accounting conventions exclude many aspects of economic importance to the business, such as the state of its order book, the technical knowledge of its staff and their ideas for new products, markets, and processes, potential sources of credit, and so on. Businesses are too complex for it to be possible to report every aspect of their affairs, particularly in the context of highly aggregated sets of accounts, but this fact makes it impossible to prescribe exactly what matters will be significant to readers from one year to the next. Hence, it is not possible to lay down exactly what will be necessary to convey a true and fair view.

Even though the precise legal status of SSAPs and FRSs is unclear, they are extensively used by company directors in preparing their accounts and by their professional staff, advisers, and auditors. Auditors also have a set of "accepted auditing standards," laid down by the CCAB Auditing Practices Board (although, just as with *GAAP*, the term *GAAS*, widely used in the United States, is not normally used in Britain). These auditing standards mainly describe established ways of handling difficult decisions that face auditors. As valuable as they are as a guide to auditor behavior, accepted auditing standards tend to leave to SSAPs and FRSs the resolution of many of the more difficult conceptual questions, such as "How does the realization principle work in this unfamiliar context?", "What is profit?", "How should joint costs be allocated and matched against revenues?", and "How should new financial instruments be accounted for?"

The list of SSAPs issued in Britain between 1970 and 1990 and FRSs since 1990 is a useful guide to those issues that accountants have needed to address as problem areas (see Table 1 for a list of current standards and Table 2 for a list of complementary publications).

1.4.3 EU Directives

The company law directives of the European Union have been adopted in British company law as they have fallen due. Britain claims a good record of compliance; thus, the Second Directive was implemented in the 1980 Companies Act, the Fourth Directive in the 1981 Companies Act, the Seventh and Eighth Directives in the 1989 Companies Act, and various other provisions have been made elsewhere to anticipate directives while they were still in draft form. Thus, the Eleventh Directive (on branch accounts) laid down new rules for the reporting of the U.K. activities of oversea companies, in force since January 1993. Britain tends to view corporate financial reporting rather differently than do some other European countries, taking a view much more similar to that in the United States, Canada, and Australia. Different philosophical traditions underlie the mainland European and international debates, although a degree of common understanding has grown over the years through such forums as the OECD Working Group on Accounting Standards and the European Accounting Federation (FEE).

The IASC (and its parent, the International Federation of Accountants, IFAC) tend, like British standard-setters, to take a utilitarian view of accounting disclosure, in which published company accounts are seen as having a particularly important role to play in financial markets; equity capital is typically raised through the stock market, rather than through investment bankers, and the need for price-sensitive information to be published accurately and rapidly to all potential market transactors underlies much of the Anglo-American thinking about disclosure. Pressure for International Accounting Standards (IASs) is seen to originate largely from the perceived need for investors in worldwide securities markets to

TABLE 1: *SSAPs and FRSs Issued 1970–1998*

SSAP 1*   Associated companies
SSAP 2   Disclosure of accounting policies
SSAP 3   Earnings per share
SSAP 4   The accounting treatment of government grants
SSAP 5   Accounting for value added tax
SSAP 6*   Extraordinary items and prior year adjustments
SSAP 7*   Accounting for changes in the purchasing power of money
SSAP 8   The treatment of taxation under the imputation system
SSAP 9   Stocks and long-term contracts
SSAP 10* Statements of source and application of funds
SSAP 11* Accounting for deferred tax
SSAP 12   Accounting for depreciation
SSAP 13   Accounting for research and development
SSAP 14* Group accounts
SSAP 15   Accounting for deferred taxation
SSAP 16* Current cost accounting
SSAP 17   Accounting for post balance sheet events
SSAP 18   Accounting for contingencies
SSAP 19   Accounting for investment properties
SSAP 20   Foreign currency translation
SSAP 21   Accounting for leases and hire purchase contracts
SSAP 22* Accounting for goodwill
SSAP 23* Accounting for acquisitions and mergers
SSAP 24   Accounting for pensions costs
SSAP 25   Segmental reporting
FRS 1   Cash flow statements
FRS 2   Accounting for subsidiary undertakings
FRS 3   Reporting financial performance
FRS 4   Capital instruments
FRS 5   Reporting the substance of transactions
FRS 6   Acquisitions and mergers
FRS 7   Fair values in acquisition accounting
FRS 8   Related party disclosures
FRS 9   Associates and joint ventures
FRS 10   Goodwill and intangible assets
FRSSE   Financial Reporting Standard for Smaller Entities

* Note: SSAPs 1, 6, 7, 10, 11, 14, 16, 22 and 23 are no longer in force; several other standards (such as FRS 1) have been amended since their first publication.

TABLE 2: *UITF Abstracts, Financial Reporting Exposure Drafts (FREDs), and Other ASB Papers Issued 1970–1998*

UITF Abstract 4   Presentation of long-term debtors in current assets (1992)
UITF Abstract 5   Transfers from current assets to fixed assets (1992)
UITF Abstract 6   Accounting for post-retirement benefits other than pensions (1992)
UITF Abstract 7   True and fair view override disclosures (1992)
UITF Abstract 9   Accounting for operations in hyper-inflationary economies (1993)
UITF Abstract 10 Disclosure of directors' share options (1994)
UITF Abstract 11 Capital instruments: issue call options (1994)
UITF Abstract 12 Lessee accounting for reverse premiums & similar incentives (1994)
UITF Abstract 13 Accounting for ESOP trusts (1995)
UITF Abstract 14 Disclosure of changes in accounting policy (1995)
UITF Abstract 15 Disclosure of substantial acquisitions (1996)
UITF Abstract 16 Income and expense subject to non-standard rates of tax (1997)
UITF Abstract 17 Employee share schemes (1997)
UITF Abstract 18 Pensions costs following the 1997 tax changes in respect of dividend income (1997)
UITF Abstract 19 Tax on gains and losses on foreign currency borrowings that hedge an investment in a foreign enterprise (1998)
UITF Abstract 20 Year 2000 issues: accounting and disclosures (1998)
UITF Abstract 21 Accounting issues arising from the proposed introduction of the euro (1998)

ASB papers that lack the force of standards:

FRED 13   Derivatives and other financial instruments: disclosures
FRED 13
(supplement) Derivatives and other financial instruments: disclosures by banks and similar institutions
FRED 14   Provisions and contingencies
FRED 15   Impairment of fixed assets and goodwill
FRED 16   Earnings per share
FRED 17   Measurement of tangible fixed assets
Operating and financial review
Interim reports
Exposure draft statement on preliminary announcements

---

be able to make comparisons among companies reporting under different disclosure regulations.

1.4.4 The British Auditing Profession

The legal framework that regulates the auditing profession in Britain is set out in the 1985 Companies Act, Part XI, Chapter V (i.e., Sections 384–394) as amended by the 1989 Companies Act, Part II (i.e., Sections 24–54).

There are six major professional bodies of accountants, which co-ordinate many of their activities through a voluntary joint committee formed in 1970, the Consultative Committee of Accountancy Bodies (CCAB). The six tend to have different functional specialties, histories, and training traditions.

The authority to sign audit reports is restricted to those members of the ICAEW, ACCA, ICAS, and ICAI (see Table 3) who hold practicing certificates from their professional bodies. Individuals and firms that meet the requirements to act as auditors are called "Registered Auditors," and they are supervised by their respective professional bodies.

Attempts to rationalize the British accountancy profession have been made ever since professional bodies first appeared in the nineteenth century. Many mergers have taken place, but an attempt to merge the six main bodies failed in 1970, after which the CCAB was itself formed to help produce some unity of purpose and policy. Other attempts since 1970 to merge some or all of the bodies have also so far failed.

From an auditing perspective, the most important CCAB committees have been the Accounting Standards Committee (until superseded by the Accounting Standards Board, which stands outside the accounting profession) and the Auditing Practices Board (APB, the status of which as an independent body is less autonomous than that of the ASB, since its business is more specifically concerned with the technical performance of auditors). The APB is likely to be obliged at some stage by the government to become independent.

Relations are close and amicable between the Accounting Standards Board and the Auditing Practices Board and their respective international counterparts, the International Accounting Standards Committee and the International Auditing Practices Committee. Care is taken to ensure consistency, whenever possible, between the standards that they each produce, although there are differences on some issues (such as deferred

TABLE 3   *CCAB Bodies Showing Those Qualified to Audit under the Companies Acts*

Name	Membership	Audit?
Institute of Chartered Accountants in England and Wales	125,000	Yes
Association of Chartered Certified Accountants	62,000	Yes
Chartered Institute of Management Accountants	44,000	No
Institute of Chartered Accountants of Scotland	14,000	Yes
Institute of Chartered Accountants in Ireland	9,000	Yes
Chartered Institute of Public Finance and Accountancy	11,000	No

taxation, see Section 3.11). Where conflict arises, the U.K. accounting and auditing standards prevail in Britain.

Despite some debate over the subject, the standard form of audit report in Britain takes a short form, generally just stating the basis for the audit opinion and confirming that the audit has been completed in accordance with auditing standards, that corporate governance arrangements are in line with the recommendations of the Cadbury Report (see Section 1.4.7), and that the accounts show a true and fair view of the state of affairs of the company at its balance sheet date and of the profits for the period then ended. Statements are published both by the auditors and by the directors setting out their respective responsibilities in respect of the accounts. (Examples are shown with the accounts of Bunzl plc on pages XXX–XXX)

The question of the legal liability of the auditor is contentious. Although the audit report is presented by the auditors to the shareholders in general meeting, and attached to the annual report and accounts circulated and published, the auditor is in a contractual relationship only with the company and owes a common law duty of care to the shareholders only as a class. This still raises the possibility that the auditor owes a wider duty of care to other parties, although it appears that the courts take a narrow view. The subject is highly controversial, however, and the legal position is still not fully resolved.

1.4.5 Company Finance and the Stock Market

The main source of finance of British companies is retained earnings. The proportion of new capital raised from this source tends to vary with the state of the economy, but in aggregate it constitutes about 65% of the capital sources shown on corporate balance sheets. Long-term finance tends to come from stockholders, either from the proceeds of new stock issues or in the form of retained profits. Short-term finance tends to come from the banking sector. Banks in Britain have been reluctant to take major equity holdings ever since the collapse of the City of Glasgow Bank in 1878, in contrast to the investment banking traditions of Japan and continental Europe. The banking sector is highly developed, with well-traded markets for all forms of security.

The heavy reliance of British companies on the stock market for long-term finance has resulted in a strong emphasis on published financial information for the use of investors. Unlike the United States, where the SEC has a prime responsibility to protect the interests of stock market investors, financial markets in Britain are largely self-regulating. The International Stock Exchange, like most of the other markets, is constituted as a private body run by its own membership, in this case the brokers who deal in stocks and shares. Whereas the government takes a close interest in the operations of financial markets, this is mainly channeled through the Bank of England, which as the government's banker has a special responsibility for financial affairs, playing an important role informally in overseeing self-regulation. Thus, the Accounting Standards Board reports to a Financial Reporting Council (the FRC), and it is quite natural for appointments to the chair of the FRC to be nominated jointly by the Governor of the Bank of England and the Secretary of State for Trade and Industry.

The Stock Exchange itself takes responsibility in Britain for supervising the rules for listing securities, which include the procedures for admission to listing and continuing obligations to regulate the conduct of companies after listing. The main source of information is the Stock Exchange "Yellow Book" a loose-leaf book that is updated at frequent and irregular intervals (for example, in October 1995 and again in 1997 to require further disclosures of directors' pensions entitlements). The Stock Exchange is also one of the leading supporters of the City of London's "Panel on Take-overs and Mergers," whose offices are located in the Exchange and which publishes the "City Code on Take-overs and Mergers." The

Stock Exchange is concerned to ensure that price-sensitive information about listed securities is made publicly available to all parties promptly, fairly, and accurately. Because this clearly includes accounting information, Stock Exchange requirements must be heeded in the case of listed companies, alongside statute law and FRC regulations. Stock Exchange requirements may go beyond the others, for example, the Yellow Book required the publication of half-yearly (unaudited) accounts covering the 6 months of each financial year well before the ASB laid down its own requirements to do so. (Some U.K. companies publish quarterly accounts on a voluntary basis, usually those that have an American listing: in such cases, the 20F form required by the SEC typically provides a fuller picture than the domestic set of accounts and has the advantage of being clearly based on historical cost rules, rather than the eclectic mixture of valuations often used in Britain.)

Although the Stock Exchange plays an important role in the regulation of listed companies, it has acquired a reputation for inactivity in enforcing accounting standards. Companies listed in the United Kingdom can at present file accounts with the Stock Exchange even though they do not comply fully with SSAPs and FRSs and lack a clean audit report. This contrasts with SEC practice in the United States, which would not accept accounts for filing if either condition were not fulfilled.

1.4.6 Substance over Form

There has long been conflict between substance and form in British corporate reporting, particularly in respect of off-balance-sheet financing. To some degree the conflict is between the legal and accounting professions, with the lawyers tending to look to strict legal form and the accountants looking to substance. While it is beyond doubt that the courts have the authority to decide what is meant by a "true and fair" view in any particular set of circumstances, in practical terms it is mainly left to accountants to develop and apply the relevant rules, and it is clear that the ASB regards the exercise of professional judgment in relation to accounts to rest with the accounting profession rather than lawyers (a view exemplified in the treatment of assets in FRS 5).

Thus, while the law insists that distributions can be made only out of "realized" profits, it is in practice left to accountants to decide what realization is to mean. Thus, for example, it seems to be legitimate for a company to realize profits on an asset by selling it to another company in the same group—perhaps a subsidiary—provided that there is a genuine transaction at no more than a fair market price. (Note that for the purposes of determining distributable profits it is the accounts of the individual company that matter, not group accounts. Unrealized intergroup profits must still be removed from group accounts. Thus, the parent company may be able in principle to declare dividends larger than reported group profits.)

Taxation plays a much looser role in relation to published company accounts in Britain than it does in most other European countries. The income figures that appear in published accounts are regarded by the Inland Revenue as the starting point for adjustments to arrive at the taxable profit. It is virtually impossible to reconcile, by using the information provided in published accounts, the amount of a company's current tax charge with its reported profit figures. This dispariaty is widening as U.K. companies are encouraged to report unrealized holding gains.

It used to be thought that taxation was an area in which form always dominated over substance, so that the strict letter of the law could be relied upon to prevail. However, the courts have held that transactions that were set up merely as devices to avoid tax could be set aside by looking through the form to the underlying purpose. The application of the principle of substance over form to tax matters has since been questioned, however, and there exists an uneasy tension in this area.

1.4.7 *The Cadbury Report on the Financial Aspects of Corporate Governance, the Hampel Report, and the Greenbury Report*

The Cadbury Committee (so named after its chairman, Sir Adrian Cadbury) was set up in May 1991 by the FRC and the accountancy profession, together with the Stock Exchange, to review "the financial aspects of corporate governance," with specific reference to listed companies. Its final report in December 1992 set out a 19-point Code of Best Practice. From mid-1993 it became mandatory under the Stock Exchange Listing Agreement for reporting companies to state their compliance with the Code and explain any noncompliance; auditors "review" compliance with these requirements in areas in which relatively objective evidence can be secured. The Code includes the following main provisions: companies were to establish effective audit committees within 2 years; directors' contracts were to be limited to a maximum of 3 years; interim reports were to be expanded to include balance sheets, and were to be subject to "review" by the auditors (not a full audit); nonaudit fees paid to auditors were to be disclosed and rotation of audit partners formalized to increase independence; and directors were to publish a statement each year declaring that the company's system of internal control is sound and that the company is a going concern. Emphasis was placed in particular on the role of nonexecutive directors (at least three) to act as independent monitors of board performance, with special responsibilities for the nomination of directors, remuneration, and the audit committee.

It was always the intention of the Cadbury Committee that its recommendations should be reviewed after 3 years, and this review was published by Sir Ronnie Hampel in 1997. The Hampel Report confirmed that the Cadbury recommendations were, in the main, working adequately, but it also expressed doubts about the desirability of applying a uniform set of governance rules to all listed companies.

Meanwhile, considerable public disquiet had been expressed about the remuneration packages awarded to the directors of newly privatized utilities, largely still in the same posts they had held before privatization but now being paid several times as much for similar duties. In response, a committee was set up in 1995 under the chairmanship of Sir Richard Greenbury to examine whether directors should be more more accountable to stockholders. The Greenbury report recommended considerable extension to disclosure requirements, particularly in the areas of directors' pension entitlements and stock options (both of which had been left largely undisclosed previously). The Stock Exchange Yellow Book was updated, making demands for fuller disclosures from listed companies as from mid-1997.

1.4.8 The Draft ASB Statement of Principles

Right from its earliest days, the Accounting Standards Board expressed its intention to publish a conceptual framework document setting out the basic assumptions underlying its standards. It chose to call this document its "Statement of Principles," and draft chapters appeared at intervals between 1991 and 1994. The first chapter published was Chapter 6, "Presentation of Financial Statements," which invited comments on a proposed form of layout even before the elements of financial statements had been defined or the underlying principles revealed. FRS 3, embodying the material of Chapter 6, was adopted by the ASB in December 1992.

This pattern has been repeated several times, with draft chapters of the Statement of Principles being published to coincide with FRSs that implement the principles that the chapters contained. The full draft Statement of Principles was not published as a single document until November 1995, when it incorporated some important changes to the earlier drafts. Public responses to the full draft were mainly unfavorable, and the ASB published a "progress paper" in July 1996, which claimed that its earlier proposals had been widely misunderstood.

The stated objectives of the Statement of Principles are (a) to assist the ASB in reviewing existing statements and developing future standards, (b) to help to reduce the number of alternative accounting treatments, (c) to assist the preparers and auditors of financial statements and (d) to assist the users in interpreting the information contained in the financial statements.

The Statement of Principles is not, and does not replace, any specific accounting standard. It consists of seven chapters, on

- Objectives of financial statements, where the needs of the various user groups are discussed
- Qualitative characteristics of financial information, which outlines primary or relevant characteristics and secondary characteristics that include comparability and understandability
- Elements of financial statements, where the essential components of each statement are identified
- Recognition, which outlines criteria for inclusion of items in the financial statements
- Measurement in financial statements, which deals with the method of valuation of assets and discusses various bases
- Presentation of financial information, which reinforces the need for a structured presentation that takes into consideration the level of detail presented
- The reporting entity, where the principles largely mirror the existing provisions of FRS 2 for the accounting treatment of subsidiary companies.

It is clear that the ASB is building on a line of conceptual thinking that stresses user needs for information that is "decision relevant."

The main points contained in the draft Statement of Principles are in fact based on the Financial Accounting Standards Board's conceptual framework study, as set out in particular in SFACs 1, 2, 5, and 6. There are close similarities, too, with the IASC's 1989 "Framework for the Preparation and Presentation of Financial Statements." The ASB was apparently much keener than either the FASB or the IASC on the adoption of current values for financial reporting, on measures to broaden the definitions of assets and (particularly) liabilities, and on the use of a Statement of Total Recognized Gains and Losses (STRGL) to report holding gains as well as operating gains and to lessen the attention paid to a single "bottom line" income figure. The ASB is much readier to encourage the adoption of discounting in financial statements, by the use of measures reflected subsequently in FASB's draft SFAC of June 1997. The ASB is also bolder in its determination to view income as the difference between the opening and closing net assets on the balance sheet, rather than accepting its conventional form as realized revenues less the costs of producing those revenues.

Although previously there has been no explicit conceptual framework in the United Kingdom, SSAP 2 and the Companies Act both endorsed the concepts of going concern, accruals (with cost matching), consistency, and prudence, all within a framework that permits either historical or current costs (see Section 3). U.K. practice has always been to permit revaluation of fixed assets when their recorded book value has been demonstrably different from any reasonable view of their current value.

The implicit rationale for this is to be found in the concept of "mean square error." This aggregates bias and variance—bias arising from reporting values that differ from those expected by readers of the accounts, and variance among the measures that arise from applying any particular measurement system. Thus, high levels of inflation produce high bias, which may outweigh the variance, and justify revaluing assets even though these current values are rather uncertain and arbitrary.

FRS 3, "Reporting Financial Performance," (1992) seeks to limit the profit and loss account to reporting operating income, as far as possible excluding holding gains on fixed assets that accrued in previous periods. The STRGL is intended to report holding gains on fixed assets, while separate statements will reconcile opening and closing shareholders' funds and show, in a separate note, historical cost profits and losses if current values have been used elsewhere in the accounts.

1.4.9 ASB Responses to Current Institutional Pressures

Recent pressure on reporting entities includes the need to disclose results that depend on particularly close relationships with external parties. FRS

8, "Related Parties," was published in October 1995, and this requires disclosure of the existence and general nature of dealings that do not reflect arm's length commercial relationships.

The challenge of accounting for complex financial instruments faces standard setters throughout the world. The ASB has urged experimentation with the use of current values for all financial instruments, which it defines broadly as: "any contract that gives rise to both a financial asset of one entity and a financial liability or equity instrument of another entity." This would extend quite considerably the principle of *marking to market*, which has already come into accepted practice in reporting the valuation of financial assets traded on active markets (despite ambiguity as to whether the gains and losses are to be treated as realized), and the proposals go much further than FASB's stop-gap SFAS-107 and 119, and its June 1996 exposure draft on accounting for derivatives.

As elsewhere in the ASB's program, it is increasingly difficult to find in any one place definitive rules to resolve any individual problem. Thus, the ASB's analysis of financial instruments tends to overlap with its discussions elsewhere of the general nature of assets and liabilities. In the absence of an accepted conceptual framework document, this means that understanding the ASB's proposals for accounting for financial instruments requires a review of FRS 5, "Reporting the Substance of Transactions" (1994), including the definition given there of assets as: "rights or other access to future economic benefits controlled by an entity as a result of past transactions or events," and of liabilities as: "obligations of an entity to transfer economic benefits as a result of past transactions or events." Both these resemble FASB definitions, but both are weakened by lack of any definitions of the terms "rights," "obligations," "transactions," and "events."

The main features of FRS 5 are its reliance on the principle that a transaction should be reported according to its *commercial effect in practice*; its definitions of rules for recognition, derecognition, and "partial derecognition"; its concern in particular with combating off balance sheet financing; and its specific attention (through Application Notes) to consignment stock, sale and repurchase agreements, debt factoring, asset securitization, and loan transfers. A further feature is its acceptance that liabilities may, under specific circumstances, be shown on the face of the balance sheet as a deduction from the assets to which they relate ("linked presentation"), recognizing that it is rare for any particular linkage to be possible between individual assets and liabilities. Thus, in-substance defeasance would be treated in this way, unless both the asset and the liability were entirely derecognized by the company with no residual rights or obligations. FRS 5 also extended the definition of subsidiary companies, by defining a new class of "quasi subsidiaries." The general requirement under FRS 5 is that transactions should be disclosed in enough detail to make sense of their underlying economic effect: in practice, there often remains considerable doubt as to what that effect may be.

2. The Form and Content of Published Financial Statements

2.1 Companies Act Schedules and "Formats"

The 1985 Companies Act, Part VII (Sections 221–262 of the act) provides regulations governing accounts and audit. The 1989 Companies Act, Part I (Sections 1–23) amends the 1985 act in some important ways.

Schedules 4–10 of the 1985 act, amended quite extensively by the 1989 act, are printed at the end of the act and set out further details of the requirements. Note that the schedules are still known by the numbers given to them by the 1985 act, even though they have been amended by the 1989 act.

2.1.1 Schedule 4 Formats

Schedule 4 of the 1985 act lays down formats (as prescribed by the European Fourth and Seventh Directives on Company Law) for the presentation of the balance sheet and profit and loss account, as discussed below.

The Balance Sheet   The schedule contains two alternative formats for the balance sheet, which differ in order. Format 1 is designed for the presentation of a balance sheet in vertical form, beginning (in contrast with American practice) with fixed assets and continuing with current assets before deducting external liabilities and provisions to produce the components of stockholders' equity. Format 2 is designed for the older two-sided form of presentation, which in Britain traditionally presented liabilities on the left and assets on the right. It is now rarely used, but assets now appear on the left and liabilities on the right. There is little difference in content except for the way that Format 1 separates into different places the creditors falling due within one year from those falling due in one year or more.

The Profit and Loss Account   The four alternative profit and loss account formats also differ according to whether they present a vertical or two-sided format. Directors may choose freely between the formats, two of these present a functional analysis of cost and revenue headings as well as showing a separate figure for gross profit, while the other two analyze the types of expenditure. The latter layout is used by Bunzl plc in the illustrative set of accounts shown at the end of this chapter, with the information divided between the consolidated profit and loss account and the notes to the accounts (particularly Note 2 "Net Operating Charges").

2.1.2 Group Accounts

Section 277 of the 1985 Companies Act, amended by Section 5 of the 1989 act, requires that any parent company shall, as well as preparing individual accounts, prepare group accounts. These comprise a consolidated balance sheet dealing with the state of affairs of the parent company and its subsidiary undertakings and also a consolidated profit and loss account dealing with the profit and loss of the parent company and its subsidiary undertakings. It is also required by FRS 1 (although not by law) to present a group cash flow statement. Under Section 5(4), however, the parent company does not usually need to publish its own separate profit and loss account but merely the consolidated profit and loss account. Small companies are exempt from the need to prepare group accounts under Section 248 of the 1985 act.

For a group, then, the current position is that disclosures that conform with ASB standards as well as the 1985 act will need to include

- A consolidated balance sheet and notes of the parent company and its subsidiaries
- A consolidated profit and loss account and related notes of the parent and its subsidiaries
- A group cash flow statement and its notes
- A group statement of total recognized gains and losses (although under current practice this typically comprises only foreign exchange gains and losses)

- A note of the historical cost profits and losses of the group
- A group reconciliation of movements in parent company shareholders' funds
- The balance sheet and profit of the parent company, together with notes.

Only the first two and the last of these items are required by the 1985 companies act.

The 1989 Companies Act (elaborated in some areas by FRSs 2 and 5) significantly altered the definition of the terms *parent* and *subsidiary*. The usual rule under the old legislation was that a company was a parent if it owned more than 50% of the shares in another company, its subsidiary. There was also an alternative rule that made it a parent if it was a member of the subsidiary and controlled the composition of its board of directors, even though it did not own more than 50% of its shares. Shares in the subsidiary that are not owned by the parent company are described as the "minority interest." Under the new legislation, the rules were extended. Now the law relates to "undertakings" that might include not only companies but also unincorporated entities. Moreover, the main criterion is now whether control is exercised. It is even possible for a parent undertaking to own no shares at all in the subsidiary (e.g., where it controls shares through a trust), and this requires the inclusion of the subsidiary in consolidated accounts even though no income comes directly to the parent. (This makes the use of the term *minority* to describe the outside shareholding rather odd, since here the "minority" would own all of the shares.)

When a company does not exercise control over another undertaking but still exercises a significant influence over it, the relationship may well give the company a "participating interest" under Section 22 of the 1989 act. Since 1970 there has been a requirement under SSAP 1 for "associated companies" to be treated differently from subsidiaries and from other investments in shares. These former rules are now reflected closely in the 1985 Companies Act, but the term *associated company* is replaced by the term *related company*, and since 1989 by *related undertaking*. Confusingly, the term *associates* is still used in the accounting standards (such as FRS 9, "Associates and Joint Ventures"). The participating interest is presumed to arise where a company owns 20% or more of the shares in another undertaking. (Because it is described as having shares, this suggests the other undertaking is a company, but a partnership, for example, could also have shares.)

There are thus three tiers of intercompany investment: (a) where a company owns a controlling interest in a subsidiary; (b) where it holds a participating interest and exercises significant influence over an associate; and (c) where it holds an interest too small to give it significant influence.

As stated above, Case (a) normally leads to the preparation of consolidated accounts, and is discussed in Section 3.2 below. Cases (b) and (c) are discussed in more detail in Section 3.10 below.

2.1.3 Additional Statements Required by FRS 3, and the "Operating and Financial Review"

FRS 3 seeks to make the income statement more informative. Not only does it require a fuller analysis of the results from continuing operations distinct from discontinued operations, but it also requires presentation of a "Statement of Total Recognized Gains and Losses" (to eliminate movements direct to reserves, by-passing the income statement), a "Note of Historical Cost Profits and Losses" (where any assets or liabilities are carried at values different from historical cost), and a "Reconciliation of Movements in Shareholders' Funds." It is not clear what actually constitutes the financial performance of the company, despite the title of FRS 3, since the new statements are intended to include various gains and losses that are by no stretch of the imagination results of managerial performance. Thus, if the directors report holdings gains in the financial statements, these are more likely to reflect external movements in the market prices of assets (and, perhaps, liabilities) than anything the company has achieved by its own efforts. The former rule required holding gains to be reported in profits once they had been realized, which at least reflected managerial decisions to sell the assets concerned (or pay off the liabilities).

Since publication of the Cadbury Report, the ASB has required listed companies to include a yearly Operating and Financial Review, somewhat similar to the Management Discussion and Analysis required in the United States.

2.2 A Specimen Set of Published Financial Statements

Shown on pages 1220-1250 is a specimen set of accounts for a British company, Bunzl plc, for the year ended December 31, 1993. These are preceded by a directors' report, presenting certain information required by the 1985 Companies Act. The statutory accounts comprise the group's consolidated profit and loss account, group balance sheet and group cash flow statement, the statement of total recognized gains, the note of historical cost profits, the reconciliation of movements in shareholders' funds, the parent company's own balance sheet, the statement of accounting policies, and notes to the accounts. There then follows a list of principal subsidiaries and associated undertakings, the statement of directors' responsibilities, the auditors' report, and (not reproduced) the report of the remuneration committee (required by the Stock Exchange listing agreement, following the recommendations of the Greenbury Report). There is, finally, a 5 year financial summary (common but not obligatory). Blunzl plc does not have a listing in the United States; however, it has a number of U.S. investors and so it also shows its consolidated profit and loss account and balance sheet converted into U.S. dollars. Because there is no new information, however, since these are prepared under U.K. generally accepted accounting principles, these are not reproduced here.

2.3   Main Features of the 1997 Bunzl Accounts

The set of accounts reproduced comprises most of the information contained in Bunzl's published 1997 "Directors' Report and Accounts." Not shown is the companion document, Bunzl's 1997 "Annual Review and Summary Financial Statement," which includes the Chairman's Statement, reviews by the chief executives reponsible for the four principal operating divisions (named in the segmental report, Note 1 to the accounts), a "Financial Review," and summary financial accounts with a separate auditor's report. With the exception of the last two items, these make up the "Operating and Financial Review" (OFR) of the company, required by the Stock Exchange but not by the 1985 act. Bunzl sends the annual review to all its stockholders, but warns that it "does not contain sufficient information to allow for a full understanding of the results of the Group and state of affairs of the Company or the Group." Some information in the annual review does not appear in the full accounts, of course; they are best read together.

   Thus, the financial review comments on several matters that are not discernable from the accounts, including a comment that "The tax charge of £44.6m represents an effective rate of 35.0% on underlying operations, the same as in 1996, and includes a charge of £1.3m on the profit on sale of discontinued operations. The overall effective rate was 35.4%. This is higher than the nominal rate UK tax rate of 31.5% principally because most of the Group's operations are in countries with higher tax rates." It is also noted that "The Group is funded by a mixture of five and seven year multi-currency committed credit facilities from 11 banks totalling £324.2m of which £110.3m was drawn down at the year end. These facilities mature between 2001 and 2003." Such details are not required by law or by standards, but this is just the sort of background that companies are urged to disclose in their OFR. There is also information on Bunzl's hedging of foreign currency positions.

The group accounts show 1997 to have been a good year, with turnover from continuing operations higher by 9% on 1996, despite the strength of the pound sterling, and operating profit from continuing operations up by a similar percentage. Profit for the financial year has risen a little faster, at 10%, while earnings per share are up from 16.4p to 17.9p.

During 1997, Bunzl made some substantial acquisitions, mainly paid for by cash. Details are set out in Note 28. Group borrowings rose as a result from £42.5 million to £118.5 million and gearing (leverage) from 14.8% to 53.2%, according to the chairman's statement; these figures cannot be seen from the accounts.

One of the major features of FRS 3, "Reporting Financial Performance," was its stress on the need to separate the results of continuing operations (including acquisitions) in the income sttements from those of discontinued operations. One effect of this has been to remove some substantial amounts of past turnover and profits from the 5-year analysis. In the case of Bunzl, the trend of sales, in particular, is markedly different, depending upon whether "total sales" or "continuing" sales are observed. For example, the 1993 sales figure of £1,519.5 million as reported in the 1993 accounts (and shown in the 2nd edition of this *Guide*) now appears as including £453.4 million of sales derived from what by 1997 were discontinued operations.

Dividends have been raised from 6.3p per share in 1996 to 6.8p in 1997. There is no requirement to publish a figure showing the maximum amount that legally can be paid out by way of dividend. Company law is complex in this area, but it is important to bear in mind that distributable profits are defined on the basis of the accounts of the company that pays the dividend and not the consolidated accounts of the group. Thus, Note 19 indicates accumulated retained group profits of £146.8 million at the end of 1997, but the parent company Bunzl plc shows £118.6 million (of which £6.8 million is described as not being available for distribution). Dividends of £30.7 million paid and proposed by Bunzl for the year are well covered by the profit attributable to shareholders of the company of £42.0 million for the year (at the foot of the note). Note 19 also comments that a separate "special reserve" of £177.2 million in the parent company balance sheet is not distributable; this apparently arose from cancelling the share premium in 1987 and 1988 once the 1985 act permitted Section 131 merger relief (see Section 3.1.4).

Note 19 also shows a debit balance of £90.4 million within group reserves under the heading "merger reserve." £117.8 million has been written off during 1997 in respect of goodwill on acquisitions made during the year. Note 28 shows that two thirds of this figure arose from the purchases of AFC and GSS. To date there is no obligation for purchased goodwill to be written off against revenue earnings. Note 19 observes that in total £322.6 million goodwill has been written off by the end of 1997, and it is safe to assume that this has been charged against reserves rather than profits. The financial review comments: "The Group will adopt FRS 10 concerning the treatment of goodwill in the 1998 accounts," so future acquisitions will be affected by the need to amortize goodwill against earnings.

It is worth noting that British practice is to show dividends declared in the year (out of earnings), whether they have been paid already or remain to be paid as a "final dividend" for the year (included in accounts payable at the year end).

The annual review includes a page of "shareholder information" that includes an analysis of shareholdings by size of holding. 4,851 out of the 5,702 shareholders in Bunzl owned 10,000 shares or fewer at the end of 1997, representing in total only 2% of issued share capital. By contrast, 75% of issued shares were held by 86 investors with 1,000,000 or more, representing institutional shareholders. This is typical of British listed companies.

2.4   Important Notes to the 1997 Bunzl Accounts

Note 1 shows the segmental analysis of sales, operating profit, and net operating assets for the years 1997 and 1996. Operations in the United States continued to produce more than 60% of group sales and operating profits, although they used less than half of group operating assets. A heavy fall in sales to the "Rest of Europe" is explained elsewhere by disposals in Germany and Italy. As required by SSAP 25, the total figure for net operating assets is reconciled to the net assets shown in the consolidated balance sheet.

Note 2 shows an analysis of net operating costs broken down into rather greater detail between continuing operations, acquisitions, and discontinued operations than the minimum requirements of FRS 3, but some of the data is needed to meet the disclosure headings required by the Schedule 4 "formats" for the profit and loss account, as explained in Section 2.1.1.

Note 4, "Taxation," shows the charge for U.K. and overseas taxes on income for the year, as required by SSAP 15, supplemented by an amount for deferred tax. As usual with U.K. companies, it is not possible to determine exactly how the tax charges have been computed, nor to reconcile them with the income figures shown.

In accordance with the current requirements of SSAP 15, deferred tax must be provided only to the extent that it is expected that an actual liability or asset will crystallize in some future period. The ASP will shortly require a change in practice (as explained in Section 3.11.3). Paragraph 34 of SSAP 15 requires reporting companies to show by way of a note "the amount of any unprovided deferred tax in respect of the period analyzed into its major components." Thus, it is possible to calculate the amount that would have been charged for the year on a "full provision" (or "comprehensive allocation") basis. It is also possible, from note 20, to find out how much would appear in an accumulated deferred taxation provision calculated on a comprehensive basis. It is also pointed out that no provision is made for any potential corporation tax liability on unrealized revaluation surpluses in respect of properties where it is expected that those properties will be held for the foreseeable future. Sensible as this seems, there is controversy over just this issue among standard setters.

Note 23 shows "net pensions cost" for the Group as £10.4 million for the year, but the pensions scheme is evidently overfunded since Note 19 refers to cumulative unrealized profits of £6.8 million relating to pensions costs included in the profit and loss account for 1997 (but not distributable). Pensions are discussed in Section 3.13, including "defined contribution " schemes that are used by Bunzl as well as the "defined benefit" schemes commonly used in the United States.

Contingent liabilities (note 21) consist almost entirely of parent company guarantees for bank borrowing by other companies in the group, doubled between 1996 and 1997 as a result, no doubt, of the acquisitions during the year.

The Bunzl accounts provide an example of good British practice; further points are noted in Section 3 below.

3. Accounting Policies and Practices in Valuation and Measurement

3.1 Introduction

It was noted earlier that Sections 226, 227, and 256 of the 1985 act (as inserted by Sections 4, 5, and 19 of the 1989 act) map out the role of accounting standards by reference to Schedule 4 of the act. Schedule 4 includes, in Parts I to VII, a great deal of information within forty dense pages. This is particularly true of Part II, "Accounting Principles and Rules."

Whereas most companies in Britain publish their accounts using historical costs, that is, on the basis set out in Part II, Section B, of the "Historical Cost Accounting Rules," they also have the power to elect to use current value accounting rules, as set out in Part II, Section C, "Alternative Accounting Rules." Previous Companies Acts have generally tried to avoid restricting the power that directors have to use any of a variety of valuation bases in preparing their accounts, and the 1985 act seeks to preserve their discretion. The 1985 act now states that fixed assets must be valued at either their purchase price or production cost, or otherwise (under the "Alternative Accounting Rules") at current value (which includes both current market value and also "current costs," a term discussed in greater detail shortly). These Alternative Accounting Rules specify that, where the Rules are adopted, all intangible fixed assets except for goodwill should be valued at their "current cost."

Companies thus have discretion whether to use the usual historical cost valuation rules and show the original purchase price or production costs of their tangible fixed assets or to adopt the Alternative Accounting Rules, whether for some or all of their fixed assets, and to revalue them to some subsequent market value or "current cost."

There is no rule at present that determines how often a fixed asset must be revalued, or if it is to be revalued at all, although the ASB has proposed that entities that revalue a class of assets should be obliged to do so every year in order to keep the valuation up to date (See Section 3.5.1).

The rules for valuing investments are even more broadly permissive. They may be valued "on any basis which appears to the directors to be appropriate in the circumstances of the company" (1985 Act, Schedule 4 Part II, paragraph 31 (3)(b)). (See also Section 3.6 below for further discussion of the valuation of property, plant, and equipment, Section 3.9 for intangible fixed assets, and Section 3.10 for fixed asset investments, that is, equity investments in other companies that are not subsidiaries.)

The term *current cost* used in the Alternative Accounting Rules has a special meaning, arising out of 14 years of debate between 1970 and 1984 over how to present accounts under conditions of inflation. In 1974 there was apparent consensus among accountants for the use of general price level adjusted historical costs (called in Britain "current purchasing power" or "constant purchasing power," abbreviated as CPP accounting). However, just as the CCAB bodies were adopting SSAP 7, "Changes in the Purchasing Power of Money," in 1974, the government set up its own Committee on Inflation Accounting. In 1975 this committee published its report (known as the Sandilands Report), which totally rejected the use of general price adjusted accounts and recommended instead a complex alternative, to be known as current cost accounting (CCA).

CCA is basically a replacement cost system, but it rejects the idea of using current replacement costs for valuing all assets since, it was argued, there are some assets in any balance sheet that are unlikely to be replaced, which should then be valued at the higher of their net realizable value and their discounted net present value. There were several attempts to produce a workable standard, but eventually a set of CCA rules was put into effect in 1980 in a temporary SSAP 16, "Current Cost Accounting." This was discontinued after a 3-year experimental period.

The set of rules in SSAP 16 was designed to show in a supplementary income statement a figure for "CCA profit" attributable to stockholders after maintaining intact the physical operating capacity of the business. Beginning with the historical cost profit figure, a supplementary CCA profit and loss account showed additional charges required to bring up to current cost levels the cost of goods sold and the year's provision for depreciation. In addition, there was an extra charge to maintain monetary working capital at a real level, thus showing an entity's CCA operating profit after maintaining the firm's operating capability intact. Finally, SSAP 16 included a complex "gearing adjustment" designed to show the share of the additional charges above those that were attributable to assets financed by loan capital (and thus not necessary to maintain the physical capital financed by stockholders' capital).

A handbook of guidance on CCA was published in 1985; however, few companies now use CCA. The main exception is the group of newly privatized utilities that must negotiate with regulatory bodies over price fixing, and thus have to justify their prices. These companies use CCA for this purpose, to reduce their reported profits and increase their capital employed.

3.2 Group Accounts

By the 1985 Companies Act Section 227(3) (as amended by the 1989 act Section 5), a company that is a parent company shall, as well as preparing individual accounts, prepare group accounts:

> The accounts shall give a true and fair view of the state of affairs as at the end of the financial year, and the profit or loss for the financial year, of the undertakings included in the consolidation as a whole, so far as concerns members of the company.

The group accounts must comply with the provisions of Schedule 4A with regard to form and content, as set out in Schedule 2 to the 1989 act. In fact, the formats are virtually the same for consolidated accounts as for individual company accounts. The 1989 act made some important changes to the law on group accounts, in particular by broadening the definition of a group as required by the European Seventh Directive, so that the key criterion is now control rather than ownership. It is now possible for certain partnerships and unincorporated joint ventures to come within consolidation requirements, so the statute now refers not to subsidiary "companies" but to subsidiary "undertakings."

Small and medium-sized groups are now exempt from the requirement to file group accounts by Sections 248–249 of the 1985 act (as amended by Section 13 of the 1989 act). Similarly, a company that is a subsidiary of a parent company within any European Union state is exempt from the need to file group accounts.

The U.K. profession has an accounting standard (FRS 2) on group accounts. This is quite short, and it adds some guidance to the statute law. FRS 5 further broadens the definition of a subsidiary undertaking to include "quasi subsidiaries," based on wider definitions of control.

3.2.1 Methods of Consolidation

The acquisition, that is, purchase, method is generally used to prepare group accounts, in which the cost of acquiring control of a subsidiary is compared with the fair value of assets acquired at that time. Merger (i.e., pooling) is used under certain conditions, discussed further in Section 3.2.4 and does not involve the use of fair values. Where the purchase is effected by the use of nonmonetary assets (usually by the issue of shares) these assets are to be valued at their fair value unless the pooling method is used. This typically means that the shares are deemed to be issued at a value in excess of par, so that a share premium or paid-in surplus arises. There is no statutory guidance as to the meaning of fair value, but it is defined by FRS 7, "Fair Values in Acquisitions Accounting," to mean open market value both for the consideration given and the assets acquired.

In general, this means valuing securities at their open market value on the day that the offer becomes unconditional. Assets and liabilities acquired should be identified and valued by using the acquirer's accounting policies. Asset valuation should employ the lower of current replacement cost at the date of acquisition and the amounts recoverable from the ownership of the assets (by sale or use). The ASB insists in FRS 7 that the calculation of fair value at acquisition should not take into account any provisions for future operating losses or reorganization costs (including plant closure costs) that may follow the acquisition. Any such future costs must be expensed against future earnings, not written off against any reserves (such as share premium on new issues of stock) created at the time of the acquisition. The difference between the cost of the acquisition and the value acquired is regarded as "goodwill" in the consolidated accounts.

Profits made by subsidiaries before takeover are regarded as part of the equity acquired; profits made after takeover are treated as part of group profits, after deduction of any amount due to minority stakeholders in the subsidiary. Unrealized intercompany profits within the group are eliminated on consolidation from group accounts. There is no guidance on how group accounting treatment should repond to the use of current values; for example, it would be logical, in a case in which current recoverable amounts were to be used for a class of assets, for this value to be marked up to recoverable amount available to the group if this was higher than the amount available to the individual subsidiary.

Several areas of group accounting practice are uncertain under current British practice; for example, it is not clear whether the elimination of unrealized intercompany profits within the group means in principle removing the whole profit recorded by the supplying member of the group or whether it is only necessary to eliminate that part that relates to the group while allowing that part relating to minority shareholders to remain. In practice, 100% elimination is usually adopted, since the group accounts are not prepared for the benefit of minority shareholders (who look instead to their company's own separate set of accounts). This treatment is consistent with a requirement of FRS 2 that insists that no goodwill on acquisition should be attributed to the minority interest.

3.2.2 *Proportional Consolidation*

Although proportional consolidation has never been adopted for use in preparing group accounts in Britain, its use was suggested in ED 50 in 1990 for use in the case of unincorporated joint ventures, as permitted by the 1985 act. Until the 1989 Companies Act it was not essential to report any more about unincorporated joint ventures than the cost of the investment and the income actually received. The use of proportional consolidation for such joint ventures was advocated in the 1990 ASB paper, "Interim Statement: Consolidated Accounts." A 1994 ASB discussion paper "Associates and Joint Ventures" proposed that proportional consolidation be used for unincorporated joint ventures (termed "strategic alliances"), but that in general the practice should be forbidden. The ASB strongly prefers the use of equity accounting, both for associates and for incorporated joint ventures, but it cannot apparently prevent the use of proportional consolidation where investors effectively own stakes in particular operating assets rather than in the venture as a whole. FRS 9 has dropped the phrase "strategic alliances" and reverted to a treatment of associates more like that in SSAP 1. The main difference is that income from associates is not to be treated as part of group operating profit, but as a separate line in the income statement following the group operating profit (and also following the income, if any, from joint ventures, which also must be reported separately under FRS 9), although the format shown in Section 2.1.1 only required the single heading "income from shares inrelated companies."

FRS 9 (paragraph 29) requires:

> The investor's consolidated balance sheet should include as a fixed asset investment the investor's share of the net assets of its associates shown as a separate item. Goodwill arising on the investor's acquisition of its associates, less any amortisation or write-down, should be included in the carrying amount for the associates but should be disclosed separately.

For joint ventures, the ASB requires the use of an expanded equity method under which the investment in the joint venture will be disaggregated in a separate note or possibly as a separate column in the group balance sheet, showing the group's share of the major classes of net assets and liabilities that the joint venture controls. The logic is that different degrees of control are exercised over subsidiaries, associates, and joint ventures, so that subsidiary assets are fully included in the group accounts, associate assets are shown only as a single line figure representing the net equity investment, and joint venture assets appear as a proportion supposedly controlled by the group, albeit jointly with others.

FRS 9 replaced the relatively simple provisions of SSAP 1, as amended by certain provisions of the 1990 "Interim Statement: Consolidated Accounts," which spelled out the equity method of investment as the cost of the investment plus the investor's share of retained profits. FRS 9 has to confront the complication that the ASB now has no clear definition of retained profits, having made the profit and loss account only one of several reports that reflect financial outcomes. Thus, associates will also require a separate line in the STRGL, and so will joint ventures, unless the information is conveyed by a note.

The definition of joint ventures has also become more complex, in particular in distinguishing these from associates. A joint venture is "an entity in which the reporting entity holds an interest on a long-term basis and is jointly controlled by the reporting entity and one or more other venturers under a contractual agreement." It is not stipulated that this agreement should be in any particular form (such as in writing), but it is noted that a reporting entity jointly controls a venture with one or more others when "none of the entities alone can control that entity but all together can do so and decisions on financial and operating policy essential to the activities, economic performance and financial position of that venture require each venturer's consent." The position is unclear if only some of these decisions need agreement among all the venturers. However, there are still cases where proportional consolidation of unincorporated joint ventures is allowed, and these may be economically important since they may include some very valuable investments in oil and mineral deposits, shared facilities, and territorial agreements where it can be argued that control is over particular assets rather than a complete undertaking.

3.2.3 Goodwill

The accounting treatment of goodwill has been a matter of great controversy in Britain. For several years, the option open under SSAP 22 to companies was either to write off goodwill by amortization against income or to write it off (eliminate it) against reserves, the latter being presented as the preferred treatment. It has been normal treatment for U.K. companies to use any of their reserves for eliminating goodwill, unless there is specific prohibition by law (as in the case of the share premium account and, probably, any revaluation reserve). The Bunzl accounts presented earlier show goodwill written off against the merger reserve.

ED 47, "Accounting for Goodwill," proposed that goodwill should be written off over its expected life, not to exceed 20 years except where, in unusual circumstances, reasons could be established for it to be written off over a period up to 40 years. The ASB has now insisted in FRS 10, "Goodwill and Intangible Assets" (1997), that all goodwill that is recognized in the accounts must be capitalized at purchase cost and amortized against income in the profit and loss account over a maximum of 20 years, except only in such cases where it can be shown that the asset has an economic life of more than 20 years. In this case, amortization will be over that longer period (possibly an indefinite life), but there must in such cases be an annual impairment review along the lines set out in FRED 15, "Impairment of Fixed Assets and Goodwill" (not yet a standard). As a practical matter, performing the impairment review will be hindered by the procedure laid down; rather than comparing book value with the aggregate future cash flows recoverable from the use of each asset (or, more plausibly, each group of complementary assets), the ASB says that book value must be compared with discounted cash flows attributable to those assets, and FRED 15 discusses ways to estimate an appropriate discount rate for the purpose. This is analyzed further in Section 3.6 below.

It is not permissible to capitalize self-generated goodwill, for example, value created by advertising products or training employees. SSAP 22, paragraph 28 specifically ruled out the inclusion of non-purchased goodwill in the balance sheets of companies or groups, but FRS 10 allows the reporting of intangibles that are purchased separately from a business, and also those that are purchased as part of a business, provided that they can be "measured reliably." The latter cannot now be written off against reserves. Thus, FRS 10 removes most of the significant distinctions between the accounting treatment of goodwill and intangibles, so that it is no longer important to be able to distinguish between them. This has reduced the effort expended on trying to identify components of an acquisition that could be capitalized, such as brands and trademarks with readily traded market values. The only remaining reason for making such a distinction is that goodwill can never be revalued upwards, whereas other intangibles may be if there is a readily ascertainable higher market value for them.

In the case of purchased goodwill, an intangible asset may arise either in the group accounts on consolidation or in the books of the acquiring company following transfer of the assets of the company acquired when it is not proposed to operate the acquired company as a subsidiary. Rather than buying the equity capital of another company, it is often the practice in Britain to buy just the assets, in particular when taking over an unlisted company, thus avoiding any unreported residual risks and claims such as product indemnity liabilities that may attach to the other party. As will be noted in Section 3.5, proposed revisions to the treatment of provisions and contingencies in FRED 14 are likely to make it more difficult to create general provisions for some of these items, so the risks of buying controlling equity interests may increase. The problem of accounting for intangibles in company accounts is discussed further in Section 3.9.

One further issue that produced extensive discussion in the derivation of FRS 10 was negative goodwill, that is, the acquisition of a business at a price that is lower than the fair values of assets acquired, rather than higher as in most cases. The ASB accepted that negative goodwill is rare, but it distinguished two distinct causes.

In most cases, the reason that a takeover succeeds at a price below the value of the net assets acquired is that there remains some residual liability for future commitments or operating losses that the acquirer cannot avoid. FRED 14 would require provisions to be set up for future operating losses only when this involves an "onerous contract"; in general, FRED 14 would require operating losses to be recognized only as they arise in future. In a takeover, recognizing these obligations, rather than ignoring them, would be likely to remove the negative goodwill. However, FRS 7, "Fair Values in Acquisition Accounting," makes this very difficult to achieve. The problem arises from the ASB's insistence than only assets and liabilities in existence at the balance sheet date are allowed to be recognized, and there is no liability in existence in the case of future operating losses. Any room the ASB may have for maneuver is further limited by FRED 14 (reviewed in Section 3.4), which insists on defining provisions in this way, as a liability. It is possible, therefore that negative goodwill may arise from this cause; it will have to be treated as if it had arisen from a bargain purchase, as below.

In the minority of cases where there genuinely has been a bargain purchase (which implies failure on the part of the vendors, say in the form of pressure due to insolvency), there is no doubt that there is some form of gain to the acquiring entity. However, this must not be taken to operating income immediately. The negative goodwill will be shown separately by the purchaser immediately below any positive goodwill in its balance sheet and deducted from it. The credit balance for negative goodwill will then be released to the profit and loss account "as the non-monetary assets are recovered, whether depreciation or sale." It is not clear what this means, but it seems to resemble the treatment of grants under SSAP 4, in Section 3.6.3, even though SSAP 4 was clearly drafted to produce cost matching.

3.2.4 Pooling

Merger accounting (i.e. pooling) was permitted by SSAP 23, where companies came together without material resources leaving the group on acquisition. Similar principles appear in FRS 6, "Acquisitions and Mergers," (1994). There is some potential confusion, since provisions described as being for merger relief have appeared separately in FRS 6 and in the 1985 and 1989 Companies Acts (now in the amended Section 131 of the 1985 act). The criteria in the act are different from those in FRS 6.

The merger provisions in Section 131 are intended to relieve companies that make an acquisition by a new issue of shares from the need to set up a share premium account (i.e., a form of compulsory, nondistributable reserve that represents the excess of issue consideration over nominal value). Section 131 allows companies to value the shares given as consideration at their nominal value and not at fair market value, thus avoiding, entirely or in part, the need to create a share premium account. In the same context, Section 132 allows them to value the assets acquired at those values at which they were carried in the books of the former owner, which helps to limit the amount that needs to appear as goodwill.

In fact it is often the case that acquisitive companies that are able to claim merger relief actually use acquisition accounting for those very same deals. Instead of showing a credit to "share premium account," however, they credit "merger reserve" with the excess of fair value over nominal value of shares issued. This merger reserve is then regarded as a proper place to write off goodwill on this, and any future, acquisition. In some cases, the debit balance shows that goodwill written off exceeds the credit balance created. (Indeed, this is true of Bunzl plc, as shown in Note 19.) The resulting debit balance is then deducted from other credit balances shown under equity.

The merger criteria in SSAP 23 and FRS 6 do not have quite the same coverage. It would be reasonable to assume that merger accounting under SSAP 23 or FRS 6 would have to be applied in all cases where merger relief is obtained under Section 131. This is not the case, however; indeed, FRS 6 does not permit merger accounting in certain cases where Section 131 has permitted "merger relief." The conditions for merger accounting are defined more narrowly. Furthermore, FRS 4 requires that the net proceeds of any share issue be credited to shareholders' funds, such proceeds being valued at the "fair value" of the net assets received by way of consideration, net of issue costs. This seems to leave the merger reserve as the only practical way to reconcile the permitted treatment under Section 131 with the financial reporting restrictions.

3.2.5 Related Undertakings

Group accounts do not merely incorporate the financial affairs of subsidiary companies. As noted in Section 3.2.2 earlier, there are other investments in the equity capital of other companies that need to be reported. Accounting for "related undertakings" (as defined in the 1985 act) or "associates" (as defined in FRS 9) typically arises where the shareholding is more than 20% but less than 50% of the shares in another entity (or, less frequently, where substantial influence is exercised over its policies even though the percentage shareholding falls outside the 20%–50% limits). There may also be investments in other companies that give ownership of less than 20% of share capital. Both these types of investment will be considered in Section 3.10.

3.3 Foreign Currency Translation

SSAP 20 addresses the translation of foreign currencies in two stages. First the financial statements are prepared for the individual companies within the group, and any transactions conducted in foreign currency are translated. Then, as a second stage, consolidated accounts are prepared for the group as a whole, with translation of the complete financial statements of foreign enterprises that are part of the group.

3.3.1 Foreign Currencies in Individual Company Accounts

Foreign currency transactions are translated into the home currency of each company at the exchange rate ruling at the date of the transaction. At the balance sheet date, monetary assets and liabilities that are denominated in a foreign currency are translated at the closing rate as of that date.

Nonmonetary assets are not restated but left at the conversion rate ruling as of the date they were originally recorded.

Differences on exchange are included in the profit and loss account for the year, except for any gain or loss arising from translation of an extraordinary item (which will be included as part of the extraordinary item) and any that reflect holding gains or losses (which appear in the STRGL). In the case of long-term monetary items, exchange gains and losses are usually taken into the profit or loss for the year; however, where there are doubts about the convertibility or marketability of the currency concerned, it may be prudent to defer recognizing such gains if the item is not yet due for settlement.

Special rules apply under SSAP 20, where investment in a foreign enterprise is financed by foreign borrowings, so that the investment is effectively "hedged" against exchange risks. In such cases, and in variants that have a similar effect, exchange gains and losses may be passed through reserves (i.e. by way of the STRGL) rather than the profit and loss account of individual companies. The issue of hedging has become much more important in recent years, partly because global markets have become more volatile but also because of sustained efforts by standard setters to come to grips with accounting for financial instruments. This area is addressed in Section 3.14.6.

3.3.2 Foreign Currencies in Group Accounts

Once the accounts for the individual enterprises have been drawn up in local currency, it is time to prepare the consolidated accounts, normally in the currency of the country in which the parent company is based. As SSAP 20, paragraph 13 states:

> The method used to translate financial statements for consolidation purposes should reflect the financial and other operational relationships which exist between an investing company and its foreign enterprises.

The standard refers to "foreign enterprises" here, rather than related companies, since the rules relate not only to subsidiaries but also to associates and even foreign branches (which may be closely integrated into the activities of the investing company or may be quite autonomous).

The closing rate/net investment method is normally used. The investment in the foreign enterprise is represented by the net worth held by the parent, rather than by the individual assets and liabilities. Such investment will usually take the form of a holding of equity capital, but it may also be in the form of a loan.

The foreign enterprise will probably have its own local borrowings, which will be repaid without having an impact on its parent overseas. The balance sheet will be translated by using the exchange rate at the balance sheet date. On the other hand, when it comes to translating items in the profit and loss account, it is permissible to choose either the closing rate or an average rate for the year, provided that whichever is selected is used consistently from one year to the next. Exchange gains or losses arising on transactions carried out by the investing company or the foreign enterprises will appear in its own profit and loss account before consolidation. But differences on exchange that arise in the course of preparing the consolidated accounts should be taken to the STRGL, not to the profit and loss account. It is not the practice in Britain to "recycle" exchange gains and losses from the STRGL to the profit and loss account when the position is eventually settled, as would be required under FASB rules.

SSAP 20 recognizes that sometimes the business activities of a foreign enterprise are so closely linked to those of the investing company that the use of the closing rate/net investment method would be misleading. In such cases it is permissible to use the temporal method (broadly, using the translation methods for the individual company referred to in Section 3.3.1).

The Bunzl accounts show a statement of the company's policy on foreign exchange translation in its Statement of Accounting Policies (item (f) "foreign currencies").

3.4 Capital and Reserves

3.4.1 Share Capital

The Companies Acts specify in detail the information that must be shown in respect of share capital, both in the balance sheet and in notes to the accounts.

3.4.2 Reserves

For many years company directors in Britain had discretion to use the term *capital reserve* to describe any credit balances that the directors regarded as nondistributable, including unrealized revaluation surpluses. The term *revenue reserve* is still used by some companies to describe profits that could in principle be regarded as available for distribution. The designations have been terms of art rather than matters of strict legal precision, conventional terms that enabled directors to signal to shareholders and others just how much might be distributed as future dividends (revenue reserves) and how much needed to be retained in the business, either as a matter of legal necessity (e.g., in the form of "share premiums," which cannot by law be distributed) or as a matter of sound business practice. Current usage is summarized below.

Common terminology used in Britain distinguishes among:

1. Expenses for a period, recorded in the books when the supplier's invoice was received

2. Accruals, the cost of which can be determined quite accurately, even though no invoice has yet been received and recorded

3. Provisions, which are estimates of costs for the current period, even though they cannot be determined with substantial accuracy

4. Reserves, which do not relate to costs of the current period but represent sums set aside out of the profits of the period to provide for future growth or for unknown contingencies

In addition to the figures that appear in the accounts, there may also be estimates shown by way of notes to the accounts to reflect contingent liabilities, those that fall due to be met if some event comes about beyond the control of the company (see also Section 3.5 below).

Although the term *capital reserves* is no longer in use, companies may set up accounts called "general reserves" or "asset replacement reserves" if they wish to earmark some part of the retained profits as being needed for permanent retention in the company. These amounts may be shown in the balance sheet formats under the heading "Reserves provided for by the articles of association." Any credit balance on the "profit and loss account" can usually be regarded as potentially distributable, although in many companies the balance is in fact too large for it to be distributed without harming the operations of the business. Moreover, such a balance does not necessarily represent the maximum amount that legally could be distributed (see Section 3.4.5 below). Retained profits are usually the major source of capital, averaging more than 65% among British companies. (In the Bunzl accounts, it represents only 58% of net assets in the consolidated balance sheet, but this is after a heavy goodwill write off in

1997; in 1996, the proportion was 77%. The parent company balance sheet shows almost 100% equity funding.) "Revaluation reserves" will be discussed briefly in Section 3.4.7.

3.4.3 Ordinary Earnings and Extraordinary Items

Another important distinction was made formerly between "ordinary" and "extraordinary" earnings, as reported in the income statement. SSAP 6, "Extraordinary Items and Prior Year Adjustments," published in 1974 and revised in 1986, gave rise to a great deal of difficulty, mainly because of the imprecise definitions of the terms used and the fact that "extraordinary items" were taken into the income statement after the ordinary earnings figure used to calculate earnings per share (EPS) under SSAP3. (Further reference is made to SSAP3 in Section 3.14.3.) SSAP 6 relied on a distinction between persistent and transient earnings. By contrast, FRS 3 seeks separate disclosure of earnings from discontinued and continuing activities.

FRS 3 redefined extraordinary items so that they have virtually disappeared from U.K. financial reports. The major component of extraordinary items used to be gains and losses on the disposal of fixed assets. Such gains and losses are now disclosed separately on the face of the profit and loss account after operating profit and before interest, except where the asset has previously been revalued (so that the gain or loss has been taken to the STRGL). It is no longer permitted to deal with these gains and losses "below the line" in calculating EPS in the profit and loss account, but they are liable to be overlooked if they appear only in the STRGL (and recycling is not permitted between the two). As noted in Section 3.5 below, ASB proposals are under consideration that would require assets and liabilities immediately before disposal to be revalued to their disposal price, so that all the holding gains/losses pass through the STRGL apart from that (arbitrary) fraction that has been written off by way of depreciation charged to profit and loss.

"Prior year adjustments" can arise under FRS 3 when changes are made in accounting policies or when fundamental errors relating to former periods are corrected. Prior period adjustments should be accounted for by restating the comparative figures for the preceding period in the primary statements and notes, and adjusting the opening balance of reserves for the cumulative effect. The cumulative effect of the adjustments should also be noted at the foot of the statement of total recognized gains and losses of the current period. The effect of prior period adjustments on the results for the preceding period should be disclosed where practicable.

3.4.4 Provisions for Taxation

Although taxation will be discussed in greater detail in Section 3.12, it is appropriate at this point to refer to two specific points. The first is that the estimated charge for corporation tax on the earnings of a year appears in the income statement, with a corresponding provision being made in the balance sheet. The amount is not known exactly at this stage: there may be various adjustments to make before a final assessment is agreed with the Inland Revenue. Moreover, there is a long time delay, under existing rules (soon to change), before the mainstream corporation tax is liable to be paid over to the authorities. It is common for two tax liabilities to be outstanding at any one balance sheet date—an amount due for payment in more than one year's time in respect of the estimated tax assessment on the current year's profit, and a further amount due for payment quite soon in respect of the tax assessment on the previous year's profits.

The second point worth noting at this point is that dividends in Britain are "declared" out of the net profits of a particular year, being proposed by the directors to the shareholders at a general meeting held after the year end to consider the results of the year. Thus, a balance sheet will usually show an amount payable in respect of the proposed dividend (often the second such dividend out of the year's earnings, with an earlier "interim" dividend paid during the course of the accounting period). Because dividend payments still currently involve payment also of a withholding tax called "advance corporation tax" (ACT), which can usually be recovered many months later against the mainstream corporation tax assessment when this falls due for payment, there can be quite large amounts of recoverable ACT paid to the Inland Revenue within 3 months or so of the dividends being declared, waiting to be offset against subsequent corporation tax assessments. Section 3.12 explains the U.K. corporate tax system and the major changes brought about by the 1997 Finance Act, No. 2.

3.4.5 Distributable Profits

It is not easy to determine the amount currently available for distribution by way of dividends. This area of law is governed by Part VIII of the 1985

Companies Act, which goes beyond the scope of this chapter. The published accounts do not show the quantum of profit that is potentially distributable, which is, broadly speaking, restricted to accumulated realized profits less accumulated realized losses of the company (not the group).

3.4.6 Redemption of Shares

It is possible for a company to repurchase its own ordinary shares (common stock) as well as preferred shares, under certain conditions laid down in Sections 159–181 of the 1985 act. The capital of the company must be preserved, however, so that a transfer of an equal amount must be made out of distributable profits to the credit of a "capital redemption reserve," unless redemption of the shares is to be paid from the proceeds of a new share issue. Shares that are redeemed are canceled and not reissued: there is no "treasury stock." Shares may, however, be held by the pensions trust (which has a separate legal identity: see Section 3.13.2).

3.4.7 Revaluation Reserves

The term revaluation reserve is used specifically for unrealized surpluses on the revaluation of fixed assets. When such assets are eventually disposed of, it used to be the practice that the amount of revaluation surplus relating to the asset disposal was transferred out of the revaluation reserve and recycled (plus any book profit or less any loss on the sale) to the credit of the profit and loss account as an extraordinary item. Since FRS 3 was issued in 1992, practice has changed. The profit or loss on disposal to be reported in the profit and loss account is now the difference between the net sale proceeds and the net carrying amount at which the asset appeared in the books immediately before sale (whether this was at historical cost, less depreciation, or at valuation). On disposal of assets that have been realued, revaluation gains included in the revaluation reserve become distributable, so these are transferred to "Other Reserves" although without being recycled through the profit and loss account.

It must be added that FRS 3 also requires a note to explain any difference between the profit and loss actually disclosed for the year and the figure that would have resulted "on an unmodified historical cost basis."

3.5 Liabilities and Provisions

In common with U.S. practice, British companies use accrual accounting in which income recognition principles first determine the timing of revenues, and costs are then matched to produce a figure for profit or loss. SSAP 2, "Disclosure of Accounting Policies," set out in 1971 a brief statement of four fundamental accounting concepts, the going concern concept, the accruals or matching concept, the consistency concept, and the prudence concept. These concepts also appear now in paragraphs 9–15, Schedule 4 of the 1985 act. It is worth noting that sales revenues are recorded in Britain at figures that exclude value added tax (VAT). SSAP 5 lays down the standard treatment of VAT, which is generally excluded both from sales revenue and also from costs unless the VAT on inputs cannot be recovered.

The term *provision* is used currently to describe a liability recognized in connection with an expense of the period for which the amount cannot yet be determined with substantial accuracy. Accumulated charges for depreciation used to be known also as provisions for depreciation, since the amount charged depends on the unexpended future life of the assets concerned; however, it is now common practice to refer to accumulated depreciation.

Contingent liabilities are less certain than provisions. They would be reflected in an expense only if some uncertain future event were to take place, with a reasonable likelihood that it will not. For example, if a claim is made against the company under warranty where the company contests liability, the chances of incurring costs may depend on the outcome of a court hearing (particularly since in Britain the losing party usually must pay the legal costs of both sides). The probability of the event occurring is sufficiently low that no definite provision is made in the current accounts, but it is sufficiently probable for it to be necessary to give information on it, by way of a note to the accounts, to give a true and fair view. SSAP 18, "Accounting for Contingencies," lays down accounting rules in more detail.

FRED 14, "Provisions and Contingencies" (June 1997), proposes major changes to the way that these terms are defined and used. Rather than provisions being "estimates of costs for the current period even though these cannot be determined with substantial accuracy," required to match costs against the revenues recorded for the period, the new definition proposes that provisions should be regarded as a form of liability that exists at the balance sheet date, so the test will not be based on matching but on whether there exists a "legal or constructive obligation to transfer economic benefits as a result of past events"; it must also be possible to estimate the amount of the obligation and the timing of its discharge within a reasonable range. There has also to be some external party to whom the obligation is owed, although it is not necessary that this party be identifiable. The provision must be created for some specific purpose, and thereafter the reporting entity is permitted to charge only that particular obligation against the provision set up in anticipation of it.

The aim of this restriction is to limit scope for directors to smooth income, a practice that the ASB abhors. The ASB does not accept that creating provisions in good faith represents a valuable way to exercise informed judgment in presenting uncertain but informative data; however, FRED 14 may lead to the sort of legalistic definitions that the ASB regards as objectionable elsewhere. There is bound to be considerable difficulty in practice in recognizing whether, and when, a "constructive" obligation exists; this, by definition, falls outside any identifiable legal commitments.

One additional type of disclosure required by the 1985 act (Schedule 4, paragraph 50) falling outside the above categories is the note of future capital commitments authorized by the directors. These used to be divided into two parts: those for which contracts have been signed and those for which contracts have not yet been signed. The need to disclose the latter was removed by statutory instrument in 1996. (See, however, the middle segment of Note 7 in Bunzl's accounts, where this useful additional information is still shown.) While this information does not show the time-scale over which the commitments extend, the information is valuable both in the context of the trend of net earnings and in assessing the liquidity of the company.

3.6 Property, Plant, and Equipment

The 1985 act Section 262(1) (as inserted by the 1989 act, Section 22) states that fixed assets are "assets of a company which are intended for use on a continuing basis in the company's activities, and 'current assets' means assets not intended for such use." Fixed assets may be tangible or intangible, and they include investments in other undertakings. The 1985 act continues a long tradition of legislation that leaves unspecified how fixed assets are to be valued and how depreciation is to be charged, but it insists that disclosure be made of the cost or valuation used to record the book value of the assets, the charge for depreciation in the current year, and the aggregate depreciation expensed to date on the assets recorded.

There is no single SSAP dedicated to the treatment of fixed assets as a class, but SSAP 12, "Accounting for Depreciation," explicitly requires depreciation to be charged on fixed assets, while SSAP 13 deals with fixed assets used for research and development, SSAP 19 deals with accounting for investment properties, and FRS 10 deals with goodwill and intangible assets. Intangible fixed assets are also discussed in Section 3.9, and investments in Section 3.10.

It was pointed out in the discussion of the historical cost vs. alternative valuation rules, in Section 3.1, that most companies in Britain publish their accounts on the basis of historical cost, although if they wish they can choose to use the Alternative Accounting Rules. These Alternative Accounting Rules allow all intangible fixed assets *except for goodwill* to be valued at their current cost. Tangible fixed assets may be valued either at current cost or, alternatively, at a market value determined at the date of their last valuation. Most British companies present fixed assets at a mixture of cost, past valuations, and current valuations.

Previous companies acts have generally tried to avoid restricting the power of directors to use any of a variety of valuation bases in preparing their accounts, and the 1985 act seeks to preserve some degree of discretion to directors. The 1985 act states that fixed assets must either (a) be valued at their purchase price or production cost, or (b) be shown, under the Alternative Accounting Rules, at some current value.

The Alternative Accounting Rules allow tangible fixed assets to be valued either at current cost or at a market value determined at the date of their last valuation. There is no rule that determines how often a fixed asset must be revalued or if it is to be revalued at all. The ASB, as shown in Financial Reporting Exposure Draft 17, "Measurement of Tangible Fixed Assets," as well as in its draft Statement of Principles, clearly favors a move to using current values throughout the accounts. However, it recognizes on pragmatic grounds that it would be impractical to move too fast. It therefore supports the use of the present modified historical cost system. In order to address what it describes as "some of the existing anomalies," the discussion paper proposed new standards to require:

1   The revaluation of properties (excluding fixed assets specific to the business)
2.   The revaluation of quoted investments
3.   The revaluation of stock of a commodity nature and long-term stock where a market of sufficient depth exists

Subject to this, SSAP 12 (on fixed asset depreciation) obviously contemplated the possibility of fixed asset revaluation: it states (SSAP 12, paragraph 5) that it "does not prescribe how frequently assets should be revalued but, where a policy of revaluing assets is adopted, the valuation should be kept up to date." Any method of calculating depreciation is acceptable, provided it allocates the charge "as fairly as possible to the periods expected to benefit from the asset's use." The rules for valuing investments have to date been even more broadly permissive. Under the Companies Acts, investments may be valued "on any basis which appears to the directors to be appropriate in the circumstances of the company" (1985 act, Schedule 4, Part II, paragraph 31 (3)(b)).

The calculation of the purchase price of a fixed asset includes those costs incidental to the shipment and installation of the asset. In the case of production costs of assets made by the company, these may include "a reasonable proportion of the costs incurred by the company which are only indirectly attributable to the production of that asset, but only to the extent that they relate to the period of production" (1985 act, Schedule 4, paragraph 26(3)(a)). Interest costs may also be included (see Section 3.6.4).

SSAP 12 requires that depreciation be charged over the life of any fixed asset whose life is of limited duration, including property. Depreciation must be charged even if the market value of such an asset increases. An exception is made under SSAP 19 in the case of investment properties. Despite the specific requirement of SSAP 12 that property be depreciated (unless it is investment property, which excludes buildings occupied either by the company or by others in the same group), it used to be quite common for companies with large property investments to ignore this requirement. Supermarkets, hotels, and similar buildings kept in a good state of repair were previously often not depreciated; the stated reason in the accounts was usually that the open market value of the property was rising faster than any deterioration in its fabric. Practice changed in this area after 1993, with the Review Panel exerting pressure on a number of large companies with major property assets.

3.6.1 Departures from Historical Cost

Some controversy has existed over the proper accounting treatment of the depreciation of fixed assets where they have been revalued. When SSAP 12 was first issued in December 1977, it was not explicit whether the amount of depreciation charged in the income statement had to be based on the revalued amount or merely on the original cost, with any extra depreciation being charged against reserves. This treatment (often called split depreciation) was favored by some companies and their accountants. This is not permitted, however, under Article 33(3) of the European Fourth Directive.

The current version of SSAP 12 is insistent:

> The accounting treatment in the profit and loss account should be consistent with that used in the balance sheet. Hence the depreciation charge in the profit and loss account for the period should be based on the carrying amount of the asset in the balance sheet, whether historical cost or revalued amount. The whole depreciation charge should be reflected in the profit and loss account. (SSAP 12, paragraph 16)

One consequence of this is that the aggregate depreciation charge to the profit and loss account in respect of any particular asset becomes arbitrary, bounded only by its historical cost at the lower limit and its replacement cost at the date of disposal as the higher limit. This arises because the allocation of depreciation to time periods is essentially arbitrary, being a joint cost of each such time period.

The question of depreciation is linked with three others: (a) the effect of revising the estimated residual lives of fixed assets; (b) the need to write down fixed assets in the event of a permanent diminution in their value; and (c) the treatment of gains and losses on disposal. These are discussed briefly in turn.

The effect of revising the estimated residual lives of fixed assets is usually that the firm will write off the unamortized book value over the remaining life as newly estimated. Only if "future results would be materially distorted" should there be an adjustment to the accumulated depreciation for years before the new estimate.

The need to write down fixed assets in the event of a permanent diminution in their value may arise perhaps as a result of obsolescence or because of a fall in demand for a product. The net book value should be written down immediately to the estimated "recoverable amount," that is to say the lower of (a) the net realizable value of an asset held for resale or (b) the amount expected to be produced by an asset in its future use as a fixed asset. FRED 15, "Inpairment of Fixed Assets and Goodwill," presents a fuller analysis, and this is discussed further at the end of this section. If it is judged to be necessary to reduce the asset value, the write-down will be against current earnings if it arises from an operational cause, or in the STRGL if it is caused by a fall in market price. It may prove difficult to identify the difference in practice. If it turns out that the reasons for making such a write-down cease to apply, it may be reversed to the extent that it is no longer necessary, with a credit to the profit and loss account.

The treatment of gains and losses on disposal involves further controversy. For those who seek consistent application of historical cost rules, the realized gain or loss on sale of fixed assets compares sale proceeds with the depreciated historical cost. If a fixed asset had been revalued, the revaluation surplus would have been taken to the credit of a revaluation reserve as an unrealized profit until the time of disposal. On sale, this is reversed, so that the surplus will enter into the calculation of the realized profit or loss on disposal.

As noted earlier, however, profit or loss on disposal of fixed assets must now be calculated as the difference between any sale proceeds and the carrying value of the asset in the books, whether this is at historical cost less depreciation or at a revaluation (FRS 3, paragraph 21).

Financial Reporting Exposure Draft 17, "Measurement of Tangible Fixed Assets," proposes that revaluation of fixed assets should mean accepting a commitment to revaluing the same assets every year, with formal valuations at intervals of not more than 3 years. This would no doubt encourage reporting entities to persist with using historical cost. The ASB has also proposed that fixed assets should normally be revalued immediately before disposal to their disposal price, so that any gains or losses compared with their book value (now called "carrying value" by the ASB) will be taken to the STRGL.

Any transfer out of revaluation reserve on disposal of a redundant asset should be shown as a movement on reserves and not included in the profit or loss on sale of the fixed asset. FRS 3, paragraph 27, requires a "statement of total recognized gains and losses" to follow the profit and loss account if there are any gains or losses or other transfers to or from reserves for the year that do not appear in the profit and loss account. This is explicitly to include (paragraph 56) any unrealized gain "such as a revaluation surplus on fixed assets."

Accordingly, the FRS requires, as a primary statement, a statement of total recognized gains and losses to show the extent to which shareholders' funds have increased or decreased from all the gains and losses recognized in the period. It follows from this perspective that the same gains and losses should not be recognized twice (for example, a holding gain recognized when a fixed asset is revalued should not be recognized a second time when the revalued asset is sold).

This means, of course, that there will be greater disjunction between reported operating profits for the year and the amount that becomes legally distributable during the year. This latter figure is strictly defined as being realized. Since revaluation gains may now bypass the profit and loss account entirely and be transferred via the STRGL to revaluation reserve (even though depreciation must be charged against operating profits on the relevant basis), realized revaluation gains now miss being reported in profits at all.

The ASB proposes to elaborate on the rule that assets with a book value ("carrying value") above their recoverable amount should be revalued downward. This in many respects just formalizes practice that goes back for centuries; it has always been the practice to value inventory, for instance, at the lower of cost price or market (net realizable) value, and fixed assets that were not expected to produce a return at least equal to their value in the books have always been written down.

What is new is the meaning placed upon the phrase "producing a return," as interpreted by the ASB in FRED 15, "Impairment of Fixed Assets and Goodwill" (June 1997). The expression has not been formally defined previously, but the idea that an asset might not be worth its book value has been associated with obsolescence or unexpected damage, and a need for prudence. This has typically meant that an asset is expected, alone or more commonly in conjunction with others, to produce a cash flow that equals its depreciated book value.

Such calculations have not traditionally been performed by discounting the cash flows, since it is not part of the accounting function to anticipate future levels of profitability in valuing assets. While depreciation involves estimating future asset lives and scrap values, it does not usually imply a need to assure readers that the assets will yield any particular rate of return.

This, however, is the implication of FRED 15, which adopts the ASB's emphasis on the balance sheet, rather than the income statement, to define impairment by comparing three alternative values at the balance sheet date. Book value must be compared with net realizable value (NRV) and with value in use and the asset must not be shown in the accounts at an amount higher than its recoverable amount (that is, the higher of NRV and value in use, also known as its economic value (EV), being the discounted cash flows it is deemed to produce).

Clearly, current assets are normally expected to have an NRV greater than EV, and fixed assets an EV greater than NRV. However, it is difficult to associate any particular cash flows with any individual asset, so it is generally necessary to identify "income generating units" that do have identifiable cash flows, and then (according to FRED 15) to discount these jointly at some appropriate post-tax rate. Impairment then may need to be identified at the level of the income generating unit, which raises difficulties about how to apportion any such reduction in value to individual assets within that group. The ASB thinks that any capitalized goodwill should be reduced first, followed by any other intangibles, and then tangible assets *pro rata.*

The approach insists that the discount rate to be used would be that appropriate to the risk attaching to the income generating unit; the implication is that any asset or group of assets that are not expected to be able to yield a return at least equal to others of the same risk class should be written down to a figure that will yield such a return.

Finally, FRED 15 accepts that, if conditions that produced the impairment are ameliorated, asset values may subsequently be written up, perhaps even to the point that the former book value is reinstated.

3.6.2 Relationship between Accounting Depreciation and Tax Allowances

There is no relationship between the book value of assets and their tax treatment (although a temporary exception to the rule is noted in Section 3.6.4); indeed, the amount charged by way of depreciation is unlikely to be the amount allowed for taxation by way of capital allowances. The Inland Revenue publishes its own scale of allowances for use with the cost of fixed assets in making an assessment of taxable profits.

3.6.3 Government Grants

The treatment of government grants is addressed in SSAP 4, "The Accounting Treatment of Government Grants." The intention is that any grants from government (whether a local or national government or the European Union) should be credited to income at the time any relevant costs are being debited. In the case of fixed assets, this means that the grant will serve to reduce the cost of using the asset year by year over its life (and not be taken as a credit in full to income in the year the grant was made or paid). SSAP 4 requires grants in respect of fixed assets to be treated as a deferred credit, to be released bit by bit as depreciation is charged. It does not permit the grant to be taken off the cost of the fixed asset so that a lower depreciation charge arises in that way. However, there is some controversy over whether the 1985 act, Schedule 4, necessarily requires the SSAP 4 treatment; some companies evidently deduct grants from the cost of fixed assets on the grounds that only the net amount really represents "cost."

3.6.4 Interest

The treatment of interest on fixed assets is addressed in the 1985 act, Schedule 4, paragraph 26(3)(b), where it is stated that there may be included in the production cost of an asset "interest on capital borrowed to finance the production of that asset, to the extent that it accrues in respect of the period of production." There is no obligation to capitalize interest; however, if directors decide to do so, Financial Reporting Exposure Draft 17, "Measurement of Tangible Fixed Assets," proposes ways in which this must be done. Such capitalization will lessen current interest charges to income but increase later depreciation charges by inclusion of interest in the cost of the asset.

Generally there is little connection between the profit or loss figure published in the income statement and the profit or loss figure used in the assessment of corporation tax. There were several years, however, in which the accounting treatment effectively determined the tax treatment of interest capitalization. In a 1966 case it was decided that the Inland Revenue was within its rights to disallow interest as a business expense in the current year where it had been capitalized as part of the costs of buildings. In a 1977 case, however, the Inland Revenue subsequently decided to change its view, and it inserted an amendment into the 1981 Finance Act (S. 38) in order to reverse the rule.

3.6.5 Investment Properties

Investment properties are covered by SSAP 19, after the requirement of SSAP 12 to depreciate freehold buildings had produced extensive disagreement. SSAP 19 requires investment properties to be carried at open market value, not necessarily appraised by a professional appraiser (valuer) but accompanied by details of the names and qualification of valuers, the bases used, and a statement whether the valuation is by an employee or officer of the company. All valuation surpluses and any deficits that are expected to be temporary should be taken to an "investment revaluation reserve" by wayt of the STRGL. However, any deficits expected to be permanent must be taken to the profit and loss account. No charge should be made for depreciation on such properties, except for properties held on lease.

FRS 3, paragraph 66 observes:

> Investment companies as defined in section 266 of the Companies Act 1985 (Companies Act investment companies) have special legal provisions regarding the recording of unrealized capital losses, with the result that their profit and loss accounts are not comparable with those of other reporting entities. In the case of such investment companies all recognized gains and losses of a capital nature should be shown only in the statement of total recognized gains and losses leaving the profit and loss account to be confined to profits available for distribution.

3.7 Leased Assets

SSAP 21, "Accounting for Leases and Hire Purchase Contracts" obliges companies that lease assets under a "finance" lease to treat the assets as though they were owned rather than leased. Hire purchase transactions are in most cases analyzed in the same way as leases. The definition of a finance lease is set out below. Any other lease is an operating lease, under which the asset does not appear in the books of the lessee, but the lease payments are shown in the income statement as they accrue. From the point of view of the lessor, the asset remains on the balance sheet and will be depreciated accordingly.

Operating leases create little difficulty. All that is necessary is that the amounts payable under the lease are allocated to the proper time periods in which the assets are used.

SSAP 21 defines a finance lease as one "that transfers substantially all the risks and rewards of ownership of an asset to the lessee." This is normally presumed to be the case if, at the outset, the present value of the minimum lease payments (including any initial payment) amounts to 90% or more of the fair value of the leased asset.

Under a finance lease the asset is valued by the lessee either at the discounted present value of the expected payments or at fair value. The latter is more logical. The discount rate under the former method is the implicit rate that equates the payments with their fair value at the start; there is little point in working out this discount rate in order to discount the payments back to yield the figure for fair value. The book value of the asset will then be depreciated over its expected life as if it had been purchased outright, taking into account any terminal residual value to be paid or received under the agreement. At the same time, a liability will be recorded of the value of the loan taken out to "buy" the asset, the loan being paid off over the life of the asset. The actual payments under the finance lease will, of course, exceed the depreciation charges, the difference representing the financing costs involved. SSAP 21 permits these financing costs to be written off against revenues, apportioned either by an actuarial method (representing a constant percentage on the outstanding balance of the loan), or on a sum of the digits or straight-line basis. The choice is basically arbitrary.

From the point of view of the lessor, the rules determining whether a lease is an operating or a finance lease are applied quite independently of how they have been applied by the lessee. (For example, the lessor may be aware of the actual cost of the asset leased, whereas the lessee may have a different idea of the fair value.) Under a finance lease, the lessor must separate the cost of the investment made in the leased asset from the "gross earnings" to be received under the lease. These "gross earnings" are the total minimum lease payments (including any initial payment and any unguaranteed residual value accruing to the lessor) less the cost of the leased asset (net of any grants receivable). The principle is that the gross earnings will be allocated on an actuarial basis to produce a constant percentage return on the net investment in the asset, reduced year by year by a proportion of rental income received. There is no particular reason in principle why an actuarial allocation pattern should be required, but a single treatment is perhaps to be be preferred to several permitted alternatives.

Disclosure of leased assets by the lessee is required by SSAP 21 as follows:

1. Policies adopted
2. Operating lease expenses for the period, divided between those for the hire of plant and machinery and all other operating leases (including property)
3. Aggregate finance charges for the period in respect of finance leases
4. Aggregate depreciation for the period on assets held either under finance leases or hire purchase contracts
5. Gross amount and accumulated depreciation in respect of each major class of asset held either under finance leases or hire purchase contracts
6. Future obligations in respect of finance leases and hire purchase contracts (which may be combined with other obligations), divided

into those payable (*a*) in the next year, (*b*) in 2 to 5 years inclusive, and (*c*) in more than 5 years

7. Operating lease commitments for payments to be made in the next year alone in respect of operating leases still to run (*a*) for no more than one year, (*b*) for 2 to 5 years, and (*c*) for more than 5 years

8. Commitments authorized but not yet started should be shown as a note under the 1985 Act, Schedule 4, paragraph 50

Disclosure of leased assets by the lessor is required by SSAP 21 as follows:

1. Policies adopted

2. Rentals receivable in the period from operating leases and (separately) from finance leases

3. Net investment in finance leases and (separately) hire purchase contracts

4. The cost of assets bought to be leased out either under finance leases or hire purchase contracts (these assets, once leased out, will be shown under "debtors" and hence will usually need to be divided between amounts due within 1 year and amounts due in more than 1 year)

5. Gross amount and accumulated depreciation in respect of each major class of asset held for the purpose of hiring under operating leases

FRS 5 notes that a leasing transaction may form only part of a larger series of transactions; in such a case it may be necessary to comply with both standards, SSAP 21 and FRS 5. (In case of conflict, it is likely that FRS 5 should take precedence.)

3.8 Oil, Gas, and Mineral Reserves

In Britain an active Oil Industry Accounting Committee (OIAC) has taken the initiative in drafting several Statements of Recommended Practice (SORPs), which have been approved (franked) by the Accounting Standards Committee. The Accounting Standards Board has announced that it will authorize certain bodies to issue their own (industry) accounting standards, and the oil and gas industry has made a start in setting its own standards.

The four oil industry SORPs are "Disclosures about Oil and Gas Exploration Activities" (April 1986), "Accounting for Oil and Gas Exploration and Development Activities" (December 1987), "Accounting for

Abandonment Costs" (June 1988), and "Accounting for Various Financing, Revenue and Other Transactions of Oil and Gas Exploration and Production Companies" (January 1991). Reference should be made to these for matters of detail. The OIAC has expressed alarm over the recent moves of the ASB to redefine provisions in FRED 14. It has been the practice in the extractive industries to build up over the years of operation a sufficient fund to pay for the deconstruction of drilling rigs and so on, and this matching of costs against revenues is specifically permitted by the European Fourth Directive, Article 20(2). The OIAC also has serious doubts about the use of discounting, proposed by the ASB in its Statement of Principles and also in a separate working paper, "Discounting in Financinal Reporting" (April 1997).

Both "full cost" and "successful efforts" methods are permitted in Britain, by SORP 2. "Cost pools" are defined geographically but will not normally cover an area smaller than a complete country. Each cost pool recorded by a full cost company will be regarded as a separate fixed asset, but each field, well, or license cost center recorded by a successful efforts company will be an individual fixed asset of that company. This is significant, for example, in deciding whether to write down the value of a fixed asset in order to reflect a permanent diminution in its value (as required by the 1985 Companies Act). Interest on capital employed may be capitalized up to the start of production.

The OIAC is unhappy with the use of historical cost accounts but reluctant to drop them in favor of current value or discounted cash flow data. Instead, it urges supplementary disclosure to guide users as to the quantities of proven reserves and similar factual information. A 1990 discussion paper "Accounting for the Value of Discovered Reserves of Oil and Gas" still expressed the view that "a comprehensive system of Value Accounting which encompasses a Profit and Loss Account and Balance Sheet, whether as primary or supplementary accounts, appears to be undesirable" (p. 40).

3.9 Intangibles (Excluding Goodwill on Consolidation)

Some discussion has already appeared in Section 3.6 of the valuation of fixed assets, which in general includes intangible and tangible fixed assets as well as investments. The 1985 act states that fixed assets must be valued either at their purchase price or production cost or, alternatively, under the Alternative Accounting Rules, at some current value. The Alternative

Accounting Rules allow all intangible fixed assets except for goodwill to be valued at their current cost.

Under the 1985 Companies Act, intangible property rights can generally be shown on the balance sheet, including purchased trademarks, patents, and so on. Indeed, SSAP 22, "Accounting for Goodwill," formerly seemed to encourage this in paragraph 13:

> Separable net assets may include identifiable intangibles such as those specifically mentioned in the balance sheet formats in the Companies Act 1985, i.e. "concessions, patents, licenses, trade marks and similar rights and assets"; other examples include publishing titles, franchise rights and customer lists. (This list of examples is not intended to be comprehensive.) Identifiable intangibles such as these form part of the separable net assets which are recorded in an acquiring company's accounts at fair value, even if they were not recorded in the acquired company's accounts.

There was, apparently, full agreement that internally generated intangibles should not be capitalized on the balance sheet but any expenditure written off as an expense against earnings.

Accounting for goodwill and intangibles is addressed in FRS 10, published in December 1997. There had previously been no standard specifically covering intangibles, although research and development has been dealt with by SSAP 13, leases by SSAP 21, and goodwill by SSAP 22. R & D and leases both continue to be covered by their respective standards.

Goodwill has been a highly contentious issue in Britain. SSAP 22 encouraged reporting entities to write off purchased goodwill against reserves; as noted above, Bunzl has done so and shows a debit balance on its merger reserve. However, this has been inconsistent since 1993 with the revised international standard, IAS 22, and many British accountants have in any case been unhappy with the treatment. When one firm buys another for a price higher than the value of the recorded assets acquired, this usually means that the purchase is still likely to represent good value for the purchaser. There is no good reason to delete the purchased goodwill entirely from the accounts.

The ASB published a discussion paper in 1993, "Goodwill and Intangible Assets," in which it sought to treat purchased intangibles as being inseparable from goodwill: it argued that the distinction between them "is often one of labeling rather than substance." The ASB used this paper to test respondents' reactions toward capitalization and amortization as against writing off the cost against reserves; no overall consensus emerged, but according to FRS 10, "more respondents favored capitalization methods than favored elimination methods."

FRS 10 requires the costs of developing intangible assets and goodwill internally to be charged as an expense as they are incurred. However, internally generated intangible assets with readily ascertainable market values may be capitalized, provided that they are clearly distinguishable from goodwill and readily measurable, and provided they belong to a homogeneous set of assets. These conditions will rarely be met.

Purchased intangibles are, in general, to be treated in the same way as goodwill in the accounts. They are to be capitalized and amortized over their useful economic lives, subject to a maximum of 20 years. However:

> There may be circumstances in which goodwill or an intangible asset can be regarded as having an indefinite life. In such circumstances, amortisation over an arbitrary period may not be an appropriate method of reflecting the depletion of the goodwill or intangible asset. This will be the case where the value of the goodwill or intangible asset is expected to be capable of continued measurement in future. In such circumstances, the Board believes that a true and fair view will be given only if the goodwill or intangible asset is not amortised, but is instead subject to annual reviews for impairment.

In practical terms, then, the distinction between goodwill and intangibles has become less important, following FRS 10, since they are to be treated similarly. But it is still true that goodwill is incapable of being revalued upward following recognition in the accounts, whereas other intangibles can be revalued if there is sufficient evidence of reliable market values. Once revalued, there will be a requirement to keep the current values up to date each year.

These assets, just like tangible assets, should never be shown as values in the balance sheet that exceed their "recoverable amount," that is to say the higher of their net realizable value and their value in use. FRED 15, "Impairment of Fixed Assets and Goodwill," was discussed in Section 3.6.1.

3.10 Equity Investments in Other Companies

It was noted in Section 3.2.5 that equity investments in other companies do not necessarily make those companies subsidiaries. The first SSAP produced by the Accounting Standards (Steering) Committee in Britain was on the subject of "Associated Companies"; SSAP 1 was originally issued in 1971 and amended in 1974 and 1982. This distinguished among three levels of investment relationships in other companies:

1. Subsidiaries (where more than 50% of the shares are owned or where control is exercised)

2. Associates (where between 20% and 50% of shares are owned or where significant influence is exercised)

3. Other investments where the degree of influence is less, usually because the participating interest is too small

FRS 2 follows the 1985 Companies Act very closely in defining parent and subsidiary undertakings in terms of control. It moves away from the criteria set out in SSAP 1, which define the three levels of investment in associates in terms of percentages of shares owned, although these percentages may still be useful in identifying the extent of control and significant influence. The 1994 ASB Discussion Paper "Associates and Joint Ventures" suggested new definitions of both the terms *participating interest* and *significant influence*, apart from introducing a new expression, *strategic alliances*, which does not appear in the new standard, FRS 9, "Associates and Joint Ventures." FRS 9 replaced SSAP 1 in 1997, and it deals with three categories of investment: (a) associates, (b) joint ventures, and (c) joint ventures that are not entities; these are all defined in terms of how control is exercised over them.

3.10.1 Subsidiaries

Subsidiaries are listed in the annual report of the parent company, and their financial results are normally consolidated in group accounts. Under certain circumstances the parent company is exempt from the need to include a particular subsidiary in group accounts. The European Seventh Directive on group accounts was embodied in the 1989 Companies Act, which restricted the right to exemption to the minimum possible under the Directive. Thus, under Section 229(3) and (4) of the 1985 act (as amended by Section 5 of the 1989 act), a subsidiary shall be excluded from consolidation because of severe long-term restrictions over the parent's right of control, or because the subsidiary is held exclusively with a view to resale, or because the activities of the subsidiary are so different from those of the group that consolidation would be incompatible with presenting a true and fair view. The wording of the last of the conditions is obscure in the act; it really applies only if the subsidiary is bound to report its affairs under separate legislation, for example, as a bank or insurance company. Group accounts were discussed in Section 3.2.

3.10.2   Associated Companies

According to FRS 9, an associate is "an entity (other than a subsidiary) in which another entity (the investor) has a participating interest and over whose operating and financial policies the investor exercises a significant influence." The test is where this significant influence is actually exercised, not whether the investor has the power to do so.

Where an investor's aggregate share in its associates or joint ventures exceeds 15% of the investor's gross assets, gross liabilities, turnover, or operating results, extra information must be disclosed beyond merely the cost of the investment plus the investor's share of retained profits (the minimum that the equity method would require). Investment in any individual associate or joint venture that exceeds 25% of the investor's assets, liabilities, turnover or operating results requires yet additional breakdown of the information, by a note showing the investor's share of asset and liability categories.

FRS 9 requires that associates be accounted for on the "equity" basis. That is to say, the cost of the investment will be shown in the books of the holding company (or the group accounts, if prepared) as a fixed asset, and whenever the associate reports profits or losses, the holding company takes its share into its own accounts (or its group accounts, if these are prepared). This means that the balance on the investment account shows the total amount currently invested in the associate, both at the time of the initial purchase and also by way of any subsequent retained profits (and reduced by any losses). When a dividend is declared, this is credited to the investment account (since less profit is retained in the associate), and debited to accounts receivable until paid.

If the value of the investment is believed to have fallen permanently below the level at which it is shown in the accounts, the value in the accounts must be written down.

The "gross equity" or "expanded equity" method is where the equity investment is augmented by way to a note showing the investor's share of particular categories of asset and liability held by the associate or joint venture concerned. This is quite similar to proportional consolidation, except that the detailed assets and liabilities are shown in a separate note and not added into the group balance sheet.

3.10.3 Other Investments

Where the holding in the other enterprise consists of a holding of shares too small to confer substantial influence, no income from the investment will be shown until a dividend is declared, when it will be credited to the income statement and included among receivables

FRS 8, "Related Party Transactions," requires disclosure of any other relationships that have the effect that transactions are not at arm's length.

3.10.4 A Note on the General Rules for Valuing Investments

The rules for valuing investments are even more broadly permissive than the rules for valuing other assets. These are usually shown at cost, but they may be valued "on any basis which appears to the directors to be appropriate in the circumstances of the company" (1985 act, Schedule 4, Part II, paragraph 31 (3)(b)). Details of the basis, and the reasons for adopting it, must be explained in a note. The definition of "investments" tends to overlap with that for "financial instruments," discussed in Section 3.14.6.

3.11 Inventories

SSAP 9 addresses the issue of valuing inventories (called "stocks" in Britain) and long-term contracts. The rules applying to long-term contracts are complex and specialized; they are summarized in Section 3.11.5.

3.11.1 Valuation Bases

Inventories are normally valued at cost or net realizable value, whichever is lower, unless the alternative valuation rules are being used, in which case stocks may be valued at current cost. According to SSAP 9, the comparison of cost and net realizable value should be done for each item of stock separately, unless this is impractical. In this context, "cost" is defined as either purchase price or direct costs of inputs plus any related production overhead that can be allocated to the goods produced or processed. The methods of identifying the costs of goods sold and the remaining inventory generally use certain simplifying conventions, rather than attempting to trace the specific movement of individual stock items.

Thus, FIFO and weighted averages are both commonly used, and other bases are occasionally found, such as the base stock method. Neither LIFO nor the base stock method is approved in SSAP 9, but there is some conflict between this and Schedule 4, paragraph 27, of the 1985 act, which permits any inventory valuation method. However, companies in Britain do not in fact use LIFO because, although permitted by the 1985 act, its use is not allowed for tax purposes; it would be permissible to use a different method for each purpose, but rather futile.

The 1985 Companies Act states that all current assets are to be treated alike regarding valuation, but of course receivables are actually valued at invoice price (less any provision for bad debts). This point is important in relation to long-term contracts, discussed in Section 3.11.5.

Inventories will be presented in the accounts subdivided into:

1. Raw materials and consumables
2. Work in progress
3. Finished goods and goods for resale
4. Payments on account

Although SSAPs require that the basis used for valuing inventories must be stated, and used consistently from one period to another, there is considerable variation in the amount of detail about inventory methods provided by companies in their statement of accounting policies.

3.11.2 Special Write-Downs for Tax

Although LIFO is not normally used by British companies because it is not allowed for tax purposes, this does not mean that the tax assessment is made on the reported net profit figure published in the accounts. In Britain, negotiations with the Inland Revenue over the tax assessment for the period may well begin with a copy of the draft accounts, but there are many items that might well be treated differently in the assessment of income for tax purposes.

3.11.3 Departures from Historical Cost

Departures from historical cost are allowed only downward where net realizable value is below cost and not upward. Upward revaluation would imply recognizing some element of profit on the goods before it was realized by being sold and invoiced to the customer (see also Section 3.11.5, however). This general rule is liable to be disregarded in certain specialized lines of business such as banking and commodity dealing, where the practice of "marking to market" is now well established in respect of dealing portfolios that have a ready market. In effect, the profit is treated as realized in these cases even though a particular buyer has not yet been identified.

3.11.4 Treatment of Overheads

The inclusion of production overheads in inventory valuation presents some difficulties in practice. There is likely to be some arbitrary judgment involved in estimating what to include in production overhead and then in how to apply this to production. SSAP 9, Appendix 1, paragraph 8, indicates that overhead allocation is to be based on the company's "normal" level of activity, which serves, if anything, to increase rather than to limit the area of discretion.

There is also the unresolved matter of whether interest may be included in defining the cost of inventory. In practice, this is more likely to present a problem in the context of long-term contracts and fixed assets, but the possibility exists in the case of inventory also.

3.11.5 Work-in-Progress under Long-Term Contracts

In 1988 the ASC revised SSAP 9 to correct anomalies that had arisen between the original version (issued in May 1975) and the 1981 Companies Act. The special rules relating to work-in-progress under long-term contracts are designed to permit profits to be recognized before the completion of the contract, which by definition could take years.

Long-term contracts are assessed individually, and the related profit is estimated by comparing turnover with related costs as the activity continues over the years, both terms being interpreted "in a manner appropriate to stage of completion of the contracts, the businesses and the industries in which they operate" (SSAP 9, paragraph 8). Disclosure is required to distinguish between costs and revenues.

If, and only if, it is considered that the outcome of the contract can be foreseen with reasonable certainty before its conclusion, attributable profit may be calculated on a prudent basis and included in current earnings, reflecting the proportion of work carried out to date and taking into account any "known inequalities of profit in the various stages of the contract" (SSAP 9, paragraph 9). If the outcome cannot be foreseen with reasonable certainty, no profit should be anticipated. If a loss is expected, the whole loss should be recognized as soon as it is foreseen, in accordance with the prudence concept (SSAP 9, paragraph 11).

SSAP 9, Appendix 3, provides further guidance on the treatment of long-term contracts. Paragraph 84 observes that "The classification of an 'amount recoverable on contracts' within debtors is a somewhat unfamiliar concept which needs careful attention." As noted in Section 3.10.1, the classification makes all the difference whether this current asset can be valued as stock (and thus at the lower of cost or net realizable value) or as debtors (i.e., receivables), which may be valued to include realized profits.

Interest may be included in defining the cost of work-in-progress under long-term contracts, as discussed in Section 3.6.4.

3.12 Taxation

When the Accounting Standards Committee began to discuss taxation (Exposure Draft 11 was issued in 1973), it apparently never questioned the possibility that taxes borne by a corporation on its profits could be regarded as a distribution of those profits to the community, as one of the parties interested in its progress. Rather, it followed the U.S. precedent and treated tax charges as an expense of running the business, even though tax charges bear virtually no relationship to input costs associated with producing revenues.

The abrupt adoption of U.S. tax accounting practices relates specifically to the treatment of deferred taxation. Before we examine this issue, however, there are particular forms of tax that appear in the accounts of British companies and that need to be explained.

3.12.1 Corporation Tax

After 1965, companies were liable to pay taxes on their net profits, by way of "corporation tax." The system of corporation tax was amended substantially with effect from April 1973 to introduce the "imputation system" in place of the "classical system." The principle was to keep company earnings from being taxed twice (once as company profits and again when distributed to stockholders as dividends as had been the case under the classical system).

The basic principle is quite simple. When a cash dividend payment is made to stockholders, withholding tax becomes payable by the company to the revenue in respect of the amount involved. Under the imputation system, this tax can be offset within certain limits against corporation tax levied on the taxable profits of the corporation. It also funds a tax credit, which the shareholder can use as partial payment of personal tax on individual income. For basic rate income tax–paying shareholders, the imputation system abolished the double taxation of dividends and was more neutral in respect of dividend distribution decisions than was the classical system. In practice, this concept of neutrality has been eroded because stockholders who are not liable to pay income tax at the basic rate (low income individuals, charities, pension funds, and some companies) are able to reclaim from the Inland Revenue the full value of the tax credit. This has created constant pressure from such shareholders for high payout ratios, and the benefits available have contributed to a substantial growth of institutional shareholding in the United Kingdom, at the expense of direct personal holders for whom the tax advantages are much lower. The imputation system is being discontinued from 1999, when company taxation will revert to the classical system. Companies will be assessed for corporation tax on the chargeable profits of the year, and this tax will be paid by quarterly instalments beginning during the year. The tax credit available to individual stockholders is being phased out over several years.

After the introduction of the imputation system, SSAP 8 came into force to provide guidance over the treatment of taxation in the accounts of companies. This will need to be replaced in due course.

Note that the 1997 Bunzl accounts were prepared when the imputation system was still in force, as it will be for accounts prepared for accounting years ending in 1998 and, in some cases,1999. There is reference in the Director's Report of Bunzl plc to the fact that dividends for the year ended December 31 1997 were paid as a "Foreign Income Dividend". This means that Bunzl was, in effect, subject to classical corporation tax, rather than the imputation system (which was not applicable to dividends paid out of foreign earnings already subject to taxation abroad).

3.12.2 *Advance Corporation Tax*

It was laid down in the 1997 Finance Act No.2 that Advance Corporation Taxation (ACT) will be discontinued in 1999. The lengthy explanation given in the second edition of this *Guide* is thus of limited value and is not reproduced here; intepretation of U.K. company accounts published for accounting years ending before mid-1999 may require reference back to the second edition.

3.12.3 *Deferred Taxation*

Accounting for deferred tax was proposed in ED 11 in 1973 and appeared in SSAP 11 in 1975. There was virtually no discussion of the need for deferred taxation in the United Kingdom; debate centered on two particular matters of detail—whether to defer on the liability method or the deferral method and whether to provide for deferred tax on a full or on a partial basis (discussed below). Apart from one or two fairly mild protests, the principle of treating tax as an expense to be "matched" to relevant revenues (rather than as an appropriation of profits, in accordance with traditional British views) was taken for granted. Clearly, the treatment of deferred tax came to Britain from the United States, where the view was well established that taxation was a charge on business (rather than on the owners of the business). The effect is to reallocate the tax effects of an accounting event in order to place those tax effects in the appropriate accounting period.

SSAP 11 adopted the "full provision" basis, and soon produced strong opposition after 1975. Companies often found themselves with huge credit balances on the deferred tax account, typically because they were usually able to write off capital expenditure for tax purposes faster than they depreciated the assets in the income statement. These produced accumulations of deferred tax credits, growing faster than any "reversals" could reduce them.

SSAP 15 in 1978 reduced the impact of deferred tax by moving to the "partial provision" basis, so that provision had to be made only where it was reasonably clear that the aggregate timing differences accumulated in any year would actually be reversed in aggregate in one or more future years.

SSAP 15 was revised in 1985 so that only the "liability" method of calculating the deferred tax provision can now be used. This means that the yearly adjustment to the deferred tax account, passing through the income statement, will be based on the tax liabilities that are expected to arise foreseeably over the next few years. Thus, for example, if an asset is revalued in the accounts by, say, £500,000 and this amount is expected to be realized on sale in the next few years, the credit to revaluation reserve of £500,000 will be reduced by the expected tax charge on that gain at the rate of corporation tax in force at the end of the year. If in subsequent years this tax rate changes, the credit to the deferred tax account will be adjusted accordingly.

In 1996, the IASC revised its IAS 12, "Accounting for Taxes on Income," to take effect for accounting periods beginning from January 1, 1998. This standard prohibits the partial provision method. The ASB is thus under pressure. British support for the partial provision method is strong, and there is some consistency in a rule that makes deferred tax provisions only for liabilities and assets that will actually lead to tax payments or savings in future periods. It is difficult to justify deferred tax balances as representing assets or liabilities in any case: it is far more difficult to do so when they represent differences between current accounting treatments and purely notional tax consequences.

However, the ASB has indicated that it accepts the need for international harmonization in this field, and that it will adopt the full provision method of deferred taxation. In a 1995 discussion paper, it suggests that the full provision method would be more palatable if discounting were allowed to be applied to the future tax effects. This may perhaps make the idea more acceptable, but it is still not clear how to apply discounting to cash flows that are very uncertain both in amount and in timing—indeed, which may well never arise at all!

3.13 Pensions

Some SSAPs have been drafted to meet new problems arising in the U.K. business environment, such as company taxation under the imputation system and accounting for value added tax. In other cases, SSAPs have followed existing U.S. practice, for example, in providing for deferred taxation. In the case of accounting for pension costs, British practice has developed in response to both pressures. From the 1960s onward, increasing numbers of British companies began providing pension schemes for the majority of their employees (not, as previously, for just their senior executives); as these schemes developed, problems of accounting for their cost were recognized in Britain as they had been in the United States from the 1950s.

The relevant U.K. standard, SSAP 24, was published in May 1988 after several years of discussions. The standard follows U.S. precedent in the sense that it seeks to match pension costs as an expense against the revenues produced at the time that the employees were working for the company. Previously, British companies had generally shown the cost of pensions as they were paid by the company. If pensions were included with current payroll costs, this meant that these costs might be shown as expenses several years—perhaps many years—after the former employees had ceased to work for the company. It was to repair this breach in the matching principle that SSAP 24 was adopted.

By comparison with U.S. requirements in FAS-87 and FAS-88, U.K. regulations are still pretty permissive at present. The ASB is likely to move to a projected unit credit method, similar to FASB requirements, but there is also pressure internationally in an entirely different direction to require pension assets and liabilities to be shown at market values on the entity's own balance sheet (as well as being reported, separately, in the accounts of the pension trust). U.K. standards at present rely upon actuarial valuations, not market values, to measure pension funding. U.K. practice presents certain institutional features that do not arise in the United States. The most obvious of these is the occurrence of "defined contribution" schemes, which began to appear in the late 1980s. Most British (and all American) schemes are "defined benefit" schemes. (The Bunzl accounts show some relevant detail in note 23.) The pension rights of employees are laid down as part of their contracts of employment and are specified as a particular pattern of benefits to be received on retirement (with modified rights arising if the employee leaves the employment of the company before retirement age). The pension benefits to be paid in each year of retirement are normally set as a fraction of the wage or salary received in the last year of employment or as an average of the last 3 years' employment. Under a defined benefit scheme, it is the employer's responsibility to make sure that funds are available to pay the pension (and any associated rights) after the employee retires. Contributions into the scheme may be made by both employees and employer or by the employer alone.

The main feature of the defined contribution scheme is that the risk attaching to funding the pension is left primarily with the employee; contributions will be made into the scheme by employees and employer, or by the employer alone, but it is left to each individual employee to make sure that the proceeds are used to buy an annuity or to make some other suitable arrangement, whatever the proceeds of the scheme may prove to be at the date of retirement.

Pension schemes have generally been set up in Britain in the form of a trust, with aims specifically to provide employee pension benefits. Thus, pension assets and liabilities do not appear in the company's own balance sheet. The company is obliged to pay its periodic contributions only to the pension trust. On the other hand, the company does have legal commitments to its employees, and any material difference between the assets of the pension scheme and its liabilities has consequences for the company, and these must be reported in its accounts, as discussed in Section 3.13.4.

Pension trustees are appointed either by the company alone or jointly by the company and employees (often through the employees' trade union representatives). The payments have been made to the trust, which has then invested them either externally, for example, with an assurance company, or internally by holding a stake in the assets of the company. Since 1992 it has been illegal to hold more than 5% of the current market value of the resources of the scheme at any one time invested in employer-related investments (i.e., in assets of the parent company or its associates).

The Social Security Act of 1990 laid down requirements for some degree of index-linking of pension schemes for inflation. As in most other areas, this act will present problems first for the actuary to the pensions scheme. It is only when the scheme is currently seen to be underfunded or overfunded that major accounting policy decisions must be made, arising from the need to decide whether to spread the effects over a number of years or to take the full impact into the current income statement.

3.13.1 Schemes Funded Externally

It has, of course, been possible for an assurance company to provide pension services to the company and its employees on a defined benefit basis. Although the assurance company, through its own actuarial staff, could then make its own estimates of the likely pension costs in future years and arrange that the necessary funds will be provided, it is in fact generally the case that the company retains responsibility for ensuring the adequacy of the scheme.

More commonly, the trustees of the company pensions scheme run their own investment portfolio, buying actuarial advice as needed to ensure that the pensions fund is being maintained at an adequate level to meet future obligations. Given the necessary economies of scale offered by a large number of employees, such a trustee scheme can employ its own expert professional staff. From the viewpoint of the employees, there may be some degree of risk when the pension trust is run by the management of their own company, relying on obscure and complex powers set out in a lengthy trust deed. There have been cases, particularly in the context of takeover bids, where the status of the pension trust and its substantial assets has been found to be unclear. The position of individual employees can also be left rather vague, even when there is little doubt that the pension scheme as a whole is well run and fully funded.

3.13.2 Schemes Funded Internally

Until 1992 it was possible for a pension trust to invest all of its funds in the company itself; indeed, it is legitimate for the trustees to receive, say, equity shares in the company rather than payments in cash. There are obvious disadvantages to this, particularly in that the portfolio held by the pension scheme is all in one security and not diversified, as finance theory requires. In the case of a pension fund, indeed, the problem of the undiversified portfolio is even worse: if the company fails, the employees lose not only income from current employment but their pensions too.

3.13.3 Defined Contribution Schemes

The idea of the defined contribution scheme seems to have been a political statement by the Conservative government in power during the 1980s, as part of its measures to encourage popular capitalism and wider holdings of equity shares. Individuals were to carry responsibilities for managing their own financial affairs, including the need to seek actuarial and investment advice to provide a pension portfolio for their old age. In principle, there are obviously economies of scale in obtaining professional advice for all employees collectively, through the pension scheme, rather than leaving it to individual employees to make their own arrangements.

From an accounting point of view, however, a defined contribution scheme has the great advantage that as soon as the agreed-upon contributions are paid into the scheme and shown as expenses in the accounts, the problem of accounting for pension costs ceases forthwith. The problems of defined benefits schemes are much greater, mainly because the actuarial risks need to be taken into account every year in deciding whether the benefits currently accruing to employees are being fully met by payments into the scheme. The next section, therefore, addresses only defined benefit schemes.

3.13.4 *Defined Benefit Schemes*

Uncertainties arise over many different variables under defined benefit schemes. How many employees are currently in the pension scheme? How long have they been with the company? How long will they stay before either retiring or leaving? What will be their likely final level of pay before retiring? What pensions or withdrawal rights do they enjoy under the scheme in either case? For how many years will they draw a pension after retirement? Do they have other rights, for example, for payments to be made to their estate in the event that they die while in service? Will the surviving spouse and dependents enjoy rights? Will rights be automatically indexed for inflation? Is there provision for any *ex gratia* increase in benefits for past, present, or future employees? What earnings can be expected on the pensions fund meanwhile?

SSAP 24 requires that "the actuarial valuation method and assumptions used for accounting purposes should satisfy the accounting objective" (paragraph 18), that is to say, the objective of making full provision over the employees' service lives for the expected costs of their pensions. This stated accounting objective is not, in fact, sufficient to produce a single, identifiable accounting treatment of pension costs. Instead, there are many different working assumptions that can legitimately be made. One important implication of making actuarial assumptions central to the accounting treatment, however, is that the treatment of pension costs becomes one of the few areas in which discounting is used under accepted British accounting principles, not of course for valuations that appear on the published balance sheet but to identify any over- or under-provided schemes.

SSAP 24 attempts to make a basic distinction between regular pension costs and variations in cost. The division between regular costs and variations in cost is fairly arbitrary in practice. The distinction means that regular costs are charged against current income, while variations in cost are generally spread over "the expected remaining service lives of the current employees in the scheme after making suitable allowances for future withdrawals" (paragraph 23). As a short-cut method, variations in cost may alternatively be spread over a period representing the average remaining service lives. Limited exceptions to this principle may arise (*a*) where substantial numbers of employees leave the pension scheme, (*b*) where pensions effects arise from a reorganization accounted for as an extraordinary item, and (*c*) under exceptional circumstances where a significant additional cost arises to the scheme that has not been allowed for in the actuarial assumptions. Under these three exceptional circumstances, prudence requires a write-off over a shorter time.

The practical effect of SSAP 24 is that analysts can now have some picture of the existence of a pension scheme and whether or not it is currently being fully funded. It is not generally possible for the effects of overfunding or underfunding to be taken to the income statement in a single year, or even over a short period of years.

An Abstract of the Urgent Issues Task Force (UITF 6, November 1992) extends the principles of SSAP 24 to noncash pension benefits.

3.14 Other Standards

3.14.1 Segmental Reporting

Reporting on the activities of the different segments of a company's business can often present problems of arbitrary allocation of costs and revenues between activities. After all, the reason for combining several activities in one company is typically that significant economies of scale exist in the exploitation of one or more common inputs. There is no way to allocate joint inputs in a way that is not arbitrary. In the rare cases of companies that are "pure" conglomerates, in which the activities are entirely independent and held as a portfolio, there is no economic logic for the company. Market investors could presumably have produced their own portfolios to give them just the same benefits.

Companies have been required to disclose segmental information in Britain for more than 20 years, even though this may well include some arbitrariness. Segmental disclosure in Britain is regulated at three levels—company law, stock exchange listing rules, and professional SSAPs. The 1967 Companies Act first required that turnover and profit before tax be analyzed in the directors' report into two or more classes when, in the opinion of the directors, these items differed substantially from one another. It also required the value of exports to be reported. The 1981 Companies Act increased these disclosure requirements. Now turnover and profits were to be split (in notes to the accounts) by principal export markets, unless the directors considered such a split would present a serious risk to the interests of the company (Schedule 4, paragraph 55, 1985 act). The emphasis is on the destination of sales, rather than sources of supply.

The Stock Exchange Listing Agreement requires an analysis by geographic region, of turnover and contribution to trading results relating to trading operations carried on by the company outside Britain and Ireland. "Contribution to trading results" might be defined differently from "profit before tax" as required by the 1985 act; moreover, the emphasis is on the countries in which business activity originates (for example, the manufacturing units from which sales originate, rather than the markets they supply). Both the 1985 act and the Listing Agreement require only geographic analysis, not line of business results. Companies often report both, however.

SSAP 25, "Segmental Reporting," was issued in1990. It extends segmental reporting requirements, both by requiring more information and also by extending the coverage of the requirements to all public companies (whether listed or not) as well as a few large private companies (see below).

Thus, the higher disclosure standards required by SSAP 25, over and above those set by company law, apply only to

1. Public limited companies

2. Holding companies that have a public company as a subsidiary

3. Banking and insurance companies

4. Private companies that exceed any two or more of the following criteria, set at 10 times the size criteria for defining medium-sized companies by Section 248 of the 1985 act. (It is likely that only 150 or so private companies will meet these criteria, out of a million private companies on the register, and out of some 16,000 estimated by the Department of Trade and Industry to be medium sized.)

FRS 3, paragraph 53 states:

> It is important for a thorough understanding of the results and financial position of a reporting entity that the impact of changes on material components of the business should be highlighted. To assist in this objective, if an acquisition, a sale or a termination has a material impact on a major business segment the FRS requires that this impact should be disclosed and explained.

SSAP 25 seeks to advise directors how to determine segments. Schedule 4, paragraph 55(2) of the 1985 act specifically states: "In this paragraph 'market' means a market delimited by geographical bounds." SSAP 25 is a little ambiguous as to how far it seeks to go beyond the act, but it certainly suggests to directors a number of factors that are more than merely geographic. Directors should consider how far different classes of business

1. Earn returns on investment out of line with the remainder of the business; or

2. Are subject to different degrees of risk; or

3. Have experienced different growth rates in the past, or have different potentials for growth in the future.

Factors that should be considered include the nature of products or services supplied and the markets for them, the nature of production processes, distribution channels for products, the way in which activities are organized by the company, and any distinctive legislative requirements relating to parts of the business. These clearly suggest an analysis by different lines of business, rather than geographic areas. However, the latter are also considered important, particularly where economic climates are regarded as notably expansionist or restrictive, where political regimes are unusually unstable, where exchange controls are restrictive, or where exchange rates fluctuate widely. Geographic proximity is not the overriding consideration in grouping territories into a single segment.

Whereas great judgment is left to the directors, SSAP 25 suggests that a segment will normally be considered significant if it contributes 10% or more of the total entity's third party turnover, or profits, or total net assets.

Segmental disclosure should show turnover, both by source and by destination, if they differ materially, divided between sales to external customers and sales to other segments of the company or group. Similarly, segmental disclosure should show operating results, which may be defined as profits or as contribution to profits (depending how far joint costs are allocated to segments) and net assets employed. Recognizing the problems that arise in practice, SSAP 25 leaves some latitude for directors to define these terms in a manner that suits their company.

3.14.2 Cash Flow Statements

SSAP 10 required that reporting entities with a turnover or income of more than £25,000 a year shall present a statement of source and application of funds, going beyond the minimum requirement of statute law. SSAP 10 laid down a standard method for preparing such a statement, derived from the income statement and balance sheet information. SSAP 10 was replaced in 1991.

FRS 1, "Cash Flow Statements," followed U.S. practice in FAS 95 (1987) and adopted a statement of cash flows rather than a statement of changes in working capital and liquid assets. FRS 1 was amended in 1996, and cash was defined more narrowly to include only cash in hand (regardless of currency) plus demand deposits less loans repayable on demand (overdrafts) from qualifying financial institutions.

It is required that the opening and closing cash balances should be reconciled with net borrowings as published in the consolidated balance sheet. In the case of Bunzl's 1997 accounts, this requires cross reference between several notes. Thus the decrease in cash over the year (£9.8 million) is reflected in the second column of note 27, which analyzes net debt. The closing balances in the fourth column of note 27 consist of five items: (a) £26.5 million cash (£20.8 "cash at bank and in hand" from the balance sheet, plus £5.7 "short term deposits" from the top row of note 12); (b) Overdrafts of £15.6 million (from the second row of note 13); (c) Debts due within one year of £13.7 million (from the 1st row of note 13); (d) Debts due after one year of £116.4 million (from the 6th row of note 15); (e) Current asset investments of £0.7 million (from the second row of note 12). The footnote to Bunzl's consolidated cash flow statement explains that the cash flows cannot be reconciled directly with the balance sheet because they have been converted for the former purpose at average exchange rates for the year and for the latter at closing rates.

FRS 1 requires the publication of a cash flow statement with all financial statements intended to give a true and fair view of financial position and profit or loss, except for "small companies" as defined in Section 246 of the 1985 act (sales below £2.8 million; balance sheet total below £1.4 million; no more than 50 employees), wholly owned subsidiaries of companies presenting an FRS 1 group cash flow statement, building societies, and mutual life assurance companies.

The cash flow statement can be prepared on either a direct or an indirect basis, that is to say, either as a summary of the cash book or derived indirectly from the opening and closing balance sheets and income statement (together with the notes). A statement reconciling the operating profit shown in the accounts with the operating cash flow figure (see below) is required under FRS 1.

Cash flows are grouped under five headings:

1. Operating cash inflow/outflow (reconciled to the operating profit before charging depreciation or interest)
2. Returns on investments and servicing of finance invested in or by the company/group (including dividends)
3. Taxation actually paid (not accrued) in the year
4. Capital expenditure on fixed assets and financial investments together with proceeds of sales of such assets
5. Acquisitions and disposals of other enterprises (associates and joint ventures)
6. Equity dividends paid
7. Management of liquid resources (excluding movements between cash balances, of course)
8. Financing activities (proceeds of issues and costs of redemptions of stocks and bonds for cash)

The statement finishes with a balance representing the increase or decrease of cash and net demand balances.

The use of published accounts to assess liquidity is still rather limited, however. The commonly used liquidity ratio comparing current assets with current liabilities gives little indication of the urgency with which those liabilities need to be met; inventories are valued at cost, rather than the realizable values they are expected to yield; the accounts give little sign how far assets of the company are charged by way of security for loans received; and finally, the accounts give no clue how far the company has available to it potential sources of liquidity, for example, in the form of overdraft facilities (for which guarantees may be forthcoming, from directors personally or from other trading partners, etc.)

3.14.3 Earnings per Share

SSAP 3 requires disclosure of earnings per share. The Bunzl accounts show, in note 6, that full dilution would not reduce EPS by as much as 5%.

One of the major aims of FRS 3 was to lessen the emphasis placed on the bottom line earnings figure in the income statement. The ASB also reduced the use of extraordinary items below the line and, hence, outside the definition of earnings for use in investment analysis. In 1993 the Institute of Investment Management and Research published new guidelines that set out ways to calculate a new "headline" earnings figure before extraordinary items (since the institute maintained that FRS 3 caused unnecessary volatility of earnings) and thus produce a new figure for sustainable earnings suitable as a basis for forecasts and EPS ratios. The Financial Times has adopted the use of the IIMR's headline earnings.

3.14.4 Post Balance Sheet Events

SSAP 17 requires disclosure of events that take place after the date of the year end but before the date on which the directors approve the accounts for publication. Both dates must be published. Briefly, if the event shows additional evidence of conditions already existing at the balance sheet date not reflected by the accounts, the accounts will have to be adjusted if the new evidence is material. If the conditions did not exist at that date, but disclosure would still be necessary in order for the reader to reach a proper understanding of the financial situation, disclosure will be made by way of a note.

3.14.5 Research and Development Expenditure

It is worth commenting again that research and development expenditure is treated quite conservatively in British accounts, both by law and under SSAP 13 (see also the comment in Section 3.9). Costs are written off against current income except for development expenditure that is pretty clearly going to be recouped.

3.14.6 Complex Financial Instruments

The fear of creative accounting has troubled the British accounting profession for many years, and some widely publicized allegations of manipulation have appeared in the press, accounting journals, newspapers, and books.

A major field for creative accounting has been complex financial instruments. These have presented opportunities to manipulate items on both the asset and liability side of the balance sheet. The ASB responded with two accounting standards in 1994. FRS 4, "Capital Instruments," concentrates on the liabilities side of the balance sheet. In particular, it aims to dispel ambiguities over the treatment of liabilities as debt, minority interests, or stockholders' funds. It does this by relying largely on the legal form of the financial instrument issued. The standard also prescribes the treatment of finance costs, by requiring that the effective interest rate be identified over the full life of the instrument, and the capitalized value set out in the accounts with annual charges of interest expensed regardless of the pattern of actual cash payments over the term of the instrument.

Capital instruments are defined as any means of raising finance, whether or not the consideration given for its issue takes the form of cash and whether or not the instrument is a transferable security or a contract between as few as two parties. FRS 4 distinguishes between equity shares (basically, those with unlimited rights to participate in profits or surplus on winding up), nonequity shares (those with some, but limited, participation rights), and other liabilities. It excludes only (*a*) warrants issued to employees under employee share schemes; (*b*) leases, which should be accounted for in accordance with SSAP 21; and (*c*) equity shares issued as part of a business combination that is accounted for as a merger.

The effect of the standard is to limit what can be shown as equity. Thus, the conversion of debt should not be anticipated, but convertible debt should be reported within liabilities and the finance cost should be calculated on the assumption that the debt will never be converted. The amount attributable to convertible debt should be stated separately from that of other liabilities. Capital instruments should be reported within shareholders' funds only if they contain no obligation at all (even contingent) to transfer economic benefits.

As for valuing debt, immediately after issue debt should be stated at the amount of the net proceeds. The finance costs of debt should be allocated to periods over the term of the debt at a constant rate on the carrying amount. All finance costs should be charged in the profit and loss account, except in the case of investment companies. The carrying amount of debt should be increased by the finance cost in respect of the reporting period and reduced by payments made in respect of the debt in that period.

The practice of treating finance costs on an annuity basis seems to be an ingrained feature of the ASB's thinking; there is little theoretical justification for making this choice when, for example, there is no corresponding requirement to depreciate fixed assets on a similar pattern. A definite rule, even if arbitrary, however, may serve to limit alternative treatments for monitoring and contracting.

FRS 5, "Reporting the Substance of Transactions," adopts the principle that the substance of transactions should dominate over their legal form. FRS 5 deals as much with assets as with liabilities. It begins by referring to the "Statement of Principles," Chapter 3, in its definition of assets and liabilities:

> Assets are rights or other access to future economic benefits controlled by an entity as a result of past transactions or events. Liabilities are an entity's

obligations to transfer economic benefits as a result of past transactions or events.

FRS 5 says that "where a transaction results in an item that meets the definition of an asset or liability, that item should be recognized in the balance sheet if there is sufficient evidence of the existence of the item (including, where appropriate, evidence that a future inflow or outflow of benefit will occur), and the item can be measured at a monetary amount with sufficient reliability." There are also rules for the "derecognition" of assets and liabilities, concerned with the removal of items from the balance sheet. FRS 5 discusses this only in the context of assets but makes a distinction among complete derecognition, no derecognition, and partial derecognition. Basically, an asset is derecognized when a transaction means the transfer of an asset to another party, together with all the significant benefits and risks relating to that asset. Partial recognition arises where, after a transaction to buy or sell an asset, some residual risks or benefits remain with the seller.

FRS 5 may impact on other standards, for example, SSAP 21 if a lease transaction is only part of a larger series of transactions.

FRS 5 also introduces an extension of the definition of subsidiary undertaking in the 1985 Companies Act. It adds the concept of the quasi-subsidiary (see Section 3.1 above).

An important feature of FRS 5 is the lengthy set of application notes in the appendix that "specify how the requirements of FRS 5 are to be applied to transactions that have certain features. For such transactions, observance of the Notes will normally be sufficient to ensure compliance with the requirements of FRS 5." These address five particular areas of practice: consignment stock, sale and repurchase agreements, factoring of debts, securitized assets, and loan transfers.

4. Expected Future Developments

4.1 The Accounting Standards Board's Future Program

The ASB was created because its predecessor, the Accounting Standards Committee, was thought to have lost credibility because of its inability to secure agreement over an inflation standard. In fact, there was probably little the ASC needed to fear on this front since the rate of inflation was falling in the late 1980s from the high levels of the 1970s towards 3% a year. Morever, the most potent pressure on standard setters tends to arise from falls in stock market prices, and in the late 1980s the stock market was in a healthy condition.

It used to be claimed that the old ASC suffered from a lack of authority, in part because its standards needed to be enforced by the six CCAB bodies upon their own members. Their councils had to be persuaded to support each new standard as it came along. It is certainly true that disciplinary action was never taken by the CCAB bodies against their members for disregarding standards. But it is also true that these same bodies felt a commitment to the standards issued in their name. Their ability to veto the issue of accounting standards was only exercised once, in 1986, and this in fact prevented a serious error: the imminent standard on foreign currency translation would have had disastrous consequences for bank dividend distributions.

The Dearing Report that led to the creation of the ASB stressed the need for a new body with formal powers of its own, and the 1989 Companies Act duly provided these. The ASB is now somewhat insulated from the need to persuade and consult as widely as the old ASC needed to do, but this presents disadvantages as well as advantages. Accountants no longer feel a sense of ownership toward standards that they no longer help to set.

While discussion papers and exposure drafts are still issued before a standard, it is now more difficult to comment helpfully at the draft stage, partly because it is more difficult to know how to pitch criticism at an appropriate level. ASB drafts may contain trivial drafting faults, inconsistencies with the wording of other standards or of company law, changes in established practice that have unpredictable effects (for better or for worse), and controversial policy innovations. Most commentators, motivated by a wish to improve proposed reforms, find it very difficult to know how far new measures are supported by a coherent and integrated work program, especially since no authoritative Statement of Principles has yet been published.

To an important extent, the ASB does not require public support for its program, having effective power to secure adherence to its standards through the Financial Reporting Review Panel. However, a major fall in stock prices in the future could potentially threaten a crisis of confidence in the ASB and undermine public and political confidence. This in turn would lead to demands for a British securities and exchange commission (perhaps on the Australian model): the ASB would then need all the friends it could muster.

4.2 International Harmonization

There is also an important agenda that is even less clearly visible to most practicing accountants than the ASB's conceptual framework, namely international harmonization. It is clear that some changes to U.K. standards (notably in the area of deferred taxation) have been driven by a wish to achieve greater international agreement and standarization. But there is little by way of recognizable due process among standard setters in negotiating international accommodations. Few people know what is going on, fewer understand the issues, and fewer still have sufficient economic incentive or effective power to intervene.

Yet the results have great significance for financial reporting globally. One has only to think of the immense cost of the initiative by the government of the People's Republic of China to require all enterprises to prepare accounts in line with international standards, particularly if this leads to the additional possibility of valuing assets and liabilities at some form of market value. Complex technical standards designed for an Anglo-American context may produce bizarre results in emerging economies.

As against this, international capital flows are still increasing, despite setbacks in the Far East, and investors need more than ever to be able to compare the results of businesses that report under different jurisdictions. The IASC looks to the International Organization of Securities Commissions to give authority to its standards, authority that it otherwise lacks from a body of international law. This authority is augmented by the willingness of individual governments to accept international standards as authoritative within their own national framework of company regulations.

The ASB supports the IASC and its work; indeed, the links between the two are close. For example, Sir David Tweedie, full-time chair of the ASB, is also a member of the IASC and chairs a number of its working parties (such as the IASC's steering group on the subject of provisions and contingencies).

This all helps to make sense of the common ground that is apparent between the conceptual frameworks of the FASB, the IASC, and the ASB. They draw on similar sources in the literature of the 1950s, and they may eventually lead to similar standards.

Whether these standards perform a valuable function is another matter. The theoretical basis on which the FASB conceptual framework project was established dates back 50 years or more. The ASB's refinements are in some respects inconsistent with it, so that, for example, the use of current market price data in published financial statements involves feedback to external readers that presupposes information that is already in the public domain. As a specific example, the wish (shared by FASB and ASB) to use discounting in calculating impairment values is interpreted by the ASB as reducing individual impaired assets, or groups of them, so that they will be sure to earn a market rate of return in future; however, the rate of return that is seen as appropriate is the observable rate put on the reported earnings of the entity, presumably as affected by the write down. The circularity is obvious. The accounts are intended, surely, as a means of triangulating market expectations, not merely mirroring them.

There needs to be a far more open and informed debate over conceptual frameworks globally, and specifically over the Statement of Principles in Britain.

Acknowledgments

The author acknowledges with thanks the help of David Matthews, Group Chief Accountant of Bunzl plc, and also of the Technical Department of the Chartered Association of Certified Accountants (ACCA), in particular Richard Martin for checking the accuracy of the technical details in this chapter. Any errors that remain are, of course, the responsibility of the author alone.

Useful Addresses

Institute of Chartered Accountants in England and Wales
Chartered Accountants' Hall
Moorgate Place
London EC2P 2BJ
Tel: +(171) 920 8100
Fax: +(171) 920 0547

Institute of Chartered Accountants of Scotland
27 Queen Street
Edinburgh EH2 1LA
Tel: +(131) 225 5673
Fax: +(131) 225 3813

Chartered Association of Certified Accountants
29 Lincoln's Inn Fields

London WC2A 3EE
Tel: +(171) 242 6855
Fax: +(171) 831 8054

Chartered Institute of Management Accountants
63 Portland Place
London W1N 4AB
Tel: +(171) 637 2311
Fax: +(171) 631 5309

Chartered Institute of Public Finance and Accountancy
3 Robert Street
London WC2N 6BH
Tel: +(171) 895 8823
Fax: +(171) 895 8825

International Accounting Standards Committee
167 Fleet Street
London EC4A 2ES
Tel: +(171) 353 0565
Fax: +(171) 353 0562

Accounting Standards Board
Holborn Hall
100 Gray's Inn Road
London WC1X 8AL
Tel: +(171) 404 8818
Fax: +(171) 404 4497

Consolidated Profit and Loss Account

for the year ended 31 December 1997

	Notes	1997 £m	1996 £m
Sales			
Existing businesses		1,604.4	1,560.2
Acquisitions		99.6	
Continuing operations		1,704.0	1,560.2
Discontinued operations		49.2	236.2
Total sales	1	**1,753.2**	**1,796.4**
Operating profit			
Existing businesses		118.1	114.6
Acquisitions		6.9	
Continuing operations		125.0	114.6
Discontinued operations		2.3	1.1
Total operating profit	1	**127.3**	**115.7**
Profit on sale of discontinued operations	29	2.2	–
Profit on ordinary activities before interest		**129.5**	**115.7**
Net interest payable	3	(3.6)	(2.2)
Profit on ordinary activities before taxation		**125.9**	**113.5**
Taxation on profit on ordinary activities	4	(44.6)	(39.7)
Profit on ordinary activities after taxation		**81.3**	**73.8**
Profit attributable to minorities		(1.1)	(0.9)
Profit for the financial year		**80.2**	**72.9**
Dividends paid and proposed	5	(30.7)	(28.1)
Retained profit		**49.5**	**44.8**
Earnings per share	6	**17.9p**	**16.4p**
Adjusted earnings per share	6	**17.6p**	**16.4p**
Dividends per share	5	**6.8p**	**6.3p**

Movements on consolidated reserves are shown in Notes 8 and 19. The Accounting Policies and Notes on pages 9 to 30 form part of these financial statements.

Consolidated Balance Sheet

at 31 December 1997

	Notes	1997 £m	1996 £m
Fixed assets			
Tangible assets	7	**174.4**	154.1
Associated undertakings	8	**11.1**	10.2
Investments	9	**4.9**	3.7
		190.4	168.0
Current assets			
Stocks	10	**170.0**	147.0
Debtors: amounts receivable within one year	11	**296.6**	282.0
Debtors: amounts receivable after more than one year	11	**13.2**	15.8
Investments	12	**9.3**	15.0
Cash at bank and in hand		**20.8**	20.6
		509.9	480.4
Current liabilities			
Creditors: amounts falling due within one year	13	**(309.7)**	(272.2)
Net current assets		**200.2**	208.2
Total assets less current liabilities		**390.6**	376.2
Creditors: amounts falling due after more than one year	14	**(117.0)**	(60.1)
Provisions for liabilities and charges	17	**(47.2)**	(24.1)
Net assets		**226.4**	292.0
Capital and reserves			
Called up share capital	18	**113.0**	111.9
Share premium account	19	**37.3**	30.5
Revaluation reserve	19	**5.7**	7.8
Merger reserve	19	**(90.4)**	25.5
Profit and loss account	19	**146.8**	102.4
Attributable share of associated undertakings' reserves	8	**10.2**	9.3
Shareholders' funds: equity interests		**222.6**	287.4
Minority equity interests		**3.8**	4.6
		226.4	292.0

Approved by the Board of Bunzl plc on 16 March 1998. A J Habgood, Chairman and J G Bason, Finance Director.

Consolidated Cash Flow Statement

for the year ended 31 December 1997

	Notes	1997 £m	1996 £m
Net cash inflow from operating activities	26	**131.0**	**155.7**
Returns on investments and servicing of finance			
Interest received		3.2	0.7
Interest paid		(4.2)	(3.3)
Dividends paid to minority shareholders		(0.3)	(0.5)
Other cash flows		(2.2)	0.3
Net cash outflow for returns on investments and servicing of finance		**(3.5)**	**(2.8)**
Tax paid		**(42.5)**	**(38.0)**
Capital expenditure and financial investment			
Purchase of tangible fixed assets		(39.9)	(37.6)
Sale of tangible fixed assets		4.8	4.8
Net cash outflow for capital expenditure and financial investment		**(35.1)**	**(32.8)**
Acquisitions and disposals			
Purchase of businesses	28	(160.3)	(78.8)
Disposal of businesses	29	57.8	–
Other acquisition and disposal cash flows		(0.2)	(3.6)
Net cash outflow for acquisitions and disposals		**(102.7)**	**(82.4)**
Equity dividends paid		**(28.0)**	**(24.3)**
Net cash outflow before use of liquid resources and financing		**(80.8)**	**(24.6)**
Management of liquid resources*		**4.3**	**(0.9)**
Financing			
Increase/(decrease) in short term loans		6.5	(5.0)
Increase in long term loans		55.0	35.4
Decrease in finance leases		(0.2)	(0.1)
Shares issued for cash		5.4	2.7
Net cash inflow from financing		**66.7**	**33.0**
(Decrease)/increase in cash		**(9.8)**	**7.5**

* Liquid resources consist of term deposits not repayable on demand.

Cash flows are stated at the average exchange rates for the year. For the purpose of calculating these cash flows, the opening and closing balance sheets have been retranslated at the average exchange rates for the year. As a result, the movements cannot be ascertained from the figures shown in the consolidated balance sheets.

Statement of Total Recognised Gains and Losses

for the year ended 31 December 1997

	Consolidated	
	1997 £m	1996 £m
Profit for the financial year	80.2	72.9
Currency translation differences on foreign currency net investments	(4.5)	(8.5)
Total recognised gains and losses for the year	**75.7**	**64.4**

Note of Historical Cost Profits and Losses

for the year ended 31 December 1997

	Consolidated	
	1997 £m	1996 £m
Reported profit on ordinary activities before taxation	125.9	113.5
Revaluation reserve movement on disposal of properties	1.6	0.7
Adjustment of depreciation to historical cost basis	0.1	0.2
Historical cost profit on ordinary activities before taxation	**127.6**	**114.4**
Historical cost profit for the year retained after taxation, minority interests and dividends	**51.2**	**45.7**

Reconciliation of Movements in Shareholders' Funds

for the year ended 31 December 1997

	Consolidated	
	1997 £m	1996 £m
Profit for the financial year	80.2	72.9
Dividends paid and proposed	(30.7)	(28.1)
Goodwill transferred to the profit and loss account from the merger reserve	1.9	–
Net transfer to reserves from the profit and loss account	**51.4**	**44.8**
Scrip dividend adjustment	0.1	1.2
Goodwill written off on acquisitions	(117.8)	(66.7)
Issue of share capital	6.3	3.9
Currency translation and other movements	(4.8)	(8.5)
Net deduction to shareholders' funds	**(64.8)**	**(25.3)**
Opening shareholders' funds	287.4	312.7
Closing shareholders' funds	**222.6**	**287.4**

Company Balance Sheet

at 31 December 1997

	Notes	1997 £m	1996 £m
Fixed assets			
Tangible assets	7	**9.1**	9.0
Investments	9	**180.0**	174.0
		189.1	183.0
Current assets			
Debtors: amounts receivable within one year	11	**235.2**	287.6
Debtors: amounts receivable after more than one year	11	**83.1**	19.6
Cash at bank and in hand		**0.2**	–
		318.5	307.2
Current liabilities			
Creditors: amounts falling due within one year	13	**(45.8)**	(54.4)
Net current assets		**272.7**	252.8
Total assets less current liabilities		**461.8**	435.8
Creditors: amounts falling due after more than one year	14	**(4.0)**	–
Provisions for liabilities and charges	17	**(11.2)**	(8.5)
Net assets		**446.6**	427.3
Capital and reserves			
Called up share capital	18	**113.0**	111.9
Share premium account	19	**37.3**	30.5
Revaluation reserve	19	**0.5**	0.5
Special reserve	19	**177.2**	177.2
Profit and loss account	19	**118.6**	107.2
Shareholders' funds: equity interests		**446.6**	427.3

Approved by the Board of Bunzl plc on 16 March 1998. A J Habgood, Chairman and J G Bason, Finance Director.

The Accounting Policies and Notes on pages 9 to 30 form part of these financial statements.

Accounting Policies

a Basis of preparation

The financial statements have been prepared under the historical cost convention, as modified by the revaluation of land and buildings, and have been prepared in accordance with applicable UK accounting standards. In order to give a true and fair view, the provisions of the Companies Act 1985 have been departed from as described in Note 19 to the financial statements.

b Basis of consolidation

The consolidated financial statements incorporate the assets and liabilities of the Company and its subsidiary undertakings at 31 December 1997 and their results for the periods during 1997 in which they were part of the Group. The consolidated financial statements include the Group's share of the results and net assets of associated undertakings owned during the financial year. Associated undertakings are those in which the Group holds a substantial shareholding and over which it is able to exercise significant influence.

c Goodwill

Goodwill, being the excess of the costs of businesses acquired over the fair value of their net tangible assets, is fully written off against the merger reserve on acquisition. In determining the profit or loss on disposal of a business, any goodwill on acquisition, net of goodwill eliminated through the profit and loss account as a result of any permanent diminution in value, is transferred to the profit and loss reserve from the merger reserve through the profit and loss account.

d Investments in subsidiary undertakings

Where the merger relief provisions of the Companies Act 1985 apply, investments of the Company are accounted for on the basis of the nominal value of shares issued as purchase consideration.

e Foreign currencies

The results of overseas subsidiary and associated undertakings have been translated into pounds sterling at average exchange rates. Assets and liabilities denominated in foreign currencies have been translated at year end exchange rates, except where a forward exchange contract has been arranged when the contracted rate is used.

Exchange differences on the retranslation of opening net worth in overseas subsidiary and associated undertakings, net of related foreign currency borrowings and foreign currency hedging contracts, together with differences arising from the use of average and year end exchange rates, have been taken to reserves. Other exchange differences are taken to the profit and loss account.

f Fixed assets

Freehold and leasehold land and buildings are included at cost or valuation on an open market existing use basis, prepared at regular intervals by qualified valuers, less accumulated depreciation. All other assets are included at historical cost, less accumulated depreciation. The profit or loss on sale of tangible fixed assets is calculated by reference to the carrying value of the assets.

g Depreciation

Fixed assets are depreciated over their estimated remaining useful lives at the following annual rates applied to original cost or subsequent valuation less estimated residual value:

Buildings   2% or life of lease if shorter
Plant and machinery   10 - 20%
Fixtures, fittings and equipment 10 - 25%

Depreciation is not provided on freehold land.

h Leases

Where the Group has substantially all the risks and rewards of ownership of an asset subject to a lease, the lease is treated as a finance lease. Future instalments payable under finance leases, net of finance charges, are included in creditors with the corresponding asset value treated as a tangible fixed asset and depreciated over the shorter of the estimated useful life or the term of the lease. All other leases are treated as operating leases and the rentals are charged to the profit and loss account as incurred.

i Sales

Sales are net sales invoiced to third parties, excluding inter company transactions, sales by associated undertakings and sales taxes.

j Stocks

Stocks are valued at the lower of cost (on a first in, first out basis) and net realisable value. For work-in-progress and finished goods, cost includes an appropriate proportion of labour and overheads.

k Deferred taxation

Deferred taxation arises from differences in the treatment of certain items for accounting and taxation purposes and is accounted for on the liability method. Provision is made to the extent that it is probable that a liability or asset will crystallise in the foreseeable future.

l Pension benefits

The Group operates both defined benefit and defined contribution pension schemes throughout the world. The funds of the principal schemes are administered by trustees, are held independently from the Group and are not included in the financial statements. Contributions paid to defined benefit schemes operated by the Group are based upon the recommendations of qualified actuaries and are charged against profits on a systematic basis over the expected remaining service lives of participating employees. Independent actuarial valuations of defined benefit schemes are made approximately every three years. Contributions paid to defined contribution schemes are charged to the profit and loss account in the period in which they arise.

Notes to the Financial Statements

1 Segmental analysis

	Sales 1997 £m	Sales 1996 £m	Operating profit 1997 £m	Operating profit 1996 £m	Net operating assets 1997 £m	Net operating assets 1996 £m
Continuing operations						
Paper and Plastic Disposables	**1,068.3**	949.9	**74.4**	69.8	**150.4**	113.8
Fine Paper	**334.8**	339.2	**20.4**	20.4	**96.6**	96.7
Filters and Tape	**179.3**	169.4	**24.4**	20.9	**76.1**	60.6
Plastic Products	**121.6**	101.7	**17.0**	14.0	**96.5**	66.0
Corporate activities			**(11.2)**	(10.5)	**(3.6)**	18.2
	1,704.0	1,560.2	**125.0**	114.6	**416.0**	355.3
Discontinued operations	**49.2**	236.2	**2.3**	1.1	**11.4**	50.9
	1,753.2	1,796.4	**127.3**	115.7	**427.4**	406.2
Country of operation						
UK	**502.1**	477.9	**39.9**	36.6	**167.0**	159.5
Rest of Europe	**79.9**	273.0	**6.7**	6.3	**20.2**	62.9
US	**1,059.9**	934.1	**82.6**	72.5	**201.4**	126.8
Rest of the world	**111.3**	111.4	**9.3**	10.8	**42.4**	38.8
Corporate activities			**(11.2)**	(10.5)	**(3.6)**	18.2
	1,753.2	1,796.4	**127.3**	115.7	**427.4**	406.2
Geographical market supplied						
UK	**448.2**	420.3				
Rest of Europe	**109.1**	297.6				
US	**1,071.4**	950.3				
Rest of the world	**124.5**	128.2				
	1,753.2	1,796.4				

Reconciliation to consolidated balance sheet

	1997	1996
Net operating assets as above	**427.4**	406.2
Interest bearing cash and investments	**12.0**	22.0
Interest bearing debt (Note 15)	**(145.7)**	(78.1)
Dividends and corporate taxes (Notes 11 and 13)	**(44.2)**	(42.2)
Provisions for deferred taxation and discontinued operations (Note 17)	**(23.1)**	(15.9)
Net assets	**226.4**	292.0

2 Net operating charges

Operating profit is stated after net operating charges of £1,625.9m (1996: £1,680.7m) analysed as follows:

	Existing businesses 1997 £m	Acquisitions 1997 £m	Discontinued operations 1997 £m	Total 1997 £m	Existing businesses 1996 £m	Discontinued operations 1996 £m	Total 1996 £m
Changes in stock of finished goods and work-in-progress	8.7	(2.2)	(14.3)	(7.8)	(5.1)	(2.9)	(8.0)
Purchases of finished goods and goods for resale	1,001.8	58.5	37.6	1,097.9	977.7	181.9	1,159.6
Raw materials and consumables	133.0	12.4	8.0	153.4	153.3	7.7	161.0
Own work capitalised	(0.5)	–	(0.1)	(0.6)	(0.6)	–	(0.6)
Employee costs (Note 24)	190.0	12.8	6.7	209.5	191.2	27.3	218.5
Depreciation	19.0	1.4	1.3	21.7	18.2	3.0	21.2
Auditors' remuneration for statutory audit	1.1	0.1	–	1.2	1.2	0.1	1.3
Hire of plant and machinery and operating lease costs	10.0	0.2	–	10.2	9.8	0.7	10.5
Property rentals	18.0	1.1	0.4	19.5	15.8	2.6	18.4
Share of profits of associated undertakings	(3.6)	–	–	(3.6)	(4.0)	–	(4.0)
Other operating expenses	109.8	8.4	7.3	125.5	88.7	14.9	103.6
Profit on sale of fixed assets	(1.0)	–	–	(1.0)	(0.6)	(0.2)	(0.8)
Net operating charges	**1,486.3**	**92.7**	**46.9**	**1,625.9**	**1,445.6**	**235.1**	**1,680.7**

Fees for non-audit work performed by the Company's auditors and their associates were £0.6m (1996: £0.3m) for the Company and its UK subsidiary undertakings and £0.3m (1996: £0.2m) for its non-UK subsidiary undertakings.

3 Net interest payable

	Consolidated	
	1997 £m	1996 £m
Interest receivable		
On bank deposits and unlisted investments	2.4	1.7
Total interest receivable	**2.4**	**1.7**
Interest payable		
On loan capital, bank loans, overdrafts and other borrowings:		
repayable within five years, not by instalments	(4.3)	(3.1)
repayable within five years, by instalments	(0.3)	(0.2)
repayable wholly or partly in more than five years	(1.4)	(0.6)
Total interest payable	**(6.0)**	**(3.9)**
Net interest payable	**(3.6)**	**(2.2)**

Notes to the Financial Statements
continued

4 Taxation

	Consolidated	
	1997 £m	1996 £m
Consolidated UK corporation tax at 31.5% (1996: 33%)	48.7	11.5
Overseas taxes	32.1	26.8
Credit for overseas tax	(40.0)	(0.7)
Associated undertakings	1.2	2.0
Deferred taxation transfers:		
accelerated capital allowances	–	(0.2)
pension arrangements and other timing differences	1.2	0.2
Total taxation for year	43.2	39.6
Credited to other reserves	1.4	0.1
Taxation on profit on ordinary activities	**44.6**	**39.7**

Deferred taxation not accounted for in the year is £0.6m (1996: £1.5m) in respect of accelerated capital allowances and £0.4m (1996: £nil) in respect of other timing differences.

5 Dividends paid and proposed

	Per share		Total	
	1997	1996	1997 £m	1996 £m
Interim paid 2 January 1998	2.3p	2.2p	10.4	9.8
Proposed final payable 1 July 1998	4.5p	4.1p	20.3	18.3
	6.8p	**6.3p**	**30.7**	**28.1**

6 Earnings per share

	1997	1996
Earnings per share calculated by dividing earnings of £80.2m (1996: £72.9m) by 448,997,470 (1996: 445,388,426), the weighted average number of ordinary shares in issue	17.9p	16.4p
Adjustment in respect of profit on sale of discontinued operations net of taxation	(0.3)p	–
Adjusted earnings per share calculated by dividing adjusted earnings of £79.2m (1996: £72.9m) by 448,997,470 (1996: 445,388,426), the weighted average number of ordinary shares in issue	17.6p	16.4p

The adjusted earnings per share calculation is presented in order to provide a more meaningful measure of the underlying performance of the Group.

The dilution in earnings per share after taking account of the exercise of all outstanding options would be less than 2%.

7 Tangible assets

Consolidated:

	Land and buildings £m	Plant and machinery £m	Fixtures, fittings and equipment £m	Total £m
Cost or valuation				
Beginning of year	66.3	162.6	54.0	282.9
Acquisitions less divestments	(4.3)	23.6	0.6	19.9
Additions	5.8	26.4	7.7	39.9
Disposals and adjustments	(3.1)	(4.4)	(0.3)	(7.8)
Currency translation movement	(1.9)	(1.5)	(0.9)	(4.3)
End of year	62.8	206.7	61.1	330.6
Depreciation				
Beginning of year	11.0	86.5	31.3	128.8
Acquisitions less divestments	0.4	15.1	(2.5)	13.0
Charge in year	1.5	14.2	6.0	21.7
Disposals and adjustments	(0.3)	(4.4)	(0.3)	(5.0)
Currency translation movement	(0.2)	(1.5)	(0.6)	(2.3)
End of year	12.4	109.9	33.9	156.2
Net book value at 31 December 1997	**50.4**	**96.8**	**27.2**	**174.4**
Net book value at 31 December 1996	55.3	76.1	22.7	154.1

The net book value of fixed assets includes assets held under finance leases and hire purchase contracts totalling £0.2m (1996: £0.4m). Accumulated depreciation of these assets amounts to £0.8m (1996: £2.0m).

The net book value of fixed assets at 31 December 1997 comprised:

	Land £m	Freehold buildings £m	Long leasehold £m	Short leasehold £m	Plant and machinery £m	Fixtures, fittings and equipment £m	Total £m
Consolidated:							
At cost	6.1	19.2	6.8	6.3	206.7	61.1	306.2
At valuation	11.1	10.8	2.5	–	–	–	24.4
Cost or valuation	17.2	30.0	9.3	6.3	206.7	61.1	330.6
Depreciation	(0.2)	(4.9)	(4.0)	(3.3)	(109.9)	(33.9)	(156.2)
Net book value at 31 December 1997	**17.0**	**25.1**	**5.3**	**3.0**	**96.8**	**27.2**	**174.4**

Notes to the Financial Statements
continued

7 Tangible assets continued

The historical cost and the related depreciation of the tangible fixed assets are:

	Land and buildings £m	Plant and machinery £m	Fixtures, fittings and equipment £m	Total £m
Historical cost	57.1	206.7	61.1	324.9
Depreciation	(12.4)	(109.9)	(33.9)	(156.2)
Net book value at 31 December 1997	44.7	96.8	27.2	168.7
Net book value at 31 December 1996	51.0	76.1	22.7	149.8

Future capital expenditure

	1997 £m	1996 £m
Commitments not provided for	2.3	2.7
Expenditure authorised but not contracted for	1.8	2.6
	4.1	5.3

Bunzl plc:

Cost or valuation

	Land £m	Freehold buildings £m	Short leasehold £m	Fixtures, fittings and equipment £m	Total £m
Beginning of year	6.8	1.6	0.4	0.9	9.7
Additions	0.5	0.2	–	0.1	0.8
Disposals	(0.3)	(0.2)	–	–	(0.5)
End of year	7.0	1.6	0.4	1.0	10.0

Depreciation

	Land £m	Freehold buildings £m	Short leasehold £m	Fixtures, fittings and equipment £m	Total £m
Beginning of year	–	0.1	0.1	0.5	0.7
Charge in year	–	–	0.1	0.2	0.3
Disposals	–	(0.1)	–	–	(0.1)
End of year	–	–	0.2	0.7	0.9
Net book value at 31 December 1997	7.0	1.6	0.2	0.3	9.1
Net book value at 31 December 1996	6.8	1.5	0.3	0.4	9.0

8 Associated undertakings

	Consolidated	
	1997 £m	1996 £m
Share of post-acquisition reserves at beginning of year	9.3	8.9
Share of current year profit after taxation	2.4	2.0
Dividend paid in year	(0.6)	(0.7)
Currency translation and other movements	(0.9)	(0.9)
Share of post-acquisition reserves at end of year	10.2	9.3
Cost of investments	0.9	0.9
Investment in associated undertakings	**11.1**	**10.2**

The principal associated undertaking is shown on page 30. All associated undertakings were unlisted in 1997.

9 Investments held as fixed assets

	Own shares £m	Unlisted £m	Total £m
Consolidated:			
Beginning of year at cost less provisions	0.8	2.9	3.7
Additions	0.4	0.8	1.2
End of year at cost less provisions	**1.2**	**3.7**	**4.9**

Own shares are ordinary shares of the Company held by the Group in an employee benefit trust. The purpose of this trust is to hold shares in the Company for subsequent transfer to certain senior employees and the executive directors under the Long Term Incentive Plan and the Share Partnership Plan, full details of which are set out in the Report of the Remuneration Committee on pages 32 to 37.

The assets, liabilities and expenditure of the trust have been incorporated in the Group's financial statements. At 31 December 1997 the trust held 1,475,835 (1996: 935,269) shares with an aggregate nominal value of £0.4m (1996: £0.2m) and market value of £3.5m (1996: £2.2m).

Notes to the Financial Statements
continued

9 Investments held as fixed assets continued

Bunzl plc:

	Own shares £m	Investments in subsidiary undertakings £m	Total £m
Beginning of year at cost less provisions	0.5	173.5	174.0
Additions	0.2	27.9	28.1
Disposals	–	(22.1)	(22.1)
End of year at cost less provisions	**0.7**	**179.3**	**180.0**

The investments in subsidiary undertakings at 31 December 1997 are stated net of provisions of £10.9m (1996: £3.5m). Principal subsidiary undertakings are listed on page 30.

10 Stocks

	Consolidated 1997 £m	1996 £m
Raw materials and consumables	28.5	23.9
Work-in-progress	4.5	3.3
Finished goods and goods for resale	137.0	119.8
	170.0	**147.0**

11 Debtors

Amounts receivable within one year

	Bunzl plc 1997 £m	1996 £m	Consolidated 1997 £m	1996 £m
Trade debtors	1.6	0.7	246.4	240.0
Amounts owed by subsidiary undertakings	232.9	286.1		
Other debtors	0.1	0.1	21.2	15.9
Prepayments and accrued income	0.5	0.6	20.5	18.0
Corporate taxes	0.1	0.1	8.5	8.1
	235.2	**287.6**	**296.6**	**282.0**

Amounts receivable after more than one year

	Bunzl plc 1997 £m	1996 £m	Consolidated 1997 £m	1996 £m
Amounts owed by subsidiary undertakings	73.3	4.4		
Pension fund prepayment	9.8	10.2	11.2	14.5
Advance corporation tax recoverable	–	5.0		
Other debtors			1.9	1.1
Corporate taxes			0.1	0.2
	83.1	19.6	**13.2**	15.8
	318.3	307.2	**309.8**	297.8

12 Investments held as current assets

	Consolidated	
	1997 £m	1996 £m
Short term deposits repayable on demand	5.7	9.7
Liquid resources	0.7	5.3
Investments	2.9	–
	9.3	15.0

Investments at 31 December 1997 comprised:

	Unlisted £m
Consolidated:	
Beginning of year at cost less provisions	–
Additions	2.9
End of year at cost less provisions	**2.9**

13 Creditors

Amounts falling due within one year

	Bund plc		Consolidated	
	1997 £m	1996 £m	1997 £m	1996 £m
Loans	–	5.0	13.7	9.5
Overdrafts	–	–	15.6	8.7
Payments received on account	–	–	0.2	0.1
Trade creditors	0.2	0.1	157.8	154.9
Amounts owing to subsidiary undertakings	12.8	12.1		
Dividends proposed	30.7	28.1	30.7	28.1
Corporate taxes	–	7.0	22.1	22.4
Other taxation and social security contributions	0.1	0.2	4.0	5.2
Other creditors	–	–	20.8	11.1
Accruals and deferred income	2.0	1.9	44.8	32.2
	45.8	54.4	309.7	272.2

14 Creditors

Amounts falling due after more than one year

	Bund plc		Consolidated	
	1997 £m	1996 £m	1997 £m	1996 £m
Loans (Note 15)	3.7	–	116.4	59.9
Accruals and deferred income	0.3	–	0.6	0.2
	4.0	–	117.0	60.1

Notes to the Financial Statements
continued

15 Loans and overdrafts

	Bunzl plc 1997 £m	Bunzl plc 1996 £m	Consolidated 1997 £m	Consolidated 1996 £m
Falling due after more than one year				
Wholly repayable within five years	–	–	66.0	15.6
Wholly repayable in more than five years	–	–	46.1	43.3
Repayable by instalments				
Instalments due within five years	3.7	–	0.4	0.6
Instalments due after more than five years	–	–	3.9	0.3
	3.7	–	4.3	0.9
Obligations under finance leases	–	–	–	0.1
Loans falling due after more than one year	3.7	–	116.4	59.9
Loans falling due within one year	–	5.0	29.3	18.2
Total loans and overdrafts	3.7	5.0	145.7	78.1
The total borrowings are repayable:				
within one year	–	5.0	29.3	18.2
between one and two years	–	–	1.0	1.0
between two and five years	–	–	65.4	15.3
after more than five years	3.7	–	50.0	43.6
	3.7	5.0	145.7	78.1
Obligations under finance lease included above are repayable:				
within one year	–	–	–	0.1
between one and five years	–	–	–	0.1
	–	–	–	0.2

The aggregate of bank loans and overdrafts is £141.8m (1996: £77.7m). Loans amounting to £1.5m (1996: £3.8m) are secured by either fixed or floating charges on various assets of the relevant companies.

The bank loans are drawn for various periods and at various interest rates linked to US dollar LIBOR. Bank loans of £110.3m (1996: £57.3m) which are repayable within one year have been drawn under committed facilities and can be refinanced on maturity from these same facilities. Accordingly, dependent upon the term of the relevant facility under which they have been drawn, £64.2m (1996: £14.0m) of these loans has been classified as repayable between two and five years and £46.1m (1996: £43.3m) has been classified as repayable after more than five years.

16 Currency and interest rate analysis of net assets and borrowings

The Group's borrowings and net assets (excluding borrowings) by currency at 31 December 1997 were:

	Net assets by currency of operation £m	Gross borrowings £m	Forward foreign exchange contracts £m	Net investments £m
Sterling	135.5	(12.3)	58.2	181.4
US dollar	159.1	(121.9)	(33.5)	3.7
Other	73.9	(11.5)	(24.9)	37.5
	368.5	**(145.7)**	**(0.2)**	**222.6**

The borrowings are at floating rates and include sterling and US dollar denominated bank borrowings that bear interest at rates based on LIBOR. The interest rate exposure is managed by using interest rate options.

17 Provisions for liabilities and charges

	Bund plc 1997 £m	Bund plc 1996 £m	Consolidated 1997 £m	Consolidated 1996 £m
Pensions	–	–	0.8	0.9
Discontinued operations	2.4	3.1	14.4	6.7
Deferred taxation (Note 20)	1.9	1.4	8.7	9.2
Other	6.9	4.0	23.3	7.3
	11.2	**8.5**	**47.2**	**24.1**

£17.9m of other provisions at 31 December 1997 relate to acquisitions.

	Pensions £m	Discontinued operations £m	Deferred taxation £m	Other £m	Consolidated Total £m
Movements					
Beginning of year	0.9	6.7	9.2	7.3	24.1
Charge in year	0.2	8.5	1.2	1.0	10.9
Acquired/(disposed)	–	–	(6.5)	18.4	11.9
Amounts utilised or transferred in year	(0.2)	(0.7)	4.6	(3.4)	0.3
Currency translation movement	(0.1)	(0.1)	0.2	–	–
End of year	**0.8**	**14.4**	**8.7**	**23.3**	**47.2**

Notes to the Financial Statements
continued

18 Share capital

	1997 £m	1996 £m
Authorised: 680 million (1996: 680 million) ordinary shares of 25p each	170.0	170.0
Issued and fully paid ordinary shares of 25p each	113.0	111.9

Number of ordinary shares in issue	1997	1996
Beginning of year	447,665,539	444,324,142
Issued during year:		
acquisitions	1,097,421	552,187
option exercises	3,095,384	2,135,587
scrip dividends	120,194	653,623
End of year	451,978,538	447,665,539

Details of share options granted and exercised during 1997 and those outstanding at 31 December 1997 under the Company's Savings Related Share Option Scheme (1981), the Sharesave Scheme (1991), the Executive Share Option Scheme (No.2) and the 1994 Executive Share Option Scheme are set out in the following table.

	1997 Grants		1997 Exercises		Options outstanding at 31.12.97	
	Number	Price (p)	Number	Price (p)	Number	Price (p)
Savings Related Scheme (1981)			207,568	68-103	-	-
Sharesave Scheme (1991)	895,457	178-198	896,900	72-190	3,690,209	72-198
Executive Scheme (No.2)			1,807,916	84-169	3,441,535	84-169
1994 Executive Scheme	2,206,500	222-260	183,000	212-239	5,958,352	170-260
	3,101,957		**3,095,384**		**13,090,096**	

The outstanding options are exercisable at various dates up to October 2007.

19 Movements on reserves

Consolidated:

	Share premium account £m	Revaluation reserve £m	Merger reserve £m	Profit and loss account £m
Beginning of year	30.5	7.8	25.5	102.4
Premium on share issues and on exercise of share options	6.8			(1.6)
Scrip dividend adjustment				0.1
Revaluation reserve movement on disposal of properties		(1.6)		1.6
Goodwill written off on acquisitions			(117.8)	
Goodwill transferred to the profit and loss account from the merger reserve			1.9	
Dividends from associated undertakings				0.6
Transfers		(0.1)		0.1
Currency translation movement		(0.4)		(3.5)
Retained profit (excluding associated undertakings)				47.1
End of year	**37.3**	**5.7**	**(90.4)**	**146.8**

As at 31 December 1997 the cumulative amount of goodwill written off to reserves in respect of acquisitions, net of goodwill attributable to subsidiary undertakings disposed of, was £322.6m (1996: £206.7m) and has been written off directly to the merger reserve.

Included within the merger reserve is £177.2m, being the special reserve of the Company.

Currency (losses)/profits of £(2.7)m (1996: £0.2m) relating to foreign currency exchange contracts and borrowings to finance investment overseas have been included within the currency translation movement in the profit and loss account.

Bunzl plc:

	Share premium account £m	Revaluation reserve £m	Special reserve £m	Profit and loss account £m
Beginning of year	30.5	0.5	177.2	107.2
Premium on share issues and on exercise of share options	6.8			
Scrip dividend adjustment				0.1
Retained profit				11.3
End of year	**37.3**	**0.5**	**177.2**	**118.6**

As permitted by Section 230 of the Companies Act 1985, the profit and loss account of the Company has not been separately presented in these financial statements.

The profit attributable to shareholders included in the accounts of the Company is £42.0m (1996: £45.2m).

As permitted under paragraph 15 of Schedule 4 to the Companies Act 1985, the directors consider it appropriate to depart from paragraph 12(a) of Schedule 4 to the Companies Act 1985 having implemented SSAP24 – 'Accounting for Pension Costs'. As a result, cumulative unrealised profits of £6.8m (1996: £6.9m) relating to pension costs have been included in the profit and loss account. This amount is not considered to be distributable.

The special reserve arose from the cancellation of the share premium account in 1987 and 1988 and at the present time is not considered to be distributable.

Notes to the Financial Statements
continued

20 Deferred taxation

	Bunzl plc		Consolidated	
	1997 £m	1996 £m	1997 £m	1996 £m
Accelerated capital allowances	–	–	4.1	4.4
Pension provisions and other timing differences	3.0	3.4	7.3	11.8
Advance corporation tax recoverable	(1.1)	(2.0)	(2.7)	(7.0)
	1.9	1.4	8.7	9.2

The potential liability for deferred taxation not provided above is:

	Bunzl plc		Consolidated	
	1997 £m	1996 £m	1997 £m	1996 £m
accelerated capital allowances	–	–	4.1	3.4
other timing differences	(0.6)	(0.6)	(2.0)	(2.9)
capital gains on disposal of properties	–	–	1.6	6.4
	(0.6)	(0.6)	3.7	6.9

Deferred tax has been accounted for in respect of future remittances of the accumulated reserves of overseas subsidiary undertakings to the extent that such distributions are anticipated. No provision has been made for potential corporate taxation on the unrealised revaluation surpluses in respect of properties which are expected to be held for the foreseeable future.

21 Contingent liabilities

	Bunzl plc		Consolidated	
	1997 £m	1996 £m	1997 £m	1996 £m
Bank guarantees	113.1	59.3	0.8	1.8
Other items	–	–	1.8	5.8
	113.1	59.3	2.6	7.6

The bank guarantees of the Company are guarantees provided on behalf of subsidiary undertakings. Other items principally comprise trade and other guarantees.

22 Directors' ordinary share interests

The interests of the directors at 31 December 1997 in the share capital of the Company were:

	Ordinary shares	
Ordinary shares	31.12.97	1.1.97
A J Habgood	265,473	261,314
A P Dyer	22,485	22,485
L C McQuade	13,195	12,834
D M Williams	64,450	60,920
P E Cushing	5,500	5,500
S G Williams	5,279	5,135
J G Bason	5,037	5,000
	381,419	373,188

The share interests shown above include the non-beneficial interests of Mr A J Habgood in 89,500 ordinary shares and of Mr D M Williams in 1,308 ordinary shares. Details of directors' options over ordinary shares and awards made under the Company's Long Term Incentive Plan and Share Partnership Plan are set out in the Report of the Remuneration Committee on pages 32 to 37. Since 31 December 1997 Mr D M Williams has acquired 26,041 ordinary shares as a result of an exercise of options under the Sharesave Scheme (1991). No other changes to the directors' ordinary share interests shown in this Note and the Report of the Remuneration Committee have taken place between 31 December 1997 and 16 March 1998.

23 Pensions

The Group operates both defined benefit and defined contribution pension schemes throughout the world. The funds of the principal schemes are administered by trustees and are held independently from the Group.

The net pension cost for the Group was £10.4m (1996: £8.9m) of which £8.4m (1996: £7.3m) was in respect of principal defined benefit schemes which provide benefits based on final pensionable salary. This cost is assessed in accordance with the advice of independent qualified actuaries.

Valuations of the principal UK defined benefit schemes were carried out as at 6 April 1997. The actuarial assumptions used in calculating the regular pension cost for these schemes are in line with those used for the funding calculations. The regular pension cost of the principal UK defined benefit schemes is adjusted for the amortisation of the difference between the actuarial surpluses and the prepayment on the balance sheet over the remaining service lives of current employees and is offset by interest arising on the surpluses.

The results of the most recent actuarial valuations of the principal defined benefit schemes were:

	UK	US
Date of most recent valuations	6.4.97	1.1.97
Method used	Projected unit method	Projected unit method
Main assumptions:		
Investment return/return on assets per annum	8.5%	8.0%
Salary increases per annum	6.0%	5.0%
Market value of investments at last valuation date	£87.5m	£29.1m
Level of funding, being the actuarial value of assets expressed as a percentage of the accrued service liabilities after allowing for expected increases in earnings	101-103%	88-114%

The Group operates other schemes overseas in accordance with local practice and legislation. Some of these schemes are externally funded, while others are internally funded, the amount set aside being shown in provisions for liabilities and charges.

19 Movements on reserves

Consolidated:

	Share premium account £m	Revaluation reserve £m	Merger reserve £m	Profit and loss account £m
Beginning of year	30.5	7.8	25.5	102.4
Premium on share issues and on exercise of share options	6.8			
Scrip dividend adjustment				(1.6)
Revaluation reserve movement on disposal of properties		(1.6)		0.1
Goodwill written off on acquisitions				1.6
Goodwill transferred to the profit and loss account from the merger reserve			(117.8)	
Dividends from associated undertakings			1.9	0.6
Transfers		(0.1)		0.1
Currency translation movement		(0.4)		(3.5)
Retained profit (excluding associated undertakings)				47.1
End of year	37.3	5.7	(90.4)	146.8

As at 31 December 1997 the cumulative amount of goodwill written off to reserves in respect of acquisitions, net of goodwill attributable to subsidiary undertakings disposed of, was £322.6m (1996: £206.7m) and has been written off directly to the merger reserve.

Included within the merger reserve is £177.2m, being the special reserve of the Company.

Currency (losses)/profits of £(2.7)m (1996: £0.2m) relating to foreign currency exchange contracts and borrowings to finance investment overseas have been included within the currency translation movement in the profit and loss account.

Bunzl plc:

	Share premium account £m	Revaluation reserve £m	Special reserve £m	Profit and loss account £m
Beginning of year	30.5	0.5	177.2	107.2
Premium on share issues and on exercise of share options	6.8			
Scrip dividend adjustment				0.1
Retained profit				11.3
End of year	37.3	0.5	177.2	118.6

As permitted by Section 230 of the Companies Act 1985, the profit and loss account of the Company has not been separately presented in these financial statements.

The profit attributable to shareholders included in the accounts of the Company is £42.0m (1996: £45.2m).

As permitted under paragraph 15 of Schedule 4 to the Companies Act 1985, the directors consider it appropriate to depart from paragraph 12(a) of Schedule 4 to the Companies Act 1985 having implemented SSAP24 – 'Accounting for Pension Costs'. As a result, cumulative unrealised profits of £6.8m (1996: £6.9m) relating to pension costs have been included in the profit and loss account. This amount is not considered to be distributable.

The special reserve arose from the cancellation of the share premium account in 1987 and 1988 and at the present time is not considered to be distributable.

Notes to the Financial Statements
continued

20 Deferred taxation

	Bunzl plc 1997 £m	1996 £m	Consolidated 1997 £m	1996 £m
Accelerated capital allowances	–	–	4.1	4.4
Pension provisions and other timing differences	3.0	3.4	7.3	11.8
Advance corporation tax recoverable	(1.1)	(2.0)	(2.7)	(7.0)
	1.9	1.4	8.7	9.2

The potential liability for deferred taxation not provided above is:

	Bunzl plc 1997 £m	1996 £m	Consolidated 1997 £m	1996 £m
accelerated capital allowances	–	–	4.1	3.4
other timing differences	(0.6)	(0.6)	(2.0)	(2.9)
capital gains on disposal of properties	–	–	1.6	6.4
	(0.6)	(0.6)	3.7	6.9

Deferred tax has been accounted for in respect of future remittances of the accumulated reserves of overseas subsidiary undertakings to the extent that such distributions are anticipated. No provision has been made for potential corporate taxation on the unrealised revaluation surpluses in respect of properties which are expected to be held for the foreseeable future.

21 Contingent liabilities

	Bunzl plc 1997 £m	1996 £m	Consolidated 1997 £m	1996 £m
Bank guarantees	113.1	59.3	0.8	1.8
Other items	–	–	1.8	5.8
	113.1	59.3	2.6	7.6

The bank guarantees of the Company are guarantees provided on behalf of subsidiary undertakings. Other items principally comprise trade and other guarantees.

22 Directors' ordinary share interests

The interests of the directors at 31 December 1997 in the share capital of the Company were:

Ordinary shares

	Ordinary shares 31.12.97	1.1.97
A J Habgood	265,473	261,314
A P Dyer	22,485	22,485
L C McQuade	13,195	12,834
D M Williams	64,450	60,920
P E Cushing	5,500	5,500
S G Williams	5,279	5,135
J G Bason	5,037	5,000
	381,419	373,188

The share interests shown above include the non-beneficial interests of Mr A J Habgood in 89,500 ordinary shares and of Mr D M Williams in 1,308 ordinary shares. Details of directors' options over ordinary shares and awards made under the Company's Long Term Incentive Plan and Share Partnership Plan are set out in the Report of the Remuneration Committee on pages 32 to 37. Since 31 December 1997 Mr D M Williams has acquired 26,041 ordinary shares as a result of an exercise of options under the Sharesave Scheme (1991). No other changes to the directors' ordinary share interests shown in this Note and the Report of the Remuneration Committee have taken place between 31 December 1997 and 16 March 1998.

Notes to the Financial Statements
continued

24 Directors and employees

The number of persons employed by the Group at 31 December 1997 and the average number employed during the year were:

	1997 Year end	1997 Average	1996 Year end	1996 Average
Paper and Plastic Disposables	3,685	3,281	3,040	2,835
Fine Paper	1,280	1,230	1,209	1,185
Filters and Tape	2,269	2,041	1,980	1,880
Plastic Products	2,536	1,920	1,892	1,932
Corporate activities	62	62	61	61
Continuing operations	9,832	8,534	8,182	7,893
Discontinued operations	212	454	952	938
	10,044	8,988	9,134	8,831

	Continuing operations 1997 £m	Discontinued operations 1997 £m	Total 1997 £m	Continuing operations 1996 £m	Discontinued operations 1996 £m	Total 1996 £m
Consolidated:						
Employee costs						
Wages and salaries	177.1	6.2	183.3	167.5	22.8	190.3
Social security costs	15.5	0.3	15.8	15.1	4.2	19.3
Pension costs (Note 23)	10.2	0.2	10.4	8.6	0.3	8.9
	202.8	6.7	209.5	191.2	27.3	218.5

	1997 £m	1996 £m
The total emoluments of the directors of the Company included above were:		
Non-executive directors	0.1	0.1
Executive directors:		
remuneration excluding performance related elements	1.1	0.8
performance related elements	0.4	0.2
pension contributions	–	–
	1.6	1.1

More detailed information concerning directors' emoluments is set out in the Report of the Remuneration Committee on pages 32 to 37. The aggregate of the amount of gains made by directors on the exercise of share options during the year was £283,701 (1996: £nil). Mr J G Bason was appointed as a director on 1 December 1996 and his emoluments included in the above table for 1996 are therefore only in respect of the period from his date of appointment to 31 December 1996.

25 Operating lease commitments

At 31 December 1997 the Group had the following annual commitments under non-cancellable operating leases:

	Land and buildings 1997 £m	Other 1997 £m	Land and buildings 1996 £m	Other 1996 £m
expiring within one year	2.5	1.2	1.0	1.2
expiring between one and five years	8.2	6.3	4.6	6.8
expiring after five years	23.3	0.6	10.4	0.8
	34.0	**8.1**	**16.0**	**8.8**

26 Reconciliation of operating profit to net cash inflow from operating activities

	Consolidated	
	1997 £m	1996 £m
Operating profit	127.3	115.7
Adjustments for non-cash items:		
depreciation	21.7	21.2
share of profits of associated undertakings	(3.6)	(4.0)
others	(1.5)	1.0
Dividend from associate	0.6	0.7
Working capital movement:		
stocks	(5.5)	9.3
debtors	(10.0)	(4.2)
creditors	5.0	16.6
Other cash movements	(3.0)	(0.6)
Net cash inflow from operating activities	**131.0**	**155.7**

27 Analysis of net debt

	1.1.97 £m	Cash flow £m	Exchange movements £m	31.12.97 £m
Cash at bank and in hand	30.0	(2.8)	(0.7)	**26.5**
Overdrafts	(8.8)	(7.0)	0.2	**(15.6)**
	21.2	(9.8)	(0.5)	**10.9**
Debt due within one year	(9.0)	(6.5)	1.8	**(13.7)**
Debt due after one year	(59.8)	(55.0)	(1.6)	**(116.4)**
Finance leases	(0.2)	0.2	–	**–**
	(69.0)	(61.3)	0.2	**(130.1)**
Current asset investments	5.3	(4.3)	(0.3)	**0.7**
	(42.5)	**(75.4)**	**(0.6)**	**(118.5)**

Notes to the Financial Statements
continued

28 Acquisitions

The principal acquisitions made during the year were American Filtrona Corporation (AFC), acquired on 23 September 1997, and the Grocery Supply Systems and related businesses (GSS) of Unisource, acquired on 20 October 1997.

Acquisitions have been accounted for under the acquisition method of accounting and contributed £6.9m to operating profit in 1997.

On acquisition the net assets and liabilities of the businesses acquired were adjusted to reflect their fair values to the Group. The fair value adjustments are provisional and will be finalised in the 1998 financial statements.

A summary of the effect of the acquisition of AFC is detailed below:

	Book value at acquisition £m	Revaluation £m	Consistency of accounting policy £m	Other £m	Fair value of assets acquired £m
Fixed assets	15.1	3.3			18.4
Stocks	9.3	(0.1)			9.2
Debtors	20.3	(2.0)			18.3
Creditors	(15.2)	(1.1)			(16.3)
Cash	31.3				31.3
Provisions for liabilities and charges	(0.5)	(3.0)	(0.3)	(9.1)	(12.9)
Taxation	(0.5)	(0.4)	0.1	1.5	0.7
	59.8	(3.3)	(0.2)	(7.6)	48.7
Goodwill					65.6
Consideration, satisfied by cash					114.3

The principal fair value adjustments are as follows:

The adjustments in respect of fixed assets principally comprise the revaluation of freehold properties which have been valued on an open market, existing use basis by qualified valuers.

The revaluation of debtors reflects the write down to their estimated realisable value.

The adjustments to creditors and provisions for liabilities and charges include amounts relating to the reassessment of potential liabilities that were not fully recognised in the balance sheet on acquisition. These include potential workers' compensation and other legal claims and environmental clean up costs.

The taxation adjustments include the recognition of a deferred tax asset for anticipated relief on fair value adjustments partially offset by a reassessment of tax liabilities.

28 Acquisitions continued

The trading results of AFC in the previous financial year and the period up to the date of acquisition were:

	Period to 22.9.97 £m	Year ended 31.12.96 £m
Sales	90.8	123.1
Operating profit	7.2	11.4
Profit before taxation	8.1	12.4
Taxation	(2.9)	(4.5)
Profit after taxation	5.2	7.9

There were no material gains or losses in these periods other than those recognised in the profit and loss account.

During the period from acquisition to the end of the year AFC contributed £2.4m to the Group's net cash inflow from operating activities, paid £1.0m in respect of taxation and spent £2.4m in respect of capital expenditure.

A summary of the effect of the acquisition of GSS is detailed below:

	Book value at acquisition £m	Provisional fair value adjustments			Fair value of assets acquired £m
		Revaluation £m	Consistency of accounting policy £m	Other £m	
Fixed assets	4.2	1.0			5.2
Stocks	15.9		(0.5)		15.4
Debtors	10.3		(0.5)		9.8
Creditors	(10.0)				(10.0)
Provisions for liabilities and charges				(4.5)	(4.5)
Taxation				1.5	1.5
	20.4	1.0	(1.0)	(3.0)	17.4
Goodwill					13.7
Consideration, satisfied by cash					31.1

The principal fair value adjustment relates to the establishment of a provision in respect of onerous property lease commitments.

Prior to acquisition, GSS was part of Unisource. However only certain of its assets and liabilities were acquired and, as a result, it is not practical to provide details of the trading results in the previous financial year to 30 September 1997 and in the period up to acquisition.

Notes to the Financial Statements
continued

28 Acquisitions continued

A summary of the effect of all acquisitions is detailed below:

| | Book value at acquisition £m | Provisional fair value adjustments | | | Fair value of assets acquired £m |
		Revaluation £m	Consistency of accounting policy £m	Other £m	
Fixed assets	22.6	4.3	(0.1)	(0.1)	26.7
Stocks	36.6	(0.1)	(0.9)		35.6
Debtors	45.0	(2.0)	(0.5)	(0.1)	42.4
Creditors	(31.6)	(1.2)		(0.1)	(32.9)
Cash	31.3				31.3
Net bank overdrafts	(13.2)				(13.2)
Provisions for liabilities and charges	(1.1)	(3.0)	(0.3)	(14.0)	(18.4)
Taxation	(1.2)	(0.4)	0.1	2.9	1.4
	88.4	(2.4)	(1.7)	(11.4)	72.9
Goodwill					117.8
Consideration					190.7

Satisfied by:	
Shares allotted	2.6
Cash consideration	178.4
Deferred consideration	9.7
	190.7

The net outflow of cash in respect of the acquisition of businesses was:

	AfC £m	GSS £m	Other £m	Total £m
Cash consideration	114.3	31.1	33.0	178.4
(Cash)/overdrafts of businesses acquired	(31.3)	–	13.2	(18.1)
Net outflow of cash in respect of the acquisition of businesses	**83.0**	**31.1**	**46.2**	**160.3**

In late February 1998, the Group purchased an additional 15% shareholding in its subsidiary undertaking Filtrona Española SA from Mr Adolfo Pfeiffer Tovar, a director of the company, thereby taking its total shareholding to 90%. The consideration paid was 180 million pesetas (£0.7 million). The net assets of Filtrona Española SA at 31 December 1997 were £7.2 million.

29 Disposals

Bunzl Italia SpA and Wilhelm Seiler GmbH were sold in February 1997. Stag Plastics Ltd and Webster Plastics Inc were sold in January and February 1998 respectively. The effect of the disposals on the net assets of the Group at 31 December 1997 was:

	£m
Fixed assets	(19.6)
Stocks	(15.7)
Debtors	(33.9)
Creditors	23.7
Net bank overdrafts	14.0
Net assets disposed of	(31.5)
Goodwill previously written off to the merger reserve	(1.9)
Disposal provisions	(8.2)
Net cash proceeds	43.8
Profit on sale of discontinued operations	**2.2**

Disposal provisions relate principally to potential obligations under the relevant sale agreements.

The net inflow of cash in respect of the disposals made in 1997 was:

	£m
Net cash proceeds	43.8
Net bank overdrafts disposed of	14.0
Net inflow of cash in respect of the disposals	**57.8**

Up to the date of disposal the businesses sold during the year produced a net cash outflow from operating activities of £3.9m, paid £0.3m in respect of servicing of finance and £0.1m in respect of taxation and spent £0.1m on capital expenditure.

Principal Subsidiary and Associated Undertakings

Subsidiary undertakings	Country of incorporation
Paper and Plastic Disposables	
Bunzl Disposables UK Ltd*	
Alpha Supplies Ltd*	
Bunzl Australia Ltd	Australia
Bunzl Distribution USA Inc	USA
Fine Paper	
Bunzl Fine Paper Ltd*	
GB Goldman Paper Co	USA
The Paper Group Inc	USA
Filters and Tape	
Filtrona Filter GmbH	Germany
Filtrona International Ltd*	
P.P. Payne Ltd*	
Filtrona Holdings Corp	USA
Plastic Products	
Bunzl Plastics Inc	USA
Bunzl Plastics Ltd*	
Filtrona Brasileira Indústria e Comércio Ltda	Brazil
Corporate activities	
Bunzl Finance plc*	
Bunzl USA Inc	USA
Associated undertakings	
Filters and Tape	
Filtrati SpA (49%)	Italy

The companies named above are the principal subsidiary and associated undertakings of Bunzl plc as at 31 December 1997 and are included in the consolidated financial statements of the Group. They are incorporated in England and Wales and are wholly owned, unless otherwise stated. The investments in these companies, as shown above, relate to ordinary shares or common stock. The principal country in which each company operates is the country of incorporation. The principal activities of the business areas are reviewed on pages 10 to 19 of the Annual Review and Summary Financial Statement.

*direct subsidiary undertakings of Bunzl plc

Statement of Directors' Responsibilities

Company law requires the directors to prepare financial statements for each financial year which give a true and fair view of the state of affairs of the Company and the Group and of the profit or loss for that period. In preparing those financial statements, the directors are required to:

- select suitable accounting policies and then apply them consistently;

- make judgements and estimates that are reasonable and prudent;

- state whether applicable accounting standards have been followed, subject to any material departures disclosed and explained in the financial statements;

- prepare the financial statements on the going concern basis unless it is inappropriate to presume that the Group will continue in business.

The directors are responsible for maintaining proper accounting records which disclose with reasonable accuracy at any time the financial position of the Company and to enable them to ensure that the financial statements comply with the Companies Act 1985. They have general responsibility for taking such steps as are reasonably open to them to safeguard the assets of the Group and prevent and detect fraud and other irregularities.

Auditors' Report

To the members of Bunzl plc
We have audited the financial statements on pages 4 to 30. We have also examined the amounts disclosed relating to emoluments, share options, long term incentive scheme and share partnership plan interests and directors' pension entitlements which form part of the Report of the Remuneration Committee on pages 32 to 37.

Respective responsibilities of directors and auditors
As described above, the Company's directors are responsible for the preparation of financial statements. It is our responsibility to form an independent opinion, based on our audit, on those financial statements and to report our opinion to you.

Basis of opinion
We conducted our audit in accordance with auditing standards issued by the Auditing Practices Board. An audit includes examination, on a test basis, of evidence relevant to the amounts and disclosures in the financial statements. It also includes an assessment of the significant estimates and judgements made by the directors in the preparation of the financial statements and of whether the accounting policies are appropriate to the Group's circumstances, consistently applied and adequately disclosed.

We planned and performed our audit so as to obtain all the information and explanations which we considered necessary in order to provide us with sufficient evidence to give reasonable assurance that the financial statements are free from material misstatement, whether caused by fraud or other irregularity or error. In forming our opinion we also evaluated the overall adequacy of the presentation of information in the financial statements.

Opinion
In our opinion the financial statements give a true and fair view of the state of affairs of the Company and the Group as at 31 December 1997 and of the profit of the Group for the year then ended and have been properly prepared in accordance with the Companies Act 1985.

KPMG Audit Plc
Chartered Accountants
Registered Auditor
London
16 March 1998

Five Year Review

	1997 £m	1996 £m	1995 £m	Before goodwill 1994 £m	Goodwill* 1994 £m	1994 £m	1993 £m
Sales							
Continuing operations	1,704.0	1,560.2	1,486.7	1,290.2		1,290.2	1,066.1
Discontinued operations	49.2	236.2	271.8	332.0		332.0	453.4
Total sales	1,753.2	1,796.4	1,758.5	1,622.2		1,622.2	1,519.5
Operating profit							
Continuing operations	125.0	114.6	103.1	80.4		80.4	59.4
Discontinued operations	2.3	1.1	5.7	6.5		6.5	4.8
	127.3	115.7	108.8	86.9		86.9	64.2
Permanent diminution in goodwill*					(49.7)	(49.7)	
Total operating profit	127.3	115.7	108.8	86.9	(49.7)	37.2	64.2
Profit/(loss) on sale of discontinued operations	2.2				(35.0)	(35.0)	1.1
Profit on ordinary activities before interest	129.5	115.7	108.8	86.9	(84.7)	2.2	65.3
Net interest payable	(3.6)	(2.2)	(2.6)	(7.1)		(7.1)	(9.5)
Profit/(loss) on ordinary activities before taxation	125.9	113.5	106.2	79.8	(84.7)	(4.9)	55.8
Taxation on profit on ordinary activities	(44.6)	(39.7)	(37.5)	(28.0)		(28.0)	(20.5)
Profit/(loss) on ordinary activities after taxation	81.3	73.8	68.7	51.8	(84.7)	(32.9)	35.3
Profit attributable to minorities	(1.1)	(0.9)	(1.2)	(0.9)		(0.9)	(1.0)
Profit/(loss) for the financial year	80.2	72.9	67.5	50.9	(84.7)	(33.8)	34.3
Earnings per share	17.9p	16.4p	15.5p			(8.0p)	8.3p
Adjusted earnings per share	17.6p	16.4p	15.5p			12.0p	8.3p
Dividends per share	6.8p	6.3p	5.8p			5.0p	4.1p
Shareholders' funds per share	49.3p	64.2p	70.4p			57.3p	55.0p
Net assets employed							
Fixed assets	190.4	168.0	159.6			145.7	143.6
Net current assets and other liabilities	36.0	124.0	158.7			103.8	94.8
Net assets	226.4	292.0	318.3			249.5	238.4
Financed by							
Shareholders' funds: equity interests	222.6	287.4	312.7			243.9	232.8
Minority equity interests	3.8	4.6	5.6			5.6	5.6
	226.4	292.0	318.3			249.5	238.4

* Goodwill 1994. The loss on sale of discontinued operations of £35.0m comprised the elimination of goodwill less a small premium on net asset value. Additionally, £49.7m of goodwill relating to past acquisitions was considered irrecoverable by the directors and was also eliminated.

Country Highlights
ICELAND

Common Legal Forms of Companies

The most common legal form of company is the limited liability company, which is of two types depending on size. Most large concerns are operated as limited liability companies, which must have at least two shareholders and share capital of ISK 4,000,000 or more; the abbreviation is HF (Iccl. hlutafélag). The other type is primarily for smaller concerns, and they are organized as private limited liability companies, which can have one shareholder or more and minimum share capital is ISK 500,000; the abbreviation is EHF (Icel. einkahlutafélag). Other forms of companies are state-owned companies, cooperative companies, companies organized as partnerships, and single proprietorships.

Sources of Financial Reporting Requirements

The primary source of financial reporting requirements is the Financial Reporting Act of 1994, which is based on the Fourth Directive from the European Union. Other sources are pronouncements issued by the Icelandic Accounting Standards Board and its predecessor the Committee on Accounting Procedures of the Association of State Authorized Accountants. Additionally, the standards issued by the International Accounting Standards Committee can be used as a source for an accounting practice.

Corporate Taxation

The two primary taxes are the income tax and the net worth tax. The income tax is currently 33% of taxable income and the net worth tax is 1.45% on total owners' equity excluding capital stock. Corporations have various options to postpone taxation of profits, mostly additional depreciation of fixed assets. Cash dividends are deductible for income tax purposes up to 7% of the nominal value of capital stock. Other important taxes are social security taxes, which are between 4% and 6.3% of total salaries and wages to employees, depending on type of operation. The value-added tax is 24.5% on the sales value of most products and services. A lower rate of 14% is applied to food, utilities, and hotel room rentals, etc.

Auditing Requirements

Companies that fulfil one or more of four requirements must be audited by a state authorized public accountant. These requirements are: total assets exceed ISK 100 million, capital stock in excess of ISK 50 million, total revenues exceed ISK 200 million, and total number of employees is more than 50. Additionally, the financial accounts of all companies registered on the Icelandic Stock Exchange, commercial banks, insurance companies, pension funds, and municipalities must be audited by a state authorized public accountant.

Organization of the Accounting and Auditing Professions

The Association of State Authorized Public Accountants is a voluntary organization whose aims are to promote quality services of its members. For this purpose the association holds regular conferences on professional issues and annually appoints committees that are responsible for the advancement of the various professional services. To qualify as a state authorized accountant an applicant must hold a university degree in accounting, have completed a training program of 3 years, and successfully pass four qualifying examinations in accounting practice, accounting theory, auditing, and taxation. The current membership is 220 auditors. No associations for accounting professionals currently exist in industry, that is, for cost and management accountants.

Constitution and Legal System

Iceland is a republic with a parliamentary government. Members of parliament (*Althingi*) are elected by popular vote in a multiparty system. All governments since Iceland became independent in 1944 have been coalition governments. The powers of the legislative and executive branches are vested in the president, parliament, and government. According to the Constitution the president exercises authority through the ministers; he or she is therefore outside politics. The judiciary is based on two levels of courts—district courts and the supreme court. The rules of procedure are based to a large extent on Scandinavian and German principles.

Currency

The currency is the Icelandic krona, abbreviated ISK. The rate of exchange for 1 US$ was 72 ISK at the end of 1997.

Official Languages

The official and only language is Icelandic, which has remained relatively unchanged for centuries. Icelandic is a Nordic language of Germanic origin.

ICELAND

Stefan Svavarsson,
University of Iceland

1. Background

1.1 Introduction

Iceland is an island located in the North Atlantic Ocean, some 103,000 square kilometers in size, with a population of 270,000. Approximately 170,000 people live in the capital, Reykjavík, and the neighboring municipalities situated in the southwest of the island. The island was settled in the late 9th century by Norwegians, although there are also some indications of Irish hermits living in the country at that time.

The country became a fully independent republic in 1944, when it terminated its union with Denmark. Previously, Iceland had been granted limited home rule in 1874, becoming an autonomous state with monarchial ties to Denmark in 1918. At the time Iceland became a fully independent nation, it had been under Norwegian and Danish rule for almost seven hundred years. The parliament of Iceland, Althingi, was established in 930, making it the oldest parliament in the world.

The main economic activities of the country have been based on agriculture and fisheries. Major technological advances in these areas resulted in marked improvements in the living conditions after the turn of the century. Additionally, the economy has gradually changed from the two basic industries to a more modern industrial structure.

The present economy is primarily based on the use of renewable natural resources—that is, the fishing banks, hydroelectric and geothermal power, and the grasslands that support the livestock industry. The economy depends largely on the fisheries and fish processing, even though the relative share of fisheries in the occupational distribution is small. Currently, fisheries and fish processing account for some 12% of the labor force, whereas the services sector, government services, and commerce account for 21%, 18%, and 14%, respectively. Agriculture is about 5%. The fisheries sector accounts for almost 80% of all goods exports, and these exports make up 33% of GDP.

Most companies in Iceland are small; between 200 and 300 companies employ 60 or more people. Holdings in the majority of companies are limited to a few shareholders, but interest in public companies has increased since the stocks and bonds market opened in the early 1980s. At the end of 1997 the approximate value of bonds outstanding (2/3) plus the capitalization of the stock market (1/3) was 452 billion ISK (1 USD = 72 ISK), compared with an estimated GDP of 521 billion ISK for 1997.

Of the three commercial banks in Iceland, two are state owned. The state-owned banks were converted into limited liability companies at the end of 1997, and the plan is to privatize these banks over the next few years. By far the largest bank is *Landsbanki Íslands* (National Bank of Iceland), which had outstanding loans and marketable bonds in excess of 95 billion ISK at the end of 1997, accounting for 35% of total bank loans and marketable bonds, including the holdings of savings and loans institutions. The investment funds had total outstanding loans in the amount of 300 billion ISK at the end of 1997.

1.2 Historical Background

Iceland's cultural and historical ties with the other Nordic countries have greatly influenced its economic and legal environment. In fact, most of the laws governing business operations have been based on similar laws in the other Nordic countries, particularly Denmark. A brief review of the historical developments will clarify this.

1.2.1 Bookkeeping Act

The first public document on accounting was a decree from the King of Denmark in 1787. This document described briefly which accounting records were to be kept by individuals engaged in business. The first Act on Bookkeeping (*Bókhaldslög*) was enacted in 1911. It included a fairly detailed description of the accounting records that were to be used. Additionally, the law stipulated that companies were to prepare a balance sheet at the end of every fiscal year; no mention was made of a profit and loss account.

Technical advances in the maintenance of accounting records led to revisions in the Bookkeeping Act in 1938 and again in 1968. The Bookkeeping Act of 1938 allowed for assets to be stated at their market value; this was probably the first rule issued on financial reporting in Iceland. In practice, however, this rule was seldom used by companies.

The 1968 Act specified for the first time in Icelandic legislation a number of rules concerning the recording and valuation of financial statement items. This law was mainly based on similar laws in Denmark and Norway. The Bookkeeping Act of 1968 introduced for the first time two important accounting concepts. First, the annual accounts were to be prepared in conformity with good accounting practice. And second, the accounts should give a "fair representation" of the operating activities of companies; oddly enough, that phrase applied only to the profit and loss account.

A new Bookkeeping Act was enacted in 1994 in view of Iceland's obligations with respect to provisions under the agreement establishing the European Economic Area (EEA). The new act is based on the provisions of the 4th Directive of the European Union. In addition to this new law on bookkeeping, a separate act on annual financial statements, the Financial Reporting Act (*Ársreikningalög*) of 1994, was passed, which will be discussed in some detail in Section 3.1.

1.2.2 Companies Act

The first Companies Act (*Hlutafélagalög*) was enacted in 1921. The act was almost silent on accounting. The only requirements of the law were that an annual statement of revenues and expenses be prepared as well as a balance sheet.

The Companies Act of 1978 was the result of efforts in all the Nordic countries to harmonize the legal environment for limited liability companies. Previously, the other Nordic countries had passed legislation based on this project. The adoption of this law was a major event in the development of accounting in Iceland. The Act contained a separate chapter on accounting, which was almost a verbatim translation of the same chapter of the Danish Companies Act.

A new Companies Act, however, was enacted in 1995, implementing major changes in Icelandic company law. The new Act is not to the same extent based on similar Nordic law as was previous legislation. This new Act does not contain a separate chapter on financial statements since the requirements for financial reports are covered by a separate law.

1.2.3 Financial Reporting Act

The Financial Reporting Act of 1994 is based on the 4th Directive of the European Union. The main provisions of the the Financial Reporting Act of 1994 will be discussed in Section 3.

1.2.4 Income Tax Act

In Iceland, as in most countries, the Income Tax Act (*Lög um tekju- og eignarskatt*) has greatly influenced financial reporting. Until quite recently, the income concept of the tax law was synonymous with accounting income. In fact, the accounting reports of companies were a mere by-product of their tax returns. This has gradually been changing, particularly following the enactment of the Companies Act of 1978 and the Income Tax Act in the same year. The provisions of the Income Tax Act that have influenced financial reporting will be explained below, particularly those provisions dealing with inflation.

Before 1978 the tax law was largely based on the historical cost concept of accounting. However, several revisions to the law allowed for revaluation of fixed assets. Curiously enough, fixed assets were to be stated at their estimated selling price when calculating the net worth tax. Despite this explicit requirement, tax authorities silently consented to the cost concept for the purpose of levying the net worth tax. Additionally, the tax law allowed for several other corrections because of the effects of inflation. They were partial adjustments which were, in fact, inadequate to deal with the problem for either tax or accounting purposes.

2. Publication and Auditing

In this section the legal requirements for the publication of annual accounts as well as auditing requirements will be discussed briefly.

2.1 Publication of Annual Accounts

According to the Financial Reporting Act, the annual accounts of all companies must be filed with the Registry of Companies. A regulation accompanying the law specifies the form and content of the financial statements, and all companies satisfying certain limits must comply with the provisions of the regulations. Other companies can send to the Registry Office an abbreviated version of the financial statements if two of the following three requirements are not met. The limits specified are: total assets of 200 million ISK, operating revenues of 400 million ISK, and a minimum total number of employees 50.

This obligation to disclose the financial statements of all companies is, of course, a major change in Icelandic practice. Previously, only those companies whose shares were available to the general public had to file their annual accounts with the Registry Office. At the discretion of the Registry Office, certain individual companies could previously also be obliged to file their annual accounts.

The Iceland Stock Exchange in Reykjavík (*Verðbréfaþing Íslands*) has been operating since 1986. For the first few years it was run under the auspices of the Central Bank of Iceland, but since July 1, 1993 the exchange has been independently operated. The operating rules of the Exchange are in conformity with EU directives for listing of public companies. The board of directors of the Exchange has the responsibility of overseeing its operations, including the trading of shares of listed companies. Additionally, the Bank Inspectorate of the Central Bank has monitoring duties. At the end of 1997 only about 50 companies were trading their shares through the Exchange or on the over-the-counter market.

The Stock Exchange has issued some requirements for the publication of annual accounts, all of which conform to the requirements of the law and good accounting practice as described in the next section. The Exchange has the authority to issue specific rules on accounting, but has not done so to date. One requirement of the Exchange in this regard is the inclusion of a cash-flow statement in the annual accounts, which was not a requirement before the enactment of the Financial Reporting Act of 1994; good accounting practice, however, called for such a statement. Listed companies must file their annual accounts with the Exchange; such accounts must be audited. Additionally, the Exchange requires at least semi-annual statements, but more frequent publication of interim statements is recommended. The interim statements need not be audited.

Lastly, the annual accounts of companies owned and operated by the national government or municipalities must be published and made available to the public.

2.2 Auditing

A new law on auditing, or rather State Authorized Accountants, was enacted in 1997. The previous law was enacted in 1976. The new law was enacted to comply with the provisions of the 8th Directive of the European Union. The new law provides for a monitoring organization on auditing activities in the country, and it also contains certain requirements for the continuing education of auditors. Additionally, the new law provides for certain rules regarding the ownership of auditing firms and their operations, including a provision for mandatory professional liability insurance.

In order to be qualified as a State Authorized Accountant one must fulfill the following requirements:

- An applicant for the professional examinations must have graduated from the Department of Business Administration of the University of Iceland, with a major area of specialization in accounting and auditing, or have received comparable education from another institution of higher learning.
- An applicant, after having successfully completed the above educational requirements, must work for an auditing firm for a minimum period of three years.
- In order to receive a certificate as a State Authorized Accountant, issued by the Minister of Finance, an applicant must successfully complete four examinations with a minimum grade of 75% in each. The tests are in accounting practice, accounting theory, auditing, and taxation.

The Financial Reporting Act of 1994 requires that certain companies' annual accounts be audited by State Authorized Accountants if one of the following conditions pertains:

- the share capital of a company is at least 50 million ISK,
- total assets exceed 100 million ISK,
- total revenues exceed 200 million ISK,
- the number of employees exceeds 50.

In addition, many other accounting entities must be audited by State Authorized Accountants. Various laws govern the operations of the relevant entities. For example, pension funds, insurance companies, commercial banks, savings banks, and municipalities are required by law to have their annual accounts audited by professional accountants.

3. Accounting Principles and Practices

As indicated earlier, financial reporting in Iceland is primarily based on the Financial Reporting Act, the Income Tax Act, and opinions of the accounting profession. In this section the influence of each of these factors, including a comment on the Accounting Standards Board, will be discussed in some detail.

3.1 Financial Reporting Act

The basic requirements of the Act are summarized below. As previously indicated, it is based on the 4th Directive from the European Union. There are, however, certain deviations from the Directive, which will be explained.

3.1.1 Annual Accounts

According to the Financial Reporting Act of 1994, annual accounts should include a balance sheet, a profit and loss account, a fund flow statement, and notes. The board of directors must prepare a separate report, which also forms a part of the annual accounts.

Where applicable, companies must prepare consolidated accounts, and the legal requirements for such are more or less in conformity with the provisions of the 7th Directive of the European Union.

3.1.2 Basic General Requirements of the Financial Reporting Act

Company annual accounts must comply with the provisions of the law and provide a true and fair view of the operating performance and financial condition of a company. Additionally, and this is an addition to the requirements of the 4th Directive, the annual accounts must be in conformity with good accounting practice. To the extent that the annual accounts, based on legal requirements and good accounting practice, do not provide a true and fair view of a company's affairs, additional information must be supplied in the notes. In other words, a company cannot change the figures in the basic financial statements, if they do not provide a true and fair view, because the derogation to this effect allowed for in the 4th Directive (under exceptional conditions) was not, oddly enough, translated into the Icelandic law.

The regulations accompanying the Financial Reporting Act prescribe the format for the basic financial statements, i.e. the balance sheet and profit and loss account. With this new format, which became effective for 1997, the presentation of the financial statements, particularly the balance sheet, changed materially compared with previous practice and law. Before 1997 the balance sheet showed current assets ahead of fixed assets and current liabilities and long-term liabilities ahead of owners' equity. This order of presentation has now been changed to comply with the provisions of the 4th Directive; this can be seen in the accompanying illustrative annual accounts at the end of this chapter. The regulations allow for deviations from the basic format if the presentation of the accounts does not show a true and fair view.

The Financial Reporting Act provides for the following general rules: (a) the accounts are based on the premise of a going concern, (b) the accounts must be prepared having regard to the principle of consistency, (c) the principle of conservatism should be adhered to, (d) the accounts must be prepared on the basis of the accrual basis of accounting, and it is specifically stipulated that the cash basis of accounting is not appropriate, and (e) the accounts must be made comparable to the previous year's financial accounts. These basic accounting principles have not previously been explicitly required under accounting law in Iceland; however, the legal requirements of good accounting practice under previous laws would have included those basic principles.

3.1.3 Basic Valuation Rules and Disclosure Requirements

In this section the basic rules concerning the most important items in the financial accounts will be discussed briefly.

Fixed assets. The basic valuation rule for fixed assets is that the book value of such assets should not exceed the historical cost or the restated historical cost. The basic valuation rule according to the 4th Directive is historical cost. Icelandic practice has, however, been based on the general price level method of accounting for inflation, and therefore it was felt that the valuation rule of restated historical cost had to be added to the Icelandic law.

If the book value of fixed assets is materially higher than their real value, the fixed assets accounts must accordingly be adjusted to reflect the lower value. This writing-down of fixed assets is in addition to the regular depreciation on account of wear and tear, but it need not be recorded unless a permanent diminution in value of the relevant fixed asset has occurred.

Conversely, the fixed assets can also be valued at real value (market value), even though this may be higher than book value, if such a real value is materially and permanently higher than the book value that is based on restated historical cost. To the extent that an Icelandic company uses this option it must credit a separate revaluation account under owners' equity with corresponding entries to account for tax obligations on such a higher value. This separate revaluation account is to be kept distinctly separate from the revaluation account, which is credited for the annual restatement of historical cost of fixed assets on the basis of general inflation. Previous law in Iceland was generally interpreted in such a fashion that only annual restatement based on general inflation was allowed for, that is, valuation based on real value in excess of restated historical cost is a new option in Icelandic financial accounting. Few examples can be cited of companies using the option given.

Depreciation on fixed assets is to be based on restated historical cost over the estimated useful life of the assets. However, if companies use the option of valuing fixed assets at a higher value, that is, market value, depreciation in the profit and loss account is limited to the depreciation charge on restated historical cost. That means that the depreciation on the excess value must be charged to the separate revaluation account under owners' equity, with a corresponding entry to lower the tax deferral obligation.

Fixed assets constructed by a company must, according to the Financial Reporting Act, include under cost materials, direct labor costs and variable overhead costs, but the company has the option of either including or excluding a share of fixed overheads. The company also has the option of either expensing or capitalizing the interest costs relating to the construction of fixed assets. Should a company use the latter option, it must supply information in the notes on the amounts involved and methods used.

Intangible assets. The cost of intangible assets can either be expensed or capitalized. According to the law, intangibles include, in addition to such assets as patents, copyrights, and goodwill, research and development costs. Should a company capitalize such assets, they must be amortized over a period of no more than five years, unless the useful life of the assets is longer, in which case the useful life may be used for amortization purposes. It should be noted that the law does not provide for a maximum period of amortization. It is the general opinion of Icelandic accounting professionals that these requirements do not permit the charging of goodwill directly to reserves under owners' equity, an option that appears to be allowed under European Union rules.

Investments in shares and bonds. Investments in shares and bonds should be classified either as short-term or long-term assets. Short-term investments in shares and bonds should be stated at either historical or market cost, whichever is lower, but short-term investments can be stated at market value if the investments are traded on the Icelandic securities market or some other public market. The law and the related regulations are not clear, however, on the treatment of an increase or decrease in the book value of such investments. Generally, such valuation changes are charged or credited to the profit and loss account.

The accepted practice for long-term equity investments is to value them at restated historical cost. Permanent valuation decreases should be recognized, but valuation increases are normally not recorded. An exception to that rule can be found in the accounting practices of investment companies that value long-term equity investments at market value and record the excess of market value over restated historical cost in a separate account under owners' equity: unrealized gains in share investments. If the market value of such investments is lower than the restated historical cost, the valuation decrease is expensed; correspondingly, subsequent increases are credited to the profit and loss account up to the restated historical cost. Deferred tax liabilities are recognized to the extent that market value of long-term investments may result in taxable income. Long-term investments in debt securities are, on the other hand, recorded at historical cost, that is, using the effective rate of interest for recognizing income on such investments.

The law allows for the equity method of accounting for investments in shares. That method is rarely used, except, of course, for the share of a parent company in subsidiary companies.

Inventories. Inventories are to be valued based on cost or market value, whichever is the lower. Icelandic law allows for the weighted average cost of inventories or last purchase price (which does not appear to be an option under the Fourth Directive nor according to good accounting practice). The law does not specify which cost-flow assumption can be used for valuing inventories. In view of the inflation adjustments made in Icelandic accounts, however, it is the general opinion of accounting professionals that the last in, first out (LIFO) assumption of cost flows is neither acceptable nor necessary.

If companies use market value for valuing inventories, and this is lower than cost, this should be accounted for in the notes accompanying the annual accounts if the differences are material. In the case of manufacturing companies, the cost of inventories may or may not include fixed overheads, which, in effect, means that for the purposes of the financial statement variable costing is allowed even though that has never been, up to the enactment of the Financial Reporting Act of 1994, an acceptable Icelandic practice. Most concerns use full absorption costing, however, for valuing inventories despite that option, which, in fact, appears to be a literal translation of the Fourth Directive.

Provision for contingencies. A new provision is included in the law on financial reporting regarding contingent liabilities. Such liabilities are to be recognized to the extent that they have accrued. According to the law, it is not necessary for the accrual of such obligations that they be precisely measureable, nor is it a requirement that the due dates be certain. The only requirement is that the probable future payment be reasonably certain. This is a new accounting requirement in Icelandic law; previous practice recognized such obligations to some extent, but they were based on the notion of good accounting practice. It should be noted in this connection that Icelandic practice has never accepted the building up of unspecified reserves (as liabilities).

This new accounting requirement makes the recording of pension liabilities obligatory, whereas under previous law notes on pension obligations were sufficient. The same does not apply, however, to tax deferral obligations since the law specifically allows for such obligations to be disclosed in the notes accompanying financial reports without being recorded.

Owners' equity accounts. The new Financial Reporting Act of 1994 is quite specific on the itemization of the various owners' equity accounts. Because Icelandic accounts are based on the general price level model of accounting for inflation, a clear distinction should be made between owners' contributions and the entities' own funds. Normally, share capital is stated in terms of par values, and the same applies to the account representing paid-in capital in excess of par. For that reason a balancing account is sometimes used that, together with the two accounts representing owners' contributions, would show the real value of shareholders contributions in terms of current prices. The remaining owners' equity accounts would therefore show the retained entity earnings (i.e. realized income) in terms of the current price level, in addition to revaluation accounts for assets stated at values exceeding restated historical cost (i.e. unrealized income). Despite the general requirements of the law concerning the separation of the two basic components of shareholders' equity here being discussed, many companies do not make a distinction between these components of owners' equity, which makes the financial reports more difficult to interpret.

Taxes on income and net worth. The law provides for either of two methods to account for taxes on income. Until recently most companies have used the taxes payable method, that is, recording only taxes that are currently due. In the past few years, however, many companies have recorded deferred taxes as well, even though the law does not require the recording of such obligations. The law does, on the other hand, require the full disclosure of deferred tax liabilities in notes. Obviously, therefore, both methods can be found in practice.

The new law requires the interperiod allocation of taxes; it has not been common practice in Icelandic annual accounts to use that method of allocating taxes, and it has not been used with respect to taxes on net worth nor on the tax savings on cash dividends (cash dividends are deductible to some extent for Icelandic companies).

Extraordinary items and prior period adjustments. According to the new Financial Reporting Act, a separation should be made in the profit and loss account between continuing operations and nonrecurring or extraordinary activities. The statement format for the profit and loss account presented in the regulations accompanying the law requires extraordinary items to be presented net of tax at the bottom of the statement, so that profits from continuing operations after tax can be shown separately. The same requirement applies to prior period adjustments, indicating that such items must be shown in the profit and loss account. The law does not, in other words, allow for either the charging or crediting of prior period adjustments directly to the retained earnings account under owners' equity, which, however, is the benchmark treatment according to international standards.

Notes to the annual accounts. A separate paragraph in the Financial Reporting Act stipulates which notes are to be included in the annual accounts. The following is a summary of the main requirements of the law:

(a) Share ownership in other companies, including information on the ownership percentage as well as the names of the companies in question.

(b) Information on the methods used to account for inflation.

(c) Specification of fixed assets including information on the official assessment values and insurance values of buildings.

(d) Information about pension obligations.

(e) Information on the effects of any changes in the valuation methods of assets and liabilities.

(f) Information on the tax position of a company, including information on the tax benefits of operating losses carried forward, and the amount of deferred tax assets and liabilities, to the extent that such items are not recorded.

(g) Information on commitments and contingent liabilities, including information on the amount of debt that is secured by assets. Information on assets and liabilities denominated in foreign currency or linked to an index must also be provided. A payment schedule for long-term debt over the next five years must be provided in the notes.

(h) Information on assets and liabilities relating to transactions between subsidiaries and/or their parent company.

Directors' report. The Financial Reporting Act requires a specific report by the directors of limited liability companies. As a minimum the report shall include information on the number of employees, total salaries and wages, bonuses paid to directors, and the percentage share of those shareholders with holdings in excess of 10%. The report shall also contain the proposal of the board of directors for the payment or nonpayment of dividends. Additionally, the directors' report shall provide information on the financial condition and operating results of the company, to the extent that such information is relevant but not included in the balance sheet and profit and loss account. The company, however, can opt not to divulge such information if to do so would be to the company's competitive disadvantage.

3.2 The Income Tax Act

Enacted in 1978, the current Income Tax Act has since been revised on several occasions. This Act takes into account the effects of general inflation on the measurement of operating performance and financial position and is based on the general purchasing power model of accounting. It was necessary to change the Income Tax Act in 1978 to take into consideration the effects of inflation. Previously, as mentioned above, partial adjustments were made to compensate for the effects of inflation on accounting measurements. During the 1970s the general rate of inflation was approximately 40% per annum, so obviously there was a great need to abandon the historical cost model of accounting for tax purposes. During the 1980s the comparable rates of inflation were around 30% per annum on the average. Currently, however, the annual rate of inflation is much lower, with the average for the first few years of the 1990s being less than 5%. Despite this recent trend, the inflation model of the tax law is still intact.

Throughout the 1970s the Income Tax Act was used for both tax and financial reporting. In fact, most companies made no distinction between tax and financial accounting. Obviously, therefore, the provisions of Income Tax Acts have greatly influenced the content of annual financial accounts. Keeping in mind the inflation rates in Iceland through the 1970s, it is obvious that financial reporting was not of great value, since it was based on the conventional wisdom of accounting, that is, the historical cost principle. The Income Tax Act of 1978 had great impact on the quality of financial reporting. It is, therefore, informative to examine the most important provisions of the Income Tax Act to see how they influenced annual accounts. The following four sub-sections explain the fundamental issues.

3.2.1 Restatement of Fixed Assets

The Income Tax Act of 1978 took effect in 1979. The act provides for the cost of fixed assets to be restated on the basis of average changes in the construction cost index between the year of reporting and the previous year. This method of calculating the changes in price levels was changed in 1991; now the restatement factor is based on changes in the index during the year of reporting. This index was chosen since it was commonly used for sundry restatement calculations, and it also reflects general price level movements adequately. In 1996 the consumer price index was substituted for the construction cost index.

In 1979 the cost of fixed assets purchased before that year was retroactively restated to the price level in 1979. From then on the restatement of fixed assets has been performed as follows:

1. the cost of fixed assets is not restated during the year of purchase, regardless of when within the year of purchase the assets were acquired;

2. the book value of fixed assets at the beginning of a year is restated annually and such restatement is credited to the revaluation account; both the restated original cost at the beginning of a year and accumulated depreciation are restated; and

3. the book value of fixed assets sold during a year is restated, regardless of when within that year the assets were sold.

According to the law, probably for the sake of simplicity, a full year's depreciation is to be taken during the year of purchase of fixed assets, and no depreciation is to be recorded during the year of sale, regardless of when within the year the respective assets were purchased or sold. Depreciation is charged to the profit and loss account on the basis of the restated historical cost.

3.2.2 Gain/Loss on the Sale of Fixed Assets

If fixed assets are sold, the calculation of gain or loss on the sale is based on the restated historical cost. Gain or loss is based on the selling price, on the one hand, and the book value of the asset sold, on the other hand. The book value is determined as the book value at the beginning of the year of sale restated for general price changes during the year of sale. As indicated above, no depreciation is charged during the year of sale. The same calculation also applies to the sale of investments in the shares of other companies. The basic purpose is to tax only real income on the sale of fixed assets.

3.2.3 Indexation of Monetary Items and Foreign Exchange Rate Variations

According to the Income Tax Act, indexation on monetary assets and liabilities must be credited or charged to the profit and loss account. The law also provides for assets and liabilities linked to a domestic index to be stated in terms of the price level at the balance sheet date. The corresponding increases (or decreases) in the book value of the respective items are to be charged or credited to the profit and loss account.

The same also applies to assets and liabilities denominated in foreign currency. The exchange rate differences are charged or credited to the profit and loss account. The law requires that the value of foreign assets and liabilities be calculated at the rates of exchange prevailing on the date of the balance sheet.

3.2.4 Gain/Loss on Net Monetary Position

The Income Tax Act provides for the effects of general inflation on monetary items to be calculated in the following fashion. The calculation is based on the net monetary position of a company at the beginning of the year of reporting. If monetary assets exceed monetary liabilities, a loss is recognized, and conversely, a gain is indicated if monetary liabilities exceed monetary assets. For this purpose the same index is used as for the restatement of fixed assets. For example, if monetary liabilities exceed monetary assets by 10 million ISK, and the average change in the construction cost index was 20%, the gain on net monetary position would be 2 million ISK. This gain is recognized in computing taxable income, and it is debited to the revaluation account. Conversely, a loss on the net monetary position is credited to the revaluation account and charged to the profit and loss account.

In calculating the net monetary position, inventories are treated as a monetary asset. This practice recognizes that the cost of goods sold needs to be adjusted during inflationary periods. All monetary assets are included in this calculation, but to the extent that a company may have used its option to defer income tax payments and written down the nominal value of debtors outstanding by 5%, the assets have to be adjusted for such tax deferral allocation. On the liabilities side, all items are included except for the estimated taxes on income and net worth at the end of the previous period. Finally, loans to and from company directors are excluded from this calculation if such assets and liabilities are non-interest-bearing or have abnormally low interest rates.

In summary the purposes of calculating the net price level adjustment on monetary items are as follows:

- to recognize the loss of holding monetary assets of fixed amounts that are non-interest-bearing;
- to recognize the gain of owing liabilities of fixed amounts that are non-interest-bearing;
- to eliminate the indexation of assets and liabilities that are linked to a domestic index;
- to eliminate the foreign exchange differences on assets and liabilities denominated in a foreign currency;
- to allow for a correction of the cost of goods sold based on the inventory level at the beginning of the reporting period.

The accuracy of this calculation of the gain/loss on monetary items depends on how representative the beginning balance of the monetary position of a particular company is for the remainder of the year of reporting. Again, as was indicated above in connection with the restatement of fixed assets, the lawmakers opted for a simple rule for this calculation. Both simplifications can lead to an overstatement or understatement of the operating performance of a company; this, therefore, can lead to over- or undertaxation. The accounting profession recognized these errors and recommended a more precise model for financial statement purposes. The next subsection will describe this model in some detail.

3.3 The Influence of the Accounting Profession

With increased demand for higher quality financial reporting, the accounting profession recognized the need for more uniformity in accounting. Therefore, the accounting profession set up a Committee on Accounting Procedure (*Reikningsskilanefnd*) in 1976. The bylaws of the Icelandic Association of State Authorized Accountants (*Félag löggiltra endurskoðenda*, FLE) state that the committee is responsible for issuing recommendations on accounting.

As indicated previously, before the 1980s annual accounts were more or less identical in substance with the tax returns of companies. This emphasis on the tax law gradually began to change in the late 1970s through the efforts of the accounting profession. The single most important event that changed the emphasis was the enactment of the Companies Act of 1978, but the Income Tax Act, oddly enough, was also instrumental in raising the quality of financial reports, since it allowed for better methods to deal with inflation. A brief summary of the most important documents issued by the Committee on Accounting Procedure follows. The committee opted to issue opinions rather than firm recommendations, as required by the bylaws of the profession. Partly, this was a result of the experimental stage that the profession felt prevailed in financial accounting.

The summary below clearly demonstrates that the accounting profession has been the primary force in making financial reports comply with the general provisions of the Companies Act and the Financial Reporting Act, that is, fair representation and, thus, divorcing financial accounting from income tax accounting.

3.3.1 The Format Statement of 1980

The Committee's first opinion in 1980 has probably influenced financial reporting in Iceland more than any other document on accounting. Basically, the opinion sugggested a new format for the presentation of annual accounts, which was based on the new Companies Act and Income Tax Act. The new format was widely accepted; in fact, many non-profit-making organizations adopted the format even though it may not always have been appropriate.

The new format, for the most part, conformed to the presentational requirements of the Companies Act. This was, at least, true for the balance sheet and the notes that became more common than before. The format for the profit and loss account was based on the one-page format with various subtotals that became popular in Icelandic accounts in the early 1970s; this format is not required by the Companies Act, but the Act did specify that certain items be shown separately.

It is noteworthy that the Committee's recommendation did not follow certain requirements of the law. For example, the Companies Act specified that transfers to and from untaxed reserves were to be expensed (or credited) to the profit and loss account. The committee, however, did not recommend such a format, since it felt that the overriding requirement of the law, that is, fair presentation of operating performance, could not be achieved if such allocations to tax reserves were entered in the profit and loss account. The Companies Act was changed on this point to conform with practice in 1989 when the law was revised.

The Committee on Accounting Procedure suggested that interest income and expenses be shown separately in the profit and loss account. The indexation on bonds payable, exchange rate fluctuations, and the price level adjustment on monetary items were also to be included under this heading. The purpose was to show separately in the profit and loss account the net real cost of interest to companies. With that presentation, however, it would have been more appropriate to classify the price level adjustment for inventories with the cost of goods sold under operating expenses. That, however, was generally not done, although some accountants included that information in the notes accompanying the annual accounts.

This statement format of 1980 will now, in some respects, be abandoned with the enactment of the Financial Reporting Act of 1994, which became effective for 1997. A few changes will be made to the profit and loss account, particularly concerning the presentation of extraordninary items, but major changes are being made in the balance sheet as discussed above.

3.3.2 The Opinion on Price Level Corrections

As indicated above, the Income Tax Act of 1978 resulted in a major improvement in the calculation of profits and net worth compared with the period prior to 1979. Actually, it is safe to say that accounting reports in Iceland in the 1970s, excluding 1979, were quite misleading because they were based on the historical cost model during periods of hyperinflation. But even though the Income Tax Act raised the quality of accounting reports, the accounting profession realized that the tax model was rather simple and could lead to errors of reporting operating performance and net worth. For that reason the Committee on Accounting Procedure issued an opinion on price level corrections in 1982. This opinion was revised in 1985 to make the concepts of profit and net worth more precise. Most large and medium-sized companies in Iceland adhere to these recommendations. Some companies, however, have not followed the committee's recommendations. So, in effect, there are two different concepts of operating performance being used, and both are considered good accounting practice; one is in conformity with the law, while the other is based on the accounting profession's recommendations. The following is a summary of the committee's recommendations:

- Nonmonetary assets are stated in terms of the purchasing power of the monetary unit as of the balance sheet date. This means that the cost of fixed assets is restated from the price level at the date of purchase to the price level at the date of reporting.

- Depreciation is recorded in the profit and loss account at the mid-period price level, but accumulated depreciation in the balance sheet is stated in terms of the price level on the date of the balance sheet.
- The gain or loss on the net monetary position is based on the monetary position as of the beginning of the year of reporting as well as the balance at year-end, taking into consideration changes in that position during the accounting period. To reflect the net effect of inflation on monetary items, the gain/loss on monetary items is calculated in terms of the purchasing power of the monetary unit at the average price level for the operating period.
- The cost of goods sold shall be calculated taking into consideration the effects of inflation on inventories. The cost of goods sold shall include a price level correction in order to state the expense item in terms of mid-period prices. Inventories included on the balance sheet shall be restated to the price level as of the balance sheet date.
- A reconciliation shall be made between owners' equity at the beginning of the year of reporting and the balance in owners' equity accounts at the end of the reporting period. Such a reconciliation shall be presented in the notes accompanying the annual accounts in terms of the monetary unit at the price level as of the date of the balance sheet.
- Lastly, the Committee on Accounting Procedure recommended that the monetary value of share capital be shown in the annual accounts in terms of the measuring unit on the balance sheet date. Any excess of total owners' equity over that amount would represent the undistributed remaining profits of a company; and conversely, if share capital restated exceeds total owners' equity, such difference would represent a net accumulated deficit as of the balance sheet date.

As can be deduced from these rules, no profit is recognized in the profit and loss account unless a company is able to maintain the real purchasing power of its owners' equity, that is, when general price level movements have been considered.

As indicated above, most companies adhere to the committee's recommendations. There are, however, several cases in which companies have opted to restate the cost of fixed assets in terms of changes in specific prices rather than general prices. Additionally, some companies have used a concept of capital maintenance, which relies on a concept of profit as operating capacity rather than the financial capital concept.

3.3.3 *Other Opinions of the Accounting Profession*

The Committee has issued several other opinions. As far as possible they have been based on the standards issued by the International Accounting Standards Committee. The Association of State Authorized Accountants is a member of that international body. The committee has also issued opinions on matters that are peculiar to the Icelandic accounting environment. Following is a list of issues with which the committee has dealt:

- Presentation of financial accounts (1980)
- Accounting for the effects of inflation (1982/85)
- Fund flow statements; working capital and cash (1986)
- Accounting for financing leases (1987)
- Accounting for investments in stocks and bonds (1988)
- Accounting for the divergence between exchange rate fluctuations and general inflation (1989)
- Accounting practices of interim financial statements (1990)
- Accounting for prior period adjustments, extraordinary items, and accounting principles changes (1990)
- Accounting for inventories of fish processing plants (1990)
- Accounting for fishing quotas (1991)
- Accounting for investments of investment companies (1991)
- Accounting for certain items in the accounts of municipalities (1991)
- Accounting for income taxes (1991)

3.3.4 *The Accounting Standards Board*

At the end of 1991 the Parliament of Iceland (*Althingi*) passed a law adding a new provision to the Bookkeeping Act of 1968. With this change in the law, an Accounting Standards Board (*Reikningsskilaráð*) was established which is responsible for issuing standards on financial accounting. The board has five members nominated as follows: the Association of State Authorized Accountants (1 member), the Department of Business Administration of the University of Iceland (1 member), and the Chamber of Commerce (1 member). One member is appointed by the Minister of Finance, and the fifth member is the Auditor General of Iceland.

The Accounting Standards Board has issued two pronouncements to date. The first one concerned the basic principles and concepts of financial accounting, and the second was on the treatment of inventories in financial statements. Additionally, the Board has prepared draft opinions on several other issues, for example, the cash flow statement, pension liabilities, investments in shares and bonds and deferred taxes. The drafts have, however, not been publicized because of difficulties in finding proper procedures resulting in harmony between accounting law and accounting rules issued by the Board.

At the time of this writing the Board is considering whether to formally adopt standards issued by the International Accounting Standards Committee as good accounting practice in the country. The Board is of the opinion that conflicts may exist between current law and the international standards, and it is considering how to deal with that issue. The Board has received legal opinion that according to Icelandic law it does not have the power to set accounting rules that are in conflict with the Financial Reporting Act. This became evident when the Board intended to issue rules on investments in shares and bonds that would effectively have eliminated options available in the law. The Board withdrew, therefore, its proposals and it is instead considering implementing the international standards by means of translating the substantive rules (or standards) into Icelandic along with a major portion of the accompanying background material and implementation guidelines.

4. Future Developments

With the Financial Reporting Act, few changes can be expected in financial accounting practice over the next few years. A committee of experts, however, is currently examining the continuation of inflation accounting in the country for both tax and financial reporting purposes. The committee is expected to issue its first opinion by the middle of 1998 and a final report in early 1999. Because current inflation rates are at only 2–4%, some company officials have demanded the abandonment of inflation accounting. Accounting professionals are divided on this issue; some feel that a valid case can be put forward in favor of continuing the inflation-adjusted accounting model, while others feel that financial accounting should revert to conventional accounting with its assumptions of stable monetary units, particularly in view of accounting conventions in neighboring countries where inflation may even be higher than in Iceland.

Useful Addresses

Association of State Authorized Accountants,
(Félag löggiltra endurskoðenda),
Sudurlandsbraut 6,
108 Reykjavík,
Iceland.
Tel. 354-568-8118
Fax 354-568-8139

Accounting Standards Board,
Reikningsskilaráð,
Skúlagötu 57,
105 Reykjavík,
Iceland.
Tel. 354-561-4121
Fax 354-562-4546

Financial statements for Hampidjan Plc.
(Fishing gear manufacturer in Iceland)

Directors' Report

The financial statements of Hampidjan Plc. and the group accounts for the company, including the following subsidiaries: Balmar Fios Lda. in Portugal, Walvis Trawl Ltd. in Namibia, and DNG-Sjovelar Ltd., are prepared, in all material respects, based on the same accounting policies used in prior year. The share ownership is 90% for Balmar, 75% for DNG-Sjovelar, and 100% for Walvis Trawl. The financial statements include adjustments for the effects of general inflation on fixed assets and monetary items. These adjustments are based on changes in the consumer price index which rose by 2.02% in 1997. The notes include an account of the effects of the subsidiaries' net income and owners' equity on the parent financial accounts.

Group
Total sales amounted to 1,347 million ISK, a decrease of 4% as compared with last year. Total number of employees was 218 for 1997 as compared with 231 in 1996. Salaries and wages including various payroll expenses amounted to 389 million ISK of which payroll expenses amounted to 44 million ISK.

Parent
The net income for 1997 amounted to 65 million ISK which is 10 million ISK lower than budgeted for the year. Total sales amounted to 1,141 million ISK which is 13% lower than the year before and 11% lower than budgeted for the year. Number of employees was 135 in 1997 as compared with 145 in 1996. Salaries and wages amounted to 286 million ISK including payroll expenses in the amount of 30 million ISK.

Stockholders' equity amounted to 978 million ISK at the end of 1997 and the equity ratio was 55%. Capital stock was 487 million ISK at the end of 1997 and the ratio of total capital stock to total shareholders' equity was 2.01. The market price for the company's shares, however, was 2.96 at the end of 1997.

The number of shareholders was 628 at year-end 1997 as compared with 579 at year-end 1996. No single shareholder owns more than 10% of the shares outstanding.

The board of directors proposes that a 7% cash dividend be paid in 1998 on the nominal value of capital stock on the date of the annual meeting.

The board of directors and the general manager hereby confirm the financial statements for the company and the group accounts for 1997.

Reykjavik, February 13th 1998.

Board of directors:
Bragi Hannesson
Árni Vilhjálmsson
Baldur Guðlaugsson
Sigurður Egilsson
Sigurgeir Guðmannsson

General manager:
Gunnar Svavarsson

Auditor' Report

To the board of directors and shareholders of Hampidjan Plc.

We have audited the accompanying balance sheet of Hampidjan Plc. as of December 31st 1997, and the related statements of income and cash flows for the year then ended including notes 1-14 for the parent and group accounts. These financial statements are the responsibility of the management of Hampidjan Plc. Our responsibility is to express an opinion on these financial statements based on our audit.

We conducted our audit in accordance with generally accepted auditing standards. Those standards require that we plan and perform the audit to obtain reasonable assurance about whether the financial statements are free of material misstatement. An audit includes examining, on a test basis, evidence supporting the amounts and disclosures in the financial statements. An audit also includes assessing the accounting principles used and significant estimates made by management, as well as evaluating the overall financial statement presentation. We believe that our audit provides a reasonable basis for our opinion.

In our opinion the financial statements give a true and fair view of the financial position of the company as of December 31st 1997, and the results of its operations and its cash flows for the year then ended in accordance with financial reporting laws and good accounting practice.

Reykjavik, February 13th 1998.

BDO Endurskodun Ltd.

Ómar H. Björnsson,
State Authorized Public Accountant

Rekstrarreikningur árið 1997
Tölur eru í þúsundum króna

Income statement for 1997
Figures are in '000 ISK

	Group 1.997	Group 1.996	Parent 1.997	Parent 1.996	
Rekstrartekjur					**Operating revenues**
Seldar vörur	1.347.349	1.410.188	1.141.485	1.307.720	Sales
Aðrar tekjur	25.049	17.912	14.306	17.912	Other income
	1.372.398	1.428.100	1.155.791	1.325.632	
Rekstrargjöld					**Operating expenses**
Hráefni	576.221	542.927	622.463	669.049	Raw materials used
Vinnulaun við framleiðslu	312.098	313.768	229.007	236.604	Payroll expense, production
Ýmis kostnaður	361.237	351.887	264.656	263.218	Operating expenses
Afskriftir	70.214	77.467	31.582	35.091	Depreciation
Birgðabreyting afurða	(18.905)	(24.433)	(26.419)	(12.821)	Change in inventories
Vaxtagjöld (-tekjur) af hr. veltufé	(24.432)	(4.783)	(30.690)	(11.625)	Net interest on working capital
	1.276.433	1.256.833	1.090.599	1.179.516	
Hagnaður fyrir vexti af langt.skuldum	95.965	171.267	65.192	146.116	Net inc. before interest on long-term debt
Vextir af langtímaskuldum	(12.774)	(21.427)	(9.774)	(17.637)	Interest on long-term debt
Hagnaður af reglulegri starfsemi	83.191	149.840	55.418	128.479	
Aðrar tekjur og (gjöld)					**Other income and (expenses)**
Hlutdeild í afkomu dótturfélaga	0	0	18.903	2.814	Share of subsidiaries´ income
Söluhagnaður eigna	0	8.570	0	8.570	Profit on sale of assets
	0	8.570	18.903	11.384	
Hagnaður fyrir tekju- og eignarskatt	83.191	158.410	74.321	139.863	Profit before taxes
Eignarskattur	3.747	4.217	3.542	4.201	Net worth tax
Tekjuskattur	14.429	48.377	5.764	29.846	Income tax
	18.176	52.594	9.306	34.047	
Hagnaður ársins	65.015	105.816	65.015	105.816	Net income for the year

Efnahagsreikningur Tölur eru í þúsundum króna					Balance sheet Figures are in '000 ISK
Eignir	Group 1.997	Group 1.996	Parent 1.997	Parent 1.996	**Assets**
Fastafjármunir					**Fixed assets**
Aðrar eignir					*Other assets*
Langtímakostnaður	1.174	5.999	0	0	Long-term costs
Varanlegir rekstrarfjármunir					*Property, plant and equipment*
Fasteignir	438.391	446.669	362.911	364.626	Real estate
Vélar og tæki	263.407	245.684	188.244	153.272	Machinery and equipment
	701.798	692.353	551.155	517.898	
Áhættufjármunir					*Investments*
Eignarhlutar í öðrum félögum	381.763	371.567	588.634	571.717	Shares of other companies
Skuldabréf og langtímakröfur	13.980	10.411	34.893	37.283	Bonds
	395.743	381.978	623.527	609.000	
Fastafjármunir samtals	1.098.715	1.080.330	1.174.682	1.126.898	**Total fixed assets**
Veltufjármunir					**Current assets**
Birgðir					*Inventories*
Hráefnabirgðir	147.134	140.871	104.357	100.316	Raw materials
Afurðabirgðir	221.624	203.316	170.010	140.361	Finished goods
	368.758	344.187	274.367	240.677	
Skammtímakröfur					*Receivables*
Viðskiptamenn	260.884	211.932	220.413	203.999	Accounts receivable
Víxlar og skuldabréf	78.191	100.867	78.191	87.511	Notes receivable
	339.075	312.799	298.604	291.510	
Sjóður og bankainnstæður	34.439	69.637	16.862	65.379	*Cash on hand and bank deposits*
Veltufjármunir samtals	742.272	726.623	589.833	597.566	**Total current assets**
Eignir samtals	1.840.987	1.806.953	1.764.515	1.724.464	**Total assets**

	Group	Group	Parent	Parent	
31. desember 1997 Tölur eru í þúsundum króna					**as at December 31st 1997** Figures are in '000 ISK
Skuldir og eigið fé	1.997	1.996	1.997	1.996	**Liabilities and owners' equity**
Eigið fé					**Stockholders' equity**
Hlutafé	487.106	405.921	487.106	405.921	Capital stock
Annað eigið fé	491.356	544.340	491.356	544.340	Other owners' equity
	978.462	950.261	978.462	950.261	
Skuldir					**Liabilities**
Skuldbindingar					*Commitments*
Tekjuskattsskuldbinding	62.987	56.337	62.987	56.337	Deferred taxes payable
Veðsetningar og ábyrgðir					Commitments
	62.987	56.337	62.987	56.337	
Langtímaskuldir					*Long-term liabilities*
Veðskuldir í íslenskum krónum	28.843	37.065	24.594	21.329	Mortgage payable - denom. in ISK
Veðskuldir í erlendum gjaldmiðli	372.523	398.897	306.474	344.116	Mortgage payable - foreign currency
	401.366	435.962	331.068	365.445	
Afborganir á næsta ári	(35.727)	(47.214)	(27.772)	(35.287)	Current maturities
	365.639	388.748	303.296	330.158	
Skammtímaskuldir					*Current liabilities*
Innlendir lánardrottnar	50.804	77.565	43.276	65.347	Accounts payable - domestic
Erlendir lánardrottnar	87.626	89.471	91.377	101.828	Accounts payable - foreign
Afurða- og útflutningslán	252.260	158.307	252.260	158.307	Bank loans
Afborganir á næsta ári	35.727	47.214	27.772	35.287	Current maturities
Ógreidd opinber gjöld	7.482	39.050	5.085	26.939	Accrued taxes payable
	433.899	411.607	419.770	387.708	
Skuldir samtals	862.525	856.692	786.053	774.203	**Total liabilities**
Skuldir og eigið fé samtals	1.840.987	1.806.953	1.764.515	1.724.464	**Total liabilities and stockholders' equity**

Sjóðstreymi 1997

Tölur eru í þúsundum króna	Group 1.997	Group 1.996	Parent 1.997	Parent 1.996	Cash flow for 1997 Figures are in '000 ISK
Handbært fé frá rekstri					**Cash flow from operating activities**
Hagnaður ársins	65.015	105.816	65.015	105.816	Net income for the year
Rekstrarliðir sem ekki hreyfa handbært fé:					*Items not affecting cash*
Afskriftir	70.214	77.467	31.582	35.091	Depreciation
Verðbætur og gengism. á langtímalán	(13.539)	2.122	(5.660)	5.386	Indexation on long-term loans
Hækkun tekjuskattsskuldbindingar	5.308	10.221	5.308	10.221	Increase in deferred taxes payable
Reiknaðar tekjur vegna verðlagsbreytinga	(1.662)	(1.672)	(3.012)	(2.396)	Net gain on total monetary position
Aðrar tekjur dótturfélaga	(8.744)				Other income of subsidiaries
Hlutdeild í afkomu dóttufélaga			(18.903)	(2.814)	Share in subsidiaries' income
	116.592	193.954	74.330	151.304	
Óreglulegir liðir:					*Extraordinary items:*
Hagnaður af sölu eigna		(8.772)		(8.570)	Gain on sale of fixed assets
Veltufé frá rekstri	116.592	185.182	74.330	142.734	Working capital from operations
Breyting rekstrartengdra liða:					*Changes in short-term items*
Skammtímakröfur, lækkun (hækkun)	(23.936)	(54.624)	(4.753)	(62.154)	Debtors, decrease (increase)
Birgðir, lækkun (hækkun)	(24.571)	(72.394)	(33.689)	(28.286)	Inventories, decrease (increase)
Skammtímaskuldir, hækkun (lækkun)	33.779	62.409	39.577	55.682	Short-term debt, increase (decrease)
Handbært fé frá rekstri	101.864	120.573	75.465	107.976	Cash flow from operations
Fjárfestingahreyfingar					**Investing activities**
Áhættufjármunir og langtímakröfur					*Investments*
Hlutabréf, breyting	(1.780)	(88.551)	(1.936)	(97.930)	Changes in share investment
Hluthafalán til dótturfélaga			5.322	(9.652)	Stockholders loans, change
Skuldabréf, breyting	(14.392)	19.056	(13.754)	18.282	Bonds, change
Varanlegir rekstrarfjármunir					*Property, plant and equipment*
Fasteignir	(11.864)	(28.611)	(8.069)		Real estate
Vélar, áhöld og bifreiðar	(62.067)	(60.416)	(46.059)	(48.271)	Machinery and equipment
Seldir fastafjármunir	6.873	14.794		14.438	Sales price of fixed assets
Ógr. af söluverði fastafj., breyting	9.359	(12.000)	9.359	(12.000)	Uncoll.sell. price of fixed assets, change
Fjárfestingahreyfingar	(73.871)	(155.728)	(55.137)	(135.133)	Investing activities
Fjármögnunarhreyfingar					**Financing activities**
Selt nýtt hlutafé	3.920				Capital stock sold
Tekin ný langtímalán	17.716	163.589	5.121	149.566	New long-term loans
Arður greiddur til hluthafa	(40.592)	(32.474)	(40.592)	(32.474)	Cash dividends
Afborgun langtímalána	(44.235)	(81.026)	(33.374)	(46.208)	Repayment of long-term loans
Fjármögnunarhreyfingar	(63.191)	50.089	(68.845)	70.884	Financing activities
Hækkun (lækkun) á handbæru fé	(35.198)	14.935	(48.517)	43.727	Increase (decrease) in cash
Handbært fé í ársbyrjun	69.637	54.702	65.379	21.652	Cash balance beginning of year
Handbært fé í árslok	34.439	69.637	16.862	65.379	**Cash balance at end of year**

Notes to the financial statements
(A summary of the main notes)

Accounting policies

1. The financial statements are in all material respects based on accounting policies consistent with those applied in the previous year. The financial statements consist of group accounts and accounts for the parent company. The financial statements for the foreign subsidiaries are made consistent with the accounting policies for the parent with regard to the adjustments to account for the effects of inflation.

2. Minority interest in subsidiaries' net income is included in the group income statement and the minority interest in equity is included among long-term debt. Intercompany transactions have been eliminated in the group accounts. The effects of the subsidiaries on the net income and equity of the group is as follows (figures are in '000 ISK):

	Share	Net income	Equity
Hampidjan Plc., Reykajvik		46,112	765,884
Balmar Fios Lda. , Portugal	90%	11,413	160,014
DNG –Sjovelar, Ltd., Akureyri	74%	6,982	49,938
Walvis Trawl Ltd., Namibia	100%	508	2,626
Total		65,015	978,462

3. The effects of general inflation on the operation and financial position of the company have been calculated and entered into the financial statements. The consumer price index rose by 2.02% in 1997.

  *   The historical cost of fixed assets is restated annually to account for changes in general prices. For this purpose the consumer price index is used. The fixed assets of foreign subsidiaries are converted in Icelandic krona using the relevant exchange rates prevailing at the end of year.
  *   Depreciation of fixed assets is based on restated historical cost and is calculated on a straight-line basis as follows:

	Depreciation rates	Salvage value
Real estate	3-8%	10%
Machinery and equipment	8-25%	0-12%

  *   The effects of general inflation on monetary assets and liabilities are calculated and recorded in the financial statements. For this purpose inventories are treated as monetary assets. The net inflation adjustment amounts to 1.7 million ISK for the group and 3.0 million ISK for the parent. The calculated inflation adjustment reflects the depreciation of monetary assets and liabilities during inflation and the adjustment is included in cost of sales and financial income and financial expense. The counterbalancing entry for the restatement of fixed assets and the calculated adjustments for the effects of inflation on monetary items are charged or credited to the revaluation account under owner' equity.

4. The nominal value of accounts receivable and other short-term claims is written down by 85 million ISK. The balance in the provision for uncollectible accounts was increased by 5 million ISK in 1997, and additionally another 8.1 million ISK was charged to the income statement.

5. Assets and liabilities denominated in foreign currencies are converted to ISK using the prevailing rate at the end of the year. Operating revenues and operating expenses of foreign subsidiaries are converted to ISK using the average foreign currency rates for the year.

6. Inventories are valued at cost or market,whichever is the lower.

Investments

7. The investment in other companies' capital stock is as follows (figures are in '000 ISK):

| | Group accounts | | Parent company | |
	Par value	Book value	Par value	Book value
Subsidiaries			114,266	212,578
Companies on the Stock Exchange	214,830	368,059	214,830	368,059
Other companies	14,255	13,704	9,566	7,997
	229,085	381,763	338,662	588,634

The investments are carried at restated historical cost or market value whichever is the lower. The market value of investment in stock on the Icelandic Stock Exchange is approximately 808 million ISK. (The investments are itemized pr. company in the Icelandic financial statements).

Property, plant and equipment

8. Changes in the accounts for property, plant and equipment can be analysed as follows for 1997 (figures are in '000 ISK):

	Real estate	Equipment
Group accounts:		
Book value at Jan. 1st. 1997	446,669	245,684
Restatement	5,691	(1,156)
Investments	11,864	62,070
Retired, sold	(3,553)	(188)
Depreciation	(22,280)	(43,003)
Book value at Dec. 31st 1997	438,391	263,407
Parent company accounts:		
Book value at Jan. 1st. 997	364,626	153,272
Restatement	7,292	3,419
Investments	8,069	46,059
Depreciation	(17,076)	(14,506)
Book value at Dec. 31st. 1997	362,911	188,244

The depreciation charged to operations in the group accounts includes, in addition to the above depreciation, amortization of long-term costs in the amount of 4.9 million ISK.

The insurance value of machinery and equipment in the group account amounts to 1,330 million ISK as compared with 789 million ISK for the parent. The official assessment value of real estate amounts to 270 million ISK and the insurance value for the same is 783 million ISK. The assessment value of sites amounts to 62 million ISK.

Long-term liabilities

9. The long-term debt of the company consists of the following (figures are in '000 ISK):

	Group accounts	Parent company
ISK loans:		
Indexed loans (cost of int. 3-9%)	28,095	24,594
Non-indexed loans (cost of int. 12%)	748	
Foreign loans:		
USD loans (cost of int. 7.7%)	52,332	52,332
JPY loans (cost of int. 2.5-3.3%)	24,129	24,129
DEM loans (cost of int. 4.2%)	3,484	3,484
ECU loans (cost of int. 6.1-6.8%)	226,528	226,529
SDR loans (cost of int. 6-8%)	30,815	0
	366,131	331,068
Minority interest	35,235	0
Total long-term debt at Dec. 31st 1997	401,366	331,068

The amortization schedule for long-term debt over the next few years is as follows (figures are in '000 ISK):

	Group	Parent
Repayments in 1998	35,727	27,772
Repayments in 1999	31,487	24,846
Repayments in 2000	31,468	26,382
Repayments in 2001	31,753	28,067
Repayments in 2002	31,827	29,916
Later	203,869	194,085
	366,131	331,068

Income tax matters

10. The deferred tax liability is due to timing differences for depreciation and provisions for accounts receivable. Changes in the tax liability were as follows for 1997 (figures are in '000 ISK):

	Group	Parent
Deferred tax liability at Jan. 1st 1997	56,337	56,337
Indexation on liability	1,342	1,342
Accrued taxes for the year	14,428	5,764
Taxes payable for the year	(9,120)	(456)
Deferred tax liability at Dec. 31st 1997	62,987	62,987

Shareholders' equity

11. At the end of 1997 authorized shares amounted to 487.5 million ISK but issued and outstanding shares were 487.1 million ISK. Changes in shareholders' equity can be analysed as follows for the group financial statements (figures are in ' 000 ISK):

	As per financial statements	In terms prices at year - end 1997
Shareholders' equity at Jan. 1st 1997	950,261	969,501
Cash dividends	(40,592)	(40,999)
Net income for the year	65,015	65,667
Restatement of fixed assets, net of gain on monetary items	2,872	
Other - reconciling adjustments	906	(15,707)
Shareholders' equity at Dec. 31st 1997	978,462	978,462

The beginning balance in shareholders' equity of 950.3 million ISK is equivalent to 969.5 million ISK in terms of the price-level at the end of the year, taking into account the change in consumer prices which rose by 2.02% in 1997.

Mortgages and commitments

12. The company's assets have been pledged as security for liabilities in the amount of 603 million ISK for the group and 569 million ISK for the parent company. The book value of the relevant assets is 716 million ISK and 588 million ISK, respectively.

Financial income and financial expense

13. The cost of long-term financing and interest on short-term assets and liabilities can be analysed as follows for 1997 (figures are in '000 ISK):

	Group	Parent
Interest, indexation and exchange rate differences on long-term debt	21,730	17,954
Gain on monetary position, long-term component	(8,956)	(8,180)
Net real interest cost - long-term debt	12,774	9,774
Net interest income less gain on short- term monetary position	(24,432)	(30,690)
Net real financial (income) expense	(11,658)	(20,916)

Other items

14. The remuneration paid to the company directors and general management amounted to 28.6 million ISK in 1997.

Country Highlights
NORWAY

Common Legal Forms of Companies
Joint-stock companies
General and limited partnerships
Sole proprietorship

Sources of Financial Reporting Requirements
The Joint-Stock Companies Act of 1976 (New companies legislation
effective from 1999)
The Accounting Act of 1977 (New accounting legislation effective from
1999)
Norwegian Accounting Standards
The Oslo Stock Exchange

Corporate Taxation
The Tax Act of 1911
The Corporate Tax Act of 1991

Auditing Requirements
The Auditing Act of 1964
The Joint-Stock Companies Act of 1976
Norwegian Standards of Auditing and Auditing Practice Statements

Organization of the Accounting and Auditing Professions
The Norwegian Institute of State Authorized Public Accountants
The Norwegian Association of Registered Accountants

Constitution and Legal System
Constitution of 1814
Constitutional monarchy
Parliamentarism
Combination of civil law and common law

Currency
Norwegian Krone (NOK)

Official Language
Norwegian

NORWAY

Atle Johnsen
Norwegian School of Economics and Business Administration, Bergen
Aasmund Eilifsen
Norwegian School of Economics and Business Administration, Bergen

1. Background

1.1 Introduction

Financial reporting in Norway is regulated by legislation. Accounting legislation is modest and may best be characterized as constituting a legal framework for accounting principles to be applied in practice. The basic principle of accounting legislation in Norway is the general requirement that annual accounts shall be prepared in accordance with good accounting practice.

Good accounting practice is a dynamic concept, allowing practice to develop as economic conditions change and business firms undertake new kinds of transactions and face new accountable events. In this dynamic setting, accounting theory and research, both domestic and international, are intended to guide good practice.

A legal framework rather than detailed rules leaves room for the exercise of professional judgment. Inherent in Norwegian accounting legislation is an implicit conceptual framework, which may best be described as historical cost accounting theory. The basic concepts and principles of this theory underlie good accounting practice and govern professional judgment in a given situation. Good accounting practice, therefore, means compliance with basic accounting principles and the legal framework as well as general acceptance.

Interpretation of the concept of good accounting practice has challenged parties interested in financial reporting (the Accounting Advisory Council, the Norwegian Institute of State Authorized Public Accountants, the Norwegian Society of Financial Analysts, and the Accounting Committee at the Oslo Stock Exchange) to express their opinions. In 1989 the Norwegian Accounting Standards Board was established under the initiative of the Oslo Stock Exchange and the Norwegian School of Economics and Business Administration. Given the limited resources available in

Norway, it was considered desirable to pool the competence and resources of interested parties into one body and thus pave the way for better standards.

In 1990 the Ministry of Finance appointed an Accounting Act Committee to draft proposals to revise existing accounting legislation.

In 1992 the Committee submitted an important subreport on accounting for income taxes. Primarily as a consequence of the Tax Reform of 1992, which changed the relationship between financial reporting and tax accounting, the accounting legislation was changed to introduce deferred tax liabilities and assets into Norwegian financial statements beginning in 1992.

In 1995 the Accounting Act Committee presented its main report. In general, the Accounting Act drafted by the Committee is a continuation of Norwegian and leading international accounting tradition. The report addresses necessary changes in the legislation to comply with the EC Directives. Harmonization of accounting legislation with the EC Directives is a constraint to facilitate harmonization with international accounting standards. Liberal interpretations of the Directives in the context of leading practice and accounting standards in member states have been necessary. The report has been subject to hearing by a number of important groups of users and preparers of financial information.

In March 1998 the Government submitted its proposed new accounting legislation. The proposed Accounting Act is, with minor exceptions, in line with the Committee's draft. The Government's support of the Committee's report in general makes it an important source of interpretations. The Storting (Norway's national assembly) is expected to enact an Accounting Act in June 1998. The new accounting legislation is expected to be effective from the beginning of 1999.

1.2 Accounting Legislation

1.2.1 Historical Development

The first legal rules for bookkeeping in Norway go back to 1874, when certain kinds of businesses were required to keep accounts for the protection of creditors. The law did not regulate valuation or financial statements, but the bookkeeping rules were in force for more than a hundred years. The Tax Act of 1911 stipulated that taxable income be calculated on the basis of accounting income. The Tax Act Committee, therefore, simultaneously drafted a proposal for an Accounting Act that included valuation rules, but it was never enacted. Another curiosity worth mentioning is the requirement of the Trade Act of 1935 that assets be valued at "true value."

In 1959 the Accounting Act Committee was appointed. Although the Accounting Act was enacted almost 20 years later, in 1977, and adapted to intermediate changes in companies legislation, the report of the Accounting Act Committee is the foundation of Norwegian accounting legislation and is an implicit conceptual framework for the interpretation of good accounting practice.

Traditionally, accounting rules have been formulated in companies legislation. The first Joint-Stock Companies Act of 1910 adopted the concept of prudence in valuation by requiring the preparation of annual accounts in accordance with "orderly and prudent business practice." The next Joint-Stock Companies Act of 1957 strengthened the regulation of accounts by including valuation rules and rules on specification of financial statements. Parent companies were also required to prepare a consolidated balance sheet. For the present debate on the general requirements to annual accounts, it is of interest to note a requirement in the law to draw up the income statement to present correctly the results of the company's operations and the law permitting departure if disclosed.

The Nordic Council decided in 1962 to harmonize companies legislation, and a common Nordic proposal was drafted. The Norwegian version was published in 1970.

1.2.2 Present Accounting Legislation

The third Joint-Stock Companies Act was enacted in 1976. This law includes a chapter on annual accounts. Without doubt, the common Nordic accounting rules are influenced by the Report of the Accounting Act Committee in Norway. The Accounting Act was enacted one year later, in 1977. The Accounting Act also applies to joint-stock companies except for the chapter on annual accounts. The regulation of annual accounts in the two laws is similar, and the inclusion of accounting rules in the Joint-Stock Companies Act is, in fact, unnecessary. This has been recognized by new legislation for joint-stock companies enacted in 1997, which does not include accounting rules. The new companies legislation will be effective from the same date as the new accounting legislation, probably January 1, 1999.

The present legislation on annual accounts includes valuation rules, contents and format of financial statements, consolidated financial statements, supplementary information, and disclosure in the board of directors' report. The valuation rules are general rules for current and fixed assets, respectively, and shall apply to all assets. Special valuation rules apply to intangible assets like goodwill and the costs of research and development; treasury stocks; discount, costs incurred in connection with the arrangement of borrowings, and losses on long-term liabilities; and the cost of equity financing. For the items involved, the special rules modify the general valuation rules.

Current assets shall be measured at the lower of cost or fair value. *Fair value* is defined as net realizable value, unless another value is appropriate according to good accounting practice. An exception allows income recognition for long-term manufacturing contracts as work on a contract progresses. Fixed assets shall be measured at cost. Depreciation is required according to a rational depreciation plan. If the fair value of a fixed asset is lower than the carrying amount, and the reason for the impairment of value is other than temporary, a write-down of the asset is required if it is necessary according to good accounting practice. Except for long-term receivables, the law does not allow reversal of a previous write-down in the case of a subsequent increase in value. Although the legislation basically prohibits writing up of fixed assets, they may be written up under certain restrictions.

1.2.3 Legal Framework

The legislation on annual accounts does not contain a detailed set of rules and can best be characterized as constituting a legal framework. The basic principle that annual accounts shall be prepared in accordance with good accounting practice leaves room for professional interpretation and application of theory and international accounting principles. It also allows dynamic practice in a changing environment. The general requirement that preparation must be in accordance with good accounting practice, however, is not an overriding principle. Practice also must be in accordance with the individual rules. Some specific rules explicitly permit departure, however, if such a departure is in accordance with good accounting practice, notably the definition of fair value for current assets and the format rules of the financial statements. In fact, these are examples of regulated override. In implementing the EC Directives in the proposed

Accounting Act, Norway has used the member state option to regulate the override.

Changes of accounting principles and methods violating the written law must be accompanied by changes in legislation. A time-consuming process, legislation delays the evolution of financial reporting in Norway. The primary objective of updating the legal framework was neglected by the Ministry of Trade, which was more concerned with enlarging the domain of legal regulation. Since 1987 the Ministry of Finance has been in charge of the accounting legislation. The proposed Accounting Act represents continued adherence to a legal framework.

1.3 Implicit Conceptual Framework

Inherent in accounting legislation is an implicit conceptual framework. The foundation of financial accounting in Norway is historical cost theory. The Report of the Accounting Act Committee published in 1962 contains a discussion of the concepts of historical cost accounting, which also underlie the valuation rules in the law. In recent years many controversial questions have been raised for which no direct answers are to be found, either in legislation or in recommendations or standards. The Oslo Stock Exchange has taken a strong position in favor of interpretation and application of concepts of the implicit conceptual framework. This view has been controversial, however. Lawyers and accountants who have limited familiarity with accounting theory have argued that the Oslo Stock Exchange has gone too far in that direction.

Historical cost accounting is often more appropriately described as transaction-based accounting. The reason is that transactions are the basis for recognition and measurement. Determination of when a transaction occurs or whether a transaction has occurred at all is crucial for revenue recognition. Substance and economic reality, rather than legal form, shall be accounted for. It has been the experience of the Oslo Stock Exchange that agreements for the sale of buildings, property, and ships often include elements changing the economic reality of the transaction, and the stock exchange has issued guidelines to ensure that financial statements report the substance. The guidelines published in the annual Accounting Bulletins deal with agreements for sale and leaseback, exchange of assets, sale and repurchase agreements, and sales subject to various options.

The treatment of executory contracts is related to the concept of transactions. Executory contracts usually are not recorded. The Oslo Stock Exchange has encouraged listed companies in the shipping sector to adopt a practice of recognizing shipbuilding contracts as assets and liabilities. Besides providing useful information about business risk, the recognition of contracts would be in accordance with fundamental definitions of transactions, assets, and liabilities.

Measurement of the transaction price is of vital importance to the historical cost system. The consideration in a sale transaction, the cost in a purchase transaction, or the consideration in an equity capital transaction basically is the fair value of the consideration at the transaction date. For interest-free credit sales, the Accounting Advisory Council has stated that the nominal amount be discounted if the effect is material. This statement has raised the consciousness of the time value of money in accounting. Several accounting standards now mandate discounting when it is appropriate.

The Accounting Act Committee of 1959 stated that the primary function in accounting is measurement of periodic income. The focus on income determination requires proper matching of expenses with revenues. The matching concept is a key element in the conceptual framework. Examples of important interpretations of the matching concept are an opinion of the Oslo Stock Exchange on expense recognition of maintenance costs and a statement from the Accounting Advisory Council on decommissioning costs.

The concept of prudence should be interpreted in the context of uncertainty. This means one should exercise caution in making estimates under conditions of uncertainty to avoid overstating assets or income and understating liabilities or expenses. It does not imply the creation of hidden reserves. Efforts to eliminate and reduce risk, like hedging, basically should be reflected in the financial statements. A well-known application of prudence is the principle of lower of cost or market value.

Other concepts inherent in the legislation are the consistency concept, the all-inclusive income concept, and the assumption of going concern. *Consistency* means consistent application of principles and methods from one period to the next. As a corollary, if a change is made, the fact of the change and its effect should be disclosed. To ensure comparability, consistency over time should be combined with uniformity in application of principles and methods. The *all-inclusive income concept* requires that all items that have an effect on equity, other than contributions from and contributions to owners, should be included in the income statement of the current period. Exceptions are adjustments resulting from so-called fundamental accounting reforms, which should be reported by adjusting opening retained earnings.

The present state of accounting regulation in Norway, characterized by a legal framework, including the concepts of good accounting practice and standard setting at an early stage, makes the implicit conceptual framework and authoritative interpretations of it the most important part of the regulations.

The implicit conceptual framework is elaborated in the report of the Accounting Act Committee, including the relation to the EC Directives. The proposed Accounting Act includes a chapter of basic accounting principles.

1.4 Good Accounting Practice

The report of the Accounting Act Committee of 1959 explained the concept of *good accounting practice* and proposed that the concept be introduced in legislation to replace the old term "orderly and prudent business practice." Although the new accounting legislation was not enacted until 1976 and 1977, the Norwegian Institute of State Authorized Public Accountants in 1970 started to work on recommendations for good accounting practice. This professional accountancy body published 17 recommendations from 1978 to 1988. The recommendations purported to be no more than guides to good practice. Several recommendations were prepared in close cooperation with the Norwegian School of Economics and Business Administration. The recommendations included important areas like foreign currency, leasing, and write-down of fixed assets. Interpretation of the concept of good accounting practice has also provoked other parties interested in financial reporting to express their opinions. The Ministry of Trade (later the Ministry of Finance) appointed an Accounting Advisory Council to issue statements on good accounting practice. The Norwegian Society of Financial Analysts has issued guidelines for the preparation and analysis of financial statements. Since the middle of the 1980s the Accounting Committee at the Oslo Stock Exchange has taken a leading role by reviewing the annual reports of the listed companies and by publishing Accounting Bulletins. In 1985 the Oslo Stock Exchange appointed an ad hoc committee to issue a recommendation for equity accounting and propose changes in legislation making possible the application of the equity method. The committee had a broad composition of

representatives, including preparers of financial statements, financial analysts, and professional accountants, as well as members of the Accounting
Committee of the Oslo Stock Exchange. Another broadly composed ad
hoc committee was appointed two years later to issue a recommendation
on accounting for business combinations.

The experience with broadly representative committees to issue recommendations to good accounting practice covering controversial and important areas was a major step in the direction of establishing a standard-
setting body. The field of those involved was radically widened, better and
more diversified expertise was available, and the Oslo Stock Exchange
gave the recommendations authoritative support.

The report of the Accounting Act Committee includes a comparison of
the concept of good accounting practice and the concept of true and fair
view. The Committee concludes that the true and fair view is a dynamic
concept similar to the concept of good accounting practice. The proposed
Accounting Act includes the traditional general requirement that the annual accounts shall be prepared in accordance with good accounting
practice.

1.5 Norwegian Accounting Standards

The Norwegian Accounting Standards Board (NASB) was established in
1989 for the purpose of publishing financial accounting standards. Behind
the standard-setting body are the following organizations: The Oslo Stock
Exchange, the Norwegian School of Economics and Business Administration, the Norwegian Institute of State Authorized Public Accountants, the
Norwegian Association of Registered Accountants, the Norwegian Society of Financial Analysts, and the Norwegian Association of MBA Graduates. This cooperation provides access to a wide range of resources and
competence, as well as ensuring that a broad range of views and interests
are reflected in published standards. In 1997 the Confederation of Norwegian Business and Industry joined the NASB to strengthen the influence of
the preparers of financial statements on standard setting.

The standard-setting process involves development of exposure drafts,
which are submitted to a wide range of bodies for comment. The comments received are evaluated before a preliminary standard, which has the
status of recommended practice, is published. The Oslo Stock Exchange
has encouraged the listed companies to take the lead in adopting exposure
drafts and preliminary standards in their financial statements. Final stan-

dards are published only after the preparers and users of financial statements have obtained practical experience with the preliminary standards and have had the opportunity to comment on their experience to the NASB. In 1992 the NASB published three final standards: NAS 1, Inventory, NAS 2, Long-term Manufacturing Contracts, and NAS 3, Contingencies and Post-Balance Sheet Events. Although standards have no legal status, the Oslo Stock Exchange has stated in *Accounting Bulletin 1992* that listed companies are expected to apply Norwegian Accounting Standards. In 1997 the NASB published NAS 4, Government Grants. The NASB has postponed issuing further final standards pending the new accounting legislation.

In addition to the final standards, the NASB has issued preliminary standards on extraordinary items, income taxes, investments in associated companies and subsidiaries, interests in joint ventures, pension costs, cash flow statement, segment reporting, related party disclosures, interim financial reporting, and earnings per share. The NASB has also published discussion papers covering revenue recognition, financial instruments disclosures, and environmental reporting. Current projects include financial instruments, foreign currency, consolidated financial statements, fusion and fission, intangibles, impairment of fixed assets, the board of directors' report, and an update of recommendations on good accounting practice. Recently, the NASB has initiated a project on good acocunting practice for small entities.

At the inception the NASB faced some strategic decision problems. Ideally, a new body should begin by issuing a statement of basic concepts and principles as did the ASB in Britain. In practice, the Board considered the substantive problems existing in financial reporting to be quite serious. The review of annual reports conducted by the Accounting Committee at the Oslo Stock Exchange revealed an urgent need for specific standards. The all-volunteer Norwegian standard-setting body, without a research staff of its own, does not have the resources to explore as does the ASB or the FASB. The standards therefore must be short and not very detailed. In arriving at conclusions, the standard setters have in their minds the implicit conceptual framework inherent in the legislation. They also rely on foreign standards, research reports, and literature.

The elaboration on the implicit conceptual framework in the report of the Accounting Act Committee and the drafted basic accounting principles will constitute the conceptual framework for the standard setting. The Government has expressed support for the conceptual framework as well as for the standard setting.

1.6 The Internationalization of Financial Reporting

The internationalization of Norwegian business and the globalization of the capital markets contribute to the necessity of internationalization of financial reporting. Norwegian companies listed on foreign stock exchanges must report in accordance with foreign or International Accounting Standards (IAS). At the Oslo Stock Exchange, the investments of foreign investors account for approximately one-third of the total market value. This also calls for the application of international accounting principles. The Oslo Stock Exchange encourages disclosure of IAS or U.S. GAAP information as supplements in the annual reports of Norwegian companies. This type of information may be presented in different forms: Complete financial statements with notes, income statement and balance sheet with disclosure of the accounting principles applied, or reconciliation of income and equity under Norwegian and international accounting principles.

The annual report of Norsk Hydro is an interesting example of the internationalization of financial reporting in Norway. Hydro is listed in Oslo, on other European stock exchanges, and since 1985 on the New York Stock Exchange. Besides the disclosure requirements following from listings, it is of primary concern for Hydro to present financial information for the main areas of business on a comparable basis with other companies operating internationally. Hydro presents two sets of consolidated financial statements, one prepared in accordance with Norwegian accounting legislation and good accounting practice, the other prepared in accordance with U.S. GAAP. The individual financial statements for the parent company are prepared in accordance with Norwegian accounting principles only. The editorial layout of the annual report has been subject to changes to facilitate comparability for investors. Hydro now presents the two sets of consolidated financial statements accompanied by common notes. The notes include disclosures required by U.S. GAAP, as well as disclosures in accordance with Norwegian requirements, and are an integral part of both sets of financial statements. The description of accounting principles applies to both sets, and differences are specified. The final note, summarizing and explaining the main differences, provides a reconciliation of income and equity under Norwegian and U.S. accounting principles. Other financial information, including information for the industry segments, is presented in accordance with U.S. GAAP.

With a view toward the internationalization of financial reporting, the NASB will work for harmonization of accounting standards. The Board applauds the IASC's comparability project and overall improvement process. Of even greater importance from the perspective of the NASB is the establishment of international cooperation among national standard setters. The idea of developing a common conceptual basis on which national standard setting bodies can issue their own accounting standards seems promising and should help lead to a prospective harmonization.

1.7 The Relationship between Financial Accounting and Tax Accounting

Fundamentally, the preparation of financial statements according to the valuation rules in the accounting legislation and good accounting practice should be independent of the computation of taxable income. Accounting income, however, has been the basis for the computation of taxable income. Special tax rules developed to meet particular objectives have usually resulted in a figure for taxable income that was lower than that for accounting income. The positive timing differences have been recognized as untaxed reserves in the Nordic format of financial statements. The dependence of taxable income on accounting income has had adverse effects on accounting practice, both in terms of the application of accounting principles and the making of accounting estimates.

The Tax Reform Committee in 1989 proposed a taxable-income concept independent of accounting income. In addition to specific measurement rules, two basic principles for income measurement were proposed, a realization principle and a nondeduction principle for "provisions according to good accounting practice." The basic principles were not defined or explained. The most serious weakness of the proposed set of rules for income measurement was the elimination of the fundamental concept of matching.

The enacted Tax Reform of 1992 kept the dependence on accounting income but included the nondeduction rule for "provisions according to good accounting practice." This apparent inconsistency has caused uncertainty in the arena of tax reform.

From an accounting point of view, computation of taxable income will still affect the application of accounting principles and the making of accounting estimates, even if the specific measurement rules of the tax code have limited the scope of the latter. The tax reform caused an increased frequency of negative differences between accounting income and taxable income. Negative differences between carrying amount and tax base cannot be handled in the Nordic format of financial statements. In line with the subreport on accounting for income taxes from the Accounting Act Committee, the accounting legislation was changed in 1992 to introduce deferred tax liabilities and assets into financial statements. The NASB simultaneously published a preliminary accounting standard for income taxes.

The Accounting Act Committee has made proposals that clarify and restrict the financial reporting alternatives of accountable transactions and events. If legislated, this will in some cases imply that the preferable reporting alternative of the entity for tax purposes will no longer be accepted in the financial reporting. To avoid unintentional effects on payable income tax of the proposed accounting changes, the Committee proposed to expand the number of specific rules for income taxation in the tax code. Some changes in the tax code have already been effected, and the Government has signaled its intentions to consider further adjustments of the tax code.

1.8 Auditing

The Auditing Act of 1964 and the 1976 Joint-Stock Companies Act set out the legal requirements for the statutory audit. Quite parallel to the requirement in the accounting legislation to prepare the annual accounts in accordance with good accounting practice, the auditing legislation refers to *good auditing practice* as the general requirement in conducting an audit. A Norwegian statutory auditor is either state authorized or registered. A state authorization is needed to conduct auditing in listed and larger-sized companies.

Good auditing practice is meant to be a dynamic concept representing the view at any time on the conduct of audits of competent auditors with a high sense of integrity. Within the legal auditing framework and in compliance with any detailed legal rules, the reference to good auditing practice intends to allow the conduct of an audit to develop as economic conditions, user needs, and auditing technology change. The Joint-Stock Companies Act requires all joint-stock companies to engage a state-authorized or registered auditor. The Auditing Act specifies the same requirement for other businesses, other than small personal ones. A state authorization is required for the auditing of joint-stock companies that have more than 200 employees, all listed companies, and some companies in specific fields such as insurance and financial services. Further, the legislation contains provisions concerning the education and practical training of auditors, the appointment and resignation of the auditor, the auditor's independence and professional ethics, the auditor's access to the client's files and other relevant information, the auditor's reporting, professional confidentiality, the auditor's legal liability, and possible legal sanctions against the auditor.

On behalf of the Ministry of Finance, the Banking, Insurance and Securities Commission supervises the profession and licenses the statutory auditors. In addition, the Ministry has appointed an Auditing Advisory Council. Although auditing is regulated by legislation, the government has relied on the profession's self-regulation, especially in matters related to the conduct of an audit.

The Norwegian Institute of State Authorized Public Accountants acts as the professional body of the currently more than 1500 state-authorized auditors. The Institute promulgates rules of professional ethics and auditing standards of good auditing practice. With effect from January 1 1998, the auditing profession has adopted the set of International Standards of Auditing as the national standards. As already mentioned, the state-authorized auditors have been strongly involved in developing good accounting practice and take an active part in the standard-setting process within the NASB. The Norwegian Association of Registered Accountants organizes about half the approximately 2,400 registered auditors, mainly acting as spokesman for its members.

Since 1973, the Norwegian School of Economics and Business Administration has run the national graduate program in accounting and auditing, which lasts 15 months. The candidates enrolled in the program hold a degree in business administration (i.e., they have completed a four-year program at university level) or have passed the examinations required for registered auditors. The School has hired leading practitioners and foreign academicians to teach together with the staff in the comprehensive full-time program. In addition to passing rigorous examinations in the program, the candidates need two years of practical training to become eligible for state authorization.

Registered auditors have completed a three-year program in business administration with emphasis on accounting and auditing at regional colleges, and must have two years of practical training.

The Auditing Act Committee of 1994 submitted in January 1997 a report to the Ministry of Finance with proposals for a general revision of the auditing legislation, including proposals to bring the legislation in line with the EC Directives. Although a number of legal adjustments are proposed, the proposals generally signal continuity in auditing legislation. At present it is an open question when any new legislation resulting from the Committee's proposals will be effective.

2. The Form and Content of Published Financial Statements

The legal annual accounts comprise the income statement and the balance sheet, including the notes, the board's report, and, if required by law, consolidated statements, constituting a composite whole. All statements must include comparative figures for the past year. Listed companies, companies with total assets exceeding NOK 10 million, or more than 200 employees (i.e., "large-sized companies") must comply with more extensive disclosure rules, most significantly, to prepare a statement of changes in financial position and interim reports.

According to the proposed Accounting Act, the financial statements also include the cash flow statement. Interim reporting is proposed not to be a part of the legal reporting requirements. Oslo Børs requires such reporting for listed companies, and the NASB has issued a preliminary standard on interim reporting.

The Accounting Act Committee has drafted a system for simplification by introducing differentiation in the accounting regulation. The simplification is justified by a cost-benefit consideration. The legal framework will be general and apply to all companies. For large companies, extended disclosure is required in the notes. Small companies have options to prepare simplified statements and notes and apply simplified valuation rules.

2.1 The Format of the Income Statement

The primary focus of financial reporting in Norway is information about earnings and its components. The introductory paragraph to the legal format of the income statement is a general requirement with respect to the presentation of the components of earnings.

The format of the income statement is vertical, grouping revenues and expenses (including gains and losses) as operating, financial, or extraordinary. The main groups and income concepts in the statement are:

- Operating revenues and expenses
- Operating income
- Financial items
- Ordinary income (income before extraordinary items)
- Extraordinary items
- Income before taxes
- Income taxes
- Earnings (income for the year)

Income before taxes is either ordinary, that is, net operating and financial items, or extraordinary.

The preliminary NAS on extraordinary items is restrictive. Extraordinary items are material income and expenses deriving from events and transactions distinct from, or only incidentally related to, the business's ordinary activities and expected to occur irregularly. Consequently, any gains or losses related to the sale of fixed assets are normally classified as part of ordinary income. Following the all-inclusive income concept more strictly than the international standards, the effects of changes in accounting principles and correction of a fundamental error that relates to prior periods are included in the income statement and classified as extraordinary. However, the effect of the introduction of a fundamental accounting reform is adjusted directly to the opening retained earnings. The proposed Accounting Act has exemptions from the all-inclusive income concept to bring Norwegian practice in line with international practice.

2.2 The Format of the Balance Sheet

The balance sheet is of the classic two-sided form, assets on the left side, arranged from cash to fixed assets, and grouped into current and noncurrent. Liabilities are arranged and grouped correspondingly.

The presentation of equity in the individual financial statements of a company is related to the regulation of capital and reserves and restrictions on dividends and other distributions in the companies legislation. To facilitate this regulation, the equity presented in the balance sheet is divided into restricted and unrestricted capital. Restricted capital includes paid-in capital in excess of par value, part of retained earnings, and the revaluation reserve. This presentation of equity is not applied in the consolidated balance sheet (see Section 2.5). In the proposed Accounting Act the equity is divided into paid-in capital and retained earnings.

Any noncapitalized pensions liabilities, mortgages, and guarantees must be specified in the extension of the balance sheet.

In addition to the main groups in the income statement and the balance sheet, the format rules include a detailed subdivision of the items. During the past decade it has become customary practice to combine items. The format rules have been interpreted to allow the combination of items, where such combination makes for greater clarity, provided that the items so combined are dealt with separately in the notes.

In the new accounting legislation the format of the income statement and the balance sheet will be adapted to the format requirements of the EC Directives.

2.3 The Notes

The notes are an integral part of the financial statements. Legislation sets the specific minimum disclosure requirements. However, the listed companies have increasingly expanded the information given in notes. This development is driven by the general legal requirement for the board's report to provide information, not given in the financial statements, of importance for assessing the company's financial position and income.

Most listed companies now describe thoroughly the accounting principles applied in their financial statements. The Oslo Stock Exchange has strongly encouraged this evolution and has in several Accounting Bulletins made recommendations on the disclosure of accounting policies.

Although the legislation requires only so-called large-sized companies to prepare a statement of changes in financial position, other companies often present such a statement voluntarily. However, there is no specific legal layout of the statement. In the late 1980s practice adopted a cash flow statement. This innovation, influenced by the FASB, was recommended by the financial analysts and the Oslo Stock Exchange. Listed companies now commonly present the cash flow statement immediately after the two basic financial statements.

The financial statements in the proposed Accounting Act also include a cash flow statement. The proposed Accounting Act does not regulate the content of the cash flow statement, which is supposed to be developed by good accounting practice. The NASB has issued a preliminary standard for the cash flow statement. This standard has not achieved general acceptance. (See the cash flow statement of the Orkla Group at the end of the chapter.)

2.4 The Board of Directors' Report

The board of directors' report should provide information of importance for assessing the company's financial position and income not included in the financial statements and notes. This basic requirement for the content of the report reflects the fact that the report is an integral part of the annual accounts and is vital for the disclosure. Disclosure should also be made of post-balance-sheet events that do not affect the condition of assets or liabilities at the balance sheet date but are of importance for making the financial statements useful.

For the parent company in a group, the report focuses on the group as an economic entity.

The proposed Accounting Act separates the board of directors' report and the annual accounts and introduces a distinction between disclosure in the report and notes. A general requirement to provide information necessary for assessing the company's financial position and income, not given in the financial statements, is introduced for the notes.

2.5 Consolidated Financial Statements

The objective of reporting consolidating financial statements is to present the companies in the group as if they were an economic entity. A group exists if a company, the parent company, has control of another company, the subsidiary. Control is defined in the legislation to exist if a company has a majority of the shareholders' voting rights or through ownership or agreement exercises dominant influence and has a considerable stake in operating income.

Consolidated financial statements comprise the consolidated income statement and the consolidated balance sheet, including the notes. The legislation requires the preparation of consolidated financial statements to be in accordance with good accounting practice and requires the legal formats to be used, suitably amended. The latter permits simplified presentation of equity in the consolidated balance sheet. Basically, the valuation rules for the individual statements apply to the consolidated statements, as does the implicit conceptual framework, implying uniform rules to be used for the whole group. The legal requirement of the consolidated statements to be a summary of the individual statements of the group has been interpreted to mean application of the same principles used in the individual statements, for the parent company as well as for each subsidiary. In fact, when different acceptable principles are used, the statements should not be changed before consolidation.

The effect on accounting income of the conformity requirement in the tax legislation, although reduced by the tax reform, can be an incentive to use other principles of valuation in the consolidated statements, where tax is not relevant. The Accounting Act Committee has proposed the implementation of the member state option in Article 29 of the Seventh Directive to permit other principles of valuation in the consolidated statements. However, the Government has not submitted a similar proposal to the Storting (Norway's national assembly).

Specific legislation on the consolidation of financial statements, being quite modest, also requires intercompany transactions and unrealized gains to be eliminated and any noncontrolling interest's part of the group's equity to be presented separately in the balance sheet. The 1988 recommendation on accounting for business combinations (see Section 3.7) supplements the legal framework and has strongly influenced consolidation practice.

For the listed companies there has been a development in focusing on the consolidated statements. The individual statements of the parent company are now commonly prepared in accordance with minimum requirements and presented as secondary to the consolidated statements of the group. The Oslo Stock Exchange has encouraged this development.

2.6 Additional Content in the Annual Reports

Some companies, notably the listed ones, present financial highlights, key figures, summaries of five or more years' data, and various financial ratios in the annual reports. Financial summaries for segments according to line of business or market are disclosed by the listed companies, typically reporting figures like net sales, operating income, ordinary income, and total assets. Different definitions are encountered and practice varies. The NASB has issued a preliminary standard on segment reporting. The Norwegian Society of Financial Analysts has issued guidelines for the preparation of various ratios for analysis of financial statements.

3. Accounting Policies and Practices in Valuation and Income Measurement

3.1 Current Assets

The accounting legislation applies the lower of cost or market principle to all current assets. For current investments, any unrealized losses are therefore recognized as expense. However, current securities may be valued on an aggregate portfolio basis if the securities are managed as one portfolio with respect to risk and return. The Oslo Stock Exchange has requested the companies to supplement the legal minimum specifications in the notes with the market values of the securities.

Legislation defines fair value as net realizable value, unless another value is appropriate according to good accounting practice. NAS 1, Inventory, prescribes net realizable value to be the appropriate value for inventory. The standard defines net realizable value as estimated future selling price in the ordinary course of business, less estimated costs of disposal and completion. Each item of inventory is normally valued separately. The cost of manufactured goods is variable costs plus some elements of fixed costs. FIFO or weighted averages are recommended for the calculation of cost of goods sold.

NAS 2, Long-term Manufacturing Contracts, recommends that revenue and related costs be recognized in the income statements as the contract activity progresses, often referred to as the percentage of completion method. The standard sets the specific terms for the application. In the case of considerable uncertainty as for profit and completion, the standard recommends the method with a zero estimate of profit. Although the general valuation rules allow the completed contract method, its use is discouraged.

The Accounting Act Committee has proposed marketable financial current assets as part of a trading portfolio to be valued at fair value.

3.2 Long-Term Investments

Long-term investments are usually carried at cost. A decline in value, other than temporary, is recognized as expense if it is necessary according to good accounting practice. Good accounting practice is interpreted to allow valuation on an aggregate portfolio basis if appropriate. When a long-term investment is of individual importance to the investor, however, it must be valued individually. A reduction in the carrying amount is not reversed.

Accounting for investments in associated companies and subsidiaries is discussed in Section 3.8.

The general valuation rules for fixed assets in the proposed Accounting Act include a reversal rule for income recognition of previous write-downs. According to the report of the Accounting Act Committee, changes in market values are considered not to be temporary.

3.3 Intangible Assets

Intangibles assets are valued according to the general valuation rules for fixed assets. Exceptions are goodwill acquired when a business is purchased, and costs of research and development, which may be capitalized and amortized according to special valuation rules.

Goodwill on consolidation, calculated as the difference between the cost of acquisition and the value of the net assets acquired, should be capitalized and is the dominating intangible asset in the financial reports. The amortization period should not exceed 5 years unless a longer period, not exceeding 20 years, can be justified. The legal amortization rule was changed in 1992. Some companies seem to apply 20 years as the general rule in the amortization of goodwill.

The costs of research and development may be capitalized under certain restrictions and normally amortized over a maximum of 5 years. However, no specific measurement rule exists in the tax code for research and development costs. Consequently, there is a tax incentive to expense these costs as incurred in the financial statements.

The Accounting Act Committee proposed to eliminate all special valuation rules modifying the general valuation rules. In response to the hearing, the Government has proposed special valuation rules for costs of research and development and purchased goodwill. The costs of research and development may be expensed as incurred. The amortization period for purchased goodwill shall not exceed 20 years.

3.4 Property, Plant, and Equipment

Accounting legislation requires depreciation in accordance with a rational depreciation plan. In practice, the straight-line depreciation plan dominates. The oil and gas industry uses the unit-of-production method. The general legal requirement to write down fixed assets also applies to property, plant, and equipment. The legislation permits revaluation of fixed assets under certain restrictions. Although the Oslo Stock Exchange has discouraged listed companies from writing up fixed assets, it occurs occasionally for property and plant. The Accounting Act Committee has proposed prohibition against writing up fixed assets.

3.5 Income Taxes

The preliminary NAS on income taxes follows the general principles of the SFAS 109 and is widely adopted. The main differences from SFAS 109 are related to the method used for netting temporary differences and tax losses carried forward, and the restrictions laid down for the recognition of a deferred tax asset.

Annual income tax expense is recognized on an accrual basis and consists of taxes payable and the periodic deferred tax. The calculation starts out in the balance sheet, identifying temporary differences between accounting and tax values of assets and liabilities. The approach, referred to as the liability method, implies the tax rules at the balance sheet date to be used in the calculations, and the effect of any changes in the taxation rules to be recognized as tax expense immediately. Calculations are on a full provision basis in nominal terms. However, deferred tax acquired when a business combination is purchased should be measured at present value, although undiscounted values are accepted for practical reasons. Temporary differences comprise timing differences and other temporary differences between accounting values and the tax basis. Apart from some special transactions based on continuity for tax purposes, and revaluations of fixed assets in accordance with the restrictions of accounting legislation, accounting for business combinations by the purchase method is the major source of other temporary differences.

The calculation of deferred tax applies an integral approach. The positive and negative timing differences expected to reverse within the same time horizon and tax losses carried forward are combined, and deferred tax is calculated on a net basis. A net positive difference gives rise to a deferred tax liability, and a negative difference gives rise to a deferred tax asset. According to the legislation, however, a deferred tax asset can be recorded only under certain restrictions. Specifically, the realization of tax benefits must be very likely, and the recognized tax asset must not exceed the deferred tax liability recorded in the same balance sheet.

The Accounting Act Committee has proposed to eliminate this special valuation rule for deferred tax assets, and also suggested a net presentation of deferred tax liability or asset.

3.6 Pensions

The accounting legislation makes no preference for incorporating pension liabilities in the financial statements or disclosing such liabilities in the extension of the balance sheet. However, more detailed information on pension plans is, in any case, required in the notes. The legal rules have been interpreted to apply only to pension liabilities funded internally. For pension plans administered by independent pension trusts or insurance companies, no pension liabilities were recognized, and only prepaid premiums made for tax purposes were recorded as long-term receivables in the balance sheet. The expenses comprised the annual premiums less the interest earned on the prepaid premiums.

Accounting for pension costs has been one of the most mixed and confusing areas in financial reporting in Norway. Flexibility within the legal framework, the influence of the tax legislation, the absence of a national standard, and technical issues may explain this historical situation. The NASB issued a preliminary standard on pension costs in 1994. The standard had at that time already been implemented by a few listed companies. The standard is coherent with the general lines in the foreign and international standards on pension accounting like SFAS 87/88, SSAP 24, and the revised IAS 19, and makes a distinction between defined contribution and defined benefits plans. In Norway most pension plans are defined benefits plans.

According to the new accounting legislation all companies, except small entities, shall recognize pension liabilities.

3.7 Business Combinations

The recommendation on accounting for business combination covers the consolidation of a parent company and its subsidiaries, as well as legal mergers. It prescribes two accounting methods, the purchase method and the pooling-of-interests method, as acceptable but not as alternatives. The basic principle of the recommendation is that the accounting method shall reflect the economic reality of the combination: a transaction or continuity. Basically, the recommendation is an elaborate interpretation of the transaction concept. A business combination should be accounted for under the purchase method when it is an acquisition transaction. In the rare circumstances of a uniting of interests, the pooling-of-interests method should be used. There has been a general understanding, however, that the regulation of mergers in the present Joint-Stock Companies Act, based on a principle of continuity, implicitly requires the pooling-of-interest method to be used in the case of a legal merger. The Accounting Act Committee has proposed valuation rules for fusion (legal merger) to remedy this situation.

3.8 Investments in Associated Companies and Subsidiaries

An initiative of the Oslo Stock Exchange in 1985 resulted in a recommendation on equity accounting and later on an amendment in legislation introducing the admittance to use the equity method in the consolidated statements for investments in associated joint-stock companies. A significant influence in another company qualifies the investee to be an associated company. If an investor holds 20% or more of the voting power of the investee, the investor normally does have significant influence. In the individual financial statements, the valuation rules of the legislation prohibit the use of equity accounting for investments in associates and subsidiaries organized as joint-stock companies.

The NASB issued a preliminary standard on equity accounting in 1993. The standard recommends that the equity method be used in the consolidated statements as well as in the individual statements for valuation of investments in associated companies and subsidiaries. However, the standard recognizes the present restriction in legislation on the use of the method.

The proposed Accounting Act includes valuation rules for general application of equity accounting.

3.9 Interests in Joint Ventures

The NASB issued a preliminary standard on accounting for interests in joint ventures in 1994. The standard recommends the proportionate method, in Norway called the *gross method* and internationally often referred to as *proportional consolidation,* as the appropriate treatment of interests in joint ventures. Joint ventures may be jointly controlled operations, assets, or entities. For interests in jointly controlled entities, application of the gross method is restricted. There is a general understanding that the legal framework does not allow the method to be used for interests in joint-stock companies in the individual statements, but the method may be used in the consolidated statements. The proposed Accounting Act includes valuation rules for general application of the gross method.

3.10   Foreign Currency

Measurements of foreign currency transactions apply the exchange rate at the date of transaction. The valuation of items denominated in a foreign currency is regulated by the valuation rules in the accounting legislation. A recommendation of good accounting practice interprets the legal framework for monetary items. Unrealized losses are expensed and unrealized gains are deferred. Hedging should be considered in the calculation of unrealized losses. Hedging includes balance sheet items and off-balance-sheet transactions. Anticipative hedges of firm commitments are included. Some listed companies value unhedged exchange positions on an aggregate portfolio basis. For current monetary items, many listed companies apply the closing rate.

Translation of financial statements of foreign operations is not regulated. In practice, foreign balance sheets are normally translated at the closing rate and income statements at the average rate for the year. The effects of exchange rate changes on net foreign investments and transactions designed as hedges of net foreign investments are adjusted directly to equity. For foreign operations that are integral parts of the operations of the reporting company, the temporal method is used for translation of the financial statements.

The Accounting Act Committee has proposed monetary items in foreign currency to be valued at the closing rate.

4. Future Developments

The report from the Accounting Act Committee was completed in 1995 and included proposed changes in the legislation in accordance with the EC Directives. The Government submitted its proposed new accounting legislation in March 1998. The proposed Accounting Act is, with minor exceptions, in line with the Committee's draft. The Storting (Norway's national assembly) is expected to enact an Accounting Act in June 1998.

The new accounting legislation is expected to be effective from the beginning of 1999.

The proposed Accounting Act is an update of the legal framework accommodating recent developments in accounting standards. The new accounting legislation further facilitates prospective harmonization of accounting standards.

| # Resultatregnskap

Mill. kroner	Note	1997	1996	1995
Driftsinntekter	1	**30.970**	25.998	21.977
Forbruk av råvarer, halvfabrikata og handelsvarer	9	**(12.618)**	(11.500)	(9.691)
Lønn og andre personalkostnader	2	**(6.734)**	(5.474)	(4.650)
Andre tilvirknings-, salgs- og adm. kostnader	5	**(7.425)**	(5.798)	(4.882)
Av- og nedskrivninger goodwill	15	**(419)**	(283)	(157)
Ordinære av- og nedskrivninger	12, 15	**(1.342)**	(1.047)	(940)
Andre inntekter og kostnader	12	**181**	20	127
Driftsresultat		**2.613**	1.916	1.784
Resultat fra tilknyttede selskaper	14	**442**	97	76
Finansposter, netto	6	**(394)**	(398)	(451)
Porteføljegevinster		**876**	816	481
Resultat før skattekostnad og minoriteter		**3.537**	2.431	1.890
Skattekostnad	7	**(863)**	(641)	(434)
Minoriteter	24	**(112)**	(38)	(24)
Årets resultat		**2.562**	1.752	1.432
Resultat pr. aksje (kroner)	Side 30-31	**53,7**	36,9	30,2
Resultat pr. aksje fullt utvannet (kroner)	Side 30-31	**53,2**	36,5	29,8

Profit and Loss Account

Amounts in NOK million	Notes	1997	1996	1995
Operating revenues	*1*	**30,970**	25,998	21,977
Raw materials, work in progress and finished goods	*9*	**(12,618)**	(11,500)	(9,691)
Wages and other personnel costs	*2*	**(6,734)**	(5,474)	(4,650)
Other manufacturing, selling and administrative expenses	*5*	**(7,425)**	(5,798)	(4,882)
Goodwill amortisation and write-downs	*15*	**(419)**	(283)	(157)
Ordinary depreciation and write-downs	*12, 15*	**(1,342)**	(1,047)	(940)
Other revenues and costs	*12*	**181**	20	127
Operating profit		**2,613**	1,916	1,784
Profits from associated companies	*14*	**442**	97	76
Financial items, net	*6*	**(394)**	(398)	(451)
Portfolio gains		**876**	816	481
Profit before taxes and minority interests		**3,537**	2,431	1,890
Taxes	*7*	**(863)**	(641)	(434)
Minority interests	*24*	**(112)**	(38)	(24)
Profit for the year		**2,562**	1,752	1,432
Earnings per share (NOK)	*Page 30-31*	**53.7**	36.9	30.2
Earnings per share fully diluted (NOK)	*Page 30-31*	**53.2**	36.5	29.8

| # Balanse

Mill. kroner	Note	1997	1996	1995
EIENDELER				
Betalingsmidler	8	**1.222**	1.063	1.416
Porteføljeinvesteringer mv.	4	**8.188**	6.512	5.866
Kunde- og andre kortsiktige fordringer	5	**4.744**	3.400	4.001
Varebeholdninger	9	**3.076**	2.744	2.938
Omløpsmidler		**17.230**	13.719	14.221
Andeler i tilknyttede selskaper	14	**1.911**	1.061	1.212
Aksjer og andeler i andre selskaper	10	**103**	91	93
Andre formuesmidler	3	**1.364**	637	389
Goodwill, immaterielle eiendeler mv.	15	**5.656**	3.704	3.776
Varige driftsmidler	15	**10.601**	7.284	7.005
Anleggsmidler		**19.635**	12.777	12.475
Eiendeler		**36.865**	26.496	26.696
GJELD OG EGENKAPITAL				
Kortsiktig rentebærende gjeld	16, 17	**1.463**	726	3.399
Kortsiktig rentefri gjeld	11	**7.244**	5.308	5.440
Kortsiktig gjeld		**8.707**	6.034	8.839
Langsiktig rentebærende gjeld	16, 17	**14.216**	9.344	8.159
Langsiktig rentefri gjeld	18	**1.823**	1.445	1.371
Langsiktig gjeld		**16.039**	10.789	9.530
Minoritetsinteresser	24	**478**	183	131
Aksjekapital		**1.233**	1.219	1.219
Annen egenkapital		**10.408**	8.271	6.977
Egenkapital	23	**11.641**	9.490	8.196
Gjeld og egenkapital		**36.865**	26.496	26.696
Gjeld sikret med pant	20	**128**	167	239
Garantiansvar og andre forhold	20, 21, 22	**1.089**	830	447

Balance Sheet

Amounts in NOK million	Note	1997	1996	1995
ASSETS				
Cash and bank deposits	8	**1,222**	1,063	1,416
Portfolio investments etc.	4	**8,188**	6,512	5,866
Accounts and other short-term receivables	5	**4,744**	3,400	4,001
Inventories	9	**3,076**	2,744	2,938
Current assets		**17,230**	13,719	14,221
Interests in associated companies	14	**1,911**	1,061	1,212
Shares and investments in other companies	10	**103**	91	93
Other long-term receivables	3	**1,364**	637	389
Goodwill	15	**5,656**	3,704	3,776
Fixed assets	15	**10,601**	7,284	7,005
Long-term assets		**19,635**	12,777	12,475
Total assets		**36,865**	26,496	26,696
LIABILITIES AND EQUITY				
Short-term interest-bearing debt	16, 17	**1,463**	726	3,399
Short-term interest-free debt	11	**7,244**	5,308	5,440
Current liabilities		**8,707**	6,034	8,839
Long-term interest-bearing debt	16, 17	**14,216**	9,344	8,159
Long-term interest-free debt	18	**1,823**	1,445	1,371
Long-term liabilities		**16,039**	10,789	9,530
Minority interests	24	**478**	183	131
Share capital		**1,233**	1,219	1,219
Other equity		**10,408**	8,271	6,977
Equity	23	**11,641**	9,490	8,196
Liabilities and equity		**36,865**	26,496	26,696
Mortgages	20	**128**	167	239
Guarantees and other commitments	20, 21, 22	**1,089**	830	447

ORKLA-KONSERNET | **Kontantstrømanalyse** [1]

Mill. kroner	Note	1997	1996	1995
INDUSTRIOMRÅDET:				
Driftsresultat		2.510	1.851	1.764
Av- og nedskrivninger		1.862	1.319	1.276
Endring netto driftskapital		(172)	420	(572)
Kontantstrøm fra driften	Side 32-33	4.200	3.590	2.468
Salg varige driftsmidler		212	236	779
Fornyelses- og miljøinvesteringer	15, side 32-33	(1.738)	(1.203)	(1.035)
Fri kontantstrøm fra driften		2.674	2.623	2.212
Betalte finansposter, netto		(565)	(613)	(437)
Fri kontantstrøm fra Industriområdet		2.109	2.010	1.775
Kontantstrøm fra Investeringsområdet før netto kjøp/salg av aksjer og eiendom		168	312	(33)
Betalte skatter og utbytter		(999)	(762)	(616)
Diverse kapitaltransaksjoner, valutakursendringer etc.		762	204	(311)
Konsernets selvfinansieringsevne		2.040	1.764	815
Ekspansjonsinvestering, Industriområdet	15, side 32-33	(5.935)	(664)	(3.765)
Netto kjøp/salg porteføljeinvesteringer		(874)	301	321
Netto kjøp/salg av eiendommer (Investeringsområdet)		(120)	(37)	40
Netto kontantstrøm		(4.889)	1.364	(2.589)
Endring brutto rentebærende gjeld		5.609	(1.488)	2.866
Endring likvide midler/rentebærende fordringer		(720)	124	(277)
Endring netto rentebærende gjeld		4.889	(1.364)	2.589
Netto rentebærende gjeld	17	13.667	8.778	10.142

1) Orkla har valgt å beholde sin tidligere presentasjonsform som hovedkontantstrøm oppstilling, men viser foreløpig Norsk RegnskapsStandard (NRS) kontantstrømanalyse i note 13.

Kontantstrøm fra driften gir uttrykk for den brutto kontantstrøm konsernet genererer fra Industriområdet, korrigert for endringer i binding av midler til driftskapital.

Fri kontantstrøm fra driften representerer industriområdets brutto rentebetjenings- og ekspansjonsevne når nåværende aktivitetsnivå er opprettholdt gjennom fornyelses- og miljøinvesteringer.

Fri kontantstrøm fra Industriområdet viser områdets ekspansjonsevne etter at renter på gjelden er betalt, men før betalt skatt og utbytte.

Konsernets selvfinansieringsevne representerer det beløpet konsernet kan ekspandere for uten at netto rentebærende gjeld øker.

Netto kontantstrøm viser konsernets nedbetalingsevne/lånebehov etter gjennomførte ekspansjonsinvesteringer, netto kjøp/salg av aksjer og eiendommer.

| Cash flow Statement [1]

Amounts in NOK million	Note	1997	1996	1995
INDUSTRY AREA:				
Operating profit		**2,510**	1,851	1,764
Depreciation and write-downs		**1,862**	1,319	1,276
Changes in net working capital		**(172)**	420	(572)
Cash flow from operations	*Page 32-33*	**4,200**	3,590	2,468
Sale of fixed assets		**212**	236	779
Replacements expenditure and environmental investments	*15, page 32-33*	**(1,738)**	(1,203)	(1,035)
Free cash flow from operations		**2,674**	2,623	2,212
Financial items, net		**(565)**	(613)	(437)
Free cash flow from Industry area		**2,109**	2,010	1,775
Cash flow from Investment area before net purchases/sales of shares and properties		**168**	312	(33)
Taxes and dividends paid		**(999)**	(762)	(616)
Miscellaneous capital transactions, foreign exchange differences, etc.		**762**	204	(311)
Group's self-financing capacity		**2,040**	1,764	815
Expansion investments in industrial activities	*15, page 32-33*	**(5,935)**	(664)	(3,765)
Net purchase/sale of portfolio shares		**(874)**	301	321
Net purchase/sale of properties (Investment area)		**(120)**	(37)	40
Net cash flow		**(4,889)**	1,364	(2,589)
Change in gross interest-bearing debt		**5,609**	(1,488)	2,866
Change in liquid assets/interest-bearing receivables		**(720)**	124	(277)
Change in net interest-bearing debt		**4,889**	(1,364)	2,589
Net interest-bearing debt	17	**13,667**	8,778	10,142

1) Orkla has decided to keep its previous cash flow statement as the main presentation. However, the cash flow statement according to Norwegian Accounting Standards Board (NASB) is presented in note 13.

Cash flow from operations expresses the gross cash flow generated by the Industry area, adjusted for changes in funds employed in providing working capital.

Free cash flow from operations represents the gross interest payment capacity of the Industry area and the ability to expand when the current level of activity has been maintained through replacement and environmental investments.

Free cash flow from Industry area shows the Industry area's ability to expand after financial items, before taxes and dividends paid.

Group's self-financing capacity represents the amount the Group can use for expansion investments without increasing net interest-bearing debt.

Net cash flow shows the Group's ability to repay debt/borrowing requirement after expansion investments and net purchase/sale of portfolio shares/properties.

The Group Accounts

1995. Orkla buys the food products companies Procordia Food and Abba Seafood from Volvo and establishes a joint venture with Volvo for their combined beverages businesses through Pripps Ringnes including 50 % of Baltic Beverages Holding (BBH). Pripps Ringnes buys a 20.5 % interest in the Finnish beverages company Oy Hartwall Ab. Media's investments in Poland are increased. Orkla sells its beverages investments in Poland. The Coca-Cola cold drink companies in Norway and Sweden are sold. In addition Norgro, Høvellast, Dacapo and Smaks Salater, together with 50 % of Helly-Hansen are sold.

1996. Orkla Media's involvement in Poland is further increased through the purchase of 51 % of Rzeczpospolita, one of Poland's leading newspapers, and in addition the papers printing company Warsaw-Print (50.8 %). Orkla Foods sells Österberg and Löfquist in Sweden, Beauvais Catering in Denmark as well as Abba Germany and the production operations in Denmark. The Kalas brand was sold in December. BBH increases activities in Russia and Ukraine. The Chemicals division and the Chinese Kaishantun establish a joint venture for production of lignin-based products. It is decided that Frionor and Norway Seafood should merge, and the group's stake is transferred to Financial Investments. The sale of Hansa Brewery is agreed upon.

The Orkla Group in its present form was established through mergers between Orkla Industrier A.S and Borregaard A.S in 1986 and between Orkla Borregaard and Nora Industrier A.S in 1991. The Group has concentrated its activities in three main areas: Branded Consumer Goods, Chemicals and Financial Investments. Since 1990 the Group has developed as follows:

1991. Orkla Beverages establishes operations in Poland in co-operation with The Coca-Cola Company. Purchase of Daishowa Chemicals (USA) makes Borregaard LignoTech the world's largest lignin producer. The Vanillin area is strengthened through coopera-tion with the Italian company EniChem through EuroVanillin (50-50). Orkla Media acquires Sunnmørsposten, Haugesunds Avis and Romsdals Budstikke.

1992. Purchase of 27 % of Frionor who sells fish and seafood in more than 30 countries. The interest was later increased to more than 50 %. 49 % of the shares in Göteborgs Kex was acquired. Option to acquire the remaining 51 %. Orkla Media and Norske Egmont establish a joint company, Hjemmet Mortensen, for magazines.

1993. Orkla Foods purchases BOB Industrier, a leading Swedish supplier of jams, squashes, etc. The Chemicals area acquires Metsä-Serlas' lignin business in Finland. The acquisition expands the prod-uct range and provides increased access to the markets in Eastern Europe. New plant for the production of lignin completed in Octo-ber. Orkla Media acquires a minority interest in Bergens Tidende and establishes at the same time strategic minority holdings in a total of 6 Polish newspapers. Orkla Media's shares in TVNorge was sold.

1994. Orkla Brands acquires the remaining 51 % of Göteborgs Kex and Kantolan in Finland is acquired. Orkla Media purchases 91.5 % of the shares in Drammens Tidende & Buskerud Blad and acquires 87.5 % of shares in Varden and strengthens its position in Poland. The Chemicals area purchases the difenols business in Italy, the remainder of EuroVanillin, together with 55 % of Taicang (China). At the same time the Chemicals area continues its growth through further investments in a new fine chemicals plant in Norway while the polymer business is sold. The Group sells its holding in the Emo group.

1997. In February Orkla acquires Volvo's 55 % financial inter-est in Pripps Ringnes and achieves 100% [1] control. BBH expands further in Lithuania and Russia. Orkla Foods buys 65 % of the Polish food manufacturer Kotlin. Orkla Foods also takes over the Check pizza company Guseppe, effective from 1 January 1998. Ringstads Ferskvare (formerly Stabburet Ferskvare) was sold. Orkla Media acquires Østlendingen AS (51 %). They acquire deci-sive majority in Østlandets Blad and has agreed to buy 49 % of the Swedish newspaper Norrländska Socialdemokraten. Orkla Media also buys several small newspapers in the eastern part of Norway. Forbrukerkontakt is sold. Chemicals buys the fine chemicals busi-ness PolyOrganix. Specialty Chemicals also establishes a joint ven-ture company with Sappi Saiccor for the production of lignin-based products in South Africa. The Orkla Group establishes a 50/50 joint venture company KiMs Asia, which will introduce KiMs snacks to Southeast-Asia.

[1] **PRO FORMA INFORMATION 1996**

Pripps Ringnes has been included 100 %. Goodwill amortisation due to the take-over has been booked with the same amount in 1996 as in 1997.

Amounts in NOK million	1997	1996
Operating revenues	30,970	29,989
Operating costs	(26,777)	(26,130)
Goodwill amortisation and write-downs	(419)	(424)
Ordinary depreciation and write-downs	(1,342)	(1,313)
Operating profit before other revenues and costs	2,432	2,122

The Group accounts for 1997 are in accordance with principles and classifications used previously. From 1997 1. year instalment of long term liabilities is entered as a long term debt. Earlier this used to be classified as short term debt.

GENERAL
The Group accounts show the consolidated result and financial position of the parent company Orkla ASA and its interests in other companies. Interests in *companies* where the Group exerts a dominant influence are consolidated 100 % in accordance with the purchase method. The minority interests' share of profit after tax are presented separately. *Interest in jointly controlled limited companies* are presented using the proportionate consolidation method. *Interests in associated companies* where the Group has a strategic interest and significant influence (20-50 %), are included based on the equity method. Assets defined as «Financial Investments» are valued at the *cost method* irrespective of the share of equity.

The Group's cost prices for assets and liabilities in subsidiaries, joint ventures and associated companies are used as a basis for recording results in the Group accounts. The Group's equity comprises the parent company's equity and retained earnings subsequent to the above-mentioned companies becoming subsidiaries, less amortisation on amounts paid for tangible assets and goodwill in excess of book values and less minority interests.

ACCOUNTING AND CONSOLIDATION PRINCIPLES
Each of the company accounts consolidated in the Group have been prepared using consistent accounting and valuation principles, and the presentation of captions in the profit and loss account and balance sheet has been made using uniform definitions.

Shares in subsidiaries are eliminated and the cost price of the shares is replaced by the company's assets and liabilities, valued at the cost price to the Group. The difference between the purchase price for the shares and the company's aggregate equity capital at the date of acquisition is analysed and primarily allocated to those of the company's assets (or liabilities) which have values different from the book value. Any residual value is being treated as goodwill in the Group accounts. The remaining equity of the aquired company together with the minority share of excess values is presented as minority interests.

The Group's interests in jointly controlled companies are eliminated using the same principles as for subsidiaries. Orkla's share of each caption is included within the Group accounts (proportionate consolidation method, see note 19).

Investments in associated companies are valued in accordance with the equity method and the Group's share of the results after amortisation of goodwill is added to the cost of the investment. The treatment of goodwill in associated companies is based on the same principles as for subsidiaries, see note 14.

Foreign subsidiaries which are not an integrated part of the parent company are translated using the exchange rate at 31.12. for the balance sheet and monthly average exchange rates for the profit

and loss account. Translation differences are charged directly against equity. Monetary items on the balance sheets of foreign subsidiaries which operate as an integrated part of the parent company are translated on the basis of the exchange rate at 31.12, while the exchange rate on the transaction date is used for non-monetary items. In the profit and loss account, depreciation and the cost of materials are translated using the historic rate while other items are translated using monthly average exchange rates. Translation differences are recorded under the caption «Other financial items».

In countries defined as hyperinflationary, the accounts have been inflation adjusted. Depreciation and the book value of operating assets are translated at the exchange rate in effect on the date of acquisition. The profit and loss account is translated using monthly average exchange rates. Other balance sheet items are translated at the year-end exchange rate. Translation differences are recorded under the caption «Other financial items». In markets where no normal market for hedging exist due to political control of exchange rates and de/revaluations Orkla uses exchange rates adjusted for expected effect of such conditions.

CLASSIFICATION, VALUATION AND ACCRUAL PRINCIPLES
The Group accounts are founded on the basic accounting principles accrual, matching and going concern. The accounts also rely on consistent definitions and the principle of congruence. Historical cost and prudence prevail when estimating values. The Orkla Group focuses substance over form reporting and detailed information about single incidents through the year.

Classification of current assets in the accounts is determined as all assets related to the conversion cycle, receivables due within one year and «assets not intended to be permanently retained or used in the business». Other assets are fixed assets. The difference between short and long-term liabilities is determined at one year prior to the maturity date.

Operating revenue is revenue after deduction of discounts, VAT, and all other government fees.

Valuation of current assets is made at the lower of original cost and market value. Fixed assets are valued at original cost less accumulated ordinary depreciation. If the market value of a fixed asset has suffered a permanent diminution, it is written down. Investments in associated companies are valued in accordance with the equity method (se above).

Accounts receivable are valued at expected realisable value. The Group's aggregate provision for bad debts on accounts receivable is stated in Note 5.

Inventories of materials are valued at the lower of cost or market value based on the FIFO principle. Finished goods and goods in process are valued at cost of processing. A provision is made for obsolescence.

Shares and other investments which represent financial investments, separate from the Group's strategic industrial investments, are classified as current assets and valued on the basis of the portfolio principle. The portfolio is managed as a whole and an adjustment in value is only made if the aggregate holdings have a lower value than original cost. Individual investments in the portfolio which have incurred a long-term fall in value are written down. Long-term shareholdings and other interests which are not treated as investments in associated companies are recorded using the cost method. The cost method means that shares/interests are recorded in the balance sheet at cost and cash payments received are treated as dividends.

Fixed assets are capitalised and depreciated if they have a useful economic life in excess of 3 years and a cost price in excess of NOK 15,000. Maintenance of fixed assets is recorded as an operating cost, whereas expenditure on additions or improvements are capitalised and depreciated in line with the corresponding asset. Asset replacements are capitalised. Except from new systems and upgrading of existing systems, all computer and IT-equipment cost due to the transition to the Year 2000 are being expensed. Excess values arising from mergers are allocated in the Group accounts to the relevant fixed assets and depreciated accordingly. Fixed assets are depreciated on a straight line basis using the following rates: buildings 2-4 %, machinery and fixtures 7-15 %, transport equipment and reusable bottles and crates 15-25 % and computer equipment 16-33 %.

Research and development (R&D). R&D-costs are expensed through the year.

Goodwill. On acquiring another company for a consideration which exceeds the value of the individual assets, the difference, to the extent it represents an economic value, is recorded in the balance sheet as goodwill. Goodwill is amortised over its expected useful life, based on calculations made at the time of purchase, but never over more than 20 years. The value of goodwill is written down if the market value is considered to be less than the book value and the reduction is considered permanent.

Pension matters. Accounting for pension costs is in accordance with the preliminary Norwegian accounting standard on pension costs. Pension costs and liabilities are calculated by actuaries using assumptions as to discount rates, future salary adjustments, state pension benefits, future returns and actuarial calculations on deaths and voluntary departures etc. The pension funds are valued in the balance sheet at market value less net pension liabilities. Any overfunding is recorded in the balance sheet to the extent it is likely that it can be utilised. Changes in pension liabilities due to alterations in the terms of pension plans are allocated to the profit and loss account over the estimated average remaining working life of pensionable employees. Changes in pension assets and liabilities due to changes in and deviations from the calculation assumptions (estimate changes) are allocated to the profit and loss account over the estimated average remaining working life of pensionable employees if the differences exceed 10 % of the gross pension liability (or pension assets if larger). Unamortised differences are disclosed in note 2.

Foreign exchange. The treatment of foreign exchange in the Group differs between hedged and unhedged items. «Hedged» means that the economic effect of fluctuations in the relevant currency has been minimalised. Balance sheet items which hedge each other are presented at the rate on the balance sheet date while balance sheet items which are hedged by off-balance sheet financial instruments are presented using the hedge rate. Debt hedged by assets in equal currency is also booked at hedge rate. Hedging transactions undertaken to hedge contractual cash flows are valued together with those cash flows while any loss on hedging transactions which do not cover contractual cash flows is expensed under the caption «Financial items». Unhedged foreign exchange positions are treated in aggregate on a portfolio basis. If there is an overall un-realised net loss on the portfolio it is expensed but unrealised net gains are not recorded as income.

Taxes. The tax charge is based on the financial result and consists of the aggregate of taxes payable and changes in deferred tax. Deferred tax is calculated at the nominal tax rate for timing differences arising between accounting and tax values.

Cash flow statement. Orkla has decided to use the previous format of the cash flow statement setup as the main presentation. The reason is that the new prelimenary standard from NASB does not have a corresponding section with informative summary accounts of the operating units. Cash flow statement NASB, see note 13.

1 Operating profit

Amounts in NOK million	1997	1996	1995
Sales in Norway	13,848	11,682	11,242
Sales in Sweden	8,076	6,887	4,186
Sales in Denmark	1,499	1,474	1,213
Sales in Finland and Iceland	553	560	375
Sales in Nordic region	23,976	20,603	17,016
Sales in the rest of Western-Europe	2,489	2,671	2,815
Sales in Eastern-Europe	2,383	970	697
Sales in Asia	776	562	453
Sales in the rest of the world	716	752	622
Sales outside the Nordic region	6,364	4,955	4,587
Total sales	30,340	25,558	21,603
Miscellaneous operating revenues	630	440	374
Operating revenues	30,970	25,998	21,977
Sales in EU-countries	*12,474*	*11,428*	*8,380*

Revenues on an operating unit level are presented at page 32-33, «Summary Account of the Operating Units».

2 Wages and other personnel costs

Wages and other personnel costs consist of costs directly related to the remuneration of employees and officers, costs related to pension arrangements for both present and past employees and government employment taxes. The costs consist of:

Amounts in NOK million	1997	1996	1995
Wages and holiday pay	(5,368)	(4,401)	(3,833)
Other remuneration	(59)	(22)	(31)
Employment tax	(1,079)	(873)	(666)
Pension costs	(228)	(178)	(120)
Wages and other personnel costs	(6,734)	(5,474)	(4,650)

Pension matters

Most employees in the Group are members of the Group service pension schemes. As at 31.12.1997, a total of 17,696 present employees were members of the service pension schemes. In addition the service pension schemes include 5,939 previous employees. The service pension schemes are defined as «net schemes» which do not bind the Group to liabilities arising from any changes in benefits from State's social security fund. The Norwegian pension plans are treated as defined benefit and defined contribution pension plans. Pension plans in Sweden are treated both as defined benefit pension plans, and in Denmark as defined contribution pension plans.

In addition, the Group has pension liabilities which are not managed by outside insurance company. These relate to early retirement pensions, discretionary pensions to early retired employees, pensions with a pension base higher than the Taxes Act maximum limit, pensions to previous board members and pensions to people who for various reasons have not been included in the service pension schemes which are to be paid by the Group. 3,961 people are covered by these schemes.

Several of the Group's insured pension schemes are overfunded. The overfunding has been evaluated, and it is assumed in the accounts that all overfunding is capable of being utilised due to the fact that some uninsured schemes can be covered from these funds, known future liabilities and the steady development which is taking place in the Group's business and organisation.

The pension charge for the year is calculated by an independent actuary based on information as at 1.1.1997. It is adjusted for any subsequent material changes. Pension costs and liabilities in foreign countries are calculated by actuaries based on local accounting principles, and

assumptions as at 1.1.1997. Adjustments are made for material divergence from Norwegian general accepted accounting principles. Norway represents 84 % and Sweden represents 14 % of gross pension liability in the Group.

Orkla's legal obligations are not influenced by the accounting treatment.

Assumptions:

	Norway	Sweden
Discount rate	6 %	8 %
Future salary adjustment	3 %	5 %
Average remaining working life	15 years	15 years
Pension adjustment/G-adjustment (Soc. sec.)	2 %	4 %
Return on pension funds	7 %	.
Estimated return 1997	10 %	.

Composition of net pension cost

Amounts in NOK million	1997	1996	1995
Present value of this year's pension benefits (including employement tax)	(165)	(132)	(104)
Interest cost on pension liability	(202)	(157)	(133)
Expected return on pension funds	182	142	130
Amortisation of deferred liability due to differences between plan/assumptions	(7)	0	0
Net pension cost benefit plans	(192)	(147)	(107)
Contribution plans	(36)	(31)	(13)
Net pension cost	(228)	(178)	(120)

Composition of net pension liability

Amounts in NOK million	31.12.97	31.12.96	31.12.95
Gross pension liability	(3,454)	(2,711)	(2,521)
Pension funds (market value)	2,815	2,188	2,032
Actual net pension liability	(639)	(523)	(489)
Unamortised differences from plan assump.	(33)	30	34
Net pension liability	(672)	(493)	(455)
Capitalised net pension liability	(884)	(662)	(616)
Capitalised net pension assets	212	169	161

Composition of pension funds (market value)

	31.12.97	31.12.96	31.12.95
Liquid assets	1 %	2 %	3 %
Money market investments	2 %	3 %	3 %
Bonds	48 %	48 %	48 %
Loans	11 %	16 %	16 %
Shares	27 %	24 %	23 %
Property	11 %	7 %	7 %
Total pension funds	100 %	100 %	100 %

Approximately 17 % of pension funds are managed by the company's own pension funds and 83 % by life insurance companies.

3 Other long-term receivables

Amounts in NOK million	1997	1996	1995
Loan board members, employees etc. [1]	74	61	65
Pension assets	212	169	161
Deferred tax allowance	110	79	69
Other long-term receivables	968	328	94
Total	1,364	637	389

1) In addition loan to board members, employees etc. are included in other short-term receivables with NOK 30 million. Employees are allowed a NOK 7 million guarantee.

4   Portfolio Investments, etc.

Financial Investments is one of the Group's three strategic business areas. The securities are managed as a portfolio. The portfolio represents financial investments in its entirety and such is separated from the Group's strategic industrial investments. The portfolio is character-ised by a focus on large individual holdings and has historically had a long term nature. However, there are no directions regulating the Financial Investments' timing of a sale of shares in any given company.

Amounts in NOK million	Number of shares/interests	Book value	Market value	Share owned %
Owned of Orkla ASA				
Norwegian listed shares				
Bank/Insurance				
BN-bank	293,900	43	59	3.0
DnB	7,791,500	190	275	1.2
Sparebank NOR Gr.f.b	616,200	150	160	2.4
Storebrand Ord.	37,648,956	567	1,995	10.0
Industry				
Adresseavisen	325,931	72	169	17.1
Aker RGI A	1,028,708	120	138 }	1.7
Aker RGI B	277,331	32	34 }	
Alcatel STK	255,762	33	91	3.0
Avantor	1,393,300	85	100	8.3
Braathens SAFE	810,600	61	60	2.5
Dyno	4,623,262	518	659	18.1
Elkem	12,474,867	486	1,254	25.3
Elkjøp	201,150	43	55	2.8
Gyldendal	127,295	5	38	5.4
Hafslund A	5,107,155	172	227 }	6.7
Hafslund B	2,634,100	106	93 }	
Håg	1,598,100	33	104	16.7
Kverneland	894,733	113	110	10.0
Kværner A	1,994,978	378	751 }	4.7
Kværner B	43,500	16	15 }	
Nera	5,426,250	179	224	8.2
NetCom	5,212,772	26	954	11.1
Norsk Hydro	539,500	158	196	0.2
Norske Skog A	104,710	24	22 }	1.1
Norske Skog B	305,686	55	61 }	
Norway Seafoods	11,831,299	328	269	16.9
Nycomed Amersham A	1,731,096	281	482	1.4
Raufoss	775,172	69	89	10.3
Rica Hotell	2,054,600	49	118	8.6
Saga Petroleum B	300,000	40	34	0.2
Scana	1,876,164	85	75	8.8
Schibsted	2,962,231	244	379	4.3
SensoNor	2,364,450	106	57	9.9
Steen & Strøm	2,767,061	139	291	9.9
Ulstein Holding	250,000	21	29	1.2
Miscellaneous		110	78	
Shipping				
Awilco B	302,500	29	26	0.7
Benor Tankers	1,247,900	39	68	5.8
Bergesen A	1,854,492	251	324 }	3.8
Bergesen B	1,028,823	158	178 }	
Farstad	700,000	21	29	1.5
First Olsen Tankers	371,200	18	24	1.9
Fred Olsen Energy	503,500	73	77	0.9
Leif Høegh	280,800	26	44	0.9
ProSafe	367,275	60	59	4.6
Ugland Nordic Shipping	418,064	18	29	5.8
Miscellaneous		24	21	
Investment Funds				
Omega Investment Fund	1,951	39	138	
Miscellaneous		11	17	
Total Norwegian listed shares		**5,904**	**10,779**	
Foreign listed shares				
Nordic				
Astra A	600,000	66	77	
Bure	2,667,500	91	259	4.9
Chips Pref. [1]	417,476	52	226	12.5
Danisco	70,000	28	29	0.0
Hartwall A [2]	80,200	8	49	0.7

Amounts in NOK million	Number of shares/interests	Book value	Market value	Share owned %
Owned by Orkla ASA continued				
Huhtamaki I	85,000	20	26	
KCI Konecranes	463,403	12	113	3.1
Kesko	300,000	29	35	
Lindex	1,339,428	30	301	9.7
Nokia A	180,000	74	94	0.1
Vostok Nafta	500,000	22	32	
Miscellaneous		215	219	
Other countries				
Brunswick Russ. Emerg	257,732	18	18	
Baan NV	80,000	19	19	
Intel	42,000	5	22	
Peoplesoft	110,000	22	31	
Rurik Inv. - SDR	3,000,000	20	46	
Russian Capital App	50,000	37	26	
Russian Growth Fund	18,195	27	38	
SAP Ord.	12,000	17	27	
SAP Pref.	11,000	14	26	
Storebrand Scu EVF A	51,101	50	70	
Zeneca Group	75,000	17	19	
Miscellaneous		226	296	
Total foreign listed shares		**1,119**	**2,098**	
Total listed shares		**7,023**	**12,877**	
Unlisted shares, options and other securities				
Berlingske Officin	234,200	96	101	10.9
Carl Aller	6,500	50	50	3.6
Chips Stamm.	52,245	11	28	1 6
CityMail	44,348	25	25	8.6
Dagbladet A	101,466	37	58 }	14.4
Dagbladet Pref.	71,677	23	41 }	
Eiendomsspar	223,444	33	50	3.0
Helly Hansen Holding	3,267,000	0	181	30.0
Holberg Ind. Ord.	520,750	33	33	30.0
Holberg Ind. Pref.	71,944	52	52	40.0
MTV Oy	806	27	27	
Offshore Heavy Tran.	4,294,474	43	43	10.0
Scala	1,151,800	40	34	8.8
Telia Overseas AB	866,520	84	84	13.1
Miscellaneous		189	183	
Total unlisted shares, options and other sec.		**743**	**990**	
Limited partnerships				
Industrikapital 94	13,908,045	113	113	
Industrikapital 97	8,348,452	67	67	
Miscellaneous		85	82	
Total limited partnerships, current assets		**265**	**262**	
Convertible bonds				
Aker RGI	75,000,000	75	222	0.1
Miscellaneous		7	7	
Total convertible bonds owned by Orkla ASA		**82**	**229**	
Loss on hedging, recorded in balance sheet			**-20**	
Shares owned by Group companies				
First Olsen T.	500,000	35	32	2.5
Miscellaneous		40	40	
Total shares owned by Group companies		**75**	**72**	
Total portfolio investments		**8,188**	**14,410**	

1) See note 10.
2) See note 14.

5 Other manufacturing, selling and administrative expenses

Amounts in NOK million	1997	1996	1995
Freight costs	(946)	(924)	(808)
Energy costs	(684)	(483)	(437)
Repair and maintenance costs	(725)	(615)	(526)
Advertising	(1,705)	(1,290)	(956)
Other	(3,365)	(2,486)	(2,155)
Total	(7,425)	(5,798)	(4,882)

Accounts receivables at 31.12. are shown less a provision for bad debts. The reserve for bad debts is included in «Other» above. The reserve has developed as follows:

Amounts in NOK million	1997	1996	1995
Bad debt reserve at 1.1.	59	61	76
Realised losses	(25)	(24)	(37)
Provision for bad debts	44	22	22
Bad debt reserve at 31.12.	78	59	61

6 Financial items, net

Amounts in NOK million	1997	1996	1995
Dividends	298	342	203
Interest income	177	179	268
Interest expenses	(875)	(885)	(887)
Net foreign exchange gains/losses	(36)	3	(10)
Other financial items, net	42 [1]	(37)	(25)
Financial items, net	(394)	(398)	(451)

1) incl. gain from sale of Hansa Brewery of NOK 61 million.

7 Taxes

Amounts in NOK million	1997	1996	1995
Taxes payable in Norway	(649)	(425)	(331)
Taxes payable abroad	(315)	(136)	(87)
Total taxes payable	(964)	(561)	(418)
Change in deferred tax Norway	120	(20)	(54)
Change in deferred tax abroad	(19)	(60)	38
Total change in deferred tax [1]	101	(80)	(16)
Total tax charge	(863)	(641)	(434)
Taxes in % of «Profit before taxes and minorities»	24.4	26.4	23.0

1) See note 18.

8 Cash and bank deposits

Amounts in NOK million	1997	1996	1995
Unrestricted deposits	697	734	463
Restricted deposits	87	90	140
Group bank account system	253	130	103
Short-term receivables	185	109	710
Total cash and bank deposits	1,222	1,063	1,416

9 Inventories and cost of goods sold [1]

Amounts in NOK million	1997	1996	1995
Raw materials	1,244	1,104	1,188
Goods in process	241	172	143
Finished goods and merchandises	1,591	1,468	1,607
Total	3,076	2,744	2,938
Orkla Foods	1,360	1,400	1,613
Orkla Beverages	371	144	119
Orkla Brands	380	362	392
Orkla Media	38	29	22
Chemicals	861	737	694
Others	66	72	98
Total	3,076	2,744	2,938

1) No single raw material represented more than 5 % of total cost of goods sold in 1997.

10 Shares and investments in other companies

Amounts in NOK million	Number of shares	Book value	Share owned %
Owned by Orkla ASA			
AB Chips OY [2]	187,500	60	10,0
Owned by Group companies			
Harvik Rubber Ind. [1]	2,400,000	6	30,0
Solo [1]	1,420	1	71,0
Norsk Avfallshåndtering	4,330	4	2,0
Miscellaneous		25	
Total shares		96	
Miscellaneous interests in partnerships [3]		7	
Total Group		103	

1) Evaluation of the Group's influence and strategic intention led to the conclusion that it would not be correct to present the interest as «associated companies».
2) Interest in voting share capital. In addition to the above item, the Financial Investments area owns shares in AB Chips OY recorded as current assets. In total the company owns 13.9 % of the voting share capital and 19.6 % of the total share capital of AB Chips OY.
3) Of which owned by Orkla ASA: ANS Høgset (7.2 %) NOK 2 million.

11 Short-term interest-free liabilities

Amounts in NOK million	1997	1996	1995
Accounts payable	1,847	1,402	1,538
State duties, taxes, holiday pay etc.	1,753	1,383	1,423
Accrued unassessed taxes	826	511	403
Allocated to dividend	426	339	290
Other short-term liabilites	2,392	1,673	1,786
Total	7,244	5,308	5,440

12   Other revenues and costs [1]

Other revenues and costs represent items classified in the operating profit of a special character which are material to the Group. These have been split out and grouped on a separate line in order to provide better comparability on the other lines in the profit and loss account.

Amounts in NOK million	1997	1996	1995
Of this:			
Gains on sale. Gains in 1997 includes Ringstads Ferskvare, Forbrukerkontakt and building Lillogaten	86	·	369
Net settlement and structur costs in winding up the agreement with The Coca-Cola Company [2]	171	·	(80)
Restructuring, write-downs in Brands and Chemicals	(64)	·	·
Social security tax due to options, bonus plan established in 1993	(12)	·	·
Gains on sale of fixed assets in Abba Tyskland		20	·
Restructuring costs related to the business in Abba Seafood		·	(162)
Total	**181**	**20**	**127**
Of this:			
Write-downs fixed assets	(116)	·	(172)
Write-downs intangible assets	-	·	(19)
Total write-downs	**(116)**	**·**	**(191)**

1) In addition non-recurring items are included in «profits from associated companies» with NOK 303 million (see note 14) and in «financial items» with NOK 61 million (45 % of profit from sale of Hansa).
2) See note 22.

13   Cash flow in accordance with the new preliminary standard from NASB

Amounts in NOK million	1997	1996	1995
Profit before taxes	3,537	2,431	1,890
Taxes paid	(799)	(448)	(355)
Changes in working capital and other adjustments	158	442	(336)
Depreciation and write-downs	1,877	1,330	1,288
Reversal of gains and associated companies	(1,449)	(983)	(947)
Cash flow from operating activities	**3,324**	**2,772**	**1,540**
Investments in fixed assets	(2,315)	(1,388)	(1,309)
Other long-term investments	(4,394)	(414)	(3,438)
Sales of assets	220	252	241
Other sales	117	116	663
Net purchases/sales of portfolio shares	(874)	301	321
Cash flow from investing activities	**(7,246)**	**(1,133)**	**(3,522)**
Dividends paid	(324)	(289)	(243)
Increased long-term debt	4,914	4,231	6,352
Payment of long-term debt	(1,486)	(3,194)	(3,892)
Changes in short-term financing	1,562	(2,489)	174
Long-term receivables	(600)	(230)	·
New equity	18	·	·
Cash flow for financing activities	**4,084**	**(1,971)**	**2,391**
Other changes	(3)	(21)	(66)
Change in cash and bank deposits	159	(363)	343
Cash and bank deposits 1.1.97 [1]	1,063	1,416	1,073
Cash and bank deposits 31.12.97 [1]	1,222	1,063	1,416

1) For specification, see note 8.

See cash flow statement page 12 and general accounting principles page 15.

14   Interests in associated companies

Amounts in NOK million	Share owned %	Original costprice at 1.1.	Book value at 1.1.	Additions/ disposals during the year	Share [1] of profit	Dividends received/ price ad-justment	Book value 31.12.97	Goodwill amorti-sation in 1997	Book value of goodwill at 31.12.
Jotun A.S	41.8	145	550	5	366	(27)	894	(3)	31
Oy Hartwall Ab	20.5	157	165	440	28	2	635	(29)	384
Asker og Bærums Budstikke A.S	30.5	75	82	·	9	(5)	86	(2)	25
Bergens Tidende A.S	28.4	67	97	-	5	(2)	100	(1)	11
A/S Østlandets Blad	62.9	25	30	(29)	-	(1)	-	-	-
Norsk Telegrambyrå A.S	22.1	3	16	-	-	-	16	-	-
Mediaselskaper Polen	·	12	12	-	1	-	13	(1)	4
K/S Swan Sea	35.0	23	7	-	18	(20)	5	-	-
K/S Knutsen Bøyelaster III	28.0	20	9	-	4	-	13	-	-
Norgesbuss Invest A.S	25.1	18	27	14	3	-	44	-	3
Orkla Exolon K/S	42.3	4	29	-	2	-	31	-	-
Oskar Sylte A.S	44.0	4	9	11	7	(3)	24	(1)	2
Miscellaneous	·	19	28	28	(1)	(5)	50	(1)	11
Total		**572**	**1,061**	**469**	**442**	**(61)**	**1,911**	**(38)**	**471**

1) Share of profit includes gain from Jotuns sale of Jotun Polymer (NOK 283 million) and gain from sale of vessels in K/S Swan Sea (NOK 20 million).

Main figures for the major associated companies (100 % figures):

Amounts in NOK million	1997 [1]	1996	1995
Jotun			
Operating revenues	5,250	5,294	4,872
Operating profit	462	372	280
Total assets	3,535	3,564	3,387

1) Preliminary figures.

Amounts in FIM million	1997 [1]	1996	1995
OY Hartwall Ab			
Operating revenues	2,648	2,000	1,723
Operating profit	568	238	85
Total assets	2,353	1,954	1,690

15 Fixed assets and goodwill, intangible assets, etc.

Fixed assets

Amounts in NOK million	Accumulated cost at 1.1.	Re-valuations at 1.1.	Written down at 1.1.	De-preciation at 1.1.	Book value at 1.1.	Addi-tions[a] in 1997	Dis-posals in 1997	Ordinary de-preciation and write-downs in 1997	Book value 31.12.97
Machinery, vehicles	9,577	-	(13)	(5,932)	3,632	2,588	(124)	(1,229)	4,867
Buildings and plant	3,724	120	(35)	(1,367)	2,442	1,560	(82)	(209)	3,711
Commercial property	253	-	-	(63)	190	327	(22)	(18)	477
Other real estate	434	61	(8)	(23)	464	115	(9)	(2)	568
Construction in progress	554	-	-	-	554	407	-	-	961
Prepaid costs relating to new con.	2	-	-	-	2	15	-	-	17
Total	14,544	181	(56)	(7,385)	7,284	5,012	(237)	(1,458)	10,601
Goodwill and intangible assets	4,642	-	(115)	(823)	3,704	2,371	-	(419)	5,656
Total	19,186	181	(171)	(8,208)	10,988	7,383	(237)	(1,877)	16,257

Goodwill etc. divided on major acquisitions

	Year of acquisition, amortisation time	Write-downs in 1997[1]	Amorti-sation in 1997[1]	Book value at 31.12.97
Pripps Ringnes 55 %	1997: 17 years	-	(129)	2,065
Procordia Food/Abba Seafood	1995: 20 years	-	(108)	1,908
Gøteborgs Kex	1994: 20 years	-	(17)	260
Bob Industrier	1993: 20 years	-	(13)	211
Rzeczpospolita	1996: 10 years	-	(21)	174
Drammens Tidende og Buskeruds Blad	1994: 20 years	-	(10)	152
Odense Marcipan	1990: 20 years	-	(12)	139
Miscellaneous		(16)	(93)	747
Total		(16)	(403)	5,656

1) Debited operating profit, see in addition note 14 for total goodwill amortisation in associated companies.

[a] Matching of additions 1997 against cash flow statement (see page 12)

Additions 1997			7.383
Replacement expenditures and environmental investments		1.738[1]	
Expansion investments	5.935		
Of this associated companies	(471)	5.464[2]	
Replacement expenditures Financial Investments area	9		
Real estate investments	136	145	
Change in accounts payable investments	94		
Foreign exchange-rate conversion effect	(19)		
Without cash flow effect	(39)	36	7.383

1) Largest single project: Orkla Trykk, chloralkali plant, new detergent factory and production equipment Nidar.
2) Largest single project: Full take over of Pripps Ringnes (NOK 4,404 million), acquisition of PolyOrganix, new pizzafactory Stranda, acquisition of Taopin, acquisition of Kotlin, acquisition of Østlendingen and capacity improvement in BBH (nearly SEK 370 million).

Investments in and disposals of fixed assets and goodwill

	Investments in:					Disposals at sales price:				
Amounts in NOK million	1993	1994	1995	1996	1997	1993	1994	1995	1996	1997
Machinery, vehicles	1,000	1,275	1,565	1,085	2,588	82	165	542	163	199
Buildings and plants	633	568	663	230	1,560	27	247	560	52	97
Commercial property	1	19	65	23	327	-	37	10	53	29
Other real estate	71	24	26	31	115	7	7	70	39	27
Construction in progress	98	(102)	7	213	407	-	-	-	-	-
Prepaid costs relating to new con.	8	(1)	(7)	1	15	-	-	-	-	-
Goodwill, etc.	341	658	2,431	211	2,371	-	-	-	109	62
Total	2,152	2,441	4,750	1,794	7,383	116	456	1,182	416	414

16 Loans

The Group's interest-bearing debt by type and maturity

Amounts in NOK million	Balance at 31.12.97	Maturity 1998	1999	2000	2001	2002	After 2002
Certificates [1]	500	500	-	-	-	-	-
Bond issues [1]	6,095	-	232	502	371	1,150	3,840
Bank loans	8,771	837	574	37	4,303	2,733	287
Mortgage institutions, insurance companies	115	17	9	9	53	5	22
Miscellaneous	198	184	2	3	-	-	9
Total interest-bearing debt	15,679	1,538	817	551	4,727	3,888	4,158
Unutilised drawing facilities	2,530	-	-	1,610	744	176	-

1) Bond issues are described separately in this note.

The average time to maturity at 31.12.1997 on the Group's interest-bearing debt was 4 years, compared to 5 years at 31.12.1996. Corresponding figures for the Group's unutilised drawing facilities was 3 years and 5 years, respectively.

Orkla ASA has a group bank account system with Den norske Bank, Christiania Bank og Kredikasse, Svenska Handelsbanken and Skandinaviska Enskilda Banken. Nora Danmark AS has a group bank account system with Unibank. The accounts of Orkla ASA and Nora Danmark AS are the only accounts directly settled with the banks and all subsidiaries' accounts are treated as intercompany receivables and payables. At 31.12.1997 the aggregate deposits were NOK 253 million, while the total drawing rights totalled to NOK 1,012 million.

Orkla may not sell shares in the following companies without the consent of the lenders in the long-term international bank loans: Borregaard Industries Ltd, Lilleborg A.S, Orkla Foods A.S and Procordia Food Förvaltning AB.

Bond issues publicly quoted (Orkla ASA) at 31.12.1997

ISIN	Coupon	Term	Currency	Out-standing
	Amounts in million			
NO 185855	10.00 %	1981/1999	NOK	31[1]
NO 185861	9.40 %	1993/2000	NOK	500
NO 185862	7.75 %	1993/2003	NOK	500
NO 185863	6.10 %	1994/2002	NOK	500
NO 185866	8.00 %	1995/2002	NOK	650
NO 185867	7.40 %	1995/2005	NOK	1,000
NO 185868	7.05 %	1996/2003	NOK	1,000
NO 185869	5.00 %	1997/1999	NOK	200
NO 185871	5.70 %	1997/2003	NOK	300
SE 312050	9.00 %	1996/2004	SEK	400
SE 418915	6.00 %	1997/2001	SEK	200

1) Convertible bonds, see note 23.

Certificates at 31.12.1997

ISIN	Coupon	Term	Currency	Out-standing
	Amounts in million			
NO 251176	4.00 %	14.11.97-16.2.98	NOK	250
NO 251177	4.20 %	14.11.97-14.5.98	NOK	250

The coupon does not reflect the Group's interest costs, as there are various interest rate swaps.

---

17 Currency and interest rate risk management

The loan portfolio's foreign exchange and interest fixing distribution, (including hedging transactions)

Amounts in NOK million	Balance at 31.12.97	Next interest rate fixing				After 2001	Average (years)
		1998	1999	2000	2001		
NOK	8,375	6,094	1,031	500	750	-	1,1
SEK	3,917	3,453	-	464	-	-	0,7
USD	1,197	868	-	329	-	-	1,0
FIM	1,134	1,134	-	-	-	-	0,3
DKK	552	552	-	-	-	-	0,3
Others	504	504	-	-	-	-	0,3
Total interest-bearing debt	15,679	12,605	1,031	1,293	750	-	0,9
Liquid assets	(1,222)	(1,222)	-	-	-	-	
Other interest-bearing rec.	(790)	(790)	-	-	-	-	
Net interest-bearing debt	13,667	10,593	1,031	1,293	750	-	

The average remaining interest period for Orkla's debt (including hedging transactions) was at 31.12.1997 0.9 years, compared to 1.8 years at 31.12.1996. In January 1998, the interest rate of debt equalling NOK 500 was fixed for 5 years.

Interest rate management
The objectives of the Orkla Group's interest rate management is to follow the general trends in the market rates and to make dispositions to moderate the market fluctuations. The loan portfolio's fixed interest structure is shaped by the choice of the interest rate structure on the Group's borrowings and by the use of interest rate derivatives.

Currency risk management
Exposure related to balance sheet items and shares in operations abroad are hedged through continuos adjustments of the loan portfolio's currency composition. Foreign exchange risk exposure related to balance sheet items is generally eliminated through financial hedging activities. Exposure related to shares in operations outside Norway is minimised by adjusting the composition of the loan portfolio in accordance with the relative importance of the respective currencies.
Hedging activites related to balance sheet items and shares in activities outside Norway are supplemented with/by hedging of the Group's operations. Exposure related to future cash flows in current contracts are normally hedged 100 per cent. Additional expected cash flows in currencies other than NOK are hedged for up to a limited period only, and only when the probability of realising such cash flows is deemed to be sufficiently high.

Outstanding foreign exchange contracts[1] and currency options[2] related to hedging of operating exposure

Amounts in million Purchase currency	Amount	Sale currency	Amount
NOK	359	USD	51
NOK	10	JPY	175
NOK	20	GBP	2
NOK	8	FRF	6
NOK	31	FIM	23
NOK	1	ESP	15
NOK	99	DEM	24
SEK	4	USD	1
SEK	8	NOK	8
SEK	11	GBP	1
SEK	29	FRF	22
SEK	46	FIM	32
SEK	47	DKK	41
SEK	17	DEM	4
DEM	4	USD	2
DEM	2	ITL	1,692
DEM	1	DKK	3
DKK	33	NOK	34
DKK	20	GBP	2
USD	10	DKK	64
CHF	7	NOK	35
CHF	3	DEM	4
ITL	16,230	USD	9
ITL	5,122	NOK	21
ATS	9	NOK	6
NLG	4	NOK	14
MYR	4	NOK	4
FIM	25	USD	5

1) Forward foreign exchange contracts are agreements for purchasing or selling currencies in specific future periods.
2) Currency options are agreements where the buyer of the option has a right to purchase or sell a specific currency at a specific price on a specific future date.

The volum of outstanding forward contracts and currency options related to hedging of operating exposure totalled NOK 1.034 million as of 31.12.1997, compared with NOK 543 million as of 31.12.1996.

18 Long-term interest-free liabilities

Amounts in NOK million	1997	1996	1995
Pension liabilities [1]	884	662	616
Deferred tax	831	709	641
Other long-term debt	108	74	114
Total	1,823	1,445	1,371

1) Pension liabilities are classified as interest-free because interests are presented together with other pension costs under salaries.

Deferred tax

The table below shows the correlation between the Group's profit for accounting purposes and taxes payable. These differences occur mainly due to a gap between accounting values and tax values. Deferred tax/ deferred tax allowances represent the timing difference multiplied with the nominal tax rate.

The table shows how the Group's deferred tax base is composed, in order to indicate when deferred taxes will fall due for payment. Net positive timing differences mean that the tax which relates to positive and negative timing differences which will fall due in the same time period is presented together. Negative differences which either relate to pensions or cannot be reversed in the same period are presented separately.

Amounts in NOK million	1997	1996	1995
Net positive timing differences:			
Short-term receivables	(60)	(53)	(58)
Shares	(175)	(56)	(177)
Inventories	65	65	87
Other short-term items	(208)	(229)	(89)
Total short-term items	(378)	(273)	(237)
Fixed assets	2,824	2,308	2,181
Net pension funds	198	163	154
Other long-term items	387	262	372
Total long-term items	3,409	2,733	2,707
Losses carried forward	(38)	(50)	(213)
Base for calculation of deferred tax	2,993	2,410	2,257
Deferred tax	842	709	641
Deferred tax allowances on surplus tax on waterfall/energy production	(11)	-	-
Total deferred tax	831	709	641
Negative timing differences which can not be set off:			
Net pension liabilities	330	195	162
Other negative differences not set off	53	92	76
Base for calculation of deferred tax allowances	383	287	238
Deferred tax allowances	110	79	69
Net deferred tax	721	630	572
Change in deferred tax [1]	(91)	(58)	(209)
Effect of accounting reform pensions	-	(10)	-
Purchase of new companies, conversion diff. etc.	192	(12)	193
Change in deferred tax profit and loss account	101	(80)	(16)

1) This include: Deferred tax allowances on adjusted new value on power plant NOK 40 million, deferred tax allowances on surplus tax on waterfall/energy production NOK 12 million and transitional effect new shipping tax NOK 26 million.

19 Jointly controlled limited companies

The Group's main jointly controlled limited companies comprise Baltic Beverages Holding (50 %), Hjemmet Mortensen (50 %) and Rzeczpospolita (51 %) and are included line by line in the financial statements. In a specification of the main captions, operating revenues, operating profit and total assets, the amounts will appear as the following:

Amounts in NOK million	1997	1996	1995
Operating revenues			
Pripps Ringnes	-	3,265	3,072
Hjemmet Mortensen	488	461	448
Rzeczpospolita-group	199	129	-
Baltic Beverages Holding [1]	1,263		
Operating profit			
Pripps Ringnes	-	300	230
Hjemmet Mortensen	71	54	39
Rzeczpospolita-group	34	13	-
Baltic Beverages Holding [1]	443		
Total assets			
Pripps Ringnes	-	2,475	2,661
Hjemmet Mortensen	436	367	224
Rzeczpospolita-group	319	302	-
Baltic Beverages Holding [1]	1,213		

1) Baltic Beverages Holding is owned 50-50 by Pripps Ringnes and Hartwall. In addition Pripps Ringnes owns 20.5 % in Hartwall. This 20.5 % interest is presented as an associated company.

20 Mortgages and guarantees

Amounts in NOK million	1997	1996	1995
Liabilities secured by mortgages	128	167	239
Mortgaged assets:			
Machinery, vehicles, etc.	1,235	668	769
Buildings and plant	646	567	709
Other real estate	67	58	61
Construction in progress	168	273	82
Inventories, etc.	87	67	65
Total book value	2,203	1,633	1,686
Guarantees, etc.:			
Joint and several guarantees	7	48	48
Subscribed, uncalled limited partnership capital	525	132	210
Other guarantee liabilities [1]	557	650	189
Total guarantee liabilities	1,089	830	447

1) Includes guarantee limits for Orkla Finans of NOK 250 million (NOK 170 million in 1996 and NOK 141 million in 1995).

21 Other issues

Orkla Foods has an obligation to purchase additional shares in Dragsbæk Margarinefabrik A.S (50 %) and Margarinefabriken Blume IS (50 %). Orkla's existing holdings were acquired in 1989 for approximately NOK 45 million. The price for additional shares will be based on indexation of this amount, adjusted for the development in earnings during the three years prior to the obligations/right being exercised. Final aquisiton must be finalized before 2006.

The minority shareholders in KiMs in Denmark hold an agreement which, under certain circumstances, allow them to increase their share from 6 % to 20 % without making further payments.

Due to a current litigation between AB Pripps Bryggerier and the Swedish customs regarding export to Russia the government has stated a claim of SEK 55 million. This claim is not considered to be justified by the Group management.

22   Long-term cooperating agreements

The Unilever agreement
Orkla has a cooperation agreement with Unilever relating to detergents and personal products. This agreement, which was originally signed in 1958, was renegotiated in February 1995. The renegotiated agreement maintains the cooperation based on the same main business principles as previously, and runs until 2014.

The Coca-Cola Company (TCCC) agreement
On 28.1.1997 Pripps Ringnes and TCCC agreed to a controlled settlement of both parts co-operative activities in Norway and Sweden during the period 1997-98. So far the settlement is running according to the agreement. A revenue of NOK 171 mill. occurs under «other revenues and costs» (see Note 12). This represents 45 % of both received compensation from TCCC and necessary allowance and write-downs due to restructuring costs of the activities in Norway. 55 % of this amount has been accounted for during the added value analysis done during take-over. In 1995 the Swedish business accordingly expensed SEK 200 mill. in accordance with the settlement of the TCCC-agreement.

PepsiCo-agreement
In June 1997 Pripps Ringnes and PepsiCo agreed that Pripps Ringnes should start licence production, distribution and sales of Pepsi products to the Swedish market. The agreement will be effective from no later than 1.1.2001 because PepsiCo's agreement with the current licenceholder expires on that date. The agreement runs for a 20 year period with an option of additional 5 years.

23   Development in equity over the last 5 years

Amounts in NOK million	Share capital	Legal reserve	Restricted reserve	Free reserve	Orkla ASA	Group reserve	Total
Equity at 1.1.1993	1,219	565	132	1,410	3,326	2,511	5,837
Adjustment reserves at 1.1. and cash payment	.	(7)	7	(15)	(15)	.	(15)
Profit for the year Orkla ASA	.	.	.	8	8	(8)	.
Group transfer received	.	.	.	818	818	(818)	.
Allocation to dividend	.	.	.	(192)	(192)	.	(192)
Allocation to legal reserve and free reserves	.	15	(36)	21	.	.	.
Group profit for the year	.	.	.	.	.	984	984
Write-down own shares in Oktav Invest	.	.	.	.	.	(28)	(28)
Conversion difference foreign subsidiaries etc.	.	.	.	.	.	(13)	(13)
Equity at 31.12.1993	1,219	573	103	2,050	3,945	2,628	6,573
Profit for the year Orkla ASA	.	.	.	198	198	(198)	.
Entries resulting from introduction of new pension standard	.	6	.	51	57	(57)	.
Group transfer received	.	.	.	711	711	(711)	.
Allocation to dividend	.	.	.	(236)	(236)	.	(236)
Allocation to legal reserve and free reserves	.	77	(36)	(41)	.	.	.
Group profit for the year	.	.	.	.	.	1,149	1,149
Charge as a result of the introduction of new pension standard	.	.	.	.	.	(285)	(285)
Conversion difference foreign subsidiaries etc.	.	.	.	.	.	28	28
Equity at 31.12.1994	1,219	656	67	2,733	4,675	2,554	7,229
Profit for the year Orkla ASA	.	.	.	2,217	2,217	(2,217)	.
Group transfer received	.	.	.	814	814	(814)	.
Allocation to dividend	.	.	.	(283)	(283)	.	(283)
Allocation to legal reserve and free reserves	.	318	(36)	(282)	.	.	.
Group profit for the year	.	.	.	.	.	1,432	1,432
Adjustment due to the merger between Pripps Ringnes	.	.	.	.	.	(182)	(182)
Conversion difference foreign subsidiaries etc.	.	.	.	.	.	0	0
Equity at 31.12.1995	1,219	974	31	5,199	7,423	773	8,196
Profit for the year Orkla ASA	.	.	.	535	535	(535)	.
Group transfer received	.	.	.	741	741	(741)	.
Allocation to dividend	.	.	.	(330)	(330)	.	(330)
Allocation to legal reserve and free reserves	.	164	(31)	(133)	.	.	.
Group profit for the year	.	.	.	.	.	1,752	1,752
Adjustment pension liability	.	.	.	.	.	(26)	(26)
Conversion difference foreign subsidiaries etc.	.	.	.	.	.	(102)	(102)
Equity at 31.12.1996	1,219	1,138	.	6,012	8,369	1,121	9,490
Profit for the year Orkla ASA	.	.	.	676	676	(676)	.
Group transfer received	.	.	.	615	615	(615)	.
Allocation to dividend	.	.	.	(410)	(410)	.	(410)
Allocation to legal reserve and free reserves	.	242	.	(242)	.	.	.
Share issue related to employees' 1993 bonus programme	14	.	.	.	14	4	18
Group profit for the year	.	.	.	.	.	2,562	2,562
Conversion difference foreign subsidiaries etc.	.	.	.	.	.	(19)	(19)
Equity at 31.12.1997	1,233	1,380	.	6,651	9,264	2,377	11,641

Share capital development

Amounts in NOK Date/year	Number of shares	Par value	Type of issue	Amount (mill.)	Ratio	Correction factor [1]	Issue price	Share capital (mill.)
31.12.1987	7,216,997	100				5.32		721.7
1988	14,433,994	50	split		2:1	2.42		721.7
1988	15,558,110	50	bonus issue	56.2	1:10	2.42		777.9
1988	12,365,274	50	amortization	159.6		2.42		618.3
31.12.1988	12,365,349	50	conversion			2.42		618.3
1989	13,275,874	50	internat. offering	45.5		2.42	365,00	663.8
31.12.1989	13,339,097	50	conversion	3.2		2.42		667.0
1990	26,678,194	25	split		2:1	1.10		667.0
1990	29,346,582	25	bonus issue	66.7	1:10	1.10		733.7
1990	31,646,582	25	internat. offering	57.5		1.10	230,00	791.2
1990	31,886,582	25	merger	6.0		1.10		797.2
31.12.1990	31,894,938	25	conversion	0.1		1.10		797.4
1991	44,314,828	25	merger	310.5		1.10		1,107.9
31.12.1991	44,314,895	25	conversion			1.10		1,107.9
1992	48,746,384	25	bonus issue	110.8	1:10			1,218.7
31.12.1992	48,746,384	25						1,218.7
31.12.1993	48,747,241	25	conversion					1,218.7
31.12.1994	48,747,241	25						1,218.7
31.12.1995	48,747,241	25						1,218.7
31.12.1996	48,747,241	25						1,218.7
31.12.1997	49,333,393	25	bonus issue	14.8				1,233.3

1) The correction factor is multiplied by the number of old shares to make these figures comparable to the number of shares in 1997.

The Board is authorized until the Annual General Meeting in 1999 to issue up to 3.3 million new shares without preferential right for existing shareholders.

The Annual General Meeting of 10 May 1994 decided to allocate options for maximum 650,000 B-shares to a subscription price of NOK 25. In this connection, in May 1997 options equivalent to 586,152 B-shares were redeemed. Remaining options equivalent to 51,533 B-shares may be exercised by 1 May 1999.

Own shares and convertible bonds

Amounts in 1,000	Par value	Number of shares	Book value
Shares owned by:			
A/S Drammen Kjexfabrik	3,283	131,330	-
Rederi-A/S Orkla	4,183	167,319	-
Chr. Salvesen & Chr. Thams's Comm. A/S	-	14	-
Oktav Invest A.S [1]	25,128	1,005,139	-
Total shares held in treasury	32,594	1,303,802	-
Convertible bonds owned by:			
A/S Drammen Kjexfabrik	30,097	2,149,785	132,423
Orkla ASA	413	29,500	4,463
Total convertible own bonds [2]	30,510	2,179,285	136,886
Total	63,104	3,483,087	136,886

1) Oktav Invest ownes 1,256,424 shares in Orkla ASA and Orkla ASA ownes 80 % of Oktav Invest.
2) Orkla holds convertible bonds with a nominal value of NOK 30.5 million. The nominal value of the total issued convertible bonds is NOK 30.6 million. The conversion price is NOK 14.00 per share. The loan expires on 31 December 1999.

Managers on different levels in the Orkla Group held pr. 31.12.1997 options at 44.360 shares with an average strike price NOK163,54. 38.360 expired 3.2.1998. Social security tax due to the value of these options has been expensed.

The Orkla-Group has a cashbonus-system, and the valuation is tied to the development of Orklas A-shares performance on the Norwegian stock exchange. This agreement includes about 30-40 managers. Each cashbonus is tied for a period of 3 years minimum. The cut off in change in value and corresponding social security tax has been expensed.

Accruals amounting to NOK 60 million have been recorded pr. 31.12.1997 in connection with these agreements.

24 **Minority interests**

Amounts in NOK million	1997	1996	1995
Minority interests on:			
Depreciation	38	25	33
Operating profit	167	53	33
Profit before taxes and minority interests	172	54	33
Taxes	60	16	9
Development in minority interests:			
Minority interests at 1.1.	183	131	213
Minorities' share of 1997 profit	112	38	24
Increase due to establishment of new companies	220	51	26
Decrease due to further acquisition of shares in group companies	(7)	(24)	(130)
Balance of dividends to minorities and share of profit as well as conversion differences	(30)	(13)	(2)
Minority interests at 31.12.	478	183	131
Minority interests relate to:			
Orkla Foods	37	38	52
Orkla Beverages	309	87	30
Orkla Brands	5	4	3
Orkla Media	67	19	15
Chemicals	16	13	13
Others	44	22	18
Total	478	183	131

Revisors beretning til Generalforsamlingen i Orkla ASA

Vi har revidert årsoppgjøret for Orkla ASA for 1997 som viser et årsresultat på 676 mill. kroner for morselskapet og et årsresultat på 2.562 mill. kroner for konsernet. Årsoppgjøret, som består av styrets beretning, resultatregnskap, balanse, kontantstrømanalyse, noter og konsernoppgjør, er avgitt av selskapets styre og konsernsjef.

Vår oppgave er å granske selskapets årsoppgjør, regnskaper og behandlingen av dets anliggender for øvrig.

Vi har utført revisjonen i henhold til gjeldende lover, forskrifter og god revisjonsskikk. Vi har gjennomført de revisjonshandlinger som vi har ansett nødvendige for å bekrefte at årsoppgjøret ikke inneholder vesentlige feil eller mangler. Vi har kontrollert utvalgte deler av grunnlagsmaterialet som underbygger regnskapspostene og vurdert de benyttede regnskapsprinsipper, de skjønnsmessige vurderinger som er foretatt av ledelsen, samt innhold og presentasjon av årsoppgjøret. I den grad det følger av god revisjonsskikk har vi gjennomgått selskapets formuesforvaltning og interne kontroll.

Styrets forslag til disponering av årets resultat tilfredsstiller de krav aksjeloven stiller.

Etter vår mening er årsoppgjøret gjort opp i samsvar med aksjelovens bestemmelser og gir et forsvarlig uttrykk for selskapets og konsernets økonomiske stilling pr. 31.12.1997 og for resultatet av virksomheten i regnskapsåret i overensstemmelse med god regnskapsskikk.

Oslo, 24. mars 1998
Arthur Andersen & Co.

Finn Berg Jacobsen
Statsautorisert revisor

Audit Report to the
Annual General Meeting of Orkla ASA

We have audited the annual accounts of Orkla ASA for 1997, showing profit for the year of NOK 676 million for the company and profit for the year of NOK 2,562 million for the Group. The annual accounts, which consist of the Board of Directors' report, statement of income, balance sheet, cash flow statement, notes and the corresponding consolidated financial statement, are the responsibility of the Board of Directors and the Group Chief Executive.

Our responsibility is to examine the company's annual accounts, its accounting records and the conduct of its affairs.

We have conducted our audit in accordance with applicable laws, regulations and generally accepted auditing standards. We have performed the auditing procedures we considered necessary to determine that the annual accounts are free of material errors or omissions. We have examined, on a test basis, the accounting material supporting the financial statements, the appropriateness of the accoutning principles applied, the accounting estimates made by management and the overall presentation of the annual accounts. To the extent required by generally accepted auditing standards we have also evaluated the company's asset management and internal controls.

The allocation of profit for the year and equity transfers as proposed by the Board of Directors, complies with the requirements of the Joint Stock Companies Act.

In our opinion, the annual accounts have been prepared in conformity with the Joint Stock Companies Act and present fairly the company's and the Group's financial position as of 31 December 1997 and the result of its operations for the fiscal year in accordance with generally accepted accounting principles.

Oslo, 24 March 1998
Arthur Andersen & Co.

Finn Berg Jacobsen
State Authorised Public Accountant (Norway)

Country Highlights
SWITZERLAND

Common Legal Forms of Companies
- Limited companies [*Aktiengesellschaft* (AG), *société anonyme* (SA), *società anonima*], 52%
- Partnerships without legal personality, 36%
- Partnerships with legal personality, 5%
- Cooperatives, 5%
- Others, 2%

Sources of Financial Reporting Requirements
- Legal source: Code of Obligations [*Obligationenrecht, Code des Obligations, Codice delle Obligazioni*] (Swiss company law), articles 662–670 and 957–964.
- Other source: Accounting and Reporting Recommendations (ARR) issued by the *Fachkommission für Empfehlungen zur Rechnungslegung* (FER). ARR approved by the Swiss Exchange admission board are mandatory for Swiss listed companies.

Corporate Taxation
- Three levels of taxation: Confederation, cantons, and communes
- Considerable differences in taxation among cantons
- Normal rate of value-added tax: 6.5 %

Auditing Requirements
- Only limited companies must be audited.
- Small firms may be audited by nonqualified persons. Higher professional standards required for listed companies and large firms. Bank auditors must fulfill additional qualifications and be certified by the Federal Banking Commission.
- Auditors certify that financial statements comply with the law and the company's articles of incorporation. In addition, auditors of listed companies must check that consolidated accounts comply with the Swiss Exchange listing rules and certify that these statements give a true and fair view of the company's assets, liabilities, and financial position.

Organization of the Accounting and Auditing Profession
- Certified accountants and auditors are members of the Swiss Institute of Certified Accountants and Tax Consultants (*Treuhand*

Kammer, Chambre Fiduciaire, Camera Fiduciaria), which delivers the legally protected title of Certified Accountant (*Diplomierter Wirtschaftsprüfer, Expert-comptable diplômé, Esperto-contabile diplomato*).

- Applicants must have several years of professional experience in an audit firm and pass an examination.

Currency

Swiss Franc (SFr or CHF).

Official Languages

- German, French, and Italian.
- Relative importance (percentage of residents with corresponding mother language):

  German: 64%
  French: 19%
  Italian: 8%
  Others: 9%

SWITZERLAND

Bernard Raffournier
University of Geneva, Geneva, Switzerland

1. Background

1.1 The Legal, Institutional, and Economic Environment of Accounting

Switzerland is a confederation of 26 cantons, all of which have considerable political, economic, and fiscal autonomy. The power to legislate is shared among the federal state, the cantons, and more than 3,000 communes. Switzerland has three official languages: German, French, and Italian. The currency is the Swiss franc (SFr).

Federal laws constitute a common basis assuring a basic level of homogeneity within the country. To a large extent, they are included in the Civil Code (*Zivilgesetzbuch—Code Civil—Codice Civile*), the Code of Obligations (*Obligationenrecht—Code des Obligations—Codice delle Obligazioni*) and the Penal Code (*Strafgesetzbuch—Code Pénal—Codice Penale*). Every canton and commune may, within the limits of its own powers, promulgate additional laws.

The main political characteristic of Switzerland is its system of direct democracy, which enables citizens to have a say on any administrative or legislative project. This system gave rise to the initiative and referendum rights.

The initiative right makes it possible for a sufficient group of electors to propose a change in the Constitution and, in some cantons, a new law. The referendum right enables the people to oppose the implementation of a new federal or cantonal law by submitting the project to a referendum.

These popular rights theoretically preclude the implementation of any governmental project that does not have the people's agreement. A recent example was the negative result of the referendum on the participation of Switzerland in the European Economic Area. However, an increase in the number of initiatives in recent years has lead to a high level of abstention, which often makes it possible for well-organized lobbying groups to block decisions detrimental to their personal interests.

The public sector is limited to specific industries (public transport, essentially). As in most European countries, there is a move toward privatization of industries that traditionally belonged to the public sector (e.g. telecommunications). Nevertheless, the economy is far from perfectly liberal because there are severe restrictions on competition. Some activities (agriculture in particular) are protected from international competition by guaranteed high prices. The main obstacle to competition, however, is the existence of many cartels of producers, importers, and distributors that contribute to keeping prices higher than in comparable countries. These cartels are perfectly legal, although a law has been adopted to prevent abuses. In addition, many cantonal regulations often preclude suppliers outside the canton from bidding for public-sector orders.

For many years, the Swiss economic and political life has been dominated by discussions on the place of Switzerland in Europe and on its relationship with the European Union (EU). Several years ago, the government decided that Switzerland should participate in the European Economic Area in order to prepare for future membership in the EU. Legislation was revised with this perspective in order to make it compatible with European Directives. After a referendum rejected Swiss adhesion to the European Economic Area in 1992, the federal government entered into negotiations with the EU in order to arrive at limited agreements on issues such as education, research, and transport. At the time of writing, this process is not yet completed. In any event, Switzerland remains largely dependent on the EU because 80% of its imports and 62% of its exports are with EU member states. In the field of accounting, a consequence of this influence is that many companies draw up their financial statements in accordance with the 4th and 7th EC Directives.

1.2 The Sources of Accounting Regulation

In the sphere of accounting, Switzerland has been, for a long time, a poorly regulated country. Until 1984, the only source of accounting regulation was the Code of Obligations (CO), part of Swiss company law, which contains some general accounting principles that apply to all enterprises (articles 957–964) and more detailed rules for companies limited by shares (articles 662–670).

The preceding version of company law dated back to 1936 and included only a few provisions concerning accounting. Its main features were the prohibition of valuation bases other than historical cost and the authorization of hidden reserves practically without limitation. For the rest, the law stated that accounting had to comply with usual business practices.

As far back as the early 1970s, a revision was undertaken that ended in 1991 with the adoption of articles 620–763 of the Code of Obligations. The aim of the revision was:

- To increase transparency

- To strengthen the protection of shareholders

- To improve the structure and functioning of companies

- To facilitate the raising of capital

- To prevent abuses

The new company law includes several provisions concerning accounting and goes much further than the initial regulation. More detailed accounting rules have been adopted, and disclosure requirements have been largely expanded. The law was implemented on July 1, 1992, except for articles governing consolidated financial statements, which became effective one year later.

A second source of accounting regulation was introduced in 1984 with the creation of the Foundation for Accounting and Reporting Recommendations (*Fachkommission für Empfehlungen zur Rechnungslegung* [FER]— *Fondation pour les recommandations relatives à la présentation des comptes*—*Fondazione per le racommandazioni concernenti la presentazione dei conti*). The objective of this standard-setting body, created on the initiative of the Swiss Institute of Certified Accountants and Tax Consultants, is to establish Accounting and Reporting Recommendations (ARR) in order to harmonize accounting practices, improve comparisons, and increase the quality of financial statements in Switzerland. Members represent such interests as auditing firms, industry, banks and insurance companies, employers and employee organizations, financial analysts and stock exchanges, universities, public administration, and other parties interested in accounting.

As of December 1997, 16 recommendations have been issued and 3 are in process (Table 1). Despite being strongly inspired by IASC standards, ARR are much less detailed and prescriptive than corresponding IAS, probably because their achievement needs a more complete consensus

TABLE 1   *FER Recommendations*

Recommendations issued

ARR No. 0   Objectives, subjects, and procedures of the Accounting and Reporting Recommendations

ARR No. 1   Components of individual company accounts and consolidated financial statements

ARR No. 2   Consolidated financial statements

ARR No. 3   Generally accepted accounting standards

ARR No. 4   The translation of financial statements expressed in foreign currencies for consolidation purposes

ARR No. 5   Valuation directives for consolidated financial statements

ARR No. 6   Funds flow statement

ARR No. 7   Presentation and format of the consolidated balance sheet and income statement

ARR No. 8   Notes to the consolidated financial statements

ARR No. 9   Intangible assets

ARR No. 10   Off-balance sheet transactions

ARR No. 11   Taxes in the consolidated financial statements

ARR No. 12   Presentation of interim statements

ARR No. 13   Accounting for leases by the lessee

ARR No. 14   Consolidated financial statements of insurance companies

ARR No. 15   Transactions with related parties

Projects

ARR No. 16   Pension costs

ARR No. 17   Inventories

ARR No. 18   Tangible assets

among conflicting interests. Compliance with ARR is optional, except for listed companies (see below).

The *Swiss Handbook of Auditing*, published by the Swiss Institute of Certified Accountants and Tax Consultants, is the third source of accounting harmonization. It provides, for all the headings of financial statements, more precise guidelines than the FER recommendations.

Stock exchange authorities have played a minor role in the evolution of accounting and disclosure practices because their requirements for listed companies have, for a long time, been quite limited. A possible explanation was that the Swiss market was dominated by banks, which could easily obtain inside information. Things began to change in 1996, when the three existing bourses of Switzerland (Zürich, Geneva, and Basel) merged into a single electronic market (the Swiss Exchange). At the same time, new listing rules were adopted, which require that Swiss listed companies comply with ARR that have been approved by the Swiss Exchange admission board. ARR Nos. 1–8, 12, and 14 have already been included in the listing rules and other ARR will probably follow. In addition, the admission board will be associated in the elaboration process of new FER recommendations in order to avoid possible rejection of these standards by stock exchange authorities. Foreign companies are not required to comply with ARR. For them, financial statements prepared in conformity with international accounting standards (IAS) or national regulation of most developed countries are sufficient.

Financial reporting of banks and bank-like finance companies is regulated by the Swiss federal banking law and monitored primarily through the Federal Banking Commission.

Because of the permissiveness of national accounting and disclosure rules, financial statements that satisfy only Swiss regulations are much less informative and reliable than those of foreign companies. That is probably why, for many years, large Swiss firms have been voluntarily complying with foreign rules, in particular EC Directives and IASC standards. At present, about 40% of Swiss listed companies declare their consolidated accounts in conformity with IAS, and the proportion of firms that follow EC Directives is even greater. To the extent that ARR are largely based on IAS, their inclusion in the listing rules of the Swiss Exchange will not have a significant impact on the accounting and disclosure practices of large firms.

1.3   Taxation

Consistent with the structure of the political system, the Confederation, the cantons and municipalities have their own tax jurisdictions. All have the power to levy taxes within certain limits. Taxation may thus vary considerably from canton to canton and even from commune to commune. The system has become so complex that a harmonization of cantonal and communal taxes has been undertaken. This process is expected to be completed by the end of the year 2000.

The main federal taxes are the direct federal tax and the value-added tax (VAT). The direct federal tax is assessed on the income of individuals and the revenues of enterprises. In 1995, a value added tax was introduced in place of the former sales tax. Its normal rate is 6.5%.

Direct taxes on revenues and income provide the main part of the resources of cantons. A breakdown of federal, cantonal, and communal taxes is as follows:

Taxes on income and wealth of individuals	53%
Taxes on income and capital of companies	11%
VAT and other consumption taxes	30%
Other taxes	6%
	100%

Total taxes as percentage of gross domestic product amount to 19%.

1.4   Auditing

1.4.1   The Role of Auditors

The auditing requirements for companies are stated by the Code of Obligations (articles 727–731a). Auditors are elected by the general meeting of shareholders for a maximum period of three years. Renewals are permitted without limitation. The general meeting of shareholders may remove them at any time.

Auditors must be independent from the board of directors or from any majority shareholder. They must also be independent from any company within the same group, if a shareholder or creditor so requests.

Auditors must have the necessary qualifications with regard to the company to be audited. In fact, small firms may be audited by nonqualified persons, but higher professional standards are required if the company has bonds outstanding, is listed on a stock exchange, or exceeds a certain size (total assets greater than 20 million SFr, revenues greater than 40 million SFr, more than 200 employees). Bank auditors must fulfill additional qualifications and be certified by the Federal Banking Commission.

The role of auditors is to ascertain whether accounting records, financial statements, and proposals for profit appropriation comply with the law and the company's articles of incorporation. In their report to the meeting of shareholders, the auditors recommend the approval, with or without qualification, or the rejection of the financial statements.

Auditors of companies that are required to be audited by specially qualified professionals must provide the board of directors with a report explaining the conduct and the results of the audit.

Consolidated financial statements of companies that are required to prepare such statements must be audited by specially qualified professionals, who must ascertain whether these statements comply with the law and principles governing consolidation. Auditors of listed companies must also check that consolidated accounts comply with the listing rules of the Swiss Exchange and certify that these statements give a true and fair view of the company's assets, liabilities, and financial position.

1.4.2 The Auditing Profession

Because the auditing profession is not protected by law, anybody may practice as an independent accountant. Nevertheless, most qualified auditors are members of the Swiss Institute of Certified Accountants and Tax Consultants *(Schweizerische Kammer der Bücher-, Steuer- und Treuhandexperten—Chambre suisse des experts comptables, fiduciaires et fiscaux—Camera svizzera dei periti contabili, fiduciari e fiscali,* in abbreviated form *Treuhand Kammer—Chambre Fiduciaire—Camera Fiduciaria),* which is the only organization authorized to deliver the legally protected title of Certified Accountant *(Diplomierter Wirtschaftsprüfer—Expert-comptable diplômé—Esperto-contabile diplomato).*

Applicants must have several years of professional experience in an audit firm and pass an examination for which they generally prepare in a school managed by the Institute. Although no academic degree is required, more and more young certified accountants hold a university degree.

2. The Form and Content of Published Financial Statements

2.1 Disclosure Requirements

2.1.1 Contents of the Annual Report

Before Swiss company law was revised, legal disclosure requirements were quite limited. The only constraint was to prepare once a year a balance sheet and a profit and loss account. Notes to the accounts were not mandatory, and the law did not even mention consolidated financial statements.

Things have considerably changed since the implementation of the revised company law (July 1, 1992). The Code of Obligations (article 662) now requires the board of directors to prepare individual financial statements, a management report, and in some cases, consolidated financial statements. Financial statements consist of the profit and loss account, the balance sheet, and the notes to the accounts. ARR No. 1 adds the funds flow statement to the list of mandatory components.

The management report must discuss the business operations and the financial and business condition of the company. It also indicates any increase in capital during the period and quotes the auditors' opinion on the financial statements (CO, article 663d).

Some large companies voluntarily disclose additional information, in particular a value-added statement and information concerning employees.

2.1.2 The Consolidated Financial Statements

If a company controls, by a majority of votes or any other means, one or more companies, consolidated financial statements must be prepared (CO, article 663e). It is noteworthy that the term "any other means" theoretically extends the obligation of consolidated financial statements to horizontal groups, that is, groups in which control does not result from internal financial linkages but from the existence of a common management.

To be exempted from the duty to prepare consolidated financial statements, a corporation, together with its subsidiaries and during two consecutive years, must not exceed two of the following thresholds :

- Total assets of 10 million Sfr,
- Sales of 20 million Sfr,
- Average of 200 employees per annum (CO, article 663e).

A corporation already included in the consolidated financial statements of a parent company is also exempted from preparing its own consolidated financial statements, provided the statements of the parent corporation have been prepared and audited according to Swiss or equivalent foreign requirements (CO, article 663f). The provisions of the 7th EU Directive are generally considered as equivalent foreign requirements.

In any event, consolidated financial statements are mandatory if the following conditions apply:

- The company has bonds outstanding;
- The shares of the corporation are listed on a stock exchange;
- Shareholders whose combined holdings represent at least 10 percent of the capital-stock so request;
- The statements are necessary to provide as reliable a determination as possible of the company's financial condition and income (CO, article 663e).

2.1.3 Interim Statements

Issuers of listed equity securities are obliged to publish an interim report on the first six months of each business year. Its content is regulated by ARR No. 12, which states that this report should contain information necessary to give the ability to form a judgment about the development of the business and the performance of the company. More specifically, such explanations should:

- Make reference to factors that had a material influence on the company's financial position and results of operations for the reporting period;
- Disclose extraordinary income and expenses (quantified if they have a material effect on the reported profit or loss)
- Allow a comparison with the corresponding period of the previous business year.

The interim statement must at least disclose, for the reporting period and the corresponding period of the previous business year:

- Net sales of goods and services
- Profit or loss before or after taxes

Financial information must be prepared on the basis of the same accounting principles as the annual financial statements. The interim statement does not need to be audited.

2.1.4 Publication of Financial Statements

Companies that have bonds outstanding or whose shares are listed on a stock exchange must either publish their individual and consolidated financial statements in the Swiss Gazette of Commerce or send a copy of them to any interested person (CO, article 697h). These documents must also be lodged with the admission board of the Swiss Exchange within six months after the end of the fiscal period (listing rules, article 64).

Unlisted companies must make their financial statements available for inspection only by creditors who have a legitimate interest. Disputes are settled in court.

When mandatory, the interim report must be published within four months of the end of the relevant period (listing rules, article 65).

Bank and bank-like finance companies must submit an annual report to the Federal Banking Commission. This detailed and comprehensive report must adhere to the specific format designed by the Commission. It includes, among other things, a detailed analysis of the balance sheet and of the income statement.

2.2 The Balance Sheet

There is no legal format for the balance sheet. It may be presented horizontally (in columns) or vertically (in a list). The order of classification does not matter; current assets and short term liabilities may be presented first or after fixed assets and owners' equity.

Before the company law was revised, the balance sheet of some firms conveyed little information, many items being grouped under the same heading. A minimum structure is now required by law. According to the Code of Obligations (article 663a), the balance sheet must distinguish among current assets, fixed assets, liabilities, and equity. These headings must also be broken down as follows:

- Current assets:
  —cash and cash equivalents
  —accounts receivable from sales of goods and rendering of services
  —other accounts receivable
  —inventories
- Fixed assets:
  —investments
  —property, plant and equipment
  —intangibles
- Liabilities:
  —accounts payable for deliveries of supplies and services rendered
  —other short term liabilities
  —long term liabilities
  —provisions for risks and expenses
- Equity:
  —capital
  —legal and other reserves
  —net income

In addition, the following items must be shown separately:

- Capital not paid in
- Aggregate amount of participations
- Accounts receivable from and liabilities to other companies of the same group or shareholders who hold a participation in the company
- Accrued assets and liabilities
- Net loss

The balance sheet must also include the accounting numbers for the preceding year.

ARR No. 7 provides a format for consolidated financial statements. The main difference with regard to legal provisions is that current and noncurrent (long term) liabilities should be separately disclosed.

2.3 The Profit and Loss Account (Income Statement)

In past years, the income statement was sometimes quite limited. Some firms did not even mention sales, making their profit and loss account begin with gross margin.

Since the implementation of the "new" Code of Obligations (article 663), the profit and loss account includes operating and nonoperating revenues and expenses, as well as extraordinary gains and expenses. Its minimum structure is as follows:

- Revenues:
  —sales of goods and rendering of services
  —financing revenues
  —gains from the sale of fixed assets
- Expenses:
  —purchases of materials and goods
  —labor expenses
  —financing expenses
  —depreciation

No particular format is required. The income statement may still be presented in columns or in a list, and revenues and expenses may be classified by nature or by function, but it must mention the corresponding accounting numbers for the preceding year. Both presentations are also allowed for the consolidated income statement (ARR No. 7).

2.4 The Notes to the Accounts

2.4.1 Legal Provisions

Before the company law was revised, the only information to be disclosed in addition to the balance sheet was the fire insurance value of tangible assets. The primary aim of this information was to enable readers of financial statements to appreciate the extent of hidden reserves in fixed assets.

Article 663b of the Code of Obligations greatly extended the list of items that must be disclosed in the notes to the accounts. These items are:

- The aggregate amount of sureties, guarantees and security interests in favor of third parties
- The aggregate amount of assets pledged, mortgaged, or assigned to secure commitments of the company and assets subject to a reservation of title
- The aggregate amount of debts resulting from leasing agreements not recorded in the balance sheet
- The fire insurance value of tangible assets
- Liabilities to pension funds
- The amounts, interest rates, and maturity dates of bonds issued by the company
- Any participation that is material for the determination of the company's financial condition and earnings
- The aggregate amount of reductions of reserves for replacement costs and additional hidden reserves if such amount exceeds the aggregate amount of newly established reserves of this kind and if the consequence is a significantly more favorable income
- Information about items that have been revalued and the amount of this revaluation
- Information about the acquisition, sale, and number of its own shares held by the company, including those held by another corporation in which the company holds a majority interest, and the conditions governing the acquisition or sale of the company's own shares
- The amount of an authorized or conditional increase of capital

In addition, companies whose shares are listed on a stock exchange must disclose the identity and participation of major known shareholders. Groups of shareholders bound by a voting agreement and individual shareholders are deemed to be major shareholders if they hold more than 5% of all voting rights (CO, article 663c).

Nevertheless, article 663h of the Code of Obligations states that information that may be detrimental to the company or the group in a material respect may be omitted, provided the auditors are informed about the reasons for noninclusion.

The law does not require companies to disclose their valuation policies or changes in valuation policies. The reason is probably to be found in the existence of hidden reserves. Nevertheless, the obligation to disclose the net variation of hidden reserves makes manipulations of income figures more apparent.

Companies that prepare consolidated financial statements must also disclose notes to these statements. They must specify the consolidation and valuation principles used (CO, article 663g). If a company deviates from these principles, it must disclose such deviations and include the information necessary for an analysis of the group's financial condition and earnings.

2.4.2 The FER Recommendations

The FER has issued two recommendations on the notes to the consolidated financial statements. ARR No. 8 requires information exceeding legal requirements, in particular:

- A description of consolidation principles (consolidation method, currency translation, treatment of internal profits, etc.)
- A description of valuation principles and changes of these principles
- Information on the scope of consolidation
- The evolution of tangible fixed assets and their accumulated depreciation
- A breakdown of sales by regions and by activities
- Information on research and development activities and subsequent (post balance sheet) events

ARR No. 10, applicable on or after January 1, 1998, is devoted to off balance sheet transactions, including derivative financial instruments.

According to this recommendation, contingent liabilities and other commitments with a maturity of more than one year must be valued and disclosed in the notes. The reported amounts should be segregated in:

- Guarantees, guarantee obligations, and creations of lien in favor of third parties
- Other measurable commitments with a contingency character
- Other commitments and contingencies.

At the balance sheet date, the open amounts of derivative financial instruments have to be disclosed, together with the related valuation principles. The disclosure should be detailed as follows:

- Interest instruments
- Currency instruments
- Other derivatives

The total of the contract values and the total of the positive or negative replacement costs have to be disclosed separately for each category.

The valuation rules for derivative financial instruments and the corresponding treatment in the income statement follow the purpose of the transaction:

- If the transaction is made for hedging purposes, the same valuation principle as that used for the underlying hedged position has to be applied.
- Trading transactions are stated on a mark-to-market basis at each balance sheet date.
- A transaction with other motives must be valued according to the lower of cost or market principle.

2.4.3 *The Extent of Disclosure*

In practice, the extent of the notes to the financial statements varies considerably among firms. Some companies disclose notes quite similar to those of competitors within the EU, while others comply only with legal requirements.

In 1990 and 1992, that is, before the implementation of the new company law, I conducted research into the extent of information in the annual reports of a sample of Swiss publicly traded firms by computing an index on the basis of requirements of the 4th EC Directive. This index could take values ranging from 0 (no disclosure) to 100 (full conformity with the 4th Directive). The results are given in Table 2.

Since these studies have been made, the extent of disclosure has, on average, increased, but there are still large variations among firms.

2.5 The Statement of Changes in Financial Position

A statement of changes in financial position, or a cash flow statement, is not legally required. The Code of Obligations does not even mention it. Nevertheless, ARR No. 1 of the FER makes this statement an integral part

TABLE 2	*Disclosures by Swiss Listed Companies*	
Disclosure index	*1990 Data* *(53 companies)*	*1992 Data* *(161 companies)*
Maximum	82.8	96.3
Minimum	8.7	8.3
Mean value	43.3	41.8

of the financial statements. It argues that information concerning funds flows must be shown in a specific statement if not clearly evident from other parts of the annual report.

The FER has issued a recommendation on the statement of changes in financial position. According to this standard (ARR No. 6), the purpose of this statement is to describe funds flows arising from operating, investing, and financing activities. Flows from operating activities must be separately disclosed.

ARR No. 6 does not require this statement to be centered on changes in cash and cash equivalents. Other funds concepts may be chosen, in particular:

- Cash and cash equivalents less short-term financial liabilities
- Net monetary current assets (cash and cash equivalents plus accounts receivable less short-term financial liabilities)
- Net financial position (cash and cash equivalents plus financial accounts receivable less financial liabilities).

Working capital is, however, considered less appropriate.

In practice, more and more companies disclose a statement of changes in financial position. For example, in 1993, among a sample of 57 Swiss listed companies, only seven did not present such a statement. The most commonly used format is a cash-flow statement, as shown below :

Fund whose changes are described:

Cash and cash equivalents	40	(80%)
Net financial position	5	(10%)
Working capital	5	(10%)
	50	

2.6 The Auditors' Report

The auditors must present to the annual general meeting of shareholders a written report in which they recommend the approval, with or without qualification, or the rejection of the financial statements (CO, article 729). This report must name all persons who have conducted the audit and confirm that the qualification and independence requirements are met.

If the company is required by law to prepare consolidated financial statements, the auditors must also ascertain whether these statements comply with the law and the rules of consolidation (CO, article 731a).

The financial statements of Georg Fischer, reproduced in the appendix to this chapter, are representative of the recent effort of many Swiss firms to comply with International Accounting Standards and provide high-quality information.

3. Accounting Policies and Practices in Valuation and Income Measurement: Implications for the Analyst

3.1 Hidden Reserves

In Switzerland, as in other countries, some enterprises may be tempted to smooth their income by means of hidden reserves. Several motives have been advanced to explain the creation of hidden reserves, such as:

- Tax reduction
- Protection against competitors
- Prevention of excessive dividend claims prejudicial to the internal financing of the firm's growth
- Prevention of excessive claims of employees
- Prevention of prejudicial stock price movements after a decrease in earnings.

The main difference is that, in Switzerland, the creation of hidden reserves is expressly allowed by law. The Code of Obligations (article 669) states that hidden reserves may be created in order to ensure prosperity to the enterprise or to distribute dividends as constant as possible. The only constraint is that these reserves must be reported to the auditors. As a result, Swiss companies make large use of hidden reserves by recognizing excessive depreciation of assets or creating unjustified provisions.

By definition, the extent of hidden reserves in financial statements is difficult to assess. An economic journal, however, in collaboration with a Swiss securities rating company, published from 1989 to 1992 a ranking of the most profitable Swiss companies, based on an estimation of their "true" (undistorted) income. In some cases, reported income represents less than 25% of estimated real earnings.

When confronted with the financial statements of Swiss companies, analysts must be conscious of the widespread use of hidden reserves.

3.2 Group Accounts

Group accounts are not subject to specific legal provisions. The Code of Obligations states that consolidated financial statements must conform to the same principles as individual accounts (CO, article 663g). The only specific requirement concerns the notes to the group statements, which must include a description of the consolidation and valuation principles used and, in case of changes, the information necessary for an analysis of the group's financial position and earnings.

Recommendations on consolidation and consolidation principles can be found in the FER standards and, to some extent, in the *Swiss Handbook of Auditing*.

3.2.1 The Scope of Consolidation

The scope of consolidation is defined neither by law nor by professional standards. ARR No. 2 does not specify conditions for inclusion in the scope of consolidation. It only mentions, as possible criteria, majority of voting rights, control, and uniform management. Companies can use either an extended conception of control, as in the EU, or a more limited one, as in the United States.

In fact, most Swiss companies limit the scope of consolidation to subsidiaries in which they have a majority interest. Among exceptions are Nestlé, whose main criterion is effective management, and Holderbank, which extends the scope of consolidation to enterprises, control of which results from an agreement.

Cases of exclusions are not better specified. ARR No. 2 cites, as examples of possible exclusions, companies that are not material to the consolidated financial statements or whose activities are too different from those of the group as a whole. In practice, the main reason put forward for the exclusion of certain subsidiaries is small size or immateriality. Other reasons are dissimilar activities from the rest of the group or severe restrictions impairing the ability to transfer funds to the parent.

ARR No. 2 stipulates that nonconsolidated investments must be recorded at cost, at proportional intrinsic value, or according to the equity method.

3.2.2 The Methods of Consolidation

According to ARR No. 2, the only method of consolidation is full consolidation. Swiss companies conform to generally accepted principles of consolidation:

- Subsidiaries under control are consolidated under the full consolidation method.

- Associates in which the parent holds directly or indirectly voting rights of 20% or more are accounted for using the equity method.

- Companies held at less than 20% are recorded at cost.

Joint ventures are generally accounted for under proportional consolidation. Examples are Bobst, Electrowatt, Holderbank, Motor Columbus, Nestlé, Rieter, and Sika. Other firms prefer to use the equity method or even maintain their interests in joint ventures at cost.

3.2.3 Intercompany Transactions

ARR No. 2 states that intercompany assets and liabilities, as well as expenses and income from intercompany transactions, must be eliminated. Dividends from consolidated subsidiaries are specifically mentioned.

In practice, intercompany assets and liabilities are always eliminated. Some companies omit eliminating intercompany profits included in inventories, generally on the grounds that they are immaterial.

3.2.4 The Consolidation of Capital

Until recently, many Swiss companies used the former German method for the consolidation of capital. Under this method, the carrying value of investments in subsidiaries is eliminated against the corresponding part of the reported capital and reserves of the subsidiary at each balance sheet date, with any difference being reported as "consolidation difference." There is no restatement of the subsidiary's assets and liabilities to fair values at the acquisition date.

This method is no longer allowed by ARR No. 2, which requires the elimination of the participation against the corresponding share of the subsidiary's equity at the date of acquisition. Given that ARR are now part of the Swiss Exchange listing rules, no listed firm should henceforward use the former German method. Nevertheless, this method can still be used by unlisted companies.

Capital may be consolidated by using two alternative methods:

- The "purchase" method, whereby the cost of an acquisition is accounted for by restating the identifiable assets and liabilities of the subsidiary to their fair value at the date of acquisition
- The "pooling of interests" method, under which the combined assets, liabilities, and reserves of the parent and its subsidiary are recorded at their existing carrying amounts

There is no legal or professional requirement concerning this issue, and most companies do not even indicate which method they use. On the basis of information disclosed in annual reports, it seems, however, that companies generally use the "purchase" method.

3.2.5 The Treatment of Goodwill

Goodwill represents the excess of the cost of acquisition over the fair value of the net identifiable assets of the subsidiary at the date of acquisition. It either can be recognized as an asset in the consolidated financial statements or immediately adjusted against shareholder's interests.

ARR No. 2 does not take a position on how goodwill should be accounted for. It only mentions that its treatment must be disclosed in the notes. More recently, ARR No. 9 has shown a preference for capitalization since this recommendation states that *"in principle, goodwill must be capitalized.*" Nevertheless, the alternative treatment is allowed, provided that the effects of a theoretical capitalization and amortization are disclosed in the notes.

As in other countries where both treatments are allowed, most Swiss companies have for a long time deducted goodwill from equity, probably to avoid a decrease of income in subsequent years because of goodwill amortization. Listed companies have recently exhibited a move toward capitalization, as shown in Table 3. This evolution is probably a consequence of the adoption of revised IAS 22, which prohibits deduction from reserves.

When recorded as an asset, goodwill is amortized over its "useful life," which varies from 5 to 40 years.

3.3 Foreign Currency Translation

3.3.1 Translation of Financial Statements in Foreign Currencies

ARR No. 4 indicates that translation of financial statements of foreign subsidiaries may be achieved by one of the following methods:

- The closing/current rate method
- The temporal method
- The monetary/nonmonetary method

TABLE 3 *Accounting Treatment of Goodwill by Swiss Listed Companies*

	1992	1993	1994	1995
Capitalization	23	31	40	66
Deduction from reserves	61	61	62	36
Subtotal	84	92	102	102
Undetermined	1			
No consolidated financial statements	17	10		
Total	102	102	102	102

The first two methods are similar to those described in IAS 21.

Under the closing rate method, all balance sheet items other than shareholders' equity are translated at the closing rate, whereas revenues and expenses are converted at the closing rate or at a periodic average rate. Translation differences arising on the translation of the balance sheet are taken into the shareholders' equity; those resulting from the translation of revenues and expenses at an average rate may be either recognized in income or taken to shareholders' equity.

The temporal method introduces a distinction between monetary items, which are translated at the closing rate; and nonmonetary items, converted at the historical rate or, in the case of valuation adjustments, at the rate existing on the date of the revaluation. Revenues and expenses are translated at the rate that existed when the transaction occurred, except depreciation, which is converted at the same rate as the corresponding balance sheet items. All translation differences are normally recognized in income.

The monetary/nonmonetary method differs from the temporal method by the fact that all nonmonetary items are translated at historical cost whether or not their value has been adjusted. The other difference is that translation differences can be either recorded in the profit and loss account or taken to shareholders' interests. ARR No. 4 describes a variant whereby inventories are classified as monetary items and thus translated at the closing rate.

ARR No. 4 does not provide rules for the choice of translation methods. It just indicates that a combination of methods should be avoided, except when the net investment approach is used. According to this approach defined in IAS 21, the translation method depends on the nature of the operating and financing activities of the subsidiary:

- For companies with a high degree of autonomy, the closing/current rate method should be used.
- Financial statements of companies whose activities form an integral part of the parent should be translated by using the temporal method.

These rules can be applied but they are not mandatory.

In practice, a small number of groups refer to well-defined translation methods. Most of them use exclusively the closing/current rate method, translating assets and liabilities at the closing rate and revenues and expenses at an average annual rate. Translation differences are generally taken to shareholders' interests.

3.3.2 *Translation of Foreign Currency Transactions*

The only available reference for translation of foreign currency transactions is the *Swiss Handbook of Auditing*. According to this book (§2.2931), transactions in foreign currencies should be recorded at the exchange rate existing at the date of the transaction (benchmark treatment), but many alternative rates can be used, as the rate at the settlement date, the closing rate, and an average or fixed rate.

In the balance sheet, receivables and liabilities in foreign currencies must be converted at the closing rate. Translation differences on the same currency and whose maturity is similar must be compensated. The resulting net difference should be recognized in income in case of loss and deferred if favorable.

In practice, most companies translate foreign currency items at the closing rate and recognize differences, favorable or not, in income. Some corporations mention that exchange differences on long-term intercompany investments are taken to retained earnings.

There is no provision concerning forward contracts but several firms indicate that foreign currency receivables and payables covered by forward contracts are translated at contracted future rates.

3.4 Capital and Reserves

3.4.1 *Share Capital*

In the new company law, the minimum share capital has been increased to 100,000 SFr. Simultaneously, the minimum per value of shares has been reduced from 100 to 10 SFr because the market value of the individual shares of many publicly traded companies had become too high compared with international standards.

There are two types of shares: bearer shares and registered shares. The main difference between them concerns the means of transfer. Bearer shares may be transferred by simple physical delivery, whereas transferring registered shares requires registration of the acquirer in the company's share ledger and, possibly, the company's consent.

Companies may also issue shares with preferential rights, consisting, in particular, of supplementary or cumulative dividends, participation in the distribution of assets remaining upon liquidation, and preemptive rights for newly issued shares.

Companies may hold their own shares up to an aggregate par value of 10% of total capital (i.e. share capital + participation capital). The corresponding voting rights are suspended as long as the company hold these shares.

A necessary condition for the acquisition of its own shares is that the company has available reserves at least equal to the amount of funds necessary for the acquisition. At the time of the acquisition, this amount is transferred to a special reserve (reserve for own shares), which will be released only when these shares are sold or canceled.

3.4.2 Participation Capital

In addition to share capital, many companies issue participation capital represented by participation certificates. In past decades, these certificates, essentially nonvoting shares, have became a popular tool for financing publicly held companies. Holders of participation certificates are not entitled to vote, but their pecuniary rights are at least the same as those of common shareholders.

There is no minimum amount, but participation capital must not exceed twice the amount of share capital.

3.4.3 Reserves

There are three types of reserves:

- General reserve
- Special reserves
- Statutory and additional reserves

The general reserve is required by law. The Code of Obligations states that 5% of the annual profit must be allocated to the general reserve until it equals 20% of paid-in capital. After this level has been attained, additional allocations must be made, notably an amount of 10% of all dividends paid in excess of a primary dividend corresponding to 5% of the annual profit. The use of the general reserve is mainly restricted to the covering of losses.

Two special reserves are also prescribed by law. They are the reserve for own shares (see above) and the revaluation reserve (see below).

The articles of incorporation may provide that additional reserves be set up and specify their purpose and use.

3.5 Liabilities and Provisions

The main issue under liabilities and provisions concerns hidden reserves. According to the *Swiss Handbook of Auditing* (§2.2624), hidden reserves cannot be created by recording fictitious liabilities in the balance sheet, but excessive and even unjustified provisions may be constituted practically without limitation.

3.6 Property, Plant, and Equipment

3.6.1 Valuation

In individual financial statements, fixed assets must be valued at historic acquisition or manufacturing costs net of the necessary depreciation (CO, article 665). Any deviation from historical costs is prohibited.

The only exception is for companies whose accumulated losses exceed half of capital and statutory reserves. In that case, the Code of Obligations (article 670) allows a revaluation of real property and participations up to the current acquisition or manufacturing costs. The revaluation difference must be taken to a special reserve (revaluation reserve), which may be reduced only by a conversion into share capital, a write-down, or the sale of the corresponding assets (CO, article 671b).

Although they are not subject to special legal provisions, a generally accepted opinion is that consolidated financial statements may be prepared with alternative valuation bases. ARR No. 5 states that possible valuation bases for consolidated accounts are historical cost and current cost. It adds that current cost may be based on actual current cost, replacement cost, or a similar cost basis. The only condition is that uniformity and consistency are ensured. The valuation basis is considered uniform if it is used for all companies being consolidated and for all items in the consolidated financial statements. Deviations from uniformity and consistency are allowed only when objectively motivated and disclosed.

In their consolidated financial statements, several companies depart from historical costs for the valuation of fixed assets. The extent of revaluation differs greatly among firms, revalued assets being :

- Land only
- Real estate (land and buildings)

- All tangible assets
- Tangible assets less real estate

Revaluation methods also are quite diverse. Some companies apply price indexes while others use market values or both methods.

3.6.2 Depreciation

The basis for depreciation is generally the acquisition or manufacturing cost. A residual value is rarely deducted. Depreciation may also be based on replacement cost. All depreciation methods may be used (e.g. straight-line, declining balance). Depreciation may also be based on the quantity of goods produced by the asset (units of production method).

Useful lives of assets should normally be chosen in accordance with the general objective of financial statements, which is to provide an "as reliable as possible" measure of the company's position and earnings. In practice, the choice is largely influenced by other considerations, in particular taxation and hidden reserves.

In Switzerland, tax rules are closely aligned with accounting principles. An expense may be deducted for taxation purpose only if recognized in income. Tax considerations may thus have a considerable influence on the choice of useful lives of fixed assets, firms tending to increase depreciation in order to minimize taxes.

Hidden reserves generally have a large impact on depreciation. Firms willing to create hidden reserves often choose to overestimate the depreciation of fixed assets. Alternatively, those willing to cancel hidden reserves in order to increase their profits tend to reduce the annual depreciation charge. If necessary, they may even reverse depreciation charged in previous years, provided the resulting carrying amount does not exceed the value of the asset, estimated on a going concern basis.

As a result of hidden reserves, it is not exceptional in individual statements to find land with a nil carrying value, buildings depreciated at obviously excessive rates, or equipment entirely depreciated in the year of acquisition.

By comparison with the fire insurance value of fixed tangible assets, which must be disclosed in the notes to the accounts, it is possible to have a rough view of the amount of hidden reserves contained in property, plant, and equipment.

Because consolidated financial statements are not subject to special valuation rules, hidden reserves should have an impact on them too. However, this impact is probably less than on individual statements for several reasons. First, because group accounts are not considered for tax purposes, companies are less motivated to maintain hidden reserves in these statements. Second, because the consolidated financial statements are the result of an aggregation of several individual companies' accounts, they can hardly be used to evaluate the performance of a particular subsidiary. Hidden reserves are thus less necessary to protect a company from competitors. Finally, whereas individual accounts are mainly used on a national basis, consolidated statements of large companies are more directed to international users. They thus should comply with international standards prohibiting hidden reserves. In addition, reporting abnormally low earnings would place Swiss companies at a competitive disadvantage for obtaining financing on international markets.

Unfortunately, it is impossible to validate these assumptions empirically because, with a few exceptions, firms do not reveal whether hidden reserves have been excluded from their consolidated financial statements. However, depreciation rates disclosed in the notes to the group accounts seem generally close to real useful lives.

3.6.3 Special Issues

The composition of acquisition or manufacturing costs is not defined either by law or by the FER.

Concerning borrowing costs, the *Swiss Handbook of Auditing* notes that interest related to the construction of buildings and equipment may be incorporated in the cost of these assets (§2.28 M). It also considers that fixed government grants should be deducted from the cost of corresponding assets.

3.7 Assets Whose Services Are Acquired by Means of Leases

According to the *Swiss Handbook of Auditing*, leases must be accounted for as follows :

- Operating leases should always be charged to income.
- Finance leases may be either charged to income or reflected in the balance sheet of the lessee.

The distinction is based on criteria used by international standards (transfer of ownership by the end of the lease term, lease containing a bargain purchase option, lease term for major part of the useful life of the asset, etc.).

When a finance lease is recorded as an asset, IAS 17 applies:

- At the inception of the lease, an asset and a liability are recorded at an amount equal to the fair value of the lease property.
- Subsequent rentals are apportioned between the finance charge and the reduction in the outstanding liability.
- The asset is depreciated on a systematic basis consistent with the depreciation policy adopted for assets owned by the lessee.

The notes must mention the aggregate amounts of obligations arising from leasing agreements not recorded in the balance sheet (CO, article 663b).

In consolidated financial statements, finance leases must be recorded as assets and shown separately (ARR No. 13).

3.8   Oil, Gas, and Other Mineral Resources

Oil, gas, and other mineral resources are of little importance in Switzerland, so there is no specific standard that applies to them.

3.9   Intangible Assets

3.9.1 Property Rights and Development Costs

The treatment of intangible assets is regulated by ARR No. 9, which applies to development costs, as well as intellectual property rights and goodwill.

According to this recommendation, internally generated intangibles may be capitalized only if they meet conditions similar to those imposed by IASC exposure drafts E 50 and E 60 (the intangible should provide future economic benefits, its cost must be identifiable and measurable separately, and the company has financial resources necessary for its completion). ARR No. 9 considers that internally generated goodwill cannot "generally" be capitalized.

For acquired intangibles, the only condition to be recorded as assets is to provide future economic benefits to the company over several years. When intangibles are designed for subsequent marketing, measurable benefits exist if there is a market for such assets. As examples of intangibles that can be capitalized, ARR No. 9 mentions, among others, licenses, patents, trademarks, copyrights, models, plans, exploration rights, software, customer lists. On the other hands, it considers that training costs and restructuring expenses cannot generally be recorded as assets, nor can costs for basic and applied research.

Capitalized intangibles are valued at the lower of cost or net realizable value. They must be amortized over their useful live, usually using the straight line method. If the useful life cannot be determined reliably, the amortization period should not exceed 5 years, unless a longer period up to a maximum of 20 years can be justified. ARR No. 9 adds that the useful life of intangibles relating to individuals cannot be longer than 5 years.

The carrying amount of intangible assets should be reviewed periodically. If a permanent impairment in value has occurred, the carrying amount must be written down to the new recoverable amount.

In practice, internally generated intangibles are rarely capitalized and in most companies (in particular large chemical and pharmaceutical firms such as Novartis and Roche), development costs are charged to income when incurred.

3.9.2 Other Deferred Costs

The Code of Obligations (article 664) enables companies to defer to future periods foundation costs, capital increase costs, and organization costs, provided they are recorded as separate items and written off within 5 years. This opportunity is practically never used in consolidated financial statements.

3.10 Participating Interests

In individual financial statements, participations are subject to the general valuation rules of assets. They must be valued at acquisition cost less necessary write-downs (CO, article 665). The use of the equity method is prohibited.

Participations exceptionally may be revalued in conformity with CO article 670 when the holding company has cumulative losses exceeding half its share capital and statutory reserves (see Section 3.5.1 above).

In group accounts, nonconsolidated participations are valued at cost or by the equity method. The choice depends on the percentage of voting rights held. Most companies use the following rules:

- Participations from 20% to 50% of voting rights: equity method
- Participations less than 20% of voting rights: acquisition cost

3.11 Inventories

The Code of Obligations (article 666) states that inventories must be valued at the lower of historical cost (acquisition or manufacturing costs) and net realizable value. Hidden reserves may be constituted for inventories as well as for other assets.

According to the *Swiss Handbook of Auditing*, manufacturing costs include overhead expenses other than those related to administrative and selling activities. The allocation of fixed production overhead should be based on the capacity of the facilities. Borrowing interests may be considered part of production overhead.

Most companies include at least a part of indirect costs in the valuation of inventories. Nevertheless, some firms value finished goods at the direct cost of production.

Work-in-progress whose production period exceeds one year may be accounted for under the percentage of completion method, whereby revenue is recognized in income as the contract activity progresses. This method is widely used by firms engaged in long-term contracts. Some companies simultaneously apply this method and the completed contract method, under which revenue is recognized only when the contract is completed or substantially completed.

All costs formulas may be used for the purpose of assigning costs to inventories (average cost, FIFO, LIFO, highest in—first out, fixed costs, etc.). In practice, only the first two methods are widely used. Some companies use them simultaneously for different sets of goods.

A write-down of one-third of historical cost may be deducted for tax purpose. Unfortunately, it is generally impossible to know to what extent this opportunity has been used.

In consolidated financial statements, alternatives to historical cost may be used. According to ARR No. 5, inventories may be valued at actual current cost, replacement cost, or on a similar cost basis. This opportunity is rarely used. The main exception was Ciba-Geigy, which until 1992 valued its inventories at indexed prices.

3.12 Taxation

Swiss companies are taxed on income and on equity. In a group, every company is taxed separately; there is no group taxation system based on consolidated earnings. Pure holdings are generally exempted from income taxation and taxed on equity at reduced rates.

Taxation methods differ among cantons and are relatively complex. Many cantons have, for a long time, assessed taxes on last year's profit or on the average taxable income of two successive years. Anticipating a harmonization law that will be implemented by the end of the year 2000, most of them have recently passed to a system where taxes are based on current year's income, as in most other countries.

The basis for income taxation is net income adjusted for expenses exceeding common business practices. Tax adjustments consist mainly of reversing hidden reserves to income. Other adjustments are generally not significant because firms often align their accounting choices to tax standards. Depending on cantons, fiscal losses may be deducted in arriving at taxes to be paid in a future period ranging from 2 to 7 years.

Taxes are not based on income only. They also depend on return on equity. For example, an income of 100,000 SFr will be more heavily taxed in a company whose equity is 500,000 SFr than in another with capital and reserves of 1,000,000 SFr.

Until 1997, the federal income tax was computed at rates between 3.63% and 9.8% of taxable income. These rates have been recently replaced by a unique rate of 8.5%. Most cantonal rates are much higher.

Companies are also taxed on equity. Taxable equity includes capital and reported and hidden reserves. Cantonal rates vary from 0.26% to 0.9%. The federal tax, which was 0.08% of taxable capital, was suppressed in 1998.

In Switzerland, there is a close relationship between taxation and financial reporting. Because taxes are based on accounting income, temporary differences between taxable income and accounting income reported in individual financial statements are rare. Consequently, firms do not generally report deferred taxes in their individual accounts.

In consolidated financial statements, values are adjusted to give a true and fair view of the financial position of the company. These adjustments, as well as the elimination of intercompany transactions, give rise to temporary differences, which makes it necessary to recognize deferred taxes in accordance with ARR No. 11.

As in IAS 12, this recommendation adopts a balance sheet approach. Temporary differences are defined as differences between the values of balance sheet positions calculated according to group accounting policies and the values calculated on a tax basis that will give rise to a tax charge or a tax reduction when they are dissolved in the future.

All future income tax effects must be considered in the calculation of deferred taxation ("comprehensive method"). Deferred taxes resulting from a revaluation of assets must be recognized in the balance sheet and separately explained in the notes. Taxes payable on undistributed profits of subsidiaries and associated companies are not accrued unless these profits are expected to be distributed.

Deferred tax assets and liabilities should be calculated at the tax rates that are expected to apply when the asset is realized or the liability is settled, in conformity with the liability method. If these rates cannot be determined, current tax rates are used.

Deferred taxes must be calculated separately for each period and each tax entity. Tax assets and tax liabilities may be netted only if they relate to the same tax entity. A deferred tax asset may be shown in the balance sheet only when it is probable that enough taxable profit will exist in the future to allow the corresponding tax saving to be realized.

3.13 Pensions

In Switzerland, pensions are funded by a two-level system. At the age of 65 (men) or 62 (women), individuals are entitled to a basic pension corresponding to what is considered the minimum living wage. Funds necessary for the payment of pensions to people already retired are provided by the contributions of enterprises and employees to a fund managed by the federal state.

Additional retirement benefits result from plans supplied by contributions of enterprises and employees to separate funds. In the private sector, these plans are defined contribution schemes. This means that amounts to be paid as retirement benefits are determined by reference to contributions to these funds together with investment earnings thereon.

Because of the characteristics of the Swiss pension scheme, most firms do not have to create a provision for pension costs.

Contributions to the State-managed fund are based on wages of people currently employed. The rates are the result of an equilibrium between retired and working people in the entire country. Because there is no direct link between them and the position of a particular firm, contributions just have to be charged to income along with corresponding wages.

Contributions to the other funds are also recognized as expenses at the time of payment. As long as there is no increase in the firm's obligations, no provision is necessary.

4. Expected Future Developments

In recent years, there has been a considerable movement toward better transparency and more disclosure by Swiss companies. This change is the result of an increase in legal requirements (new company law), the development of national accounting standards (FER recommendations), the emergence of new accounting and disclosure requirements for listed companies, and a voluntary effort on the part of some companies willing to comply with international standards. This movement will probably continue and even intensify in the future.

At the professional level, several new ARR are being prepared. Whereas the first FER recommendations were rather permissive and allowed several different treatments, recent ARR are more stringent. This evolution, which can be seen as a consequence of the IASC effort to reduce options in accounting standards, will probably be maintained. Future ARR should thus be more and more prescriptive and detailed.

Paradoxically, this movement will have little effect on the reporting and disclosure practices of large Swiss companies, which for many years have been basing their disclosure policies on international standards, rather than on national regulation. Medium-sized companies will be more concerned by the development of ARR and the increase of the Swiss Exchange disclosure requirements. Small unlisted companies will probably continue to depart occasionally from generally accepted principles, as long as ARR are not compulsory. For these enterprises, the end of hidden reserves cannot be expected in the foreseeable future.

The only event that could cause a thorough change in the accounting practices of small firms would be the adhesion of Switzerland to the European Union, with the resultant implementation of the 4th and 7th Directives. Given the people's rejection of the European Economic Area, the federal government will not propose such an initiative before a clear majority favorable to this project has emerged. According to polls, this condition is far from being met.

Useful Addresses

Treuhand Kammer (Swiss Institute of Certified Accountants and Tax Consultants)
Limmatquai 120
CH—8001 Zürich
Tel.: +41 (0)1 267 75 75
Fax: +41 (0)1 267 75 85

Swiss Exchange
Selnaustrasse 30
Postfach
CH—8021 Zürich
Tel.: +41 (0)1 229 21 11
Fax: + 41 (0)1 229 22 40
http://www.swx.ch

Financial Statements

Financial and accounting topics

Since 1993 Georg Fischer accounting methods have complied with the International Accounting Standards (IAS), whose current state of development already ensures a high degree of disclosure and clarity. Georg Fischer basically follows the ongoing developments in these standards, at the same time adhering to the principle of accounting continuity. For greater clarity, a separate statement of changes in equity and minority interests is included in this report immediately after the consolidated income statement. The following notes explain the effects of structural changes in the Georg Fischer financial statements:

Additions to the scope of consolidation during the year under review included the Mecatool Group, which belongs to the AGIE CHARMILLES Peripheral Products division. Also included are the following small companies: George Fischer Pty Ltd, Oakleigh, Rematech Comércio e Representações Ltda, São Paulo, AGIE CHARMILLES Holding SAS, Palaiseau, and George Fischer Investments Ltd, Coventry.

OWL Ltd Logistics Systems, Buchs, and Verkehrstechnik AG, Schaffhausen, were divested per year-end 1997 from the Plant Engineering and Automotive Products Groups respectively, but remained fully consolidated in the 1997 accounts. The Lock Technology activities sold at the end of 1996 is no longer included in accounts for the 1997 business year. The aforementioned changes in the scope of consolidation have little effect on comparability with the previous year. On the other hand, income and cash flow of the AGIE Group were included only for the last quarter of 1996 as against full-year inclusion for 1997.

As in the previous year, the two 50/50 joint ventures Georg Fischer Disa and Kubota Georg Fischer are quota-consolidated.

Minority interests disclosed in the balance sheet and income statement mainly comprise public shareholdings in AGIE CHARMILLES, a listed company fully consolidated in the Georg Fischer Corporation. Due to the subscribed capital increase of 1997, income from minority interests is higher than the previous year.

In 1997 a project was launched for improving the quality and availability of reporting and accounting information. First fruits of this project were reflected in earlier completion of the 1997 accounts, and in 1998 it will be continued with a view to further time savings and ongoing quality improvement. Ultimate goal is the immediate availability of reliable business data at all times.

As of January 1, 1999, Eurocurrency will become a reality likewise for the Georg Fischer Corporation, with corresponding impact on our business activities and accounting. The necessary preparations were therefore started during the year under review, and the first measures have already been taken in this connection. By the end of 1998 we shall be ready for the new situation.

Notes to the consolidated financial statements

Corporate accounting and consolidation principles

General

The consolidated financial statements fairly present the net assets, financial position and results from operations of the Georg Fischer Corporation. The consolidated annual accounts are based on the financial statements of the Georg Fischer corporate subsidiaries for the year ended December 31, prepared in accordance with corporate accounting principles.

Since 1993 the consolidated financial statements comply with the International Accounting Standards (IAS). Segment assets and results are not disclosed as required by IAS. The consolidated financial statements further comply with the fourth and seventh directives of the European Union, Swiss shareholding law and the accounting principles of the Listing Rules of the Swiss Exchange.

Principles of consolidation

The consolidated financial statements include both those of Georg Fischer Ltd (holding company) and those of all Swiss and foreign subsidiaries in which the holding company holds directly or indirectly a participation and which are subject to Georg Fischer corporate management responsibility. Assets, liabilities, revenues and expenditures of these companies are fully consolidated. All transactions between corporate subsidiaries (accounts receivable, accounts payable, income and expenses) are eliminated upon consolidation. Minority interests included in equity and results of consolidated companies are presented separately.

Joint ventures in which Georg Fischer Ltd has a direct or indirect participation of 50%, and whose management is not solely controlled by the Georg Fischer Corporation,

are included in the consolidated financial statements using the proportionate consolidation method.

Companies in which the Georg Fischer Corporation has a minority interest of 20% or more are included in the consolidated financial statements using the equity method of accounting. The Corporation's share in the net assets of these companies is therefore presented as non-consolidated investments on the consolidated balance sheet, while its share in the net results is included in the consolidated income statement under Income from non-consolidated investments.

Companies in which the Corporation has an interest of less than 20%, and certain immaterial investments, are stated at cost less any valuation adjustment deemed necessary.

The effect of deletions from the scope of consolidation is dealt with in the income statement.

Consolidation is based on the purchase method, whereby the purchase price of a subsidiary is eliminated at the time of acquisition against shareholders' equity determined according to uniform corporate valuation principles.

Since 1995 a therefrom remaining goodwill is capitalized and amortized over a useful life of maximum 20 years, subject to any additional write-downs due to specific conditions.

Foreign currencies

The financial statements of corporate subsidiaries denominated in foreign currencies are translated into Swiss francs as follows:

- Balance sheets at year end rates
- Income statements at average rates for the year under review

- Cash flow statements at average or year end rates for the year under review

Any resulting translation adjustments are directly credited or debited to shareholders' equity and therefore do not give rise to any profit impact.

Exchange differences with regard to transactions and balance sheet amounts denominated in foreign currencies are credited or debited. Translation differences resulting from equity-like corporate loans denominated in foreign currencies are credited or debited to shareholders' equity. The exchange rates applied for translation of the major currencies used within the Corporation are presented under note 2.

Cash flow statement

The cash flow statement is based on the actual changes in cash and cash equivalents. The effects of foreign currency translation and changes in scope of consolidation are presented separately.

Principles of valuation

General

Assets and liabilities included in consolidation are valued according to uniform corporate accounting principles. The corporate accounts are prepared on an acquisition or production cost basis with the exception of marketable securities, certain non-consolidated investments and investment properties, of which the valuation principles are disclosed below. Income and expenses are recognized using the accrual principle of accounting.

Cash and cash equivalents
Cash and cash equivalents include cash on hand, postal and bank accounts and fixed-term deposits up to 90 days, which are stated at nominal value.

Securities

Marketable securities are stated at market value as of balance sheet date.

Accounts receivable
Accounts receivable are presented net of allowances for general and specific credit risks.

Inventories

Inventories are stated at the lower of cost (purchase price or production cost) and net realizable value. Production costs include direct labour and materials used, as well as a commensurate share of related overhead costs. Provisions are established to cover any risks arising from obsolescence. Profits capitalized in inventories purchased from corporate subsidiaries are eliminated upon consolidation.

Advance payments made to suppliers are added to inventories, whilst advance payments received from customers on orders in progress are deducted.

Tangible fixed assets

Tangible fixed assets, except for investment properties, are stated at cost less appropriate depreciation. Depreciable assets are written off on a straight line basis over their estimated useful lives as follows:

Buildings 20 to 40 years
Machinery   3 to 15 years
Others (vehicles,
EDP equipment, etc.)   3 to 5 years

Assets of relatively minor value are charged directly to the income statement.

Investment properties are stated at prudent market values less deferred taxes. Market values are reviewed periodically by corporate and external experts.

Assets acquired under long-term lease contracts are capitalized and depreciated in the same way as other tangible fixed assets. The related lease installments outstanding are presented under liabilities.

Financial assets
Financial assets comprise non-consolidated participations and other financial investments. The non-consolidated investments comprise those designated in the list of subsidiaries on pages 33 to 35 with "E" (equity valuation basis)or "B" (book value on a cost basis). Valuation of such investments is set out under Principles of Consolidation (see page 13). Accounts receivable and payable, total liabilities and net profit of the companies concerned are insignificant when compared to the consolidated amounts.

Other financial investments are stated at the lower of cost and market.

Intangible assets
Intangible assets such as royalties, patents and similar rights are amortized on a straight line basis over a maximum period of 5 years. Intangible assets also include goodwill (see principles of consolidation).

Research and development
All research and development expenses are recognized in the income statement when incurred. For practical reasons, such expenses are not calculated or disclosed.

Provisions
Provisions include the following:

Services yet to be rendered
Work due related to revenue already recognized.

Taxes
Tax obligations not yet finally assessed, and deferred taxes. Deferred taxes are provided for at the enacted tax rate according to IAS 12 revised, except when tax losses brought forward are available to offset the expected liabilities.

Pension fund obligations
Any pension fund obligations payable by corporate subsidiaries to their employees (mainly in the case of German subsidiaries), see note 18.

Restructuring and other obligations
Guarantees, sureties, restructuring projects and various other risks. Restructuring costs are provided for in the year of resolution and recognized as part of the non-operating result.

Revaluation surplus
The effect of revaluation of investment properties is included in revaluation surplus, taking account of deferred taxes. Revaluation surplus related to a sale of a property is transferred to retained earnings without affecting income.

Georg Fischer Konzern

Konsolidierte Bilanz per 31. Dezember 1997

Aktiven	Erläute-rungen	1997 Mio. SFr.	%	1996 Mio. SFr.	%
Umlaufvermögen					
Flüssige Mittel		211		176	
Wertschriften		67		20	
Forderungen aus Lieferungen					
und Leistungen	(3)	570		530	
Übrige Forderungen	(4)	149		79	
Vorräte	(5)	420	1 417	53	497	1 302	49
Anlagevermögen	(6)				
Liegenschaften	(7)	628		654	
Übrige Sachanlagen		525		558	
Nicht konsolidierte Beteiligungen	(6)	52		54	
Übrige Finanzanlagen	(8)	23		54	
Immaterielle Anlagen	(9)	54	1 282	47	36	1 356	51
Total Aktiven			2 699	100		2 658	100

Passiven

	Erläute-rungen	1997 Mio. SFr.	%	1996 Mio. SFr.	%
Fremdkapital	(10)				
Kurzfristiges Fremdkapital					
Banken		106		229	
Hypotheken		5		11	
Personalvorsorge-Einrichtungen		7		17	
Verbindlichkeiten aus Lieferungen					
und Leistungen		221		201	
Übriges kurzfristiges Fremdkapital	(12)	159	498	18	169	627	23
Rückstellungen	(13)		477	18		447	17
Längerfristiges Fremdkapital					
Banken		383		390	
Hypotheken		22		43	
Anleihen	(11)	333		245	
Personalvorsorge-Einrichtungen		29		44	
Übriges längerfristiges Fremdkapital		6	773	29	25	747	28
			1 748	65		1 821	68
Minderheitsanteile			104	4		66	3
Eigenkapital	(14)				
Aktienkapital		327		327	
Kapitalreserven (Agio)		80		80	
Reserven für eigene Aktien		12		2	
Neubewertungsreserven		127		146	
Konzernreserven		301	847	31	216	771	29
Total Passiven			2 699	100		2 658	100

Georg Fischer Corporation

Consolidated balance sheet as at December 31, 1997

Assets	Notes	1997 million Sfr.	%	1996 million Sfr.	%
Current assets					
Cash and cash equivalents		211		176	
Securities		67		20	
Trade accounts receivable	(3)	570		530	
Other accounts receivable .	(4)	149		79	
Inventories	(5)	420	1 417	53	497	1 302	49
Fixed assets	(6)				
Land and buildings	(7)	628		654	
Machinery and equipment		525		558	
Non-consolidated investments	(6)	52		54	
Other financial assets	(8)	23		54	
Intangible assets	(9)	54	1 282	47	36	1 356	51
Total assets			2 699	100	2 658	100

Liabilities and shareholders' equity

	Notes	1997 million Sfr.	%	1996 million Sfr.	%
Liabilities	(10)				
Current liabilities					
Banks		106		229	
Mortgages		5		11	
Pension funds ·		7		17	
Trade accounts payable		221		201	
Other accounts payable	(12)	159	498	18	169	627	23
Provisions	(13)		477	18		447	17
Long-term liabilities					
Banks		383		390	
Mortgages		22		43	
Debenture loans	(11)	333		245	
Pension funds		29		44	
Other accounts payable		6	773	29	25	747	28
			1 748	65		1 821	68
Minority interests			104	4		66	3
Shareholders' equity	(14)				
Share capital		327		327	
Share premium		80		80	
Reserve for own shares		12		2	
Revaluation surplus		127		146	
Retained earnings		301	847	31	216	771	29
Total liabilities and shareholders' equity			2 699	100		2 658	100

Georg Fischer Konzern

Konsolidierte Erfolgsrechnung 1997

	Erläute-rungen	1997 Mio. SFr.	%	1996 Mio. SFr.	%
Umsatz	(22)	3 076		2 568	
Bestandesänderungen Vorräte		−45		15	
Übriger betrieblicher Ertrag	(23)	61		53	
Ertrag		3 092	100	2 636	100
Vorleistungen					
Material und Fabrikate		−1 251		−1 027	
Dienstleistungen		−591		−546	
Wertschöpfung		1 250	40	1 063	40
Personalaufwand	(24)	−902		−812	
Abschreibungen auf					
Anlagevermögen	(6)	−131		−109	
Diverse Aufwendungen	(25)	−27		−12	
Betriebserfolg vor Zinsen und Steuern		190	6	130	5
Finanzergebnis	(26)	−40		−37	
Ausserbetriebliches Ergebnis	(27)	−5		13	
Ergebnis aus nicht konsolidierten					
Beteiligungen		1		1	
Konzernergebnis vor Ertragssteuern		146	5	107	4
Ertragssteuern	(28)	−19		−22	
Konzernergebnis inkl. Minderheitsanteile		127	4	85	3
Minderheitsanteile		−13		−7	
Konzernergebnis		114	4	78	3

Georg Fischer Corporation

Consolidated income statement 1997

	Notes	1997 million Sfr.	%	1996 million Sfr.	%
Sales	(22)	3 076		2 568	
Change in work in progress and finished goods		−45		15	
Other operating income	(23)	61		53	
Income		3 092	100	2 636	100
Expenditure on					
Materials and products		−1 251		−1 027	
External services		−591		−546	
Value added		1 250	40	1 063	40
Personnel expenses	(24)	−902		−812	
Depreciation and amortization	(6)	−131		−109	
Other operating expenses	(25)	−27		−12	
Operating profit before interest and taxes		190	6	130	5
Financial result	(26)	−40		−37	
Non-operating result	(27)	−5		13	
Income from non-consolidated investments		1		1	
Profit before taxes		146	5	107	4
Income taxes	(28)	−19		−22	
Profit after taxes		127	4	85	3
Minority interests		−13		−7	
Net profit		114	4	78	3

Georg Fischer Konzern

Eigenkapitalnachweis 1997

(ohne Minderheitsanteile)

in Mio. SFr.

	Aktien-kapital	Kapital-reserven (Agio)	Reserven für eigene Aktien	Neube-wertungs-reserven	Konzern-reserven (ohne Währungs-differenzen)	Währungs-differenzen kumulativ	**Eigen-kapital**
Stand 1. 1. 1997	327	80	2	146	220	−4	771
Konzernergebnis					114		114
Dividende					−29		−29
Währungsumrechnung						−9	−9
Übrige Veränderungen			10	−19	9		0
Stand 31. 12. 1997	327	80	12	127	314	−13	847

vgl. Erläuterung 14

Minderheitsanteile 1997

in Mio. SFr.	**Minderheits-anteile**
Stand 1. 1. 1997	66
Ergebnis	13
Dividende	−3
Währungsumrechnung	−8
Kapitalerhöhung AGIE CHARMILLES	36
Stand 31. 12. 1997	104

Georg Fischer Corporation

Changes in equity 1997

(excl. minority interests)

in million Sfr.

	Share capital	Share premium	Reserve for own shares	Re-valuation surplus	Retained earnings (excl. currency translation differences)	Cumulative currency translation differences	**Total equity**
Balance at Jan. 1, 1997	327	80	2	146	220	−4	**771**
Net profit					114		**114**
Dividends					−29		**−29**
Foreign currency translation						−9	**−9**
Other changes			10	−19	9		**0**
Balance at Dec. 31, 1997	327	80	12	127	314	−13	**847**

see note 14

Minority interests 1997

in million Sfr.

	Minority interests
Balance at Jan. 1, 1997	**66**
Net profit	**13**
Dividends	**−3**
Foreign currency translation	**−8**
Capital increase of AGIE CHARMILLES	**36**
Balance at Dec. 31, 1997	**104**

Georg Fischer Konzern

Konsolidierte Geldflussrechnung 1997

	Erläute-rungen	1997 Mio. SFr.		1996 Mio. SFr.	
Konzernergebnis inkl. Minderheitsanteile		127		85	
Abschreibungen auf Anlagevermögen (+)		131		109	
Übriger nicht liquiditätswirksamer Aufwand (+)		47		40	
Übriger nicht liquiditätswirksamer Ertrag (–)		–39	266	–54	180
Cash-flow			**266**		**180**
Zunahme (–), Abnahme (+) Vorräte		83		–23	
Zunahme (–), Abnahme (+) Forderungen aus Lieferungen und Leistungen		–36		–45	
Zunahme (–), Abnahme (+) übrige Forderungen		–70		20	
Zunahme (+), Abnahme (–) Verbindlichkeiten aus Lieferungen und Leistungen		19		–6	
Zunahme (+), Abnahme (–) Rückstellungen und übriges unverzinsliches Fremdkapital		55	51	7	–47
Geldfluss aus Geschäftstätigkeit			**317**		**133**
Zugänge von Sachanlagen (–)	(6)	–116		–157	
Zugänge von nicht konsolidierten Beteiligungen (–)	(6)	–9		–4	
Zugänge von übrigen Finanzanlagen und immateriellen Anlagen (–)	(6)	–34		–69	
Abgänge von Sachanlagen (+)		27		40	
Abgänge von nicht konsolidierten Beteiligungen (+)		12		0	
Abgänge von übrigen Finanzanlagen und immateriellen Anlagen (+)		44		0	
Zugänge (–), Abgänge (+) von Wertschriften		–47		13	
Zugänge (–), Abgänge (+) Konsolidierungskreis	(1)	–4		–84	
Geldfluss aus Investitionstätigkeit		–127	**–127**	–261	**–261**
Saldo Innenfinanzierung			**190**		**–128**
Gewinnausschüttungen (–)		–32		–23	
Aufnahme (+), Rückzahlung (–) Obligationenanleihe	(11)	88		–10	
Kapitalerhöhung AGIE CHARMILLES		36		0	
Zunahme (+), Abnahme (–) übriges verzinsliches Fremdkapital		–244		174	
Geldfluss aus Finanzierungstätigkeit		–152	**–152**	141	**141**
Zunahme (+), Abnahme (–) flüssige Mittel aus Währungsdifferenzen			–3		20
Total Geldfluss			**35**		**33**
Bestand Flüssige Mittel Anfang Geschäftsjahr (+)			176		143
Bestand Flüssige Mittel Ende Geschäftsjahr			**211**		**176**

Georg Fischer Corporation

Consolidated cash flow statement 1997

	Notes	1997 million Sfr.		1996 million Sfr.	
Profit after taxes		127		85	
Depreciation and amortization (+)		131		109	
Other expenses not involving the movement of funds (+)		47		40	
Other income not involving the movement of funds (–)		–39	266	–54	180
Cash flow			**266**		**180**
Additions (–) or reductions (+) to inventories		83		–23	
Additions (–) or reductions (+) to trade accounts receivable		–36		–45	
Additions (–) or reductions (+) to other accounts receivable		–70		20	
Additions (+) or reductions (–) to trade accounts payable		19		–6	
Additions (+) or reductions (–) to provisions and other non-interest-bearing liabilities		55	51	7	–47
Cash flow from operating activities			**317**		**133**
Additions to tangible fixed assets (–)	(6)	–116		–157	
Investments in non-consolidated companies (–)	(6)	–9		–4	
Investments in other financial assets and intangible assets (–)	(6)	–34		–69	
Proceeds from disposals of tangible fixed assets (+)		27		40	
Proceeds from disposals of non-consolidated companies (+)		12		0	
Proceeds from disposals of other financial assets and intangible assets (+)		44		0	
Additions (–) or reductions (+) to securities		–47		13	
Additions (–) or reductions (+) to scope of consolidation	(1)	–4		–84	
Cash flow from investing activities		**–127**	**–127**	**–261**	**–261**
Balance of internal financing			**190**		**–128**
Distribution of profit (–)		–32		–23	
Debenture loan issue (+), repayment (–)	(11)	88		–10	
Capital increase of AGIE CHARMILLES		36		0	
Additions (+) or reductions (–) to other interest-bearing liabilities		–244		174	
Cash flow from financing activities		**–152**	**–152**	**141**	**141**
Effect of exchange rate changes			–3		20
Net cash flow			**35**		**33**
Cash and cash equivalents at beginning of year (+)			176		143
Cash and cash equivalents at end of year			**211**		**176**

Other notes to the consolidated financial statements

Changes in scope of consolidation
The fully consolidated subsidiaries are listed with the respective shareholdings on pages 33 to 35. During the year under review the scope of consolidation changed as follows:

Fully consolidated subsidiaries:

Additions	Disposals
per Jan. 1, 1997 Mecatool Group George Fischer Pty Ltd, Oakleigh Rematech Comércio e Representações Ltda, São Paulo George Fischer Investments Ltd, Coventry	per Dec. 31, 1997 Buss Ltd, Pratteln (cf. additions per Dec. 31, 1997) OWL GmbH Logistik-Consulting, Friedrichshafen
per Sept. 30, 1997 AGIE CHARMILLES Holding SAS, Palaiseau	
per Dec. 31, 1997 from division of Buss Ltd, Pratteln, into legally independent business units: – Buss Compounding Systems Ltd, Pratteln – Buss CPS Chemical Process Systems Ltd, Pratteln – Buss MDL Erection Services Ltd, Pratteln – Buss Immobilien und Service AG, Pratteln	

Additions and reductions to the scope of consolidation in the cash flow statement comprise Sfr. 4 million net from acquisition and disposal of consolidated companies. They are disclosed net of cash and cash equivalents acquired or disposed.

Foreign exchange rates

		Average rates Sfr.		Year-end rates Sfr.	
		1997	1996	1997	1996
1	US$	1.45	1.23	1.454	1.349
1	S$	0.98	0.88	0.865	0.965
1	£	2.37	1.93	2.409	2.282
100	DM	83.73	82.10	81.27	86.85
100	FF	24.87	24.10	24.29	25.75
100	LIT	0.085	0.080	0.083	0.088
100	OES	11.90	11.70	11.55	12.34
100	YEN	1.20	1.14	1.119	1.162

Trade accounts receivable
The allowance for doubtful debts deducted from trade accounts receivable amounts to Sfr. 32 million (previous year Sfr. 28 million).

Other accounts receivable

Note 4

in million Sfr.	1997	1996
Taxes recoverable	79	45
Collateral, guarantee deposits	5	6
Other accounts receivable	47	16
Deferred expenses and accrued income	18	12
Total	149	79

Inventories (including advances)

Note 5

in million Sfr.	1997	1996
Inventories	546	624
[of which raw materials and components]	[136]	[150]
[of which work in progress]	[163]	[205]
[of which finished goods and goods for resale]	[247]	[269]
Advance payments made to suppliers	10	18
Advance payments received from customers	−136	−145
Total	420	497

The allowance deducted from inventories amounts to Sfr. 80 million
(previous year Sfr. 73 million).

Movements of fixed assets

Note 6

in million Sfr.	Land and buildings for business purposes	Investment properties	Machinery and equipment	Other tangible fixed assets	Assets under construction	Leased assets	Total tangible fixed assets	Non-consolidated investments	Other financial assets	Intangible assets	Total fixed assets 1997	Total fixed assets 1996
Cost or revalued amounts												
As per January 1	713	294	912	375	81	2	2 377	54	54	39	**2 524**	2 153
Additions	10		46	24	36		116	9	12	22	**159**	230
Disposals	−4	−29	−32	−24	−1		−90	−12	−42	−2	**−146**	−137
Changes in scope of consolidation	2						2				**2**	153
Reclassifications, other changes	37	7	43	2	−89		0			1	**1**	0
Foreign currency translations	−13	−6	−20	−5	1		−43	1	−1	−1	**−44**	125
As per December 31	745	266	949	372	28	2	2 362	52	23	59	**2 496**	2 524
Accumulated depreciation												
As per January 1	−297	−56	−551	−260	0	−1	−1 165	−	−	−3	**−1 168**	−1 041
Additions	−23	−2	−75	−31			−131	−	−	−3	**−134**	−109
Disposals	1	2	28	21			52	−	−	1	**53**	92
Changes in scope of consolidation	1						1	−	−		**1**	−60
Reclassifications, other changes	−24	15	3	6			0	−	−		**0**	0
Foreign currency translation			29	5			34	−	−		**34**	−50
As per December 31	−342	−41	−566	−259	0	−1	−1 209	−	−	−5	**−1 214**	−1 168
Carrying amounts												
As per January 1	416	238	361	115	81	1	1 212	54	54	36	**1 356**	1 112
As per December 31	403	225	383	113	28	1	**1 153**	52	23	54	**1 282**	1 356

Insurance value of tangible fixed assets: Sfr. 3381 million (previous year Sfr. 3327 million)

Note 7

Changes in investment properties

in million Sfr.	1997	1996
Carrying amount before revaluation	98	92
Revaluation	127	146
Carrying amount after revaluation	225	238

The revaluation corresponds to the revaluation surplus (see "Changes in equity" on page 11) and has decreased by Sfr. 19 million compared to the previous year due to property sales.

Note 8

Other financial assets
Other financial assets include own shares amounting to Sfr. 12 million (previous year Sfr. 2 million).

Note 9

Intangible assets, goodwill
The goodwill disclosed under intangible assets amounts to Sfr. 29 million (previous year Sfr. 31 million).

Note 10

Interest-bearing liabilities

in million Sfr.		1997			1996
	Short-term	Long-term		Total	Total
Maturity date of interest-bearing liabilities	within 1 year	Up to 5 years	Over 5 years		
Banks	106	340	43	489	619
Mortgages	5	18	4	27	54
Debenture loans	0	200	133	333	245
Pension funds	7	5	24	36	61
Other interest-bearing liabilities	3	2	3	8	65
Total	121	565	207	893	1044

Currency allocation
Interest-bearing liabilities are originally denominated in the following currencies: 60% in Sfr., 15% in DM, 8% in OES, 3% in US$, 9% in £ and 5% in other currencies. With the exception of DM, financing is mostly currency-congruent.

Interest rates
About 74% of long-term liabilities are at fixed interest rates. They include interest rate swaps of Sfr. 50 million, for which Georg Fischer is the fixed rate payer.

Note 11

Debenture loans

in million Sfr.	1997	1996
Georg Fischer Ltd, Schaffhausen		
Debenture loans		
5³/₄% 1995–2000	100	100
4³/₄% 1996–2002	100	100
Debenture loans carrying options to purchase shares		
2¹/₄% 1987–1996/98	–	45
Convertible loan		
2 % 1997–2003	133	–
Total	333	245

Other accounts payable (short-term)

in million Sfr.	1997	1996
Other interest-bearing liabilities	3	46
Taxes	23	31
Welfare contributions	17	16
Other liabilities	50	27
Accrued expenses and deferred income	66	49
Total	159	169

Provisions

in million Sfr.	1997	1996
Services yet to be rendered	197	195
Taxes	108	100
[of which deferred taxes]	[77]	[75]
Pension fund obligations	86	86
Restructuring and other obligations	86	66
Total	477	447

Equity

The changes in equity are presented on page 11. For details of share capital, see "Information for investors", page 27, and "Comments on the balance sheet" of Georg Fischer Ltd, Schaffhausen, pages 29 and 30.

Contingencies

in million Sfr.	1997	1996
Contingent liabilities for discounted notes	14	6
Pending foreign exchange transactions (gross)	157	147
Obligations on sold foreign exchange options	0	24
Guarantees, sureties	30	25
Total	201	202

Guarantees and sureties relate to third party obligations in connection with normal business activities.

Financing and related risks

Off-balance-sheet transactions
Derivative financial instruments are used exclusively for hedging corporate risks in connection with interest rate and foreign currency fluctuations. Only first-class financial institutes are employed. The extent of corporate-controlled forward transactions for covering currency exchange risks depends primarily on the specific risk assessment. Corporate hedging with respect to 1997 sales amounted to approximately 50% of monthly cash receipts in foreign currencies. As of December 31, 1997, about 20% of foreign exchange risks outstanding on expected cash flows for 1998 had already been hedged.

The table below shows the forward transactions (net) in major currencies:

in million Sfr.	1997	1996
US$	58	27
£	12	15
DM	8	43
FF	4	11
Other	27	33
Total	109	129

The underlying volume of foreign currency options as per December 31, 1997, amounted to Sfr. 21 million net.

Credit risks
Current bank deposits are placed at institutes with a high credit rating. Credit risk on
trade receivables is limited due to the wide distribution of Georg Fischer customers
among different business sectors and geographical regions. There are no significant
concentrations of credit risks.

Interest risks
Interest-bearing corporate investments are mainly on a short-term basis. Securities
primarily comprise debentures with medium-term maturity. With regard to interest-
bearing liabilities and corporate debenture loans, see notes 10 and 11.

Foreign exchange risks
Forward transactions at various dates to cover foreign exchange risks on cash in-flows
during 1998 and on corporate loans amounted to Sfr. 109 million net. If these transactions
had been concluded on December 31, 1997, their value would likewise have totalled
Sfr. 109 million, thus representing a balanced result as against loss of earnings totalling
Sfr. 8 million from forward transactions in 1996. The maturities of these transactions
are spread over the next 12 months.

in million Sfr.	1997	1996
Total contractual value of forward currency transactions (obligation)	109	129
Total market value of forward currency transactions (obligation)	109	137
Overlap of obligation	0	8

Fair values
Cash and cash equivalents, securities, trade receivables and short-term loans are stated
at fair values according to IAS.

Note 17

Pledged assets
Assets pledged or restricted on title in part or whole amount to Sfr. 122 million
(previous year Sfr. 175 million).

Note 18

Pension funds
Corporate pension funds in favour of employees mainly comprise financially indepen-
dent funds and foundations. Most of these funds are based on defined benefit plans.
Pension funds are generally financed by employer and employee contributions.

Based on IAS 19 (Retirement Benefit Costs), revised in 1995, independent actuarial
valuations were carried out as of January 1, 1995, with respect to defined benefit plans
using the projected unit credit method. Parameters recommended by actuaries have
been used for determining the required provisions.

Updated actuarial valuations resulted in a surplus of pension assets over obligations
throughout the corporation of Sfr. 36 million as per December 31, 1997.

Taking into account the provisions established on initial recognition, the situation with
regard to salary-indexed pension funds is as follows:

in million Sfr.	Dec. 31, 1997	Dec. 31, 1996
Pension obligations	-275	-278
Assets	225	209
Deficit	-50	-69
Provisions	86	86
Surplus	36	17

Additional prepaid pension contributions amounting to Sfr. 23 million are available for
use by the Corporation.

Other financial commitments
At December 31, 1997, additions to tangible fixed assets amounting to Sfr. 23 million
(previous year Sfr. 30 million) were approved.

There are no material unrecognized lease commitments as defined by Art. 663b Item 3
of the Swiss Code of Obligations (operating leases).

Debt covenants were complied with.

Related parties
The members of the Board of Directors are listed on page 22. Their total fees for 1997
amounted to 1 758 registered shares of Georg Fischer (previous year Sfr. 0.58 million).

As in the previous year, there are no accounts receivable from or payable to members
of the Board of Directors or important shareholders.

Transactions with related parties are conducted exclusively at arm's length.

Events occurring after balance sheet date
OWL Ltd Logistics Systems, Buchs, and Verkehrstechnik AG, Schaffhausen, have been
divested, but remain fully consolidated in the accounts for 1997. Profit from the sale of
these companies is disclosed under "Non-operating result".

Sales

Sales by Group
in million Sfr.

	1997		1996	
Automotive Products	918	29 %	850	32 %
Piping Systems	671	21 %	592	22 %
Manufacturing Technology	909	29 %	616	23 %
Plant Engineering	674	21 %	615	23 %
	3 172	100 %	2 673	100 %
Consolidation	−56		−60	
Total billings	3 116		2 613	
Sales deductions	−40		−45	
Total sales	3 076		2 568	

Sales by geographical segment
in million Sfr.

	1997		1996	
Germany	936	30 %	793	30 %
Other EU countries	1 016	33 %	863	33 %
Switzerland	147	5 %	128	5 %
Other European countries	125	4 %	104	4 %
America	528	17 %	391	15 %
Asia, Africa, Australia	364	11 %	334	13 %
Total billings	3 116	100 %	2 613	100 %
Sales deductions	−40		−45	
Total sales	3 076		2 568	

Note 23

Other operating income

The major components of this line item are commission income, manufacturing costs capitalized for own use, gains on sale of fixed assets and licence fees. Manufacturing costs capitalized for own use amounted to Sfr. 2 million in 1997 (previous year Sfr. 3 million).

Note 24

Personnel expenses

in million Sfr.	1997	1996
Salaries and wages	737	664
Expenses for corporate pension funds	47	41
Social and welfare expenses	118	107
Total	902	812

Note 25

Other operating expenses

in million Sfr.	1997	1996
Value adjustments and provisions	9	3
Cost of disposals of current and fixed assets	11	4
Capital taxes	7	5
Total	27	12

Value adjustments and provisions include an increase in provisions of Sfr. 7 million (previous year Sfr. 7 million).

The cost of disposals of current and fixed assets mainly includes residual write-offs on operating asset disposals and partial operating asset write-offs. The corresponding sales proceeds are included in other operating income. The disposals of fixed assets resulted in a gain of Sfr. 1 million (previous year Sfr. 2 million).

Note 26

Financial result

in million Sfr.	1997	1996
Interest income	10	5
Interest expenses	−51	−39
Other financial items	1	−3
Total	−40	−37

Other financial items consist of foreign exchange differences on currency transactions which do not relate to sales of products or services. They likewise include securities yield and issuing fees.

Note 27

Non-operating result

in million Sfr.	1997	1996
Non-operating income	11	29
Non-operating expenses	−16	−16
Total	−5	13

The non-operating result comprises items which cannot be attributed to operating activities. Expenses include restructuring costs. Income comprises rental income from investment properties and gains on sale of properties and divested subsidiaries.

Income taxes

Note 28

Income taxes are calculated based on the net profit according to uniform valuation principles.

in million Sfr.	1997	1996
Current taxes	19	21
Deferred taxes	0	1
Total	19	22

Bericht des Konzernprüfers an die Generalversammlung der Georg Fischer AG, Schaffhausen

Als Konzernprüfer haben wir die auf den Seiten 9 bis 23 wiedergegebene Konzernrechnung der Georg Fischer AG, Schaffhausen, bestehend aus konsolidierter Bilanz, konsolidierter Erfolgsrechnung, konsolidierter Geldflussrechnung und Anhang der Konzernrechnung, für das am 31. Dezember 1997 abgeschlossene Geschäftsjahr geprüft. Verschiedene Jahresrechnungen von Tochtergesellschafien, die einen massgeblichen Anteil an der Konzernrechnung haben, wurden von anderen Prüfern geprüft.

Für die Konzernrechnung ist der Verwaltungsrat verantwortlich, während unsere Aufgabe darin besteht, diese zu prüfen und zu beurteilen. Wir bestätigen, dass wir die gesetzlichen Anforderungen hinsichtlich Befähigung und Unabhängigkeit erfüllen.

Unsere Prüfung erfolgte nach den Grundsätzen des Berufsstandes sowie nach den International Standards on Auditing der International Federation of Accountants (IFAC), wonach eine Prüfung so zu planen und durchzuführen ist, dass wesentliche Fehlaussagen in der Konzernrechnung mit angemessener Sicherheit erkannt werden. Wit prüften die Posten und Angaben der Konzernrechnung mittels Analysen und Erhebungen auf der Basis von Stichproben. Ferner beurteilten wir die Anwendung der massgebenden Rechnungslegungsgrundsätze, die wesentlichen Bewertungsentscheide sowie die Darstellung der Konzernrechnung als Ganzes. Wir sind der Auffassung, dass unsere Prüfung eine ausreichende Grundlage für unser Urteil bildet.

Wie im Anhang der Konzernrechnung unter den Grundsätzen der Konzernrechnungslegung auf Seite 13 erwähnt wird, sind gewisse Segmentinformationen, die nach IAS 14 vorgeschrieben sind, nicht ausgewiesen.

Gemäss unserer Beurteilung vermittelt die Konzernrechnung mit Ausnahme des oben erwähnten Punktes ein den tatsächlichen Verhältnissen entsprechendes Bild der Vermögens-, Finanz- und Ertragslage in Übereinstimmung mit den International Accounting Standards des IASC sowie der 4. und 7. EU-Richtlinie, und sie entspricht dem Gesetz sowie den Rechnungslegungsvorschriften des Kotierungsreglements der Schweizer Börse.

Der Konzernlagebericht steht im Einklang mit der Konzernrechnung.

Wir empfehlen, die vorliegende Konzernrechnung zu genehmigen.

KPMG Fides Peat

P. Hess	P. Bertschinger
Dipl. Wirtschafisprüfer	Dipl. Wirtschaftsprüfer
Leitender Revisor	Leitender Revisor

Zürich, 11. Februar 1998

Report of the Group Auditors to the General Meeting of Georg Fischer Ltd, Schaffhausen

As Group Auditors, we have audited the consolidated financial statements of Georg Fischer Ltd, Schaffhausen, and subsidiaries, presented on pages 9 to 23 and consisting of the consolidated balance sheet as of December 31, 1997, and the consolidated income and cash flow statements and notes to the consolidated financial statements for the year then ended. Certain financial statements of subsidiaries which form a material part of the consolidated financial statements have been audited by other auditors.

The consolidated financial statements are the responsibility of the Company's Board of Directors. Our responsibility is to express an opinion on these consolidated financial statements based on our audit. We confirm that we meet the Swiss legal requirements concerning professional qualification and independence.

Our audit was conducted in accordance with auditing standards promulgated in Switzerland by the profession and with the International Standards on Auditing issued by the International Federation of Accountants (IFAC). Those standards require that we plan and perform an audit to obtain reasonable assurance as to whether the consolidated financial statements are free of material misstatement. An audit includes examining, on a test basis, evidence supporting the amounts and disclosures in the consolidated financial statements. An audit also includes assessing the accounting principles used and significant estimates made by the management, as well as evaluating the overall presentation of the consolidated financial statements. We believe that our audit provides a reasonable basis for our opinion.

As mentioned in the notes on corporate accounting and consolidation principles, page 13, certain segment information as required by IAS 14 has not been disclosed.

In our opinion, except for the issue mentioned above, the consolidated financial statements give a true and fair view of the consolidated financial position, results of operations and cash flows in accordance with the International Accounting Standards of the International Accounting Standards Committee (IASC) and the fourth and seventh directives of the European Union, and are in accordance with the provisions of Swiss law and the accounting principles of the Listing Rules of the Swiss Exchange.

The directors' annual report on the corporation is consistent with the consolidated financial statements.

We recommend that the consolidated financial statements submitted to you be approved.

KPMG Fides Peat

P. Hess   P. Bertschinger
Swiss Certified Accountant   Swiss Certified Accountant
Auditor in charge   Auditor in charge

Zurich, February 11, 1998

Georg Fischer AG, Schaffhausen

Bilanz per 31. Dezember 1997

Aktiven	Erläute-rungen	1997 SFr.	1996 SFr.
Umlaufvermögen	(1)		
Flüssige Mittel		46 303 654	587 065
Wertschriften		62 981 874	5 017 070
Forderungen an Konzerngesellschaften		245 225 354	198 071 428
Übrige Forderungen		3 058 941	36 014 310
Aktive Rechnungsabgrenzungen		934 766	41 514
Total Umlaufvermögen		**358 504 589**	**239 731 387**
Anlagevermögen	(2)		
Beteiligungen		532 924 000	523 560 000
Darlehen an Dritte		141 400	
Darlehen an Konzerngesellschaften		190 518 000	179 225 285
Total Anlagevermögen		**723 583 400**	**702 785 285**
Total Aktiven		**1 082 087 989**	**942 516 672**

Passiven

Fremdkapital	(3)		
Kurzfristige Verbindlichkeiten			
Bankverbindlichkeiten		1 808 826	3 423 099
Verbindlichkeiten gegenüber Dritten		1 797 320	29 791
Verbindlichkeiten gegenüber Konzerngesellschaften		32 071 040	9 920 307
Übrige Verbindlichkeiten		645 891	20 959
Passive Rechnungsabgrenzungen		8 264 232	9 121 672
Rückstellungen		43 830 877	37 364 066
Langfristige Verbindlichkeiten			
Anleihen		332 821 400	245 000 000
Banken		70 000 000	70 000 000
Darlehen gegenüber Dritten		1 750 000	
Total Fremdkapital		**492 989 586**	**374 879 894**
Eigenkapital	(4)		
Aktienkapital		327 286 500	327 240 000
Gesetzliche Reserven			
Allgemeine Reserven		139 638 539	139 504 368
Reserve für eigene Aktien		11 923 000	1 510 000
Spezialreserve		36 677 000	22 090 000
Bilanzgewinn			
Gewinnvortrag	23 290 810		
Jahresgewinn	50 282 554	73 573 364	77 292 410
Total Eigenkapital		**589 098 403**	**567 636 778**
Total Passiven		**1 082 087 989**	**942 516 672**

Georg Fischer Ltd, Schaffhausen

Balance sheet as at December 31, 1997

Assets	Notes Sfr.	1997 Sfr.	1996 Sfr.
Current assets	(1)		
Cash and cash equivalents		46 303 654	587 065
Securities		62 981 874	5 017 070
Accounts receivable from consolidated companies		245 225 354	198 071 428
Other accounts receivable		3 058 941	36 014 310
Deferred expenses and accrued income		934 766	41 514
Total current assets		**358 504 589**	**239 731 387**
Fixed assets	(2)		
Investments in subsidiaries		532 924 000	523 560 000
Loans to third parties		141 400	
Loans to consolidated companies		190 518 000	179 225 285
Total fixed assets		**723 583 400**	**702 785 285**
Total assets		**1 082 087 989**	**942 516 672**

Liabilities and shareholders' equity

Liabilities	(3)	1997	1996
Current liabilities			
Banks		1 808 826	3 423 099
Accounts payable to third parties		1 797 320	29 791
Accounts payable to consolidated companies		32 071 040	9 920 307
Other liabilities		645 891	20 959
Accrued expenses and deferred income		8 264 232	9 121 672
Provisions		43 830 877	37 364 066
Long-term liabilities			
Debenture loans		332 821 400	245 000 000
Bank loans		70 000 000	70 000 000
Loans from third parties		1 750 000	
Total liabilities		**492 989 586**	**374 879 894**
Shareholders' equity	(4)		
Share capital		327 286 500	327 240 000
Legal reserves			
General reserves		139 638 539	139 504 368
Reserve for own shares		11 923 000	1 510 000
Special reserves		36 677 000	22 090 000
Available earnings			
Profit carried forward	23 290 810		
Profit for the year	50 282 554	73 573 364	77 292 410
Total shareholders' equity		**589 098 403**	**567 636 778**
Total liabilities and shareholders' equity		**1 082 087 989**	**942 516 672**

Erfolgsrechnung 1997

	Erläute- rungen	1997 SFr.	1996 SFr.
Ertrag	(8)		
Ertrag aus Beteiligungen		68 605 171	66 830 205
Finanzertrag		25 744 436	31 478 611
Übrige Erträge		1 039 246	1 383 693
		95 388 853	**99 692 509**
Aufwand	(9)		
Aufwand für Beteiligungen		1 320 219	13 036 802
Finanzaufwand		34 928 818	23 304 472
Übrige Aufwendungen		8 857 262	5 979 608
		45 106 299	**42 320 882**
Jahresgewinn		**50 282 554**	**57 371 627**
		95 388 853	**99 692 509**

Income statement 1997

	Notes	1997 Sfr.	1996 Sfr.
Income	(8)		
Income from investments		68 605 171	66 830 205
Financial income		25 744 436	31 478 611
Other income		1 039 246	1 383 693
		95 388 853	**99 692 509**
Expenses	(9)		
Expenses for investments		1 320 219	13 036 802
Financial expenses		34 928 818	23 304 472
Other expenses		8 857 262	5 979 608
		45 106 299	**42 320 882**
Profit for the year		**50 282 554**	**57 371 627**
		95 388 853	**99 692 509**

Notes to the financial statements

Comments on the balance sheet

Current assets   Note 1
The increase in current assets and securities is primarily attributable to the 2% convertible
bond issue. Further concentration of internal finance transactions on Georg Fischer Ltd
led to a significant rise in accounts receivable from consolidated companies.

Fixed assets   Note 2
The investments in subsidiaries of Georg Fischer Ltd are listed on pages 33 to 35
under the "Direct" column. Significant additions comprise the capital increases of AGIE
CHARMILLES Holding AG, Zug, and of George Fischer Holding Ltd, Coventry, together
with the founding of Georg Fischer Piping Systems Ltd, Shanghai. These are partially
offset by the capital reductions of Georg Fischer Management Ltd, Schaffhausen, and
Georg Fischer Immobilien AG, Schaffhausen.

The book value of affiliated companies is based on the sum of their net asset values.

Liabilities   Note 3
A breakdown of debenture loans can be found on page 18 under "notes to the consolidated financial statements". Some of the 2% bonds issued in 1997 have already been
converted.

Note 4

Shareholders' equity
– Share capital
Share capital of 327.3 million Swiss francs comprises 549 693 bearer shares at par value of Sfr. 500 each and 524 400 registered shares at par value of Sfr. 100 each. After deduction of bearer shares to the nominal value of 5 million Swiss francs, which remain at the disposal of the Board of Directors, total dividend-bearing nominal capital therefore amounts to 322.3 million Swiss francs.

– Conditional capital
The conditional capital increase of up to 35 million Swiss francs approved by the Annual General Meeting of April 19, 1995, is reserved as security for the 2% convertible bond issue 1997–2003.

Note 5

Significant shareholders
SIG Schweizerische Industrie-Gesellschaft Holding AG, Neuhausen am Rheinfall, is recorded in the share register with 100 000 registered shares.

Note 6

Own shares held by the company and by subsidiaries

	Number of shares		Total value
	Registered shares	Bearer shares	Sfr.
Balance at Jan. 1, 1997	5 792	–	1 505 920
– Purchase	15 191	6 870	18 705 892
– Sales at prevailing stock exchange rates	–12 394	–5 190	–13 948 625
– Gain on sales/value adjustments			429 345
Balance at Dec. 31, 1997	8 589	1 680	6 692 532

Own registered shares are reserved for board members' fees and annual bonus payments to senior executives.

Likewise at the disposal of the Board of Directors are bearer shares totalling 5 million Swiss francs par value.

Note 7

Contingent liabilities

	1997 Sfr.	1996 Sfr.
Total guarantees and pledges in favour of third and affiliated parties		
– Guaranteed maximum amount	658 649 164	769 486 999
– Draw-down amount	242 766 513	401 120 383

Georg Fischer Ltd belongs to the Georg Fischer value-added tax group, and thus carries joint liability to the federal tax authorities for value-added tax debts of the entire group.

Comments on the income statement

Income

Note 8

Income from investments in subsidiaries comprises dividends received from directly held subsidiaries. In the previous year this item also included income from the sale of participations.

Expenses

Note 9

Expense outlay for participations was substantially lower during the year under review, since due to their improved results no formation of provisions was necessary as in the previous year.

The decrease in financial income is attributable to currency exchange losses on loans in German marks due to strengthening of the Swiss franc.

There are no further facts present that would require disclosure according to Art. 663b of the Swiss Code of Obligations.

Note 10

Antrag des Verwaltungsrates über die Verwendung des Bilanzgewinns 1997

	1997 SFr.	1996 SFr.
Jahresgewinn	50 282 554	57 371 627
Gewinnvortrag aus dem Vorjahr	23 290 810	19 920 783
Bilanzgewinn	73 573 364	77 292 410

Antrag des Verwaltungsrates:

– Ausrichtung einer Dividende von SFr. 12.– je Namenaktie (1996: SFr. 9.–) und SFr. 60.– je Inhaberaktie (1996: SFr. 45.–)	38 674 380	29 001 600
– Zuweisung an die Spezialreserve	15 000 000	25 000 000
– Vortrag auf neue Rechnung	19 898 984	23 290 810
	73 573 364	77 292 410

Schaffhausen, 22. Januar 1998

Für den Verwaltungsrat
Der Präsident

Ulrich Bremi

Bericht der Revisionsstelle an die Generalversammlung der Georg Fischer AG, Schaffhausen

Als Revisionsstelle haben wir die Buchführung und die Jahresrechnung (Bilanz, Erfolgsrechnung und Anhang) der Georg Fischer AG, Schaffhausen, für das am 31. Dezember 1997 abgeschlossene Geschäftsjahr geprüft.

Für die Jahresrechnung ist der Verwaltungsrat verantwortlich, während unsere Aufgabe darin besteht, diese zu prüfen und zu beurteilen. Wir bestätigen, dass wir die gesetzlichen Anforderungen hinsichtlich Befähigung und Unabhängigkeit erfüllen.

Unsere Prüfung erfolgte nach den Grundsätzen des Berufsstandes, wonach eine Prüfung so zu planen und durchzuführen ist, dass wesentliche Fehlaussagen in der Jahresrechnung mit angemessener Sicherheit erkannt werden. Wir prüften die Posten und Angaben der Jahresrechnung mittels Analysen und Erhebungen auf der Basis von Stichproben. Ferner beurteilten wir die Anwendung der massgebenden Rechnungslegungsgrundsätze, die wesentlichen Bewertungsentscheide sowie die Darstellung der Jahresrechnung als Ganzes. Wir sind der Auffassung, dass unsere Prüfung eine ausreichende Grundlage für unser Urteil bildet.

Gemäss unserer Beurteilung entsprechen die Buchführung und die Jahresrechnung sowie der Antrag über die Verwendung des Bilanzgewinnes Gesetz und Statuten.

Wir empfehlen, die vorliegende Jahresrechnung zu genehmigen. KPMG Fides Peat

P. Hess	A. Buck
Dipl. Wirtschaftsprüfer	Dipl. Wirtschafisprüfer
Leitender Revisor	Leitender Revisor

Zürich, 23. Januar 1998

Proposal by the Board of Directors of Georg Fischer Ltd for the distribution of available earnings for 1997

	1997 Sfr.	1996 Sfr.
Profit for the year	50 282 554	57 371 627
Profit carried forward from previous year	23 290 810	19 920 783
Available earnings	73 573 364	77 292 410
Proposal of the Board of Directors:		
– Dividend payment of Sfr. 12.– per registered share (1996: Sfr. 9.–) and Sfr. 60.– per bearer share (1996: Sfr. 45.–)	38 674 380	29 001 600
– Allocation to special reserves	15 000 000	25 000 000
– to be carried forward	19 898 984	23 290 810
	73 573 364	77 292 410

Schaffhausen, January 22, 1998

For the Board of Directors
The Chairman

Ulrich Bremi

Report of the Statutory Auditors to the General Meeting of Georg Fischer Ltd, Schaffhausen

As Statutory Auditors, we have audited the accounting records and the financial statements (balance sheet, income statement and notes) of Georg Fischer Ltd, Schaffhausen, for the year ended December 31, 1997.

The financial statements are the responsibility of the Board of Directors. Our responsibility is to express an opinion on these financial statements based on our audit. We confirm that we meet the legal requirements concerning professional qualification and independence.

Our audit was conducted in accordance with auditing standards promulgated by the profession, which require that an audit be planned and performed to obtain reasonable assurance about whether the financial statements are free from material misstatement. We have examined on a test basis evidence supporting the amounts and disclosures in the financial statements. We have also assessed the accounting principles used, significant estimates made and the overall financial statement presentation. We believe that our audit provides a reasonable basis for our opinion.

In our opinion, the accounting records, financial statements and the proposed appropriation of available earnings comply with the law and the company's articles of incorporation.

We recommend that the financial statements submitted to you be approved.

KPMG Fides Peat

P. Hess
Swiss Certified Accountant
Auditor in charge

A. Buck
Swiss Certified Accountant
Auditor in charge

Zurich, January 23, 1998

Country Highlights
TURKEY

Common Legal Forms of Companies

Turkish law recognizes seven legal forms of companies:

1. Ordinary partnership
2. General partnership
3. Limited partnership
4. Company limited by shares (corporations and joint-stock companies)
5. Partnership limited by shares
6. Limited liability partnership
7. Co-operative society

The law provides for two types of corporations: closely held corporations and publicly held corporations.

The Capital Market Law covers publicly held corporations, including companies that offer their securities to the public, brokers operating in the capital market, unit trusts, and other capital market establishments

Sources of Financial Reporting Requirements

The Turkish Commercial Code is foremost among sources of financial reporting requirements for companies. Another source of significance with respect to the capital market, capital market institutions, and public companies is the Capital Market Law. Secondary sources are decrees having the force of law, decrees of the Council of Ministers, and Communiqués of the Capital Market Board.

Corporate Taxation

All companies limited by shares (joint-stock companies), limited liability partnerships, co-operatives, state enterprises, undertakings owned by associations and foundations, joint ventures, and mutual trusts are subject to corporation tax under the Capital Market Law.

Auditing Requirements

The Turkish Commercial Code, Capital Market Law, and Law on Co-operative Societies are the legal bases for auditing requirements. Companies limited by shares and co-operative societies are audited by an internal auditor, or a committee of auditors, which is a statutory organ of the company but is not required to have professional expertise in the field. However, banks, financial leasing companies, publicly held companies, and institutions of the capital market are obliged to undergo independent auditing, which must be performed by a member of the Independent Auditing Institutions.

Organization of the Accounting and Auditing Professions

Organization of the accounting and auditing profession has been regulated by Law No. 3568 Concerning Independent Accounting, Financial Consulting and Sworn Financial Consulting, dated 1989. This law brought about the Union of Chambers of Independent Accountants, Financial Consultants and Sworn Financial Consultants.

Constitution and Legal System

The constitutional system is based on the Constitution of 1982. The structure of public authority in Turkey is founded on the principle of separation of legislative, executive, and judicial powers. Legislative power is vested in the Grand National Assembly of Turkey. The Assembly consists of 550 deputies elected by universal suffrage by the nation. The executive power consists of the President of the Republic and the Council of Ministers. Judicial powers are vested in the courts. The judiciary is divided into four categories: (i) constitutional, (ii) administrative, (iii) ordinary, and (iv) special courts such as courts for land registrations and courts for labor disputes.

Currency

Turkish Lira

Official Language

Turkish

TURKEY

Unal Tekinalp
Center for Research and Practice in European Law
University of Istanbul

1. Background

1.1 Historical Overview

The enactment of legislation concerning independent accounting and financial reporting, as well as the development of the accounting and auditing profession in Turkey have taken place rather recently. Consequently, the contribution of such legislation to accounting regulation or self-regulation has not been substantial.

Accounting law in Turkey has not experienced a development parallel to company law and has remained under the influence of taxation law, lacking any distinct character. In 1982, however, the Capital Market Law (CML) was enacted, and the Capital Market Board (CMB) was established. Consequently, accounting law entered a new phase of development.

Although the first draft law for regulation of the accounting and auditing professions had been prepared as early as 1932, it was only put into force in 1989, by Law No. 3568 concerning Independent Accounting, Financial Consulting and Sworn Financial Consulting (the "Independent Accounting Law"). Pursuant to the provisions of the Independent Accounting Law, the Union of Chambers of Independent Accountants, Financial Consultants, and Sworn Financial Consultants were established. The delay was caused by the long struggle between the accounting and auditing specialists on one side and lawyers on the other. Specific rules concerning auditing were enacted in 1987.

The communiqués issued by the CMB and the Central Bank of the Turkish Republic should be regarded as partial efforts at regulation. However, there has been a certain degree of overlap between the above-mentioned regulations and the Independent Accounting Law.

1.2 Development of Company Law

Legislation (in the modern sense) concerning commercial law and companies was enacted for the first time in the Ottoman Empire with the *Kanunname-i-Ticaret* (literally "Commercial Code") in 1850. It was based on the French Code of Commerce of 1870.

The mid 1920s were a time of innovation, when the social, political, and cultural landscape of Turkey began to undergo fundemental changes. A series of legal reforms took place in 1926. Under these reforms, Ottoman law was replaced by a system based on various European models, such as the Swiss Civil Code and Code of Obligations, the Halien Penal Code, and the German Code of Penal Procedure. This was the climate in which the Commercial Code of 1926 was born. This code contains only a few provisions concerning accounting, such as accounting books, the obligation to keep accounting books, and obligations of certification.

The present Turkish Code of Commerce (TCC), dated 1957, which superseded the Turkish Code of Commerce of 1926, is not based on the philosophy of disclosure, and therefore it also does not regulate financial reporting. The main features of the TCC are valuation principles and the authorization of hidden reserves practically without limitation.

With the 1938 passage of the "Law on Organization, Administration and Auditing of State Economic Enterprises that are Fully Owned by the State" (Law No. 3460), state enterprises were regarded as a whole rather than being considered one by one. Even so, provisions for the preparation of consolidated financial statements were not stipulated.

Law No. 3460 (1938) began a process of development for public enterprises from the standpoint of the introduction and improvement of generally acceptable principles of accounting and also of financial reporting and auditing.

At present, state enterprises are governed by Decree Law No. 233 (1983), which provides that the accounts of state enterprises, companies, and their subsidiaries be kept in such a manner as to present well-ordered information on financial conditions, operations, costs, and investments (Article 33.1); they should be drawn up in accordance with a certain model (Article 34.1); and the balance sheet and other statements should be published in the official Gazette after they have been audited and approved by the Grand National Assembly (Article 34.3). With the enactment of the Tax Laws in 1949 and 1950, an accounting jurisprudence was created in

Turkey, aimed at determining the tax base in the most accurate manner. Through the numerous amendments that were subsequently made, such an accounting law became firmly established in Turkey, as a result of the fact that the Tax Procedure Law is a "code" that fully discloses the principles of accounting and balance sheet preparation as well as valuation principles.

Regarding the banking sector, neither the Law for Protection of Bank Deposits No. 2243 (1933), nor Banking Law No. 2999 (1936), which superseded the former, covered the subjects of financial reporting and disclosure to a great extent, but the disclosure principle was introduced to a limited extent with Banking Law No. 7129, which came into force in 1958. Under Banking Law No. 3182 (1985), which is currently in force, and other related legislation, the scope of the disclosure principle has since been widened and the trends are in that direction.

Banks are obliged to prepare their accounts, annual balance sheets, and profit and loss accounts in accordance with the uniform accounts plan, standard-type balance sheet and profit and loss account models, and their notes. These models were prepared by the Turkish Banks Association and came into force with the approval of the Under Secretariat for the Treasury and Foreign Trade of the Prime Ministry. This rule applies to the branch offices of foreign banks in Turkey as well.

Similar regulations govern insurance companies. The accounts plan that banks should apply, its explanations, as well as generally accepted accounting principles and their applications and the accounts plan related to overdue claims were published in 1985.

The CML, which covers companies that offer their securities to the public, companies whose ownership is available to the public at large, that is, joint-stock and public limited companies (Article 11), brokers operating in the capital market (Articles 31–34), and unit trusts (Article 35) founded according to the open-end principle, constituted another milestone in the jurisprudence of accounting in Turkey.

The CML adopted as its model the Securities and Exchange Act of the United States and created an agency called the Capital Market Board, or CMB, resembling the U.S. Securities and Exchange Commission and which was equipped with vast powers that included indicating the accounting standards to be applied by corporations covered by the CML.

The main objective of the CML was to establish the control of the CMB over new issues of securities to the public and the requirement for corporations to obtain permission from the said authority for such a purpose, and to enlarge the scope of application of the disclosure principle and to enhance its effectiveness.

Thus, a rapid development of a wide scope was achieved in the law governing corporations, at least from the points of view of both disclosure and financial reporting. Under the CML, companies that offer to the public such securities as commercial paper, debentures, share certificates, or bonds, or the number of whose shareholders is established to be more than one hundred and thus are considered to be public companies, will be obliged to draw up their balance sheets and profit and loss accounts according to the forms and principles to be established by the CMB (Article 16).

This authority of the CMB is not confined to determining the layouts of the financial statements; it also covers the laying down of accounting principles to be observed. The CMB discharged that duty in 1983 with the publication of the "Communiqué on Principles Governing Standard Financial Statements and Reports" and, in 1984, the "Unified Chart of Accounts."

The "Communiqué on Principles and Rules Appertaining to Financial Statements and Reports in the Capital Market" (January 1989), which was generally well received, was complemented by the "Communiqué on Principles and Rules Appertaining to Intermediate Financial Statements" (July 1989). The latter was amended by the publication of the "Standard Unified Chart of Accounts Plan and the Principles for Application of the Plan" (1989). Detailed regulation was introduced in 1992 by the "General Communiqué Concerning Implementation of the Accounting System" by the Ministry of Finance.

1.3 The Evolution of Current Accounting Thought

The provisions of the Turkish Code of Commerce (TCC) that have been subject to justified criticism are those concerning auditing (Articles 347–359). The principal points of criticism have been the following: the internal auditor (or committee of auditors), which is a statutory requirement, was not required to be an expert in the field; the auditor or the committee of auditors were not, in practice, able to perform their auditing duties consistently; it is impossible with a few auditors to fulfill the principle of having the auditing function carried out by a team that should consist of members complementing one another.

However, because the provisions relating to auditors were contained not only in the section of the TCC relating to auditors but also in other parts of the TCC, and that they have been assigned such other duties as calling the general meeting of shareholders, inserting items in the agenda, hearing complaints, and, when required, representing the company in courts of law in addition to their auditing duties, it has been difficult to change the system.

In spite of all these difficulties, the view that a corporation should be audited by an expert institution that is independent of the company has become ever more generally accepted.

When the CMB published its "Regulations on Auditing by Independent Auditor in the Capital Market" in 1987, the first step was taken toward the application of auditing practice in its full sense, notwithstanding the legal and practical difficulties that may arise with two sources of auditing. True, the Banking Law had already introduced the employment of expert auditors to the Turkish legal system, but that slight improvement was not sufficient to eliminate all the drawbacks of the system. In fact, immediately after the publication of the Regulations, the Central Bank issued its Communiqué Serial No. 1 on Bank Audits (1987).

With a view to firmly establishing independent auditing institutions, the CMB issued Communiqué Serial X, No. 3, on "General Principles Appertaining to Independent Auditing Establishments and Auditors" (June 1987), "Communiqué on Principles and Rules Appertaining to Independent Auditing Work and Reporting" (1987), and their attachments, which were prepared in considerable detail.

1.4 The Present Accounting Environment

The role of law in the determination of accounting requirements had been quite limited before the 1980s. Until that time, the influence of fiscal auditors and of the Ministry of Finance inspectors had been considerable. In their audits of tax returns and accounting records, they made their examinations and drew up their reports for the Ministry of Finance, often from the standpoint of generally accepted accounting principles, and created the establishment of some accounting standards, albeit from a taxation standpoint.

At present, the influence of these inspectors and auditors continues on statutory and self-regulatory bodies. One reason is that the said bodies have recruited their own specialized personnel from among the inspectors and auditors, who also became partners with many of the international auditing companies that commenced operating in Turkey in the 1970s.

Today also, the great majority of those who are allowed to operate under Law No. 3568 as chartered financial advisors and who are empowered to perform auditing functions consist of the above-mentioned inspectors and auditors. The question remains whether those who in the past always performed audits with the fiscal interests of the government in mind will be able to give a new character, not dominated by tax considerations, to generally acceptable accounting principles in Turkey.

Since 1982, the CMB has been functioning as a law-making body in this respect under the authority granted to it by law. The characteristic feature of the communiqués published by the CMB has been the philosophy of disclosure embedded in its provisions. The rules they have laid down are aimed at realizing disclosure both through the substance (i.e., the contents) of the financial statements and their form (i.e., the layout of the statements), as well as the procedure for their being made public.

There is no doubt that the CMB took into account the EC Fourth Directive and that its principles and provisions have had a significant influence on the drafting of the CMB's communiqués. Communiqué Series XI, No. 1 (O.J. No. 20064, January 29, 1989), contains accounting principles parallel to the Fourth Directive, among them the principle of the "true and fair view." However, this was not laid down as an explicit superior rule (the true and fair view override), and an explicit indication of that principle in Turkish legislation would not necessarily entail its full application in practice, because that principle can enjoy full application only with the full implementation of the Fourth Directive and the establishment of the concept of a "true and fair view."

The other communiqués of the CMB concerning accounting standards and financial reporting are given in the appendix.

2. The Form and Content of Published Financial Statements

The disclosure philosophy, as explained above, is a recent phenomenon in Turkey and has been applied to only a limited number of corporations. State economic enterprises that are closed to the outside world and make their financial reporting to a closed circle are not included.

As for corporations that are not covered by the CML and are subject only to the TCC, the possibility of applying the disclosure principle to them is almost negligible. The TCC is inadequate in this respect because the relevant provisions of the TCC were borrowed from the Code of Obligations of Switzerland, which at that time failed to incorporate the disclosure principle and has only recently been amended in this direction.

2.1 Turkish Code of Commerce

The TCC does not put forward specimens of financial statements that companies must conform to and has not included any provisions about financial reporting, even at a minimum level. The principles governing the drawing-up of balance sheets were limited to the provisions in its Article 75 such that "the balance sheets and income statements should be drawn up in the Turkish currency and in a clear, complete and easily understandable manner."

Since Turkish balance sheet jurisprudence has remained under the influence not of traditional auditing practice but of taxation law, however, even this inadequate provision could not be fully observed in practice. That inadequate provision also applies to partnerships with limited liability and partnerships limited by shares, the latter being quite rare. It must be pointed out, however, that no legal provisions existed, in particular for partnerships with limited liability, regarding accounting and the balance sheet, which are entirely dominated by taxation law.

Needless to say, the TCC, which has not included the disclosure principle even at the minimum scale, does not recognize the "true and fair view" doctrine. On the other hand, in academic texts, the necessity of adopting the disclosure principle as well as the true and fair view doctrine has been pointed out since the 1960s.

From 1987 onward, changes have started to take place with the communiqués. Both the CMB and the Ministry of Finance have issued regulations concerning financial reporting and accounting standards that are in compliance with the directives of the EU. These are Communiqué XI/1 and Communiqué No. 1 concerning implementation of the Unified Chart of Accounts.

2.2 Communiqué XI/1

Communiqué XI/1, which is in force at present, has, on the one hand, introduced detailed rules on the subject of financial statements, such as balance sheet principles, financial reporting, and disclosure and, on the other hand, provides specimens that should be used as a guide for such financial statements as balance sheet, profit and loss account, and cash flow table. Furthermore, the minimum data that should be included in the reports of the board of directors and of auditors have been indicated by the CMB.

Finally, a specimen "cost of sales table," to be drawn up by intermediary companies, and "profit distribution table" have been provided in the attachment to this Communiqué.

Although Communiqué XI/1 and Communiqué No.1 have reduced the differences between Turkish Legislation and International Accounting Standards, the differences arising from Turkish tax legislation persist.

2.2.1 *Basic Concepts of Accounting*

Section 1 of Communiqué No. XI/1 lays down certain basic concepts of accounting. Thirteen basic concepts are stated, some of which are valuation rules concerning:

- Going concern
- Consistency from year to year
- Prudence
- Accruals
- Separate valuation of the components of asset and liability items
- Correspondence of the opening balance sheet for one year with that of the closing balance sheet for the preceding year

In addition, Section 1 stipulated certain concepts such as the concepts of full disclosure, materiality principle, social responsibility, impartiality, substance over form, entity, and the kind of currency and measurement of cost.

Full Disclosure (Presentation and Disclosure) In the definition of the concept of full disclosure, it was stated that "the full disclosure concept means that the financial statements should be clear and comprehensible enough to enable the persons or institutions that will use such statements to reach decisions." Developments that may take place in the future, however, have been required to be included (Article 10), and the accuracy of financial statements has been laid down as a requirement (Article 47). Communiqué XI/1 embodies the true and fair view principle of the EC Fourth Directive in its Articles 4.4, 5, 10–14, and 47. It is certain, however, that Communiqué XI/1 does not regard that principle as an overriding rule, as expressed in Articles 2.4 and 2.5 of the Fourth Directive.

Materiality   Materiality concepts have been defined in Communiqué XI/1 in such a form as to be considered within the scope of the full disclosure principle. According to the definition, the relative significance of an accounting item or financial phenomenon must be at a level in which its value can influence the analysis to be made on the basis of the financial statements and the decision to be reached. It is a condition that significant items and financial phenomena and other points of importance should be included in the financial statements (Article 11).

Taking Article 47 into consideration on the accuracy of financial statements, we can say that the true and fair view principle has been expressed in this provision.

The accuracy of financial statements requires that:

1. While they are in accordance with the generally accepted accounting principles and the accounting standards published by the CMB, they also reflect any exceptional facts.

2. They have been prepared in accordance with the accounting policies chosen by the undertakings with the purpose of conforming to generally accepted accounting principles and to the standards published by the CMB.

3. Together with their footnotes and attachments, they are satisfactory, clear, understandable, and suitable for interpretation.

4. The significant developments are stated in sufficient detail and reflect important points and developments.

Social Responsibility   The principle of *social responsibility* relates to conforming to generally accepted accounting principles and standards of bookkeeping and acting within the framework of the aim of enlightening individuals and various institutions and of the objectives of disclosure in a consciousness of social responsibility. The basic responsibility of the managers of undertakings and of accounting departments is to prepare the relevant data in an accurate and correct form and to present them for the use of interested parties (Article 12).

The Principle of Impartiality   *Impartiality* means that the presentation of financial and accounting information and the financial statements should be of such content and in such a form that they may be of use to everyone. Such information and financial statements may not be prepared or offered in such a way as to allow only some people to use them to meet their requirements (Article 13.1).

The Principle of Substance over Form *Substance over form* means that substance, rather than the legal form, should be taken as the basis for reflecting operations on the accounting records and in their analyses. In case a difference arises between the form and the substance in the application of a principle or a rule, precedence should be given to the substance in principle (Article 14).

Communiqué XI/1 of the CMB has provided a legal basis that ensures widespread application of generally accepted accounting principles. Although it is assumed in some academic texts that the requirement laid down in Article 75 of the TCC that the balance sheets of undertakings should be drawn up according to "commercial principles" means that the generally accepted accounting principles have been adopted in Turkish jurisprudence under a legal provision, Communiqué XI/1 is much more explicit in this respect and assumes that the general accounting principles are the accounting standards contained in the directives issued by the CMB; or the principles that conform to accounting concepts generally used in the same business sector for undertakings of comparable size and that are generally approved in academic circles in connection with points that have not been regulated by CMB, or those adopted in international standards (Article 4.4).

At the end of this chapter are English and Turkish versions of specimen balance sheet, profit and loss account, funds flow, and cash flow tables to be prepared by companies covered by the regulations of the CMB, including intermediary firms. Communiqué XI/1 states that disclosure will be required not only in financial statements, but also in their footnotes and annexes (Article 46a).

2.2.2 Reporting of Material Events

The CMB issued the communiqué "Serial: Vlll, No: 20, Disclosure of material events" in 1993. This communiqué requires that events that may affect the value of capital market instruments or investment decisions be disclosed.

The communiqué has specially determined some material events to be disclosed:

1. Changes in control of the company
2. Acquisition or disposition or leasing of fixed assets
3. Changes in operations (starting a new operation or cessation of an existing one, disputes in court, etc.)

4. Changes in investments
5. Changes in the company's financial situation such as new issues or losing half of the net capital
6. Acquisition or disposition of subsidiaries, undertakings, joint ventures
7. Changes in management, such as the appointment or registration of managers, managerial disputes in court

The communiqué also requires the company's managers and shareholders who control more than 10% of the company's shares to disclose their trading of those shares within the first week of the following month. Extraordinary changes in value or volume of the stock and any rumor or publication about the company and its securities are recognized as material events to be disclosed.

The company and related parties should also disclose the material events that are not specifically mentioned in the communiqué but materially affect the value of the stock. Written disclosure should be sent to the CMB and to the related stock exchange in the case of its shares being traded on a stock exchange, to be disclosed by the CMB and stock exchange. Disclosure should be clear and understandable and not misleading. After it is sent to the CMB and the stock exchange, the information can then be sent to the press.

3. Accounting Policies and Practices in Valuation and Income Measurement: Implications for the Analyst

3.1 Group Accounts

Turkish jurisprudence does not contain provisions concerning group accounts either in the TCC, which includes company law, or in the legislation concerning taxation. Some groups of companies prepare consolidated balance sheets; such balance sheets, however, are not filed with any authority but are used for the self-evaluation of such groups. They are often used in connection with joint ventures and other collaborative efforts involving foreign companies, for the purpose of giving the prospective partner an idea of the financial situation of the group.

There is no uniform method for the consolidation of balance sheets that some groups draw up for their own purpose. The analysis of Price Waterhouse in this respect is as follows:

The acquisition or purchase method is the only method we have seen used in Turkey with goodwill in consolidation being capitalized and amortized over three to five years. Goodwill is generally only recognized in consolidation. While theoretically possible we have not seen either the merger or pooling method or the "Former German" method. However, in the acquisition or purchase method, if it is deemed that assets are overvalued, in consolidation they are revalued downward thus reducing or eliminating goodwill.

> Proportional consolidation whereby there is a line-by-line consolidation based on the actual ownership control percentage, thus eliminating the need to separately set up minority interest, rather than using 100 percent and then setting up minority interest, is not normally used. However, it can be used in a joint venture condition.
>
> Equity accounting is used when ownership is between 20 percent and 50 percent. Goodwill is not normally recognized by the investor. Of course if the investor group has goodwill which is being amortized this will lower the annual change in equity to be equitized.

Güven Coopers and Lybrand's analysis of major differences between Turkish law and IAS and generally recognized accounting principles is as follows: Consolidation or the equity method is not required or envisaged by either company law or the tax legislation. Thus, in accounting for business combinations, neither the acquisition (or purchase method) nor the merger (or pooling of interests method) is legally recognized. On the legal amalgamation or fusion of companies, the assets and liabilities of the liquidated company are transferred at balance sheet values, and shares are issued to the shareholders of the liquidated company. Otherwise the rules for liquidation apply.

These comments should, however, be understood in light of the CMB's Communiqué XI/10 related to the "Communiqué Concerning Principles and Rules Related to Preparation of Consolidated Financial Statements in the Capital Markets" issued in 1992. The main points of the Communiqué can be summarized as follows:

1. Communiqué XI/10 does not oblige groups to prepare consolidated financial statements. However, the groups that include any enter-

prise subject to the CML should prepare their consolidated financial statements according to the procedures detailed in the communiqué if they disclose any consolidated information to the public.

2. The reason for this regulation is the impossibility of obliging the parent companies that are not subject to CML. Thus, it satisfies the need for a true and fair view in any public disclosure by such a group of companies. In fact, the crux is related to the Commercial Law in general.

3. Parent company, subsidiary, and group concepts are defined basically by considering the facts of Turkish enterprises and groups, and the EEC's Seventh Directive [83/359, O.J. 1983, L 193/1], which deals with consolidated accounts so that the relationship between a parent company and a subsidiary is not obtained only by a majority of voting shares but also by the controlling management.

4. According to Communiqué XI/10, a group is: a community of parent company and its subsidiaries that, despite being legally independent of one another, are related in terms of capital, management, and control and that, regardless of their field of activity, are centrally coordinated under the control of the parent company in the areas of planning, organization, management, and finance.

5. To provide complete and comprehensive information about the group as a whole, the parent company will prepare consolidated accounts and financial statements that consolidate the other group companies into the parent company's financial statements.

6. There is no exception for the group companies to be included in the scope of consolidation, regardless of their location or activities.

7. Because in Turkish enterprises the parent company–subsidiary relationship forms during the establishment stage, and the acquisition of subsidiaries through takeovers in the secondary market is rarely seen, and because of the difficulties in calculating goodwill by going back to the acquisition date, in the Communiqué, goodwill has been calculated as in item No. 8.

8. If there is any share belonging to any group company within any group company's capital and share premiums (paid-in surplus), these shares and the related paid-in surplus and their cost value in the investor company's book should be netted off. In this procedure if the cost value is more, the difference is recognized as positive goodwill and shown as a deduction from reserves in the consolidated statements, but if the cost value is less, the difference is

recognized as negative goodwill and shown as an addition to reserves in the consolidated statements.

9. In the consolidated balance sheet, the paid-in capital account is the parent company's paid-in capital. None of the subsidiary's paid-in capital is included in the consolidated balance sheet. Only if the subsidiaries have shares of the parent company, would the paid-in capital of the consolidated balance sheet be less than the paid-in capital of the parent company.

10. If the group companies have capital liabilities (capital subscriptions due), the related capital receivables should be netted off.

11. The financial statements of the group companies that are not subject to the CML should be revised according to the accounting standards of the CMB (banks and insurance companies may be excepted from such a requirement).

12. Consolidated financial statements are the combination of all the financial statements of the enterprises in the group in which capital participations, receivables, payables, income, and expense accounts belonging to group companies are netted-off.

13. Shares of paid-in capital and profit and loss accounts that belong to minority shareholders should be shown separately.

14. When the companies forming the group (and thus subject to consolidation) have such varied activities that a consolidation would cause unreasonable results, group companies can be categorized in terms of their activities, such as production companies, service companies, financial companies, and trading companies.

15. To allow a true and fair view to the public, all additional and necessary information should be provided in the footnotes.

16. Disclosure of the consolidated financial statements and related information is not obligatory. Only when the groups disclose their consolidated financial statements should they prepare their financial statements, according to Communiqué XI/10. Companies subject to the CML should submit these statements to the CMB within 6 working days.

3.2 Foreign Currency Translation

There is no common practice in connection with the translation of financial statements of foreign subsidiaries and equity participations (associated companies) for consolidated or equity accounting. This is because the preparation of consolidated financial statements is not widespread, and so far, Turkish companies have not had a significant number of subsidiaries or equity participations in foreign countries. The practice in this respect has been limited to a small number of foreign branch offices of banks and subsidiaries of some construction companies and a few large holding companies. The fact that the draft of the communiqué of the CMB concerning consolidation has left the subsidiaries situated abroad outside the scope of consolidation has been a point of criticism.

The analysis of Price Waterhouse in this respect is as follows:

> Equity participations are normally translated using a variation of the closing rate-net investment method or the monetary-nonmonetary method.

Foreign subsidiaries in consolidation are normally dealt with by using either a variation of the temporal method, primarily fixed assets at historical rates and other items at closing rates, or translate all assets and liabilities at the closing rate.

In all cases that we have seen, both for equity participations and subsidiaries the translation difference is taken to the income statement.

Foreign currency denominated financial assets or liabilities are almost always converted at the closing rate. This would be different if an appropriate forward contract existed, but in Turkey they do not normally exist.

Again the translation gain or loss is reflected in the income statement.

3.3 Capital and Reserves

3.3.1 Capital

Turkish legislation regulating companies limited by shares (corporations) assumes two kinds of capital: capital fixed in advance and authorized capital.

Capital Fixed in Advance (Predetermined Capital or Basic Capital) Regulated by the TCC, capital fixed in advance is a kind of arrangement whereby the whole of the amount of capital is subscribed by the shareholders before the registration of the company's foundation or before its increase of capital, 25% of the capital being paid in by the shareholders. Thus, the remaining 75% becomes the liability of the subscribers. The significance of this arrangement from the standpoint of accounting jurisprudence is that it gives rise to three concepts: capital, called-up capital, and uncalled capital.

The TCC and the CML are in conflict with regard to the treatment of the uncalled portion of capital fixed in advance. The TCC requires that the capital fixed in advance should be entered in the liabilities side of the balance sheet at its nominal value, and the uncalled portion thereof should be shown on the assets side as a separate item (Article 463.1 and 2).

On the other hand, it is stated in Communiqué Series XI/1 of the CMB and in the balance sheet format attached to it that the total of the capital mentioned in a company's statutes should be included among the liabilities at its nominal value, with the uncalled portion shown as a deduction under the heading "capital subscriptions" and not in the assets as stated in the TCC.

Authorized Capital Authorized capital is regulated under the CML. Such a system of capital formation may be applied only by public companies. Such companies, however, also have the option to choose the system of capital fixed in advance. In the authorized capital system, the amount of issued capital is included in the capital and reserves section of the balance sheet, and the authorized capital is indicated as a footnote.

3.3.2 Reserves

Reserves in Turkish jurisprudence are regulated in detail by the provisions relating to companies limited by shares. These provisions are also applied to partnerships with limited liability (TCC 534) and partnerships limited by shares (TCC 476.2). There are no provisions in the legislation governing person-based companies or ordinary partnerships. Reserves are not regulated under any provisions of taxation law, however.

Reserves are defined in the Turkish law on companies limited by shares as the net worth of the possessions (net assets) exceeding capital. This definition also covers hidden reserves, because Turkish law, following the Swiss law on which it is modeled, has allowed the keeping of hidden reserves. Article 458 of the TCC explicitly allows companies to set aside hidden reserves, and Articles 460, 461, and 462.2 have allowed evaluation of fixed assets at any figure up to their initial price; that is, fixed assets must be carried in the balance sheet at no higher than their purchase price, less depreciation (TCC 460, 461, 462.2—the so-called *Hochstwertprinzip* in Swiss Law). Although an attempt was made with Communiqué Series XI/1 of the CMB to prevent companies limited by shares that come under the CML from setting aside hidden reserves, by requiring them to adopt the system of using a fixed historical price, owing to the provisions of Article 458 of the TCC, that attempt did not bear fruit. Because of both Article 458 of the TCC and the possibility of valuing assets at a level up to the extent of their historical value, the doctrine of true and fair view, which is present in Communiqué XI/1 of the CMB, has become a source of equivocation.

It needs to be pointed out that under the Fourth Directive, hidden reserves are not considered compatible with giving a true and fair view. The 1986 directive (No. 86/635/ECC) on the financial reporting of financial and credit institutions allows the use of hidden reserves only as a member state option pending further harmonization. This should not be interpreted as signifying that the use of hidden reserves is generally considered compatible with the financial statements giving a true and fair view in the European Union.

Under Turkish legislation, reserves may be examined from various standpoints of (a) whether it is mandatory to set them aside, (b) the purpose for which they are allocated, and (c) disclosure criteria.

Mandatory Reserves   According to the criterion of mandatory reserves, reserves are divided into two categories: legal and optional.

Legal reserves are those that are required by law to be set aside, and their use is regulated by law. Acting contrary to the rules laid down by law for this purpose would constitute a legal offense and might entail a liability on the part of the Board of Directors (TCC 336) or an annulment of the resolution concerned of the shareholders' meeting (TCC 381). The prequisite for declaring a dividend for shareholders, or adopting a resolution for payment of remuneration to Directors out of the annual profit, is that the statutory reserve should have been set aside first (TCC 472).

Statutory reserves consist of two groups: retained earnings (earned surplus) and capital surplus. It is obligatory to set aside one-twentieth of the net profit each year until these retained earnings add up to one-fifth of the capital (TCC 466.1). In Turkish practice, this is designated the "first allocation." The TCC calls this item in the balance sheet "general reserves" (TCC 466.1). Moreover, the TCC requires another allocation of reserves, called in practice the "second allocation." The second allocation is mandatory in the case of companies declaring a dividend for shareholders in excess of 5% of the annual profit, or even if a smaller dividend has been declared, in the event of remuneration being allocated to "other persons sharing the profit," such as directors, owners of founders' shares, company employees, or foundations. Otherwise, a second allocation would not be made (TCC 466.1.N.3). Unlike the first allocation, the second allocation of reserves has no limit. As long as conditions permit, the second allocation may be made no matter what amount has been reached.

Under Turkish law, capital surplus will come into being in either of two circumstances:

1. Shares may be issued at a price exceeding their par value, that is, at a premium. When there is such an issue, the part of the premium that is not allocated to capital redemption or to charity will be set aside as a statutory reserve (TCC 466.2.N.1).

2. The Board of Directors will apply a special procedure to the shareholder who fails to pay in the part of the capital he has subscribed to. Pursuant to Article 407.2 the Board may forfeit the title to shares and the partial payment of a defaulting shareholder and issue new shares in place of those that are forfeited. The partial payments will be kept by the company. The amount kept by the company and the proceeds of the subsequent sales will constitute reserves and, after losses that may have been realized on the replacement shares are deducted, must be placed in the general reserve fund.

Optional reserves will be set aside according to the provisions in the Statute or under a resolution adopted at a shareholders' meeting (TCC 467, 469.2). Reserves set aside under the resolution of shareholders are called "extraordinary reserves" in practice. The TCC has not set a limit to the reserves to be set aside under the company statute. The limit set down on the reserves to be set aside under shareholders' resolution is quite vague and its scope is wide. The company in general meeting may, before declaring a dividend, create reserve funds other than or exceeding those prescribed by law or articles if such a course seems to be desirable in order to ensure the continued prosperity of the company or the equalization of dividends (TCC Article 469.2).

The Purpose of Reserves   Reserves may be divided into two categories: (a) reserves whose purpose has not been specified and (b) those whose purpose has been specified. Reserves whose purpose has not been specified may be used for any legitimate purpose. If a purpose has not been specified, however, companies are bound by the purposes indicated in Article 469.2 of the TCC, mentioned above in connection with optional reserves. It is a widespread practice in Turkey to distribute optional reserves as dividends from time to time. It is doubtful, however, whether such a practice is motivated by any social considerations other than the aim of declaring stable dividends. The TCC does not contain an explanation of the objective for setting up dividends. The TCC does not contain an explanation of the objective for setting aside statutory reserves, but the objective for a part of the "general reserves" has been explained.

The law states that the funds in the general reserves may be used exclusively for making up for losses or for carrying on the company's operations in difficult times, taking measures for preventing unemployment or alleviating its consequences, as long as the general reserves do not exceed one-half of the company's capital (TCC 469.2).

There is freedom of choice in spending the general reserves exceeding the limit set down in the law and in spending the other statutory reserves. Many academics are of the opinion that it is permissible to distribute statutory reserves as dividends, benefiting from the above-mentioned freedom.

As far as a share premium (paid-in surplus) is concerned, however, there is no doubt that the law has indicated that it should be used only for redemption of capital (TCC 466.2.N.1).

For reserves whose purpose has been specified, the purpose to which reserves are to be allocated may be shown either in the statute or by the General Assembly. In such a case, the reserves can be spent only for the specified purpose. If they are to be spent for another purpose, the statute or the resolution of the shareholders in the general meeting must be amended. However, the resolution of the shareholders in this respect must not be contrary to the principle of good faith; otherwise it would be annulled (TCC 381).

The law has allowed the creation of mutual assistance funds and other similar organizations with the use of the reserves under statute or shareholders' decision and, thus, has emphasized its social character once more.

Disclosure Criterion According to the third criterion, reserves may be classified as (*a*) apparent (or disclosed) reserves and (*b*) hidden reserves.

The statutory and optional reserves make up the apparent reserves. Those reserves set aside by revaluing the assets at a value lower than their actual value at the balance sheet date, or by other means, make up the hidden reserves. According to the TCC, an undervaluation in the balance sheet of the assets of the company at the date of the balance sheet and the creation of other hidden reserves by the directors are permissible if this seems desirable for assuring the continued prosperity of the company or the equalization of dividends.

Other means of creating hidden reserves include high rates of depreciation allowance and provisions. It is not permissible to set aside hidden reserves by showing fictitious debts or by failing to show some assets in the balance sheet.

The administration must inform the auditor about the creation or an application of hidden reserves (TCC Article 458). The Board of Directors is responsible to the internal auditor regarding where the hidden reserves are spent (TCC 458.2).

3.4 Liabilities and Provisions

According to the definition in the TCC, provisions are "Probable losses whether from the execution of contracts involving delivery or acceptance on the part of the company or from similar current transactions, [which] shall be provided for in the balance sheet by reserves" (TCC 465).

It can be seen that provisions may not cover a general purpose. The TCC has indicated a narrow scope for the purpose of provisions, although it has not been restrictive. In other words, provisions may be set aside not in connection with all kinds of loss risks but only "for losses that may arise in future from obligations to deliver or take delivery or similar commitments in the future."

In order to be allowed to set aside a valid provision, the relation between its purpose and any "loss" should not be overlooked. Provisions may not be set aside for probable expenses.

Even though it is not explicitly indicated in Article 465.2 of the TCC, the provisions against losses in value of certain asset items of the balance sheet are of the same character. Likewise, provisions set aside for legal disputes, losses arising from transactions at exchanges for future deliveries, any guarantees supplied to customers, insurance risks, losses arising from foreign exchange and various penalties, as well as amounts set aside for renewal of fixed assets in franchised companies, for expenses that would be distributed among several years and for pensions or severance payments, are of the same character.

Provisions are of two categories: (a) those that are set aside from the annual profit, and (*b*) those that are set aside in a manner to decrease the profit during the year. Those mentioned in Article 465.2 of the TCC pertain, as a rule, to those set aside from the annual profit, because the term *reserve* has been used for them. That article can be regarded as covering the first category mentioned above only through a broad interpretation.

Provisions are the conventional means used for setting aside hidden reserves. When provisions are released, that is, when the foreseen risk does not materialize, they are converted into reserves. It would be more appropriate to use the term *reverting to their original character* in describing this process, because the law clearly indicates that provisions are "reserves" (TCC 465).

On the other hand, the Tax Procedure Law N.213 defines provisions very narrowly. According to this law, provisions are amounts set aside to cover losses or expenses that have occurred or that may occur in the future and that constitute a liability for the company whose exact amount is not definitely established (Article 288). A matter of controversy among academics and specialists interested in tax jurisprudence is whether an undertaking may set aside provisions at will and deduct them from income for tax purposes. The opinion of the majority is that the provisions set aside may be deducted from taxable income only in cases in which the tax laws clearly allow them to do so. Those cases, on the other hand, are highly limited in number. The fiscal offices and the State Council have permitted the deduction of provisions for severance pay of employees, in spite of arguments against this in academic texts. The CMB, on the other hand, regards such items as provisions.

3.5 Property, Plant, and Equipment

3.5.1 Historical Cost Basis

According to tax law, property, plant, and equipment are stated at historical cost (Tax Procedure Law, Article 269). As explained earlier, the TCC allows evaluation of property, plant, and equipment at any figure up to their historical price. Following the TCC,

Fixed assets used in conduct of the business, such as land, buildings, power installations and machines, means of transport, implements and furniture must not be valued in the balance sheet at a higher figure than their purchase or cost price and appropriate depreciation must be written off.

The same rule applies to rights, concessions, letters, patents, processes of manufacture, licenses, trademarks and similar actual assets (TCC 460).

Historical cost is defined in a manner similar to GAAP, except that companies are free to either capitalize or to treat the financing costs related to capital expenditures as an expense, even after the related assets are placed in use.

In accordance with a change in the tax legislation dated and enacted in 1983 (Law No. 2791), revaluation of fixed assets, particularly of property, plant, and equipment, is permitted. Revaluation of land is not permitted. Property, plant, and equipment held throughout the year and the related accumulated depreciation are devalued in accordance with the regulations of the Ministry of Finance and Customs at a rate specified each year that is in line with the official inflation rate. The rates used for revaluation purposes have generally been lower than the rates of inflation.

The increase in the net book value of the said assets is permitted to be added to shareholders' equity, giving companies the option of issuing capital shares, which are called "gratis shares," for the amount of the revaluation (Tax Procedure Law Article 298). In the case of revaluation of the fixed assets a portion of financing expenses is not tax-deductible.

3.5.2 Depreciation of Fixed Assets

Depreciation of fixed assets is controlled by the Ministry of Finance. Standardized rates are published by this Ministry, but the tax authorities have the power to accept higher rates if they can be justified in special circumstances. Both normal and accelerated depreciation methods are accepted and used. The taxpayer may choose either the straight-line or the declining balance method. Since January 1, 1995, taxpayers using the straight-line method have been able to apply any rate of depreciation up to 20%. Some of the depreciation methods are not in conformity with the IAS, for instance, a full year's depreciation must be allowed in the year of acquisition to avoid any loss of depreciation for tax purposes in future periods; and a 5-year depreciation period is allowed for plant and equipment.

Buildings are depreciated at rates between 2% and 6% per year. Other tangible and intangible assets, except land, are depreciated principally over 4 years by using either the straight-line or the double declining-balance method. A change from straight-line depreciation to the declining-balance method is not permitted, but the opposite change is possible.

3.5.3 Government Grants

Cash grants can be deducted from the asset base, thereby reducing the depreciable base, or the base distributed to shareholders. This is not in conformity with the IAS rules.

Such distributions take place in fact simply because during the investment years it is likely that new investments face operating losses, in which case such government grants can be passed on to individual shareholders with absolutely no tax effect, and such funds can be reinvested by means of capital increase, thereby keeping the asset base of depreciable assets the same, although the cash grant has been granted, thereby not reducing the depreciable base.

3.5.4 Interest Charges

Interest charges are capitalized during the years of investment. However, whenever the investment period is completed and operations start, even though the loan is long term, the interest charges associated with the operating years can either be treated as expense or capitalized. Interest capitalized during the investment period appears in the income statement by means of depreciation of the assets concerned. According to the tax legislation, care must be taken that interest on those loans associated with specific assets is included or capitalized with those assets.

3.5.5 Real Estate Development

Turkish law does not contain any provisions concerning real estate development in the TCC, in the legislation concerning taxation, or in the capital market regulations.

3.6 Leases

Turkey has a special body of regulation on leases (Law on Financial Rentals of June 1985). Almost without exception, financial leases are considered off-balance-sheet borrowing, and that is the way they are reported. However, audited statements may recognize such leases as financial obligations within the balance sheet. Finance lease contracts provide a purchase option, and there is a fixed minimum lease term. Operating lease contracts are treated as normal rent and do not fall under the body of legislation governing leases. No distinctions exist as to legal and economic ownership for leasing operations, and the lessor remains the owner of the leased assets for legal and tax purposes.

Therefore, there is no distinction of lease contracts between finance and operating lease for tax purposes, and the accounting treatment follows the tax treatment; the lessor must capitalize the asset and bears the depreciation; the installments paid by the lessee are expenses to the profit and loss account.

3.7 Oil, Gas, and Other Mineral Resources

There is no specific reference to the full cost or the successful efforts methods, or their acceptability, exclusively for oil and gas activities. Instead, accounting practices permitted for tax purposes apply (i.e., income tax method).

3.8 Intangible Assets

The Turkish Commercial Code has allowed valuation of legally protected intellectual property rights, such as patents, copyrights, trade names, brand names, and know-how at any figure up to the historical cost (TCC Article 460.2) (see Section 3.5).

According to tax legislation, legally protected intangible assets are stated at cost, to be amortized over their useful lives. If their useful lives cannot be identified clearly, such assets are amortized over 5 years.

Capitalization of establishment or formation costs is optional; nonpatented patents, know-how reflected in the development costs of products or computer software, and brand names are not recognized as assets.

3.9 Participating Interests

Long-term investments are stated at cost plus reserves distributed by way of bonus shares. No consolidation or equity accounting is performed for equity participations.

In practice, provisions of most sorts, and in particular provisions to reduce securities to net realizable value, are not usually made since Turkey is an inflationary country. Securities are almost always valued at cost. For both fixed assets and securities, interest charges and losses on foreign exchange liabilities are often included in the determination of cost. This can occur even after assets come into use.

3.10 Inventories

The most frequently used valuation methods for inventories are average cost and FIFO. The LIFO method can be used only if and when the company's records prove that last purchases have been used or sold first.

Write-downs for tax purposes only should be ignored. Of course, proper accounting valuation write-downs should be made, including provisions for obsolescence and damaged goods.

Normally there are no departures from historical cost, except as above. Sometimes the latest invoice method is used, but this should not be accepted.

Appropriate production and related administrative overheads are included in inventory cost.

Because of the inflationary environment and frequent renegotiations that take place in Turkey, for contract work-in-process most companies we have seen use the completed contract method; the percentage of completion method would be desirable.

3.11 Taxation

The most important taxes are as follows:

1. Taxes on income
   — Corporation (income) tax
   — Personal income tax (includes withholding on payments abroad)
2. Taxes on wealth
   — Inheritance and gift taxes
   — Motor vehicle tax
   — Property tax

3. Taxes on expenditure
   — Value added tax (VAT)
   — Banking and insurance transactions taxes
   — Stamp duty taxes
   — Municipality taxes
4. Transfer taxes
   — Deed registry tax
   — Vehicle purchase tax

The principal taxes are corporation tax, income tax, VAT, and customs duties; the other taxes are all minor, both from the point of view of the revenue raised and from that of their effect on business transactions. No income taxes are imposed by provincial municipal authorities.

Corporation Tax   The taxation of corporations has been changed with a new law effective January 1, 1994. This new law introduces taxation of corporations in two stages. In the first stage corporate income is subject to corporation tax. In the second stage the distributable profit, *regardless of whether it is distributed*, is subjected to income-withholding-tax.

The corporate earnings listed below are fully exempt from tax, that is, they are neither subject to the first stage corporation nor the second stage income tax:

1. Dividends received from resident full liability taxpayer corporations

2. Premium obtained from the sale of share certificates by the issuing company above the face value (emission premium)

3. Profits earned from putting the production facilities and the related real estate as capital in kind in a new company established to invest under an investment incentive certificate and added to the paid-in capital of the company in the year the profit is realized

4. Dividends received from
   — Investment funds (excluding foreign currency investment funds) with portfolios holding a minimum of 25% of the total portfolio in stocks
   — Dividends received from venture (risk) capital investment funds
   — Dividends received from real estate investment funds

The components of corporate earnings listed below are exempt from the corporation tax (first stage taxation) but are subject to withholding tax at the rates indicated (second stage taxation)

1. Profits earned from the sale of participation shares and real estate and added to the share capital in the same year: 10%
2. Profits earned from the sale of pre-emptive rights: 10%.

An investment allowance (see below) is deductible for Stage 1 purposes but not for Stage 2.

Stage 1: The first tax to be paid is a corporate tax, the rate of which is 25%. There exists an additional fund levy to be paid on the calculated corporate tax at the rate of 10%. Exemptions, including investment allowance, tourism revenue, and dividend from Mutual Funds and Investment Companies, are permitted for social and economic purposes. The corporate tax cannot be less than 20% of the corporate income before the deduction of exceptions, which is called the minimum corporate tax. However, investment allowance is also exempt from the 20% corporate tax. Prior year losses may be deduced or carried forward for a maximum of 5 years.

In addition to the investment allowance, the deductions and exemptions listed below are subject neither to 25% nor to 20% corporate tax.

1. Dividends received from resident full liability taxpayer corporations
2. Financing fund provision
3. Profits earned from the sale of pre-emptive rights and premium obtained from the sale of share certificates by the issuing company above the face value (emission premium)
4. Profits earned from the sale of equity participations and immovables as well as from contributing the production facilities and the related real estates as capital in kind in a new company established to invest under an investment incentive certificate and added to the paid-in capital of the company in the year the profit is realized.

Phase II (Income-withholding-tax): In the second stage the corporate income less deductions (including previous years' losses carried forward and the corporation tax computed) is regarded as distributable profit and subjected to withholding tax. The basic rate of withholding tax is 20%

(plus 10% fund surcharge). For public companies (i.e. corporations that have offered a minimum of 15% of their capital to the public and registered with the Capital Market Board), it is charged at 10% (plus 10% fund surcharge). Although the basic rate is 20%, some components of the corporate income are charged at lower rates, and interest from government bonds and treasury bills is exempt.

Total tax burden on corporate income: Disregarding the exemption and profits subject to withholding tax at rates other than 20%, total tax on corporate income is 44% for nonpublic companies and 35.75% for public companies as shown below.

	Public Co.	Nonpublic	
1	1.000.0	1.000.0	Corporate income
2	(250.0)	(250.0)	Corporation tax (1.000x25%)
3	(25.0)	(25.0)	Fund surcharge (10% of line 2)
4	750.0	750.0	Corporate income subject to withholding tax (1000-250)
5	(75.0)	(150.0)	Withholding tax (750 x 10% for public; 750x20% for nonpublic)
6	(7.5)	(15.0)	Fund surcharge (10% of line 5)
7	357.5	440.0	Total tax payable (Lines 2+3+5+6)
8	642.5	560.0	Net corporate income after tax (Line 1–7)
9	35.75%	44%	Total tax burden (Line 7/Line 1)

However second stage corporation tax (income-withholding-tax) is regarded as dividend tax in respect of double taxation treaties signed by Turkey.

Income Determination For corporate tax purposes, a corporation's income is calculated in accordance with the provisions of personal income tax.

Both limited and fully taxpayer (unlimited) companies are entitled to revalue their fixed assets, excluding land sites and other intangible assets (e.g., royalties and founding expenditures) in accordance with the index published annually by the Ministry of Finance.

According to tax laws, inventories must be valued at their actual cost. If the cost cannot be determined on an individual basis, then a moving-average determination is acceptable. The LIFO method can also be used. However, taxpayers are obliged to apply LIFO for at least 5 years. If LIFO is used, a percentage of financing expenses is not tax deductible for tax purposes.

Certain expenses, including formation expenses, expenses of issuing shares, and the start-up costs of business operations, are deductible. Hidden distributions of profits are not deductible. Furthermore, if the company revalues its fixed assets or values its stock according to the LIFO method, a certain percentage (15%–20%) of financial expenses are not deductible. However, manufacturing companies are not within the scope of this limitation.

Investment Allowance   The investment allowance is defined in the income tax law. The purpose of this incentive is to encourage investment generally; thus, it can be deducted from taxable income. Investment incentive allowances are granted to companies and individuals at rates between 20% and 100% of the cost of specified assets, which are listed in a "General Encouragement Table" published annually in the Official Gazette.

Special Provisions   There is no special provision for capital gains. Gains resulting from sales of fixed assets subject to depreciation are taxed at the normal rate, and gains are not taxable when proceeds are reinvested in new fixed assets.

Value Added Tax   A Value Added Tax (VAT) was introduced in Turkey on October 25, 1984, effective from 1985. VAT Law No. 3065 adopted an EC-type VAT. All commercial, industrial, agricultural, and professional activities are included in the scope of this tax.

The VAT is levied at rates varying from 1% to 40%, with a basic rate of 15%. The rates are as follows:

- Leasing, 1%
- Basic food, 8%
- Natural gas, 8%
- Luxury goods, 23% (Mainly fur, jewelry, perfumes, cosmetics, household equipment, appliance, cars, and pleasure boats)
- Luxury cars, 40%

Banking and the activities of insurance companies are exempt from VAT.

3.11.3 The Taxation of Individuals

All individuals resident in Turkey are liable for personal income tax on their worldwide income, according to the personal Income Tax Law dated December 31, 1960, No.193.

3.12 Pensions

Employee pension schemes involving defined contribution or benefit plans are uncommon in Turkey. Under the Turkish Social Security Law, all employees (except agricultural workers, the self-employed, civil servants, and employees of some large banks) are covered by the social security system, which, as well as other benefits, includes a retirement pension. In accordance with existing labor law, companies are required to make lump sum payments to employees whose employment is terminated because of retirement or for reasons other than resignation or misconduct. However, the lump sum payments cannot be expensed until paid.

4. Expected Future Developments

We can predict that the adoption of international accounting standards and the development of financial reporting in Turkey will be multifaceted and comprehensive and will accelerate in the coming years. These developments will underline the importance of the "true and fair view" and the disclosure principles, leading to standards of higher quality from both a scientific and a result-oriented approach. Moreover, they will extend to all companies limited by shares and not only those under the ambit of the CML. It is unlikely that new arrangements in this respect will cover partnerships limited by shares, and partnerships with limited liability, which are not common in Turkey (unlike Germany and France). The existence of government bills for amendment of both CML and TTC, and the fact that the bill for amending CML is now in the last phase before enactment, are all indications verifying the above expectations. Another significant indication is the ever widening incidence of auditing.

Another important development is that an authority (agency) will be created to impose accounting standards when the CML is amended.

Turkey has great hopes invested in the implementation of Act 3568. In order for these hopes to be realized, however, the construction and practice of this act must be free of the "all is for taxes" mentality.

Appendix A

Additional Communiqués of the Capital Market Board on Auditing Standards and Financial Reporting

XI/2: Principles of the Chart of Account and Principles for the Application of this Plan (O.J. No. 20064, November 29, 1989)

XI/3: Communiqué on the Principles and Rules Related to Intermediate Financial Statements (O.J. No. 20233, July 26, 1989)

XI/4: Communiqué Concerning the Amendment of Some Articles of Communiqué Concerning the Principles and Rules Related to Financial Statements and Reports in the Capital Market (O.J. No. 20387, December 29, 1989)

XI/6: Communiqué Concerning the Principles and Rules Related to the Financial Statements and Reports of Investment Funds (O.J. No. 20447, February 28, 1990)

XI/7: Communiqué Concerning Principles of the Chart of Accounts Related to Intermediary Institutions (O.J. No. 21128, January 31, 1992)

XI/10: Communiqué Concerning Principles and Rules Related to the Preparation of Consolidated Financial Statements in the Capital Market (O.J. No. 21185, March 28, 1992)

XI/11: Communiqué Concerning a General Explanation on the Determination of the Requiremenets of Preparing Financial Statements and Reports, the Public Disclosing thereof, and the Auditing of Companies and Establishments Subject to the Capital Market Law (O.J. No. 21146, February 18, 1992).

Appendix B: Financial Statements

Mali Sonuçlar (Milyon TL)

	1993	1994	1995	1996	1997
Net Satışlar	2.677.002	5.443.179	12.782.931	24.571.051	46.065.876
Cari Aktifler	1.103.708	3.433.245	7.773.737	15.436.487	27.198.972
Sabit Kıymetler	2.167.641	4.271.964	7.850.192	13.827.681	30.017.791
Amortismanlar	1.081.811	1.933.782	3.674.975	6.718.604	14.264.821
Toplam Aktifler	2.275.897	5.779.636	11.962.331	23.283.028	43.702.227
Öz Varlıklar	1.255.086	3.506.661	7.761.501	16.217.696	29.567.151

Toplam Aktifler
(Milyar TL)

Net Satışlar
(Milyar TL)

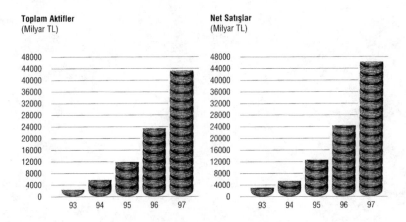

Öz Varlıklar
(Milyar TL)

Sabit Kıymetler
(Milyar TL)

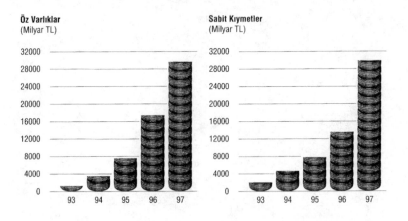

Financial Results (Million TL)

	1993	1994	1995	1996	1997
Net Sales	2,677,002	5,443,179	12,782,931	24,571,051	46,065,876
Current Assets	1,103,708	3,433,245	7,773,737	15,436,487	27,198,972
Fixed Assets	2,167,641	4,271,964	7,850,192	13,827,681	30,017,791
Depreciation	1,081,811	1,933,782	3,674,975	6,718,604	14,264,821
Total Assets	2,275,897	5,779,636	11,962,331	23,283,028	43,702,227
Net Worth	1,255,086	3,506,661	7,761,501	16,217,696	29,567,151

Total Assets
(Billion TL)

Net Sales
(Billion TL)

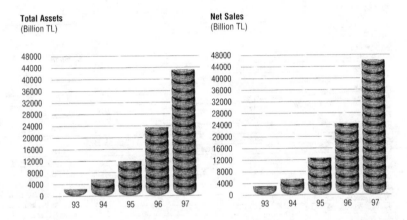

Net Worth
(Billion TL)

Fixed Assets
(Billion TL)

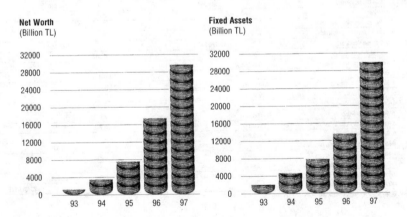

C- FİNANSAL YAPIYA İLİŞKİN BİLGİLER

Brisa Bridgestone Sabancı Lastik Sanayi ve Ticaret A.Ş.
31 Aralık 1997 Tarihli Ayrıntılı Bilanço (MİLYON TL)

AKTİF (VARLIKLAR)

	Cari dönem 31.12.1997		Önceki dönem 31.12.1996	
I. DÖNEN VARLIKLAR		27.198.972		15.436.487
A. Hazır değerler		4.574.267		4.308.613
1. Kasa	645		182	
2. Bankalar	4.573.622		4.308.431	
B. Menkul Kıymetler		2.463.009		1.599.083
1. Kamu Kesimi Tahvil Senedi ve Bonoları	2.463.009		1.541.619	
2. Diğer Menkul Kıymetler	0		57.464	
C. Kısa Vadeli Ticari Alacaklar		10.141.423		5.147.441
1. Alıcılar	4.796.100		1.942.683	
2. Alacak Senetleri	5.480.105		2.919.966	
3. Verilen Depozito ve Teminatlar	8.805		85	
4. Diğer Kısa Vadeli Alacaklar	202.014		424.432	
5. Alacak Reeskontu (-)	(323.633)		(119.127)	
6. Şüpheli Alacaklar Karşılığı (-)	(21.968)		(20.598)	
D. Diğer Kısa Vadeli Alacaklar		172.444		616.075
1. Kısa Vadeli Diğer Alacaklar	172.444		616.075	
E. Stoklar		6.813.809		3.678.539
1. İlk Madde ve Malzeme	3.091.057		1.514.970	
2. Yarı Mamuller	444.922		317.454	
3. Mamuller	2.293.214		1.509.522	
4. Emtia	460.225		165.474	
5. Diğer Stoklar	0		0	
6. Verilen Sipariş Avansları	524.391		171.119	
F. Diğer Dönen Varlıklar		3.034.020		86.736
II. DURAN VARLIKLAR		16.503.255		7.846.541
A. Uzun Vadeli Ticari Alacaklar		18.792		13.351
1. Alıcılar	6		6	
2. Alacak Senetleri	19.240		10.550	
3. Verilen Depozito ve Teminat	302		231	
4. Uzun Vadeli Diğer Alacaklar	11.077		8.037	
5. Alacak Senetleri Reeskontu (-)	(11.833)		(5.473)	
B. Finansal Duran Varlıklar		702.050		702.050
1. İştirakler	702.050		702.050	
2. İştiraklere Sermaye Taahhütleri	0		0	
3. Diğer Finansal Duran Varlıklar	0		0	
C. Maddi Duran Varlıklar		15.720.243		7.083.442
1. Arazi ve Arsalar	26.455		1.343	
2. Yerüstü ve Yeraltı Düzenleri	334.298		193.132	
3. Binalar	5.235.016		2.844.418	
4. Makine, Tesis ve Cihazlar	20.457.857		10.149.397	
5. Taşıt Araç ve Gereçleri	258.143		163.130	
6. Döşeme ve Demirbaşlar	259.319		114.608	
7. Birikmiş Amortismanlar (-)	(14.264.821)		(6.718.604)	
8. Yapılmakta Olan Yatırımlar	1.968.332		55.745	
9. Verilen Sipariş Avansları	1.445.644		280.273	
D. Maddi Olmayan Duran Varlıklar		32.727		25.635
1. Haklar	6.956		7.213	
2. Diğer Maddi Olmayan Duran Varlıklar	25.771		18.422	
E. Diğer Duran Varlıklar		29.443		22.063
AKTİF (VARLIKLAR) TOPLAMI		43.702.227		23.283.028

Ekteki dipnotlar bu mali tabloların ayrılmaz bir parçasıdır.

C- FINANCIAL REVIEW

Brisa Bridgestone Sabancı Lastik Sanayi ve Ticaret A.Ş.
Balance Sheet as of December 31, 1997 and 1996 (Million TL)

ASSETS

		Current Period Dec 31, 1997		Previous Period Dec 31, 1996	
I.	CURRENT ASSETS		27,198,972		15,436,487
A.	Liquid Assets		4,574,267		4,308,613
	1. Cash on Hand	645		182	
	2. Cash in Banks	4,573,622		4,308,431	
B.	Marketable Securities		2,463,009		1,599,083
	1. Government Debentures, Notes and Bonds	2,463,009		1,541,619	
	2. Other Marketable Securities	0		57,464	
C.	Short-term Commercial Receivables		10,141,423		5,147,441
	1. Customers	4,796,100		1,942,683	
	2. Notes Receivable	5,480,105		2,919,966	
	3. Deposits and Guarantees Given	8,805		85	
	4. Other Short-term Receivables	202,014		424,432	
	5. Discount on Notes Receivable (-)	(323,633)		(119,127)	
	6. Provision for Doubtful Receivables (-)	(21,968)		(20,598)	
D.	Other Short-term Receivables		172,444		616,075
	1. Short-term Other Receivables	172,444		616,075	
E.	Inventories		6,813,809		3,678,539
	1. Raw Materials	3,091,057		1,514,970	
	2. Semi-Finished Products	444,922		317,454	
	3. Finished Products	2,293,214		1,509,522	
	4. Goods for Resale	460,225		165,474	
	5. Other Inventories	0		0	
	6. Advances on Purchase Orders	524,391		171,119	
F.	Other Current Assets		3,034,020		86,736
II.	FIXED ASSETS		16,503,255		7,846,541
A.	Long-term Commercial Receivables		18,792		13,351
	1. Customers	6		6	
	2. Notes Receivable	19,240		10,550	
	3. Deposits and Guarantees Given	302		231	
	4. Other Long-term Receivable	11,077		8,037	
	5. Discount on Notes Receivable (-)	(11,833)		(5,473)	
B.	Long-term Financial Investments		702,050		702,050
	1. Equity Investments in Affiliates	702,050		702,050	
	2. Capital Commitments to Affiliates	0		0	
	3. Other Financial Fixed Assets	0		0	
C.	Tangible Fixed Assets		15,720,243		7,083,442
	1. Land	26,455		1,343	
	2. Infrastructure	334,298		193,132	
	3. Buildings	5,235,016		2,844,418	
	4. Plant, Machinery and Equipment	20,457,857		10,149,397	
	5. Vehicles	258,143		163,130	
	6. Furniture and Fixtures	259,319		114,608	
	7. Accumulated Depreciation (-)	(14,264,821)		(6,718,604)	
	8. Investments in Progress	1,968,332		55,745	
	9. Advances on Purchase Orders	1,445,644		280,273	
D.	Intangible Fixed Assets		32,727		25,635
	1. Rights	6,956		7,213	
	2. Other Intangible Fixed Assets	25,771		18,422	
E.	Other Fixed Assets		29,443		22,063
	TOTAL ASSETS		43,702,227		23,283,028

PASİF (KAYNAKLAR)

		Cari dönem 31.12.1997		Önceki dönem 31.12.1996	
I.	**KISA VADELİ BORÇLAR**		**12.413.550**		**6.184.188**
A.	**Finansal Borçlar**		783.341		10.557
	1. Banka Kredileri	780.000		0	
	2. Uzun Vadeli Kredi C. Yıl Taksit ve Faizleri	3.341		10.557	
	3. Tahvil Anapara Taksitleri ve Faizleri	0		0	
	4. Diğer Finansal Borçlar	0		0	
B.	**Ticari Borçlar**		2.532.239		1.599.461
	1. Satıcılar	2.441.603		1.178.399	
	2. Borç Senetleri	0		200.000	
	3. Alınan Depozito ve Teminatlar	90.636		37.584	
	4. Diğer Ticari Borçlar	0		200.197	
	5. Borç Reeskontu (-)	0		(16.719)	
C.	**Diğer Kısa Vadeli Borçlar**		2.670.510		1.072.115
	1. Ortaklara Borçlar	6.208		2.226	
	2. Ödenecek Giderler	53.155		29.960	
	3. Ödenecek Vergi, Harç ve Diğer Kesintiler	723.273		250.431	
	4. Kısa Vadeli Diğer Borçlar	1.887.874		789.498	
D.	**Alınan Sipariş Avansları**		134.100		128.057
E.	**Borç ve Gider Karşılıkları**		6.293.360		3.373.998
	1. Vergi Karşılıkları	5.798.045		3.371.694	
	2. Diğer Borç ve Gider Karşılıkları	495.315		2.304	
II.	**UZUN VADELİ BORÇLAR**		1.721.526		881.144
A.	**Finansal Borçlar**		0		3.341
	1. Banka Kredileri	0		3.341	
B.	**Borç ve Gider Karşılıkları**		1.721.526		877.803
	1. Kıdem Tazminatı Karşılıkları	1.721.526		877.803	
III.	**ÖZ SERMAYE**		29.567.151		16.217.696
A.	**Sermaye**		7.441.875		1.063.125
B.	**Sermaye Taahhütleri (-)**		0		0
C.	**Emisyon Primi**		4.903		4.903
D.	**Yeniden Değerleme Değer Artışı**		5.719.050		6.680.618
	1. Duran Varlıklardaki Değer Artışı	5.719.050		6.680.618	
	2. İştiraklerdeki Değer Artışı	0		0	
E.	**Yedekler**		4.491.096		1.639.370
	1. Yasal Yedekler	865.013		426.857	
	2. Özel Yedekler	0		0	
	3. Olağanüstü Yedekler	3.564.109		1.169.149	
	4. Maliyet Artış Fonu	61.974		43.364	
F.	**Dönem Kârı (Net)**		11.910.227		6.829.680

PASİF (KAYNAKLAR) TOPLAMI			**43.702.227**		**23.283.028**

LIABILITIES

		Current Period Dec 31, 1997		Previous Period Dec 31, 1996	
I.	SHORT-TERM LIABILITIES		12,413,550		6,184,188
A.	Financial Liabilities		783,341		10,557
	1. Bank Credits	780,000		0	
	2. Current Payments and Interest Due on Long-term Loans	3,341		10,557	
	3. Payments and Interest Due on Bonds	0		0	
	4. Other Financial Payables	0		0	
B.	Commercial Payables		2,532,239		1,599,461
	1. Suppliers	2,441,603		1,178,399	
	2. Notes Payable	0		200,000	
	3. Deposits and Guarantees Received	90,636		37,584	
	4. Other Commercial Payables	0		200,197	
	5. Discount on Notes Payable (-)	0		(16,719)	
C.	Other Short-term Payables		2,670,510		1,072,115
	1. Payables to Shareholders	6,208		2,226	
	2. Accrued Expenditures	53,155		29,960	
	3. Tax and Levies Payable	723,273		250,431	
	4. Short-term Other Payables	1,887,874		789,498	
D.	Advances on Orders Received		134,100		128,057
E.	Provisions		6,293,360		3,373,998
	1. Tax Provisions	5,798,045		3,371,694	
	2. Provisions for Other Debts and Expenses	495,315		2,304	
II.	LONG-TERM LIABILITIES		1,721,526		881,144
A.	Financial Liabilities		0		3,341
	1. Bank Credits	0		3,341	
B.	Provision For Debts and Expenses		1,721,526		877,803
	1. Provision for Retirement and Severence Pay	1,721,526		877,803	
III.	EQUITY		29,567,151		16,217,696
A.	Capital		7,441,875		1,063,125
B.	Capital Commitments (-)		0		0
C.	Share Premium		4,903		4,903
D.	Revaluation Fund		5,719,050		6,680,618
	1. Revaluation of Fixed Assets	5,719,050		6,680,618	
	2. Revaluation of Equity Investments	0		0	
E.	Reserves		4,491,096		1,639,370
	1. Legal Reserves	865,013		426,857	
	2. Special Reserves	0		0	
	3. Extraordinary Reserves	3,564,109		1,169,149	
	4. Cost Increase Fund	61,974		43,364	
F.	Net Profit For The Year		11,910,227		6,829,680
	TOTAL LIABILITIES AND EQUITY		43,702,227		23,283,028

Brisa Bridgestone Sabancı Lastik Sanayi ve Ticaret A.Ş.
31 Aralık 1997 Tarihli Ayrıntılı Gelir Tablosu (MİLYON TL)

		Cari dönem 31.12.1997		Önceki dönem 31.12.1996
A.	Brüt Satışlar		52.933.997	27.210.806
	1. Yurtiçi Satışlar	43.453.061		21.253.912
	2. Yurtdışı Satışlar	9.480.936		5.956.894
	3. Diğer Satışlar			
B.	Satışlardan İndirimler (-)		(6.868.121)	(2.639.755)
	1. Satıştan İadeler (-)	(139.326)		(61.674)
	2. Satış İskontoları (-)	(6.118.433)		(2.295.556)
	3. Diğer İndirimler (-)	(610.362)		(282.525)
C.	Net Satışlar		46.065.876	24.571.051
D.	Satışların Maliyeti		(24.370.947)	(13.436.487)
	BRÜT SATIŞ KÂRI		21.694.929	11.134.564
E.	Faaliyet Giderleri (-)		(5.935.979)	(2.537.440)
	1. Araştırma ve Geliştirme Giderleri (-)	(496.180)		0
	2. Pazarlama, Satış ve Dağıtım Giderleri (-)	(3.411.090)		(1.573.999)
	3. Genel Yönetim Giderleri (-)	(2.028.709)		(963.441)
	ESAS FAALİYET KÂRI		15.758.950	8.597.124
F.	Diğer Faaliyetlerden Gelirler ve Kârlar		4.222.399	2.444.702
	1. Faiz ve Diğer Temettü Gelirleri	1.201.937		379.514
	2. Faaliyetle ilgili Diğer Gelirler ve Kârlar	3.020.462		2.065.188
G.	Diğer Faaliyetlerden Giderler ve Zararlar (-)		(946.023)	(581.152)
H.	Finansman Giderleri (-)		(421.918)	(33.997)
	1. Kısa Vadeli Borçlanma Giderleri (-)	(418.856)		(20.593)
	2. Uzun Vadeli Borçlanma Giderleri (-)	(3.062)		(13.404)
	FAALİYET KÂRI		18.613.408	10.426.677
I.	Olağanüstü Gelirler ve Kârlar		169.988	629.751
	1. Önceki Dönem Gelir ve Kârları	94.306		526.215
	2. Diğer Olağanüstü Gelirler ve Kârlar	75.682		103.536
J.	Olağanüstü Giderler ve Zararlar (-)		(1.075.124)	(310.418)
	1. Çalışılmayan Dönem Giderleri ve Zararları (-)	(944.452)		43.569
	2. Önceki Dönem Gider ve Zararları (-)	(76.420)		215.026
	3. Diğer Olağanüstü Giderler ve Zararlar (-)	(54.252)		51.823
	DÖNEM KÂRI		17.708.272	10.746.010
K.	Ödenecek Vergi ve Diğer Yasal Yükümlülükler (-)		(5.798.045)	(3.916.330)
	NET DÖNEM KÂRI		11.910.227	6.829.680

Ekteki dipnotlar bu mali tabloların ayrılmaz bir parçasıdır.

Brisa Bridgestone Sabancı Lastik Sanayi ve Ticaret A.Ş.
Income Statement for the Year Ending December 31, **1997** (Million TL)

		Current Period Dec 31, 1997		Previous Period Dec 31, 1996
A.	**Gross Sales**	**52,933,997**		**27,210,806**
	1. Domestic Sales	43,453,061	21,253,912	
	2. Export Sales	9,480,936	5,956,894	
	3. Other Sales			
B.	**Reductions to Sales (-)**	**(6,868,121)**		**(2,639,755)**
	1. Sales Returns (-)	(139,326)	(61,674)	
	2. Sales Discounts (-)	(6,118,433)	(2,295,556)	
	3. Other Reductions (-)	(610,362)	(282,525)	
C.	**Net Sales**	**46,065,876**		**24,571,051**
D.	**Cost of Sales (-)**	**(24,370,947)**		**(13,436,487)**
	GROSS SALES PROFIT	**21,694,929**		**11,134,564**
E.	**Operational Expenses (-)**	**(5,935,979)**		**(2,537,440)**
	1. Research and Development Expenses (-)	(496,180)	0	
	2. Marketing, Sales and Distribution Expenses (-)	(3,411,090)	(1,573,999)	
	3. General Administrative Expenses (-)	(2,028,709)	(963,441)	
	ACTUAL OPERATIONAL PROFIT	**15,758,950**		**8,597,124**
F.	**Income and Profit From Other Activities**	**4,222,399**		**2,444,702**
	1. Interest and Other Dividend Income	1,201,937	379,514	
	2. Other Income and Profit Related to Activities	3,020,462	2,065,188	
G.	**Expenses and Losses From Other Activities (-)**	**(946,023)**		**(581,152)**
H.	**Financing Expenses (-)**	**(421,918)**		**(33,997)**
	1. Short-term Loan Expenses (-)	(418,856)	(20,593)	
	2. Long-term Loan Expenses (-)	(3,062)	(13,404)	
	OPERATIONAL PROFIT	**18,613,408**		**10,426,677**
I.	**Extraordinary Income and Profit**	**169,988**		**629,751**
	1. Previous Year's Income and Profit	94,306	526,215	
	2. Other Extraordinary Income and Profit	75,682	103,536	
J.	**Extraordinary Expenses and Losses (-)**	**(1,075,124)**		**(310,418)**
	1. Inoperative Period Expenses and Losses (-)	(944,452)	(43,569)	
	2. Previous Year's Expenses and Losses (-)	(76,420)	(215,026)	
	3. Other Extraordinary Expenses and Losses (-)	(54,252)	(51,823)	
	PROFIT FOR THE YEAR	**17,708,272**		**10,746,010**
K.	**Tax and Other Levies Payable (-)**	**(5,798,045)**		**(3,916,330)**
	NET PROFIT FOR THE YEAR	**11,910,227**		**6,829,680**

The attached notes are an integral part of these financial statements

Brisa Bridgestone Sabancı Lastik Sanayi ve Ticaret A.Ş.
Notes to the Balance Sheets as of
December 31, 1997 and 1996 (Million TL)

1) COMPANY'S FIELD OF ACTIVITY:
Production and sales of all types of tyres.

2) SHAREHOLDERS HOLDING OVER 10% OF CAPITAL:

Name	Share %	Amount (Million TL)
Bridgestone Corporation	42.86	3,189,273
H.Ö. Sabancı Holding A.Ş.	16.60	1,235,346
Akbank A.Ş.	10.36	770,763

3) RIGHTS OF PREFERRED SHARES:
In accordance with the Company's
Charter, as of December 31, 1996 and
1997, 5% of the year's profits are
distributed to holders of founding
preferred shares, which are 100 shares
and have only the right to profit sharing.

4) REGISTERED CAPITAL CEILING:
Registered capital ceiling:
25,000,000

5) CAPITAL INCREASES DURING THE YEAR:
Capital was increased by 6,378,750
million which was entirely covered by the
Fixed Assets Revaluation Fund.

6) MARKETABLE SECURITIES OTHER THAN SHARES ISSUED DURING THE YEAR:
None

7) MARKETABLE SECURITIES REPRESENTING PAID-OFF DEBTS DURING THE YEAR:
None

8) CHANGES IN TANGIBLE FIXED ASSETS DURING THE YEAR:
a) Cost of tangible fixed assets
purchased, produced or built: 5,566,368
b) Fixed Assets sold or scrapped: 720
c) Revaluation increase during the year
5,423,238

Revaluation of fixed assets (+)	9,956,840
Revaluation of accumulated depreciation (-)	(4,533,602)

d) Type, total amount, start and
completion date, and percentage of
completion of Investments in Progress

Type of Investment	: Expansion – Modernization
Start Date	: 01.09.1995
Completion Date	: 31.12.2001
Total Investment	: $145,000,000
% complete	: 32%

9) INVESTMENT DEDUCTION FROM THE TAX BASE FOR THE CURRENT AND FUTURE YEARS: 3,634,820

Investment Deduction for the current year : 3,634,820

Investment Deduction for future years :

10) RECEIVABLE/PAYABLE RELATIONS BETWEEN THE COMPANY AND ITS SHAREHOLDERS, AFFILIATES and SUBSIDIARIES:

	Receivables		Payables	
	Commercial	Non-Com.	Commercial	Non-Com.
SHAREHOLDERS	(Million TL)	(Million TL)	(Million TL)	(Million TL)
Group Firms	1,580,977	33,994	313,127	7,681
Shareholders	122,769	65,287	240,924	32,067*
Subsidiaries	-	-	-	-
Affiliates	-	-	94,424	-

* 6,208 million TL of the 32,067 million TL non-commercial payables to
Shareholders is their dividend payment.

11) ACCOUNTING PRINCIPLES AND VALUATION PROCEDURES IN EFFECT:

a) Accounting Principles in Effect
The Company prepares its financial
statements and reports in accordance
with the principles and rules set out in
the Capital Market Board Regulation
Circular Series XI/I and amendments
thereto.

b) Notes Receivable and Payable
Company values its notes receivable and
notes payable (including post-dated
checks) in accordance with the 80% rate
set by the Central Bank.

c) Unsecured Receivables and Liabilities
Due to the fact that the Company's
receivables and liabilities which are
unsecured by promissory notes do not
exceed a three-month period, they are not
subject to discounting.

d) Inventories
The Company values its inventories at the
lower of cost of acquisition or the net
recoverable value. Costs of raw
materials, goods and other inventories
are determined using the moving average
cost method; semi-finished and finished
products are valued using the monthly
average cost method.

e) Tangible Fixed Assets

To account for the high rate of inflation in Turkey, the Company follows the optional policy of not valuing tangible fixed assets using the historical cost method. Instead, the Company revalues its tangible fixed assets (except land) using the Ministry of Finance promulgated revaluation ratio, reset each year. As of December 31, 1997 the official revaluation rate applied to tangible fixed assets is 80.4%.

Tangible fixed assets are depreciated using the following ratios. Fixed assets acquired in 1997 are handled using the accelerated depreciation method.

	Ratio (%)
Infrastructure	4-10
Buildings	2-4
Machinery, Plants and Equipment	10-20
Vehicles	20
Furniture and Fixtures	10-20

f) Foreign Currency Assets and Liabilities

Foreign currency assets and liabilities are valued at year end using the Central Bank foreign currency purchasing rates and the equivalent Turkish Lira totals are presented in the attached Balance Sheet.

g) Retirement and Severance Pay

The Company calculates its retirement and severance pay liability which will be paid to employees in the future in accordance with the Employment Law and sets aside a provision for this liability in accordance with Capital Market Board regulations. The retirement and severance pay ceiling as of December 31, 1997 is set at 104,734,375 TL.

h) Financial Fixed Assets

The Company values its financial fixed assets at their cost of acquisition.

i) Income and Expenditures

Income and expenditures are recorded on the accrual basis when the service is completed or the goods are delivered. Price differences which are attributable to sales in previous periods are accounted for in the current period.

12) EVENTS OCCURRING AFTER THE BALANCE SHEET DATE:

RETIREMENT AND SEVERANCE PAY:
As of January 1, 1998 the retirement and severance pay ceiling has been increased to 149,990,000 TL.

SOCIAL SECURITY CEILING:
As of January 1, 1998 the social security ceiling has been increased to 82,964,100 TL.

13) CONTINGENT LIABILITIES:

From Court cases opened by the Company	-
From Court cases opened against the Company	468 (Million TL)

14) ACCOUNTING ESTIMATES CHANGES:

None

15) MORTGAGES OR GUARANTEES AGAINST ASSETS:

Mortgages given: 563,350

16) INSURANCE ON ASSETS:

61,039,270

FIXED ASSET	INSURED VALUE (MILLION TL)
BUILDINGS	5,784,192
PLANTS, MACHINERY AND EQUIP.	28,569,180
VEHICLES	200,310
FURNITURE AND FIXTURES	5,678,412
INVENTORIES	9,661,159
INVESTMENTS IN PROGRESS	11,146,017

17) MORTGAGES OR GUARANTEES RECEIVED :

3,371,035

Received from	Type of Mortgage/Guar.	Receivable
Agent	Letters of Guarantee	1,635,504
Agent	Mortgage	1,697,026
Shipping Customers	Letters of Guarantee	36,165
Automotive Customers	Letters of Guarantee	2,340

18) CONTINGENT COMMITMENTS NOT LISTED IN THE BALANCE SHEET:

Type of Commitment	Amount
Expansion Incentive	$ 118,208,677
Letters of Guarantee Given	1,060,664 TL

19) BLOCKED BANK DEPOSITS:

None

20) MARKETABLE SECURITIES WITH RECORDED VALUES UNDER THE STOCK MARKET VALUE:

None

21) MARKETABLE SECURITIES ISSUED BY PARTNERSHIPS, AFFILIATES AND SUBSIDIARIES:

None

22) BREAKDOWN OF "OTHER" ACCOUNTS IN THE FINANCIAL STATEMENTS OVER 20% OF THE SUB-TOTAL OR 5% OF ASSETS:

Liabilities	(Million TL)	(Million TL)
1. Short-term Liabilities		
C. Other Short-term Liabilities		
4. Short-term Other Liabilities		1,887,874
- Refundable VAT	1,386,737	
- Royalties	423,534	
- Other	77,603	

23) PERSONNEL RECEIVABLES / PAYABLES IN OTHER RECEIVABLES AND OTHER SHORT- AND LONG-TERM PAYABLES OVER 1% OF ASSETS:

The total of receivables due from and payables to personnel does not exceed 1% of total assets.

24) DOUBTFUL RECEIVABLES DUE FROM SHAREHOLDERS, AFFILIATES AND SUBSIDIARIES:

None

25) DOUBTFUL RECEIVABLES:

21,968

26) EQUITY INVESTMENTS:

	Affiliate Investment (Million TL)	Ratio (%)
Enerjisa Elektrik Üretim A.Ş.	702,050	36.95

27) FREE SHARES EARNED FROM AFFILIATES AND SUBSIDIARIES:

None

28) EASEMENTS ON LAND AND BUILDINGS:

None

29) REVALUATION ON FIXED ASSETS IN PAST THREE YEARS:

Year	Revaluation
31.12.1997	5,423,238
31.12.1996	2,996,869
31.12.1995	2,199,847

30) FOREIGN CURRENCY ASSETS, RECEIVABLES AND PAYABLES:

	For. Cur.	Amount	Ext. Rate	TL Equivalent
Liabilities	$	5,790,760.18	204,750	1,185,658
	JY	41,984,545.96	1,578	66,252
	DM	1,860,699.19	114,240	212,566
	£	36,457.69	338,870	12,354
	ECU	525.00	224,870	118
	LIT	28,359,535.00	115.70	3,281
Receivables	$	1,553,553.73	204,750	318,090
	JY	125,666.00	1,578	198
	DM	218,364.30	114,240	24,946
	LIT	1,005,186,581.77	115.7	116,300
Banks	$	17,669,497.06	204,750	3,617,830
	JY	1,760,234.69	1,578	2,778
	DM	112,474.41	114,240	12,849
	£	2,318.83	338,870	786

31) LIABILITIES INCURRED BY THE COMPANY ON BEHALF OF ITS SHAREHOLDERS, AFFILIATES OR SUBSIDIARIES:

None

32) AVERAGE NUMBER OF PERSONNEL BY CATEGORY:

Union	1,054
Non-Union	349
Total	**1,403**

33) OTHER MATTERS SUBSTANTIALLY AFFECTING THE FINANCIAL STATEMENTS:

None

Brisa Bridgestone Sabancı Lastik Sanayi ve Ticaret A.Ş.
Notes to Income the Statement for 1997 (Million TL)

1) DEPRECIATION, DEPRECIATION AND DEPLETION EXPENSES FOR THE PERIOD: 3,037,483
a) Depreciation Expenses 3,029,888
    aa) Normal Depreciation Expenses 2,223,687
    ab) Depreciation attributing to Revaluation 806,201
b) Depletion Expenses 7,595

2) DISCOUNTING AND PROVISION EXPENSES FOR THE PERIOD: 1,197,278
Discounting on Notes Receivable 352,185
Provision for Retirement and Severance Pay 843,722
Provision for Doubtful receivables 1,371

3) TOTAL FINANCING EXPENSES FOR THE PERIOD: 421,918
a) Charged to production costs -
b) Charged to tangible fixed assets -
c) Charged directly to expenses 421,918

4) TOTAL OF THE YEAR'S FINANCING EXPENSES RELATING TO SHARE-HOLDERS, SUBSIDIARIES AND AFFILIATES: 418,828
Akbank : 418,828

5) PURCHASES FROM AND SALES TO SHAREHOLDER, SUBSIDIARY AND AFFILIATE FIRMS:

	Purchases (Million TL)	Sales (Million TL)
Shareholders		
Kordsa	4,133.904	-
Bridgestone Corporation	-	2,634,705
Affiliates		
Enerjisa	196,722	-

6) INTEREST, RENT AND SIMILAR PAYMENTS TO AND FROM SHARE-HOLDER, SUBSIDIARY AND AFFILIATE FIRMS:

	Rent Paid
to Shareholder H.Ö.Sabancı Holding	121.908

7) SALARIES AND OTHER EMOLUMENTS TO THE COMPANY'S EXECUTIVES: 167,063

8) CHANGE IN DEPRECIATION METHODOLOGY FROM PREVIOUS PERIOD AND ITS EFFECT (+) OR (-):
The accelerated depreciation method was used in the calculation of depreciation on fixed assets purchased in 1997 and investments in progress.
Using this method led to 860,261 million TL more in depreciation.

9) INVENTORY COST CALCULATION SYSTEMS AND METHODS:
System: Phased costing system
Method: for raw materials, goods for resale and other stock: moving average cost method; for semi-finished products and finished products: monthly weighted average cost method.

10) WHETHER A COMPLETE OR PARTIAL STOCK INVENTORY WAS TAKEN:
The Company conducted an inventory of its stocks as of December 31, 1997. VEGA participated in the inventory and the necessary tests were accomplished.

11) WHETHER ANY OF THE INDIVIDUAL IN-COUNTRY OR OUT-OF-COUNTRY SALES OF GOODS, SCRAP AND THE LIKE OR SALE OF SERVICES TOTALED OVER 20% OF GROSS SALES:
None.

12) INFORMATON REGARDING ANY INCENTIVES OR SUPPORTS FOR SALES:
The Company applies various discounts and premiums in its sales, depending on market conditions. In addition, the Company received an export incentive totalling 16,384 million TL for exports in previous years and accounts for this in its Previous Year's Income and Profits Account.

13) INCOME AND EXPENSES RELATING TO THE PREVIOUS PERIOD

Previous Year Income and Profits		94,307
- Foreign Currency Exchange Profits	38,944	
- Export Incentives	28,024	
- Research–Development Incentives	15,939	
- Agency Commissions	2,513	
- Other Income and Profits	8,887	
Previous Year Expenses and Losses		76,420
- Export Expenses	52,563	
- Foreign Currency Exchange Losses	19,493	
- Insurance Expenses	2,538	
- Other Expenses	1,826	

Brisa Bridgestone Sabancı Lastik Sanayi ve Ticaret A.Ş.
31 Aralık 1997 Tarihli Fon Akım Tablosu (MİLYON TL)

	Cari dönem 31.12.1997		Önceki dönem 31.12.1996	
A. FON KAYNAKLARI		25.584.017		13.053.556
1. Faaliyet Kârından Sağlanan Kaynak	22.272.126		11.918.127	
a) Faaliyet Kârı	18.613.407		10.426.677	
b) Amortismanlar (+)	2.093.030		1.045.039	
c) Fon Çıkışı Gerektirmeyen Diğer Gid. (+)	1.690.289		460.797	
d) Fon Girişi Sağlamayan Gelirler (-)	(124.600)		(14.386)	
2. Olağanüstü Kârdan Sağlanan Kaynak		0		629.751
a) Olağanüstü Kâr	0		629.751	
b) Fon Çıkışı Gerektirmeyen Diğer Gid. (+)	0			
c) Fon Girişi Sağlamayan Gelirler (-)	0			
3. Dönem Varlıklar Tutarında Azalış		0		
4. Duran Varlıklar Tutarında Azalış		0		
5. Kısa Vadeli Borçlarda Artış		3.293.281		464.758
6. Uzun Vadeli Borçlarda Artış		0		
7. Sermaye Artırımı (Nakit Karşılığı)		0		
8. Emisyon Primi		0		
9. Maliyet Artış Fonu		18.610		40.920
B. KAYNAK KULLANIMLARI		25.584.017		13.053.556
1. Faaliyet Zararından Dolayı Kaynak Kullanımı		0		0
a) Faaliyet Zararı	0			
b) Amortismanlar (+)	0			
c) Fon Çıkışı Gerektirmeyen Diğer Gid. (-)	0			
d) Fon Girişi Sağlamayan Diğer Gelirler (+)	0			
2. Olağanüstü Zarardan Dolayı Kaynak Kullanımı		(39.317)		297.664
a) Olağanüstü Zarar	905.136		310.418	
b) Fon Çıkışı Gerektirmeyen Gid. (-)	(944.453)		(12.754)	
c) Fon Girişi Sağlamayan Gelirler (+)	0			
3. Ödenen Vergi ve Benzerleri		3.916.330		1.480.422
4. Ödenen Temettüler		3.996.563		1.388.885
5. Dönen Varlıkların Tutarındaki Artışlar		11.423.725		8.144.536
6. Duran Varlıkların Tutarındaki Artışlar (Yeniden Değerleme Hariç)		6.283.375		1.731.493
7. Kısa Vadeli Borçlarda Azalış		0		
8. Uzun Vadeli Borçlarda Azalış		3.341		10.556
9. Sermayede Azalış		0		
NET İŞLETME SERMAYESİNDE DEĞİŞİM				
1. Net İşletme Sermayesinde Artış		8.130.444		7.679.778

Ekteki dipnotlar bu mali tabloların ayrılmaz bir parçasıdır.

Brisa Bridgestone Sabancı Lastik Sanayi ve Ticaret A.Ş.
Funds Flow Statement for the Year Ending December 31, 1997 and 1996 (Million TL)

		Current Period Dec 31, 1997		Previous Period Dec 31, 1996	
A. SOURCES			25,584,017		13,053,556
1. From Operational Profit		22,272,126		11,918,127	
a) Operational Profit	18,613,407		10,426,677		
b) Depreciation (+)	2,093,030		1,045,039		
c) Other Non-Fund Expenses (+)	1,690,289		460,797		
d) Non-Fund Income (-)	(124,600)		(14,386)		
2. From Extraordinary Profit		0		629,751	
a) Extraordinary Profit	0		629,751		
b) Non-Fund Expenses (+)	0		0		
c) Non-Fund Income (-)	0		0		
3. Decrease in Current Assets		0		0	
4. Decrease in Fixed Assets		0		0	
5. Increase in Short-term Liabilities		3,293,281		464,758	
6. Increase in Long-term Liabilities		0		0	
7. Capital Increase (In cash)		0		0	
8. Share Premium		0		0	
9. Cost Increase Fund		18,610		40,920	
B. FUNDS USE			25,584,017		13,053,556
1. Due to Operational Loss		0		0	
a) Operational Loss	0		0		
b) Depreciation (+)	0		0		
c) Other Non-Fund Expenses (-)	0		0		
d) Other Non-Fund Income (+)	0		0		
2. Due to Extraordinary Loss		(39,317)		297,664	
a) Extraordinary Loss	905,136		310,418		
b) Non-Fund Expenses (-)	(944,453)		(12,754)		
c) Non-Fund Income (+)	0		0		
3. Taxes and Levies Paid		3,916,330		1,480,422	
4. Dividends Paid		3,996,563		1,388,885	
5. Increase in Current Assets		11,423,725		8,144,536	
6. Increase in Fixed Assets (ex. Reval.)		6,283,375		1,731,493	
7. Decrease in Short-term Liabilities		0		0	
8. Decrease in Long-term Liabilities		3,341		10,556	
9. Capital Decrease		0		0	
CHANGE IN NET OPERATIONAL CAPITAL					
1. Net Increase in Working Capital			8,130,444		7,679,778

(The attached notes are an integral part of these financial statements.)

Brisa Bridgestone Sabancı Lastik Sanayi ve Ticaret A.Ş.
31 Aralık 1997 Tarihli Nakit Akım Tablosu (MİLYON TL)

	Cari dönem 31.12.1997		Önceki dönem 31.12.1996	
A. Dönem Başı Nakit Mevcudu		4.308.613		1.895.848
B. Dönem İçi Nakit Girişleri		47.076.651		26.527.138
1. Satışlardan Elde Edilen Nakit		40.643.630		22.951.197
a) Net Satış Hasılatı	46.065.876		24.571.051	
b) Alacaklardaki (Satışlardan Kaynaklanan) Azalışlar	0			
c) Alacaklardaki (Satışlardan Kaynaklanan) Artışlar (-)	(5.422.246)		(1.619.854)	
2. Diğer Faaliyetlerden Gelirler ve Kârlardan				
Dolayı Sağlanan Nakit		4.222.399		2.243.997
3. Olağanüstü Gelir ve Kârlardan Sağlanan Nakit		169.988		629.751
4. Kısa Vadeli Borçlardaki Artış (Alımlarla İlgili Olmayan)		2.040.634		542.381
a) Menkul Kıymet İhraçlarından	0		0	
b) Diğer Artışlar	2.040.634		542.381	
5. Uzun Vadeli Borçlardaki Artış (Alımlarla İlgili Olmayan)		0		0
a) Menkul Kıymet İhraçlarından	0		0	
b) Diğer Artışlar	0		0	
6. Sermaye Artırımından Sağlanan Nakit		0		0
7. Diğer Nakit Girişleri				159.812
C. Dönem İçi Nakit Çıkışları		46.810.997		24.114.373
1. Maliyetlerden Kaynaklanan Nakit Çıkışı		23.832.137		13.218.234
a) Satışların Maliyeti	24.370.946		13.436.487	
b) Stoklardaki Artış	3.135.270		1.792.431	
c) Borçlardaki (Alımlardan Kaynaklanan) Azalış	0		0	
d) Borçlardaki (Alımlardan Kaynaklanan) Artış (-)	(1.263.204)		(1.054.356)	
e) Amortisman ve Karşılıklar gibi Nakit Çıkışı				
Gerektirmeyen Giderler (-)	2.410.875		(956.328)	
f) Stoklardaki Azalış (-)	0		0	
2. Faaliyet Giderlerinden Dolayı Nakit Çıkışı		4.943.752		2.094.034
a) Araştırma ve Geliştirme Giderleri	496.180		0	
b) Pazarlama, Satış ve Dağıtım Giderleri	3.411.090		1.573.999	
c) Genel Yönetim Giderleri	2.028.709		963.441	
d) Nakit Çıkışı Gerektirmeyen Giderler (-)	(992.227)		(443.406)	
3. Diğer Faaliyetlerden Giderler ve Zararlardan				
Dolayı Nakit Çıkışı		592.468		438.020
a) Diğer Faaliyetlerle İlgili Giderler ve Zararlar	946.023		581.152	
b) Nakit Çıkışı Gerektirmeyen Giderler ve Zararlar (-)	(353.555)		(143.132)	
4. Finansman Giderlerinden Dolayı Nakit Çıkışı		395.257		30.551
5. Olağanüstü Giderler ve Zararlardan Dolayı Nakit Çıkışı		130.671		266.847
a) Olağanüstü Giderler ve Zararlar	1.075.124		310.418	
b) Nakit Çıkışı Gerektirmeyen Giderler ve Zararlar (-)	(944.453)		(43.571)	
6. Duran Varlık Yatırımları Nedeniyle Nakit Çıkışı		6.292.065		1.731.493
7. Kısa Vadeli Borçların Ana Para Ödemeleri				
(Alımlarla İlgili Olmayan)		0		1.113.549
a) Menkul Kıymet Anapara Ödemeleri	0		0	
b) Diğer Ödemeler	0		1.113.549	
8. Uzun Vadeli Borçların Anapara Ödemeleri				
(Alımlarla İlgili Olmayan)		10.557		28.986
a) Menkul Kıymet Anapara Ödemeleri	0		0	
b) Diğer Ödemeler	10.557		28.986	
9. Ödenen Vergi ve Benzerleri		3.916.330		1.480.422
10. Ödenen Temettüler		3.996.563		1.388.885
11. Diğer Nakit Çıkışları		2.701.197		2.323.352
D. Dönem Sonu Nakit Mevcudu (A+B-C)		4.574.267		4.308.613
E. Nakit Artışı / (Azalışı)		265.654		2.412.765

Ekteki dipnotlar bu mali tabloların ayrılmaz bir parçasıdır.

Brisa Bridgestone Sabancı Lastik Sanayi ve Ticaret A.Ş.
Cash Flow Statement for the period ending December 31, 1997 and 1996 (Million TL)

		Current Period Dec 31, 1997		Previous Period Dec 31, 1996
A.	**CASH AT START OF YEAR**		4,308,613	1,895,848
B.	**CASH INPUTS DURING YEAR**		47,076,651	26,527,138
	1. Cash from Sales	40,643,630		22,951,197
	a) Net Sales Revenues	46,065,876		24,571,051
	b) Decrease in Sales Receivables	0		0
	c) Increase in Sales Receivables (-)	(5,422,246)		(1,619,854)
	2. From Other Activity Income and Profit	4,222,399		2,243,997
	3. From Extraordinary Income and Profit	169,988		629,751
	4. Increase in Short-term Debts (Non-purchase related)	2,040,634		542,381
	a) Marketable Security Export	0		0
	b) Other Increases	2,040,634		542,381
	5. Increase in Long-term Debts (Non-purchase related)	0		0
	a) From Marketable Security Export	0		0
	b) Other Increases	0		0
	6. Cash from Capital Increase	0		0
	7. Other Cash Inputs			159,812
C.	**CASH OUTFLOWS DURING YEAR**		46,810,997	24,114,373
	1. Cash Outflows due to Costs	23,832,137		13,218,234
	a) Cost of Sales	24,370,946		13,436,487
	b) Increases in Inventory	3,135,270		1,792,431
	c) Decreases in Sales Payables	0		0
	d) Increases in Sales Payables (-)	(1,263,204)		(1,054,356)
	e) Non-Fund Outflow Expenses (-)	(2,410,875)		(956,328)
	f) Decreases in Inventory (-)	0		0
	2. Cash Outflows due to Operational Expenditures	4,943,752		2,094,034
	a) Research & Development Expenditures	496,180		0
	b) Marketing, Sales & Distribution Expenditures	3,411,090		1,573,999
	c) General Administrative Expenditures	2,028,709		963,441
	d) Expenditures Not Requiring Cash Outflow (-)	(992,227)		(443,406)
	3. Other Activity Expenditures & Losses	592,468		438,020
	a) Other Activity Expenditures & Losses	946,023		581,152
	b) Non-outflow Expenditures & Losses (-)	(353,555)		(143,132)
	4. Outflow due to Financing Expenditures	395,257		30,551
	5. Extraordinary Expenditures and Losses	130,671		266,847
	a) Extraordinary Expenditures & Losses	1,075,124		310,418
	b) Expenditures & Losses Not Requiring Cash Outflow (-)	(944,453)		(43,571)
	6. Funds Outflow due to Investment in Fixed Assets	6,292,065		1,731,493
	7. Short-term Debt Principal & Interest			
	(Non-purchase Related)	0		1,113,549
	a) Marketable Securities Principal Payments	0		0
	b) Other Payments	0		1,113,549
	8. Long-term Debt Principal Payments			
	(Non-purchase Related)	10,557		28,986
	a) Marketable Securities Principal Payments	0		0
	b) Other Payments	10,557		28,986
	9. Taxes and Levies Paid	3,916,330		1,480,422
	10. Dividends Paid	3,996,563		1,388,885
	11. Other Cash Outflows	2,701,197		2,323,352
D.	**CASH AT END OF YEAR (A+B-C)**		4,574,267	4,308,613
E.	**CASH INCREASE**		265,654	2,412,765

(The attached notes are an integral part of the financial statements.)

Brisa Bridgestone Sabancı Lastik Sanayi ve Ticaret A.Ş.
1997 Dönemi Mali Oranlar Tablosu

	Cari dönem 31.12.1997	Önceki dönem 31.12.1996
1- Likidite Oranları		
1- Cari Oran: (Dönen Varlıklar / Kısa Vadeli Borçlar)	2.19	2.50
2- Asit Test Oranı: (Dönen Varlıklar - Stoklar / Kısa Vadeli Borçlar)	1.64	1.90
II- Mali Bünye Oranları:		
1- Toplam Borçların / Toplam Aktiflere: (Borçlar Toplamı / Aktif Toplamı)	0.32	0.30
2- Öz Sermayenin / Toplam borçlara: (Öz Sermaye / Borçlar Toplamı)	2.09	2.30
III- Faaliyet ve Kârlılık Oranları		
1- Satışların Kârlılık Oranı: (Net Dönem Kârı /Net Satışlar)	0.26	0.28
2- Aktiflerin Kârlılık Oranı: (Net Dönem Kârı / Toplam Aktifler)	0.27	0.29
3- Özkaynakların Kârlılık Oranı: (Net Dönem Kârı / Özkaynaklar)	0.67	0.73

Mali Yapı ile İlgili Önlemler:
Şirketimiz sağlıklı ve güçlü mali bünyesi ile 1997 yılını da başarılı bir şekilde tamamlamıştır.

Brisa Bridgestone Sabancı Lastik Sanayi ve Ticaret A.Ş.
1997 Financial Ratios

	Current Period Dec 31, 1997	Previous Period Dec 31, 1996
1- Liqudity Ratios		
1- Current Ratio (current assets/short term debts)	2,19	2,50
2- Acid Test Ratio (current assets-inventories/short term debts)	1,64	1,90
II- Financial Structure Ratios		
1- Total Debts/Total Assets	0,32	0,30
2- Net Worth/Total Debts	2,09	2,30
III- Ratios of Operation and Profitability		
1- Ratio of Profitability of Sales (net term profit/net sales)	0,26	0,28
2- Ratio of Profitability of Assets (net term profit/total assets)	0,27	0,29
3- Ratio of Profitability of Net Worth (net term profit/net worth)	0,67	0,73

Measures Relevant to Financial Structure
With its healthy and powerful structure, our Company completed the term in question succesfully in 1997.

III. Kâr Dağıtım Önerisi

Yönetim Kurulu olarak 1.1.1997 - 31.12.1997 döneminde yaratılmış bulunan 17.708.271.875.196.- TL kârın Esas Mukavelenamemizin 28. maddesi mucibi Kurumlar Vergisi, Gelir Vergisi Stopajı, Fon Payı ve Birinci tertip Yasal Akçe tenzil edildikten sonra kalan 11.024.812.919.437.- TL kârın aşağıda tabloda görüldüğü şekilde:

Brisa Bridgestone Sabancı Lastik Sanayi ve Ticaret A.Ş.
31 Aralık 1997 Kâr Dağıtım Tablosu (MİLYON TL)

	Cari dönem 31.12.1997		Önceki dönem 31.12.1996	
A. DÖNEM KÂRININ DAĞITIMI				
1. Dönem Kârı		17.708.272		10.746.010
2. Geçmiş Yıllar Zararları (-)				
3. Ödenecek Vergiler (-)		5.798.045		3.916.330
- Kurumlar Vergisi	3.778.723		2.706.458	
- Gelir Vergisi Kesintisi	1.492.227		852.478	
- Diğer Vergi ve Benzerleri	527.095		357.394	
4. Birinci Tertip Yasal Yedek (-)		885.414		0
5. Net Dağıtılabilir Dönem Kârı		11.024.813		6.829.680
6. Ortaklara Birinci Temettü (-)		6.397.820		3.952.891
- Adi Hisse Senedi Sahiplerine	5.512.406		3.415.590	
- İmtiyazlı Hisse Senedi Sahiplerine	885.414		537.301	
7. Yönetim Kuruluna Temettü (-)		90.000		36.000
8. Ortaklara İkinci Temettü (-)		69.000		7.672
- Adi Hisse Senedi Sahiplerine	69.000		7.672	
- İmtiyazlı Hisse Senedi Sahiplerine	0		0	
9. İkinci Tertip Yasal Yedek (-)		687.192		438.156
10. Olağanüstü Yedek (-)		3.780.801		2.394.961
B. HİSSE BAŞINA KÂR				
1. Adi Hisse Senedi Sahiplerine (TL /%)	1.481 / 148		6.424 / 642.4	
2. İmtiyazlı Hisse Senedi Sahiplerine (TL)				
C. HİSSE BAŞINA KÂR PAYI				
1. Adi Hisse Senedi Sahiplerine (TL /%)	750 / 75		3.220 / 322	
2. İmtiyazlı Hisse Senedi Sahiplerine (TL)	8.854.135.937		5.373.005.218 TL	

tefrikine ve 7.441.875.000.000.- TL sermayeyi temsil eden hisse senetleri için %75 oranında temettü payı ile imtiyazlı hisse senetleri ve Yönetim Kurulu kâr paylarının 30.03.1998 tarihinden itibaren dağıtılmasına karar vermenizi teklif eder, saygılarımızı sunarız.

Yönetim Kurulu adına
Başkan

Sakıp SABANCI

III. Proposal for Profit Distribution

The Board of Directors hereby submits and kindly requests resolution for distribution beginning from March 31,1997 of the profit worth TL 11,024,812,919,437 after Corporate Tax, Withholding, Defense Industry Support Fund and 1st Legal Reserve deductions from the profit worth TL 17,708,271,875,196 generated in the period 01.01.1997 - 31.12.1997 according to Article 28 of Articles of Association as given below:

Brisa Bridgestone Sabancı Lastik Sanayi ve Ticaret A.Ş.
Profit Distribution Statement for the period ending December 31, 1997 and 1996 (Million TL)

		Current Period Dec 31, 1997		Previous Period (*) Dec 31, 1996
A. DISTRIBUTION OF PROFIT FOR THE PERIOD				
1. Year's Profit		17,708,272		10,746,010
2. Previous Year's Losses (-)		0		0
3. Taxes Payable (-)		(5,798,045)		(3,916,330)
- Corporate Taxes and Funds	3,778,723		2,706,458	
- Income Tax Withholding and Funds	1,492,227		852,478	
- Other Taxes and Levies	527,095		357,394	
4. First Legal Reserve (-)		(885,414)		0
5. Net Distributable Profit for the Year		11,024,813		6,829,680
6. First Dividend to Shareholders (-)		(6,397,820)		(3,952,891)
- Holding Ordinary Shares	5,512,406		3,415,590	
- Holding Preferred Shares	885,414		537,301	
7. Dividend to the Board of Directors (-)		(90,000)		(36,000)
8. Second Dividend to Shareholders (-)		(69,000)		(7,672)
- Holding Ordinary Shares	69,000		7,672	
- Holding Preferred Shares	0		0	
9. Second Legal Reserve (-)		(687,192)		(438,156)
10. Extraordinary Reserve (-)		(3,780,801)		(2,394,961)
B. PROFIT PER SHARE				
1. on Ordinary Shares (TL /%)		1,480 / 148		6,424 / 642,4
2. on Preferred Shares (TL)				
C. DIVIDEND PER SHARE				
1. on Ordinary Shares (TL /%)		750 / 75		3,220 / 322
2. on Preferred Shares (TL)		8,854,135,937		5,373,005,218

where 75% of dividend on shares representing TL 7,441,875,000,000 of capital and their usufruct and shares of Board of Directors.

Respectfully yours,
for the Board of Directors
Chairman

Sakıp SABANCI

Denetçi Raporu Özeti

Brisa Bridgestone Sabancı Lastik Sanayi ve Ticaret A.Ş.

Ünvanı	: Brisa Bridgestone Sabancı Lastik San. ve Tic. A.Ş.
Merkezi	: İstanbul
Sermayesi	: 7.441.875.000.000.-TL
Faaliyet Konusu	: Taşıt tekerlek lastikleri imalatı ve satışı

- Denetçilerin adı ve görev
süreleri, ortak veya şirketin
personeli olup olmadıkları

: Yalçın Küçükertunç - Hitoshi Saito -
İsmail Opan. Görev süremiz 1 yıldır.
Şirket ortaklığımız yoktur.
Şirket personeli değiliz.

- Katılınan Yönetim Kurulu ve
yapılan Denetleme Kurulu
Toplantılarının sayısı

: 4 defa Yönetim Kurulu'na katılınmış,
6 defa Denetleme Kurulu Toplantısı
yapılmıştır.

- Ortaklık hesapları, defter ve
belgeleri üzerinde yapılan
incelemenin kapsamı, hangi
tarihlerde inceleme yapıldığı
ve varılan sonuç

: Vergi Mevzuatı ve Ticaret Hukuku
açısından 3., 6., 9., 12. ayların
ilk haftalarında tetkik ve kontrol
yapılmış, tenkide değer bir
hususa rastlanmamıştır.

- Türk Ticaret Kanunu'nun 353'üncü
maddesinin 1'inci fıkrasının 3 numaralı
bendi gereğince ortaklık veznesinde
yapılan sayımların sayısı ve sonuçları

: 4 kere kasa sayımı yapılmış ve mevcut
kayıtlara uygun bulunmuştur.

- Türk Ticaret Kanunu'nun 353'üncü
maddesinin 1'inci fıkrasının 4 numaralı
bendi gereğince yapılan inceleme
tarihleri ve sonuçları

: Her ayın ilk iş gününde yapılan
incelemelerde mevcut kıymetli
evrakın defter kayıtlarına
uygun olduğu tespit edilmiştir.

- İntikal eden şikayet ve yolsuzluklar
ve bunlar hakkında yapılan işlemler

: Herhangi bir şikayet intikal etmemiştr.

Brisa Bridgestone Sabancı Lastik Sanayi ve Ticaret Anonim Şirketi'nin 1.1.1997 - 31.12.1997 dönemi hesap ve işlemlerini
Türk Ticaret Kanunu, ortaklığın esas sözleşmesi ve diğer mevzuat ile genel kabul görmüş muhasebe ilke ve standartlarına göre incelemiş
bulunmaktayız.

Görüşümüze göre içeriğini benimsediğimiz 31.12.1997 tarihi itibariyle düzenlenmiş bilanço, ortaklığın anılan tarihteki gerçek mali durumunu,
1.1.1997 - 31.12.1997 döneme ait kâr/zarar tablosu, anılan döneme ait faaliyet sonuçlarını gerçeğe uygun ve
doğru olarak yansıtmakta; kâr dağıtım önerisi yasalara ve ortaklık esas sözleşmesine uygun bulunmaktadır.

Bilançonun ve gelir tablosunun onaylanmasını ve Yönetim Kurulu'nun aklanmasını oylarınıza arz ederiz. 27.01.1998

DENETLEME KURULU

Yalçın KÜÇÜKERTUNÇ   Hitoshi SAITO   İsmail OPAN

Auditors' Report Summary

To The General Assembly of Brisa Bridgestone Sabancı Lastik Sanayi ve Ticaret A.Ş.

Title	:	Brisa Bridgestone Sabancı Lastik San. ve Tic. A.Ş.
Center	:	İstanbul
Capital	:	TL 7,441,875,000,000
Field of Activity	:	Manufacturing and sales of vehicle tyres

- Name and duty period of Auditors and relation with company; as shareholder or personnel

: Yalçın Küçükertunç -Hitoshi Saito - İsmail Opan. Duty period is one year. We are not shareholders and personnel of the company.

- Number of Auditors' Committee meetings, and participated board meetings

: Number of participated board meetings was 4. Number of auditors' committee meetings was 6

- Scope of studies on partnership accounts, records and documents, date of studies and conclusion

: From the side of Tax Regulations and the Commercial Code, in the first weeks of the 3rd, 6th, 9th and 12th months controls and investigations were made and nothing to be criticised was found.

- Number and conclusions of cash counts which is made according to sub paragraph 3 of paragraph 1 of Article 353 of the Turkish Commercial Code

: 4 times cash counts were made and it was found in line with existing records.

- The date and conclusion of investigation which is made according to sub paragraph 4 of paragraph 1 of Article 353 of the Turkish Commercial Code

: In the investigation made in the first working day of every month it was determined that existing securities were in accordance with records.

- Complaints and irregularities received and actions to be taken

: There were no complaints and irregularities.

Ve have examined Brisa Bridgestone Sabancı Lastik Sanayi ve Ticaret A.Ş.'s accounts and procedures for the 1.1.1997 - 31.12.1997 period as required by the Turkish Commercial Code, the Articles of Association of the Company other regulations and generally accepted accounting principles and standards.

In our opinion, the enclosed balance sheet prepared as of 31.12.1997 shows the financial position of the Company at the date mentioned above; income statement for 1.1.1997 - 31.12.1997 period, reflects the actual and accurate results of the Company's activities; profit distribution proposal is appropriate to partnership of Articles of Association and Legislation.

We herewith submit the balance sheet and income statement for your approval and release the Board of Directors. 27.01.1998

<u>AUDITORS' COMMITTEE</u>

Yalçın KÜÇÜKERTUNÇ   Hitoshi SAITO   İsmail OPAN

Brisa Bridgestone Sabancı Lastik Sanayi ve Ticaret A.Ş.'nin
1997 Hesap Dönemine Ait Bağımsız Denetçi Raporu

Brisa Bridgestone Sabancı Lastik Sanayi ve Ticaret A.Ş.'nin 31 Aralık 1997 tarihi itibariyle düzenlenmiş bilançosunu ve bu tarihte sona eren hesap dönemine ait gelir tablosunu incelemiş bulunuyoruz.

İncelemelerimiz, genel kabul görmüş denetleme ilke, esas ve standartlarına uygun olarak yapılmış ve dolayısıyla hesap ve işlemlerle ilgili olarak muhasebe kayıtlarının kontrolü ile gerekli gördüğümüz diğer denetleme yöntem ve tekniklerini içermiştir.

Görüşümüze göre, söz konusu mali tablolar Brisa Bridgestone Sabancı Lastik Sanayi ve Ticaret A.Ş.'nin 31 Aralık 1997 tarihindeki gerçek mali durumunu ve bu tarihte sona eren hesap dönemine ait gerçek faaliyet sonucunu, uygulanan mevzuata ve bir önceki hesap dönemi ile tutarlı bir şekilde uygulanan genel kabul görmüş muhasebe ilkelerine uygun olarak doğru bir biçimde yansıtmaktadır.

VEGA BAĞIMSIZ DENETİM VE
YEMİNLİ MALİ MÜŞAVİRLİK A.Ş.
AGN INTERNATIONAL

Erciş KURTULUŞ
Sorumlu Başdenetçi

İstanbul, 09.02.1998

Brisa Bridgestone Sabancı Lastik Sanayi ve Ticaret A.Ş.
Independent Auditor's Report
For the Year Ending December 31, 1997

We have audited the attached Balance Sheet of Brisa Bridgestone Sabancı Lastik Sanayi ve Ticaret A.Ş. as of December 31, 1997 and the related Income Statement for the year then ended. Our examination was conducted in accordance with generally accepted auditing standards and accordingly included such tests of the accounting records and calculations and other auditing procedures considered necessary in the circumstances.

In our opinion, the attached Balance Sheet and Income Statement fairly present the financial position of Brisa Bridgestone Sabancı Lastik Sanayi ve Ticaret A.Ş. as of December 31, 1997 and the results of its operations for the year then ended in conformity with regulations and generally accepted accounting principles promulgated by the Capital Market Board, applied on a consistent basis.

VEGA BAĞIMSIZ DENETİM VE
YEMİNLİ MALİ MÜŞAVİRLİK A.Ş.
AGN INTERNATIONAL

Erciş KURTULUŞ
Senior Auditor Charge

Istanbul, 09.02.1998

EASTERN EUROPE: OVERVIEW

Derek Bailey
Thames Valley University,
London, England

In the second edition it was observed that "this is a time of extraordinarily rapid and fascinating change in accounting in Eastern Europe." During the past decade strenuous efforts have been made by the former socialist countries to advance the integration of the European homeland through the transformation of their socioeconomic systems.

Many of those countries have entered into agreements of association with the European Commission for the purpose of securing eventual accession to the single market of the EU. Some of the associated countries (Czech Republic, Estonia, Hungary, Poland, Slovakia, and Slovenia) have entered into the process of negotiation for accession to the European Union, although negotiations are expected to be protracted.

For all the associated countries, necessary measures of accounting reform are contained in the White Paper issued in May 1995 by the European Commission. The direction of accounting reform has been preordained: harmonization with the EU accounting directives and, so it would seem, at least cognizance of the international accounting standards. Are accounting texts in error, then, in arguing that effective accounting systems are designed knowingly with respect to specific socioeconomic environments?

A number of countries (i.e. those not traumatized by past, present, or prospective warfare) have made considerable efforts to legislate, to a greater or lesser extent, for the EU accounting directives (although implementation and enforcement are separate considerations).

Of course, if an authentic translation of the EU accounting directives into the national language is absent, as is so for many of the smaller countries, it is difficult to comprehend how due legal process has come to be observed; how legislators have satisfied themselves that the laws debated and adopted are appropriate; and how accounting and auditing personnel, independently and authoritatively, have become informed on the new responsibilities arising from European accounting harmonization.

Nevertheless, it is for the European Commission to determine, in the course of the negotiations for eventual accession to the single market of the EU, whether compliance with the accounting directives has been achieved and an adequate national regulatory system has been established.

However, statutory financial statements cannot be expected to be used as in the member states of the EU until well-functioning and stable market economies, effective corporate governance, and efficient capital markets are in being. Indeed, it is problematic whether, in the testing conditions of system design and construction (i.e. the introduction of new political systems, legal systems, institutional structures, economic and social organizations; in short, a new way of living) and continuing systemic instability (evidenced by acute economic and financial difficulties, bank failures and stock exchange turbulence) it is prudent to proceed beyond an objective legally orientated regular and orderly presentation to a subjective true and fair presentation in the compilation of financial statements.

The immaturity of new institutional arrangements and the presence of irregular business practices and illegitimate business activities might counsel caution, or prudence in the advocacy and adoption of sophisticated and ill-understood accounting principles and practices. There is not only uncertainty surrounding many transactions but pervasive uncertainty concerning the functioning of the transforming socioeconomic system.

Depending on the robustness of the national regulatory systems, prevalent corruption (and, in extreme instances, the criminalization of business practice) may invade the integrity of the financial statements. Further, weak trust relations, cemented by corrupt practices, erode the relevance of financial statements. (At least initially firm trust relations may be restricted to *nomenklatura* networks enduring from the old society).

In these circumstances attention (e.g. as expressed through new accounting legislation) may well be directed to the construction of a properly documented and verifiable accounting record. The statutory financial statements may be required to be firmly grounded in the accounting record of transactions. Hence, legal compliance in practice becomes a primary consideration in their compilation and verification. And the creation of a properly documented accounting record may well be given at least as much attention as financial reporting in the course of accounting reform. Criminal sanctions, up to and inclusive of imprisonment, concentrate the mind wonderfully on legal compliance and inhibit the independent exercise of subjective judgment. In these matters the relative public standing of an established legal profession and an embryonic and struggling accounting profession may be telling.

Notwithstanding foreign pressures for accounting change, the existing societal conditions, rather than market conditionss, may affect the thrust of accounting reform. The induction of civic and business responsibility, the creation of a well-ordered and tax-paying business community may bring about a paradoxical situation in which a borrowed accounting reform, designed for the markets, is subordinated to state purposes.

Thus, the accounting reform legislation may extend impartially to all economic entities: not only companies but also partnerships and sole proprietorships, and other kinds of undertakings and economic entities. The accounting legislation may apply with but little discrimination to both public and private companies, and to large and small companies. But such an approach to accounting reform is readily comprehensible, given the urgent necessity of raising tax revenue and as long as public access to the statutory financial statements remains problematic.

These considerations, as do the external pressures, cause accounting change to flow downward from governments to enterprises (i.e. as in the command economies). At what point does ministerial supervision and ministerial direction (e.g. of professional associations) become indistinguishable? Should auditors be subordinated to tax inspectors? Should accounting rules be an adjunct of taxation rules? Circumstances temper the nature of accounting discourse. Underlying the discourse are conflicting conceptions of the role of the accountant, as well as the auditor, in society. That is, to serve the general interest of society (however that may be defined, as in the command economy) or the particular interests of the business community? Arguments at contention in the discourse may well turn on differing perceptions of the new socioeconomic system being developed (e.g. laissez faire market economy or social market economy?).

How commercially useful are the statutory finacial statements during the transitional period? It has been observed that "an enterprise viable at market prices might have negative net assets . . . administratively adjusted book values may have no necessary relationship to the market value of the capital assets." And, there is the seemingly intractable problem of the new currencies being pegged artificaly to the stable currencies of one or other of the major trading powers.

Perhaps not surprisingly, foreign investors have tended to prefer financial statements reworked by an international accounting firm to be in accord with international accounting principles and practices and expressed in one of the working languages of the EU. That is, nonstatutory financial statements are preferred to the statutory financial statements.

It is an occurrence that raises an interesting question. Suppose an international arbitration tribunal (e.g. comprising arbitrators nominated by the International Chamber of Commerce) was obliged to take into consideration, as pertinent and material to the proceedings, some part of the content of the annual financial statements relating to a company in one or another of the associated countries. Would the tribunal defer to the statutory financial statements (i.e. legally recognized documents within the national jurisdiction where the company conducts its operations) or to the nonstatutory financial statements (i.e. preferred by the international business community but lacking legal recognition within that same national jurisdiction)?

There is another interesting question. Is the introduction of legislation, in response to an EU accounting directive, requiring, under legal penalty, accountants and auditors to comply with an undefined and seemingly undefinable, rule, such as a true and fair view, compatible with the obligations assumed by the associated countries when signing the European Convention on Human Rights? The Convention Article 7 upholds a fundamental tenet of the rule of law, namely, that the content of the law is reasonably comprehensible so that individuals may regulate their conduct to ensure compliance with their obligations under the law. Is it reasonable to require compliance with an operating rule that remains undefined when it is transferred to a country far removed, both in traditions and experiences, from the customary region of application?

On the new stock exchanges the dealings in securities have been characterized by short term trading rather than long term investment considerations. Given the prevailing low level of domestic saving, activity on the stock exchanges has been dominated by foreign capital. The volatile ebb and flow of foreign liquid capital has caused turbulence on some of the stock exchanges. In these conditions the demand of stock operators is concentrated on current information. Dated information (e.g. as contained in annual financial statements) is heavily discounted. It is access to business gossip (i.e. inside information) that matters, as it did for dealings in the securities of merchant venturers long ago in London coffee houses and, earlier, on the Rialto.

The international financial institutions have required the national and commercial banking sector in a number of countries (i.e. where crises of the banking sysyem have occurred) to comply with the international accounting standards and to use for audits the services of the international accounting firms. In consequence, the desirability of adherence to the international accounting standards is entering the consciousness of the national, or domestic, accounting community and is tending to eclipse other perspectives (e.g. adherence to the EU accounting directives). The practicalities of so doing are a separate matter.

It may be that public access to the annual financial statements of companies is associated with the longevity and stability of the institutional structures of a given country, even if tempered by other factors (e.g. a laissez faire market economy compared with a social market economy).

In a number of countries the spirit, springing from the Treaty of Rome, that informs the EU accounting directives is not recognized. The Statutory financial statements of companies, even when filed with a national registry, are neither accessible (i.e. may be read) nor available (i.e. copies acquired) in the public domain. (Poland is a notable exception. A public reference library containing runs of the statutory financial statements of quoted companies has been opened in Warsaw. Of course, to accord with the EU accounting directives, these financial statements are necessarily in the Polish language).

Whereas in some countries there may exist a transitional difficulty (e.g. because of the inadequacy of the resources at the disposal of the national registry) elsewhere there seems to be a general resistance to openness, or transparency, concerning the annual financial statements.

A common view among the new breed of entrepreneurs is that a corollary of private ownership over economic resources is privacy over their financial affairs, extending to a reluctance to make disclosures to shareholders, bankers, and state authorities. The state enterprises, protected from bankruptcy, revealed their financial statements to the state authorities, but why should enterprises in private ownership be expected to behave in a like manner?

A further difficulty, mentioned already, is that the filing requirement for statutory financial statements distingushes inadequately between different kinds of companies for these statements to come into the public domain.

The disclosure of the financial statements into the public domain may not be beneficial, especially for the smaller and more vulnerable companies. Racketeers may be encouraged to impose higher illicit taxation demands, made real by the power of illegal but effective punitive sanctions.

However, two separate filing requirements, one for state purposes (and not publicly accessible) and one for commercial purposes (and publicly accessible) is impracticable, especially for smaller and impoverished countries.

The placing of statutory financial statements in the public domain may be motivated by two quite different public policy objectives:

1. The enhancement of effective competition in a market economy (i.e. the commercial objective, as in a laissez faire market economy)

2. The realization of public accountability in a democratic society (i.e. the political objective, as in a social market economy)

Which of these two objectives is pursued determines:

A. The nature and extent of the disclosure (i.e. the information revealed in the statutory financial statements)
B. The range of business undertakings affected.

In the United States there is a practical distinction between the business affairs of:

1. The larger, listed (or quoted) corporations. The SEC regulates the filing, examination, and public availability of their statutory financial statements, i.e. annual accounts, being a matter of general interest and the subject of federal legislation.
2. The smaller, unlisted companies, traditionally regarded as a private affair and regulated separately by the legislation of the individual states of the Union.

Principally, even if not exclusively, in the United States attention is directed to the entry into the public domain of the financial statements of companies raising funds through the stock exchanges supervised by the SEC. The scope of the tasks undertaken by the FASB has been affected and, in its turn, has influenced the work of the IASC.

In Western Europe, and particularly in the EU, a contrasting approach has been adopted, influenced in part by a different and troublesome historical experience. In pursuance of the goal expressed in the Treaty of Rome, 1972, Art. 54(3)(g), the First and Fourth Company Law Directives provide for the public availability (i.e. to all third parties or, in other words, all citizens) of minimum equivalent financial information by all companies in competition with one another throughout the member states of the EU. (The draft Fifth Company Law Directive was directed to the realization of the same goal. However, reaction to the draft directive varied, depending upon whether the ethos of a laissez faire market economy or the ethos of a social market economy characterized the stance taken by particular member states).

However, the Fourth Directive was drafted primarily for quoted companies, apparently, and either absentmindly or through osmosis came to be extended to all companies.

That might not matter in relatively homogeneous Western Europe, comprising principally mature and stable market economies. It could be otherwise for relatively heterogenous Central and Eastern Europe, comprising nascent and immature market economies at different stages in the transformation from command economies. The extension of accounting legislation, designed and applied in one socioeconomic environment, to a different socioeconomic environment might well require careful deliberation, and its outcome is a matter for speculation.

A phased approach to accounting reform (with respect to placing the statutory financial statements of companies in the public domain) might have been worthy of consideration for the countries undergoing socioeconomic transformation. For example, concerning:

quoted companies	raising capital on the European stock market
quoted companies	raising capital on the domestic stock exchange
other companies	raising capital from the public
smaller companies	in which management and ownership are not separated

And a phased approach implies an approach suited to the specific conditions of a given country.

Assuming that European accounting harmonization (i.e. compliance with the EC accounting directives) were to be achieved throughout the former socialist countries would the public accessibility of statutory financial statements, in the national languages, at national registries in distant locations promote the realization of effective business communication in a European-wide single market? Or, would it be an expression of the triumph of bureaucratic purblindness over commercial realism? A practical demonstration of the inadequacy of a national solution to a European problem?

A provisional European solution to the European problem might be suggested tentatively: the public availability of the statutory financial statements for all the companies quoted on European stock exchanges, in one or other of the working languages of the EU, at European registries in selected major European financial centers (e.g. Frankfurt-am-Main, London, Paris) (cf. the SEC in the United States).

Such a solution could well have lessened the burden of accounting reform, especially for the smaller and less well endowed countries immersed in the wide ranging complexities of socioeconomic transformation.

And as the prospective date for admission to the EU continues to hover over a distant horizon, a more measured approach to accounting reform could have been contemplated by the countries undergoing socioeconomic transformation.

BALTIC STATES

Jaan and Lehte Alver
Estonian Business School, Tallinn, Estonia
Jonas Mackevicius
Vilnius University, Vilnius, Lithuania
Vilma Paupa
University of Latvia, Riga, Latvia
Derek Bailey
Thames Valley University, London, England

1. Background

1.1 History

The Baltic States, comprising Estonia, Latvia, and Lithuania, cover an area of 175,000 square kilometres along the southeast shores of the Baltic Sea.

The total population of the Baltic States is approximately 8 million. There are considerable differences among the three countries (e.g., with respect to ethnic origin, language, religious inclination, and historical experience). The Estonians, for example, have an affinity with the Finns, and Lithuania and Poland have had close historical ties.

The tribal peoples of Estonia and Latvia were conquered by western European invaders in the thirteenth century. Lithuania resisted foreign aggression, and in the following century became a major multi-national and religiously tolerant power. In 1385 the Grand Duchy of Lithuania entered into a union with Poland.

The possession of the Baltic States remained a matter of contention among the great powers. Between 1710 and 1795 the Baltic States were absorbed into the Russian Empire and, by 1917, had become a backward and impoverished agrarian region of Europe, evidenced by a high level of emigration.

The independence of the Baltic States was recognized internationally in 1920, lost in 1940, and recovered in 1991. In 1940 and, following German occupation in 1941–1944, the Baltic States were incorporated into the USSR. During that period substantial industrialization occurred: large plants, built to serve all-Union needs, drew in migrating workers from other parts of the USSR. The urban population rose to 70%. The failure to achieve economic autonomy within the USSR led to a successful struggle for the recovery of independence. The ensuing severe economic difficulties created an urgent necessity for extensive restructuring of political, economic, and social institutions with the goal of creating viable market economies. Jurisdictional disputes (e.g. over access to natural resources) have hindered the development of economic co-operation among the Baltic States. The three countries seek a form of economic integration with the stable market economies of Northern and Western Europe.

Until 1939 the German-speaking communities played a leading role in the commerce of Estonia and Latvia. Russian was the principal language used in the conduct of economic activities, including accounting, from 1944 until the late 1980s. Estonian, Latvian, and Lithuanian are now the official languages of the Baltic states. Russian continues to be used widely, and English is increasingly being used in business affairs.

1.2 Legal Background

In Lithuania the provisional law on the Principles of Accounting 1992, although not repealed, has been supplanted by decrees and other secondary legal measures issued by the Ministry of Finance. In both Estonia and Latvia transitional measures have been replaced by primary legislation; in Estonia by the Accounting Act 1994 and in Latvia by the Law on Accounting 1994 and the Law on Annual Reports 1994.

Estonia has a tradition of codified law, evidenced by a commercial code, and an emphasis on due legal process, whereas in Lithuania there is a greater reliance upon accounting change through executive action. In both Latvia and Lithuania there have been swift attempts to assimilate through legal measures Western European models of financial reporting, whereas there has been a pronounced American influence upon accounting reform in Estonia.

In all the Baltic States, nationally inspired primary legislation has been concerned with the creation of an authenticated accounting record as the foundation for financial reporting by all enterprises (e.g., for levying taxes and the collecting statistics). Primary accounting laws are applicable to all enterprises except the smallest (below the VAT threshold), although in Lithuania secondary legislation concerning financial reporting is restricted to enterprises that have the status of a legal person.

Throughout the Baltic States statutory financial statements are required to be filed in the national languages. In Estonia, and possibly in Latvia, accounting and financial reporting continue to be undertaken in the Russian languages in some enterprises. In Estonia, but not in Latvia, auditing may be undertaken in the Russian language, the financial statements subsequently being translated into Estonian before filing.

The Ministry of Finance occupies a significant role in the development of accounting regulation in each country. Under the Ministry of Finance an Accounting Board has been established in Estonia and Lithuania. National charts of accounts have been promulgated by the Ministry of Finance in Latvia and Lithuania.

1.3   Business Background

The principal forms of business enterprise are private (closed) and public (open) limited liability companies, general and limited partnerships, and sole proprietorships. The majority of businesses are private companies or sole proprietorships. Many of the small and medium-sized enterprises are short lived because of an insufficiency of entrepreneurial and managerial skills and market volatility. Despite the predominance of small and medium-sized enterprises, and the inadequacy of managerial and accounting skills, there has been negligible attempt to specify appropriate reporting and auditing regimes.

Public companies in Estonia and Lithuania have both supervisory and management boards. Stock exchanges have been opened in Tallinn, Riga, and Vilnius (the capital cities of Estonia, Latvia, and Lithuania, respectively). Because of the low level of activity, some have advocated a single capital market for the Baltic States, as well as the development of a common trading area.

1.4   Audit Profession

In Estonia the Auditing Board, set up in 1991 and under the supervision of the Ministry of Finance, is responsible for the administration of an examination leading to conferring the designation of licensed auditor. The Board is responsible for monitoring the activities of licensed auditors and a number of auditing standards, derived from internationally acceptable auditing practice, have been issued. Licences are no longer issued to auditing firms (a consequence of a state de-regulation initiative). There is no association of auditors.

The development of a domestic auditing capacity has occurred more slowly in Latvia and Lithuania. The Law on Sworn Inspectors 1995 was adopted in Latvia, the term "sworn inspector" being the official designation for auditor. An Examining Commission and a Licensing Commission have been set up under the supervision of the Ministry of Finance. Also in 1995 the system of examinations was introduced. Licences are issued to both individuals and auditing firms.

Lithuania has seen controversy concerning the respective roles of tax inspector and auditor and false starts to the creation of a domestic auditing capacity. As a consequence, a number of unofficial associations of persons engaged in auditing developed. An Accounting and Auditing Board was set up by the Ministry of Finance, although until 1997 only preparatory work was undertaken. Because of the dearth in the supply of authorized auditors, the buoyant demand for accounting service generally has generated a supply of unlicensed auditors.

2. The Form and Content of Annual Financial Statements

Within the Baltic States the question of public accessibility to companies' annual financial statements has not been resolved. The annual accounts comprise:

1. Balance sheet

2. Profit and loss account

3. Appropriation account (Lithuania) or statement of discretionary profit appropriations or treatment of loss (Estonia and Latvia)

4. Cash flow statement (Lithuania)

5. Notes to the annual accounts, with the inclusion of the annual report (Lithuania) and cash flow statement (Estonia)

6. Annual report (Estonia and Latvia)

7. Audit opinion (Estonia and Latvia). Hitherto audit has been optional in Lithuania.

2.1 Balance Sheet

On the balance sheet the current year's profit is shown net of all appropriation (Lithuania) or before discretionary appropriations (Estonia and Latvia).

In Latvia and Lithuania the general format of the balance sheet follows closely the specification of the EC Fourth Directive. In the former country:

1. Formation expenses are not distinguished.

2. Loans to company personnel are shown under financial fixed assets as well as under current assets.

3. Work-in-progress and work-in-progress for third parties (i.e. sub-contracted work) are distinguished.

4. Draught animals and productive cattle are shown as a separate item under current assets.

5. Amounts owed to subsidiaries and amounts owed to associated companies are distinguished.

6. Company tax is distinguished from the item "other creditors including tax and social security contributions."

7. Unpaid dividends for earlier years are shown as a separate item.

In a Lithuanian balance sheet:

1. Formation expenses are classified into the following four groups:
   • Alteration to capital and formation of enterprise costs
   • Loan issue costs
   • Other formation costs
   • Reorganization costs

2. Land is distinguished from buildings.

3. Means of transportation are distinguished.

4. Leasing and similar rights appear as a separate item under tangible fixed assets.

5. Amounts receivable after one year from trade and other debtors are distinguished.

6. Finished products and goods purchased for resale are distinguished.

7. Shares in affiliated undertakings are not distinguished under current assets.

8. Reserves are separated into available for distribution and not available for distribution, the legal reserve being shown separately.

9. Financing (grants and subsidies) appears as a separate item.

10. Provisions for taxation are divided into unexpected tax charges and other tax charges.

11. Provisions for major repairs and large-scale maintenance are shown as a separate item.

12. Postponed taxes are classified into

    (a) on capital and subsidies
    (b) others

13. Taxes, accrued remuneration, and social security contributions are shown as a single item.

2.2 Profit and Loss Account

Both the cost of sales model and the total operating costs model (i.e. as permitted by the EU Fourth Directive) of the profit and loss account may be used in Estonia and Latvia but only the cost of sales model is used in Lithuania.

Not shown as separate items on a Lithuanian profit and loss account are:

- Income from participating interests
- Value adjustments in respect of financial assets held as current assets

Tax on extraordinary profit or loss is not shown as a separate item in either Latvia or Lithuania.

Profit is shown net of tax (Estonia and Latvia) or net of all appropriations after the completion of the appropriation account (Lithuania). In Estonia and Latvia a statement of appropriation of profit or treatment of loss is prepared. That statement may be incorporated into the annual report or the notes to the accounts in Latvia. The creation of a legal reserve is required in all the Baltic States.

2.3 Cash Flow Statement

The authorized format for the obligatory cash flow statement in Lithuania is as follows:

- Cash flow from operating activities
- Cash flow from investing activities

- Cash flow from financial activities
- Cash flow from extraordinary activities
- Increase/decrease in net cash flow
- Cash at beginning of period
- Cash at end of period

In Estonia the cash flow statement is to be included in the notes to the accounts and to show the cash flow from each of operating, investing, and financing activities separately, no specific format having been stipulated.

A cash flow statement has not been required in Latvia.

2.4   Notes to the Accounts

The requirements for additional information to be shown in the notes to the accounts (or elsewhere for Latvia) vary among the Baltic States, but do include:

- Structure of share capital
- Loans expressed in national and foreign currencies (Lithuania)
- Loans, mortgages, guarantees to shareholders (Latvia)
- Secured and unsecured loans
- Security given for loans
- Debts guaranteed by the government (Lithuania)
- Provisions and allowances (Estonia and Lithuania)
- Deferred and accrued liabilities (Estonia and Lithuania)
- Commitments for taxes and remuneration (Lithuania)
- All taxes, payable and paid
- Tax reductions and rebates (Latvia)
- Amounts in special accounts (Lithuania)
- Contingent liabilities
- Fixed assets
- Inventory write-downs (Estonia)
- Off-balance sheet assets (Estonia)
- Segmental reporting
- Accounting methods employed

- Changes in financial statement formats or accounting methods (Estonia).

The purpose of some of the notes would seem to be to catch items that could well, but may not, have been shown in the financial statements. The requirements for notes to the accounts are best regarded, perhaps, as an exhortation to good and, possibly, desired practice.

2.5 Annual Report

The annual report is required to cover:

1. General state of the enterprise (Lithuania)
2. Research and development activities
3. Significant events occurring during (Estonia) or after (Latvia and Lithuania) the financial year
4. Planned events (Estonia) and new capital investment (Latvia)
5. Future trends (Latvia)
6. Current conditions (Lithuania) or financial difficulties (Latvia) affecting the future of the enterprise
7. Proposed Accommodation with Creditors (Latvia)

2.6 Audit

In Estonia an audit is carried out by a licensed auditor, who is required to confirm that the accounting is organized in accordance with the legislation and good accounting practice. The audit opinion contains the sentences: "The annual report is the responsibility of the management. Our responsibility is to express an opinion on their annual report based on our audits."

Audit responsibility for the substance of the annual report (the term embracing all elements of the annual accounts in Estonia) may be problematic.

In Latvia the sworn inspector is required to ascertain that the accounting system, financial statements, and annual report conform with the legislation and, if the audit is satisfactory, to prepare an audit opinion that the accounting books, financial statements, and annual report "present fairly

. . . the financial position . . . in accordance with generally accepted accounting principles . . . ." For small Latvian enterprises an audit committee may undertake the audit.

The Law on the Principles of Accounting 1992 provides for audits to be optional in Lithuania.

There is no requirement for an audit report in any of the Baltic States.

2.7   Filing

In Estonia the annual accounts are required to be filed with the national register and to be made accessible to interested persons.

In Latvia the annual accounts are required to be filed with the State Financial Inspection Board and to be made accessible to the general public.

In Lithuania the annual accounts are filed with the Department of Statistics and the Taxation Office.

2.8   Publication

Publication, in the sense of public access to the annual accounts of companies, is not regarded as a current issue in Latvia and Lithuania.

From 1997 the annual accounts of some companies have been accessible publicly, primarily for legal rather than commercial purposes, at the registries in Estonia.

3. Accounting Policies and Practices in Valuation and Income Measurement

In general terms, all transactions are to be evidenced by validated documents, the latter providing content for the accounting records, which, in turn, provide content for the financial statements. More particularly, the accounting records and the financial statements are to be prepared in accordance with:

- Good accounting practice or, alternatively, in the right and correct manner (Estonia)
- Good accounting practice and the legal provisions (Latvia)
- Laws and executive acts (Lithuania)

The financial statements are required:

- To fairly present the entity's assets, liabilities, owners' equity, and financial result (Estonia)
- To present a clear and precise picture of the assets, liabilities, and financial results (Latvia)
- To be clear and understandable, neutral and reliable, reflecting the material and financial reality (Lithuania)

In doing so use is to be made of:

- Internationally accepted accounting assumptions and principles (Estonia)
- Going concern, matching, prudence, consistency (Latvia)
- Going concern, accrual accounting (Lithuania)

Deviations from the provisions of the law are permitted in exceptional instances, for example:

- To fairly present (Estonia)
- To give an explanation (Latvia)
- If otherwise the correct position cannot be provided (Lithuania)

In all the Baltic States fixed assets are to be valued at acquisition cost or production cost, the latter to include the costs of bringing the item to a serviceable condition. Interest on borrowed sums is to be included in cost (Latvia and Lithuania). If the market value of a tangible asset exceeds its cost and is substantial and likely to persist, the item may be revalued, the difference being taken to a revaluation reserve. A comparable loss in value of a tangible fixed asset or a long-term financial asset may be written off. An upward revaluation of long-term financial assets is permitted but not of land (Latvia). Elsewhere the situation is uncertain. The revaluation reserve may not be attributed to income (Latvia and Lithuania).

Essential improvements to tangible long-term assets are to be capitalized (Lithuania) but only if the useful life is extended or capacity increased or output costs reduced or quality improved (Estonia).

Formation and organization costs may be capitalized and written off over 5 years. In general, intangible fixed assets (e.g. goodwill) are to be written off over the same period. For purchased concessions, patents, licences, and trademarks, the period of write-off may be extended to 20 years (Estonia).

Development costs may be capitalized, given the resources to complete the project and it is likely to generate revenue, and written off over 5 years (Estonia). Such restrictions upon the application of a basic rule are uncommon.

Current assets are to be valued on the balance sheet at the lower of cost or net realisable value (Estonia) or market price (Latvia); and at actual acquisition or production cost (Lithuania).

Inventories are to be recorded at acquisition or production cost, FIFO or average cost methods may be used (Estonia and Latvia), and also LIFO (Lithuania), and on that basis shown on the balance sheet (Estonia). If the effect is to show the cost of inventories at less than market value, the difference is to be shown in the notes (Lithuania) or any difference from market value is to be shown in notes to the accounts (Latvia).

Contracts in progress are to be valued at actual expenditures plus a proportion of profit, but an excess of cost over contract price is to be written off (Lithuania).

Interest on borrowed sums for financing inventories or contracts are to be capitalized if the acquisition or completed period exceeds one year (Lithuania).

If a loan is repayable at an amount greater than received, the difference is shown as a separate asset and amortized over the period of the loan (Latvia).

Debts should be shown on the balance sheet net of uncollectible amounts (Estonia and Latvia). Disputed debts should be shown on the balance sheet as entered into the accounting records (Lithuania). There should be a provision for doubtful debts (Latvia and Lithuania).

Securities held as current assets and with a fluctuating value are to be shown at market value (Latvia).

Foreign currency balances are to be valued in accordance with the official rate of exchange as at the date of the balance sheet (Lithuania).

4. Expected Future Developments

Since the Baltic States recovered their independence, accounting reform has proceeded independently and separately in each of the Baltic Republics so that accounting diversification has occurred. The extent to which the provisions of accounting legislation are observed is problematic, given the inadequacy of the domestic auditing capacity.

Complaints by shareholders of a lack of accounting information are not unknown, and the concept of commercial secrecy tends to reinforce a reluctance, stemming from perceptions of the prerogatives of private property ownership, to divulge accounting information.

The eventual emergence of a unified capital market and stock exchange for the Baltic States could lead to a common approach being adopted for the annual accounts of listed companies. There has been some contemplation, at one stock exchange, of a future availability of annual accounts through the Internet as the only medium of publication.

Hitherto accounting reform has been driven by a need to satisfy state purposes rather than commercial purposes, although the influence of foreign advocacy on accounting reform is evident. A consequence has been some bewilderment among accounting personnel concerning the purpose of accounting reform. Accounting in the context of a market economy may well remain a matter of puzzlement in the absence of an adequate informative literature in the Estonian, Latvian, and Lithuanian languages. Some Western accounting materials are accessible only in Russian or, for some Lithuanians, the Polish languages.

The primary need is possibly for consolidation of the progress thus far attempted.

THE CZECH REPUBLIC

Jan Dolezal
BDO CS s.r.o., Prague

1. Background

1.1 Accounting Background

The development of accounting systems in the Czech Republic has undergone several substantial changes of direction during the twentieth century. During the first 45 years of the century, there was a strong influence from the accounting practice and accounting principles used in the German-speaking countries of Europe. Law No. 116/1946, "On Uniform Organization of Accounting in Enterprises," laid down accounting practice in the period 1946–1952, emphasizing the utilization of accounting information for purposes of enterprise direction. This was the period in which the construction of a centrally directed and centrally planned economy began, and there was a corresponding influence on the accounting system. The first steps toward uniformity of accounting in the economy were made. Financial accounting, operational (internal) accounting, and auxiliary accounting (including payroll, inventories, etc.) were separate parts of this system.

In 1953 a system of registration in the national economy was introduced by Law No. 41/1952, "On Principles of Accounting Registration." This system, used during the period 1953–1965, was based on practice in the Soviet Union. It was predetermined primarily to meet the demands of centralized direction of the economy, and thus weakened the economic functions of accounting and the independence of enterprises. Historical costs were used for the valuation of assets, and the demands of costing were emphasized over external reporting considerations.

Further development of centrally organized and widely understood information systems came about with three new pieces of legislation in 1971: Law No. 21/1971, "On Uniform Social-Economic Information System," Government Decree No. 153/1971, "On Information System of Enterprises," and the Federal Ministry of Finance Decree No. 154/1971, "On Accounting."

From 1971, accounting in Czechoslovakia was organized by the Federal Ministry of Finance. The ministry stipulated the basic accounting principles and bookkeeping regulations, including formats of financial statements, as well as regulations for checking and approving the annual financial statements of organizations. Financial accounting and cost accounting formed a system that used the same pricing and other principles.

In keeping their accounts (drawing up their schedule of accounts and keeping records of their economic operations), enterprises proceed according to the chart of accounts and the directive to the chart of accounts. This chart of accounts, containing general accounts, is obligatory for enterprises. Enterprises must choose from it and include in their charts of accounts all accounts relating to their activity. In selected sections of the chart of accounts (classes of accounts and groups of accounts), organizations may form accounts and analytical accounts according to their own needs, especially with regard to intra-enterprise management.

Since 1989, and consistent with broader political and economic changes, accounting legislation has been updated. Government Decree No. 136/1989, "On Information Systems of Enterprises," and the Federal Ministry of Finance Decree No. 23/1990, "On Accounting," introduced greater independence for enterprises in cost accounting and stimulated the wide application of computers. This law is now valid in both separated states—in the Czech Republic and the Slovak Republic.

Basic principles of the Fourth and Seventh EU Directives were embodied in this law, thereby substantially changing the previous regulations and accounting practice. These changes concern especially valuation principles, preparation, publication, and auditing of financial statements and other parts of the accounting system.

1.2 The Auditing Profession

For a long time, the balance sheet and income statements of Czech and Slovak enterprises were approved by senior administrators or by central authority (ministry). Laws approved during 1989 and 1990 introduced independent auditing of the annual statements and economic activity of certain legal forms of enterprises, by one or two (in the case of enterprises with foreign capital participation) independent auditors. Business law and the law on accounting require the audit of financial statements for all stock companies and large limited liability companies or cooperatives (with turnover exceeding 40 million Czech crowns or equity exceeding 20 million Czech crowns). The distinction between stock companies and limited liability companies is precisely as in German law. A similar distinction is incorporated into the Polish Commercial Code and may be compared with the distinction between public companies and private companies in the United Kingdom.

The audit includes checking whether

1. The annual financial statements (consolidated financial statements) give a true and fair view of the assets, liabilities, equity, financial position, and income of the company

2. The accounting records are kept fully and properly

After checking the annual statements and the economic activity of the enterprise, the auditors prepare a written report. Until 1993, the scope of the report and other more detailed provisions concerning auditors and their activity were detailed in Federal Ministry of Finance Decree No. 63/1989.

Law No. 526/1992, "On the Auditors and the Chamber of Auditors in Czech Republic," prepares a basis for auditing to the level that is used in the developed countries. This law includes the qualification requirements for auditors (in the case of foreign persons, if they meet the requirements of their own particular country, an examination in Czech accounting and tax law is required), the scope of auditors' duties, the appointment and revocation of auditors, and the assessment of their qualifications and work.

Today the Czech auditing profession is headed by the Chamber of Auditors, which was founded in February 1993. The Chamber is a member of both IFAC and FEE. Members of the Chamber are both certified auditors (there were about 1200 of them in 1997) and assistant auditors. The Chamber of Auditors organizes the examinations and education of its members and prepares Czech national auditing standards on the basis of international ones. The first twenty national auditing standards concerning all major areas of the audit were prepared and published and came into effect on or before January 1, 1998.

2. The Form and Content of Published Financial Statements

For many years the content of financial reporting was influenced by the command economy with its centralized direction. Therefore, the contents, formats, and system of approval of financial statements were not compatible with those used in Western Europe and other countries with a market economy.

Enterprises (including joint ventures within the Czech Republic) must file financial statements in the structure, extent, and terms stated by the Federal Ministry of Finance (since 1993, the Czech Ministry of Finance) in Decree Nr. V/l–31 388/1992. As of 1998, enterprises must present the following financial reports:

- Profit and loss account
- Balance sheet
- Notes to the accounts (including cash flow statement)

In the Czech Republic, uniform financial statements for profit-making organizations are used. Different financial statements are required from nonprofit organizations, banks, insurance companies, and small businesses. In the conditions of the newly developing market economy and for East-West joint ventures, the problem of the publication of data on their operations is of fundamental importance to enterprises. The law on accounting requires publication of financial statements for all stock companies and large limited liability companies or cooperatives (with turnover exceeding 40 million Czech crowns or equity exceeding 20 million Czech crowns). The Ministry of Finance gives the precise layout of financial statements for different types of businesses and also the minimal structure of published statements. These represent a simplification of the obligatory state formats of the balance sheet and income statement.

Financial statements are filed with the tax collection office (together with two copies of the tax return) and the statistical authority. Abbreviated financial statements are published in a special journal *Obchodní věstník*. Copies of the annual report containing the financial statements are filed with the special organization *Národní informači středisko*.

To give a better view on the development of company operations, items in the financial statements show figures not only for the last period (year), but also for the preceding year.

The content of the notes to the accounts is established by the Ministry of Finance Decree of September 8, 1993. Full notes are obligatory for enterprises that must be audited. Abbreviated notes can be presented by other (small) companies.

Full notes include:

1. General information—description and organization of the company, information on shareholders holding greater than 20% of shares, detailed information on participations in the group companies greater than 20%, the number and structure of employees, including personnel cost, salaries, and benefits of the members of management and supervisory boards, loans and guarantees given to the shareholders and members of the management and supervisory boards

2. A description of accounting policies and principles—valuation of assets and contents of inventory prices, changes in valuation, depreciation and accounting methods, including reasons for these changes and the effect on individual items of the balance sheet and profit and loss account, calculation of adjustments to individual items of assets, transfer of foreign currency items into Czech crowns

3. Additional information for the financial statements:
   - Tangible and intangible fixed assets—broken up into major groups such as property and plant, vehicles, and office equipment, and showing cost and accumulated depreciation
   - Leased assets—total expected payment, actual payment made up to the balance sheet date, payments expected within one year and after one year
   - Changes in fixed assets
   - Assets not shown in the balance sheet—for example, low-priced assets
   - Assets with market value substantially higher than book value
   - Investments (number and par value of shares shown by type and issuer and with gains from these shares)
   - Receivables—overdue part, intercompany receivables, receivables covered by guarantees
   - Changes in stockholders' equity
   - Distribution of profits
   - Description of shares issued
   - Liabilities—overdue part, intercompany liabilities, liabilities covered by guarantees, contingent liabilities

- Commitments
- Provisions—changes during the accounting period
- Revenues by segments
- Cost of research and development
- Explanation of material events occuring after balance sheet date
4. Cash flow statement—A presentation of consolidated financial statements is required by the accounting law for companies with a participation greater than 20% in other companies.

In January 1994, the consolidation rules were issued by the Ministry of Finance. These consolidation rules are based on the Seventh EU Directive of June 13, 1983 on consolidated accounts. Consolidation is obligatory for groups with total sum of equity exceeding 300 million Czech crowns and total turnover exceeding 600 million Czech crowns. The consolidation is not obligatory for a parent company that is a subsidiary of another company headquartered abroad and consolidating its accounts according to the Seventh Directive. The method of full consolidation is used for subsidiaries and the equity method for affiliated companies. The consolidation difference (goodwill or "badwill") occuring in the first year of consolidation can be written off within one year or over a period of 5 years.

The requirements for the disclosure of financial information are not affected by stock companies being listed or quoted on the Prague Stock Exchange. As a precondition for a listing, however, stock companies are required to prepare much more detailed information. Since 1993 listed stock companies have been required to present audited half-yearly financial statements.

In accordance with Czech business law, the financial statements are approved by an annual meeting of shareholders, as is the decision on the appropriation of profits.

3. Accounting Policies and Practices in Valuation and Income Measurement: Implications for the Analyst

Foreign accountants and accounting firms studying the financial reports of Czech enterprises should bear in mind the following accounting policies and practices in valuation and income measurement.

3.1 Capital and Reserves

Until 1992 state enterprises were the most common legal form of enterprise. Until 1990 state enterprises presented the following compulsory items of capital:

1. Fund of fixed assets: reflecting the original value of property, plant, and equipment diminished by accumulated depreciation and loans used for the purchase of property, plant, and equipment. This item did not include the value of land.

2. Fund of current assets: the part of capital received from the state that was devoted to current assets. Its amount could be increased when necessary by transfer from the development fund, and vice versa.

3. Securities and investments fund: the par value of purchased securities and investments in other companies. Its amount equaled the amount of securities and investments included in assets.

4. Development fund: a reserve for the future development of the enterprise. It contained accumulated depreciation not yet used, the amount of income devoted to future development of the enterprise, and the estimated future cost of research.

In 1991, all the above funds of state enterprises merged into one single item, known as equity.

By 1994, in the process of privatization, most state enterprises were converted to share companies or limited liability companies.

The minimum subscribed capital is 1,000,000 Czech crowns for a share corporation and 100,000 Czech crowns for a limited liability company. Sole proprietorships and partnerships have no given limits of capital.

Two types of reserves exist—capital and revenue reserves. Capital reserves consist of:

1. The premium paid in connection with the issuance of new shares or received by conversion of convertible debentures

2. Other capital input that does not form a part of share capital

3. Received gifts or state subsidies (these items remain in the balance sheet and are not written off)

The reserve fund is an obligatory general reserve for all forms of enterprise (except for sole proprietorships). In a stock corporation, this fund is created from the profit after tax at the rate of at least 20% of the profit in the first year (but not more than 10% of the stockholders' equity) and 5% in following years until the amount of this fund reaches the level of 20% of total shareholder equity. In a limited liability company, this fund is created from the profit after tax at the rate of at least 10% of the profit in the first year (but not more than 5% of the stockholders' equity) and 5% in following years until the amount of this fund reaches the level of 10% of total shareholder equity.

There are other possible statutory reserves—social reserve and bonus reserve, which are optional for joint ventures and privatized companies (formerly mandatory for state enterprises). Bonus reserve can be used to allow the participation of the staff in the company profit.

3.2 Liabilities and Provisions

Since 1993 a distinction has been made between long-term and short-term liabilities and provisions. Current portions of long-term liabilities are not measured and disclosed separately.

Provisions include legal and other provisions. Legal provisions are deductible for tax purposes and are precisely stipulated by law No. 593/ 1992, "On Provisions for Measurement of the Income Tax Basis." Legal provisions include:

- Provisions for bad debt (up to 100%), when the debtor is declared bankrupt
- Provisions for repairs of plant and equipment
- Special bank provisions (for standard loans, 1% of the average amount of these loans; for classified loans, from 1% to 20%; for guarantees given, 2%)
- Special insurance provisions (non-life insurance—up to 60% of premium)
- Provisions for overdue loans (20% for loans overdue for more than 6 months but less than 1 year, 33% for loans overdue for more than 1 year)

Other provisions depend on decisions of the enterprise, and they are not tax deductible.

The structure of liabilities includes:

- Long-term liabilities (including accounts and notes payable, bonds, and prepayments received)
- Short-term liabilities (including accounts and notes payable, prepayments received, wages payable, tax payable, deferred taxes)
- Bank loans (subdivided into short-term and long-term loans)
- Other liabilities (deferred expenses, prepaid revenues, differences in exchange rates)

Provisions are based on appropriate calculations. Liabilities and issued bonds are measured at par value.

3.3 Property, Plant, and Equipment

Until 1991, in the Czech Republic, property, plant, and equipment accounts did not include land. For a long time land was considered to be property of the state and thus not measured and registered in accounts. Today land is already included in the assets and accounts of companies at prices given by a decree. These prices may differ from the market value of a particular piece of land.

Equipment and machines must be included only when their cost is higher than 10,000 Czech crowns. Equipment under this limit can be shown in the balance sheet or transferred directly into expense. This choice depends on management. Property, plant, and equipment (except for land) are measured at original cost; only when purchased from another enterprise that used the asset before must it be revalued at the second purchase cost. The replacement value is used only for property, plant, and equipment received as a gift, received free after the termination of a financial leasing contract, or newly found during stock-taking. Machines and equipment under 10,000 Czech crowns can be written off in the expense immediately after being purchased.

In the balance sheet fixed assets are disclosed subdivided into tangible, intangible, and financial assets. The depreciation charge in property, plant, and equipment is normally calculated on a straight-line basis. The percentage of depreciation depends on the class of asset and its useful life, given by an internal instruction of the enterprise. For tax purposes, depreciation rates are given for individual classes of property, plant, and equipment by

Law No. 586/1992, "On the Income Tax." In this law separate rates for straight-line and accelerated depreciation are shown.

Estimated useful lives are normally as follows:

Freehold buildings	45 years
Plant and machinery	8–15 years
Motor vehicles	4 years
Fixtures and fittings	8 years
Computer equipment	4 years
Computer software	4 years
Office equipment	4 years

3.4 Assets Acquired by Means of Leases

Assets acquired by means of leases are not included as assets on the balance sheet of the lessee. They are registered separately and treated as off-balance-sheet items. According to Czech accounting principles, any initial down payment is booked as a current asset and written off over the period of the leasing contract, and the monthly payment installments are charged to the profit and loss account. In the cases of both operational and financial leasing, the assets are shown and depreciated in the accounts of the lessor.

The leasing rules are dominated by tax regulations. Financial leasing exists when:

- The lease period exceeds 40% of the depreciation period given in the tax law and exceeds the minimal period of 3 years (the minimal period is 8 years for immovables).
- The purchase price at the end of the leasing period is not higher than book value if the straight-line depreciation method was used.

3.5 Oil, Gas, and Other Mineral Resources

Until 1992 oil, gas, and other mineral resources were not included in the assets of the enterprises. They were considered to be state property. Since 1993 they have been included in the land account and land price (when purchased). This amount is decreased as the resource is extracted, and the depletion is booked in expenses.

3.6 Participations

Investments in other companies are measured at purchase price (purchase cost without expenses related to the purchase, such as commissions). Investments in subsidiaries, in associated companies, and in other companies are disclosed separately.

3.7 Inventories

Materials are measured from the moment of purchase up to the time of their consumption at cost, including transport and handling costs. When bought from various enterprises for different prices, the materials are measured and disclosed at actual cost. Since January 1, 1993 only the average cost and FIFO methods of valuation of inventories have been allowed. Work in progress and finished goods are measured at planned or actual cost (full or direct). Provision is made, where necessary, for obsolescent and slow-moving stock and poor quality raw materials.

3.8 Taxation

Companies and enterprises must pay taxes to the state budget, as laid down by law. Since 1993 substantial taxation changes have been approved in the Czech Republic. The principal method of direct taxation is income tax at the rate 35% of taxable profit. Taxable income can be different from commercial income (shown in the profit and loss account). Two major reasons exist:

1. Temporal differences—different accounting and tax depreciation methods and rates, provisions that are not recognized for tax purposes
2. Definite differences—expenses that are not recognized for tax purposes and income taxed by the paying company (e.g., dividends, bond interest)

Deferred tax has been introduced in the Czech Republic. However, the deferred tax liability or receivable is derived only from differences between the accounting and tax depreciation of fixed assets.

In addition, enterprises pay a payroll tax for every employee. The amount of this tax depends on the earnings of the employee, the number of children and other persons dependent on the employee, and so on.

In 1993 a value added tax (VAT) was introduced, and this tax is paid by enterprises. Two rates of VAT are used—22% for goods and 5% for services, with some exceptions allowed in the law.

The taxation system also includes:

- A consumption tax, levied on petrol, spirits, wine, beer, and tobacco products
- An immovables tax, levied on land and buildings
- A road tax, levied on cars and trucks used for business purposes
- An inheritance tax, gift tax, and tax on transfer of immovables

3.9 Pension Costs

In the Czech Republic, social security for the old age of workers and other staff is provided by the state budget, and secutity for illness is provided by special insurance companies. Companies pay special transfers for pension costs (including unemployment insurance) to the state budget. Its level amounts to 26% of payroll paid by the company and 9% paid by the employee. Additional voluntary pension insurance can be obtained by payments to special pension funds.

3.10 Intangibles

Until 1990 Czechoslovak financial or accounting legal regulations did not recognize intangible assets as a special form of property. Therefore, in balance sheets there were no such items as patents, licenses, trademarks, or goodwill. Some intangible assets (e.g., patents) could be treated as a special category of deferred charges.

Since 1991 partially, and fully since 1993, the idea has been accepted to show intangible assets in the accounts of enterprises. Since 1993 a more detailed structure of intangible assets greater than 20,000 Czech crowns (40,000 Czech crowns since 1996) has been presented: organization cost, intangible results of research activities, software, rights, and other intangible assets. Amortization of these intangibles is included during the useful life of the latter, up to a maximum of 5 years (8 years for tax purposes). Purchased intangible assets less than 40,000 Czech crowns can be treated as an expense.

Purchased intangibles are measured at cost (inclusive of expenses related to the purchase, such as transportation expense, commission). Lower of cost or replacement value is used for the valuation of self-produced intangible assets.

In the process of privatization, goodwill may occur on the balance sheet. It arises if assets are received or purchased at a price different from book value in the accounts of the selling company. This goodwill (or badwill in the case of negative difference) is amortized in the expense (or in the income) over a period of 15 years.

4. Expected Future Developments

Since the revolution in November 1989, the economy, accounting practice, financial reporting, and accounting systems in the Czech Republic have been in a phase of rapid evolution toward the European level common for a market economy. Fundamentally new legislation on accounting and taxation has been in effect since January 1993. The taxation burden has gradually been diminished. In 1997 the income tax rate decreased from 49% to 35%, and further decrease of direct taxes can be expected. Tax relief for foreign investors such as tax holidays has been proposed.

Accounting principles and procedures and financial reporting reflect the influence of International Accounting Standards (IAS) and the EU Directives. Further harmonization with IAS and EU Directives is found in the new law on accounting, which should take effect in 1999. Some reporting and valuation principles, including leasing contracts and investments, will be changed.

An auditors' opinion on financial reports has become obligatory for most larger enterprises. Further growth in the number of auditors and the organization of their activity is likely. These measures will raise the prestige of the accountancy profession to the level common in developed countries.

Useful Address

Komora auditorů České republiky
(Chamber of Auditors in the Czech Republic)
Opletalova 55/57
111 21 Praha 1
post box 772
Czech Republic
Tel. +4202-2421 2670
Fax. +4202-2421 1905

Financial Statements (from a Czech company, 1997)

ROZVAHA

v tis. Kč

	1996	1997
Aktiva celkem	209 102	246 002
Stálá aktiva	79 481	86 944
- nehmotný investiční majetek	504	1 508
- hmotný investiční majetek	78 977	85 436
- finanční investice		
- podílové cenné papíry a vklady v podnicích ve skupině		
- ostatní finanční investice		
Oběžná aktiva	128 458	154 314
- zásoby	64 670	76 230
- dlouhodobé pohledávky		
- krátkodobé pohledávky	51 956	79 159
- finanční majetek	11 832	- 1 075
Ostatní aktiva	1 163	4 744
Pasíva celkem	209 102	246 002
Vlastní jmění	124 007	138 130
- základní jmění	104 589	104 589
- kapitálové fondy	-	1 058
- fondy tvořené ze zisku	11 532	10 208
- hospodářský výsledek minulých let	7 886	7 886
- hospodářský výsledek účetního období		14 389
Cizí zdroje	83 791	107 200
- zákonné rezervy		
- jiné rezervy		
- dlouhodobé závazky		
- krátkodobé závazky	47 589	60 600
- bankovní úvěry a výpomoci	36 202	46 600
- dlouhodobé bankovní úvěry		
- krátkodobé bankovní úvěry a výpomoci	36 202	46 600
Ostatní pasíva	1 304	672

BALANCE SHEET (IN THOUSAND CZECH CROWNS)

	1996	*1997*
Total assets	209,102	246 002
Fixed assets	79,481	86,944
- intangible fixed assets	504	1,508
- tangible fixed assets	78,977	86,436
- financial investments		
- participating interests in affiliated undertakings		
- other investments		
Current assets	128,458	154,314
- inventories	64,670	76,230
- long-term accounts receivable		
- short-term account receivable	51,956	79,159
- financial assets, cash	11,832	- 1,075
Other assets	1,163	4,744
Total liabilities	209,102	246,002
Equity	124,007	138,130
- capital stock	104,589	104,589
- capital reserves	—	1,058
- revenue reserves	11,532	10,208
- undistributed profit of previous years	7,886	7,886
- profit for current year		14,389
Liabilities	83,791	107,200
- legal provisions		
- other provisions		
- long-term accounts and notes payable		
- short term accounts and notes payable	47,589	60,600
- bank loans	36,202	46,600
- long-term bank loans		
- short-term bank loans	36,202	46,600
Other liabilities	1,304	672

Výkaz zisků a ztrát

	1997
Tržby za prodej zboží	7 973
Náklady vynaložené na prodané zboží	7 788
+ Obchodní marže	185
Výroba	209 194
Tržby za prodej vlastních výrobků a služeb	206 265
Změna stavu vnitropodnikových zásob vlastní výroby	763
Aktivace	2 165
Výrobní spotřeba	140 982
+ Přidaná hodnota	68 396
Osobní náklady	21 596
Daně a poplatky	295
Jiné provozní výnosy	4 289
Jiné provozní náklady	6 007
Odpisy nehmotného a hmotného investičního majetku	8 728
Zúčtování rezerv, opravných položek a	
časového rozlišení provozních výnosů	
Tvorba rezerv, opravných položek a časového	
rozlišení provozních nákladů	
* Provozní hospodářský výsledek	36 060
Finanční výnosy	328
Finanční náklady	6 521
Zúčtování rezerv a opravných položek do finančních výnosů	
Tvorba rezerv a opravných položek na finanční náklady	
* Hospodářský výsledek z finančních operací	- 6 193
Splatná daň z příjmů za běžnou činnost	14 620
Odložená daň z příjmů za běžnou činnost	
** Hospodářský výsledek za běžnou činnost	15 247
Mimořádné výnosy	2 388
Mimořádné náklady	3 246
Splatná daň z příjmů z mimořádné činnosti	
Odložená daň z příjmů z mimořádné činnosti	
*Mimořádný hospodářský výsledek	- 858
***Hospodářský výsledek za účetní období	14 389

PROFIT AND LOSS ACCOUNT

	1997
Sales of goods	7,973
Cost of sales	7,788
+ Gross Margin	185
Production	209,194
Sales of own products and services	206,265
Changes in work in progress and in finished goods	764
Production for own consumption	2,165
Cost of production	140,982
+ Value added	68,397
Staff expenses	21,596
Taxes	295
Other production income	4,289
Other production expenses	6,007
Depreciation and amortization	8,728
Use of provisions and deferred expenses	
Creation of provisions and accrued expenses	
* Operating profit or loss	36,060
Financial revenues	328
Financial expenses	6,521
Use of provisions and deferred financial expenses	
Creation of provisions and accrued financial expenses	
* Financial profit or loss	-6,193
Tax payable from operations	14,620
Deferred tax from operations	
*Net profit or loss on ordinary activities	15,247
Extraordinary revenues	2,388
Extraordinary expenses	3,246
Tax payable on extraordinary operations	
Deferred tax on extraordinary operations	
* Profit or loss on extraordinary operations	-858
*** Profit or loss for accounting period	14,389

Zpráva auditora

určená akcionářům společnosti ABC, a. s.

Provedli jsme v souladu se Zákonem o auditorech a Komoře auditorů České republiky a s auditorskými směrnicemi, jež vydala Komora auditorů České republiky, ověření účetní závěrky společnosti ABC, a.s. sestavené k 31. 12. 1997.

Za sestavení účetní závěrky je odpovědný statutární orgán společnosti. Naší úlohou je vyjádřit na základě auditu výrok o této účetní závěrce. Auditorské směrnice požadují plánovat a provést audit tak, aby auditor získal přiměřené ujištění o tom, že účetní závěrka neobsahuje významné nesprávnosti. Audit zahrnuje výběrové ověření úplnosti a průkaznosti částek a informací uvedených v účetní závěrce a posouzení použitých účetních postupů a významných odhadů provedených společností a rovněž posouzení celkové prezentace účetní závěrky. Jsme přesvědčeni, že provedený audit poskytuje přiměřený podklad pro vyjádření našeho výroku.

Podle našeho názoru, účetní závěrka ve všech významných ohledech věrně zobrazuje v souladu se Zákonem o účetnictví a účetními předpisy platnými v České republice majetek, závazky a vlastní jmění společnosti ABC, a. s. a její výsledek hospodaření dosažený za rok 1997.

V Praze, dne 31. ledna 1998

B D O C S s. r. o.   Doc. Ing. Jan Doležal, CSc.
Kvestorská 2   číslo dekretu 0070
140 00 Praha 4
Licence KA ČR číslo 18

Auditors' Report

Auditors' report to the members of ABC, a.s.

We have audited the financial statements of ABC, a.s. for the year ended December 31, 1997 in accordance with the Law on Auditors and Chamber of Auditors of the Czech Republic and in accordance with the auditing standards issued by the Chamber of Auditors of the Czech Republic.

The accounting and financial statements are the responsibility of the company's managment. Our responsibility is to express an opinion on these financial statements. Auditing standards require that the audit is planned and performed to obtain reasonable assurance about whether the financial statements are free from material misstatements.

In our opinion, the financial statements give in all material respects a true and fair view of the assets, liabilities, and financial position of ABC, a.s. as at December 31, 1997 and result for the year then ended in accordance with the Law on accounting and accounting standards valid in the Czech Republic.

Prague, January 31, 1998
BDO CS s.r.o.
Certified Accountants and Consultants
Kvestorská 2
Praha 4
License CACR no. 18

HUNGARY

Maria Borda
EU PHARE
Financial Sector Development Program
Ministry of Finance, KPMG Hungary

1. The History of Accounting Development

The development of Hungarian accounting can be divided into three periods:

1. During the nineteenth and the first half of the twentieth centuries Hungarian accounting was strongly influenced by Western European countries.
2. Between 1948 and 1988, accounting developments were geared to the requirements of a centrally planned economic system.
3. Since 1988 the transition to a market economy has had to be facilitated by new accounting functions. In January of 1992 a new accounting law, basically in line with EC Directives and International Accounting Systems, was introduced, based on its preparation started in 1989.

Before discussing the three periods, this chapter gives an overview of the legal infrastructure of Hungarian accounting.

1.1 Development of the Legal Framework of Accounting

The Budapest Commodity and Security Exchange was established in 1864. The first company law in Hungary, the so-called Commercial Law No. XXXVII/1875, came into force in 1875. This law incorporated an act relating to shares as well.

The first law on notes was enacted in 1890, the issuance of bonds first being regulated by an act of 1897, and the first law on mortgages having been passed in 1876. At the beginning of the twentieth century, together with most other developed capitalist countries, Hungary became a signatory to the Hague Treaty on Notes. A special law (No. V/1930) on private limited companies was enacted in 1930. By enactment of these laws, the legal standards of business life in Hungary corresponded to European norms generally.

In 1989, after a 40-year break, Hungary had the most developed legal framework in Eastern Europe for privatization and joint ventures. To create a real market economy, the overwhelming proportion of state property rights have been transferred to the private sector. The announced goal of the government is that the proportion of state property be reduced from 90% in 1989 to about 30%–40% in the next few years. In 1993, 50% of the GDP came from the private sector. By 1998, 80% of state property had been privatized.

In 1989, Hungary was the first Eastern bloc country to establish Western European legal standards of business, by enacting Law No. VI/1988 on business associations, and Law No. XXIV/1988 on investment by foreigners in Hungary. The latter permitted special tax benefits in favor of foreign participants. Unified Entrepreneurs' Profit Taxes Law No. XI/1988 could result in tax holidays of up to 5 years and 60% tax benefit for another 5 years for companies to which foreigners have contributed more than 30% of the capital, if the company operated specific manufacturing enterprises or in the hotel industry. The last year in which foreigners could enjoy the special tax benefit was 1993. The last year of tax benefits allowable under this program is 2003. Since 1994 a tax break has been granted for any investors in companies in which exports are increased or new jobs are created or for investments of at least HUF 1 billion. Law No XIII/1989 on the transformation of business organizations and companies also has great significance for privatization. The main purpose of the law is to provide rules for the transformation of state-owned companies into business associations, declaring simultaneously the principle of general (legal) succession. Furthermore, it provides rules for the transformation of a company into another type of company, including mergers and split-ups.

The Hungarian Stock Exchange—facilitated by Law No. VI/1990 on Securities and the Stock Exchange—was the first to reopen in Central and Eastern Europe. On the basis of Law No. VII/1990, the National Property Agency—a policy advisory and review body—was established to ensure that state assets are sold at "fair" prices.

In 1992 a state holding company was established by Law No. LIII/1992 for the management and sale of state assets. Backing the transformation law, valuation decree No. 30/1989 established the principles of initial share pricing and net asset valuation. In 1992 after the rapid change of legal environment, this decree was replaced by Law No. LIV/1992 on the privatization of state property.

A two-tier banking system could be introduced as a result of Law No. LX/1991 on the National Bank of Hungary and Law No. LXIX/1991 on commercial banks and banking activities, both of which came into force on December 1, 1991. They were based on the EC Banking Directives. A set of amendments to the banking law came into force on December 31, 1993. A very strict law, Law No. IL/1991 on bankruptcy, liquidation, and final accounts, was introduced in 1992.

As Hungary's economy is restructured, its national economy will be brought into the world market. In addition to greater exports to developed capitalist countries, Hungary must attract foreign capital and, along with it, modern technology.

Joint ventures are considered to be among the most important vehicles of privatization and foreign investment in Hungary. In 1989 the number of joint ventures grew from about 300 to more than 1000. By 1991 the number of joint ventures with more than 50 employees had increased to 11,000. In 1991–1993 the amount of capital invested in Hungary was as great as the total for all the other former eastern bloc countries.

In Hungary, the law on accountancy has occupied a central place in accounting regulations. The first law on accountancy was incorporated within the Commercial Law of 1875. After the Second World War, responsibility for accounting regulation lay with the Ministry of Finance. In 1968, during the period of central economic planning, Law No. 33/1968 on accountancy came into force. It was followed by Law No. II/1979 on public finances, which included the regulation of accounting and auditing.

When the new conditions of economic development came into existence, the old accounting model did not work. A need arose to introduce accounting standards consistent with the generally accepted accounting principles used in the developed market economies. The new law, Law No. XVIII/1991 on accounting, was introduced on January 1, 1992. Law No. CVIII/1993, which amended Law No. XVIII/1991 on accounting, came into force in January 1994. Further amendments to the accounting law included Law No. XX/1995, Law No. CXV/1996, and Law No. CXXX/1997.

The provisions of the new laws were worked out by the accounting department of the Ministry of Finance, taking into consideration the opinions of future users of accounting information, such as the World Bank, academics, experts from international accounting firms, foreign and domestic accounting and auditing associations, and the worldwide accounting profession.

Today the function of accounting in Hungary is to facilitate the creation of a market economy through privatization and joint ventures. To meet this requirement, radical accounting changes are needed. The new law brings into accounting practice the essential technical and conceptual changes.

1.2 The Development of Accounting Theory to the End of the Second World War and Influences from Other Countries

During the nineteenth century and the first half of the twentieth century, the development of Hungarian accounting was deeply influenced by practice in other European countries, especially Germany. At that time in Europe, different accounting theories, different allocation techniques of the costs to products, unit cost calculation methods, and theories on balance sheets were developed. The most notable theorists were Hügli, Schär, Schmalenbach, Niklisch, Mellerovich, Schmidt, and Kosiol.

Various account theories were used for the development of the chart of accounts. According to the two account line theory, which was worked out by Hügli (1887), Schär (1888), and Niklisch (1911), asset and liability accounts are differentiated. The balance sheet is based on the two account line theory. The third account line is the group of cost accounts for detailed recording of the operating costs. The fourth account line is the group of net income accounts. The profit and loss statement is based on the four account line theory (Schmalenbach, 1927). The current chart of accounts in Hungary is based on Schmalenbach's related theory.

The different balance sheet theories—dynamic, static, and organic—concern the relationships between the goal of setting a balance sheet and the asset valuation methods. The goal of setting a balance sheet can be to show the realized result—profit or loss—of a given period, the current value of invested assets, or both of these. Generally, according to these theories, the term *realized result* represents the difference between the selling price of an item and its acquisition cost. This is the conventionally reported "gross margin" according to generally accepted accounting principles.

The difference between the current replacement cost of an item and its acquisition cost, termed "holding gain or loss," is considered "nonrealized profit or loss." When the goal is to show the realized profit or loss of a given period in the balance sheet, the actual acquisition cost of assets—

their historical cost—should be used in the valuation process. This "dy-namic" balance theory can be classified as either classical (Schmalenbach) or "cash-oriented" (Kosiol).

If the goal of setting a balance sheet is to show the current market value of invested assets, their replacement cost should be used in the valuation process. The related balance sheet theory is called static (Niklisch). When-ever the goal of setting a balance sheet is to show both the realized result of a period and the current value of the invested asset, the double valuation method should be used. This means parallel use for acquisition and re-placement costs in the valuation process. This is the "organic" theory (Schmidt). This method is used to separate "realized profit" from the profit that comes from price changes, a concern during periods of high inflation. The theoretical basis of the balance sheet and income statement in Hun-gary is the classical dynamic balance sheet theory.

Although the aforementioned directions in accounting theory in Conti-nental Europe were necessary and useful, to some extent they neglected the managerial approach and failed to assist the planning function of management. Whereas managerial accounting developed quickly in West-ern Europe in the late 1940s and 1950s, in Hungary the accounting field was influenced primarily by Soviet experience, where accounting was subordinated to central planning.

1.3   Accounting and Auditing under the Central Planning System (1948–1988)

During the period when the national economy was under direct central control, the main tasks of accounting were to provide factual data on the economic activity of enterprises, to measure and control fulfillment of the planned targets at both enterprise and national levels, to provide informa-tion for sectoral and national aggregations, and for the derivation of national indices.

Accounting became a tool for macro-level monitoring of the firm. In providing data for reliable planning and control decisions at the national level, however, accounting was successful only to certain degree. The main limitation was that accounting lost its original function as showing a true and fair view of the financial position and net income generation of a company. Instead of that accounting provided production and national income statistics. A further limitation of accounting was that in the ab-sence of market mechanism, money and prices could not fulfil their function in macro-economic structural decision making. As a result, accounting valuations lost their objective basis, missing the self-regulation force of a market.

Under the central planning system, accounting failed the function of providing information for managerial decision-making and could not serve as an efficient micro-managerial tool.

Financial statements supplied data that could be summarized to provide a general view of the aggregate activities by region, industry, and the entire economy. In order to achieve this, uniformly applicable normative rules of bookkeeping were laid down by detailed regulations.

The scheme of accounts determined the rules for the general ledger and the basic requirements of physical accounts. According to the pre-1992 Accounting Law, the Minister of Finance regulated by decrees the bookkeeping system of all Hungarian firms and public organizations through a General Compulsory Scheme of Accounts. The basic documentation systems, a product cost-tracing system, and the principles of financial statements, valuation methods, and disclosure of financial statements were also regulated. Accounting rules were strongly influenced by tax regulation and other elements of economic regulation.

The contents of the closing financial statements were strictly regulated and the preprinted formats obligatory. The ordinary annual financial report consisted of a balance sheet, an income statement (in summary and in detail), a profit distribution statement (for taxation), a statement of costs detailed by type, and other statements of supplementary information.

The financial report had to be presented to the Board of Directors or to the General Meeting. The Board of Directors or the General Meeting was authorized to accept the balance sheet and the stated profit or loss and the profit distribution.

The acceptance and approval of the balance sheet were documented by the signature of the head of the authorizing body (i.e., the chair of the Board of Directors or the General Meeting). The approved balance sheet, together with the income statement, had to be lodged with the Court of Registration by May 31 of the year after the accounting period. Copies of the deposited documents also had to be filed with the local tax authority.

Under this old accounting legislation, the approved balance sheet, the ledger statements supporting the balance sheet, and the inventory and analytical records were audited by the tax authority within financial and economic audits but could be revised by the company itself under a system of self-audit. Financial audits and self-audits were carried out to verify the validity and completeness of the approved balance sheet, the profit distribution, and the settlements due within the central budget and to ensure compliance with inventory-taking and valuation rules.

State financial auditing extended to economic activity as a whole and the analysis of the success of financial and economic decisions, as well as the impact of economic regulations. It helped the central and the enterprise-level leadership in the assessment of management activity and in the evaluation of decisions taken or missed.

Under financial audits, the Taxes and State Financial Audit Board examined:

1. The business organization's balance sheet and income statement to verify that the assets and the profit or loss of business activities were included to reflect a true picture of the business and that accounting, bookkeeping, and the system of documentation comply with legislative provisions

2. Compliance with the rules pertaining to the payment of taxes and other fiscal liabilities toward the state and the use of budgetary subsidies (for example, consumer and producer price subsidies) (Since January 1991 these subsidies have been significantly reduced.)

The Board carried out financial audits of each business organization, usually every second year. The state auditors included their findings that required action on the part of the authorities in protocols. The protocol played a similar role to that of the audit report in the case of companies that were audited by an independent auditor. The content and form of the protocol was defined by Law No. II/1979 on public finance. An audited company might comment on the contents of the protocol orally at the closing meeting or in writing within days of receiving the protocol.

Auditing started from the requirements of both rational flexibility and strict formal discipline, as required by economic activity. Auditing had to help maintain economic and auditing order, as well as detect abuses that might occur.

Under the "New Economic Mechanism" of the 1970s and 1980s, attempts were made to introduce innovative changes. For example, some domestic prices were allowed to approximate to world prices, the administrative regulation of wages and salaries was abolished, and value-added taxation and personal income taxes were adapted. Under the centralized economic system, however, none of them achieved the desired results. Now the goal is to move from the centralized economic system to a true market economy.

1.4 The Accounting and Auditing Profession Today

1.4.1 Current Influence of the Former Overregulated Accounting System on the Accounting Profession; Changing Approach

The former overregulated accounting system has a strong influence on the current accounting profession. During the past 40 years accountants in Hungary had to follow strict rules, prescribed in detail. They had no time to consider things, and there was no room for consideration. Accountants did not have the opportunity to build an accounting and reporting system that would fit the goals and strategies of their companies. Under such circumstances, the accountants within management usually have been regarded as low skilled technicians, or "bookkeepers:' The entire profession lost its reputation, so it was not able to attract the most talented young people.

The new accounting regulation, in line with the EU Directives, has absolutely different characteristics. The law forms the underlying basis of financial reporting. The principles of the law can not be considered as detailed obligatory rules, and neither do they cater to all accounting possibilities. The new law requires accountants to apply a new approach in their everyday work. They must make decisions to meet the principles of the new laws. To use the acquisition cost of the assets is no longer the only possibility for accounting valuation. In certain cases, accountants must make their best estimation for stating the market value of assets.

Accountants also must consider the time value of money when making accounting decisions. When setting the accounting policy of a company, they have to be not only bookkeepers but economists and marketing experts and to cope with the strategic requirements of the company at the same time. In 1992 a 2-week course on the new accounting law was not enough to equip accountants with what they need to cope with and manage the change to the new approach. Accounting reform needs to be accomplished in the minds of accountants, which takes longer.

This process should be facilitated by the necessary institutional framework development of the accounting profession.

1.4.2 *The Auditing Profession*

The traditions of the Hungarian auditing profession date from 1932, when the Association of Hungarian Auditors (AHA) was founded. During the period of central planning, the independent audit function did not find its place within the existing economic structure, and the AHA was not active. The recent significant economic changes in Hungary created the need for control over the professional, educational, and ethical standards of accountants. In 1987 the AHA was reestablished and soon became internationally accepted.

A national professional organization of accountants, the AHA has taken part since 1988 in the annual congress of the European Accounting Association. In 1992 the AHA became a member of the International Federation of Accountants (IFAC). Meetings are in process with the *Fédération des Experts Comptables Européens* (FEE). AHA has become an associated member of FEE. AHA, with 2500 members, has been considered a basis for the development of an independent auditing profession in Hungary.

Decree No. 46/1992 on Independent Audit defined the required qualification process for a Hungarian Chartered Accountant.

After the necessary examinations was passed, the "degree" of Registered Hungarian Chartered Accountant was given by the Ministry of Finance.

In 1991 the AHA changed its name to Hungarian Chamber of Auditors (HCA). But the change was only formal, a strong self-standing professional body of the auditors was missing at that time.

1.4.3 *Institutional Development of Accountancy Profession*

In 1992 the EU PHARE Financial Sector Development Program, represented by the Ministry of Finance PHARE Program Management Unit (MoF PHARE PMU) wished to encourage and assist the accountancy profession to establish appropriate professional bodies that corresponded with current EU practices.

The structure of the accountancy profession should have been designed to maximise its contribution to the wealth creation process in the economy.

In Phase 1 in 1993 a review was taken on the operations of accounting, auditing, and tax advisory associations in six EU member states to determine the different systems established for ensuring the best development of bookkeeping, accounting, auditing, and tax advisory practice at all levels nationally. Upon findings of the review, the consultant was asked to recommend a system appropriate to the development of the Hungarian bookkeeping, accounting, auditing, and tax advisory professions at all levels, existing structure and financial realities, made in close co-operation with relevant representatives of the Hungarian professions.

As a result, it was agreed that independent self-supporting professional bodies should be established. Therefore the Association of Accountants and the Association of Tax Advisors were established, whereas the Hungarian Chamber of Auditors, having been established in 1987, needed further development.

In Phase 2, integrated three-year business plans and directives were prepared in line with the EC best practice for each organization to set their objectives, tasks and activities to meet their members' professional needs.

In Phase 3, Standard Agreements were signed between the MoF Phare PMU and the professional bodies to finance the implementation of tasks and activities described in the business plans. Under the necessary professional approach the professional bodies should be vital for modern, efficiently operating market economies.

In order to establish and maintain efficiently and effectively operating professional bodies (to EU standards), the professional bodies have to cover the following tasks. The most important functions that should be provided by the professional bodies are:

- To combine the forces of the membership in order to represent professional interest

- To provide, organize and initiate training for the profession and to ensure that the members keep up with the developments of the profession

- To elaborate codes of ethics

- To set up professional standards and supervise their implementation

- To provide a constant review of accounting, auditing, and taxation legislation and to advise authorities for amendment or updating

- To harmonize with similar EU organizations

These organizations have to provide a stable and reliable background for its members by:

- showing well-balanced economic performance
- securing the necessary financial background for professional training
- widening and developing international professional contacts
- developing recruitment activity among new possible members

1.4.4 Implementation of Business Plans of Professional Bodies

The implementation of the Standard Agreements started in May 1996 in the case of the Tax Advisors and in September 1996 in the case of the Accountants and the Auditors.

The organizations faced a difficult situation. Due to the Phare administration procedure and the late signing of the Standard Agreements, the approved three year business plans had to be implemented practically in half time. That meant severe time constrains and additional efforts on the side of the organizations.

The joint budget of the three organizations (managed of course separately by each body) was MECU 1.430, which was fully committed and disbursed by the end of the period of 1997.

Apart from the available Phare assistance, the institutions utilized their own funds as well for the implementation of their plans. These funds came in as membership fees and were increasing as the project was developing.

When procuring goods and services, the institutions observed the Phare procurement rules as outlined in the Standard Agreements through the utilization of the Phare Manual on the Decentralized Implementation System.

All three business plans dealt with the same headings, which is obvious at institutional development projects at organizations of very similar professions. The division of the budget headings followed also this pattern. Therefore the following main items were dealt with in the financial plans:

- foundation
- representation
- membership services
- training
- administration
- other fundable operational expenses

This would indicate that joint projects could be initiated and implemented between two or even three organizations. In fact this idea came up in Phase 1 of the Phare project. But the practice showed, that it did not work. The organizations did not show much interest to cooperate with each other at that stage.

The possible creation of a common service unit as a technical means to provide differentiated services to and for the professional bodies to cover their common function seemed to be logical.

A summary of main achievements in the course of the implementation of their business plans of all three professional bodies is given below.

1.4.5. Association of Accountants

The Association of Accountants was established in the second half of 1995. In this process the recommendations of the business plan were taken into account to a large extent. This organization has the biggest potential in respect of the number of members, since over 50,000 professionals can be listed as having professional links to the association.

The actual membership reached 2,500 by the end of the project period. With the expanding services offered, the Association hopes to increase its membership significantly in the forthcoming years.

The association was founded without any previous initiatives, following the example of similar European institutions and taking into account the findings and recommendations of the studies and the business plans.

The original business plan envisaged the foundation of only three regional organizations, in the first years of operation. In the course of 1996 they were established in all counties, thus the full country network has been built up giving good basis for future development.

The association has put emphasis onto the development of the members' journal, which is being published on a regular basis from August 1997, and the library.

The association, having an attracting effect toward the potential membership, considered the training element of the business plan as the most important. The training comprised courses on different topics, related to the everyday work of accounting specialists. The project was tendered, the winner, the College of Finance and Accountancy, has held 97 courses that lasted 223 days with more than 3,000 participants. Its positive effect showed up in the second half of 1997, when the number of members rose by about 10%.

Since this association has the shortest period of existence, its international relations are less developed than those of the other two bodies. In the future members could gain positive experience on the operation of similar EU country based organizations. The gradual development of international connections is a high priority.

1.4.6 Association of Tax Advisors

The association had its roots in the club of tax advisors, operating in the framework of a training and publishing company for about three years. At founding the association was following the pattern worked out in the business plan.

The mission statement of the association declares the Chamber as the desired form of organization and certain steps have been already taken toward it. At this stage one can forecast it will happen in one or two years' time.

Because tax advising is the narrowest profession, it can plan with a total membership of about 2,000 plus the tax advisory companies (about 200), as the business plan found. The Association has mobilized around 1,400 members by the end of the second year of operation (1997).

After furnishing and equipping their headquarters, the development of the library went on representing a serious amount of up to date information related to the tax advisory profession.

The highest attention was devoted to the training sub-projects, since the Association considered it as the basic element in the way of providing the necessary tools for the everyday work and development of the tax advisors.

A consistent examination system and the related training materials have been worked out. In the future they will be upgraded as required. Another important element of their activity is building and strengthening international contacts with their partner organizations through out the world.

1.4.7 Chamber of Auditors

The business plan of the Chamber of Auditors included the preparation of draft law on the Hungarian Chamber of Auditors and the auditing activity.

This Act was being discussed for over two years and is of vital importance for the auditing profession. The Parliament passed it in the summer of 1997.

After the acceptance of the new Act No. LV/1997 on the Hungarian Chamber of Auditors and the auditing activity, the actions related to the implementation of the Standard Agreement have accelerated.

The new Chamber had to be re-established, following the tight deadlines set by the law. In six months the whole available budget was committed and disbursed observing the Phare rules. The regional organizations also had to be re-established, but having set up them earlier meant easier solutions. The re-established HCA has 4800 full and part time members.

The elaboration of curricula and examination syllabuses of chartered accountants, as well as preparation of training program, has been accounted as the most important project of their business plan. The content of HCA training program is consistent with the requirements of the Eight Council Directive of European Commission (No. 84/253 EU Directive). The subjects of the chartered accountants qualification and examination system are defined in the appendix of the Law No. LV/1997. The Ministry of Finance delegated its previous responsibility in the field to the HCA.

Another crucial project was the preparation of the Hungarian auditing standards, based on the International Standards of Audit. They will serve as basis for the HCA to elaborate and introduce the National Auditing Standards in 1998.

Under the Law No. LV/1997:

- Membership is compulsory for individuals wishing to provide an audit service

- Legal authority of HCA is exercised by the Minister of Finance

- Preconditions for starting the study for earning the chartered accounting degree are as follows:

  a. university degree earned at universities taught accounting, finance and control subjects

  b. 3 years of practical experience in the field of accounting, finance or control

  c. clean record

  d. degree of certified (balance sheet) accountant

- The qualification of Hungarian Chartered Account is given by the HCA.

Summing up the procedures describing above it can be stated that the institutional development of the accountancy profession can not be declared finished.

The present development of accounting, tax advising and auditing professions should facilitate the EU accession procedure of Hungary.

1.5 The Accounting System Today

1.5.1 Goal of the New Law on Accountancy

The purpose of the law on accountancy is to introduce accounting regulations in line with international accounting principles, ensuring the production of information that is sufficiently comprehensive and accurate to enable a true and fair view of the income-generating capabilities, development of the net assets and financial position of an economic entity to be shown. The law defines the reporting and bookkeeping requirements of those subject to its legislation and the basic principles to be followed in the course of the preparation of the financial reports and of bookkeeping (based on internationally accepted principles). It establishes rules for independent auditing and disclosure and the publication data of financial statements.

1.5.2 Scope and Effective Date of the New Legislation

The requirements of the act extend to

1. Entrepreneurs
2. Budgetary organizations
3. Other organizations
4. The National Bank of Hungary

The act defines *entrepreneurs* as every such natural person, legal entity, or economic organization not being a legal entity pursuing in its own name and upon its own risks manufacturing activities or providing services for compensation for the purposes of making a profit and accumulating wealth in a businesslike manner, including financial and insurance institutions. *Budgetary organizations* shall include the central budgetary organization, local government, institutions, and associations founded thereby, the trustee of the social security fund, and the separated state financial fund. *Other organizations* include housing cooperatives, condominiums, social organizations, public bodies, special interest groups, legal entities of churches, foundations, investment funds, public utility companies, public companies and other organizations as defined in separate legal regulations. Under the last amendment to the accounting Law No. CXXX/1997, the scope of the law does not extend to foreign entrepreneurs who have a majority holding or a 100% stake in a business operating but not registered in Hungary and does not extend to the commercial representation offices of foreign enterpreneurs..

Law No. XVIII/1991 on accounting came into effect on January 1, 1992; Section 8 on the consolidated annual report is supposed to come into effect in January 1995. Law No. CVIII/1993, which amends Law No. XVIII/1991 on accounting came into force in January 1994. It brought forward the effective date of the introduction of the consolidated annual reporting requirements.

The further amendments to the Law No. XVIII/1991 are as follows:

The Law No. XX/1995, which came into force on April 7, 1995, includes two basic changes. First, it introduced the opportunity of revaluation of intangible, tangible assets as well as the shares and participations in accordance with the market value of the assets.

The amount exceeding the book value of the above assets may be shown in asset side of the balance sheet as value correction and as valuation reserve in the amount equal to the value correction within the equity.

Second, sections 41/c–41/d of the Law provides rules for the conversion of the figures, shown in the balance sheet of the annual report or simplified annual report, from foreign exchange to HUF or from HUF to foreign exchange, relevant to the entrepreneurs of duty free zones or other entrepreneurs register in Hungary, defined in the section 41/b (1) of this Law.

The Law No. CXV/1996 is effective January 1, 1997. It includes new elements, reducing the differences between IAS and the Hungarian accounting law, within the limits of EU Directives. The most important new elements of the Law are as follows:

- introduction of additional basic accounting principles,
- accounting for previous years' errors,
- accounting for interest on securities,

- increasing number of elements of assets' acquisition and production costs,
- accounting for transfer of funds,
- changes in equity,
- accounting treatment for unrealized revaluation losses,
- accounting for provisions,
- accounting for financial leasing,
- cash flow statement as required part of the notes.

The most important change introduced by the Law No. CXXX/1997 are as follows:

- the scope of the accounting law extends to subsidies of foreign entrepreneurs registered outside of Hungary,
- the new accounting issues of foreign subsidiaries,
- publication requirements,
- statutory audit requirements.

1.5.3 *The New Approach*

Generally Accepted Accounting Principles (GAAP) form the underlying basis of financial reporting by most reporting entities in countries that have an established system of financial reporting. These principles are not rigid regulations, and neither do they cater to all accounting possibilities. They have generally been used by countries to develop their own system of financial reporting and/or regulation. They have evolved over a considerable period of time to enable a greater degree of comparability among financial reports of different years, of different companies, and of different countries.

These principles usually establish what would be reasonable accounting practice and what would generally lead to accounts presenting a true and fair view of their financial position at a point in time and results over a period of time. They have a certain breadth, and where there is a choice between two or more reasonable policies, companies may select their own accounting policies from those detailed in the general principles. The use of different accounting principles affects a set of financial statements, and companies are therefore required to disclose the accounting principles used in preparing their financial statements.

The 1992 accounting law enacted in Hungary had the following characteristics:

1. It was based on internationally accepted accounting principles, although it did not seek to introduce all these principles.
2. There was an element of choice. The new regulations enable companies to select the appropriate principles on which to establish their accounting information system. The degree of choice permitted by law was, however, restricted.
3. A new relationship arose between accounting and tax regulations. The regulations became independent of each other. The taxable income and the tax amount to be paid were defined by the profit tax law. Accounting income is defined by the accounting law.

1.5.4 European Community Standards as a Basis for the Accounting Law

Accounting law has been based on the Fourth, Seventh, and Eighth Directives of the Council of European Communities. It also takes into consideration International Accounting Standards issued by the International Accounting Standards Board and International Auditing Guidelines. The Fourth Directive includes the regulation of financial statements of limited liability corporations. The Seventh Directive lays down the basic rules pertaining to the preparation of consolidated financial statements. The Eighth Directive covers the appointment and qualification of persons responsible for carrying out the statutory audits of accounting documents.

The Fourth Directive contains the central requirement for the role of financial statements. It prescribes two different balance sheet formats and four different formats for the income statement. Member states may prescribe one of the formats or permit companies to choose one of the formats for themselves. The layout of the balance sheet presentation, called horizontal format, is prescribed by Article 9 of the Fourth Directive, which is used most commonly in the majority of continental European countries. It is shown in Figure 1 at the end of the chapter. The other layout, prescribed by Article 10, is called the vertical format and is most common in the United Kingdom. The new Hungarian law stipulates that all companies must adopt the balance sheet format of Article 9.

The income statement formats prescribed by the directive present the total cost model and the cost of sales models either vertically or horizontally. The new law permits companies to adopt the model that is considered to be the most appropriate to the nature of the business. The model must, however, be presented vertically. The two models are presented in Figures 4 and 5. The total cost model is based on the principle of the gross income statement, which derives from Continental European practice. The cost of sales model follows the functional approach of classification of expenses. In Anglo-Saxon practice usually the cost of sales model is used; in Western Europe either of the models is applied.

2. The Form and Content of Published Financial Statements

2.1 The Objective of Financial Reporting

The predominant objective of financial statements is to provide information on the financial performance of the company upon which management, present and future investors, creditors, and other interested parties may base their decisions. Companies shall prepare a report on their economic resources and the claims on them (net assets, financial position and operating performance, net income) during a period, supported by their accounting records.

2.2 Differentiation of Financial Reports According to the Size and Method of Bookkeeping

The type of report required by a company is determined by its size and method of bookkeeping. There are three different types of report:

1. Annual Report
2. Simplified Annual Report
3. Simplified Balance Sheet

The reports prepared are the responsibility of the entity and its authorized representatives. The accounting period is based on the calendar year.

Financial reporting should include explanations and interpretations to help users understand the financial information provided. Supporting notes and the business report satisfy this objective. In 1992 and 1993 the content of the financial statements was determined by Figures 1–4 and further breakdown was not permitted. Since 1994 further breakdown and analysis have been permitted if they are considered helpful to the reader.

2.2.1 Annual Report

A company that operates a double-entry bookkeeping system and that meets two of the three criteria detailed below in two consecutive years is required to prepare an annual report. The criteria are as follows:

1. Total assets of at least HUF 150 million
2. Annual net sales of at least HUF 300 million
3. Average number of employees exceeds 100 in any given year

The annual report consists of a balance sheet, an income statement, notes to the accounts, and a business report. The structure, format, and contents of the annual report must be consistent from one year to the next to ensure true comparability. Comparative figures are to be shown for both the balance sheet and the income statement.

Assets and liabilities in the balance sheet and revenues and expenditures in the income statement are to be shown gross and are not to be netted off. The annual report shall be prepared in a clear and transparent form, in the structure and form prescribed by law. It shall be prepared in the Hungarian language and in thousand forints.

2.2.2 Simplified Annual Report

Companies that operate a double-entry bookkeeping system but do not meet the size criteria referred to above are required only to produce a simplified annual report. This consists of a balance sheet and an income statement, as shown in Figures 2 and 4 or 5 and notes to the accounts.

2.2.3 Simplified Balance Sheet

An entrepreneur—whose net sales do not exceed HUF 50 million in two consecutive years—keeping single-entry books must prepare a simplified balance sheet with an accounting reference date of December 31 and breakdown of profit or loss for the calendar year. The simplified balance sheet must be prepared in the form prescribed by the new legislation, on the basis of properly maintained account books. The format of the simplified balance sheet is shown in Figure 6 in accordance with the amendment Law No. CXV/1996..

In the simplified balance sheet, depreciation and any loss of value of intangible goods and tangible assets shall be accounted for, irrespective of whether the result is a profit or a loss. Equity consists of subscribed capital, capital reserve accumulated retained earnings and simplified balance sheet profit or loss for the financial year.

The accumulated retained earnings represents the amount of accumulated profits accounted for from the commencement of business excluding the profit of loss for the given financial year.

Specific reserves to cover guarantee obligations are not required. The amount of any dividends due to the owners, the amount of liabilities not related to the supply of goods and services, or raising of loans, as well as any tax liabilities not paid, shall be shown among short-term liabilities.

Because of the cash basis of accounting, prepaid and accrued expenses and deferred income are not applicable and may not be presented in the balance sheet. The simplified balance sheet must be supported by an inventory taking.

Double-Entry Bookkeeping All companies except those in which net sales do not exceed HUF 50 million in two consecutive years, the budgetary organizations, and the National Bank of Hungary must maintain double-entry account books. Ledger accounts are classified, and the double-entry bookkeeping standards are summarized in the uniform chart of accounts. Under the new law, however, the application of the uniform chart of accounts is no longer mandatory. The main goal of the chart is to facilitate the organization of bookkeeping and financial reporting.

The chart lays down nine classes of accounts and, within them, the groups of accounts and their types. Classes 1–4 include the balance sheet accounts, Classes 1–3 the assets accounts, and Class 4 the accounts of equities, specific reserves, and liabilities. Classes 5, 8, and 9 include data needed for the presentation of income statements.

Class 5 is used for recording operating costs by types. It contains all the material costs, labor, labor-related costs, depreciation allowance, and other costs. Labor-related costs include social insurance and contributions to the unemployment fund. This accounting of costs by types provides the basic data for the national economic information system in accordance with the new law.

In Class 6, overhead (indirect) costs used to be collected by departments. Class 7 has been used for accounting for direct costs by products. Under the new system, Classes 6 and 7 are no longer required but may be used as previously or as management determines. For example, these classes may be used to establish responsibility/cost centers within the organization.

Class 8 includes accounts for expenses. It specifies the accounts for recording direct costs and various other cost of sales that are not represented in the direct cost of products or services, financial and extraordinary expenses, and profit tax levied. Class 9 accounts for sales, other revenue, and revenue from financial transactions and extraordinary revenue.

The Chart of Accounts at Company Level A company shall establish a chart of accounts, which must be based on the uniform chart of accounts determined by the act. The use of account classes as determined by the act is compulsory, although a company may choose to increase account categories within the standard classes. The goal of the company chart of accounts is to facilitate preparation of the financial statements required by the accounting law, taking into consideration the specific goals of company management and the specific conditions of the company.

Single-Entry Bookkeeping Entrepreneurs who are required to produce only a simplified balance sheet and whose annual net sales revenue does not exceed HUF 50 million in two consecutive years may keep single-entry account books. Single-entry bookkeeping is basically a record of cash receipts and payments. The increase or decrease in cash results in changes in revenue or expenses, or in accounts receivable or in accounts payable or in owner's capital.

The journal ledger and analyzed cash book are considered to be the most usual methods of single-entry bookkeeping. In the journal ledger, the input and output general sales tax items are always recorded separately. Because only cash-in and cash-out transactions are recorded in the journal ledger, it must be supplemented by the physical (analytical) records, which provide information for preparing the simplified balance sheet.

2.3 The Content of Financial Statements in the Annual Report

2.3.1 Balance Sheet

In 1988, important changes were made in the required content and structure of the balance sheet. The distinction between funds for current assets, fixed assets, and other special funds, which characterized the period 1946–1987, was dominated in favor of a homogeneous "funds for assets" account. In the long run, this treatment facilitates the establishment of an interest in asset values. Instead of a segmented view of asset categories, corporate leadership could now focus on the effective management of the entire asset base.

Since 1989 customers' advance payments have been registered on the liabilities side as an accrual, the opposite of the previous practice, when they had been netted out against accounts receivable. Another change has been made by taking the intangible assets (this category was introduced in 1988) out of the gross value of fixed assets and putting them under a separate balance sheet account title.

As a result of these changes, the Hungarian balance sheet of the early 1990s resembles more closely than previously that of the Anglo-Saxon and World Bank model.

The balance sheet lists the assets according to mobility (liquidity) and the liabilities according to solvency due date, in descending order.

The prescribed format of balance sheet under the new accounting law is shown in Figure 1 at the end of the chapter.

Assets   Assets should be classified as long-term assets, current assets, or prepaid expenses and accrued income. The classification of assets between long-term assets and current assets is based on the business purpose and expected use of the assets. Assets that are expected to be realized in cash, sold, or consumed within one year are to be considered current assets.

Long-term assets. Long-term assets comprise (a) intangible assets, (b) tangible assets, and (c) financial assets. *Intangible assets* include rights, concessions, intellectual goods, and goodwill. Research and development costs and foundation and reorganization expenses may be capitalized and presented as intangible assets if they have the potential for providing the company with a future benefit. In the case of capitalization of foundation expenses, dividends shall not be paid unless the after-tax profits and the accumulated retained earnings, adjusted by the amount of loss carried forward, exceed the amount of the capitalized foundation and reorganization expenses not yet written off.

Tangible assets. Tangible assets include land, forests, plant buildings, technical equipment, machines, vehicles, plant and shop furnishings, and other equipment.

Financial assets. Financial assets are long-term investments in equity shares of other companies acquired to obtain control over a company or to obtain a long-term interest in the earnings of a subsidiary. Such assets also include other long-term investments and long-term loans granted.

Current assets. Assets that are expected to be realized in cash, sold, or consumed within one year are current assets. Current assets include inventories, receivables, marketable securities, and monetary assets.

Prepaid expenses and accrued income. Prepaid expenses and accrued income include expenditures incurred in the accounting period but that relate to the following accounting period and income earned in the accounting period but not received until the following accounting period.

Owners' Equity and Liabilities   The liability side of the balance sheet must be presented under the following classifications: owners' equity, specific reserves, liabilities, and accrued expenses and deferred income.

Owner's equity. In line with Law No. CXV/1996 the owners equity includes:

1. Subscribed capital
2. Subscribed but unpaid capital
3. Capital reserve (share premium account)
4. Accumulated retained earnings (profits)
5. Evaluation reserve
6. Balance sheet profit or loss for the financial year

Subscribed capital is that part of equity that is registered or will be registered as such by the Court of Registration. Within the subscribed capital should be shown separately.

a. owners' share repurchased at face value
b. the amount of capital increase, capital decrease of share or limited liability companies which have not yet been registered with the Court of Registration.

Among the items of equity any issued but unpaid capital shall be shown separately as a negative figure.

Capital reserve may include the following items:

- The difference between the par and issued value of the shares
- The amount of capital permanently transferred by the founders to the company

- Decrease or increase in the issued capital against or from the capital reserve
- The amount of capital permanently transferred by other companies to the company
- The value of share-vouchers subscribed by cooperative members and asset-notes acquired by employees and other increase or decrease of capital reserve based on legal provisions

Accumulated retained earnings comprise the opening accumulated retained earnings plus the balance sheet profit for the previous period, less brought-forward losses amortized through retained earnings, plus or minus accumulated retained earnings transferred to or from legal provisions, less the amount transferred to subscribed capital, less the amount used for dividend or profit sharing of the period, and related taxed incurred.

Valuation Reserve can be shown in Equity in amount which equal to the value correction of Invested assets.

Balance sheet profit or loss for the financial year is the after-tax profit or loss, increased by the amount of accumulated retained earnings used for dividend or profit sharing of the given period and reduced by the whole amount of the declared dividend or profit sharing. This should equal the profit figure in the income statement. Dividend cannot be paid from subscribed capital.

Specific reserves. Under the new system, a category of specific reserve has been created. The concept of a specific reserve allows for the provision for certain anticipated losses and expenses and can allow for the deferral of the recognition of gains or profits until they are certain to be realized.

Specific reserves may be deducted from the amount of profit before tax. They should cover potential losses from receivables overdue, bad debts, and advance payments made, and to cover obligations of early retirement pension and redundancy payments. Specific reserves may be created to cover guarantee obligations. If the entity does not create such reserves, all guarantee obligations should be classified and disclosed in a note to the accounts. The amount of such reserves shall be detailed in a note.

Insurance companies may form specific reserves to cover long-term obligations and to balance out damage fluctuations between years. The risk reserve requirements pertaining to financial institutions have been regulated by a separate law, Law on banks and banking activities.

Liabilities. Liabilities are classified as short or long term. Short-term liabilities are loans and credits received with a maturity of less than a year and include the portion of long-term liabilities to be repaid within one year of the accounting date. The amount of the latter shall be disclosed in a note. Short-term liabilities include advance payments received from customers, shown as noncash liabilities.

Long-term liabilities are due more than one year after the accounting date.

Accrued expenses and deferred income. Accruals and deferred income should be used to account for cash receipts received before the balance sheet date but which relate to revenues arising in the next accounting period, costs relating to the current accounting period that will be invoiced in the next period, claims arising from damages, penalties for defaults relating to the current period that have been enforced or submitted against the firm between the accounting date and the preparation of accounts (payments for damages and legal costs that become known during this period), and proposed bonus payments and related social security contributions for both employee and executive staff relating to the current period.

Under the new system, the executive bonus payment will not be separated from the nonexecutive one. The amount of bonuses announced but not paid will be shown in the balance sheet as accruals.

2.3.2 Income Statement (Profit and Loss Account)

The income statement shows the balance sheet profit or loss as the after tax profit or loss of regular and extraordinary activities of the firm, increased by the amount of accumulated retained earnings used for the dividend or (profit-sharing) of the year and reduced by the announced dividend amount. The statement contains the total revenue of the enterprise (i.e., receipt from sales and other income), as well as the total expenses (costs of sales, overhead costs not distributed to products, so-called period costs, and other expenses).

Two models are used in developing the income statement permitted by the law. These are the total cost model and the cost of sales model. The prescribed format for the total cost model is shown in Figure 4.

The main categories of this format and their relationship can be described as follows:

1. Net sales and other revenues
2. Changes in self-produced inventory and work in progress plus capitalized self-manufactured fixed assets

3. Gross production value (1 + 2)

4. Material and material-type expenditures

5. Value added production (3 − 4)

6. Labor and labor-related costs plus depreciation allowance plus other costs plus other expenditures

7. Profit or loss of business activity (5 − 6)

8. Profit or loss of financial transactions

9. Profit or loss from regular business activities (7 + 8)

10. Extraordinary profit or loss

11. Profit before tax (9 + 10)

12. Tax payment liability

13. After-tax profit

14. Amount of accumulated retained earnings used for dividend or profit sharing of the period

15. Dividend or profit sharing of the period announced

16. Balance sheet profit or loss for the financial year (13 + 14 − 15)

The gross income statement presents the opportunity for calculation of value added production, which is widely used in western European countries.

The other format of income statement is the cost of sales model. It is shown in Figure 5.

If the cost of sales model is used, the structure of the income statement is usually based on a functional approach. This means that in showing the profit of the period against net sales, the manufacturing costs of the products and services sold, the marketing costs of the period, and finally, the general administration expenses of the period are all detailed.

In the old practice, the cost of sales model was used, but the functional approach was not followed. Hungarian companies, following the principle of direct costing, tried to separate fixed and variable costs within the income statement, or at least to separate them directly and indirectly by tracing the costs of products and services. Unlike Western practice, the direct costs of goods sold included direct marketing costs of products and services as well manufacturing costs.

Under the new system, if the cost of sales model is used, marketing costs are now separated from the direct costs of sale and are disclosed within indirect costs of sale as sales costs. Financial revenues and expenses should be disclosed separately from the other components of the old category of other revenue and expenses. Specific provisions may now be made for anticipated losses from doubtful debts and receivables overdue and to cover obligations under early retirement pension and redundancy payment guarantee. These provisions are to be charged in the income statement as other expenses. The distinction of profits and losses from ordinary and extraordinary activities has also been introduced. The profit tax charged on the period is also recorded as other expenses.

2.3.3 Notes to the Accounts

The notes to the accounts contain the additional information necessary for providing a reliable, true and fair view of the net assets, financial position, and net income disclosed in the balance sheet and income statement. They contain both numerical data and explanatory text.

The notes disclose the accounting policies adopted by the company from the alternatives offered by law and the effect of the applied methods on net assets, the financial position, and net income. For example, the notes provide detailed information on depreciation rates of tangible and intangible assets. They also contain details of the major shareholders of the company, the number of the company's employees, research and development costs, and the profit tax liability.

The notes should also give information on the portion of any liabilities in the balance sheet that are due in more than 5 years and details of any mortgages or guarantees entered into by the company. Any contingent liabilities that require disclosure in order to give a full picture of the company's position but that are not included in the balance sheet should also be included.

The notes should also include details of the gross opening value of intangible assets and tangible assets, the increase or decrease in these assets, the accumulated depreciation, and depreciation charged for the year, by balance sheet items.

The Hungarian legislation of 1992, like the Fourth EU Directive, does not meet the requirement of international accounting standards to produce a statement of cash flows as part of the accounts package. This statement reports the major sources and uses of cash. It explains how the financing, investing, and operating activities of a firm affect the cash balance for a period, and it is considered to be of great importance to both creditors and investors and the company management itself.

In international practice according to the latest developments, less emphasis is placed on profitability in the form of a single earnings figure (earnings per share) and more upon viability in the form of cash flow information. A business may be profitable in the sense that it is selling its products or service at prices greater than the cost of providing them or making gains by holding assets whose value is appreciating, but unless it is able to convert its "profits" into cash, it will not survive. The Hungarian accounting practice missed the cash flow approach, and an economy in transition to a market economy cannot fail to be aware of cash flows.

Under the amendment Law No. CXV/1996 the notes should include the cash flow statement at least with the contents as specified in the schedule in Figure 9. The development of cash flow statement is based on the indirect method.

2.3.4 Business Report

The business report must include a fair review of the position of the company's business and its development. It should cover significant events, particularly those that take place after the balance sheet date. Details relating to the purchase of a company's own shares and of the company's research and development policy should be given. The business report should be compatible with the view presented by the rest of the accounts.

2.3.5 Filing and Publication under the New Legislation

All companies incorporated in the Trade Register keeping double- or single-entry books must file their annual reports, containing the auditor's report, if applicable, as well as the proposal or resolution pertaining to the use of the after-tax profit, with the Court of Registration by May 31 of the year following the accounting period.

Under the new legislation of 1992, all companies limited by shares, limited companies with prime capital in excess of HUF 50 million, single-person limited liability companies, and firms issuing bonds, as well as any other company that so desires, must publish their financial reports containing the auditor's report and the notes to the accounts but not the business report.

The requirement to publish financial statements became gradually more stringent. Since January 1, 1994, all companies with net sales revenues in excess of HUF 1 billion have been required to publish their statements. After January 1, 1996, all companies with net sales revenues in excess of

HUF 300 million, and since January 1, 1998 all companies keeping double-entry books, are required to publish their statements containing the auditor's report with the exception of companies with net sales revenues less than HUF 50 million and whose annual report was prepared by certified accountant (the late exception was introduced by Law No. CXXX/1997).

2.4 Review of the Financial Report

Under the new legislation, the balance sheet must be signed by a person authorized to represent the entity. The financial report must be presented to the board of directors and/or the general meeting. The financial report with the profit distribution, the dividend proposal, and profit tax amount are presented to the ultimate decision-making body of the business organization—the general meeting—with comments by the supervisory committee and the auditor, where mandatory audit is required. The board of directors, or the general meeting, is authorized to accept the balance sheet and the profit or loss statement, and the profit distribution (the size of dividend payment, the amount of profit tax, settlement of losses). The deadline for filing the financial report, audited where a mandatory audit is required, is May 31 following the end of the accounting period. The deadline for reporting to the tax authority is May 31 following the end of the accounting period.

Under the new legislation, the name and content of the former state financial and economic auditing shall be changed. It is known as tax auditing and shall have a limited scope. It does not cover management's economic decision making but checks that the accounting income calculation conforms to accounting legislation and that the taxable income is in accordance with tax requirements. The self-audit system used by companies is basically unchanged.

Under the tax legislation concerning the approved balance sheet, the ledger statements supporting the balance sheet, the inventory, and analytical records may be audited by the tax authority under tax audits and revised by the company itself under self-audit.

Tax audits and self-audits are carried out to verify the validity and completeness of the approved balance sheet, the profit distribution, and the due settlements with the central budget, and compliance with inventory-taking and tax valuation rules. If it is found during the tax audit or self-audit that the balance sheet is wrong, the necessary adjustments must be made on the basis of the relevant provisions in force during the period when the error was made.

The Law No. CXV/1966 introduced the differentiation between accounting of significant and nonsignificant amount of errors detected by the external or self-audit. Error of significant amount is identified if it exceeds 1% of grand total of balance sheet or HUF 500 million. Error of significant amount will be shown in separated columns in both balance sheet and the profit or loss account. The error of nonsignificant amount shall constitute a part of the data of the profit or loss account in the subject year.

2.5 The Function of Independent Auditors

The overall goal of independent auditing is to assess the performance of management in its strategic decision making and to provide audited information upon which external users of the accounts, for example, shareholders, lenders, and potential investors, may base their decisions. The charter of a business association may stipulate that the conduct of management be audited by an independent auditor instead of, or in addition to, the supervisory committee.

It is mandatory to appoint independent auditors for companies limited by shares and for one-person limited liability companies, and for limited liability companies with a stock capital of more than HUF 50 million and every company keeping double entry books with net sales exceeding HUF 50 million. Independent auditors must have been qualified as chartered accountants and registered with the Hungarian Chamber of Auditors. There should be no family connections or business ties between the auditor and the client company. The auditors must be independent in order to be impartial in undertaking their duties. In the case of the transformation of a state-owned enterprise into a business association or one form of company into another form of company or in the case of their liquidation, the transforming balance sheet or final account also should be audited by an independent auditor in accordance with the Law on Transformation, the Company Law, and the Law on Sale of State Properties. If a company limited by shares decides to publicly trade its securities, the main financial statements should be audited by an independent auditor as well. In accordance with the Law on Securities and Stock Exchange, the company prospectus should include these audited financial statements.

The auditor's function is to examine the report presented to each general meeting or board meeting—especially the balance sheet and the whole financial report—and make sure they contain valid figures and comply with legislative provisions.

The auditor has access to the company's books, may seek information from executives and employees, and may examine the company's pay office, portfolio and inventories, agreements, and bank accounts. The auditor must attend the board meeting or general meeting and give an opinion on the audited balance sheet and reports. If the auditor finds that the company's capital may be expected to decrease significantly, or if there is any other such fact for which executives may be held liable, the auditor must let the supervisory committee know and may, at the same time, request that the ultimate decision-making body of the company be convened.

A primary function of the auditor is to review and certify the balance sheet and the balance sheet report and give an opinion. For this purpose, the auditor must examine the balance sheet and the financial report impartially and thoroughly and in turn countersign the reviewed balance sheet. The auditor may refuse to countersign if the balance sheet and financial report contain false figures, if the form in which they have been prepared violates legislative provisions, or if deliberate fraud has occurred. The auditor should draw attention to any unfavorable change in capital, financial position, or profitability. The auditor has a duty of confidentiality to the client with respect to the facts, data, and business information that come to the auditor's attention in the course of the audit.

The auditor must prepare an audit report, in writing, on the financial report review, the income statement, and the statement of profit distribution in compliance with respective legislative provisions that the capital, assets, and liabilities in the balance sheet and the company's revenues, costs, expenses, and profit or loss in the income statement reflect a true and fair picture and comply with the relevant legislative provisions. To illustrate the standard form audit report agreed with the Draft National Auditing Standards, an actual example of an audit report is shown below.

Auditor's Report for the Stockholders—XYZ Hungaria Kft.

We have audited the accompanying balance sheet of XYZ Hungaria Kft. "the Company" as of 31 December 1997 and the related profit and loss account and supplement (collectively "the financial statement") for the period then ended included in the Company's 1997 Annual Report. The Annual Report is the responsibility of management.

Our responsibility is to express an opinion on the financial statements on the basis of our audit and to assess whether the related accounting information contained in the Business Report included in the Annual Report is consistent with that contained in the financial statements. We conducted our audit in accordance with the applicable laws and regulations in force in Hungary and with the National Standards on

Auditing. Those standards require that we plan and perform the audit to obtain reasonable assurance about whether the financial statements are free of material misstatement. An audit includes examining, on a test basis, evidence supporting the amounts and disclosures in the financial statements. An audit also includes assessing the accounting principles used and significant estimates made by management, as well as evaluating the overall financial statement presentation. Our work with respect to the Business Report was limited to the aforementioned scope, and did not include a review of any information other than that drawn from the audited accounting records of the Company. We believe that our work provides a reasonable basis for our opinion. In our opinion:

The Annual Report has been compiled in accordance with Law XVIII on Accounting and with general accounting principles in Hungary. The Annual Report provides a true and fair view of the financial position of the Company as of 31 December 1993 and the results of its operations for the year ended.

Budapest, 7 May 1998.
(Translation of the original statutory version which has been signed.)
HCA Name
Hungarian Chartered Accountant

3. Accounting Policies and Practices in Valuation and Income Measurement

3.1 Principles and Theories behind Accounting Policies and Practices

The old accounting system broadly conformed to the principles of the accrual basis of accounting. The effects of business transactions were generally recognized when they occurred, regardless of when the cash was actually received or paid. An example, however, of the failure to apply the accrual accounting principle consistently was in the area of bad debts. By using historical cost valuations without applying the principle of prudence, the conventional financial statements failed to reflect the result of management's decisions in the company's current economic environment.

Under the new legislation the financial report is prepared by using generally accepted accounting principles. These includes the principles of:

• Going concern

• Completeness

• Truth

- Lucidity
- Consistency
- Continuity
- Accrual/matching
- Prudence
- Gross settlement
- Individual valuation
- Time deferral

The Law No. CXV/1996 introduced the principles of materiality and substance over form and cost–benefit comparison. In the developed market economies, the accounting concept of prudence exerts a significant influence on profit measurement and the accounting methods used in the preparation of financial statements. It renders accounting "entrepreneur friendly." However, the concept of prudence should not be used for the creation of hidden reserves.

The new Hungarian accounting legislation has, with some few exceptions, been drawn up in accordance with the principle of prudence The exceptions are gradually eliminated by the amendments to the law. At the creation of provisions for bad debt Law No. CXV/1996 introduced the necessity of qualification of customers and debtors instead of qualification of Accounts Receivable. Earlier the creation of provision was allowed if the receivable was overdue.

Even the application of direct costing valuation of manufactured stock is considered to be more prudent than the full absorption costing methods, more commonly used in Anglo-Saxon countries.

3.2 Participations, Consolidation Policy, Group Accounts

3.2.1 *Accounting Methods for Participations*

In developed market economies there are three basic methods used in accounting for long-term investments.

1. Cost method or lower of cost or market value method
2. Equity method
3. Consolidation

The determination of the method of accounting for long-term investments depends on the purpose of the investment and on the percentage of voting stock that the investing company owns.

The Hungarian law on business association identifies types of long-term investments:

1. When the company has a majority holding or exercises decisive control over a second company, the holding company is known as the parent company. The majority owned company is defined as a holding that exceeds 50% of the subscribed capital carrying voting rights in the subsidiary, called the subsidiary.

2. A significant holding is held by the parent company that has significant influence over the control of another company and where the value of its investment exceeds 25% of the subscribed capital of the other company but does not exceed 50%.

3. Mutual participation exists between two limited companies if each of them has acquired the shares amounting to more than one quarter part of the registered capital of the other one or if more than one quarter part of the votes are due to it in the general assembly of the other limited company.

Cost Method or Lower of Cost or Market Value Method   Under the new legislation, companies having a minority participation (the percentage of voting stock less than 25%) in another company will account for the investment using the cost method. Under the cost method an investor records its investments at acquisition cost. The investor recognizes as income only dividends received. In the balance sheet such investments are valued at the lower of cost or market value. Any write-down in the value of the investment is shown under financial expenses in the income statement.

Securities Shown among Current Assets   If the security is listed on the Stock Exchange and the market value is permanently (for at least one year preceding the balance sheet preparation date) below cost as of the preparation date of balance sheet, the price listed on the Stock Exchange as of the balance sheet date should be used. If the security is not listed on the Stock Exchange and the market value is below cost as of the preparation date of the balance sheet, this lower market value as of the preparation date is to be used.

Companies having a majority holding or exercising decisive control over subsidiaries, with the exceptions defined above, should prepare a consolidated annual report. This involves the production of consolidated accounts designed to present a true picture of the group of companies' transactions with third parties. To this end, all intercompany balances are eliminated, together with any intragroup sales and the effect of intercompany transfers of fixed assets.

When significant holding is held, the equity method is used. For consolidation of mutual participations, proportional consolidation is applied.

3.2.2 Overview: The Scope of Group Accounts

Under international business practice, the main advantages of consolidation include the following:

1. A reduction in the financial risk of operating a single business unit of legally separated companies
2. To meet more effectively the requirement of tax legislation, especially in the case of foreign subsidiaries
3. To expand or diversify with the minimum of capital investment

In pre-1992 Hungarian accounting practice, different methods of consolidation, such as acquisition or purchase, merger or pooling, or the "former German method" had not yet been introduced. Increasing national and international economic integration resulted in the growing importance of the introduction of consolidation.

In Hungary under Law No. XVIII/1991 on accounting and Law No. CVIII/1993, which amended the law on accounting, the requirement of consolidation came into effect on January 1, 1994.

A parent company need not prepare a consolidated financial report if:

1. The parent company is itself a subsidiary of a company that is seated in Hungary
2. On the balance sheet date in 2 consecutive years preceding the subject year, two of the following three indices do not exceed the following limits:
   a. The balance-sheet grand total does not exceed HUF 500 million.
   b. The annual net revenue does not exceed HUF 1,000 million.
   c. The average number of employees in the subject year does not exceed 250 persons.

When defining the above indices, the added figures of the parent company and subsidiaries before consolidation shall be taken into consideration.

It is not mandatory to involve a subsidiary in the preparation of the consolidated annual report if:

- It would cost an unreasonable amount of money
- The investment has been acquired for the sole purpose of resale and classified as a current asset in the parent company balance sheet
- Legal restrictions prevent the parent company from exercising its right
- Without consolidation the financial report will provide a true and fair view on the financial position and result of the company

The exemptions defined above shall not apply to parent companies that are financial institutions or insurance companies or if on the balance sheet date the shares of the parent companies or their subsidiaries are publicly traded.

Consolidated financial statements, however, are not the basis either for taxation or for profit distribution.

The consolidated annual report consists of a consolidated balance sheet, a consolidated profit and loss account, and consolidated summary notes. The balance sheet and profit and loss account of a consolidated annual report differ from the balance sheet (Figure 2) and profit and loss account (Figures 4 and 5) of an annual report in accordance with Figures 7 and 8.

Under the Law No. CXV/1996 a parent company shall deposit its consolidated annual report with the exception of business report but containing the auditor's report with the Court of Registration by Sept. 30 of the year following the accounting period, and also shall publish with the same deadline.

3.2.3 Steps for Preparation of the Consolidated Annual Report

In the course of the preparation of the consolidated annual report, the following shall be performed:

- Any adjustments arising from the use of different evaluation methods, for assessing the items of the consolidated balance sheet and profit and loss account (that is, a standard evaluation method shall be used)

- Conversion into forints of the items of the balance sheets and profit and loss accounts drawn up in foreign currencies
- Capital consolidation
- Debt consolidation (canceling any receivables and liabilities existing between the companies involved in consolidation)
- Omission of interim results (canceling any profit and loss items arising from transactions between the companies involved in consolidation that are included in the value of assets)
- Consolidation of revenues and expenditures (canceling any revenues and expenditures arising from transactions between the companies involved in consolidation)
- Consolidation of jointly managed enterprises
- Capital consolidation of associated enterprises
- Definition of tax difference due to consolidation

3.2.4 Foreign Currency Translation for Consolidation

For translating items of financial statements drawn up in a foreign currency of a subsidiary, the following exchange rate can be applied:

1. The exchange rate prevailing at the date selected in accordance with the accounting law for items in the balance sheet (with the exception of the balance sheet profit amount). This value, however, cannot be higher than the value calculated at the official foreign exchange medium rate published by National Bank of Hungary as of the balance sheet date.

2. The official foreign exchange medium rate published by the National Bank of Hungary as of the balance sheet date for all items of the balance sheet. The balance sheet profit also shall be valued at this rate.

3. For items of the profit and loss account:
   - Depreciation, loss in value, material-type expenses at the exchange rate applying to the corresponding balance sheet items
   - The balance sheet profit valuation shown above
   - The monthly rate—at the end of month for the rest of the items of the profit and loss account

Translation differences are recorded:

- Partly in the preliminary balance sheet of the given company as a change (adjustment) in equity
- Partly in the preliminary profit and loss account of the given company as other revenues and/or other expenses

The adjustments, arising from different evaluation methods, are recorded in the same way as translation differences.

3.2.5 Capital Consolidation

The primary method of capital consolidation is the Anglo-Saxon purchase or acquisition method. The value of the share due to the parent company from the subsidiary shall be taken at the amount of the parent's ownership ratio. There are two methods: the book value method and the current value method.

According to the book value method, the book values in the individual balance sheets (as adjusted as a result of the application of identical valuation principles) are compared with the cost of the investment. If a debit balance arises, this must be allocated to the relevant balance sheet headings—attachable to the assets and liabilities—in the proportion of shares held. Any amount remaining is to be recorded as goodwill on the asset side of the balance sheet. In the case of a credit balance, the hidden reserves are attachable to the assets and the hidden debts are attachable to the liabilities. The remaining credit balance arising must be recorded as a consolidation difference on the liability side of the balance sheet (negative goodwill, or "badwill").

According to the current value method, the subsidiaries' book values are replaced by updated value at the date of acquisition of the share, or the first time the subsidiary is involved in consolidation. In that case, hidden reserves are fully reflected. After the revaluation, however, the proportional net equity of the subsidiary is not allowed to exceed the cost of the investment. Thus, no "badwill" can arise from applying method 2.

Any debit or credit balances between proportional net equity and the acquisition cost of the shares are classified as goodwill or "badwill." Disclosed hidden reserves relating to other shareholders are dealt with by inclusion in the minority interest.

Goodwill arising at the time of the first consolidation is amortized systematically over the years that are likely to benefit (maximum years: 15).

The capital consolidation difference entered among liabilities may be accounted to the credit of the profit if it is certain that at the consolidated balance sheet date this difference amount is a realized profit.

The difference between the shares from the affiliate shareholders' equity due to the parent company and the calculated shares at the time of the first consolidation should be shown in the consolidated balance sheet as a correction of the shareholders' equity.

When the consolidated annual report is prepared, the number of shares from the shareholders' equity of the affiliate not due to the parent company must be shown among the liabilities—separately within the shareholders' equity—in the consolidated balance sheet as minority interest (shares of external members, other owners).

The law offers several options to companies with regard to capital consolidation. The preferred capital consolidation method will probably be the book value method because of its simplicity.

3.2.6 Proportional and Equity Consolidation

For consolidation of jointly managed enterprises—companies have the ownership right on an equal basis—the proportional consolidation method can be used. When a significant holding is held by the parent company, the equity method of long-term investment can be applied for the consolidation of associated enterprises.

If proportional consolidation is applied, the same principles as for capital consolidations are to be followed. The consolidation differences are handled as described above.

When the equity method is used, the given share in the subsidiary shall be entered in a separate line of the parent company balance sheet.

3.2.7 Debt and Income (Revenues and Expenses) Consolidation

The elimination of intercompany debt, of intercompany revenues and expenses, as well as of intercompany profits and losses in principle follows the requirements of the Seventh EU Directive.

3.2.8 Record of Corporate Tax Difference due to Consolidation

Timing differences incurred in connection with consolidation measures (e.g., intercompany profit elimination) must be addressed by recording deferred tax. If the tax payable based on the individual profit and loss accounts is more than the tax payable according to the consolidated profit and loss account, then the difference shall be entered separately in the consolidated balance sheet as a deferred profit tax liability and in the consolidated profit and loss account as tax difference.

3.2.9 Summary of the Consolidation Procedure

The consolidated balance sheet is prepared in the following way:

1. The investment account in the parent company's balance sheet is eliminated and replaced with the individual assets and liabilities of the subsidiary.
2. Intercompany receivables and payables are eliminated.
3. The minority interest in the subsidiary's net assets is shown among equities.

The consolidated income statement is prepared in the following way:

1. Sales and purchases of goods and services between the parent and its subsidiaries (purchases for the buying company and sales for the selling company) are eliminated.
2. Income and expenses on loans receivable or bond indebtedness between the parent and its subsidiaries are eliminated.
3. Items related to the transfer of participation and dividends between the parent and its subsidiaries are eliminated. The amount of the minority interest in the subsidiary's income is the result of multiplying the subsidiary's net income by the minority's percentage of ownership. Typically, the minority's interest in the subsidiary's income appears as a deduction in calculating consolidated net income.

Consolidated income, therefore, comprises the parent's net income and that of its subsidiaries, less the minority interest and adjusted for the effect of any intercompany transactions.

When consolidated accounts are analyzed, particular attention should be given to notes regarding foreign currency translation and tax differences.

The accounting law introduced the consolidation requirement effective January 1, 1994. The theory and practice of consolidation were totally new for the majority of practitioners. Course materials and hand-outs must have been prepared, and courses were to be organized to impart new knowledge to accountants. The University of Economics and Hungarian Chamber of Auditors have launched a course on consolidation. EU PHARE also funded a Train-the-Trainer course on consolidation.

3.3 Foreign Currency Translation

Foreign currency transactions are restricted because the domestic currency—the Hungarian forint—is not fully convertible. The currency, however, is actually convertible for commercial purposes. The import is fully liberalized.

The accounting law established the exchange rate mechanism until full convertibility is achieved. In accordance with the law, foreign cash contributions should be valued at the middle rate of the National Bank of Hungary in force when the cash contribution or the actual payment was made (historical rate). As the foreign currency is used, the difference between the historical and the ongoing rate—the selling rate at the date of use—is no longer accounted for against the capital reserve but against profit or loss (1997).

Foreign currency cash balances are valued in the balance sheet at their book value. If their forint value, calculated at the buying rate advertised by the financial institution authorized to perform foreign exchange transactions and performing the given transaction, on the last day of the accounting period is less than their book value, they will be valued at the closing rate. If the forint value of currencies that are not transferable or listed by the financial institution authorized to perform foreign exchange transactions is calculated at the free market rate valid on the last day of the accounting period at less than their book value, the calculated value shall be used.

Accounts receivable in foreign currencies are valued at the buying rate advertised by the financial institution authorized to perform foreign exchange transactions and performing the given transaction on the contractual date of payment, if the given currency rate has not decreased and the cash has not been collected as of the date the balance sheet is prepared. If the currency rate described above has decreased, the closing buying rate will be used. If cash has been collected as of the date the balance sheet is prepared, the buying rate advertised by the given financial institution on the settlement of payment will be used for valuation of the receivables.

Accounts payable in foreign currencies are valued at the selling rate advertised by the financial institution authorized to perform foreign exchange transactions and performing the given transaction on the contractual day of payment if the given currency rate is decreasing or has not changed and the debt has not been repaid as of the date of the balance sheet preparation. If the given currency rate is increasing, the closing selling rate described above shall be used.

If payment has been made by the date the balance sheet is prepared, accounts payable are valued at the selling rate advertised by the given financial institution valid on the day of the financial performance.

3.4 Capital and Reserves

In 1988 the homogeneous "funds for property" account was introduced. The general fund and changes in the general fund were differentiated within the homogenous property fund. The general fund balance sheet account title referred to registered property value. The other account covered the changes in the general fund, including, for example, the net profit for the period and other changes in the property value that had not yet been registered. In 1989 additional changes were introduced. The existing general fund became the founder's property, the so-called registered capital, and the increases in the general fund were renamed the accumulated property fund, similar to accumulated retained earnings in Anglo-Saxon practice.

Since 1992 accounting law has required the following structure of the owner's equity account:

- Registered (subscribed) capital
- Capital reserve (share premium account)
- Accumulated retained earnings (result reserve)
- Loss carried forward from previous years
- Balance sheet profit or loss for the financial year

In 1997 accounting law introduced the following structure of equity:

- Subscribed (registered) capital
- Subscribed but unpaid capital
- Capital reserve (share premium account)
- Accumulated retained earnings (profits)
- Evaluation reserve
- Balance sheet profit or loss for the financial year

Company Law defines the minimum amount of foundation capital (as registered capital) for limited companies and companies limited by shares. The subscribed capital can be shown within the equity whether or not registration has happened yet. Subscribed capital and capital reserve are defined as a nondistributable element of the owner's equity. As a result of the 1997 modification to the accounting law, all transfers of funds must be accounted for in the profit and loss account and can no longer be treated as direct transfers to reserves. Cash, state subsidies and other contributions of assets can only be transferred to capital or profit reserve in cases specifically stated by law. The revaluation reserves as unrealized revaluation surpluses creates a new element of equity introduced in 1995. The opportunity of revaluation of long life assets can be considered as a treatment of inflation impact within the balance sheet. The revaluation difference can not be depreciated even against the revaluation reserve.

Result reserve can be available for supplementing the balance sheet profit if it is not tied up in accordance with the accounting or another law and the amount of equity following this transaction exceeds the amount of the registered capital.

3.5 Liabilities and Provisions

Liabilities and provisions are valued in the balance sheet at their book value. If the repayable amount of a liability is higher than the amount received, the repayable amount shall be entered in the balance sheet among other liabilities. The difference between the repayable and received amount shall be shown among prepaid expenses.

When loans and other liabilities in foreign currency are revalued at year end, the amount of any foreign exchange loss is usually charged to the profit and loss account. However the law of 1996 permits, but does not require, companies to defer recognition of unrealized exchange losses on loans or bonds raised for the purpose of financing long term investments. The deferred unrealized loss will be shown in the balance sheet as prepaid expense.

Outstanding commitments and contingencies should be disclosed in the notes to accounts.

The category of provisions was introduced by the new accounting legislation. Provisions shall be reported among the liabilities, such as specific provisions created from pretax profit in line with the Fourth EU Directive. Planning for provision for bad debt usually is based on the grouping of accounts receivable on the basis of their maturity. Creation of provision has to be based on qualification of the debtors.

3.6 Property, Plant, and Equipment

Property, plant, and equipment are valued at historical cost. Under the old legislation, no departure from the historical cost basis was permitted. The straight-line, time, and production depreciation methods were used. The norms for depreciation used to be compulsory. The new law brought the depreciation of tangible assets within the scope of managerial decision making.

For financial reporting any kind of depreciation rate can be used that reflects the useful life of the asset. The amount of depreciation above the planned depreciation amount shall be accounted for in the period if the market value at balance sheet preparation date is less than the book value of the asset. There is a difference between depreciation requirements for financial reporting and tax reporting, because the depreciation norms are obligatory when prescribed by the tax law. If the depreciation rates used for financial reporting differ from the tax rate, the difference should be shown within the notes to accounts.

Interest charges on loans for ongoing investments are capitalized as part of the cost of property and plant. That type of interest charge does not affect the net income of the account year. After the plant is brought into operation, the interest charge is recorded as a period expense against the revenues of the periods concerned.

Since 1997 the acquisition cost includes the items related closely to the acquisition of the asset such as duties payable, pre-charged but nondeductible VAT. Revaluation of properties, plants and equipment is allowed.

3.7 Land

The valuation of land depends on when it was purchased. During the past 40 years at one time it used to be recorded without value. The law on land ownership was enacted in 1994. The accounting techniques should be used in accordance with the new land law (for example, under Accounting for Mortgages).

3.8 Leased Assets

In Hungarian practice, the capital or finance lease accounting method has not been introduced by the new accounting legislation in 1992. All leases were considered operating leases. This helped managers in the use of off-balance sheet financing. However, the law did require disclosure in the notes of off-balance sheet financing. In 1997 accounting for finance leases was introduced by the law.

Under the IAS rental transactions which are concluded for the major part of asset's useful life can qualify as finance leases. Transactions where the present value of the minimum rental fees at the beginning of rental is greater than or equal to the fair value of the leased assets also qualify as finance leases. These rules apply regardless of whether ownership title is eventually transferred or not.

The definition of finance lease given by bank legislation does not cover the above cases clearly which makes the qualification of lease difficult. Also the uncertainty of present value calculation creates problems for the practitioners.

3.9 Oil, Gas, and Other Mineral Resources

In the case of oil, gas, and other mineral resources, depletion is based on the value of the natural resource.

3.10 Intangible Assets

Intangible assets, purchased or self-generated, are valued at cost. Before 1992 there was no amortization of intangible assets, which hindered their wider use. This was legislated for by the new law.

Amortization rates defined by the law are as follows:

- Rights and concessions are written off over 6 years or longer.
- Research and development costs, as well as foundation and reorganization costs, are written off over a period of 5 years or less.
- Patents, license, and other intellectual product costs are written off over the useful life of the assets.
- Goodwill shall be written off over a period of 5 years or more up to a period of 15 years. Disclosure is required if the amortization period is more than 5 years.

The purchase cost of rights and concessions can be capitalized and written off over a period of 6 years or longer.

Under international standards research and development costs are usually expensed unless certain conditions are satisfied (IAS 9).

3.11 Inventories

The valuation of inventories is based on historical costs. Before 1989, for the valuation of purchased inventory, the so-called standard cost adjusted by the actual price difference was widely used. FIFO was also allowed as a cost flow assumption for merchandise inventory. Self-produced inventories were valued at factory unit cost, later at direct unit cost.

Under the new law, the actual acquisition cost, LIFO and FIFO cost flow assumptions, or the weighted average method are to be used for the valuation of purchased inventory. The purchase cost includes the purchase price reduced by any discount, increased by any extra charge related to the purchase or delivery cost, taxes, and customs charges. Since 1997 the nondeductible VAT, and any fees and duties connected with the purchase charged by the authorities are included in the purchase cost.

Under the new law, the direct unit cost continues to be used for the valuation of self-produced goods, but it cannot include any selling costs. The direct unit cost includes material costs, wage expenditures, and costs that have been verifiably closely related to manufacture or product. No provision is allowed for slow-moving or obsolete items of inventory, own and purchased.

If the market value of inventories has declined below cost as of the date of the balance sheet, the lower of cost and net realizable value should be shown in the balance sheet. The losses in value, defined above, should be recorded as other costs (Figure 4, line VII; and Figure 5, line 07).

Under long-term contracts the direct cost of unfinished construction and installation may be defined by proportioning on the basis of the degree of performance and the customer's certificate.

The difference of the year-end closing and opening stock shall be taken into consideration as change in self-manufactured assets (Figure 4, line 04).

3.12 Taxation

In Hungary, the reported income and taxation income of companies used to be the same. The distinction between taxable income and accounting income was introduced by the new accounting legislation. Tax liability is the annual amount of tax liability payable for profits on the basis of the tax return. The state uses all possible means for increasing the state budget receipt. The profit tax law strictly defines the components of taxable income and the adjustments necessary to the accounting incomes to get the taxable income. The most relevant components are as follows:

- Depreciation rates of fixed assets
- The level of creation of and the titles of specific reserves
- Representation costs rated to be accounted for taxable income

Accelerated depreciation rates are usually not allowed for taxation. The system of investment incentives is increasingly exercised. Generally, a certain negative deferred profit tax effect exists that is not recorded. In 1998 the general corporate tax rate is 18%, and the dividend tax rate is 20%. Advance tax payment should be made by companies on the basis of the actual profit generation of the previous year. In 1998 the maximum personal income tax rate is 42% on gross incomes over HUF 550,000 per annum.

In 1998 the general VAT rate is 25%, with the exception of previously zero rated items, including most foodstuffs, which became taxable at 12%.

3.13 Social Security, Pension, and Health Care Contribution

In Hungary the social contribution and pension system developed under the centralized planning system. The amount of contribution used to be defined centrally. During the past years great development went on in the building the new elements of social security system based on private ownership. The private investment funds now compete with each other.

The 1998 rate of social security contribution is 42% and the contribution to the unemployment fund is 4%. Both are paid by business organizations and are considered cost elements. Employees pay a pension contribution of 7% (6% is paid to the private pension funds and 1% to the central social security fund), a health care contribution of 3%, and a contribution to the unemployment fund of 1.5%, calculated on gross wages and salaries. Accounting for Pension plan is applied.

4. Expected Future Developments

4.1 Harmonization between Company and Accounting Laws

In March of 1998 the Hungarian EU accession talks began. The first stage of the talks is devoted to harmonization between the Hungarian and EU legal frameworks. This harmonization is facilitated by elaboration of the amendment to Company Law No. CXLIV/1997 and Law No. CXLV/1997 on Registration of Firms, coming into force in June of 1998. The short-term accounting expectation now is to create harmony between the new company and registration laws and accounting legislation. The amendment to the accounting law will include:

- Accounting issues of new rules for the registration of firms
- A requirement to provide dividend advance payment (capital maintaining)
- Accounting regulations for the transformation of companies from one form to another, including final accounts and liquidation

4.2 Accounting Regulation Development

To facilitate the accession of Hungary to the EU, to bring the economy into the world market, and to increase foreign capital invested, it is essential that financial statements be prepared according to internationally accepted standards. In order to comply with international and European Union standards, Hungary has engaged in an aggressive accounting and auditing transition.

In 1992 the goal of the new accounting legislation was to define the requirements concerning firms' accounting procedures and financial reporting systems in the new conditions of the economy. The new law, which was based on the Fourth, Seventh, and Eighth Directives of the Council of the European Union, approached the internationally accepted principles of accountancy. The adaptation of the EU directives has continued to be influenced by German accounting practice. When Hungary made its choice of those alternatives offered by the directives, it chose the Continental European model. The German federal government provided a great help on the implementation of consolidation policy under the amendment accounting Law No. CVIII/1993.

A majority of the changes enacted by the amendments during 1992–1998 strengthened the development into the direction of international accounting principles, while simultaneously resulting in the accounting law covering more and more detailed regulations. This led to the contradiction that if practitioners want to follow the main principles of the law they often have to violate the detailed regulations and vice versa.

The development of Hungarian accounting regulatory framework creates one of the most important mid-term future accounting tasks. Internationally, there are two basic approaches to the way accounting regulations are established. Under the first approach accounting practices are governed by laws and decrees. This was the method prevailing in the EU, as well as in the majority of Continental European countries. Germany and Austria represent the traditional examples. The second approach is based on self-regulation by the accounting profession through a standard-setting procedure. This method was identified in Ireland, the United Kingdom, the United States, Canada, Australia, and New Zealand. A third model is a mixture of the above two approaches. It has a primarily legal character but relies to a large extent on the self-regulation of the profession. France, Belgium, and the Netherlands could be identified as traditional examples, but Germany also has made an important movement in the direction of this third approach. A standard-setting body has been proposed recently there.

Analyzing the development of the international accounting regulation framework, we can conclude that it shows strengthening of the self-regulation element. The creation of self-regulation of the profession in Hungary would facilitate that the law provides only the principal framework of accounting regulation and the detailed regulations are given by the accounting standards.

Hungary has begun to prepare for the establishment of a National Standard-Setting Body. The project is funded by EU Phare Financial Sector Development Program. The National Standard-Setting Body will elaborate the national financial accounting standards. The question is what kind of national standards need to be elaborated.

It is obvious that during the past few years there has been an increased tendency toward international harmonization of accounting standards. The major goal of the new accounting strategy of the European Commission has been to establish conformity between IASs and EU Accounting Directives facilitating world economic integration. Also, to reduce the costs borne by reporting companies that must comply with the different accounting requirements in each country in which they operate, International Accounting Standards have been developed. In order to meet the challenge of internationalization and globalization of business and of the interpenetration of capital markets, the Hungarian national standards should be in agreement with the international accounting standards.

The statutory audit should provide the necessary enforcement for effectiveness of these standards in everyday practice. Also, the role of the professional bodies should be strengthened in the implementation procedure of the standards. This requires the further strengthening of the accounting and auditing professions to become an effective driving force within the financial sector.

Financial Statements

Figure 1
HUNGARIA KFT

MÉRLEG/ESZKÖZÖK	1996.12.31. eFt	1997.12.31. eFt
01. **A. BEFEKTETETT ESZKÖZÖK**	132,225	139,047
02. **1. IMMATERIÁLIS JAVAK**		
03. VAGYONI ÉRTÉKÛ JOGOK		
04. ÜZLETI VAGY CÉGÉRTÉK		
05. SZELLEMI TERMÉKEK		
06. KISÉRLETI FEJLESZTÉS AKTIVÁLT ÉRTÉKE		
07. ALAPÍTAS-ÁTSZERVEZÉS AKTIVÁLT ÉRTÉKE		
08. **II. TÁRGYI ESZKÖZÖK**	132,225	139,047
09. INGATLANOK	50,755	49,704
10. MÛSZAKI BERENDEZÉSEK, FELSZERELÉSEK, JÁRMÛVEK	74,423	88,848
11. EGYÉB BERENDEZÉSEK, FELSZERELÉSEK, JÁRMÛVEK	7,047	495
12. BERUHÁZÁSOK		
13. BERUHÁZÁSOKRA ADOTT ELÕLEG		
14. **III. BEFEKTETETT PÉNZÜGYI ESZKÖZÖK**		
15. RÉSZESEDÉSEK		
16. ÉRTÉKPAPÍROK		
17. ADOTT KÖLCSÖNÖK		
18. HOSSZÚ LEJÁRATÚ BANKBETÉTEK		
19. **B FORGÓESZKÖZÖK**	68,337	107,844
20. **1. KÉSZLETEK**	11,827	12,943
21. ANYAGOK	11,822	12,834
22. ÁRUK		
23. KÉSZLETEKRE ADOTT ELÕLEGEK	5	99
24. ÁLLATOK		
25. BEFEJEZETLEN TERMELÉS ÉS FÉLKÉSZ TERMÉKEK		
26. KÉSZTERMÉKEK		10
27. **II. KÖVETELÉSEK**	29,247	63,918
28. KÖVETELÉSEK ÁRUSZÁLLÍTÁSBÓL ÉS SZOLGÁLTATÁSBÓL	7,729	37,730
29. VÁLTÓKÖVETELÉSEK		
30. JEGYZETT, DE MÉG BE NEM FIZETETT TÕKE		
31. ALAPÍTÓKKAL SZEMBENI KÖVETELÉSEK		
32. EGYÉB KÖVETELÉSEK	21,518	26,188
33. **III. ÉRTÉKPAPÍROK**		

12

34.	ELADÁSRA VÁSÁROLT KÖTVÉNYEK		
35.	SAJÁT RÉSZVÉNYEK, ÜZLETRÉSZEK, ELADÁSRA VÁS. RÉSZV.		
36.	EGYÉB ÉRTÉKPAPÍROK		
37.	**IV. PÉNZESZKÖZÖK**	27,263	30,979
38.	PÉNZTÁR, CSEKK	10	885
39.	BANKBETÉTEK	27,253	30,094
40.	**C. AKTÍV IDÕBELI ELHATÁROLÁSOK**	1,667	678
41.	**ESZKÖZÖK ÖSSZESEN:**	202,229	247,565
42.	**D. SAJÁT TÕKE**	152,410	152,410
43.	I. JEGYZETT TÕKE	152,410	152,410
44.	II. JEGYZETT, DE MÉG BE NEM FIZETETT TÕKE (-)		
45.	III. TÕKETARTALÉK		
46.	IV. EREDMÉNYTARTALÉK		
47.	V. ÉRTÉKELÉSI TARTALÉK		
47/a.	VI. MÉRLEG SZERINTI EREDMÉNY		
48.	**E. CÉLTARTALÉKOK**		4,663
49.	1. CÉLTARTALÉK A VARHATÓ VESZTESÉGEKRE		4,363
50.	2. CÉLTARTALÉK A VÁRHATÓ KÖTELEZETTSÉGEKRE		300
51.	3. EGYÉB CÉLTARTALÉKOK		
52.	**F. KÖTELEZETTSÉGEK**	49,819	61,076
53.	**I. HOSSZÚ LEJÁRATÚ KÖTELEZETTSÉGEK**	27,092	
54.	BERUHÁZÁSI ÉS FEJLESZTÉSI HITELEK		
55.	EGYÉB HOSSZÚ LEJÁRATÚ HITELEK		
56.	HOSSZÚ LEJÁRATRA KAPOTT KÖLCSÖNÖK		
57.	TARTOZÁSOK KÖTVÉNY-KIBOCSATÁSBÓL		
58.	ALAPÍTÓKKAL SZEMBENI KÖTELEZETTSÉGEK	27,092	
59.	EGYÉB HOSSZÚ LEJÁRATÚ KÖTELEZETTSÉGEK		
60.	**II. RÖVID LEJÁRATÚ KÖTELEZETTSÉGEK**	22,727	61,076
61.	VEVÕTÕL KAPOTT ELÕLEGEK		
62.	KÖTELEZETTSÉGEK ÁRUSZÁLLÍTÁSBÓL ÉS SZOLGÁLTATÁSBÓL	8,239	33,419
63.	VÁLTÓTARTOZÁSOK		
64.	RÖVID LEJÁRATÚ HITELEK		
65.	RÖVID LEJÁRATÚ KÖLCSÖNÖK		
66.	EGYÉB RÖVID LEJÁRATÚ KÖTELEZETTSÉGEK	14,488	27,657
67.	**G. PASSZÍV IDÓBELI ELHATÁROLÁSOK**		29,416
68.	**FORRÁSOK ÖSSZESEN:**	202,229	247,565

Figure 2
Hungaria KFT Balance Sheet
at 31 December 1997

Assets		31 December, 1996 (THUF)	31 December, 1997 (THUF)
01	A. Invested Assets		
02	I. Intangible Assets		
03	Rights/Concessions		
04	Goodwill		
05	Intellectual Goods		
06	Capitalised Research and Development		
07	Capitalised Formation and Reorganisation Expenses		
08	II. Tangible Assets	132,225	139,047
09	Land and Buildings	50,755	49,704
10	Plant and Machinery	74,423	88,848
11	Other fixtures, fittings tools and equipment	7,047	495
12	Tangible Assets under construction		
13	Advance Payments Towards Investments		
14	III. Financial Assets		
15	Participating Interest		
16	Long term investments in shares and securities		
17	Loans Granted		
18	Long term bank deposits		
19	B. Current Assets	68,337	107,840
20	I. Stocks (Inventories)	11,827	12,943
21	Raw materials	11,822	12,8322
22	Commodities		
23	Advance payments on stocks	5	99
24	Animals		
25	Work in progress		
26	Finished goods	0	10
27	II. Receivables	29,247	63,918
28	Accounts receivable	7,729	37,730
29	Bills of exchange		
30	Capital subscribed not yet paid		
31	Claims against founders		

32	Other receivables	21.518	26,188
33	III. Securities		
34	Bonds bought for resale		
35	Shares bought for resale		
36	Other securities		
37	IV. Monetary Assets	27,263	30,979
38	Cash, Cheques	10	885
39	Bank Deposits	27,253	30,094
40	C. Prepaid Expenses and Accrued Income	1,667	678
41	**TOTAL ASSETS**	202,229	247,565
42	D. Owner's Equity	152,410	152,410
43	I. Subscribed Capital	152,410	152,410
44	II. Subscribed but unpaid capital (-)		
45	III. Capital Reserves		
46	IV. Accumulated Retained Earnings		
47	V. Evaluation reserve		
47/a	VI. Balance Sheet profit or Loss for the financial year		
48	E. Specific Reserves	0	4,663
49	Reserves for expected losses	0	4,363
50	Reserves for expected obligations	0	300
51	Other Specific Reserves		
52	F. Liabilities	49,819	61,076
53	I. Long Term Liabilities	27,092	0
54	Investments and Developments credits		
55	Other long term credits		
56	Long Term loans		
57	Bonds Payable		
58	Obligations to founders	27,092	0
59	Other long term liabilities		
60	II. Short Term Liabilities	22,727	61,076
61	Advance payments form customers		
62	Accounts payable	8,239	33,419
63	Bills of exchange		
64	Short Term Credits		
65	Short Term Liabilities		
66	Other Short Term Liabilities	14,488	27,657
67	G. Accruals and Deferred income	0	29,416
68	**TOTAL LIABILITIES**	202,229	247,565

Figure 3

EREDMÉNYKIMUTATÁS	1996	1997
	eFt	*eFt*
01. BELFÖLDI ÉRTÉKESÍTÉS NETTÓ ÁRBEVÉTELE	208,123	456.495
02. EXPORT ÉRTÉKESÍTÉS NETTÓ ÁRBEVÉTELE		1.508
I. ÉRTÉKESÍTÉS NETTÓ ÁRBEVÉTELE	208,123	458,003
II. EGYÉB BEVÉTELEK	157	5,438
03. SAJÁT ELÕÁLLÍTÁSÚ ESZKÖZÖK AKTIVÁLT ÉRTÉKE		
04. SAJÁT TERMELÉSÛ KÉSZLETEK ÁLLOMÁNYVÁLTOZÁSA		
III. AKTIVÁLT SAJÁT TELJESÍTMÉNYEK ÉRTÉKE		
05. ANYAGKÖLTSÉG	141,332	354,770
06. IGÉNYBE VETT ANYAGJELLEGÛ SZOLGÁLTATÁSOK ÉRTÉKE	630	3,616
07. ELADOTT ÁRUK BESZERZÉSI ÉRTÉKE		
08. ALVÁLLALKOZÓI TELJESÍTMÉNYEK ÉRTÉKE		
IV. ANYAGJELLEGÛ RÁFORDÍTÁSOK	141,962	358,386
09. BÉRKÖLTSÉG	3,316	7,474
10. SZEMÉLYI JELLEGÛ EGYÉB KIFIZETÉSEK	1,203	2,209
11. TÁRSADALOMBIZTOSÍTÁSI JÁRULÉK	1,402	3,147
V. SZEMÉLYI JELLEGÛ RÁFORDÍTÁSOK	5,921	12,830
VI. ÉRTÉKCSÖKKENÉSI LEÍRÁS	8,046	15,833
VII. EGYÉB KÖLTSÉGEK	4,963	18,004
VIII. EGYÉB RÁFORDÍTÁSOK	257	8,029
A. ÜZEMI (ÜZLETI) TEVÉKENYSÉG EREDMÉNYE	47,131	50,359
12. KAPOTT KAMATOK ÉS KAMAT JELLEGÛ BEVÉTELEK	3,315	6,179
13. KAPOTT OSZTALÉK ÉS RÉSZESEDÉS		
14. PÉNZÜGYI MÛVELETEK EGYÉB BEVÉTELEI		
IX. PÉNZÜGYI MÛVELETEK BEVÉTELEI	3,315	6,179
15. FIZETETT KAMATOK ÉS KAMATJELLEGÛ BEVÉTELEK	8	1,660
16. PÉNZÜGYI BEFEKTETÉSEK LEÍRÁSA		
17. PÉNZÜGYI MÛVELETEK EGYÉB RÁFORDÍTÁSAI		
X. PÉNZÜGYI MÛVELETEK RÁFORDÍTÁSAI	8	1,660
B. PÉNZÜGYI MÛVELETEK EREDMÉNYE	3,307	4,519
C. SZOKÁSOS VÁLLALKOZÓI EREDMÉNY	50,438	54,878
XI. RENDKÍVÜLI BEVÉTELEK	86	285
XII. RENDKÍVÜLI RÁFORDÍTÁSOK		106
D. RENDKÍVÜLI EREDMÉNY	86	179
E. ADÓZÁS ELÕTTI EREDMÉNY	50,524	55,057
XIII. ADÓFIZETÉSI KÖTELEZETTSÉG		
F. ADÓZOTT EREDMÉNY	50,524	55,057
18. EREDMÉNYTART. IGÉNYBEVÉTELE OSZT-RA, RÉSZES-RE		
19. FIZETETT (JÓVÁHAGYOTT) OSZTALÉK ÉS RÉSZESEDÉS	50,524	55,057
G. MÉRLEG SZERINTI EREDMÉNY	0	0

Figure 4

Hungaria Kft.
Profit and Loss Account, Version "A"
For the year ended 31 December 1997

Profit and Loss Account	1996	1997
01 Net domestic sales revenues	208,123	456,495
02 Net export sales revenues	0	1,508
I Net sales revenues (01+ 02)	208,123	458,003
II Other revenue	157	5,438
03 Capitalised value of self- manufactured assets		
04 Changes in stock of self-manufactured assets		
III Capitalised value of own performance (03+ 04)		
05 Materials costs	141,332	354,770
06 Value of material-type services used	630	3,616
07 Purchase value cost of goods sold		
08 Value of subcontractors' performance		
IV Material-type expenditures (05 + 06+ 07+ 08)	141,962	358,386
09 Labor costs	3,316	7,474
10 Other payments to personnel	1,203	2,209
11 Social security contributions	1,402	3,147
V Labor related costs (09+10+11)	5,921	12,830
VI Depreciation allowance	8,046	15,833
VII Other costs	4,963	18,004
VIII Other expenses	257	8,029
A Profit or loss from business activity (I+II+III+IV+V+VI+VII+VIII)		
12 Interest received and	3,315	6,179
13 Dividend and participation received		
14 Other revenue from financial transactions		
IX Revenue from financial transactions (12+13+14)	3,315	6,179
15 Paid interest and interest-	8	1,660
16 Write-off of financial transactions		
17 Other expenditure on financial transactions		
X Expenditure on financial transactions (15+16+17)	8	1,660
B Profit or loss from financial transactions (IX–X)	3,307	4,519
C Regular business profit or loss (+–A+ –B)	50,438	54,878
XI Extraordinary revenue	86	285
XII Extraordinary expenditure	0	106
D Extraordinary profit or loss (XI–XII)	86	179
E Profit or loss before tax (+–C+ –D)	50,524	55,057
XIII Tax payment liability		
F After tax profit or loss (+ –E–XIII)		
18 Use of accumulated retained earnings for dividends or participation		
19 Dividend and participation announced	50,524	55,057
G Balance sheet profit or loss for the financial year (+-F+18–19)	0	0

NOTES TO THE BALANCE SHEET

Tangible fixed assets

Buildings and equipment are recorded at cost less accumulated depreciation. Depreciation is calculated on a monthly basis using the straight line method at rates based on the expected useful lives of the respective assets, and in accordance with the rates laid down in the Act LXXXI of 1996 on Company Tax, appendix 2. These rates are shown below:

Category of asset	*Depreciation rates*
Machinery and equipment	14.5%
Real estate	3 %

The assets used in conjunction with the blowing machine are depreciated over 3 years, which is the estimated useful life of the machine as prescribed in the law.

Tangible assets purchased for under 30 THUF are expensed to the profit and loss in full and registered in Class 0 in the Chart of Accounts.

The general ledger is supported by a manual fixed asset register showing cost, accumulated depreciation, net book value, and depreciation charged in the period for each asset. The register is generated from the same source documentation as the general ledger.

The company performs a physical count of tangible assets and ensures that the value is accurate every two years. In the intervening time the value and quantity of the assets are based on the amounts recorded in the manual fixed asset register.

The cost of "contributions in kind" are detailed in the listings and the joint venture agreement.

The additions to fixed assets for the year ended 1997 are detailed below:

Asset category	*THUF*
Real estate	556
Machinery and equipment	21,746
Vehicles	353
	22,655

Included within the machinery and equipment category are capitalised costs of 15,123 THUF relating to the lease of the B-40 bottle blowing machine.

Tangible fixed assets in 1997

Cost	*Real estate equipment machinery and fittings*	*Technical equipment and vehicles*	*Other*	*Total Cost*
1 January 97	*(THUF)*	*(THUF)*	*(THUF)*	*(THUF)*
Additions	51,821	81,976	200	133,997
Small value assets	556	21,746	353	22,655

31 December 97	0	10,000	0	10,000
Accumulated Depreciation	52,377	113,722	553	166,652
1 January 97	1,066	10,706	0	11,772
Charge for the year	1,607	14,168	58	15,833
31 December 97	2,673	24,874	58	27,605
Net book value				
31 December 97	49,704	88,848	495	139,047

Inventories

Inventories are valued at the lower of cost, determined on a "first in first out" basis, and net realisable value.

Raw material purchases were made from foreign companies. Inventory at the 31 December 1997 was valued using the exchange rate in effect on the invoice date.

In compliance with Hungarian legislation, custom duties of 2,395 THUF have been included within the valuation of closing stock. The detailed stock listing reconciles to the stock accounts in the general ledger. The company holds copies of:

— the purchase invoice;

— delivery notes which details the number of bottles delivered; and

— minutes indicating unusual stock movements

All stock items were expensed on the date of purchase. The company maintained minimum stock levels to meet production requirements.

Movements in stock are vouched to delivery notes and sales invoices. A physical stock count is done on a monthly basis because of the high turnover of stock. The stocktake was completed as at 31 December 1997. The finished goods stock levels maintained are low as Hungary manufactures bottles to sales orders.

Receivables, liquid assets and prepaid expenses

The receivables from sales can be found in the debtors ledger account. Receivables due from the joint venture owners have been classified under other debtors in accordance with the Hungarian accounting law.

Included in the Balance Sheet line for trade debtors are outstanding balances from joint venture owners, holding a combined shareholding of 4.4%. This amounted to 37,730 THUF.

Hungarian Accounting law requires intercompany balances to be shown in other short term receivables. The year end balance of company B, which has a shareholding of 56% in company Hungaria Kft., has been classified here.

As well as debtors ledger a separate ledger is kept for all sales, for VAT recording purposes.

Included in other receivables are amounts owed from employees.

Hungaria Kft. has two bank accounts with OKHB Rt, a settlement account and a foreign exchange transaction account.

Equity and liabilities

Equity

The issued share capital of Hungaria Kft. is 152,410 of which 39.6% is held by a foreign investor.

Liabilities

Separate general ledger accounts are maintained for foreign and domestic creditors.

The company accounted for customs duty payables, local government taxes, and payroll creditors on a timely basis. Payments were made on their due dates.

No corporate income taxes have been provided for in the financial statements of Hungaria Kft. as the result of a legislated tax holiday applicable to companies which operate in certain "Activities of Special Importance" and which meet minimum capital and foreign ownership thresholds. As a result the company is free from the obligation to pay corporation tax and technical development fund tax.

At 31 October 1997 the company circularised its creditors and reconciled the replies to the company's accounting records.

Included in other short-term liabilities is a liability due to company B of 945 THUF. Intercompany balances should be disclosed in this category under Hungarian Accounting Law.

A provision of 4,363 THUF for doubtful debtors was made in the financial statements of Hungaria. This is in compliance with Hungarian Accounting Law.

Liquidity position analysis
1. Current assets in proportion of short term liabilities:

31 Dec. 1996	31 Dec. 1997
3:1	1.76:1

2. Short-term liabilities in proportion of equity:

31 Dec, 1996	31 Dec, 1997
11.24%	24.67%

Information regarding the Profit and Loss Account
Version "A" of the profit and loss account was used by Hungaria Kft.

Subsequent event

At the shareholders' General Meeting on 9 March 1998 board members fees of 150 THUF and management bonuses of 123 THUF were approved. An additional social security and unemployment insurance liability resulted from the bonus approval of 60 THUF. The resulting profit after tax figure of 55,057 THUF was distributed as a dividend.

Types of cost

Costs were accounted for and grouped in accordance with version A: Costs were matched to revenues earned in the correct accounting period in accordance with the accruals concept.

Direct costs include the customs and transportation fees.

Costs that have been separately identified include:

— cost of energy
— consumables for materials
— other materials
— depreciation of assets with a value under 30 THUF

Other and extraordinary expenses

Extraordinary revenues and expenses have been recorded in Class 8 and 9. This is in compliance with the Hungarian accounting law. The extraordinary income and costs relate to claims and penalties received from and paid to insurance companies.

Sales and other revenues

The majority of net sales for the year ended 31 December are domestic sales. Sales to foreign companies have not been significant in 1997.

Monthly reconciliations are performed between the total sales value and the number of units sold. The VAT payable on these sales is also reconciled on a monthly basis.

Other revenues:	(THUF)
Exchange rate gain	5,171
Other	267
Total	5,438

Other costs:	*(HUF)*
Stationary	86,629
Newspapers and publications	56,558
Postage	159,770
Other supplies	5,685,900
Costs of public utilities	1,283,318
Statistical dues	10,275,350
Insurance fees	456,475
Total	18,004,000

Other expenses:	*(THUF)*
Education fund tax	110
Local tax	1,394
Unemployment contributions	320
Provisions	4,663
Loss from exchange rate differences	1,507
Interest on late payments	35
Total	8,029

Analysis of profit

	1996	1997	*Difference*
	(THUF)	*(THUF)*	*(THUF)*
Trading profit	47,131	50,359	3,228
Profit on financial transactions	3,307	4,519	1,212
Profit on ordinary activities	50,438	54,878	4,440
Extraordinary profit	86	179	93
Profit after taxation	50,524	55,057	4,533
Retained profit of the year	0	0	0

Analysis of revenues

	1996	1997	1997/1996 (%)
	(THUF)	*(THUF)*	
Net domestic sales	208,123	456,495	219
Net external sales	0	1,508	
Other revenues	157	5,438	
Total	208,280	463.441	

Analysis of costs and expenses

Costs *and expenses*	1996 (THUF)	1997 (THUF)	1997/1996 (%) (THUF)
Cost of raw materials	141,332	354,770	251
Material-type cost	630	3,616	574
Wages and salaries	3,316	7,474	225
Other staff emoluments	1,203	2,209	184
Social insurance contribution	1,402	3,147	224
Depreciation	8,046	15,833	197
Other costs	4,963	18,004	363
Other expenses	257	8,029	3,124

Wages and salaries

The average number of people employed by Hungaria Kft. for the year ended 1997 was 11. These employees were grouped as follows:

(THUF)

1 staff managing director
1 staff commercial manager
1 staff administrator
1 staff part-time worker chief account
7 staff manual workers
Distribution of wages and salaries

Manual workers	5,759
Intellectual workers	1,715
Total	7,474

The cash flow statement of Hungaria Kft. is presented in Figure 9.

Figure 5
Income Statement Format
(Cost of Sales Model)

Version B
01 Net domestic sales revenue
02 Net export sales revenue
   I Net sales revenues (01+ 02)
   II Other revenues
03 Direct prime costs of sale
04 Purchase value of goods sold, value of subcontractor's performance
   III Direct costs of sale (03+ 04)
05 Sales costs
06 Administration costs
07 Other general overheads
   IV Indirect costs of sale (05 + 06+ 07)
   V Other expenses and expenditures
   A/ Profit or loss from business activities
   (I+II–III–IV–V)
The remainder of the format corresponds to lines 12–19, IX–XIII and B–G of Version A.

Figure 6
Simplified Balance Sheet

Assets
A.   Investments
     I. Intangible goods
     II. Tangible assets
     III. Financial investments
B.   Current assets
     I. Inventories
     II. Receivables, of which:
        —receivables from cash out items,
        —receivables not related to monetary movements
        Less: general turnover tax payable and has not been entered in tax return
     III. Securities
     IV. Cash

Liabilities
C.   Equity
     I. Subscribed capital
     II. Capital reserves

III. Accumulated retained earnings
IV. Simplified balance sheet profit or loss
D. Reserve
E. Specific reserves
F. Liabilities
   I. Long-term liabilities
   II. Short-term liabilities
   Less: deductible general turnover tax not yet accounted for the central budget

Figure 7

*Additional Information Required for
the Consolidated Balance Sheet*

Reference is made to classifications shown in Figure 2.
The following additional details shall be given:

A/III/1. Participation
A/III/2. Shares in other companies as long term investment
A/III/3. The lines of loans given to

—company with majority holding
—company with a significant holding
—other companies

A/III/4. Long term bank deposits
B/II/5. Other receivables due from

—company having a majority holding
—company having a significant holding
—other companies

B/III/1. Bonds bought for resale
B/III/2. Own shares, participations
B/III/3. Other securities held in

—company having a majority holding
—company having a significant holding
—other companies

B/III/2. Own shares and other shares, purchased for resale, from

—company having a majority holding
—company having a significant holding
—other companies

D/I/1. Issued capital

—ssued by companies involved in consolidation
—issued by jointly managed enterprises
—issued by associated enterprises
—repurchased own shares, business shares

F/I/6. Other long-term liabilities

—companies involved in consolidation
—jointly managed enterprises
—associated enterprises
—other entrepreneurs

F/II/6. Other short-term liabilities

—companies involved in consolidation
—jointly managed enterprises
—associated enterprises
—other entrepreneurs

Figure 8

*Additional Information for
the Consolidated Income Statement*

Reference is made to the classifications shown in Figure 4.
The following details shall be given:

01 Net domestic sales revenue
02 Net export sales revenue
II. Other revenue from
12 Interest received and interest-related revenues
13 Dividend and profit-sharing received
15 Paid interest and interest-related payments
19 Dividend and profit-sharing paid (approved)

The above-listed items shall be detailed in a breakdown by

—companies involved in consolidation
—jointly managed enterprises
—associated enterprises
—other entrepreneurs

Figure 9

HUNGARIA Kft.

Cash Flow Statements

for the year ended 31 December 1997

		THUF
I. Cash flows from operation (rows 1–13)		
1. Profit or loss before tax	+ –	55.057
2. Depreciation	+	15.833
3. Loss in value accounted for	+	
4. Difference between creation and use of provision	+ –	4.663
5. Profit or loss from sales of invested assets	+ –	
6. Change in accounts payable	+ –	25.180
7. Change in other short-term liabilities	+ –	13.169
8. Change in accrued expenses and deferred income	+ –	29.416
9. Change in account receivable	+ –	(34.671)
10. Change in other current assets	+ –	(1.116)
11. Change in deferred expenses and accrued income	+ –	989
12. Tax paid	–	
13. Dividends paid	–	(55.057)

	THUF
I. Cash flows from operation	*53.463*

II. Cash flows from investments (rows 14–16)		
14. Purchase of invested assets	–	(22.655)
15. Sale of invested assets	+	
16. Dividends received	+	
II. Cash flows from investments		(22.655)

III. Cash flow from financial transactions (rows 17–22)		
17. Cash receipt from issuing shares, bonds and liquid asset taken over definitively	+	
18. Borrowing (increase)	+	
19. Withdrawal of shares	–	
20. Repayment of bonds	–	
21. Repayment of loans	–	(27.092)
22. Liquid assets handed over definitively	–	
III. Cash flow from financial transactions		(27.092)

IV. Total net cash flows (rows + –I+ –II+ –III)	3.716

POLAND

Alicja Jaruga
Lodz University, Lodz, Poland
and
Derek Bailey
Thames Valley University, London, England

1. Background

1.1 History

The Commonwealth (*Rzeczpospolita*) of Poland-Lithuania was a major political and economic power in Europe during the 15th to 17th centuries. The keeping of methodical accounting records may be traced back to the 15th century. To this period belong the oldest preserved inventory schedules and account books of the large landed estates and municipalities. The earliest extant merchant books, covering the period 1421–1454, belonged to Jan Pis of Gdansk (a Hanseatic seaport). The first commercial and accounting manuals appeared in the 1530s.

There is early evidence of the influence of accounting principles developed in Northern Italy. For two generations accounting and related records of the Royal Salt Mine in Wieliczka were maintained by an Italian family.

The royal (state) treasury was separated from the court (household) treasury in the 16th century. The Polish Seym (Parliament) approved the separation, elements of state accounting emerged, and in 1591 the treasury tribunal was constituted.

During a process of reform, the first state budget was passed by the Seym in 1768. The constitution of May 3, 1791 established a right for the Seym to approve public revenues and expenditures. The Polish Constitution of Third May ("the first constitution of its type in Europe" and the first to be written after the American Constitution) and Polish budgeting served as a model for other European countries.

Opposition to the reform process led to the progressive partition of Poland by Russia, Prussia, and Austria in 1773, 1793, and 1795 and the loss of independence. Thereafter the legislation of these powerful countries had a measurable effect on the regularization of accounting practice in partitioned Poland.

The arrival of Napoleon in Poland resulted in the creation of the self-governing Grand Duchy of Warsaw (1807–1815) and his defeat in the creation of the Congress Kingdom of Poland (1815–1864) with the Russian Tsar as King. The Napoleonic Commercial Code was adopted in the Grand Duchy in 1808 and, later, in the Congress Kingdom. This Commercial Code remained in operation until 1934 in the Second Polish Republic (1918–1939).

An institutionalized market for commodities and securities, established in 1817 in Warsaw, the capital of the Congress Kingdom, played a significant role. The books of exchange brokers were initially examined by the magistrate of a commercial court.

In the parts of Poland directly incorporated into the Russian Empire, its commercial laws (Volumes X and XI of the collection of laws) were applied.

In the parts of Poland administered by the German and Austro-Hungarian empires, the German Commercial Code (*Handelsgesetzbuch*) was applied. The Shares Regulation 1899 authorized chambers of industry and commerce to compile lists of proper persons ("accounting experts") for the verification of the statutes and reports of joint-stock companies, reflecting the growing importance of foreign capital. In 1907 the Polish Association of Accountants was established, although its influence on accounting regulation was slight.

In the latter part of the 19th century industrialisation and commercialisation, especially after the peasantry was granted land ownership rights and the growth of credit institutions contributed to the gradual regularization of accounting practice.

Apart from broadly drawn commercial codes, the main source of accounting regularization was fiscal, as the rules for taxation increasingly influenced accounting practice. This fact was readily apparent by the early decades of the 20th century, when rates of taxation increased considerably, and the natural conflict of interest between business enterprises and the fiscal authorities appeared.

The creation of the independent Second Republic, in 1918, required the reintegration of the diverse business and accounting practices that had grown up during the one and a quarter centuries of the tripartite partition. In 1934 the Polish Commercial Code was introduced.

Accounting continued to be regulated generally by the new commercial code, although precedence was ceded to the needs of taxation through fiscal legislation. In practice there was an obligation to prepare two sets of financial statements: one for commercial purposes and one for taxation purposes, the latter being a restatement of the former. Accounting was affected also by criminal, civil, and bankruptcy laws.

The influence of the Warsaw Stock Exchange on accounting was negligible because the low level of private saving delayed the development of a capital market. The annual financial statements of listed companies were required to be audited and published.

The annual financial statements of other joint-stock companies were verified by auditors and copies lodged with a provincial court and the Ministry of Industry and Trade. Some annual financial statements were published in abbreviated form in journals (e.g. *Monitor Polski*).

At the request of a business partner, the annual financial statements could be examined and revised by an auditor or auditors appointed by a commercial court.

A registered merchant was obliged to present a financial statement to a commercial court at the end of the financial year.

From the late 1980s, with the recognition of the inevitability of the emergence and expansion of a market economy, there was a renewed interest in the business and accounting practices of the Second Republic. For example, the 1934 Commercial Code, which fell into disuse after 1948 but was not revoked, was gradually reactivated.

Since 1939 there have been three successive waves of influence on accounting in Poland: German, Soviet, and West European. During the so-called Fourth Partition of Poland (1939–1944) the German system of compulsory uniform accounting was extended into the regions under German occupation. The Soviet accounting system was introduced into the regions incorporated into the USSR.

In 1944 the Polish state was reestablished within transplanted frontiers, and during the remainder of the 1940s the German experience had a significant influence on accountancy. The first uniform accounting plan, introduced in 1946, was inspired by the German model.

Later, in 1951–1953, the mixed economy was replaced by a centrally planned economy and the adoption of Soviet economic planning and financing methods led to the introduction of the Soviet accounting plan. Reform of the accounting plan was undertaken in 1959, 1974 (influenced in part by French experience of a uniform accounting system), and 1985.

In the late 1950s the qualifications for state authorized accountant were introduced.

The Polish accounting system came under the direct administration of the Ministry of Finance. In place of general principles of accounting, derived from the commercial code and taxation legislation, obligatory and uniform measures of accounting were introduced by financial law. The financial law explicitly covered the scope of financial accounting to a considerable extent. Accountancy was reduced to economic record keeping. The emphasis was placed on legal form. The financial statements, although unpublished, were used for such purposes as national statistics generation, performance measurement, and price setting within the context of central economic planning.

The failure to achieve an effective reform of the centrally planned economy led, at the close of the 1980s, to its dismantling and to the radical transformation of the entire socioeconomic system. The objectives were the creation of a social market economy and its integration into the wider global economy, with the prospect of admission to the internal market of the European Union. New institutions were required, such as commercial banks and a stock exchange, and the ownership of state enterprises had to be transferred and new private enterprises created. State subsidies for enterprises were severely restricted or eliminated, prices were decontrolled, and currency convertibility was introduced so that a market mechanism could be integrated into the transformed economic system.

The transformation of the economic system created a need to restructure accounting and financial reporting. The then existing accounting requirements had been determined mainly by state authorities, and the first phase of restructuring was carried out under the direction of the Accounting Department of the Ministry of Finance. The Ministry adopted an Accounting Decree, effective from January 1, 1991. The decree stipulated new formats for the financial statements and a new approach to the determination of net result. In a departure from earlier practice, the draft decree had been opened for discussion and evaluation by the Association of Accountants in Poland (*Stowarzyszenie Ksiegowych w Polsce*) (reestablished in 1956) and by academics before its promulgation by the Ministry of Finance.

In the same year the Audit and Publication of Financial Statements and Expert Auditors and their Self-Regulation Acts were adopted.

Both the Accounting Decree and the Audit Act, being interim measures, were superseded by later legislation.

1.2 Legal Framework

Poland, like most European countries, has a system of codified law. The Commercial Code of 1934 remains in force, although some of its provisions have been either revoked or modified to suit contemporary needs. Provision is made for the creation of civil, unlimited, and limited partnerships. In addition, the Commercial Code provides for the creation of private, or closed, companies and public, or open, companies. In Polish legislation these are known as limited liability companies and joint stock companies, respectively. The former may, and the latter must, establish a supervisory board in addition to the management board (i.e. board of directors). The basic rules for accounting and financial reporting by companies contained in the Commercial Code (Articles 244–253 and 418–430) have been repealed by new legislation.

The Accounting Act of 1994 provides for the comprehensive reform of accounting, financial reporting, and auditing. The purpose of the Act is the regularization of accounting and the procedures for the audit of financial statements by qualified auditors (Article 1). Sections of the Act deal with bookkeeping (Articles 11–25), inventorization (Articles 26–27), valuation of assets and liabilities and calculation of net result (Articles 28–44), financial statements of an entity (Articles 45–54), financial statements of a capital group (Articles 55–63), auditing and publication (Articles 64–70), accounting archives protection (Articles 71–76), criminal responsibility (Articles 77–79), and sundry matters.

The provisions of the Act extend to nearly all economic entities (e.g. sole proprietorships and partnerships with an annual net income of at least 400,000 ECU (Article 2.1.2) and are not confined to companies. For this reason the generic term used in the Act is *entity* (Article 3.1.1) and not *company*.

The Accounting Act was complemented by the Expert Auditors and their Self-Regulation Act of 1994. In the following year the Ministry of Finance adopted a decree concerning the specific principles for the preparation of consolidated financial statements.

The principal forms of taxation are corporate and personal income tax and value added tax. The rate of corporate income tax, now 36%, is scheduled to fall to 32% at the end of the century. Frequent changes to the complex taxation regulations impact accounting. (Since 1995 deferred tax has entered into accounting).

The arrangements for social security, including pensions, differ greatly from those customary in Western Europe. The overall rate of contribution, based on payroll cost, is now 45%, and the total contributions are transferred to the State Social Security Institution.

1.3 Audit Profession

In Poland the audit profession is subject to the Expert Auditors and their Self-Regulation Act of 1994. These professionals are known as expert auditors (*biegli rewidenci*).

The earlier 1991 Act established the National Chamber of Expert Auditors (*Krajow Izba Bieglych Rewidentow*). The National Chamber is supervised by the Ministry of Finance (i.e. is a constituted authority with respect to statutory audits in accordance with the EC Eighth Directive, Article 2.2).

The bodies under the National Chamber are:

- National Congress
- National Council
- National Audit Committee
- National Disciplinary Court
- National Disciplinary Attorney

The National Council maintains the register of expert auditors, who are persons of Polish nationality possessing full legal rights. To be included in the register an approved person is required to have:

- Obtained a higher education
- Undertaken 2 years of recognized professional practice
- Completed a 2-year apprenticeship under the direction of an expert auditor
- Successfully passed the expert auditor examinations
- Obtained an expert auditor diploma

The conduct of the expert auditor examinations and the oversight of professional practice and apprenticeship are undertaken by the Commission, which is convened for a 4-year term by the National Council in agreement with the Minister of Finance and acting under approved regulations.

The expert auditor is comparable to a statutory auditor (i.e., as described in the EU Eighth Directive, Article 2.1 (a)).

The former state authorized accountants have been given an opportunity to register as expert auditors, given appropriate practical experience and training, although only 6,400 of a total of more than 50,000 are engaged in accounting work. All have been members of the Association of Accountants in Poland.

More than 8,000 names have been entered into the register by the National Council, by which are published:

- A list of practicing expert auditors
- A list of entities entitled to audit financial statements

The entities, in addition to sole practitioners, entitled to audit consist of unlimited and limited partnerships, civil partnerships, and incorporated entities (i.e. legal persons), given an appropriate complement of expert auditors.

More than 1,600 accounting firms, including affiliates of the leading international accounting firms, undertake auditing in Poland.

1.4 Securities Commission

The Securities Commission was established by the Public Trading in Securities and Trust Funds Act of 1991 and charged with responsibility for matters relating to public trading in securities, in particular:

- Supervision of the observance of the rules for fair trading and competition in the field of public trading in securities
- Instigation, organization, and implementation of measures for ensuring the effective operation of the securities market
- Co-operation with other organizations and institutions and participants in the public trading of securities with the aim of informing the economic policy of the state for the development of the securities market
- Popularization of knowledge of the principles of the operation of a securities market.

The tasks of the Securities Commission include supervision of the activities of stockbrokers and the Warsaw Stock Exchange (opened in 1991). In tackling these tasks the Securities Commission has been heavily influenced by the Securities and Exchange Commission of the United

States. Quoted companies are required to provide a flow of financial information (e.g. quarterly, half-yearly, and provisional annual results, as well as annual financial statements) to the Securities Commission. This is likely to have a significant impact on the quality and content of the financial statements of publicly quoted companies.

Approximately 150 companies are now quoted on the Warsaw Stock Exchange. The Exchange has been described as "very transparent for foreign investors," and the annual financial statements for quoted companies are readily available in Warsaw.

1.5 Uniform Charts of Accounts

Although used throughout the period 1940–1989, there is now no intention to introduce an obligatory uniform chart of accounts. However, the Accounting Act of 1994 requires each entity to prepare its own chart of accounts (Article 10.1.1). Model charts of accounts may be used to unify the principles of grouping economic operations and to reduce the work of the entity in creating its own chart of accounts (Article 83.1). Model charts of accounts may be determined (Article 83.2) by:

1. The Securities Commission for quoted companies
2. The Ministry of Finance for other entities

Formats for reporting by capital groups are contained in appendixes to the Consolidation Decree of 1995.

1.6 Simplified Financial Statements

Simplified annual financial statements may be prepared by small entities not exceeding two of the following criteria (Article 50.2):

Average number of employees	50 persons
Total balance sheet assets at the end of the financial year	1 million ECU
Net sales from goods, products and financial operations for the year	2 million ECU

Capital groups not exceeding two of the above criteria by a factor of three need not prepare consolidated financial statements (Article 56.1).

2. The Form and Content of Published Financial Statements

The accounting books and financial statements for all entities must be prepared in the Polish language and the Polish currency (Article 9).

2.1 Single Entity

The financial statements for an entity comprise (Article 45.2):

- Balance sheet
- Profit and loss account
- Additional information (i.e. notes to the financial statements) as set out in Appendix 7 to the Accounting Act.

In addition, public companies and private, other than small, companies are required to provide a cash flow statement (Article 45.3). The management boards of all companies are required to prepare an annual report on the operations of the entity during the year (Article 49.1). The single vertical format for the balance sheet and the four alternative formats for the profit and loss account are specified in appendixes to the Act.

2.1.1 Balance Sheet

The format of the balance sheet was changed significantly by the Accounting Decree of 1991 and, in general, confirmed by the later Accounting Act.

The new format approximates the format specified in the EU Fourth Directive, although there are differences. Relations with affiliated undertakings are not distinguished. Also not distinguished are debtors and creditors, classified under current but falling due for settlement after one year. Instead, all debtors and creditors to be settled after one year are classified as long term (Article 3.1.19).

2.1.2 Fixed Assets

Tangible and intangible fixed assets are distinguished. The former embraces property owned or co-owned, machinery, equipment, means of transportation, and livestock with an expected useful life of at least one year, whether used by the entity or provided for the use of another entity on the basis of a rental or similar agreement. Also included are fixed assets used but not owned if, on the basis of other regulations (i.e. taxation regulations), they are eligible for depreciation or amortization by the given entity (Article 3.1.11). In practice, all rental agreements are treated as operating leases although leasehold improvements are capitalized.

Intangible assets are defined (Article 3.1.13) as property rights acquired by an entity and which may be of economic benefit. Included are co-operative ownership of rights to premises and copyrights, inventions, patents, trademarks, and comparable items, with an expected useful life in excess of one year, used by the entity or elsewhere used on the basis of a rental or similar agreement. Perpetual usufruct of land (excess of the initial fee over the annual fee) although otherwise not capitalized.

In addition, intangible assets includes:

- Organizational expenses incurred in connection with the establishment or further capitalization of a public company
- Goodwill
- Development costs

In the Act development is defined as research, or knowledge otherwise gained, that may be used for the production of new or significantly improved and clearly defined products or processes.

2.1.3 Financial Assets

Financial assets include shares, stocks, and securities, provided they are held for other than trading, and long-term loans.

2.1.4 Current Assets

Current assets are not defined but include inventory, debtors, marketable securities, and monetary assets. Tangible current assets are defined as materials purchased for own use or for production, work-in-progress, saleable finished output, and goods purchased for resale (Article 3.1.14).

Marketable securities include own shares or stock for resale. Monetary assets denotes cash and cash equivalents held in domestic and foreign currencies and includes foreign bills maturing within 3 months (Article 3.1.15).

2.1.5 Equity and Liabilities

Equity and liabilities are classified under the five headings of capital; provisions; long-term liabilities; short-term liabilities and special funds; and accrued costs and deferred revenues.

2.1.6 Capital

Capital (or own fund) comprises:

- Share capital
- Subscribed share capital unpaid
- Supplementary capital
- Asset revaluation reserve
- Other reserve capital
- Retained earnings
- Net profit or loss for the financial year

Supplementary capital includes share premium, legal reserves created by law, company's notarial deed (i.e. a combined memorandum and articles of association) or other agreements and capital surcharges (i.e. additional capital temporarily introduced by shareholders). The creation of a legal reserve by public companies is stipulated in the Commercial Code, Article 427.1.

The net profit or loss for the financial year is shown as a separate item because its appropriation depends on approval at the forthcoming annual general meeting of shareholders. The amount shown on the balance sheet must be equal to the net result less obligatory charges (i.e. before discretionary appropriations) shown on the profit and loss account. The major obligatory charge is for tax.

2.1.7 Provisions

Provisions for corporate or personal income tax are separated from other provisions. This first group of provisions accommodates temporary timing differences resulting from the recognition of income earned or cost incurred at different points in time under the Accounting Act and under the income tax regulations (Article 37.3). Provision must be made for deferred tax liabilities, whereas amounts recoverable may be acknowledged.

Other provisions are intended to provide for risks known to the entity, possible losses, and the financial implications of other incidents (Article 7.1.5) and, in particular (Article 37.1):

- Debtors overdue (e.g. arising from insolvency and payment is unlikely within the next six months)
- Disputed debtors

(In both instances the provisions are to be restricted to the amounts not covered by guarantee or other collateral).

- Certain or probable losses on business transactions in progress
- Financial implications of legal proceedings in progress (if the loss may be estimated reliably).

2.1.8 Long-Term Liabilities

Long-term liabilities are classified into (1) debt, bonds, and other securities, (2) bank loans, and (3) other. *Long term*, within this context is not defined but, by inference, would seem to refer to any period in excess of 12 months.

2.1.9 Short-Term Liabilities and Special Funds

Short-term liabilities are classified under nine headings, including:

- Tax, customs duties, and social insurance liabilities
- Accrued remuneration

Special funds are created in accordance with the requirements of national legislation (e.g., employees' fund).

2.1.10 Profit and Loss Account

A choice of four formats for the profit and loss account (two each for the cost of sales model and the total operating costs model is prescribed in appendixes to the Accounting Act. The structure of the profit and loss account, under the cost of sales model and in a simplified form, is as follows:

Sales revenue
Cost of sales
  Gross profit
Selling and administrative costs
  Profit on sales
Other operating revenues and costs
  Operating profit/loss
Financial revenues and costs
  Gross profit/loss from economic activity
Extraordinary gains and losses
  Gross profit/loss
Obligatory charges on gross profit
  Net profit/loss

The obligatory charges comprise income tax and transfer to legal reserves.

2.1.11   Notes to the Accounts

The notes to the accounts are intended to contain information not otherwise disclosed and provide explanations necessary for the financial statements to present fairly and clearly the assets, financial situation, financial result, and profitability of an entity (Article 48.1). In particular the notes should provide:

1. Explanations of the valuation methods applied, methods used in the preparation of the financial statements, and reasons for any changes compared with the preceding year

2. Supplementary information on the assets, liabilities, and equity shown in the balance sheet and on items in the profit and loss account

3. Any other significant or material information necessary to understand the balance sheet and the profit and loss account

4. Proposed appropriation of profit or treatment of loss

5. Basic information concerning the entity's employees and board(s)

The additional information to be provided is itemized in Appendix 7. Among the information required is:

- The value of land under perpetual usufruct
- The value of fixed assets not depreciated and used under rental, leasing, or other agreements
- Liabilities to the budgets of the state or local government arising from the ownership of buildings
- Analysis of liabilities according to the maturity dates of outstanding payments:
  (a) up to 1 year
  (b) 1 to 5 years
  (c) over 5 years
- List of prepayments, accruals, and deferred revenues
- List of types of liabilities secured on the entity's assets
- Contingent liabilities inclusive of bills of exchange, warranties
- Explanation of unplanned depreciation charges
- Amount of inventory value adjustments arising from fall in sales value
- Reconciliation between the taxable income (as determined under taxation legislation) and the overall gross profit/loss (as shown on the profit and loss account)
- Information on extraordinary gains and losses analyzed under Acts of God and other causes
- Income tax on extraordinary profit or loss
- Deferred tax liability

2.1.12 Cash Flow Statement

With the exception of exempted entities (Articles 45.3 and 64.1), a cash flow statement is required to be prepared according to the format provided in Appendix 8 to the Accounting Act (Article 48.3).

The general structure of the cash flow statement is as follows:

- Cash flow from operating activities
- Cash flow from investing activities

- Cash flow from financing activities
- Net change in monetary assets
- Monetary assets at the beginning of the financial year
- Monetary assets at the end of the financial year

The format presupposes the use of the indirect method of computation.

2.1.13 Annual Report

The management boards of all entities are required to prepare an annual report on the entity's operations during the financial year (Article 49.1). The annual report is required to include information on (Article 49.2):

1. Major events, including capital investments having a significant impact on the operations of the entity and taking place during the financial year or so expected in a subsequent year
2. Projected development of the entity
3. Major achievements in research and technical development
4. Current and expected financial conditions

2.1.14 Audit

The audit of the annual financial statements is required for (Article 64.1):

- Public companies
- Private companies that exceed two of the following criteria in the financial year preceding the financial year for which the financial statements are prepared:
  — Average number of employees: 50 persons
  — Total balance sheet assets at the end of the financial year: 1 million ECU
  — Net sales from goods, products and financial operations for the year: 3 million ECU

(Note the difference from the criteria given in Article 50.2).

Private companies not satisfying the criteria are required to be audited once every 3 years (Article 64.3.1).

In addition audits are required for:

- Annual consolidated financial statements (Article 64.1)
- Financial statements of public companies prepared as at the date of a merger or takeover (Article 64.3.2).

The objective of the audit is for the auditor to provide a written opinion, together with an audit report, on whether the financial statements are correct (*prawidlowe*) and provide a clear (*jasno*) and fair (*rzetelne*) presentation of the assets, financial situation, financial result, and profitability of the entity (Article 65.1).

The written audit opinion is required to state whether the examined financial statements (Article 65.2):

- Have been prepared on the basis of properly maintained accounting books
- Have been prepared in accordance with the principles contained in the Accounting Act
- Have been prepared in conformity, as to their form and content, with the legislation, notarial deed, and the agreements binding upon the entity
- Present fairly and clearly all the information significant for an assessment of the entity

The audit report is required to include (Article 65.4):

- General characteristics of the entity
- Confirmation that the desired information, explanations, and statements were received
- Assessment of the adequacy of the accounting system and the related internal control procedures
- A description of each balance sheet and profit and loss account item or group of items
- Presentation of the assets, financial situation, financial result, and profitability of the entity
- Presentation of events having a significant negative impact on the situation, especially if endangering the continuity of the entity

- Any violations of legislation or the notarial deed or agreements entered into by the entity.

The written audit opinion and the audit report must be derived from documentary audit evidence such that a later reviewing auditor would be able to judge the appropriateness of that opinion (Art 65.5).

2.1.15 Filing and Publication

The annual financial statements, the decision on their approval (i.e., by a general meeting of shareholders), the appropriation of the net profit or treatment of the net loss, and the annual report, together with (when required to be prepared) the written audit opinion for all companies should be lodged with the relevant court of registration or commercial registry (Article 69.1).

For public companies and the larger private companies, the balance sheet, profit and loss account, cash flow statement, written audit opinion, and the decisions on the approval of the financial statements and the appropriation of the net profit, or the treatment of the net loss, should be submitted for publication in the official journal *Monitor Polski B* (Article 70).

Thus, small private companies are exempt from the publication, as distinct from the filing, requirement.

2.2 Capital Group

A capital group, comprising a parent entity and its subsidiary and associated entities, is required to prepare consolidated financial statements in such manner as to represent the group as a single entity (Article 55.1).

The consolidated financial statements comprise:

- Consolidated balance sheet
- Consolidated profit and loss account
- Consolidated cash flow statement
- Additional information (i.e., notes to the consolidated financial statements)
- Report on the group's activities

For the purposes of consolidation the methods to be used are (Article 57.1):

For subsidiary entity: full consolidation method

For associated entity: equity method

But for a subsidiary with wholly dissimilar activities, the equity method is to be used (Article 47.2).

Consolidated financial statements are not required for any subsidiary or associated entity if (Article 56.2):

- The entity was purchased for resale
- The values contained in the financial statements of the entity are insignificant compared with those contained in the financial statements of the parent entity
- Control over the entity is limited to less than one year or is otherwise restricted

The difference arising on setting off the purchase value to the parent entity against the market value of the net assets acquired in the subsidiary is to be disclosed as goodwill on consolidation or as capital reserve on consolidation (Article 58.2). According to the Accounting Act, Article 58.5, these balances are to be written off within 5 years.

Also to be eliminated on consolidation are (Article 58.3):

- Reciprocal debts and liabilities
- Revenues and costs resulting from transactions among the consolidated entities
- Profits or losses arising from the inter-entity transactions of the consolidated entities
- Dividends paid to, and received by, the parent entity

The consolidation entities are required to apply identical methods for valuation and the preparation of the financial statements. Where it is not so appropriate adjustments should be made to the financial statements of the entities concerned before consolidation (Article 60).

Financial statements subject to consolidation that are expressed in foreign currencies should be translated into Polish currency using the principles specified in Article 51.3 (and explained in the next section) (Article 60.3).

The notes attached to the consolidated financial statements, in addition to the information specified in Appendix 7, should include (Article 61):

- A list of the entities making up the capital group
- A description of the methods used in the valuation and calculation of items included in the consolidated financial statements
- Analysis of sales revenue by activities and geographic markets
- Effect of changes in the capital group

The approved manner of consolidation is set out more fully in the Decree on the Specific Principles for the Preparation of Consolidated Financial Statements issued by the Minister of Finance in 1995.

3. Accounting Policies and Practices in Valuation and Income Measurement

The compilation of the accounting books is required to be (Article 24):

- Fair: Entries reflect the actual position of the entity
- Accurate: Entries are complete and correct on the basis of approved accounting evidence
- Verifiable: Allow for the verification of the correctness of the entries and balances
- Up-to-date: Enable the mandatory financial statements and other statements, tax returns and other financial settlements to be prepared in due time

Accounting, defined to embrace financial reporting, is required to be conducted properly to ensure the fair and clear disclosure of the assets, financial situation, financial result, and profitability of the entity (Article 4.1). Provided the purpose is not jeopardized, the accounting principles may be applied in a simplified manner (Article 4.3). All relevant business transactions are to be separately and properly disclosed in the accounting records (Article 8.1). In so doing there must be observed prudence (Article 8.1) in order not to overstate the profit (Article 7.1).

Individual assets and liabilities are to be valued and recorded at the prices (costs) actually incurred on their purchase (production) and with prudence (Article 7). There is to be no set-off of different types of items

(Article 7.3). In the valuation of assets and liabilities and in the determination of the net result, it is assumed that the business of the entity will continue as a going concern in the foreseeable future unless contradicted by the actual status or legal status of the entity (Article 5.2).

The accounting principles adopted should be used continuously and in a consistent manner (Article 5.1), with all revenues and associated costs for a given year recorded irrespective of the dates of receipts and payments (Article 6). However, operational revenues and extraordinary profits should be recognized only when virtually certain (Article 7.1.3).

As of the balance sheet date the assets and liabilities should be valued as follows (Article 28):

Tangible and intangible fixed assets	At purchase price, or production cost or revaluation, reduced by depreciation
Investments in progress Shares in other entities Long-term securities	At purchase price, or production cost less any permanent reduction in value
Tangible current assets	At purchase price or production cost
Short-term securities (for resale)	At cost but not higher than realizable value
Promissory notes Debentures	At realizable value, any differ ence from purchase price being recorded as financial income or financial cost
Debtors and creditors, including loans	At amounts actually receivable or payable
Money assets Capital (funds); securities issued Other assets and liabilities	At nominal value

The purchase price of an imported good includes all costs for bringing the item to a usable condition and any public and legal charges (Article 28.2.1).

If it is not possible to determine the purchase price of an asset, or if an asset is received as a gift, it is to be valued at the sale price of an identical or similar product (Article 28.2.1). If the production cost of an asset is unknown, it is to be valued at the sale price of an identical or similar product less the normal profit (Article 28.2.2).

The net realizable value is defined (Article 28.3) as the selling price (excluding VAT) less discounts, rebates, excise duty, completion costs, and selling costs, but increased by any subsidy due. Otherwise the net realizable value is to be estimated.

The net book value and accumulated depreciation of tangible fixed assets may be revalued (e.g., to reflect, although not necessarily fully, the effect of inflation) by ministerial direction contained in separate regulations. The revaluation should not exceed the economically justified value of the asset (Article 31.4). The difference arising on revaluation is to be taken to an asset revaluation reserve and, upon disposal of the asset, transferred to reserve capital or a similar account (Article 31.5).

Depreciation (Article 32) should be based on the current depreciation plan (i.e., specified rates and amounts of annual depreciation for particular tangible fixed assets). The depreciation rates may be modified to take into account:

- The number of shifts worked
- The rate of technological and economic progress
- Productive capacity
- Legal and other restrictions on working life
- Estimated net salvage value
- Depreciation rates contained in taxation regulations or sectoral guidelines

The valuation and depreciation of intangible fixed assets should be undertaken in a similar manner to tangible fixed assets (Article 33.1).

Development costs, formation expenses, and goodwill are to be written off in not more than 5 years (Article 33.3 and 33.4). When the purchase price of an entity is lower than the market value of the assets acquired, the difference is to be treated as deferred income (and not as a capital reserve) and is to be written off in not more than 5 years (Article 33.4). Both goodwill and deferred income may be eliminated over a longer period than 5 years when justified (Article 33.4).

Provided the estimated production cycle does not exceed 3 months, the work-in-progress may be valued at direct material cost or direct production cost or (if the total assets and net result are not distorted) not at all (Article 34.1).

The value of tangible current assets recorded at standard costs during the year should be appropriately adjusted at the date of the balance sheet (Article 34.2). Planned production cost may be used for the valuation of work-in-progress and finished goods, given that the difference between planned and actual cost is insignificant and the net realizable value is not exceeded (Article 34.2).

With respect to tangible current assets and short-term securities (intended for resale), if the purchase price or production cost varies for identical or near identical items, they may be valued at weighted average price, first in first out (FIFO), last in first out (LIFO), or actual price (Article 34.4).

Tangible current assets having suffered a loss of utility should be valued at net realizable value (Article 35.1). For finished products and goods bought for resale, the equivalent loss may be recognized over a period not exceeding 5 full financial years from the date of purchase or production (Article 35.2).

The share capital of companies is to be recorded at the amount shown in the contractual agreement (e.g. notarial deed) and recorded in the commercial register, called up but unpaid contributions being shown as such on the balance sheet (Article 36.2).

Grants, subsidies, and contributions (allowances) for capital investment and development are to be recorded as deferred income (given they are not required to be treated as capital increments by virtue of other legislation) and to be recognized as income in parallel with the relevant depreciation charges or development costs (Article 40).

Transactions expressed in foreign currencies are to be translated and recorded as follows (Article 30.2):

1. Concerning monetary assets, shares, and securities: at actual rate of exchange for purchase or sale
2. Concerning other assets and liabilities: at average rate of exchange at the date of the transaction

Items expressed in foreign currencies are to be translated for inclusion in the balance sheet as follows (Article 30.1):

1. Shares in other entities, long-term securities, and cash held in entities dealing in foreign currencies: at actual rate of exchange for purchase but not higher than the average rate of exchange as at the date of the balance sheet
2. Other assets and liabilities: at the average rate of exchange as at the date of the balance sheet

Where an entity has internal organizational units (e.g., branches or divisions) located outside Poland that prepare their own financial statements, these last should be incorporated into the financial statements of the entity by using the average rate of exchange as at the date of the balance sheet (Article 51.3).

For the consolidation of foreign subsidiaries currency translation is to be made for:

1. Profit and loss account: at average rate of exchange
2. Balance sheet: at closing rate of exchange

Any difference arising on the foreign currency translation is to be taken to capital reserve or goodwill (without offset if more than one foreign subsidiary). The average rate of exchange to be used is as determined by the National Bank of Poland (Article 30).

Differences arising on foreign currency translations:

1. At the time of the settlement of transactions
2. On the valuation of monetary assets, shares, and securities at the date of the balance sheet

are to be treated as financial costs or financial revenues (Article 30.4).

Differences arising on foreign currency translations caused through the valuation of assets and liabilities other than monetary assets, shares, and securities if:

1. Positive: are to be treated as deferred income
2. Negative: are to be treated as a financial cost (Article 30.5).

4. Expected Future Developments

New programs for accounting education have been adopted in universities and vocational schools and by professional training institutions. Strenuous efforts are needed to change the mentality of accountants to adjust to the commercial environment of a competitive market economy and to increase accountants' knowledge and understanding in international accounting principles and practices. Further changes are necessary in the hitherto prevailing accounting philosophy.

Both the accounting profession and accounting academics have been deeply involved in commenting on drafts of the legislation affecting accounting and auditing. In addition, representatives of the legal profession have participated in monitoring the consistency of the new legislation and its relationship to other laws.

Increased attention is likely to be given to the development of accounting standards, especially for quoted companies, and recently a Committee on Accounting Standards was established.

Transparency (both with respect to the information contained within, and the public access to, the statutory financial statements) seems to be well developed in comparison with prevailing European practice.

Not without reason has such progress been achieved. An interest in the problem of accounting in market economies was aroused once the inevitability of the insertion of a market mechanism into the general structure of the socialist economy was recognized. As long ago as the late 1970s, the Association of Accountants in Poland attempted to establish enduring relations with Western European accounting institutions (e.g. ICAEW in London and the UEC in Brussels) and in 1984 became a member of IFAC. However, the National Chamber of Expert Auditors remains unaffiliated with FEE.

Progress by accounting academics was achieved through exchange programs between Polish and Western (i.e. American, British, German, and French) universities, the first being set up in the mid-1970s. Through these channels more recently the accounting profession was provided with Polish translations of the International Accounting Standards and the EC accounting directives and introduced to management accounting. The British Know How Fund, and its special project for accounting, had a great impact on the reshaping of accounting education and the development of new accounting rules.

The policy, advanced by the government, of seeking an early entry to the process of European economic integration provided a strong stimulus for the assimilation of the EC accounting directives (and, in 1990, influenced the drafting of the Accounting Decree that came into force at the beginning of the following year).

Although a comprehensive reform of accounting, financial reporting, and auditing has been effected, its practical effect has still to be measured fully. Therefore, continuing refinement of accounting legislation may be expected, arising from the experience of the implementation and enforcement of the new laws and as the Polish economy integrates into the wider European market.

Acknowledgment

Thanks are due to Marek Schroeder for his timely assistance.

Useful Addresses

Ministry of Finance
Department of Accounting
ul. Swietokrzyska 12
00-916 Warszawa
Poland

National Chamber of Expert Auditors
(Krajowa Izba Bieglych Ksiegowych)
00-172 Warszawa
ul. Dzika 19/23
Poland

Accounting Standards Committee
Foundation for Capital Market Standards Development
Plac Powstancow Warszawy 1
00-950 Warszawa
Poland

Financial Statements

Format of Polish Financial Statements (from 1997)

Balance Sheet

Aktywa	**Assets**
A. Majątek trwały	A. Fixed assets
I. Wartości niematerialne i prawne	I. Intangible assets
1. Koszty organizacji poniesione przy założeniu lub późniejszym rozszerzeniu spółki akcyjnej	1. Organizational costs incurred in connection with the start-up or expansion of a joint stock company
2. Koszty prac rozwojowych	2. Development costs
3. Wartość firmy	3. Goodwill
4. Inne wartości niematerialne i prawne	4. Other intangibles
5. Zaliczki na poczet wartości niematerialnych i prawnych	5. Prepayment for intangibles
II. Rzeczowy majątek trwały	II. Tangible fixed assets
1. Grunty własne	1. Land (own)
2. Budynki i budowle	2. Buildings and structures
3. Urządzenia techniczne i maszyny	3. Machinery and technical equipment
4. Środki transportu	4. Transportation equipment
5. Pozostałe środki trwałe	5. Other fixed assets
6. Inwestycje rozpoczęte	6. Investments (capital) in progress
7. Zaliczki na poczet inwestycji	7. Prepayments for (capital) investments
III. Finansowy majątek trwały	III. Financial assets
1. Udziały i akcje	1. Shares and stocks
2. Papiery wartościowe	2. Securities
3. Udzielone pożyczki długoterminowe	3. Long-term loans
4. Inne składniki finansowego majątku trwałego	4. Other financial fixed assets
IV. Należności długoterminowe	IV. Long-term receivables
B. Majątek obrotowy	B. Current assets
I. Zapasy	I. Inventory
1. Materiały	1. Materials
2. Półprodukty i produkty w toku	2. Semi-finished products and work in progress
3. Produkty gotowe	3. Finished products
4. Towary	4. Trade goods
5. Zaliczki na poczet dostaw	5. Prepayments for inventory
II. Należności i roszczenia	II. Receivables and claims
1. Należności z tytułu dostaw i usług	1. Trade receivables
2. Należności z tytułu podatków dotacji i ubezpieczeń społecznych	2. Receivables from State budget: taxes, subsidies, social insurance

3. Należności
   wewnątrzzakładowe
4. Pozostałe należności
5. Należności dochodzone na
   drodze sądowej
III. Papiery wartościowe
   przeznaczoe do obrotu
   1. Udziały lub akcje własne do
      zbycia
   2. Inne papiery wartościowe
IV. Środki pieniężne
   1. Środki pieniężne w kasie
   2. Środki pieniężne w banku
   3. Inne środki pieniężne (weksle,
      czeki obce itp.)
C. Rozliczenia międzyokresowe
   kosztów
   1. Czynne rozliczenia
      międzyokresowe kosztów
   2. Inne rozliczenia
      międzyokresowe
Suma aktywów

3. Intra-company receivables

4. Other receivables
5. Receivables in litigation

III. Marketable securities (for
   trading)
   1. Own shares or stocks for sale

   2. Other securities
IV. Monetary assets
   1. Cash in hand
   2. Cash at bank
   3. Other monetary assets (bills,
      external cheques, etc.)
C. Prepayments

   1. Prepaid expenses

   2. Other prepaid items

Total assets

Pasywa
A. Kapitał (fundusz) własny
  I. Kapitał (fundusz) podstawowy
  II. Należne, lecz nie wniesione
    wkłady na poczet kapitału
    podstawowego (wielkość
    ujemna)
  III. Kapitał (fundusz) zapasowy
    1. Ze sprzedaży akcji powyżej
      ich wartości nominalnej
    2. Tworzony ustawowo
    3. Tworzony zgodnie ze statutem
      lub umową

    4. Z dopłat wspólników

    5. Inny
  IV. Kapitał (fundusz) rezerwowy z
    aktualizacji wyceny
  V. Pozostałe kapitały (fundusze)
    rezerwowe
  VI. Nie podzielony wynik finansowy
    z lat ubiegłych
    1. Zysk (wielkość dodatnia)
    2. Strata (wielkość ujemna)
  VII. Wynik finansowy netto roku
    obrotowego
    1. Zysk netto (wielkość
      dodatnia)
    2. Strata netto (wielkość ujemna)
    3. Odpisy z wyniku finansowego
      biczącego roku obrotowego

B. Rezerwy
    1. Rezerwy na podatek
      dochodowy od osób prawnych
      lub osób fizycznych
    2. Pozostałe rezerwy
C. Zobowiązania długoterminowe
    1. Długoterminowe pożyczki,
      obligacje i inne papiery
      wartościowe
    2. Długoterminowe kredyty
      bankowe
    3. Pozostałe zobowiązania
      długoterminowe
D. Zobowiązania krótkoterminowe i
   fundusze specjalne
  I. Zobowiązania krótkoterminowe
    1. Pożyczki, obligacje i papiery

Equity and Liabilities
A. Capital (fund)
  I. Share capital (fund)
  II. Subscribed but unpaid capital
    (negative amount)

  III. Supplementary capital
    1. Share premium
    2. Statutory reserve (created by
      law)
    3. Statutory (created on the basis
      of articles of association, or
      agreement)
    4. Capital surcharges (additional
      temporary capital introduced
      by shareholders)
    5. Other
  IV. Asset revaluation reserve

  V. Other reserve capital (funds)

  VI. Retained earnings
    1. Profit (positive amount)
    2. Loss (negative amount)

  VII. Net profit or loss for the
    financial year
    1. Net profit (positive amount)

    2. Net loss (negative amount)
    3. Appropriations from the
      profit (loss) account for the
      current financial year

B. Provisions
    1. Provisions for corporate or
      personal income tax

    2. Other provisions
C. Long-term liabilities
    1. Long-term debt, bonds, and
      other securities

    2. Long-term bank loans

    3. Other long-term liabilities

D. Short-term liabilities and Special
   funds
  I. Short-term liabilities
    1. Loans, bonds and securities

wartościowe
2. Kredyty bankowe
3. Zaliczki otrzymane na poczet
   dostaw
4. Zobowiązania z tytułu dostaw
   i usług
5. Zobowiązania wekslowe
6. Zobowiązania z tytułu
   podatków, ceł, ubezpieczeń
   społecznych
7. Zobowiązania z tytułu
   wynagrodzeń
8. Zobowiązania
   wewnątrzzakładowe
9. Pozostale zobowiązania
   krótkoterminowe
II. Fundusze specjalne
E. Rozliczenia międzyokresowe i
   przychody przyszłych okresów
   1. Bierne rozliczenia
      międzyokresowe kosztów
   2. Przychody przyszłych okresów
Suma pasywów

2. Bank loans
3. Prepayments received for
   goods and services
4. Trade payables

5. Bills of exchange payable
6. Taxes, customs duties, social
   insurance liabilities

7. Salary payables

8. Intra-company liabilities

9. Other short-term liabilities

II. Special funds
E. Accrued costs and deferred income

   1. Accrued costs

   2. Deferred income
Total equity and liabilities

Income Statement

Koszty i straty	Costs and Losses
A. Koszty działalności operacyjnej	A. Operating costs
I. Wartość sprzedanych towarów i materiałów	I. Cost of sales of trade goods and materials
II. Zużycie materiałów i energii	II. Cost of materials and energy consumed
III. Usługi obce	III. External services
IV. Podatki i opłaty	IV. Taxes and fees
V. Wynagrodzenia	V. Salaries
VI. Świadczenia na rzecz pracowników	VI. Employee benefits
VII. Amortyzacja	VII. Depreciation
VIII. Pozostałe	VIII. Other
B. Zysk ze sprzedaży	B. Gross profit from sales
C. Pozostałe koszty operacyjne	C. Other operating costs
I. Wartość sprzedanych sprzedanych składników majątku trwałego	I. Net book value of fixed assets sold
II. Pozostałe koszty operacyjne	II. Other operating costs
D. Zysk na działalności operacyjnej	D. Operating profit
E. Koszty finansowe	E. Financial costs
I. Odpisy aktualizujące wartość finansowego majątku trwałego oraz krótkoterminowych papierów wartościowych	I. Provisions and write-offs in respect of financial fixed assets and short-term securities
II. Odsetki do zapłacenia - w tym dla jednostek zależnych i stowarzyszonych	II. Interest payable - including subsidiary and associated entities
III. Pozostałe	III. Others
F. Zysk brutto na działalności gospodarczej	F. Gross Profit on economic acitvity
G. Straty nadzwyczajne	G. Extraordinary losses:
H. Zysk brutto	H. Gross profit
I. Obowiązkowe obciążenia wyniku finansowego	I. Obligatory charges on gross profit
I. Podatek dochodowy od osób prawnych lub osób fizycznych	1. Personal or corporate income tax
II. Pozostałe obowiązkowe obciążenia	2. Other obligatory charges
J. Zysk netto	J. Net Profit
Przychody i zyski	Income and Profits
A. Przychody ze sprzedaży i zrównane z nimi	A. Sales revenue and similar items
I. Przychód ze sprzedaży produktów	I. Revenue from sales of products
II. Zmiana stanu produktów (zwiększenie-wartość dodatnia, zmniejszenie-wartość ujemna)	II. Change in stock and work in progress (increase-negative amount, decrease-positive amount)

III. Przychód ze sprzedaży towarów
i materiałów
IV. Koszt wytworzenia świadczeń na
własne potrzeby jednostki
B. Strata ze sprzedaży
C. Pozostałe przychody operacyjne
  I. Przychody ze sprzedaży
  składników majątku trwałego
  II. Dotacje
  III. Pozostałe przychody operacyjne
D. Strata na działalności operacyjnej
E. Przychody finansowe
  I. Dywidendy z tytułu udziałów-w
  tym od jednostek zależnych i
  stowarzyszonych
  II. Odsetki uzyskane
  III. Pozostałe
F. Strata brutto na działalności
gospodarczej
G. Zyski nadzwyczajne
H. Starata brutto
I. Strata netto

III. Revenue from sales of trade
goods and raw materials
IV. Cost of work performed by the
entity for its own needs
B. Loss from sales
C. Other operating revenue
  I. Revenue from sales of fixed
  assets
  II. Subsidies
  III. Other operating revenue
D. Operating loss
E. Financial income
  I. Dividends-including dividends
  from subsidiaries and associated
  entities
  II. Interest earned
  III. Other
F. Gross loss on economic activity

G. Extraordinary gains
H. Gross loss
I. Net loss

COMMONWEALTH OF INDEPENDENT STATES (CIS): OVERVIEW

Derek Bailey
Thames Valley University,
London, England

The dismantling of the administrative arrangements for centralized planning in 1988–1989 extinguished the rationale for the existence of the multi-national USSR as a centrally planned economy. The Baltic States (Estonia, Latvia, and Lithuania) seceded from the USSR, and in September 1991, their independence gained international recognition. In the following December the USSR itself dissolved into a number of independent countries: four in Europe (Belarus, Moldova, Russia, and Ukraine), three in Transcaucasia (Armenia, Azerbaijan, and Georgia), and the remainder in Central Asia (Kazakhstan, Kirghizia, Tadzhikistan, Turkmenistan, and Uzbekistan). In recognition of common economic and political interests, these countries, with the exclusion of the Baltic States, gradually came together in a loose association called the Commonwealth of Independent States (CIS).

In the Baltic States (as is so for other countries that have entered into agreements of association with the European Commission for the purpose of seeking accession to the single market of the European Union), accounting reform has progressed sufficiently far for the annual financial statements to have become recognizably akin, at least formally, to those encountered in international accounting practice. It may be observed that progress in accounting reform being undertaken is dependent upon success in the creation of democratic (representative) institutions and a competitive market economy.

The situation is different, however, for at least some of the successor states to the USSR (e.g. Belarus, Russia, and Ukraine) in which the socioeconomic transformation is proceeding more slowly and with greater hesitancy. In these countries, the accounting and reporting system, originally created at the beginning of the nineteen-thirties to serve the needs of the centrally planned economy, has been modified but neither radically reformed nor abandoned.

The evidently growing, although conceivably temporary, divergence in the pace of accounting change may be attributed to a number of causes.

The USSR arose through the collapse, in 1917, of the Tsarist autocracy of the Russian Empire under the impact of war and revolution. Within the Russian Empire serfdom had not been abolished until 1861. Although initially growing slowly, from 1890 the pace of industrialization and economic development increased. Thus, the capitalist mode of production had existed within the Tsarist autocracy for but a short period.

Within Russia, and down the centuries, the relevance of Western European models of development has been debated keenly and endlessly because of the difference in historical experience between the two parts of Europe (i.e., the Tartar-Mongol Yoke rather than the Renaissance and the Reformation).

In the CIS countries new institutional structures are being created, but problems of their organization, functioning, and integration remain unresolved. The effective disengagement of the polity from the economy presents continuing difficulties. Political considerations tend to weigh heavily on economic, and commercial, decision making. The needs of the state (e.g. with respect to raising revenue for the state budget) tend to dominate over the desired requirements for the market in determining the direction, rate, and extent of accounting change.

In these unsettled conditions a precipitate rate of accounting change (in reaction to foreign-pressures) might lead to accounting uniformity being displaced by accounting disarray. It could occur if the pace of accounting change did not correspond to the needs of the transforming socioeconomic system and, simultaneously, the capacity for retraining accounting personnel (and their capacity for absorbing and applying new ways of accounting) became exhausted.

BELARUS

Dmitri Pankov
Belarussian State Economics University, Minsk, Belarus
and
Derek Bailey
Thames Valley University, London, England

1. Background

1.1 History

The Belarussian state emerged initially as the Principality of Polotsk-Minsk during the early decades of the 11th century when Kievan Rus, the original Russian state, was fragmented under the impact of civil war. A distinct Belarussian identity evolved during the centuries when Muscovite Russia was under the Mongol-Tartar yoke (1240–1480). From the 13th century the Belarussian lands were absorbed steadily into the Grand Duchy of Lithuania and, in the late 18th century, incorporated fully into the Russian Empire. After a failed attempt in 1918 to establish an independent republic, Belarus was constituted a union republic within the USSR. Belarus became independent at the end of 1991 when the USSR was dissolved.

During the Soviet era (1918–1991) Belarus was integrated completely into the political, economic, and accounting systems required by the centrally planned socialist economy.

The main features of the unified socialist accounting system were:

- Unified chart of accounts prescribed by the Ministry of Finance USSR and applied in all economic entities
- Centralized and authoritative regulation by the Ministry of Finance USSR for all kinds of accounting practices and the recording of transactions
- Unified general ledger, subsidiary ledgers, and accounting documentation
- Unified treatment of accounting data

In the absence of preparatory work before independence the pace of accounting reform inevitably would be measured.

Belarus covers an area of 208,000 square kilometres. The population of 10.2 million comprises Belarussians (77%), Russians (13%), Poles (4%), and other minorities (6%). Two-thirds of the population is urban.

In 1990 industrial production made up 60% of GNP. The principal products consisted of machinery, trucks, tractors, and radios and electronic equipment, for the most part being destined for use within the USSR.

1.2 Legal Background

Until 1994 regulations concerning accounting, reporting, and accounting inspection inherited from the USSR continued to be used in Belarus. In that year new legislation, prepared under the direction of the Ministry of Finance, was adopted by the Belarussian Duma (parliament). The Accounting Law of 1994 and the Auditing Law of 1994 came into operation at the beginning of the following year and are intended to replace the old regulations. The new legislation, in general terms, represents an interim, and not a final, stage in accounting reform.

The Accounting Law determines the theoretical, methodological, and organizational bases for the system of accounting in Belarus. The provisions of the law are binding on all types of enterprises conducting business activities within the country. The law consists of thirty-one paragraphs grouped into seven chapters dealing with:

1. General provisions
2. Governmental regulation of accounting and reporting
3. Organization of enterprise accounting
4. Reporting
5. Rules of valuation and accounting
6. Documentation and recording
7. Criminal responsibility

Accounting continues to come under the direction and regulation of the Department for Accounting Methodology of the Ministry of Finance. The Accounting Law specifies the Council of Ministers as the ultimate authority in the process for the creation and supervision of accounting standards, rules, and other legal norms and instructions.

The Accounting Law establishes the extent of the competence of the chief executive in the field of accounting and the scope of the professional rights and responsibilities of the chief accountant.

The new laws have been supplemented by official instructions for:

- Depreciation
- Revaluation of assets
- Preparation of financial statements

1.3 Taxation Regime

The system of taxation is extremely complicated and has a strong influence on both accounting and reporting.

In 1998 the State Taxation Inspectorate issued the binding "List of Expenses for Inclusion in Costs for the Determination of Taxable Income." The main purpose for issuing such a tax regulation was to ensure the proper realization in practice of the accounting principle "matching costs and revenues" and the separation of costs (i.e. chargeable against current revenue before the assessment of tax) from investments. The list specifies the kind of expenditures that, within given norms and limits, are not subject to taxation. All other expenditures must be met out of the net profit remaining after the deduction of all taxes. The effect of the tax regulations has been to determine the composition of costs.

Because calculations for the various taxes are based on different formulas, it has become necessary to create special accounting data for tax purposes. There are two categories of state budgetary taxes:

1. Centralized (i.e. republican) taxes paid to the central state budget
2. Local (i.e. municipal) taxes paid to the budget of the relevant territorial authority

In addition there are the extra-budgetary taxes raised for special needs, such as:

- Agricultural Producers Support Fund
- Housing Maintenance Support Fund
- Kindergartens Support Fund

The general scheme for the determination of the various tax liabilities is set out below:

1. Total sales
2. Less tax on sales of products and work
3. Less tax on sales of services
4. Less tax for Agricultural Producers Support Fund (1% of total sales)
5. Less tax for Housing Maintenance Support Fund (0.5% of total sales)
6. Less excise duty (from 10% to 80% of total sales, depending on the class of commodities sold)
7. Net sales $(1 - 2 - 3 - 4 - 5 - 6)$ for the calculation of value added tax
8. Less costs allowed as shown on the List of Expenses for Inclusion in Costs for the Determination of Taxable Income
9. Added Value $(7 - 8)$
10. Less value added tax (10% to 20% of added value depending on the nature of the sales)
11. Less labor costs
12. Less contributions to Social Security Fund and Unemployment Fund
13. Less depreciation
14. Total costs $(8 + 11 + 12 + 13)$
15. Profit (loss) from sales of products, work, and services $(7-14)$
16. Profit (loss) from sales of other assets
17. Profit from sales of stocks, bonds, securities, and other valuable paper
18. Balance sheet profit (loss) $(15 + 16 + 17)$
19. Less property tax
20. Less income tax (15% to 30% of balance sheet profit net of property tax)
21. Net profit (loss) $(18 - 19 - 20)$

22. Less payments for fines, penalties

23. Net profit (loss) for utilization (i.e. appropriation) (21 − 22)

Of the various taxes the most significant are value added tax and income tax. The weight of current taxation on enterprises is very heavy and in many instances is equal to 75% to 80% of income.

1.4 Chart of Accounts

Three unified charts of accounts have been developed and authorized by the Ministry of Finance for:

- Business enterprises
- Financial institutions
- Nonprofit budget financed organizations

The use of the appropriate chart of accounts is obligatory.

The chart of accounts provides the foundation for the system of accounting in Belarus. The principal objectives are:

1. Unified accounting methodology for the entire national economy
2. Economically relevant classification and grouping of information on the business activities of enterprises
3. Unified approach to cost calculation, control, and the analysis of general microeconomic indicators
4. Comparability of accounting methodology and accounting data for different enterprises

The Chart of Accounts for Business Enterprises came into force on January 1, 1993. The Chart contains 100 synthetic (or aggregation) accounts and 60 subaccounts grouped into ten classes. The account classes reflect the sequence of business operations (i.e. as in the national chart of accounts used in the USSR).

The charts of accounts are integral to the implementation of the national plan of accounts. Thus, the use of the account numbers, as shown in the relevant chart of accounts, is essential for the implementation of the double entry accounting methodology, processing of accounting documents, and recording transactions in the subsidiary and general ledgers.

1.5 Business Background

The conduct of economic activities by business enterprises is governed by several special economic laws introduced in recent years, such as the Commercial Companies Law, Joint Stock Companies Law, Property Law, and Leasing Law.

Business enterprises are permitted to be based on the following types of property ownership:

(a) state
(b) public
(c) private
(d) mixed

With respect to legal status, business enterprises may be organized as sole proprietorships, partnerships (also known as co-operatives), and companies. In addition there are joint ventures (i.e. with foreign participation) and foreign-owned companies.

Of the total number of economic entities, 60% are in the state sector and 40% in the non-state sector of the national economy. The former consist primarily of industrial enterprises, whereas the latter mostly comprise trading, service, and agricultural enterprises.

The composition of enterprises in the non-state sector is as follows:

	%
Sole proprietorships	14.5
Partnerships	2.8
Companies	18.5
Enterprises with foreign participation	3.5
Leasing enterprises	12.8
Collective farms	30.6
Other enterprises	17.3
	100.0

1.6 Professional Organization

The Belarussian Association of Accountants (*Belarusskaya assotsiatsiya bukhgalterov*, BAB) was founded in 1991. Members of the association:

- Act as consultants to the Ministry of Finance in the development of accounting methodology
- Provide expert opinion to the law courts on accounting matters
- Provide protection to accountants being sued
- Provide advisory services to accountants working in enterprises

The association has the right to participate in the drafting of accounting regulations. It has also been preparing for the introduction of a scheme for the national certification of accounting specialists based on the model for a chartered or public certified accountant. In 1999 the association will commence holding the examinations for the new qualification.

The Chamber of Auditors (*Palata auditorov*) also was established in 1991. Since 1992 the Chamber has been providing a national certification for auditors.

The Auditing Law of 1994 gave a start to the professionalization of auditing activities. The principal requirements for the granting of an auditor's licence by the Chamber are:

- Completion of a university education in economics, accounting, finance, or business administration
- Five years of practical experience as an accountant, controller, or auditor
- Successful completion of the Chamber's set of examinations (comprising accounting theory and practice, reporting and auditing, business law, taxation, and privatization)

2. The Form and Content of Accounting Statements

Because accounting reform in Belarus is at an interim stage (i.e. in transformation from reporting for the socialist economy to reporting for the market economy), use of the term *financial statement* may be misleading and, therefore, the term *accounting statement* has been used.

Accounting records and accounting statements are prepared customarily in the Russian language, although the use of the Belarussian language, hitherto confined to rural areas, is being encouraged.

The Ministry of Finance issues obligatory instructions concerning the formats and contents, forms to be used, and procedures to be followed in the preparation of accounting statements. There are monthly, quarterly, and annual reporting cycles, with deadlines of 15 days, 30 days, and three calendar months, respectively, for submission of the appropriate accounting statements. There is a common financial year (ending on December 31).

Since 1994 all business enterprises (i.e. irrespective of the form of ownership and irrespective of size) have been required to prepare the following accounting statements:

- Form 1. Balance sheet (quarterly)
- Form 2. Report of profits and losses (quarterly)
- Form 3. Appendix to the balance sheet (annually)
- Special tax forms (monthly)

Each accounting statement is required to be signed by the executive director and the chief accountant.

2.1 Balance Sheet

The balance sheet is prepared as at the beginning of the first day following the end of the reporting period (i.e. April 1, July 1, October 1, and January 1).

The assets and financial sources (i.e. owners' equity and liabilities) are grouped in the balance sheet as follows:

Active Assets	*Passive Sources*
1. Long term (tangible) assets	1. Sources of owned assets
2. Intangible assets	2. Long term financial liabilities
3. Current assets	3. Creditors and other liabilities

Also shown on the face of the balance sheet are the memoranda (or so-called off balance sheet) accounts.

2.2 Report of Profits and Losses

The equivalent of the income statement comprises five discontinuous sections:

1. Financial result
2. Utilization (i.e. appropriation) of profit
3. Payments to budget
4. Payments to extra budgetary and other funds
5. Movement of financial resources for capital investment and other financial investments

In the first section is shown the net profit (inclusive of any state subsidy for covering losses) or net loss before appropriations. There are distinguished:

- Net result from sales of products, work, and services
- Net result from other sales (e.g. from disposal of fixed and current assets)
- Net result from dealings in securities

There is provided in the second section a list of the appropriations of profit (for payment to the state budget, creation of reserve funds and other purposes), showing the year end position.

In the third section are shown the amounts due and paid for thirteen kinds of payments (taxes, duties, and economic sanctions) to the state budget. These include property tax, profit tax, value added tax, extraordinary tax, and employees' tax.

In the fourth section are shown the largely obligatory payments to the extra-budgetary and other funds under ten headings. For each there is shown amount due, enterprise spending, and amount transferred to the fund.

In the fifth section is shown the movement of the financial resources at the disposal of the enterprise, a distinction being made between owned and attached assets financing.

2.3 Appendix to the Balance Sheet

The appendix consists of four separate sections:

1. Composition and movement of basic means (i.e., tangible fixed assets)
2. Composition and movement of nonmaterial (i.e., intangible) assets

3. Financial investment

4. Movement of funds and other resources

In the first, second, and fourth sections there are shown the opening balances, additions, reductions, and closing balances under fifteen, six, and a minimum of six headings, respectively. In the third section long-term and short-term investment are distinguished under four headings, the opening and closing balances being shown.

2.4 Annual Report

The annual accounting statements are supplemented by an annual report for the purpose of providing additional data for the exposure, clarification, and evaluation of the main factors having a significant influence on the financial results and the financial position of the enterprise. Therefore, comments and explanations on the results of the business activities should be added.

2.5 Audit

An annual audit is obligatory for joint stock (i.e. open) companies, joint venture companies, and foreign-owned companies.

2.6 Filing and Publication

There is no requirement to file the annual accounting statements, annual report, and auditor's opinion (if any) with a commercial registry. There are no requirements for their general disclosure, or publication, whether to the general public or, more narrowly, to investors.

Accessibility to the annual, and other, accounting statements is usually a matter of either managerial policy or private arrangement.

2.7 Presentation

The stipulated accounting statements are required to be presented:

- For all enterprises: to State Taxation Inspectorate and local taxation inspectorate

- For non-state enterprises: to owners and founders (e.g. major stock-holders, partners)
- For state enterprises: to
  - (a) Certain ministries (e.g. for national economy, industry, agriculture, trade, etc), or
  - (b) Some other relevant administrative authority (e.g. department of state, industrial group, committee, etc). depending on the hierarchical structure of governmental administrative (managerial) control.

In certain instances the accounting statements must be sent to particular state authorities charged with providing strict control over some aspect of business activities, for example: Ministry of Foreign Economic Relations, Chamber for State Control, Taxation Investigative Police, local municipal authority, law courts, and banks.

3. Accounting Policies in Valuation and Income Measurement

The Accounting Law of 1994 introduced the concept of accounting policy into accounting theory and practice of Belarus. In the Law are given brief rules for the valuation of items shown in the balance sheet:

- Tangible fixed assets and intangible assets: initial actual cost less depreciation
- Raw and processed materials, purchased semi-finished products, components (in sets and completed): actual historical cost, including all sorts of expenses incurred in acquisition and delivery
- Work-in-progress: actual cost
- Finished products: actual production cost

In the balance sheets for retail companies the item "goods for resale" is to be shown at purchase price. The difference between the purchase price and the retail price (i.e. the mark-up margin) is to be shown on the face of the balance sheet as a memorandum amount. Outstanding balances with debtors and creditors are shown at amounts to be received or paid, bad debts not being shown as a separate item. Assets (e.g. cash, debtors) expressed in foreign currencies are to be translated into Belarussian roubles at the official rate of exchange at the date of the balance sheet as given by the Belarussian National Bank.

In the determination of income the recognition of revenues may be based on either the cash or accrual method. For inclusion in the costs of production, the fixed assets are to be depreciated in accordance with the centrally determined and authorized norms. Inventories may be charged to the costs of production by using any of the specific price, weighted average price, FIFO, or LIFO methods.

4. Expected Future Developments

Having been a constituent of the centrally planned economy of the USSR for many decades exerts a profound effect on the course of socioeconomic change in Belarus. That fact has a significant effect on the pace of feasible accounting change.

Moreover, the future for accounting change in Belarus bears a close relation to the development of political and economic links with Russia and other countries belonging to the Commonwealth of Independent States (CIS). In general terms, there is a desire to maintain a degree of accounting harmonization among this group of countries.

In 1996 the special accounting working group of representatives from each of the countries belonging to the CIS prepared the drafts of two documents:

- General Principles of Reporting for Commercial Organizations
- General Provisions for the Preparation of Financial Statements by Commercial Organizations

Belarus has, as have other CIS countries, declared its appreciation of the need for acceptance of the principles of international accounting and its intention to develop its accounting and reporting system to be in agreement with international principles, concepts, and assumptions applied in accounting, such as accounting entity, adequate disclosure, consistency, going concern, realization, and matching.

Following a consideration of the draft documents, a unified format and content for the balance sheet and income statement was recommended.

There is supposed to be a recomposition of the contents, and a regrouping, of the accounts to make possible the compilation of the balance sheet with a new structure as follows:

Assets	*Owners' Equity and Liabilities*
Non-current assets	Equity capital and reserves
	Minority interest
	Noncurrent liabilities
Current assets	Current liabilities

The greatest changes are intended for the income statement. The aim is to begin using an international format to disclose clearly gross profit, operating income, taxable income, and net income (after tax).

The task of implementing a new version of the income statement is almost wholly dependent on the development of a new taxation code, for which the requirements still must be determined.

An important step in the development of accounting and reporting theory and methodology has been the preparation for the introduction into the practice of accounting, from 1999, of the cash flow statement. Until now the cash flow statement has not been used in Belarus. Use of the cash flow statement will require a complete reconciliation with the balance sheet and the income statement.

To obtain the legal authority to implement the projected changes to the balance sheet and income statement, the Ministry of Finance has submitted a set of proposals to the Belarussian Duma for incorporation into a new version of the Accounting Law.

There are proposals for the elaboration of a new hierarchy of accounting regulations comprising:

1. Laws
2. Standards
3. Supplementary instructions
4. Explanations

Such an important innovation as national accounting standards remains underdeveloped. For the first time in the history of Belarus, a project began in 1997 to create national accounting standards. The project is being undertaken in conjunction with the European Commission's TACIS scheme, the ICAEW, and the British Foundation for Accountancy and Financial Management. So far three standards have been prepared:

- General Accounting Principles
- Accounting for Leases
- Accounting for Marketable Securities

In preparation for 1998 are standards for

- Accounting for Inflation
- Accounting and Reporting for Cash Flow

Future accounting development in Belarus is likely to proceed by steady incremental steps.

Useful Addresses

Ministry of Finance
Department of Accounting Methodology
Sovetskaya Street 7
220048 Minsk
Belarus

Belarussian Association of Accountants
c/o Belarussian State Economics University
Department of Accounting, Room 216
Partizan Avenue 27
220172 Minsk
Belarus

RUSSIAN FEDERATION

Yaroslav V. Sokolov
St. Petersburg Institute of Commerce and Economics
Valery V. Kovalev
St.Petersburg Institute of Commerce and Economics
Svetlana M. Bychkova
St.Petersburg State Agricultural University
Irina A. Smirnova
St.Petersburg Institute of Commerce and Economics

1. Background

1.1 A Brief History of Accounting in Russia

Over the course of eleven centuries, Russia was transformed from a number of city states and principalities in Eastern Europe into a European power encompassing a huge land area and culturally diverse peoples. An enduring problem has been the creation of administrative structures for the effective governance of such a diverse state, while simultaneously promoting economic progress sufficient for supporting its upkeep. Consequently, accounting has been perceived as an administrative control device rather than a business tool.

The history of accounting in the Russian lands may be divided into four periods:

1. 862–1700: The emergence and development of accounting systems based on single entry
2. 1700–1917: The adoption of double-entry bookkeeping from Western Europe
3. 1917–1985: The adaptation of double-entry bookkeeping to the requirements of a centrally planned socialist economy
4. 1985–present: The attempt to modify Soviet accounting in order to be in agreement with international accounting practice

The first period, extending from the foundation of the city state of Novgorod to the introduction of the Westernizing reforms of Peter I, was shaped by the adoption of Christianity (988), the introduction of the Cyrillic alphabet, the promulgation of the first code of law *Russkaya Pravda* (1016), and the influence of the Russian Orthodox Church. The monasteries acquired substantial holdings of land and serfs. Monastic accounting, a form of single-entry record keeping originating in the Eastern Roman Empire, was progressively developed.

The second period commenced with the attempt by Peter I to end the isolation of Russia by modernizing the country through a process of Westernization. His successors continued the development of his innovations through the adoption of mercantile regulations (1727), the establishment of the first Russian bank (1733), the formation of the first joint-stock company (1757), and the publication in Russian, under the title *Key to Commerce* and from an English translation, of the first book on double-entry bookkeeping (1783). The first original Russian books on the subject were published in 1809, and by 1917 a total of 1356 books on accounting had been published. Bookkeeping was adapted to Russian conditions. In the 19th century, a convertible gold rouble was introduced, as well as taxes on profits and the obligatory publication of the balance sheets of quoted joint-stock companies. These developments provided increasing opportunities for accounting specialists, although no professional associations were established.

The third period was characterized by fundamental changes in all socioeconomic relationships in an attempt to accelerate development after the overthrow of the Tsarist autocracy. The system of accounting was repeatedly transformed as follows:

- 1917–1918: An attempt at national economic stabilization through extensive nationalization of business undertakings and the spread of budgetary accounting
- 1918–1921: Establishment of the regime of "war communism" and centralized control of industry and distribution of all resources and products through allocation and rationing. There was an attempt to combine total accountability with the abolition of money. Monetary accounting ceased.
- 1921–1929: Introduction of the "new economic policy," signaling the establishment of a mixed economy and the restoration of traditional double-entry accounting
- 1929–1953: The construction of the framework of a socialist economic system and the deformation of basic accounting principles

- 1953–1985: The adaptation of accounting to the requirements of a centrally planned economy

The consequence of these changes was the implementation of a system of unified socialist accounting throughout the USSR, the main features of which were:

- A rigid hierarchical structure of the national economic system
- A unified chart of accounts
- The centralized regulation of accounting practice and authoritative prescription of accounting entries for typical transactions
- The unification of primary documentation and uniform treatment of accounting data
- Formats for authorized financial statements prescribed by the Ministry of Finance
- The absence of independent audit and its substitution by strict intra-departmental control

The fourth period was marked by the failure of an attempt to radically reform the Soviet economic system and its subsequent disintegration. As a result, the question of restructuring the national economy arose and, with it, the question of the reorganization of the accounting system. By 1985, it had become evident that the established accounting system was inadequate for the reflection of actual economic processes and even distorted economic reality. It became apparent that all the better accounting practices hitherto developed elsewhere would have to be introduced. The recent period may be regarded as characterized by the gradual adaptation of Soviet accounting to the accounting principles and practices generally accepted in the Western economies.

Apart from the Baltic states, and especially during the period of independence in 1918–1939, the accounting experience was common to all the constituent republics of the USSR. As a result of the disintegration of the USSR at the end of 1991, the pace of accounting change began to vary among the successor republics.

A reformation of the economic structure of the Russian Federation (the major successor state of the former USSR) involves a transformation from the centrally planned (or administrative command) economy into a market economy. The reforms are in full progress and are having a profound effect on the development of accounting and auditing. In their adaptation to the changing needs of the transforming economic structures, accounting and auditing are required to solve a number of new theoretical and practical problems and to play significant roles in the economy of the country.

1.2 Regulation of Accounting in Russia

The centralization of accounting methodology derives largely from former Soviet political and economic legislation. The necessity for organizing a single accounting and statistical system and the leading role of the Council of Ministers of the USSR in the tasks was established by the Soviet constitution. The Council of Ministers was required "to carry out measures" for the organization of accounting and statistics in the country. To that end, there were approved by decree:

- *Regulation on Documents and Records for Accounting in Enterprises and Economic Organizations* (1961)
- *Regulation on Accounting Statements and Balance Sheets* (1979)
- *Regulation on Chief Accountants* (1980)
- *All-Union Chart of Accounts.*

The final version of the All-Union Chart of Accounts, in the conditions of the centrally planned economy, was issued in 1985 and used until 1992. Thus, there were no special accounting laws in the country, and accounting practice was totally regulated by these documents. They were supplemented by special orders issued periodically by the Ministry of Finance. Since 1991, the legal requirements for accounting have begun to change.

Accounting has been regulated traditionally by a set of normative documents issued by the Ministry of Finance. Therefore, the Ministry has had to play a leading role in the process of accounting reform. The early 1990s was the time when the influence of Anglo-American accounting thought began to spread in Russia. It occurred mainly through personal contacts between specialists from the United States and the United Kingdom and representatives of the Ministry of Finance. But, for Russia, it was quite natural to start accounting reform with a radical change of the All-Union Chart of Accounts that actually provides the foundation for accounting methodology in the country.

The first steps in creating the framework of new accounting legislation were taken in the early 1990s. The following principal normative accounting documents, which were new for the most part, were issued at that time:

- *Regulation on Accounting and Reporting in the Russian Federation,* approved by the government of the Russian Federation on February 16, 1992
- *Regulation on Cost Allocation and Requirements for the Calculation of Taxable Income,* approved by the government of the Russian Federation on August 5, 1992
- *National Uniform Chart of Accounts,* approved by the Ministry of Finance of Russia on December 19, 1991

Several drafts of the accounting and auditing laws, worked out by different bodies, were published for discussion during that time. The leading role of the Ministry of Finance in the licensing of accountants and auditors and in the working out of methodological regulations and instructions was preserved in the various drafts.

Until now accounting in Russia has been regulated by different governmental bodies, although the level of centralization has been steadily decreasing. This is evident from the variety of methods that can be used in practice for the creation of accounting rules (see Table 1).

TABLE 1. *System of Accounting Regulation in Russia*

Level of Authority	Normative Documents	Bodies Responsible for Development
Level I—legislative	Federal laws, Government acts, President's decrees	Parliament of Russia, Government of Russia, President of Russia
Level II—normative	Accounting standards	Ministry of Finance of Russia, Central Bank of Russia
Level III—methodical	Normative acts (other than accounting standards), method-instructions instructions	Ministry of Finance of Russia, State and municipal authorities
Level IV—organizational	Intra-firm regulations (orders, guidelines, manuals, etc.) within the accounting policy of a company	Businesses, consulting firms

Examples of documents from the different levels of authority are:

Level I: The Civil Code of the Russian Federation, federal laws "On Accounting," "On Limited Liability Companies," etc.

Level II: Regulation on Accounting and Reporting in the Russian Federation, National Chart of Accounts, national accounting standard "Accounting Policy for an Enterprise," etc.

Level III: Current instructions and manuals, such as, "On the procedure for net equity valuation," instructions defining the content and structure of annual and quarterly financial statements, etc.

Level IV: Orders, instructions, and manuals worked out and used in a company, such as the order "On Accounting Policy" that should be issued annually in every company and signed by its director.

Although the Russian accounting system has a direct influence on accounting principles and methods, there is another system, of indirect influence, based on the laws and regulations reflecting the tax aspects of accounting. It includes, among others, the laws "On the Profit Tax of Enterprises and Organizations," "On Value-Added Tax," Regulation on Cost Allocation and Requirements for the Calculation of Taxable Income.

A set of the principal normative documents governing accounting practice has been worked out already.

Every year changes are made to the Uniform Chart of Accounts. A sizeable number of current instructions, particularly connected with taxation, are issued periodically. Although the basic requirements concerning financial statements have been described in the Accounting standard "Financial Statement of a Company," twice yearly the Ministry of Finance issues special orders that are supplemented by instructions concerning the prescribed formats of quarterly and annual financial statements (with only minor changes from previous formats).

The law "On Accounting," issued in 1996, is the most important document of the accounting reform. Its acceptance means that in Russia the unconditional adoption of the Anglo-American accounting model is *not* considered to be the best way to reform the national accounting system. The law consists of four chapters: I—General Provisions, II—Basic Requirements of Accounting Procedures. Accounting Documents and their Registration, III—Reporting, and IV—Final Provisions.

The contents of the Law on Accounting may be summarized as follows:

I. General Provisions

The first chapter gives a definition of accounting and formulates the main goals as:

(a) Providing full and reliable information about a company to both internal and external users

(b) Providing information needed for the implementation of the control function

(c) Preventing negative results of business activity and discovering internal reserves and means for supporting the financial stability of a company.

The law confirms that the legislation dealing with accounting consists of the law "On Accounting" (by which the unified juridical and methodological framework of accounting is established) and other federal laws, Presidential decrees, and Governmental decrees. The main goals of this legislation are:

(a) Establishing the unified methods and procedures for use in accounting practice

(b) Mandating the presentation of reliable and comparable information about a company's assets and its profits and losses

All companies and organizations operating in Russia, as well as branches and representative offices of foreign companies, should follow the Accounting Law unless some other law foreseen by international treaties is signed by the Russian Federation. Individuals undertaking business activity without forming a juridical entity must follow Russia's taxation legislation.

Federal laws may delegate the right of accounting regulation to certain official bodies that, within their competence, can work out and approve for use:

• Charts of accounts and instructions for their use (for example, the Central Bank of Russia is responsible for development of the unified chart of accounts for banks; the Ministry of Finance for businesses)

- National accounting standards for explaining the principles, rules, and methods for accounting and reporting
- Other regulations and manuals

II. Basic Requirements of Accounting Procedures. Accounting Documents and Their Registration

Assets owned by a company should be registered apart from assets that belong to third parties and are only managed by the company. The meaning of the word "apart" can be interpreted in a different manner but here it means that assets not owned by a company should be registered outside the double-entry system, that is, by using off-balance-sheet accounts. However, this article means that any type of leased assets (in the case of both finance and operating leases) must be shown in the double-entry system of a lessor. Assets acquired or produced must be valued at cost; assets obtained free of charge must be valued by using market prices. Fixed assets should be depreciated (amortized). Transactions in foreign currencies should be shown in roubles using the exchange rates declared by the Central Bank of Russia at the date of transaction implementation.

III. Reporting

All companies (except nonprofit organizations financed from federal, municipal, or local budgets) must prepare the following financial statements:

- The Balance Sheet
- Profit and Loss Account
- Supplements to these statements as prescribed by normative documents,
- Audit Opinion confirming reliability of accounts (if an obligatory audit is required by legislation)
- Explanatory Note

The financial year in Russia coincides with the calendar year for all companies.

Financial statements should be presented to:

(a) Owners

(b) The local office of the State Committee on Statistics of the region where the company is registered

The law regulates the procedure for the publication of accounts. This is a new step in Russian accounting practice. The financial statements should be presented to the agencies of the State Committee on Statistics and from there made available to all external parties interested in the business activity of a company. The cost of copying the reported data should be paid by the receiver of the information.

The publication of the accounts is made only after:

- Audit implementation
- Approval of the accounts at the owners' annual meeting

To some extent, the rules of publication are regulated by the Federal Commission for Securities and the Capital Market (FCSCM). According to its decree "On additional data that should be obligatorily published by a publicly held company," approved on May 8, 1996, such a company must publish additionally:

- Data about net assets and equity
- Number of shareholders
- Information about the body responsible for the registration of pre-ferred stock of the company

According to Article 4 of Paragraph 13, if the owners of a company believe that the rules and methods prescribed by accounting regulation do not allow the presentation of a true view about the company, there may be a deviation from these rules. In that case, such deviations should be explained in the Explanatory Note.

IV. Final Provisions

The Law states that responsibility for the evasion of accounting, as well as for the deterioration of financial statements and the violation of their proper presentation, falls on the directors of the company and any other persons responsible for organization and implementation of accounting.

The Regulation on Accounting and Reporting 1992 was worked out in 1991 by the Ministry of Finance of Russia on behalf of the government of Russia. Some changes and supplements to the regulation were approved by the Ministry of Finance during the following years. The Regulation determines the methodological and organizational aspects of accounting in Russia and is applicable to all types of enterprises doing business in the country. For the five years after its publication, the Regulation was the most important normative act for accounting practitioners because it corresponded to their methodological backgrounds. The Regulation outlined the methodological aspects of accounting already in use in Russia. On the other hand, it does supplement in many places other accounting legislation and clarifies some matters not detailed elsewhere in the law.

The Regulation on Accounting and Reporting consists of four chapters: I. General provisions, II. Basic principles of accounting practice, III. The organizational structure of accounting, IV. Reporting.

The proposal to work out a set of national accounting standards was accepted by both the official authorities and academics. Therefore, in 1993 the Ministry of Finance decided to start work on their preparation. The leading role in the development of accounting standards is taken by the Department on the Methodology of Accounting and Reporting (DMAR) of the Ministry of Finance.

The typical procedure for the development of a national accounting standard is as follows:

1. DMAR appoints someone to prepare a draft for a standard. Sometimes several drafts are prepared by different specialists.

2. The draft is presented to the Council on the Methodology of Accounting for discussion. (The Council is a nongovernmental professional organization founded in 1994 by the order issued by the Ministry of Finance. It consists of approximately 90 persons who are representatives of some governmental bodies, businesses, and universities from different parts of Russia; its destination is to be an advisory board to DMAR; it has meetings in Moscow at least twice a year).

3. After the first discussion at the meeting of the Council, the draft for an accounting standard is usually revised and published in the main professional journal *Accounting* for review by all specialists. Their comments are also published in the journal.

4. The person responsible for the draft reviews all remarks and develops a new draft for presentation to the Council. After the draft is approved, it is presented by DMAR to a Deputy Minister of Finance for signing and subsequent publication.

In 1994 the first accounting standard "Accounting Policy for an Enterprise" (PBU I/94) was approved by the Ministry of Finance. Of all the accounting standards it is the most significant. All accounting practitioners are familiar with the details of its contents. The reason is that, in accordance with the Regulation on Accounting and Reporting, all companies must make an annual declaration of their accounting policy. That is, a special order, signed by the director of a company, must set out certain aspects of the accounting policy to be followed during the coming year. These aspects are dealt with in the accounting standard "Accounting Policy for an Enterprise," being divided into:

(a) Methodical aspects of accounting policy

(b) Organizational aspects of accounting policy

The former signifies the practices employed in the construction of entries into the accounting records.

The expression "accounting policy" has been newly introduced into Russian accounting practice as a portmanteau term. That is, it embraces not only the practices used in the compilation of accounting records but also the organization of the accounting system and the accounting aspects of managerial control.

1.3 National Uniform Chart of Accounts for Businesses

In Western countries each company has a certain freedom, to a greater or lesser extent, in the design of its own set of accounts to reflect the nature of its business and the needs of its management in directing that business. In Russia this process in many aspects is regulated centrally. There is a tradition of using a uniform charts of accounts created by the state authorities. The use of the chart of accounts has been obligatory.

The uniform chart of accounts for businesses, consisting of "synthetic" (i.e. main or summary) accounts and subaccounts and accompanied by a description of the economic meaning of each account, is issued by the ministry of Finance as a special document entitled "The Uniform Chart of

Accounts for Businesses and Instructions for its Use." On the basis of the uniform chart, each enterprise may create as needed its own set of "analytic" (i.e. supporting) accounts to supplement the synthetic accounts.

The uniform chart of accounts has been used for working out centrally some typical accounting entries recommended for use by practitioners when recording various kinds of transactions (economic operations). Collections of these accounting entries have been prepared as instructional manuals and published by the Ministry of Finance. In fact there have been dozens of such recommended entries, and not all of them are beyond dispute. However, practitioners have been forced to follow the recommendations, making them, in effect, obligatory.

From time to time the chart of accounts, or the set of recommended entries, has been corrected, clarified, or expanded. The chart of accounts is used also in the preparation of the financial statements (e.g. each of the lines on Form No. 1 for the balance sheet contains the numbers of the synthetic accounts to be aggregated on that line).

The chart of accounts can be considered the most important element of the accounting system in Russia because it determines accounting practice and other elements of the system. The essence of the accounting system used in Russia can be understood easily by analyzing the system and its chart, which provide the following:

- An interrelated classification, grouping, and generalization of information about business activities of enterprises

- A unified methodological basis for the organization of accounting in the whole national economy

- An effective system of control of indicators for business activities

- Comparability of accounting procedures used and information generated in the accounting systems of different enterprises

- A common understanding that, for accountants, simplifies the transition from one industry to another

The first uniform chart of accounts appeared in Russia in the 1920s. It was intended for industries only and was revised periodically. Thus, the industrial chart of accounts for 1940 included 124 accounts and 80 subaccounts; the chart for 1954 included 79 accounts and 142 subaccounts; the chart for 1959 included 71 accounts and 92 subaccounts; and the chart for 1968 included 82 accounts and 106 subaccounts. In 1961 the first All-

Union Uniform Chart of Accounts for businesses was created and put into operation. It was obligatory for all types of enterprises excluding nonprofit organizations and banks. With only insignificant changes the chart was used in accounting practice until 1992.

Experts from the United Nations took part in the creation of the initial version of the new All-Union Chart of Accounts published in 1991. It complied in its main aspects with the internationally used general accounting principles. The final version of the All-Union Chart of Accounts was issued by the Ministry of Finance USSR in its decree No. 56, dated November 1, 1991. The decree ordered that the bookkeeping of all enterprises be carried out in accordance with the requirements of the new chart of accounts as from the beginning of 1992. The transition from the old All-Union Uniform Chart of Accounts to the new (now) National Uniform Chart of Accounts (renamed because of the dissolution of the USSR) was made during the year. There are now several charts of accounts for profit-orientated companies, the most important being for businesses and for banks.

The National Uniform Chart of Accounts consists of about 100 accounts and 60 subaccounts grouped into 10 main sections. Each account has its own number (code), which is used in accounting ledgers and transactions. The synthetic accounts have two-digit numbers and the off-balance-sheet accounts have three-digit numbers. The account numbers are authorized by the Ministry of Finance and cannot be changed by a company. Some account numbers are not now in use but may be used in future revisions of the chart. Because of their complexity, most accounts are divided into subaccounts. Each account or subaccount can be divided further into analytic accounts (e.g. accounts according to the number of suppliers).

Accounts included in the first nine sections, which are called balance sheet accounts, are used in double-entry accounting. Section No. 10 includes special off-balance sheet accounts reflecting various kinds of transactions that should be recorded outside the double-entry system.

The ten sections of the National Uniform Chart of Accounts are:

Section 1	Long Term Assets and Other Investments
Section 2	Production Inventory
Section 3	Production Expenses
Section 4	Finished Products, Goods and Sales
Section 5	Monetary Assets

Section 6   Settlements (Receivables and Payables)

Section 7   Financial Results and Profit Utilisation

Section 8   Funds and Reserves

Section 9   Bank Credits and Financing

Section 10   Off Balance Sheet Accounts

1.4 Auditing

Auditing, as the term is understood in the Western countries, did not exist in the USSR, nor has it ever existed in Russia. Throughout the history of Russia the pervasive power of the state and the absence (or very limited existence) of private ownership made impossible the emergence of an auditing profession. The notion of an independent controller was absolutely alien to the consciousness of administrators, managers, and professionals. While understanding that their performance had to be monitored, they believed that the evaluator should report what he was told, rather than what he believed or had discovered about an organization's activities.

Nor did government officials have any use for independent auditors. They regarded all subordinate enterprises as being under their full control and would not have wanted an outsider to investigate their operations. Because Russia continued to be a country of administrative law rather than civil law, where vertical ties have always prevailed over horizontal ties, the concepts of "control" and "controller" were used instead of "audit" and "auditor." The term "revision" (inspection) also was widely used.

The situation did not begin to change until 1987–1990 when the decentralized reform of the economic system of the USSR was attempted. In 1987 the initial general regulations governing joint ventures with Western companies were issued. The regulations required conformity with Western (internationally received) practice in that audits were to be performed "for a fee by Soviet auditing commercial organizations." At this time the international accounting firms began opening offices in Russia. These were organized as joint venture companies with Russian partners (e.g. representatives of the Ministry of Finance, members of various external economic departments, and accounting specialists).

In 1988 the Law on Co-operatives, enabling the development of small scale private enterprises, was adopted. The pioneers of business consultancy began their activities. Their first work was the preparation of legal charters for all kinds of co-operatives. Later these business consultancies undertook the official registration of privatization documents on behalf of directors who wished to become the owners of state enterprises. Then they became the auditors to the newly registered private enterprises.

The principal documents governing auditing activities at the present time are as follows:

(a) The President of the Russian Federation, by decree N 2263, dated December 22, 1993 and titled "Concerning Auditing Activities in the Russian Federation," approved Temporary Rules for Auditing Activities in the Russian Federation (The Temporary Rules define the fundamental legal principles for the conduct of auditing activities in the Russian Federation and are expected to remain in force until the adoption of the proposed audit law.)

(b) The Government of the Russian Federation,

(i) by decree N 482, dated May 6, 1993, approved the regulations:

—Concerning the Approval of the Normative Documents for the Regulation of Auditing Activities in the Russian Federation

—The Procedure for Conducting Attestation for the Right to Perform Auditing Activities

—The Procedure for Issuing Licences for the Right to Perform Auditing Activities

(ii) by decree N 1355, dated December 7, 1994, approved the regulation "On the Main Criteria of Economic Entities to be Subject to Compulsory Annual Auditing" (The regulation has been amended by decree N 408, dated April 25, 1995.)

(c) The Commission for Auditing Activities, on February 9, 1996, approved the "Order on the Compilation of the Audit Report on the Annual Accounting Report."

The Temporary Rules define the fundamental legal principles for carrying out auditing activities in the Russian Federation until adoption of the proposed audit law. Auditing is defined as an entrepreneurial activity of auditors (or auditing firms) involving the independent nondepartmental inspection of accounting reports and balance sheets, payment and settlement documents, tax declarations, and other financial obligations and commitments of economic entities, as well as the provision of other auditing services.

The principal objective of auditing activities is to establish the authenticity of the accounting (financial) reports of economic entities and the conformity of the financial and economic operations carried out by those entities to the normative acts that are current in the Russian Federation.

Audits may be compulsory or voluntary. Compulsory audits are carried out in instances that are directly established by the legislative acts of the Russian Federation. Audits are compulsory for public joint-stock companies, banks, insurance companies, stock exchanges, investment institutions (i.e. investment funds and their holding companies), charitable funds, joint-ventures, and other companies with revenue more than 500,000 MS or total assets in excess of 200,000 MS. (MS is equal to the amount of the minimum monthly salary not subject to taxation. In August 1997 MS was equal to 83490 roubles; $1 = 5900 roubles.)

Any enterprise, and its directors, evading the compulsory audit can be taken to court and fined. The amount of the fine can vary from 100 MS to 500 MS for enterprises and from 50 MS to 100 MS for their director.

Auditing may be carried out by auditing firms (including foreign auditing firms and joint ventures) and certified auditors who hold a special license and are listed in the State Register of Auditors and Auditing Firms. An auditing firm may have any form of organization recognized by law except that of a public joint stock company. Independent auditors and auditing firms may not carry on any kind of business unrelated to accounting, auditing, financial analysis, or consulting. In addition to performing audits, auditors and auditing firms may provide services associated with arranging, restoring, and maintaining accounting (financial) records, compiling income declarations and accounting (financial) reports, analyzing economic and financial activities, and assessing the value of the assets and liabilities of economic entities, consulting on matters relating to financial, tax, banking, and other economic legislation of the Russian federation, and the provision of training and other services associated with their type of activity.

Auditors (and auditing firms) may engage in auditing activities only after receiving a license granting permission to engage in such activities.

It is anticipated that four different kinds of license will be issued for the auditing of:

- Banks, insurance companies
- Stock exchanges
- Investment funds
- All other enterprises

The agency that has licensed a certain auditor or auditing firm may verify the quality of the audit, if considered necessary, either on its own initiative or at the request of the client audited or at the request of the public prosecutor.

The license of an auditor or an auditing firm may be canceled by the issuing body for any of the reasons specified in the Temporary Rules, such as an adverse court decision or repeated unqualified audits. A firm or an individual auditing without a license may be prosecuted. The profits realized from such unauthorized audit activity must be refunded. In addition, the firm can be fined from 500 MS to 1000 MS (with corresponding amounts for an individual).

Authorities that are authorized to issue licenses to engage in auditing activities shall have the right to appeal to an arbitration court for the liquidation of that legal entity.

Auditors (and auditing firms) bear liability, in accordance with established procedure, for violating the legislation of the Russian Federation in carrying out auditing activities.

All physical persons who wish to engage in auditing activities either independently or within an auditing firm shall undergo attestation (certification).

According to these documents (i.e. the Temporary Rules for Auditing Activities and Decree N482) attestation to the right to carry out auditing activities is carried out with the aim of ensuring the professional execution by auditors of their duties.

Persons having an economics or legal (higher or intermediate special) education and who have worked for not less than three of the past five years as an auditor, specialist of an auditing organization (or auditing firm), accountant, economist, inspector, manager of an enterprise, member of the staff of a scientific body or teacher in an economics field can be admitted for attestation.

Persons convicted by a court sentence involving punishment in the form of the deprivation of the right to hold certain posts or to engage in certain activities in the field of financial and economic relations may not be admitted for attestation.

Persons who have successfully passed attestation shall receive a standard auditor's qualification certificate. The qualification certificate must be issued within one month of the day of attestation. In the event that a person who has been attested does not commence work as an auditor within 2 years of receiving the qualification certificate, the certificate loses its force.

The result of the audit is an auditing report having legal significance for all legal entities and physical persons.

There are four types of report:

1. Unqualified positive report. The auditor considers the financial statements are true and fair.
2. Qualified positive report. The auditor considers the financial statements are true and fair apart from some nonmaterial matters.
3. Negative report. The auditor considers the financial statements are not true and fair.
4. Disclaimer of an opinion. The auditor is unable to express an opinion in any circumstances.

In fact, there does exist an additional form of report that officially is considered to be a sub-type of the unqualified positive report. In the appendix to the Order on the Compilation of the Audit Report it is described as an "unqualified positive report (in the existence of serious doubt about the possibility of the economic entity to continue its activity and fulfil its obligations for a period of at least twelve months from the end of accounting period)." In other words, the auditor is sure that today the financial statements are true and fair, but he cannot give a guarantee that the enterprise will not be bankrupt within a year. This is a type of audit report that contradicts the entire theory of auditing but was adopted because of the serious economic situation in the country.

The signs by which the auditor is able to make this type of report are the following:

1. Repeated material losses or instability of current assets
2. Inability of the company to cover in time its debts
3. Loss of big clients arising from uninsured disastrous circumstances
4. Juridical investigation with unpredictable results
5. Disagreements with tax inspection concerning the payment of tax
6. Guarantees on obligations of third parties

The auditor's report must consist of three parts:

1. An introductory section in which are shown the name, address, and telephone number of the auditing firm and the names of all the auditors involved in the audit. Also shown is the name of the agency

that licensed the auditing firm and the registration number and expire date of the license.

2. An analytical section giving the name of the firm audited, the accounting period, the quality of accounting and internal control, and any material misstatements and any deviations from the accounting regulations

3. An opinion section outlining the conclusion based on the results of the audit examination

Each page of the auditor's report must be signed by the auditor and sealed with his or her stamp. In addition, the auditor's report must be signed by the manager of the auditing firm (the person who has been authorized to sign for the firm and seal with the auditing firm's stamp). The opinion section may be presented by the business enterprise audited to all parties interested in its activities.

The Commission on Auditing Activities intends to produce thirty auditing standards. At the beginning of 1998 only eleven had been issued. All are closely related to the accepted international standards.

All standards are divided into three groups:

1. General (qualification of auditor, independence, etc.)

2. Field work (planning, investigation, and appraisal of accounting and internal control, audit evidence, etc.)

3. Reporting (types of financial statement under audit, its correspondence to normative documents, framework of report). There are audit planning, engagement letter, audit evidence, using the work of an expert, audit sampling, documenting of auditing, auditor's activity in revealing distortion of the financial statement, investigation and estimation of accounting and internal control systems in the audit process, date of signing the audit report and reflection (in this document) of post-balance sheet events, order of composition of audit report about the financial statement, written information of auditor to the management of the economic entity about the results of auditing

The specific feature of the Russian auditing standards is that all are obligatory for fulfilment by auditing firms (auditors) except those points of a standard designated as only recommendations.

In the most recent times some of the problems connected with strengthening the accounting and auditing profession were solved. In particular:

1. A comparison of the Russian and Western charts of accounts revealed no great differences. (Therefore, the proposed new Russian accounting and auditing standards have a strong correspondence with those applied in Western Europe.)
2. Special training and certifying centers for auditors have been created.
3. The professional associations in Moscow, St. Petersburg, and regional centers are fast developing.
4. New regulations on auditing have been issued.

1.5 Taxation

The basic principles of taxation in the Russian Federation are formulated in the Constitution accepted on December 12, 1993. According to Article 57, it is obligatory to pay the legally levied taxes and duties. The laws levying new taxes or worsening the position of taxpayers have no retroactive effect.

The system of taxes paid to the federal budget and the general principles of taxation in the Russian Federation are to be set out in a federal law (item 3 of Article 75 of the Constitution). At the present time the general principles of taxation (such as the rights, responsibilities, and duties of taxpayers), and also the comprehensive list of taxes and levies are determined in the Law dated December 27, 1991, No. 2118-1 "On the Bases of the Taxation System in the Russian Federation." The public authorities at all levels of administration have no right to introduce surtaxes and obligatory deductions (privileges) that are not stipulated by the legislation of the Russian Federation or to increase the rates of levied taxes or tax payments.

All taxes of the Russian Federation are divided into three groups:

- Federal;
- Regional (the taxes of republics within the structure of the Russian Federation, its territories, and autonomous regions)
- Local

The collection of federal taxes is regulated by special laws for each tax (except the transport tax installed by the decree of the President, dated December 22, 1993, No. 2270 "On Some Changes in Taxation and the Interrelations of Budgets of Various Levels").

The instructions and methodical recommendations for application of taxation legislation are issued by the State Taxation Service in agreement with the Ministry of Finance of the Russian Federation and have the most important significance in taxation regulation. The implementation of large numbers of sub-law acts is characteristic of taxation arrangements in the Russian Federation.

Federal taxes (including the rates and tax privileges) are set only by acts in the form of laws and decrees on taxation. The normative acts of appropriate bodies are defined by these acts. The change in the method of taxation for specific taxes is carried out by modifications and additions to the act of the Russian Federation in force for the specific tax. Modifications to the taxation system and the granting of tax privileges not stipulated by Russian taxation legislation are not permitted.

The system of taxation is functioning without change until the acceptance of a special decision on tax reform. Proposals on taxation reform can be introduced not later than 3 months before the beginning of the corresponding financial year.

The Russian State Taxation Service is the uniform monitoring system for the observance of tax laws, for the regularity of calculation, the completeness and timeliness of tax payments, and other obligatory payments to the appropriate budget. The rights and responsibilities of the taxation authority are determined by the Law dated March 21, 1991, N 943-1 "On the State Taxation Service of RSFSR," and also by Articles 14 and 16 of the Law "On the Framework of the Taxation System in the Russian Federation."

The Russian Taxation Police is the law enforcement body and a constituent of the economic safety maintenance forces of the Russian Federation, in exposing, preventing, and suppressing tax crimes and offences. The legal foundations, the principles for their organization and activities, and the structure and authority of federal bodies of the tax police are determined in the Law dated June 24, 1993, N5238-1 "On the Federal Bodies of the Taxation Police."

The taxation system of Russia in its general structure and principles of construction largely corresponds to the systems prevailing for the taxation of legal persons and citizens in Western market economies.

The taxation of the profits and incomes of legal persons is regulated by:

1. The internationally recognized tax treaties of the Russian Federation
2. The Law dated December 27, 1991, No. 2116-1 "On the Taxation of the Profit of Enterprises and Organizations"

3. The instructional and methodical documents of the State Taxation Service issued on their basis

4. The Regulation on Production Cost Allocation and the Requirements for Financial Results Calculation.

The object of taxation is the gross profit of the enterprise reduced (or enlarged) according to the requirements of the Law On the Taxation of the Profit of Enterprises and Organizations.

Gross profit = *Profit from sales of production (works, services)*
+ Profit from sales of fixed capital assets
+ Profit from sales of other property
+ Nonoperational income – nonoperational expenses

The list of nonoperational income and expenses, and also the costs to be included in production cost for the purposes of taxation, is given in the Regulation on Cost Allocation.

2. The Form and Content of Published Financial Statements

Accounting in Russia has always consisted of three related parts (bookkeeping, statistical accounting, and operative accounting) for the following reasons:

- The differing objectives of the organizations to which the reports are presented
- Differing degrees of accuracy and volume of data used
- Different time constraints of the accounting information

The organizational structure of the accounting system has determined the different types of statements to be used. Bookkeeping and statistical statements are systematized sets of correlated accounting data, prepared in accordance with special rules and presented to designated organizations outside the business. Operative accounting statements are not subject to form, structure, and presentation regulations and are intended for use within the enterprise.

Because of the most recent changes in the political and economic environment in Russia, bookkeeping statements (also called financial statements) have become in reality the sole reliable means of communication between enterprises and external organizations. Financial statements are uniform, and the order of their approval, preparation, and presentation is regularly ruled on by the Ministry of Finance of Russia.

The main aspects of financial statement presentation are determined by the following documents:

- Law "On Accounting"

- Regulation on Accounting and Reporting in the Russian Federation

- Accounting standard Financial Statement of an Organization. (PBU 4/96)

In addition, twice annually, the Ministry of Finance issues instructions "On the annual (quarterly) financial statements" that explain the content of the annual (quarterly) accounts and the way of their preparation. Blank forms for all financial statements are created by the Ministry of Finance.

Accounting statements must be prepared by companies annually and quarterly. Currently the annual reporting includes the following formats of financial statements that must be prepared by all enterprises (except nonprofit organizations, insurance companies, and banks):

- The Balance Sheet (Form No. 1)

- Profit and Loss Account (Form No. 2)

- Explanations to the Balance Sheet and P&L Account:
  —Capital Movement Statement (Form No. 3)
  —Cash Flow Statement (Form No. 4)
  —Supplement to the Balance Sheet (Form No. 5)

- Explanatory Note

- Specialized Forms

- Statement about the Utilization of Financial Means Received from the Budget

- Audit Opinion (if necessary)

The quarterly reporting for all enterprises consists of three statements:

- Balance Sheet
- Profit and Loss Account
- Statement about the Utilization of Financial Means Received from the Budget.

The first five forms are the most common because they are prepared by all enterprises. The Regulation permits branch ministries and governmental departments of Russia and the republics to create some additional specialized reporting forms reflecting the peculiarities of their subordinate enterprises. That is, these enterprises must prepare only the specialized forms. These additional forms must be co-ordinated with the Ministry of Finance. The "Statement about the Utilization of Financial Means Received from the Budget" must be prepared if an enterprise received financial help from the state, republic, or municipal budgets.

An explanatory note usually consists of 15 to 20 pages, and its content traditionally was not prescribed except that it had to clarify and explain the basic factors that influenced the financial results as well as the main aspects of the financial condition of the enterprise. Nevertheless, some recommendations about the content of the explanatory note have been outlined in the accounting standard PBU 4/96. According to this document, information about the most significant items (their amounts at the beginning of the year, at year end, and their movements) should be disclosed in the note.

The annual reports are presented to:

- The owners of the enterprise as identified in its fundamental (statutory) documents, and the senior level of administration within the industrial ministry
- The state tax inspectors (required not by the Law "On Accounting" but by the legislation on taxation)
- Other state authorities authorized by legislation to control some aspect of the business activity of enterprises (for example, financial institutions providing for the financing of some expenses from the state budget).

Banks, insurance companies, investment funds, and nonprofit organizations have their own formats for the financial statements and manner of annual report presentation that are regulated accordingly by the Russian Federation, the Russian Insurance Supervision Service, and the State Property Committee with the consent of the Ministry of Finance of Russia.

3. Rules for Valuation and Income Measurement

3.1 Capital and Financial Investments

The following are examples of capital investments:

- Construction works

- The acquisition of fixed assets, equipment, and tools

- Expenses of geological exploration and drilling

- Expenses of working the land and the resettlement of people in connection with the construction of new enterprises

Investments are reflected in a balance sheet according to the actual expenses of the builder (supplier). Investments in other enterprises within Russia, capital participations in enterprises abroad, investment in the securities of other enterprises, as well as other financial investments, are reflected in the balance sheet according to the actual costs of an investor enterprise.

3.2 Fixed Assets and Intangible Assets

Fixed assets include buildings; structures; transmitting devices; machines and equipment; vehicles; tools, production implements, accessories, equipment (apart from those items that in accordance with the current rules belong to the current assets); draft and breeding livestock irrespective of their value; perennial plants; and other assets such as library stocks, museum valuables, and zoo animals. Fixed assets also include expenditures incurred for the improvement of soils (amelioration, reclamation, irrigation, and other works) and for rented buildings, structures, equipment, and other such long-lived items.

Before being commissioned into permanent operation, capital construction projects, being in temporary operation, are not included as fixed assets. In accounts and balance sheets, expenses on such projects are entered as uncompleted capital construction (account #08).

Plots of land, deposits of mineral resources, and forests and reservoirs given to enterprises are not reflected in balance sheets unless legislation specifically requires that they should be.

Buildings and structures for which construction has been completed, installed equipment, and finished capital construction projects are included as fixed assets after approval of all expenses relating to delivery, assembly, and installation of equipment. Capital investment in perennial plants, as well as in the improvement of soils, is incurred on the areas accepted for exploitation, irrespective of whether or not the whole complex of works is completed.

Completed capital expenditure on rented buildings, structures, equipment, and other objects is included by the lessee in his own fixed assets as a sum of actual expenses. Upon the expiration of the lease term, these expenses, if so envisaged by the lease agreement, are transferred to the lessor, who includes them as increased initial value of the corresponding objects.

Fixed assets are reflected in the balance sheet by a sum equal to their actual initial costs. The initial value can be changed only if the item was reconstructed, additionally equipped, or partly liquidated.

The following items are not classed as fixed assets and are included as current items (low-value and short-life items):

- Items whose service life is less than one year irrespective of their value

- Items whose original cost is less than a certain limit declared in the present regulation (currently, this limit is 100,000 roubles, and it is assumed that in the future it can be corrected annually on January 1 according to the annual rate of inflation; directors of enterprises are permitted to reduce this limit); this condition does not affect agricultural machines, tools, or mature draft and breeding livestock

- Special items for fishing (trawls, seines, fishing nets, drag nets, etc.), irrespective of their value and useful life

- Special instruments and special devices, irrespective of their value

- Perennial plants, grown in nurseries as planting out material

- Young animals and feeding animals, poultry, rabbits, beasts of burden, and bee swarms, as well as experimental animals

- Items designated for hire, irrespective of their value

- Special clothes, footwear, and bedding, irrespective of their value and useful life

Intangible assets include the rights to use land, water resources, and other natural resources, industrial property as well as intellectual property, and other similar rights. Intangible assets are reflected in the balance sheet in the sum of expenses incurred for their acquisition, including expenses on preparation for use.

Fixed assets are depreciated according to the centrally established norms into costs of production or operation. Intangibles must be amortized into expenses over the period benefited, not to exceed 10 years or the business life of an enterprise according to norms established at the enterprise. Low-value and short-life items are amortized into expenses in one of two ways: (a) 50% of their cost is depreciated immediately when the items are transferred for use and the remaining 50% (excluding scrap value) when said objects are written off, or (b) 100% of the cost is depreciated immediately when they are transferred for use. Items whose cost is less than one-twentieth of the above-mentioned limit are depreciated immediately when they are transferred for use.

3.3 Raw Materials, Materials, Finished Products, and Commodities

Raw materials, materials, fuel, purchased semi-products and completed parts, spare parts, and other material valuables are reflected in balance sheet at their actual cost, including all expenses incurred in their acquisition and delivery for storage. Computing the unit costs can be made by one of the following methods:

- Weighted averaged cost

- First-in, first-out (FIFO)

- Last-in, first-out (LIFO)

Finished products are reflected in the balance sheet by a sum equal to their actual production costs.

At retail trade establishments, goods are entered in the balance sheet at their retail (sale) prices, while at wholesale warehouses, trading depots, and wholesale supplying organizations, it is done on the basis of retail prices or purchasing values. The difference between purchasing values and retail prices is entered in the balance sheet as a separate item.

Valuables whose market prices have decreased during the reporting year as well as items that have become partially obsolete are reflected in the balance sheet by a sum equal to the prices of their estimated realization. The difference is charged against the results of economic activity.

3.4 Unfinished Production and Expenses of Future Periods

In industries with large-scale or mass production it is admissible to assess incomplete production by normative (planned) net cost. In enterprises making one-of-a-kind or special-order products, unfinished production is reflected in the balance sheet by actual net cost.

Expenses incurred in the period under review but subject to liquidation in subsequent periods are reflected in the balance sheet as a separate item, as prepaid expenses. Such expenses are to be written off in due time.

3.5 Funds and Reserves

The statutory capital, representing the resources required at the foundation of the enterprise for the conduct of its economic activities, is shown as a separate item on the balance sheet. Also shown separately is the amount owing by participants (founders) in respect of contributions to capital.

Enterprises may create a reserve fund to meet unforeseen losses and expenses. A provision for doubtful debts may be created on the basis of a survey of debtors made at the end of the year. At the end of the following year, any unused portion of the provision is added to that year's profit.

In order to achieve an even spread of future expenses in the costs of production or operating expenses, enterprises are allowed to create reserves to meet:

- Future payments to workers going on holiday

- Payments of annual bonuses for length of service

- Expenses incurred on repairs of fixed assets

- Production expenses incurred on preparatory work in seasonal branches of industry

- Future expenses incurred on repair of objects for hire

3.6 Settlements with Debtors and Creditors; Other Items of a Balance Sheet

Debtors and creditors are shown on the balance sheet in the amounts shown in the accounting records and accepted as correct. Within the prescribed period, discrepancies concerning the amounts due and owing must be referred to the other party for agreement.

Amounts shown in the balance sheet as amounts due to, or owing by, financial organizations, banks, and higher administrative organizations should be mutually reconciled and agreed. It is forbidden to show unreconciled amounts on the balance sheet.

Assets held through the foreign currency accounts of enterprises, and also the balances for debtors and creditors and other financial assets expressed in foreign currencies, are translated into Russian currency for inclusion in a balance sheet. For foreign currency translation purposes, the rate of exchange quoted by the Central Bank of the Russian Federation on the first day after the end of the reporting period is used.

Fines, penalties and sanctions, either admitted by the debtor or imposed by a decision of a court, arbitrator, or some other authority, are written off to expenses immediately unless otherwise decided. Before their payment, or receipt, these amounts are shown in the balance sheets of the payer, or payee, as creditors or debtors, respectively.

Bad debts and other debts recognized as unrecoverable by the enterprise are written off at the discretion of the head of the enterprise and charged against the provision for doubtful debts; or, if no provision for doubtful debts has been created, they are charged to expenses or against reserves. The writing off of a bad debt as a result of a debtor's insolvency does not imply a cancellation of the obligation. From the time of the write-off the bad debt should be recorded in a memorandum (off-balance sheet) account for a period of 5 years to provide for the possibility of subsequent recovery.

Amounts unsettled on creditor accounts for which the debt recovery period has expired are transferred either to profit or to the special purpose funds of the enterprise.

3.7 Profit (Loss) of an Enterprise

The final financial result of the economic activities of the enterprise is measured as the difference between total revenues (from the sale of products, work, and services; from the sale of fixed assets and other property of the enterprise; and from other sales) and the matching expenses. For revenue recognition, enterprises may use either the cash basis or the accrual basis. The recognition of revenue for the year ahead in the current year may be disclosed, at the discretion of the enterprise, in the section on accounting policy in the annual report.

4. Expected Future Developments

From the beginning of the 1990s the transition to a market economy has led to an understanding of the necessity for changes in accounting. The Department of Accounting and Reporting Methodology of the Ministry of Finance of the Russian Federation developed a special program for the reform of the accounting system.

The starting point of the reformation of the accounting system in Russia is the State Program for the Transition of the Russian Federation to International Practice in the System of Accounting and Statistics as Required for the Development of the Market Economy. The program was approved by a decision of the Supreme Soviet of the Russian Federation on October 23, 1992. For the realization of the program systems of accounting in Russia and in the developed countries were analyzed and compared. The result of the work was the Program for the Reform of the Accounting System, approved by the Bureau of the Methodological Accounting Council under the guidance of the Ministry of Finance.

The process of transition to the international accounting standards should be realized in several stages by the year 2000. The duration of the period is caused by the necessity for (1) the reconstruction in accordance with international requirements not only of accounting legislation but also civil law, tax law, and other laws; (2) the accumulation of practical experience in new business conditions. The direct application of many international accounting standards and regulations is impossible for legal reasons: an absence of equivalent norms and terminology in Russian laws and Government Decrees.

At the preliminary stage a general approach to the development of normative documents was devised. A systemic structure of normative accounting regulation was determined, and a list of twenty basic standards was composed. Moreover, the nature of the connections between accounting and taxation was analyzed, and the problem of state and professional regulation of accounting was investigated.

Most important was the question of a model for the development of Russian accounting: Should it be the model of a particular country or the international standards for financial statements? In analyzing the possibility of applying the international accounting standards in Russia the experts of the Ministry of Finance were mindful of the following considerations:

1. The economy of Russia is becoming an organic part of the world economic system.

2. The opportunity to use a world experience of rules formulation is appearing.

Russian specialists knew at the initial stage that the international standards were not intended to regulate accounting and reporting in separate countries, nor to be used directly in practice. The purpose of the international standards is the harmonization of national accounting and reporting systems among countries for increasing the consumer quality of the financial statements.

Therefore the application of the international standards was considered desirable. The international standards should be used:

1. In the creation of the concept of accounting in a market economy to ensure the correspondence of the financial statements of Russian and Western companies

2. In the development of national accounting standards

It is an approach spread widely across the world. This is one of the reasons why the national frameworks of accounting standards are very similar to the international framework.

Transition to the international standards is a long-term process because many changes in accounting, tax, and law regulations are needed. New instructions should be developed for the application of the accounting standards and its correspondence to the Civil Code and tax requirements. Moreover, the application of any internationally adopted decision is possible only in the situation of its correspondence to the actual Russian model of the market economy. In other words, the international standards of financial reporting may not be used directly in developing the national system of accounting regulations but should be adapted to the Russian socioeconomic situation.

It is the approach used for the framework of the Program for the Reform of the Accounting System in Russia. The purpose of this document is the development of an accounting system adequate to the new type of economic relations in the Russian economy. It means the creation of a national system of accounting that should (1) be based on Russian accounting and legal practice; (2) achieve maximum correspondence with the requirements of the international accounting standards.

The objectives of the accounting reform program in Russia are:

1. To bring the accounting system into correspondence with the new economic reality and to ensure its functioning through a coherent restructuring of accounting rules and regulations. The approach to its realization includes, in particular:

   —Noncontradiction of the Russian system to world-recognized approaches to accounting and reporting

   —Creating the model for co-existence and correspondence of the accounting and tax systems

   —Changing the order of formation of the financial results including the structure of costs

   —Introducing procedures for the correction of accounting data because of inflation

   —Changing the permitted methods for the valuation of assets and liabilities

   —Creating a mechanism for ensuring the openness (publicity) of financial statements

   —Forming a system of independent financial control (audit)

2. To reform the system for the normative regulation of accounting. The main purpose of regulation should be to ensure access of all interested users to true and fair financial statements. The overall approach includes in particular:

   —Reorientation of normative regulation from the accounting process to the financial statements

   —Regulation of financial accounting but not the managerial function

   —Correspondence of the normative regulations with the professional recommendations

   —Application of the international standards to the national standards development

The modern institutional construction of the accounting regulating system involves a combination of governmental and professional regulation. Through the formation of the accounting profession in response to new economic conditions, the role and degree of involvement of the professional organizations is continually increasing.

The main intention of the general approach is ensuring the stable development of accounting. The prevention or moderation of the consequences of risk during the development of the system requires:

—Continuous monitoring of the factors that govern these risks

—Creation of the system of social-state control for monitoring the observance of accounting regulations

—Provision of information for making decisions on financial and economic problems while ensuring the stable development of the accounting system

3. To form the accounting profession in correspondence with the requirements of the new economic situation. In a market economy the accountant should be transformed from a bookkeeper (who registers the economic facts and carries out a subsequent analysis) to the highly educated economist (who is able not only to understand and assess each fact of economic activity but to forecast and suggest ways of future development). The main prerequisite for this change is a structuring of the accounting profession.

The overall approach includes in particular:

—Creation of a number of authoritative and representative institutions

—Formation of the system for professional certification of accountants and auditors

—Participating in the activities of the appropriate international professional organizations (IFAC and others)

—Development and diffusion of the norms of professional ethics

—Organization of social control for professional activities, etc.

The implementation of this approach will lead representatives of the accounting profession to reappraise their role and place in the structure of management and in society in order to realize the purpose of the accounting profession in the stable development of the economy.

Necessary, although not sufficient, prerequisites are the emergence of interested users of accounting information and effective owners of enterprises and other economic resources. A general reform of the accounting system is possible only for the poste restante provision of accounting information.

The implementation of the accounting reform program in Russia has commenced, although its successful completion will require a number of years.

Acknowledgment

With thanks to Derek Bailey for editorial assitance.

Annex

Appendix No. 1 to Order No. 97 of the Ministry of Finance of the Russian Federation of November 12, 1996 WITH AMENDMENTS AND ADDITIONS TO THE STANDARD FORMS FOR ANNUAL ACCOUNTING REPORTS, made on the base of the Order No. 81n of the Ministry of Finance of the Russian Federation of November 21, 1997 Approved by the Ministry of Finance of the Russian Federation for Annual Accounting Reports for 1997

BALANCE SHEET

for_____199__

	Codes
Form No. 1 according to *OKUD*	0710001
Date (year, month, day)	
Organization .... according to *OKPO*	
Sector (type of activity) .... according to *OKONKh*	
Organizational and legal form .... according to *KOPF*	
State property administration body .... according to *OKPO*	
Unit of measurement .... according to *SOEI*	
Control amount	

Address _____

_____

Date sent	
Date received	
Deadline for submission	

ASSETS	Line code	At year beginning	At year end
1	2	3	4

I NON-CURRENT ASSETS

Intangible assets (04, 05):	110		
Including:			
—organizational expenses	111		
—patents, licences, trademarks (service marks), other rights and assets similar to those listed	112		
Fixed assets (01, 02, 03):	120		
Including:			
—land plots, and sites for the use of natural resources	121		
—buildings, installations, machinery and equipment	122		
Incomplete construction (07, 08, 61)	130		
Long-term financial investments (06, 82)	140		
Including:			
—investments in subsidiaries	141		
—investments in associates	142		
—investments in other organizations	143		
—loans granted to organizations for a period of more than 12 months	144		
—other long-term financial investments	145		
Other non-current assets	150		
Total for Section I	190		

II CURRENT ASSETS

Stocks and supplies	210		
Including:			
—raw materials, other materials and other similar valuables (10, 15, 16)	211		
—rearers and fatteners (11)	212		
—low-value and short-life items (12, 13, 16)	213		
—expenditures on work-in-progress (handling costs) (20, 21, 23, 29, 30, 36, 44)	214		
—finished products and goods for resale (40, 41)	215		
—goods despatched (45)	216		
—deferred expenses (31)	217		

ASSETS	Line code	At year beginning	At year end
1	2	3	4
—other stocks and supplies and expenditures	218		
Value added tax on acquired valuables (19)	220		
Accounts receivable (payments in respect of which are expected more than 12 months after the accounting date)	230		
Including:			
—customers and clients (62, 76, 82)	231		
—bills of exchange receivable (62)	232		
—indebtedness of subsidiary and dependent companies (78)	233		
—advances issued (61)	234		
—sundry debtors	235		
Accounts receivable (payments in respect of which are expected within 12 months after the accounting date)	240		
Including:			
—customers and clients (62, 76, 82)	241		
—bills of exchange receivable (62)	242		
—indebtedness of subsidiary and associates (78)	243		
—indebtedness of participants (founding parties) in respect of contributions to the charter capital (75)	244		
—advances issued (61)	245		
—sundry debtors	246		
Short-term financial investments (56, 58, 82)	250		
Including:			
—investments in dependent companies	251		
—own shares purchased from shareholders	252		
—other short-term financial investments	253		
Monetary resources	260		
Including:			
—cash (50)	261		
—settlement accounts (51)	262		
—currency accounts (52)	263		
—other monetary resources (55, 56, 57)	264		
Other current assets	270		
Total for Section II	290		

ASSETS	Line code	At year beginning	At year end
1	2	3	4

III LOSSES

Uncovered losses of previous years (88)	310		
Uncovered losses for the accounting year	320	X	
Total for Section III	390		
BALANCE (total of lines 190 + 290 + 390)	399		

LIABILITIES	Line code	At year beginning	At year end
1	2	3	4

IV CAPITAL AND RESERVES

Charter capital (85)	410		
Additional capital (87)	420		
Reserve capital (86)	430		
Including:			
—reserve funds which are formed in accordance with legislation	431		
—provisions which are formed in accordance with the foundation documents	432		
Accumulation funds (88)	440		
Social fund (88)	450		
Special-purpose financing and receipts (96)	460		
Undistributed profit of previous years (88)	470		
Undistributed profit for the accounting year	480	X	
Total for Section IV	490		

V LONG-TERM LIABILITIES

Borrowed resources (92, 95)	510		
Including:	510		
—bank credits repayable more than 12 months after the accounting date	511		
—other loans repayable more than 12 months after the accounting date	512		
Other long-term liabilities	520		
Total for Section V	590		

LIABILITIES	Line code	At year beginning	At year end
1	2	3	4

VI SHORT-TERM LIABILITIES

Borrowed resources (90, 94)	610		
Including:			
—bank credits	611		
—other loans	612		
Accounts payable	620		
Including:			
—suppliers and contractors (60, 76)	621		
—bills of exchange payable (60)	622		
—indebtedness to subsidiary and associates (78)	623		
—labour payment (70)	624		
—social insurance and social security (69)	625		
—indebtedness to the budget (68)	626		
—advances received (64)	627		
—sundry creditors	628		
Settlements in respect of dividends (75)	630		
Deferred income (83)	640		
Consumption funds (88)	650		
Provisions for future expenses and payments (89)	660		
Other short-term liabilities	670		
Total for Section VI	690		
BALANCE (total of lines 490 + 590 + 690)	699		

Director   Chief Accountant

Approved by the Ministry of Finance of the
Russian Federation for 1997 Annual Accounting Reports

PROFIT AND LOSS ACCOUNT
for_____199__

	Codes
Form No. 2 according to *OKUD*	0710002
Date (year, month, day)	
Organization .... according to *OKPO*	
Sector (type of activity) .... according to *OKONKh*	
Organizational and legal form .... according to *KOPF*	
State property administration body .... according to *OKPO*	
Unit of measurement .... according to *SOEI*	
Control amount	

INDICATOR	Line code	For the accounting period	For the same period in the preceding year
1	2	3	4
Receipts (net) from the sale of goods, products, work and services (less value added tax, excise duty and similar compulsory payments)	010		
Cost of production of the sale of goods, products, work and services	020		
Commercial expenses	030		
Management expenses	040		
Profit (loss) from sales (lines (010 – 020 – 030 – 040))	050		
Interest receivable	060		
Interest payable	070		
Income from participation in other organizations	080		
Other operating income	090		
Other operating expenses	100		
Profit (loss) from financial and economic activity (lines 050 + 060 – 070 + 080 + 090 – 100)	110		
Other non-sale income	120		
Other non-sale expenses	130		
Profit (loss) for the accounting period (lines (110 + 120 – 130))	140		
Taxation on profit	150		
Diverted resources	160		
Undistributed profit (loss) for the accounting period (lines (140 – 150 – 160))	170		

Director   Chief Accountant

INDEX

A

AA. *See* Accountant-administratieconsulent
Abridged accounts, Spain, 834, 836
Absorption costing
  Denmark, 217
  in Marnmark, 188
ACCA. *See* Chartered Association of Certified Accountants
Accademia Italiana de Economia Aziendale (AIDEA), 541
Accelerated depreciation, Italy, 585
Access, Italy, 540
Accountancy law, Hungary, 1399
Accountant-administratieconsulent (AA), Netherlands, 695
Accountants
  Iceland, 1258–1259
Accounting. *See also* Full-cost method; Successful efforts accounting
  in central planning system (Hungary), 1500–1503
  commercial and tax in Germany, 361–362
  concepts (Turkey), 1407–1409
  development in Italy, 523–534
  Eastern Europe, 1458–1463
  equity (Greece), 473
  financial vs. tax (Norway), 1297–1298
  Italy, 546–554
  for leases. *See* Leases
  for oil, gas, and mineral resources. *See* Oil, gas, and other mineral resources
  Portugal, 802–814
  and taxation (Italy), 583–586
Accounting Act
  Norway, 1288, 1289, 1310–1311
  Poland, 1568
  Sweden, 1080–1081, 1110
Accounting Act and Decree (France), 297, 304, 310
Accounting Act Committee, Norway, 1288, 1289, 1292, 1309, 1310
Accounting Advisory Council, Norway, 1287, 1292
Accounting and Reporting Recommendations, Switzerland, 1335
Accounting Board, Sweden, 1082–1083, 1085
Accounting Committee, at Oslo Stock Exchange, 1287
Accounting concepts, Luxembourg, 681
Accounting Decree (Belgium), 112
Accounting depreciation, and tax allowances (United Kingdom), 1187

Accounting directives. *See* EU Directives
Accounting Directives Law, Germany, 21, 358, 394
Accounting firms, Denmark, 189
Accounting guidelines, Netherlands, 701
Accounting income. *See* Income
Accounting information, presenting (Spain), 826–836
Accounting Law
  Belarus, 1599–1600, 1608, 1610
  Hungary, 1501
  Poland, 1567–1568, 1587–1588
Accounting legislation. *See* Law(s)
Accounting Plan
  France, 822
  Spain, 821–822
Accounting principles and practices
  Austria, 48–60
  Hungary, 1528–1529
  Iceland, 1259–1274
  Luxembourg, 679–685
  Netherlands, 719
  Portugal, 819–839
  statement of (Spain), 844
  Sweden, 1089–1110
  Switzerland, 1334
  Republic of Ireland, 897, 903–950
  valuation and income measurement, Greece, 471–480; Netherlands, 720–753; Spain, 842–858; United Kingdom, 1164–1215, Baltic States, 1472–1474
Accounting policy
  changes in (Netherlands), 749
Accounting profession
  Greece, 464–465
  Hungary, 1503–1510, 1544–1546
  Iceland, 1269–1274
  Italy, 546–554, 573–575
  Portugal, 810–814
  Republic of Ireland, 891–892
  and stock exchange (Spain), 840–841
  Sweden, 1081–1083
  United Kingdom, 1139–1140
Accounting regulations. *See* Accounting rules; Law(s); Regulation(s)
Accounting requirements, of holding companies (Luxembourg), 676–677
Accounting rules
  Denmark, 197
  France, 294–297
  Germany, 360–361
  introduction to European, 1–28
  national, 1–2